METRIC CONVERSION CHARTS

VOLUME

USA	CANADA
1 teaspoon	5 ml
1 tablespoon	15 ml
¼ cup	60 ml
⅓ cup	80 ml
½ cup	120 ml
⅔ cup	160 ml
¾ cup	180 ml
1 cup	240 ml
1 pint	475 ml
1 quart	.95 liter
1 quart plus ¼ cup	1 liter
1 gallon	3.8 liters

TEMPERATURE

TO CONVERT FROM FAHRENHEIT TO CELSIUS: SUBTRACT 32, MULTIPLY BY 5, THEN DIVIDE BY 9

32°F	0°C
212°F	100°C
250°F	121°C
325°F	163°C
350°F	176°C
375°F	190°C
400°F	205°C
425°F	218°C
450°F	232°C

WEIGHT

USA	CANADA
1 ounce	28.3 grams
4 ounces	113 grams
8 ounces	227 grams
12 ounces	340.2 grams

PAN VOLUMES

PAN SIZE	APPROXIMATE VOLUME
2½" by 1½" muffin pan cup	½ cup
8½" by 4½" by 2½" loaf pan	6 cups
9" by 5" by 3" loaf pan	8 cups
8" by 8" by 1½" baking pan	6 cups
9" by 9" by 1½" baking pan	8 cups
9" by 1" pie plate	4 cups
11" by 7" by 1½" baking pan	8 cups
13" by 9" by 2" baking pan	15 cups
15½" by 10½" by 1" jelly roll pan	16 cups

MEASURING PANS

TO GET AN ACCURATE MEASUREMENT OF YOUR BAKEWARE, FOLLOW THE GUIDELINES BELOW

Pan Volume: Using a measuring cup, fill a baking pan to the rim with water, just short of overflowing. The number of cups needed to fill the pan equals the cup volume of the pan. If you have a pan with a removable bottom, substitute granulated sugar for water.

Pan Size: With a ruler, measure the length and width of a pan across its top from one inside edge to the opposite inside edge. Holding ruler perpendicular to pan, measure the depth of a pan on the inside of the pan from the bottom to the rim.

THE GOOD HOUSEKEEPING COOKBOOK

1,275 RECIPES *from* AMERICA'S FAVORITE TEST KITCHEN

SUNDAY DINNER COLLECTOR'S EDITION

HEARST BOOKS
New York

HEARST BOOKS
New York

An Imprint of Sterling Publishing
387 Park Avenue South
New York, NY 10016

ISBN 978-1-61837-137-9

Good Housekeeping
Editor in Chief: Rosemary Ellis
Creative Director: Courtney Murphy
Food Director: Susan Westmoreland
Nutrition Director: Samantha B. Cassetty, MS, RD
Kitchen Appliances & Food Technology Director: Sharon Franke
Home Appliances & Cleaning Products Director: Carolyn E. Forté

Layout Designer: MG Design
Photography credits on page 751

The Good Housekeeping Cookbook Seal guarantees that the recipes in this cookbook meet the strict standards of the Good Housekeeping Research Institute. The Institute has been a source of reliable information and a consumer advocate since 1900, and established its seal of approval in 1909. Every recipe has been triple-tested for ease, reliability, and great taste.

Distributed in Canada by Sterling Publishing
c/o Canadian Manda Group, 165 Dufferin Street
Toronto, Ontario, Canada M6K 3H6
Distributed in the United Kingdom by GMC Distribution Services
Castle Place, 166 High Street, Lewes, East Sussex, England BN7 1XU
Distributed in Australia by Capricorn Link (Australia) Pty. Ltd.
P.O. Box 704, Windsor, NSW 2756, Australia

For information about custom editions, special sales, and premium and corporate purchases, please contact Sterling Special Sales at 800-805-5489 or specialsales@sterlingpublishing.com.

Manufactured in China

2 4 6 8 10 9 7 5 3 1

www.sterlingpublishing.com

WELCOME

Dear Home Cook,

Welcome to our special Sunday dinner edition of the *Good Housekeeping Cookbook*.

You've probably heard that study after study shows that sitting down to a family dinner is one of the very best habits you can develop. Everyone tends to eat healthier, children are less likely to have emotional and behavioral problems (and get better grades!), and it's a wonderful opportunity to relax and connect as a family. But for many of us—myself included—creating that time out can be a challenge. Perhaps one of you often works late, or your kids have sports practice what seems like every night of the week, or the prep work just feels daunting. Whatever the obstacles, it can be more than a little tricky to pull off this wonderful ritual.

So let us help. We've put together 52 menus, one for every week of the year. Each includes a main dish, two sides, and dessert. The menus are organized seasonally to provide lighter, fresh offerings in the spring, plenty of grilling ideas for the summer, and heartier meals to prepare during the colder months. You can follow along with our plan, or pick and choose as you please—and we also give you pointers for putting together your own menu.

"Sunday dinner" is just a catchphrase for a meal that can happen any night of the week—and it's about more than what's on your plate. This is a time for creating special memories with your entire family, and we have plenty of ideas for including everyone in the process, even young children. We'll show you simple strategies and shortcuts for planning the meal, from choosing the menu to going grocery shopping for yummy and nutritious ingredients.

The next step is prepping the dinner, and this book is chock-full of tips and tricks to keep things moving smoothly, whether your kindergartener is measuring flour or your teen is chopping vegetables. We run through the basics of setting a simple but festive table, and you'll find real-world strategies for banishing electronics from your table time so you can enjoy your meal and really connect with each other.

Once you're in the habit of preparing a special weekly menu, dip into the rest of the recipes—1,275 in all! Each one has been triple-tested to work at the renowned *Good Housekeeping* test kitchens, and you'll find dishes of every variety, as well as an entire chapter on quick and easy weeknight meals.

We hope this cookbook, and the meals you make from it, will help make your family life both sweeter and more satisfying.

Happy cooking!

With best wishes,

Rosemary Ellis
Editor-in-Chief

CONTENTS

SPRING

Spring meals begin to transition into lighter fare, and they take advantage of fresh produce beginning to appear at the market. We've got you covered for the holidays, too, with delicious brisket for Passover and zesty pineapple-glazed ham for Easter.

Chinese Dumplings, page 49

Roman Chicken Sauté with Artichokes, page 158

Vegetable Chowder, page 56

Eggs Stuffed with Smoked Salmon and Cucumbers, page 39

Sliced Citrus with Lemon-Lime Syrup, page 607

Healthy Caesar Salad, page 477

Pasta Primavera, page 258

Mixed Pea Pod Stir-Fry, page 418

Scallop and Asparagus Stir-Fry, page 217

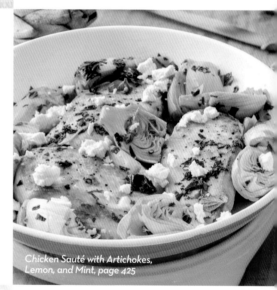

*Chicken Sauté with Artichokes,
Lemon, and Mint, page 425*

Strawberry Cheese Pie, page 663

SUMMER

Summer is a great time to eat outdoors, of course, and this section is packed with ideas to get you grilling. We also seize the opportunity to enjoy in-season corn and tomatoes, plus berries, peaches, and watermelon.

Red Wine and Rosemary Porterhouse, page 347

Southern Fried Chicken, page 171

Classic Strawberry Shortcakes, page 616

MENU 17

....

Pork Tenderloin
Cutlets with
Plum Glaze 355

Cantaloupe and
Cucumber Salad 483

Asian Rice. 288

Fruit Crisp. 602

Peach Cobbler, page 619

MENU 18

....

Cold-Poached
Salmon Steaks with
Watercress Sauce 195

Vichyssoise 60

Mediterranean
Rice Salad. 488

Peach Cobbler 619

Tuscan White-Bean Bruschetta, page 40

MENU 19

....

Grilled Chicken
Breasts Saltimbocca. . 364

Honeydew and
Lime Soup. 61

Zucchini Ribbons
with Mint. 433

Fire-Roasted
Nectarines 621

Grilled Chicken Breasts Saltimbocca, page 364

MENU 20

....

Penne
with Pesto. 254

Tuscan White-
Bean Bruschetta 40

Grilled Vegetable
Stack 382

Watermelon Bowl 471

Grilled Sweet Potatoes, page 385

MENU 21

....

Brisket with Chunky
BBQ Sauce 350

Three-Bean
Salad 480

Grilled Sweet
Potatoes 385

Apricot Upside-
Down Cake 634

MENU 22

Deep Dish Peach-Berry Pie, page 666

MENU 23

*Fresh Salmon Burgers
with Capers and Dill, page 210*

MENU 24

Summer Squash and Chicken, page 370

MENU 25

Greek Peasant Salad, page 481

MENU 26

FALL

Fall brings heartier meals with cooler weather. You and your family can warm up with delicious flank steak, thyme-roasted chicken, breaded pork tenderloin, and more.

Spaghetti and Meatballs, page 267

MENU 27

MENU 28

MENU 29

Lacy Parmesan Crisps, page 249

Brownie Pudding Cake, page 610

Chicken with Rosemary Dumplings, page 168

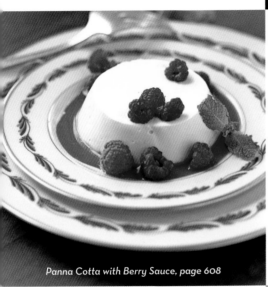

Panna Cotta with Berry Sauce, page 608

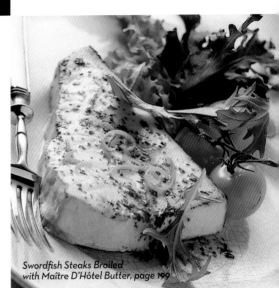

*Swordfish Steaks Broiled
with Maître D'Hôtel Butter, page 199*

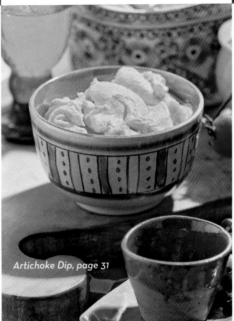

Artichoke Dip, page 31

Sunday Dinner XIII

Thyme-Roasted Chicken and Vegetables, page 156

Green-Apple Salad with Endive and Radicchio, page 548

Candied Sweet Potatoes, page 437

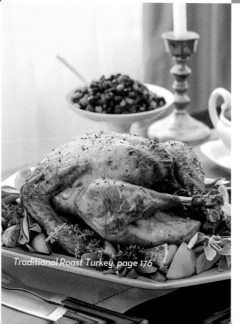

Traditional Roast Turkey, page 176

WINTER

Winter is a time for celebration: enjoy short ribs dinner for Hanukkah and a special roast for Christmas. When the holidays are over, our easy and flavorful meals will carry you through until spring.

MENU 40

Sufganiyot, page 551

MENU 41

MENU 42

Country Captain Casserole, page 166

Quick Cream of Broccoli Soup, page 54

Butternut-Apple Soup, page 52

Quick Minestrone, page 64

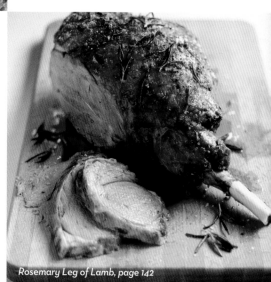

Rosemary Leg of Lamb, page 142

Chocolate Cream Pie, page 668

MENU 48

Baked Scrod with Fennel
and Potatoes 203

Hearty Mushroom-
Barley Soup 67

Lemon-Cranberry
Shortbread 685

*Roast Chicken with
Forty Cloves of Garlic, page 155*

MENU 49

Roast Chicken with
Forty Cloves of Garlic . 155

Warm Farro Salad
with Roasted
Vegetables 299

Parmesan
Potatoes 426

Crème Caramel 603

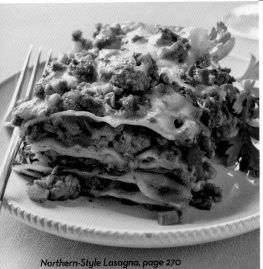

Northern-Style Lasagna, page 270

MENU 50

Northern-Style
Lasagna 270

Mixed Greens with
Pears and Pecans 475

Oranges with
Caramel 462

Almond
Crescents 692

Crème Caramel, page 603

MENU 51

Panfried Scallops 217

Baby Romaine
with Fennel
and Citrus 479

Mashed Potatoes with
Garlic and Lemon 422

Chocolate Raspberry
Thumbprints 699

Oranges with Caramel, page 462

MENU 52

Ginger-Glazed Duck . . . 183

Warm Quinoa
and Broccoli
Salad with Carrot-
Ginger Dressing 301

Citrus Carrots 189

Gingerbread 635

SUNDAY DINNER

STARTING A NEW TRADITION

It's time for your family to start a new tradition (or maybe revive an old one that got lost somewhere along the way): bringing back Sunday dinner. This isn't just about what you eat at the end of the week. This is the meal where your family gathers around the table and enjoys a full dinner of a main dish, two sides, and dessert. This is the time you all set aside to be with one another without distractions—no television, no texting, no phone calls, no homework. This is when you linger at the table, savoring not just the delicious food, but also each other's company.

No one is exempt from the busy pace of today's life. Between work, school, friends, sports, and club activities, it's no wonder family dinner often involves calling out for pizza or ordering from a drive-through window. Maybe a cozy night is where you all eat sandwiches together while watching your favorite show. It's all part of how we live now. Prepackaged foods can be a huge help to a busy family, and sometimes it's easier to leave a pot of stew on the stove and let everyone help themselves. But consider setting aside one night—just one—each week where you put in the extra effort to slow down, prepare a special meal, and enjoy it together.

We call this meal "Sunday dinner" in remembrance of days past. For many American families, a typical Sunday consisted of church services followed by a big meal. Sunday dinner was usually served around 2 or 3 in the afternoon—later than lunch, but several hours earlier than the typical weeknight dinner. Sunday is, of course, a wonderful night to make a special family meal, and a logical time to reflect on the past

week and gear up for what's ahead. But if your Sundays are eaten up by soccer games and birthday parties, catching up on work or training for a 10K race, you have plenty of other options—six, to be exact.

You can cook Sunday dinner any night of the week. At first glance, Monday may seem like an odd choice, but a family dinner can be a great way to kick off the week. Tuesdays and Thursdays might be the only nights your family has free. Wednesday provides something to look forward to midweek as you get over the "hump." Friday is a wonderful night for a family meal, and follows the Jewish tradition of the Sabbath dinner, which marks the transition from the workweek to a more restful time. Saturday offers many of the same advantages as Sunday, and if you eat in the late afternoon, you can still have a date night with your spouse—or bring out the board games or DVDs and extend dinner into a whole family evening. Or maybe you'll mix it up and take each week as it comes.

ENJOY DELICIOUS DINNERS

This book provides a year's worth of menus as suggestions for your Sunday dinner. Each meal includes a main course, two side dishes, and dessert. In many of the menus, you can serve one of the sides—soup or salad, for example—as a starter. Menus provide a mix of meals on the lighter side (Menu 9: Broiled Salmon Steaks, Salsa Verde, Mixed Pea Pod Stir-Fry, Vanilla Pound Cake), heartier ones (Menu 14: Red Wine and Rosemary Porterhouse, Grilled Caesar Salad, Crumb-Topped Tomatoes, Chocolate Fondue with Fruit), and somewhere-in-the-middle options (Menu 28: Fennel-Crusted Bluefish, Red Potato Salad, Braised Leeks, Brownie Pudding Cake). All the dinners are nutritious and well balanced. Not only did *Good Housekeeping*'s team of test-kitchen experts work on these recipes, so too did our resident R.D. And remember that this is a special, once-weekly meal. It's a time to enjoy.

Some meals use a particular ingredient in more than one dish. For example, Menu 7 features Tomato and Ricotta Salata Bruschetta and Lemon-Ricotta Cheesecake, while Menu 52 includes Warm Quinoa and Broccoli Salad with Carrot-Ginger Dressing, Ginger-Glazed Duck, and Gingerbread. We've designed the menus so that if you are buying a special ingredient, you won't have to stare at it in your refrigerator or pantry and wonder what to do the rest. But remember, you have more than 1,000 recipes right at your fingertips. If you get your hands on some beautiful fresh mint for the Zucchini Ribbons with Mint in Menu 19, try making the Mint Melon Cups (page 455) later in the week. If your family likes the sage in the Tuscan White Beans with Sage in Menu 30, grill up Citrus-Sage Chicken (page 365) and enjoy the same flavor in a very different main dish.

If you really get into the swing of things and want to prepare a special meal on other nights of the week, it couldn't be easier to put together your own menu. Start by looking at the Table of Contents. Is your family in the mood for pork (Meat, page 94)? Do you want to use your slow cooker (Soups, Stews & One-Pot Meals, page 50)? Is it a perfect night to grill (Grilling, page 344)? Once you've picked your main dish, start thinking about the starter and sides. You'll want a good balance of protein, grains, and fruits and vegetables. Think about texture and color contrasts; aim for a mix of creamy and crunchy textures. Many of our recipes suggest a perfect pairing, and you can also take a look at what you have on hand. We can put an abundance of greens to good use with Salads & Salad Dressings (page 472). If your pantry is overflowing, turn to Beans, Rice & Other Grains (page 278) for inspiration. And if you want to get something on the table fast, Quick & Easy Weeknight Meals (page 306) will be your salvation.

EXPLORE SEASONAL MENUS

We have arranged the menus seasonally, tuning in to how we tend to eat throughout the year: lighter fare in the spring, when so many fresh vegetables reappear in the market; plenty of outdoor dining ideas for summer; heartier meals when it cools off in fall; and robust, warming dishes for winter. We also offer fresh takes on traditional holiday dinners. You can follow chronologically and let us do the work for you, or mix and match according to your family's preferences. And the best thing about this cookbook is that there is ample room for experimentation—we have 1,275 recipes inside! If you love the sides in a particular menu but your family is in the mood for, say, seafood instead of steak, simply turn to Fish & Shellfish (page 190) and pick from one of dozens of options.

The menus are designed for a family of four, but you can often double the recipes if your household is bigger or if you're inviting friends or extended family. If you usually have a table of five or six, consider doubling the recipes and enjoying the leftovers during the rest of the week. Page through the rest of the book and let your instincts lead you. Extra roast chicken could be used in Chicken and Rice Soup (page 293) or Asian Chicken Salad (page 322).

One final word: We don't expect you to do it all yourself. This meal is a family affair, and that includes every part of it—planning, prepping, cleaning up, and, of course, eating. We've got plenty of ideas and tips to help you involve everyone, from toddlers to teens, to make this a truly special time.

Dinner recipes include options that are made with meat, poultry, and seafood—plus vegetarian dishes, too. The menus star in-season fruits and vegetables, such as asparagus in spring and fennel in fall.

Grilled Sweet Potatoes, page 385

Pasta Primavera, page 258

Thyme-Roasted Chicken and Vegetables, page 156

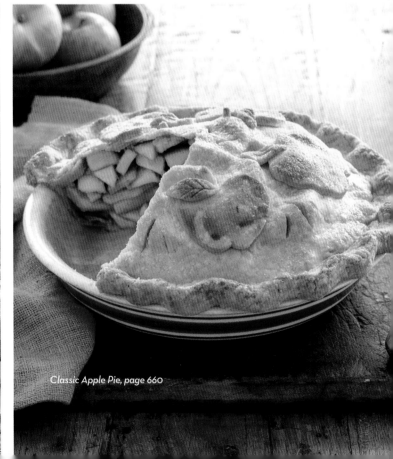
Classic Apple Pie, page 660

PLANNING THE MEAL

First things first: Who can help you with what this week? Not only will extra hands make meal prep easier, you'll also boost opportunities for family bonding. You can rotate assignments so that everyone is involved each week, or you can designate one start-to-finish aide for the day. Or you can throw everyone in and make it a true group effort! Whatever you choose, keep it fun and educational. Look for ways to bring your family together before you even get to the table.

CHOOSE THE MENU

There are many ways to go about selecting your supper for a particular week. Your first and simplest option is to decide yourself. You can follow our suggestions by matching up the date on the calendar with the corresponding seasonal menu.

If it's the first week of July, for example, you are about five menus into the Summer section, or Menu 18. If that particular meal doesn't feel right, look at the ones around it for something more appealing. But there are no rules. Pick the one you like best that week.

You may also want to decide based on what you have on hand. If it's spring and you grabbed a batch of asparagus from your farmers' market earlier in the week, an obvious choice is Menu 12, which features Scallop and Asparagus Stir-Fry.

You can also be more inclusive in your menu selection and bring in some or all of your family to help you decide. If you have a designated helper for the meal, let her or him take the lead. If you want everyone to have a say, gather together and read the possibilities aloud or even email to get each person's input.

STOCK YOUR PANTRY

Keeping a well-stocked pantry and refrigerator will make it easier to cook all your meals, not just Sunday dinner. Do a quick scan of your kitchen each week. If you're out of or running low on any staples, replenish your supply. If you have a lot of ingredients already on hand, you'll find yourself calling out for pizza less and less often.

A well-stocked pantry will make meal preparation easier.

DRY GOODS

Onions, garlic, shallots Store these in a net bag or open basket (not in plastic), in a cool, dry spot, and they'll last a month. Red, yellow, and sweet onions are handy to have. Don't mingle onions and spuds; they emit gases that shorten each other's lives.

Potatoes, sweet potatoes Store as onions above, keeping separate. Scrub well, and you can skip the peeling step for most recipes.

Beans Mainstays are cannellini, pinto, and black beans, as well as chickpeas. For no-fuss, high-protein dishes, fold these into a tortilla or puree into a soup.

Tomatoes Fire-roasted will jump-start Tex-Mex meals; peeled whole tomatoes are a shortcut to sauces as fresh as summer.

Roasted peppers An adaptable add-in. Toss with garlic and capers and serve with toasted Italian bread slices for an insta-bruschetta, or sauté with sherry, chicken, and capers.

Chicken broth This superstar staple boosts the flavor of sauces, stews, and sautés. Low-sodium varieties are the heart-healthiest.

Tuna Water-packed is a lean choice. Keep a couple of cans of oil-packed white albacore, too: It's stellar in sauces and Niçoise salad.

Olives Improve salads, sauces, pizzas, and pastas. Choose briny, green, or rich, ripe ones from Italy, Greece, or France.

Chipotle chiles Spicy and smoky. Packed in adobo sauce, a tangy-hot tomato puree—just a teaspoon adds fieriness to dishes.

Salsa Amazingly versatile: It can sub for butter on baked potatoes and for ketchup on a burger. Or spoon over fish, then broil.

Marinara sauce Go beyond pairing with pasta: Use as a pan sauce for pork or turkey cutlets, to poach eggs, or to make minestrone.

Coconut milk This is a staple of Thai and Indian cuisine, as the mildness cuts heat. Light versions are best—just as creamy, but with half the fat.

GRAINS

Polenta Ready in five minutes. Tasty with marinara and cheese, or with sausage.

Couscous Precooked, so it's weeknight-speedy. Serve with stews or as a simple side (see page 302).

Quinoa Use this fiber-rich protein in pilafs and salads instead of rice.

Oats Use to stretch meatballs and meatloaf, or to coat oven-fried chicken.

Pasta Stock a range of shapes and sizes. Whole grain varieties are healthiest.

Rice Buy in bulk, then pop in the freezer—it will keep for up to a year in the cold. Plain cooked rice will last a week in the fridge.

Bulgur Quicker than rice—a mild, nutty side dish, perfect with pork or salmon.

HERBS, SPICES, AND CONDIMENTS

Spices and seeds You can't beat the taste of fresh herbs, but may not want to buy a massive bunch of rosemary when you need only a sprig. Keep a full rotation of never-fail dried seasonings, including thyme, oregano, dill, tarragon, rosemary, chili powder, cumin, coriander, curry, cinnamon, red pepper, and fennel seeds. Ditch dried herbs after two years, when the flavor nosedives.

Salt and pepper Never be without this dynamic duo. If a recipe calls for coarse or kosher salt and you're using table salt, reduce the quantity a little (and vice versa). Freshly ground black pepper has more of a pop.

Liquid condiments Have these basics at the ready: olive oils, vegetable oils, balsamic vinegar, red wine vinegar, soy sauce, Worcestershire sauce, and hot sauce. If you want to branch out a bit, keep a couple of olive oils on hand—extra-virgin is great for dressing and drizzling, while regular costs less and is fine for sautés. Sunflower and safflower oil are neutral and will not impart any unwanted flavor to your dishes. Experiment with champagne and sherry vinegars to jazz up your meals, and periodically splurge on a specialty bottle for fantastic taste.

BAKING

Leaveners After opening, baking powder keeps for six to 12 months, baking soda for two years.

Sugars Pack granulated, confectioners', and light and dark brown into airtight containers. To prevent brown sugar from hardening, add an apple slice to the container (change it monthly).

Flours Store all-purpose, whole wheat, and cake in airtight containers. Whole wheat flour should be refrigerated. The oils in the whole grains become rancid within a few months.

Chocolate Stock unsweetened cocoa and unsweetened and semi-sweet chocolate chips.

Cupcake liners Pleated greaseproof liners come in every size and style.

Cornstarch For in-a-pinch cake flour, swap two tablespoons of cornstarch for all-purpose flour for every cup of flour.

Vanilla extract Although it's pricier, the all-natural extracts beat artificial for flavor.

FRIDGE

Tube of tomato paste If a recipe calls for a few spoonfuls, this easy-squeeze tube is less wasteful than opening a whole can. This is double-concentrated, with an intense tomato-ness.

Reduced-fat mayonnaise For a go-to glaze for broiled fish, mix with mustard or horseradish.

Capers Their salty sharpness perks up fish, pasta, or chicken.

Mango chutney, apricot jam, marmalade The sugars in the fruits caramelize during cooking, so these are great as fuss-free glazes. Slather straight from the jar onto pork or poultry before grilling or broiling.

Mustard A can-do condiment, whether it's a grainy Dijon, a full-bodied brown, or a more mellow yellow. Enlivens everything from cream sauces to vinaigrettes.

Hoisin sauce Try its chile-spiced sweetness in Asian dishes and dipping sauces.

Pickles Chop cornichons into tuna salad, or sweet pickles into potato salad.

Milk, yogurt, sour cream Group dairy items together on the middle shelves.

Eggs Avoid putting egg trays in the door—temps are too warm. Leave in the carton and place on a back shelf, where it's consistently colder.

Vegetables Don't wash before putting in the fridge. Leave in the supermarket's plastic produce bags and keep in the crisper. The only exception: celery. Wrap it in foil, and the stalks will stay colorful and crunchy for several weeks.

Cantaloupe, apples Segregate these ethylene emitters from produce sensitive to the gas, such as lettuces and parsley.

Lemons, limes, oranges Unbeatable for brightening up dishes, citrus fruit can be stored for up to two weeks with zero fall-off in flavor.

Cheese Semi-hard and hard cheeses will last for weeks. If mold develops, just trim one inch around moldy spots and rewrap tightly in clean waxed paper or plastic.

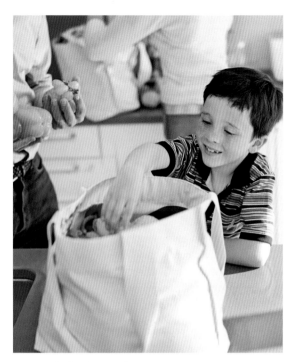

Shopping for food can teach your child a lot.

GO SHOPPING

Shopping for Sunday dinner can be its own event, or you can fold it into your regular trip for stocking up. Either way, note the ingredients for each recipe in the menu, then check to see what you have on hand (see "Stock Your Pantry," page xxiii). When you make your shopping list, group like items (particularly if you are using the same ingredient for two or more dishes) so that you don't have to double back in the store. And why not bring your assistant along? This is a wonderful opportunity to educate your children on nutrition, economics, and even geography.

If you're shopping just for Sunday dinner, this is a great time to try an ethnic store or the farmers' market. If you live in an area with a butcher, a greenmarket, and/or a fishmonger, try making a separate trip for at least one of your ingredients—you might be pleasantly surprised at the difference in quality. It can also be fun to make this into an event: You can treat your helper to lunch, or fold in a visit to the park or aquarium.

NUTRITIONAL RECOMMENDATIONS

Many of us remember, and still live by, the old food pyramid. But the U.S. Department of Agriculture has developed a new set of recommendations, and our menus are designed with them in mind. Your plate should be half full of fruits and vegetables, and the remaining half should be split between proteins and grains, with a small amount of dairy (you can learn more at www.choosemyplate .gov). See pages 15–17 for more nutritional insight plus information on the food groups.

Talk with your family honestly about their likes, dislikes, and habits. Agree that once a week, at Sunday dinner, you will eat a balanced meal that resembles the Choose My Plate model. Talk about the wide variety of foods you'll be trying all year, and the different ways you will flavor vegetables and grains. Encourage everyone to take at least one bite of everything, and explain that you might make great discoveries along the way. Perhaps you'll find out you love Brussels sprouts— especially when they're made with bacon (Menu 32).

GOING ORGANIC

Eating organic foods has taken off in recent years. Organic foods are farmed or otherwise produced without synthetic pesticides, chemical fertilizers, irradiation, industrial solvents, or chemical food additives. The USDA organic seal covers fresh and processed agricultural food products, including crops and livestock.

More and more people are also eating locally grown, in-season fruits and vegetables and what's known as a "farm-totable" approach. This is a personal decision, of course, and it can also be a fluid one. You may shop at the farmers' market three weeks out of the month, but then grab a package of asparagus imported from Peru from the supermarket in the middle of October.

Organic food is more expensive than nonorganic because the farming methods are more labor intensive. If you like the idea of shopping organic but can't decide whether it's worth it, see the box at left. It highlights which foods you should buy organic whenever possible.

Our menus are organized to reflect what's in season at various times of the year, but our selections don't follow an absolute rule, and neither should you. If your family is craving a particular vegetable and you can get ahold of it at your supermarket, go for it. Better out of season than not at all!

VEGETABLES AND FRUITS

Our menus feature plenty of vegetables, and many are old favorites, such as mushrooms and potatoes, prepared in both familiar and innovative ways. But we also offer opportunities to branch out a little with, for example, celery root and fennel.

Shopping with children is a great way to get them excited about vegetables. Start by reading the buying tips for your vegetable of the week. For example, if you need to pick up broccoli (page 394), you'll learn that you need to look for firm stalks with tightly closed dark green flowerets, and that you should avoid stalks that are yellowing or blooming. Once you're at the market, enlist your assistant to help you pick out the best specimens, and talk about how excited you are to eat them. He or she will be much more likely to take at least a few bites at dinner.

Want more info? See page 387 for tips on buying, storing, and preparing vegetables, and check out the alphabetical listings to find specifics on availability and peak season, as well as particular pointers for more than 50 vegetables.

Fruit can liven up a dish or provide a tart counterpoint to rich flavors. A healthy diet includes two to four servings of fruit per day, but many families struggle to fit them in. Our menus include plenty of fruit: You'll find them in the desserts, of course, but also in salads and as accompaniments to main dishes. Many traditional dishes pair fruit with meat, poultry, or seafood; classic examples are pork chops with applesauce, lemon chicken, and fish with mango salsa. Don't be afraid to experiment with fruit at all your meals, even if it's just a small serving on the side.

WHEN TO CHOOSE ORGANIC

The Environmental Working Group has noted that the following foods have the highest concentrations of pesticide residue:

Apples	Cherry tomatoes
Strawberries	Summer squash
Grapes	Kale
Celery	Collard greens
Spinach	Peaches and nectarines
Cucumbers	
Potatoes	Bell peppers and hot peppers

If you have the option of buying organic for these foods and don't mind spending a little extra, these are your best bets. Note that many items at farmers' markets are not USDA-approved "organic," but the growers follow the same processes. Don't be afraid to ask.

Foods with the lowest amount of pesticide residue include:

Corn	Asparagus
Onions	Eggplant
Pineapple	Kiwi
Avocado	Grapefruit
Cabbage	Cantaloupe
Sweet peas	Sweet potatoes
Papaya	Mushrooms
Mango	

If you want to buy organic only when absolutely necessary, you can choose the nonorganic options for these foods without worrying too much about your family's health.

Kids are more likely to eat veggies that they chose themselves.

See page 447 for smart hints on buying, storing, and preparing vegetables, and dip into the alphabetical listings to find specifics on availability and peak season, as well as details on enjoying 30+ types of fruit.

DAIRY

Cheese can be one of those ingredients that really kicks up a dish's flavor and makes it a memorable treat. You can find tips on buying and storing cheese, as well as a glossary to help you sort out all the yummy varieties, on pages 242–243.

Eggs make an appearance in many of the recipes on our menus. Sometimes they are front and center, like Eggs Stuffed with Smoked Salmon and Cucumbers in Menu 4, while in other dishes you'll need one or two to bring the terrific flavors and textures together. And, of course, you almost always need eggs for baked desserts. See pages 225–226 for your complete guide to the care and handling of eggs.

MEAT

Our menus feature a wide array of meats, from beef to pork to lamb. And while we have dozens of tasty options, meal prep and shopping can be a challenge if you have an older child who is questioning the ethics of eating meat. Don't shy away from discussions. Talk to vegetarian-leaning teens about alternative sources of protein, such as beans and grains (see page xxix). Make a vegetarian Sunday supper regularly—our Pasta Primavera (Menu 7) or Penne with Pesto (Menu 30) are great places to start.

See pages 95–97 for information on buying, storing, and cooking meat, as well as meat safety information. Popular beef cuts are pictured on page 98; veal cuts are on page 116; pork cuts are on page 125; and lamb cuts are on page 140. You'll also find roasting times through the chapter.

POULTRY

Who doesn't love chicken? You'll find it sautéed, roasted, and grilled—plus irresistible recipes for duck and turkey, too.

See pages 149–151 for information on getting to know your poultry, shopping choices, fresh versus frozen, handling and storage, safely thawing, and roasting times.

SEAFOOD

Fish is appearing more and more frequently on American dinner tables, as families are embracing it as a healthy source of lean protein. Our menus feature an abundance of seafood, and we've mixed it up to include the usual suspects, like salmon and shrimp, but also scallops, scrod, catfish, bluefish, snapper…and more.

See pages 191–193 for information on buying and storing fish and shellfish, as well as cooking tips and glossaries.

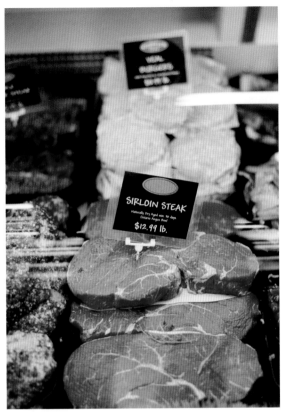

Confused about cuts of meat? See Chapter 4 for help.

PASTA

Many families enjoy pasta during the week—it's quick and easy. But don't discount it as a possibility for Sunday dinner. The noodles in our menus are paired with everything from a mushroom-rich fettucine (Menu 46) to a hearty lasagna with meat sauce (Menu 50).

See pages 251–252 for information on buying and storing pasta, a glossary, and tips on cooking.

BEANS, RICE, AND OTHER GRAINS

Beans and many grains provide a major source of healthy protein (to get top-notch nutrition, serve them together—see page 279). You'll find baked, white, and garbanzo in our menus, and more! Rice has long been a standby in many kitchens, but we keep it from being boring by dressing it up with ingredients such as lemon and coconut. Grains are a great base for many flavors, and a fun and easy way to explore in the kitchen. We also include quinoa and couscous in our menus, but feel free to experiment and try something else—the glossary on 287 will help you keep them all straight.

See pages 279–280 for information on soaking and cooking beans, as well as the glossary. The sections on rice and other grains are on pages 285–287.

. . . .

HOW MUCH TO BUY?

Here are some common ingredients and the amount of food they yield for your recipe. To see even more, go to the inside back cover of this book.

. . . .

INGREDIENTS	YIELD
Bacon, 16-ounce package, diced, cooked	1 ½ cups, pieces
Beans, dry, 1 cup	2 to 2 ½ cups cooked
Butter or margarine, 1 pound	4 sticks or 2 cups
Cheddar cheese, 4 ounces	1 cup shredded
Chicken, 3 pounds, cooked	2 ½ cups, diced meat
Couscous, uncooked, 1 cup	2 ½ cups cooked
Flour, 1 pound	3 ½ cups
Mushrooms, fresh, ½ pound	scant 1 cup sliced and cooked
Peas, green, fresh, 1 pound shelled	1 cup
Rice, 1 cup, regular long-grain	3 cups, cooked
Spaghetti, 8 ounces	4 cups cooked

PUT AWAY FOOD

If your pantry and refrigerator are on the cluttered and disorganized end of the spectrum, a logical time to spruce things up is when you're unloading the makings for Sunday dinner. You don't have to tackle the whole job at once: Organize the fridge one week and the pantry the next, or just take it shelf by shelf each week.

Scan your fridge, and be sure to discard any food that has spoiled or gotten moldy, as well as leftovers that no one has eaten in the past two days. Open the pantry and throw away any open boxes of staples that are more than six months old. If you spot canned goods that you've had for more than a year, donate them to a food pantry or shelter, or add to an emergency preparedness kit. When you begin to put things back in the cupboard, group similar items together (like cereal with grains), and get in the habit of placing all food labels facing front. And be sure to put your assistant to good use. Even children who don't yet read can group together recognizable items like cereal boxes, or they can carefully ferry sealed, nonbreakable items to the counter or table for you to sort.

Label your ingredients for Sunday dinner so you don't lose track of them.

DRY GOODS

If you aren't cooking right away and prefer to put away dry ingredients for Sunday dinner, label the package so you don't lose track of it (and so no one else in your family gets into it). Your assistant can mark SUNDAY DINNER on a strip of masking tape or a Post-it note.

Store boxed dry goods by type. If an item is in an odd-shaped package, such as dried beans or rice, you may want to transfer it to a clear, airtight container. (This is a great task for an older child, and a younger one can do it by using a small scoop or even a spoon.)

PRODUCE

Store produce in a refrigerator bin or countertop basket until you're ready to prep it. Sturdy vegetables like carrots, celery, and winter squashes can be prepped a day ahead and refrigerated.

Wash produce just before you're going to eat it. Rinse under warm water, and scrub well with a clean produce brush. You can set aside the clean items in a colander and dry bigger ones (such as zucchini) with paper towels or a clean dishtowel. Do this even for foods with thick skin, like avocado and cantaloupe, as their exteriors may carry bacteria from traveling and handling. Put aside your designated Sunday dinner ingredients in a labeled bowl so no one eats them before their time.

MEAT, FISH, POULTRY

If you're cooking within a day or two, store your meat, seafood, or poultry in the refrigerator. If you shop several days before Sunday dinner, stow the item in the freezer with a label. Put a reminder note on the refrigerator to move it to the fridge the night before, or set an alert on your smartphone or tablet.

PREPPING THE MEAL

Once you've bought the food and put it away, get started on preparing the meal, even if you won't do any actual cooking until another day. To begin, get yourself accustomed to the idea of having an assistant in the kitchen. This can be an adjustment, especially if you are used to cooking alone and have come to think of it as a time to relax and contemplate. Perhaps you enjoy a glass of wine while preparing a meal, or use that time to listen to a radio program or podcast. Focus on the positive. It is just one night a week, and prepping and cooking with your kids is a great way to educate them on how to make healthy choices—and you've already laid the groundwork at the market! You're also teaching them to feed themselves, which will cut way back on fast food and takeout when they are on their own. And, perhaps best of all, children of any age are far more likely to eat what they've had a hand in preparing.

There are many ways to make prepping the meal a fun experience. Don matching aprons and prepare a special snack or drink, and play your assistant's favorite music to keep things lively. Talk to younger children about your own family dinners when you were young, and use the alone time to catch up with adolescents who have begun asserting their independence. Be sure to tell them how happy you are to be working together. This is the time to create special memories.

PLAN SCHEDULE

Work with your assistant to come up with a schedule for cooking dinner. Check each recipe for make-ahead items, and decide whether you want to take advantage of that option or do it all at once. (Baked desserts are a good idea to make the day before or morning of.) Write out a schedule of what needs to happen when. For example, if you're planning a

4 o'clock roast chicken dinner, your schedule might look like this:

3:00 Put chicken in oven
3:15 Peel vegetables
3:30 Put vegetables in oven
3:35 Start making salad

Use a timer: With all the multi-tasking it's easy to forget to check on things. You can put an older child in charge of setting alerts on his or her smartphone or a family computer or tablet. If you have a wall clock in your kitchen, younger children can get a time-telling lesson if you include a sketch of where the big and little hands should be. If you have only digital clocks, coach him or her to keep an eye on it and notify you when it's time for the next step. (Don't let this be your only reminder, however!)

COOK

Roll up your sleeves—it's finally time to cook. Make sure you have your recipe pages right at hand, either by marking the pages with Post-it notes or making photocopies beforehand.

Every recipe has steps youngsters can handle, such as washing, organizing, measuring, and mixing.

READ THROUGH THE RECIPE

Before you do anything else, read through the recipe and make sure you have all the ingredients on hand. (If you're running low on something, measure it out just to be sure. When in doubt, send your spouse or a driving-age child to the market.) This is a great task for your assistant to help you with, as you can read the list of ingredients while she or he places them on the work surface (or vice versa). You can either group together items for each dish, or keep like with like—vegetables together, oils and spices together, grains together. The second approach may be more helpful with menus that use the same ingredient in more than one dish.

Younger children can search for items by description, or you can have them make tick marks next to each item as you set it aside. This is also a great way to practice alphabet skills, as you can spell an item for your child, or ask him or her to spell for you.

WASH AND PEEL

If you haven't washed your fruits and vegetables, now is the time to do it. You should also peel, pit, and core as needed. Remove meat, fish, and poultry from its packaging and pat dry with paper towels to remove any residual moisture, which can prevent a nice sear or crust from forming. Wash well all work surfaces, cutting boards, utensils, and hands that come into contact with these items.

MEASUREMENTS

Liquid and dry measuring cups are not interchangeable; be sure to use the right one for all your ingredients. Children of all ages will enjoy scooping and leveling ingredients. Coach them never to measure an ingredient over the food bowl—if your hands slip, you could end up with half a cup of salt in a recipe that requires only a teaspoon. For more tips on measuring, see pages 11–12.

Unless your children are in their teens, you may want to handle all of the cutting yourself.

There is only one drawback to the mise en place, but it's a big one: extra cleanup. At the very least, you will have a few extra ramekins or bowls to unload from your dishwasher. If you decide you want to try it, or that it's a good idea for a particular menu (see below), ask for extra help to wash and put away the containers as you cook.

The mise en place does have its benefits. Organizing your ingredients in advance saves you time when cooking because the prep work is already done. You simply transfer the contents of the container into the proper pan or pot, and this is usually easier for younger assistants than, say, scraping an ingredient off the cutting board.

Incorporating a mise en place can be especially helpful when you are working with a menu that has several components prepared on the stove, as you can monitor your pans constantly without having to turn away to measure.

CUTTING

Unless your children are in their teens, you may want to handle all of the cutting yourself. But you can employ a younger assistant to scoop a chopped ingredient into a bowl (be sure to hold or place the knife far from little hands), and you can talk about what you're doing. Are you mincing, coarsely chopping, or doing something in between? Why would one recipe call for something to be cubed, while another calls for matchstick strips? If you do entrust your helper with knife work, take a moment to review the basics (see page 12).

MISE EN PLACE

Mise en place is a French term that refers to organizing and arranging your ingredients before cooking. In addition to washing, peeling, and chopping, as explained above, each one is measured and placed in an individual container.

ENJOYING THE MEAL

At long last, it's time to take off your apron, sit down, and enjoy the fruits of your labor. But a successful family dinner is about more than just the food, so follow these tips for an all-around wonderful meal. Bon appétit!

SET THE TABLE

If you keep your dining table free of clutter, setting it shouldn't take longer than a few minutes. If your family tends to stow items on the table, implement a new rule that on the morning of Sunday dinner, everyone has to gather and put away his or her things. You may have already assigned this task to one of your children as a household chore, but rotating it to your assistant, especially a younger one, is a good learning experience.

You can keep things simple, or get as fancy as you'd like—this is a great time to use a beautiful tablecloth or pretty placemats, or to bring out the wedding china you adore but hardly ever seem to use. If your family is on the larger side or you are having guests, ask your assistant to make place cards to mix things up. This can be as simple as a Post-it note. If you're really feeling ambitious, check out "Setting A Proper Table" on page 20. Otherwise, just cover the basics (you can even draw a sketch for younger children to follow):

Plate Center in front of the diner's chair; don't place too close to the edge of the table.

Salad bowl/plate or soup bowl On top of the dinner plate; you can also place to the side, especially if your family is in the habit of eating salad or soup with or after the main course.

Napkin To the left of the dinner plate.

Fork On top of the napkin.

Knife To the right of the dinner plate.

Spoon To the right of the knife. If your meal has no dishes that require a spoon, skip it and save yourself the extra cleanup.

Glass Above the dinner plate and to the right.

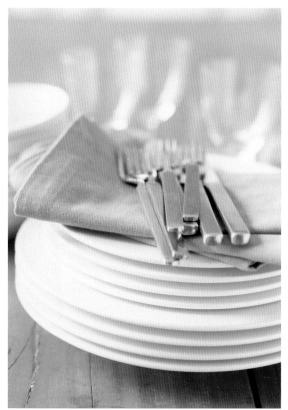

Cloth napkins can add a special touch to Sunday dinner.

FAMILY DISCUSSIONS

If your family is not in the habit of sitting down to dinner regularly, here's how to jump-start a conversation. Each week, pick a different family member to determine a Sunday dinner topic to discuss—this could range from an upcoming election to *Dora the Explorer.* If your family includes a broad age range, or is on the smaller side, have everyone come up with an idea, and cover them all.

Ask everyone at the table talk about her or his previous week. If a particular reminiscence sparks a longer discussion, just go with it—you always have next week's Sunday dinner to catch up.

Chatting about the upcoming week is a great way to bring your family together and plan ahead. Perhaps you didn't realize that two of your children need to be in different areas at the same time—can you carpool with another parent? Your spouse may be looking at a few late nights at the office, and you can adjust your meal plans accordingly. Younger children will benefit from a discussion of what their week will look like—and you can gently correct a 4-year-old who expects to have a play date every afternoon of the week.

Bread Feel free to skip bread plates, but if having one will make the dinner plate less messy, place above the dinner plate and to the left.

CHECK IN PERSONAL DEVICES

Unplug your family to help the conversation flow. Nothing curtails a special dinner faster than the sound of your spouse's ringtone or the sight of your 12-year-old furiously texting under the table. No matter what your policy is every other night of the week, insist on this rule for Sunday dinner: *No personal devices at the table.* Designate a drawer, basket, bowl, or even an empty shoebox that all family members can stash their turned-off personal devices in; have your assistant collect electronics.

CLEANING UP

Now that you've finished eating, here's how to make quick work of the aftermath.

TABLE

Your first step is to clear away the dishes between dinner and dessert. Have your spouse or an older child clear away each setting while you're getting dessert ready. Ask him or her to scrape the dishes into the garbage or down the disposal, and to stack them up the plates and bowls and place the silverware into the sink or a large serving bowl.

When the entire meal is over, clear away the rest of the table, then have a family member gather up the tablecloth, placemats and napkins if wash-able, and any dishtowels from the kitchen. He or she should place the bundle in the washing machine and start the load, or ask an adult to do it. If your table linens have suffered through the inevitable spills and splashes, keep a stain stick or spray handy in the kitchen for pretreating.

DISHES

If you don't have a dishwasher, be sure to have at least one helper in the kitchen to handle drying and putting away while you wash (or vice versa). If you do have a dishwasher, plan ahead so it's empty, or almost empty, before you start cooking Sunday dinner so you have plenty of room and don't have to rearrange and wrestle with your dishes.

LOADING IT RIGHT: DISHWASHER KNOW-HOW

A dishwasher can be the most helpful cleanup tool in the kitchen, but be sure to give your youngsters (and possibly your spouse?) a crash course in proper loading so that you don't have to redo a creative arrangement:

• *Pre-rinse dishes* if they're going to sit in the dishwasher all day or overnight or select the quick rinse cycle. If you're running a cycle right away, just scrape off the food and leave it at that.

• *Secure all plastics.* If you don't, they may flip and fill with water or fall onto the heating element and melt.

• *Never stack items.* The water spray won't be able to reach (or clean) the dish that's on top.

BOTTOM RACK

• *Load plates and bowls* so that the dirty side faces the water spray. Pots, pans, and casseroles should angle down for the best cleaning results.

• *Watch out for utensils with long, thin handles.* They might slip and keep the spray arm from spinning.

• *Make sure the spoons don't nest together.* Place some handles up and others down so that all surfaces get washed.

• *Tuck flat pans and platters* along the sides and back of the rack. Never place them in front, by the door—they'll keep the detergent from reaching the dishes. (*Tip*: For extra side space, move your flatware basket to the center if possible.)

• *Always separate your stainless steel and silver* (or silver-plated) flatware. If the two types touch in the wash, a reaction may occur and the silver could pit.

TOP RACK

• *Place glasses and mugs* between the tines—never on top. The tip of the prong can leave a water spot.

• *Arrange wineglasses carefully.* To help prevent breakage, don't let them touch one another or the top of the dishwasher.

• *Angle cups* as much as the rack design will allow to

keep water from pooling on the base of the upside-down cups. Still got puddles? Unload the bottom rack first to avoid the drip-down.

Detergent Do's: Powders, liquids, and packets can all clean well. But the detergent has to be fresh or it won't do the job. A good rule of thumb: Buy only what you can use up within two months. And you should always store it in a cool, dry spot (not under the sink, where the detergent can clump or deteriorate).

KITCHEN

Once you've taken care of the dishes, spend a few minutes tending to the rest of the kitchen with an older helper:

Work surfaces Wipe down all your countertops.

Stovetop and oven Clean off any spills on the stove or in the oven.

Pots and pans Dry and put away larger items that you washed by hand.

Dishtowels, kitchen sponge Put out fresh dishtowels and toss your kitchen sponge, dampened well, in the microwave for two minutes to kill bacteria.

Sink Sprinkle or spray cleanser in your sink and give it a quick scrub.

Once you're done, turn off the lights, hug your assistant, and bask in the afterglow of a wonderful meal. Now turn the page and get cooking!

1
BASICS

EQUIPMENT

A well-equipped kitchen is a must for cooking delicious meals. You can accomplish a lot with a good set of knives and a few well-chosen pots and pans. Just remember, you often get what you pay for. High-quality utensils, made from durable materials, last longer, so buy the best you can afford.

Stainless steel is easy to clean and not too heavy, but it isn't a very good conductor of heat; an aluminum or copper core is often added to improve its heat-conducting properties. By contrast, copper is an excellent conductor of heat and copper pots are gorgeous, but the pots must be polished and can be very heavy. Cast iron and aluminum are inexpensive and excellent heat conductors. Unfortunately, they react to acidic ingredients, such as tomatoes and wine, but they are also available enamel-coated.

ON THE STOVE

Here is a list of basic pots and pans that every kitchen should be equipped with:

Saucepan Three or four saucepans with lids, ranging from 1 to 4 quarts. They should be between 3½ to 4 inches deep, so you can stir without spilling food over the side.

Dutch oven These pots are ideal for braising roasts and stews on top of the stove as well as in the oven. A 5- to 6-quart Dutch oven is the most useful.

Skillets You'll need at least three sizes: small (8-inch), medium (9- to 10-inch), and large (12-inch).

Saucepot This wide, deep pot can be used for soups and stews. A 5-quart saucepot that has a tight-fitting lid is versatile.

Stockpot A tall, narrow, 6- to 8-quart stockpot can be called into action to cook many foods, including pasta, soups, stocks, lobster, and corn on the cob.

Basic cooking equipment: steamer, saucepans, grill pan, Dutch oven, thermometers, skillets, double boiler

Double boiler A saucepan topped with another covered saucepan; food is gently cooked in the top pan by water simmering in the bottom pan.

Grill pan This ridged skillet acts as a stovetop grill. Food can be cooked with little or no added fat; the ridges allow any rendered fat to drip away as the food cooks.

Griddle This flat metal pan can be heated on top of the stove to cook pancakes, French toast, cheese sandwiches, and bacon. Electric models (some have nonstick surfaces) are also available.

IN THE OVEN

Some of the most popular materials for bakeware include enameled cast iron (easy to clean and a good heat conductor), enameled steel (a reasonably priced, lightweight choice for roasting pans), stainless steel (moderately heavy and durable), aluminum (often laminated to create a nonstick surface), heat-resistant glass (a popular, inexpensive choice), and glass-ceramic (which can go from oven to freezer). Earthenware and stoneware are good for long, slow baking, like stews or beans.

Cake pans that have a dull heat-absorbing finish, such as aluminum, produce the best cakes. Avoid shiny metals, such as stainless steel, which reflect the heat, and dark metal pans, which absorb heat too quickly. When it comes to baking bread, choose heavy aluminum or dark metal pans for the best texture and a well-browned crust.

How to Measure a Pan

To measure a baking dish or pan, measure across the top of the dish from inside edge to inside edge. Measure the depth on the inside of the dish from the bottom to the rim.

Essential Bakeware Roundup

Baking dish A large, fairly shallow oval or rectangular dish with sides about 2 inches high; usually glass or ceramic. It's good to have a variety of sizes, but 10" by 15", 13" by 9", and 11" by 7" are the most commonly used.

Baking pan Similar to a baking dish but made of metal; the sides are 1½ to 2 inches high. You'll want an 8-inch square, a 9-inch square, and a 13" by 9" pan.

Bundt pan Sometimes called a fluted tube pan. A

Basic baking and roasting pans: metal loaf pan, oval baking dish, jelly-roll pan, cookie sheet, roasting pan and rack, round cake pan, square baking pan, springform pan

10-inch, 12-cup size is good for most needs.

Cake pan Layer cakes are usually baked in 8- or 9-inch round pans (you'll need two or three of each); baking pans are used for rectangular and square cakes.

Casserole Round, oval, square, or rectangular, this lidded dish can be glass, ceramic, or enameled metal.

Cookie sheets For the best air circulation and for even browning, choose shiny, heavy, metal cookie sheets with one or two slightly raised sides. Double-thick insulated pans protect against overbrowning. Nonstick surfaces are another option.

Custard cups Purchase glass cups or ceramic ramekins with a 6-ounce capacity.

Jelly-roll pan Use a standard aluminum 15½" by 10½" pan for jelly-roll cakes.

Loaf pan Standard sizes are 9" by 5" and 8½" by 4½". There is a substantial volume difference between the two.

Muffin tins To bake muffins and cupcakes, use standard 2½" by 1¼" muffin-pan cups; 1¾" by 1" mini muffin-pan cups are nice to have too.

The recipes in this book have been perfected for use at sea level. At higher altitudes, adjustments in the cooking time, temperature, and ingredients could be necessary.

At sea level, water boils at 212°F. With each additional 500 feet of altitude, the boiling point drops 1°F. Even though the boiling point is lower, it takes longer to generate the heat required to cook food. Therefore, at high altitudes, foods boiled in water (such as pasta and beans) will take longer to come to a boil and will require longer cooking times than our recipes suggest. The processing times for canning foods and the blanching times for freezing vegetables will vary, too.

At high altitudes, cake recipes may need slight adjustments in the proportions of flour, leavening, liquid, eggs, etc. These adjustments will vary from recipe to recipe, and no set guidelines can be given. Many cake mixes now carry special directions on the label for high-altitude preparation.

High altitudes can also affect the rising of doughs and batters, deep-frying, candy making, and other aspects of food preparation. For complete information and special recipes for your area, call or write to the home agent at your county cooperative extension office or to the home economics department of your local utility company or state university.

Pie plate The standard size is 9" by 1"; deep-dish pie plates are 9½" by 1½" or 9½" by 2". Glass, dark metal, and aluminum pans yield crisp, nicely browned piecrusts.

Roasting pan A large deep pan typically made of stainless steel, enameled steel, or aluminum. A rectangular roasting pan with a rack is the most useful.

Springform pan 9" by 3" and 10" by 2½" are the ones most often called for.

Tart pan A shallow metal pan with fluted sides and a removable bottom that comes in many shapes and sizes: 9" by 1" and 11" by 1" round pans are the most common.

Tube pan Comes in 9- and 10-inch diameters.

UTENSIL CENTRAL

In addition to pots and pans, every kitchen needs other helpful tools. Here are some we find indispensable:

Bristle brushes Use one for cleaning pots and one for scrubbing vegetables.

Colander Choose a large colander with a stable footed base; the more holes it has, the more quickly food can drain.

Cooling racks If you bake a lot of cookies, you should have at least two large wire racks. Bakers who like to make layer cakes should have three or four small round racks.

Corkscrew A tool used to remove the corks from wine bottles. They are available at most kitchenware stores in a range of prices.

Cutting boards Plastic boards are lightweight and easy to clean in the dishwasher, but wooden boards are extremely durable and don't attract or retain any more bacteria than plastic ones.

Grater This flat or box-shaped tool can grate (small holes), shred (large holes), or slice (large slots). We love Microplane® graters for their sharpness and ease of use.

Measuring cups For liquids, use clear glass or plastic cups with pouring spouts. It's useful to have two sizes: a 1-cup measure for smaller amounts and a 2- or 4-cup measure for larger amounts. To measure dry ingredients accurately, use metal or plastic cups that come in nested sets of ¼ cup, ⅓ cup, ½ cup, and 1 cup.

Measuring spoons Come in nesting sets; stainless-steel spoons are the most durable. Most sets include ¼ teaspoon, ½ teaspoon, 1 teaspoon, and 1 tablespoon.

Mixing bowls Stainless-steel bowls are the most versatile because they react quickly to changes in temperature. Glass or ceramic bowls work well to insulate rising yeast dough.

Rolling pins Heavy pins, either hardwood or marble, work best for rolling out dough.

Sieve/strainer A wire sieve can be used to sift ingredients or strain liquids. Buy a few sizes with different mesh gauges.

Spatulas To turn food, use heatproof or metal spatulas (pancake turners). Rubber spatulas are used for mixing and folding; they're not heatproof. Silicon spatulas are heatproof. And a long, narrow metal spatula is a must for frosting cakes.

Thermometers Meat thermometers are vital when roasting meats and poultry, and many options are available. Instant-read thermometers, which register up to 220°F, are very accurate. Probe-type thermometers give a digital reading on a unit that is placed outside the oven. Candy thermometers register temperatures up to 400°F and can be used for candy making and deep-frying. An oven thermometer is the best way to accurately check the temperature of an oven, because control dials and thermostats are notoriously inaccurate. Optional, but nice to have, are freezer and refrigerator thermometers.

Tongs Spring-action tongs are the best for picking up foods and for turning meats without piercing them.

Vegetable peeler Swivel-blade peelers remove less peel than fixed-blade peelers; they conform to the shape of the food.

Whisk Use the right whisk for the job. A medium-size whisk is good for sauces, vinaigrettes, and batters. Flat paddle-shaped whisks are perfect for getting into the corners of roasting pans when making pan gravies. Large balloon-shaped whisks are ideal for beating air into heavy cream or egg whites.

Nice-to-Have Extras

Adjustable-blade slicer Use to slice, cut into matchstick strips, and waffle-cut. Adjustable-blade slicers range from the classic and pricey metal mandoline to lightweight plastic models that do a great job for much less money.

Apple corer This cylindrical tool neatly cores whole apples as well as pears. Buy the largest size because it will easily remove all the core.

Egg beater This hand-powered mixer can also be used for whipping cream. It's low-tech but useful.

Ice-cream maker Available in manual and electric models; some have insulated liners that must be frozen overnight.

Juicer Use for extracting fruit and vegetable juices. One of the most practical models is a simple ridged cone that easily juices citrus fruits. Small electric versions are great when you need a large quantity of juice.

Kitchen scissors For cutting kitchen string, snipping fresh herbs, and trimming artichoke leaves. Shears, which are larger and spring-loaded, make cutting up poultry simple. Buy sturdy models made of stainless steel.

Melon baller Besides scooping perfect globes of melon (and potatoes), this tool neatly cores halved apples and pears.

Mortar and pestle Use for grinding spices and herbs. You crush with the pestle (the batlike tool) in the mortar (the bowl).

Pastry bag For decorating cakes and pies, forming spritz cookies, and creating beautifully shaped pastries. Disposable plastic pastry bags don't retain odors and flavors as plastic-lined canvas bags do.

Pastry blender This tool's metal wires easily cut cold fat into flour for tart dough, pastry dough, biscuits, and scones.

Pastry brush Use to brush dough with melted butter or beaten egg and to apply glazes; also great for dusting excess flour from dough. When buying, look for well-anchored natural bristle brushes in widths of 1 to 1½ inches.

Potato masher Perfect for cooked potatoes and other root vegetables and for turning cooked beans into a chunky puree.

Ruler Keep a ruler in the kitchen for measuring pans and pastry shapes as well as for other tasks.

Salad spinner Uses centrifugal force to dry greens, preventing dressed salads from getting watered down.

Skewers A must for kabobs. Always soak wooden and bamboo skewers in water for 30 minutes before using to prevent them from burning on the grill.

Steamer The collapsible metal style easily fits into various-sized pots and pans. There is also a version that consists of a saucepan with a perforated bowl-like insert that allows the steam to penetrate. Bamboo steamers fit into woks.

Zester Pulled across the peel of citrus fruit, it removes the colorful, flavorful outer layer, leaving the bitter pith behind.

Sharpening Up on Knives

The importance of good knives cannot be overemphasized. Poorly made knives make cutting and chopping tiresome work, while good knives will enable you to whip through these jobs with ease. If you take good care of your fine knives, they'll last a lifetime.

High-carbon stainless steel, an alloy that contains a large proportion of carbon, makes excellent knives that sharpen well. Some cooks prefer carbon-steel knives because they hold a very sharp edge, but they also corrode and stain easily. Knives that purport to never need sharpening have two drawbacks: The blades are finely serrated, so their ridges can tear food instead of cutting it. When the knives eventually do need sharpening, it isn't possible.

Before buying a knife, hold it in your hand to see if it feels comfortable. The best knives are made of a solid piece of metal (called the tang) that goes all the way through the handle. The extra weight of the tang gives a knife better balance.

Using the proper knife for each kitchen chore is more efficient and will make the job easier, ultimately saving you time in preparation. These knives should be in every well-run kitchen:
• Chef's knife (for slicing, chopping, and mincing)
• Paring knife (for fruits and vegetables)
• Long serrated knife (for slicing breads, cakes, and thin-skinned fruits and vegetables)
• Carving knife (for slicing meats). It often comes in a set with a carving fork.

• Thin-bladed boning knife (for trimming fat and cutting poultry and meat)
• Slicing knife (for cutting thin slices of meat). It has a scalloped edge and a round tip, so you won't poke a hole in the roast
• Heavy cleaver (for cutting up poultry)

COOKING BASICS

If you master just a few fundamental cooking skills, you will be assured success in the kitchen. Measuring ingredients may be a simple task, but if performed carelessly, it may mean the difference between success and failure. Learn how to chop, slice, and cut properly and your meal preparation time will be reduced. And remember, as with other skills, practice makes perfect.

MEASURING BASICS

Measure ingredients carefully, and you'll get consistent results each time you prepare a recipe. Every kitchen needs liquid measuring cups, dry measuring cups, and measuring spoons.
• For liquids, use clear glass measuring cups with pouring spouts. Place the cup on a level surface and add the desired amount of liquid; bend down to check the accuracy of the measure at eye level (do not lift up the cup).
• For dry ingredients, use standard-size metal or plastic cups that can be leveled off.
• Nesting sets of graduated measuring spoons are used to measure both liquid and dry ingredients.

Basic measuring cups and spoons: 1-, 2-, and 4-cup glass measuring cups, set of dry measuring cups, set of measuring spoons

We use the "spoon-and-sweep" method for measuring dry ingredients such as flour, sugar, and cocoa. To measure flour, for example, stir it with a fork or whisk to aerate it (flour tends to pack down during storage). Lightly spoon the flour into a dry measuring cup to overflowing, then level it off with the straight edge of a knife or narrow metal spatula: Don't pack the flour or shake the cup. If a recipe calls for 1 cup sifted flour, sift the flour, then spoon it into the cup. If you need 1 cup flour, sifted, measure the flour and then sift. Do not "dip and sweep" (use the measuring cup to scoop the flour); it packs too much flour into the cup.

Butter and margarine come in premarked sticks, so there's no need to use a measuring cup. Use the markings on the wrapper to measure the desired amount, then cut it off. One 4-ounce (¼ pound) stick of butter or margarine equals 8 tablespoons or ½ cup.

Ingredients such as vegetable shortening, butter, and brown sugar, should be firmly packed (pressed) into dry measuring cups or spoons and then leveled off.

Before measuring sticky ingredients, such as corn syrup or molasses, coat the measuring cup or spoon with vegetable oil or nonstick cooking spray, so the item can slide out easily.

If you have any doubts about the volume of a baking dish or casserole, pour a measured amount of water into the dish, right up to the top. Or double-check a baking pan's dimensions with a ruler; even a 1-inch difference can affect your baking success.

CUTTING BASICS

For the best results, use a chef's knife, and sharpen it on a steel before each use. To prevent the cutting board from slipping, place a damp towel underneath. Hold the knife handle in your right hand near the blade. Your thumb should be on the left side of the handle and your fingers close together and wrapped around the other side of the handle.

In this book, we coarsely chop, slice, cube, cut into matchstick strips, finely chop, and mince. Here's how:

Coarsely chop To cut food into ½- to ¾-inch irregular pieces: When chopping, the tip of the knife remains on the cutting board; the knife handle is raised and lowered in a rocking motion while the knife is moved from left to right. If necessary, tuck under the fingers of your left hand and carefully push the food toward the blade.

Chop To cut food into small irregular pieces about the size of peas: Roughly cut up the food, then move the knife through the food until you have the desired size.

Finely chop To chop food into very small irregular pieces, less than ¼ inch.

Mince To cut into tiny irregular pieces, less than ⅛ inch. We use this term only for ginger.

Cube To cut into ½-inch blocks: First cut the food lengthwise into ½-inch-thick slices. Stack the slices and cut into ½-inch-wide sticks. Then cut crosswise into ½-inch cubes.

Matchstick strips First, cut the food into slices 2 inches long and ⅛ inch thick. Stack the slices; cut lengthwise into ⅛-inch-wide sticks.

FOOD SAFETY AND STORAGE

Use these guidelines to help keep the food in your kitchen wholesome and safe to eat.

RULES OF FOOD SAFETY

Keep It Clean

Good old-fashioned cleanliness is the best safeguard against harmful bacteria. Keep a clean kitchen. Always wash and dry your hands before handling food. Frequently wash kitchen towels, dishcloths, and sponges. Rinse fruits and vegetables thoroughly before eating. Sterilize cutting boards once a week in a solution of 1 tablespoon bleach per 1 gallon water.

Avoid Cross-Contamination

Don't put cooked meat (or any ready-to-eat food) on a plate that has been in contact with raw meat, poultry, or fish. It's a good idea to have several cutting boards: one for raw meats, poultry, and fish; one for vegetables and cheese; and perhaps a third for fruits, nuts, and chocolate.

Cook It Right

To kill harmful bacteria that may be present in raw eggs, fish, poultry, and meat, it's essential to cook these foods thoroughly. The United States Department of Agriculture recommends cooking them to at least 160°F. At this temperature, however, food (especially meat) may be cooked beyond your preference. If you cook it less, some risk is involved, so the choice is ultimately a personal one. An instant-read thermometer is the easiest way to check for doneness. To check visually, follow these guidelines: Cook red meat to at least medium-rare, pork until the juices run clear and the meat retains just a trace of pink, poultry until the juices run clear, fish just until opaque throughout, and egg yolks and whites until thickened and set. Always cook ground meat until no pink remains. When cooking egg-based sauces, be sure the final temperature is no lower than 160°F.

Keep Hot Foods Hot and Cold Foods Cold

The safe zones for storing food are below 40°F and above 140°F. Keep food below or above these temperatures, and you'll discourage bacterial growth (bacteria love a moist, warm environment). Don't leave food out at room temperature for longer than two hours. In hot weather, protein foods such as chicken, egg salad, or any food containing mayonnaise should not be left out of the refrigerator for more than one hour. It's also unwise to cook food in stages. For example, don't partially cook fish, poultry, or meat, then return to it later to finish cooking. Even when food is stored in the refrigerator between the cooking stages, safe temperatures may not be maintained and bacteria could develop.

Treat Leftovers with Respect

Refrigerate leftovers as soon as possible. Divide large amounts among smaller containers for quicker cooling. Date all leftovers so you know how long you've had them. If you have any doubt about a food's freshness, throw it out.

REFRIGERATOR KNOW-HOW

Don't take your refrigerator for granted. Help it do its job by following a few simple rules:

Be sure the temperature of your refrigerator remains between 33° and 40°F; use a refrigerator thermometer for extra insurance. To prevent spoilage, store foods on a

---

HOW LONG WILL IT KEEP?

Foods frozen for longer than the recommended times aren't harmful—they just won't be at their peak flavor and texture.

FOOD	TIME IN FREEZER (0°F)
Milk	3 months
Butter	6 to 9 months
Cheese, hard (Cheddar, Swiss)	6 months
Cheese, soft (Brie, Bel Paese)	6 months
Cream, half-and-half	4 months
Sour cream	don't feeze
Eggs (raw yolks, whites)	1 year
Frankfurters (opened or unopened packages)	1 to 2 months
Luncheon meats (opened or unopened packages)	1 to 2 months
Bacon	1 month
Sausage, raw, links or patties	1 to 2 months
Ham, fully cooked (whole, half, slices)	1 to 2 months
Ground or stew meat	3 to 4 months
Steaks	6 to 12 months
Chops	3 to 6 months
Roasts	4 to 12 months
Chicken or turkey, whole	1 year
Chicken or turkey, pieces	9 months
Casseroles, cooked, poultry	4 to 6 months
Casseroles, cooked, meat	2 to 3 months
Soups and stews	2 to 3 months
Fish, lean (cod, flounder, haddock)	6 months
Fish, fatty (bluefish, mackerel, salmon)	2 to 3 months
Fish, cooked	4 to 6 months
Fish, smoked	2 months in vacuum pack
Shrimp, scallops, squid, shucked clams, mussels, oysters	3 to 6 months
Pizza	1 to 2 months
Breads and rolls, yeast	3 to 6 month
Breads, quick	2 to 3 months
Cakes, unfrosted	3 months
Cheesecakes	2 to 3 months
Cookies, baked	3 months
Cookie dough, raw	2 to 3 months
Pies, fruit, unbaked	8 months
Pies, custard or meringue-topped	don't freeze
Piecrust, raw	2 to 3 months
Nuts, salted	6 to 8 months
Nuts, unsalted	9 to 12 months

rotating basis: Place newly stored items at the back of the shelves and move older items to the front.

Store meat, fish, and poultry on a plate to catch any drips; if you don't plan to cook them within two days, freeze them immediately. Never store eggs in the open egg compartment in the refrigerator door; it's too warm. Eggs should be kept in their original container to prevent them from absorbing the odors of other foods. For this same reason, store cheese, cream, milk, yogurt, margarine, and butter tightly closed in their containers or packaging or wrap airtight.

PANTRY STORAGE

Unless otherwise noted, these pantry staples fare best in a cool, dry place. For more information on ingredients such as flour, pasta, and grains, see the specific chapter introductions.

Baking powder Once opened, it will keep for up to six months. To test its effectiveness, add ½ teaspoon to ½ cup warm water; it should bubble vigorously.

Bread crumbs Store dried bread crumbs for up to six months or, for better flavor, refrigerate for up to two years.

Honey Lasts indefinitely; if it crystallizes, remove the lid and place the jar in a bowl of hot water. Stir until the crystals dissolve.

Hot pepper sauce Refrigerate after opening.

Olive oil Keep in a cool, dark place for up to six months. Don't buy more than you can use; it can turn rancid, especially if stored in a warm place.

Pancake syrup It will keep for up to nine months (if stored longer, the syrup will thin and the flavor will weaken).

Peanut butter Unopened it will hold for a year in your cupboard. Refrigerate after opening to keep it from becoming rancid.

Soy sauce Unopened it will keep for one year. Once opened, refrigerate to keep for an additional year.

Spices and dried herbs Store in opaque containers in a cool, dark place (not near the stove) for up to one year. After that, herbs and spices begin to lose their flavor. It's a good idea to write the date of purchase on the label. Sniff before using: If the aroma is weak, discard and buy a new supply.

Vegetable oil Store in a cool, dark place for up to six months.

Vinegar Unopened it will keep indefinitely. The sediment that sometimes appears is harmless; strain off the vinegar, if you wish. Once opened store for up to six months. Vinegar with added flavorings, such as herbs, should be strained into a clean bottle as soon as the vinegar level drops below the top of the ingredients.

STORING FRESH HERBS

Most fresh herbs are highly perishable, so buy them in small quantities. To store for a few days, immerse the roots or stems in 2 inches of water. Cover with a plastic bag; refrigerate.

To dry fresh herbs (this works best with sturdy herbs like rosemary and thyme), rinse lightly and pat dry with paper towels. Hang them upside down, in bunches, in a dry, dark place. When the leaves become brittle (it typically takes from a few days up to one week), pick them off and discard the stems. Store the dried leaves in a tightly covered opaque container in a cool, dry place.

To freeze herbs, rinse lightly, pat dry, and remove the stems. Place them in plastic containers or heavy-duty zip-tight plastic bags. When frozen, herbs darken, but their flavor remains. There's no need to thaw frozen herbs; add them directly to the pot. Or place a few herbs (leaves only) in each section of an ice cube tray. Add enough water to cover; freeze. Unmold and store the cubes in heavy-duty zip-tight plastic bags. Add the cubes to simmering soups, sauces, or stews.

TAKING FOOD ON THE ROAD

Whenever food is removed from the refrigerator, it can easily warm to temperatures that encourage bacterial growth. But with some planning, you can avoid potential problems.

For picnics, use two small coolers rather than one large one. Use one cooler for nonperishables, such as fruit and beverages, and the other for perishable items, such as meats, poultry, salads, and cheese. Remember: A cooler cannot make foods colder than they already are, so chill foods thoroughly before placing them in the cooler. To preserve the chill, don't open the lid for longer or more often than necessary.

Double-wrap meat and poultry in zip-tight plastic bags so the juices don't leak out and contaminate other foods. Pack perishable items, like meat, next to the ice packs. Delicate items, such as green salads and slaws, should be stored away from the ice to prevent freezing.

Thermal carrying bags are the most convenient way to transport hot foods, but a cooler can also maintain the temperature of hot foods for a few hours. If you are bringing a hot dish to a party, heat it until piping hot. Wrap the covered dish in a thick layer of newspaper to insulate it and keep the heat in, then place in a cooler that isn't much bigger than the dish.

EATING WELL

The message is simple: Eat well to stay well. The good news is that you don't need a graduate degree in nutrition to eat healthfully on a daily basis. What follows are some guidelines and information to help you make informed decisions about what you and your family should eat to maintain a balanced diet.

DIETARY GUIDELINES FOR AMERICANS

• Consume a variety of nutrient-dense foods and beverages within the basic food groups. Choose foods that limit your intake of saturated and trans fats, cholesterol, added sugars, salt, and alcohol.

USING THE NUTRITIONAL VALUES IN THIS BOOK

At the bottom of each recipe, you'll find nutritional information. To aid you in using this information, see "Nutrients: The Big Three" (page 16) and "Understanding Food Labels" (right) for the recommended daily nutrient levels. Aim to balance higher-fat recipes with leaner accompaniments. For example, serve lasagna with a green salad tossed with lowfat dressing, skim milk, and fresh fruit for dessert.
• Our nutritional calculations do not include any optional ingredients or garnishes.
• When alternative ingredients are given (such as margarine), our calculations are based on the first item listed.
• Unless otherwise noted, whole milk has been used.

UNDERSTANDING FOOD LABELS

Food labels help you make informed choices about the foods to include in your diet.

The Percent Daily Values reflect the percentage of the recommended daily amount of a nutrient in a serving (based on 2,000 calories daily). You can "budget" your intake of nutrients by adding up these percentages. For example, the label below shows a food containing 13 percent of the daily value for fat. If the next food you eat has a 10 percent daily value for fat, you've already had 23 percent of your total fat allowance for the day. When it comes to fat, saturated fat, sodium, and cholesterol, try to keep the daily values below 100 percent. Aim for 100 percent of fiber, vitamins A and C, calcium, and iron. (Other vitamins and minerals may also appear on labels.)

The Daily Values footnote includes a chart that shows some Daily Values for diets containing 2,000 and 2,500 calories. Your own daily values may be higher or lower.

Food labels are required to have an ingredients list. The ingredients are listed in descending order according to their weight. This enables you to easily discern which food products contain larger amounts of ingredients that are healthful.

Nutrition Facts
Serving Size 2 pieces (29g)
Servings Per Container 15

Amount Per Serving	
Calories 150	Calories from Fat 80

	% Daily Value*
Total Fat 8g	**13%**
Saturated Fat 5g	**27%**
Cholesterol 25mg	**8%**
Sodium 115mg	**5%**
Total Carbohydrate 18g	**6%**
Dietary Fiber 0g	**0%**
Sugars 6g	
Protein 2g	

Vitamin A 0%	•	Vitamin C 0%
Calcium 2%	•	Iron 2%

* Percent Daily Values are based on a 2,000 calorie diet.

• Engage in regular physical activity and reduce sedentary activities to promote health, psychological well-being, and a healthy body weight.

• Consume 2 cups of fruit and 2½ cups of vegetables (dark green and orange-colored vegetables, legumes, and starchy vegetables) each day for a 2,000-calorie diet, adjusting the amount as needed.

• Consume three or more 1-ounce-equivalent servings of whole grains each day.

• Consume 3 cups of fat-free or low-fat milk or equivalent dairy products per day.

• Derive less than 10 percent of your calories from saturated fat and less than 300mg of cholesterol per day. Avoid trans fats.

• Keep your total fat intake between 20 and 35 percent of your calories, with most fats coming from polyunsaturated and monounsaturated sources, such as fish, nuts, and vegetable oils.

• Choose fiber-rich fruits, vegetables, and whole grains each day.

• Consume less than 2,300mg (about 1 teaspoon) of sodium each day.

• Women who choose to drink alcohol should limit themselves to one drink per day; men should limit themselves to no more than two drinks per day.

For the complete recommendations, go to www.healthierus.gov/dieteryguidelines.

NUTRIENTS: THE BIG THREE

Our bodies need three essential nutrients: carbohydrates, proteins, and fats.

Carbohydrates The right kind of carbohydrates is the mainstay of a well-balanced diet. "Good" carbohydrates include fruits, vegetables, and whole grains. Carbohydrates come in many forms. They can be made up of dietary fiber, starch, or sugar. Diets rich in dietary fiber have been shown to have a reduced risk of coronary heart disease, among other benefits, and research indicates that whole-grain eaters are thinner than people who eat few whole-grain foods. Fiber, which is found in the bran layer of some grains, including whole wheat, is credited with some of the health benefits of whole grains. When whole wheat is processed to make white flour, the healthful bran layer is removed, along with the disease-fighting antioxidants in the bran. The latest government recommendations are that at least half of your grains should be whole grain (see "How to Spot a Whole Grain," opposite).

The starch and sugar in carbohydrates supply the body with the energy it needs for normal body functions, including brain functions, heartbeat, breathing, and digestion, as well as for exercise such as walking, running, and cycling. When carbohydrates are digested, they become blood sugar (glucose), which is then used as fuel in our bodies. In general, the less sugar you eat the better. This doesn't, however, include the naturally occurring sugar in fruit, milk, or yogurt. You need to limit the *added* sugar that comes from sweeteners, including white sugar, brown sugar, honey, maple syrup, high-fructose corn syrup, dextrose, sucrose, fruit juice concentrate, and other sweeteners. Remember that starch is an important part of a balanced diet. Look for good carbs, such as whole-wheat pasta, whole-grain polenta, buckwheat, and oatmeal.

Unfortunately, it is not always easy to tell if a product is a whole grain–rich food. So here are some clues:

• Look for the word *whole* in the ingredients list.

• See where the whole grain falls in the list of ingredients. Remember that ingredients are listed in order of their weight: If a whole grain is listed first and is the only grain, there is a lot of whole grain in the product. If the first ingredient is *wheat flour* (which is really white flour), followed by some sort of sweetener, then *whole-wheat flour* is not the dominant grain.

• Check the amount of dietary fiber. In general, 100-percent whole-grain products should have at least 2 grams of fiber per ounce (29 grams) or per 80 calories; crackers at least 3 grams fiber per ounce; pasta at least 5 grams of fiber per 2 ounces dried. *For more information, go to* www.wholegrainscouncil.org.

Proteins The body needs protein to produce new body tissue. They are also a great weight-loss friend, as protein helps keep you feeling full for hours after eating. Too much protein, however, is unhealthy; it can stress the kidneys, and if it comes from fatty meat, it is also filling you with saturated fat. Beef, chicken, fish, pork, lamb, and other meats and tofu and other soy products are the richest sources of protein. Beans (black, pinto, etc.), lentils, cheese, milk, and yogurt are the next highest. A small amount of protein can also be found in grains, bread, and other starches and in vegetables. Ideally, your plate should look like this: half-filled with vegetables or fruits, a quarter with starches, and another quarter with protein-rich foods (and a little fat).

Fats The government guideline for fat consumption is 20 to 35 percent of your total daily calories, which is a wide range. Much more important than the total fat is the amount of saturated and trans fat in your diet. Here's what you need to know about these fats:

When an excess of saturated fat is consumed, it raises your blood cholesterol level, increasing your risk of heart disease and stroke. Saturated fat is found naturally in foods, but it is especially concentrated in fatty animal-based foods, such as butter and chicken skin and in some oils, such as palm and coconut. Even "good" oils like olive and canola contain a little saturated fat, so you can't avoid it entirely. For a heart-healthy diet you should derive less than 10 percent of your total calories from saturated fat, which is a maximum of 15 grams of saturated fat daily, based on a 1,500-calorie diet.

Even worse than saturated fat is trans fat, which not only raises the LDL ("bad cholesterol") but also lowers the HDL ("good cholesterol"). It is formed by a process called hydrogenation, which turns oils into semisolids like margarine and shortening. On the ingredients list these oils appear as partially hydrogenated oils or shortening and are reflected in the trans fat total on the Nutrition Facts label. It is important to keep your intake of trans fat low. Here are some tips:
• Use canola or olive oil whenever possible.
• Limit—or avoid—processed foods made with partially hydrogenated oils, or with oils high in saturated fat (palm, palm kernel, coconut) or with butter.
• Use "0 trans" or "trans fat–free" margarine.

HOW TO INTERPRET PACKAGE INFORMATION

While the Nutrition Facts label can tell you a lot about a food, you need to check the ingredients list to see what you're really eating. Is your breakfast cereal made with whole grains or does your favorite salad dressing contain oil that is high in saturated fat, for example.

By law, ingredients lists must be ordered by weight. The heaviest ingredient goes first, followed by the next heaviest, and so on. It is not a good sign if sugar is the first ingredient in a cereal or when bad fats like partially hydrogenated soybean and cottonseed oils are the third ingredient listed on a can of biscuit dough.

HOW TO SPOT A WHOLE GRAIN

To help you when shopping for whole grains, here are the words you should look for in the ingredients list:

IT'S A WHOLE GRAIN IF IT'S CALLED:	IT'S NOT A WHOLE GRAIN IF IT'S CALLED:
Brown (also black, red, purple) rice	Corn flour or cornmeal
Buckwheat	Enriched flour
Bulgur (cracked wheat)	Multigrain (this means various grains, not necessarily whole)
Millet	Pumpernickel
Quinoa	Rice or rice flour
Sorghum	Rye flour or rye
Triticale	Stone-ground wheat (it needs to say "stone-ground whole wheat")
Whole-grain corn	Unbleached wheat flour
Whole oats and oatmeal	Wheat or wheat flour
Whole rye	Wheat germ (not a whole grain but very good for you)
Whole spelt	Whole barley (pearl barley; not a whole grain but very good for you)
Whole wheat	
Wild rice	

Below is a list of common phrases found on many food packages:

Cholesterol free or No cholesterol Don't be fooled by the words *No cholesterol* written across the label of a jar of peanut butter or bottle of canola oil. If you turn to the Nutrition Facts label, you'll see that no brand of either food has cholesterol—and never did! Only foods of animal origin contain cholesterol. But manufacturers hope you don't know that.

Light This word is used to describe fat content, taste, or color. If the manufacturer is describing the fat content as "light," the product has at least 50 percent less fat than the original. The label must also say "50% less fat than our regular product." "Light" olive oil, on the other hand, describes the oil's color. The oil is as caloric as regular olive oil but has been processed to remove some of its flavor. A muffin mix can say "light and fluffy" as a way to describe its texture or consistency.

Low-fat or Fat-free Low-fat products must contain 3 grams or less fat per serving and fat-free products must have less than 0.5 grams of fat per serving. But check the number of calories—that number could be very high. It is easy to gain lots of weight eating fat-free cookies because they are loaded with sugar.

Low sodium or Light in sodium This means that the sodium was cut by at least 50 percent over the original product. Be careful when using a "low" version of a super-high-sodium food such as soy sauce or soup. You can still end up consuming a lot of sodium. Check the numbers on the Nutrition Facts label.

Sugar-free, No added sugars, Without added sugars A sugar-free chocolate candy may not contain a speck of sugar, but it's still got plenty of fat and calories. Be sure to check out the Nutrition Facts label to know how many calories and grams of saturated fat you're consuming.

Sweetened with fruit juice, Fruit juice sweetener, or Fruit juice concentrate These sweeteners are made by reducing fruit juice—usually grape juice—into a sticky sweetener. These sweeteners are not nutritious; they are just like sugar.

KEEP IT LIGHT

In general, animal products are higher in fat than plant foods, but it's not necessary to cut out all meat and dairy products to keep your fat intake reasonable. Low-fat dairy foods, lean and well-trimmed meat, and skinless poultry provide the same amounts of vitamins and minerals as their fattier counterparts. Skinless poultry, fish, dry beans, and split peas are the "slimmest" foods in this category. By removing the skin from poultry, you reduce the fat by almost one half. Most seafood is low in fat and also contains beneficial omega-3 oils, which have been linked to lowering blood cholesterol. Dry beans also provide the body with fiber, which is necessary for digestion.

You can enjoy red meat if you choose lean cuts and trim away all the visible fat (marbled fat cannot be trimmed away). Here are some good choices:
• Beef eye round, top round, tenderloin, top sirloin, flank steak, top loin, ground beef. Choose ground sirloin; it's 90 to 93 percent lean.
• Veal cutlets (from the leg) and loin chops
• Pork tenderloin, boneless top loin roast, loin chops, and boneless sirloin chops
• Lamb, boneless leg (shank portions), loin roast, loin chops, leg cubes for kabobs

Trimming the Fat
Here are some suggestions to make trimming excess fat from your diet easier:
• Choose lean cuts of meat and trim off all the visible fat before cooking. Remove skin from poultry before or after cooking.
• Broil meat on a rack so the fat can drip away.
• Substitute ground chicken or ground turkey for ground beef. Look for ground turkey breast or chicken breast; otherwise, it may contain skin and therefore have as much fat as ground beef.
• Substitute protein-packed dried legumes, like beans and lentils, for meat in casseroles.
• Chill soups and stews overnight so you can remove all the hardened fat from the surface.
• Be skimpy with fat. Use nonstick pans and nonstick cooking spray, or "sauté" in a small amount of broth or water. Don't just pour oil into a skillet; it's easy to add too much. Measure or use a pastry brush to coat pans with a thin layer of oil. When baking, coat pans with a

spritz of nonstick cooking spray instead of oils or fats. (Kitchenware shops now carry oil sprayers you can fill with your favorite oil.)

• Experiment with lowfat or skim milk, lowfat sour cream and cheese, and nonfat yogurt: they provide the same amounts of calcium and protein as the whole-milk varieties but with less fat or none at all.

• When making dips, substitute nonfat plain yogurt for sour cream.

• Use fresh herbs and zesty seasonings liberally.

• Choose angel food cake instead of pound cake, especially when making cake-based desserts like trifle.

• To reduce fat and cholesterol, you can substitute 2 egg whites for 1 whole egg in recipes, but don't substitute egg whites for all the whole eggs when baking; the dessert will have better texture and flavor if you retain a yolk or two.

• Replace sour cream with buttermilk or yogurt in recipes for baked goods.

ENTERTAINING

Everyone loves a party, but the trick is to ensure that the cook has a good time, too. Whether you're planning a casual backyard barbecue, an elegant dinner, or a holiday buffet, a few simple strategies will guarantee you stress-free entertaining.

THINK AHEAD

• All good parties are well organized. Start with a few lists: a guest list, a menu, a shopping list, and a menu preparation timetable.

• Invite guests two to three weeks ahead. Depending on the event you may want to specify the appropriate dress, the type of food that will be served, and the expected duration of the party.

• Simplicity is the key to a successful menu, especially when you're expecting a large number of guests. The majority of the dishes should be those you've cooked and enjoyed in the past. Take advantage of dishes that taste even better when made ahead. It's also smart to include some dishes that freeze well.

• Look for food preparation time-savers. For example, if you're making a shrimp dish, purchase peeled, deveined shrimp instead of cleaning them yourself.

• Let the menu reflect the time of year. Use seasonal fruits and vegetables whenever possible. They will be at their peak of flavor and reasonably priced.

• Be sure you have a well-stocked bar with plenty of choices for nondrinkers. And keep lots of ice on hand—even more than you think you'll need.

• At least one week before the party, check your supply of chairs, glasses, serving dishes, and utensils. Consider the space needed to enable guests to circulate easily and, if necessary, shift or remove furniture.

BUFFET BASICS

Buffets are great for carefree entertaining; just put out the food and keep the bowls and platters full. But don't leave food out at room temperature for longer than two hours, and be sure to replenish the table with fresh platters you've prepared in advance.

• One of the easiest ways to entertain is to create a menu of room-temperature dishes. Hot buffets, on the other hand, should have one centerpiece dish with simple side dishes.

• Keep desserts simple; cakes and cookies that can be eaten out of hand, for example.

• Avoid traffic jams at the buffet table. If possible, place the table in the center of the room, so guests can serve themselves from both sides of the table. Provide two serving utensils for each bowl or tray. Bundle the forks and napkins together and place at both ends of the buffet.

DINNER-PARTY STRATEGIES

When planning the menu for a dinner party, it is important that the flavors, colors, textures, and richness of the food be well balanced. Follow a creamy soup with a simple roast, and avoid repeating ingredients and flavors. Also, consider the amount of time you'll need to spend in the kitchen. Soups, stews, casseroles, mousses, sorbets, and baked goods can be made ahead. Try not to have more than two dishes that require your last-minute attention.

Formal table setting: dinner plate, salad plate, bread plate, salad fork, dinner fork, soup spoon, dinner knife, dessert fork, dessert spoon, butter knife, white wine glass, red wine glass, water glass

SETTING A PROPER TABLE

There is a proper way to set a table. To begin, place a dinner plate at each setting. Top with a salad plate. If serving soup, place the soup bowls on top of the salad plates. Set the bread plates to the left of the dinner plates above the forks. Napkins go either to the left of the forks or in the center of the dinner plates.

Flatware is arranged in a common-sense way, in the order used, beginning farther away from the plate. Forks are placed on the left, while knives (cutting edge facing the plate) and spoons are on the right. If you are serving soup, the soup spoons are placed to the right of the knives. If you are serving salad, the salad forks are set to the left of the dinner forks. Butter knives may be placed right on the butter plates.

If you have enough flatware and room on the table, the dessert forks and spoons can be placed above the dinner plates (see photo above). Otherwise, set out the dessert flatware with the dessert. And don't forget to provide teaspoons for coffee or tea.

• If serving only one wine, place the wineglasses slightly above the dinner knives and set the water glasses to their left. If also serving wine to accompany the first course, place those glasses to the right of the primary wineglasses.

WINE

When choosing a beverage to complement a meal, there's no reason to restrict yourself to wine. Although wine can be suave and elegant or simple and refreshing, when food is spicy or very robust it can overwhelm or compete with a wine unless you choose very carefully. What follows is all you need to know to get you started choosing, serving, and enjoying wine with ease.

KNOW YOUR WINES

There are two kinds of wine: red (which includes rosé) and white. Wine is described primarily by its relative sweetness. A dry wine lacks natural sugars (but it still can be perceived as fruity), a semidry wine generally tastes sweet, and a sweet wine is very sweet.

White wines range from very dry (Manzanilla sherry) to very sweet (Tokay), while red wines are usually dry (except for some kosher-type wines). In general, wines are named either for the predominant grape used in production (cabernet sauvignon) or for the region of production (Chianti). A wine is judged by three basic components: its color, aroma (bouquet), and taste. White wines range in color from pale yellow-green to straw yellow to deep gold, whereas red wines range from purplish red to ruby red.

What is a good wine? Any wine you enjoy drinking. Let your eyes, nose, and mouth be your guides.

White Wines

Chardonnay One of the most popular wines, chardonnay is produced the world over. Most chardonnays are buttery, fruity, and fairly dry; they are often aged in oak. Chardonnays that have been aged in small oak barrels (sometimes new ones) are often characterized as being "oaky," a quality that can mask a wine's lovely fruity qualities. Serve with summer foods, such as grilled salmon or chicken, as well as with roasted chicken or fish.

Gewürztraminer A specialty of Alsace, France, although it's produced in other countries as well. It is a spicy wine that can be dry or semisweet. If dry, serve with fish, poultry, or spicy foods. If sweet, serve with fruit desserts.

Riesling This wine has a floral fragrance with hints of honey. Late-harvest Riesling is produced from superripe grapes that are intensely sweet, making it one of the world's most delicious wines. German Rieslings are much sweeter than Alsatian Rieslings. They are excellent with Chinese food, lightly spiced food, and roast chicken. Alsatian Rieslings are ideal summertime wines.

Sauvignon Blanc A refreshing, clean-flavored wine with a grassy, herbaceous aroma. It is sometimes labeled *fumé blanc*. Serve with poultry, fish, or shellfish.

Red Wines

Beaujolais A pleasant, light-bodied, fruity French wine that goes well with meats and poultry.

Beaujolais Nouveau A light, fruity wine that is seven to nine weeks old and is released for sale on the third Thursday of November. It is an ideal wine to serve at Thanksgiving.

Bordeaux Some of the greatest wines in the world are from the Bordeaux region in France. These wines are rich and fragrant and known for their ability to age well. Roast goose, lamb, and other red meats are the perfect partners.

Burgundy Wines from the Burgundy region of France are elegant, highly prized, and among the most expensive in the world. Burgundys, made from 100 percent pinot noir grapes, are lighter in body and color than some other red wines. They bear no resemblance to the typical California Burgundy. Enjoy with salmon, red meat, pork, poultry, and game.

Cabernet Sauvignon Produced in many countries, this well-known wine is full-bodied and can be complex, with hints of spice and ripe fruit. It complements hearty meats, poultry, and stews.

Chianti One of the most famous Italian wines, true Chianti is Tuscan. This sturdy, dry wine goes nicely with tomato-based pasta dishes, steaks, hamburgers, and pizza.

Merlot Rich, fragrant, and smooth bodied, this wine is easy to like. Serve with robust foods such as lamb, sausages, stews, braises, and Cornish hens.

Pinot Noir This intensely flavored wine is now produced in Oregon and California—often with great success. The wine can be light or full bodied. It goes with almost any food but is especially good with salmon, poultry, pork, veal, ham, and cheese.

Zinfandel Originally grown in Europe, "zin" has become a uniquely California wine. It has a spicy, fruity, slight raspberry flavor. It can stand up to hearty foods, such as steaks, lamb, veal chops, game birds, and hamburgers.

Other Wines

Madeira, Sherry, and Port These are wines that have been fortified with a spirit (usually brandy) to increase their alcohol content. They are usually enjoyed after a meal, although dry sherry is often sipped before dinner as an apértif.

Rosé This light-bodied wine is made from red grapes: The grape skins are left on just long enough to produce the desired pink color. (Inexpensive rosés are often tinted.) Serve well chilled, before dinner or with lighter foods.

Sparkling Wine These bubbly wines range from slightly sweet to dry. Champagne is the most famous (even though we often use the term to mean any sparkling wine). True champagne is produced only in the Champagne region of France by the traditional *méthode champenoise,* but other countries also make fine sparklers, too. Sparkling wines go with every food, including dessert.

SERVING WINE

Serving wine at the proper temperature helps to bring out all its flavor. Red wine is often served too warm, while white wine is often served too cold, which makes it difficult to fully appreciate them. Red wine should be served at cool room temperature. If it's too warm, place it in a bucket of ice water for five minutes. Some young and fruity reds, such as Beaujolais, are best when slightly chilled. White wines and sparkling wines should be served well chilled but not so cold that their delicious flavors are hidden. To quick-chill white or sparkling wine, submerge the bottle in a bucket or pot filled with half ice and half water. Or wrap the bottle in several thicknesses of wet paper towels and place in the freezer for 20 to 30 minutes or until chilled. (Check to make sure the wine doesn't freeze.)

Wine is traditionally served in stemmed glasses: The large flat base allows you to swirl the wine, which helps release its aroma and flavor. When drinking wine, hold the glass by the stem. This is especially important with chilled wines; it prevents the heat from your hand from warming the wine. Glasses should be filled one-half to two-thirds full to leave enough room for swirling.

Exposing wine to air lets it "breathe" and release its flavor, but simply uncorking the bottle doesn't do much—the wine needs to be poured. If you wish, decant it (pour it into a decanter) before serving. (If decanting an aged wine, leave any sediment in the bottle.)

PAIRING WINE WITH FOOD

There really aren't any strict rules when it comes to pairing wine with food, but try to match the intensity of the flavors. For example, serve a light wine with a delicate entrée and a robust wine with a full-flavored dish. Gewürztraminer is a good match for gingery Asian dishes, while zinfandel can stand up to the spicy flavors of Mexican food. An easy way to pair wine with food is to serve a wine from the same region or country as the recipe you are preparing. For example, a paella is best enjoyed with a Spanish wine, while pasta with tomato sauce is ideally matched with an Italian red wine.

Here are a few rules of thumb: Red wines go well with meats, roast chicken, salmon, tomato-based pasta dishes, and hard cheeses (like Parmesan). White wines are a good match for delicately flavored fish, skillet poultry dishes, vegetable dishes, cheese-based pasta dishes, and soft and semisoft cheeses.

COOKING TERMS GLOSSARY

Al dente Italian for "to the tooth," describes perfectly cooked pasta: just tender and with a slight resistance.

Baste To spoon or brush a liquid over food to keep it moist during cooking. The liquid can be a sauce, marinade, broth, melted butter, or pan juices.

Beat To briskly mix or stir a mixture with a spoon, whisk, fork, or electric mixer.

Blanch To cook food (usually fruits or vegetables) briefly in boiling water, then plunge into ice water to stop the cooking. It locks in the color, texture, and flavor. Blanching is used to loosen tomato and peach skins (for peeling) and to mellow the saltiness or bitterness of certain foods.

Blend To mix ingredients until smooth or completely combined.

Blind bake To bake a piecrust before it's filled. To prevent the dough from puffing up during baking, the pastry dough is lined with foil and filled with pie weights or dry beans; they are removed shortly before the end of the baking time to allow the crust to color.

Boil To heat a liquid until bubbles break vigorously on the surface (water boils at 212°F). It also means to cook food, such as pasta or potatoes, in a boiling liquid.

Braise To cook food by first browning it in fat, then covered, on top of the stove or in the oven, in a small amount of liquid. This slow method tenderizes tough cuts of meat by breaking down their fibers and develops their flavor.

Broth A thin, clear liquid produced by simmering in water vegetables, poultry, meat, or fish (on the bone). Broth is used as a base for soups, stews, sauces, and many other dishes. Canned broth is a convenient substitute for homemade.

Brown To cook over high heat, usually on top of the stove, to brown food.

Butterfly To split food, such as shrimp or boneless leg of lamb, horizontally, cutting almost all the way through, then opening it up (like a book) to form a butterfly shape. It exposes a more uniform surface area so food cooks evenly and quickly.

Caramelize To heat sugar until it becomes syrupy and golden to deep amber in color. Sugar-topped desserts like crème brûlée are caramelized under the broiler or with a propane torch. Onions become caramelized when slowly cooked until golden brown and very tender.

Core To remove the seeds or tough woody centers from fruits such as apples, pears, and pineapple and from vegetables such as cabbage and fennel.

Cream To beat butter, margarine, or other fat until it's creamy looking or with sugar until it's fluffy and light. This technique beats in air, creating light-textured baked goods.

Crimp To decoratively pinch or press the edges of a single piecrust or to seal the edges of a double-crusted pie so the filling doesn't seep out during baking.

Curdle To coagulate or separate into solids and liquids. Egg- and milk-based mixtures can curdle if heated too quickly, overcooked, or combined with an acid, such as lemon juice.

Cut in To work a solid fat, such as shortening, butter, or margarine, into dry ingredients using a pastry blender or two knives scissor-fashion until the pieces are the desired size.

Deglaze To scrape up the flavorful browned bits from the bottom of a skillet or roasting pan in which meat or poultry has been cooked by adding water, wine, or broth and stirring while gently heating.

Devein To remove the dark intestinal vein of shrimp. The shrimp is first peeled, then a lengthwise slit is made along the back, exposing the vein so that it can be removed.

Dollop A spoonful of soft food, such as pesto, yogurt, whipped cream, or crème fraîche.

Dot To scatter bits of butter or margarine over a pie filling, casserole, or other dish before baking. It adds richness and flavor and helps promote browning.

Dredge To lightly coat with flour, cornmeal, or bread crumbs. Meats and fish are dredged before cooking to create a crisp, browned exterior.

Drippings The melted fat and juices that collect in a pan when meat or poultry is cooked. Drippings form the base for gravies and pan sauces.

Drizzle To pour melted butter, oil, syrup, melted chocolate, or other liquid back and forth over food in a fine stream.

Dust To coat lightly with flour (greased baking pans) or with confectioners' sugar or cocoa (cakes and pastries) or another powdery ingredient.

Emulsify To bind liquids that usually can't blend easily, such as oil and vinegar. The trick is to slowly add one liquid, usually the oil, to the other while mixing vigorously. Natural emulsifiers, such as egg yolks or mustard, are often added to vinaigrettes or sauces to emulsify them for a longer period.

Ferment To bring about a chemical change in foods and beverages that is caused by enzymes in bacteria or yeasts. Beer, wine, yogurt, buttermilk, vinegar, cheese, and yeast breads all get their distinctive flavors from fermentation.

Flour As a verb, means to coat food, a surface, or a baking pan with flour.

Fold To combine a light mixture (such as beaten egg whites, whipped cream, or sifted flour) with a heavier mixture (such as a cake batter or the base of a soufflé) without deflating either. A rubber spatula is the best tool to use for folding.

Fork-tender A degree of doneness for cooked vegetables and meats. When the food is pierced with a fork, there is only a very slight resistance.

Glaze To coat food by brushing with melted jelly, jam, or barbecue sauce or to brush piecrust with milk or beaten egg before baking.

Grill To cook food directly or indirectly over a source of heat (usually charcoal, briquettes, or gas) or in a special ridged pan.

Julienne To cut food, especially vegetables, into thin, uniform matchstick strips about 2 inches long.

Knead To work dough until it's smooth and elastic, either by pressing and folding with the heel of the hand or by working it in a heavy-duty electric mixer with a dough hook. Kneading develops the gluten in flour, an elastic protein that gives yeast breads their structure.

Leavening An agent that causes dough or batter to rise. Common leaveners include baking powder, baking soda, and yeast. Natural leaveners are air (when beaten into eggs) and steam (in popovers, éclairs, and cream puffs).

Marinate To flavor and/or tenderize a food by letting it sit in a liquid (such as lemon juice, wine, or yogurt) and, often, oil, herbs, or spices. When a marinade contains an acid, the marinating should be done in a nonreactive container.

Panfry To cook food in a small amount of fat in a skillet until browned and cooked through.

Parboil To partially cook food in boiling water. Carrots are often parboiled before they're added to other foods that take less time to cook.

Pare To cut away the skin or rind of a fruit or vegetable. A vegetable peeler or paring knife (a small knife with a 3- to 4-inch blade) is usually used.

Pasteurize To kill the bacteria in milk, fruit juices, or other liquids by heating to a moderately high temperature, then rapidly cooling it. All milk sold in the U.S. is pasteurized. Ultrapasteurized (UHT) milk is subjected to very high temperatures—about 300°F— and vacuum-packed for extended storage. It will keep without refrigeration for up to six months but must be refrigerated once it's opened. Ultrapasteurized cream is not vacuum-packed; it must be refrigerated.

Pinch The amount of a powdery ingredient, such as salt, pepper, or a spice, you can hold between your thumb and forefinger; about $\frac{1}{16}$ teaspoon.

Pipe To force a food, such as frosting, whipped cream, or mashed potatoes, through a pastry bag fitted with a pastry tip in a decorative manner or to shape meringues or éclairs. You can also use a plastic bag with a corner snipped off.

Poach To cook food in a gently simmering (barely moving) liquid: The amount and type of liquid will depend on the food being poached.

Pound To flatten to a uniform thickness using a meat mallet, meat pounder, or rolling pin. Meat and poultry is pounded to ensure even cooking. Pounding also tenderizes tough meats by breaking up hard-to-chew connective tissue.

Preheat To bring an oven or broiler to the desired temperature before cooking food.

Prick To pierce a food, such as a piecrust or a potato, usually with a fork, to prevent it from puffing up or bursting during cooking/baking.

Proof To dissolve yeast in a measured amount of warm water (105° to 115°F), sometimes with a small amount of sugar and then set it aside until foamy to make sure that it is "active."

Punch down To deflate yeast dough after it has risen fully. It is not necessary to literally "punch" down the dough; it needs only to be gently deflated.

Puree To mash or grind food until completely smooth, usually in a food processor, blender, sieve, or food mill.

Reduce To rapidly boil a liquid, such as a sauce, wine, or stock, until it has reduced in volume in order to concentrate the flavor.

Render To slowly cook animal fat or skin until the fat separates from its connective tissue. It is strained before being used. The crisp brown bits left in the pan are called cracklings.

Roast To cook in an uncovered pan in the oven by dry heat. Roasted food develops a well-browned exterior. Tender cuts of meat, poultry, and fish are suitable for roasting, as are many vegetables.

Rolling boil A full constant boil that cannot be stirred down.

Sauté To cook food quickly in a small amount of hot fat in a skillet; the term derives from the French word *sauter* ("to jump").

Scald To heat a liquid, such as cream or milk, just until tiny bubbles appear around the edge of the pan.

Score To make shallow cuts (usually parallel or crisscross) in the surface of food before cooking. This is done mainly to facilitate flavor absorption, as in marinated meats, chicken, and fish, but sometimes also for decorative purposes on hams. The tops of breads are often scored to enable them to rise (during baking) without bursting.

Sear To brown meat, fish, or poultry quickly by placing over very high heat.

Shave To cut wide, paper-thin slices of food, such as Parmesan cheese or chocolate.

Shred To cut, tear, or grate food into narrow strips or pieces.

Shuck To remove the shells of oysters, mussels, scallops, or clams.

Sift To press ingredients, such as flour or confectioners' sugar, through a sifter or sieve. Sifting incorporates air and removes lumps, which helps ingredients to combine more easily.

Simmer To cook food in a liquid over low heat (at about 185°F). A few small bubbles should be visible on the surface.

Skim To remove fat or froth from the surface of a liquid, such as broth, boiling jelly, or soup. A skimmer, a long-handled metal utensil with a flat mesh disk or perforated bowl at one end, is the ideal tool for the job.

Soft peaks When cream or egg whites are beaten until they stand in peaks that bend over at the top when the beaters are lifted.

Steam To cook food, covered, over a small amount of boiling water. The food is usually set on a rack or in a basket. Since it's not immersed in water, the food retains more of its nutrients, color, and flavor than it would with other cooking methods.

Stiff peaks When cream or egg whites are beaten until they stand in firm peaks that hold their shape when the beaters are lifted.

Stir-fry To cook pieces of food quickly in a small amount of oil over high heat, stirring and tossing almost constantly. Stir-frying is used in Asian cooking; a wok is the traditional pan, although a large skillet will do just as well.

Temper To warm food gently before adding it to a hot mixture so it doesn't separate or curdle.

Tender-crisp The ideal degree of doneness for many fresh vegetables: They're tender but still retain some of their crunch.

Toast To brown bread, croutons, whole spices, or nuts in a dry skillet or in the oven. Toasting enhances the flavor of nuts and facilitates removal of the skin from hazelnuts.

Toss To lift and drop pieces of food quickly and gently with two utensils, usually to coat them with a sauce (as for pasta) or a dressing (as for salad).

Whip To beat an ingredient (especially heavy or whipping cream) or mixture rapidly to incorporate air and increase volume. You can use a whisk, egg beater, or electric mixer.

Whisk To beat ingredients (such as heavy or whipping cream, eggs, salad dressings, or sauces) with a fork or whisk to mix, blend, or incorporate air.

Zest To remove the flavorful colored part of citrus skin. Use the fine holes of a grater, a zester, or a vegetable peeler, avoiding the bitter white pith underneath.

INGREDIENTS GLOSSARY

Almond paste A firm but pliable confection made of ground almonds and confectioners' sugar mixed with glucose, corn syrup, or egg white. Available in cans or tubes, almond paste is similar to *marzipan*, which is sweeter and softer. If almond paste seems hard, microwave on High for a few seconds to soften.

Amaretti cookies Crisp, round almond-flavored Italian cookies, found at Italian grocers and specialty food stores. They often come tissue-wrapped in pairs and packed into pretty tin boxes.

Calvados An apple brandy made in the Normandy region of France. Applejack is a good substitute.

Capers The flower buds of a bush native to parts of the Mediterranean and Asia. They are usually dried and then pickled in a vinegar brine. Also available at specialty food stores are capers packed in salt, which have a purer flavor. Capers should be rinsed under cold water and drained before using.

Chili powder A blend of ground dried mild chiles and ingredients such as cumin and garlic powder. Ground dried chiles without added seasonings are also available and sometimes labeled chile powder.

Chipotles en adobo Dried, smoked red jalapeño peppers canned in a thick chile puree called *adobo*. Handle these chiles and their sauce with care; they are very hot and can easily burn your skin. Leftover *chipotles en adobo* can be frozen. Freeze individual chiles with some sauce on a waxed paper–lined cookie sheet until firm, then remove from the waxed paper and store in a heavy-duty zip-tight plastic bag for up to three months. *Chipotles en adobo* can be found in Latino markets and many supermarkets.

Chorizo A spicy pork sausage seasoned with chiles and garlic. Spanish-style chorizo is a firm, smoked link sausage. Do not substitute Mexican-style fresh chorizo.

Cilantro A pungent green herb, popular in Asian and Latino cooking; sometimes called fresh coriander or Chinese parsley. It is often sold with the roots still attached; the roots are sometimes chopped and used as a seasoning.

Cinnamon sticks Used to garnish hot beverages. They can also be simmered in a liquid to release their warm, spicy flavor.

Coconut milk An unsweetened infusion of shredded coconut meat and water that is strained and canned. It is not interchangeable with cream of coconut, which is rich, sweet, and used in desserts and tropical mixed drinks.

Cornichons Tiny gherkinlike cucumbers that are pickled in a tart brine. Small dill pickles are an acceptable substitute if the cornichons are to be chopped and used in a sauce.

Crab boil A mix of herbs and spices (such as mustard seeds, whole allspice, peppercorns, bay leaves, and dried chiles) that is sometimes added to the water in which crab, shrimp, or lobster is cooked.

Curry powder Widely used in Indian cooking, the blend of spices and heat intensity can greatly vary. A typical curry powder can contain up to twenty different spices, including turmeric, cardamom, red chiles, black pepper, and cumin. Madras-style curry powder, available in supermarkets, is a reliable moderately spicy blend.

Durum A hard wheat that is ground to make semolina flour, which is used for pasta.

Espresso coffee powder, instant Available at Italian grocers and many supermarkets, it is a convenient way to add rich, deep-roasted coffee flavor to food and beverages.

Fish sauce An integral flavoring in Southeast Asian cooking, it is made from fermented fish. Also known as *nam pla* (Thai) and *nuoc nam* (Vietnam); the Philippine version, *pastis,* has a much milder flavor. Store at cool room temperature in a dark place; it will keep for about one year.

Five-spice powder A favorite seasoning in Chinese cooking; it is usually a blend of equal parts cinnamon, cloves, fennel, star anise, and Szechwan peppercorns.

Hoisin sauce This sweet, thick sauce is made from a base of soybeans. Refrigerate after opening. Often used in Chinese barbecue sauces for chicken and ribs.

Juniper berries Fragrant dried blue-black berries that are used as a seasoning and the main flavoring in gin. They can usually be found in spice shops and specialty food stores. If unavailable, stir 1 to 2 tablespoons of gin into the finished dish during the last five minutes of cooking.

Kirsch Also called *kirschwasser* (German for "cherry water"), a clear brandy distilled from cherry juice and pits. (This type of clear spirit made from fruit is called *eau-de-vie.*) Often used to flavor fondues and desserts.

Mango chutney A sweet and spicy condiment that is often served with curries. Major Grey's is made in the British style, slightly sweeter than Indian chutneys.

Maple syrup, pure Maple sap that has been boiled down until syrupy. It has a delicious subtle flavor that is incomparable. Maple-flavored syrup is made from a liquid such as corn syrup mixed with a small amount of pure maple syrup. Pancake syrup is corn syrup with natural or artificial maple extract added.

Marsala A fortified wine, originally from Sicily but also produced in California; available sweet (best for desserts) and dry (use in savory dishes).

Miso A highly concentrated fermented soybean paste made from a combination of soybeans and grain that is widely used in Japanese cooking and made in different strengths. *Red miso* has the strongest flavor; *golden* is fairly mild; and *white miso* is mellow and slightly sweet. Look for miso in natural food stores and Asian markets.

Molasses A by-product of sugar refining, molasses is the liquid that remains after the sugar crystals are extracted. Molasses can be sulphured or unsulphured. Light molasses is from the first boiling (refining) and has a mild flavor. Dark molasses is from the second boiling and is darker and less sweet. Blackstrap molasses, from the third boiling, is bitter.

Mustard, Dijon This prepared mustard gets its distinctive flavor from a special blend of mustard seeds and white wine. There are many different brands, with varying heat levels, so when you find a brand you like, stick with it.

Old Bay seasoning An aromatic, somewhat hot blend of ground spices that is popular with cooks in the Chesapeake Bay area, especially for seafood dishes.

Olives The fruit of the olive tree is naturally very bitter and must be processed to make it edible. There are many olive varieties, and the finished product depends on the ripeness of the fruit and the type of processing. While each has a particular flavor, many are interchangeable. Black olives include the tiny Niçoise, the gray-black Gaeta, the vinegar-cured Kalamata (also available pitted), and the pleasantly bitter, wrinkled, oil-cured Moroccan. Picholine and manzanilla are two popular green olives. To remove the pits from olives, use an olive or cherry pitter. Or put the olives on a work surface, place the flat side of a large knife on top of one olive, and press down to lightly crush the olive; remove the pit.

Olive oil Pressing tree-ripened olives produces the prized liquid we know as olive oil. Its flavor, color, and fragrance depend on the region of origin and the quality of the harvest. In general, extra-virgin olive oil, from the first pressing, is full-flavored, bright green to green-gold in color, and best used on salads or other dishes where its taste can be most appreciated. Regular olive oil (sometimes called pure olive oil) is from a subsequent pressing and has a milder but still distinctive fruity flavor; it's a good cooking oil. "Light" olive oil has been specially treated to remove much of the characteristic olive taste; it is not lower in fat.

Pancetta An unsmoked bacon that is rolled into a cylinder and sliced to order. It is used in Italian dishes. Pancetta is available at Italian delicatessens, specialty food stores, and some supermarkets. Substitute regular smoked bacon, if necessary.

Pepper The world's most popular spice, peppercorns are the dried berries of a perennial vine. They come in three colors: black, white, and green. Black pepper is picked just before the berry ripens; the skin turns black when dried. White pepper is the ripened berry with the skin removed; it has a milder flavor than black pepper. Green peppercorns are soft, underripe berries, usually preserved in brine. Freshly ground pepper has an incomparable flavor, so it's worth the investment to purchase a good-quality pepper mill (grinder). Some recipes call for coarse-cracked pepper (also called butcher's grind), but it's just as easy to crush your own peppercorns in a mortar with a pestle or on a work surface with a heavy skillet.

Pine nuts From the pinecones of certain pine trees, these small, elongated ivory-colored nuts are sometimes called *pignoli* or *piñon.* They turn rancid easily; store in the refrigerator for up to three months or freeze for up to nine months.

Porcini mushrooms, dried These members of *Boletus edulis* are imported from Italy and have a rich, earthy flavor; the French variety, called *cèpes,* are more expensive. They must be rehydrated in hot water before use. After soaking, rinse them under cold running water to remove any grit. Use the flavorful soaking liquid to add extra mushroom flavor. Available in specialty food stores and Italian markets.

Prosciutto A cured, aged, air-dried ham with a firm texture and delicious salty flavor. Imported Italian prosciutto, available at quality grocers and butchers, has a milder flavor than the domestic variety.

Salt There are so many kinds of salt available, it's easy to take this familiar ingredient for granted. Each has a different level of saltiness, so it's helpful to understand the differences. We tested our recipes with fine-grained table salt, which has additives that keep it free flowing. Iodized salt is table salt that has been treated with iodine (which helps prevent hyperthyroidism). Kosher salt has no additives. Some cooks prefer it for its mild flavor and its coarse texture, which makes it easy to pick up for sprinkling. Sea salt is also less salty than common table salt. If you use kosher or sea salt in your cooking, you will need a larger quantity. Grayish rock salt is not a food-quality salt but is used in old-fashioned ice-cream makers and as a bed upon which to bake and serve stuffed oysters and clams.

Savoiardi Long, crisp, Italian-style ladyfingers that are usually layered with a moist filling to soften them, as in tiramisù.

Semolina A coarse, sandlike grind of durum wheat used to make pasta and some breads.

Sesame oil, Asian Dark brown-orange in color, this oil is pressed from roasted sesame seeds. It is generally used as a seasoning, not a cooking oil.

Soy sauce Made from fermented soybeans and roasted wheat or barley, this dark, salty sauce is indispensable in Asian cooking. There are many different versions, and some can be quite salty. Use a reliable Japanese brand.

Star anise A star-shaped spice with eight points, each containing a seed. Often used in Chinese cooking, it has a delicate licorice flavor.

Tahini Sesame seeds ground into a thick paste; stir well to incorporate the oil that rises to the top. Available at natural food stores and most supermarkets.

Tapenade A French olive paste seasoned with anchovies, herbs, and garlic and used as a condiment. The Italian version is called *olivada.*

Tomatoes, dried Often referred to as "sun-dried" tomatoes but rarely dried in the sun anymore, these intensely flavored dehydrated tomatoes are processed by more commercial methods. They can be purchased loose packed or packed with oil in a jar. Loose-packed dried tomatoes should be soaked in boiling water to cover until softened, then drained.

Vinegar Bacterial activity can turn some liquids into vinegar; *vin aigre* means "sour wine." *Cider vinegar,* made from apple juice, is a popular vinegar. *Distilled white vinegar* has a strong flavor but is preferred for pickling because it doesn't darken food. Red and white wines are also made into vinegars. The more expensive vinegars are produced by an ancient process that slowly turns the wine sour, instead of by inoculating them with fast-acting bacteria. *Tarragon vinegar* is white wine that has been infused with tarragon. *Balsamic vinegar* is made from semidry Trebbiano grapes, so the resulting vinegar has a sweet note. Most supermarket varieties are tasty, but they aren't true balsamic vinegars, which are aged for years in wood caskets and are quite expensive. *Malt vinegar,* a British favorite, is a mild vinegar made from malted barley.

Wonton wrappers Delicate thin squares of wheat noodles, they can be stuffed to make wontons or other dumplings or ravioli. Look for them in the refrigerated section of the supermarket or at Asian grocery stores. Wrap leftover wrappers in plastic wrap and heavy-duty foil and freeze for up to one month.

2
....
APPETIZERS

Appetizers serve two important roles: They whet one's appetite and set the tone for the meal that follows. A stylish sit-down dinner calls for elegant appetizers that look and taste special, while dips and chips are perfect for a backyard barbecue. At a cocktail party, on the other hand, the hors d'oeuvres *are* the meal, so you'll need to offer a tempting selection. But some of our favorite appetizers are simply snacks, nibbles, and munchies that are meant to be served without ceremony and simply enjoyed.

HOW TO MANAGE THE MENU

• Prepare appetizers in advance whenever possible.
• Serve only one or two appetizers that require last-minute attention.
• For appetizers that require last-minute assembling, prepare the separate components ahead of time and chill until serving time.
• Plan on only one or two hot appetizers unless you have more than one oven.
• Be sure to serve some appetizers that are work-free, such as nuts or cheese.
• Figure on about ten to twelve appetizers per person if no meal follows. Otherwise, allow five or six pieces.

DO-AHEAD STRATEGIES

Vegetables for crudités can be prepared up to one day ahead. Wrap radishes, cherry tomatoes, cucumber, and celery in damp paper towels and refrigerate in plastic bags. Cut up asparagus, broccoli, green beans, and cauliflower and boil until tender-crisp. Drain, rinse under cold water, and pat dry. Refrigerate as above.

Dips and spreads can often be made up to several days ahead and refrigerated.

Pâtés and terrines taste best if made one to two days ahead. Meat pâtés can be frozen for up to two months. Defrost overnight in the refrigerator.

Pastry appetizers can be frozen, raw or baked, for up to one month. Layer them in baking pans, separating the layers with waxed paper, then double wrap in foil. Arrange baked pastries on cookie sheets and reheat at 350°F for about 10 minutes. Bake frozen raw pastries as the recipe directs, allowing extra baking time.

Tea sandwiches make excellent appetizers. Make them up to four hours ahead and arrange in jelly-roll pans. Separate the layers with damp paper towels, cover securely with plastic wrap, and refrigerate.

TIPS FOR SERVING WITH STYLE

Be thoughtful. Appetizers should be easy to handle without being messy, easy to eat without utensils, and require no more than a couple of bites.

Make it pretty. Arrange cut-up vegetables on a tray or in a large basket lined with plastic wrap and covered with leafy salad greens.

Be creative. Serve dips and spreads in hollowed-out loaves of bread or cabbages.

Be dramatic. Add height by placing platters on inverted baking dishes covered with colored napkins.

Make it flavorful. Remove cold appetizers from the refrigerator about thirty minutes before serving.

Perfect Guacamole (recipe page 32)

ROASTED RED PEPPER DIP

....

Fresh roasted red peppers are what make this dip special, so don't substitute the ones that come in a jar. Roasting peppers is easy to do. If you've never done it, this is the perfect opportunity. Once you've tasted them, you'll wonder why you waited so long.

Prep: 45 minutes

- 4   red peppers, roasted (page 419)
- ½   teaspoon ground cumin
- ½   cup walnuts, toasted
- 2   slices firm white bread, torn into pieces
- 2   tablespoons raspberry or balsamic vinegar
- 1   tablespoon olive oil
- ½   teaspoon salt
- ⅛   teaspoon ground red pepper (cayenne)
       toasted pita bread wedges

1. Cut roasted peppers into large pieces. In small skillet, toast cumin over low heat, stirring constantly, until very fragrant, 1 to 2 minutes.

2. In food processor with knife blade attached, process walnuts until ground. Add roasted peppers, cumin, bread, vinegar, oil, salt, and ground red pepper; puree until smooth. Transfer to bowl. If not serving right away, cover and refrigerate up to 4 hours. Serve with toasted pita bread wedges. Makes about 2 cups.

Each tablespoon: About 23 calories, 0g protein, 2g carbohydrate, 2g total fat (0g saturated), 0mg cholesterol, 46mg sodium.

Roasted Red Pepper Dip

ROASTED EGGPLANT DIP WITH HERBS

....

The fresh flavors of lemon and mint are a perfect match for the baked eggplant in this Mediterranean-style dip.

Prep: 15 minutes plus cooling and draining
Roast: 1 hour

- 2   small eggplants (1 pound each)
- 2   garlic cloves, thinly sliced
- 2   tablespoons olive oil
- 4   teaspoons fresh lemon juice
- 1   teaspoon salt
- ¼   teaspoon ground black pepper
- 2   tablespoons chopped fresh parsley
- 2   tablespoons chopped fresh mint
       toasted pita bread wedges

1. Preheat oven to 400°F. With knife, cut slits all over eggplants; insert garlic slices in slits. Place eggplants in jelly-roll pan and roast until collapsed and tender, about 1 hour.

2. When cool enough to handle, cut eggplants in half. Scoop out flesh and place in colander set over bowl; discard skin. Let drain 10 minutes.

3. Transfer eggplant to food processor with knife blade attached. Add oil, lemon juice, salt, and pepper; pulse to coarsely chop. Add parsley and mint, pulsing to combine. Spoon into bowl; cover and refrigerate up to 4 hours. Serve with toasted pita bread wedges. Makes about 2 cups.

Each tablespoon: About 14 calories, 0g protein, 2g carbohydrate, 1g total fat (0g saturated), 0mg cholesterol, 74mg sodium.

BABA GANOUSH
Prepare as directed above. Omit parsley and mint. Stir in **½ teaspoon ground cumin, ¼ cup tahini (sesame seed paste), and ½ cup low-fat plain yogurt.**

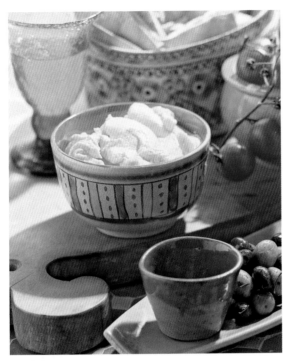
Artichoke Dip

ARTICHOKE DIP

···

Serve this simple dip along with crisp toasted wedges of pita bread. An assortment of olives and cherry tomatoes makes a tasty accompaniment.

Prep: 10 minutes

- 1 lemon
- 1 can (13.75 ounces) artichoke hearts, drained
- ¼ cup light mayonnaise
- ¼ cup freshly grated Parmesan cheese
- 2 tablespoons olive oil

1. From lemon, grate ½ teaspoon peel and squeeze 2 teaspoons juice.

2. In food processor with knife blade attached, puree lemon peel and juice, artichoke hearts, Parmesan, and oil until smooth. Transfer to serving bowl. If not serving right away, cover and refrigerate up to 3 days. Makes about 1¼ cups.

Each tablespoon: About 30 calories, 1g protein, 1g carbohydrate, 3g total fat (1g saturated), 2mg cholesterol, 70mg sodium.

HUMMUS

···

Middle Eastern dips, such as hummus, once seemed exotic, but now they're familiar old friends. Tahini is readily available at health food stores and supermarkets.

Prep: 15 minutes plus chilling

- 4 garlic cloves, peeled
- 1 large lemon
- 1 can (15 to 19 ounces) garbanzo beans, rinsed and drained
- 2 tablespoons tahini (sesame seed paste, page 27)
- 3 tablespoons olive oil
- 2 tablespoons water
- ½ teaspoon salt
- ⅛ teaspoon ground red pepper (cayenne)
- ½ teaspoon paprika
- 2 tablespoons chopped fresh cilantro (optional) pita bread wedges olives

1. In 1-quart saucepan, heat *2 cups water* to boiling over high heat. Add garlic and cook 3 minutes to blanch; drain.

2. From lemon, grate 1 teaspoon peel and squeeze 3 tablespoons juice. In food processor with knife blade attached, combine beans, tahini, garlic, lemon peel and juice, oil, water, salt, and ground red pepper. Puree until smooth. Transfer to platter; cover and refrigerate up to 4 hours. To serve, sprinkle with paprika and cilantro, if using. Serve with pita bread wedges and olives. Makes 2 cups.

Each tablespoon: About 28 calories, 1g protein, 2g carbohydrate, 2g total fat (0g saturated), 0mg cholesterol, 54mg sodium.

MEZE

TEST KITCHEN TIP

Meze, little savory dishes to be nibbled before a meal or with drinks, are a tradition in Greece, Turkey, and the Middle East. Try any of the following with pita or French bread, along with feta cheese chunks, olives, radishes, sliced cucumbers, or tomato wedges: Roasted Red Pepper Dip, Tzatziki, or Hummus.

PERFECT GUACAMOLE

(Pictured on page 28)

....

Our favorite avocados for guacamole are the varieties with thick, pebbly, green skin such as Hass, Pinkerton, and Reed. While guacamole is usually served as a dip, it is also a great accompaniment for fajitas or tacos.

Prep: 15 minutes

1   jalapeño chile, seeded and finely chopped
⅓ cup loosely packed fresh cilantro leaves, chopped
¼ cup finely chopped sweet onion such as Vidalia or Maui
½ teaspoon salt
2   ripe avocados
1   plum tomato
    plain tortilla chips

1. In mortar, combine jalapeño, cilantro, onion, and salt; with pestle, grind until mixture becomes juicy and thick (onion can still be slightly chunky).

2. Cut each avocado lengthwise in half around seed. Twist halves in opposite directions to separate. Slip spoon between pit and fruit and work pit out. With spoon, scoop fruit from peel onto cutting board.

3. Cut tomato crosswise in half. Squeeze halves to remove seeds and juice. Coarsely chop tomato.

4. If mortar is large enough, add avocado and chopped tomato to onion mixture in mortar. (If mortar is small, combine avocado, tomato, and onion mixture in bowl.) Mash slightly with pestle or spoon until mixture is blended but still somewhat chunky.

5. Guacamole is best when served as soon as it's made. If not serving right away, press plastic wrap directly onto surface of guacamole to prevent discoloration and refrigerate up to 1 hour. Serve with chips. Makes about 1¾ cups.

Each tablespoon: About 25 calories, 0g protein, 1g carbohydrate, 2g total fat (0g saturated), 0mg cholesterol, 45mg sodium.

WARM LAYERED BEAN DIP

....

This colorful dip is always a hit. The pinto bean, Jack cheese, and salsa layers can be assembled several hours in advance, then baked just before serving.

Prep: 35 minutes   Bake: 12 minutes

2   garlic cloves, peeled
1   can (15 to 19 ounces) pinto beans, rinsed and drained
2   green onions, finely chopped
1   tablespoon tomato paste
1   tablespoon water
4   ounces Monterey Jack cheese, shredded (1 cup)
1   cup mild to medium salsa
2   avocados, each cut in half, pitted, and peeled
¼ cup chopped fresh cilantro
3   tablespoons finely chopped red onion
2   tablespoons fresh lime juice
½ teaspoon salt
1   cup sour cream
    tortilla chips

1. Preheat oven to 350°F. In 1-quart saucepan, heat *2 cups water* to boiling over high heat. Add garlic and cook 3 minutes to blanch; drain. With flat side of chef's knife, mash garlic; transfer to medium bowl and add beans, half of green onions, tomato paste, and water. Mash until well combined but still slightly chunky. Spread in bottom of 9-inch glass pie plate.

2. Sprinkle cheese over bean mixture, then spread salsa on top. Bake until piping hot, about 12 minutes.

3. Meanwhile, in medium bowl, mash avocados just until slightly chunky. Stir in cilantro, red onion, lime juice, and salt. Spoon avocado mixture over hot dip mixture and spread sour cream on top. Sprinkle with remaining green onions. Serve with tortilla chips. Makes about 5½ cups.

Each tablespoon: About 22 calories, 1g protein, 1g carbohydrate, 2g total fat (1g saturated), 3mg cholesterol, 61mg sodium.

TZATZIKI

In Greece, this is served as a dip with pita bread or as a cold sauce to accompany grilled fish or chicken.

Prep: 20 minutes plus overnight to drain, plus chilling

- 2 cups (16 ounces) plain low-fat yogurt
- ½ English (seedless) cucumber, not peeled, seeded and finely chopped, plus a few very thin slices
- 1½ teaspoons salt
- 1 to 2 garlic cloves, chopped
- 1 tablespoon chopped fresh mint or dill plus additional sprigs
- 1 tablespoon extra-virgin olive oil
- ½ teaspoon red wine vinegar
- ¼ teaspoon ground black pepper

1. Spoon yogurt into sieve lined with cheesecloth or coffee filter set over bowl; cover and refrigerate overnight. Transfer drained yogurt to medium bowl and discard liquid.

2. Meanwhile, in colander set over bowl, toss chopped cucumber with 1 teaspoon salt. Let drain at least 1 hour at room temperature, or cover and refrigerate up to 8 hours. In batches, wrap chopped cucumber in kitchen towel and squeeze to remove as much liquid as possible. Pat dry with paper towels, then add to bowl with yogurt.

3. With flat side of chef's knife, mash garlic to a paste with remaining ½ teaspoon salt. Add garlic, chopped mint, oil, vinegar, and pepper to yogurt and stir to combine. Cover and refrigerate at least 2 or up to 4 hours. Serve chilled or at room temperature, topped with cucumber slices and mint sprigs. Makes about 1¼ cups.

Each tablespoon: About 17 calories, 1g protein, 1g carbohydrate, 1g total fat (0g saturated), 1mg cholesterol, 182mg sodium.

HERBED YOGURT-CHEESE DIP

Prepare yogurt as in Step 1. Stir in **1 garlic clove,** crushed with garlic press, **¾ cup chopped fresh basil, 1 tablespoon olive oil,** and **½ teaspoon salt.** Serve with crackers or cut-up vegetables. Makes about 1 cup.

5 IDEAS FOR . . . ENGLISH CUCUMBERS

If you've never tried one of these lo-o-o-ong, sweet, thin-skinned cukes, you're in for a treat. There's no need to peel 'em, since they're not waxed, and no need to seed, as they're virtually seedless. Our recipes call for one-half to two 13- to 14-ounce cucumbers.

CUCUMBER CANAPÉS

Cut one-half cucumber into 24 thin slices. Arrange on work surface and top each slice with ¼ teaspoon pesto. Crumble 1 ounce goat cheese and sprinkle on top of canapés. Makes 24.

MELON 'N' CUKE SALSA

In large bowl, combine 1 cucumber, peeled and cut into ¼-inch pieces; 2 cups ripe melon chunks (¼-inch pieces); 1 jalapeño chile, seeded and finely chopped; 3 tablespoons fresh lime juice; 2 tablespoons chopped fresh basil leaves; and ¼ teaspoon salt. Makes 4½ cups.

COOL-AS-A-CUKE BUTTERMILK SOUP

In blender, puree until smooth: 2 peeled, chopped cucumbers, 1 cup buttermilk, ½ cup loosely packed fresh mint leaves, ½ teaspoon salt, and ⅛ teaspoon ground black pepper. Stir in 1 cup buttermilk. Serve soup chilled; garnish with snipped fresh chives and chopped mint leaves. Makes 4¼ cups.

MEDITERRANEAN TUNA

In large bowl, combine 1 cucumber cut into ¾ inch chunks; 2 cans (5 ounces each) drained and flaked chunk light tuna in water; ⅓ cup pitted Kalamata olives, chopped; 2 small tomatoes, chopped; and 3 tablespoons olive oil vinaigrette. Stir until blended. Serve over greens or on toasted baguette. Makes 5 cups.

SCANDINAVIAN SHRIMP SALAD

In large bowl, combine 1 very thinly sliced cucumber; 1 pound cooked, shelled large shrimp; ½ cup reduced-fat sour cream; ¼ teaspoon freshly grated lemon peel; 2 tablespoons fresh lemon juice; 2 tablespoons chopped fresh dill; ¼ teaspoon salt; and ⅛ teaspoon ground black pepper. Serve on rye toast. Makes 4 cups.

TAPENADE

....

This Provençal olive spread can be enjoyed on crisp bread or crackers or as a condiment for fish or chicken.

Prep: 20 minutes

- 2 garlic cloves, peeled
- 1½ cups Gaeta or Kalamata olives, pitted
- ½ cup pimiento-stuffed olives
- 1 tablespoon olive oil
- 1 teaspoon fennel seeds
- 1 teaspoon freshly grated orange peel

1. In 1-quart saucepan, heat *2 cups water* to boiling over high heat. Add garlic and cook 3 minutes to blanch; drain.

2. In food processor with knife blade attached, combine olives, oil, fennel seeds, orange peel, and garlic; process until chopped. Transfer to bowl; cover and refrigerate up 3 days. Makes about 1¼ cups.

Each tablespoon: About 41 calories, 0g protein, 2g carbohydrate, 4g total fat (0g saturated), 0mg cholesterol, 264mg sodium.

MARINATED MIXED OLIVES

....

This assortment of olives is an inviting addition to any antipasto tray. If you have an orange on hand, mix its peel with—or use instead of—the lemon peel.

Prep: 10 minutes plus standing and marinating
Cook: 5 minutes

- ¼ cup extra-virgin olive oil
- 2 teaspoons fennel seeds, crushed
- 4 small bay leaves
- 2 pounds assorted Mediterranean olives, such as Niçoise, picholine, or Kalamata
- 6 strips (3" by 1" each) lemon peel
- 4 garlic cloves, crushed with side of chef's knife

1. In 1-quart saucepan, heat oil, fennel seeds, and bay leaves over medium heat until hot but not smoking. Remove saucepan from heat; let stand 10 minutes.

2. In large bowl, combine olives, lemon peel, garlic, and oil mixture. Cover and refrigerate, stirring occasionally, at least 24 hours or up to several days to blend flavors. Store in refrigerator up to 1 month. Drain to serve. Makes about 6 cups.

Each ¼ cup: About 107 calories, 1g protein, 3g carbohydrate, 10g total fat (1g saturated), 0mg cholesterol, 680mg sodium.

SWEET AND SPICY NUTS

....

Packaged in pretty jars or cellophane bags, these treats are a perfect hostess gift.

Prep: 15 minutes plus cooling
Bake: 25 minutes

- 1 cup sugar
- 2 teaspoons salt
- 1 teaspoon ground cumin
- 1 teaspoon ground cinnamon
- 1 teaspoon coarsely ground black pepper
- ½ teaspoon ground red pepper (cayenne)
- 1 large egg white
- 6 cups raw unsalted nuts, such as walnuts, pecans, natural almonds, and/or cashews

1. Preheat oven to 325°F. Grease two 15½" by 10½" jelly-roll pans.

2. In small bowl, combine sugar, salt, cumin, cinnamon, black pepper, and red pepper; stir until blended. In large bowl, with wire whisk, beat egg white until foamy. Add nuts to egg white; stir to coat evenly. Add sugar mixture; toss until nuts are thoroughly coated.

3. Divide nut mixture between prepared jelly-roll pans, spreading evenly. Bake, stirring twice during baking, until golden brown and dry, 25 to 27 minutes. With slotted spoon, transfer nuts to waxed paper; spread in single layer. Cool. Store in airtight container at room temperature up to 1 month. Makes about 8 cups.

Each ¼ cup: About 165 calories, 4g protein, 11g carbohydrate, 12g total fat (2g saturated), 0mg cholesterol, 150mg sodium.

HOT CRABMEAT SPREAD

....

The topping of sliced almonds adds another layer of rich flavor and an unexpected crunch to this crowd-pleasing spread.

Prep: 10 minutes   Bake: 22 minutes

- 3 tablespoons sliced almonds
- 1 container (8 ounces) lump crabmeat
- 1 package (8 ounces) cream cheese, softened
- 3 tablespoons minced onion
- 1 tablespoon milk
- ½ teaspoon prepared white horseradish
- ¼ teaspoon salt
- ⅛ teaspoon coarsely ground black pepper
    assorted crackers

1. Preheat oven to 375°F. Spread almonds in 8-inch square metal baking pan. Bake 2 to 3 minutes or until lightly toasted. Pick through crabmeat to remove any pieces of shell, making sure not to break up meat.

2. In bowl, stir cream cheese, onion, milk, horseradish, salt, and pepper until blended. Gently stir in crabmeat. Spread mixture into shallow 9-inch ceramic or glass baking dish.

3. Sprinkle almonds over crabmeat mixture. Bake 20 to 25 minutes or until edges brown and center begins to bubble. Serve hot with crackers. Makes about 12 servings.

Each serving: About 40 calories, 2g protein, 1g carbohydrate, 3g total fat (2g saturated), 0mg fiber, 17mg cholesterol, 70mg sodium.

SHRIMP RILLETTES

....

This rich, pâté-like spread is served cold as an appetizer on bread or toast. To make ahead, freeze rillettes in jars or ramekins up to three weeks. Make sure to place jars in freezer-weight plastic storage bags, or wrap ramekins well in foil before freezing. Before serving, thaw in refrigerator overnight. Present rillettes with a French baguette or assorted crackers.

Shrimp Rillettes

Prep: 15 minutes plus chilling   Cook: 3 minutes

- 6 tablespoons butter (no substitutions), softened
- 1 pound shelled and deveined shrimp
- 2 tablespoons brandy or dry sherry
- ¼ teaspoon ground red pepper (cayenne)
- 2 tablespoons fresh lemon juice
- ¼ teaspoon salt

1. In 10-inch skillet, heat 2 tablespoons butter on medium-high until melted. Add shrimp and cook 2 minutes or until shrimp turn opaque throughout, stirring frequently. Add brandy and cook 30 seconds. Transfer shrimp mixture to food processor with knife blade attached; pulse until finely chopped.

2. To shrimp mixture in processor, add ground red pepper, lemon juice, remaining 4 tablespoons butter, and salt; pulse until evenly blended.

3. Transfer shrimp mixture to 3 small jars and cover with plastic wrap, pressing wrap directly onto surface of shrimp mixture. Refrigerate at least 8 hours to blend flavors or up to 3 days. Let stand 30 minutes at room temperature before serving. Makes 1¾ cups, or three 6-ounce jars of 6 servings each.

Each serving: About 75 calories, 6g protein, 0g carbohydrate, 5g total fat (3g saturated), 0g fiber, 55mg cholesterol, 125mg sodium.

Potato Halves with Smoked Salmon and Dill

POTATO HALVES WITH SMOKED SALMON AND DILL

....

For ease of arranging and serving, cut a thin slice from the rounded side of each potato half before steaming so it will sit flat on your serving platter.

Prep: 20 minutes   **Cook: 10 minutes**

- 18 baby red potatoes (1½ pounds), cut in half
- 2 tablespoons water
- 1 tablespoon olive oil
- ½ teaspoon salt
- ¼ teaspoon coarsely ground black pepper
- ¼ cup reduced-fat sour cream
- 4 ounces sliced smoked salmon, cut into 36 pieces
- 1 tablespoon snipped fresh dill

1. In microwave-safe large bowl, place potatoes and water. Cover bowl with vented plastic wrap, and microwave on High 5 to 6 minutes or until just fork-tender.

2. Meanwhile, prepare outdoor grill for direct grilling over medium heat.

3. Transfer potatoes to jelly-roll pan. Brush potatoes all over with olive oil, and sprinkle with salt and pepper. Place potatoes on hot grill grate; cook 5 to 6 minutes or until lightly charred on both sides, turning once.

4. Arrange potato halves, rounded sides down, on serving plate. Top each with about ¼ teaspoon sour cream, 1 piece salmon, and some dill. Makes 12 appetizer servings.

Each serving: About 75 calories, 3g protein, 12g carbohydrate, 2g total fat (1g saturated), 1g fiber, 4mg cholesterol, 290mg sodium.

EASY AÏOLI

Aïoli (ay-OH-lee), a garlic mayonnaise from Provence, is the classic condiment for Bouillabaisse (page 72). It's wonderful as a dip for vegetables and as a sauce for fish or lamb.

Prep: 5 minutes plus cooling
Cook: 20 minutes

- 1⅛ teaspoons salt
- 1 head garlic, separated into cloves
- ½ cup mayonnaise
- 2 teaspoons fresh lemon juice
- ½ teaspoon Dijon mustard
- ⅛ teaspoon ground red pepper (cayenne)
- ¼ cup extra-virgin olive oil

1. In 2-quart saucepan, combine *4 cups water* and 1 teaspoon salt; heat to boiling over high heat. Add garlic and boil until garlic has softened, about 20 minutes. Drain. When cool enough to handle, squeeze soft garlic from each clove into small bowl.

2. In blender, puree garlic, mayonnaise, lemon juice, mustard, remaining ⅛ teaspoon salt, and ground red pepper until smooth. With blender running, through hole in cover, add oil in slow, steady stream until mixture is thickened. Transfer to bowl; cover and refrigerate up to 4 hours. Makes about ¾ cup.

Each tablespoon: About 112 calories, 0g protein, 2g carbohydrate, 12g total fat (2g saturated), 5mg cholesterol, 276mg sodium.

CREAM CHEESE TO THE RESCUE

TEST KITCHEN TIP

Unexpected guests? For an almost-instant spread, place an 8-ounce block of cream cheese on a serving platter and spread generously with hot pepper jelly, mango chutney, olive paste (olivada), or salsa. Or, in a food processor with the knife blade attached, puree cream cheese with marinated dried tomatoes, roasted peppers, pickled jalapeño chiles, prepared horseradish, or grated onion; season with coarsely ground pepper. (If you wish, thin the spread with milk to make a dip.) No crackers? Toast some bread and cut into triangles.

SALMON PÂTÉ

This combination of fresh and smoked salmon brings elegance to a Sunday brunch buffet, while the microwave and food processor make preparation easy.

Prep: 10 minutes plus chilling
Cook: 2 minutes

- 1 lemon
- 1 piece salmon fillet (8 ounces), skin removed
- ¼ teaspoon salt
- ⅛ teaspoon ground black pepper
- 2 tablespoons water
- 8 ounces smoked salmon
- 3 tablespoons butter or margarine, softened
- 2 tablespoons reduced-fat cream cheese
- 2 tablespoons chopped fresh chives
  toast rounds or unsalted crackers

1. From lemon, grate 1 teaspoon peel. Cut lemon in half. From 1 lemon half, squeeze 1 tablespoon juice; cut other lemon half into 3 slices. Set peel and juice aside.

2. Sprinkle salmon fillet with salt and pepper to season both sides. Place in microwave-safe shallow bowl or glass pie plate. Top salmon with lemon slices and water. Cook, covered, in microwave oven on High 2 minutes. Let stand, covered, 2 minutes longer. Remove salmon from liquid and place in medium bowl; flake with fork and set aside to cool.

3. Meanwhile, in food processor with knife blade attached, pulse smoked salmon, butter, Neufchâtel, and lemon peel and juice just until smooth (do not overprocess). Gently stir smoked salmon mixture and 1 tablespoon chives into flaked salmon in bowl just until combined. Wrap remaining chives in plastic wrap and refrigerate for garnish later. Spoon salmon pâté into serving bowl or crock; cover and refrigerate for at least 2 hours or overnight.

4. To serve, let pâté stand at room temperature 30 minutes or until soft enough to spread. Garnish pâté with remaining chives. Serve with toast rounds or crackers. Makes about 2 cups.

Each tablespoon: About 30 calories, 3g protein, 0g carbohydrate, 2g total fat (1g saturated), 0g fiber, 6mg cholesterol, 180mg sodium.

CHICKEN LIVER PÂTÉ

....

This silky-smooth pâté is seasoned the traditional way—with thyme and brandy. For the best flavor, refrigerate at least three hours before serving.

Prep: 25 minutes plus chilling
Cook: 20 minutes

2 tablespoons butter or margarine
1 small onion, finely chopped
1 garlic clove, finely chopped
1 pound chicken livers, trimmed
2 tablespoons brandy
½ cup heavy or whipping cream
½ teaspoon salt
¼ teaspoon dried thyme
¼ teaspoon ground black pepper
   assorted crackers, toast, or thinly sliced apples

1. In 10-inch skillet, melt butter over medium-high heat. Add onion and cook, stirring frequently, until tender and golden, about 10 minutes. Stir in garlic and chicken livers and cook until livers are lightly browned but still pink inside, about 5 minutes. Stir in brandy; cook 5 minutes.

2. In blender or in food processor with knife blade attached, puree chicken-liver mixture, cream, salt, thyme, and pepper until smooth, stopping blender occasionally and scraping down side with rubber spatula.

3. Spoon mixture into small bowl; cover and refrigerate at least 3 hours or up to overnight. Let stand 30 minutes at room temperature before serving. Serve with crackers, toast, or apples. Makes about 1½ cups.

Each tablespoon: About 54 calories, 4g protein, 1g carbohydrate, 4g total fat (2g saturated), 92mg cholesterol, 75mg sodium.

SMOKED TROUT PÂTÉ

....

This smoky spread is easily prepared in a food processor.

Prep: 25 minutes

3 whole smoked trout (1¼ pounds total)
1 container (8 ounces) whipped cream cheese
¼ cup low-fat mayonnaise dressing
3 tablespoons fresh lemon juice
⅛ teaspoon ground black pepper
1 tablespoon finely chopped fresh chives
   or green onion
   cucumber slices and assorted crackers

1. Cut head and tail from each trout; discard along with skin and bones. In food processor with knife blade attached, puree trout, cream cheese, mayonnaise dressing, lemon juice, and pepper until smooth.

2. Spoon trout mixture into medium bowl; stir in chives. Cover and refrigerate up to overnight if not serving right away. Before serving, let stand 15 minutes at room temperature to soften. Serve with cucumber slices and crackers. Makes about 3 cups.

Each tablespoon: About 32 calories, 2g protein, 1g carbohydrate, 2g total fat (1g saturated), 7mg cholesterol, 101mg sodium.

WHAT ELSE CAN IT DO?
EGG SLICER

Making precise slices of softer, smaller foods is a snap, literally, with this tool designed to hold slippery, hard-cooked eggs in its cradle as the wires cut through. (Cleanup is just as speedy—use a kitchen brush and warm, soapy water.) It can:

• Quick-slice soft fruits and vegetables such as peeled kiwis, hulled strawberries, white or cremini mushrooms, and pitted olives.
• Create perfect rounds from soft cheeses, like fresh mozzarella balls and goat cheese.
• Make even pats from a stick of butter.

EGGS STUFFED WITH SMOKED SALMON AND CUCUMBERS

....

Make the filling up to a day before, then stuff the eggs well before your guests arrive. These light, fresh flavors are the perfect accompaniment to a spring celebration.

Prep: 30 minutes plus chilling   Cook: 15 minutes

- 10 large eggs
- 2 ounces smoked salmon, finely chopped (⅓ cup)
- 3 tablespoons light mayonnaise
- ¼ cup finely chopped cucumber
- 2 teaspoons chopped fresh dill plus sprigs for garnish
- ⅛ teaspoon ground black pepper

1. In 4-quart saucepan, place eggs and enough *cold water* to cover by at least 1 inch; heat to boiling on high. Immediately remove saucepan from heat and cover tightly; let stand 15 minutes. Pour off hot water, and run cold water over eggs to cool. Peel eggs.

2. Slice eggs lengthwise in half. Gently remove yolks and place in medium bowl; with fork, break yolks into chunks. Reserve 1 tablespoon chopped salmon and add remaining salmon to egg yolks. Add mayonnaise, cucumber, chopped dill, and pepper; gently stir until combined. (Egg-yolk mixture and egg whites can now be covered separately and refrigerated up to 24 hours.)

3. Place egg whites on serving dish or in jelly-roll pan lined with paper towels (to prevent eggs from rolling). Spoon about 1 tablespoon egg-yolk mixture into each egg-white half. Top eggs with reserved chopped salmon. Cover eggs and refrigerate up to 4 hours. Just before serving, garnish with dill sprigs. Makes 20 appetizer servings.

Each serving: About 50 calories, 4g protein, 1g carbohydrate, 3g total fat (1g saturated), 0g fiber, 108mg cholesterol, 70mg sodium.

Eggs Stuffed with Smoked Salmon and Cucumbers

TOMATO AND RICOTTA SALATA BRUSCHETTA

....

Bruschetta is toasted Italian bread that is rubbed with garlic and drizzled with olive oil. It's often topped with savory ingredients to make a simple appetizer. Here we use ripe tomatoes and ricotta salata, a lightly salted and pressed sheep's milk cheese. Ricotta salata can be found at Italian markets and specialty food stores.

Prep: 25 minutes

1 loaf (8 ounces) Italian bread, cut on diagonal into ½-inch-thick slices

8 garlic cloves, each cut in half

1 pound ripe plum tomatoes (6 medium), seeded and cut into ½-inch pieces

1 tablespoon finely chopped red onion

1 tablespoon chopped fresh basil

4 ounces ricotta salata, feta, or goat cheese, cut into ½-inch pieces

2 tablespoons extra-virgin olive oil

2 teaspoons balsamic vinegar

¼ teaspoon salt

¼ teaspoon coarsely ground black pepper

1. Preheat oven to 400°F. Place bread slices on cookie sheet and bake until lightly toasted, about 5 minutes. Rub one side of each toast slice with cut side of garlic.

2. Meanwhile, in bowl, gently toss tomatoes, onion, basil, cheese, oil, vinegar, salt, and pepper until combined.

3. To serve, spoon tomato mixture on garlic-rubbed side of toast slices. Makes 16 bruschetta.

Each bruschetta: About 79 calories, 2g protein, 9g carbohydrate, 4g total fat (1g saturated), 6mg cholesterol, 236mg sodium.

TUSCAN WHITE-BEAN BRUSCHETTA

Prepare toast as directed (left) but prepare topping as follows: In bowl, with fork, lightly mash **1 can (15½ to 19 ounces) white kidney beans (cannellini),** rinsed and drained, with **1 tablespoon fresh lemon juice.** Stir in **1 tablespoon olive oil, 2 teaspoons chopped fresh parsley, 1 teaspoon minced fresh sage, ¼ teaspoon salt,** and **⅛ teaspoon coarsely ground black pepper.** Just before serving, spoon mixture over garlic-rubbed side of toast slices. Sprinkle with **1 teaspoon chopped fresh parsley.** Makes 16 bruschetta.

Each bruschetta: About 33 calories, 2g protein, 4g carbohydrate, 1g total fat (0g saturated), 0mg cholesterol, 77mg sodium.

POKER CHIPS

....

Save on cleanup by lining the cookie sheets with heavy-duty foil or parchment paper.

Prep: 10 minutes plus cooling   Bake: 8 minutes

½ cup olive oil

1 tablespoon freshly grated Parmesan or Pecorino-Romano cheese

1 tablespoon chili powder

1 teaspoon ground cumin

1 package (12 ounces) white or whole-wheat pitas

1. Preheat oven to 425°F. In cup, with fork, mix oil, Parmesan, chili powder, and cumin.

2. With knife or kitchen shears, carefully split each pita. Brush insides of pita halves lightly with oil mixture. Cut each half into 8 wedges.

3. Transfer pita wedges to two ungreased cookie sheets (wedges can overlap slightly). Place cookie sheets on two oven racks and bake pita chips until edges are golden, 8 to 10 minutes. Watch carefully, as they can burn quickly.

4. Transfer cookie sheets to wire racks and cool completely. Store chips in airtight container up to 1 week. Makes 8 dozen chips.

Each chip: About 20 calories, 0g protein, 2g carbohydrate, 1g total fat (0g saturated), 0mg cholesterol, 20mg sodium.

Tomato and Ricotta Salata Bruschetta and Tuscan White-Bean Bruschetta

BAKED RICOTTA WITH TOMATO VINAIGRETTE

....

Once baked and allowed to set, the squares of ricotta cheese make a nice substitute for medallions of goat cheese or even polenta wedges.

Prep: 15 minutes plus standing   Bake: 1 hour

- 2 lemons
- 1 container (32 ounces) part-skim ricotta cheese
- ³/₄ teaspoon salt
- ³/₈ teaspoon ground black pepper
- ½ teaspoon Dijon mustard
- ¼ cup olive oil
- 4 plum tomatoes, coarsely chopped
- 1 bag (5 to 6 ounces) baby greens

1. Preheat oven to 375°F. From lemons, grate 1 teaspoon peel and squeeze 3 tablespoons juice. Set aside. Spray 9-inch glass or ceramic pie plate with nonstick cooking spray.

2. In medium bowl, stir lemon peel, ricotta, ½ teaspoon salt, and ¼ teaspoon pepper until blended. Spread ricotta mixture evenly in prepared pie plate. Bake 1 hour or until cheese is lightly browned. Let stand 10 minutes to allow cheese to set. Slice into 12 wedges.

3. Meanwhile, in medium bowl, whisk together lemon juice, Dijon, ¼ teaspoon salt, and ⅛ teaspoon pepper. Whisk in olive oil in slow steady stream until blended. Stir in chopped tomatoes.

4. To serve, place 1 ricotta wedge along with some greens on each of 12 serving plates. Top greens and ricotta with tomato vinaigrette. Makes 12 first-course servings.

Each serving: About 155 calories, 9g protein, 6g carbohydrate, 11g total fat (4g saturated), 1g fiber, 23mg cholesterol, 245mg sodium.

Baked Ricotta with Tomato Vinaigrette

SAVORY BLUE CHEESE, WALNUT, AND DATE RUGELACH

....

Filling cream cheese dough with a mixture of blue cheese, walnuts, and dates turns rugelach into delicious pastries that go perfectly with a glass of red or white wine.

**Prep: 40 minutes plus chilling and cooling
Bake: 30 minutes**

- 1 cup butter or margarine (2 sticks), softened
- 1 package (8 ounces) cream cheese, softened
- 2 cups all-purpose flour
- ½ teaspoon salt
- 1½ cups walnuts
- 4 ounces blue cheese, cut into small pieces
- 48 pitted dates (about 12 ounces)
- 1 large egg white
- 1 teaspoon water

1. Prepare dough: In large bowl, with mixer at medium speed, beat butter and cream cheese until creamy, occasionally scraping bowl with rubber spatula. Reduce speed to low; gradually beat in flour and salt just until blended, occasionally scraping bowl.

2. Divide dough into 4 equal pieces; shape each into a disk. Wrap each disk in plastic wrap and refrigerate until dough is firm enough to roll, at least 4 hours or overnight. (Or place dough in freezer 1 hour if using butter, 1 hour 30 minutes if using margarine.)

3. In food processor with knife blade attached, process ½ cup walnuts until finely chopped; transfer to small bowl and reserve. In same food processor bowl, process blue cheese and remaining 1 cup walnuts just until a coarse mixture forms.

4. Preheat oven to 350°F. Line two large cookie sheets with foil; grease foil.

5. On lightly floured surface, with floured rolling pin, roll one disk of dough into 10-inch round. (If dough is too cold to roll, let stand 5 to 10 minutes at room temperature to soften slightly.) With pastry wheel or knife, cut dough into 12 equal wedges (do not separate). Beginning 1 inch from edge, sprinkle ½ cup blue-cheese mixture in 2-inch-wide ring, leaving dough in center exposed. Place 1 whole date horizontally on wide curved end of each wedge. Starting at wide end, roll up each wedge, jelly-roll fashion. Place rugelach, point side down, 1 inch apart, on cookie sheet. Repeat with remaining dough (one disk at a time), blue-cheese mixture, and dates.

6. In small bowl, lightly beat egg white with water. With pastry brush, brush rugelach with egg-white mixture and sprinkle evenly with reserved walnuts.

7. Bake until golden, 30 to 35 minutes, rotating sheets between upper and lower racks halfway through baking. With wide spatula, immediately transfer rugelach to wire racks to cool. Store in airtight container up to 3 days, or in freezer up to 3 months. Makes 48 appetizers.

Each appetizer: about 125 calories, 2g protein, 10g carbohydrate, 9g total fat (4g saturated), 18mg cholesterol, 115mg sodium.

EASY SPICY CHEESE STRAWS

Called paillettes *(little straws) in French, these twisted strips of pastry are perfect with cocktails or wine. Feel free to substitute your favorite hard grating cheese for the Cheddar. Parmesan and Asiago are good choices. Frozen puff pastry makes preparation a breeze.*

Prep: 30 minutes   Bake: 20 minutes per batch

- 1 tablespoon paprika
- ½ teaspoon dried thyme
- ¼ to ½ teaspoon ground red pepper (cayenne)
- ¼ teaspoon salt
- 1 package (17¼ ounces) frozen puff-pastry sheets, thawed
- 1 large egg white, lightly beaten
- 8 ounces sharp Cheddar cheese, shredded (2 cups)

1. Grease two large cookie sheets. In small bowl, combine paprika, thyme, ground red pepper, and salt.

2. Unfold 1 puff-pastry sheet. On lightly floured surface, with floured rolling pin, roll pastry into 14-inch square. Lightly brush with egg white. Sprinkle half of paprika mixture on pastry. Sprinkle half of Cheddar on half of pastry. Fold pastry over to cover cheese, forming rectangle. With rolling pin, lightly roll over pastry to seal layers together. With pizza wheel or knife, cut pastry crosswise into ½-inch-wide strips.

3. Preheat oven to 375°F. Place strips ½ inch apart on prepared cookie sheets, twisting each strip twice to form spiral and pressing ends against cookie sheet to prevent strips from uncurling. Bake cheese straws until golden, 20 to 22 minutes. With spatula, carefully transfer to wire racks to cool.

4. Repeat with remaining puff-pastry sheet, egg white, paprika mixture, and cheese. Store in airtight container up to 1 week. Makes about 48 cheese straws.

Each straw: About 78 calories, 2g protein, 5g carbohydrate, 5g total fat (2g saturated), 5mg cholesterol, 68mg sodium.

QUICK QUESADILLAS

....

Serve as an accompaniment to Spicy Black Bean Soup (page 62) or as the first course for a Southwest-themed barbecue.

Prep: 10 minutes   Bake: 5 minutes

8   (7- to 8-inch) flour tortillas
1   jar (7 ounces) roasted red peppers, drained and thinly sliced
2   small green onions, thinly sliced
4   ounces Pepper Jack cheese, shredded (1 cup)
³⁄₄ cup loosely packed fresh cilantro leaves

1. Preheat oven to 400°F. Place 4 tortillas on large cookie sheet. Sprinkle one-fourth of roasted peppers, green onions, cheese, and cilantro on each tortilla; top with remaining tortillas to make 4 quesadillas.

2. Bake quesadillas until heated through, about 5 minutes. Cut each quesadilla into 8 wedges. Serve warm. Makes 32 appetizers.

Each wedge: About 45 calories, 2g protein, 5g carbohydrate, 2g total fat (1g saturated), 4mg cholesterol, 74mg sodium.

---

5 IDEAS FOR . . . BAKED TORTILLA CHIPS

Put away the salsa and guacamole—these crisps aren't just for dipping. Here are clever ways to turn even the broken bits at the bottom of the bag into your new secret ingredient. (Our recipes call for baked chips, which have 20 fewer calories per ounce, as well as less fat—but use traditional chips if you prefer.)

CHILES RELLENOS PIE

Preheat oven to 350°F. Drain 2 cans (4 to 4½ ounces each) whole green chiles. Slit each chile on 1 side; open flat and pat dry. Grease 9½-inch deep-dish pie plate; use chiles to line bottom. In bowl, whisk 5 large eggs with 1½ cups reduced-fat (2%) milk and ½ cup finely chopped fully cooked chorizo (2 ounces); pour over chiles. Top with 2 cups coarsely crushed tortilla chips. Bake 40 minutes or until set in center. Serves 6.

MEXICAN COCKTAIL MEATBALLS

Preheat oven to 425°F. From 1 jar (16 ounces) picante sauce, measure ⅓ cup and place in medium bowl. Mix in 1 pound ground beef, ½ cup crushed tortilla chips, ¼ cup chopped fresh cilantro, 2 tablespoons water, and 1 large egg. Scoop into 1-inch balls; place on foil-lined cookie sheet. Bake 20 minutes to cook through. In microwave-safe serving bowl, heat remaining picante sauce in microwave on High 1 to 2 minutes, until hot. Place meatballs in sauce; provide cocktail picks for serving. Serves 8.

TOMATO AND CORN SOUP

In saucepan, heat 1 tablespoon olive oil over medium heat. Add 1 chopped small onion and cook 8 minutes or until lightly browned and tender, stirring often. Add 2 cans (14 to 14½ ounces each) reduced-sodium chicken broth, 1 can (14½ ounces) diced tomatoes with chiles, and 1 package (10 ounces) frozen corn kernels; heat to boiling. Spoon into 4 bowls. Divide 1 cup coarsely crushed tortilla chips among bowls to top soup. Serves 4.

PIZZA BITES

Preheat oven to 425°F. Arrange 40 bite-size tortilla chip cups on large cookie sheet. (If using regular tortilla chips, which are larger, place on 2 cookie sheets.) In bowl, stir 1 cup shredded Italian cheese blend with 2 tablespoons store-bought pesto. Spoon cheese mixture onto chips. Slice 10 grape tomatoes into 4 pieces each; place 1 on each pizza bite. Bake 6 minutes to melt cheese. Serves 8.

CHILAQUILES

Preheat oven to 350°F. In 8-inch-square glass baking dish coated with nonstick cooking spray, layer half of each of the following ingredients: 2 cups shredded cooked chicken or turkey, 1⅓ cups thick and chunky salsa, 1 can (15 to 19 ounces) rinsed and drained black beans, 1 cup shredded Mexican cheese blend, and 3 cups coarsely crushed tortilla chips. Repeat layering. Bake 40 minutes to heat through. Serves 6.

CHORIZO AND BLACK BEAN NACHOS

....

These are serious nachos for chile lovers. Be sure to use fully cooked chorizo links, not soft bulk-style chorizo.

Prep: 20 minutes   Bake: 5 minutes per batch

- 36 unbroken large tortilla chips
- 3 large ripe plum tomatoes, cut into ¼-inch pieces
- ⅓ cup chopped fresh cilantro
- ¼ teaspoon salt
- 1 tablespoon vegetable oil
- 1 fully cooked chorizo sausage (3 ounces), finely chopped, or ¾ cup finely chopped pepperoni (3 ounces)
- 1 medium onion, finely chopped
- 1 garlic clove, finely chopped
- ½ teaspoon ground cumin
- 1 can (15 to 19 ounces) black beans, rinsed and drained
- 4 ounces Monterey Jack cheese, shredded (1 cup)
- 2 pickled jalapeño chiles, very thinly sliced

1. Preheat oven to 400°F. Arrange as many tortilla chips as will fit in single layer on two ungreased large cookie sheets. In small bowl, combine tomatoes, cilantro, and salt.

2. In 10-inch skillet, heat oil over medium heat. Add chorizo, onion, garlic, and cumin; cook, stirring, until onion is tender, about 5 minutes. Stir in beans and heat through.

3. Place 1 tablespoon bean mixture on each tortilla chip. Sprinkle cheese over beans and top each nacho with 1 slice jalapeño. Bake until cheese begins to melt, about 5 minutes.

4. Spoon about 1 teaspoon tomato mixture on each nacho. Transfer nachos to platter. Makes 36 nachos.

Each nacho: About 51 calories, 2g protein, 4g carbohydrate, 3g total fat (1g saturated), 5mg cholesterol, 112mg sodium.

CUBANO QUESADILLAS

....

Our take on the classic pressed sandwich adds a touch of the Southwest. Low-fat tortillas make for a lighter bite with all the flavor of the original.

Prep: 18 minutes   Cook: 2 minutes

- 8 (6-inch) low-fat tortillas
- ¼ cup yellow mustard
- 4 ounces thinly sliced Black Forest ham
- 8 sandwich-cut dill pickle slices
- 4 ounces thinly sliced roast pork from the deli
- 4 ounces thinly sliced part-skim Swiss cheese

1. Prepare outdoor grill for directly grilling over medium heat.

2. Brush 1 side of each tortilla with mustard. Evenly divide ham, pickles, pork, and cheese between 4 tortillas, placing them on top of mustard. Top with remaining tortillas, mustard side down, pressing firmly.

3. With large metal spatula, place quesadillas on hot grill grate and cook 2 to 3 minutes or until tortillas on both sides are browned and Swiss cheese melts, carefully turning quesadillas once. Transfer quesadillas to large cutting board; let stand 1 minute. Cut each quesadilla into 4 wedges to serve. Makes 8 appetizer servings.

Each serving (2 wedges): About 190 calories, 15g protein, 18g carbohydrate, 6g total fat (2g saturated), 1g fiber, 27mg cholesterol, 640mg sodium.

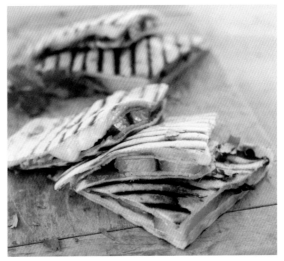

Cubano Quesadillas

MINI GOUGÈRES

··

In French bistros, diners are often presented with a small napkin-lined basket or plate filled with these cheese puffs known as gougères. Once you become familar with making the choux paste (batter), these puffs are sure to become part of your repertoire.

Prep: 20 minutes **Bake:** 30 minutes

- 6 ounces Gruyère or Swiss cheese
- 1 cup water
- 6 tablespoons butter or margarine, cut up
- 1½ teaspoons Dijon mustard
- ½ teaspoon hot pepper sauce
- ¼ teaspoon salt
- 1 cup all-purpose flour
- 4 large eggs

1. Preheat oven to 400°F. Grease and flour two large cookie sheets. Shred Gruyère to equal 1 cup; finely dice remaining cheese.

2. In 3-quart saucepan, heat water, butter, mustard, hot pepper sauce, and salt to boiling. Remove saucepan from heat. With wooden spoon, vigorously stir in flour all at once until mixture forms ball and leaves side of pan.

3. Add eggs, one at a time, beating well after each addition, until batter is smooth and satinlike. Stir in shredded and diced cheese. Drop batter by rounded teaspoons, about 2 inches apart, onto prepared cookie sheets.

4. Bake 30 to 35 minutes, rotating sheets between upper and lower racks halfway through baking, until deep golden. Transfer puffs to wire racks to cool. Serve warm or at room temperature. Makes about 48 puffs.

Each puff: About 60 calories, 3g protein, 3g carbohydrate, 4g total fat (2g saturated), 34mg cholesterol, 65mg sodium.

CHEDDAR CURRY PUFFS

Prepare gougères as directed above, but use **Cheddar cheese** in place of Gruyère cheese. Add **2 teaspoons curry powder,** ½ **teaspoon ground coriander,** and ½ **teaspoon ground cumin** to water mixture in Step 2. Makes about 48 puffs.

BUFFALO-STYLE CHICKEN WINGS

··

Here's a broiled version of one of America's favorite appetizers. Serve with plenty of napkins!

Prep: 15 minutes **Broil:** 20 minutes

- 4 ounces blue cheese, crumbled (1 cup)
- ½ cup sour cream
- ¼ cup mayonnaise
- ¼ cup milk
- ¼ cup chopped fresh parsley
- 1 tablespoon fresh lemon juice
- ½ teaspoon salt
- 3 pounds chicken wings (18 wings), tips discarded, if desired
- 3 tablespoons butter or margarine
- ¼ cup hot pepper sauce
- 1 medium bunch celery, cut into sticks

1. Preheat broiler. In medium bowl, combine blue cheese, sour cream, mayonnaise, milk, parsley, lemon juice, and ¼ teaspoon salt. Cover and refrigerate.

2. Arrange chicken wings on rack in broiling pan; sprinkle with remaining ¼ teaspoon salt. Broil 5 inches from heat source 10 minutes. Turn wings and broil until golden, 10 to 15 minutes longer.

3. Meanwhile, in small saucepan, melt butter with hot pepper sauce over low heat, stirring occasionally; keep hot.

4. In large bowl, toss wings with seasoned butter to coat all sides. Arrange chicken wings and celery on platter along with blue-cheese sauce and serve. Makes 18 appetizers.

Each appetizer (without wing tip): About 169 calories, 10g protein, 3g carbohydrate, 13g total fat (5g saturated), 39mg cholesterol, 349mg sodium.

MINI REMOULADE CRAB CAKES

••••••••••••••••••••••••••••••••

Crab cakes are a universal favorite. These luscious morsels can be prepared up to several hours ahead and refrigerated. Reheat just before serving.

Prep: 25 minutes   Bake: 20 minutes

- 2 tablespoons butter or margarine
- 1 small onion, finely chopped
- ½ red pepper, finely chopped
- 1 stalk celery, finely chopped
- ¼ cup light mayonnaise
- 1 tablespoon sour cream
- 2 teaspoons grainy Dijon mustard
- ½ teaspoon freshly grated lemon peel
- ¼ teaspoon salt
- ⅛ teaspoon ground red pepper (cayenne)
- 1 pound lump crabmeat, picked over
- 1 cup fresh bread crumbs (about 2 slices bread)
  Lemon Sauce (below)

1. In 10-inch skillet, melt butter over medium heat. Add onion, red pepper, and celery. Cook, stirring frequently, until vegetables are tender, about 10 minutes. Let cool.

2. In large bowl, stir mayonnaise, sour cream, mustard, lemon peel, salt, and ground red pepper until blended; stir in crabmeat and bread crumbs just until mixed. Cover and refrigerate 30 minutes.

3. Meanwhile, prepare Lemon Sauce.

4. Preheat oven to 400°F. Lightly grease two cookie sheets. Drop level tablespoons crab mixture, pressing lightly, on prepared cookie sheets. Bake until golden brown, about 15 minutes. Top each crab cake with about ½ teaspoon lemon sauce. Serve hot. Makes about 50 mini crab cakes.

LEMON SAUCE

In small bowl, stir together ¼ **cup light mayonnaise, ¼ cup sour cream, 1 teaspoon freshly grated lemon peel, 1 tablespoon fresh lemon juice, pinch salt,** and **pinch ground red pepper (cayenne)** until blended. Makes about ½ cup.

Each crab cake with sauce: About 28 calories, 2g protein, 1g carbohydrate, 2g fat (1g saturated), 12mg cholesterol, 71mg sodium.

MAIN-DISH CRAB CAKES

Prepare crab cakes (left) but divide crab mixture into 8 portions, about ½ cup each, and shape each into a 3-inch cake. Place on greased cookie sheet. Bake until golden brown, about 20 minutes, gently turning cake over with spatula halfway through baking. Serve with Lemon Sauce (opposite), if desired.

Each crab cake: About 138 calories, 12g protein, 5g carbohydrate, 7g fat (3g saturated), 68mg cholesterol, 366mg sodium.

PROSCIUTTO-WRAPPED ASPARAGUS

••••••••••••••••••••••••••••••••

Delicate, succulent asparagus is the perfect foil for salty prosciutto. You can assemble these early in the day and bake them at the very last minute.

Prep: 25 minutes   Bake: 10 minutes

- 24 thick asparagus spears, trimmed and peeled
- 12 thin slices prosciutto (5 ounces)
- ½ cup freshly grated Parmesan cheese
- ¼ teaspoon coarsely ground black pepper

1. In 5-quart Dutch oven, heat *3 quarts water* to boiling over high heat. Add asparagus; cook 3 minutes to blanch. Drain; rinse with cold running water. Pat dry with paper towels.

2. Preheat oven to 450°F. Working in batches, spread out prosciutto on cutting board; cut each slice lengthwise in half and separate slightly. Evenly sprinkle 1 teaspoon Parmesan on each prosciutto strip. Place 1 asparagus spear at end of 1 strip; wrap prosciutto in spiral along length of asparagus (don't cover asparagus tip). Transfer to jelly-roll pan. Repeat with remaining prosciutto, Parmesan, and asparagus. Sprinkle with pepper. If not serving right away, cover and refrigerate up to 6 hours.

3. Bake prosciutto-wrapped asparagus 10 minutes. Transfer to paper towels to drain. Arrange on platter and serve warm. Makes 24 appetizers.

Each appetizer: About 28 calories, 3g protein, 1g carbohydrate, 2g total fat (1g saturated), 6mg cholesterol, 148mg sodium.

SHRIMP COCKTAIL

....

Everyone loves to dip shrimp into sauce; it's fun and it's tasty. So here are two sauces that are very different but equally delicious.

Prep: 25 minutes plus chilling
Cook: 17 minutes

- 1 lemon, thinly sliced
- 4 bay leaves
- 20 whole black peppercorns
- 10 whole allspice berries
- 2 teaspoons salt
- 24 extra-large shrimp (1 pound), shelled and deveined (page 221)
      Southwestern-Style Cocktail Sauce (below)
      Mustard Dipping Sauce (right)
- 12 small romaine lettuce leaves
- 24 (7-inch) bamboo skewers

1. In 5-quart Dutch oven, combine *2 quarts water,* lemon, bay leaves, peppercorns, allspice berries, and salt; heat to boiling. Cover and boil 15 minutes.

2. Add shrimp and cook just until opaque throughout, 1 to 2 minutes. Drain and rinse with cold running water to stop cooking. Cover and refrigerate shrimp up to 24 hours.

3. Prepare Southwestern-Style Cocktail Sauce and/ or Mustard Dipping Sauce.

4. Just before serving, place bowls of sauces in center of platter; arrange romaine leaves around bowls, leaf tips facing out. Thread each shrimp on a bamboo skewer and arrange skewers on romaine. Makes 8 first-course servings.

Each serving without sauce: About 51 calories, 10g protein, 1g carbohydrate, 1g total fat (0g saturated), 70mg cholesterol, 141mg sodium.

SOUTHWESTERN-STYLE COCKTAIL SAUCE

In bowl, stir **1 cup bottled cocktail sauce, 2 tablespoons chopped fresh cilantro, 2 teaspoons minced jalapeño chile,** and **2 teaspoons fresh lime juice** until well combined. Cover and refrigerate up to 24 hours. Makes about 1 cup.

Each tablespoon: About 18 calories, 0g protein, 4g carbohydrate, 0g total fat (0g saturated), 0mg cholesterol, 191mg sodium.

MUSTARD DIPPING SAUCE

In small serving bowl, stir **1 cup reduced-fat sour cream, 3 tablespoons grainy Dijon mustard, 3 tablespoons chopped fresh parsley, ¼ teaspoon freshly grated lemon peel, ¼ teaspoon salt,** and **⅛ teaspoon coarsely ground black pepper** until well combined. Cover and refrigerate up to 24 hours. Makes about 1 cup.

Each tablespoon: About 28 calories, 1g protein, 1g carbohydrate, 2g total fat (1g saturated), 5mg cholesterol, 111mg sodium.

PROSCIUTTO WITH MELON

....

The marriage of sweet ripe melon and salty prosciutto is a classic combination. Imported prosciutto di Parma, available at Italian grocers and specialty food markets, is much milder than the domestic varieties of this ham. It's worth seeking out.

Prep: 10 minutes

- 1 small honeydew melon or 1 medium cantaloupe, chilled
- 4 ounces prosciutto, thinly sliced
      freshly ground black pepper

1. Cut melon in half through stem end and remove seeds. Cut each half into 4 wedges; cut off rind.

2. Arrange 2 melon wedges on each of four plates; arrange prosciutto to side of melon. Sprinkle pepper on each serving. Makes 4 first-course servings.

Each serving: About 150 calories, 9g protein, 22g carbohydrate, 4g total fat (1g saturated), 23mg cholesterol, 548mg sodium.

PROSCIUTTO WITH OTHER FRUIT

Prepare as directed but substitute **8 large green or black figs,** each cut in half, or **2 medium papayas,** peeled, seeded, and sliced, for melon.

CHINESE DUMPLINGS

···

Steamed dumplings are fun to make at home. Have them for brunch; it's the way the Chinese enjoy them.

Prep: 45 minutes   Cook: 10 minutes

- 2 cups packed sliced Napa cabbage (Chinese cabbage)
- 8 ounces ground pork
- 1 green onion, finely chopped
- 1½ teaspoons minced, peeled fresh ginger
- 2 tablespoons soy sauce
- 1 tablespoon dry sherry
- 2 teaspoons cornstarch
- 36 wonton wrappers (9 ounces)
- 1 large egg white, beaten
   Soy Dipping Sauce (right)

1. Prepare filling: In 2-quart saucepan, heat *1 inch water* to boiling over high heat. Add cabbage and heat to boiling. Cook 1 minute; drain. Immediately rinse with cold running water to stop cooking. With hands, squeeze out as much water from cabbage as possible. Finely chop cabbage. Squeeze out any remaining water from cabbage; place in medium bowl. Stir in pork, green onion, ginger, soy sauce, sherry, and cornstarch until well blended.

2. Arrange half of wonton wrappers on waxed paper. With pastry brush, brush each wrapper lightly with egg white. Spoon 1 rounded teaspoon filling into center of each wrapper. Bring two opposite corners of each wonton wrapper together over filling; pinch and pleat edges together to seal in filling. Repeat with remaining wrappers, egg white, and filling.

3. In deep nonstick 12-inch skillet, heat *½ inch water* to boiling over high heat. Place all dumplings, pleated edges up, in one layer in skillet. With spatula, move dumplings gently to prevent them from sticking to bottom of skillet; heat to boiling. Reduce heat; cover and simmer until dumplings are cooked through, about 5 minutes.

4. Meanwhile, prepare Soy Dipping Sauce.

5. With slotted spoon, transfer dumplings to platter. Serve with dipping sauce. Makes 36 dumplings.

Each dumpling without sauce: About 40 calories, 2g protein, 5g carbohydrate, 1g total fat (1g saturated), 5g cholesterol, 103g sodium.

SOY DIPPING SAUCE

In small serving bowl, stir ¼ **cup soy sauce,** ¼ **cup seasoned rice vinegar or white wine vinegar,** and **2 tablespoons peeled fresh ginger,** cut into very thin slivers, until blended. Makes about ½ cup.

Each teaspoon: About 4 calories, 0g protein, 1g carbohydrate, 0g total fat (0g saturated), 0mg cholesterol, 221mg sodium.

Chinese Dumplings

3

SOUPS, STEWS & ONE-POT MEALS

Whether made on the stovetop or in a slow cooker, soups, stews, and chilis are the very essence of one-pot cooking, and, as you would expect, have a lot in common. They are all made in one pot, they taste even better a day or so later, and they are as easy to cook up in small amounts as in large potfuls, especially if you utilize a slow cooker! Even better, they make almost a complete meal. Begin with a crisp green salad, add some fresh bread, and dinner is served. How easy is that?

In this chapter, you will find recipes from all corners of the globe, including Vietnamese Noodle Soup (page 68), Gazpacho with Cilantro Cream (page 60), Moroccan Vegetable Stew (page 78), Hungarian Pork Goulash (page 87), Provençal Beef Stew (page 79), and Pasta e Fagiole with Sausage (page 66). **Slow-cooker specialties, from Tomatillo Pork (page 88) to Sweet and Tangy Braised Chuck Roast (page 90), are all indicated with the following symbol: 🝧 . To achieve one-pot perfection, see 10 Helpful Tips for the Slow Cooker (page 89).**

SOUP

Soups are infinite in variety and exceptionally versatile. A soup can be a light and elegant first course, a substantial rib-sticking meal-in-a-pot, or a refreshing cooler on a summer's day. It can be a crystal-clear golden liquid, a silky smooth and creamy puree, or thick with vegetables, noodles, and a protein, such as chicken or beef. Some soups are always served cold, like gazpacho, and some are always served hot, such as split pea soup. And others are so versatile that they are just as delicious hot, cold, or at room temperature. Whatever your preference, there is a soup to suit your taste.

STEW

Warming, hearty, and always satisfying, stews are perfect cold-weather food. Stews can be made with chicken, pork, beef, veal, or fish that has been cut into small pieces or hearty chunks. And while some stews are laden with a variety of vegetables, others contain only one or two. The liquid can be as varied as the ingredients themselves: water, broth, tomato juice, and wine, or a combination can all work in a stew. Served up in large shallow bowls with hunks of bread for sopping up all the flavorful juices, a stew is comfort food of the first order.

CHILI

Just who cooked up the first chili is in dispute, but many chili aficionados believe credit must go to the Texas trail cooks who fed the cowboys while "winning the West." In fact, by 1880 eating a "bowl of red" was commonplace in cities like San Antonio. In this chapter we offer a tasty variety of all-American chilis. Some are made with chunks of beef, others with ground beef, and one is made with tasty pieces of pork. Our Cincinnati Chili (page 86) gets served up on a bed of spaghetti, while the New Mexican Green Chili (page 86) is a bold pot of pork shoulder chunks, onions, jalapeños, cumin, cayenne, fresh tomatillos, and poblanos that speaks of the best of the Southwest.

South-of-the-Border Chicken Soup (recipe page 67)

APPLE AND PARSNIP SOUP

This creamy soup takes delicious advantage of autumn's bounty. The puree is light, yet rich and flavorful with no need for cream.

Prep: 15 minutes   Cook: 20 minutes

- 1 package (32 ounces) chicken broth
- 2 cups water
- 1 tablespoon olive oil
- 2 large shallots, finely chopped (1/2 cup)
- 1 stalk celery, finely chopped
- 2 pounds McIntosh or Braeburn apples (4 to 6 medium), peeled, cored, and chopped
- 1 pound parsnips, peeled and chopped
- 1/4 teaspoon dried thyme
- 1/2 teaspoon salt
- 1/4 teaspoon pepper
  roasted, hulled pumpkin seeds for garnish

1. In covered 2-quart saucepan, heat chicken broth and water to boiling over high heat.

2. Meanwhile, in 5- to 6-quart saucepot, heat oil over medium heat. Add shallots and celery, and cook about 5 minutes or until softened and lightly browned. Add apples, parsnips, thyme, salt, and ground black pepper, and cook 1 minute.

3. Add hot broth mixture to saucepot; cover and heat to boiling over high heat. Reduce heat to low and simmer, covered, 6 to 7 minutes or until parsnips are very tender.

4. Spoon one-third of apple mixture into blender; cover, removing center part of lid to let steam escape. Lay a paper towel over top and puree until smooth. Pour puree into bowl. Repeat with remaining mixture. Return to saucepot to reheat. Garnish with pumpkin seeds to serve. Makes about 9 cups or 6 appetizer servings.

Each serving: About 160 calories, 3g protein, 34g carbohydrate, 3g total fat (0g saturated), 6g fiber, 0mg cholesterol, 600mg sodium.

Tip: If you have an immersion blender, use it to puree soup right in the pot.

BUTTERNUT-APPLE SOUP

Nothing can match a pureed vegetable and cream soup for texture and this subtly sweet combination of squash and apples just proves the point.

Prep: 15 minutes   Cook: 40 to 45 minutes

- 2 tablespoons vegetable oil
- 1 small onion, chopped
- 2 medium butternut squash (1 3/4 pounds each), peeled, seeded, and cut into 3/4-inch pieces
- 3/4 pound Golden Delicious apples (2 medium), peeled, cored, and coarsely chopped
- 1 can (14 1/2 ounces) vegetable broth or 1 3/4 cups Vegetable Broth (page 71)
- 1 1/2 cups water
- 1 teaspoon freshly chopped fresh thyme or 1/4 teaspoon dried thyme
- 1 teaspoon salt
- 1/8 teaspoon coarsely ground black pepper
- 1 cup half-and-half or light cream

1. In 4-quart saucepan, heat oil over medium heat. Add onion and cook until tender and golden, about 10 minutes. Stir in squash, apples, broth, water, thyme, salt, and pepper; heat to boiling over high heat. Reduce heat to low; cover and simmer, stirring often, until squash is very tender, 20 to 25 minutes.

2. Spoon one-third of squash mixture into blender; cover, with center part of cover removed to let steam escape, and puree until smooth. Pour puree into bowl. Repeat with remaining mixture.

3. Return puree to saucepan; stir in half-and-half. Heat through over medium heat, stirring occasionally (do not boil). Makes about 9 cups or 8 first-course servings.

Each serving: About 175 calories, 3g protein, 28g carbohydrate, 7mg total fat (3mg saturated), 11mg cholesterol, 525mg sodium.

SPICY CURRIED CARROT SOUP

Prepare as directed but substitute **2 pounds carrots,** peeled and cut into 2-inch pieces, for squash. Increase broth to 2 cans. In Step 1, omit thyme and **add 2 teaspoons curry powder,** and **2 teaspoons grated fresh ginger.** Omit half-and-half. Makes about 8 cups or 8 first-course servings.

Butternut-Apple Soup

CREAM OF ASPARAGUS SOUP

For the most flavor, choose the thickest asparagus you can find for this creamy soup. If you wish, garnish each serving with a sprinkling of snipped fresh chives or chopped tarragon or parsley.

Prep: 10 minutes   Cook: 25 to 30 minutes

- 2 tablespoons butter or margarine
- 1 medium onion, chopped
- 12 ounces asparagus, trimmed and cut into 1-inch pieces (3 cups)
- 3 tablespoons all-purpose flour
- ¼ teaspoon salt
- ⅛ teaspoon ground black pepper
- 1 can (14½ ounces) chicken or vegetable broth or 1¾ cups Chicken Broth (page 70) or Vegetable Broth (page 71)
- 1 cup half-and-half or light cream

1. In 3-quart saucepan, melt butter over medium heat; add onion and cook, stirring frequently, until tender and golden, about 10 minutes. Add asparagus; cook 1 minute.

2. Stir in flour, salt, and pepper until blended. Gradually stir in broth; heat to boiling, stirring constantly. Reduce heat; cover and simmer until asparagus is tender, 5 to 10 minutes.

3. Spoon half of mixture into blender; cover, with center part of cover removed to let steam escape, and puree until smooth. Pour into bowl. Repeat with remaining mixture.

4. Return puree to saucepan; stir in half-and-half. Heat through (do not boil). Serve soup hot, or cover and refrigerate to serve chilled later. If chilled soup is too thick, stir in some milk. Makes about 5 cups or 4 first-course servings.

Each serving: About 194 calories, 6g protein, 14g carbohydrate, 14g total fat (8g saturated), 38mg cholesterol, 657mg sodium.

CREAM OF CAULIFLOWER OR BROCCOLI SOUP

Prepare as directed above but substitute **3 cups small cauliflower or broccoli flowerets** for asparagus. Use **1¼ cups half-and-half or light cream** and add **dash of ground red pepper**. If desired, stir in **4 ounces sharp Cheddar cheese,** shredded (1 cup) and **½ teaspoon Dijon mustard** when heating through. Makes about 5 cups or 4 first-course servings.

CREAM OF MUSHROOM SOUP

Prepare as directed above but substitute **1 pound mushrooms,** trimmed and sliced for asparagus. Makes about 4½ cups or 4 first-course servings.

QUICK CREAM OF BROCCOLI SOUP

....

Frozen vegetables are picked and processed so quickly they often retain more nutrients than fresh ones. Many frozen vegetables are easily transformed into a satisfying soup. If broccoli is not one of your favorites, try one of the variations.

Prep: 5 minutes   Cook: 20 minutes

- 1 tablespoon butter or margarine
- 1 medium onion, chopped
- 1 package (10 ounces) frozen chopped broccoli
- 1 can (14½ ounces) chicken broth or 1¾ cups Chicken Broth (page 70)
- ¼ teaspoon dried thyme
- ⅛ teaspoon salt
- ⅛ teaspoon ground black pepper
- pinch ground nutmeg
- pinch ground red pepper (cayenne; optional)
- 1½ cups milk
- 2 teaspoons fresh lemon juice

1. In 3-quart saucepan, melt butter over medium heat. Add onion and cook, stirring occasionally, until tender, about 5 minutes. Add frozen broccoli, broth, thyme, salt, pepper, nutmeg, and ground red pepper, if using; heat to boiling over high heat. Reduce heat and simmer 10 minutes.

2. Spoon half of mixture into blender; cover, with center part of cover removed to let steam escape, and puree until smooth. Pour into bowl. Repeat with remaining mixture.

3. Return puree to saucepan; stir in milk. Heat through, stirring often (do not boil). Remove from heat and stir in lemon juice. Makes about 3¾ cups or 4 first-course servings.

Each serving: About 130 calories, 6g protein, 12g carbohydrate, 7g total fat (4g saturated), 21mg cholesterol, 594mg sodium.

QUICK CREAM OF CORN SOUP

Prepare as directed above but substitute **1 package (10 ounces) frozen whole-kernel corn** for broccoli; if you like, add **¾ teaspoon chili powder** after cooking onion and cook 30 seconds before adding broth.

QUICK CREAM OF PEA SOUP

Prepare as directed (left) but substitute **1 package (10 ounces) frozen peas** for broccoli; if you like, add **¼ teaspoon dried mint leaves** with broth.

QUICK CREAM OF ASPARAGUS SOUP

Prepare as directed (left) but substitute **1 package (10 ounces) frozen asparagus** for broccoli; if you like, add **¼ teaspoon dried tarragon** with broth.

CALDO VERDE

....

In Portugal, this delicious soup gets its rich green color from finely shredded Galician cabbage, which is sold in the outdoor markets. Kale, readily available in supermarkets, makes a fine substitute. If you like, sprinkle the soup with ½ cup finely chopped fully cooked spicy smoked sausage, such as linguiça or chorizo.

Prep: 15 minutes   Cook: 40 to 45 minutes

- 2 tablespoons olive oil
- 1 large onion (12 ounces), chopped
- 3 garlic cloves, finely chopped
- 2½ pounds all-purpose potatoes (8 medium), peeled and cut into 2-inch pieces
- 2 cans (14½ ounces each) chicken broth or 3½ cups Chicken Broth (page 70)
- 3 cups water
- 1 teaspoon salt
- ¼ teaspoon coarsely ground black pepper
- 1 pound kale, tough stems and veins trimmed and leaves very thinly sliced

1. In 5-quart Dutch oven, heat oil over medium heat. Add onion and garlic; cook until onion is golden, about 10 minutes. Add potatoes, broth, water, salt, and pepper; heat to boiling over high heat. Reduce heat; cover and simmer until potatoes are tender, about 20 minutes.

2. Mash potatoes in broth, keeping potatoes lumpy.

3. Stir in kale; simmer, uncovered, until kale is tender, 5 to 8 minutes. Makes about 10 cups or 5 main-dish servings.

Each serving: About 251 calories, 7g protein, 41g carbohydrate, 7g total fat (1g saturated), 0mg cholesterol, 1,187mg sodium.

PASTA E PISELLI

Here is a quick weeknight version of pasta e fagiole. In season, use fresh peas (piselli). Cook them in the broth until tender before adding the pasta.

Prep: 10 minutes plus cooking pasta
Cook: 20 minutes

- 2 tablespoons olive oil
- 3 garlic cloves, crushed with side of chef's knife
- 1 can (14½ ounces) diced tomatoes
- 2 cans (14½ ounces each) chicken broth or 3½ cups Chicken Broth (page 70)
- ½ cup water
- ¼ cup loosely packed fresh basil leaves, coarsely chopped
- 8 ounces mixed pasta, such as penne, bow ties, or elbow macaroni (2 cups), cooked as label directs
- 1 package (10 ounces) frozen peas, thawed freshly grated Parmesan cheese

1. In nonreactive 4-quart saucepan, heat oil over medium heat. Add garlic; cook, stirring frequently, until golden, about 2 minutes.

2. Add tomatoes with their juice, broth, water, and basil; heat to boiling. Reduce heat; cover and simmer 5 minutes. Discard garlic.

3. Stir in pasta and peas; heat through. Serve with grated Parmesan. Makes about 10 cups or 5 main-dish servings.

Each serving without Parmesan: About 317 calories, 12g protein, 51g carbohydrate, 8g total fat (1g saturated), 0mg cholesterol, 1,044mg sodium.

POTATO AND LEEK SOUP

By cutting out the heavy cream that is traditionally in this recipe, we reduced both the total fat and saturated fat by 4 grams each and dropped the cholesterol by a not-too-shabby 24 milligrams.

Prep: 15 minutes   Cook: 28 minutes

- 1½ pounds leeks (about 3 large)
- 1 tablespoon olive oil
- 1 tablespoon butter or margarine
- 12 ounces all-purpose potatoes, peeled and cut into ½-inch pieces
- 2 cans (14 to 14½ ounces each) reduced-sodium chicken broth
- 1 sprig plus 1 tablespoon chopped fresh dill
- ½ teaspoon salt
- ⅛ teaspoon ground black pepper
- 1 cup whole milk
- 2 teaspoons fresh lemon juice

1. Cut off roots and trim dark green tops from leeks. Discard any tough outer leaves. Cut each leek lengthwise in half, then crosswise into ¼-inch-wide slices. Rinse leeks thoroughly in large bowl of cold water, swishing to remove sand. Transfer leeks by hand to colander to drain. Repeat process, changing water several times, until all sand is removed.

2. In 4-quart saucepan, heat oil and butter on medium until butter melts. Add leeks and cook 8 to 10 minutes or until tender, stirring occasionally. Stir in potatoes, broth, dill sprig, salt, and pepper. Cover and heat to boiling on high. Reduce heat to low; simmer 15 minutes or until potatoes are very tender.

3. Ladle potato mixture into blender in 3 batches; cover, removing center part of lid to let steam escape. Lay a paper towel over top and puree until smooth. Pour each batch of puree into bowl. Return to same saucepan and stir in milk; heat through. Stir in lemon juice and serve, garnishing with chopped dill. Makes 6 first-course servings.

Each serving: About 140 calories, 4g protein, 20g carbohydrate, 6g total fat (2g saturated), 2g fiber, 6mg cholesterol, 515mg sodium.

FRENCH ONION SOUP

....

Onions, slowly cooked until deep brown and cara-melized, give this classic its distinctive flavor. Great for a party, this recipe is easily doubled; simply cook the onions in two skillets.

Prep: 10 minutes   Cook/Bake: 2 hours

4 tablespoons butter or margarine
6 medium onions, thinly sliced
¼ teaspoon salt
4 cups water
1 can (14½ ounces) beef broth or
   1¾ cups Brown Beef Stock (page 71)
¼ teaspoon dried thyme
4 diagonal slices (½-inch thick) French bread
4 ounces Gruyère or Swiss cheese, shredded (1 cup)

1. In nonstick 12-inch skillet, melt butter over medium-low heat. Add onions and salt and cook, stirring occasionally, until onions are very tender and begin to caramelize, about 45 minutes. Reduce heat to low and cook, stirring frequently, until onions are deep golden brown, about 15 minutes longer.

2. Transfer onions to 5-quart Dutch oven. Add ½ cup water to same skillet and heat to boiling, stirring until browned bits are loosened from bottom of skillet. Add to onions in Dutch oven. Add remaining 3½ cups water, broth, and thyme to onions and heat to boiling over high heat. Reduce heat and simmer 30 minutes.

3. Preheat oven to 450°F. Arrange bread slices on cookie sheet and bake until lightly toasted, about 5 minutes. Place four ovenproof bowls in jelly-roll pan for easier handling. Spoon soup evenly into bowls and top with toasted bread, slightly pressing bread into soup. Sprinkle Gruyère evenly on top. Bake until cheese has melted and begins to brown, 12 to 15 minutes. Makes about 5 cups or 4 first-course servings.

Each serving: About 402 calories, 15g protein, 37g carbohydrate, 22g total fat (13g saturated), 64mg cholesterol, 887mg sodium.

VEGETABLE CHOWDER

....

If you have your own vegetable garden or if you live near a farmers' market, you will want to make this luscious soup to take advantage of the fresh summer produce.

Prep: 15 minutes   Cook: 30 minutes

2 tablespoons olive oil
1 large onion (12 ounces), chopped
3 cups water
3 medium zucchini and/or yellow summer squashes
   (about 8 ounces each), coarsely chopped
2 red and/or yellow peppers, coarsely chopped
3 large ripe tomatoes (2 pounds), coarsely chopped
3 large garlic cloves, crushed with garlic press
½ teaspoon fennel seeds
2 teaspoons salt
¼ teaspoon ground black pepper
   sliced fresh basil leaves for garnish

1. In 5-quart saucepot or Dutch oven, heat oil over medium-high heat. Add onion and cook until tender and lightly browned, about 10 minutes. Add water, zucchini and/or yellow squashes, peppers, tomatoes, garlic, fennel seeds, salt, and black pepper; heat to boiling. Reduce heat to medium and cook, uncovered, until vegetables are tender, about 20 minutes.

2. Spoon one-third of the mixture into blender; cover, with center part of cover removed to let steam escape, and puree until smooth. Pour puree into bowl. Repeat with remaining mixture.

3. To serve hot, return soup to same clean saucepot and heat through. To serve cold, cover and refrigerate at least 4 hours. Garnish with sliced basil. Makes about 9 cups or 6 main-dish servings.

Each serving: About 120 calories, 4g protein, 18g carbohydrate, 5g total fat (1g saturated), 0mg cholesterol, 795mg sodium.

SUMMERTIME CORN CHOWDER

A basket of warm Buttermilk Biscuits (page 559) and thickly sliced ham are all that's needed to complete the menu for a real summertime treat.

Prep: 25 minutes   **Cook: 35 to 40 minutes**

6	medium ears corn, husks and silk removed
4	slices bacon, cut into ½-inch pieces
1	medium red onion, chopped
1	jalapeño chile, seeded and finely chopped
1	garlic clove, finely chopped
2	tablespoons all-purpose flour
½	teaspoon salt
⅛	teaspoon ground black pepper
1	pound red potatoes (6 medium), cut into ½-inch pieces
2	cans (14½ ounces each) chicken broth or 3½ cups Chicken Broth (page 70)
2	cups half-and-half or light cream
2	small ripe tomatoes (8 ounces), peeled, seeded, and chopped
	thinly sliced basil leaves

Summertime Corn Chowder

1. Cut kernels from corncobs (about 3 cups), reserving 3 corncobs; discard remaining corncobs.

2. In 5-quart Dutch oven, cook bacon over medium heat until browned. With slotted spoon, transfer bacon to paper towels to drain; crumble.

3. To bacon drippings in Dutch oven, add onion and jalapeño and cook, stirring, until onion is tender, about 5 minutes. Add garlic; cook 1 minute longer. Stir in flour, salt, and pepper; cook, stirring, 1 minute.

4. Stir in potatoes, reserved corncobs, broth, and half-and-half; heat to boiling over high heat. Reduce heat; cover and simmer until potatoes are tender, 10 to 15 minutes.

5. Discard corncobs; stir in reserved corn kernels and heat through. Transfer chowder to warm tureen. Stir in tomatoes and sprinkle with bacon and basil. Makes about 9½ cups or 8 first-course servings.

Each serving: About 272 calories, 7g protein, 29g carbohydrate, 15g total fat (7g saturated), 30mg cholesterol, 693mg sodium.

CHILLED TUSCAN-STYLE TOMATO SOUP

••••••••••••••••••••••••••••••••••••••

Summer in a bowl: the uncooked version of Papa al Pomodoro, *Italy's famous bread-thickened tomato soup.*

Prep: 15 minutes plus chilling   Cook: 1 minute

- 1 teaspoon olive oil
- 1 clove garlic, minced
- 3 ounces country-style bread, cut into 1-inch cubes (2 cups)
- 3 pounds ripe tomatoes (9 medium), cut into quarters
- ¼ cup loosely packed fresh basil leaves, chopped, plus additional leaves for garnish
- 1 teaspoon sugar
- ½ teaspoon salt

1. In small skillet, heat oil on medium until hot. Add garlic and cook 1 minute, stirring. Remove skillet from heat.

2. In food processor with knife blade attached, pulse bread until coarsely chopped. Add tomatoes and garlic; pulse until soup is almost pureed. Pour soup into bowl; stir in chopped basil, sugar, and salt. Cover and refrigerate until well chilled, at least 2 hours or overnight. Garnish each serving with basil leaves. Makes about 6 cups or 4 first-course servings.

Each serving: About 145 calories, 5g protein, 28g carbohydrate, 3g total fat (1g saturated), 4g fiber, 0mg cholesterol, 445mg sodium.

---

5 IDEAS FOR . . . TOMATO-VEGETABLE JUICE

No matter which brand of tomato-veggie juice you prefer, the typical 8-ounce glassful delivers two healthy servings of vegetables.

ALPHABET SOUP

In 5-quart saucepot, combine 1 package (32 ounces) chicken broth, 4 cups vegetable juice, 1 package (16 ounces) frozen mixed vegetables, ½ teaspoon Italian seasoning, and ¼ teaspoon ground black pepper. Cover saucepot; heat to boiling. Stir in 1 cup uncooked alphabet pasta or orzo. Simmer soup, uncovered, on medium low 8 minutes or until pasta and vegetables are tender. Serves 6.

PECORINO-PEPPER BISCUITS

Prepare 1 batch all-purpose pancake-and-baking mix as label directs for drop biscuits with following alterations: Stir ¼ cup freshly grated Pecorino-Romano cheese and ¼ teaspoon coarsely ground black pepper into dry mix, and substitute vegetable juice for milk. Drop dough by scant ¼ cup onto ungreased large cookie sheet and bake as label directs. Makes 9 biscuits.

SPICY RED RICE

In 3-quart saucepan, heat 2 teaspoons vegetable oil, cook 1 large onion, chopped, on medium 6 minutes or until softened. Stir in ¾ cup long-grain white rice and ¼ teaspoon dried rosemary; cook 1 minute. Stir in 3 cup spicy vegetable juice and ¼ teaspoon salt; heat to boiling. Cover and simmer on low 20 to 24 minutes, until rice is tender and liquid is absorbed. Stir in ½ cup toasted slivered almonds. Serves 4.

SPANISH MEATBALLS

In 12-inch skillet, combine 3 cups vegetable juice, 2 tablespoons seasoned dried bread crumbs, and ½ teaspoon each ground cumin and smoked paprika; heat to boiling. Simmer, uncovered, on medium low 18 minutes to thicken slightly. Meanwhile, in bowl, mix 1 pound lean (90%) ground beef with ⅓ cup seasoned dried bread crumbs, ⅓ cup vegetable juice, and ½ teaspoon smoked paprika. Shape into 1-inch balls; drop into hot sauce, and simmer 12 to 14 minutes or until cooked through. Serve over rice. Serves 4.

SAUSAGE CHILI

Remove casings from 1 package (1¼ pounds) turkey Italian sausage links and crumble. In 5-quart Dutch oven, cook sausage and 2 chopped medium onions, on medium 8 minutes or until onions soften. Stir in 1½ tablespoons chili powder; cook 2 minutes. Add 4 cups spicy vegetable juice; heat to boiling. Simmer, uncovered, on low 15 minutes. Stir in 2 cans (15 to 19 ounces each) red kidney beans, rinsed and drained; heat through. Serves 6.

Cool Cucumber Soup

COOL CUCUMBER SOUP

···

Homemade curry oil adds a taste of the tropics to this summer favorite.

Prep: 25 minutes plus chilling   Cook: 3 minutes

- 2 English (seedless) cucumbers (about 12 ounces each), peeled
- 1 small garlic clove, crushed with garlic press
- 2 cups (16 ounces) plain low-fat yogurt
- ½ cup low-fat (1%) milk
- 1 tablespoon fresh lemon juice
- 1¼ teaspoons salt
- 2 tablespoons olive oil
- ½ teaspoon curry powder
- ½ teaspoon ground cumin
- ¼ teaspoon crushed red pepper
- 1 small tomato, chopped
- 1 tablespoon sliced fresh mint leaves

1. Prepare soup: Cut enough cucumber into ¼-inch pieces to equal ½ cup; reserve for garnish. Cut remaining cucumbers into 2-inch pieces. In food processor with knife blade attached or in blender, puree large cucumber pieces, garlic, yogurt, milk, lemon juice, and salt until almost smooth. Pour mixture into medium bowl; cover and refrigerate until cold, at least 2 hours.

2. Meanwhile, prepare curry oil: In small saucepan, heat oil over low heat. Stir in curry powder, cumin, and crushed red pepper; cook until fragrant and oil is hot, about 3 minutes. Remove saucepan from heat; strain curry oil through sieve into cup.

3. Prepare garnish: In small bowl, combine tomato and reserved cucumber.

4. To serve, stir soup and ladle into bowls. Garnish each with spoonful of cucumber mixture; sprinkle with mint and drizzle with curry oil. Makes about 4 cups or 4 first-course servings.

Each serving: About 170 calories, 8g protein, 15g carbohydrate, 9g total fat (2g saturated), 8mg cholesterol, 830mg sodium.

VICHYSSOISE

This elegant soup, traditionally served cold, is just as delicious hot (just call it cream of potato and leek soup). Either way, serve it in small cups, and be sure to garnish with a sprinkling of snipped fresh chives.

Prep: 20 minutes plus chilling   Cook: 55 minutes

- 4   medium leeks (1¼ pounds)
- 2   tablespoons butter or margarine
- 1   pound all-purpose potatoes (3 medium), peeled and thinly sliced
- 2   cans (14½ ounces each) chicken broth or 3½ cups Chicken Broth (page 70)
- ½   cup water
- 1   teaspoon salt
- ¼   teaspoon ground black pepper
- 1   cup milk
- ½   cup heavy or whipping cream

1. Cut off roots and trim dark green tops from leeks; cut each leek lengthwise in half. Cut enough of white and pale green parts crosswise into ¼-inch pieces to equal 4½ cups. (Reserve any leftover leeks for another use.) Rinse leeks in large bowl of cold water, swishing to remove sand; transfer to colander to drain, leaving sand in bottom of bowl.

2. In 4-quart saucepan, melt butter over medium heat; add leeks and cook, stirring occasionally, 8 to 10 minutes. Add potatoes, broth, water, salt, and pepper; heat to boiling over high heat. Reduce heat; cover and simmer 30 minutes.

3. Spoon half of mixture into blender; cover, with center part of cover removed to let steam escape, and puree until smooth. Pour into bowl. Repeat with remaining mixture.

4. Stir milk and cream into puree. To serve hot, return soup to same clean saucepan and heat through over low heat (do not boil). To serve cold, cover and refrigerate at least 4 hours or until very cold. Makes about 8 cups or 8 first-course servings.

Each serving: About 161 calories, 4g protein, 14g carbohydrate, 10g total fat (6g saturated), 32mg cholesterol, 778mg sodium.

GAZPACHO WITH CILANTRO CREAM

Recipes for this full-flavored, uncooked tomato-based soup abound. Ours is topped with a dollop of cilantro-spiked sour cream, a tasty combination.

Prep: 30 minutes plus chilling

- 2   medium cucumbers (8 ounces each), peeled
- 1   yellow pepper
- ¼   small red onion
- 2   pounds ripe tomatoes (5 medium), peeled, seeded, and chopped
- ½   to 1 small jalapeño chile, seeded
- 3   tablespoons fresh lime juice
- 2   tablespoons extra-virgin olive oil
- ¾   plus ⅛ teaspoon salt
- ¼   cup reduced-fat sour cream or plain low-fat yogurt
- 1   tablespoon milk
- 4   teaspoons chopped fresh cilantro

1. Chop half of 1 cucumber, half of yellow pepper, and all of onion into ¼-inch pieces; set aside. Cut remaining cucumbers and yellow pepper into large pieces.

2. In blender or in food processor with knife blade attached, puree large pieces of cucumber and yellow pepper, tomatoes, jalapeño, lime juice, oil, and ¾ teaspoon salt until smooth. Pour puree into bowl; add cut-up cucumber, yellow pepper, and onion. Cover and refrigerate until well chilled, at least 6 hours or up to overnight.

3. Prepare cilantro cream: In small bowl, stir sour cream, milk, cilantro, and remaining ⅛ teaspoon salt until smooth. Cover and refrigerate.

4. To serve, top soup with dollops of cilantro cream. Makes about 5 cups or 4 first-course servings.

Each serving: About 156 calories, 4g protein, 17g carbohydrate, 10g total fat (2g saturated), 6mg cholesterol, 545mg sodium.

Spring Pea Soup

HONEYDEW AND LIME SOUP

∙∙∙∙∙∙∙∙∙∙∙∙∙∙∙∙∙∙∙∙∙∙∙∙∙∙∙∙∙∙∙∙∙∙∙∙∙∙

This chilled soup starts a summer meal off with a refreshing mix of surprising flavors. Choose a melon that is fully ripe for a smooth consistency.

Prep: 10 minutes, plus chilling

- 1   honeydew melon (5 pounds), chilled, cut into 1-inch chunks (8 cups)
- ¼   cup fresh lime juice
- ¼   cup loosely packed fresh cilantro leaves
- 1   teaspoon jalapeño hot sauce
- ⅛   teaspoon salt

1. In blender, pulse melon with lime juice, cilantro, hot sauce, and salt until pureed. Transfer soup to large bowl or pitcher; cover and refrigerate 2 hours or until chilled. Stir before serving. Makes about 6 cups or 6 servings.

Each serving: About 85 calories, 1g protein, 23g carbohydrate, 0g total fat, 2g fiber, 0mg cholesterol, 80mg sodium.

SPRING PEA SOUP

∙∙

As bright and green as the season, this soup has a fresh flavor that complements any celebratory meal. If you can't find edible flowers, garnish with pea shoots or a sprig of mint.

Prep: 12 minutes   Cook: 23 minutes

- 2   tablespoons butter or margarine
- 2   large shallots, thinly sliced (¾ cup)
- 1   carton (32 ounces) reduced-sodium chicken broth
- 2   cups water
- 2   bags (16 ounces each) frozen peas, thawed
- 1   large all-purpose potato (8 ounces), peeled and cut into 1-inch chunks
- ½   cup loosely packed fresh mint leaves, chopped
- ¾   teaspoon salt
- ¼   teaspoon ground black pepper
- 3   tablespoons fresh lemon juice
- 10   nasturtium flowers for garnish (optional, see Tip)

1. In 4-quart saucepan, heat butter on medium-low until melted. Add shallots and cook 10 to 12 minutes or until very tender.

2. Add broth, water, peas, potato, half of chopped mint, salt, and pepper; heat to boiling on high. Reduce heat to medium; simmer mixture 10 minutes, stirring occasionally.

3. Spoon half of mixture into blender; cover, removing center part of lid to let steam escape. Lay a paper towel over top and puree until smooth. Pour puree into medium bowl. Repeat with remaining mixture. Return soup to saucepan, and reheat on medium if necessary. Stir in lemon juice and remaining mint.

4. To serve, spoon soup into 10 serving bowls; garnish with nasturtiums if using. Makes 10 first-course servings.

Each serving: About 120 calories, 6g protein, 19g carbohydrate, 3g total fat (1g saturated), 5g fiber, 0mg cholesterol, 475mg sodium.

Tip: Nasturtiums and other edible flowers can be found in the produce section of better supermarkets and at farmers' markets.

CLASSIC BLACK BEAN SOUP

....

True to the classic, we flavor this soup with ham and dry sherry.

Prep: 20 minutes plus soaking beans
Cook: 2 hours 30 minutes

- 3 tablespoons olive oil
- 3 large carrots, peeled and chopped
- 3 medium onions, chopped
- 3 stalks celery with leaves, chopped
- 4 garlic cloves, peeled
- 2 bay leaves
- ½ teaspoon dried thyme
- 1 pound dry black beans, soaked and drained (page 279)
- 2 smoked ham hocks (1½ pounds)
- 10 cups water
- 1 teaspoon coarsely ground black pepper
- ½ cup chopped fresh parsley
- 3 tablespoons dry sherry
- 2 teaspoons salt
- 12 paper-thin lemon slices

1. In 5-quart Dutch oven, heat oil over medium heat. Add carrots, onions, and celery and cook, stirring occasionally, until vegetables are tender, about 10 minutes. Add garlic, bay leaves, and thyme; cook 1 minute.

2. Add beans, ham hocks, water, and pepper to Dutch oven; heat to boiling over high heat. Reduce heat and simmer until beans are very tender, about 2 hours. Discard ham hocks and bay leaves.

3. Spoon one-fourth of bean mixture into blender; cover, with center part of cover removed to let steam escape, and puree until very smooth. Pour puree into bowl. Repeat with remaining mixture. Return puree to Dutch oven and stir in sherry, salt, and all but 2 tablespoons parsley. Cook 5 minutes.

4. To serve, ladle soup into bowls, garnish with lemon slices, and sprinkle with remaining parsley. Makes about 13 cups or 12 first-course servings.

Each serving: About 207 calories, 10g protein, 32g carbohydrate, 5g total fat (1g saturated), 2mg cholesterol, 788mg sodium.

SPICY BLACK BEAN SOUP

....

Canned beans make this soup a snap to prepare, and a zingy blend of spices gives it south-of-the-border sass.

Prep: 10 minutes   Cook: 30 minutes

- 1 tablespoon vegetable oil
- 1 medium onion, chopped
- 2 garlic cloves, finely chopped
- 2 teaspoons chili powder
- 1 teaspoon ground cumin
- ¼ teaspoon crushed red pepper
- 2 cans (15 to 19 ounces each) black beans, rinsed and drained
- 2 cups water
- 1 can (14½ ounces) chicken broth or 1¾ cups Chicken Broth (page 70)
- ¼ cup coarsely chopped fresh cilantro lime wedges

1. In 3-quart saucepan, heat oil over medium heat. Add onion and cook, stirring occasionally, until tender, 5 to 8 minutes. Stir in garlic, chili powder, cumin, and crushed red pepper; cook 30 seconds. Stir in beans, water, and broth; heat to boiling over high heat. Reduce heat and simmer 15 minutes.

2. Spoon one-third of mixture into blender; cover, with center part of cover removed to let steam escape, and puree until smooth. Pour puree into bowl. Repeat with remaining mixture. Sprinkle with cilantro and serve with wedges of lime. Makes about 6⅔ cups or 6 first-course servings.

Each serving: About 137 calories, 7g protein, 19g carbohydrate, 4g total fat (0g saturated), 0mg cholesterol, 563mg sodium.

SPLIT PEA SOUP WITH HAM

·····················

This hearty old-fashioned favorite is a perfect pick-me-up on a cold blustery day.

Prep: 10 minutes   Cook: 1 hour 15 minutes

- 2 tablespoons vegetable oil
- 2 white turnips (6 ounces each), peeled and chopped (optional)
- 2 carrots, peeled and finely chopped
- 2 stalks celery, finely chopped
- 1 medium onion, finely chopped
- 1 package (16 ounces) dry split peas, rinsed and picked through
- 2 smoked ham hocks (1½ pounds)
- 8 cups water
- 1 bay leaf
- 1 teaspoon salt
- ¼ teaspoon ground allspice

1. In 5-quart Dutch oven, heat oil over medium-high heat. Add turnips, if using, carrots, celery, and onion; cook, stirring frequently, until carrots are tender-crisp, about 10 minutes. Add split peas, ham hocks, water, bay leaf, salt, and allspice; heat to boiling over high heat. Reduce heat; cover and simmer 45 minutes.

2. Discard bay leaf. Transfer ham hocks to cutting board; discard skin and bones. Finely chop meat. Return meat to soup. Heat through. Makes 11 cups or 6 main-dish servings.

Each serving: About 343 calories, 21g protein, 52g carbohydrate, 7g total fat (1g saturated), 3mg cholesterol, 1,174mg sodium.

GERMAN LENTIL SOUP

Prepare as above, but omit turnips. Substitute **1 pound lentils,** rinsed and picked over, for peas, and substitute ½ **teaspoon thyme** for allspice.

CURRIED LENTIL SOUP

·····················

Based on an Indian classic, this thick and hearty soup is bound to become a staple in your soup repertoire. Lentils, unlike other dried legumes, don't require pre-soaking, so this can be prepared in less time than most other bean soups.

Prep: 30 minutes   Cook: 1 hour

- 2 tablespoons olive oil
- 4 carrots, peeled and finely chopped
- 2 large stalks celery, finely chopped
- 1 large onion (12 ounces), finely chopped
- 1 medium Granny Smith apple, peeled, cored, and finely chopped
- 1 tablespoon grated, peeled fresh ginger
- 1 large garlic clove, crushed with garlic press
- 2 teaspoons curry powder
- ¾ teaspoon ground cumin
- ¾ teaspoon ground coriander
- 1 package (16 ounces) lentils, rinsed and picked through
- 5 cups water
- 2 cans (14½ ounces each) vegetable or chicken broth or 3½ cups Vegetable Broth (page 71) or Chicken Broth (page 70)
- ¼ cup chopped fresh cilantro
- ½ teaspoon salt
  plain low-fat yogurt

1. In 5-quart Dutch oven, heat oil over medium-high heat. Add carrots, celery, onion, and apple; cook, stirring occasionally, until lightly browned, 10 to 15 minutes.

2. Add ginger, garlic, curry powder, cumin, and coriander; cook, stirring, 1 minute.

3. Add lentils, water, and broth; heat to boiling over high heat. Reduce heat; cover and simmer, stirring occasionally, until lentils are tender, 45 to 55 minutes. Stir in cilantro and salt. To serve, top soup with dollops of yogurt. Makes about 10 cups or 5 main-dish servings.

Each serving without yogurt: About 434 calories, 27g protein, 69g carbohydrate, 7g total fat (1g saturated), 0mg cholesterol, 966mg sodium.

MINESTRONE WITH PESTO

······································

Freshly made pesto adds body and richness to this soup. During the summer, when basil is plentiful and well priced, make up a double or triple batch of our home-made pesto. Pack it into a jar, top it off with a thin layer of olive oil to keep it nice and green, then put the lid on. Refrigerate for up to several months.

Prep: 20 minutes plus soaking beans   Cook: 1 hour

- 8 ounces dry Great Northern beans (1⅓ cups), soaked and drained (page 279)
- 2 tablespoons olive oil
- 3 carrots, peeled and cut into ¼-inch-thick slices
- 2 stalks celery, cut into ¼-inch-thick slices
- 1 large onion (12 ounces), finely chopped
- 2 ounces pancetta or bacon, finely chopped
- 1 pound all-purpose potatoes (3 medium), peeled and chopped
- 2 medium zucchini (8 ounces each), each cut lengthwise into quarters, then crosswise into ¼-inch-thick slices
- ½ medium head savoy cabbage (1 pound), thinly sliced
- 1 large garlic clove, crushed with garlic press
- 1 can (14½ ounces) diced tomatoes
- 2 cans (14½ ounces each) chicken broth or 3½ cups Chicken Broth (page 70)
- 1 cup water
  Pesto (right) or ½ cup store-bought pesto
- ½ teaspoon salt

1. In 4-quart saucepan, combine beans and enough *water to cover by 2 inches;* heat to boiling over high heat. Reduce heat; cover and simmer, stirring occasionally, until beans are tender, 40 minutes to 1 hour. Drain beans.

2. Meanwhile, in nonreactive 5-quart Dutch oven, heat oil over medium-high heat. Add carrots, celery, onion, and pancetta; cook, stirring occasionally, until onions begin to brown, about 10 minutes. Add potatoes, zucchini, cabbage, and garlic; cook, stirring constantly, until cabbage has wilted. Add tomatoes with their juice, broth, and water; heat to boiling over high heat. Reduce heat; cover and simmer until vegetables are tender, about 30 minutes.

3. Meanwhile, prepare pesto.

4. In blender or in food processor with knife blade attached, puree ½ cup beans with 1 cup soup mixture until smooth. Stir puree, remaining beans, and salt into soup; heat to boiling. Reduce heat; cover and simmer 10 minutes. Garnish with dollops of pesto. Makes about 13 cups or 6 main-dish servings.

PESTO

In blender, puree ⅔ **cup packed fresh basil leaves, ¼ cup freshly grated Parmesan cheese, ¼ cup olive oil, 1 tablespoon water,** and **¼ teaspoon salt** until smooth.

Each serving with pesto: About 444 calories, 18g protein, 53g carbohydrate, 20g total fat (4g saturated), 9mg cholesterol, 1,204mg sodium.

QUICK MINESTRONE

Prepare as directed (left) omitting Step 1 and use **2 cans (15 to 19 ounces each) Great Northern beans,** rinsed and drained, for soaked beans. Add beans with tomatoes.

SOUP SAVVY

Here are some of the most popular types of soups:

BISQUE: A classic French soup with a rich, creamy texture. It is usually made from shellfish and thickened with rice.

BROTH: A flavorful liquid made from simmered meat, fish, or poultry and/or vegetables.

CHOWDER: Hearty and chunky, this soup is chock-full of fish, shellfish, and/or vegetables. Clam chowder has been popular in New England since colonial times.

CONSOMMÉ: Broth that has been clarified into a crystal-clear liquid.

GUMBO: One of the signature dishes of Cajun cooking, gumbo is a thick soup that can contain chicken, duck, seafood, or ham and vegetables such as tomatoes, onion, bell peppers, and celery. It is thickened with a roux (a browned butter and flour mixture), okra, and/or filé (ground sassafras leaves) and is served over white rice.

STOCK: Similar to broth but made from bones, often roasted, that are simmered with water and/or vegetables.

PASTA E FAGIOLI WITH SAUSAGE

···

Pasta e fagioli, Italian pasta and bean soup, becomes a meal-in-a-pot with the addition of sweet sausage and fresh spinach. Using canned beans speeds up cooking.

Prep: 15 minutes   Cook: 1 hour

- 1 pound sweet Italian-sausage links, casings removed
- 1 tablespoon olive oil
- 2 medium onions, chopped
- 2 garlic cloves, crushed with garlic press
- 1 can (28 ounces) plum tomatoes
- 2 cans (14½ ounces each) chicken broth or 3½ cups Chicken Broth (page 70)
- 2 cups water
- 3 cans (15 to 19 ounces) Great Northern or white kidney (cannellini) beans, rinsed and drained (page 279)
- 6 ounces ditalini or tubetti pasta (1 rounded cup)
- 5 ounces spinach, washed and dried very well, tough stems trimmed, and leaves cut into 1-inch-wide strips freshly grated Parmesan cheese (optional)

1. Heat nonreactive 5-quart Dutch oven over medium-high heat until very hot. Add sausage and cook until well browned, breaking up sausage with side of spoon. Transfer sausage to bowl.

2. Reduce heat to medium; add oil to Dutch oven. Add onions and cook until tender and golden, about 10 minutes. Add garlic; cook 1 minute. Add tomatoes with their juice, breaking them up with side of spoon.

3. Add broth and water; heat to boiling over high heat. Reduce heat; cover and simmer 15 minutes. Add beans and heat to boiling; cover and simmer 15 minutes longer. Add sausage and heat through.

4. Meanwhile, in 4-quart saucepan, cook pasta as label directs, but do not salt to water; drain.

5. Just before serving, stir spinach and cooked pasta into soup. Serve with Parmesan, if you like. Makes about 16 cups or 8 main-dish servings.

Each serving: About 558 calories, 28g protein, 65g carbohydrate, 22g total fat (7g saturated), 43mg cholesterol, 1,432mg sodium.

Pasta e Fagioli with Sausage

GARNISHING SOUP

As delicious as soup is, almost any bowl of soup will be enhanced by an added splash of color or a bit of extra flavor. Chopped fresh herbs are the simplest of all garnishes. Choose an herb that complements the soup's flavor and color. For the best results, chop or snip fresh herbs just before using. Pureed soups can accommodate other kinds of garnishes. The smooth texture of a pureed bean or tomato soup calls out for a sprinkling of grated Parmesan cheese or crumbled bacon. Pureed vegetable soups are often topped with a drizzle of heavy cream.

SOUTH-OF-THE-BORDER CHICKEN SOUP

(Pictured on page 50)

....

We give this rich homemade soup a Latin accent with lime and cilantro, and serve it with chunks of buttery avocado and crisp tortilla chips.

Prep: 25 minutes   Cook: 1 hour

- 8 medium all-purpose potatoes (2½ pounds)
- 1 chicken (4 pounds), cut into 8 pieces
- 3 large stalks celery, each cut into thirds
- 3 carrots, peeled and each cut into thirds
- 2 medium onions, not peeled, each cut into quarters
- 10 cups water
- 10 sprigs plus ¼ cup chopped fresh cilantro
- 2 bay leaves
- 1 teaspoon whole black peppercorns
- 1 can (15¼ to 16 ounces) whole-kernel corn, drained
- 2 teaspoons salt
- ¼ cup fresh lime juice (about 2 large limes)
- 2 ripe medium avocados, cut into ½-inch pieces
  tortilla chips
  lime wedges

1. Peel 3 potatoes. In 8-quart Dutch oven, combine chicken, peeled potatoes, celery, carrots, onions, water, cilantro sprigs, bay leaves, and peppercorns; heat to boiling over high heat. Reduce heat; cover and simmer until chicken loses its pink color throughout and vegetables are tender, 35 to 45 minutes. Transfer chicken and potatoes to separate bowls.

2. Strain broth through sieve into large bowl; discard vegetables. Skim and discard fat from broth; return broth to same clean Dutch oven. Mash cooked potatoes with 1 cup broth; stir mashed-potato mixture into broth in Dutch oven.

3. Peel and chop remaining 5 potatoes. Add potatoes to broth; heat to boiling over high heat. Reduce heat; cover and simmer until potatoes are tender, about 10 minutes.

4. Meanwhile, discard skin and bones from chicken; cut chicken into bite-size pieces. Stir chicken, corn, and salt into broth; heat through.

5. Just before serving, stir lime juice and chopped cilantro into soup. Serve with avocado, tortilla chips, and lime wedges. Makes about 16 cups or 8 main-dish servings.

Each serving without garnishes: About 344 calories, 28g protein, 34g carbohydrate, 12g total fat (2g saturated), 76mg cholesterol, 772mg sodium.

HEARTY MUSHROOM-BARLEY SOUP

....

A real rib-sticker. Get a head start by cooking the barley the day before, then cool and refrigerate until needed.

Prep: 20 minutes   Cook: 1 hour

- ¾ cup pearl barley
- 8 cups water
- 2 tablespoons olive oil
- 3 stalks celery, cut into ¼-inch-thick slices
- 1 large onion (12 ounces), chopped
- 1½ pounds mushrooms, trimmed and thickly sliced
- 2 tablespoons tomato paste
- 5 carrots, peeled and each cut lengthwise in half, then crosswise into ¼-inch-thick slices
- 2 cans (14½ ounces each) beef broth or 3½ cups Brown Beef Stock (page 71)
- ¼ cup dry sherry
- 1½ teaspoons salt

1. In 3-quart saucepan, combine barley and 4 cups water; heat to boiling over high heat. Reduce heat; cover and simmer 30 minutes. Drain.

2. Meanwhile, in 5-quart Dutch oven, heat oil over medium-high heat. Add celery and onion; cook, stirring, until golden, about 10 minutes. Increase heat to high; add mushrooms and cook, stirring occasionally, until liquid has evaporated and mushrooms are lightly browned, 10 to 12 minutes.

3. Reduce heat to medium-high; add tomato paste and cook, stirring, 2 minutes. Add barley, carrots, broth, sherry, salt, and remaining 4 cups water; heat to boiling. Reduce heat; cover and simmer until carrots and barley are tender, 20 to 25 minutes. Makes about 12 cups or 10 first-course servings.

Each serving: About 133 calories, 5g protein, 21g carbohydrate, 4g total fat (1g saturated), 1mg cholesterol, 684mg sodium.

VIETNAMESE NOODLE SOUP

....

Although Vietnamese soup is traditionally served with thinly sliced beef, our variation uses chicken breast meat. The flat, wide rice noodles (bahn pho) can be purchased in the Asian section of some grocery stores or in Asian markets.

Prep: 20 minutes   Cook: 25 minutes

4 ounces flat dried rice noodles or linguine

3 green onions, thinly sliced on diagonal

2 garlic cloves, peeled

6 basil sprigs

6 sprigs plus 2 tablespoons chopped fresh cilantro

4 cans (14½ ounces each) low-sodium chicken broth or 7 cups Chicken Broth (page 70)

1 teaspoon coriander seeds

1 cinnamon stick (3 inches)

2 large skinless, boneless chicken breast halves (1 pound)

4 medium mushrooms, trimmed and sliced

   mint sprigs

   lime wedges (optional)

1. In large bowl, soak rice noodles in enough *warm water to cover* 20 minutes, or cook linguine as label directs. Drain.

2. Meanwhile, in 3-quart saucepan, combine one-third of green onions, garlic, basil and cilantro sprigs, broth, coriander seeds, and cinnamon stick; heat to boiling over high heat. Reduce heat; cover and simmer 10 minutes. Strain through sieve set over bowl; discard solids. Return broth to saucepan.

3. Cut chicken breast halves on diagonal into thin strips. Stir chicken, drained noodles, mushrooms, and remaining green onions into broth; heat to boiling over high heat. Reduce heat; cover and simmer until chicken loses its pink color throughout, about 3 minutes. Sprinkle with chopped cilantro and top with mint sprigs. Serve with lime wedges, if you like. Makes about 9 cups or 4 main-dish servings.

Each serving: About 269 calories, 30g protein, 27g carbohydrate, 2g total fat (0g saturated), 66mg cholesterol, 1,107mg sodium.

TURKEY SOUP

....

What's the Friday after Thanksgiving without turkey soup? Use your favorite vegetables to personalize this simple recipe.

Prep: 15 minutes plus overnight to chill
Cook: 5 hours

6 carrots, peeled

3 stalks celery

   roasted turkey carcass, plus 2 cups cooked turkey meat, finely chopped

2 medium onions, each cut into quarters

5 parsley sprigs

1 garlic clove, peeled

¼ teaspoon dried thyme

½ bay leaf

6 quarts water

1¼ teaspoons salt

1 cup regular long-grain rice, cooked as label directs

2 tablespoons fresh lemon juice or 1 tablespoon dry sherry

1. Cut 2 carrots and 1 stalk celery into 2-inch pieces. In 12-quart stockpot, combine turkey carcass, carrot and celery pieces, onions, parsley sprigs, garlic, thyme, bay leaf, and 6 quarts water or enough water to cover; heat to boiling over high heat. Skim foam from surface. Reduce heat and simmer, skimming occasionally, 4 hours.

2. Strain broth through colander set over large bowl; discard solids. Strain again through sieve into several containers; cool. Cover and refrigerate overnight.

3. Remove and discard fat from surface of broth; measure broth and pour into 5-quart saucepot. If necessary, boil broth over high heat until reduced to 10 cups to concentrate flavor.

4. Cut remaining 4 carrots and remaining 2 stalks celery into ½-inch pieces; add to broth with salt. Heat soup to boiling. Reduce heat and simmer until vegetables are tender, about 15 minutes. Stir in cooked rice and turkey; heat through, about 5 minutes. Remove from heat and stir in lemon juice. Makes about 13 cups or 12 first-course servings.

Each serving: About 113 calories, 10g protein, 12g carbohydrate, 2g total fat (1g saturated), 21mg cholesterol, 355mg sodium.

BEEF-VEGETABLE SOUP

An old-fashioned crowd-pleaser, this soup can be made a day ahead, but for the most vibrant color, stir in the peas just before serving. You'll have plenty of soup here—the leftovers freeze well.

Prep: 30 minutes plus soaking beans
Cook: 1 hour 45 minutes

1   tablespoon vegetable oil
2   pounds bone-in beef shank cross cuts, each 2 inches thick, trimmed
2   medium onions, chopped
3   garlic cloves, finely chopped
⅛   teaspoon ground cloves
4   large carrots, peeled and chopped
2   stalks celery, chopped
½   small head green cabbage (8 ounces), cored and chopped (5 cups)
4   cups water
1   can (14½ ounces) beef broth or 1¾ cups Brown Beef Stock (page 71)
2   teaspoons salt
½   teaspoon dried thyme
½   teaspoon ground black pepper
8   ounces dry large lima beans (1¼ cups), soaked and drained (page 279)
1   pound all-purpose potatoes (3 medium), peeled and cut into 1-inch pieces
1   can (14 to 16 ounces) tomatoes, chopped
1   cup frozen whole-kernel corn
1   cup frozen peas
¼   cup chopped fresh parsley

1. In nonreactive 8-quart saucepot, heat oil over medium-high heat until very hot. Add beef, in batches, and cook until well browned, transferring meat to bowl as it is browned. Reduce heat to medium; add onions and cook, stirring, until tender, about 5 minutes. Stir in garlic and cloves and cook 30 seconds. Return beef to saucepot; add carrots, celery, cabbage, water, broth, salt, thyme, and pepper; heat to boiling. Reduce heat; cover and simmer until beef is tender, about 1 hour.

2. Meanwhile, in 4-quart saucepan, combine beans and enough *water to cover by 2 inches;* heat to boiling over high heat. Reduce heat; cover and simmer until beans are just tender, about 30 minutes; drain.

3. Add potatoes and beans to saucepot; heat to boiling. Cover and simmer 5 minutes. Stir in tomatoes with their juice; cover and simmer until potatoes are tender, about 10 minutes longer.

4. With slotted spoon, transfer beef to cutting board. Cut beef into ½-inch pieces, discarding bones and gristle. Return beef to saucepot and add frozen corn and peas; heat through. Spoon into bowls and sprinkle with parsley. Makes about 15½ cups or 8 main-dish servings.

Each serving: About 278 calories, 24g protein, 35g carbohydrate, 6g total fat (1g saturated), 30mg cholesterol, 955mg sodium.

STORING SOUPS AND STOCK

• Soup and stock should be quickly cooled before storing in the refrigerator or freezer. To cool down a pot of soup or stock, place the pot in a sink filled with ice water and let stand, stirring until tepid. Or pour the soup into small containers and cool for thirty minutes, then refrigerate.

• Stocks and most soups freeze well in airtight containers for up to three months. Be sure to leave at least ½ inch of headspace to allow for expansion. Freezing may diminish some of a soup's flavor, so be sure to taste the soup and adjust the seasoning before serving.

• Soup enriched with cream, yogurt, or eggs cannot be frozen because it will curdle when reheated; the soup base can be frozen, however. Prepare the soup just up to the point of adding the cream, yogurt, or eggs. Freeze like any other soup, then thaw and reheat, adding the enrichment at the last minute—just long enough to heat through. Do not allow the soup to boil, or it may curdle.

CHICKEN BROTH

....

Nothing beats the flavor of homemade chicken broth. Make it in large batches and freeze in containers for up to four months. Our recipe has an added bonus: The cooked chicken can be used in casseroles and salads.

Prep: 10 minutes plus cooling
Cook: 4 hours 30 minutes

1   chicken (3 to 3½ pounds), including neck (giblets reserved for another use)
2   carrots, peeled and cut into 2-inch pieces
1   stalk celery, cut into 2-inch pieces
1   medium onion, cut into quarters
5   parsley sprigs
1   garlic clove
½   teaspoon dried thyme
½   bay leaf
3   quarts water

1. In 6-quart saucepot, combine chicken, chicken neck, carrots, celery, onion, parsley, garlic, thyme, bay leaf, and 3 quarts water or enough water to cover; heat to boiling over high heat. Skim foam from surface. Reduce heat and simmer 1 hour, turning chicken once and skimming.

2. Remove from heat; transfer chicken to large bowl. When cool enough to handle, remove skin and bones from chicken. (Reserve chicken for another use.) Return skin and bones to Dutch oven and heat to boiling. Skim foam; reduce heat and simmer 3 hours.

3. Strain broth through colander into large bowl; discard solids. Strain again through sieve into containers; cool. Cover and refrigerate to use within 3 days, or freeze up to 4 months.

4. To use, skim and discard fat from surface of broth. Makes about 5 cups.

Each cup: About 36 calories, 3g protein, 4g carbohydrate, 1g total fat (1g saturated), 3mg cholesterol, 91mg sodium.

PRESSURE COOKER CHICKEN BROTH

In 6-quart pressure cooker, place all ingredients for Chicken Broth but use only **4 cups water.** Following manufacturer's directions, cover pressure cooker and bring up to high pressure (15 pounds). Cook 15 minutes. Remove cooker from heat and allow pressure to drop 5 minutes, then follow manufacturer's directions for quick release of pressure. Strain broth through colander into large bowl; discard solids. Strain again through sieve into containers; cool. Meanwhile, remove skin and bones from chicken; discard. (Reserve chicken for another use.) Cover broth and refrigerate to use within 3 days, or freeze up to 4 months. To use, skim and discard fat from surface of broth. Makes about 5½ cups or 6 first-course servings.

BROTH

TEST KITCHEN TIP

Homemade stock is a wonderful ingredient to have on hand, but don't underestimate the convenience and quality of canned broth. Supermarkets carry an assortment of canned broths, including chicken, beef, and vegetable, not to mention reduced-sodium, no-salt-added, and fat-free.

CHICKEN BROTH is used a lot in our test kitchens, but we sometimes dilute one 14½-ounce can of broth with ¾ cup water. This step is entirely optional, but we think it softens the intense flavor of canned broth.

LOW-SODIUM AND NO-SALT-ADDED BROTHS are recommended in recipes when regular canned broth would oversalt the finished dish. This is especially true in dishes where the cooking liquid evaporates substantially. When using homemade broth or stock, add salt to taste.

FAT-FREE BROTH is healthful, but it's just as easy to remove the fat from canned broth yourself. Freeze the unopened can of broth for one or two hours to solidify the thin layer of surface fat. Open the can, lift off the fat, and discard.

BOUILLON CUBES AND POWDERS don't have as natural a flavor as homemade or canned broths, so while cubes and powders are convenient, broth has the flavor edge.

BROWN BEEF STOCK

For a richer, meatier flavor, use four pounds of beef bones and one pound of oxtails.

Prep: 5 minutes   Cook: 7 hours 30 minutes

- 5 pounds beef bones, cut into 3-inch pieces
- 2 medium onions, each cut in half
- 3 carrots, peeled and each cut in half
- 2 stalks celery, each cut in half
- 13 cups water
- 1 small bunch parsley
- 1 bay leaf
- ½ teaspoon dried thyme

1. Preheat oven to 450°F. Spread beef bones, onions, carrots, and celery in large roasting pan (17½" by 11½"). Roast, stirring every 15 minutes, until well browned, about 1 hour.

2. With tongs, transfer browned bones and vegetables to 6-quart saucepot. Carefully pour off fat from roasting pan. Add 1 cup water to roasting pan and heat to boiling, stirring until browned bits are loosened from bottom of pan; add to pot. Add remaining 12 cups water, parsley, bay leaf, and thyme to pot. Heat to boiling over high heat, skimming foam from surface. Reduce heat and simmer, skimming foam occasionally, 6 hours.

3. Strain broth through colander into large bowl; discard solids. Strain again through fine-mesh sieve into containers. Cool. Cover and refrigerate to use within 3 days, or freeze up to 4 months.

4. To use, skim and discard fat from surface of stock. Makes about 5 cups.

Each cup: About 39 calories, 5g protein, 5g carbohydrate, 0g total fat (0g saturated), 0mg cholesterol, 73mg sodium.

VEGETABLE BROTH

The optional fennel and parsnip add a natural sweetness to the flavor. For an Asian-flavored broth, add minced lemongrass, minced fresh ginger, or chopped fresh cilantro.

Prep: 25 minutes   Cook: 2 hours

- 4 large leeks
- 2 to 4 garlic cloves, not peeled
- 13 cups water
  salt
- 1 large all-purpose potato, peeled, cut lengthwise in half, and thinly sliced
- 1 small fennel bulb, trimmed and chopped (optional)
- 3 parsnips, peeled and thinly sliced (optional)
- 2 large carrots, peeled and thinly sliced
- 3 stalks celery with leaves, thinly sliced
- 4 ounces mushrooms, trimmed and thinly sliced
- 10 parsley sprigs
- 4 thyme sprigs
- 2 bay leaves
- 1 teaspoon whole black peppercorns
  ground black pepper

1. Cut off roots and trim dark green tops from leeks; thinly slice leeks. Rinse leeks in large bowl of cold water, swishing to remove sand; transfer to colander to drain, leaving sand in bottom of bowl.

2. In 6-quart saucepot, combine leeks, garlic, 1 cup water, and pinch salt; heat to boiling. Reduce heat to medium; cover and cook until leeks are tender, about 15 minutes.

3. Add potato, fennel if using, parsnips if using, carrots, celery, mushrooms, parsley and thyme sprigs, bay leaves, peppercorns, and remaining 12 cups water. Heat to boiling; reduce heat and simmer, uncovered, at least 1 hour 30 minutes.

4. Taste and continue cooking if flavor is not concentrated enough. Season with salt and pepper to taste. Strain broth through fine-mesh sieve into containers, pressing on solids with back of wooden spoon to extract liquid; cool. Cover and refrigerate to use within 3 days, or freeze up to 4 months. Makes about 6 cups.

Each cup: About 19 calories, 1g protein, 4g carbohydrate, 0g total fat (0g saturated), 0mg cholesterol, 9mg sodium.

BOULLABAISSE

Ask Provençal cooks how to make bouillabaisse and you'll get a different and passionate response each time. When preparing this classic fisherman's stew, use at least three different kinds of fish with textures ranging from firm to flaky; add the most fragile fish to the pot last. Serve with bread toasts and generous dollops of the aïoli. C'est magnifique!

Prep: 1 hour   Cook: 1 hour

- 3   leeks (1 pound)
- 2   tablespoons olive oil
- 1   large fennel bulb (1½ pounds), trimmed and thinly sliced
- 1   medium onion, chopped
- 2   garlic cloves, finely chopped
      pinch ground red pepper (cayenne)
- 1   cup dry white wine
- 2   bottles (8 ounces each) clam juice
- 1   can (14 to 16 ounces) tomatoes
- 1   cup water
- 3   strips (3" by 1" each) orange peel
- ½   bay leaf
- ¾   teaspoon salt
- ¼   teaspoon dried thyme
- ⅛   teaspoon ground black pepper
      Easy Aïoli (page 37)
- 1   pound monkfish, dark membrane removed, cut into 1-inch pieces
- 1   dozen medium mussels, scrubbed and debearded (page 215)
- 1   pound cod fillet, cut into 1-inch pieces
- 1   pound medium shrimp, shelled and deveined (page 221)
- 2   tablespoons chopped fresh parsley
- 1   loaf French bread, thinly sliced and lightly toasted

1. Cut off roots and trim dark green tops from leeks; cut each leek lengthwise in half, then crosswise into thin slices. Rinse leeks in large bowl of cold water, swishing to remove sand; transfer to colander to drain, leaving sand in bottom of bowl.

2. In nonreactive 5-quart Dutch oven, heat oil over medium heat. Stir in leeks, fennel, and onion; cook, stirring occasionally, until vegetables are tender, about 15 minutes. Add garlic and ground red pepper and cook 30 seconds.

3. Add wine and heat to boiling; boil 1 minute. Stir in clam juice, tomatoes with their juice, water, orange peel, bay leaf, salt, thyme, and black pepper, breaking up tomatoes with side of spoon; heat to boiling. Reduce heat and simmer 20 minutes. Discard bay leaf.

4. Meanwhile, prepare Easy Aïoli.

5. Increase heat to medium-high. Stir in monkfish; cover and cook 3 minutes. Stir in mussels; cover and cook 1 minute. Stir in cod and shrimp; cover and cook until mussels open and fish and shrimp are just opaque throughout, 2 to 3 minutes longer. Discard any mussels that have not opened.

6. To serve, ladle bouillabaisse into large shallow soup bowls; sprinkle with parsley. Spoon aïoli onto toasted French bread and float in bouillabaisse. Makes 11 cups or 6 main-dish servings.

Each serving without toast or Easy Aïoli: About 312 calories, 42g protein, 17g carbohydrate, 8g total fat (1g saturated), 149mg cholesterol, 835mg sodium.

A BRIEF HISTORY OF CHOWDER

In the 16th and 17th centuries, fish chowder was enjoyed by the French as well as by the native Americans. In America, by 1751, recipes for fish chowder began to appear in newspapers. Many were prepared by "layering chowder ingredients." Each ingredient was placed in a pot in a layer of uniform thickness, then slowly cooked. By the mid-18th century, chowder was a mainstay throughout the Northeast. Clams and other shellfish were added to chowders largely because of their great availability, as all one had to do along the shore was to dig them up. When the 1896 edition of the *Boston Cooking School Cookbook* contained three recipes for chowder, it was clear that chowder was here to stay.

LOBSTER BISQUE

....

When you serve lobster, save the shells and cooking liquid and make this splendid soup the next day.

Prep: 15 minutes   Cook: 1 hour 15 minutes

- 2 tablespoons butter or margarine
- 1 medium onion, chopped
- 1 carrot, peeled and chopped
- 1 stalk celery, chopped
- 1 garlic clove, finely chopped
- 3 tablespoons tomato paste
  leftover shells and heads from 4 steamed lobsters
- 2 tablespoons cognac or brandy
- 6 cups water
- 2 bottles (8 ounces each) clam juice or 2 cups cooking liquid from steaming lobsters
- 3 parsley sprigs
- ⅛ teaspoon dried thyme
  pinch ground nutmeg
  pinch ground red pepper (cayenne)
- 3 tablespoons all-purpose flour
- ¾ cup heavy or whipping cream

1. In 12-quart nonreactive stockpot, melt butter over medium heat. Add onion, carrot, celery, and garlic and cook until onion is tender, about 5 minutes. Stir in tomato paste.

2. Increase heat to high and add lobster shells; cook, stirring occasionally, 5 minutes. Stir in cognac and cook until liquid has evaporated. Add water, clam juice, parsley, thyme, nutmeg, and ground red pepper; heat to boiling. Reduce heat; cover and simmer 30 minutes.

3. Strain soup through sieve into 4-quart saucepan; discard solids. Heat to boiling over high heat; boil until reduced to 5 cups, 10 to 15 minutes.

4. In small bowl, with wire whisk, whisk flour into cream until blended and smooth. Gradually whisk cream mixture into soup; heat just to boiling, whisking constantly. Reduce heat and simmer 2 minutes. Makes about 5½ cups or 4 first-course servings.

Each serving: About 258 calories, 3g protein, 12g carbohydrate, 22g total fat (14g saturated), 77mg cholesterol, 441mg sodium.

MANHATTAN CLAM CHOWDER

....

Chowder clams are flavorful but tough and must be chopped after cooking. Substitute cherrystone clams, if you like; there's no need to chop them.

Prep: 30 minutes plus cooling   Cook: 50 minutes

- 5 cups water
- 3 dozen chowder or cherrystone clams, scrubbed (page 214)
- 5 slices bacon, finely chopped
- 1 large onion (12 ounces), finely chopped
- 2 large carrots, peeled and finely chopped
- 2 stalks celery, finely chopped
- 1 pound all-purpose potatoes (3 medium), peeled and finely chopped
- ½ bay leaf
- 1¼ teaspoons dried thyme
- ¼ teaspoon ground black pepper
- 1 can (28 ounces) plum tomatoes
- 2 tablespoons chopped fresh parsley
- ¾ teaspoon salt

1. In nonreactive 8-quart saucepot, heat 1 cup water to boiling over high heat. Add clams; heat to boiling. Reduce heat; cover and simmer until clams open, 5 to 10 minutes, transferring clams to bowl as they open. Discard any clams that have not opened.

2. When cool enough to handle, remove clams from their shells and coarsely chop. Strain clam broth through sieve lined with paper towels into bowl.

3. In same clean saucepot, cook bacon over medium heat until browned; add onion and cook until tender, 5 minutes. Add carrots and celery; cook 5 minutes.

4. Add clam broth to bacon mixture in saucepot. Add potatoes, remaining 4 cups water, bay leaf, thyme, and pepper; heat to boiling. Reduce heat; cover and simmer 10 minutes. Add tomatoes with their liquid, breaking them up with side of spoon, and simmer 10 minutes longer.

5. Stir in chopped clams and heat through. Discard bay leaf and sprinkle with parsley. Taste for seasoning; add salt as needed. Makes about 12 cups or 12 first-course servings.

Each serving: About 117 calories, 5g protein, 12g carbohydrate, 6g total fat (2g saturated), 12mg cholesterol, 342mg sodium.

NEW ENGLAND CLAM CHOWDER

· ·

Clam chowder, New England's signature seafood dish, derives its name from chaudière, the French word for "cauldron." The saltiness of clams and salt pork varies; taste the soup before serving and season if needed.

Prep: 25 minutes plus cooling   Cook: 45 minutes

  1   cup water
1½   dozen large littleneck clams (about 4 pounds),
       scrubbed (page 214)
  3   slices bacon, chopped
  1   medium onion, finely chopped
  1   tablespoon all-purpose flour
  ¼   teaspoon ground black pepper
  1   pound all-purpose potatoes, (3 medium), peeled
       and chopped
  2   cups half-and-half
  1   cup milk
  ¾   teaspoon salt or to taste

1. In a 5- to 6-quart saucepot, heat water to boiling over high heat. Add clams; heat to boiling. Reduce heat slightly; cover and simmer until clams open, 5 to 10 minutes. Transfer clams to a bowl as they open. Discard any clams that have not opened.

2. When cool enough to handle, remove clams from their shells and coarsely chop. Discard shells. Strain clam broth through sieve lined with paper towels into measuring cup; if necessary add enough *water* to equal 2 cups.

3. In same clean saucepot, cook bacon over medium heat until lightly browned. With slotted spoon, remove bacon to paper towels. Add onion to drippings in pot; cook, stirring occasionally, until tender, about 5 minutes. Stir in flour and pepper until blended; cook 1 minute. Gradually stir in clam broth until smooth. Add potatoes; heat to boiling. Reduce heat; cover and simmer until potatoes are tender, about 15 minutes.

4. Stir in half-and-half, milk, and chopped clams; heat through (do not boil). Stir in bacon. Taste for seasoning; add salt as needed. Makes about 6 cups.

Each cup: About 371g calories, 18g protein, 24g carbohydrate, 22g total fat (11g saturated), 77mg cholesterol, 534mg sodium.

YANKEE COD CHOWDER

Prepare as directed (left) omitting water and clams. Follow Step 3 through stirring in flour and pepper and cooking for 1 minute. Stir in **3 bottles (8 ounces each) of clam broth** until smooth. Add potatoes and cook as directed. Add **1 pound cod fillet,** cut into 1½-inch pieces, to pot. Cover and simmer until fish is just opaque throughout, 2 to 5 minutes. Stir in half-and-half; omit milk. Heat through (do not boil). Stir in bacon. Taste for seasoning; add salt as needed. Makes about 8½ cups.

Each cup: About 259 calories, 14g protein, 15g carbohydrate, 16g total fat (7g saturated), 56mg cholesterol, 590mg sodium.

HEALTHY NEW ENGLAND CLAM CHOWDER

· ·

To slim this dish—by more than half the calories and cholesterol—we trimmed the bacon, swapped reduced-fat milk for cream, and stirred in flour in place of several starchy potatoes.

Prep: 20 minutes   Cook: 35 minutes

1½   cups water plus more for broth
 12   large cherrystone or chowder clams, scrubbed
       (page 214)
  2   slices bacon, chopped
  1   medium onion, chopped
  1   medium carrot, chopped
  1   stalk celery, chopped
  2   tablespoons all-purpose flour
  1   large potato (12 ounces), peeled and cut into
       ½-inch chunks
  2   cups reduced-fat (2%) milk
  ⅛   teaspoon ground black pepper
  1   tablespoon finely chopped fresh chives

1. In 4-quart saucepan, heat water to boiling on high. Add clams; return to boiling. Reduce heat to medium low; cover and simmer 10 minutes or until clams open, transferring clams to bowl as they open. Discard any unopened clams.

2. Into 4-cup liquid measuring cup, strain clam broth through sieve lined with paper towel. Add water to broth to equal 2½ cups total.

3. Rinse saucepan to remove any grit. In same saucepan, cook bacon on medium until browned. With slotted spoon, transfer bacon to paper towels to drain, leaving bacon fat in pan. Add onion, carrot, and celery to pan, and cook 9 to 10 minutes or until tender, stirring occasionally. Meanwhile, remove clams from shells and coarsely chop.

4. Stir flour into vegetable mixture; cook 1 minute, stirring. Gradually stir in clam broth. Add potato; heat to boiling. Cover; simmer on low 12 minutes or until potato is tender, stirring occasionally. Stir in milk, clams, pepper, and bacon; heat through (do not boil). Sprinkle with chives to serve. Makes 6 servings.

Each serving: About 180 calories, 8g protein, 20g carbohydrate, 9g total fat (4g saturated), 2g fiber, 21mg cholesterol, 155mg sodium.

SAN FRANCISCO-STYLE SEAFOOD STEW

······························

Sometimes called cioppino, *this dish is a favorite of the city's Italian-American community and seafood lovers everywhere. Use the toasts to soak up the delectable broth.*

Prep: 20 minutes   Toast/Cook: 30 minutes

- 1 sourdough baguette
- 2 tablespoons olive oil
- ¼ teaspoon coarsely ground black pepper
- 1 medium onion, chopped
- 1 medium red pepper, chopped
- 2 cloves garlic, crushed with press
- ½ cup dry white wine
- 1 can (28 ounces) whole tomatoes in juice
- 1 cup water
- ⅛ teaspoon crushed red pepper
- ½ cup loosely packed fresh parsley leaves, chopped
- 1 pound large mussels, scrubbed and beards removed (page 215)
- ¾ pound striped bass fillet, skin removed, cut into 1½-inch pieces
- ½ pound large shrimp, shelled and deveined (page 221)
- ¼ cup loosely packed fresh basil leaves, chopped

1. Preheat oven to 400°F. Cut enough bread on the diagonal to make eight ½-inch-thick slices. Wrap remaining bread; reserve for another use. Place bread slices on cookie sheet. Brush with 1 tablespoon oil and sprinkle with black pepper. Toast bread in oven 8 to 10 minutes or until golden.

2. Meanwhile, in 5- to 6-quart Dutch oven, heat remaining 1 tablespoon oil over medium-high heat until hot. Add onion, red pepper, and garlic; cook 6 to 8 minutes or until very tender and browned, stirring frequently. Add wine; heat to boiling. Boil 1 to 2 minutes or until wine reduces by half. While vegetables are cooking, pour tomatoes with their juice into medium bowl; with kitchen shears, chop tomatoes.

3. Stir tomatoes with their juice, water, and crushed red pepper into Dutch oven; cover and heat to boiling. Add parsley, mussels, striped bass, and shrimp; heat to boiling. Reduce heat to medium-low and simmer, covered, 8 to 10 minutes or until striped bass and shrimp are opaque and mussels open, stirring occasionally.

4. Remove Dutch oven from heat. Discard any mussels that have not opened. Stir basil into stew. Serve with sourdough toasts. Makes about 10 cups or 4 main-dish servings.

Each serving: About 425 calories, 37g protein, 41g carbohydrate, 13g total fat (2g saturated), 5g fiber, 149mg cholesterol, 850mg sodium.

San Francisco-Style Seafood Stew

ANDOUILLE-SHRIMP GUMBO

··

This is one of the best gumbos around. Chock-full of chicken, andouille sausage, shrimp, vegetables, and rice, including the holy trinity of onion, green pepper, and celery, this is perfect party food.

Prep: 30 minutes   Cook: 1 hour 10 minutes

⅓ cup plus 1 tablespoon vegetable oil
½ cup all-purpose flour
2 celery stalks, chopped
2 garlic cloves, minced
1 medium green pepper, chopped
1 medium onion, chopped
2 cans (14½ ounces each) chicken broth or 3½ cups Chicken Broth (page 70)
1 can (14½ ounces) stewed tomatoes
1 pound skinless, boneless chicken thighs, cut into thin strips
½ pound andouille or chorizo sausage, cut into ¼-inch-thick slices
6 ounces okra, cut into ½-inch-thick slices
1 cup loosely packed fresh parsley leaves, chopped
1 tablespoon minced fresh thyme leaves
1 tablespoon minced fresh sage leaves
¾ teaspoon salt
½ teaspoon coarsely ground black pepper
4 cups water
1 pound medium shrimp, shelled and deveined (page 221), with tail part of shell left on
1 cup long-grain white rice, cooked as label directs

1. In 6-quart saucepot, heat ⅓ cup oil over medium-low heat until hot. Gradually stir in flour until blended and cook, stirring, until mixture is dark brown, about 15 minutes.

2. Meanwhile, in nonstick 12-inch skillet, heat remaining 1 tablespoon oil over medium heat until hot. Add celery, garlic, green pepper, and onion and cook, stirring occasionally, until vegetables are tender.

3. When flour mixture is ready, gradually stir in broth until blended and smooth. Add stewed tomatoes, chicken, andouille, okra, parsley, thyme, sage, salt, black pepper, cooked vegetables, and water; heat to boiling over high heat. Reduce heat to low; simmer, uncovered, 40 minutes.

4. Skim off fat and discard. Add shrimp and cook, uncovered, until shrimp turn opaque throughout, about 5 minutes longer.

5. Ladle gumbo into large bowls. Top with a scoop of hot rice. Makes about 11 cups or 6 main-dish servings.

Each serving: About 525 calories, 40g protein, 46g carbohydrate, 19g total fat (6g saturated), 169mg cholesterol, 1,515mg sodium.

MUSSELS IN SAFFRON-TOMATO BROTH

··

Serve steaming bowls of these mussels with hunks of country-style bread to sop up all of the savory juices.

Prep: 20 minutes   Cook: 30 minutes

3 tablespoons olive oil
2 garlic cloves, crushed with side of chef's knife
1 small bay leaf
½ teaspoon loosely packed saffron threads
⅛ to ¼ teaspoon crushed red pepper
1 can (14½ ounces) diced tomatoes
1 bottle (8 ounces) clam juice
½ cup dry white wine
5 dozen medium mussels, scrubbed and debearded (page 215)

1. In nonreactive 8-quart saucepot, heat oil over medium heat. Add garlic and cook until golden. Add bay leaf, saffron, and crushed red pepper; cook, stirring, 1 minute.

2. Add tomatoes with their liquid, clam juice, and wine; heat to boiling over high heat. Reduce heat; cover and simmer 20 minutes.

3. Add mussels; heat to boiling over high heat. Reduce heat to medium; cover and simmer until mussels open, about 5 minutes, transferring mussels to bowl as they open. Discard bay leaf and any mussels that have not opened. To serve, transfer mussels and broth to large soup bowls. Makes 4 main-dish servings.

Each serving: About 219 calories, 16g protein, 10g carbohydrate, 13g total fat (2g saturated), 34mg cholesterol, 642mg sodium.

MOROCCAN VEGETABLE STEW

....

Spiced with cinnamon and crushed pepper, sweetened with dried plums, and served over couscous, this typical Moroccan stew (called a tagine) is as rich and satisfying as any meat dish.

Prep: 15 minutes   Cook: 40 minutes

- 1 tablespoon olive oil
- 1 medium butternut squash (about 2 pounds), peeled and cut into 1-inch pieces
- 2 carrots, peeled and cut into 1/4-inch-thick slices
- 1 medium onion, chopped
- 1 can (15 to 19 ounces) garbanzo beans, rinsed and drained
- 1 can (14 1/2 ounces) stewed tomatoes
- 1/2 cup pitted prunes, chopped
- 1/2 teaspoon ground cinnamon
- 1/2 teaspoon salt
- 1/8 to 1/4 teaspoon crushed red pepper
- 1 1/2 cups water
- 1 cup couscous (Moroccan pasta)
- 1 1/4 cups vegetable or chicken broth
- 2 tablespoons chopped fresh cilantro or parsley

1. In nonstick 12-inch skillet, heat oil over medium-high heat. Add squash, carrots, and onion and cook, stirring frequently, until onion is tender and golden, about 10 minutes.

2. Stir in garbanzo beans, tomatoes, prunes, cinnamon, salt, crushed red pepper, and water; heat to boiling. Reduce heat; cover and simmer until all vegetables are tender, about 30 minutes.

3. Meanwhile, prepare couscous as label directs, but use broth in place of water.

4. To serve, stir cilantro into stew and spoon over couscous. Makes 4 main-dish servings.

Each serving: About 474 calories, 14g protein, 95g carbohydrate, 6g total fat (1g saturated), 0mg cholesterol, 1,022mg sodium.

CHICKEN BOUILLABAISSE

....

Serve in oversized soup bowls with a dollop of garlic mayonnaise (see Easy Aïoli, page 37) and thickly sliced French bread toasts.

Prep: 1 hour   Bake: 30 minutes

- 1 tablespoon olive oil
- 8 large bone-in chicken thighs (2 1/2 pounds), skin and fat removed
- 2 large carrots, peeled and finely chopped
- 1 medium onion, finely chopped
- 1 large fennel bulb (1 1/2 pounds), cut into 1/4-inch-thick slices
- 1/2 cup water
- 3 garlic cloves, finely chopped
- 1 can (14 1/2 ounces) diced tomatoes
- 1 can (14 1/2 ounces) chicken broth or 1 3/4 cups Chicken Broth (page 70)
- 1/2 cup dry white wine
- 2 tablespoons anisette (anise-flavored liqueur; optional)
- 1/4 teaspoon dried thyme
- 1/4 teaspoon salt
- 1/8 teaspoon ground red pepper (cayenne)
- 1 bay leaf
  pinch saffron threads

1. In 5-quart Dutch oven, heat oil over medium-high heat until very hot. Add chicken, in batches, and cook until golden brown, about 5 minutes per side, using slotted spoon to transfer chicken pieces to bowl as they are browned.

2. Add carrots and onion to Dutch oven and cook over medium heat, stirring occasionally, until tender and golden, about 10 minutes. Transfer mixture to bowl with chicken.

3. Preheat oven to 350°F. Add fennel and water to Dutch oven, stirring until browned bits are loosened from bottom of pot. Cook over medium heat, stirring occasionally, until fennel is tender and browned, about 7 minutes. Add garlic and cook 3 minutes.

4. Return chicken and carrot mixture to Dutch oven. Add tomatoes with their juice, broth, wine, anisette, if using, thyme, salt, ground red pepper, bay leaf, and saffron; heat to boiling. Cover and bake until juices run clear when thickest part of chicken is pierced with tip of knife, about 30 minutes. Discard bay leaf. Makes 4 main-dish servings.

Each serving: About 317 calories, 36g protein, 18g carbohydrate, 11g total fat (2g saturated), 135mg cholesterol, 1,036mg sodium.

PROVENÇAL BEEF STEW (DAUBE)

In southern France, food is often flavored with garden-fresh tomatoes, olives, garlic, fresh orange peel, and a variety of herbs, including lavender. We suggest serving our robust Provençal-inspired stew with boiled potatoes and lots of crusty bread for soaking up all of the delicious sauce.

Prep: 15 minutes   Cook: 2 hours 30 minutes

 2 pounds lean boneless beef chuck, trimmed and cut into 2-inch pieces
 4 teaspoons olive oil
 1 large onion (12 ounces), chopped
 2 carrots, peeled and chopped
 2 garlic cloves, finely chopped
 1 can (14 to 16 ounces) tomatoes
 2 cups dry red wine
 4 strips (3" by ³⁄₄" each) orange peel
 3 whole cloves
 1 teaspoon salt
 ¼ teaspoon ground black pepper
 ¼ teaspoon dried thyme
 1 bay leaf
 2 tablespoons chopped fresh parsley

1. Pat beef dry with paper towels. In nonreactive 5-quart Dutch oven, heat 2 teaspoons oil over medium-high heat until very hot. Add half of beef and cook until well browned, using slotted spoon to transfer meat to bowl as it is browned. Repeat with remaining 2 teaspoons oil and remaining beef.

2. Reduce heat to medium. Add onion and carrots to Dutch oven and cook, stirring occasionally, until tender, about 5 minutes. Stir in garlic and cook until very fragrant, about 30 seconds. Stir in tomatoes with their juice, breaking them up with side of spoon. Add wine, orange peel, cloves, salt, pepper, thyme, bay leaf, and beef; heat to boiling over high heat.

3. Reduce heat; cover and simmer 2 hours to 2 hours 30 minutes, until meat is very tender. With slotted spoon, transfer meat to serving bowl and keep warm. Skim and discard fat from stew liquid.

4. Increase heat to medium-high and boil liquid 10 minutes to concentrate flavors. Discard bay leaf and spoon liquid over meat. Sprinkle with parsley. Makes 6 main-dish servings.

Each serving: About 292 calories, 30g protein, 11g carbohydrate, 14g total fat (4g saturated), 95mg cholesterol, 601mg sodium.

STEW SAVVY

A few simple steps are the keys to success when making stew.
- Always use a heavy pot, such as a Dutch oven, which promotes even cooking.
- When browning meat or vegetables, first pat them dry. Always add meat to the hot oil without crowding the pan, so that it browns rather than steams. Give meat or vegetables a chance to brown before turning, which will create browned bits on the bottom of the pan that will add rich flavor.
- Add enough liquid to cover or almost cover the ingredients.
- Cook stews slowly on top of the stove over low heat to tenderize the meat.
- Quicker-cooking ingredients, such as potatoes and peas, are usually added near the end of the cooking time, so they don't get overcooked.

BOEUF BOURGUIGNON

....

This classic French dish has become an American fixture. Begin with a salad of mixed baby greens dressed with vinaigrette and end with chocolate mousse topped with whipped cream—typical bistro fare.

Prep: 30 minutes   Cook: 2 hours 45 minutes

- 2 slices bacon, chopped
- 2 pounds lean boneless beef chuck, trimmed and cut into 1½-inch pieces
- 2 teaspoons vegetable oil
- 1 large onion (12 ounces), chopped
- 2 carrots, peeled and chopped
- 2 garlic cloves, finely chopped
- 2 tablespoons all-purpose flour
- 2 teaspoons tomato paste
- 2 cups dry red wine such as Pinot Noir
- ½ bay leaf
- 1 teaspoon plus pinch salt
- ¼ teaspoon plus pinch ground black pepper
- 1 pound small white onions, peeled
- 3 tablespoons butter or margarine
- 1 teaspoon sugar
- 1 cup water
- 1 pound mushrooms, trimmed and cut into quarters if large

1. In nonreactive 5-quart Dutch oven, cook bacon over medium heat until just beginning to brown. With slotted spoon, transfer bacon to medium bowl.

2. Pat beef dry with paper towels. Add 1 teaspoon oil to Dutch oven and increase heat to medium-high. Add beef, in batches, to bacon drippings and cook until well browned, using slotted spoon to transfer beef as it is browned to bowl with bacon. Add remaining 1 teaspoon oil if necessary.

3. Reduce heat to medium. Add chopped onion, carrots, and garlic to Dutch oven; cook until onion and carrots are tender, about 8 minutes. Stir in flour; cook 1 minute. Stir in tomato paste; cook 1 minute. Add wine, bay leaf, 1 teaspoon salt, and ¼ teaspoon pepper, stirring until browned bits are loosened from bottom of oven.

4. Return beef and bacon to Dutch oven; heat to boiling. Reduce heat; cover and simmer until beef is very tender, about 1 hour 30 minutes. Remove bay leaf. Skim and discard fat.

5. Meanwhile, in 10-inch skillet, combine small white onions, 1 tablespoon butter, sugar, and water; heat to boiling. Reduce heat; cover and simmer until onions are just tender, about 10 minutes. Remove cover and cook over medium-high heat, swirling pan occasionally, until water has evaporated and onions are golden. Transfer to bowl; keep warm.

6. In same skillet, melt remaining 2 tablespoons butter over medium-high heat. Add mushrooms and remaining pinch each salt and pepper; cook, stirring, until mushrooms are tender and liquid has evaporated. Stir onions and mushrooms into stew. Makes 6 main-dish servings.

Each serving: About 415 calories, 33g protein, 20g carbohydrate, 23g total fat (9g saturated), 116mg cholesterol, 261mg sodium.

A GLOSSARY OF MEAT STEW

Meat stews are enjoyed around the world. Here are some of the most famous:

BEEF BOURGUIGNON: This French beef stew is flavored with onions, mushrooms, and bacon.

BEEF CARBONNADE: A Belgian stew that contains dark beer and caramelized onions.

BLANQUETTE DE VEAU: A rich, creamy veal stew, so named because the meat is not browned.

DAUBE: In France, daubes are often baked in a pot known as a *daubière*.

GOULASH: Called *gulyás* in its native Hungary, this stew is flavored with paprika.

NAVARIN: A French stew made with lamb and usually onions, potatoes, turnips, and herbs.

STIFADO: A Greek stew prepared with lamb or beef, flavored with tomatoes and oregano, and baked in a casserole.

MOROCCAN-STYLE LAMB WITH COUSCOUS

....

This sweet but slightly spicy stew is served on a bed of couscous, grain-shaped semolina pasta.

Prep: 20 minutes   Cook: 1 hour 45 minutes

- 2 pounds boneless lamb shoulder, trimmed and cut into 1¼-inch pieces
- 2 tablespoons olive oil
- 2 garlic cloves, finely chopped
- 1½ teaspoons ground cumin
- 1½ teaspoons ground coriander
- 1 large onion (12 ounces), cut into 8 wedges
- 1 can (14½ to 16 ounces) stewed tomatoes
- 1 cinnamon stick (3 inches)
- 1¼ teaspoons salt
- ¼ teaspoon ground red pepper (cayenne)
- 1 cup water
- 2 pounds sweet potatoes (3 large), peeled and cut into 2-inch pieces
- 2 cups couscous (Moroccan pasta)
- 1 can (15 to 19 ounces) garbanzo beans, rinsed and drained
- 1 cup dark seedless raisins
- ¼ cup chopped fresh cilantro

1. Pat lamb dry with paper towels. In nonreactive 5-quart Dutch oven, heat 1 tablespoon oil over medium-high heat until very hot. Add half of lamb and cook until browned, using slotted spoon to transfer meat to bowl as it is browned. Repeat with remaining 1 tablespoon oil and remaining lamb.

2. To drippings in Dutch oven, add garlic, cumin, and coriander; cook 30 seconds. Return lamb to Dutch oven. Stir in onion, tomatoes, cinnamon stick, salt, ground red pepper, and water; heat to boiling over high heat. Reduce heat; cover and simmer, stirring occasionally, 45 minutes. Stir in sweet potatoes; cover and simmer 30 minutes longer.

3. Meanwhile, prepare couscous as label directs.

4. Add garbanzo beans and raisins to Dutch oven. Cover and cook, stirring once or twice, until lamb and vegetables are tender, about 5 minutes longer.

5. Just before serving, stir in cilantro. Serve lamb stew on couscous. Makes 8 main-dish servings.

Each serving: About 570 calories, 33g protein, 81g carbohydrate, 13g total fat (3g saturated), 75mg cholesterol, 651mg sodium.

VEAL AND MUSHROOM STEW

....

In this recipe, the veal is slowly simmered with mushrooms and a touch of sweet Marsala wine until tender. Peas are added for their subtle sweetness and color.

Prep: 30 minutes   Bake: 1 hour

- 1½ pounds boneless veal shoulder, cut into 1½-inch pieces
- ¾ teaspoon salt
- ¼ teaspoon ground black pepper
- 3 tablespoons vegetable oil
- 1 pound white mushrooms, trimmed and cut in half
- ¼ pound shiitake mushrooms, stems removed
- ½ cup water
- ⅓ cup dry Marsala wine
- 1 package (10 ounces) frozen peas, thawed

1. Preheat oven to 350°F. Pat veal dry with paper towels. Sprinkle veal with salt and pepper. In nonreactive 5-quart Dutch oven, heat 2 tablespoons oil over medium-high heat until very hot. Add half of veal and cook until browned, using slotted spoon to transfer meat to bowl as it is browned. Repeat with remaining veal (without additional oil).

2. In Dutch oven, heat remaining 1 tablespoon oil over medium-high heat. Add white and shiitake mushrooms and cook, stirring occasionally, until lightly browned.

3. Return veal to Dutch oven; stir in water and Marsala, stirring until browned bits are loosened from bottom of pan. Heat veal mixture to boiling.

4. Cover Dutch oven and bake, stirring occasionally, until veal is tender, 1 hour to 1 hour 15 minutes. Stir in peas and heat through. Makes 6 main-dish servings.

Each serving: About 249 calories, 26g protein, 12g carbohydrate, 11g total fat (2g saturated), 94mg cholesterol, 448mg sodium.

CREAMY VEAL STEW

....

Known in France as **Blanquette de Veau**, *this velvety stew is perfect just the way it is. It can, however, be accented with 2 tablespoons chopped fresh tarragon and 2 tablespoons lemon juice, stirred in with the cream.*

Prep: 35 minutes   Bake: 1 hour 15 minutes

2 pounds boneless veal shoulder, cut into 1½-inch pieces
¼ cup all-purpose flour
1 teaspoon salt
¼ teaspoon ground black pepper
2 tablespoons plus 2 teaspoons vegetable oil
1 cup dry white wine
2 medium onions, chopped
1 cup chicken broth
1 bay leaf
¼ teaspoon dried thyme
¼ cup heavy or whipping cream

1. Preheat oven to 350°F. Pat veal dry with paper towels. On waxed paper, combine flour, salt, and pepper. Coat veal with seasoned flour, shaking off excess.

2. In nonstick 12-inch skillet, heat 1 tablespoon oil over medium-high heat until very hot. Add half of veal and cook until browned, using slotted spoon to transfer meat to bowl as it is browned. Repeat with 1 tablespoon oil and remaining veal. Add wine to skillet and heat to boiling, stirring until browned bits are loosened from bottom of skillet; remove from heat.

3. In nonreactive 5-quart Dutch oven, heat remaining 2 teaspoons oil over medium heat. Add onions and cook until tender, about 5 minutes. Stir in veal, broth, bay leaf, thyme, and pan-juice mixture from skillet. Heat to boiling; cover and bake until veal is tender, about 1 hour 15 minutes. Discard bay leaf; stir in heavy cream. Makes 6 main-dish servings.

Each serving: About 285 calories, 31g protein, 10g carbohydrate, 13g total fat (4g saturated), 139mg cholesterol, 696mg sodium.

LAMB NAVARIN

....

Celebrate spring with this vegetable-laden classic French ragoût.

Prep: 20 minutes   Cook: 2 hours

3 pounds boneless lamb shoulder, trimmed and cut into 1-inch pieces
2 tablespoons butter or margarine
2 small onions, each cut into quarters, then crosswise into slices
1½ cups dry white wine
1½ cups chicken broth
1 cup water
6 sprigs plus 2 tablespoons chopped fresh parsley
2 thyme sprigs or ¼ teaspoon dried thyme
2 bay leaves
4 garlic cloves, finely chopped
½ teaspoon salt
¼ teaspoon ground black pepper
8 ounces peeled baby carrots (1⅓ cups)
2 small turnips (4 ounces each), peeled and cut into ¾-inch pieces
8 ounces pearl onions, peeled (1 cup)
1½ pounds asparagus, trimmed and cut into 2-inch lengths
2 teaspoons sugar

1. Pat lamb dry with paper towels. In nonreactive 5-quart Dutch oven, melt butter over medium heat. Cook lamb, in batches, until well browned, using slotted spoon to transfer meat to bowl as it is browned. Add onions to Dutch oven and cook, stirring, until tender, about 5 minutes. Add wine, broth, water, parsley sprigs, thyme sprigs, bay leaves, and lamb to pot; heat to boiling over high heat. Reduce heat; cover and simmer 15 minutes. Add garlic, salt, and pepper and simmer 30 minutes longer.

2. Add carrots, turnips, and pearl onions to Dutch oven; partially cover and cook until lamb is tender, about 30 minutes longer. Stir in asparagus and cook until vegetables are tender, 5 to 10 minutes longer.

3. With slotted spoon, transfer meat and vegetables to deep dish and keep warm. Boil stew liquid over medium-high heat until it has reduced and thickened, about 10 minutes.

4. Discard parsley and thyme sprigs and bay leaves. Stir in sugar. Taste for seasoning; add salt as needed. Spoon stew liquid over meat and vegetables and sprinkle with parsley. Makes 8 main-dish servings.

Each serving: About 312 calories, 39g protein, 14g carbohydrate, 11g total fat (5g saturated), 117mg cholesterol, 500mg sodium.

COUNTRY BORSCHT STEW

....

Unlike cold beet borscht, this hearty richly flavored version is loaded with cabbage, carrots, parsnips, and succulent beef short ribs. Served hot, it is sure to warm you on even the coldest of winter days.

Prep: 1 hour 15 minutes   Bake: 2 hours

- 2 bunches beets (1³/₄ pounds without tops)
- 1 medium head red cabbage (about 2³/₄ pounds)
- 5 pounds beef chuck short ribs
- 1 pound carrots, peeled and each cut lengthwise in half, then crosswise into 1-inch-thick pieces
- 1 pound parsnips, peeled and each cut lengthwise in half, then crosswise into 1-inch-thick pieces
- 1 large onion (12 ounces), cut into 1-inch pieces
- 2 teaspoons salt
- 1 teaspoon caraway seeds, crushed
- ¼ teaspoon ground cloves
- 1 carton (32 ounces) chicken broth or 4 cups Chicken Broth (page 70)
- 2 bay leaves
- ½ cup loosely packed fresh dill sprigs, chopped sour cream (optional)

1. Trim tops, if any, from beets. Peel and shred beets (you should have about 6½ cups shredded beets). Cut cabbage into quarters; remove and discard core. Cut cabbage into ½-inch slices.

2. Heat 8-quart Dutch oven over medium-high heat until hot. Pat beef ribs dry with paper towels. Add beef in batches and cook until well browned on all sides, 5 to 6 minutes per batch, using tongs to transfer meat to medium bowl as it is browned. (You may need to reduce heat to medium if fat in Dutch oven begins to smoke.) Preheat oven to 325°F.

3. Reduce heat to medium. Discard all but ¼ cup drippings in Dutch oven. Add carrots, parsnips, onion, salt, caraway seeds, and cloves; cook, stirring occasionally, until vegetables are golden, about 10 minutes. Add cabbage and cook, stirring frequently, until wilted, about 10 minutes.

4. Return meat with its juices to Dutch oven; stir in broth, bay leaves, and beets. Heat to boiling over high heat, stirring until browned bits are loosened from bottom of Dutch oven. Cover and bake until meat is fork-tender, 2 hours to 2 hours 15 minutes.

5. Remove stew from oven. With tongs, transfer short-rib meat and bones to large bowl to cool slightly. Discard bay leaves. Skim and discard fat. When short ribs are cool enough to handle, cut meat into 1-inch pieces; discard bones and fat.

6. Return meat to Dutch oven. Heat over medium heat until hot. Stir in dill. To serve, ladle borscht into shallow soup bowls and top with sour cream, if you like. Makes about 16 cups or 12 main-dish servings.

Each serving: About 525 calories, 22g protein, 22g carbohydrate, 39g total fat (16g saturated), 82mg cholesterol, 830mg sodium.

Country Borscht Stew

FIVE-SPICE BRAISED PORK AND CABBAGE

....

In this dish, a generous amount of five-spice powder adds a lot of exotic flavor with very little effort. The powder, found in supermarkets, usually consists of equal parts of cinnamon, cloves, fennel seeds, star anise, and Szechuan peppercorns.

Prep: 1 hour   Bake: 1 hour 30 minutes

  4 pounds boneless pork shoulder, trimmed and
     cut into 2-inch pieces
  2 tablespoons brown sugar
  1 tablespoon Chinese five-spice powder
  1 tablespoon vegetable oil
  1 teaspoon grated fresh orange peel
 3/4 teaspoon salt
  1 medium head green cabbage (about 2½ pounds)
  1 large onion (12 ounces), cut in half, then
     sliced crosswise
  1 piece (3 inches) peeled fresh ginger,
     cut into slivers
  1 can (14½ ounces) chicken broth or
     1¾ cups Chicken Broth (page 70)
 ¼ cup soy sauce
  2 tablespoons seasoned rice vinegar or
     cider vinegar
     long-grain white rice (optional)
 ¼ cup cornstarch
  3 tablespoons water

1. Pat pork dry with paper towels. In large bowl, toss pork with brown sugar, five-spice powder, oil, orange peel, and salt until evenly coated. Set aside.

2. Remove tough outer leaves from cabbage. Cut cabbage into 4 wedges; remove and discard core. Cut cabbage into 2-inch pieces. Set aside.

3. Heat 6- to 8-quart Dutch oven over medium-high heat until hot. Add pork, in batches, and cook until well browned, 4 to 7 minutes, adding more oil if necessary, and transferring pork with slotted spoon to medium bowl as it is browned. (You may need to reduce heat to medium if oil begins to smoke.) Preheat oven to 325°F.

4. Reduce heat to medium. To fat remaining in Dutch oven, add onion and ginger, and cook, stirring frequently, until tender, about 5 minutes. Add cabbage and cook, stirring frequently, until cabbage wilts, 6 to 8 minutes. Add broth, soy sauce, and vinegar, and stir until browned bits are loosened from bottom of Dutch oven. Return pork with its juices to Dutch oven; heat to boiling.

5. Cover and bake until meat is fork-tender, about 1 hour 30 minutes.

6. About 30 minutes before serving, prepare rice, if you like.

7. Skim and discard fat from stew. In cup, combine cornstarch and water. Heat stew to boiling over medium heat. Stir in cornstarch mixture; heat to boiling. Boil until stew thickens slightly, about 1 minute. Serve with rice, if you like. Makes about 11 cups or 8 main-dish servings.

Each serving: About 455 calories, 49g protein, 19g carbohydrate, 20g total fat (6g saturated), 162mg cholesterol, 1,210mg sodium.

MOLE CHILI CON CARNE

....

From the word molli, *which means "concoction," comes mole, a favorite sauce in Mexico that is probably prepared in as many ways as there are cooks who make it. Mole is a rich-tasting, reddish brown sauce, one of whose unlikely ingredients—chocolate—contributes body without making the sauce sweet.*

Prep: 1 hour 10 minutes   Bake: 1 hour 45 minutes

  2 pounds boneless pork shoulder, trimmed and
     cut into 1-inch pieces
  2 pounds boneless beef chuck, trimmed and
     cut into 1-inch pieces
  2 teaspoons vegetable oil
  6 garlic cloves, crushed with press
  2 medium onions, chopped
  1 tablespoon ground coriander
  1 tablespoon ground cumin
  1 tablespoon paprika
 1½ teaspoons chipotle chile powder
 ½ teaspoon ground cinnamon
  3 cans (15 to 19 ounces each) pink beans and/or red
     kidney beans
  1 can (28 ounces) diced tomatoes

1 cup water
2 squares (2 ounces) unsweetened chocolate, chopped
1½ teaspoons salt
warm corn tortillas (optional)

1. Pat pork and beef dry with paper towels. In 6- to 8-quart Dutch oven, heat oil over medium-high heat until very hot. Add meat in batches and cook until well browned, 5 to 6 minutes, adding more oil if necessary and using slotted spoon to transfer meat to medium bowl as it is browned. (You may need to reduce heat to medium if oil in Dutch oven begins to smoke.) Preheat oven to 325°F.

2. Reduce heat to medium. Add garlic, onions, coriander, cumin, paprika, chipotle chili powder, and cinnamon to drippings in Dutch oven, and cook, stirring frequently, until onion is tender, about 5 minutes.

3. Return meat with its juices to Dutch oven. Stir in beans with their liquid, tomatoes with their juice, water, chocolate, and salt; heat to boiling over high heat, stirring until browned bits are loosened from bottom of Dutch oven.

4. Cover and bake until meat is fork-tender, 1 hour and 45 minutes to 2 hours. Skim and discard any fat. Spoon chili into bowls and serve with tortillas, if you like. Makes about 15 cups or 10 main-dish servings.

Each serving: About 525 calories, 55g protein, 34g carbohydrate, 19g total fat (7g saturated), 146mg cholesterol, 1,335mg sodium.

Mole Chili con Carne

NEW MEXICAN GREEN CHILI

At New Mexico's chile stands, green chiles are as popular as red ones. Tomatillos, which resemble small, hard green tomatoes and are covered with papery husks, are sold fresh and canned. Dark green poblano chiles are sometimes called fresh ancho chiles, but don't confuse them with dried anchos.

Prep: 30 minutes   Bake: 2 hours 30 minutes

- 1   bunch cilantro
- 3   garlic cloves, finely chopped
- 1½   teaspoons salt
- 2   pounds boneless pork shoulder, trimmed and cut into ³⁄₄-inch pieces
- 2   medium onions, chopped
- 3   serrano or jalapeño chiles, seeded and finely chopped
- 1   teaspoon ground cumin
- ¼   teaspoon ground red pepper (cayenne)
- 2   pounds tomatillos, husked, rinsed, and cut into quarters
- 4   poblano chiles or 2 green peppers, roasted (page 419), seeded, and cut into 1-inch pieces
- 1   can (15¼ to 16 ounces) whole-kernel corn, drained
      sour cream (optional)
      warm flour tortillas (optional)

1. Preheat oven to 325°F. Chop enough cilantro leaves and stems to equal ¼ cup; chop and reserve another ¼ cup cilantro leaves for garnish. With side of chef's knife, mash garlic and salt to paste; transfer to 5-quart Dutch oven. Add pork, onions, serranos, cilantro leaves and stems, cumin, and ground red pepper; toss to combine. Cover and bake 1 hour.

2. Stir in tomatillos and roasted poblanos. Cover and bake until pork is very tender, 1 hour 30 minutes to 2 hours longer.

3. Skim and discard fat. Stir in corn and heat through. Sprinkle with reserved cilantro and serve with sour cream and tortillas, if you like. Makes 6 main-dish servings.

Each serving: About 378 calories, 34g protein, 27g carbohydrate, 16g total fat (5g saturated), 103mg cholesterol, 802mg sodium.

CINCINNATI CHILI

This dish is served many ways all over Cincinnati. A "three-way" is over spaghetti with shredded Cheddar on top. Add chopped onion, and it becomes a "four-way." For a "five-way," add cooked red kidney beans.

Prep: 25 minutes   Cook: 3 hours

- 2   teaspoons vegetable oil
- 2   medium onions, chopped
- 2   teaspoons finely chopped garlic
- 2   pounds ground beef chuck
- 2   tablespoons chili powder
- 1   tablespoon ground cumin
- 1   teaspoon ground cinnamon
- 1   teaspoon salt
- ½   teaspoon dried oregano
- ½   teaspoon ground red pepper (cayenne)
- 2   cans (16 ounces each) tomatoes
- 1   can (14½ ounces) beef broth or 1³⁄₄ cups Brown Beef Stock (page 71)
- 1½   cups water
- ½   square (½ ounce) unsweetened chocolate, chopped
- 1   package (16 ounces) spaghetti or linguine

1. In nonreactive 5-quart Dutch oven, heat oil over medium heat. Add onions and cook, stirring occasionally, until tender, about 5 minutes. Transfer to small bowl; set aside. Add garlic to Dutch oven; cook 1 minute longer. Transfer to bowl with onions.

2. In same Dutch oven, cook ground beef over high heat, breaking up meat with side of spoon, until meat is browned. Discard fat. Stir in chili powder, cumin, cinnamon, salt, oregano, and ground red pepper; cook 1 minute longer.

3. Add tomatoes with their juice to Dutch oven, breaking them up with side of spoon. Stir in broth, water, chocolate, browned beef, and onion-garlic mixture; heat to boiling. Reduce heat; cover and simmer 2 hours 30 minutes. Remove cover and simmer until thickened, about 30 minutes longer.

4. Meanwhile, cook pasta as label directs. Drain. Serve chili over pasta. Makes 8 main-dish servings.

Each serving without spaghetti: About 270 calories, 26g protein, 12g carbohydrate, 14g total fat (5g saturated), 71mg cholesterol, 756mg sodium.

TWO-ALARM CHILI

....

If you like really hot chili, increase the pickled jalapeño and ground red pepper to your taste. Here cocoa is the secret ingredient that balances the seasonings.

Prep: 20 minutes   **Cook: 35 minutes**

- 1 tablespoon olive oil
- 1 medium onion, chopped
- 2 garlic cloves, finely chopped
- 2 green peppers, chopped
- 2 pounds ground beef chuck
- 3 pickled jalapeño chiles, seeded and finely chopped (2 tablespoons)
- 3 tablespoons chili powder
- 2 teaspoons unsweetened cocoa
- 1¼ teaspoons salt
- ¾ teaspoon ground coriander
- ½ teaspoon dried oregano
- ¼ teaspoon ground red pepper (cayenne)
- 1 can (14 to 16 ounces) tomatoes, chopped

1. In nonstick 12-inch skillet, heat oil over medium heat. Add onion and garlic and cook, stirring occasionally, until onion is tender, about 5 minutes. Add green peppers and cook, stirring, until tender-crisp, about 5 minutes longer.

2. Add ground beef and cook, breaking up meat with side of spoon, until meat is no longer pink. Stir in pickled jalapeños, chili powder, cocoa, salt, coriander, oregano, and ground red pepper; cook 1 minute. Add tomatoes with their juice and heat to boiling. Reduce heat and simmer, stirring occasionally, until slightly thickened, 15 to 20 minutes longer. Makes 6 main-dish servings.

Each serving: About 326 calories, 33g protein, 10g carbohydrate, 18g total fat (6g saturated), 94mg cholesterol, 758mg sodium.

HUNGARIAN PORK GOULASH

....

Old-world recipes for goulash often include sauerkraut. Look for plastic bags of fresh sauerkraut in the refrigerated section of the supermarket. Do not use the canned variety; it's too sour. Serve with egg noodles to sop up all the delectable sauce.

Prep: 20 minutes   **Bake: 1 hour 30 minutes**

- 2 tablespoons vegetable oil
- 2 large onions (12 ounces each), chopped
- 1 garlic clove, finely chopped
- ¼ cup paprika, preferably sweet Hungarian
- 2 pounds boneless pork shoulder blade roast (fresh pork butt), trimmed and cut into 1½-inch pieces
- 1 bag (16 ounces) sauerkraut, rinsed and drained
- 1 can (14½ ounces) diced tomatoes
- 1 can (14½ ounces) beef broth or 1¾ cups Brown Beef Stock (page 71)
- ½ teaspoon salt
- ¼ teaspoon ground black pepper
- 1 container (8 ounces) sour cream

1. Preheat oven to 325°F. In nonreactive 5-quart Dutch oven, heat oil over medium heat. Add onions and cook, stirring frequently, 10 minutes. Stir in garlic; cook until onions are very tender, about 5 minutes longer.

2. Add paprika to onions, stirring well; cook 1 minute. Add pork, sauerkraut, tomatoes with their juice, broth, salt, and pepper; heat to boiling over high heat. Cover and bake until pork is tender, about 1 hour 30 minutes.

3. Remove stew from oven. Stir in sour cream. Heat through over medium heat (do not boil). Makes 6 main-dish servings.

Each serving: About 450 calories, 33g protein, 17g carbohydrate, 28g total fat (11g saturated), 120mg cholesterol, 1,135mg sodium.

LOW 'N' SLOW PULLED PORK

Pork shoulder blade roast is known as a cheap cut of meat. But when slow-cooked for hours in a sweet and tangy sauce, it becomes meltingly tender.

Prep: 20 minutes   Slow cook: 8 hours on low

- 1   medium onion, chopped
- ½   cup ketchup
- ⅓   cup cider vinegar
- ¼   cup packed brown sugar
- ¼   cup tomato paste
- 2   tablespoons sweet paprika
- 2   tablespoons Worcestershire sauce
- 2   tablespoons yellow mustard
- 1½ teaspoons salt
- 1¼ teaspoons ground black pepper
- 4   pounds boneless pork shoulder blade roast (fresh pork butt), cut into 4 pieces
- 12 soft sandwich buns or ciabatta rolls, warmed
      dill pickles (optional)
      potato chips (optional)
      hot sauce (optional)

1. In 4½- to 6-quart slow-cooker pot, stir onion, ketchup, vinegar, brown sugar, tomato paste, paprika, Worcestershire, mustard, salt, and pepper until combined. Add pork to sauce mixture and turn to coat well with sauce.

2. Cover slow cooker with lid and cook pork mixture on low setting as manufacturer directs, 8 to 10 hours or until pork is very tender.

3. With tongs, transfer pork to large bowl. Turn setting on slow cooker to high; cover and heat sauce to boiling to thicken and reduce slightly.

4. While sauce boils, with 2 forks, pull pork into shreds. Return shredded pork to slow cooker and toss with sauce to combine. Cover slow cooker and heat through on high setting if necessary.

5. Spoon pork mixture onto bottom of sandwich buns; replace tops of buns. Serve with pickles, potato chips, and hot sauce if you like. Makes 12 sandwiches.

Each serving: About 475 calories, 31g protein, 29g carbohydrate, 26g total fat (9g saturated), 2g fiber, 107mg cholesterol, 760mg sodium.

Low 'n' Slow Pulled Pork

TOMATILLO PORK

Tomatillos, also called Mexican green tomatoes, are the main ingredient in salsa verde. They bring a bright hint of lemon to this set-and-forget dish.

Prep: 10 minutes
Slow cook: 8 hours on low or 5 hours on high

- 1   large bunch cilantro
- 3   garlic cloves, sliced
- 2   pounds small red potatoes (about 8), cut into quarters
- 1   bone-in pork-shoulder roast (about 3 pounds), well trimmed
- 1   jar (16 to 18 ounces) salsa verde (green salsa)

1. From bunch of cilantro, remove and set aside 15 large sprigs. Remove enough leaves from remaining cilantro to equal ½ cup, loosely packed. Refrigerate leaves to sprinkle over pork after cooking.

2. In 4½- to 6-quart slow-cooker pot, combine cilantro sprigs, garlic, and potatoes. Place pork on top of potato mixture. Pour salsa over and around pork. Cover slow cooker with lid and cook as manufacturer directs on low setting 8 to 10 hours (or on high setting 5 to 5½ hours).

3. Transfer pork to cutting board and slice. Transfer pork and potatoes to warm deep platter. Skim and discard fat and cilantro from cooking liquid. Spoon cooking liquid over pork and potatoes. Sprinkle reserved cilantro leaves over pork. Makes 8 main-dish servings.

Each serving: About 300 calories, 25g protein, 27g carbohydrate, 9g total fat (3g saturated), 2g fiber, 79mg cholesterol, 295mg sodium.

LATIN-STYLE BEEF (ROPA VIEJA)

··

Our richly spiced slow-cooker version of the classic Latin-American stew.

Prep: 20 minutes
Slow cook: about 9 hours on low or 6 hours on high

- 1 can (14½ ounces) diced tomatoes
- 1 tablespoon capers, drained
- 1 tablespoon ground cumin
- ½ teaspoon ground cinnamon
- 1 teaspoon salt
- 3 garlic cloves, sliced
- 2 large red, yellow, and/or green peppers, sliced
- 2 large pickled jalapeño chiles, sliced
- 1 medium onion, cut in half and sliced
- 1 fresh beef brisket (about 3 pounds)
  warm tortillas and/or cooked white rice
  with parsley (optional)

1. In 4½- to 6-quart slow-cooker pot, combine tomatoes with their juice, capers, cumin, cinnamon, and salt. Add garlic, peppers, jalapeños, onion, and brisket; stir to coat brisket and vegetables with tomato mixture. Cover slow cooker with lid and cook as manufacturer directs on low setting 9 to 10 hours (or on high setting 6 to 6½ hours).

2. With slotted spoon, transfer brisket and vegetables to large bowl. With 2 forks, shred brisket along the grain into fine strips. Skim and discard fat from cooking liquid. Stir cooking liquid into brisket mixture. Serve brisket mixture with tortillas and/or rice if you like. Makes 8 main-dish servings.

Each serving: About 400 calories, 35g protein, 7g carbohydrate, 25g total fat (9g saturated), 2g fiber, 109mg cholesterol, 690mg sodium.

10 HELPFUL TIPS FOR THE SLOW COOKER

• Less tender cuts of meat and poultry—such as pork and lamb shoulder, chuck roast, beef brisket, and poultry legs—are best suited for slow cooking. Skim and discard fat from cooking liquid when done.

• Fish and other seafood are not a good fit unless they are added in the last hour of cooking.

• Avoid using ground meat; long, slow cooking, compromises its texture, giving it a mealy, sandy quality.

• Slow cooking tends to intensify flavorful spices and seasonings such as chili powder and garlic, so use them conservatively. Dried herbs may lose flavor, so adjust seasonings at the end of cooking. If you're using fresh herbs, save some to toss in at the last minute for best flavor.

• For richer flavor in stews, sprinkle meat and poultry with flour and brown in skillet before slow cooking. Scrape up browned bits in skillet and add to the pot to help thicken sauce and enhance flavor.

• To make cleanup easier, use slow-cooker pot liners.

• For even cooking, fill slow-cooker pot at least halfway—but never to the brim. For soups and stews, leave about 2 inches of space between food and lid.

• Resist stirring the pot because meat and vegetables may break up.

• If your recipe produces more liquid than you want, remove solids with a slotted spoon to a serving dish and keep warm. Turn slow-cooker temperature to high; cook remaining liquid, uncovered, to reduce to desired thickness.

• Most recipes can be prepped the night before—all you have to do in the morning is toss in ingredients and flip the switch on the slow cooker! Premeasure ingredients, precut vegetables, trim meats, and mix liquids and seasonings. Refrigerate components separately in bowls or zip-tight plastic bags.

🍲 SHORT RIBS WITH ROOT VEGETABLES

....

When cooked slowly in a flavorful liquid, short ribs become meltingly tender and the meat will literally fall off the bones. Look for meaty ribs about 2 to 4 inches long; ribs cut similar in size will cook more evenly.

Prep: 35 minutes
Slow cook: 8 hours on low or 5 hours on high

- 3 pounds bone-in beef chuck short ribs
- 1 teaspoon salt
- ½ teaspoon ground black pepper
- 2 large parsnips (about 4 ounces each), peeled and cut into 1-inch chunks
- 1 medium turnip (about 8 ounces), peeled and cut into 1-inch chunks
- 1 bag (16 ounces) peeled baby carrots
- 1 jumbo onion (about 1 pound), coarsely chopped
- 4 large garlic cloves, thinly sliced
- 1 teaspoon dried thyme
- 2 cups dry red wine
- ¼ cup tomato paste

1. Heat 12-inch skillet over medium-high heat until hot. Add ribs to skillet and sprinkle with ½ teaspoon salt and ¼ teaspoon pepper. Cook ribs about 10 minutes or until well browned on all sides, turning occasionally.

2. Meanwhile, in 5- to 6-quart slow-cooker pot, place parsnips, turnip, and carrots.

3. Transfer ribs to slow cooker on top of vegetables. Discard drippings in skillet. Reduce heat to medium; add onion to skillet and cook about 8 minutes or until browned, stirring frequently. Stir in garlic and thyme and cook 1 minute, stirring constantly. Add wine and heat to boiling over high heat, stirring to loosen browned bits from bottom of skillet. Remove skillet from heat and stir in tomato paste, ½ teaspoon salt, and ¼ teaspoon pepper.

4. Pour wine mixture over ribs in slow cooker. Cover slow cooker with lid and cook as manufacturer directs on low setting, 8 to 10 hours (or on high setting 4 to 5 hours) or until meat is fork-tender and falling off the bones.

5. With tongs, transfer ribs to deep platter; discard bones if you like. With spoon, skim and discard fat from sauce in slow cooker. Spoon vegetables and sauce over ribs. Makes 6 main-dish servings.

Each serving: About 655 calories, 27g protein, 24g carbohydrate, 50g total fat (21g saturated), 5g fiber, 114mg cholesterol, 535mg sodium.

🍲 SWEET AND TANGY BRAISED CHUCK ROAST

....

Gingersnap cookies and raisins balance vinegar to give a sweet-and-sour flavor to the classic chuck roast. Slow cooking makes this tough cut tender and yields a rich, delicious sauce.

Prep: 10 minutes
Slow cook: about 8 hours on low or 6 hours on high

- 6 (2-inch) gingersnap cookies, finely crushed into crumbs
- 2 cups (about half 16-ounce bag) peeled baby carrots
- 2 large stalks celery, cut crosswise into 2-inch pieces
- 1 medium onion, cut into 1-inch pieces
- 1 cup dry red wine
- 2 tablespoons red wine vinegar
- ¼ cup raisins
- 1 teaspoon salt
- ½ teaspoon ground black pepper
- 1 boneless beef chuck roast (about 2 pounds)

1. In 4½- to 6-quart slow-cooker pot, combine gingersnap crumbs, carrots, celery, onion, wine, vinegar, raisins, salt, and pepper. Place chuck roast on top of vegetables. Cover slow cooker with lid and cook as manufacturer directs on low setting 8 to 10 hours (or on high setting 6 to 6½ hours) or until roast is very tender.

2. Place roast on warm platter. Skim and discard fat from cooking liquid. Serve roast with vegetables and sauce. Makes 6 main-dish servings.

Each serving: About 360 calories, 25g protein, 17g carbohydrate, 21g total fat (8g saturated), 2g fiber, 83mg cholesterol, 540mg sodium.

🍲 AFRICAN SWEET POTATO AND PEANUT STEW

··

A hearty meatless stew that's packed with protein and filled with flavor.

Prep: 25 minutes
Slow cook: about 8 hours on low or 4 hours on high

- 3 garlic cloves, peeled
- 2 cups loosely packed fresh cilantro leaves and stems
- 1 can (28 ounces) diced tomatoes
- ½ cup creamy or chunky peanut butter
- 2 teaspoons ground cumin
- ½ teaspoon ground cinnamon
- ¼ teaspoon ground red pepper (cayenne)
- ¾ teaspoon salt
- 1 cup water
- 3 pounds sweet potatoes (4 medium), peeled and cut into 2-inch chunks
- 1 can (15 to 19 ounces) garbanzo beans, rinsed and drained
- 1 package (16 ounces) frozen whole or cut green beans

1. In blender or food processor with knife blade attached, blend garlic, cilantro, tomatoes with their juice, peanut butter, cumin, cinnamon, ground red pepper, and salt until pureed.

2. Into 4½- to 6-quart slow-cooker pot, pour peanut-butter mixture; stir in water. Add sweet potatoes and garbanzo beans; stir to combine. Cover slow cooker with lid and cook as manufacturer directs on low setting 8 to 10 hours (or on high setting 4 to 5 hours) or until potatoes are very tender.

3. About 10 minutes before sweet-potato mixture is done, cook green beans as label directs. Gently stir green beans into stew. Makes about 11 cups or 6 main-dish servings.

Each serving: About 495 calories, 16g protein, 83g carbohydrate, 13g total fat (3g saturated), 12g fiber, 0mg cholesterol, 1,105mg sodium.

🍲 RED-COOKED TURKEY THIGHS WITH LEEKS

··

Braising the flavorful thigh meat in soy sauce results in the deep, reddish-brown color that gives this classic Asian cooking method its name.

Prep: 20 minutes
Slow cook: about 8 hours on low or 4 hours on high

- 4 large leeks (about 2 pounds)
- ½ cup dry sherry
- ⅓ cup soy sauce
- ¼ cup packed brown sugar
- 2 tablespoons minced, peeled fresh ginger
- 1 teaspoon Chinese five-spice powder
- 3 small turkey thighs (about 1 pound each), skin removed
- 3 garlic cloves, crushed with press
- 2 cups (about half 16-ounce bag) peeled baby carrots

1. Cut off roots and dark-green tops from leeks. Discard tough outer leaves. Cut each leek lengthwise in half then crosswise in half. Rinse leeks in large bowl of cold water, swishing to remove sand. Transfer leeks to colander. Repeat several times, until no sand remains. Drain well.

2. In 4½- to 6-quart slow-cooker pot, combine sherry, soy sauce, sugar, ginger, and five-spice powder. Add leeks, turkey, garlic, and carrots, and toss to coat with soy mixture. Cover slow cooker with lid and cook as manufacturer directs on low setting 8 to 10 hours (or on high setting 4 to 5 hours).

3. Transfer turkey and vegetables to deep platter, removing and discarding turkey bones. Skim and discard fat from cooking liquid. Spoon cooking liquid over turkey and vegetables. Makes 6 main-dish servings.

Each serving: About 355 calories, 41g protein, 24g carbohydrate, 10g total fat (3g saturated), 2g fiber, 112mg cholesterol, 1,005mg sodium.

LATIN CHICKEN WITH BLACK BEANS AND SWEET POTATOES

While lean breast meat would become tough over the long cooking time, thighs will be juicy and delicious.

Prep: 15 minutes
Slow cook: 8 hours on low or 4 hours on high

- 3 pounds bone-in skinless chicken thighs
- 2 teaspoons ground cumin
- ¼ teaspoon salt
- ¼ teaspoon ground black pepper
- 1 teaspoon smoked paprika or ½ teaspoon chopped chipotle chiles in adobo sauce
- ½ teaspoon ground allspice
- 1 cup chicken broth
- ½ cup salsa
- 3 large cloves garlic, crushed with press
- 2 cans (15 to 19 ounces each) black beans, rinsed and drained
- 2 pounds sweet potatoes, peeled and cut into 2-inch chunks
- 1 roasted red pepper from a jar, cut into strips (1 cup)
- ⅓ cup loosely packed fresh cilantro leaves, chopped lime wedges

1. Sprinkle chicken thighs with ½ teaspoon cumin, salt, and pepper. Heat 12-inch nonstick skillet over medium-high heat until hot; add chicken thighs and cook until well browned on all sides, about 10 minutes. Transfer chicken to plate. Remove skillet from heat.

2. In same skillet, combine smoked paprika, allspice, chicken broth, salsa, garlic, and remaining 1½ teaspoons cumin.

3. In 6-quart slow cooker, combine beans and sweet potatoes. Place chicken on top of potato mixture in slow cooker; pour broth mixture over chicken. Cover slow cooker with lid and cook as manufacturer directs on low setting 8 hours (or on high 4 hours).

4. With tongs or slotted spoon, remove chicken pieces to large platter. Gently stir roasted red pepper strips into potato mixture. Spoon mixture over chicken. Sprinkle with cilantro and serve with lime wedges. Makes 6 main-dish servings.

Each serving: About 415 calories, 36g protein, 61g carbohydrate, 6g total fat (1g saturated), 12g fiber, 107mg cholesterol, 875mg sodium.

CHICKEN TAGINE

A tagine is a Moroccan stew of meat or poultry served over couscous. The traditional tagine pot is made of clay, with a flat bowl for a base and a cone-shaped top. A slow-cooker, while less dramatic, is a fine substitute.

Prep: 20 minutes
Slow cook: 8 hours on low or 4 hours on high

- 1 medium butternut squash (1½ pounds), peeled and cut into 2-inch chunks (see Tip)
- 2 medium tomatoes, coarsely chopped
- 1 medium onion, chopped
- 2 cloves garlic, crushed with press
- 1 can (15 to 19 ounces) garbanzo beans, rinsed and drained
- 1 cup chicken broth
- ⅓ cup raisins
- 2 teaspoons ground coriander
- 2 teaspoons ground cumin
- ½ teaspoon ground cinnamon
- ½ teaspoon salt
- ¼ teaspoon ground black pepper
- 3 pounds bone-in skinless chicken thighs
- 1 box (10 ounces) plain couscous
- ½ cup pitted green olives

1. In 6-quart slow cooker, combine squash, tomatoes, onion, garlic, beans, broth, and raisins. In cup, combine coriander, cumin, cinnamon, salt, and pepper. Rub spice mixture all over chicken thighs; place chicken on top of vegetable mixture. Cover slow cooker with lid and cook as manufacturer directs on low setting 8 hours (or on high 4 hours).

2. About 10 minutes before serving, prepare couscous as label directs.

3. To serve, fluff couscous with fork. Stir olives into chicken mixture. Serve chicken mixture over couscous. Makes 6 main-dish servings.

Each serving: About 545 calories, 39g protein, 80g carbohydrate, 9g total fat (2g saturated), 10g fiber, 107mg cholesterol, 855mg sodium.

Tip: To peel butternut squash, lay it on its side. Using a sharp knife, cut crosswise into 2-inch rounds. Place rounds flat-side down and cut away the peel. Scoop out seeds and cut as desired.

4
....
MEAT

Meat is the major source of protein in the American diet, so it is important to know how to choose it and cook it properly.

BUYING MEAT

All meat in the United States is inspected by the United States Department of Agriculture (USDA) to ensure that it is safe to eat and free of disease, although some diseases, such as *E. coli* and salmonella, cannot be detected by the naked eye.

Grading is a voluntary procedure, and the grade given to any particular piece of meat reflects its tenderness: The higher the grade, the more tender the meat. There are different criteria for grading beef, lamb, and veal. In general, meat is graded according to age (the older the animal, the tougher the flesh) and the amount of marbling (streaks or flecks of fat within the flesh). This internal fat melts into the meat during the cooking process, moistening and flavoring the meat; the external fat that surrounds chops and steaks can be trimmed away.

The meat available to consumers is graded prime, choice, and select or good. Beef has the largest number of grading levels because the degree of tenderness varies much more from cut to cut. Lamb is also graded but veal only occasionally. Pork is rarely graded because only the highest grade is sold to consumers. One good bit of advice: Always buy the highest grade of meat you can afford.

STORING MEAT

Always store raw meat in the coldest part of the refrigerator (usually the bottom shelf), away from cooked and ready-to-eat foods. Place the meat on a plate or tray to catch any drips. Refrigerate uncooked meat for up to two days or freeze for up to six months. Ground meat can be refrigerated for one or two days or frozen for up to three months.

For short-term storage (up to two days in the refrigerator or up to two weeks in the freezer), leave raw meat in its original store wrapping. For longer freezing, or if the wrapping is torn, carefully rewrap the meat in freezer wrap or heavy-duty foil, pressing out all the air. Stack steaks, chops, and patties between sheets of freezer paper before wrapping. Label each package with the name of the cut, the number of servings, and the date.

Thaw frozen meat, on a plate to catch any drips, overnight in the refrigerator, not at room temperature. Do not refreeze uncooked meat or the texture will suffer. And for best results, do not freeze meat, raw or cooked, for longer than three months. Large roasts, however, can be frozen for up to one year.

COOKING TECHNIQUES

The USDA recommends that all meat be cooked until well-done (160°F) to kill any bacteria that could cause illness. We sometimes recommend cooking temperatures that are below this figure, because some meat tastes best cooked medium-rare or medium. Food-borne illnesses are relatively rare and usually affect only infants, the elderly, or people with weak immune systems. The degree to which you cook meat is a matter of personal taste, but also keep in mind for whom you are cooking.

Roasting

There is only one way to guarantee that meat is roasted to the desired doneness: Use a meat thermometer. Always insert a thermometer into the center or thickest part of the roast without touching any bone or fatty sections. Boneless roasts are tied to help them keep their shape during roasting. In our recipes, we sometimes place boneless roasts on a rack in the roasting pan so the heat can circulate under the meat, preventing the meat from cooking in its juices. Not all boneless roasts need to be cooked on racks, however. Tenderloin and some loin roasts cook so quickly that they don't have time to create juices. Rib roasts and other bone-in cuts come with their own natural built-in racks. Always remove a roast from the oven when it reaches 5° to 10°F less than the desired temperature, as the temperature will continue to rise as the meat stands. It is not necessary to cover the meat; the density of the hot roast will keep it from cooling too quickly. A foil tent would only trap the steam and soften the roast's delicious crusty exterior.

Panfrying and Sautéing

These fastest of cooking methods yield quick, tasty results. Before sautéing, pat the meat dry with paper towels so it can easily brown. Be sure to use a heavy-bottomed skillet so the heat is conducted evenly. We don't advise using a nonstick skillet; its slick surface inhibits the formation of a good crust. And don't crowd the meat in the pan or it will steam instead of brown. Cook over medium-high to high heat to sear the meat and give it rich flavor.

Braising and Stewing

Few dishes satisfy as much as a long-simmered stew or braised pot roast. The key is to be patient when slow simmering tough cuts of meat: It takes a long time for the collagen in the meat to melt and for the meat to become fork-tender. The key word here is "simmering." Tip: Do not let the liquid cook at more than a slow simmer or the meat will end up dry and tough.

Braising is usually done in a Dutch oven: a sturdy pot with a tight-fitting lid and a handle at each side that can go from the stovetop to the oven (and directly to the table if you like). Enameled cast-iron Dutch ovens are somewhat expensive but can last a lifetime. Old-fashioned, less expensive cast-iron Dutch ovens work equally well.

Broiling and Grilling

These dry-heat cooking methods are close cousins. In broiling, the heat source is on top of the food, while in grilling, the heat source is below. Whether broiled or grilled, the food gets caramelized from the intense heat, which greatly contributes to its flavor. To make up for the lack of delicious smoky flavor when broiling, we like to use a flavorful marinade or dry rub. See Grilling, page 344.

Always preheat a broiler on high for about ten minutes. Stoves with separate broiling units have adjustable broiler racks that enable them to be positioned as close to or as far away from the heating element as desired. Electric ovens that double as broilers are problematic. There is usually only one upper-rack position that is close to the heating element, but it is sometimes farther away than the ideal distance. This makes preheating especially important.

Carving Meat

Steaks and roasts benefit from a resting period before being served. This allows time for the internal juices to get redistributed throughout the meat, making the meat juicy and firming it for easier carving. Steaks

MEAT THERMOMETERS

TEST KITCHEN TIP

OLD-FASHIONED MEAT THERMOMETER: Inserted into the meat before cooking and is left in the meat while it is being roasted.

INSTANT-READ THERMOMETER: Inserted into the meat for an almost immediate reading, then removed.

PROBE THERMOMETER: The desired temperature is set on a display and a probe is inserted into the meat. When the desired temperature is reached, an alert sounds. Allows you to roast meat to an exact temperature without having to open the oven to check.

should be transferred to a warm platter to keep them from cooling off, but they only need to stand for a minute or two before being served. Average-size roasts (about three pounds) should stand for ten minutes, and larger roasts for up to fifteen minutes.

For safety's sake, it's a good idea to place a towel under the carving board to prevent it from moving. Always carve with a sharp, thin-bladed knife and use a two-tine meat fork to steady the roast. Carve across the grain, not parallel to the fibers of the meat; this produces shorter fibers, making the meat more tender.

MEAT SAFETY

When handling any raw meat, keep it separate from other ingredients until ready to combine. If the meat comes in contact with the work surface, the surface should be thoroughly washed, along with your hands, knives, and any other utensils in hot, soapy water.

Do not allow raw meat to stand at room temperature longer than one hour. Some cookbooks suggest letting meat stand out until it reaches room temperature so the meat will roast more evenly. We don't agree. We use refrigerator-temperature meat for all of our recipes. If you are serving cooked meat as part of a buffet, do not let it stand at room temperature longer than two hours.

BEEF

Beef is still America's favorite meat. Whether you're enjoying a grilled steak, a juicy burger, or a savory stew, beef's deep, hearty flavor is sure to come through.

Buying Beef
Choose meat that is bright to deep red; any fat should be creamy white. As with all meat, color is a good indicator of quality. Cut edges should look freshly cut and moist—never wet. Vacuum-packed beef is darker and often looks more purple than red. Last, remember that the names of steaks and roasts often vary from state to state: A "strip steak" in California is known as a "shell steak" in New York.

ROASTING TIMES FOR BEEF

This roasting chart gives guidelines for cooking a variety of cuts from medium-rare to well-done when cooking without a recipe. Start with meat at refrigerator temperature. Remove a roast from the oven when it reaches 5° to 10°F below desired doneness; temperature will continue to rise as it stands.

CUT	OVEN TEMPERATURE	WEIGHT	APPROXIMATE COOKING TIME (MINUTES PER POUND)		
			MEDIUM-RARE (135°–140°F)	MEDIUM (145°–155°F)	WELL-DONE (OVER 160°F)
Rib roast	325°F	4 to 6 pounds	24 to 30 minutes	30 to 36 minutes	34 to 38 minutes
(chine bone removed)		6 to 8 pounds	15 to 20 minutes	22 to 26 minutes	27 to 30 minutes
Rib-eye roast	350°F	4 to 6 pounds	15 to 20 minutes	18 to 22 minutes	20 to 24 minutes
Whole tenderloin	450°F	4 to 5 pounds	40 to 60 minutes (total time)		
Half tenderloin	450°F	2 to 3 pounds	35 to 50 minutes (total time)		
Round tip roast	325°F	3 to 4 pounds	25 to 30 minutes	30 to 35 minutes	35 to 38 minutes
		6 to 8 pounds	22 to 25 minutes	26 to 32 minutes	30 to 35 minutes
Eye round roast	325°F	2 to 3 pounds	20 to 25 minutes	25 to 30 minutes	30 to 35 minutes

POPULAR BEEF CUTS

Beef rib roast, small end

Also called standing rib roast *(roast)*.

Beef rib-eye roast

Large center muscle of rib with bones and seam fat removed *(roast)*.

Beef bottom round roast

Also called beef bottom round pot roast; suitable for roasting if high quality *(braise, roast)*.

Beef chuck shoulder pot roast, boneless

Also called boneless cross-rib pot roast *(braise)*.

Beef chuck short ribs

Also called flanken short ribs *(braise)*.

Beef top loin steak

Also called shell, strip, New York, club, and Delmonico steak. Also available boneless *(broil, grill, panfry)*.

Beef loin porterhouse steak

Includes tenderloin at least 1¼ inches in diameter *(broil, grill, panfry)*.

Beef rib-eye steak

Boneless steak also called fillet or Spencer steak; cut from beef rib-eye roast. Also available bone-in *(broil, panfry)*.

Beef round top round steak

Also known as London broil. Best when marinated *(broil, grill)*.

Beef loin tenderloin roast

Cut from tenderloin muscle; very tender, boneless, with very little (or no) fat covering. Also called beef tenderloin *(roast)*.

BEEF RIB ROAST WITH CREAMY HORSERADISH SAUCE

....

If you like, reserve the fat from the pan drippings to make Yorkshire Pudding (right), then prepare an au jus sauce. Add 2 cups of homemade Brown Beef Stock (page 71) to the pan drippings and bring to a boil, scraping up all the flavorful browned bits.

Prep: 25 minutes   Roast: 3 hours

1   (4-rib) beef rib roast from small end (7 pounds), trimmed and chine bone removed

3   tablespoons whole tricolor peppercorns (red, green, and black)

1   teaspoon salt
    Creamy Horseradish Sauce (below)

1. Preheat oven to 325°F. In medium roasting pan (14" by 10"), place rib roast, fat side up. In mortar, with pestle, crush peppercorns with salt. Use to rub on fat side of roast.

2. Roast beef until meat thermometer inserted in thickest part of meat (not touching bone) reaches 140°F, about 3 hours. Internal temperature of meat will rise to 145°F (medium) upon standing. Or roast until desired doneness.

3. When roast is done, transfer to warm large platter and let stand 15 minutes to set juices for easier carving. Meanwhile, prepare Creamy Horseradish Sauce. Makes 10 main-dish servings.

Each serving without sauce: About 317 calories, 39g protein, 1g carbohydrate, 16g total fat (7g saturated), 113mg cholesterol, 322mg sodium.

CREAMY HORSERADISH SAUCE

In small bowl, combine **1 jar (6 ounces) white horseradish,** drained, **½ cup mayonnaise, 1 teaspoon sugar,** and **½ teaspoon salt.** Whip **½ cup heavy or whipping cream;** fold into horseradish mixture. Makes about 1⅔ cups.

Each tablespoon: About 49 calories, 0g protein, 1g carbohydrate, 5g total fat (2g saturated), 9mg cholesterol, 74mg sodium.

YORKSHIRE PUDDING

Preheat oven to 450°F. In medium bowl, with wire whisk, combine **1½ cups all-purpose flour** and **¾ teaspoon salt.** Add **1½ cups milk** and **3 large eggs,** beaten. Beat until smooth. Pour **3 tablespoons drippings** from roast beef pan into small metal baking pan (13" by 9"); bake 2 minutes. Remove pan from oven and pour batter over drippings. Bake until puffed and lightly browned, about 25 minutes. Cut into squares. Makes 8 accompaniment servings.

Each serving: About 183 calories, 6g protein, 20g carbohydrate, 8g total fat (4g saturated), 90mg cholesterol, 246mg sodium.

CARVING A RIB ROAST

The chine bone should be removed by your butcher so you can carve the roast between the rib bones. Carving will be easier and the meat will be juicier if the roast stands at least 15 minutes after you have removed it from the oven.

Place the roast, rib side down, on cutting board. With a carving knife, make a vertical cut toward the ribs, cutting a slice about ¼ inch thick.

Release the slice by cutting horizontally along the top of the rib bone. Transfer the slice to a warm platter.

Repeat to cut more slices. As each rib bone is exposed, cut it away from the roast and add to the platter. This will make it easier to carve the remaining meat.

BEEF EYE ROUND AU JUS

Roast some herbed new potatoes at the same time. And for the tenderest results, do not roast this cut to more than medium rare.

Prep: 30 minutes   **Roast:** 1 hour 10 minutes

- 1 beef eye round roast (4½ pounds), trimmed
- 1½ teaspoons salt
- ½ teaspoon dried thyme
- ¼ teaspoon ground black pepper
- 2 tablespoons olive oil
- 1 bag (16 ounces) carrots, peeled and cut into 2" by ¼" matchstick strips
- 1 pound leeks (3 medium), white and light green parts, cut into 2" by ¼" matchstick strips
- 4 garlic cloves, thinly sliced
- 1¼ cups dry red wine
- ½ cup water
- 1 bay leaf

1. Preheat oven to 450°F. In small bowl, combine salt, thyme, and pepper; use to rub on roast. In 10-inch skillet, heat oil over medium-high heat until very hot. Add beef and cook until browned on all sides, about 10 minutes. Transfer beef to nonreactive medium roasting pan (14" by 10").

2. Add carrots, leeks, and garlic to skillet and cook, stirring occasionally, until carrots are tender, about 7 minutes. Arrange vegetable mixture around beef.

3. Roast beef 25 minutes. Add wine, water, and bay leaf to roasting pan. Turn oven control to 325°F and roast until meat thermometer inserted in center of roast reaches 140°F, about 45 minutes longer. Internal temperature of meat will rise to 145°F (medium) upon standing. Or roast until desired doneness. Remove and discard bay leaf.

4. When roast is done, transfer to warm large platter and let stand 15 minutes to set juices for easier slicing. To serve, cut roast into thin slices and serve with vegetables. Makes 12 main-dish servings.

Each serving: About 232 calories, 33g protein, 6g carbohydrate, 8g total fat (2g saturated), 76mg cholesterol, 358mg sodium.

STUFFED BEEF TENDERLOIN WITH MUSHROOM GRAVY

This is a real showstopper that's great for entertaining. We gild the lily by dressing up this already exquisite roast with a melt-in-your-mouth stuffing.

Prep: 45 minutes   **Roast/Cook:** 1 hour

Spinach-Mushroom Stuffing (opposite)
- 2 teaspoons chopped fresh thyme
- 1 teaspoon salt
- 1 teaspoon coarsely ground black pepper
- 1 whole beef tenderloin, trimmed (4 pounds)
- 2 tablespoons butter or margarine
- ¼ cup plain dried bread crumbs
- 1 can (14½ ounces) chicken broth or 1¾ cups Chicken Broth (page 70)
- 2 tablespoons dry vermouth
- 8 ounces mushrooms, trimmed and sliced
- 2 tablespoons all-purpose flour

1. Prepare Spinach-Mushroom Stuffing; set aside.

2. Preheat oven to 425°F. In small bowl, combine thyme, salt, and pepper; use to rub on tenderloin. Turn thinner end of meat under tenderloin to make meat an even thickness. With sharp knife, cut 1½-inch-deep slit in tenderloin, beginning 2 inches from thicker end of meat and ending 2 inches from opposite end.

3. Spoon Spinach-Mushroom Stuffing into slit in tenderloin. With string, tie tenderloin at 2-inch intervals to help hold its shape. Place stuffed tenderloin on rack in large roasting pan (17" by 11½"); roast tenderloin 30 minutes.

4. Meanwhile, in 1-quart saucepan, melt 1 tablespoon butter over low heat. Remove saucepan from heat; stir in bread crumbs.

5. Remove tenderloin from oven; sprinkle breadcrumb topping over stuffing. Roast tenderloin until meat thermometer inserted in center of meat reaches 140°F, about 10 minutes longer. Internal temperature of meat will rise to 145°F (medium) upon standing. Or roast until desired doneness. Transfer tenderloin to warm platter and let stand 10 minutes to set juices for easier slicing.

6. Meanwhile, prepare mushroom gravy: Add ½ cup broth and vermouth to drippings in roasting pan; stir over low heat until browned bits are loosened from bottom of pan. Pour drippings mixture into 4-cup measuring cup; let stand until fat separates from meat juice. Skim and discard fat from meat-juice mixture. Add remaining broth and enough water to equal 2½ cups; set aside.

7. In 12-inch skillet, melt remaining 1 tablespoon butter over medium-high heat. Add mushrooms and cook until golden and liquid has evaporated, about 12 minutes. Stir in flour. Gradually stir meat-juice mixture into mushrooms and cook, stirring constantly, until gravy has thickened slightly and boils; boil 1 minute.

8. To serve, remove string and cut tenderloin into slices. Serve with mushroom gravy. Makes 10 main-dish servings.

Each serving with gravy: About 371 calories, 35g protein, 8g carbohydrate, 21g total fat (10g saturated), 114mg cholesterol, 679mg sodium.

SPINACH-MUSHROOM STUFFING

In 12-inch skillet, melt **4 tablespoons butter or margarine** over medium-high heat; add 1 pound mushrooms, coarsely chopped, and cook until golden and liquid has evaporated, 12 to 15 minutes. Stir in **2 tablespoons dry vermouth;** cook 1 minute longer. Remove skillet from heat; stir in **1 package (10 ounces) frozen chopped spinach,** thawed and squeezed dry, **2 tablespoons freshly grated Parmesan cheese, 2 tablespoons plain dried bread crumbs, 1 teaspoon chopped fresh thyme, ¼ teaspoon salt,** and **½ teaspoon coarsely ground black pepper.** Cool.

SAUCES FOR BEEF TENDERLOIN

 TEST KITCHEN TIP

Béarnaise Sauce (page 503) is perfect with Roasted Beef Tenderloin. Cilantro Sauce (page 504) is a good choice for the Asian-Flavored Tenderloin. For the Southwestern-Flavored variation, try either Cilantro Sauce or Tomato Salsa (page 507) or Orange-Fennel Salsa (page 507).

ROASTED BEEF TENDERLOIN

Beef tenderloin can be brushed with a mixture of spices and fresh herbs of your choice. Served hot or at room temperature, it's perfect party fare.

Prep: 5 minutes   Roast: 50 minutes

- 2 tablespoons butter or margarine, melted
- 2 teaspoons Worcestershire sauce
- 1 teaspoon salt
- 1 teaspoon coarsely ground black pepper
- 1 whole beef tenderloin (5 pounds), trimmed and tied

1. Preheat oven to 450°F. In small bowl, combine butter, Worcestershire, salt, and pepper. Brush mixture on tenderloin.

2. Place tenderloin in 15½" by 10½" jelly-roll pan and roast until meat thermometer inserted in center of meat reaches 140°F, about 50 minutes. Internal temperature of meat will rise to 145°F (medium) upon standing. Or roast until desired doneness.

3. Transfer tenderloin to warm platter and let stand 15 minutes to set juices for easier slicing. Makes 12 main-dish servings.

Each serving: About 251 calories, 29g protein, 0g carbohydrate, 14g total fat (6g saturated), 92mg cholesterol, 276mg sodium.

SOUTHWESTERN-FLAVORED TENDERLOIN

In small bowl, combine **1 tablespoon vegetable oil, 1 teaspoon honey, 1 tablespoon chili powder, 2 teaspoons ground cumin, 1 teaspoon salt,** and **¼ teaspoon dried oregano,** crumbled. Brush mixture on tenderloin instead of butter mixture; roast as directed.

ASIAN-FLAVORED TENDERLOIN

In small bowl, combine **2 teaspoons soy sauce, 2 teaspoons Asian sesame oil, 1 teaspoon honey, 1 teaspoon Chinese five-spice powder, ¼ teaspoon ground ginger,** and **⅛ teaspoon ground red pepper (cayenne).** Brush mixture on tenderloin instead of butter mixture; roast as directed.

ROPA VIEJA

....

In Spanish, ropa vieja means "old clothes." The stew is simmered a long time so the meat can be shredded into thin strips resembling tattered fabric.

Prep: 45 minutes   Cook: 3 hours 30 minutes

- 1 beef flank steak (1³/₄ pounds)
- 1 medium onion, coarsely chopped
- 1 carrot, peeled and coarsely chopped
- 1 bay leaf
- 2 teaspoons salt
- 5 cups water
- 4 teaspoons olive oil
- 1 large onion (12 ounces), sliced
- 1 red pepper, cut into ¹/₂-inch-wide strips
- 1 yellow pepper, cut into ¹/₂-inch-wide strips
- 1 green pepper, cut into ¹/₂-inch-wide strips
- 3 garlic cloves, crushed with garlic press
- 3 serrano or jalapeño chiles, seeded and finely chopped
- ¹/₄ teaspoon ground cinnamon
- 1 can (14 to 16 ounces) tomatoes
- capers

1. Cut flank steak crosswise into thirds. In nonreactive 5-quart Dutch oven, combine flank steak, chopped onion, carrot, bay leaf, 1 teaspoon salt, and water; heat to boiling over high heat. Reduce heat; cover and simmer until meat is very tender, 2 hours 30 minutes to 3 hours. Remove Dutch oven from heat. Remove cover and let flank steak stand 30 minutes.

2. In 12-inch skillet, heat oil over medium-high heat. Add sliced onion, red, yellow, and green peppers, and remaining 1 teaspoon salt; cook, stirring often, until vegetables are tender, about 15 minutes. Stir in garlic, serrano chiles, and cinnamon; cook 30 seconds. Stir in tomatoes with their juice, breaking them up with side of spoon, and cook 5 minutes.

3. With slotted spoon, transfer beef to large bowl; strain broth. Set aside 2 cups broth (reserve remaining broth for another use). Using two forks, shred beef into fine strips.

4. Stir 2 cups broth and shredded meat into pepper mixture and simmer, stirring occasionally, 10 minutes. Sprinkle with capers to serve. Makes 6 main-dish servings.

Each serving: About 246 calories, 25g protein, 10g carbohydrate, 12g total fat (4g saturated), 57mg cholesterol, 779mg sodium.

BRISKET WITH MUSHROOMS

....

Humble beef brisket becomes a company dish when combined with a heady combination of fresh and dried mushrooms and served with a rich red wine sauce. To prepare at Passover, use matzoh meal instead of flour.

Prep: 1 hour 30 minutes   Bake: 2 hours 30 minutes

- ³/₄ cup boiling water
- ¹/₂ ounce dried porcini mushrooms (¹/₂ cup)
- 8 ounces small shiitake mushrooms, stems removed
- 8 ounces white mushrooms, trimmed
- ¹/₄ cup vegetable oil
- 1 fresh beef brisket (4 pounds), well trimmed
- 4 medium red onions, sliced
- 2 garlic cloves, sliced
- 3 tablespoons all-purpose flour
- 1 can (14¹/₂ ounces) beef broth or 1³/₄ cups Brown Beef Stock (page 71)
- 1 cup dry red wine
- ¹/₄ cup brandy
- 4 large fresh sage leaves
- 1 bay leaf
- 1¹/₂ teaspoons fresh thyme
- ¹/₂ teaspoon salt
- ¹/₄ teaspoon coarsely ground black pepper
- ¹/₄ cup chopped fresh parsley

1. In small bowl, pour boiling water over porcini mushrooms; let stand 30 minutes.

2. With slotted spoon, remove porcini, reserving mushroom liquid. Rinse mushrooms to remove any grit, then chop. Strain liquid through sieve lined with paper towels; set aside.

3. Preheat oven to 325°F. In 8-quart Dutch oven, heat oil over medium-high heat until very hot. Add brisket and cook until browned, about 10 minutes. Transfer brisket to platter; set aside. Add onions to Dutch oven and cook over medium heat, stirring occasionally, until lightly browned, about 15 minutes. Stir in garlic and cook 30 seconds. Stir in flour and cook, stirring until golden brown, about 2 minutes.

4. Return brisket to Dutch oven. Stir in porcini mushrooms, mushroom liquid, shiitake and white mushrooms, broth, wine, brandy, sage leaves, bay leaf, thyme, salt, pepper, and 2 tablespoons parsley. Heat to boiling over high heat. Cover and place in oven. Bake until brisket is tender, about 2 hours 30 minutes.

5. Transfer meat from Dutch oven to warm platter; let stand 15 minutes. Skim and discard fat from liquid in Dutch oven. Discard sage leaves and bay leaf. Heat liquid in pot to boiling over high heat. Reduce heat to medium; cook, uncovered, until thickened, about 15 minutes.

6. Slice brisket thinly across the grain. Stir remaining 2 tablespoons parsley into brisket liquid. Spoon some over meat; pass remaining liquid separately. Makes 10 main-dish servings.

Each serving: About 333 calories, 34g protein, 12g carbohydrate, 16g total fat (4g saturated), 90mg cholesterol, 447mg sodium.

COOKING BEEF

To cook a tender piece of beef, it's best to match the cut of meat to the right cooking technique.

BROILING, GRILLING, AND PANFRYING: Choose porterhouse steak, T-bone steak, London broil (top round), top loin, rib-eye, sirloin steak, tenderloin, flank steak, skirt steak, cube steak, minute steak, and ground beef.

BRAISING AND STEWING: Choose chuck roast, brisket, short ribs, shin (shank cross cuts), and oxtails. Cubes for stew are usually cut from boneless chuck or bottom round, but chuck gives the moistest results. Bone-in cuts add flavor and body to stews.

ROASTING: Choose standing rib roast, tenderloin, rib-eye, eye round, and tri-tip.

COUNTRY POT ROAST

....

This is blue-ribbon country cooking. To give the home-style sauce a bit more body and flavor, we puree half of the vegetables.

Prep: 25 minutes   Bake: 3 hours

- 1 tablespoon vegetable oil
- 1 boneless beef chuck cross-rib pot roast or boneless chuck eye roast (4 pounds), trimmed
- 1 large onion (12 ounces), coarsely chopped
- 1 carrot, peeled and coarsely chopped
- 1 stalk celery, coarsely chopped
- 2 garlic cloves, finely chopped
- 1 can (15 ounces) crushed tomatoes
- ½ cup chicken broth
- 1 teaspoon salt
- ½ teaspoon dried thyme, crumbled
- ¼ teaspoon ground black pepper
- 1 bay leaf

1. Preheat oven to 350°F. In nonreactive 5-quart Dutch oven, heat oil over high heat until very hot. Add roast and cook until browned. Transfer roast to plate.

2. Add onion, carrot, and celery to Dutch oven and cook over medium-high heat until lightly browned. Add garlic; cook, stirring constantly, until fragrant, about 20 seconds.

3. Return roast to Dutch oven; add tomatoes, broth, salt, thyme, pepper, and bay leaf; heat to boiling. Cover and place in oven. Bake, turning roast once, until roast is tender, about 3 hours.

4. When roast is done, transfer to large platter and keep warm. Discard bay leaf. Skim and discard fat from liquid in Dutch oven. Transfer half of vegetables and liquid to blender; cover, with center part of cover removed to let steam escape, and puree until smooth. Pour pureed mixture into Dutch oven and stir until combined; heat to boiling. Cut meat into thin slices and serve with vegetables and sauce. Makes 8 main-dish servings.

Each serving: About 304 calories, 35g protein, 6g carbohydrate, 15g total fat (5g saturated), 114mg cholesterol, 573mg sodium.

GRILLADES

....

This New Orleans–style smothered steak is often served with grits for breakfast. We like it for lunch and dinner, too.

Prep: 15 minutes   Cook: 1 hour

- 4   beef minute steaks (6 ounces each)
- ½   teaspoon salt
- ¼   teaspoon ground black pepper
- 3   teaspoons vegetable oil
- 1   medium onion, chopped
- 1   green pepper, chopped
- 1   stalk celery, chopped
- 2   garlic cloves, finely chopped
- 1   can (14 to 16 ounces) tomatoes in puree
- 1   cup beef broth
- 1   teaspoon Worcestershire sauce
- 2   bay leaves
- 1   tablespoon red wine vinegar

1. Sprinkle beef with salt and black pepper. In nonstick 12-inch skillet, heat 1 teaspoon oil over medium-high heat until very hot. Add steaks and cook until browned, about 2 minutes per side, transferring steaks to plate as they are browned.

2. Add remaining 2 teaspoons oil to skillet; reduce heat to medium. Add onion and cook, stirring, 5 minutes. Add green pepper, celery, and garlic; cook, stirring, 3 minutes longer. Add tomatoes with their puree, breaking them up with side of spoon. Stir in broth, Worcestershire, and bay leaves. Increase heat to high; heat to boiling.

3. Return steaks to skillet and reduce heat. Cover and simmer 40 minutes. Transfer steaks to platter; keep warm. Increase heat to high; stir in vinegar and heat to boiling. Boil until sauce has thickened, about 5 minutes. Discard bay leaves. To serve, spoon sauce over steaks. Makes 4 main-dish servings.

Each serving: About 437 calories, 37g protein, 13g carbohydrate, 26g total fat (9g saturated), 107mg cholesterol, 772mg sodium.

FLANK STEAK WITH RED ONION MARMALADE

....

This juicy panfried steak, topped with a sweet and tangy red onion mixture, is an easy weeknight dish to put together.

Prep: 10 minutes   Cook: 35 minutes

- 3   tablespoons butter or margarine
- 2   medium red onions (1 pound), thinly sliced
- 3   tablespoons distilled white vinegar
- 3   tablespoons sugar
- 1   teaspoon salt
- 1   beef flank steak (1½ pounds)
- ¼   teaspoon coarsely ground pepper

1. In nonstick 12-inch skillet, melt 2 tablespoons butter over medium heat. Add onions and cook, stirring occasionally, until tender, about 15 minutes. Stir in vinegar, sugar, and ½ teaspoon salt. Reduce heat and simmer 5 minutes. Spoon red onion marmalade into small bowl; keep warm.

2. Wash skillet and wipe dry. Sprinkle steak with pepper and remaining ½ teaspoon salt. In skillet, melt remaining 1 tablespoon butter over medium-high heat. Add steak and cook 6 to 8 minutes per side for medium-rare or until desired doneness.

3. Slice steak and serve with red onion marmalade. Makes 6 main-dish servings.

Each serving: About 281 calories, 24g protein, 14g carbohydrate, 14g total fat (7g saturated), 72mg cholesterol, 150mg sodium.

NEW ENGLAND BOILED DINNER

(Pictured on page 94)

....

Gently simmering the meat for hours creates its melt-in-your-mouth quality. If you like, substitute turnips or parsnips for the rutabaga, or add a few additional potatoes so you can make Corned Beef Hash (opposite) with the tasty leftovers.

Prep: 15 minutes   Cook: 3 hours 30 minutes

- 1 corned beef brisket (4 to 4½ pounds)
- 1 medium onion studded with 4 whole cloves
- 8 cups water
- 8 medium all-purpose potatoes (2½ pounds), peeled and each cut in half
- 8 carrots, peeled and each cut in half
- 1 small rutabaga (2 pounds), peeled and cut in half, each half cut into 8 wedges
- 1 small green cabbage (2 pounds), cut into 8 wedges
- 2 tablespoons chopped fresh parsley
   Dijon mustard
   bottled white horseradish

1. In 8-quart Dutch oven, place brisket, clove-studded onion, and water and heat to boiling over high heat. With slotted spoon, skim and discard foam from surface. Reduce heat; cover and simmer until brisket is tender, 2 hours 30 minutes to 3 hours.

2. Add potatoes, carrots, and rutabaga to Dutch oven; heat to boiling over high heat. Reduce heat; cover and simmer until vegetables are tender, about 30 minutes.

3. With slotted spoon, transfer brisket and vegetables to deep large platter; keep warm.

4. Heat liquid remaining in Dutch oven to boiling over high heat. Add cabbage; heat to boiling. Cover and boil until cabbage is tender, about 5 minutes.

5. Slice brisket very thinly across the grain. Transfer sliced meat to platter with vegetables. Place cabbage wedges on platter, sprinkle parsley on vegetables, and serve mustard and horseradish alongside. Makes 8 main-dish servings.

Each serving: About 587 calories, 35g protein, 43g carbohydrate, 31g total fat (10g saturated), 157mg cholesterol, 1,887mg sodium.

CORNED BEEF HASH

....

A breakfast tradition, especially with a freshly poached egg on top. By adding chopped cooked beets to the mixture, you get Red Flannel Hash, a Yankee classic. Purchase cooked corned beef or use leftovers from New England Boiled Dinner (left).

Prep: 15 minutes   Cook: 25 minutes

- 3 tablespoons butter or margarine
- 1 large onion (12 ounces), chopped
- 2 cups chopped lean cooked corned beef
- 2 cups chopped cooked all-purpose potatoes
- ¼ teaspoon coarsely ground pepper
- 1 tablespoon chopped fresh parsley

1. In 10-inch skillet, melt butter over medium heat. Add onion and cook, stirring often, until tender, about 5 minutes.

2. Stir in corned beef, potatoes, and pepper until well combined. Cook, pressing hash down firmly with spatula, until bottom of hash has browned, about 15 minutes.

3. With spatula, turn hash over one small section at a time. Press down with spatula and cook until second side has browned, 5 to 10 minutes longer. Sprinkle with parsley. Makes 4 main-dish servings.

Each serving: About 337 calories, 23g protein, 21g carbohydrate, 18g total fat (9g saturated), 89mg cholesterol, 947mg sodium.

RED FLANNEL HASH

Prepare as directed, adding **1 cup finely chopped cooked beets** with corned beef, potatoes, and pepper.

FILET MIGNON WITH ROQUEFORT

....

We switched the traditional rib-eye steak for a lean filet mignon and cooked it in only 2 teaspoons olive oil. The Roquefort cheese topping is so luxuriously flavorful that just a tablespoon per serving is enough.

Prep: 5 minutes   Cook: 10 minutes

- 2 teaspoons olive oil
- 4 beef tenderloin steaks (1 inch thick), trimmed of fat (4 ounces each)
- ½ teaspoon salt
- ¼ teaspoon coarsely ground black pepper
- 1 ounce Roquefort cheese, crumbled (¼ cup)

1. In 12-inch skillet, heat oil on high until hot. On waxed paper, evenly season steaks, on both sides, with salt and pepper.

2. Add steaks to skillet and cook 10 minutes for medium-rare or until desired doneness, turning over once. Transfer steaks to 4 dinner plates; top with Roquefort. Makes 4 main-dish servings.

Each serving: About 205 calories, 25g protein, 0g carbohydrate, 11g total fat (4g saturated), 0g fiber, 63mg cholesterol, 470mg sodium.

STEAK SUCCESS

The easiest way to check the doneness of steak is to cut into its center. You can also use the "touch test." The longer a steak cooks, the firmer the meat becomes as its juices evaporate. Press the steak in the center. If the steak is somewhat soft, it is medium-rare. If it bounces back slightly, the steak is medium. If firm, the steak is well-done.

Filet Mignon with Roquefort

FILET MIGNON WITH MUSTARD-CAPER SAUCE

....

A well-browned exterior is the key to maximum flavor with sautéed beef. Be sure to cook it over high heat.

Prep: 5 minutes   Cook: 20 minutes

- 4 beef tenderloin steaks (filet mignon), 1½ inches thick (6 ounces each)
- ½ teaspoon salt
- ¼ teaspoon coarsely ground black pepper
- 1 tablespoon olive oil
- 3 tablespoons finely chopped shallots
- ⅓ cup dry white wine
- ⅓ cup beef broth
- ⅓ cup heavy or whipping cream
- 3 tablespoons capers, drained
- 1 tablespoon Dijon mustard
- ¼ cup chopped watercress leaves plus additional leaves

1. Sprinkle steaks with salt and pepper. In nonstick 12-inch skillet, heat oil over high heat until very hot. Add steaks and cook, without turning, until browned, about 7 minutes. Turn steaks and cook 7 minutes longer for medium-rare or until desired doneness. Transfer to plates; keep warm.

2. Add shallots to drippings in skillet; cook 30 seconds. Stir in wine; cook, stirring, until browned bits are loosened from bottom of skillet. Stir in broth and boil 1 minute. Stir in cream; boil 1 minute longer. Stir in capers, mustard, and chopped watercress.

3. To serve, spoon sauce over meat and garnish with watercress. Makes 4 main-dish servings.

Each serving: About 334 calories, 27g protein, 3g carbohydrate, 22g total fat (9g saturated), 105mg cholesterol, 799mg sodium.

STEAK AU POIVRE

Prepare as directed but in Step 1 use **2 tablespoons crushed black peppercorns.** In Step 2 omit shallots, broth, capers, and mustard; stir in wine and **2 tablespoons brandy,** stirring until browned bits are loosened. Stir in cream and boil until thickened. Replace watercress with **1 tablespoon chopped fresh parsley.**

STEAK WITH RED WINE SAUCE

Try this simple sauce with any panfried beef, from burgers to filet mignon. It is thickened with a little butter at the end, a French cooking technique that rounds out the wine and enriches the sauce. (Do not use margarine; it will not thicken the sauce.)

Prep: 5 minutes   Cook: 20 minutes

- 2 teaspoons vegetable oil
- 4 boneless beef strip (shell) steaks, 1 inch thick (8 ounces each)
- ½ teaspoon salt
- ¼ teaspoon ground black pepper
- ¼ cup finely chopped shallots
- 1 cup dry red wine
   pinch dried thyme, crumbled
- 2 tablespoons butter, cut into pieces
- 2 teaspoons chopped fresh tarragon or flat-leaf parsley

1. In 12-inch skillet, heat oil over medium-high heat until very hot. Sprinkle steaks with salt and pepper. Cook 5 to 6 minutes per side for medium-rare or until desired doneness. Transfer steaks to warm platter.

2. Discard drippings from skillet. Add shallots to pan and cook, stirring, until tender, about 1 minute. Add wine and thyme; heat to boiling over high heat. Boil until sauce has reduced to ⅓ cup, about 5 minutes. Remove pan from heat; stir in butter, stirring just until incorporated.

3. Cut steaks into thin slices. Transfer to warm platter; pour sauce on top and sprinkle with tarragon. Makes 4 main-dish servings.

Each serving: About 436 calories, 49g protein, 3g carbohydrate, 24g total fat (10g saturated), 145mg cholesterol, 179mg sodium.

Tangerine-Beef Stir-Fry

TUSCAN PAN-SEARED STRIP STEAK

Tuscan cooks know all it takes to bring out the flavor of a rich cut of beef is a squeeze of fresh lemon juice.

Prep: 5 minutes   Cook: 12 minutes

- 4 boneless beef strip (shell) steaks, 1 inch thick (8 ounces each)
- 2 teaspoons olive oil
- 1 tablespoon chopped fresh rosemary or 1 teaspoon dried rosemary, crumbled
- 1 teaspoon salt
- 1 teaspoon coarsely ground black pepper
- 4 lemon wedges

1. Heat 12-inch skillet over high heat until very hot. Brush steaks with olive oil. In small bowl, combine rosemary, salt, and pepper. Use to rub on steaks.

2. Place steaks in skillet; reduce heat to medium-high. Cook steaks 7 minutes; turn and cook 5 minutes longer for medium-rare or 7 minutes longer for medium. Serve with lemon wedges. Makes 4 main-dish servings.

Each serving: About 375 calories, 49g protein, 1g carbohydrate, 18g total fat (6g saturated), 129mg cholesterol, 699mg sodium.

TANGERINE-BEEF STIR-FRY

The secret to a perfect stir-fry is to have all your ingredients sliced and prepped.

Prep: 25 minutes   Cook: 20 minutes

- 2 to 3 tangerines
- ¼ cup dry sherry
- 1 tablespoon grated peeled fresh ginger
- 1 teaspoon Asian sesame oil
- 1 teaspoon plus 1 tablespoon cornstarch
- 2 tablespoons low-sodium soy sauce
- 1 beef flank steak (about 1 pound), cut crosswise into ⅛-inch-thick slices
- 4 teaspoons vegetable oil
- 1 large red pepper, thinly sliced
- 6 ounces snow peas, strings removed
- 3 green onions, cut into 1-inch pieces
- ¼ cup water

1. With vegetable peeler, remove peel in strips from tangerines. Using small knife, remove any white pith from peel; set peel aside. Cut remaining pith from tangerines. Working with tangerines 1 at a time, hold over 2-cup liquid measuring cup to catch juice and cut on either side of membranes to remove each segment, allowing fruit and juice to drop into cup. Into same measuring cup, squeeze juice from remaining membranes until fruit and juice mixture equals ½ cup. Discard seeds, if any. Stir in sherry, ginger, sesame oil, and 1 teaspoon cornstarch; set aside. In medium bowl, mix soy sauce and remaining 1 tablespoon cornstarch. Add beef and toss to coat; set aside.

2. In 12-inch skillet, heat 2 teaspoons vegetable oil over medium-high heat until hot. Add tangerine peel and cook 2 to 3 minutes or until lightly browned. Transfer peel to large bowl.

3. To same skillet, add red pepper, snow peas, and green onions, and toss to coat with oil; cook 1 minute. Add water and cook about 2 minutes longer or until vegetables are tender-crisp, stirring frequently. Drain vegetables and transfer to bowl with peel.

4. To same skillet, add 1 teaspoon vegetable oil and heat until very hot. Add half of beef mixture and cook 2 minutes or until beef is lightly browned, stirring frequently. Transfer to bowl with vegetables. Repeat with remaining 1 teaspoon vegetable oil and beef mixture.

5. Add juice mixture to skillet and heat to boiling; boil 1 minute. Return beef mixture to skillet; heat through. Makes 4 main-dish servings.

Each serving: About 330 calories, 25g protein, 17g carbohydrate, 18g total fat (6g saturated), 59mg cholesterol, 385mg sodium.

FAJITAS

Fajitas are ideal party fare. Serve with your favorite salsa, homemade if time permits (pages 506–508).

**Prep: 15 minutes plus marinating
Cook/Broil: 20 minutes**

- 3 tablespoons fresh lime juice
- 3 tablespoons fresh orange juice
- ¾ teaspoon salt
- ½ teaspoon dried oregano, crumbled
- 1 beef skirt steak (1¾ pounds)
- 1 tablespoon olive oil
- 2 medium onions, thinly sliced
- 2 garlic cloves, thinly sliced
- 3 large red peppers, cut into ½-inch-thick strips
- 1 large green pepper, cut into ½-inch-thick strips
- 2 teaspoons finely chopped pickled jalapeño chile
- 12 (6-inch) flour tortillas

1. In cup, combine lime and orange juices, ½ teaspoon salt, and oregano. Transfer to ziptight plastic bag; add meat, turning to coat. Seal bag, pressing out as much air as possible. Refrigerate beef 1 hour to marinate, turning bag once.

2. Preheat broiler. Meanwhile, in 12-inch skillet, heat oil over medium heat. Add onions and garlic and cook, stirring frequently, until onions are tender, about 5 minutes. Add red and green peppers, jalapeño, and remaining ¼ teaspoon salt; cook, stirring frequently, until red and green peppers are tender, about 7 minutes.

3. Place meat on rack in broiling pan. Broil steak 6 inches from heat source 3 to 4 minutes per side for medium-rare or until desired doneness. Cut meat into thin slices across the grain and serve with tortillas and pepper mixture. Makes 6 main-dish servings.

Each serving: About 418 calories, 30g protein, 34g carbohydrate, 17g total fat (6g saturated), 66mg cholesterol, 531mg sodium.

GROUND BEEF

Some of America's favorite dishes start with ground beef: meat loaf, meatballs, burgers, chili, and casseroles, and that's just the beginning. Its popularity is well-deserved: It delivers big-time flavor at relatively low cost.

Buying and Storing

The label on ground beef often denotes the percentage of lean meat to fat, but sometimes the cut of meat is also listed. You can buy ground chuck, which is about 80 percent lean; ground sirloin, which is 90 to 95 percent extra-lean; and ground round, which at 85 percent lean is juicy, flavorful, and the most popular cut. If meat is labeled "ground beef," it comes from a combination of cuts and is only 70 percent lean. Keep in mind that the amount of fat in ground beef affects the moistness and texture of the cooked dish, so you will get different results when using ground chuck, ground round, or ground sirloin.

Ground beef should be cherry red. Don't worry if the meat in the center looks darker than the meat on the exterior. The darker color comes from a lack of oxygen. When exposed to the air, this darker meat will become redder.

E. coli, a strain of potentially deadly bacteria, has been found in mass-produced meat patties. To guard against this bacteria, always purchase ground beef from a reliable source and shape your own burgers.

Cooking Ground Beef Safely

Disease-causing bacteria like *E. coli* contaminate only the surface of food, so the inside of a roast or steak is not affected. The bacteria are killed when the outside of the food is exposed to high temperatures, when grilling and roasting, for example. When beef is ground, any outer surface contamination gets mixed throughout the meat. The bacteria on the surface of a grilled burger may be killed, but unless the interior of the meat is cooked to 160°F, dangerous bacteria can still be present. To eliminate this danger, always cook ground beef until well-done. When pressed in the center, a burger or patty should feel firm and spring back.

DANISH MEATBALLS

....

These tender meatballs have a creamy sauce just made for spooning over noodles or rice. If you wish, serve the meatballs as they do in Denmark, with a dollop of lingonberry preserves.

Prep: 25 minutes   Cook: 15 minutes

- 1½ pounds ground beef chuck or ground meat for meat loaf (beef, pork, and veal)
- ½ cup plain dried bread crumbs
- 1 large egg
- ¼ cup chopped fresh flat-leaf parsley
- 2 tablespoons chopped fresh dill
- 1 tablespoon grated onion
- 1 teaspoon salt
- ¼ teaspoon ground black pepper
- ⅛ teaspoon ground nutmeg
- 2 tablespoons butter or margarine
- 2 tablespoons all-purpose flour
- 1½ cups milk
- 1 cup low-sodium chicken broth
  lingonberry preserves (optional)

1. In large bowl, combine ground beef, bread crumbs, egg, parsley, dill, onion, salt, pepper, and nutmeg just until well blended but not overmixed. Shape mixture into 24 meatballs, handling meat as little as possible.

2. In 12-inch skillet, melt butter over medium-high heat. Add meatballs and cook until browned, using slotted spoon to transfer meatballs to clean large bowl as they are browned. Discard all but 2 tablespoons drippings from skillet.

3. Stir flour into drippings in skillet; cook over medium heat, stirring, 1 minute. Gradually add milk and broth; cook, stirring constantly, until mixture has thickened and boils.

4. Add meatballs to skillet; heat to boiling. Reduce heat; cover and simmer 10 minutes. Serve with lingonberry preserves, if desired. Makes 6 main-dish servings.

Each serving: About 330 calories, 28g protein, 12g carbohydrate, 19g total fat (9g saturated), 125mg cholesterol, 991mg sodium.

MEXICAN MEATBALLS

....

If chipotle chiles are hard to find locally, substitute 1 seeded and minced jalapeño chile and ¹/₄ teaspoon liquid smoke.

Prep: 30 minutes   Cook: 45 minutes

- 1¹/₂ pounds ground beef chuck
- ³/₄ cup plain dried bread crumbs
- 1 large egg
- 3 garlic cloves, finely chopped
- 1 teaspoon salt
- ¹/₂ teaspoon ground black pepper
- ¹/₄ cup water
- 1 can (28 ounces) tomatoes
- 1 chipotle chile in adobo (page 25)
- 2 teaspoons vegetable oil
- 1 small onion, finely chopped
- 1 teaspoon ground cumin
- 1 cup chicken broth
- ¹/₄ cup chopped fresh cilantro

1. In large bowl, combine ground beef, bread crumbs, egg, one-third of garlic, salt, pepper, and water just until well blended but not overmixed. Shape mixture into 1-inch meatballs, handling meat as little as possible.

2. In blender, puree tomatoes with their juice and chipotle chile until smooth.

3. In nonreactive 5-quart Dutch oven, heat oil over medium heat. Add onion and cook, stirring often, until tender, about 5 minutes. Stir in cumin and remaining garlic; cook 30 seconds. Stir in tomato mixture and broth; heat to boiling over high heat.

4. Add meatballs; heat to boiling. Reduce heat and simmer 30 minutes. To serve, sprinkle with cilantro. Makes 6 main-dish servings.

Each serving: About 318 calories, 28g protein, 18g carbohydrate, 15g total fat (5g saturated), 106mg cholesterol, 1,001mg sodium.

GREEK MEATBALLS

....

These baked meatballs are prepared with a winning combination of beef and lamb, a touch of mint, and some feta cheese. Offer some Tzatziki (page 33) alongside, if you like.

Prep: 20 minutes   Bake: 20 minutes

- 1 pound ground beef chuck
- 1 pound lean ground lamb
- 1 cup fresh bread crumbs (about 2 slices bread)
- 2 large eggs
- 4 ounces feta cheese, finely crumbled (1 cup)
- 3 bunches green onions, finely chopped (1 cup)
- ¹/₄ cup chopped fresh flat-leaf parsley
- 2 garlic cloves, finely chopped
- 1 tablespoon dried mint, crumbled
- 2 tablespoons olive oil
- 1 tablespoon red wine vinegar
- ¹/₂ teaspoon salt
- ¹/₄ teaspoon ground black pepper

1. Preheat oven to 425°F. In large bowl, combine ground beef, ground lamb, bread crumbs, eggs, feta, green onions, parsley, garlic, mint, oil, vinegar, salt, and pepper just until well blended but not overmixed.

2. Shape mixture into scant ¹/₄-cup meatballs, handling meat as little as possible. Place 1 inch apart in two jelly-roll pans. Bake until cooked through, 20 to 25 minutes. Makes 8 main-dish servings.

Each serving: About 365 calories, 26g protein, 5g carbohydrate, 27g total fat (11g saturated), 143mg cholesterol, 425mg sodium.

STUFFED TOMATOES WITH LEAN GROUND BEEF

....

Make a meal from garden-fresh tomatoes and the traditional flavors of Greece: mint, cinnamon, and a crumble of feta cheese.

Prep: 25 minutes   Cook: 35 minutes

- ½ cup quick-cooking (10-minute) brown rice
- 1 tablespoon olive oil
- 1 medium onion (6 to 8 ounces), chopped
- 1¼ pounds lean (90%) ground beef
- ⅓ cup loosely packed fresh mint leaves, chopped, plus mint sprigs for garnish
- ½ teaspoon ground cinnamon
- ¼ teaspoon salt
- ¼ teaspoon ground black pepper
- 6 large tomatoes (10 ounces each)
- ½ cup crumbled feta cheese (2 ounces)
- ¼ cup panko (Japanese-style bread crumbs)

1. Preheat oven to 425°F. In 3-quart saucepan, cook rice as label directs.

2. Meanwhile, in 12-inch nonstick skillet, heat oil on medium 1 minute. Add onion, and cook 10 to 12 minutes or until lightly browned and tender. Stir in ground beef, half of chopped mint, cinnamon, salt, and pepper. Cook 5 to 6 minutes or until beef loses its pink color throughout, breaking up meat with spatula and stirring occasionally. Stir in remaining chopped mint.

3. While ground beef cooks, cut each tomato horizontally in half. With melon baller or spoon, scoop out tomato pulp; place in large bowl. Remove 1 cup tomato pulp from bowl and chop. Discard remaining pulp or save for another use. Return chopped pulp to bowl. Add rice, feta cheese, and beef mixture; stir until well blended.

Stuffed Tomatoes with Lean Ground Beef

4. In 15½" by 10½" jelly-roll pan, place hollowed-out tomato halves, cut sides up. Mound scant ½ cup beef filling in each tomato half; sprinkle with panko. Bake tomatoes 25 to 30 minutes or until crumbs are browned and filling is heated through. Garnish with mint sprigs. Makes 6 main-dish servings.

Each serving: About 270 calories, 26 protein, 21g carbohydrate, 10g total fat (3g saturated), 4g fiber, 50mg cholesterol, 285mg sodium.

TAMALE PIE

....

This tamale pie has a velvety soft cornmeal top and bottom crust. If you prefer firm slices, be sure to let it rest for at least 25 minutes before serving.

Prep: 25 minutes   **Bake:** 45 minutes

- 2 teaspoons vegetable oil
- 1 medium onion, chopped
- 1 pound ground beef chuck
- 1 tablespoon chili powder
- 1 teaspoon ground cumin
- 1 cup medium-hot salsa
- 1 can (15¼ to 16 ounces) whole-kernel corn, drained
- 4 cups water
- 1 cup cornmeal
- 1 teaspoon salt
- 2 ounces Cheddar cheese, shredded (½ cup)

1. Preheat oven to 350°F. In nonstick 12-inch skillet, heat oil over medium-high heat; add onion and cook until tender and golden, about 5 minutes. Stir in ground beef and cook, breaking up meat with side of spoon, until meat is browned, about 5 minutes. Skim and discard any fat. Stir in chili powder and cumin and cook 2 minutes longer. Remove from heat and stir in salsa and corn.

2. In 2-quart saucepan, heat water to boiling. With wire whisk, gradually whisk in cornmeal and salt. Cook over medium heat, whisking frequently, 5 minutes.

3. Pour half of cornmeal mixture into shallow 2-quart casserole. Spoon beef mixture over cornmeal; spoon remaining cornmeal over beef and sprinkle Cheddar on top. Bake 45 minutes. Remove casserole from oven and let stand 15 to 25 minutes before serving. Makes 6 main-dish servings.

Each serving: About 334 calories, 21g protein, 33g carbohydrate, 13g total fat (5g saturated), 57mg cholesterol, 1,026mg sodium.

SUSAN'S MEAT LOAF

....

This delicious basic meat loaf is from the "Susan, Our Teenage Cook" series, which ran in Good Housekeeping *for decades. Ground chuck makes it tender and tasty.*

Prep: 15 minutes   **Bake:** 1 hour

- 2 pounds ground beef chuck
- 2 large eggs
- 2 cups fresh bread crumbs (about 4 slices bread)
- 2 green onions, finely chopped
- 1 medium onion, finely chopped
- ¾ cup ketchup
- ¼ cup milk
- 2 tablespoons bottled white horseradish
- 1½ teaspoons salt
- 1 teaspoon dry mustard

1. Preheat oven to 400°F. In large bowl, combine ground beef, eggs, bread crumbs, green onions, onion, ¼ cup ketchup, milk, horseradish, salt, and dry mustard just until well blended but not overmixed.

2. Spoon mixture into 9" by 5" metal loaf pan, pressing firmly. Spread remaining ½ cup ketchup on top of loaf. Bake 1 hour. Let stand 10 minutes to set juices for easier slicing. Makes 8 main-dish servings.

Each serving: About 283 calories, 27g protein, 15g carbohydrate, 13g total fat (5g saturated), 125mg cholesterol, 845mg sodium.

MEAT LOAF DONE JUST RIGHT

It's important to cook a meatloaf just until cooked through so that it remains moist and tasty. In our recipes we give the exact time needed to cook up a flavorful loaf. But you can also use an instant-read thermometer, which is the most fail-safe way to determine doneness for ground meat in loaves and in patties. Insert the thermometer into the thickest portion of the loaf or in the middle, inserting it halfway in. For patties, insert it horizontally until it reaches the center. The thermometer should read 160°F. Be sure to wash it before you reinsert it if needed.

Cajun Meat Loaf

CAJUN MEAT LOAF

....

This spicy meat loaf is for those who like a bit of kick in their comfort food.

Prep: 20 minutes   Bake: 1 hour 15 minutes

2   tablespoons butter or margarine
2   carrots, peeled and finely chopped
1   large onion (12 ounces), chopped
1   large stalk celery, chopped
1   small green pepper, finely chopped
2   garlic cloves, crushed with garlic press
2   pounds ground meat for meat loaf
    (beef, pork, and veal)
2   large eggs
1   cup fresh bread crumbs (about 2 slices bread)
½   cup plus 2 tablespoons ketchup
¼   cup milk
1   tablespoon Worcestershire sauce
2   teaspoons salt
1   teaspoon ground cumin
½   teaspoon dried thyme
½   teaspoon ground nutmeg
½   teaspoon ground red pepper (cayenne)
½   teaspoon coarsely ground black pepper

1. In nonstick 12-inch skillet, melt butter over medium heat. Add carrots, onion, celery, and green pepper and cook, stirring occasionally, until vegetables are tender, about 15 minutes. Add garlic and cook 1 minute longer. Set aside to cool slightly.

2. Preheat oven to 375°F. In large bowl, combine ground meat, eggs, bread crumbs, ½ cup ketchup, milk, Worcestershire, salt, cumin, thyme, nutmeg, ground red pepper, black pepper, and cooked vegetable mixture just until well blended but not overmixed.

3. In 13" by 9" baking pan, shape meat mixture into 10" by 5" loaf, pressing firmly. Brush remaining 2 tablespoons ketchup on top of loaf. Bake 1 hour 15 minutes. Let stand 10 minutes to set juices for easier slicing. Makes 8 main-dish servings.

Each serving: About 364 calories, 24g protein, 14g carbohydrate, 23g total fat (10g saturated), 149mg cholesterol, 961mg sodium.

VEAL

Veal has always been regarded as one of the finest meats, and it is associated with some very elegant dishes. This lean, delicate meat resembles poultry more than beef, and it has a versatility that lends itself to a variety of seasonings and cooking techniques. But remember, veal requires a bit of extra attention to keep it from becoming overcooked and dried out.

Buying Veal

Veal calves are raised for eight to sixteen weeks. In order to maintain the meat's delicate texture, the calves are never subjected to excessive movement. The finest and most expensive veal is *milk-fed*, either their mother's milk or a special milk formula. Milk-fed veal is rarely labeled as such but can be recognized by its pale pink, almost white color.

Grain-fed veal comes from older calves that were raised on grain or grass. It has a deep rosy pink color and a slightly stronger flavor than milk-fed veal. This veal is sometimes labeled "calf" but more often it is just labeled "veal."

When buying veal at the supermarket, let your eye be your guide. Look for meat that is fine-textured and pale. While marbling in beef is desirable, veal should have very little marbling, and what fat there is should be firm and very white. The bones of milk-fed veal have reddish marrow. Prime veal is usually milk-fed, whereas grain-fed veal is usually graded choice. Veal marketed under brand names is rarely graded.

Veal cutlets are readily available but vary in quality. The cutlets are ideally cut from a single muscle, usually the top or bottom round. If they are cut from two or three muscles, they will curl when cooked.

Storing Veal

Because veal is a moist meat, it is fairly perishable. Large cuts and stew meat will only keep for two days, tightly wrapped, in the refrigerator. Be sure to cook veal cutlets the day of purchase.

Cooking Veal

Broiling, Grilling and Panfrying For broiling or grilling, choose thick chops and steaks so they won't dry out. Veal cutlets, which are thin, are usually panfried.

ROASTING TIMES FOR VEAL

(OVEN TEMPERATURE OF 325°F)

Start with meat at refrigerator temperature. Remove roast from oven when it reaches 5°F below desired doneness; temperature will continue to rise as roast stands.

MEAT CUT	THERMOMETER READING	APPROXIMATE COOKING TIME (MINUTES PER POUND)
Boneless shoulder roast	160°F	35 to 40 minutes
Leg rump or round roast (boneless)	160°F	35 to 40 minutes
Boneless leg roast	160°F	25 to 30 minutes
Rib roast	160°F	30 to 35 minutes

Best Bets: Shoulder or blade steaks, loin or rib chops, ground veal, and cutlets.

Braising and Stewing Bone-in pieces are especially suited to braising and stewing. Veal stew meat, cut from the neck or shoulder, is readily available and delicious.

Best Bets: Shanks, shank cross cuts (osso buco), arm (shoulder) or blade steak, breast, and shoulder.

Roasting Veal roasts are generally very lean, so you'll get juicier results by cooking them to only 155°F, since the temperature will rise as it stands. Veal breast and shoulder roasts should be cooked until well done and tender.

Best Bets: Rib roast, loin roast, round, shoulder roast, and breast.

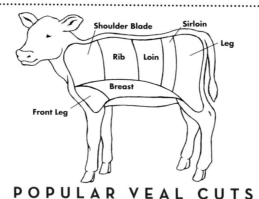

Shoulder Blade · Sirloin · Leg · Rib · Loin · Breast · Front Leg

POPULAR VEAL CUTS

Veal shoulder roast, boneless

Shoulder cut with bones removed; rolled and tied to keep its shape *(braise, roast)*.

Veal breast

Also called breast of veal. Contains lower ribs, lean meat, and layers of fat, making it juicy and flavorful *(braise, roast)*.

Veal breast riblets

Also called veal riblets; long, narrow cuts containing rib bones with thin fat covering *(braise)*.

Veal shoulder blade steak

Also called veal shoulder steak or veal shoulder chop *(braise, panfry)*.

Veal rib chops

Contain big rib-eye muscle. Expensive and tasty *(braise, panfry, grill, broil)*.

Veal loin chops

Muscles include top loin and tenderloin *(braise, panfry, grill, broil)*.

Veal top loin chops

Same as veal loin chops except do not contain tenderloin *(braise, panfry, grill, broil)*.

Veal cutlets

Very lean, thin, boneless slices from leg that are pounded thinly. Also called scallopini *(braise, panfry)*.

Veal shank crosscuts

Cut crosswise from hindshank, usually 1 to 2½ inches thick. Also called osso buco *(braise)*.

VEAL SHOULDER CHOPS, OSSO BUCO STYLE

....

After a quick and easy browning in one pot, these gourmet veal chops—meatier than the veal shanks in traditional Osso Buco—are simmered with crushed tomatoes, herbs, and white wine until tender and oh-so-flavorful.

Prep: 30 minutes   Cook: 2 hours 10 minutes

- 1 tablespoon olive oil
- 4 pounds bone-in veal shoulder chops
- ½ teaspoon salt
- ¼ teaspoon ground black pepper
- 4 medium carrots, chopped
- 3 medium stalks celery, thinly sliced
- 2 medium onions, chopped
- 4 cloves garlic, finely chopped
- 1 can (14½ ounces) whole tomatoes in juice
- 1 cup dry white wine
- 1 can (14 to 14½ ounces) chicken broth or 1¾ cups Chicken Broth (page 70)
- 1 bay leaf
- 1 package (10 ounces) frozen peas, thawed
- ½ teaspoon grated fresh lemon peel plus additional for garnish

Veal Shoulder Chops, Osso Buco Style

1. Preheat oven to 350°F. In wide-bottom 6-quart Dutch oven, heat oil over medium-high heat until very hot. Sprinkle veal chops with salt and pepper to season both sides. Add veal chops to Dutch oven in 3 batches, and cook 8 to 9 minutes per batch or until veal is browned on both sides, turning over once. Transfer veal to plate once it is browned.

2. After all veal is browned, add carrots, celery, onions, and garlic to Dutch oven, and cook on medium 12 minutes or until vegetables are lightly browned and tender, stirring occasionally.

3. Return veal and any juices from plate to Dutch oven. Stir in tomatoes with their juice, wine, broth, and bay leaf. Heat mixture to boiling on high, stirring and breaking up tomatoes with side of spoon.

4. Cover Dutch oven and place in oven. Bake 1 hour and 15 minutes or until veal is very tender when pierced with fork. Transfer veal to platter. Skim off and discard fat from liquid in Dutch oven.

5. Place Dutch oven on burner on top of range, and cook sauce on medium-high heat about 10 minutes or until slightly thickened, stirring occasionally. Add peas and ½ teaspoon lemon peel; cook 2 minutes.

6. To serve, discard bay leaf. Transfer veal to dinner plates. Spoon sauce over veal; sprinkle with additional lemon peel for garnish. Makes about 8 main-dish servings.

Each serving: About 270 calories, 38g protein, 15g carbohydrate, 6g total fat (1g saturated), 4g fiber, 141mg cholesterol, 575mg sodium.

FRUIT-STUFFED VEAL ROAST

....

Fruit is frequently included in pork stuffings, but many fruits also complement the mild flavor of veal. If you like, use one type of dried fruit, such as apples, pears, or prunes.

Prep: 35 minutes   Roast: 1 hour 20 minutes

- 2 slices firm white bread, cut into ½-inch cubes
- 4 teaspoons olive oil
- 2 shallots, finely chopped
- 1 garlic clove, finely chopped
- ½ cup mixed dried fruit, coarsely chopped
- 2 teaspoons Dijon mustard
- ¾ teaspoon salt
- ½ teaspoon dried rosemary, crumbled
- 1 boneless veal shoulder roast (2½ pounds)
- ½ cup chicken broth
- 1 Golden Delicious apple, peeled, cored, and chopped
- ¼ cup applejack brandy or Calvados
- ½ cup heavy or whipping cream

1. Preheat oven to 375°F. Place bread cubes on cookie sheet and bake until lightly browned, about 5 minutes. Transfer to medium bowl. Turn oven control to 425°F.

2. In 1-quart saucepan, heat 2 teaspoons oil over medium heat. Add half of shallots and garlic and cook, stirring, until shallot is tender, about 4 minutes; add to bowl with croutons. Add dried fruit, mustard, ¼ teaspoon salt, and ¼ teaspoon rosemary; toss to combine.

3. Using sharp knife, cut roast lengthwise three-quarters of the way through, being careful not to cut all the way through. Open and spread flat like a book. Spoon fruit mixture on roast, leaving 1-inch border all around. Roll up roast from one long side to enclose filling; tie with string at 1-inch intervals to secure. Rub ¼ teaspoon of salt and remaining ¼ teaspoon rosemary on veal.

4. Place roast in small roasting pan (13" by 9") and roast until lightly browned, about 30 minutes. Turn oven control to 375°F and roast until meat thermometer inserted in center of roast reaches 155°F, about 50 minutes longer. Internal temperature of meat will rise to 160°F (medium) upon standing. Transfer roast to warm platter and let stand 10 minutes to set juices for easier slicing.

5. Meanwhile, skim and discard fat from roasting pan. Place pan on stove, add broth and heat to boiling, stirring until browned bits are loosened from bottom of pan. Remove from heat and set aside.

6. Heat remaining 2 teaspoons oil in small skillet over medium heat. Add remaining shallots and cook, stirring frequently, until tender, about 4 minutes. Add apple and cook, stirring frequently, until tender-crisp, about 4 minutes. Remove from heat and add applejack. Return to heat and cook until liquid has evaporated. Add broth from roasting pan and heat to boiling; boil 3 minutes. Add cream and boil until sauce has slightly thickened, about 5 minutes. Stir in remaining ¼ teaspoon salt.

7. Slice veal and serve with applejack sauce. Makes 8 main-dish servings.

Each serving: About 323 calories, 30g protein, 13g carbohydrate, 15g total fat (7g saturated), 145mg cholesterol, 463mg sodium.

STUFFED BREAST OF VEAL

....

This cut of meat can always be counted on for being moist, flavorful, and easy on the wallet. Here, it is filled with the classic Sicilian combination of spinach and golden raisins. Or use our Bacon and Collard Greens Stuffing (opposite) for a change of pace. Serve the veal hot or at room temperature; either way, it will be delicious.

**Prep: 25 minutes plus cooling
Bake: 2 hours 15 minutes**

- 1 tablespoon olive oil
- 1 small onion, chopped
- 3 garlic cloves, finely chopped
- 2 packages (10 ounces each) frozen chopped spinach, thawed and squeezed dry
- 1 lemon
- ⅓ cup golden raisins
- ¾ teaspoon salt
- 1 bone-in veal breast (4 pounds), with pocket for stuffing
- 1 cup chicken broth

1. Preheat oven to 425°F. In 12-inch skillet, heat oil over medium-low heat. Add onion and garlic and cook, stirring frequently, until onion is tender, about 5 minutes. Add spinach and cook, stirring frequently, until liquid has evaporated, about 2 minutes. Remove from heat.

2. From lemon, grate ¾ teaspoon peel and squeeze 2 tablespoons juice; set juice aside. Add raisins, ½ teaspoon salt, and lemon peel to spinach. Cool to room temperature. Spoon mixture into pocket of veal.

3. Place breast, meat side up, in medium roasting pan (14" by 10"). Sprinkle remaining ¼ teaspoon salt on meat side (not rib side) of veal and roast 1 hour. Turn veal, rib side up, and pour broth and lemon juice into bottom of roasting pan. Cover veal with loose tent of foil and bake until tender, about 1 hour 15 minutes longer.

4. Transfer veal, rib side down, to cutting board and let stand 10 minutes to set juices for easier carving. Skim and discard fat from drippings in pan. Carve veal by slicing down along one rib bone. Cut away rib bone and discard, then continue carving. Transfer slices to warm platter and serve with pan juices. Makes 6 main-dish servings.

Each serving: About 425 calories, 51g protein, 13g carbohydrate, 18g total fat (6g saturated), 183mg cholesterol, 637mg sodium.

BACON AND COLLARD GREENS STUFFING
Substitute ¼ **cup minced shallots** for the onion and cook with the garlic as directed. Stir in **2 packages (10 ounces) each of thawed and squeezed dry frozen chopped collard greens** instead of the spinach. Omit the grated lemon and raisins and stir **4 slices of crisp-cooked and chopped bacon** into the greens mixture. Proceed as directed.

BRAISED VEAL CHOPS WITH TOMATOES AND PEAS

The bones in the shoulder chops contribute extra flavor and body to the sauce. Two large chops will easily feed four people.

Prep: 10 minutes   Cook: 1 hour 15 minutes

- 2 veal shoulder blade chops, 1 inch thick (1 pound each)
- 1 slice bacon, chopped
- ¼ teaspoon salt
- ⅛ teaspoon ground black pepper
- 1 medium onion, chopped
- 2 garlic cloves, finely chopped
- 1 can (14½ ounces) tomatoes in puree
- 1 cup chicken broth
- ½ cup dry white wine
- ¼ teaspoon dried sage, crumbled
- 1 cup frozen peas

1. In 12-inch skillet, cook bacon over medium-high heat until browned. With slotted spoon, transfer bacon to paper towels to drain; reserve.

2. Pat veal dry with paper towels. Sprinkle chops with salt and pepper. Cook chops in drippings in skillet over medium-high heat until browned, about 5 minutes per side. Transfer veal to plate.

3. Reduce heat to medium. Add onion to skillet and cook, stirring occasionally, until lightly browned, about 5 minutes. Stir in garlic and cook 1 minute longer. Stir in tomatoes with their puree, broth, wine, and sage and heat to boiling, breaking up tomatoes with side of spoon.

4. Return chops to skillet; cover and simmer over medium-low heat until veal is tender, about 45 minutes. Transfer veal to platter; keep warm. Add peas to skillet and cook 5 minutes. To serve, cut veal into serving portions, spoon sauce over veal, and sprinkle bacon on top. Makes 4 main-dish servings.

Each serving: About 289 calories, 35g protein, 16g carbohydrate, 9g total fat (3g saturated), 139mg cholesterol, 782mg sodium.

OSSO BUCO WITH GREMOLATA

··

This aromatic recipe from northern Italy is especially wonderful served with Creamy Polenta (page 304).

Prep: 40 minutes   Bake: 2 hours

- 4 meaty veal shank cross cuts (osso buco), each about 2 inches thick (1 pound each)
- ½ teaspoon salt
- ¼ teaspoon ground black pepper
- 1 tablespoon olive oil
- 2 medium onions, chopped
- 3 carrots, peeled and chopped
- 2 stalks celery, chopped
- 4 garlic cloves, finely chopped
- 1 can (14½ to 16 ounces) tomatoes in puree
- 1 cup dry white wine
- 1 cup chicken broth
- 1 bay leaf
- 2 tablespoons chopped fresh parsley
- ½ teaspoon freshly grated lemon peel

1. Preheat oven to 350°F. Sprinkle shanks with salt and pepper. In nonreactive 5-quart Dutch oven, heat oil over medium-high heat until very hot. Add shanks and cook until browned, about 10 minutes, transferring shanks to plate as they are browned.

2. Add onions to Dutch oven and cook over medium heat, stirring occasionally, until slightly browned, about 5 minutes. Add carrots, celery, and three-fourths of garlic; cook 2 minutes longer.

3. Return veal to Dutch oven. Stir in tomatoes with their puree, wine, broth, and bay leaf; heat to boiling over high heat. Cover and place in oven. Bake until veal is tender when pierced with fork, about 2 hours.

4. Meanwhile, prepare gremolata: In small bowl, mix parsley, lemon peel, and remaining garlic. Cover and refrigerate until ready to serve.

5. Transfer veal to platter. Heat sauce in Dutch oven to boiling over high heat; boil until it has reduced to 4 cups, about 10 minutes. Pour sauce over veal and sprinkle with gremolata. Makes 4 main-dish servings.

Each serving: About 374 calories, 53g protein, 20g carbohydrate, 8g total fat (2g saturated), 183mg cholesterol, 874mg sodium.

VEAL STEW WITH GREMOLATA

Use **2½ pounds boneless veal shoulder,** cut into 1½-inch pieces. Proceed as in Step 1 but brown veal in batches, transferring meat to bowl as it is browned. Continue as directed but bake only 1 hour 30 minutes. Makes 6 main-dish servings.

VEAL SCALLOPINI MARSALA

··

Simple, elegant, and scrumptious, this quintessential Italian dish takes only minutes to prepare.

Prep: 10 minutes   Cook: 15 minutes

- 1 pound veal cutlets
- ¼ cup all-purpose flour
- ¼ teaspoon salt
- ⅛ teaspoon coarsely ground pepper
- 3 tablespoons butter or margarine
- ½ cup dry Marsala wine
- ½ cup chicken broth
- 1 tablespoon chopped fresh parsley

1. Place cutlets between two sheets of plastic wrap or waxed paper. With meat mallet or rolling pin, pound cutlets to ⅛-inch thickness. Cut cutlets into 3" by 3" pieces. On waxed paper, combine flour, salt, and pepper; coat veal with seasoned flour, shaking off excess.

2. In 10-inch skillet, melt butter over medium-high heat. Cook veal, in batches, until lightly browned, 45 to 60 seconds per side, using tongs to transfer pieces to warm platter as they are browned; keep warm.

3. Add Marsala and broth to veal drippings in pan and cook, stirring until browned bits are loosened from bottom of skillet, until syrupy, 4 to 5 minutes. Pour sauce over veal and sprinkle with parsley. Makes 6 main-dish servings.

Each serving: About 179 calories, 17g protein, 5g carbohydrate, 7g total fat (4g saturated), 75mg cholesterol, 288mg sodium.

VITELLO TONNATO

Serve this delicious cold buffet dish with bowls of roasted red peppers, potato salad, and a variety of olives.

Prep: 20 minutes plus cooling and chilling
Cook: 1 hour 50 minutes

- 1 rolled boneless veal shoulder roast (2³/₄ to 3 pounds), trimmed and tied
- 10 anchovy fillets
- 2 garlic cloves, thinly sliced
- 3 cups water
- 1 can (14¹/₂ ounces) chicken broth or 1³/₄ cups Chicken Broth (page 70)
- 1 cup dry white wine
- 1 medium onion, thinly sliced
- 2 carrots, peeled and thinly sliced
- 1 can (6 ounces) tuna packed in oil, undrained
- ¹/₂ cup mayonnaise
- ¹/₂ cup heavy or whipping cream
- 1 tablespoon fresh lemon juice
- ¹/₂ teaspoon salt
- ¹/₄ teaspoon dried sage
- 2 tablespoons chopped fresh parsley

1. With sharp knife, make slits all over veal. Coarsely chop 2 anchovies; insert chopped anchovies and garlic into slits.

2. In nonreactive 5-quart Dutch oven, combine water, broth, wine, onion, and carrots and heat to boiling over medium heat. Add roast to Dutch oven. Reduce heat; cover and simmer until veal is tender, about 1 hour and 45 minutes.

3. Remove from heat; let veal cool in broth 1 hour, then transfer veal to plate and refrigerate to cool completely. Strain broth, reserving ³/₄ cup; discard remaining broth. Transfer reserved broth to food processor fitted with knife blade. Add tuna, mayonnaise, cream, lemon juice, salt, sage, and remaining 8 anchovies; puree until smooth.

4. Cut veal into thin slices; transfer to deep platter large enough to hold veal in one or two layers. Pour sauce over veal; cover and refrigerate at least 1 hour or up to 24 hours. Serve chilled or at room temperature, sprinkled with parsley. Makes 8 main-dish servings.

Each serving: About 401 calories, 37g protein, 3g carbohydrate, 26g total fat (7g saturated), 172mg cholesterol, 801mg sodium.

WIENER SCHNITZEL

Travelers to Vienna rarely leave without enjoying these thin, tender, breaded veal cutlets.

Prep: 15 minutes   Cook: 20 minutes

- 6 veal cutlets (1¹/₂ pounds)
- 2 large eggs
- 1¹/₃ cups all-purpose flour
- 1 teaspoon salt
- ¹/₂ teaspoon coarsely ground black pepper
- 1¹/₂ cups plain dried bread crumbs
- 4 tablespoons butter or margarine
- 6 anchovy fillets (optional)
- 2 tablespoons capers, drained
- 2 tablespoons chopped fresh parsley
- 2 lemons, each cut into 6 wedges

1. Place cutlets between two sheets of plastic wrap or waxed paper. With meat mallet or rolling pin, pound cutlets to ¹/₈-inch thickness.

2. In pie plate, beat eggs; on waxed paper, combine flour, salt, and pepper. Place bread crumbs on separate sheet of waxed paper. Coat cutlets in seasoned flour, dip in eggs, and then coat evenly with bread crumbs.

3. In 12-inch skillet, melt 2 tablespoons butter over medium-high heat. Add cutlets, a few at a time, and cook until browned, 3 to 4 minutes per side, adding remaining 2 tablespoons butter as needed. Using tongs, transfer cutlets to warm platter as they are browned.

4. To serve, top cutlets with anchovies, if using, and capers; sprinkle with parsley and garnish with lemon wedges. Makes 6 main-dish servings.

Each serving: About 348 calories, 30g protein, 25g carbohydrate, 13g total fat (6g saturated), 180mg cholesterol, 920mg sodium.

SCHNITZEL À LA HOLSTEIN
Prepare Wiener Schnitzel as directed but serve each cutlet topped with **1 fried egg.**

VEAL PARMIGIANA

....

Smothered in marinara sauce and topped with moz-
zarella cheese, this Italian-restaurant favorite is easy to
make at home.

Prep: 30 minutes   Cook: 25 minutes

- 2 cups Marinara Sauce (page 254) or bottled marinara sauce
- 1 cup plain dried bread crumbs
- ½ teaspoon salt
- ⅛ teaspoon ground black pepper
- 1 large egg
- 2 tablespoons water
- 6 veal cutlets (1½ pounds)
- 3 tablespoons butter or margarine
- ¼ cup freshly grated Parmesan cheese
- 4 ounces part-skim mozzarella cheese, shredded (1 cup)

1. Prepare Marinara Sauce, if using.

2. On waxed paper, combine bread crumbs, salt, and pepper. In pie plate, beat egg and water. Dip cutlets in egg mixture, then in bread crumbs; repeat to coat each cutlet twice.

3. In 12-inch skillet, melt butter over medium heat. Add cutlets, a few at a time, and cook until browned, about 5 minutes per side, using tongs to transfer cutlets to platter as they are browned.

4. Return cutlets to skillet. Spoon sauce evenly over cutlets. Sprinkle with Parmesan and top with mozzarella. Reduce heat to low; cover and cook just until cheese has melted, about 5 minutes. Makes 6 main-dish servings.

Each serving: About 367 calories, 35g protein, 19g carbohydrate, 17g total fat (8g saturated), 154mg cholesterol, 913mg sodium.

CHICKEN PARMIGIANA

Substitute **1½ pounds skinless, boneless chicken breast halves** for veal and prepare as directed above.

VEAL PICCATA

....

This piquant dish depends on real dairy butter for its
success. Do not use margarine; the sauce will not
thicken properly.

Prep: 10 minutes   Cook: 15 minutes

- ¼ cup all-purpose flour
- ½ teaspoon salt
- ¼ teaspoon ground black pepper
- 1 pound veal cutlets
- 4 teaspoons olive or vegetable oil
- ⅓ cup dry white wine
- 1 cup chicken broth
- 2 tablespoons fresh lemon juice
- 1 tablespoon butter
- 1 tablespoon chopped fresh flat-leaf parsley

1. Place cutlets between two sheets of plastic wrap or waxed paper. With meat mallet or rolling pin, pound cutlets to ¼-inch thickness. On waxed paper, combine flour, salt, and pepper. Coat cutlets with seasoned flour, shaking off excess.

2. In 12-inch skillet, heat 2 teaspoons oil over medium-high heat until very hot. Add half of cutlets and cook until browned, about 2 minutes. Turn cutlets and cook 1 minute longer. Using tongs, transfer cutlets to platter; keep warm. Repeat with remaining 2 teaspoons oil and remaining veal.

3. Increase heat to high and add wine to skillet, stirring until browned bits are loosened from bottom of skillet. Add broth and heat to boiling; boil until sauce has reduced to ½ cup, 4 to 6 minutes. Stir in lemon juice, butter, and parsley. When butter has melted, pour sauce over veal. Makes 4 main-dish servings.

Each serving: About 226 calories, 26g protein, 7g carbohydrate, 10g total fat (3g saturated), 96mg cholesterol, 643mg sodium.

VEAL WITH TOMATO AND ARUGULA SALAD

....

Crispy veal cutlets topped with a zesty salad offer a mouthwatering combination of contrasting colors, flavors, and textures—perfect for a late supper.

Prep: 20 minutes   Cook: 10 minutes

- 2   teaspoons fresh lemon juice
- 6   tablespoons olive oil
- 1   teaspoon salt
- ¾   teaspoon ground black pepper
- 1   large tomato (12 ounces), coarsely chopped
- 1   cup loosely packed basil leaves
- ¼   cup coarsely chopped red onion
- 1   pound veal cutlets
- 2   large eggs
- ½   cup all-purpose flour
- 1   cup plain dried bread crumbs
- 1   bunch arugula (10 ounces), trimmed

1. In medium bowl, combine lemon juice, 2 tablespoons oil, ½ teaspoon salt, and ¼ teaspoon pepper. Stir in tomato, basil, and onion; set aside.

2. Place cutlets between two sheets of plastic wrap or waxed paper. With meat mallet or rolling pin, pound cutlets to ⅛-inch thickness.

3. In pie plate, beat eggs with remaining ½ teaspoon each salt and pepper. Place flour on waxed paper; place bread crumbs on separate sheet of waxed paper. Coat cutlets in flour, dip in egg mixture, and then coat evenly in bread crumbs.

4. In 12-inch skillet, heat 2 tablespoons oil over medium-high heat until very hot. Add half of cutlets and cook about 3 minutes per side. Using tongs, transfer to platter large enough to hold cutlets in single layer; keep warm. Repeat with remaining 2 tablespoons oil and remaining veal.

5. To serve, add arugula to tomato mixture and toss to combine. Spoon on top of hot veal. Makes 4 main-dish servings.

Each serving: About 538 calories, 35g protein, 39g carbohydrate, 27g total fat (5g saturated), 195mg cholesterol, 939mg sodium.

PORK

From bacon to pork chops, from holiday ham to grilled sausage, there are many delicious ways to enjoy pork. Surprisingly, only one-third of American pork is served fresh: The rest is smoked, salted, cured, or made into tasty sausage.

Modern breeding methods have standardized pork to the degree that the various cuts are no longer graded. Simply check the label for the cut you need. And since pork is slaughtered at an early age, it is naturally tender.

Buying Pork

Look for fresh pork that's pinkish white to grayish pink (the leg and shoulder cuts tend to be darker than the loin cuts). The flesh should be firm to the touch. The amount of marbled fat should be minimal, and any external fat should be firm and white. Cured and smoked pork products, however, are darker in color due to the curing process.

Storing Pork

Fresh pork can be refrigerated, tightly wrapped, for up to two days. Cured and smoked products, if unsliced and sealed in their original packaging, will last for two weeks or longer, but only one week after being opened. Do not store according to the "purchase by" date on the package, as supermarket refrigerators are colder than those at home.

Cooking Pork Safely

Like other meats, today's pork is much leaner than in the past. Recipes used to require pork to be cooked to 170°F to prevent any possible infection from trichinosis, a disease that could be passed to humans through undercooked pork. Not only has trichinosis been eradicated from pork products, but the parasite that carries the disease is killed at 137°F. So for tender, juicy pork it should not be cooked above 160°F. The exception is large cuts like fresh ham, which should be cooked to 170°F. When carved, they will have just a hint of pink at the center (with a deeper pink color near the bone), but the juices will run clear. Cook ground pork just until no trace of pink remains in the center. And to keep pork chops juicy, cook just until the meat is opaque at the bone.

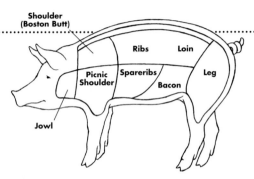

Shoulder
(Boston Butt)

Ribs   Loin

Picnic   Spareribs   Leg
Shoulder

Bacon

Jowl

POPULAR PORK CUTS

Pork shoulder arm picnic

Also called picnic or whole fresh picnic *(roast)*.

Pork shoulder arm roast

Also called pork arm roast *(roast)*.

Pork leg roast, boneless

Also called rolled fresh ham.
Also available bone-in *(roast)*.

Pork loin center rib roast

Contains loin eye muscle and rib bones;
also called pork loin roast and center cut
pork roast. Also available boneless *(roast)*.

Pork loin tenderloin

Very tender and lean; cut into slices for
panfrying or stir-frying. Also called pork
tenderloin *(roast, broil, panfry, grill)*.

Pork spareribs

Contain long rib bones with thin covering
of meat on outside of and between ribs
(roast, bake, braise, broil, grill).

Pork loin country-style ribs

Actually blade end loin chops that have been
split. Also called country-style spareribs
(roast, bake, braise, broil, grill).

Pork loin rib chops

Contain loin eye muscle and backbone.
Also called center cut chops
(braise, panfry, broil, grill).

Pork loin chops

Contain eye muscle and tenderloin separated
by T-shaped bone. Also called loin end chops
(braise, panfry, broil, grill).

Pork loin sirloin chops

From sirloin end of loin. Also called sirloin
pork chops or sirloin pork steaks *(braise,
panfry, broil, grill)*.

Pork loin sirloin cutlets

Boneless, tender slices cut from
sirloin end of loin *(braise, panfry,
broil, grill)*.

Pork loin blade chops

From blade end of loin. Also called pork loin
blade steaks *(braise, panfry, broil, grill)*.

TYPES OF HAM

Smoked ham comes from the hind leg of pork, whereas picnic ham comes from the shoulder. These hams are labeled either "partially cooked" or "fully cooked." In either case, be sure to follow the label's instructions.

Partially cooked ham must be cooked to 155°F before eating.

Fully cooked ham is ready to serve, but its flavor is much improved by heating it to an internal temperature of 130° to 140°F. It is available:
• bone-in: whole, shank, or butt portions
• semiboneless: the aitch and shank bones have been removed; only the leg bone remains
• boneless: rolled and shaped or formed

Spiral-sliced ham is ham that has been cut in one long continuous slice, and is ideal buffet food.

Canned ham is cured but not always smoked.

Boneless smoked pork shoulder (also called boneless pork butt), rolled and wrapped in a mesh stockinette that is removed before serving, is much smaller than ham. It's a great way to serve smoked pork to a small number of people.

Country hams, such as Smithfield and Virginia, are heavily salted and smoked. They should be soaked in cold water for 24 to 36 hours to remove the excess salt, then thoroughly cooked.

Prosciutto and prosciutto de Parma are cured, air-dried ham that have not been smoked. Imported and domestic prosciutto can be purchased in specialty food stores and in many supermarkets.

ROASTING TIMES FOR PORK
(OVEN TEMPERATURE OF 350°F)

Start with meat at refrigerator temperature. Remove roast from oven when it reaches 5°F below desired doneness; temperature will continue to rise 5° to 10° as roast stands.

CUT	WEIGHT	MEAT THERMOMETER READING	APPROXIMATE COOKING TIME (MINUTES PER POUND)
FRESH PORK (WITH BONE)			
Crown roast	6 to 10 pounds	160°F	25 to 30 minutes
Center loin roast	3 to 5 pounds	160°F	25 to 30 minutes
Boneless top loin roast	2 to 4 pounds	160°F	25 to 30 minutes
Whole leg (fresh ham)	10 to 14 pounds	160° to 170°F	25 to 30 minutes
Leg half, shank or butt portion	3 to 5 pounds	160° to 170°F	40 minutes
Boston butt	3 to 6 pounds	160° to 170°F	45 minutes
Tenderloin (roast at 425° to 450°F)	½ to 1½ pounds	160°F	25 to 35 minutes total
SMOKED, COOK BEFORE EATING (HEAT AT 325°F)			
Whole ham	14 to 16 pounds	160°F	15 to 18 minutes
SMOKED FULLY COOKED PORK			
Whole ham	14 to 16 pounds	130° to 140°F	1 to 1¾ hours total
Half ham	6 to 8 pounds	130° to 140°F	1 hour total

FRESH HAM WITH SPICED APPLE GLAZE

....

A whole ham will provide enough meat for your grandest dinner party. A fragrant blend of cinnamon, cloves, and nutmeg—ideal with pork—is rubbed on before roasting. Serve with several kinds of mustard.

Prep: 15 minutes   **Bake: 5 hours**

- 1 whole pork leg (fresh ham, 15 pounds), trimmed
- 2 teaspoons dried thyme
- 2 teaspoons ground cinnamon
- 2 teaspoons salt
- 1 teaspoon coarsely ground black pepper
- ½ teaspoon ground nutmeg
- ½ teaspoon ground cloves
- 1 jar (10 ounces) apple jelly
- ¼ cup balsamic vinegar

1. Preheat oven to 350°F. With knife, remove skin and trim excess fat from pork leg, leaving only a thin layer of fat.

2. In cup, combine thyme, cinnamon, salt, pepper, nutmeg, and cloves. Use to rub on pork. Place pork, fat side up, on rack in large roasting pan (17" by 11½"). Roast pork 3 hours. Cover pork loosely with tent of foil. Continue roasting until meat thermometer inserted into thickest part of pork (not touching bone) registers 150°F, about 1 hour.

3. Meanwhile, in 1-quart saucepan, heat apple jelly and vinegar to boiling over high heat; boil 2 minutes. Set aside.

4. When pork has reached 150°F, remove foil and brush pork with glaze. Continue roasting pork, brushing occasionally with remaining glaze, until meat thermometer registers 165°. (Meat near bone will be slightly pink.) Internal temperature of pork will rise to 170° upon standing.

5. When roast is done, transfer to warm large platter; let stand 20 minutes to set juices for easier carving. Makes 24 main-dish servings.

Each serving: About 298 calories, 38g protein, 6g carbohydrate, 12g total fat (4g saturated), 123mg cholesterol, 232mg sodium.

CARVING A WHOLE HAM

Place cooked ham on a cutting board. Using a carving fork to steady the ham, cut a few slices from the thin side of ham. Turn the ham over. Cut a few slices from the meaty end.

Cut out a small wedge of meat at the shank end of the ham.

Cut even slices along the ham, cutting through to the bone. Release the meat by cutting horizontally along the top of the bone. Transfer slices to a warm platter.

PORK SAUSAGE

Fresh sausage is simply seasoned ground pork that has been stuffed into casings or formed into patties; it must be cooked. **Cured and smoked sausages** sometimes require further cooking. **Andouille,** a spicy smoked sausage, is an important ingredient in Cajun cooking. **Kielbasa** (Polish sausage) is a good substitute for andouille and is delicious grilled. **Chorizo** is available fresh or smoked. It is seasoned with paprika and chiles and is used in Spanish and Mexican cooking. Many **German-style sausages,** such as bratwurst (a combination of pork and veal), are fresh sausages and must be cooked. **Dried and cured sausages,** such as salami and pepperoni, are usually presliced and don't require cooking.

PINEAPPLE-GLAZED HAM

Here's our recipe for this time-honored classic, along with two delicious glaze variations. A spiral-cut ham is an easy alternative.

Prep: 15 minutes   Bake: 2 hours 10 minutes

1   fully cooked smoked bone-in ham (14 pounds)
1   can (20 ounces) crushed pineapple, drained
1   cup packed dark brown sugar
1   tablespoon Dijon mustard

1. Preheat oven to 325°F. With sharp knife, remove skin and trim fat from ham, leaving about ¼-inch-thick layer of fat. Place ham on rack in large roasting pan (17" by 11½"). Bake ham 1 hour 45 minutes.

2. Meanwhile, prepare pineapple glaze: In medium bowl, combine pineapple, brown sugar, and mustard until blended. Remove ham from oven. Brush pineapple mixture on ham. Bake until meat thermometer inserted in thickest part of ham (not touching bone) reaches 135°F, 25 to 30 minutes longer. Internal temperature of ham will rise to 140°F upon standing. Transfer ham to warm platter and let stand 15 minutes to set juices for easier slicing. Makes 20 main-dish servings.

Each serving: About 193 calories, 21g protein, 15g carbohydrate, 5g total fat (2g saturated), 47mg cholesterol, 1,150mg sodium.

MELBA-GLAZED HAM

Prepare ham as directed but in Step 2 in small saucepan, heat ⅔ **cup peach preserves** and ½ **cup red raspberry jelly or jam** until melted and smooth. During the last thirty minutes of roasting time, brush the glaze over the ham two or three times. Makes about 1 cup.

TOMATO AND ONION GLAZED HAM

Prepare ham as directed but in Step 2 in small saucepan, melt **1 tablespoon butter or margarine** over medium heat. Add **2 tablespoons finely chopped onion** and cook until tender. Stir in **1 can (8 ounces) tomato sauce, 2 tablespoons brown sugar,** and **1 teaspoon Worcestershire sauce;** heat to boiling. Reduce heat; simmer until glaze thickens, about 5 minutes. During the last thirty minutes of roasting time, brush the glaze over the ham two or three times. Makes about 1 cup.

MORE WAYS TO ENJOY HAM

Here are just a few ways to use leftovers and to add the rich smoky flavor of ham to your meals.

ZESTY SANDWICH SPREAD
In food processor, grind enough ham to equal 2 cups. Transfer to medium bowl and stir in ½ cup sweet pickle relish, ½ cup finely chopped celery, and 1 package (3 ounces) cream cheese. Serve as sandwich spread or with unsalted crackers.

EGGS BENEDICT
For Sunday brunch, serve thinly sliced ham on a toasted English muffin, topped with poached egg and Hollandaise Sauce (page 502).

HEARTY SOUPS
Use ham bone in split-pea soup, bean soup, or lentil soup.

OPEN-FACED GRILLED SANDWICHES
Brown slices of ham and pineapple in butter or margarine. Place on toasted kaiser roll halves, top with Cheddar cheese, and broil until cheese melts.

FLAVORFUL SAUCE
Add some minced ham to White Sauce (Béchamel, page 502), and serve over chicken or vegetables.

MAIN-DISH SALADS
Toss some chopped ham into macaroni, potato, or rice salad for a tasty main dish. Or add ¼ cup chopped ham to Creamy Potato Salad (page 486).

HAM AND MELON
Arrange thinly sliced ham on thinly sliced melon wedges or other fruit to serve for breakfast, lunch, or as a first course.

HAM BISCUITS
Make biscuits (page 559). Split, spread with butter and top with thinly sliced ham.

PORK ROAST WITH FENNEL AND GARLIC

....

Our flavorful secret is a spice paste. For greater flavor absorption, rub the meat ahead of time and refrigerate for up to twenty-four hours. Bone-in cuts, such as this loin roast, take a little longer to cook than boneless cuts but are the most flavorful.

Prep: 10 minutes   Roast: 1 hour 30 minutes

- 4 garlic cloves, finely chopped
- 2½ teaspoons fennel seeds, crushed
- 1 teaspoon salt
- ½ teaspoon ground black pepper
- 2 teaspoons olive oil
- 1 bone-in pork loin roast (4 pounds), trimmed
- ⅓ cup dry white wine
- ⅔ cup chicken broth

1. Preheat oven to 450°F. In cup, combine garlic, fennel seeds, salt, pepper, and oil to make paste.

2. Place roast in small roasting pan (13" by 9") and rub fennel paste on outside of pork and between bones. Roast pork 45 minutes. Turn oven control to 350°F, cover meat loosely with tent of foil, and roast until meat thermometer inserted in thickest part of roast (not touching bone) reaches 155°F, about 45 minutes longer. Internal temperature of meat will rise to 160°F upon standing. When roast is done, transfer to warm platter and let stand 15 minutes to set juices for easier carving.

3. Meanwhile, add wine to roasting pan and heat to boiling over high heat, stirring until browned bits are loosened from bottom of pan. Add broth and heat to boiling. Remove from heat; skim and discard fat. Serve sauce with roast. Makes 8 main-dish servings.

Each serving: About 270 calories, 35g protein, 1g carbohydrate, 13g total fat (4g saturated), 99mg cholesterol, 440mg sodium.

PORK ROAST WITH FRESH SAGE
Prepare as above but substitute ¼ **cup fresh parsley, 2 tablespoons chopped fresh sage,** and ½ **teaspoon dried thyme** for fennel seeds.

FRENCH ROAST PORK

....

The spice mixture rubbed onto the pork is a classic French combination of warm spices known as **quatre épices,** *which means "four spices." We've taken the liberty of adding some thyme for a savory note. Once the pork begins roasting, the aroma of warm spices will fill your kitchen.*

Prep: 5 minutes   Roast: 1 hour

- 1 boneless pork loin roast (2 pounds), trimmed
- 1 teaspoon salt
- ¾ teaspoon dried thyme
- ½ teaspoon ground cinnamon
- ½ teaspoon ground black pepper
- ⅛ teaspoon ground nutmeg
- ⅛ teaspoon ground cloves
- ⅓ cup dry white wine
- ⅔ cup chicken broth
  applesauce

1. Preheat oven to 350°F. Pat pork dry with paper towels.

2. In cup, combine salt, thyme, cinnamon, pepper, nutmeg, and cloves. Use to rub on pork.

3. Place roast on rack in small roasting pan (13" by 9"). Roast pork until meat thermometer inserted in center of roast reaches 155°F, about 1 hour. Internal temperature of meat will rise to 160°F upon standing.

4. When roast is done, transfer to warm platter and let stand 15 minutes to set juices for easier slicing.

5. Meanwhile, add wine to roasting pan and heat to boiling over high heat, stirring until browned bits are loosened from bottom of pan. Add broth and heat to boiling; boil 2 minutes. Remove from heat; skim and discard fat. Serve pan juices and applesauce with pork. Makes 6 main-dish servings.

Each serving: About 254 calories, 33g protein, 1g carbohydrate, 11g total fat (4g saturated), 93mg cholesterol, 561mg sodium.

SPICE-BRINED PORK LOIN

Brining in a blend of kosher salt, sugar, and spices infuses this pork with wonderful flavor and keeps it tender and juicy. Allow the pork to soak in the brine for 18 to 24 hours before roasting.

Prep: 20 minutes plus marinating 18 to 24 hours
Roast: 1 hour

- 2 cups cold water
- ¼ cup sugar
- ¼ cup kosher salt
- 2 tablespoons coriander seeds
- 2 tablespoons cracked black pepper
- 2 tablespoons fennel seeds
- 2 tablespoons cumin seeds
   peel from 1 navel orange, white pith removed
- 3 cups ice
- 1 boneless pork loin roast (about 3 pounds), trimmed
- 4 garlic cloves, crushed with side of chef's knife

1. In 2-quart saucepan, heat 1 cup water, sugar, salt, coriander, pepper, fennel, cumin, and orange peel to boiling over high heat. Reduce heat to low; simmer 2 minutes. Remove saucepan from heat; stir in ice until almost melted. Stir in remaining cup water.

2. Place pork in large zip-tight plastic bag. Add garlic and brine; seal bag, pressing out excess air. Place bag in large bowl or small roasting pan and refrigerate 18 to 24 hours.

3. When ready to cook pork, preheat oven to 400°F. Remove pork from bag; discard brine (it's alright if some spices stick to pork). Place roast on rack in medium roasting pan (14" by 10"). Roast pork 1 hour to 1 hour 15 minutes or until meat thermometer inserted into center of roast reaches 150°F. Internal temperature of meat will rise to 160°F upon standing. Transfer pork to cutting board and let stand 10 minutes to allow juices to set for easier slicing.

Each serving: About 175 calories, 24g protein, 1g carbohydrate, 8g total fat (3g saturated), 67mg cholesterol, 445mg sodium.

Spice-Brined Pork Loin

COOKING PORK

Since pork is usually tender, many cuts are perfectly suitable for these cooking methods.

BROILING, GRILLING, PANFRYING AND STIR-FRYING: Many lean cuts lend themselves to these methods.
Best Bets: Tenderloin, loin, rib and loin chops, sirloin chops and cutlets, blade chops, and sausages. Spareribs are good broiled or grilled if first precooked.
BRAISING AND STEWING: Many cuts of pork stand up well to long, slow cooking in liquid.
Best Bets: Sirloin chops, blade chops, shoulder, spareribs and pork cubes for stew.
ROASTING: Use tender cuts from the loin.
Best Bets: Rib crown roast, shoulder arm roast, arm picnic roast, fresh ham, whole boneless tenderloin, bone-in and boneless loin, spareribs, and country-style ribs.

PORK LOIN WITH LEMON AND CORIANDER

···

Brining the pork loin allows you a lot of leeway in how far ahead you start your recipe—anywhere from 18 to 48 hours. For the best flavor and texture, do not leave the meat in the brine longer.

Prep: 20 minutes plus 18 to 48 hours brining
Cook: 60 minutes

- 3 lemons
- ½ cup kosher salt
- ½ cup sugar
- 3 tablespoons coriander seeds
- 3 tablespoons cracked black peppercorns
- 3 cloves garlic, crushed with side of chef's knife
- 3 cups water
- 4 cups ice cubes
- 1 boneless pork loin roast (5 pounds), trimmed of fat
   cilantro sprigs for garnish

1. Prepare brine: From 2 lemons, with vegetable peeler, remove peel in ¾-inch-wide strips. In 4-quart saucepan, heat lemon peel, salt, sugar, coriander, pepper, garlic, and 2 cups water to boiling on high. Reduce heat to medium-low and simmer 3 minutes, stirring to make sure salt and sugar dissolve. Remove saucepan from heat, add ice cubes, and stir until ice cubes almost melt; stir in remaining 1 cup water.

2. Place pork in very large (2- to 2½-gallon) zip-tight plastic bag with brine and seal, pressing out excess air. (If necessary, cut pork loin crosswise in half and use one or two 1-gallon bags.) Place bag in bowl, making sure that pork is completely covered with brine, and refrigerate pork at least 18 or up to 48 hours.

3. When ready to cook pork, preheat oven to 400°F. Remove pork from brine and place fat side up on rack in large roasting pan (17" by 11½"). Drain brine through sieve, discarding liquid. Press spices from sieve onto top of pork; discard lemon peel and garlic.

Pork Loin with Lemon and Coriander

4. Roast pork 55 to 65 minutes (pork loin will vary in length and thickness, which can affect cooking time; begin to check the pork's internal temperature at 50 minutes) or until instant-read thermometer reaches 150°F (internal temperature will rise 5°F to 10°F upon standing). Transfer pork to large platter; cover and set aside at least 10 minutes to allow juices to set for easier slicing. Cut remaining lemon into wedges; use to garnish platter with cilantro sprigs. Makes 16 main-dish servings.

Each serving: About 200 calories, 27g protein, 2g carbohydrate, 9g total fat (3g saturated), 1g fiber, 76 mg cholesterol, 425 mg sodium.

CARIBBEAN PORK ROAST

....

The seasonings that give this dish its Caribbean flavor are similar to those used in jerk cooking. The piquant sauce would also go well with grilled chicken or fish.

Prep: 10 minutes   Roast: 1 hour 20 minutes

- 1 boneless pork shoulder blade roast (fresh pork butt, 2½ pounds), trimmed
- 1½ teaspoons salt
- 1¼ teaspoons sugar
- ¾ teaspoon ground ginger
- ½ teaspoon ground allspice
- ½ teaspoon ground black pepper
- 3 teaspoons Dijon mustard
- ⅔ cup mango chutney, chopped
- 6 tablespoons fresh lime juice
- 2 tablespoons water

1. Preheat oven to 425°F. Using sharp knife, cut roast lengthwise almost in half, being careful not to cut all the way through. Open and spread flat like a book. In cup, combine salt, sugar, ginger, allspice, and pepper. Brush cut side of pork with 2 teaspoons mustard and sprinkle with half of seasoning mixture. Close pork "book" and rub remaining seasoning mixture on outside of pork. Tie roast with string at 1-inch intervals.

2. Place roast on rack in small roasting pan (13" by 9"). Roast pork 1 hour. Turn oven control to 350°F and roast until meat thermometer inserted in center of roast reaches 155°F, about 20 minutes longer. Internal temperature of meat will rise to 160°F upon standing. Let stand 10 minutes to set juices for easier slicing.

3. Meanwhile, in small bowl, combine chutney, lime juice, water, and remaining 1 teaspoon mustard. Serve sauce with sliced pork. Makes 6 main-dish servings.

Each serving: About 417 calories, 35g protein, 28g carbohydrate, 17g total fat (6g saturated), 124mg cholesterol, 1,050mg sodium.

OVEN-BARBECUED SPARERIBS

....

These sweet and sticky ribs are worth getting your fingers dirty for! Nevertheless, keep the napkins handy.

Prep: 10 minutes   Roast: 1 hour 30 minutes

- 6 pounds pork spareribs, cut into 1-rib portions
- 1 can (6 ounces) tomato paste
- ¼ cup packed brown sugar
- ½ cup water
- ¼ cup honey
- ¼ cup cider vinegar
- 2 tablespoons vegetable oil
- 1 tablespoon grated onion
- 2 teaspoons chili powder
- 2 teaspoons salt

1. Preheat oven to 325°F. Arrange spareribs in single layer in large roasting pan (17" by 11½"). Roast spareribs 1 hour.

2. Meanwhile, prepare glaze: In medium bowl, combine tomato paste with brown sugar, water, honey, vinegar, oil, onion, chili powder, and salt until well blended.

3. Brush ribs with glaze. Continue roasting ribs, brushing frequently with glaze, until ribs are tender, about 30 minutes longer. Makes 6 main-dish servings.

Each serving: About 849 calories, 53g protein, 27g carbohydrate, 59g total fat (20g saturated), 214mg cholesterol, 1,178mg sodium.

Caribbean Pork Roast

MEXICAN-STYLE SPARERIBS

....

A heady blend of tequila, orange juice, lime juice, and jalapeño pepper gives these pork ribs their personality. If you wish, the ribs can be marinated overnight.

Prep: 15 minutes   Roast: 1 hour 50 minutes

- 1 cup firmly packed fresh cilantro leaves and stems
- ½ small onion, thinly sliced
- 4 garlic cloves, crushed with garlic press
- 1 pickled jalapeño chile
- ½ cup fresh lime juice
- ¼ cup fresh orange juice
- ¼ cup tequila
- 1 tablespoon olive oil
- 2 tablespoons sugar
- ½ teaspoon dried oregano
- 3 pounds pork spareribs

1. Preheat oven to 350°F.

2. In blender, combine cilantro, onion, garlic, pickled jalapeño, lime and orange juices, tequila, oil, sugar, and oregano and puree until smooth.

3. Place spareribs in nonreactive roasting pan just large enough to hold them in single layer. Pour cilantro mixture over ribs, turning to coat well. Roast, turning ribs twice, 1 hour 30 minutes. Turn oven control to 450°F and roast ribs until very tender and richly colored, about 20 minutes longer.

4. Transfer ribs to warm platter. Skim and discard fat from sauce remaining in pan and spoon sauce over ribs. Makes 4 main-dish servings.

Each serving: About 610 calories, 40g protein, 13g carbohydrate, 44g total fat (15g saturated), 161mg cholesterol, 183mg sodium.

PULLED PORK BARBECUE

....

This easy indoor pork barbecue is so tender it can be pulled apart. For authentic smoky flavor, brown the pork on the grill.

Prep: 10 minutes plus cooling
Cook: 2 hours 45 minutes

- 3 pounds boneless pork shoulder blade roast, trimmed and tied
- ½ teaspoon salt
- ¼ teaspoon ground black pepper
- 1 tablespoon vegetable oil
- 2 cups water
- 1 cup ketchup
- ¼ cup distilled white vinegar
- ¼ cup Worcestershire sauce
- ⅓ cup packed brown sugar
- 1 tablespoon dry mustard
- ¼ to ½ teaspoon crushed red pepper
- 10 hamburger buns, split

1. Pat pork dry with paper towels. Sprinkle roast with salt and pepper. In nonreactive 5-quart Dutch oven, heat oil over medium-high heat until very hot. Add roast and cook until browned, about 5 minutes. Transfer pork to plate; discard drippings from pan.

2. Combine water, ketchup, vinegar, Worcestershire, brown sugar, dry mustard, and crushed red pepper in Dutch oven. Add pork and heat to boiling over high heat. Reduce heat; cover and simmer, turning roast every 30 minutes, 2 hours 30 minutes.

3. Transfer roast to plate and cool. Boil pot liquid until it has reduced and thickened, about 5 minutes.

4. When roast is cool enough to handle, discard strings. Separate meat into chunks, removing as much fat as possible. With hands or fork, shred meat into bite-size pieces. Return pork to Dutch oven, stirring; heat through. Serve pulled pork on hamburger buns. Makes 10 main-dish servings.

Each serving: About 408 calories, 31g protein, 37g carbohydrate, 15g total fat (4g saturated), 93mg cholesterol, 806mg sodium.

ORANGE-GLAZED PORK ROLLS

....

When you want smoky pork flavor but don't want to serve ham, roast a smoked pork shoulder roll. Its neat shape makes for easy serving, so it's no trouble to prepare several.

Prep: 5 minutes   Cook/Bake: 1 hour 50 minutes

- 2   smoked pork shoulder rolls (3 pounds each)
- ¼   teaspoon whole black peppercorns
- 1   bay leaf
- 1   jar (10 to 12 ounces) orange marmalade
- 2   tablespoons bottled white horseradish

1. Remove stockinette casing (if any) from pork rolls, if directed on label. In 8-quart saucepot, place shoulder rolls, peppercorns, bay leaf, and enough *water* to cover meat; heat to boiling over high heat. Reduce heat; cover and simmer until pork rolls are tender, about 1 hour 30 minutes.

2. Preheat oven to 350°F. In small bowl, combine orange marmalade and horseradish.

3. When shoulder rolls are done, arrange in 13" by 9" baking pan; bake, brushing occasionally with marmalade mixture, 20 minutes.

4. To serve, cut rolls into slices and arrange on warm platter. Makes 12 main-dish servings.

Each serving: About 605 calories, 33g protein, 18g carbohydrate, 44g total fat (16g saturated), 126mg cholesterol, 1,847mg sodium.

BREADED PORK TENDERLOIN

....

This recipe shows just how quickly pork tenderloin can be transformed into a delicious meal. Serve with your favorite salsa or with lemon wedges.

Prep: 20 minutes   Cook: 10 minutes

- 1   pork tenderloin (12 ounces), trimmed
- 1   large egg
- 2   tablespoons water
- ½   teaspoon salt
- ¼   teaspoon dried rosemary, crumbled
- ¾   cup plain dried bread crumbs
- 3   tablespoons vegetable oil

1. Using sharp knife, cut tenderloin lengthwise almost in half, being careful not to cut all the way through. Open and spread flat like a book. Place pork between two sheets of plastic wrap or waxed paper. With meat mallet or rolling pin, pound pork to ¼-inch thickness; cut crosswise into 4 equal pieces.

2. In pie plate, with fork, lightly beat egg, water, salt, and rosemary. Place bread crumbs on waxed paper. Using tongs, dip pork in egg mixture, then in bread crumbs. Repeat to coat each piece of pork twice.

3. In 12-inch skillet, heat oil over medium-high heat until very hot. Add pork and cook until browned and cooked through, about 5 minutes per side. Makes 4 main-dish servings.

Each serving: About 291 calories, 22g protein, 15g carbohydrate, 15g total fat (3g saturated), 108mg cholesterol, 522mg sodium.

WHAT ELSE CAN IT DO?
ZIP-TIGHT BAGS

————————

These sturdy bags, with their tight self-seals and multiple sizes (from snack to 2½ gallons), can be used for much more than mere storage.

Here, four new roles:

• Brine chicken, small turkeys, or big cuts of meat in a flavorful liquid, like Pork Loin with Lemon and Coriander, page 131.

• Crush whole spices like coriander, fennel, or cumin for a dry rub; or graham crackers for a crumb crust. Place in the bag, press out the air, seal, place on a solid, sturdy surface, and pound with a heavy flat-bottomed pan or rolling pin.

• Pour batter for pancakes or waffles with no mess. Fill a bag with pancake or waffle batter. When ready to cook, open the zipper about ½ inch and pour out first batch onto hot griddle. Reseal until ready to make more.

• Pipe ornamental icing on holiday cookies, or drizzle melted chocolate on desserts for a festive garnish. Add icing or chocolate to bag; cut a small opening in one corner and gently squeeze.

CHOUCROUTE GARNI

For sauerkraut lovers! Serve this filling, homey dish, best made during the cold winter months, with boiled potatoes, a pot of good-quality mustard, and a loaf of crusty bread.

Prep: 20 minutes   Cook: 50 minutes

- 4 slices bacon, cut into 1-inch pieces
- ¼ cup water
- 1 large onion (12 ounces), thinly sliced
- 2 McIntosh apples, each peeled, cut into quarters, and thinly sliced
- 2 bags (16 ounces each) sauerkraut, rinsed and drained
- 1½ cups fruity white wine, such as riesling
- 6 juniper berries, crushed
- 1 bay leaf
- 6 smoked pork chops, ½ inch thick (4 ounces each)
- 1 pound kielbasa (smoked Polish sausage), cut into 1½-inch pieces

1. In nonreactive 5-quart Dutch oven, combine bacon and water; cook over medium-low heat until bacon is lightly crisped, about 4 minutes. Add onion and cook, stirring frequently, until onion is tender and golden, about 7 minutes.

2. Add apples and cook until tender, about 3 minutes. Stir in sauerkraut, wine, juniper berries, and bay leaf and heat to boiling. Reduce heat; cover and simmer 15 minutes.

3. Nestle pork chops and kielbasa into cabbage mixture; cover and cook until pork is heated through and sauerkraut is tender, about 20 minutes. Discard bay leaf and serve. Makes 6 main-dish servings.

Each serving: About 524 calories, 27g protein, 19g carbohydrate, 37g total fat (13g saturated), 106mg cholesterol, 3,151mg sodium.

Choucroute Garni

POLENTA AND SAUSAGE CASSEROLE

....

Layers of creamy polenta, cheese, and a tomato-sausage sauce make this a terrific casserole for a potluck party, buffet, or brunch.

Prep: 1 hour   Bake: 35 minutes

- 8 ounces sweet Italian-sausage links, casings removed
- 8 ounces hot Italian-sausage links, casings removed
- 1 tablespoon olive oil
- 1 large onion (12 ounces), chopped
- 1 large stalk celery, chopped
- 1 carrot, peeled and chopped
- 1 can (28 ounces) plum tomatoes in puree
- 2 cups yellow cornmeal
- 1 can (14½ ounces) chicken broth or 1¾ cups Chicken Broth (page 70)
- ¾ teaspoon salt
- 4½ cups boiling water
- ½ cup freshly grated Parmesan cheese
- 8 ounces Fontina or mozzarella cheese, shredded (2 cups)

1. Prepare tomato-sausage sauce: In nonreactive 5-quart Dutch oven, cook sweet and hot sausage meat over medium-high heat, breaking up meat with side of spoon, until browned. With slotted spoon, transfer meat to bowl. Discard fat from Dutch oven.

2. Add oil to Dutch oven. Add onion, celery, and carrot and cook over medium-high heat until browned. Stir in sausage and tomatoes with their puree, breaking up tomatoes with side of spoon. Heat to boiling over high heat. Reduce heat; cover and simmer 10 minutes. Remove cover and simmer 10 minutes longer.

3. Preheat oven to 350°F. Prepare polenta: In 4-quart saucepan with wire whisk, mix cornmeal, broth, and salt. Over medium-high heat, add boiling water and cook, whisking constantly, until mixture has thickened, about 5 minutes. Whisk in Parmesan.

4. Grease 13" by 9" baking dish. Evenly spread half of polenta mixture in prepared dish; top with half of tomato-sausage sauce, then half of Fontina. Repeat with remaining polenta mixture and sauce.

5. Bake casserole 15 minutes. Sprinkle with remaining Fontina; bake until mixture is bubbling and cheese is golden, about 20 minutes longer. Let stand 15 minutes for easier serving. Makes 8 main-dish servings.

Each serving: About 466 calories, 23g protein, 38g carbohydrate, 25g total fat (11g saturated), 70mg cholesterol, 1,323mg sodium.

BALSAMIC-GLAZED PORK CHOPS

....

Balsamic vinegar is very versatile; it's not just for salad dressing. Here it's turned into a sweet-tart sauce just made for tender pork.

Prep: 5 minutes   Cook: 10 minutes

- 8 boneless pork loin chops, ½ inch thick (3 ounces each), trimmed
- ½ teaspoon salt
- ¼ teaspoon ground black pepper
- 1 tablespoon olive oil
- 3 tablespoons finely chopped shallot or onion
- ⅓ cup balsamic vinegar
- ¼ cup packed brown sugar

1. Pat pork dry with paper towels. Sprinkle chops with salt and pepper. In 12-inch skillet, heat oil over medium-high heat until hot. Cook pork 4 minutes on one side; turn and cook 3 minutes on second side. Transfer pork to platter; keep warm.

2. Increase heat to high. Stir shallot into pan juices; cook 1 minute. Stir in vinegar and sugar and cook 1 minute longer. Pour sauce over pork. Makes 4 main-dish servings.

Each serving: About 275 calories, 28g protein, 15g carbohydrate, 11g total fat (3g saturated), 76mg cholesterol, 364mg sodium.

STUFFED PORK CHOPS

The aroma of this dish will remind you of childhood trips to your grandparents for Sunday supper. If you don't have rye bread for the stuffing, use whole wheat.

Prep: 20 minutes   Cook: 30 minutes

- 4 teaspoons vegetable oil
- 1 small onion, chopped
- 1 Golden Delicious apple, peeled, cored, and chopped
- ½ teaspoon caraway seeds
   pinch dried thyme
- 2 slices rye bread, toasted and cut into ¼-inch pieces
- 2 tablespoons plus ½ cup chicken broth
- 1 tablespoon spicy brown mustard
- 4 pork loin chops, 1 inch thick (8 ounces each)
- ¼ teaspoon salt

1. In 10-inch skillet, heat 2 teaspoons oil over medium heat. Add onion and cook until tender, about 5 minutes. Add apple, caraway seeds, and thyme and cook 3 minutes longer. Transfer apple mixture to medium bowl. Wipe skillet clean.

2. Stir bread pieces, 2 tablespoons broth, and mustard into apple mixture. Pat pork dry with paper towels. Holding knife parallel to surface, cut a horizontal pocket in each chop. Stuff apple mixture into pocket of each chop and secure with toothpicks. Sprinkle with salt.

3. In 12-inch skillet, heat remaining 2 teaspoons oil over medium heat until hot. Cook chops until they just lose their pink color throughout, about 7 minutes per side. Transfer chops to warm platter.

4. Increase heat to high. Add remaining ½ cup broth to skillet and heat to boiling, stirring to loosen brown bits from bottom of pan. Boil broth until reduced to ¼ cup, 3 to 5 minutes. Pour sauce over chops. Makes 4 main-dish servings.

Each serving: About 367 calories, 39g protein, 15g carbohydrate, 15g total fat (4g saturated), 102mg cholesterol, 540mg sodium.

ITALIAN SAUSAGE AND BROCCOLI RABE

In this rustic classic, sweet sausage balances the pleasant bite of broccoli rabe. Fans of this bitter green may want to double the amount used.

Prep: 5 minutes   Cook: 30 minutes

- 1 bunch broccoli rabe (1 pound), tough ends trimmed
- 2 teaspoons salt
- 1 pound sweet Italian-sausage links, pricked with fork
- ¼ cup water
- 1 tablespoon olive oil
- 1 large garlic clove, finely chopped
- ⅛ teaspoon crushed red pepper

1. In 5-quart saucepot, heat *4 quarts water* to boiling. Add broccoli rabe and salt. Cook just until stems are tender, about 5 minutes; drain. When cool enough to handle, coarsely chop broccoli rabe.

2. Meanwhile, in 10-inch skillet, heat sausage links and water to boiling over medium heat. Cover and cook 5 minutes. Remove cover and cook, turning sausages frequently, until water has evaporated and sausages are well browned, about 20 minutes longer. Using tongs, transfer sausages to paper towels to drain; cut each sausage on diagonal in half.

3. Discard fat from skillet but do not wipe clean. To drippings in skillet, add oil, garlic, and crushed red pepper. Cook, stirring, until very fragrant, about 15 seconds. Add broccoli rabe and cook, stirring, until well coated and heated through, about 2 minutes. Stir in sausages and remove from heat. Makes 4 main-dish servings.

Each serving: About 325 calories, 19g protein, 6g carbohydrate, 25g total fat (8g saturated), 65mg cholesterol, 1,079mg sodium.

LAMB

The unique, relatively mild flavor of lamb calls for bold seasonings like garlic, rosemary, and wine or intriguing combinations of assertive, exotic spices and sweet fruits.

Buying Lamb

Americans generally prefer the milder taste of young lamb, and the good news is that most supermarket lamb is from animals six to twelve months old. Baby lamb (milk-fed lamb) is less than two months old and has a delicate flavor and pale pink color. Even though it is raised year-round, so-called spring lamb (Easter lamb) comes from slightly older sheep up to five months old. Both of these younger lambs are specialty items that are most easily found during the holiday season at ethnic butchers. Look for lamb from Australia and New Zealand in supermarkets and in butcher shops. The cuts are smaller than those of American lamb, since they come from smaller—not younger—animals, but you can count on the meat to be tender and flavorful.

When shopping for lamb, look for meat that is pinkish red. Darker meat indicates an older animal, and it will have a stronger flavor. The fat should look white, firm, and waxy. The bones should be porous and unsplintered, with a reddish tinge at the cut end. If you buy a large cut of lamb, such as a whole leg, be sure the fell (the thin membrane covering the fat) has been removed. If necessary, peel it off with the help of a sharp knife. In any case, the fat should be trimmed away so only a thin covering remains.

Storing Lamb

Lamb chops, stew meat, and roasts can be stored for up to two days in the refrigerator. Ground lamb is quite perishable, so it should be used within one day of purchase.

ROASTING TIMES FOR LAMB
(OVEN TEMPERATURE OF 350°F)

Start with meat at refrigerator temperature. Remove roast from oven when it reaches 5°F below desired doneness; the internal temperature will continue to rise as it stands.

| | | APPROXIMATE COOKING TIME (MINUTES PER POUND) | | |
| | | MEDIUM-RARE | MEDIUM | WELL-DONE |
CUT	WEIGHT	(135°-140°F)	(145°-155°F)	(OVER 160°F)
Whole leg	5 to 7 pounds	15 minutes	15 to 18 minutes	20 minutes
	7 to 9 pounds	20 minutes	20 to 23 minutes	25 minutes
Leg shank half	3 to 4 pounds	20 to 25 minutes	30 minutes	35 to 40 minutes
Leg sirloin half	3 to 4 pounds	20 to 23 minutes	25 to 30 minutes	35 minutes
Leg roast (boneless)	4 to 7 pounds	15 to 18 minutes	20 to 23 minutes	25 minutes
Rib roast or rack (roast at 375°F)	1½ to 2½ pounds	20 to 25 minutes	30 minutes	35 minutes
Crown roast, unstuffed (roast at 375°F)	2 to 3 pounds	20 minutes	25 minutes	30 minutes
Shoulder roast	4 to 6 pounds	20 minutes	25 minutes	30 minutes
Shoulder roast (boneless)	3½ to 6 pounds	35 minutes	40 minutes	45 minutes

POPULAR LAMB CUTS

Lamb rib roast

Elegant and expensive. Also called rack of lamb *(roast)*.

Lamb shoulder neck slices

Cross cuts of neck. Also called neck of lamb and bone-in lamb for stew (braise).

Lamb rib chops

Also called rack lamb chops *(broil, grill, panfry, roast, bake)*.

Lamb loin chops

Meaty area has both rib-eye muscle and tenderloin *(broil, grill, panfry)*.

Lamb leg sirloin chop

Includes three different muscles. Also called lamb sirloin steak *(broil, grill, panfry)*.

Lamb shoulder arm chops

Cut from arm portion of shoulder. Also called arm cut chops, round bone chops, or shoulder chops *(braise, broil, grill)*.

Lamb shoulder blade chops

From blade portion of the shoulder. Also called lamb shoulder chops or blade cut chops *(braise, broil, grill, panfry)*.

Lamb shanks

Cut from arm of shoulder *(braise)*.

Lamb leg whole

Also called leg of lamb; available bone-in and boneless *(roast)*.

Lamb leg shank half

Sirloin half removed. Lower half of leg and round leg bone included *(roast)*.

Lamb breast riblets

Cut from breast, contain long and narrow ribs with layers of meat and fat *(braise)*.

Lamb breast

Also called breast of lamb. Part of forequarter, containing row of ribs *(braise, roast)*.

ROAST RACK OF LAMB

....

When you feel like showing off, few dishes do it more elegantly than a classic rack of lamb. For easy carving, ask the butcher to loosen the backbone from the ribs.

Prep: 10 minutes   Roast: 20 to 25 minutes

- 2 teaspoons dried rosemary, crumbled
- 2 teaspoons olive oil
- ½ teaspoon dried thyme
- 1 large garlic clove, minced
- ½ teaspoon salt
- ¼ teaspoon freshly ground black pepper
- 2 lamb rib roasts (racks of lamb), 8 ribs each, (1¼ pounds each), trimmed

1. Preheat oven to 450°F. In a small cup, combine rosemary, oil, thyme, garlic, salt, and pepper to form a paste. Rub paste on tops (fat side) of racks. Place racks, rub side up, in a large shallow roasting pan.

2. Roast lamb until meat thermometer inserted in center of lamb (not touching bone) reaches 135° to 140°F for medium-rare, 20 to 25 minutes. Transfer to a cutting board and let stand 10 minutes to set juices. Cut between ribs to serve. Makes 4 main-dish servings.

Each serving: About 675 calories, 31g protein, 1g carbohydrate, 60g total fat (25g saturated), 145mg cholesterol, 379mg sodium.

CRUMB-TOPPED ROAST RACK OF LAMB

In small bowl, combine **1 cup fresh bread crumbs (2 slices firm white bread), 1 teaspoon olive oil, ⅛ teaspoon salt** and **⅛ teaspoon black pepper.** Follow directions for roast rack of lamb, rubbing racks with paste. After roasting lamb for 10 minutes, remove from oven. Spread **2 tablespoons Dijon mustard** over tops of racks. Press bread crumb mixture over mustard and pat to stick. Roast lamb to 135° to 140°F for medium-rare, 10 to 15 minutes longer.

CARVING A LEG OF LAMB

Cut a slice from the thin side of the leg so it can lie flat for easier carving; turn the leg cut side down. Holding the meat steady with a carving fork, make a vertical cut to the bone 1 inch from the shank. Holding the knife horizontally, cut along the top of the bone about halfway down its length.

Holding the leg steady by grasping the bone or by inserting a carving fork into the lamb, slice the meat that has been released from the bone. Make a second horizontal cut almost to the end of the leg, then slice the remaining lamb.

Turn the leg over. With the knife blade almost flat and working away from you, cut long slices following the line of the bone.

ROASTED LEG OF LAMB WITH PISTACHIO-MINT CRUST

··

To prevent the nut crust from burning, don't spread it over the roast until after it has cooked for one hour.

Prep: 30 minutes   Roast: 2 hours 15 minutes

- 1 whole bone-in lamb leg (7 pounds), trimmed
- 2 large garlic cloves, sliced
- 1½ teaspoons salt
- 2 tablespoons butter or margarine
- 1 small onion, chopped
- 1½ slices firm white bread, torn into ¼-inch pieces
- ½ cup pistachios, finely chopped
- 2 tablespoons coarsely chopped fresh mint
- ¼ teaspoon coarsely ground black pepper
- ½ cup port wine
- 3 tablespoons all-purpose flour
- 1 can (14½ ounces) chicken broth or 1¾ cups Chicken Broth (page 70)

1. Preheat oven to 325°F. Cut about a dozen ½-inch-long slits in lamb and insert slice of garlic in each. Sprinkle lamb with 1 teaspoon salt. Place lamb, fat side up, on rack in large roasting pan (17" by 11½"). Roast lamb 1 hour.

2. Meanwhile, in 10-inch skillet, melt butter over medium heat. Add onion and cook until lightly browned and tender, about 10 minutes; remove from heat. Stir in bread, pistachios, mint, remaining ½ teaspoon salt, and pepper. After lamb has roasted 1 hour, carefully pat mixture onto lamb.

3. Roast lamb 1 hour 15 to 30 minutes longer, until meat thermometer inserted in thickest part of lamb (not touching bone) reaches 140°F. Internal temperature of meat will rise to 145°F (medium) upon standing. When lamb is done, transfer to warm platter and let stand 15 minutes to set juices for easier carving.

4. Meanwhile, prepare gravy: Remove rack from roasting pan; pour pan drippings into 2-cup measuring cup. Add port to pan, stirring until browned bits are loosened from bottom of pan. Pour into drippings in cup; let stand until fat separates out. Skim 2 tablespoons fat from drippings; return to roasting pan. Discard any remaining fat.

5. With wire whisk, whisk flour into fat in roasting pan over medium-high heat until well blended. Gradually whisk in meat juice and broth and heat to boiling, stirring constantly; boil 1 minute. Pour gravy into gravy boat and serve with lamb. Makes 10 main-dish servings.

Each serving: About 404 calories, 46g protein, 8g carbohydrate, 18g total fat (7g saturated), 144mg cholesterol, 680mg sodium.

Tip: Some Indian markets and specialty stores sell shelled pistachios, or simply shell your own.

ROSEMARY LEG OF LAMB

··

The French often roast lamb that has first been rubbed with a mix of fragrant dried herbs. Here's our version—bon appétit.

Prep: 5 minutes   Roast: 1 hour 45 minutes

- 1 whole bone-in lamb leg (7½ pounds), trimmed
- ½ teaspoon dried rosemary, crumbled
- ½ teaspoon dried thyme, crumbled
- ½ teaspoon salt
- ¼ teaspoon ground black pepper

1. Preheat oven to 450°F. Place lamb in large roasting pan (17" by 11½"). In cup, combine rosemary, thyme, salt, and pepper. Use to rub on lamb.

2. Roast lamb 15 minutes. Turn oven control to 350°F and roast, basting every 15 minutes with pan juices, until meat thermometer inserted in thickest part of lamb (not touching bone) reaches 140°F, 1 hour 30 to 45 minutes longer. Internal temperature of meat will rise to 145°F (medium) upon standing. Or roast until desired doneness.

3. When lamb is done, transfer to cutting board and let stand 15 minutes to set juices for easier carving.

4. Carve lamb into slices and arrange on warm platter. Makes 10 main-dish servings.

Each serving: About 312 calories, 46g protein, 0g carbohydrate, 13g total fat (5g saturated), 145mg cholesterol, 227mg sodium.

MUSTARD-CRUSTED LAMB

·······································

All lamb has a small flap of fat and meat that covers the top of the loin. If the rack you want still has the flap, ask the butcher to cut it off for picture-perfect chops.

Prep: 35 minutes   Cook: 30 minutes

- 1 New Zealand lamb rib roast, or rack of lamb (1 pound), 8 ribs, flap trimmed
- ½ teaspoon salt
- ½ teaspoon ground black pepper
- 3 tablespoons Dijon mustard with seeds
- 2 tablespoons chopped fresh mint or basil leaves
- 4 tablespoons chopped shallots (2 medium)
- ¼ cup panko (Japanese bread crumbs)
- 3 small red potatoes (9 ounces total), each cut into 4 wedges
- 2 tablespoons cold water
- ½ bunch broccoli rabe (8 ounces), tough stem ends trimmed
- 1 teaspoon olive oil
- 3 tablespoons reduced-fat sour cream

1. Preheat oven to 425°F. Place lamb, meat side up, in small roasting pan. Sprinkle lamb with ¼ teaspoon each salt and pepper. In small bowl, stir together mustard, mint, and 2 tablespoons shallots. Reserve 2 tablespoons mustard mixture for sauce; spread remainder on lamb. Pat on panko to coat.

2. Roast lamb in oven 25 to 30 minutes for medium-rare (140°F on meat thermometer) or until desired doneness.

3. Meanwhile, fill a 4-quart saucepan with *water* and bring to boiling over high heat. In microwave-safe medium bowl, combine potatoes and cold water. Cover with vented plastic wrap, and microwave on High 4 minutes or until fork-tender. Drain; toss with ⅛ teaspoon each salt and pepper. Keep warm.

4. Add broccoli rabe to boiling water in saucepan, and cook 3 minutes. Drain well; wipe pan dry. In same saucepan, heat oil and remaining 2 tablespoons shallots over medium-high heat; add broccoli rabe and cook 2 minutes, stirring frequently. Toss with ⅛ teaspoon each salt and pepper. Keep warm.

5. Stir sour cream into reserved mustard mixture. Cut lamb into 2-rib pieces, and place 4 ribs each on 2 dinner plates along with potatoes and broccoli rabe. Serve lamb with sour cream sauce. Makes 2 main-dish servings.

Each serving: About 420 calories, 28g protein, 43g carbohydrate, 15g total fat (5g saturated), 5g fiber, 73mg cholesterol, 825mg sodium.

LAMB STEAK WITH RED PEPPER RELISH

·······································

Lamb steak, an often overlooked cut, is simply a thick crosswise slice of lamb leg that is every bit as delicious as you'd expect.

Prep: 30 minutes   Broil: 10 minutes

- ⅓ cup cider vinegar
- ¼ cup sugar
- 1¼ teaspoons salt
  - pinch dried thyme, crumbled
  - pinch fennel seeds, crushed
- 2 small red peppers, chopped
- 1 medium Golden Delicious apple, peeled, cored, and chopped
- 2 jalapeño chiles, seeded and finely chopped
- 1 center-cut lamb steak, 1 inch thick (1½ pounds), or 8 lamb loin chops, 1 inch thick (4 ounces each)

1. In 2-quart saucepan, combine vinegar, sugar, 1 teaspoon salt, thyme, and fennel seeds; heat to boiling over high heat. Add red peppers, apple, and jalapeños; heat to boiling. Reduce heat and simmer, stirring occasionally, until liquid has evaporated, 15 to 20 minutes. Keep warm.

2. Meanwhile, preheat broiler. Sprinkle lamb with remaining ¼ teaspoon salt. Place lamb on rack in broiling pan. Place pan in broiler at closest position to heat source and broil lamb 5 minutes. Turn lamb and broil 5 minutes longer for medium-rare or until desired doneness. Serve lamb with warm red pepper relish. Makes 4 main-dish servings.

Each serving: About 267 calories, 26g protein, 21g carbohydrate, 9g total fat (3g saturated), 82mg cholesterol, 799mg sodium.

LAMB SHANKS WITH WHITE BEANS AND ROASTED ENDIVE

Lamb shanks, a Mediterranean favorite, are paired with endive that is roasted in the oven at the same time as the lamb for a rich, mellow flavor.

Prep: 1 hour 30 minutes   Bake: 2 hours

White Beans and Lamb Shanks

1	package (16 ounces) dry Great Northern beans
8	small lamb shanks (about 1 pound each)
2½	teaspoons salt
1	teaspoon coarsely ground pepper
2	tablespoons vegetable oil
6	medium garlic cloves, crushed with side of chef's knife
4	carrots, peeled and cut into 1-inch pieces
1	large onion (12 ounces), coarsely chopped
¼	cup all-purpose flour
2	tablespoons tomato paste
2	cups dry white wine
1	can (14 to 14½ ounces) chicken broth or 1¾ cups Chicken Broth (page 70)
2	sprigs fresh rosemary, plus 8 sprigs for garnish

Roasted Endive

1	tablespoon olive oil
½	teaspoon salt
¼	teaspoon coarsely ground pepper
8	medium heads Belgian endive (about 1½ pounds)

1. Prepare white beans: In 4-quart saucepan, combine beans and enough *water* to cover by 2 inches; heat to boiling over high heat. Cook 3 minutes; remove from heat. Cover and set aside until beans are softened, about 1 hour. Drain and rinse beans. (Or, if you prefer, soak beans overnight in cold water. Drain and rinse.)

2. Meanwhile, prepare lamb shanks: Pat shanks dry with paper towels; sprinkle with 1 teaspoon salt and ½ teaspoon pepper. In 8-quart Dutch oven, heat oil over medium-high heat until very hot but not smoking. Add shanks, in batches, and cook, until browned, 12 to 15 minutes, using tongs to transfer shanks to large bowl as they are browned. If necessary, reduce heat to medium before adding second batch of shanks to prevent overbrowning.

3. Preheat oven to 375°F. Add garlic, carrots, and onion to Dutch oven; cook, stirring frequently, until browned and tender, about 10 minutes. Add flour, tomato paste, and remaining 1½ teaspoons salt and ½ teaspoon pepper; cook, stirring constantly, 2 minutes. Add wine and heat to boiling, stirring until browned bits are loosened from bottom of Dutch oven; boil 5 minutes. Add broth and 1 cup water; heat to boiling. Stir in beans and 2 sprigs rosemary. Return shanks to Dutch oven; heat to boiling. Cover Dutch oven and bake 1 hour.

4. Meanwhile, prepare roasted endive: In large bowl, with fork, mix oil, salt, and pepper. Trim root ends of endive and cut each lengthwise in half. Add endive to oil mixture and toss until evenly coated. Arrange endive, cut sides down, in 15½" by 10½" jelly-roll pan.

5. After 1 hour, turn shanks and replace cover. Place endive in same oven. Bake shanks and endive until meat is fork-tender and easily separates from bone and endive is very tender and bottoms begin to brown, about 1 hour.

6. When shanks are done, transfer to large bowl. Skim and discard fat from liquid in Dutch oven. Remove and discard rosemary. To serve, spoon some beans and cooking liquid onto each of 8 large dinner plates. Top each with 1 lamb shank and 2 endive halves. Garnish with a rosemary sprig. Makes 8 main-dish servings.

Each serving lamb and beans: About 725 calories, 67g protein, 46g carbohydrate, 28g total fat (11g saturated), 198mg cholesterol, 1,110mg sodium.

Each serving endive: About 30 calories, 1g protein, 3g carbohydrate, 2g total fat (0g saturated), 0mg cholesterol, 145mg sodium.

SHEPHERD'S PIE

....

Traditional shepherd's pie is made with lamb. If you use beef instead, it's called Cottage Pie. Either way, it's real comfort food.

Prep: 40 minutes   Bake: 20 minutes

- 2 pounds all-purpose potatoes, peeled and cut into quarters
- ½ cup milk
- 3 tablespoons butter or margarine
- ¼ cup plus 1 tablespoon freshly grated Parmesan cheese
- 1 teaspoon salt
- ¼ plus ⅛ teaspoon ground black pepper
- 1 medium onion, chopped
- 2 carrots, peeled and chopped
- 1 pound ground lamb
- 2 tablespoons tomato paste
- 2 tablespoons all-purpose flour
- ¼ cup dry red wine
- 1 cup chicken broth
- ¼ teaspoon dried thyme
- 1 cup frozen peas

1. Preheat oven to 425°F. In 4-quart saucepan, combine potatoes and enough *water* to cover; heat to boiling. Boil until potatoes are tender, about 20 minutes; drain and return to saucepan. With potato masher, mash potatoes with milk and 2 tablespoons butter. Stir in ¼ cup Parmesan, ½ teaspoon salt, and ¼ teaspoon pepper; set aside.

2. Meanwhile, in nonstick 10-inch skillet, melt remaining 1 tablespoon butter over medium heat. Add onion and carrots; cook until vegetables are tender, about 5 minutes. Add ground lamb and cook over medium-high heat, stirring and breaking up meat with spoon, until lamb is no longer pink, about 5 minutes. Skim and discard fat. Add tomato paste and cook, stirring, 1 minute. Add flour and cook, stirring, 1 minute longer. Stir in wine and cook until wine has evaporated. Add broth, thyme, remaining ½ teaspoon salt, and remaining ⅛ teaspoon pepper, stirring until browned bits are loosened from bottom of skillet. Heat to boiling; stir in peas.

3. Transfer lamb mixture to 9-inch deep-dish pie plate. Spoon mashed potatoes evenly on top and sprinkle with remaining 1 tablespoon Parmesan. Place on foil-lined cookie sheet and bake until slightly browned, about 20 minutes. Makes 4 main-dish servings.

Each serving: About 599 calories, 31g protein, 50g carbohydrate, 31g total fat (15g saturated), 113mg cholesterol, 1,272mg sodium.

GLAZED ROSEMARY LAMB CHOPS

....

These rosemary-scented lamb chops are broiled with an apple-jelly and balsamic-vinegar glaze. Keep this glaze in mind for pork, too.

Prep: 10 minutes   Broil: 10 minutes

- 8 lamb loin chops, 1 inch thick (4 ounces each)
- 1 large garlic clove, cut in half
- 2 teaspoons chopped fresh rosemary or ½ teaspoon dried rosemary, crumbled
- ¼ teaspoon salt
- ¼ teaspoon coarsely ground black pepper
- ¼ cup apple jelly
- 1 tablespoon balsamic vinegar

1. Preheat broiler. Rub both sides of chops with cut side of garlic; sprinkle with rosemary, salt, and pepper. In cup, combine apple jelly and vinegar.

2. Place chops on rack in broiling pan. Place pan in broiler at closest position to heat source; broil chops 4 minutes. Brush chops with half of apple-jelly mixture; broil 1 minute. Turn chops and broil 4 minutes longer. Brush chops with remaining jelly mixture and broil 1 minute longer for medium-rare or until desired doneness.

3. Transfer lamb to warm platter. Skim and discard fat from drippings in pan. Serve chops with pan juices, or drizzle with additional balsamic vinegar. Makes 4 main-dish servings.

Each serving: About 240 calories, 26g protein, 14g carbohydrate, 8g total fat (3g saturated), 82mg cholesterol, 223mg sodium.

PANFRIED CALF'S LIVER AND BACON

....

A classic combination of crispy bacon and panfried liver.

Prep: 10 minutes   Cook: 8 minutes

4 slices bacon
3 tablespoons all-purpose flour
4 slices calf's liver, ½ inch thick (1 pound)
¼ teaspoon salt
   chopped fresh parsley
1 small lemon, cut into 4 wedges

1. In 12-inch skillet, cook bacon over medium-high heat until browned. With slotted spoon, transfer bacon to paper towels to drain; keep warm.

2. Place flour on waxed paper. Coat liver with flour, shaking off excess.

3. Discard all but 1 tablespoon bacon drippings from skillet. Add liver slices to hot drippings in skillet and cook over medium-high heat until crisp and browned but slightly pink inside, 1½ to 2 minutes per side. (Don't overcook, or liver will be tough.) Sprinkle with salt.

4. Place liver and bacon on warm platter; sprinkle with parsley and serve with lemon wedges. Makes 4 main-dish servings.

Each serving: About 233 calories, 23g protein, 10g carbohydrate, 11g total fat (4g saturated), 358mg cholesterol, 331mg sodium.

OVEN-BAKED PEPPER BACON

....

The perfect way to make bacon for a crowd: in the oven! This method works best when using lean bacon, but if the bacon renders an excessive amount of fat, pour it off before switching racks.

Prep: 10 minutes   Bake: 25 minutes

1½ pounds sliced lean bacon
2½ teaspoons coarsely ground black pepper

1. Preheat oven to 400°F. Arrange bacon slices in two jelly-roll or roasting pans, overlapping the lean edge of each bacon slice with fat edge of the next. Sprinkle pepper evenly over bacon. Bake until bacon is golden brown and crisp, about 25 minutes, rotating baking pans between upper and lower oven racks halfway through baking.

2. Transfer bacon to paper towels. Keep warm until ready to serve. Makes 12 accompaniment servings.

Each serving: About 93 calories, 5g protein, 0g carbohydrate, 8g total fat (3g saturated), 13mg cholesterol, 254mg sodium.

MEAT BARGAINS

TEST KITCHEN TIP

You don't have to deplete your savings to incorporate quality meat into a meal. While less-expensive cuts often require more time to cook or marinate to keep them tender, the end result will be rich and flavorful. Here are some tips to help stretch your dinner dollar:

• Buy larger cuts of meat; they're often sold at a lower price per pound than smaller ones. Ask the butcher to cut the pork shoulder arm picnic, beef chuck shoulder, beef rump, or bottom round roast into smaller pieces, or purchase family packs of meat in bulk from a club store.

Label and freeze any portions you're not going to use right away.

• Look for the bone-in choices from less tender meats. They tend to cost less, and the bone adds a depth of flavor to stews and soups. Look for chuck blade steaks, shoulder lamb chops, veal breast, and lamb shanks.

• Don't shy away from fat. The leaner the cut, the more expensive it'll be. Fresh ham, beef chuck, and cross-rib pot roast are tender and juicy after a long braise, and the fat can easily be skimmed off after cooking.

5
POULTRY

All around the globe, poultry has found its way into just about every kitchen. It is prized for its versatility and for the ease with which it can be combined with a vast range of ingredients. Whether you are preparing chicken gumbo to be served over steamed rice, a succulent and juicy golden brown turkey to grace the holiday table, or an Italian classic like chicken cacciatore, these dishes are guaranteed to satisfy family and friends alike.

The United States Department of Agriculture inspection sticker on poultry guarantees that it was raised and processed according to strict government guidelines. Grade A birds, the most common variety in supermarkets, are the highest quality. And more than 90 percent of all broiler-fryers (chickens that range from about 2 ½ to 4 pounds) are marketed under a brand name, a further assurance of quality.

KNOW YOUR CHICKEN

Broiler-fryers Tender young birds that weigh 3 to 5 pounds. They can be roasted, fried, sautéed, grilled, or broiled.

Roasters Meaty birds that usually weigh 6 to 8 pounds and are best when roasted.

Cornish hens Small birds that weigh up to 2 pounds each. They are tasty grilled, broiled, and roasted.

Fowl Also called stewing hens, these tough older birds are available especially around the holidays. They are always braised or stewed and make the tastiest chicken broth.

Capons Neutered male chickens that weigh 8 to 10 pounds on average. They are very meaty and tender and are usually roasted.

POULTRY SHOPPING CHOICES

Organic The term *organic* is not recognized by the USDA, so it cannot appear on labels. The term can be used in advertisements to promote a brand, however. Generally, organic poultry has been raised on organically grown, antibiotic-free feed.

Free-range These birds have been raised in an environment that provides access to open spaces but not necessarily an open farmyard. This free movement allows them to develop more muscle, which contributes to fuller-flavored meat.

All-natural This simply means that the poultry has been minimally processed. Its feed was not necessarily organic and might have contained antibiotics.

Kosher Kosher birds have been processed according to Kosher dietary laws under the strict supervision of a rabbi. The procedure includes salting to draw out the blood and season the meat.

Halal If you live in an area that has a Muslim community, there is probably a Halal butcher. These birds are not fed hormones and are slaughtered manually while a special prayer is recited.

Cornish Hens Milanese (recipe page 175)

POULTRY SENSE

POULTRY	READY-TO-COOK WEIGHT	SERVINGS	STUFFING
Broiler-fryer	2½ to 4½ pounds	2 to 4	1 to 3 cups
Roasting chicken	5 to 7 pounds	5 to 7	3 to 6 cups
Capon	6 to 8 pounds	6 to 8	3 to 6 cups
Cornish hen	1 to 2 pounds	1 to 2	¾ to 1½ cups
Turkey	8 to 12 pounds	6 to 8	6 to 9 cups
	12 to 16 pounds	12 to 16	9 to 12 cups
	16 to 20 pounds	16 to 20	12 to 15 cups
	20 to 24 pounds	20 to 24	15 to 18 cups
Turkey breast	4 to 6 pounds	5 to 8	—
Turkey breast (boneless)	4 to 6 pounds	5 to 8	—
Duck	4 to 5 pounds	4	3 to 4 cups
Goose	10 to 12 pounds	6 to 8	6 to 9 cups

BUYING FRESH AND FROZEN POULTRY

Look for fresh whole birds that appear plump and have meaty breasts. Chicken sold as parts should also look plump. Poultry skin should be smooth and moist and free of bruises and pinfeathers. The color of the skin can range from creamy white to yellow, depending on the bird's feed and breed, and is not an indication of flavor or quality. In general, tenderness depends on the age of the bird.

Buy fresh poultry according to the "sell-by" date on the package. When you open the package, the chicken may have a slight odor. This is caused by oxidation and should disappear once the bird is rinsed with cold running water. If the poultry still smells, return it to the market. Be sure to avoid packages with leaks or tears.

If you buy frozen poultry, be sure the meat is rock-hard and without any signs of freezer burn, and make sure there are no ice crystals. The packaging should be tightly sealed and intact. Frozen liquid in the bottom can indicate that the bird was thawed and refrozen.

HANDLING AND STORING POULTRY

Store raw poultry in its original store wrapping on a plate to catch any leaks. If wrapped in butcher paper, remove the paper and place the bird in a large plastic bag. Keep poultry in the coldest part of the refrigerator (usually the bottom shelf), away from cooked or ready-to-eat foods and use within two days. Store uncooked giblets separately in the refrigerator and use within a day, or wrap and freeze for up to one month.

Be sure to wash your hands, the cutting board, and any utensils that have come in contact with raw poultry with hot, soapy water. To destroy germs, bleach your cutting board once a week or so with a solution of 1 tablespoon chlorine bleach to 1 gallon warm water.

Freeze raw poultry for up to six months. Ground poultry will keep in the refrigerator for one day or in the freezer for up to three months. Cool cooked poultry as quickly as possible, then cover and refrigerate up to three days, or tightly wrap and freeze for up to three months.

THAWING POULTRY SAFELY

For safety's sake, thaw poultry either in the refrigerator or by immersion in cold water—not on the kitchen counter at room temperature.

Thawing in the refrigerator This is the preferred method. Leave the bird in its original wrapper, and place it on a tray to catch any drips. As a general rule, allow about six hours per pound. For example, a 24-pound turkey will take approximately four days to thaw completely.

Thawing in cold water If there's no time to thaw the bird in the refrigerator, use this method, which takes less time but requires more attention. Place the bird (in its original wrapper or in a watertight plastic bag) in a large pan or in the sink with enough cold water to cover. (Warm water thaws poultry too quickly and can encourage bacterial growth.) Change the water every 30 minutes to maintain the temperature. Allow about 30 minutes of thawing time per pound, then add 1 hour to that total.

5 THAWING TIPS

• Frozen poultry should be thawed completely before being cooked.
• Remove giblets as soon as possible during thawing, then wrap and refrigerate.
• A bird is thawed if the ice crystals have disappeared from the body cavity and the meat is soft and the joints are flexible.
• Once thawed, cook the bird within 12 hours.
• For reasons of texture—not safety—do not refreeze thawed poultry.

ROASTING TIMES

POULTRY	READY-TO-COOK WEIGHT	COOKING TIME (UNSTUFFED)	COOKING TIME (STUFFED)
Chicken (at 350°F)	2½ to 3 pounds	1¼ to 1½ hours	1¼ to 1½ hours
	3 to 4½ pounds	1½ to 1¾ hours	1½ to 1¾ hours
	5 to 7 pounds	2 to 2¼ hours	2 to 2¼ hours
Capon (at 325°F)	5 to 6 pounds	2 to 2½ hours	2½ to 3 hours
	6 to 8 pounds	2½ to 3½ hours	3 to 4 hours
Cornish hen (at 350°F)	1 to 2 pounds	1 to 1¼ hours	1 to 1¼ hours
Turkey (at 325°F)	Variations in roasting conditions could increase indicated roasting times up to 30 minutes.		
	8 to 12 pounds	2¾ to 3 hours	3 to 3½ hours
	12 to 14 pounds	3 to 3¾ hours	3½ to 4 hours
	14 to 18 pounds	3¾ to 4¼ hours	4 to 4¼ hours
	18 to 20 pounds	4¼ to 4½ hours	4¼ to 4¾ hours
	20 to 24 pounds	4½ to 5 hours	4¾ to 5½ hours
Duck (at 350°F)	4 to 5 pounds	2½ to 2¾ hours	2½ to 2¾ hours
Goose (at 350°F)	10 to 12 pounds	2¾ to 3¼ hours	3 to 3½ hours

MAHOGANY ROAST CHICKEN

....

Give your chicken a deep amber glaze by brushing it with balsamic vinegar, brown sugar, and dry vermouth.

Prep: 10 minutes   Roast: 1 hour 15 minutes

- 1 chicken (3½ pounds)
- ¾ teaspoon salt
- ½ teaspoon coarsely ground black pepper
- 2 tablespoons dark brown sugar
- 2 tablespoons balsamic vinegar
- 2 tablespoons dry vermouth
- ¼ cup water

1. Preheat oven to 375°F. Remove giblets and neck; reserve for another use. Rinse chicken inside and out with cold running water; drain. Pat dry with paper towels. Sprinkle salt and pepper on outside of chicken.

2. With chicken breast side up, lift wings up toward neck, then fold wing tips under back of chicken so wings stay in place. Tie legs together with string. Place chicken, breast side up, on rack in small roasting pan (13" by 9"). Roast chicken 45 minutes.

3. Meanwhile, prepare glaze: In bowl, stir brown sugar, vinegar, and vermouth until sugar dissolves.

4. After chicken has roasted 45 minutes, brush with some glaze. Turn oven control to 400°F and roast chicken, brushing with glaze twice more during roasting, until chicken is deep brown, about 30 minutes longer. Chicken is done when temperature on meat thermometer inserted in thickest part of thigh, next to body, reaches 175° to 180°F and juices run clear when thigh is pierced with tip of knife.

5. Transfer chicken to warm platter; let stand 10 minutes to set juices for easier carving.

6. Meanwhile, remove rack from roasting pan. Skim and discard fat from drippings in pan. Add water to pan; heat to boiling over medium heat, stirring until browned bits are loosened from bottom of pan. Serve chicken with pan juices. Makes 4 main-dish servings.

Each serving with skin: About 446 calories, 48g protein, 7g carbohydrate, 24g total fat (7g saturated), 154mg cholesterol, 583mg sodium.

ROAST LEMON CHICKEN

....

For an easy dinner when company calls, roast an extra-large succulent chicken.

Prep: 10 minutes   Roast: 1 hour 30 minutes to 2 hours

- 1 roasting chicken or capon (7 pounds)
- 2 lemons
- 1 bunch thyme
- 2 garlic cloves
- ¾ teaspoon salt
- ½ teaspoon ground black pepper
- 1¼ cups chicken broth
- 2 teaspoons cornstarch
- 1 tablespoon cold water

1. Preheat oven to 375°F. Remove giblets and neck from chicken; reserve for another use. Pat chicken dry with paper towels.

2. From 1 lemon, cut 4 thin round slices. Cut remainder of lemon and second lemon into quarters. With fingertips, separate skin from meat on chicken breast. Place 2 lemon slices under skin of each breast half. Set aside several thyme sprigs for garnish. Place garlic cloves, lemon quarters, and remaining thyme sprigs inside cavity of chicken. Sprinkle chicken with ½ teaspoon salt and ¼ teaspoon pepper.

3. With chicken breast side up, lift wings up toward neck, then fold wing tips under back of chicken so wings stay in place. Tie legs together with string. Place chicken, breast side up, on rack in medium roasting pan (14" by 10").

4. Roast chicken, basting occasionally with pan drippings, 1 hour 30 minutes to 2 hours. When chicken turns golden brown, cover loosely with tent of foil to prevent overbrowning. Chicken is done when temperature on meat thermometer inserted in thickest part of thigh, next to body, reaches 175°F and juices run clear when thigh is pierced with tip of knife.

5. Transfer chicken to warm platter; let stand 15 minutes to set juices for easier carving.

6. Meanwhile, prepare gravy: Remove rack from roasting pan. Skim and discard fat from drippings. Add broth to pan, stirring until browned bits are loosened from pan. In cup, blend cornstarch and water. Stir cornstarch mixture into broth. Add remaining ¼ teaspoon each salt and pepper. Heat to boiling over high heat, stirring; boil 1 minute.

7. Garnish chicken with reserved thyme sprigs. Serve with gravy. Remove skin from chicken before eating, if desired. Makes 8 main-dish servings.

Each serving with skin: About 469 calories, 50g protein, 3g carbohydrate, 28g total fat (8g saturated), 156mg cholesterol, 525mg sodium.

Each serving without skin: About 291 calories, 42g protein, 3g carbohydrate, 11g total fat (3g saturated), 125mg cholesterol, 500mg sodium.

LEMON-ROASTED CHICKEN FOR A CROWD

When you need a special dish for a big party but you don't have time to fuss, turn to this tasty crowd-pleasing recipe.

Prep: 20 minutes   Roast: 1 hour 30 minutes

1½ cups fresh lemon juice (7 large lemons)
¼   cup vegetable oil
1   large onion (12 ounces), finely chopped
2   large garlic cloves, crushed with garlic press
1   tablespoon plus 2 teaspoons salt
1   tablespoon dried thyme
2   teaspoons ground black pepper
5   chickens (3 pounds each),
    each cut into quarters

1. Preheat oven to 375°F. In medium bowl, combine lemon juice, oil, onion, garlic, salt, thyme, and pepper. In two large roasting pans (17" by 11½"), arrange chicken, skin side up. Pour lemon-juice mixture over chicken.

2. Roast chicken, basting occasionally with pan juices, until juices run clear when thickest part of chicken is pierced with tip of knife, about 1 hour 30 minutes.

3. Transfer chicken to warm platters. Skim and discard fat from drippings in pan; pour pan drippings into medium bowl. Spoon some pan juices over chicken and serve chicken with remaining juices. Makes 20 main-dish servings.

Each serving: About 381 calories, 41g protein, 3g carbohydrate, 22g total fat (6g saturated), 132mg cholesterol, 706mg sodium.

CUTTING UP A RAW CHICKEN

To remove a leg, cut down between the thigh and the body. Bend the leg portion back; twist to crack the hip joint. Cut through the joint. Repeat for the other leg.

To separate the leg from the thigh, place the leg skin side down and cut through the center joint. Repeat with the other leg.

To remove a wing, pull the wing away from the body, then cut between the wing joint and the breast. Repeat with the other wing.

Using kitchen shears, cut through the rib cage along one side of the backbone from the tail to the neck. Repeat on the other side to remove the backbone in one piece.

Place the breast skin side down and cut in half by placing a heavy knife lengthwise along the center of the breastbone. Press the knife to cut through the bone and meat.

APPLE AND THYME ROAST CHICKEN

·····································

The tempting aroma of fresh apples, thyme sprigs, and allspice will fill your kitchen.

Prep: 20 minutes   Roast: 1 hour

- 1   chicken (3½ pounds)
- 2   sprigs plus 1 tablespooon chopped fresh thyme
- ¾   teaspoon salt
- ¼   teaspoon coarsely ground black pepper
- ⅛   teaspoon ground allspice
- 1   jumbo onion (1 pound), cut into 12 wedges
- ¼   cup water
- 2   teaspoons olive oil
- 2   large Granny Smith apples, each cored and cut into quarters
- 2   tablespoons applejack brandy or Calvados
- ½   cup chicken broth

1. Preheat oven to 450°F. Remove giblets and neck from chicken; reserve for another use. Pat chicken dry with paper towels.

2. With fingertips, gently separate skin from meat on chicken breast. Place 1 thyme sprig under skin of each breast half. In cup, combine chopped thyme, salt, pepper, and allspice.

3. With chicken breast side up, lift wings up toward neck, then fold wing tips under back of chicken so wings stay in place. Tie legs together with string.

4. In medium roasting pan (14" by 10"), toss onion, chopped-thyme mixture, water, and oil. Push onion mixture to sides of pan. Place chicken, breast side up, on small rack in center of roasting pan.

5. Roast chicken and onion mixture 40 minutes. Add apples to pan; roast about 20 minutes longer. Chicken is done when temperature on meat thermometer inserted in thickest part of thigh, next to body, reaches 175° to 180°F and juices run clear when thigh is pierced with tip of knife.

6. Transfer chicken to warm platter; let stand 10 minutes to set juices for easier carving.

7. Meanwhile, remove rack from roasting pan. With slotted spoon, transfer onion mixture to platter with chicken. Skim and discard fat from drippings in pan. Add applejack to pan drippings; cook 1 minute over medium heat, stirring constantly. Add broth; heat to boiling. Serve pan-juice mixture with chicken. Remove skin from chicken before eating, if desired. Makes 4 main-dish servings.

Each serving with skin: About 589 calories, 49g protein, 22g carbohydrate, 33g total fat (9g saturated), 159mg cholesterol, 708mg sodium.

Each serving without skin: About 441 calories, 43g protein, 22g carbohydrate, 20g total fat (5g saturated), 132mg cholesterol, 686mg sodium.

CARVING TIPS

TEST KITCHEN TIP

Letting the bird rest after roasting results in firmer, juicier meat that is easier to carve. Poultry should stand at least ten minutes before carving so the simmering juices can relax back into the meat. When carving, use a sharp thin-bladed knife that is long enough to slice off the breast of large birds like turkey or long-bodied birds such as duck or goose.

ROAST CHICKEN WITH FORTY CLOVES OF GARLIC

···

Slow roasting mellows garlic to a sweet nuttiness. Serve with lots of crusty bread for spreading the extra garlic.

Prep: 15 minutes   Roast: 1 hour

1	chicken (3½ pounds)
6	thyme sprigs
½	teaspoon salt
¼	teaspoon coarsely ground black pepper
40	garlic cloves (2 heads), loose papery skin discarded but not peeled
1	cup chicken broth

1. Preheat oven to 450°F. Remove giblets and neck from chicken; reserve for another use. Pat chicken dry with paper towels.

2. With fingertips, gently separate skin from meat on chicken breast. Place 2 thyme sprigs under skin of each breast half. Place remaining 2 sprigs inside cavity of chicken. Sprinkle salt and pepper on outside of chicken.

3. With chicken breast side up, lift wings up toward neck, then fold wing tips under back of chicken so wings stay in place. Tie legs together with string. Place chicken, breast side up, on rack in small roasting pan (13" by 9").

4. Roast chicken 30 minutes. Add garlic cloves to pan; roast about 30 minutes longer. Chicken is done when temperature on meat thermometer inserted in thickest part of thigh, next to body, reaches 175° to 180°F and juices run clear when thigh is pierced with tip of knife.

5. Transfer chicken to warm platter; let stand 10 minutes to set juices for easier carving.

6. Meanwhile, remove rack from roasting pan. With slotted spoon, transfer garlic cloves to small bowl. Skim and discard fat from drippings in pan. Remove and discard skin from 6 garlic cloves; return peeled garlic to roasting pan and add broth. Heat broth mixture to boiling over medium heat, stirring to loosen browned bits from bottom of pan and mashing garlic with back of spoon until well blended. Serve chicken with pan juices and remaining garlic cloves. Remove skin from chicken before eating, if desired. Makes 4 main-dish servings.

CARVING A ROAST CHICKEN
───────────────────

To remove the breast meat, using a thin sharp knife, start along one side of the breastbone, cutting down along the rib cage (scraping against the bones as you go), cutting off the breast meat in one piece. Repeat on the other side.

To carve the breast meat, holding the knife at a slight angle, cut the meat crosswise into even slices.

To remove a chicken leg, force it away from the body with a carving fork until it pops out of its socket. Separate the thigh from the body by cutting through the joint. If you like, separate the drumstick from the thigh by cutting through the center joint. Repeat on the other side. To remove the wings, cut through the joints where the wings meet the body.

Each serving with skin: About 501 calories, 50g protein, 11g carbohydrate, 28g total fat (8g saturated), 157mg cholesterol, 688mg sodium.

Each serving without skin: About 352 calories, 44g protein, 10g carbohydrate, 14g total fat (4g saturated), 129mg cholesterol, 667mg sodium.

BAKED "FRIED" CHICKEN

....

For this healthier version of fried chicken, skinless chicken pieces are dipped in a spicy bread-crumb coating and baked until crispy and golden brown. We guarantee that you won't miss the calories.

Prep: 15 minutes   Bake: 35 minutes

olive oil nonstick cooking spray
½ cup plain dried bread crumbs
¼ cup freshly grated Parmesan cheese
2 tablespoons cornmeal
½ teaspoon ground red pepper (cayenne)
1 large egg white
½ teaspoon salt
1 chicken (3½ pounds), cut into 8 pieces and skin removed from all but wings

1. Preheat oven to 425°F. Grease 15½" by 10½" jelly-roll pan with cooking spray.

2. On waxed paper, combine bread crumbs, Parmesan, cornmeal, and ground red pepper. In pie plate, beat egg white and salt.

3. Dip each piece of chicken in egg-white mixture, then coat with crumb mixture, pressing firmly so mixture adheres. Arrange chicken in prepared pan; lightly coat chicken with cooking spray.

4. Bake chicken until coating is crisp and golden brown and juices run clear when thickest part of chicken is pierced with tip of knife, about 35 minutes. Makes 4 main-dish servings.

Each serving: About 329 calories, 46g protein, 14g carbohydrate, 9g fat (3g saturated), 137mg cholesterol, 660mg sodium.

THYME-ROASTED CHICKEN AND VEGETABLES

....

In just over an hour, you can have a one-dish meal of roasted chicken with fennel, potatoes, and onion ready to bring to the table.

Prep: 20 minutes   Roast: 50 minutes

1 chicken (3½ pounds), cut into 8 pieces and skin removed from all but wings
1 pound all-purpose potatoes (3 medium), not peeled, cut into 2-inch pieces
1 large fennel bulb (1½ pounds), trimmed and cut into 8 wedges
1 large red onion, cut into 8 wedges
1 tablespoon chopped fresh thyme or 1 teaspoon dried thyme
1 teaspoon salt
½ teaspoon ground black pepper
2 tablespoons olive oil
⅓ cup water

1. Preheat oven to 450°F. In large roasting pan (17" by 11½"), arrange chicken, and place potatoes, fennel, and onion around it. Sprinkle chicken with thyme, salt, and pepper. Drizzle oil over chicken and vegetables.

2. Roast chicken and vegetables 20 minutes; baste with drippings in pan. Roast, basting once more, until juices run clear when chicken breasts are pierced with tip of knife, about 20 minutes longer. Transfer chicken breasts to platter; keep warm.

3. Continue roasting remaining chicken pieces until juices run clear when thickest part of chicken is pierced with tip of knife and vegetables are fork-tender, about 10 minutes longer. Transfer chicken and vegetables to platter with breasts; keep warm.

4. Skim and discard fat from drippings in pan. To drippings, add water; heat to boiling over medium heat, stirring until brown bits are loosened from bottom. Spoon pan juices over chicken and vegetables. Makes 4 main-dish servings.

Each serving: About 401 calories, 43g protein, 28g carbohydrate, 13g total fat (2g saturated), 124mg cholesterol, 870mg sodium.

LEMON-OREGANO CHICKEN

....

Try other citrus-herb combinations, such as lime-cilantro, lemon-basil, or orange-sage using this same preparation method.

Prep: 15 minutes   **Roast: 30 minutes**

- 3 lemons
- ¼ cup loosely packed fresh oregano leaves, chopped
- ¼ cup loosely packed fresh parsley leaves, chopped
- 1 tablespoon olive oil
- 1 teaspoon salt
- ¼ teaspoon ground black pepper
- 1 chicken (about 3½ pounds), cut into 8 pieces and skin removed from all but wings

1. Preheat oven to 450°F. Line jelly-roll pan with nonstick foil or foil coated with nonstick spray. From 2 lemons, grate 1 tablespoon peel and squeeze 3 tablespoons juice. Cut remaining lemon into wedges; set aside.

2. In large bowl, combine lemon peel and juice, oregano, parsley, olive oil, salt, and pepper. Add chicken pieces; toss to coat. Arrange chicken pieces in prepared pan.

3. Roast chicken, without turning, 30 to 35 minutes or until juices run clear when thickest part of chicken is pierced with tip of knife. Transfer to warm platter. Serve with lemon wedges to squeeze over chicken. Makes 4 main-dish servings.

Each serving: About 300 calories, 40g protein, 3g carbohydrate, 14g total fat (3g saturated), 0g fiber, 121mg cholesterol, 700mg sodium.

ROMAN CHICKEN SAUTÉ WITH ARTICHOKES

....

A quick, colorful, and light dish that comes together in minutes, this is a great antidote when the family cries "chicken again?"

Prep: 15 minutes   **Cook: 15 minutes**

- 1¼ pounds chicken-breast tenders, each cut crosswise in half, then cut lengthwise in half
- ¼ teaspoon salt
- ¼ teaspoon ground black pepper
- 3 teaspoons olive oil
- 2 cloves garlic, thinly sliced
- 1 can (13¾ to 14 ounces) artichoke hearts, drained and each cut into quarters
- ½ cup dry white wine
- ½ cup chicken broth
- 1 pint grape tomatoes
- 1 teaspoon grated fresh lemon peel plus additional for garnish
- 1 bag (5 to 6 ounces) baby arugula

1. Sprinkle chicken with salt and pepper to season all sides. In 12-inch skillet, heat 2 teaspoons oil on medium high until very hot. Add chicken and cook 8 minutes or until browned on the outside and no longer pink inside, stirring occasionally. With slotted spoon, transfer chicken to bowl.

2. To same skillet, add remaining 1 teaspoon oil. Reduce heat to medium and add garlic; cook 30 seconds or until golden. Stir in artichokes, and cook 3 to 4 minutes or until browned. Stir in wine, and cook 1 minute on medium-high heat.

3. Add chicken broth and tomatoes; cover and cook 2 to 3 minutes or until most tomatoes burst. Remove skillet from heat. Return chicken to skillet; stir in lemon peel until combined. Arrange arugula on platter; top with sautéed chicken mixture. Garnish chicken with lemon peel. Makes 6 main-dish servings.

Each serving: About 165 calories, 25g protein, 7g carbohydrate, 4g total fat (1g saturated), 1g fiber, 55mg cholesterol, 330mg sodium.

PICNIC CHICKEN WITH THREE SAUCES

....

This walnut-crusted baked chicken is delicious hot or cold, especially when dipped into one of our easy sauces.

Prep: 30 minutes   Bake: 30 minutes

olive oil nonstick cooking spray

1¾ cups walnuts (about 8 ounces)

1 cup plain dried bread crumbs

1½ teaspoons salt

¼ to ½ teaspoon ground red pepper (cayenne)

2 large eggs

8 medium bone-in chicken breast halves (4 pounds), skin removed

8 medium chicken drumsticks (1¾ pounds), skin removed

choice of sauce (opposite)

1. Preheat oven to 425°F. Grease two 15½" by 10½" jelly-roll pans with cooking spray.

2. In food processor with knife blade attached, process walnuts with ¼ cup bread crumbs until walnuts are finely ground. In medium bowl, combine nut mixture, salt, ground red pepper, and remaining ¾ cup bread crumbs; stir until well mixed. In pie plate, beat eggs.

3. Cut each chicken breast half crosswise into two pieces. One at a time, dip breast pieces and drumsticks in beaten egg, then into walnut mixture to coat evenly, pressing firmly so mixture adheres. Arrange chicken in jelly-roll pans; lightly coat chicken with cooking spray.

4. Bake chicken until golden brown and juices run clear when thickest part of chicken is pierced with tip of knife, 30 to 35 minutes, rotating pans between upper and lower oven racks halfway through baking.

5. Meanwhile, prepare sauce. Cover and refrigerate sauce if not serving right away.

6. Serve chicken hot with dipping sauce, or cool chicken slightly, cover, and refrigerate to serve cold later with sauce. Makes 12 main-dish servings.

Each serving without sauce: About 311 calories, 32g protein, 10g carbohydrate, 16g total fat (2g saturated), 113mg cholesterol, 468mg sodium.

REMOVING SKIN FROM RAW CHICKEN

To remove the skin from a chicken thigh, grasp the skin tightly and pull it off in one piece. If you like, grasp the skin with a piece of paper towel or dip your fingers into a little coarse salt to get a better grip.

To remove the skin from a drumstick, grasp the skin at the meaty end of the drumstick; pull the skin down and off the end of the drumstick. (If necessary, use a sharp knife to cut the skin off.)

To remove the skin from a chicken breast, grasp the skin at the thin end of breast and pull it off. (It is difficult to remove the skin from chicken wings—don't bother.)

BLUE-CHEESE SAUCE

In medium bowl, combine **4 ounces blue cheese,** crumbled (1 cup), **½ cup mayonnaise, ½ cup plain lowfat yogurt, ½ teaspoon hot pepper sauce,** and **¼ teaspoon coarsely ground black pepper** until blended. Makes about 1½ cups sauce.

Each tablespoon: About 53 calories, 1g protein, 1g carbohydrate, 5g total fat (1g saturated), 7mg cholesterol, 98mg sodium.

CREAMY HONEY-MUSTARD SAUCE

In medium bowl, combine **⅔ cup Dijon mustard, ¼ cup sour cream, ¼ cup honey,** and **¾ teaspoon Worcestershire sauce** until well blended. Makes about 1¼ cups sauce.

Each tablespoon: About 27 calories, 0g protein, 4g carbohydrate, 1g total fat (0g saturated), 1mg cholesterol, 197mg sodium.

APRICOT-BALSAMIC SAUCE

In medium bowl, combine **1 jar (12 ounces) apricot preserves, 2 tablespoons balsamic vinegar, 1 tablespoon soy sauce,** and **¼ teaspoon freshly grated orange peel** until well blended. Makes about 1¼ cups sauce.

Each tablespoon: About 42 calories, 0g protein, 11g carbohydrate, 0g total fat (0g saturated), 0mg cholesterol, 58mg sodium.

ASPARAGUS-CHICKEN ROULADES

....

When food is "butterflied," it is cut horizontally almost in half, then opened flat, resembling a butterfly.

Prep: 18 minutes   Cook 10 minutes

- 4 medium skinless, boneless chicken breast halves (1¼ pounds)
- 1 lemon
- 3 ounces goat cheese, softened
- ½ cup loosely packed fresh mint leaves, chopped
- ¾ pound thin asparagus, trimmed
- ¼ teaspoon ground black pepper
- ¼ teaspoon salt
- 1 tablespoon olive oil
- ½ cup chicken broth

1. Holding knife parallel to work surface and against a long side of chicken-breast half, cut chicken almost in half, making sure not to cut all the way through. Open breast half and spread flat like a book. Repeat with remaining chicken.

2. From lemon, grate ½ teaspoon peel and squeeze 1 tablespoon juice; set aside juice. In small bowl, stir goat cheese, mint, and lemon peel until mixed.

3. Spread goat-cheese mixture evenly on cut sides of breast halves. Place one-fourth of uncooked asparagus on a long side of each breast half. Roll up each breast half to enclose asparagus, allowing ends of stalks to stick out if necessary; secure with toothpicks. Sprinkle chicken roulades with pepper and salt.

4. In 12-inch skillet, heat oil over medium-high heat until hot. Add roulades and cook, covered, 9 to 11 minutes or until chicken loses its pink color throughout, turning roulades to brown all sides.

5. Transfer roulades to cutting board; keep warm. To same skillet, add broth and reserved lemon juice; heat to boiling, scraping up any browned bits. Remove skillet from heat.

6. To serve, discard toothpicks from roulades. Cut roulades crosswise into 1-inch-thick slices. Place each sliced roulade on a dinner plate; drizzle with pan sauce. Makes 4 main-dish servings.

Each serving: About 265 calories, 39g protein, 2g carbohydrate, 10g total fat (4g saturated), 92mg cholesterol, 450mg sodium.

COQ AU VIN

....

This well-known dish, which is basically chicken stewed in a red-wine sauce, is a specialty of the Burgundy region of France. Use a moderately priced California or Oregon Pinot Noir, which is made from the same grape as more expensive French Burgundy.

Prep: 45 minutes   Bake: 45 minutes

- 4 slices bacon, cut into ³/₄-inch pieces
- 4 tablespoons butter or margarine
- ¼ teaspoon salt
- ⅛ teaspoon ground black pepper
- 1 chicken (3½ pounds), cut into 8 pieces and skin removed from all but wings
- 1 small onion, finely chopped
- 1 carrot, peeled and finely chopped
- 18 pearl onions (generous 1 cup), peeled
- 10 ounces mushrooms, trimmed
- ⅓ cup all-purpose flour
- 2 cups dry red wine
- 1⅓ cups chicken broth
- 2 tablespoons tomato paste
- 1 stalk celery
- 12 sprigs plus 3 tablespoons chopped parsley
- 2 bay leaves

1. Preheat oven to 325°F. In 5-quart Dutch oven, cook bacon over medium-high heat until crisp. With slotted spoon, transfer to paper towels to drain. Reduce heat to medium and add butter to drippings in pot. Sprinkle chicken with salt and pepper. Add chicken to Dutch oven, in batches if necessary, and cook until golden brown, about 5 minutes per side, using tongs to transfer chicken pieces to bowl as they are browned.

2. Add chopped onion and carrot to Dutch oven and cook until lightly browned, about 5 minutes. With slotted spoon, transfer to bowl with chicken. Add pearl onions to Dutch oven and cook, stirring, until browned, about 6 minutes; transfer to bowl. Add mushrooms to pot and cook, stirring, until browned, about 6 minutes; transfer to bowl.

3. Add flour to Dutch oven and cook, stirring, 2 minutes. With wire whisk, whisk in ½ cup wine until smooth. Add remaining 1½ cups wine, broth, and tomato paste. Heat to boiling, whisking constantly; boil 2 minutes. Return chicken, vegetables, and three-fourths of bacon to Dutch oven.

4. With string, tie together celery, parsley sprigs, and bay leaves; add to Dutch oven. Cover and place in oven. Bake, stirring occasionally, 45 minutes.

5. When chicken is tender and sauce is slightly thickened, skim fat and discard celery bundle. Sprinkle coq au vin with remaining bacon and chopped parsley. Makes 6 main-dish servings.

Each serving: About 414 calories, 32g protein, 17g carbohydrate, 24g total fat (10g saturated), 115mg cholesterol, 645mg sodium.

CHICKEN CURRY

....

Serve curry over rice with an array of condiments. Chopped cilantro, chopped peanuts, shredded coconut, golden raisins, cucumber sticks, mango chutney, toasted slivered almonds, and sliced bananas are popular items but by no means the only possibilities.

**Prep: 15 minutes plus cooling
Cook: 1 hour 15 minutes**

- 1 chicken (3½ pounds), cut into 8 pieces
- 4 medium onions, finely chopped
- 2 carrots, peeled and finely chopped
- 2 stalks celery with leaves, finely chopped
- 8 parsley sprigs
- 1 lime
- 4 tablespoons butter or margarine
- 2 Granny Smith apples, peeled, cored, and chopped
- 3 garlic cloves, finely chopped
- 1 tablespoon curry powder
- 3 tablespoons all-purpose flour
- ½ cup half-and-half or light cream
- ⅓ cup golden raisins
- 2 tablespoons mango chutney, chopped
- 2 teaspoons minced, peeled fresh ginger
- ½ teaspoon salt
  pinch ground red pepper (cayenne)

1. In 5-quart Dutch oven, combine chicken, one-fourth onions, carrots, celery, and parsley sprigs. Add just enough *water* to cover. Heat to boiling over high heat. Reduce heat; partially cover and simmer, turning once, until chicken loses its pink color throughout, 25 to 30 minutes. Using tongs, transfer chicken to bowl. When cool enough to handle, remove and discard skin and bones; with hands, shred chicken.

2. Meanwhile, strain broth through sieve, discarding vegetables. Return broth to Dutch oven; heat to boiling and boil until reduced to 2 cups. Skim and discard fat from broth; reserve broth.

3. From lime, grate ½ teaspoon peel and squeeze 5 teaspoons juice; set aside.

4. In 12-inch skillet, melt butter over medium heat. Add remaining three-fourths onions, apples, garlic, and curry powder and cook, stirring, until apples are tender, about 10 minutes. Sprinkle with flour, stirring to blend. Gradually add 2 cups reserved broth, stirring constantly until broth has thickened and boils. Stir in lime peel and juice, half-and-half, raisins, chutney, ginger, salt, and ground red pepper. Reduce heat and simmer, stirring occasionally, 5 minutes. Add chicken and heat through. Makes 6 main-dish servings.

Each serving: About 379 calories, 30g protein, 33g carbohydrate, 14g total fat (7g saturated), 117mg cholesterol, 449mg sodium.

CUCUMBER RAITA

This classic accompaniment to Indian dishes can tame the heat of even the fiercest curry. Peel, seed, and coarsely shred 1 medium cucumber. Squeeze out as much liquid as possible. In a small bowl, combine the cucumber with 1 cup (8 ounces) plain yogurt. Season with salt and pepper. Add a tablespoon of chopped fresh mint, if you like.

CHICKEN MOLE

Mole (MO-lay) is a thick, rich, dark brown Mexican sauce traditionally made with dried chiles, spices, seeds such as pumpkin, nuts, and a touch of unsweetened chocolate. Serve with rice and crisp tortillas.

Prep: 10 minutes   Cook: 45 minutes

- 1 can (14½ ounces) diced tomatoes
- 1 can (4 to 4½ ounces) chopped mild green chiles
- ½ cup whole blanched almonds
- ½ small onion, coarsely chopped
- 1 small garlic clove, peeled
- 1 tablespoon chili powder
- 1 teaspoon ground cumin
- 1 teaspoon ground coriander
- ¾ teaspoon ground cinnamon
- ¾ teaspoon salt
- ½ teaspoon sugar
- 1 tablespoon olive oil
- 3 pounds bone-in chicken parts, skin removed from all but wings
- ½ square (½ ounce) unsweetened chocolate, chopped
- ¼ cup water
- 2 tablespoons chopped fresh cilantro

1. Prepare mole sauce: In blender or in food processor with knife blade attached, puree tomatoes, chiles, almonds, onion, garlic, chili powder, cumin, coriander, cinnamon, salt, and sugar until smooth.

2. In 12-inch skillet, heat oil over medium-high heat until very hot. Add chicken and cook until golden brown, about 5 minutes per side, using tongs to transfer chicken pieces to large bowl as they are browned.

3. Add mole sauce, chocolate, and water to skillet; cook, stirring, until chocolate melts. Return chicken to skillet; heat to boiling. Reduce heat; cover and simmer until chicken juices run clear when chicken thigh is pierced with tip of knife, 30 to 35 minutes. Sprinkle with cilantro to serve. Makes 6 main-dish servings.

Each serving: About 263 calories, 27g protein, 9g carbohydrate, 14g total fat (3g saturated), 76mg cholesterol, 617mg sodium.

SALSA VERDE ENCHILADAS

....

Store-bought rotisserie chickens make this a quick, weeknight fix; making an extra casserole to freeze for later saves even more time. With reduced-fat sour cream and cheese, we've lightened the calories, too.

Prep: 50 minutes   Cook: 20 minutes

- 2 rotisserie chickens
- 2 jars (16 to 17.6 ounces each) mild salsa verde
- 6 green onions, thinly sliced
- ¼ cup fresh lime juice (from 2 to 3 limes)
- ½ cup loosely packed fresh cilantro leaves, chopped
- 16 (6-inch) corn tortillas
- 1 container (8 ounces) reduced-fat sour cream
- ½ cup reduced-sodium chicken broth
- 1 package (8 ounces) reduced-fat (2%) shredded Mexican cheese blend (2 cups)

1. Remove meat from chickens and coarsely shred; place in medium bowl (you will need 5½ cups; reserve any extra for another use). Discard skin and bones. Stir ½ cup salsa verde into chicken to evenly coat.

2. Preheat oven to 350°F. Grease two 13" by 9" glass or ceramic baking dishes; set aside. In 12-inch skillet, heat remaining salsa verde, green onions, and lime juice to boiling over medium-high heat. Boil 2 minutes, stirring occasionally. Stir in 2 tablespoons cilantro; keep warm over very low heat.

3. With tongs, place 1 tortilla in salsa verde mixture; heat 10 seconds. Place tortilla on waxed paper; top with about ⅓ cup shredded-chicken mixture. Roll up tortilla and place, seam side down, in prepared baking dish. Repeat with remaining tortillas and chicken mixture, arranging 8 tortillas in each dish.

4. Stir sour cream and broth into remaining salsa verde mixture in skillet; spoon over filled tortillas. Cover one baking dish with foil and bake 15 minutes. Remove foil; sprinkle with 1 cup cheese and 1 tablespoon cilantro. Bake 5 minutes longer or until cheese melts. Meanwhile, sprinkle remaining cheese and cilantro over second casserole and prepare for freezing. Makes 2 casseroles with 4 main-dish servings each.

Each serving: About 465 calories, 39g protein, 36g carbohydrate, 18g total fat (7g saturated), 3g fiber, 117mg cholesterol, 785mg sodium.

CHICKEN TIKKA MASALA

....

Tender chunks of chicken in a rich sauce filled with the flavors of India. Our version puts dinner on the table in minutes.

Prep: 10 minutes   Cook: 15 minutes

- 1 cup basmati rice
- 1 tablespoon vegetable oil
- 1 medium onion, chopped
- 2 teaspoons grated peeled fresh ginger
- 1 clove garlic, crushed with press
- 2 tablespoons Indian curry paste
- 1¼ pounds skinless, boneless chicken breast halves, cut into 1-inch chunks
- ¼ teaspoon salt
- ¼ teaspoon ground black pepper
- 1 cup crushed tomatoes (from 15-ounce can)
- ½ cup half-and-half or light cream
- ¼ cup loosely packed fresh cilantro leaves, chopped, plus additional for garnish

1. Prepare rice as label directs.

2. Meanwhile, in 12-inch nonstick skillet, heat oil on medium 1 minute. Add onion and cook 6 minutes, stirring frequently. Add ginger, garlic, and curry paste; cook 3 minutes longer.

3. Add chicken, salt, and pepper and cook 2 minutes or until no longer pink on the outside, stirring occasionally. Add tomatoes; cover and cook 3 to 4 minutes longer or until chicken just loses its pink color throughout.

4. Uncover and stir in half-and-half and cilantro. Spoon rice into 4 shallow bowls; top with chicken mixture and garnish with chopped cilantro. Makes 4 main-dish servings.

Each serving: About 430 calories, 39g protein, 42g carbohydrate, 13g total fat (4g saturated), 6g fiber, 93mg cholesterol, 685mg sodium.

COUNTRY CAPTAIN CASSEROLE

···

Though the exact origin of this well-known dish is often debated, its great flavor is never in dispute.

Prep: 30 minutes   Bake: 1 hour

- 2 tablespoons plus 1 teaspoon vegetable oil
- 2 chickens (3½ pounds each), each cut into 8 pieces and skin removed from all but wings
- 2 medium onions, chopped
- 1 large Granny Smith apple, peeled, cored, and chopped
- 1 large green pepper, chopped
- 3 large garlic cloves, finely chopped
- 1 tablespoon grated, peeled fresh ginger
- 3 tablespoons curry powder
- ½ teaspoon coarsely ground black pepper
- ¼ teaspoon ground cumin
- 1 can (28 ounces) plum tomatoes in puree
- 1 can (14½ ounces) chicken broth or 1¾ cups Chicken Broth (page 70)
- ½ cup dark seedless raisins
- 1 teaspoon salt
- ¼ cup chopped fresh parsley

1. In nonreactive 8-quart Dutch oven, heat 2 tablespoons oil over medium-high heat until very hot. Add chicken, in batches, and cook until golden brown, about 5 minutes per side. Using tongs, transfer chicken pieces to bowl as they are browned.

2. Preheat oven to 350°F. In same Dutch oven, heat remaining 1 teaspoon oil over medium-high heat. Add onions, apple, green pepper, garlic, and ginger; cook, stirring frequently, 2 minutes. Reduce heat to medium; cover and cook 5 minutes longer.

3. Stir in curry powder, black pepper, and cumin; cook 1 minute. Add tomatoes with their puree, broth, raisins, salt, and chicken pieces, breaking up tomatoes with side of spoon. Heat to boiling over high heat; boil 1 minute. Cover and place in oven. Bake 1 hour. Sprinkle with parsley. Makes 8 main-dish servings.

Each serving: About 347 calories, 43g protein, 19g carbohydrate, 11g total fat (2g saturated), 133mg cholesterol, 825mg sodium.

Country Captain Casserole

ARROZ CON POLLO

From Madrid to Miami, versions of this comforting dish are served almost anywhere Spanish is spoken.

Prep: 15 minutes   Cook: 40 minutes

- 1 tablespoon vegetable oil
- 6 medium bone-in chicken thighs (1½ pounds), skin and fat removed
- 1 medium onion, finely chopped
- 1 red pepper, chopped
- 1 garlic clove, finely chopped
- ⅛ teaspoon ground red pepper (cayenne)
- 1 cup regular long-grain rice
- 1 can (14½ ounces) chicken broth or 1¾ cups Chicken Broth (page 70)
- ¼ cup water
- 1 strip (3" by ½") lemon peel
- ¼ teaspoon dried oregano
- ¼ teaspoon salt
- 1 cup frozen peas
- ¼ cup chopped pimiento-stuffed olives (salad olives)
- ¼ cup chopped fresh cilantro
  lemon wedges

1. In 5-quart Dutch oven, heat oil over medium-high heat until very hot. Add chicken and cook until golden brown, about 5 minutes per side. With tongs, transfer chicken pieces to bowl as they are browned.

2. Reduce heat to medium. Add onion and red pepper to Dutch oven and cook until tender, about 5 minutes. Stir in garlic and ground red pepper and cook 30 seconds. Add rice and cook, stirring, 1 minute. Stir in broth, water, lemon peel, oregano, salt, and chicken; heat to boiling. Reduce heat; cover and simmer until juices run clear when thickest part of chicken is pierced with tip of knife, about 20 minutes.

3. Stir in peas; cover and heat through. Remove from heat and let stand 5 minutes.

4. Transfer chicken to serving bowl. Sprinkle with olives and cilantro; serve with lemon wedges. Makes 4 main-dish servings.

Each serving: About 387 calories, 26g protein, 48g carbohydrate, 9g total fat (2g saturated), 81mg cholesterol, 927mg sodium.

CHICKEN CACCIATORE

Food prepared alla cacciatore, "hunter-style," includes mushrooms in the sauce. This dish is representative of the kind of home cooking that found its way first into Italian restaurants and then into American kitchens. Serve over wide, flat noodles.

Prep: 15 minutes   Cook: 40 minutes

- 2 tablespoons olive oil
- 1 chicken (3½ pounds), cut into 8 pieces and skin removed from all but wings
- 3 tablespoons all-purpose flour
- 1 medium onion, finely chopped
- 4 garlic cloves, crushed with garlic press
- 8 ounces mushrooms, trimmed and thickly sliced
- 1 can (14 to 16 ounces) tomatoes
- ½ teaspoon salt
- ½ teaspoon dried oregano, crumbled
- ¼ teaspoon dried sage
- ⅛ teaspoon ground red pepper (cayenne)

1. In 12-inch skillet, heat oil over medium-high heat until very hot. On waxed paper, coat chicken with flour, shaking off excess. Add chicken to skillet and cook until golden brown, about 3 minutes per side. With tongs, transfer chicken pieces to bowl as they are browned.

2. Add onion and garlic to skillet. Reduce heat to medium-low and cook, stirring occasionally, until onion is tender, about 5 minutes. Add mushrooms and cook, stirring frequently, until just tender, about 3 minutes.

3. Add tomatoes with their juice, breaking them up with side of spoon. Add salt, oregano, sage, ground red pepper, and chicken and heat to boiling over high heat. Reduce heat; cover and simmer until juices run clear when thickest part of chicken is pierced with tip of knife, about 25 minutes.

4. Transfer chicken to serving bowl. Spoon sauce over chicken. Makes 4 main-dish servings.

Each serving: About 371 calories, 44g protein, 18g carbohydrate, 13g total fat (3g saturated), 133mg cholesterol, 608mg sodium.

CHICKEN WITH ROSEMARY DUMPLINGS ~

It doesn't take hours to make a stew when you're using chicken breasts. The tender, melt-in-your-mouth dumplings make this stew a complete meal.

Prep: 15 minutes   Cook: 1 hour

- 2 tablespoons vegetable oil
- 6 large bone-in chicken breast halves (3¼ pounds), skin removed
- 4 large carrots, peeled and cut into 1-inch pieces
- 2 large stalks celery, cut into ¼-inch-thick slices
- 1 medium onion, finely chopped
- 1 cup plus 2 tablespoons all-purpose flour
- 2 teaspoons baking powder
- 1½ teaspoons chopped fresh rosemary or ½ teaspoon dried rosemary, crumbled
- 1 teaspoon salt
- 1 large egg
- 1½ cups milk
- 2 cups water
- 1 can (14½ ounces) low-sodium chicken broth or 1¾ cups Chicken Broth (page 70)
- ¼ teaspoon ground black pepper
- 1 package (10 ounces) frozen peas

1. In 8-quart Dutch oven, heat 1 tablespoon oil over medium-high heat until very hot. Add 3 chicken breast halves; cook until golden brown, about 5 minutes per side. With tongs, transfer chicken pieces to bowl as they are browned. Repeat with remaining chicken.

2. Add remaining 1 tablespoon oil to drippings in Dutch oven. Add carrots, celery, and onion and cook, stirring frequently, until vegetables are golden brown and tender, about 10 minutes.

3. Prepare dumplings: In small bowl, combine 1 cup flour, baking powder, rosemary, and ½ teaspoon salt. In cup, with fork, beat egg with ½ cup milk. Stir egg mixture into flour mixture until just blended.

4. Return chicken to Dutch oven; add water, broth, pepper, and remaining ½ teaspoon salt. Heat to boiling over high heat. Drop dumpling mixture by rounded tablespoons on top of chicken and vegetables to make 12 dumplings. Reduce heat; cover and simmer 15 minutes.

5. With slotted spoon, transfer dumplings, chicken, and vegetables to serving bowl; keep warm. Reserve broth in Dutch oven.

6. In cup, blend remaining 2 tablespoons flour with remaining 1 cup milk until smooth; stir into broth mixture. Heat to boiling over high heat; boil 1 minute to thicken slightly. Add peas and heat through. Pour sauce over chicken and dumplings. Makes 6 main-dish servings.

Each serving: About 437 calories, 46g protein, 38g carbohydrate, 10g total fat (3g saturated), 137mg cholesterol, 951mg sodium

MEDITERRANEAN CHICKEN WITH SOFT POLENTA

You can buy packages of cornmeal labeled polenta in specialty food stores, but we find that regular yellow cornmeal works—and tastes—equally good.

Prep: 15 minutes   Cook: 40 minutes

- 2 tablespoons all-purpose flour
- ¾ teaspoon salt
- ¼ teaspoon ground black pepper
- 4 medium chicken leg quarters (2¼ pounds), skin and fat removed
- 1 tablespoon olive oil
- 1 small onion, cut in half and thinly sliced
- ½ cup dry white wine
- 1 can (14½ ounces) diced tomatoes
- ½ cup Kalamata olives, pitted and coarsely chopped
- 4 strips (3" by 1" each) fresh lemon peel
- 6 sprigs fresh thyme plus additional for garnish
- 2¼ cups whole milk
- 1 can (14 to 14½ ounces) chicken broth or 1¾ cups Chicken Broth (page 70)
- 1 cup yellow cornmeal
- 2 tablespoons butter or margarine, cut into pieces
- ⅛ teaspoon ground black pepper

1. Prepare chicken: On waxed paper, combine flour, ½ teaspoon salt, and pepper. Use to coat chicken legs shaking off excess.

2. In nonstick 12-inch skillet, heat oil over medium heat until hot. Add legs and cook, turning over once, until browned, 10 to 12 minutes. With slotted spoon, transfer legs to plate.

3. To drippings in skillet, add onion and cook, stirring frequently, until golden brown, about 5 minutes. Add wine; boil until reduced by half, about 2 minutes. Add tomatoes with their juice, olives, lemon peel, 6 thyme sprigs, and remaining ¼ teaspoon salt. Return legs with any accumulated juices to skillet, stirring to coat; heat to boiling over high heat. Reduce heat to low; cover and simmer just until juices run clear when thickest part of leg is pierced with tip of knife, about 20 minutes.

4. Meanwhile, prepare soft polenta: In 3-quart non-reactive saucepan, heat milk and broth to boiling over high heat. Reduce heat to low; gradually whisk in cornmeal. Cook, stirring occasionally, until mixture is very thick, about 10 minutes. Remove saucepan from heat; stir in butter and pepper.

5. Remove lemon peel and thyme sprigs from chicken mixture. Divide polenta among 4 dinner plates; top each with 1 chicken leg and some sauce. Garnish with remaining thyme sprigs. Makes 4 main-dish servings.

Each serving: About 550 calories, 41g protein, 43g carbohydrate, 23g total fat (6g saturated), 139mg cholesterol, 1,685mg sodium.

HOW TO PIT AN OLIVE

 TEST KITCHEN TIP You can buy pitted olives, but we think that unpitted olives are more flavorful, and it is very easy to pit them. Place the olives on a cutting board. With the bottom of a small heavy saucepan, a rolling pin, or the flat side of a large chef's knife, press down hard on the olives, one at a time, to split them open. Lift out the pits with your fingers and discard.

SPICY PEANUT CHICKEN

....

This recipe is based on the cuisines of Africa. A crisp cucumber salad and jasmine or basmati rice, available in most supermarkets, are the usual accompaniments.

Prep: 15 minutes   Cook: 1 hour 10 minutes

- 1 teaspoon ground cumin
- ¼ teaspoon ground cinnamon
- 4 medium chicken leg quarters (2¼ pounds), skin and fat removed
- 1 tablespoon vegetable oil
- 1 medium onion, thinly sliced
- 1 can (28 ounces) plum tomatoes, drained, juice reserved, and coarsely chopped
- ¼ cup creamy peanut butter
- ¼ cup packed fresh cilantro leaves plus additional sprigs
- 2 garlic cloves, peeled
- ½ teaspoon salt
- ¼ teaspoon crushed red pepper

1. In cup, combine cumin and cinnamon. Use to rub on chicken.

2. In nonstick 12-inch skillet, heat oil over medium-high heat until very hot. Add chicken and cook until golden brown, about 5 minutes per side. Add onion and cook until golden, about 5 minutes.

3. Meanwhile, in blender or in food processor with knife blade attached, puree reserved tomato juice, peanut butter, cilantro, garlic, salt, and crushed red pepper until smooth.

4. Pour peanut-butter mixture and chopped tomatoes over chicken; heat to boiling. Reduce heat; cover and simmer until juices run clear when thickest part of chicken is pierced with tip of knife, about 40 minutes. Garnish with cilantro sprigs. Makes 4 main-dish servings.

Each serving: About 361 calories, 36g protein, 16g carbohydrate, 18g fat (3g saturated), 116mg cholesterol, 817mg sodium.

CHICKEN THIGHS PROVENÇAL

. . . .

The quintessentially Provençal combination of thyme, basil, fennel, and orange makes sensational chicken.

Prep: 30 minutes   Cook: 1 hour 15 minutes

2 pounds skinless, boneless chicken thighs, fat removed and each cut into quarters
¾ teaspoon salt
3 teaspoons olive oil
2 red peppers, cut into ¼-inch-wide strips
1 yellow pepper, cut into ¼-inch-wide strips
1 jumbo onion (1 pound), thinly sliced
3 garlic cloves, crushed with garlic press
1 can (28 ounces) plum tomatoes
¼ teaspoon dried thyme
¼ teaspoon fennel seeds, crushed
3 strips (3" by 1" each) orange peel
½ cup loosely packed fresh basil leaves, chopped

1. Sprinkle chicken with ½ teaspoon salt. In nonreactive 5-quart Dutch oven, heat 1 teaspoon oil over medium-high heat until very hot. Add half of chicken and cook until golden brown, about 5 minutes per side. With tongs, transfer chicken pieces to bowl as they are browned. Repeat with 1 teaspoon oil and remaining chicken.

2. Reduce heat to medium. To drippings in Dutch oven, add remaining 1 teaspoon oil, red and yellow peppers, onion, and remaining ¼ teaspoon salt. Cook, stirring frequently, until vegetables are tender and lightly browned, about 20 minutes. Add garlic; cook 1 minute longer.

3. Return chicken to Dutch oven. Add tomatoes with their juice, thyme, fennel seeds, and orange peel; heat to boiling, breaking up tomatoes with side of spoon. Reduce heat; cover and simmer until chicken loses its pink color throughout, about 15 minutes.

4. Transfer to serving bowl and sprinkle with basil to serve. Makes 8 main-dish servings.

Each serving: About 204 calories, 24g protein, 12g carbohydrate, 7g total fat (1g saturated), 94mg cholesterol, 480mg sodium.

POULE AU POT WITH TARRAGON

. . . .

Stewed chicken and vegetables is a favorite Sunday supper in France. Use the leftover broth as the base for a soup later in the week.

Prep: 15 minutes   Cook: 1 hour

3 medium leeks (about 1 pound)
1 chicken (3½ pounds), cut into 8 pieces
1 pound small red potatoes
1 bag (16 ounces) carrots, peeled and cut into 3-inch pieces
4 cups water
1 can (14½ ounces) chicken broth or 1¾ cups Chicken Broth (page 70)
½ teaspoon salt
¼ teaspoon dried thyme
¼ teaspoon ground black pepper
1 large sprig plus 1 tablespoon chopped fresh tarragon

1. Cut off roots and trim dark green tops from leeks; cut each leek lengthwise in half, then crosswise into 3-inch pieces. Rinse in large bowl of cold water, swishing to remove sand; transfer to colander to drain, leaving sand in bottom of bowl.

2. In 6- to 8-quart Dutch oven, combine leeks, chicken, potatoes, carrots, water, broth, salt, thyme, pepper, and tarragon sprig. Heat to boiling over high heat. Reduce heat; cover and simmer until chicken loses its pink color throughout, about 45 minutes.

3. With slotted spoon, transfer chicken and vegetables to serving bowl. Remove and discard skin from chicken. Skim and discard fat from broth. Pour 1 cup broth over chicken (refrigerate remaining broth for another use). To serve, sprinkle chopped tarragon on top. Makes 4 main-dish servings.

Each serving: About 472 calories, 47g protein, 44g carbohydrate, 11g total fat (3g saturated), 127mg cholesterol, 859mg sodium.

SOUTHERN FRIED CHICKEN

....

Here it is: our favorite recipe for this all-time classic. Mashed potatoes or biscuits are a must.

**Prep: 35 minutes plus chilling and standing
Cook: 40 minutes**

- 2 cups buttermilk
- 2 tablespoons hot pepper sauce
- 1 tablespoon salt
- 2 chickens (3½ pounds each), each cut into 8 pieces
- 2 cups all-purpose flour
- 1½ teaspoons baking powder
- 1 teaspoon ground black pepper
- 1 teaspoon paprika
- 5 cups vegetable oil or shortening for frying

1. In extra-large (2- to 2½-gallon) zip-tight plastic bag, combine buttermilk, hot pepper sauce, and 1 teaspoon salt. Add chicken pieces, turning to coat. Seal bag, pressing out excess air. Place bag in bowl; refrigerate 2 to 24 hours to marinate, turning bag over once.

2. In pie plate, stir flour, baking powder, pepper, paprika, and remaining 2 teaspoons salt until well mixed. Remove chicken, a few pieces at a time, from buttermilk, shaking off excess. Add chicken to flour mixture, turning to coat well. Place chicken pieces so that they do not touch one another on wire rack, set over waxed paper. Repeat with remaining chicken. Let stand until coating has set, about 15 minutes. Discard buttermilk mixture.

3. Meanwhile, preheat oven to 250°F. Line two 15½" by 10½" jelly-roll pans or large cookie sheets with paper towels. Divide oil between two 12-inch skillets, preferably electric (there should be about ½ inch oil in each skillet), and heat over medium heat until temperature reaches 360°F on deep-fry thermometer.

4. To each skillet, add 4 chicken pieces, skin side down, being careful to avoid crowding. Cover skillets and cook until chicken is light golden brown on bottom, 4 to 5 minutes. Turn pieces and cook, covered (reducing heat to medium-low if necessary to maintain a temperature of 300°F), 8 to 10 minutes longer for white meat, 13 to 15 minutes longer for dark meat, turning pieces every 4 or 5 minutes, until well browned on all sides and juices run clear when thickest part is pierced with tip of knife. Using tongs, transfer chicken pieces to jelly-roll pans lined with paper towel to drain; keep warm in oven. Repeat with remaining chicken. Makes 8 main-dish servings.

Each serving: About 545 calories, 39g protein, 25g carbohydrate, 31g total fat (6g saturated), 140mg cholesterol, 845mg sodium.

POACHED CHICKEN BREASTS WITH TWO SAUCES

Poached chicken breasts are versatile—and healthful.

POACHED CHICKEN BREASTS

In 12-inch skillet, combine 6 small skinless, boneless chicken breast halves (1¾ pounds), 1 medium onion, thinly sliced, 3 cups water, and 1 bay leaf. Heat to boiling over high heat. Reduce heat; cover and simmer 1 minute, turning chicken over halfway through cooking. Remove skillet from heat; cover and let stand 10 minutes. Transfer chicken to plate; cover loosely and refrigerate until chilled. Makes 6 servings.

TURKISH CHICKEN IN WALNUT SAUCE

In food processor with knife blade attached, process 1¼ cups toasted walnuts and 3 slices firm white bread torn into pieces, until walnuts are finely ground. Add 1 cup chicken broth, 1 small garlic clove, minced, ¾ teaspoon salt, ½ teaspoon paprika, and ⅓ teaspoon ground red pepper (cayenne); process until well combined. Chop chicken breasts then stir half of walnut sauce into chicken until combined. Spoon onto serving platter. Pour remaining sauce on top. Cover with plastic wrap and let stand 30 minutes, or refrigerate up to 8 hours. Makes 6 main-dish servings.

CHICKEN BREASTS TONNATO

In blender or in food processor with knife blade attached, blend 1 can (6½ ounces) white tuna in oil, 4 anchovy fillets, 2 tablespoons capers, drained, ¼ cup olive oil, ¼ cup fresh lemon juice, ¼ teaspoon salt, and ¾ cup reserved poaching liquid until smooth. Line platter with 1 bunch arugula or lettuce leaves. Dip each cold chicken breast half into tuna sauce to coat; arrange on arugula. Pour any remaining sauce over chicken. Garnish with lemon slices and 2 teaspoons capers. Makes 6 main-dish servings.

BONING CHICKEN BREASTS

To bone a chicken breast, remove skin if desired (page 160). Hold a knife as close as possible to the bone; move the blade along the rib bones, gently pulling the meat away from the bones with the other hand. Cut away the white tendon from the underside of the breast.

CHICKEN BREASTS WITH LEMON-CAPER SAUCE

Preparing chicken alla Francese reverses the order in which chicken is ordinarily coated. Here, the chicken is dipped first in flour and then in beaten egg. The result is deep golden chicken with a delicate, puffy coating.

Prep: 15 minutes   Cook: 20 minutes

- 4 medium skinless, boneless chicken breast halves (1¼ pounds)
- 2 tablespoons plus 1½ teaspoons all-purpose flour
- ½ teaspoon salt
- 1 large egg
- 2 teaspoons olive oil
- 2 tablespoons butter or margarine
- 2 lemons, each cut in half
- 3 garlic cloves, crushed with side of chef's knife
- ½ cup chicken broth
- ¼ cup dry white wine
- 2 tablespoons capers, drained
- 1 tablespoon chopped fresh parsley

1. Place chicken breast halves between two sheets of plastic wrap or waxed paper. With meat mallet or rolling pin, pound to ½-inch thickness. On waxed paper, combine 2 tablespoons flour and salt. In pie plate, beat egg.

2. In 12-inch skillet, heat oil over medium-high heat until very hot. Stir in 1 tablespoon butter until melted. One by one, coat each chicken breast with flour mixture, dip in egg, and add to skillet; cook 5 minutes. Reduce heat to medium, turn chicken, and cook until chicken loses its pink color throughout, 8 to 10 minutes longer. Using tongs, transfer chicken breasts to platter; keep warm.

3. From ½ lemon, cut thin slices; from remaining 1½ lemons, squeeze 2 tablespoons juice. To drippings in skillet, add lemon slices and garlic; cook, stirring, until garlic is golden. In small bowl, blend broth, wine, lemon juice, and remaining 1½ teaspoons flour until smooth; stir into mixture in skillet. Heat sauce to boiling; boil 1 minute. Stir in capers and remaining 1 tablespoon butter until butter melts. Discard garlic. Arrange lemon slices over and between chicken breasts. Pour sauce over chicken; sprinkle with chopped parsley. Makes 4 main-dish servings.

Each serving: About 287 calories, 35g protein, 7g carbohydrate, 11g total fat (5g saturated), 151mg cholesterol, 773mg sodium.

THAI CHICKEN WITH BASIL

This stir-fry is a good example of Thai cooking, which is defined by the blending of cool and hot flavors, such as cilantro, basil, ginger, garlic, and chiles.

Prep: 20 minutes plus marinating   Cook: 10 minutes

- 1 pound skinless, boneless chicken breast halves
- 3 tablespoons Asian fish sauce (nuoc nam, page 26)
- 1 tablespoon soy sauce
- 1 tablespoon brown sugar
- 2 teaspoons vegetable oil
- 1 large onion (12 ounces), cut into ¼-inch-thick slices
- 2 red or green chiles (serrano or jalapeño), seeded and cut into matchstick strips
- 2 teaspoons minced, peeled fresh ginger
- 2 garlic cloves, crushed with garlic press
- 1½ cups loosely packed fresh basil leaves

1. With knife held in slanting position, almost parallel to cutting surface, cut each chicken breast half crosswise into ¼-inch-thick slices. In medium bowl, combine fish sauce, soy sauce, and brown sugar; add chicken slices, tossing to coat. Let marinate 5 minutes.

2. In 12-inch skillet, heat oil over medium-high heat until very hot. Add chicken with marinade and cook, stirring frequently (stir-frying), until chicken loses its pink color throughout, 3 to 4 minutes. With slotted spoon, transfer chicken to bowl.

3. Add onion to marinade remaining in skillet and cook, stir-frying, until tender-crisp, about 4 minutes. Stir in chiles, ginger, and garlic; cook 1 minute longer.

4. Return chicken to skillet; heat through. Stir in basil leaves just before serving. Makes 4 main-dish servings.

Each serving: About 238 calories, 31g protein, 16g carbohydrate, 5g total fat (1g saturated), 66mg cholesterol, 784mg sodium.

Thai Chicken with Basil

GROUND CHICKEN AND GROUND TURKEY

To answer the public's demand for reduced-fat ground meats, poultry producers now offer both ground turkey and ground chicken. Each type of ground poultry has a different fat content, and since fat provides moisture and flavor, expect different results when cooking with different varieties. For example, lean ground turkey breast works well when cooked in a liquid (think along the lines of turkey meatballs in tomato sauce), but it is less successful when made into turkey burgers, where its lack of fat may make the burgers dry.

Ground chicken Made from white and dark chicken meat with skin, its fat content is about ten percent. It is an excellent all-purpose ground poultry, but any recipe prepared with this product will have a slightly softer texture than the same dish prepared with ground turkey.

Ground turkey breast Ninety-nine percent lean, this is simply white turkey breast meat, ground without any skin or fat.

Ground turkey This is a mixture of white and dark turkey meat; ground with the skin, which adds moisture. It has about seven percent fat, which is similar to the fat content of ground beef sirloin.

Ground turkey (dark meat) Usually found in the frozen section of the supermarket, packed in plastic tubes, it contains about 15 percent fat. Ground dark turkey meat may be less expensive, but it has the same fat content as ground beef round, so it doesn't offer much in the way of fat reduction.

LEANER MEATBALLS

....

Enjoy some of these tasty Italian-style meatballs with your favorite pasta and sauce, and freeze the rest. Let them cool in the pan on a wire rack, then transfer the meatballs to a jelly-roll pan and place in the freezer until frozen. Transfer them to large zip-tight plastic bags and freeze for up to one month.

Prep: 25 minutes   Bake: 15 minutes

- ⅓ cup water
- 1½ cups fresh bread crumbs (about 3 slices firm white bread)
- 1 pound lean ground beef
- 1 pound lean ground turkey meat
- 2 large egg whites
- ⅓ cup freshly grated Pecorino-Romano or Parmesan cheese
- 3 tablespoons grated onion
- 2 tablespoons chopped fresh parsley
- 1 garlic clove, minced
- 1 teaspoon salt
- ¼ teaspoon coarsely ground black pepper

1. Preheat oven to 425°F. Line 15½" by 10½" jelly-roll pan with foil and lightly grease.

2. In large bowl, pour water over bread crumbs. With hands, toss until bread is evenly moistened. Add ground beef, ground turkey, egg whites, Romano, onion, parsley, garlic, salt, and pepper; with hands, combine just until well blended but not overmixed.

3. Shape mixture into twenty-four 2-inch meatballs (for easier shaping, use slightly wet hands), handling meat as little as possible. Arrange meatballs in prepared pan and bake until lightly browned and cooked through, 15 to 20 minutes. Makes 24 meatballs.

Each meatball: About 80 calories, 8g protein, 2g carbohydrate, 4g total fat (1g saturated), 44mg cholesterol, 166mg sodium.

TURKEY MEAT LOAF

....

Thickly slice any leftover meat loaf and place between slices of hearty bread that have been spread with mango chutney for the best ever brown-bag lunch.

Prep: 15 minutes   Bake: 1 hour

- 1 tablespoon olive oil
- 1 medium onion, finely chopped
- 2 garlic cloves, finely chopped
- 2 pounds ground turkey meat
- 2 large eggs
- 1 cup fresh bread crumbs (about 2 slices firm white bread)
- ¼ cup milk
- ¼ cup mango chutney, chopped
- 2 tablespoons ketchup
- 1¼ teaspoons salt
- ½ teaspoon dried sage

1. Preheat oven to 350°F. In 6-inch skillet, heat oil over medium heat. Add onion and garlic and cook, stirring frequently, until tender, about 5 minutes. Transfer to medium bowl; cool to room temperature.

2. Add ground turkey, eggs, bread crumbs, milk, chutney, ketchup, salt, and sage to bowl; combine just until well blended but not overmixed. Spoon mixture into 9" by 5" metal loaf pan; press down gently. Cover with foil and bake until meat thermometer inserted in center of meat loaf registers 170°F, about 1 hour. Cool in pan 10 minutes; turn out onto warm platter and slice. Makes 8 main-dish servings.

Each serving: About 261 calories, 23g protein, 14g carbohydrate, 12g total fat (3g saturated), 137mg cholesterol, 657mg sodium.

CORNISH HENS

These small birds, a cross of the White Plymouth and Cornish chicken breeds, weigh between 1½ and 1¾ pounds and yield two servings. For a bird small enough for a single serving, look for *poussin* at specialty butcher shops. Pronounced "poose-AHN," these small chickens weigh about 1 pound each. You can substitute poussin for Cornish hens in most recipes, but reduce the cooking time by about one third.

CORNISH HENS MILANESE

(Pictured on page 148)

....

Gremolata, a tasty blend of chopped fresh parsley, freshly grated lemon peel, and pungent garlic, is a popular way to finish a food dish in Italy. We also love gremolata scattered over steamed green beans or new potatoes.

Prep: 5 minutes   Roast: 50 minutes

- 2   Cornish hens (1½ pounds each)
- 3   tablespoons chopped fresh parsley
- 1   teaspoon extra-virgin olive oil
- ¼   teaspoon salt
- ⅛   teaspoon ground black pepper
- 1   small garlic clove, minced
- ½   teaspoon freshly grated lemon peel

1. Preheat oven to 375°F. Remove giblets and necks from hens; reserve for another use. With poultry shears, cut each hen lengthwise in half. Rinse hen halves with cold running water; pat dry with paper towels.

2. In small bowl, combine 2 tablespoons parsley, oil, salt, and pepper. With fingertips, carefully separate skin from meat on each hen half; spread parsley mixture under skin. Place hens, skin side up, in large roasting pan (17" by 11½").

3. Roast hens, basting with drippings 3 times, until juices run clear when thickest part of thigh is pierced with tip of knife, about 50 minutes.

4. Arrange hens warm on platter. In cup, combine remaining 1 tablespoon parsley, garlic, and lemon peel; sprinkle over hens. Makes 4 main-dish servings.

Each serving: About 384 calories, 32g protein, 0g carbohydrate, 27g total fat (7g saturated), 187mg cholesterol, 236mg sodium.

CHICKEN LIVERS MARSALA

....

In this classic preparation, Marsala wine mellows and sweetens the assertive flavor of the chicken livers. Serve with rice or noodles to soak up the juices.

Prep: 15 minutes   Cook: 15 minutes

- 1   pound chicken livers, trimmed and cut in half
- 3   tablespoons butter or margarine
- ¾   teaspoon salt
- 1   medium onion, chopped
- 8   ounces mushrooms, trimmed and cut in half
- ¼   teaspoon ground black pepper
- ¼   cup dry Marsala wine
- 1   tablespoon chopped fresh parsley

1. Pat livers dry with paper towels. In 10-inch skillet, melt 1 tablespoon butter over medium-high heat. Add livers, sprinkle with ½ teaspoon salt, and cook, stirring often, until livers are browned but still pink in center, 3 to 4 minutes. Transfer livers to bowl.

2. Add remaining 2 tablespoons butter to skillet. Add onion and cook until tender, about 5 minutes. Add mushrooms, pepper, and remaining ¼ teaspoon salt and cook until mushrooms are tender. Stir in Marsala and heat to boiling. Add livers and heat through. Sprinkle with parsley. Makes 4 main-dish servings.

Each serving: About 272 calories, 22g protein, 12g carbohydrate, 13g total fat (7g saturated), 522mg cholesterol, 619mg sodium.

MARSALA WINE

Marsala, Italy's most famous fortified wine, is produced by a process similar to the one used in Spain to make sherry. Marsala is made in several different styles: **secco** (dry), **semisecco** (semisweet), and **dolce** (sweet). It is also classified based on its flavor characteristics and aging:

Fine is usually aged less than one year

Superiore is aged at least two years

Superiore Riserva is aged at least four years

Vergine e/o Soleras is aged at least five years

Vergine e/o Soleras Stravecchio or *Vergine e/o Solveras Riserva* is aged at least ten years

TURKEY

Choose your turkey by size—there is no difference in flavor or texture between a tom (male) and a hen (female). Fresh birds are especially delicious, but if you choose to buy a frozen bird, be sure to allow enough time for thorough thawing. Farm-raised wild turkey breeds, found in specialty butcher shops, have a mildly gamy flavor and are never as big or as meaty as the supermarket variety.

TURKEY PARTS

Turkey parts are readily available and can be prepared in as many ways as chicken. Whole turkey breast is a good way to feed a crowd and makes tasty leftovers for sandwiches. Turkey drumsticks, both economical and tasty, are an excellent choice for a weeknight meal. Lean turkey cutlets (boneless sliced turkey breast) cook quickly and look elegant, but take care not to overcook them or they will toughen and dry out.

TRADITIONAL ROAST TURKEY WITH GIBLET GRAVY

··

Here it is—the traditional Thanksgiving centerpiece. The chart on page 151 will tell you, in a flash, how much time you'll need to roast the perfect bird, no matter how small or how large.

Prep: 1 hour (not including stuffing)
Roast: 3 hours 45 minutes

choice of stuffing (pages 186–189)
1   turkey (14 pounds)
1½ teaspoons salt
½   teaspoon coarsely ground black pepper
    Giblet Gravy (page 178)

1. Prepare desired stuffing; set aside.

2. Preheat oven to 325°F. Remove giblets and neck from turkey; reserve for making Giblet Gravy. Rinse turkey inside and out with cold running water and drain well; pat dry with paper towels.

3. Loosely spoon some stuffing into neck cavity. Fold neck skin over stuffing; fasten neck skin to turkey back with one or two skewers.

4. Loosely spoon remaining stuffing into body cavity (bake any leftover stuffing in small covered casserole during last 30 minutes of roasting time). Fold skin over cavity opening; skewer closed, if necessary. Tie legs and tail together with string, push drumsticks under band of skin, or use stuffing clamp. Secure wings to body with string, if desired.

5. Place turkey, breast side up, on rack in large roasting pan (17" by 11½"). Sprinkle salt and pepper on outside of turkey. Cover with loose tent of foil. Roast about 3 hours 45 minutes. Start checking for doneness during last hour of roasting.

6. To brown turkey, remove foil during last hour of roasting and baste occasionally with pan drippings. Turkey is done when temperature on meat thermometer inserted in thickest part of thigh, next to body, reaches 180° to 185°F and juices run clear when thickest part of thigh is pierced with tip of knife. (Breast temperature should be 170° to 175°F, stuffing temperature 160° to 165°F.)

7. While turkey is roasting, prepare giblets and neck to use in Giblet Gravy.

8. Transfer turkey to large platter; keep warm. Let stand at least 15 minutes to set juices for easier carving.

9. Meanwhile, prepare Giblet Gravy.

10. Serve turkey with stuffing and gravy. Makes 14 main-dish servings.

Each serving without skin, stuffing, or gravy: About 143 calories, 25g protein, 0g carbohydrate, 4g total fat (1g saturated), 65mg cholesterol, 146mg sodium.

GIBLET GRAVY

Prepare giblets and neck: In 3-quart saucepan, combine **gizzard, heart, neck,** and enough **water** to cover; heat to boiling over high heat. Reduce heat; cover and simmer 45 minutes. Add **liver** and cook 15 minutes longer. Strain giblet broth through sieve into large bowl. Pull meat from neck; discard bones. Coarsely chop neck meat and giblets. Cover and refrigerate meat and broth separately.

To make gravy, remove rack from roasting pan. Strain **pan drippings** through sieve into 4-cup measuring cup or medium bowl. Add **1 cup giblet broth** to hot roasting pan and heat to boiling, stirring until browned bits are loosened from bottom of pan; add to drippings in measuring cup. Let stand 1 minute, or until fat separates from meat juice. Spoon **2 tablespoons fat** from drippings into 2-quart saucepan; skim and discard any remaining fat. Add **remaining giblet broth** and enough *water* to meat juice in cup to equal 3½ cups.

Heat fat in saucepan over medium heat. Stir in **2 tablespoons all-purpose flour** and ½ **teaspoon salt** and cook, stirring, until flour turns golden brown. With wire whisk, gradually whisk in **meat-juice mixture** and cook, whisking, until gravy has thickened slightly and boils; boil 1 minute. Stir in reserved giblets and neck meat; heat through. Pour gravy into gravy boat. Makes about 3½ cups gravy.

Each ¼ cup gravy: About 128 calories, 17g protein, 1g carbohydrate, 5g total fat (2g saturated), 153mg cholesterol, 152mg sodium.

GIBLETS

TEST KITCHEN TIP

Giblets, poultry organs that can be cooked and eaten, include the liver, heart, and gizzard; some of them may be used to enrich gravy or to make a quick, flavorful broth. (Don't add livers to broth, they will make it bitter.) Giblets are usually wrapped in a separate package along with the neck and placed in the cavity of a bird, but the content varies from producer to producer. For your holiday giblet gravy, we recommend buying giblets separately to be sure of what you are buying.

CARVING A ROAST TURKEY

Cut through the skin where the leg is attached. To remove the leg, force it away from the body with a carving fork until it pops out of the socket. Separate the thigh from the body by cutting through the joint. If you like, separate the drumstick from the thigh by cutting through the center joint. To carve the leg, slice the thigh and drumstick meat, cutting parallel to the bones. Repeat on the other side.

To carve the breast, make a horizontal cut above the wing joint along the length of the bird, making sure to cut down to the bone.

With the knife parallel to the rib cage, cut the breast meat into thin slices. Cut off the wing. Repeat on the other side.

ROSEMARY ROAST TURKEY BREAST

....

When a whole turkey is too much, use just the breast. It will make white-meat fans very happy.

Prep: 20 minutes   Roast: 2 hours 15 to 30 minutes

- 1 bone-in turkey breast (6 to 7 pounds)
- 1½ teaspoons dried rosemary, crumbled
- 1 teaspoon salt
- ¾ teaspoon coarsely ground black pepper
- 1 cup chicken broth

1. Preheat oven to 350°F. Rinse turkey breast with cold running water and drain well; pat dry with paper towels. In cup, combine rosemary, salt, and pepper. Rub rosemary mixture on both inside and outside of turkey breast.

2. Place turkey, skin side up, on rack in small roasting pan (13" by 9"). Cover turkey with loose tent of foil. Roast turkey 1 hour 30 minutes. Remove foil; roast, occasionally basting with pan drippings, 45 to 60 minutes longer. Start checking for doneness during last 30 minutes of cooking. Turkey breast is done when temperature on meat thermometer inserted into thickest part of breast (not touching bone) reaches 170°F and juices run clear when thickest part of breast is pierced with tip of knife.

3. Transfer turkey to warm platter. Let stand 15 minutes to set juices for easier carving.

4. Meanwhile, pour broth into drippings in hot roasting pan; heat to boiling, stirring until browned bits are loosened from bottom of pan. Strain pan-juice mixture through sieve into 1-quart saucepan; let stand 1 minute. Skim and discard fat. Heat pan-juice mixture over medium heat until hot; serve with turkey. Remove skin before eating. Makes 10 main-dish servings.

Each serving without skin and with pan juices: About 251 calories, 55g protein, 0g carbohydrate, 2g total fat (0g saturated), 152mg cholesterol, 428mg sodium.

TURKEY MARSALA WITH MUSHROOMS

....

Turkey cutlets are an excellent and economical substitute for veal scallopini, and this recipe proves it.

Prep: 15 minutes   Cook: 15 minutes

- 2 tablespoons butter or margarine
- 10 ounces mushrooms, trimmed and sliced
- ¾ teaspoon salt
- 1 pound turkey cutlets, large pieces cut in half
- 3 tablespoons all-purpose flour
- ¼ teaspoon ground black pepper
- 1 tablespoon olive oil
- ½ cup dry Marsala wine
- ¼ cup water

1. In 12-inch skillet, melt 1 tablespoon butter over medium-high heat. Add mushrooms and ¼ teaspoon salt; cook until mushrooms are golden brown and liquid has evaporated, about 7 minutes. With slotted spoon, transfer mushrooms to medium bowl.

2. Meanwhile, with meat mallet or between two sheets of plastic wrap or waxed paper with rolling pin, pound turkey cutlets to ¼-inch thickness. On waxed paper, combine flour, pepper, and remaining ½ teaspoon salt; use to coat cutlets, shaking off excess.

3. In same skillet, melt remaining 1 tablespoon butter with oil over medium-high heat. Add half of cutlets and cook until cutlets are golden brown and lose their pink color throughout, 1 to 2 minutes per side. Transfer cutlets to bowl with mushrooms; keep warm. Repeat with remaining cutlets.

4. To skillet, add Marsala and water; cook 1 minute. Stir in turkey cutlets and mushrooms, turning to coat with sauce. Makes 4 main-dish servings.

Each serving: About 284 calories, 30g protein, 9g carbohydrate, 10g total fat (4g saturated), 86mg cholesterol, 556mg sodium.

CURRIED SWEET POTATO SHEPHERD'S PIE

....

Our flavor-filled adaptation of the traditional casserole combines curried turkey with gingered vegetables, nestled under a savory crust of mashed sweet potatoes. Make two and freeze one, so you can enjoy any night of the week.

Prep: 1 hour   Cook: 35 minutes

   5   medium (12-ounce) sweet potatoes
   2   tablespoons vegetable oil
   2   pounds ground turkey or chicken
   2   teaspoons salt
 ⅓   cup all-purpose flour
   1   tablespoon curry powder
   1   can (14- to 14½-ounces) chicken broth or 1³/₄ cups Chicken Broth (page 70)
1½   pounds carrots, peeled and chopped
1½   pounds parsnips, peeled and chopped
   1   medium onion, chopped
   1   tablespoon grated peeled fresh ginger
   1   package (10 ounces) frozen peas
   1   cup reduced-fat (2%) milk, warmed
   2   tablespoons butter or margarine

Curried Sweet Potato Shepherd's Pie

1. Pierce potatoes all over with fork. Cook in microwave on High 15 to 17 minutes or until potatoes are tender when pierced with fork, turning potatoes over once; set aside.

2. Meanwhile, in 12-inch skillet, heat 1 tablespoon oil over medium-high heat until hot. Add turkey; sprinkle with ½ teaspoon salt and cook 5 to 6 minutes or until no longer pink, stirring and breaking up turkey with side of spoon.

3. Stir flour and curry powder into turkey in skillet; cook 1 minute, stirring. Add broth and heat to boiling. Cook 1 minute or until mixture thickens slightly. Divide turkey mixture between two 2½- to 3-quart glass or ceramic baking dishes and spread evenly.

4. Preheat oven to 375°F. Wipe skillet dry. To same skillet, add remaining 1 tablespoon oil and heat on medium until hot. Add carrots, parsnips, and onion, and cook, covered, about 15 minutes or until vegetables are browned and tender, stirring occasionally. Stir in ginger, frozen peas, and ½ teaspoon salt. Divide vegetable mixture between casseroles, spreading evenly over turkey mixture.

5. When cool enough to handle, cut potatoes in half length-wise and scoop flesh from skins into large bowl. With potato masher, coarsely mash potatoes. Stir in milk, butter, and 1 teaspoon salt; mash until well blended. Spread potatoes over vegetables.

6. Bake one shepherd's pie, uncovered, 35 to 40 minutes or until top is browned. Meanwhile, prepare second casserole for freezing. Makes 2 casseroles with 6 servings each.

Each serving: About 365 calories, 19g protein, 47g carbohydrate, 12g total fat (3g saturated), 9g fiber, 61mg cholesterol, 630mg sodium.

Tip: When microwaving sweet potatoes, it's important to use potatoes that are as uniform in size and shape as possible. Otherwise, they will not cook evenly.

TURKEY POTPIE WITH CORNMEAL CRUST

....

Chock full of turkey and vegetables, this potpie is the last word in comfort food.

Prep: 30 minutes   Bake: 35 minutes

- 1 tablespoon vegetable oil
- 1 medium rutabaga (1 pound), peeled and cut into ½-inch pieces
- 3 carrots, peeled and cut into ½-inch pieces
- 1 large onion (12 ounces), chopped
- 1 pound all-purpose potatoes (3 medium), peeled and cut into ½-inch pieces
- 2 large stalks celery, chopped
- ¾ teaspoon salt
- 1 pound cooked turkey or chicken, cut into ½-inch pieces (4 cups)
- 1 package (10 ounces) frozen peas
- 1 can (14½ ounces) chicken broth or 1¾ cups Chicken Broth (page 70)
- 1 cup milk
- ¼ cup all-purpose flour
- ¼ teaspoon ground black pepper
- ⅛ teaspoon dried thyme
  Cornmeal Crust (right)
- 1 large egg, beaten

1. Prepare potpie filling: In 12-inch skillet, heat oil over medium-high heat; add rutabaga, carrots, and onion and cook 10 minutes. Stir in potatoes, celery, and ½ teaspoon salt; cook, stirring frequently, until rutabaga is tender-crisp, about 10 minutes longer. Spoon into 13" by 9" baking dish; add turkey and peas.

2. In 2-quart saucepan, heat broth to boiling. Meanwhile, in small bowl, blend milk and flour until smooth. Stir milk mixture into broth. Add pepper, thyme, and remaining ¼ teaspoon salt; heat to boiling over high heat, stirring. Stir sauce into chicken-vegetable mixture in baking dish.

3. Prepare Cornmeal Crust. Preheat oven to 425°F.

4. On lightly floured surface, with floured rolling pin, roll dough into rectangle 2 inches longer and wider than baking dish. Arrange dough rectangle over filling; trim edge, leaving 1-inch overhang. Fold overhang under; flute. Brush crust with some egg. If desired, reroll trimmings; cut into decorative shapes to garnish top of pie. Brush dough cutouts with egg. Cut several slits in crust to allow steam to escape during baking.

5. Place potpie on foil-lined cookie sheet to catch any overflow during baking. Bake potpie until crust is golden brown and filling is hot and bubbling, 35 to 40 minutes. During last 10 minutes of baking, cover edges of crust with foil to prevent overbrowning. Makes 10 main-dish servings.

Each serving: About 416 calories, 21g protein, 42g carbohydrate, 18g total fat (5g saturated), 60mg cholesterol, 644mg sodium.

CORNMEAL CRUST

In large bowl, combine **1½ cups all-purpose flour, ¼ cup cornmeal,** and **¾ teaspoon salt.** With pastry blender or two knives used scissor-fashion, cut in **⅔ cup vegetable shortening** until mixture resembles coarse crumbs. Sprinkle **6 to 7 tablespoons cold water,** 1 tablespoon at a time, over flour mixture, mixing with fork after each addition until dough is just moist enough to hold together.

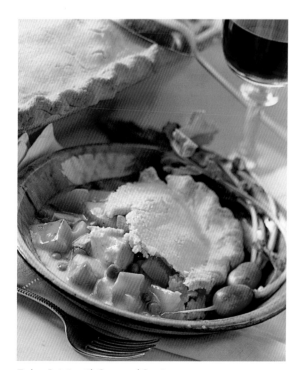

Turkey Potpie with Cornmeal Crust

TURKEY THIGHS OSSO BUCO–STYLE

....

Cooked in a manner usually reserved for veal shanks, turkey thighs make an excellent stew. Serve with soft polenta or rice pilaf.

Prep: 20 minutes   Bake: 1 hour 30 minutes

- ¼   teaspoon salt
- ¼   teaspoon ground black pepper
- 2   turkey thighs (1¼ pounds each), skin removed
- 2   teaspoons vegetable oil
- 2   medium onions, finely chopped
- 4   carrots, peeled and cut into ¾-inch pieces
- 2   stalks celery, cut into ½-inch pieces
- 4   garlic cloves, finely chopped
- 1   can (14½ ounces) tomatoes in puree
- ½   cup dry red wine
- 1   bay leaf
- ¼   teaspoon dried thyme

1. Preheat oven to 350°F. Sprinkle salt and pepper on turkey. In nonreactive 5-quart Dutch oven, heat oil over medium-high heat until very hot. Add 1 turkey thigh and cook, turning occasionally, until golden brown, about 5 minutes. With tongs, transfer thigh to plate; repeat with second thigh. Discard all but 1 tablespoon fat from Dutch oven.

2. Reduce heat to medium. Add onions to Dutch oven and cook, stirring occasionally, 5 minutes. Add carrots, celery, and garlic; cook, stirring frequently, 2 minutes longer.

3. Stir in tomatoes with puree, wine, bay leaf, and thyme, breaking up tomatoes with side of spoon; heat to boiling. Add browned turkey; cover and place in oven. Bake until turkey is tender, about 1 hour 30 minutes. Discard bay leaf. Remove turkey meat from bones and cut into bite-size pieces; return meat to Dutch oven and stir well. Makes 4 main-dish servings.

Each serving: About 323 calories, 36g protein, 24g carbohydrate, 9g total fat (3g saturated), 122mg cholesterol, 483mg sodium.

OLD-FASHIONED CREAMED TURKEY

....

This old-time favorite, sometimes called turkey hash, deserves a place in the Comfort Food Hall of Fame. You can stir in leftover cooked vegetables—carrots, peas, and potatoes are all good—along with the turkey. Spoon it over noodles, mashed potatoes, or rice.

Prep: 10 minutes   Cook: 20 minutes

- 2   tablespoons butter or margarine
- 1   small onion, finely chopped
- 3   tablespoons all-purpose flour
- 2   cups milk
- ½   teaspoon salt
- ⅛   teaspoon ground black pepper
      pinch ground nutmeg
- 8   ounces cooked turkey or chicken, cut into ½-inch pieces (2 cups)
- 2   tablespoons chopped fresh parsley

1. In 3-quart saucepan, melt butter over medium heat. Add onion and cook, stirring, until tender, about 5 minutes. Stir in flour and cook, stirring constantly, 1 minute. With wire whisk, gradually whisk in milk, salt, pepper, and nutmeg. Heat to boiling over medium-high heat, whisking. Reduce heat and simmer, whisking occasionally, 5 minutes.

2. Stir turkey into sauce and heat through. Stir in parsley and serve. Makes 4 main-dish servings.

Each serving: About 277 calories, 26g protein, 13g carbohydrate, 13g total fat (7g saturated), 87mg cholesterol, 462mg sodium.

DUCK

Most supermarket ducks are of the Pekin (Long Island) breed. While the meat is flavorful, it can also be fatty. Cutting a duck into quarters helps render the excess fat. Specialty butchers often carry Moulard or Muscovy ducks, which are leaner and meatier than the Pekin variety but also much more expensive.

GINGER-GLAZED DUCK

....

To ensure crisp, flavorful skin, this glazed duck is roasted at high heat during the last 10 minutes.

Prep: 10 minutes   Roast: 2 hours 10 minutes

- 1 duck (4½ pounds), cut into quarters, fat removed
- 3 teaspoons grated, peeled fresh ginger
- ½ teaspoon salt
- ¼ teaspoon ground black pepper
- 2 tablespoons honey
- 1 tablespoon soy sauce

1. Preheat oven to 350°F. Pat duck dry with paper towels. With two-tine fork, prick skin in several places.

2. In cup, combine 1 teaspoon ginger, salt, and pepper. Use to rub on meat side of duck quarters. Place duck, skin side up, on rack in large (17" by 11½") foil-lined roasting pan. Roast 2 hours, using spoon or bulb baster to remove fat from pan occasionally.

3. Meanwhile, in cup, combine honey, soy sauce, and remaining 2 teaspoons ginger.

4. Turn oven control to 450°F. Remove duck from oven and brush all over with ginger glaze. Return to oven and roast 10 minutes longer. Makes 4 main-dish servings.

Each serving: About 690 calories, 37g protein, 9g carbohydrate, 55g total fat (19g saturated), 163mg cholesterol, 662mg sodium.

CHIPOTLE-GLAZED DUCK

Prepare as directed but omit ginger, honey, and soy sauce. While duck roasts, press **2 tablespoons chopped canned chipotle chiles in adobo** (page 25) through sieve into small bowl; discard skin and seeds. Stir **2 tablespoons light (mild) molasses** into chipotle chiles. Proceed as in Step 4.

RED-COOKED DUCK

....

Chinese "red-cooked" food is simmered in a soy-sauce mixture that turns the food a dark reddish brown.

Prep: 25 minutes   Bake: 2 hours

- 4 green onions
- 1 duck (4½ pounds), cut into 8 pieces, fat removed
- 1 tablespoon olive oil
- ¼ cup soy sauce
- 2 tablespoons dry sherry
- 1 tablespoon minced, peeled fresh ginger
- 3 garlic cloves, each cut in half
- 1 tablespoon brown sugar
- 2 whole star anise or ½ teaspoon anise seeds
- ¼ teaspoon ground red pepper (cayenne)
- ¾ cup water

1. Preheat oven to 350°F. Cut green onions on diagonal into 1½-inch pieces.

2. Pat duck dry with paper towels.

3. In 8-quart Dutch oven, heat oil over high heat until very hot. Cook duck, in batches, until golden brown, about 8 minutes, using tongs to transfer duck pieces to large bowl as they are browned. Discard all but 1 tablespoon fat from Dutch oven. Add green onions and cook, stirring, until lightly browned, about 5 minutes.

4. Stir in soy sauce, sherry, ginger, garlic, brown sugar, star anise, ground red pepper, and water. Heat to boiling over high heat, stirring until browned bits are loosened from bottom of Dutch oven.

5. Return duck to Dutch oven. Cover and place in oven. Bake 2 hours, basting duck several times with pan liquid.

6. With tongs, transfer duck to warm deep platter. Strain sauce through sieve; skim and discard fat. Serve duck topped with sauce. Makes 4 main-dish servings.

Each serving: About 721 calories, 38g protein, 8g carbohydrate, 59g total fat (19g saturated), 163mg cholesterol, 1,293mg sodium.

SEARED DUCK BREAST WITH DRIED CHERRIES AND PORT

....

If you can only find the larger duck breasts, which weigh in at 12 to 13 ounces each, buy two of them and cook them on medium-low 20 minutes, with skin side down; turn them over and continue cooking 4 minutes longer. To serve, slice the breasts as in step 4, but give each diner the slices from half a breast.

Prep: 5 minutes   Cook: 25 minutes

- 4 boneless fresh or frozen (thawed) duck-breast halves with skin (6 ounces each)
- ¼ teaspoon salt
- ⅛ teaspoon coarsely ground black pepper
- 1 large shallot, thinly sliced
- 1 clove garlic, crushed with press
- 1 cup port wine
- 2 tablespoons balsamic vinegar
- ⅓ cup dried cherries

1. Pat duck breasts dry with paper towels. With sharp knife, cut 4 diagonal slashes, about ¼ inch deep, in skin and fat on each breast half. On sheet of waxed paper, evenly season duck breasts, on both sides, with salt and pepper.

2. In 12-inch nonstick skillet, cook breasts, skin side down, on medium 15 minutes or until skin is well browned and crispy. As breasts cook, spoon off and discard fat in skillet. Turn breasts over and cook on flesh side about 4 minutes for medium-rare or until desired doneness. Transfer breasts to cutting board; cover with foil to keep warm until ready to serve.

3. Discard all but 1 teaspoon duck fat remaining in skillet. Add shallot and cook on medium 2 to 3 minutes or until beginning to brown. Stir in garlic and cook 1 minute. Add port wine, balsamic vinegar, and cherries; heat to boiling. Boil 3 minutes or until sauce is reduced to 3/4 cup, stirring frequently.

4. To serve, thinly slice each breast and transfer to a dinner plate. Spoon port sauce over breasts. Makes 4 main-dish servings.

Each serving: About 315 calories, 28g protein, 19g carbohydrate, 13g total fat (4g saturated), 1g fiber, 155mg cholesterol, 245mg sodium.

Seared Duck Breast with Dried Cherries and Port

GOOSE

Goose is the holiday bird of choice for many families. It has dark, deep-flavored, firm-textured flesh and, when roasted properly, sports an irresistibly crisp, golden skin. A goose is a large bird that isn't very meaty, but the meat is fairly rich. Serve it in small portions, accompanied by generous helpings of stuffing.

CRISPY ROAST GOOSE WITH ORANGE SAUCE

Piercing the skin of goose helps drain off the large amount of fat and also crisps the skin. Serve with one of our homemade cranberry sauces or chutneys (pages 508–509). Pour all the flavorful fat through a fine sieve and freeze for up to four months. Use for browning potatoes.

Prep: 30 minutes   Roast: 4 hours 25 minutes

- 1 goose (12 pounds)
- 5 navel oranges, each cut in half
- 1 bunch thyme
- 4 bay leaves
- ½ teaspoon dried thyme
- 1¼ teaspoons salt
- ½ teaspoon coarsely ground black pepper
- 3 tablespoons orange-flavored liqueur
- 2 tablespoons cornstarch
- ½ cup orange marmalade

1. Preheat oven to 400°F. Remove giblets and neck from goose; reserve for another use. Trim and discard fat from body cavity and any excess skin. Rinse goose inside and out with cold running water and drain well; pat dry with paper towels. With goose breast side up, lift wings up toward neck, then fold wing tips under back of goose so wings stay in place. Place 6 orange halves, thyme sprigs, and bay leaves in body cavity. Tie legs and tail together with string. Fold neck skin over back. With two-tine fork, prick skin in several places to drain fat during roasting.

2. Place goose, breast side up, on rack in large roasting pan (17" by 11½"). In cup, combine dried thyme, 1 teaspoon salt, and pepper; rub mixture over goose. Cover goose and roasting pan with foil. Roast 1 hour 30 minutes; turn oven control to 325°F and roast 2 hours longer.

3. Meanwhile, in small bowl, from remaining 4 orange halves, squeeze ¾ cup juice. Stir in 1 tablespoon liqueur, cornstarch, and remaining ¼ teaspoon salt; set aside. In cup, mix orange marmalade with remaining 2 tablespoons liqueur.

4. With spoon or bulb baster, remove as much fat from roasting pan as possible. Remove foil and roast goose 45 minutes longer. Remove goose from oven and turn oven control to 450°F. Brush marmalade mixture over goose. Roast goose until skin is golden brown and crisp, about 10 minutes longer. Transfer goose to warm platter; let stand at least 15 minutes for juices to set for easier carving.

5. Prepare sauce: Remove rack from roasting pan. Strain pan drippings through sieve into 8-cup measuring cup or large bowl. Let stand until fat separates from meat juice; skim and reserve fat for another use (there should be about 5 cups fat). Measure meat juice; if necessary, add enough water to meat juice to equal 1 cup. Return meat juice to pan and add reserved orange-juice mixture. Heat sauce to boiling over medium heat, stirring; boil 1 minute. (Makes about 1¾ cups.) Serve sauce with goose. Remove skin before eating, if desired. Makes 10 main-dish servings.

Each serving with skin: About 810 calories, 66g protein, 5g carbohydrate, 57g total fat (18g saturated), 235mg cholesterol, 472mg sodium.

Each serving without skin: About 488 calories, 57g protein, 5g carbohydrate, 25g total fat (9g saturated), 188mg cholesterol, 440mg sodium.

Tradition often dictates a stuffed bird (especially the holiday turkey), so the juices of the bird can moisten the stuffing. But some cooks prefer to roast their birds unstuffed and heat the stuffing in a separate baking dish. If you prefer your poultry stuffed, here are some pointers on how to do it safely.

• One important rule of thumb: Remember that the stuffing is only being heated through while inside the bird and does not actually cook. Therefore, it is important that the ingredients be thoroughly cooked before being combined.

• To save time, cut up the raw stuffing ingredients the night before, then cover and refrigerate. If you wish, you can cook the vegetables and meat, then cool, cover, and refrigerate. When you're ready to put the stuffing together, reheat the cooked ingredients in a large skillet before proceeding with the recipe.

• Stuff the bird just before roasting—never in advance—and roast immediately. Use warm cooked ingredients and hot broth or stock for your stuffing. A warm stuffing will reach the safe temperature of 160°F more quickly. At this safe temperature, bacteria, including salmonella, are killed.

• Lightly stuff the body and neck cavities; do not pack. Stuffing needs room to expand during cooking. You will rarely be able to fit all of the stuffing inside the bird, so bake the extra stuffing in a covered buttered baking dish for about 30 minutes or until heated through.

• After cooking, the stuffing temperature should have reached 160°F to be safe. Check the temperature with a meat thermometer inserted deep into the stuffing. If the poultry has reached the proper temperature but the stuffing hasn't, transfer the stuffing to a buttered baking dish, cover, and continue baking until it reaches 160°F.

• Any leftover stuffing should be promptly removed from the bird (to avoid potential bacterial growth). Transfer the stuffing to a covered container and use within three days, or freeze up to one month.

SOUTHWEST CORN BREAD STUFFING

This old-style stuffing starts with moist homemade Monterey Jack corn bread. Crumble the corn bread, drizzle with chicken broth, and you've got stuffing!

Prep: 20 minutes plus cooling
Bake: 1 hour 45 minutes

- 2 cups yellow cornmeal
- 2 teaspoons baking powder
- 1 teaspoon baking soda
- 1 teaspoon salt
- 2 cups buttermilk
- ½ cup butter or margarine (1 stick), melted and cooled
- 1 can (14¾ ounces) cream-style corn
- 2 cans (4 to 4½ ounces each) chopped mild green chiles
- 8 ounces Monterey Jack cheese, shredded (2 cups)
- 4 large eggs, lightly beaten
- ½ cup chicken broth

1. Preheat oven to 350°F. Grease 13" by 9" baking pan or deep oven-safe 12-inch skillet (if skillet is not oven-safe, wrap handle with double layer of foil).

2. In large bowl, combine cornmeal, baking powder, baking soda, and salt. Stir in buttermilk, melted butter, corn, chiles, cheese, and eggs and stir until thoroughly blended. Pour batter into baking pan.

3. Bake corn bread until top is browned and toothpick inserted in center comes out clean, 60 to 65 minutes. Cool in pan on wire rack. (The cornbread can be used after cooling to make stuffing, but it will make a firmer stuffing if allowed to stale slightly. If desired, cover and reserve corn bread up to 2 days.)

4. Prepare stuffing: Crumble corn bread into large bowl. Drizzle with broth; toss to mix well. Use to stuff 12- to 16-pound turkey, or heat in baking dish and serve alongside poultry or ham: Spoon stuffing into greased 13" by 9" baking dish; cover with foil and bake in preheated 325°F oven until heated through, about 45 minutes. Makes about 11 cups stuffing.

Each ½ cup stuffing: About 161 calories, 6g protein, 15g carbohydrate, 9g total fat (5g saturated), 62mg cholesterol, 481mg sodium.

COUNTRY SAUSAGE AND CORN BREAD STUFFING

It's hard to resist this all-time favorite stuffing of pecans, sausage, and store-bought stuffing mix.

Prep: 45 minutes   Bake: 45 minutes

- 1 pound pork sausage meat
- 4 tablespoons butter or margarine
- 3 stalks celery, coarsely chopped
- 1 large onion (12 ounces), coarsely chopped
- 1 red pepper, coarsely chopped
- 1 can (14½ ounces) chicken broth or 1¾ cups Chicken Broth (page 70)
- ½ teaspoon coarsely ground black pepper
- ¾ cup water
- 1 package (14 to 16 ounces) corn bread stuffing mix
- 1½ cups pecans (6 ounces), toasted and coarsely chopped
- ¼ cup chopped fresh parsley

1. Heat 12-inch skillet over medium-high heat until very hot. Add sausage meat and cook, breaking up sausage with side of spoon, until browned, about 10 minutes. With tongs, transfer sausage to large bowl.

2. Discard all but 2 tablespoons sausage drippings. Add butter, celery, onion, and red pepper to skillet; cook, stirring occasionally, until vegetables are golden brown and tender. Stir in broth, black pepper, and water; heat to boiling, stirring until browned bits are loosened from bottom of skillet.

3. Add vegetable mixture, stuffing mix, pecans, and parsley to sausage; stir to combine well. Use to stuff 12- to 16-pound turkey, or heat in baking dish and serve alongside poultry or ham: Spoon stuffing into greased 13" by 9" baking dish; cover with foil and bake in preheated 325°F oven until heated through, about 45 minutes. Makes about 12 cups stuffing.

Each ½ cup stuffing: About 174 calories, 4g protein, 15g carbohydrate, 11g total fat (3g saturated), 13mg cholesterol, 407mg sodium.

CHESTNUT AND APPLE STUFFING

It's easiest to peel chestnuts while they're warm. Peel only a few at a time while you keep the rest hot.

Prep: 1 hour   Bake: 45 minutes

- 2 pounds fresh chestnuts
- 10 cups ½-inch cubes day-old French bread (one 16-ounce loaf)
- 6 tablespoons butter or margarine
- 2 stalks celery, sliced
- 1 medium onion, coarsely chopped
- 1¾ pounds Rome Beauty or Crispin apples (3 large), peeled, cored, and coarsely chopped
- 2 teaspoons poultry seasoning
- 1 can (14½ ounces) chicken broth or 1¾ cups Chicken Broth (page 70)
- 1 cup water
- 1 teaspoon salt

1. Preheat oven to 400°F. With sharp knife, slash shell of each chestnut. Place in jelly-roll pan and roast until shells burst open, about 20 minutes. When cool enough to handle, with paring knife, peel chestnuts. Chop chestnut meat; place in large bowl. Add bread cubes to bowl with chestnuts and toss to combine.

2. In 3-quart saucepan, melt butter over medium-high heat. Add celery and onion and cook until golden brown and tender, about 10 minutes. Add apples and poultry seasoning; cook, stirring occasionally, 2 minutes longer. Stir in broth, water, and salt; heat to boiling over high heat.

3. Pour hot vegetable mixture over chestnut mixture; stir to combine well. Use to stuff 12- to 16-pound turkey, or heat in baking dish and serve alongside poultry or ham: Spoon stuffing into greased 13" by 9" baking dish; cover with foil and bake in preheated 325°F oven until heated through, about 45 minutes. Makes about 12 cups stuffing.

Each ½ cup stuffing: About 158 calories, 3g protein, 28g carbohydrate, 4g total fat (2g saturated), 8mg cholesterol, 321mg sodium.

PARSNIPS, SWISS CHARD, AND BACON STUFFING

··

The unusual pairing of parsnips and Swiss chard with bacon will surprise and delight your family and guests.

Prep: 45 minutes   Bake: 45 minutes

- 8 ounces sliced bacon, cut into ½-inch pieces
- 1 pound parsnips, peeled and coarsely chopped
- 3 stalks celery, coarsely chopped
- 1 large onion (12 ounces), coarsely chopped
- 1½ pounds Swiss chard, tough stems trimmed and leaves cut into 2-inch pieces
- 1 can (14½ ounces) chicken broth or 1¾ cups Chicken Broth (page 70)
- ½ teaspoon coarsely ground black pepper
- 2 packages (8 ounces each) herb-seasoned stuffing mix

1. In 12-inch skillet, cook bacon over medium-low heat until browned. With slotted spoon, transfer to large bowl.

2. Discard all but ¼ cup bacon drippings from skillet. Increase heat to medium-high; add parsnips, celery, and onion and cook, stirring occasionally, until vegetables are golden and tender, about 15 minutes. Add Swiss chard; cook, stirring frequently, until chard wilts, about 2 minutes. Stir in broth and pepper.

3. Add vegetable mixture and stuffing mix to bacon in bowl; toss to combine well. Use to stuff 12- to 16-pound turkey, or heat in baking dish and serve alongside poultry or ham: Spoon stuffing into greased 13" by 9" baking dish; cover with foil and bake in preheated 325°F oven until heated through, about 45 minutes. Makes about 14 cups stuffing.

Each ½ cup stuffing: About 112 calories, 3g protein, 17g carbohydrate, 3g total fat (1g saturated), 3mg cholesterol, 390mg sodium.

NORTHWEST FRUIT STUFFING

··

The sour-cherry orchards of the Northwest are celebrated in this fruit-studded stuffing.

Prep: 40 minutes   Bake: 45 minutes

- ½ cup butter or margarine (1 stick)
- 1 large red onion, coarsely chopped
- 1 medium fennel bulb (1¼ pounds), trimmed and coarsely chopped
- 2 large pears, peeled, cored, and coarsely chopped
- 1 large Granny Smith apple, peeled, cored, and coarsely chopped
- 1½ loaves (16 ounces each) sliced firm white bread, cut into ¾-inch cubes and lightly toasted
- 1 cup chicken broth
- ⅔ cup dried tart cherries
- ½ cup golden raisins
- ⅓ cup chopped fresh parsley
- 2 teaspoons chopped fresh thyme
- 1 teaspoon chopped fresh sage
- 1 teaspoon salt
- ½ teaspoon coarsely ground black pepper

1. In 12-inch skillet, melt butter over medium-high heat. Add onion and fennel and cook, stirring occasionally, until vegetables are golden brown and tender, 10 to 12 minutes. Add pears and apple and cook 5 minutes longer. Transfer to large bowl.

2. Add bread cubes, broth, cherries, raisins, parsley, thyme, sage, salt, and pepper to bowl with pears and apple; toss to combine well. Use to stuff 12- to 16-pound turkey, or heat in baking dish and serve alongside poultry or ham: Spoon stuffing into greased 13" by 9" baking dish; cover with foil and bake in preheated 325°F oven until heated through, about 45 minutes. Makes about 12 cups stuffing.

Each ½ cup stuffing: About 151 calories, 3g protein, 24g carbohydrate, 5g total fat (3g saturated), 11mg cholesterol, 351mg sodium.

MOIST BREAD STUFFING

···

This is the traditional stuffing most of us grew up with.

Prep: 25 minutes   Bake: 45 minutes

- ½ cup butter or margarine (1 stick)
- 5 stalks celery, finely chopped
- 1 medium onion, finely chopped
- 2 loaves (16 ounces each) sliced firm white bread, cut into ¾-inch cubes
- 1 can (14½ ounces) chicken broth or 1¾ cups Chicken Broth (page 70)
- ¼ cup chopped fresh parsley
- 1 teaspoon dried thyme
- ¾ teaspoon salt
- ½ teaspoon ground black pepper
- ½ teaspoon dried sage

1. In 5-quart Dutch oven, melt butter over medium heat. Add celery and onion and cook, stirring occasionally, until tender, about 15 minutes.

2. Remove Dutch oven from heat. Add bread cubes, broth, parsley, thyme, salt, pepper, and sage; toss to combine well. Use to stuff 12- to 16-pound turkey, or heat in baking dish and serve alongside poultry or ham: Spoon stuffing into greased 13" by 9" baking dish; cover with foil and bake in preheated 325°F oven until heated through, about 45 minutes. Makes about 10 cups stuffing.

Each ½ cup stuffing: About 170 calories, 4g protein, 24g carbohydrate, 6g total fat (3g saturated), 13mg cholesterol, 473mg sodium.

Tip: For the best results, use firm white bread. If you wish, set the bread cubes out overnight so they become stale.

---

5 IDEAS FOR . . . FROZEN CONCENTRATED ORANGE JUICE

This thrifty stand-in for fresh OJ lasts up to a year in your freezer. One 12-ounce can defrosts into 1½ cups.

QUICK MARINATED PORK

Preheat oven to 475°F. In bowl, combine ½ cup thawed concentrate, 2 tablespoons reduced-sodium soy sauce, 2 teaspoons grated, peeled fresh ginger, and ⅛ teaspoon each salt and ground black pepper. Reserve ⅓ cup sauce for serving. Place remaining sauce in large zip-tight bag with 1 pork tenderloin (1½ pounds); refrigerate 10 minutes. Place pork on rack in roasting pan lined with heavy-duty foil; brush pork with some of sauce remaining in bag. Roast 13 minutes; turn pork over and brush again. Roast 13 to 15 minutes longer or until internal temperature reaches 155°F. Let stand 5 minutes before slicing. Serve with reserved sauce. Serves 4.

ORANGE-GLAZED CHICKEN

Preheat oven to 450°F. In bowl, combine ½ cup thawed concentrate, 2 tablespoons Worcestershire sauce, ¼ teaspoon ground red pepper (cayenne), and ¼ teaspoon each salt and ground black pepper. Reserve ¼ cup sauce for serving. On 15½" by 10½" jelly-roll pan lined with heavy-duty foil, arrange 1 (3½-pound) chicken cut into 8 pieces, skin removed. Brush with half of remaining sauce. Roast 10 minutes; turn chicken pieces over and brush again. Roast 8 to 10 minutes longer or until juices run clear when pierced with tip of knife. Serve with reserved sauce. Serves 4.

SUNSHINE TRIFLE

In bowl, combine 1½ cups prepared vanilla pudding and ⅓ cup thawed concentrate. In another bowl, whip ½ cup heavy cream and 1 teaspoon sugar until soft peaks form. Cut half of 10¾-ounce frozen pound cake into ½-inch cubes. In 4 (8-ounce) parfait glasses, layer cake, pudding, and cream; repeat. Chill 2 hours. Serves 4.

BREAKFAST SMOOTHIE

In blender, combine 4 ice cubes, ⅔ cup low-fat (1%) milk, ¼ cup concentrate, 1 tablespoon honey, ⅛ teaspoon vanilla extract, and 1 small ripe banana. Blend until smooth. Serves 1.

CITRUS CARROTS

In 12-inch nonstick skillet, heat 1 tablespoon butter on medium 1 minute. Add 1 pound carrots, thinly sliced, and cook 2 minutes, stirring occasionally. Add 2 tablespoons water; cover and cook 6 minutes, stirring occasionally. Uncover; add ¼ cup concentrate and ¼ teaspoon each salt and ground black pepper. Cook 1 to 2 minutes or until tender. Toss with 2 tablespoons snipped chives. Serves 4.

6
FISH & SHELLFISH

The growing popularity of fish and shellfish is hardly a surprise. Seafood is a rich source of protein, vitamins, and minerals and is low in fat. And oily fish, such as salmon and tuna, are high in omega-3 fatty acids, which can lower blood cholesterol levels.

BUYING FISH AND SHELLFISH

The surface of a whole fish should glisten but not look slimy. Ask the fishmonger to show you the gills; they should be bright red with no tinge of brown. The eyes should not be sunken, but don't worry if they are clouded over, because the eyes of some fish lose their shine soon after they are caught.

Fish fillets and steaks are often sold in plastic-wrapped trays. Look for fish that appears moist and has no gaps in the flesh, which should feel firm through the plastic. The meat of dark fish, such as tuna, should not contain any rainbow streaks.

Mollusks (including clams, mussels, and oysters), must be purchased alive because their viscera deteriorate quickly once dead. Tightly closed shells indicate the mollusks are alive, but if you tap a gaping shell and it closes, it's also fine. Don't buy mollusks with broken shells. And if a clam or mussel feels especially heavy, it could be filled with mud, so discard it. Mollusks sold out of their shells, like scallops and squid, should be as sweet smelling as an ocean breeze. And the siphons of soft-shell clams should retract slightly when touched.

Crustaceans, including crabs and lobsters, should be purchased alive from a store with a large turnover and appear lively. Fresh shrimp should also be subjected to the sniff test; black spots on the shell mean the shrimp are over the hill.

STORING FISH AND SHELLFISH

• Keep fish and shellfish as cold as possible. Have the seafood you purchase packed in ice, or place it in the same bag as your frozen food.
• Store fish in the coldest part of the refrigerator, where the temperature is between 35° and 40°F. Or store on ice: Fill a baking dish with ice, and place the wrapped seafood on top, replenishing the ice as needed. You can also cover frozen artificial ice packets with a kitchen towel and place the wrapped fish on top.
• It is especially important to keep oily fish, such as mackerel and bluefish, as cold as possible. Their high fat content means they can go rancid quickly at less-than-ideal temperatures.
• If you must freeze seafood, be sure it is very fresh, and wrap it tightly in plastic wrap and heavy-duty foil. Freeze for up to three months.
• Shellfish should also be placed in the coldest part of the refrigerator. Store live clams, mussels, and oysters in a large bowl covered with a wet towel; use within one day. Refrigerate crabs in a tightly closed heavy-duty paper bag poked with a few airholes; cook within one day of purchase. Lobsters should be cooked on the day of purchase because they don't last long once out of water. Keep them well wrapped in a wet cloth or in several layers of newspaper in the refrigerator.

Mussels with Tomatoes and White Wine (recipe page 215)

• Cooked crab and lobster should be eaten within one day of purchase. Shucked oysters and crabmeat are often pasteurized, which extends their shelf life but decreases their flavor.

COOKING SUCCESS

Here's the simple secret to cooking fish successfully: Don't overcook it. Cook it until the flesh is just opaque throughout; it will continue to cook after it has been removed from the heat.

Before cooking fillets, especially thick ones, run your fingers over the flesh to feel for any stray bones. Remove them with tweezers set aside for that purpose.

To check fish fillets or steaks for doneness, use the tip of a small knife to separate the flesh in the thickest part; it should be uniformly opaque. To check whole fish, make an incision at the backbone to see if the flesh is opaque or insert an instant-read thermometer in the thickest part near the backbone; it should read 135° to 140°F.

Before cooking clams, mussels, or oysters, scrub the shells well under cold running water to remove any surface sand and grit.

KNOW YOUR FISH

Fish is categorized two ways: by shape (round or flat) and by fat content (lean to oily). It is helpful to know the fat content, flavor, and texture of various fish so you can easily substitute one for another.

Round fish have a plump, cylindrical shape and an eye on each side of the head. The backbone runs down the center of the fish, separating the two thick fillets. Round fish are generally filleted or cut into steaks but can also be cooked whole. Common round fish include salmon, red snapper, sea bass, monkfish, and catfish.

Flatfish have wide, thin bodies with both eyes on the same side of the head. The backbone runs down the center of the fish, with two lines of bones fanning out on either side, separating the top and bottom fillets. Flatfish are usually filleted. The most common are sole, flounder, and halibut.

The fat content of a fish is a good indicator of the flavor you can expect. *Lean fish* make up the majority

THE FISH EXCHANGE

LEAN	MODERATE	OILY
Cod, Scrod	Bluefish	Bluefin tuna
Flounder	Catfish	Butterfish
Grouper	Mahi-mahi	Herring
Haddock	Rainbow trout	Lake trout
Halibut	Striped bass	Mackerel
Monkfish	Swordfish	Pompano
Ocean perch	Yellowfin tuna	Salmon
Orange roughy		Shad
Pike		Whitefish
Pollock		
Red snapper		
Rockfish		
Sea bass		
Sole		
Tilapia		
Tilefish		
Turbot		
Whiting		

of fish. They have the blandest flavor and most delicate texture. *Moderately oily fish* have a slightly higher fat content, a pleasant texture, and a mild flavor. Some fish, such as tuna, can be categorized as either moderately oily or oily, depending on the species. *Oily fish* have flesh that is strong-tasting, firm, and meaty. They are high in omega-3 fatty acids.

FISH GLOSSARY

Here is a glossary of some of the fish you are likely to find in your market.

Arctic char Very similar to salmon; usually farm-raised. Also known as salmon trout.

Bluefish A dark-fleshed, strong-flavored, oily fish. The fresher it is, the milder the flavor.

Catfish A beloved freshwater fish of the American South. Farm-raised catfish are readily available.

Cod This saltwater fish, found in both Atlantic and Pacific waters, is known for its mild flavor and white, flaky flesh. Small cod are called scrod.

Flounder A popular flatfish with white flesh, a delicate texture, and mild flavor.

Grouper Has firm, meaty, white flesh and is sold whole or filleted.

Halibut A large flatfish with firm, flavorful flesh. Often sold as fillets, but one of the few flatfish thick enough to be cut into steaks.

Mackerel An oily fish with a pronounced fish flavor. When large, it is called *Spanish mackerel.*

Monkfish A favored fish in Provence, monkfish has firm flesh and a lobsterlike flavor.

Pompano On the West Coast, pompano is called *yellowtail.* It has somewhat oily flesh and a firm texture.

Red snapper An excellent all-purpose fish and one of the few fillets firm enough to be grilled.

Salmon Much of the salmon in our markets is farm-raised, even when labeled "Atlantic" or "Norwegian." Wild salmon, such as *coho, king,* and *sockeye,* has superior flavor but is available in limited quantities.

Sole A flatfish with firm white flesh and a distinctively delicate flavor.

Striped bass Most striped bass in today's markets is a farm-raised hybrid of striped bass and white bass.

Swordfish A fish with a firm and meaty texture that is a good choice for broiling and grilling.

Trout Rainbow trout and brook trout are about 12 ounces each and serve one person.

Tuna A huge fish with plenty of muscle and flavor. The most common varieties are *bluefin, yellowfin, albacore,* and *skipjack.* Tuna is also known as *ahi* and *bonito.*

KNOW YOUR SHELLFISH

Mollusks have soft bodies that are protected by shells consisting of one or more parts. This glossary lists the most popular shellfish.

Clams. Hard-shell clams, the most common Atlantic Coast variety, are categorized by size. *Littlenecks* are the smallest, *cherrystones* are medium, and *chowder clams* are the largest.

Soft-shell clams have delicate shells that don't completely close because of the long necklike siphon that protrudes between the two halves of the shell. On the East Coast, they are usually called *steamers,* because they are so delicious when steamed. They are also know as *Ipswich* clams, so named for the location of one of the largest clam beds. West Coast soft-shell clams include the huge *geoduck* (GOO-ee-duck) and the long *razor clam.*

Mussels Most markets carry *blue mussels,* which have bluish black shells and are harvested wild or cultivated. *New Zealand green mussels* are slightly larger and have a bright green shell.

Oysters Oysters are usually named for the location of their beds: *Wellfleet, Chincoteague,* and *Apalachicola* on the East Coast and *Westcott Bay, Tomales Bay,* and the tiny *Olympia* on the West Coast are examples.

Scallops Sea scallops are gathered year round and are relatively large. Small *bay scallops* are only available in the fall and winter. *Calico scallops* are very small, but they have the least flavor and the toughest texture.

Squid Also called calamari, many fish markets sell it already cleaned.

CRUSTACEANS

Crustaceans have elongated bodies that are covered by jointed shells.

Crab On the West Coast, there is *Dungeness crab,* whose season runs from October to April. *King crab,* usually from Alaska, provides the large legs that are sold fresh or frozen. Small *blue crabs* are found along the East and Gulf Coasts. The large pieces of meat from the body are sold as lump, jumbo, or backfin crabmeat.

Soft-shell crabs Blue crabs caught during the short period after they have shed their hard shells and before their new, soft shells have hardened. They are available fresh from May to September.

Stone crabs Popular in Florida, the claws are harvested, and the rest of the crab is tossed back into the water so new claws can regenerate.

Lobster There are two types: *American (Maine) lobster,* from the North Atlantic coast, and *rock (spiny) lobster,* which is harvested off Florida, California, Australia, and New Zealand. It is usually sold as frozen lobster tail.

Shrimp More than 95 percent of the shrimp sold has been previously frozen. *Warm-water shrimp* live in tropical waters and are usually categorized by the color of their shell: pink, white, blue, or black tiger.

TARRAGON-ROASTED SALMON

....

No fish poacher? Roast a whole salmon in the oven instead. This herb-stuffed fish is a delicious dish that serves up to ten people. Any leftovers can be turned into tasty salmon cakes or salmon salad.

Prep: 10 minutes   Roast: 40 minutes

- 2 large lemons, thinly sliced
- 1 whole salmon (5½ pounds), cleaned and scaled
- 2 tablespoons olive oil
- ½ teaspoon salt
- ½ teaspoon coarsely ground black pepper
- 1 large bunch tarragon
- 1 small bunch parsley
  Caper Sauce (right)
  lemon wedges

1. Preheat oven to 450°F. Line jelly-roll pan with foil. Arrange one-third of lemon slices in row down center of pan.

2. Rinse salmon inside and out with cold running water; pat dry with paper towels. Rub outside of salmon with oil. Place salmon on top of lemon slices. Sprinkle cavity with salt and pepper. Place tarragon and parsley sprigs and half of remaining lemon slices in cavity. Arrange remaining lemon slices on top of fish. Roast salmon until just opaque throughout when knife is inserted at backbone, about 40 minutes.

3. Meanwhile, prepare Caper Sauce.

4. Carefully remove lemon slices and peel off skin from top of salmon; discard. Using two wide spatulas, transfer salmon to cutting board.

5. To serve, slide cake server under front section of top fillet and lift off fillet; transfer to warm large platter. Slide server under backbone and lift it away from bottom fillet; discard. Slide cake server between bottom fillet and skin and transfer fillet to platter. Serve with lemon wedges and caper sauce. Makes 10 main-dish servings.

Each serving without sauce: About 325 calories, 33g protein, 1g carbohydrate, 20g total fat (4g saturated), 96mg cholesterol, 213mg sodium.

SMOKED AND PROCESSED FISH

ANCHOVIES: These tiny salted fish are an important seasoning in Mediterranean cooking. They are usually found filleted, salt-cured, and canned in oil. Because most recipes call only for a few fillets, you will often have leftover anchovies; cover the can tightly with plastic wrap and use within one week. Anchovy paste is a convenient product because there is no waste. About ½ teaspoon of anchovy paste equals one fillet.

CAVIAR: Real caviar is the salted roe of sturgeon. You may see lumpfish and salmon "caviar," but they are not really caviar—they're just fish eggs. Caviar is rare, costly, and uniquely delicious. There are three categories: *beluga* (large dark gray eggs), *osetra* (medium eggs that range in color from yellow to brown), and *sevruga* (smaller eggs that are light gray).

SALT COD: Cod that has been salted and dried. Buy thick white pieces; salt cod turns gray as it ages. Salt cod is always soaked thoroughly and rinsed before cooking to remove the salt.

SMOKED SALMON: *Nova* is named after the true Nova Scotia salmon, which is rarely seen in our markets. It has been cured in brine and then smoked. *Lox* is salmon that has been pickled in a spiced brine but is not always smoked.

CAPER SAUCE

In medium bowl, mix **¾ cup sour cream, ½ cup mayonnaise, ¼ cup milk, 3 tablespoons capers,** drained and chopped, **2 tablespoons chopped fresh tarragon, ½ teaspoon freshly grated lemon peel,** and **⅛ teaspoon coarsely ground black pepper** until blended. Cover and refrigerate until ready to serve, up to two days. Makes about 1⅔ cups.

Each tablespoon: About 58 calories, 0g protein, 1g carbohydrate, 6g total fat (2g saturated), 7mg cholesterol, 90mg sodium.

COLD POACHED SALMON STEAKS WITH WATERCRESS SAUCE

....

One of the best warm-weather entrées around. Fast and easy, and you don't even have to turn on the oven.

Prep: 15 minutes plus cooling   Cook: 10 minutes

- 1 medium lemon
- 4 salmon steaks, 1 inch thick (6 ounces each)
- ³/₄ teaspoon salt
- ½ teaspoon coarsely ground black pepper
- 1 medium onion, thinly sliced
    Watercress Sauce (below)

1. From lemon, squeeze juice; reserve for Watercress Sauce. Set lemon shells aside. Rub salmon steaks evenly with salt and pepper.

2. In 12-inch skillet, heat *½ inch water* to boiling over high heat. Add salmon, onion, and lemon shells; heat to boiling. Reduce heat; cover and simmer until fish is just opaque throughout, 5 to 8 minutes. With slotted spatula, transfer fish to platter. Let cool 30 minutes, or cover and refrigerate to serve later.

3. Meanwhile, prepare Watercress Sauce.

4. Remove skin and bones from salmon, if you like. Serve with sauce. Makes 4 main-dish servings.

Each serving without sauce: About 274 calories, 30g protein, 0g carbohydrate, 16g total fat (3g saturated), 88mg cholesterol, 231mg sodium.

WATERCRESS SAUCE

In blender or in food processor with knife blade attached, puree **½ bunch watercress,** tough stems trimmed (1 cup), **½ cup sour cream, 1 tablespoon fresh lemon juice, 1 teaspoon chopped fresh tarragon** or **⅛ teaspoon dried tarragon, 1½ teaspoons sugar,** and **1 teaspoon salt** until smooth. Cover and refrigerate. Makes about ½ cup sauce.

Each tablespoon: About 35 calories, 1g protein, 2g carbohydrate, 3g total fat (2g saturated), 6mg cholesterol, 301mg sodium.

SALT-BAKED FISH

....

Baking a whole fish in a crust of kosher salt seals in the juices, guaranteeing exquisitely moist—and surprisingly unsalty—fish.

Prep: 5 minutes   Bake: 30 minutes

- 4 cups kosher salt
- 1 whole red snapper, striped bass, or porgy
    (1½ to 2 pounds), cleaned and scaled
- 1 lemon
- 3 rosemary or thyme sprigs

1. Preheat oven to 450°F. Line 13" by 9" baking pan with foil; spread 2 cups salt in bottom of pan.

2. Rinse snapper inside and out with cold running water; pat dry with paper towels. From lemon, cut 3 slices. Cut remaining lemon into wedges. Place lemon slices and rosemary in cavity of fish. Place fish on bed of salt; cover with remaining 2 cups salt. Bake until fish is just opaque throughout when knife is inserted at backbone, about 30 minutes.

3. To serve, tap salt crust to release from top of fish; discard. Slide cake server under front section of top fillet and lift off fillet; transfer to platter. Slide server under backbone and lift it away from bottom fillet; discard. Slide cake server between bottom fillet and skin and transfer fillet to platter. Serve with reserved lemon wedges. Makes 2 main-dish servings.

Each serving: About 188 calories, 37g protein, 6g carbohydrate, 3g total fat (1g saturated), 66mg cholesterol, 800mg sodium.

ROAST STRIPED BASS

Prepare as directed above substituting **1 whole striped bass (2¼ pounds),** cleaned and scaled, for snapper and omitting salt. Make diagonal slashes on each side of fish at 1-inch intervals, about ¼ inch deep. Place bass in medium roasting pan (14" by 10"). Proceed as above. Makes 4 main-dish servings.

TROUT MEUNIÈRE

···

Here's the classic way to prepare trout, along with four tasty seasoning variations. One trout per person makes a generous serving.

Prep: 10 minutes plus standing   Cook: 20 minutes

- 4 brook or rainbow trout (10 to 12 ounces each), cleaned and scaled
- 1 cup milk
- ¼ cup all-purpose flour
- ½ teaspoon salt
- 4 tablespoons vegetable oil
- ¼ cup fresh lemon juice
- 4 tablespoons butter or margarine
- ¼ cup chopped fresh parsley

1. Rinse trout inside and out with cold running water; pat dry with paper towels. Soak trout in milk 10 minutes. On waxed paper, combine flour and salt. Remove trout from milk and coat evenly with flour mixture, shaking off excess.

2. In 12-inch skillet, heat 2 tablespoons oil over medium heat until very hot. Add 2 trout and cook until just opaque throughout when knife is inserted at backbone, 4 to 5 minutes per side. Transfer to platter and keep warm. Repeat with remaining 2 tablespoons oil and remaining fish.

3. Pour off any fat remaining in skillet and wipe skillet clean with paper towels. Return skillet to heat; add lemon juice and cook 15 seconds. Add butter; cook until foamy, about 2 minutes. Stir in parsley and pour butter sauce over fish. Makes 4 main-dish servings.

Each serving: About 493 calories, 41g protein, 8g carbohydrate, 32g total fat (10g saturated), 143mg cholesterol, 468mg sodium.

TROUT WITH BROWN BUTTER AND SAGE
Prepare as directed through Step 2. In Step 3, substitute **2 tablespoons chopped fresh sage** for parsley and cook until butter is lightly browned, about 3 minutes. Add **1 teaspoon fresh lemon juice.** Pour sauce over fish.

TROUT AMANDINE
Prepare as directed through Step 2. In Step 3, omit parsley. Add **¼ cup sliced almonds** to skillet with butter and cook until almonds are golden, 2 to 3 minutes. Add **1 teaspoon fresh lemon juice.** Pour sauce over fish.

TROUT GRENOBLOISE
Prepare as directed through Step 2. In Step 3, omit lemon juice. From **1 lemon,** remove peel and white pith. Cut lemon into ¼-inch-thick slices; discard seeds. Cut slices into ½-inch pieces. After cooking butter until foamy, add lemon, **4 teaspoons capers,** and **1 tablespoon chopped fresh parsley.** Spoon sauce over fish.

TROUT WITH CORNMEAL AND BACON
Prepare as directed through Step 2, substituting **⅓ cup cornmeal** for flour in Step 1 and bacon drippings from **4 strips bacon** for oil in Step 2. Omit Step 3. Garnish fish with **crumbled cooked bacon.**

TROUT

Rainbow trout and brook trout are marketed at just the right size for single servings: between 8 and 12 ounces. They belong to the *Salmonidae* (salmon) family. Rainbow trout has a green or blue back, silvery sides covered with tiny dark spots, and a thin red strip running along each side. Brook trout, on the other hand, has a green-brown back and green sides, and its skin is mottled with yellow and red spots. Although trout is still caught in the wild, most of the trout in stores have been farmed in springwater-fed ponds. Trout is mild flavored and delicate and is best enjoyed when prepared simply as in our tasty recipes.

BROILED SALMON STEAKS

....

Broiling is a quick—and easy—way to get healthful, flavorful salmon steaks onto the dinner table in less than 15 minutes.

Prep: 3 minutes   Broil: 10 minutes

- 4 salmon steaks, 1 inch thick (6 ounces each)
- 1 teaspoon vegetable oil
     pinch salt
     pinch ground black pepper

1. Preheat broiler. Rub both sides of salmon steaks with oil and sprinkle with salt and pepper.

2. Place salmon on rack in broiling pan. Place pan in broiler, 4 inches from heat source. Broil salmon 5 minutes, then turn and broil until fish is just opaque throughout, about 5 minutes longer. Makes 4 main-dish servings.

Each serving: About 284 calories, 30g protein, 0g carbohydrate, 17g total fat (3g saturated), 88mg cholesterol, 123mg sodium.

SALMON STEAKS TERIYAKI

Prepare as above, omitting salt and pepper in Step 1. In small saucepan, combine **6 tablespoons soy sauce, ½ teaspoon Asian sesame oil, 3 tablespoons brown sugar, 1 garlic clove,** crushed, and **1 teaspoon minced, peeled fresh ginger;** heat to boiling over medium-high heat. Boil until mixture has thickened slightly, about 3 minutes. Strain through fine-mesh sieve; discard solids. In Step 2, broil salmon 3 minutes, then brush with glaze and broil 2 minutes more. Turn steaks and broil 3 minutes; brush with glaze and broil 2 minutes more. To serve, sprinkle with **2 green onions,** cut on diagonal into thin slices. Makes 4 main-dish servings.

Each serving: About 313 calories, 36g protein, 13g carbohydrate, 12g total fat (2g saturated), 93mg cholesterol, 1,550mg sodium.

PAN-SEARED TUNA

....

This is a great way to cook tuna steaks: Get the oil in the pan very hot and sear the fish very quickly. The oil in the marinade moistens the fish but adds hardly any fat at all.

Prep: 10 minutes plus marinating   Cook: 6 minutes

- 4   large lemons
- 6   tablespoons olive oil
- 6   tablespoons chopped fresh parsley
- ½   teaspoon salt
- ¼   teaspoon ground black pepper
- 4   tuna steaks, ¾ inch thick (5 ounces each)

1. From lemons, grate 1 teaspoon peel and squeeze ⅔ cup juice. In 9-inch square baking dish, with wire whisk, whisk lemon peel and juice, 3 tablespoons oil, 5 tablespoons parsley, salt, and pepper until mixed. Add tuna, turning to coat. Cover and refrigerate 45 minutes to marinate, turning occasionally.

2. In 10-inch cast-iron skillet or other heavy skillet, heat remaining 3 tablespoons oil over medium-high heat until hot. Add tuna and cook until pale pink in center (medium), about 3 minutes per side, or until desired doneness. Transfer to plates and sprinkle with remaining 1 tablespoon parsley. Makes 4 main-dish servings.

Each serving: About 246 calories, 30g protein, 1g carbohydrate, 13g total fat (2g saturated), 48mg cholesterol, 341mg sodium.

HALIBUT BRAISED IN RED WINE

Red wine does go with fish! Here the slight acidity of the wine accents the mild flavor of the halibut. Other tasty fish options include salmon and monkfish.

Prep: 10 minutes   Cook: 30 minutes

- 2 tablespoons butter or margarine
- ½ cup finely chopped shallots (3 large)
- 1 garlic clove, finely chopped
- 1 carrot, peeled and thinly sliced
- 2 cups dry red wine
- ¾ cup chicken broth
- ½ teaspoon salt
- ¼ teaspoon dried thyme
- 4 skinless, boneless halibut steaks, 1 inch thick (6 ounces each)
- 2 tablespoons chopped fresh parsley

1. In nonstick 12-inch skillet, melt 1 tablespoon butter over low heat. Add shallots and garlic and cook, stirring occasionally, until shallots are tender, about 4 minutes. Add carrot and cook 4 minutes longer. Add wine and heat to boiling over high heat; boil 2 minutes. Add broth, salt, and thyme. Slip in halibut and reduce heat to low. Cover and cook until fish is just opaque throughout, about 8 minutes. With slotted spatula, transfer fish to platter and keep warm.

2. Increase heat to high and boil wine mixture until it has reduced by half, 7 to 10 minutes. Remove from heat and swirl in remaining 1 tablespoon butter until melted. Strain sauce through fine-mesh sieve. To serve, spoon sauce over fish and sprinkle with parsley. Makes 4 main-dish servings.

Each serving: About 277 calories, 37g protein, 8g carbohydrate, 10g total fat (4g saturated), 70mg cholesterol, 643mg sodium.

SWORDFISH STEAKS BROILED WITH MAÎTRE D'HÔTEL BUTTER

Swordfish is terrific with the classic lemon-and-herb butter, but any of the other flavored butters (page 504) would be just as inviting. If you like, top each steak with a tablespoon of the herbed butter before serving.

Prep: 15 minutes   Broil: 8 minutes

- 4 teaspoons Maître d'Hôtel Butter (page 504)
- 4 swordfish steaks, 1 inch thick (6 ounces each)

1. Prepare Maître d'Hôtel Butter.

2. Preheat broiler. Place swordfish on rack in broiling pan. Spread ½ teaspoon Maître d'Hôtel Butter on each side of each fish steak. Place pan in broiler, 4 inches from heat source. Broil swordfish, without turning, until just opaque throughout, 8 to 10 minutes. Spoon pan juices over fish to serve. Makes 4 main-dish servings.

Each serving: About 217 calories, 30g protein, 0g carbohydrate, 10g total fat (4g saturated), 69mg cholesterol, 175mg sodium.

Swordfish Steaks Broiled with Maître d'Hôtel Butter

BROILED COD STEAKS MONTAUK

....

A flavored mayonnaise topping is a quick way to add punch to broiled fish.

Prep: 5 minutes   Broil: 6 minutes

¼ cup mayonnaise
½ teaspoon Dijon mustard
⅛ teaspoon salt
⅛ teaspoon ground black pepper
4 cod steaks, ½ inch thick (6 ounces each)

1. Preheat broiler.

2. In small bowl, mix mayonnaise, mustard, salt, and pepper until blended.

3. Lightly oil rack in broiling pan. Place cod on rack in broiling pan. Place pan in broiler, 4 inches from heat source. Broil cod until just opaque throughout, 5 to 7 minutes. Remove broiling pan from broiler. Brush mayonnaise mixture on fish. Return pan to broiler; broil until mayonnaise mixture is lightly browned and bubbling, 1 to 2 minutes longer. Makes 4 main-dish servings.

Each serving: About 222 calories, 27g protein, 0g carbohydrate, 12g total fat (2g saturated), 72mg cholesterol, 247mg sodium.

LEMON TOPPING

Prepare as directed but substitute **½ teaspoon freshly grated lemon peel** for Dijon mustard.

HORSERADISH TOPPING

Prepare as directed but substitute **1 teaspoon bottled white horseradish** for Dijon mustard.

DILL-PEPPER TOPPING

Prepare as directed but substitute **2 tablespoons chopped fresh dill** for Dijon mustard and **¼ teaspoon coarsely ground black pepper** for ground black pepper.

LIME-JALAPEÑO TOPPING

Prepare as directed but substitute **½ teaspoon freshly grated lime peel** for Dijon mustard and add **1 small jalapeño,** seeded and minced, to mayonnaise mixture.

PARMESAN TOPPING

Prepare as directed but substitute **2 tablespoons freshly grated Parmesan cheese** for Dijon mustard.

DRIED TOMATO TOPPING

Prepare as directed (left) but substitute **1 dried tomato,** finely chopped, for Dijon mustard.

COD VERACRUZ

....

This is fish, Mexican-style. Chile aficionados may want to add a little more cayenne pepper or hot chili powder.

Prep: 15 minutes   Cook: 35 minutes

4 tablespoons vegetable oil
1 yellow pepper, cut into thin strips
1 medium onion, thinly sliced
1 jalapeño chile, seeded and finely chopped
1 garlic clove, thinly sliced
¾ teaspoon chili powder
½ teaspoon salt
1 can (14½ to 16 ounces) tomatoes in puree
½ teaspoon ground coriander
¼ teaspoon ground cumin
⅛ teaspoon ground red pepper (cayenne)
4 cod steaks, ¾ inch thick (4 ounces each)

1. In nonstick 12-inch skillet, heat 2 tablespoons oil over medium heat. Add yellow pepper and onion and cook, stirring, until tender and golden, 15 minutes. Add jalapeño, garlic, ½ teaspoon chili powder, and ¼ teaspoon salt and cook, stirring, 3 minutes.

2. Add tomatoes with their puree and cook, breaking up tomatoes with side of spoon, until mixture has slightly reduced, about 10 minutes.

3. Meanwhile, in cup, combine coriander, cumin, remaining ¼ teaspoon each chili powder and salt, and ground red pepper. Sprinkle both sides of cod steaks with spice mixture.

4. In 10-inch skillet, heat remaining 2 tablespoons oil over medium-high heat until hot. Add cod and cook until steaks are just opaque throughout and nicely browned, 3 to 4 minutes per side. To serve, arrange fish on platter and top with warm tomato sauce. Makes 4 main-dish servings.

Each serving: About 254 calories, 19g protein, 12g carbohydrate, 14g total fat (2g saturated), 43mg cholesterol, 508mg sodium.

ROAST SALMON IN TARRAGON AND CAPERS

....

A whole salmon fillet with an herb-encrusted topping looks festive, tastes fabulous, and is surprisingly quick and easy to prepare.

Prep: 10 minutes   Roast: 30 minutes

- 3 tablespoons butter or margarine
- ⅓ cup plain dried bread crumbs
- ¼ cup loosely packed fresh parsley leaves, minced
- 3 tablespoons drained capers, minced
- 1 teaspoon dried tarragon
- 2 teaspoons freshly grated lemon peel
- ¼ teaspoon salt
- ¼ teaspoon coarsely ground black pepper
- 1 whole salmon fillet (2 to 2½ pounds)
  lemon wedges

1. Preheat oven to 450°F. Line jelly-roll pan with foil; grease foil.

2. In 1-quart saucepan, melt butter over low heat. Remove saucepan from heat; stir in bread crumbs, parsley, capers, tarragon, lemon peel, salt, and pepper.

3. Place salmon, skin side down, in prepared pan. Pat crumb mixture on top. Roast until salmon turns opaque throughout and topping is lightly browned, about 30 minutes.

4. With two large spatulas, carefully transfer salmon to platter (it's okay if salmon skin sticks to foil). Serve with lemon wedges. Makes 6 main-dish servings.

Each serving: About 325 calories, 28g protein, 5g carbohydrate, 21g total fat (4g saturated), 76mg cholesterol, 425mg sodium.

FENNEL-CRUSTED BLUEFISH

....

If you prefer to grill, rub the bluefish with the olive oil, then with the fennel mixture; grill over medium-high heat. Serve with lemon wedges.

Prep: 5 minutes   Cook: 8 minutes

- 2 teaspoons fennel seeds, crushed
- ½ teaspoon whole black peppercorns, crushed
- ½ teaspoon salt
- 4 pieces bluefish fillet (6 ounces each)
- 1 tablespoon butter or margarine
- 1 teaspoon olive oil

1. In cup, combine fennel seeds, peppercorns, and salt. Use to rub on both sides of bluefish fillets.

2. In 12-inch skillet, melt butter with oil over medium-high heat. Add bluefish and cook until fish is just opaque throughout, 4 to 6 minutes per side. Makes 4 main-dish servings.

Each serving: About 247 calories, 34g protein, 0g carbohydrate, 11g total fat (3g saturated), 108mg cholesterol, 422mg sodium.

TURNING FILLETS IN FRYING SKILLET

––––––––––––––

To turn fish fillets so they don't fall apart, use a wide slotted spatula, supporting the fillet with your fingers as you turn it.

FRIED CATFISH

Before frying, let the coated fish fillets stand for a few minutes to set the crust; it will adhere better and fry to crispy perfection.

Prep: 15 minutes plus standing **Cook:** 20 minutes

- ³/₄ cup cornmeal
- 2 tablespoons all-purpose flour
- ½ teaspoon salt
- ¼ teaspoon ground black pepper
- ¼ cup milk
- 6 catfish fillets (6 ounces each)
- 4 tablespoons vegetable oil
  lemon wedges

1. In zip-tight plastic bag, combine cornmeal, flour, salt, and pepper. Pour milk into pie plate. Dip catfish fillets, one at a time, into milk to coat well, then into cornmeal mixture, shaking bag to coat fish. Place coated catfish on wire rack set over waxed paper; set aside to dry 20 minutes.

2. In 10-inch skillet, heat 2 tablespoons oil over medium-high heat until hot. Add 3 catfish fillets to skillet and fry until just opaque throughout and golden, 4 to 5 minutes per side. Transfer to paper towels to drain. Repeat with remaining 2 tablespoons oil and remaining catfish. Serve with lemon wedges. Makes 6 main-dish servings.

Each serving: About 377 calories, 28g protein, 16g carbohydrate, 22g total fat (4g saturated), 58mg cholesterol, 255mg sodium.

CODFISH CAKES

Crisp but tender fish cakes are a great weekend supper; serve with homemade Tartar Sauce (page 504).

Prep: 30 minutes plus chilling **Cook:** 10 minutes

- 3 tablespoons vegetable oil
- 2 large stalks celery, chopped
- 1 small onion, chopped
- 1½ cups fresh bread crumbs (about 3 slices bread)
- 1 pound cod fillet
- 1 large egg, lightly beaten
- 2 tablespoons light mayonnaise
- 1 tablespoon chopped fresh parsley
- 1 teaspoon fresh lemon juice
- ¼ teaspoon hot pepper sauce
- ½ teaspoon salt
  lemon wedges

1. In 12-inch skillet, heat 1 tablespoon oil over medium heat. Add celery and onion and cook, stirring occasionally, until onion is tender and lightly browned, about 10 minutes. Remove skillet from heat.

2. Place two thirds of bread crumbs on waxed paper. Place remaining crumbs in medium bowl. With tweezers, remove any bones from cod. With large chef's knife, finely chop fish; add to bowl with bread crumbs. Stir in celery-onion mixture, egg, mayonnaise, parsley, lemon juice, pepper sauce, and salt until well combined.

3. Shape fish mixture into four 3-inch patties (mixture will be very soft and moist). Refrigerate patties until firm, at least 30 minutes. Wipe skillet clean.

4. Use bread crumbs on waxed paper to coat patties, patting crumbs to adhere. In same skillet, heat remaining 2 tablespoons oil over medium-low heat until hot. Add patties to skillet and cook until browned and cooked through, 5 to 6 minutes per side. Serve with lemon wedges. Makes 4 main-dish servings.

Each serving: About 298 calories, 24g protein, 15g carbohydrate, 16g total fat (2g saturated), 105mg cholesterol, 565mg sodium.

COD, CABBAGE, AND BACON IN PARCHMENT

....

Curly savoy cabbage is more delicate than plain green cabbage and goes well with the subtle flavor of cod.

Prep: 20 minutes   Bake: 20 minutes

- 2 slices bacon, chopped
- 2 teaspoons vegetable oil
- ½ head (¾ pound) savoy cabbage, thinly sliced (6 cups)
- ½ plus ⅛ teaspoon salt
- ¼ plus ⅛ teaspoon ground black pepper pinch dried thyme
- 4 thick pieces cod fillet (6 ounces each)
- 4 squares (12 inches each) cooking parchment or foil
- 1 tablespoon butter or margarine, cut into very small pieces

1. Preheat oven to 400°F.

2. In 12-inch skillet, cook bacon over medium-low heat until browned. With slotted spoon, transfer to paper towels to drain. Discard drippings from skillet; wipe skillet clean.

3. In same skillet, heat oil over high heat. Add cabbage, ½ teaspoon salt, ¼ teaspoon pepper, and thyme; cook, stirring, until cabbage is tender. Stir in bacon.

4. With tweezers, remove any bones from cod. Place one-fourth cabbage mixture on one half of each parchment square. Place fillets on top of cabbage. Sprinkle fillets with remaining ⅛ teaspoon each salt and pepper and evenly dot with butter.

5. Fold unfilled half of parchment over cod. To seal packets, beginning at a corner where parchment is folded, make ½-inch-wide folds, with each new fold overlapping the previous one, until packet is completely sealed. Packet will resemble half-circle. Place packets in jelly-roll pan. Bake 20 minutes (packets will puff up and brown). Cut packets open to serve. Makes 4 main-dish servings.

Each serving: About 232 calories, 33g protein, 7g carbohydrate, 8g total fat (3g saturated), 84mg cholesterol, 567mg sodium.

BAKED SCROD WITH FENNEL AND POTATOES

....

Here's a simple dish that needs only a crisp green salad to become a complete meal.

Prep: 15 minutes   Bake: 55 minutes

- 1½ pounds red potatoes (4 large), not peeled, thinly sliced
- 1 medium fennel bulb (1 pound), trimmed and thinly sliced, feathery tops reserved
- 1 garlic clove, finely chopped
- 2 tablespoons olive oil
- ¾ plus ⅛ teaspoon salt
- ½ teaspoon coarsely ground black pepper
- 4 pieces scrod fillet (5 ounces each)
- 1 large ripe tomato (8 ounces), seeded and chopped

1. Preheat oven to 425°F.

2. In shallow 2½-quart baking dish, toss potatoes, fennel, garlic, oil, ¾ teaspoon salt, and ¼ teaspoon pepper until well combined; spread evenly in baking dish. Bake, stirring once, until vegetables are tender and lightly browned, about 45 minutes.

3. With tweezers, remove any bones from scrod. Sprinkle scrod with remaining ⅛ teaspoon salt and remaining ¼ teaspoon pepper. Arrange on top of potato mixture. Bake until fish is just opaque throughout, 10 to 15 minutes.

4. Sprinkle with tomato and garnish with reserved fennel tops. Makes 4 main-dish servings.

Each serving: About 335 calories, 30g protein, 35g carbohydrate, 8g total fat (1g saturated), 61mg cholesterol, 679mg sodium.

SCROD WITH LEMON-GARLIC BREAD CRUMBS

....

Want an easy way to bake up flaky scrod fillets? Top them with lots of garlicky bread crumbs.

Prep: 20 minutes   **Bake:** 10 minutes

- 2 tablespoons butter or margarine
- 1 garlic clove, finely chopped
- 1 cup fresh bread crumbs (about 2 slices bread)
- 4 pieces scrod or cod fillet (6 ounces each)
- 2 tablespoons fresh lemon juice
- ½ teaspoon salt
- 1 tablespoon chopped fresh parsley
  lemon wedges

1. Preheat oven to 450°F. In 10-inch skillet, melt butter over medium heat. Add garlic; cook until golden. Add bread crumbs and cook, stirring frequently, until lightly toasted. Remove skillet from heat.

2. With tweezers, remove any bones from scrod. In 13" by 9" baking dish, arrange fillets in single layer; sprinkle with lemon juice and salt. Press bread-crumb mixture onto fillets. Bake until fish is just opaque throughout, 10 to 15 minutes.

3. Sprinkle scrod with parsley and serve with lemon wedges. Makes 4 main-dish servings.

Each serving: About 231 calories, 32g protein, 8g carbohydrate, 7g total fat (4g saturated), 89mg cholesterol, 517mg sodium.

OVEN-FRIED FISH

....

Here's a reduced-fat method for getting crispy fish without lots of oil. To keep the fat profile low, serve with Tartar Sauce (page 504), made with lowfat mayonnaise or simply sprinkle the fish with malt vinegar. For fish and chips, serve with crisp Oven Fries (page 425) and malt vinegar.

Prep: 10 minutes   **Bake:** 12 minutes

- 2 teaspoons vegetable oil
- ¼ cup all-purpose flour
- ½ teaspoon salt
- ¼ teaspoon ground red pepper (cayenne)
- 2 large egg whites
- 1 cup plain dried bread crumbs
- 1 pound flounder or sole fillets, cut on diagonal into 1-inch-wide strips

1. Preheat oven to 450°F. Grease cookie sheet with oil; set aside.

2. On waxed paper, combine flour, salt, and ground red pepper. In shallow bowl, beat egg whites just until foamy. On separate sheet of waxed paper, place bread crumbs. Coat flounder strips with seasoned flour, shaking off excess. Dip strips into egg white, then coat in bread crumbs, patting crumbs to adhere. Arrange fish strips on prepared cookie sheet.

3. Place cookie sheet on lowest oven rack and bake fish 5 minutes. With wide spatula, turn fish. Bake until just opaque throughout and golden, 4 to 5 minutes longer. Makes 4 main-dish servings.

Each serving: About 267 calories, 27g protein, 26g carbohydrate, 5g total fat (1g saturated), 54mg cholesterol, 642mg sodium.

ASIAN-STYLE FLOUNDER BAKED IN PARCHMENT

....

Baking in parchment packets is a simple way to seal in the juices and the flavor of delicate fish. Substitute foil for the parchment paper, if necessary.

Prep: 15 minutes   Bake: 8 minutes

- 2 large green onions
- 2 tablespoons soy sauce
- 2 tablespoons seasoned rice vinegar
- 4 flounder fillets (6 ounces each)
- 4 sheets (12" by 15" each) cooking parchment or foil
- 2 teaspoons grated, peeled fresh ginger

1. Cut green onion tops into 2" by ¼" matchstick strips; reserve for garnish. Thinly slice white part of green onions.

2. In small bowl, combine soy sauce and vinegar.

3. Preheat oven to 425°F. Place 1 flounder fillet on one half of each parchment sheet. Sprinkle with ginger and sliced green onions; drizzle with soy-sauce mixture. Fold unfilled half of parchment over fish. To seal packets, beginning at a corner where parchment is folded, make ½-inch-wide folds, with each new fold overlapping previous one, until packet is completely sealed. Packet will resemble half-circle. Place packets in jelly-roll pan. Bake 8 minutes (packets will puff up and brown).

4. Cut packets open and garnish fish with reserved green-onion strips. Makes 4 main-dish servings.

Each serving: About 170 calories, 33g protein, 3g carbohydrate, 2g total fat (0g saturated), 82mg cholesterol, 802mg sodium.

WHOLE FLOUNDER IN PARCHMENT

Prepare as above, but use a **3-pound whole flounder,** cleaned and scaled, and 2 sheets 24" by 12" of parchment or foil. Preheat oven to 400°F. Line rimmed baking pan with parchment paper. Follow Steps 1 and 2. Place fish on parchment in pan. Sprinkle with ginger and sliced green onions; drizzle with soy-sauce mixture. Top with second sheet of parchment. To seal fish, beginning at one corner, make ½-inch-wide folds, with each new fold overlapping previous one, until packet is sealed. Roast fish about 30 minutes, or until fish is just opaque when knife is inserted at backbone. Cut parchment open and using two wide slotted spatulas, transfer fish to large platter. Pour pan juices over fish and garnish with reserved green-onion strips. Makes 4 main-dish servings.

BAKED FLOUNDER WITH SAVORY CRUMB TOPPING

....

Need a fast and flavorful midweek supper recipe? Our tasty flounder is the answer. If you don't have an open bottle of dry white wine, substitute dry vermouth or reduced-sodium chicken broth.

Prep: 15 minutes   Bake: 10 minutes

- 1½ cups fresh bread crumbs (about 3 slices bread)
- 2 tablespoons chopped fresh parsley
- ¼ cup dry white wine
- 4 flounder fillets (5 ounces each)
- ¼ teaspoon salt
- ¼ cup mayonnaise

1. Preheat oven to 400°F. In 10-inch skillet, toast bread crumbs over medium heat, stirring frequently, until golden, about 10 minutes. Remove from heat and stir in parsley.

2. Pour wine into 13" by 9" baking dish; add flounder fillets, turning to coat. Arrange fillets, skinned side up, in dish, tucking thin ends under. Sprinkle with salt and spread mayonnaise on top. Gently pat bread-crumb mixture over mayonnaise. Bake until fish is just opaque throughout and topping has crisped, about 10 minutes. Makes 4 main-dish servings.

Each serving: About 295 calories, 29g protein, 11g carbohydrate, 13g total fat (2g saturated), 76mg cholesterol, 452mg sodium.

PARMESAN CHEESE FILLETS

Prepare as directed above but use only ⅔ **cup plain dried bread crumbs** and add ⅓ **cup freshly grated Parmesan cheese** to bread-crumb mixture.

SESAME SEED FILLETS

Prepare as directed above but use only ¾ **cup plain dried bread crumbs** and add ¼ **cup sesame seeds** to bread-crumb mixture.

ROLLED SOLE STUFFED WITH CRAB

....

For a stress-free dinner party, stuff and roll up the sole fillets and refrigerate for up to four hours before baking them. The sauce can also be prepared several hours ahead, then reheated gently just before serving.

Prep: 20 minutes   Bake: 25 minutes

- 2 tablespoons butter or margarine
- 4 tablespoons finely chopped shallots
- 8 ounces lump crabmeat, picked over
- ½ cup fresh bread crumbs (about 1 slice bread)
- 1 tablespoon chopped fresh parsley
- 2 teaspoons fresh lemon juice
- ½ plus ⅛ teaspoon salt
- ⅛ teaspoon plus pinch ground black pepper
- 6 sole or flounder fillets (6 ounces each)
- 1 can (14 to 16 ounces) tomatoes, drained
- ¼ cup heavy or whipping cream
- 1 teaspoon chopped fresh tarragon or parsley

1. Preheat oven to 400°F. Grease 13" by 9" baking dish; set aside.

Rolled Sole Stuffed with Crab

2. In nonstick 10-inch skillet, melt 1 tablespoon butter over medium heat. Add 2 tablespoons shallots and cook until tender, about 2 minutes. Transfer to medium bowl. Add crabmeat, bread crumbs, parsley, lemon juice, ¼ teaspoon salt, and ⅛ teaspoon pepper to shallots; toss with fork until evenly combined.

3. Sprinkle skinned side of sole fillets with ¼ teaspoon salt. Spoon crabmeat mixture evenly over fillets. Roll up fillets and place, seam side down, in prepared baking dish. Bake until fish is just opaque throughout, about 25 minutes.

4. Meanwhile, in blender, puree tomatoes until smooth. In same 10-inch skillet, melt remaining 1 tablespoon butter over medium heat. Add remaining 2 tablespoons shallots and cook until tender, about 2 minutes. Add pureed tomatoes, remaining ⅛ teaspoon salt, and remaining pinch pepper; increase heat to high and cook, stirring frequently, until liquid has almost evaporated, about 5 minutes. Stir in cream and heat to boiling. Remove from heat and stir in tarragon.

5. With wide slotted spatula, transfer fish to warm platter. Stir any juices in baking dish into sauce; spoon sauce over fish. Makes 6 main-dish servings.

Each serving: About 298 calories, 41g protein, 7g carbohydrate, 11g total fat (5g saturated), 144mg cholesterol, 665mg sodium.

CRABMEAT: DELICIOUS DELICACY

 Although live crabs are often available at the fish counter, buying cooked crabmeat is easiest way when you need to use the meat as a recipe ingredient.

LUMP OR BACKFIN consists of large whole lumps from the body and backfin. It is very expensive and tasty.
SPECIAL CRABMEAT is made up of lump crabmeat and flaked meat from the rest of the body.
FLAKED CRABMEAT contains all of the meat from the body but no lump meat.
CLAW CRABMEAT is meat from the claws.

Crabmeat is sold fresh by the half pound and pound. It should have a sweet aroma and look moist and snowy white. Canned crabmeat is good in a pinch, but it lacks the special flavor of the fresh.

PORTUGUESE-STYLE MONKFISH

....

Here, chunks of firm monkfish are cooked in a spicy sausage-tomato sauce until tender. Serve over rice or pasta.

Prep: 25 minutes   Cook: 40 minutes

- 1 tablespoon olive oil
- 1 medium onion, chopped
- 3 garlic cloves, finely chopped
- 1 fully cooked chorizo sausage (3 ounces), cut lengthwise into quarters, then crosswise into thin slices
- 1 red pepper, chopped
- ⅔ cup chicken broth
- 1 can (14 to 16 ounces) tomatoes, chopped
- ¼ teaspoon salt
- ¼ teaspoon crushed red pepper
- 1½ pounds monkfish, dark membrane removed, cut into 1-inch pieces
- ¼ cup chopped fresh parsley

1. In nonstick 10-inch skillet, heat oil over medium-low heat. Add onion and garlic and cook, stirring frequently, until onion is tender, about 5 minutes.

2. Add chorizo and chopped red pepper and cook, stirring frequently, until pepper is tender, about 5 minutes. Add broth and heat to boiling. Stir in tomatoes with their juice, salt, and crushed red pepper; heat to boiling.

3. Add monkfish to skillet. Reduce heat; cover and simmer until monkfish is tender, about 10 minutes. With slotted spoon, transfer monkfish to bowl. Increase heat to high and boil liquid until sauce has reduced and thickened, about 5 minutes. Return fish to skillet and stir in parsley. Makes 4 main-dish servings.

Each serving: About 308 calories, 32g protein, 11g carbohydrate, 15g total fat (4g saturated), 61mg cholesterol, 781mg sodium.

RED SNAPPER IN PARCHMENT WITH TOMATOES AND BASIL

....

Here, the snapper juices mingle with the tomatoes and basil in a parchment packet to create a fabulous sauce.

Prep: 25 minutes   Bake: 15 minutes

- 1 tablespoon butter or margarine
- 1 large garlic clove, finely chopped
- 1 pound ripe plum tomatoes, seeded and chopped (2 cups)
- ¼ plus ⅛ teaspoon salt
- ¼ teaspoon ground black pepper
- ⅓ cup chopped fresh basil
- 4 red snapper fillets (6 ounces each), skin removed
- 4 squares (12 inches each) cooking parchment or foil

1. Preheat oven to 400°F.

2. In 12-inch skillet, melt butter over medium-high heat. Add garlic and cook 30 seconds. Add tomatoes, ¼ teaspoon salt, and ⅛ teaspoon pepper. Cook, stirring frequently, until liquid has almost evaporated, about 5 minutes. Remove from heat and stir in basil.

3. With tweezers, remove any bones from snapper fillets. Place 1 fillet, skinned side down, on one half of each parchment square. Sprinkle with remaining ⅛ teaspoon each salt and pepper; top with tomato mixture.

4. Fold unfilled half of parchment over fish. To seal packets, beginning at a corner where parchment is folded, make ½-inch-wide folds, with each new fold overlapping previous one, until packet is completely sealed. Packet will resemble half-circle. Place packets in jelly-roll pan. Bake 15 minutes (packets will puff up and brown). Cut packets open to serve. Makes 4 main-dish servings.

Each serving: About 207 calories, 33g protein, 6g carbohydrate, 5g total fat (2g saturated), 65mg cholesterol, 359mg sodium.

BAKED SALMON FILLETS

Thick center-cut pieces of salmon bake in about 20 minutes. If using thinner pieces cut nearer the tail, check after 15 minutes. There are many sauces that go well with baked salmon; try Salmoriglio Sauce (page 505) or a fruit salsa (pages 506–508).

Prep: 5 minutes   **Bake: 15 minutes**

- 4 pieces salmon fillet with skin (6 ounces each)
- 1 teaspoon olive oil
- 1/8 teaspoon salt
- 1/8 teaspoon ground black pepper

1. Preheat oven to 400°F and grease 13" by 9" baking dish.

2. With tweezers, remove any bones from salmon fillets. Arrange fillets in prepared baking dish; rub with oil and sprinkle with salt and pepper. Bake until salmon is just opaque throughout, 15 to 20 minutes. Makes 4 main-dish servings.

Each serving: About 331 calories, 34g protein, 0g carbohydrate, 21g total fat (4g saturated), 100mg cholesterol, 174mg sodium.

SAUCES FOR FISH

Unlike meat and poultry dishes, where pan sauces are often created from the cooking juices, many fish sauces are separate recipes. For a Mediterranean touch, try Salmoriglio Sauce (page 505) or Salsa Verde (page 505). Some favorite mayonnaise-based sauces include Tartar Sauce (page 504), and Easy Aïoli (page 37). Salsas, such as Olive and Lemon or Orange-Fennel (pages 506–507), are excellent condiments for grilled fish, or top fish with a pat of Olive Butter or Ginger-Cilantro Butter (page 504).

SALMON AND LENTILS

A sprightly lemon dressing is spooned over flavorful salmon and lentils. Serve a green vegetable on the side.

Prep: 10 minutes   **Cook/Bake: 50 minutes**

- 1 cup lentils, rinsed and picked through
- 2 1/4 cups water
- 3/4 plus 1/8 teaspoon salt
- 4 pieces salmon fillet with skin (6 ounces each)
- 1 teaspoon plus 2 tablespoons olive oil
- 1/8 plus 1/4 teaspoon coarsely ground black pepper
- 1 lemon
- 1 teaspoon Dijon mustard
- 4 teaspoons chopped fresh tarragon
- 1 tablespoon butter or margarine
- 1/4 cup finely chopped shallots
- 1/4 cup chopped fresh parsley

1. Preheat oven to 400°F. In 2-quart saucepan, combine lentils, water, and 1/2 teaspoon salt; heat to boiling over high heat. Reduce heat; cover and simmer until lentils are tender, 20 to 30 minutes. Drain.

2. Meanwhile, grease 13" by 9" baking dish. With tweezers, remove any bones from salmon. Arrange fillets in single layer in prepared baking dish. Rub with 1 teaspoon oil and sprinkle with 1/8 teaspoon each salt and pepper. Bake until fish is just opaque throughout, 15 to 20 minutes.

3. While salmon is baking, prepare dressing: From lemon, grate 1/2 teaspoon peel and squeeze 2 tablespoons juice. In small bowl, with wire whisk, whisk together lemon juice, mustard, and remaining 1/4 teaspoon salt. Gradually whisk in remaining 2 tablespoons oil, then stir in 2 teaspoons tarragon.

4. In 10-inch skillet, melt butter over medium heat. Add shallots and cook, stirring, 2 minutes. Stir in lentils, lemon peel, and remaining 1/4 teaspoon pepper. Remove from heat and stir in parsley and remaining 2 teaspoons tarragon. Spread lentil mixture on platter. Arrange salmon on top of lentils and spoon dressing over salmon. Makes 4 main-dish servings.

Each serving: About 582 calories, 48g protein, 30g carbohydrate, 30g total fat (7g saturated), 108mg cholesterol, 604mg sodium.

Salmon and Lentils

FRESH SALMON BURGERS WITH CAPERS AND DILL

....

Our lemon-caper sauce is easy as well as delicious. It also makes a tasty sandwich spread and is a great dipper for shrimp and scallops.

Prep: 25 minutes   Grill: 6 minutes

- 1 large lemon
- ¼ cup light mayonnaise
- 1 tablespoon capers, drained and coarsely chopped
- 1 pound salmon fillet, skin removed
- ¼ cup loosely packed fresh dill, chopped
- 2 green onions, thinly sliced
- ½ cup plain dried bread crumbs
- ¾ teaspoon salt
  nonstick cooking spray
- 4 whole-wheat hamburger buns, split and toasted
  green-leaf lettuce leaves

1. Prepare grill pan or outdoor grill for direct grilling.

2. Meanwhile, from lemon, grate 1 teaspoon peel and squeeze 1 tablespoon juice.

3. In small bowl, stir lemon juice, ½ teaspoon lemon peel, mayonnaise, and capers until blended. Set lemon-caper sauce aside. Makes about ⅓ cup.

4. With tweezers, remove any bones from salmon. With large chef's knife, finely chop salmon; place in medium bowl. Add dill, green onions, ¼ cup bread crumbs, salt, and remaining ½ teaspoon lemon peel; gently mix with fork until combined. Shape salmon mixture into four 3-inch round burgers.

5. Sprinkle both sides of burgers with remaining bread crumbs; pat gently to adhere. Spray both sides of burgers with nonstick spray.

6. Place burgers on grill over medium heat. Cook burgers 6 to 8 minutes for medium or until desired doneness, turning once.

7. Serve burgers on buns with lettuce and lemon-caper mayonnaise. Makes 4 main-dish servings.

Each serving: About 380 calories, 27g protein, 34g carbohydrate, 15g total fat (3g saturated), 65mg cholesterol, 990mg sodium.

SALMON TERIYAKI BURGERS

Prepare as above, but omit lemon-caper sauce. In Step 3, substitute **½ cup diced water chestnuts, ¼ cup teriyaki sauce,** and **¼ teaspoon crushed red pepper** for dill, green onions, bread crumbs, salt, and lemon peel. Do not sprinkle burgers with bread crumbs. Proceed as directed. To serve, place burgers on buns with lettuce and spoon **1 tablespoon hoisin sauce** over each.

FIVE-SPICE SALMON FILLETS

....

Chinese five-spice powder adds an intriguing hint of licorice to rich salmon.

Prep: 5 minutes   Cook: 8 minutes

- 4 pieces salmon fillet (4 ounces each), skin removed
- 2 teaspoons Chinese five-spice powder
- 1 teaspoon all-purpose flour
- ½ teaspoon salt
- ¼ teaspoon cracked black pepper
- 2 teaspoons vegetable oil

1. With tweezers, remove any bones from salmon fillets. On waxed paper, combine five-spice powder, flour, salt, and pepper. Use to rub on both sides of fillets.

2. In nonstick 10-inch skillet, heat oil over medium heat until hot. Add salmon; cook until just opaque throughout, 4 to 5 minutes per side. Makes 4 main-dish servings.

Each serving: About 222 calories, 21g protein, 2g carbohydrate, 14g total fat (3g saturated), 63mg cholesterol, 353mg sodium.

SNAPPER LIVORNESE

....

Vibrant with olives, capers, and basil, this preparation works beautifully with any lean white fish.

Prep: 10 minutes   Cook: 25 minutes

- 1 tablespoon olive oil
- 1 garlic clove, finely chopped
- 1 can (14 to 16 ounces) tomatoes
- ⅛ teaspoon salt
- ⅛ teaspoon ground black pepper
- 4 red snapper fillets (6 ounces each)
- ¼ cup chopped fresh basil
- ¼ cup Kalamata or Gaeta olives, pitted and chopped
- 2 teaspoons capers, drained

1. In nonstick 10-inch skillet, heat oil over medium heat. Add garlic and cook just until very fragrant, about 30 seconds. Stir in tomatoes with their juice, salt, and pepper, breaking up tomatoes with spoon. Heat to boiling; reduce heat and simmer 10 minutes.

2. With tweezers, remove any bones from snapper fillets. Place fillets, skin side down, in skillet. Cover and simmer until fish is just opaque throughout, about 10 minutes. With wide slotted spatula, transfer fish to warm platter. Stir basil, olives, and capers into tomato sauce and spoon over snapper. Makes 4 main-dish servings.

Each serving: About 250 calories, 36g protein, 6g carbohydrate, 8g total fat (1g saturated), 63mg cholesterol, 571mg sodium.

REMOVING PIN BONES

Run your fingers along each fillet to check for pin bones. Use tweezers or pin-nose pliers (set aside for that purpose) to pull them out. Or use a sharp knife to cut along each side of the strip of bones and remove it.

Snapper Livornese

KEDGEREE

....

A traditional British breakfast dish, kedgeree is also delicious for brunch or supper.

Prep: 35 minutes   Bake: 30 minutes

1 tablespoon butter or margarine
1 small onion, chopped
¾ teaspoon curry powder
1½ cups regular long-grain rice
3 cups water
1 teaspoon salt
¼ teaspoon coarsely ground black pepper
1 pound smoked haddock fillet (finnan haddie)
1 lemon
4 large hard-cooked eggs, coarsely chopped
¼ cup chopped fresh parsley
½ cup heavy or whipping cream

1. In 2-quart saucepan, melt butter over medium heat. Add onion and cook until tender, about 5 minutes. Stir in curry powder and rice. Add water, salt, and pepper; heat to boiling. Reduce heat; cover and simmer, without stirring or lifting lid, until rice is tender and all liquid has been absorbed, about 20 minutes. Transfer to large bowl.

2. Meanwhile, in 10-inch skillet, combine smoked haddock fillet with enough *water* to cover; heat to boiling. Reduce heat and simmer just until haddock begins to flake, 5 to 10 minutes. Drain and cool slightly.

3. Preheat oven to 350°F. From lemon, grate ½ teaspoon peel and squeeze 1 tablespoon juice; add lemon peel and juice to rice, fluffing with fork. Flake haddock, discarding any skin or bones. Add fish, eggs, and parsley to rice, tossing gently. Transfer to 13" by 9" baking dish, spreading evenly; drizzle cream over top. Cover with foil and bake 30 minutes. Makes 6 main-dish servings.

Each serving: About 406 calories, 27g protein, 42g carbohydrate, 14g total fat (7g saturated), 232mg cholesterol, 0mg sodium.

BRANDADE

....

A little of this flavorful, velvety Provençal hors d'oeuvre goes a long way. Spread on thin slices of toasted bread.

**Prep: 20 minutes plus 24 to 36 hours to soak cod
Cook: 20 minutes**

1 pound salt cod fillets
1 large baking potato (12 ounces), peeled and thinly sliced
3 garlic cloves, peeled
1 cup heavy or whipping cream
   pinch ground nutmeg
2 tablespoons extra-virgin olive oil
   thinly sliced French bread, toasted

1. In medium bowl, combine salt cod fillets and enough *cold water* to cover generously. Cover and refrigerate, changing water several times, 24 to 36 hours. Drain and rinse well.

2. In 3-quart saucepan, combine potato, garlic, and *3 cups water;* heat to boiling over high heat. Reduce heat and simmer until potato is tender, 12 to 15 minutes. Drain, reserving 1 cup water. Mash potato and garlic until almost smooth. Transfer mixture to medium bowl.

3. Meanwhile, in clean 3-quart saucepan, combine cod and enough *water* to cover; heat to boiling. Reduce heat and simmer until fish can be flaked with fork, 5 to 10 minutes; drain. When cool enough to handle, discard any skin or bones. Transfer cod to food processor with knife blade attached and pulse until flaked.

4. In clean 3-quart saucepan, heat cream over low heat. With wooden spoon, stir in cod, potato mixture, reserved potato water, and nutmeg; stir until well combined. With wire whisk, gradually whisk in oil. Serve with toast. Makes 4 cups or 12 first-course servings.

Each ¼ cup without toast: About 216 calories, 25g protein, 5g carbohydrate, 11g total fat (5g saturated), 85mg cholesterol, 0mg sodium.

PORTUGUESE-STYLE SALT COD

They say that the Portuguese have 365 ways to cook salt cod. This is certainly one of the best.

Prep: 35 minutes plus 24 to 36 hours to soak cod
Cook/Bake: 1 hour 20 minutes

- 1 pound salt cod fillets
- ¼ cup olive oil, preferably extra-virgin
- 3 small onions, thinly sliced
- 2 garlic cloves, thinly sliced
- 1 pound (5 small) all-purpose potatoes
- 1 can (28 ounces) tomatoes, drained and chopped
- ¼ cup plus 1 tablespoon chopped fresh parsley
- ¼ teaspoon salt
- ¼ teaspoon ground black pepper
- 2 large hard-cooked eggs, each cut lengthwise into quarters
- 16 oil-cured black olives, pitted
- 2 teaspoons capers, drained

1. In medium bowl, combine salt cod fillets and enough *cold water* to cover generously. Cover and refrigerate, changing water several times, 24 to 36 hours. Drain and rinse well.

2. In 3-quart saucepan, combine cod and enough *water* to cover; heat to boiling. Reduce heat and simmer until fish can be flaked with fork, 5 to 10 minutes; drain. When cool enough to handle, discard any skin or bones and coarsely flake cod.

3. Meanwhile, in 10-inch skillet, heat oil over medium heat. Add onions and garlic and cook, stirring, until very tender and golden, about 10 minutes. With slotted spoon, transfer onions to bowl. Pour oil in skillet into cup; reserve.

4. In 5-quart Dutch oven, combine potatoes and enough salted *cold water* to cover; heat to boiling. Cook just until potatoes are tender when pierced with fork, about 20 minutes. When cool enough to handle, peel potatoes and cut into thin slices.

5. Preheat oven to 350°F. Lightly oil 8-inch square baking dish. In dish, layer potatoes, tomatoes, ¼ cup parsley, half of onions, cod, and remaining onions, lightly sprinkling each layer with salt and pepper. Bake until golden and heated through, about 35 minutes.

6. To serve, drizzle with reserved oil. Arrange eggs on top and sprinkle with olives, capers, and remaining 1 tablespoon parsley. Makes 4 main-dish servings.

Each serving: About 697 calories, 80g protein, 39g carbohydrate, 25g total fat (4g saturated), 279mg cholesterol, sodium n/a.

CHINESE STEAMED CLAMS

Serve this Asian-inspired dish with steamed white rice so all of the flavorful broth can be enjoyed.

Prep: 10 minutes   Cook: 10 minutes

- 1 tablespoon vegetable oil
- 2 green onions, finely chopped
- 1 tablespoon minced, peeled fresh ginger
- 1 garlic clove, finely chopped
- 2 dozen cherrystone or littleneck clams, scrubbed (page 214), or mussels, scrubbed and debearded (page 215)
- ½ cup water
- 3 tablespoons dry sherry
- 2 tablespoons soy sauce
- 2 tablespoons chopped fresh cilantro

In 8-quart saucepot, heat oil over high heat. Add green onions, ginger, and garlic; cook until green onions are tender, about 1 minute. Add clams, water, sherry, and soy sauce; heat to boiling. Reduce heat; cover and simmer 5 to 10 minutes, transferring clams to large platter as they open. Discard any clams that have not opened. Pour broth over clams on platter and sprinkle with cilantro. Makes 4 first-course servings.

Each serving: About 131 calories, 14g protein, 5g carbohydrate, 4g total fat (1g saturated), 36mg cholesterol, 576mg sodium.

SCRUBBING AND SHUCKING CLAMS

Scrub the clams well under cold running water to remove all the grit.

Protecting your hand with a folded towel, hold the clam with the "hinge" facing you; wedge the thin edge of a clam knife between the shells.

Slide the knife around to separate the shells.

Open the shell. Cut the clam meat away from the top shell; discard the top shell.

Slide the knife underneath the meat in the bottom shell to release it.

STEAMED SOFT-SHELL CLAMS

....

A great appetizer or main dish to have with an ice-cold beer on a hot summer day!

Prep: 5 minutes   Cook: 10 minutes

6 dozen steamer (soft-shell) clams
    melted butter or margarine (optional)

1. In very large bowl or in kitchen sink, place clams and enough *cold water* to cover; drain. Repeat rinsing and draining until sand no longer falls to bottom of bowl.

2. In steamer or 8-quart saucepot fitted with rack, heat enough *water* to cover pan bottom to boiling over high heat. Place clams on rack in steamer. Reduce heat; cover and steam until clams open, 5 to 10 minutes, transferring clams to bowl as they open. Discard any clams that have not opened.

3. Strain clam broth through sieve lined with paper towels and pour into 6 soup cups or mugs.

4. To eat, with fingers, pull clams from shells by neck; peel off and discard black sheath that covers neck. Dip clams first in broth to remove any sand, then into melted butter, if you like. When sand has settled to bottom, broth can be sipped, if desired. Makes 6 first-course servings.

Each serving without butter: About 76 calories, 13g protein, 3g carbohydrate, 1g total fat (0g saturated), 35mg cholesterol, 57mg sodium.

MUSSELS WITH TOMATOES AND WHITE WINE

(Pictured on page 190)

···

This saucy dish should be served with plenty of good crusty bread for dipping.

Prep: 20 minutes   Cook: 25 minutes

- 1   tablespoon olive or vegetable oil
- 1   small onion, chopped
- 2   garlic cloves, finely chopped
- ¼   teaspoon crushed red pepper
- 1   can (14 to 16 ounces) tomatoes
- ¾   cup dry white wine
- 4   pounds large mussels, scrubbed and debearded (right)
- 2   tablespoons chopped fresh parsley

1. In nonreactive 5-quart Dutch oven, heat oil over medium heat. Add onion and cook until tender and golden, 6 to 8 minutes. Add garlic and crushed red pepper and cook 30 seconds longer. Stir in tomatoes with their juice and wine, breaking up tomatoes with side of spoon. Heat to boiling; boil 3 minutes.

2. Add mussels; heat to boiling. Reduce heat; cover and simmer until mussels open, about 5 minutes, transferring mussels to large bowl as they open. Discard any mussels that have not opened. Pour mussel broth over mussels and sprinkle with parsley. Makes 8 first-course or 4 main-dish servings.

Each first-course serving: About 104 calories, 9g protein, 6g carbohydrate, 3g total fat (1g saturated), 18mg cholesterol, 277mg sodium.

MOULES À LA MARINIÈRE

Prepare as above, substituting **butter** for olive oil, if you like, and **⅓ cup chopped shallots** for onion. Omit crushed red pepper and tomatoes; use **1½ cups dry white wine.** Proceed as directed.

SCRUBBING AND DEBEARDING MUSSELS

Scrub mussels well under cold running water. To debeard, grasp the hairlike beard firmly with your thumb and forefinger and pull it away, or scrape it off with a knife.

(Cultivated mussels usually do not have beards.)

PANFRIED OYSTERS

··

Large plump oysters work best in this seaside favorite.

Prep: 15 minutes   Cook: 10 minutes

- 1   pint shucked oysters, drained
- ⅔   cup finely crushed saltine crackers
- 2   tablespoons butter or margarine
- 2   tablespoons vegetable oil
      lemon wedges

1. Gently pat oysters dry with paper towels. Place cracker crumbs on waxed paper and coat oysters with crumbs.

2. In 10-inch skillet, heat 1 tablespoon butter and 1 tablespoon oil over medium-high heat until hot. Add half of oysters to skillet and cook until golden brown, 2 to 3 minutes per side. Repeat with remaining butter, oil, and oysters. Serve with lemon wedges. Makes 4 first-course servings.

Each serving: About 249 calories, 10g protein, 13g carbohydrate, 17g total fat (5g saturated), 85mg cholesterol, 353mg sodium.

SCALLOPED OYSTERS

....

Bake these delectable crumb-topped oysters in individual ramekins, if you have them, or in a shallow 2½ quart baking dish. The baking time will depend on the depth of the dish.

Prep: 40 minutes   Bake: 15 minutes

- 10 slices firm white bread, torn into 1-inch pieces
- 4 tablespoons butter or margarine, melted
- 1½ pints shucked oysters with their liquid
- ¾ cup heavy or whipping cream
- ¼ teaspoon salt
- ⅛ teaspoon coarsely ground black pepper
- 2 tablespoons chopped fresh parsley

1. Preheat oven to 400°F. Place bread pieces in jelly-roll pan and drizzle with melted butter, tossing to coat evenly. Toast bread in oven, stirring occasionally, until crisp and golden, about 25 minutes.

2. Meanwhile, drain oysters, reserving liquid, and refrigerate. In 1-quart saucepan, heat oyster liquid to boiling over high heat. Reduce heat to medium and cook until oyster liquid has reduced to 3 tablespoons, about 5 minutes. Add cream, salt, and pepper; heat to boiling. Remove saucepan from heat.

3. In large bowl, gently combine toasted bread pieces, oysters, and parsley. Spoon mixture into eight 12-ounce ramekins, dividing it evenly. Pour about 2 tablespoons cream mixture over each. Bake just until edges of oysters begin to curl, about 15 minutes. Makes 8 first-course servings.

Each serving: About 288 calories, 10g protein, 22g carbohydrate, 18g total fat (10g saturated), 99mg cholesterol, 436mg sodium.

SCALLOPS PROVENÇAL

....

A hint of orange peel gives this tomato sauce a flavor reminiscent of southern France. If you wish, make the sauce in advance and reheat at serving time. You can substitute bay scallops for the sea scallops.

Prep: 20 minutes   Cook: 20 minutes

- 1 large leek (8 ounces)
- 2 tablespoons olive oil
- 2 garlic cloves, finely chopped
- 1 can (14 to 16 ounces) tomatoes, chopped
- 1 teaspoon salt
- ½ teaspoon freshly grated orange peel
   pinch ground red pepper (cayenne)
- 1 pound sea scallops
- ¼ cup all-purpose flour

1. Cut off roots and trim dark green tops from leek; cut lengthwise in half, then crosswise into thin slices. Rinse in large bowl of cold water, swishing to remove sand; transfer to colander to drain, leaving sand in bottom of bowl.

2. In nonstick 10-inch skillet, heat 1 tablespoon oil over medium heat. Add leek and garlic and cook, stirring frequently, until leek is tender, about 7 minutes. Add tomatoes with their juice, ½ teaspoon salt, orange peel, and ground red pepper; heat to boiling. Reduce heat and simmer until sauce has thickened slightly, about 5 minutes.

3. Meanwhile, pull off and discard tough crescent-shaped muscle from each scallop. Pat scallops dry with paper towels. Cut each scallop horizontally in half if large.

4. In 12-inch skillet, heat remaining 1 tablespoon oil over medium-high heat until hot. Place flour on waxed paper and coat scallops with flour, shaking off excess. Sprinkle remaining ½ teaspoon salt on scallops. Add scallops to skillet and cook, stirring, until just opaque throughout and lightly golden, about 4 minutes. Stir in sauce and heat through. Makes 4 main-dish servings.

Each serving: About 227 calories, 21g protein, 17g carbohydrate, 8g total fat (1g saturated), 37mg cholesterol, 944mg sodium.

SCALLOP AND ASPARAGUS STIR-FRY

....

Tossing this dish with chopped basil just before serving adds a pleasing touch of fresh flavor. With steamed rice, you have a complete meal.

Prep: 20 minutes   Cook: 15 minutes

- 1 pound sea scallops
- 2 tablespoons reduced-sodium soy sauce
- 1 tablespoon minced, peeled fresh ginger
- 2 tablespoons vegetable oil
- 2 garlic cloves, thinly sliced
- 1½ pounds asparagus, trimmed and cut into 2-inch pieces
- ¼ teaspoon crushed red pepper
- ½ cup loosely packed fresh basil leaves, chopped, plus additional leaves

1. Pull off and discard tough crescent-shaped muscle from each scallop. In bowl, toss scallops with 1 tablespoon soy sauce and ginger.

2. In 12-inch skillet, heat 1 tablespoon oil over medium-high heat. Add garlic and cook, stirring often, until golden. With slotted spoon, transfer garlic to medium bowl.

3. Add asparagus and crushed red pepper to skillet and cook, stirring frequently (stir-frying), until asparagus is tender-crisp, about 7 minutes. Transfer asparagus to bowl with garlic.

4. Add remaining 1 tablespoon oil to skillet; add scallop mixture and stir-fry until scallops are just opaque throughout, 3 to 5 minutes.

5. Return asparagus and garlic to skillet, along with remaining 1 tablespoon soy sauce; heat through. Add chopped basil, tossing to combine. Spoon mixture onto warm platter and top with basil leaves. Makes 4 main-dish servings.

Each serving: About 204 calories, 24g protein, 10g carbohydrate, 8g total fat (1g saturated), 37mg cholesterol, 487mg sodium.

Scallop and Asparagus Stir-Fry

PANFRIED SCALLOPS

....

Try these during the fall and winter months, when small bay scallops are in season. Otherwise, substitute sea scallops and increase the cooking time accordingly.

Prep: 5 minutes   Cook: 5 minutes

- 1 pound bay scallops
- 2 tablespoons olive oil
- ½ teaspoon salt
- 2 tablespoons chopped fresh parsley
- 4 lemon wedges

Pat scallops dry with paper towels. In 12-inch skillet, heat oil over medium-high heat until hot. Add scallops to skillet and sprinkle with salt. Cook, stirring, until just opaque throughout, about 4 minutes. Add parsley and toss. Serve with lemon wedges. Makes 4 main-dish servings.

Each serving: About 160 calories, 19g protein, 3g carbohydrate, 8g total fat (1g saturated), 37mg cholesterol, 473mg sodium.

CRAB BOIL

A big pot of spiced boiled crabs, a Chesapeake Bay tradition, is a delicious but messy affair. Cover the table with newspaper and have lots of big napkins on hand. Serve with coleslaw and rolls. (If you want to cook crab so you can pick the meat for another recipe, omit the crab boil seasoning and red pepper.)

Prep: 8 minutes   Cook: 40 minutes

- 2 medium onions, coarsely chopped
- 1 carrot, peeled and coarsely chopped
- 1 stalk celery, coarsely chopped
- 1 lemon, sliced
- ½ cup crab boil seasoning
- 1 tablespoon crushed red pepper
- 1 tablespoon salt
- 1 gallon (16 cups) water
- 1 can or bottle (12 ounces) beer
- 2 dozen live hard-shell blue crabs, rinsed

1. In 12-quart stockpot, combine onions, carrot, celery, lemon, crab boil seasoning, crushed red pepper, salt, water, and beer. Heat to boiling over high heat; cook 15 minutes.

2. Using tongs, transfer crabs to stockpot. Cover and heat to boiling; boil 5 minutes (crabs will turn red). With tongs, transfer crabs to colander to drain, then place on warm platter.

3. To eat crab, twist off claws and legs, then crack shell to remove meat. Break off flat pointed apron from underside of crab; remove top shell. Discard feathery gills. With kitchen shears or hands, break body in half down center. With fingers or lobster pick, remove meat. Makes 4 main-dish servings.

Each serving: About 123 calories, 24g protein, 0g carbohydrate, 2g total fat (0g saturated), 119mg cholesterol, 1,410mg sodium.

Panfried Soft-Shell Crabs

CLEANING SOFT-SHELL CRABS

Soft-shell crabs are sometimes available already cleaned, but it is better to do it yourself at home, because crabs begin to spoil once their viscera are removed. To clean, with kitchen shears, cut across each crab ¼ inch behind the eyes; discard front portion. Cut off the flat pointed "apron" on the underside. Bend back the top shell on each side and snip off the spongy gills. Rinse with cold running water; pat dry with paper towels.

PANFRIED SOFT-SHELL CRABS

Here's the classic way to prepare soft-shell crabs so they're crispy outside and moist inside.

Prep: 30 minutes   Cook: 12 minutes

- ½ cup all-purpose flour
- ¾ teaspoon salt
- ½ teaspoon ground black pepper
- 8 live soft-shell crabs (6 ounces each), cleaned
- 4 tablespoons butter or margarine
  lemon wedges

1. On waxed paper, combine flour, salt, and pepper. Coat crabs with seasoned flour, shaking off excess.

2. In 12-inch skillet, melt 2 tablespoons butter over medium heat until hot; add 4 crabs and cook until golden, 3 to 4 minutes per side. Transfer crabs to platter and keep warm. Repeat with remaining butter and remaining crabs. Serve with lemon wedges. Makes 4 main-dish servings.

Each serving: About 256 calories, 19g protein, 12g carbohydrate, 15g total fat (8g saturated), 188mg cholesterol, 1,207mg sodium.

STEAMED LOBSTER

Quite simply, a seafood lover's dream.

Prep: 5 minutes   Cook: 20 minutes

- 2 live lobsters (1¼ to 1½ pounds each)
- 4 tablespoons butter or margarine, melted
- 2 teaspoons fresh lemon juice

1. In 12-quart stockpot, heat *1½ inches water* to boiling over high heat. Plunge lobsters, headfirst, into boiling water. Cover and heat to boiling; steam 12 minutes. With tongs, transfer lobsters to colander to drain, then place on platter.

2. Combine melted butter and lemon juice; transfer to small cups for dipping lobster.

3. To eat lobster, twist off claws and legs. With lobster cracker, nut cracker, or hammer, crack large claws; remove meat. Separate legs at joints; push out meat. Twist to separate tail from body. Reserve any red roe (coral) and greenish liver (tomalley) separately, if desired. With kitchen shears, cut down along center of underside of tail; gently remove meat. Lift bony portion behind small legs from shell; with lobster pick or fork, remove small nuggets of meat. Dip lobster into lemon butter. Makes 2 main-dish servings.

Each serving with butter: About 340 calories, 29g protein, 2g carbohydrate, 24g total fat (15g saturated), 162mg cholesterol, 760mg sodium.

SHRIMP CURRY

This is a mildly seasoned curry prepared in the French style with cream. Serve over rice, if you like.

Prep: 20 minutes   Cook: 12 minutes

- 2 tablespoons butter or margarine
- 2 garlic cloves, finely chopped
- 2 teaspoons minced, peeled fresh ginger
- 2 teaspoons curry powder
- ½ teaspoon ground coriander
- ½ teaspoon ground cumin
- ¾ cup heavy or whipping cream
- 1 teaspoon salt
- 1 medium zucchini (8 ounces), cut lengthwise in half, then crosswise into thin slices
- 1 pound medium shrimp, shelled and deveined (opposite)
- ½ teaspoon ground black pepper
- 2 tablespoons chopped fresh cilantro

1. In 2-quart saucepan, melt 1 tablespoon butter over medium heat. Add garlic, ginger, curry powder, coriander, and cumin; cook, stirring, 1 minute. Stir in cream and ½ teaspoon salt; increase heat to high and boil until curry sauce has thickened, about 5 minutes.

2. In 10-inch skillet, melt remaining 1 tablespoon butter over medium-high heat. Add zucchini and cook, stirring, until zucchini begins to brown, 2 to 3 minutes. Stir in shrimp, pepper, and remaining ½ teaspoon salt; cook, stirring, until shrimp are just opaque throughout, about 2 minutes. Stir shrimp and zucchini into curry sauce; sprinkle with cilantro. Makes 4 main-dish servings.

Each serving: About 318 calories, 21g protein, 5g carbohydrate, 24g total fat (14g saturated), 216mg cholesterol, 797mg sodium.

THAI SHRIMP

Spoon this chunky shrimp-and-vegetable mixture over fragrant jasmine rice.

Prep: 30 minutes   Cook: 15 minutes

- 2 medium limes
- 3 teaspoons vegetable oil
- 1 small onion, finely chopped
- 1 small red pepper, thinly sliced
- 2 teaspoons grated, peeled fresh ginger
- ⅛ to ¼ teaspoon ground red pepper (cayenne)
- 4 ounces medium mushrooms, cut into quarters
- ½ teaspoon salt
- 1 can (13¾ to 15 ounces) light coconut milk (not cream of coconut)
- 1 pound large shrimp, shelled and deveined (opposite)
- 2 ounces snow peas, strings removed and cut into 2" by ¼" matchstick strips
- ⅓ cup loosely packed fresh cilantro leaves

1. From limes, with vegetable peeler, peel six 1" by ¾" strips of peel; squeeze 2 tablespoons juice. Set aside.

2. In nonstick 12-inch skillet, heat 2 teaspoons oil over medium heat. Add onion and cook until tender, about 5 minutes. Add sliced red pepper and cook 1 minute. Stir in ginger and ground red pepper; cook 1 minute. Transfer onion mixture to small bowl.

3. In same skillet, heat remaining 1 teaspoon oil over medium heat. Add mushrooms and salt and cook until tender and lightly browned, about 5 minutes. Stir in coconut milk, lime peel and juice, and onion mixture and heat to boiling. Add shrimp and cook until shrimp are opaque throughout, about 2 minutes. Stir in snow peas and cilantro. Makes 4 main-dish servings.

Each serving: About 222 calories, 20g protein, 11g carbohydrate, 11g total fat (4g saturated), 140mg cholesterol, 456mg sodium.

SHRIMP ÉTOUFFÉE

....

Étouffée means "smothered" in Cajun French, and that's just what these shrimp are—smothered in a scrumptious sauce loaded with peppers, onions, and celery—and plenty of flavor.

Prep: 30 minutes   **Cook: 1 hour**

4	tablespoons butter or margarine
¼	cup all-purpose flour
1	yellow pepper, chopped
2	medium onions, chopped
2	stalks celery with some leaves, chopped
2	garlic cloves, finely chopped
3	cups water
3	tablespoons tomato paste
2	bay leaves
1½	teaspoons salt
¾	teaspoon chili powder
¼	teaspoon dried thyme
¼	teaspoon ground black pepper
1½	pounds medium shrimp, shelled and deveined (below)
1	cup chopped green onions (5 medium)
¼	cup plus 2 tablespoons chopped fresh parsley
1	cup regular long-grain rice, cooked as label directs

1. In 4-quart Dutch oven, melt butter over medium heat. With wooden spoon, gradually stir in flour until blended and cook, stirring constantly, until flour mixture is color of peanut butter; do not let burn. Add yellow pepper, onions, celery, and garlic. Cook, stirring frequently, until onions are tender, about 5 minutes. Stir in water and tomato paste and heat to boiling. Add bay leaves, salt, chili powder, thyme, and black pepper; reduce heat and simmer 30 minutes.

2. Stir in shrimp, green onions, and ¼ cup parsley. Return to simmer and cook 3 minutes. Remove from heat, cover, and let stand 10 minutes. Discard bay leaves and sprinkle étouffée with remaining 2 tablespoons parsley. Serve with hot rice. Makes 6 main-dish servings.

Each serving without rice: About 229 calories, 21g protein, 15g carbohydrate, 10g total fat (5g saturated), 161mg cholesterol, 882mg sodium.

CRAWFISH ÉTOUFFÉE

Prepare as directed but substitute **1 pound fresh or frozen cooked crawfish tail meat** for shrimp.

Each serving without rice: About 217 calories, 20g protein, 14g carbohydrate, 9g total fat (5g saturated), 155mg cholesterol, 797mg sodium.

SHELLING AND DEVEINING SHRIMP

With kitchen shears or a small knife, cut the shrimp shell along the outer curve, just deep enough into the flesh to expose the dark vein.

Peel back the shell from the cut and gently separate the shell from the shrimp. Discard the shell (or use to make fish stock).

Remove the vein with the tip of a small knife; discard. Rinse the shrimp with cold running water. Pat dry with paper towel.

SHRIMP TEMPURA

....

Shrimp tempura waits for no one—it gets soggy quickly. Serve as soon as the shrimp are lifted out of the pot and drained.

Prep: 25 minutes   Cook: 15 minutes

vegetable oil for frying

Dipping Sauce

- ⅓ cup chicken broth
- 3 tablespoons soy sauce
- 2 tablespoons water
- 1 tablespoon plus 1 teaspoon seasoned rice vinegar
- 2 teaspoons sugar
- 1 teaspoon minced, peeled fresh ginger

Batter

- ¾ cup ice-cold water
- 1 cup cake flour (not self-rising)
- 1 teaspoon baking powder
- ¼ teaspoon salt

- 1 pound large shrimp, shelled, deveined, and butterflied (page 221 and right)

1. In 5-quart Dutch oven, heat 2½ inches vegetable oil until temperature reaches 400°F on deep-fat thermometer.

2. Meanwhile, in small saucepan, combine broth, soy sauce, 2 tablespoons water, vinegar, sugar, and ginger; heat to boiling over high heat. Boil 2 minutes. Strain through sieve into small bowl and keep dipping sauce warm.

3. Pour ice-cold water into medium bowl; sift flour, baking powder, and salt into water. With fork, stir just until barely incorporated; a few lumps may remain.

4. Dip 4 shrimp at a time into batter to coat lightly. Allowing excess batter to drip off, add shrimp to hot oil and fry, turning once or twice, until coating is very pale golden, 1 to 2 minutes. With slotted spoon, transfer shrimp to paper towels to drain. Serve immediately with warm dipping sauce. Makes 4 main-dish servings.

Each serving: About 309 calories, 22g protein, 27g carbohydrate, 12g total fat (2g saturated), 140mg cholesterol, 1,355mg sodium.

BEER-BATTERED FRIED SHRIMP

Prepare as above, omitting Step 2. In Step 3, omit baking powder and substitute **1 cup beer** for water and proceed as directed. Serve shrimp with Tartar Sauce (page 504). Makes 6 first-course servings.

BUTTERFLYING SHRIMP

Remove the shell, leaving the tail segment in place. With kitchen shears or a small knife, cut the shrimp along the outer curve, about three-fourths of the way through the flesh.

Spread the flesh open and remove the dark vein with the tip of the knife. Rinse the butterflied shrimp with cold running water.

SHRIMP AND POTATOES IN FETA-TOMATO SAUCE

....

Feta cheese gives this Greek-style dish a tangy finish.

Prep: 20 minutes   Cook: 50 minutes

- 1 tablespoon olive oil
- 2 medium onions, chopped
- 1½ pounds all-purpose potatoes, peeled and cut into 1-inch pieces
- 1 large garlic clove, finely chopped
     pinch ground red pepper (cayenne)
- ¾ cup water
- ½ teaspoon salt
- 1 can (14 to 16 ounces) tomatoes
- 1 pound medium shrimp, shelled and deveined (page 221)
- 4 ounces feta cheese, crumbled (1 cup)
- ¼ cup chopped fresh dill

1. In nonstick 10-inch skillet, heat oil over medium heat. Add onions and cook, stirring frequently, until tender and golden, about 10 minutes.

2. Add potatoes and cook, stirring, until potatoes begin to brown, about 10 minutes. Stir in garlic and ground red pepper and cook 30 seconds. Stir in water and salt; cover and cook until potatoes are almost tender, about 10 minutes.

3. Add tomatoes with their juice, breaking up tomatoes with side of spoon. Cook, uncovered, until liquid has thickened slightly, about 10 minutes.

4. Stir in shrimp and feta. Cover and cook until shrimp are opaque throughout, 3 to 5 minutes. Remove from heat and stir in dill. Makes 4 main-dish servings.

Each serving: About 359 calories, 27g protein, 37g carbohydrate, 11g total fat (5g saturated), 165mg cholesterol, 926mg sodium.

FRIED CALAMARI FRA DIAVOLO

....

Crispy golden-fried squid is served with a tomato dipping sauce that is often as spicy as the devil (fra diavolo means "brother devil"). Or simply serve with lemon wedges, if you prefer.

Prep: 10 minutes   Cook: 25 minutes

- 1 tablespoon olive oil
- 2 garlic cloves, crushed with side of chef's knife
- ⅛ to ¼ teaspoon crushed red pepper
- 1 can (14 to 16 ounces) tomatoes
- ¾ teaspoon salt
- 1 pound cleaned squid
- ⅔ cup all-purpose flour
- 1 cup water
     vegetable oil for frying

1. In nonreactive 1-quart saucepan, heat olive oil over medium heat. Add garlic and crushed red pepper; cook until garlic is golden, about 30 seconds. Add tomatoes with their juice and ½ teaspoon salt, breaking up tomatoes with side of spoon; heat to boiling. Reduce heat; cover and simmer 10 minutes. Keep warm.

2. Rinse squid with cold running water and gently pat dry with paper towels. Slice squid bodies crosswise into ¾-inch rings. Cut tentacles into pieces if large.

3. To make batter, in small bowl, with fork, mix flour and water until smooth. In 10-inch skillet, heat ½ inch vegetable oil over medium heat until very hot. (A small piece of bread dropped into oil should sink, then rise to top and begin bubbling.) In small batches, drop squid into batter. Allowing excess batter to drip off, add squid to hot oil. Fry, turning to brown on all sides, until golden, about 2 minutes. With slotted spoon, transfer squid to paper towels to drain; sprinkle with remaining ¼ teaspoon salt. Serve with tomato sauce for dipping. Makes 4 first-course servings.

Each serving: About 325 calories, 21g protein, 25g carbohydrate, 16g total fat (2g saturated), 264mg cholesterol, 660mg sodium.

7

EGGS & CHEESE

EGGS

There is an old saying that "The egg is to cuisine what the article is to speech." Like the little words that help to provide a sentence with structure, the humble egg is taken for granted. Without eggs, cakes would be tough and flat, custards wouldn't set, a meringue would be just a pile of sugar, soufflés wouldn't puff, mayonnaise wouldn't thicken, meat loaves would crumble, and breakfast just wouldn't be the same. The egg is an indispensable, invaluable ingredient that no kitchen can do entirely without. It is a good source of protein, iron, and vitamins. And while whole eggs and egg yolks are relatively high in fat and cholesterol, egg whites are completely fat and cholesterol free.

SALMONELLA AND EGGS

Raw eggs pose a health concern because they can be contaminated with salmonella, a bacterium that can cause food poisoning. Salmonella is killed at 160°F, so be sure to cook eggs to at least that temperature (this is easily reached with scrambled eggs, "over-hard" fried eggs, custards, and other favorite egg dishes). Certain people, such as the elderly, infants, pregnant women, and those with compromised immune systems, are especially susceptible to infection and should not eat undercooked eggs. After handling raw eggs, thoroughly wash your hands and any utensils that have come in contact with the eggs with hot, soapy water.

Pasteurized eggs Available in the dairy case, these eggs are free from salmonella, *E. coli*, and listeria. Cook them the way you would any other eggs.

Egg substitutes These products, which are pasteurized and salmonella free, are used by people with special dietary needs. Liquid egg substitute (colored egg whites) can be substituted for whole eggs, but don't expect the rich flavor real eggs deliver.

Dehydrated egg whites and meringue powder No need to overcrowd the refrigerator with cartons or to separate fresh eggs for meringue recipes. Just follow the reconstituting directions on the package.

CHOOSING EGGS

As defined by the United States Department of Agriculture, eggs that are sold are sized and graded. An egg's grade is based on many factors, including the appearance of the shell, the quality of the interior of the egg, and the size of the air pocket at the top of the egg (usually determined by candling, a process in which the egg is held against a strong light to illuminate its interior). The grades are as follows:

Grade AA eggs With firm, high yolks and thick whites, they are the best choice for frying, poaching, and cooking in the shell.

Grade A eggs Fine all-purpose eggs with whites that are thinner than those of Grade AAs. They are good for baking.

Grade B eggs These have the thinnest white. They are rarely available to the consumer.

The *chalaza*, the thin white cord that attaches the yolk to the shell, is especially prominent in a very fresh egg and disappears as an egg ages. (When making a custard, you may want to strain the custard to remove the chalazae, which become hard when cooked.)

Overnight Baked French Toast (recipe page 240)

The size of an egg is determined by its weight. Eggs are graded jumbo, extra large, large, medium, and small. All of the recipes in this book use large eggs unless otherwise noted. Using the right size egg is important, especially in recipes that call for a large number.

An eggshell's color is determined solely by the breed of hen. Cooks in the Northeast often prefer brown eggs, but they are no different from the white variety. It is important, however, that the eggshells be clean and uncracked; never buy cracked eggs. Before purchasing eggs, move them in the carton to make sure they haven't cracked and stuck.

STORING EGGS

Eggs should be stored in their carton in a cool part of the refrigerator. The open egg compartment on the refrigerator door is not the ideal place, because it is exposed to warm air every time the door is opened. Also, keep eggs away from strong-smelling foods, such as cheese or onions. Aromas and flavors can easily pass through an egg's thin shell, which is another good reason to keep eggs in their protective carton. To keep the yolks centered, store eggs pointed end down. If stored at around 40°F, eggs will keep for about one month.

The Sell-By Date Keep eggs refrigerated until ready to use, because they deteriorate quickly at room temperature. As fresh eggs age, their thick translucent whites thin out and their round firm yolks flatten. For poaching and frying, use very fresh eggs, because they hold their shape the best. The carton "sell-by" date is the easiest way to tell how old eggs are: It can never be more than thirty days past the packing date. Some states show the packing date in Julian numbers, which run from 001 (January 1) to 365 (December 31).

The Buoyancy Test If you don't have the egg carton and want to check for freshness, all you need is a glass of water. As an egg ages, its liquid begins to evaporate, making the air space at the top of the egg bigger and the egg increasingly buoyant. When placed in a glass of water, a fresh egg will sink to the bottom, a slightly older egg will stand upright, and an old egg will float. As a last resort, there's always the smell test. Break the egg into a saucer and give it a sniff. An egg should have no odor at all or smell absolutely clean and slightly sweet. There's no mistaking the aroma of a bad egg.

Egg Yolk Color The color of an egg yolk can range from yellow to orange. It is determined solely by the hen's diet and is not an indication of taste or freshness. You will sometimes see a small blood spot on an egg yolk. This is caused by a ruptured blood vessel and does not denote freshness. If desired, it can easily be removed with the tip of a knife.

SEPARATING EGGS

To separate an egg, sharply tap the eggshell along its middle to make a crosswise crack. With your thumbs, gently pull open the shell along the crack, letting some of the white run into a bowl. Slowly transfer the yolk back and forth from one half-shell to the other, being careful not to break the yolk on any sharp shell edges, until all the white has run into the bowl. If any yolk does get into the whites, it can sometimes be removed with a small spoon or the edge of an eggshell.

BEATING EGG WHITES

When beating egg whites, keep in mind that their volume will increase six to nine times, so use a large enough bowl. The bowl and the beaters must be absolutely clean; even the tiniest bit of fat will prevent peaks from forming. Stainless-steel or glass bowls do the best job. A little cream of tartar will stabilize egg whites, but salt discourages foaming.

Room-temperature egg whites beat to the fullest volume. Let chilled whites stand for 30 minutes to warm up. Or, place the bowl of egg whites into a separate bowl of hot water; stir for one or two minutes.

If a recipe says to beat egg whites until "foamy" or "frothy," beat them until they form a mass of tiny clear bubbles. For "soft peaks," beat until the whites form soft rounded peaks that droop when the beaters are lifted.

For "stiff glossy peaks," beat until the whites form peaks that hold their shape when the beaters are lifted but are still moist. Overbeaten whites look lumpy and watery—there is no way to salvage them.

How sugar is added to egg whites is crucial. Sugar should be added gradually so it has time to dissolve. Beat the egg whites to the soft peak stage, then begin adding the sugar, about 2 tablespoons at a time, beating until the whites are stiff and glossy.

BASIC OMELETS

....

A well-made omelet can be a quick supper or a satisfying breakfast. Mix up a batch of eggs, prepare your fillings, and you're ready for quick assembly-line production. For lower-fat omelets, use 4 large eggs and 8 egg whites.

Prep: 5 minutes plus preparing filling
Cook: 2 minutes per omelet

choice of filling (right and page 228)
8 large eggs
½ cup water
½ teaspoon salt
4 teaspoons butter or margarine

1. Prepare filling; keep warm. In medium bowl, with wire whisk, beat eggs, water, and salt.

2. In nonstick 10-inch skillet, melt 1 teaspoon butter over medium-high heat. Pour ½ cup egg mixture into skillet. Cook, gently lifting edge of eggs with heat-safe rubber spatula and tilting pan to allow uncooked eggs to run underneath, until eggs are set, about 1 minute. Spoon one-fourth of filling over half of omelet. Fold unfilled half of omelet over filling and slide onto warm plate. Repeat with remaining butter, egg mixture, and filling. If desired, keep omelets warm in 200°F oven until all omelets are cooked. Makes 4 main-dish servings.

Each omelet without filling: About 183 calories, 13g protein, 1g carbohydrate, 14g total fat (5g saturated), 435mg cholesterol, 455mg sodium.

CREAMY MUSHROOM FILLING

In nonstick 10-inch skillet, melt **1 tablespoon butter or margarine** over medium heat. Add **1 medium onion,** finely chopped; cook until tender, about 5 minutes. Stir in **8 ounces mushrooms,** trimmed and thinly sliced, **¼ teaspoon salt,** and **⅛ teaspoon ground black pepper;** cook until liquid has evaporated. Stir in **¼ cup heavy cream;** boil until thickened, about 3 minutes. Stir in **2 tablespoons chopped fresh parsley.** Use one-fourth mushroom mixture for each omelet.

Each filled omelet: About 291 calories, 15g protein, 8g carbohydrate, 23g total fat (11g saturated), 463mg cholesterol, 637mg sodium.

BLACK BEAN AND SALSA FILLING

In nonstick 10-inch skillet, cook **1 cup canned black beans,** rinsed and drained, and **1 cup medium-hot salsa** over medium heat, stirring frequently, until liquid has evaporated. Divide black-bean mixture, **1 ripe medium avocado,** peeled and chopped, and **¼ cup sour cream** among omelets.

Each filled omelet: About 365 calories, 17g protein, 18g carbohydrate, 25g total fat (9g saturated), 442mg cholesterol, 1,307mg sodium.

RED PEPPER AND GOAT CHEESE FILLING

In nonstick 10-inch skillet, melt **2 teaspoons butter or margarine** over medium heat. Add **2 red peppers,** thinly sliced, and **¼ teaspoon salt;** cook until tender and lightly browned. Add **1 garlic clove,** finely chopped; cook 1 minute. Divide red pepper, **2 ounces goat cheese,** and **½ cup loosely packed, trimmed and torn arugula** among omelets.

Each filled omelet: About 257 calories, 16g protein, 3g carbohydrate, 20g total fat (10g saturated), 452mg cholesterol, 692mg sodium.

Basic Omelet with Garden-Vegetable Filling

GARDEN-VEGETABLE FILLING

In nonstick 10-inch skillet, heat **1 tablespoon olive oil** over medium heat. Add **1 small onion,** chopped, **1 small zucchini (6 ounces),** chopped, **1 small yellow pepper,** chopped, **½ teaspoon salt,** and **⅛ teaspoon ground black pepper;** cook until vegetables are tender, about 10 minutes. Stir in **2 ripe plum tomatoes,** chopped, and **¼ cup chopped fresh basil;** heat through. Use one-fourth mixture for each omelet.

Each filled omelet: About 239 calories, 14g protein, 7g carbohydrate, 17g total fat (6g saturated), 435mg cholesterol, 749mg sodium.

WESTERN FILLING

In nonstick 10-inch skillet, heat **1 tablespoon olive oil** over medium heat. Add **1 small onion,** chopped, **1 green pepper,** chopped, **8 ounces mushrooms,** trimmed and thinly sliced, and **¼ teaspoon salt;** cook until vegetables are tender and liquid has evaporated, about 10 minutes. Add **4 ounces sliced ham,** finely chopped (1 cup), and heat through. Use one-fourth filling for each omelet.

Each filled omelet: About 294 calories, 19g protein, 8g carbohydrate, 21g total fat (7g saturated), 452mg cholesterol, 974mg sodium.

EGG WHITE OMELET

Prepare filling. Blend **2 tablespoons skim milk** and **1 tablespoon all-purpose flour** until smooth. Whisk in **4 large egg whites, ½ teaspoon salt,** and **¼ teaspoon**

ground turmeric if using. In nonstick 8-inch skillet, heat **2 teaspoons olive oil** over medium heat. Add egg white mixture and cook until just set, about 2 minutes. Spoon filling, if using, over half of omelet. Continue as for Basic Omelets (page 227). Makes 1 main-dish serving.

Each omelet without filling: About 186 calories, 16g protein, 9g carbohydrate, 9g total fat (1g saturated), 1mg cholesterol, 1,393mg sodium.

SCRAMBLED EGGS WITH CREAM CHEESE

....

These rich and creamy scrambled eggs are not everyday fare. This is a great large-batch recipe for brunch, but it is easily halved.

Prep: 10 minutes   Cook: 10 minutes

- 14 large eggs
- ¼ teaspoon ground black pepper
- 3 tablespoons butter or margarine
- 2 packages (3 ounces each) cream cheese, cut into 1-inch cubes

1. In large bowl, with wire whisk, beat eggs and pepper until well blended.

2. In nonstick 12-inch skillet, melt butter over medium heat; add eggs. With heat-safe spatula, gently push egg mixture as it begins to set to form soft curds.

3. When eggs are partially cooked, top with cream cheese. Continue cooking, stirring occasionally, until eggs have thickened and no visible liquid egg remains. Serve on warm platter. Makes 8 main-dish servings.

Each serving: About 243 calories, 13g protein, 2g carbohydrate, 20g total fat (10g saturated), 407mg cholesterol, 217mg sodium.

SCRAMBLED EGGS WITH CREAM CHEESE AND SALMON

Prepare as directed above but sprinkle **4 ounces smoked salmon,** chopped, over eggs with cream cheese. To serve, top with **¼ cup chopped green onions.**

Each serving: About 260 calories, 15g protein, 2g carbohydrate, 21g total fat (10g saturated), 410mg cholesterol, 501mg sodium.

BASIC FLUFFY OMELET

Beaten egg whites give this oven-baked omelet extra lift. For a cheese omelet, sprinkle top with shredded cheese during the last minute of baking.

Prep: 10 minutes   **Cook/Bake: 15 minutes**

- 4 large eggs, separated
- 2 tablespoons water
- ⅛ teaspoon salt
- 1 tablespoon butter or margarine

1. Preheat oven to 350°F. In medium bowl, with mixer at high speed, beat egg whites until stiff peaks form when beaters are lifted. In large bowl, with mixer at high speed, beat egg yolks, water, and salt until egg-yolk mixture has thickened. With rubber spatula, gently fold one-third of beaten egg whites into egg-yolk mixture. Fold in remaining egg whites until just blended.

2. In oven-safe nonstick 10-inch skillet (if skillet is not oven-safe, wrap handle with double layer of foil), melt butter over medium-low heat. Add egg mixture and cook until top has puffed and underside is golden, about 3 minutes.

3. Place skillet in oven. Bake until top of omelet is golden and center springs back when lightly touched with finger, about 10 minutes.

4. To serve, loosen omelet from skillet and slide onto warm platter. Makes 2 main-dish servings.

Each serving: About 200 calories, 13g protein, 1g carbohydrate, 16g total fat (7g saturated), 441mg cholesterol, 331mg sodium.

SPAGHETTI FRITTATA

This is a great way to use up leftover pasta, even if it is coated with tomato sauce. (You'll need about 3 cups of cooked pasta.)

Prep: 20 minutes   **Cook/Broil: 10 minutes**

- 6 large eggs
- ¼ cup milk
- ⅓ cup freshly grated Parmesan cheese
- ¼ cup chopped fresh basil
- ½ teaspoon salt
- ¼ teaspoon ground black pepper
- 6 ounces thin spaghetti, broken in half and cooked as label directs
- 1 tablespoon olive oil

1. Preheat broiler. In large bowl, with wire whisk, beat eggs, milk, Parmesan, basil, salt, and pepper until well blended. Add pasta and toss to combine.

2. In oven-safe nonstick 10-inch skillet (if skillet is not oven-safe, wrap handle with double layer of foil), heat oil over medium-low heat. Add pasta-egg mixture, pressing lightly with spatula to flatten. Cook until mixture is almost set in center, about 10 minutes. Place skillet in broiler 6 inches from heat source. Broil until frittata is set, about 1 minute.

3. To serve, loosen frittata from skillet and slide onto warm platter; cut into 4 wedges. Makes 4 main-dish servings.

Each serving: About 347 calories, 19g protein, 34g carbohydrate, 14g total fat (5g saturated), 327mg cholesterol, 545mg sodium.

QUICK NO-COOK FILLINGS FOR OMELETS

Here are delicious flavor combos to suite every taste.
- Mango chutney and sour cream
- Diced avocado, salsa, and sour cream
- Chopped tomato and pesto
- Chopped smoked salmon, cubed cream cheese, and capers

- Chopped tomato, crumbled feta cheese, and dill
- Chopped smoked turkey, thinly sliced red onion, and cubed Brie cheese
- Diced ham, chopped green onions, and shredded Pepper Jack cheese
- Ricotta cheese, berries, and confectioners' sugar
- Chopped fresh herbs, green onions, and sour cream

CLASSIC CHEESE SOUFFLÉ

....

An all-American soufflé made with sharp Cheddar cheese. To gain the most height, don't overfold the cheese mixture before pouring it into the soufflé dish.

Prep: 20 minutes   Bake: 55 minutes

- 2 tablespoons plain dried bread crumbs or freshly grated Parmesan cheese
- 4 tablespoons butter or margarine
- ¼ cup all-purpose flour
- 1½ cups milk, warmed
- 8 ounces sharp Cheddar cheese, shredded (2 cups)
- ¼ teaspoon salt
- ⅛ teaspoon ground red pepper (cayenne)
- 5 large eggs, separated
- 1 large egg white

1. Preheat oven to 325°F. Grease 2-quart soufflé dish; sprinkle evenly with bread crumbs.

2. Prepare cheese sauce: In heavy 2-quart saucepan, melt butter over low heat. Add flour and cook, stirring, 1 minute. With wire whisk, gradually whisk in warm milk. Cook over medium heat, stirring constantly with wooden spoon, until sauce has thickened and boils. Reduce heat and simmer, stirring frequently, 3 minutes. Stir in Cheddar, salt, and ground red pepper; cook, stirring, just until cheese has melted and sauce is smooth. Remove saucepan from heat.

3. In bowl, with wire whisk, lightly beat egg yolks; gradually whisk in ½ cup hot cheese sauce. Gradually whisk egg-yolk mixture into cheese sauce in saucepan, stirring rapidly to prevent curdling. Pour cheese mixture back into bowl.

4. In large bowl, with mixer at high speed, beat 6 egg whites until stiff peaks form when beaters are lifted. With rubber spatula, gently fold one-third of beaten egg whites into cheese mixture. Fold in remaining whites just until blended.

5. Pour mixture into prepared soufflé dish. If desired, to create top-hat effect (center will rise higher than edge), with back of spoon, make 1-inch-deep indentation all around top of soufflé about 1 inch from edge of dish. Bake until soufflé has puffed and is golden brown and knife inserted 1 inch from edge comes out clean, 55 to 60 minutes. Serve hot. Makes 6 main-dish servings.

Each serving: About 356 calories, 18g protein, 9g carbohydrate, 27g total fat (15g saturated), 246mg cholesterol, 519mg sodium.

GRUYÈRE-SPINACH SOUFFLÉ

Prepare as directed (left) but substitute **8 ounces Gruyère cheese** for Cheddar and stir **1 package (10 ounces) frozen chopped spinach,** thawed and squeezed dry, into cheese mixture before folding in beaten egg whites. Substitute **pinch ground nutmeg** for ground red pepper.

Each serving: About 372 calories, 21g protein, 11g carbohydrate, 27g total fat (15g saturated), 248mg cholesterol, 446mg sodium.

SOUTHWESTERN SOUFFLÉ

Prepare as directed (left) but substitute **8 ounces Monterey Jack cheese** for Cheddar and stir **½ cup chopped cooked ham** into cheese mixture before folding in beaten egg whites.

Each serving: About 366 calories, 21g protein, 9g carbohydrate, 27g total fat (15g saturated), 253mg cholesterol, 662mg sodium.

HOW MANY? HOW MUCH?

——————

If you are measuring eggs by volume, use these amounts:

1 large egg white	=	about 2 tablespoons
1 large egg yolk	=	about 1 tablespoon
5 large eggs	=	about 1 cup
8 large egg whites	=	about 1 cup

CRUSTLESS LEEK AND GRUYÈRE QUICHE

....

A quiche without a crust? Don't worry—the delicate custard is so smooth and tasty you'll never miss the pastry. And did we mention that by losing it, we've saved you 200 calories and 13 grams fat per serving?

Prep: 20 minutes   Bake: 30 minutes

- 1 pound leeks (about 3 medium)
- 1 tablespoon olive oil
- ½ teaspoon salt
- 6 large eggs
- 2½ cups whole milk
- 1 tablespoon cornstarch
- ¼ teaspoon coarsely ground black pepper
- 4 ounces Gruyère cheese, shredded (1 cup)

1. Preheat oven to 350°F. Grease 10-inch quiche dish or 9½-inch deep-dish pie plate. Cut off roots and trim dark green tops from leeks. Discard any tough outer leaves. Cut each leek lengthwise in half, then crosswise into ¼-inch-wide slices. Rinse leeks thoroughly in large bowl of cold water, swishing to remove sand. With hands, transfer leeks to colander to drain. Repeat process, changing water several times, until all sand is removed. Shake colander several times to remove excess water from leeks.

2. In 12-inch nonstick skillet, heat oil on medium 1 minute. Add leeks and ¼ teaspoon salt, and cook 12 to 14 minutes or until leeks are tender and browned, stirring frequently. Transfer leeks to prepared quiche dish and spread evenly.

3. Meanwhile, in bowl, with wire whisk, beat eggs, milk, cornstarch, ¼ teaspoon salt, and pepper until well blended.

4. Pour egg mixture over leeks in dish. Sprinkle with Gruyère. Bake 30 to 35 minutes or until knife inserted in center comes out clean. Cool on wire rack for 5 minutes. Makes 6 main-dish servings.

Each serving: About 260 calories, 16g protein, 11g carbohydrate, 17g total fat (8g saturated), 1g fiber, 247mg cholesterol, 375mg sodium.

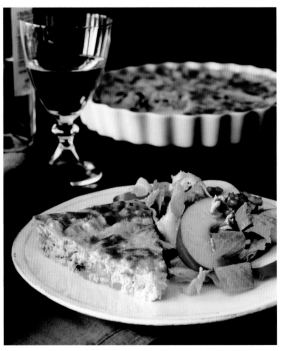

Crustless Leek and Gruyère Quiche

SOUTHWESTERN RICE AND CORN FRITTATA

....

A hearty, one-skillet dish that's perfect for a weeknight supper or a Sunday brunch. Or cut the frittata into smaller wedges and serve it as a game-day snack.

Prep: 25 minutes   Bake: 20 minutes

- 1 package (8 to 9 ounces) precooked whole-grain brown rice (scant 2 cups)
- 4 teaspoons olive oil
- 1 small onion, chopped
- 1 jalapeño chile, seeded and finely chopped
- 1 garlic clove, finely chopped
- 1 cup frozen corn kernels
- 8 large eggs
- ¼ cup milk
- ¼ cup loosely packed fresh cilantro leaves, chopped
- ½ teaspoon salt
- ½ cup shredded Mexican cheese blend
  prepared salsa (optional)

1. Heat brown rice as label directs.

2. Meanwhile, preheat oven to 400°F. In oven-safe nonstick 10-inch skillet, heat 2 teaspoons oil over medium heat until hot. Add onion and cook 4 to 5 minutes or until lightly browned, stirring occasionally. Stir in jalapeño and garlic; cook 30 seconds, stirring. Add corn and cook 1 minute or until corn is thawed, stirring occasionally. Transfer corn mixture to bowl.

3. In large bowl, with wire whisk, beat eggs, milk, cilantro, and ½ teaspoon salt until well blended. Stir in rice, corn mixture, and cheese.

4. In same skillet, heat remaining 2 teaspoons oil over medium heat until hot. Pour in egg mixture; cover and cook 3 minutes or until egg mixture starts to set around the edge.

5. Remove cover and place skillet in oven; bake 20 minutes or until knife inserted 2 inches from edge comes out clean. Remove frittata from oven; let stand 5 minutes.

6. To serve, loosen frittata from skillet; slide onto warm platter. Cut into wedges; serve with salsa if you like. Makes 6 main-dish servings.

Each serving: About 245 calories, 13g protein, 19g carbohydrate, 14g total fat (5g saturated), 2g fiber, 293mg cholesterol, 355mg sodium.

Breakfast Tortilla Stack

BREAKFAST TORTILLA STACK

···

Here's a breakfast that will keep you full all morning. Packed with whole-grain fiber and protein, yet low in fat, it's a delicious way to start the day off right. Makes a great afternoon snack, too.

Prep: 25 minutes   Cook: 5 minutes

- ¼ cup chopped red onion
- 2 ripe medium tomatoes, chopped
- ¼ cup loosely packed fresh cilantro leaves, chopped
- 4 large eggs
- 4 large egg whites
- ¼ teaspoon salt
- ¼ teaspoon ground black pepper
- 1 cup fat-free refried beans
- ¼ teaspoon ground chipotle chile
- 4 (7-inch) whole-wheat tortillas

1. Prepare salsa: In cup of ice water, soak chopped onion 10 minutes; drain well. In small bowl, combine onion, tomato, and cilantro; set aside.

2. In medium bowl, with wire whisk or fork, beat whole eggs, egg whites, salt, and pepper until blended.

3. Spray 10-inch nonstick skillet with cooking spray; heat on medium 1 minute. Pour egg mixture into skillet; cook about 5 minutes or until egg mixture is set but still moist, stirring occasionally.

4. Meanwhile, in microwave-safe small bowl, mix beans and chipotle chile. Cover with vented plastic wrap; heat in microwave on High 1 minute or until hot.

5. Place stack of tortillas between damp paper towels on microwave-safe plate; heat in microwave on High 10 to 15 seconds to warm. To serve, layer each tortilla with eggs, beans, and salsa. Makes 4 main-dish servings.

Each serving: About 200 calories, 13g protein, 29g carbohydrate, 4g total fat (1g saturated), 13g fiber, 160mg cholesterol, 635mg sodium.

CHIVE AND GOAT CHEESE FRITTATA

....

A frittata is an Italian omelet in which the ingredients are mixed with the eggs rather than folded inside. The frittata is often slipped under the broiler to brown the top. Ours is packed with the delicious flavors of tangy goat cheese, ripe tomato, and fresh chives.

Prep: 15 minutes   Cook/Bake: 20 minutes

- 8 large eggs
- ⅓ cup milk
- ½ teaspoon salt
- ⅛ teaspoon freshly ground pepper
- 1 ripe medium tomato, chopped
- 2 tablespoons snipped fresh chives
- 1 tablespoon butter or olive oil
- 1 package (3½ ounces) goat cheese

1. Preheat oven to 375°F. In medium bowl, with wire whisk, beat eggs, milk, salt, and pepper until well blended. Stir in tomato and chives.

2. In oven-safe nonstick 10-inch skillet (if skillet is not oven-safe, wrap handle with a double layer of foil), melt butter over medium heat. Pour in egg mixture. Drop tablespoons of goat cheese on top of egg mixture, cook, without stirring, until egg mixture begins to set around edge, 3 to 4 minutes.

3. Place skillet in oven; bake until frittata is set, 8 to 10 minutes. To serve, loosen frittata from skillet and slide onto warm platter; cut into 4 wedges. Makes 4 main-dish servings.

Each serving: About 262 calories, 18g protein, 4g carbohydrate, 19g total fat (9g saturated), 447mg cholesterol, 552mg sodium.

POTATO AND HAM FRITTATA

Prepare egg mixture as directed above but omit tomato, chives, and goat cheese. Cut **2 large red potatoes** into ½-inch pieces. Coarsely chop **1 medium onion.** Heat oil in skillet over medium heat. Add potatoes and onion; cover and cook, stirring occasionally, until potatoes are tender, about 12 minutes. Stir in **4 ounces cooked ham,** finely chopped (1 cup). Cook 2 minutes. Spread potato mixture evenly in skillet. Pour egg mixture into skillet and follow remaining cooking directions.

ASPARAGUS AND ROMANO FRITTATA

Omit tomato, chives, and goat cheese. Prepare egg mixture as directed. Cut **1 pound asparagus** into 1-inch pieces. Thinly slice **4 green onions.** Melt butter in skillet over medium-high heat. Stir in asparagus; cook 4 minutes. Reduce heat to medium, add onions, cook 2 minutes, stirring. Spread vegetable mixture in skillet. Stir **½ cup freshly grated Pecorino-Romano cheese** into eggs and pour into skillet. Cook as directed.

QUICHE LORRAINE

....

This is the classic version that put quiche on the culinary map in the 1970s.

Prep: 35 minutes   Bake: 55 minutes

Pastry Dough for 1-Crust Pie (page 534)

- 4 large eggs
- 2 cups milk
- ½ teaspoon salt
- ⅛ teaspoon ground black pepper
  pinch ground nutmeg
- 4 slices bacon, cooked and crumbled
- 4 ounces Gruyère or Swiss cheese, shredded (1 cup)

1. Prepare Pastry Dough for 1-Crust Pie. Preheat oven to 425°F. Use dough to line 9-inch pie plate. Line pie shell with foil and fill with pie weights or dry beans. Bake 10 minutes. Remove foil with weights; bake until golden, 5 to 10 minutes longer. Cool on wire rack. Turn oven control to 350°F.

2. In medium bowl, with wire whisk, beat eggs, milk, salt, pepper, and nutmeg until well blended. Sprinkle bacon and Gruyère over bottom of crust; pour egg mixture over bacon and cheese.

3. Place pie plate on foil-lined cookie sheet to catch any overflow. Bake until knife inserted in center comes out clean, 55 to 60 minutes. Cool on wire rack 15 minutes. Serve hot or at room temperature. Makes 8 main-dish servings.

Each serving: About 304 calories, 12g protein, 18g carbohydrate, 20g total fat (10g saturated), 149mg cholesterol, 439mg sodium.

MUSHROOM QUICHE

Prepare and bake Pastry Dough. Prepare egg mixture as directed but omit bacon and Gruyère. In 10-inch skillet, melt **2 tablespoons butter or margarine** over medium-high heat. Add **8 ounces mushrooms, trimmed and very thinly sliced, 2 tablespoons finely chopped onion, ¼ teaspoon salt, ⅛ teaspoon coarsely ground black pepper,** and **pinch dried thyme;** cook, stirring frequently, until mushrooms are tender and liquid has evaporated, about 10 minutes. Add to egg mixture, stirring to mix. Pour into piecrust. Proceed with Step 4, but reduce baking time to 45 to 50 minutes.

ASPARAGUS QUICHE

Prepare and bake Pastry Dough. Prepare egg mixture as directed but omit bacon. Trim **1 pound asparagus** and cut into ¾-inch pieces (2½ cups). In 2-quart saucepan, heat *4 cups water* to boiling over high heat. Add asparagus and cook until tender, 6 to 8 minutes; drain. Rinse asparagus with cold running water; drain. Spread asparagus over bottom of crust and sprinkle with Gruyère; pour egg mixture over. Proceed with Step 4, but reduce baking time to 40 to 45 minutes.

BITE-SIZE BACON QUICHES

Prepare Pastry Dough for 2-Crust Pie (page 533). On lightly floured surface, with floured rolling pin, roll dough ⅛ inch thick. Using 3-inch round cookie cutter, cut dough into 36 circles, rerolling trimmings. Line thirty-six 1¾-inch mini muffin-pan cups with dough circles. Cover and refrigerate. Prepare egg mixture as directed, using **2 eggs, 1 cup milk,** and **¼ teaspoon salt.** Divide bacon and cheese evenly among pastry cups. Spoon a scant tablespoon egg mixture into each cup. Bake until egg mixture is set, about 25 minutes. Remove quiches from pans and serve hot. Makes 36 bite-size quiches.

Each serving: About 90 calories, 3g protein, 6g carbohydrate, 6g total fat (3g saturated), 24mg cholesterol, 105mg sodium.

HUEVOS RANCHEROS

....

Hungry ranchers know that this Mexican country-style egg dish is an excellent source of energy before a long, hard workday.

Prep: 10 minutes   **Cook/Bake:** 20 minutes

- 1 tablespoon vegetable oil
- 1 medium onion, coarsely chopped
- 1 garlic clove, finely chopped
- 1 jalapeño chile, seeded and finely chopped
- 1 can (14 to 16 ounces) tomatoes
- ¼ teaspoon salt
- 4 (6-inch) corn or flour tortillas
- 3 tablespoons butter or margarine
- 4 large eggs
- 2 tablespoons sour cream
- 1 tablespoon chopped fresh cilantro
- 1 ripe medium avocado, pitted, peeled, and cut crosswise into thin slices

1. Preheat oven to 350°F. In nonreactive 2-quart saucepan, heat 1 tablespoon oil over medium-high heat. Add onion, garlic, and jalapeño and cook, stirring occasionally, until onion is tender, about 5 minutes. Stir in tomatoes with their juice and salt; heat to boiling over high heat, breaking up tomatoes with side of spoon. Reduce heat; cover and simmer, stirring occasionally, 5 minutes.

2. Wrap tortillas in foil; place in oven until heated through, about 10 minutes.

3. Meanwhile, in 10-inch skillet, melt butter over medium heat. Break 1 egg into small cup and, holding cup close to skillet, slip egg into skillet; repeat with remaining eggs. Reduce heat to low; cook slowly, spooning butter over eggs to baste them and turning eggs to cook on both sides, until egg whites are completely set and egg yolks begin to thicken but are not hard.

4. Place tortillas on warm plates; place 1 fried egg on each tortilla and spoon 2 tablespoons tomato sauce over each. Top with some sour cream and sprinkle with cilantro; garnish with avocado slices. Serve with remaining tomato sauce. Makes 4 main-dish servings.

Each serving: About 403 calories, 11g protein, 25g carbohydrate, 31g total fat (10g saturated), 239mg cholesterol, 521mg sodium.

HEALTHY MAKEOVER
EGGS BENEDICT

....

Velvety, egg-and-butter-rich hollandaise makes this brunch favorite irresistible but unkind to both arteries and waistlines. We lightened its load by substituting in a lemony white sauce (cutting the per-serving saturated fat from 10 grams to 3 and the cholesterol by more than 100 milligrams) and bumped up the fiber with spinach and whole-wheat muffins.

Prep: 35 minutes   Cook: 25 minutes

- 1 lemon
- 2 tablespoons butter or margarine
- 2 tablespoons all-purpose flour
- 1 cup low-fat (1%) milk, warmed
   pinch salt
- ⅛ teaspoon ground black pepper
- 4 slices (4 ounces) low-sodium ham
- 1 tablespoon distilled white vinegar
- 8 large eggs
- 4 whole-wheat English muffins
- 1 bag (9 ounces) baby spinach
   chives and lemon peel for garnish

1. Preheat oven to 350°F. Fill teakettle with water; heat to boiling on high.

2. Meanwhile, prepare sauce: From lemon, grate ½ teaspoon peel and squeeze 2 tablespoons juice. In 1-quart saucepan, melt butter on low. Add flour and cook 1 minute, stirring. With wire whisk, gradually whisk in milk. Cook on medium, stirring, until sauce thickens and boils. Reduce heat; simmer, stirring, 5 minutes. Remove from heat; stir in lemon peel and juice, a pinch salt, and ⅛ teaspoon freshly ground black pepper. Keep warm. Makes 1 cup.

3. Meanwhile, halve ham slices; in 12-inch skillet, cook on medium 5 minutes, turning once. Remove; keep warm. To same skillet, add vinegar and 1½ inches boiling water; keep at gentle simmer.

4. Break 1 egg into cup; holding cup at water's surface, slip in egg. Repeat with 3 more eggs; cook 3 to 5 minutes or until whites are set. With slotted spoon, transfer eggs to paper towel–lined plate. Repeat with remaining eggs.

Healthy Makeover Eggs Benedict

5. While eggs are cooking, toast muffin halves in oven 10 minutes or until golden. Cook spinach as label directs.

6. To serve, top each muffin half with 1 piece ham, divide spinach among all halves, and finish with 1 egg and 2 tablespoons sauce on each. Makes 4 servings.

Each serving: About 435 calories, 32g protein, 35g carbohydrate, 19g total fat (3g saturated), 5g fiber, 470mg cholesterol, 970mg sodium.

CLASSIC EGGS BENEDICT

....

This brunch classic serves eight, allowing one egg and one muffin half per diner (if you're serving friends or family with large appetites, however, it will serve four).

Prep: 25 minutes   Cook: 10 minutes

Hollandaise Sauce (page 502)

8   slices Canadian bacon

4   English muffins, split and toasted

8   large eggs

1. Prepare Hollandaise Sauce; keep warm.

2. In jelly-roll pan, arrange toasted English muffins in single layer and top each with slice of Canadian bacon; keep warm.

3. Poach eggs: In 12-inch skillet, heat *1½ inches water* to boiling. Reduce heat to medium-low. Break 1 egg into small cup; holding cup close to surface of water, slip into simmering water. Repeat with remaining eggs. Cook until egg whites have set and egg yolks begin to thicken but are not hard, 3 to 5 minutes.

4. Place jelly-roll pan with bacon-topped English muffins next to poaching eggs. With slotted spoon, carefully remove eggs, one at a time, from water and very briefly drain (still held in spoon) on paper towels; set 1 egg on top of each slice of Canadian bacon. Spoon Hollandaise Sauce over. Serve hot. Makes 8 main-dish servings.

Each serving: About 311 calories, 15g protein, 15g carbohydrate, 21g total fat (10g saturated), 337mg cholesterol, 786mg sodium.

BASIC CREPES

....

These delicate pancakes can be stuffed with one of our fillings or rolled up with some jam. The crepes can be prepared up to one day ahead; wrap a stack tightly in plastic wrap and refrigerate.

Prep: 5 minutes plus chilling   Cook: 25 minutes

3   large eggs

1½   cups milk

4   tablespoons butter or margarine, melted

²/₃ cup all-purpose flour

½   teaspoon salt

1. In blender, blend eggs, milk, 2 tablespoons butter, flour, and salt until smooth, scraping down sides of blender. Transfer batter to medium bowl; cover and refrigerate at least 1 hour or up to overnight to allow flour to absorb liquid.

2. Heat 10-inch skillet over medium-high heat. Brush bottom of skillet lightly with some remaining butter. With wire whisk, throughly mix batter to blend well. Pour scant ¼ cup batter into skillet; tilt pan to coat bottom completely with batter. Cook crepe until top is set and underside is lightly browned, about 1½ minutes.

3. With heat-safe rubber spatula, loosen edge of crepe; turn. Cook until second side has browned, about 30 seconds. Slip crepe onto waxed paper. Repeat with remaining batter, brushing pan lightly with butter before cooking each crepe and stacking crepes between sheets of waxed paper. Makes about 12 crepes.

Each crepe: About 97 calories, 3g protein, 7g carbohydrate, 6g total fat (3g saturated), 68mg cholesterol, 166mg sodium.

CREPES WITH PIPÉRADE FILLING

....

In the Basque region, which straddles the mountainous Spanish-French border, pipérade is a favorite component of egg dishes.

Prep: 45 minutes   Cook/Bake: 45 minutes

Basic Crepes (page 237)
1 tablespoon olive oil
1 medium onion, thinly sliced
1 red pepper, thinly sliced
1 yellow or green pepper, thinly sliced
¾ teaspoon salt
1 garlic clove, finely chopped
⅛ teaspoon ground red pepper (cayenne)
1 can (14 to 16 ounces) tomatoes
3 ounces Gruyère cheese, shredded (¾ cup)
1 tablespoon chopped fresh parsley

1. Prepare Basic Crepes. Set aside 8 crepes. (Reserve remaining crepes for another use.) Preheat oven to 400°F.

2. In 10-inch skillet, heat oil over medium heat. Add onion, red and yellow peppers, and salt; cover and cook until vegetables are tender, about 15 minutes. Stir in garlic and ground red pepper; cook 30 seconds. Add tomatoes with their juice, breaking them up with side of spoon. Cook, uncovered, until juices have thickened, about 15 minutes.

3. Place crepes on surface; sprinkle one slightly rounded tablespoon of Gruyère over each crepe, leaving 1-inch border. Spread generous ¼ cup filling down center of each crepe. Roll up crepes and place, seam side down, in shallow 2-quart baking dish. Bake until heated through, about 15 minutes. Sprinkle with parsley. Makes 4 main-dish servings.

Each serving: About 360 calories, 15g protein, 25g carbohydrate, 23g total fat (11g saturated), 159mg cholesterol, 1,019mg sodium.

CREPES FILLED WITH APPLES AND GRUYÈRE

....

Apples and Gruyère, a match made in heaven, make an easy but delicious crepe filling.

Prep: 45 minutes   Cook/Bake: 10 minutes

Basic Crepes (page 237)
1 tablespoon butter or margarine
2 Golden Delicious apples, each peeled, cored, and cut into 16 wedges
4 ounces Gruyère cheese, shredded (1 cup)

1. Prepare Basic Crepes. Set aside 8 crepes. (Reserve remaining crepes for another use.) Preheat oven to 400°F. Grease large cookie sheet.

2. In 10-inch skillet, melt butter over medium-high heat. Add apples and cook, stirring frequently, until tender and beginning to brown, about 5 minutes.

3. Place crepes on surface; sprinkle one-fourth of Gruyère over half of each crepe. Place one-fourth of apples over Gruyère. Fold crepes over to enclose filling; place on prepared cookie sheet. Bake until cheese melts, about 5 minutes. Makes 4 main-dish servings.

Each serving: About 372 calories, 15g protein, 23g carbohydrate, 25g total fat (14g saturated), 174mg cholesterol, 457mg sodium.

CREPE FILLINGS

Here are some other tasty fruit and cheese combinations for filling crepes.

STRAWBERRIES AND GOAT CHEESE: Use 2 cups hulled and sliced strawberries and 8 ounces of fresh (mild) goat cheese. Prepare as directed above but cook the strawberries only until slightly softened, about 2 minutes.

RED PLUMS AND SWISS CHEESE: Use 4 large plums and 4 ounces Swiss cheese. Prepare as directed above.

BLUEBERRIES AND RICOTTA CHEESE: Use 2 cups blueberries and 8 ounces ricotta cheese. Prepare as directed above, but cook the blueberries just until slightly softened, about 3 minutes.

PUFFY APPLE PANCAKE

....

Caramelized apples are an easy and delicious enhancement for our basic puffy pancake.

Prep: 15 minutes   Cook/Bake: 30 minutes

- 2   tablespoons butter or margarine
- ½   cup plus 2 tablespoons sugar
- ¼   cup water
- 6   medium Granny Smith or Newtown Pippin apples (2 pounds), each peeled, cored, and cut into 8 wedges
- 3   large eggs
- ¾   cup milk
- ¾   cup all-purpose flour
- ¼   teaspoon salt

1. Preheat oven to 425°F. In oven-safe 12-inch skillet (if skillet is not oven-safe, wrap handle with double layer of foil), combine butter, ½ cup sugar, and water; heat to boiling over medium-high heat. Add apples; cook, stirring occasionally, until apples are golden and sugar mixture begins to caramelize, about 15 minutes.

2. Meanwhile, in blender or in food processor with knife blade attached, blend eggs, milk, flour, remaining 2 tablespoons sugar, and salt until smooth.

3. Pour batter over apples. Place skillet in oven and bake until pancake has puffed and is golden, about 15 minutes. Serve hot. Makes 6 main-dish servings.

Each serving: About 301 calories, 6g protein, 54g carbohydrate, 8g total fat (4g saturated), 121mg cholesterol, 181mg sodium.

SIMPLE PUFFY PANCAKE

Prepare as directed above but omit apple mixture in Step 1. In Step 3, add **2 tablespoons butter or margarine** to skillet and heat in oven until melted. Pour batter into skillet and bake as directed. Serve filled with a mixture of fresh berries and bananas, or a simple drizzle of maple syrup. Makes 6 main-dish servings.

FRENCH TOAST

....

If you like, try adding a pinch of cinnamon, nutmeg, orange peel, and/or vanilla extract to the egg mixture.

Prep: 5 minutes   Cook: 15 minutes

- 3   large eggs
- ¾   cup milk
- ⅛   teaspoon salt
- 4   tablespoons butter or margarine
- 8   slices (½ inch thick) sourdough or other firm white bread
    softened butter or margarine, maple syrup, or honey

1. Preheat oven to 250°F. In pie plate, with wire whisk, beat eggs, milk, and salt until well blended. In nonstick 12-inch skillet, melt 2 tablespoons butter over medium-high heat.

2. Dip 4 bread slices, one at a time, in beaten egg mixture to coat both sides well. Place in skillet and cook until browned, about 4 minutes per side. Transfer to cookie sheet; keep warm in oven. Repeat with remaining 2 tablespoons butter and remaining 4 bread slices. Serve hot with butter, maple syrup, or honey. Makes 4 main-dish servings.

Each serving without butter, syrup, or honey: About 341 calories, 11g protein, 32g carbohydrate, 18g total fat (10g saturated), 197mg cholesterol, 605mg sodium.

EGG SIZE EQUIVALENTS

Almost any size egg can be used for frying, scrambling, hard-cooking, and poaching. For baking and custards, however, large-size eggs are usually used. To substitute one size egg for another, follow our guidelines.

EGG SIZE EQUIVALENTS

LGE	JUMBO	X-LGE	MED	SMALL
1	1	1	1	1
2	2	2	2	3
3	3	2	3	4
4	3	4	5	5
5	4	4	6	7
6	5	5	7	8

OVERNIGHT BAKED FRENCH TOAST

(Pictured on page 224)

....

With its glorious brown-sugar crust, this rich, eggy French toast is a beautiful choice for company—and it's made with very little effort. Garnish with a sprinkling of confectioners' sugar and fresh berries.

Prep: 10 minutes plus overnight to chill

Bake: 1 hour

12 slices firm white bread
6 large eggs
2 cups milk
1 teaspoon vanilla extract
¼ teaspoon ground cinnamon
¼ teaspoon ground nutmeg
   pinch salt
½ cup packed brown sugar
4 tablespoons butter or margarine, softened
1 tablespoon maple syrup

1. Arrange bread slices in four stacks in 8-inch square baking dish.

2. In blender, combine eggs, milk, vanilla, cinnamon, nutmeg, and salt and blend until mixture is smooth. Slowly pour egg mixture over bread slices; press bread down to absorb egg mixture, spooning egg mixture over any uncoated bread. Cover and refrigerate overnight.

3. Preheat oven to 350°F. In small bowl, stir brown sugar, butter, and maple syrup until combined. Spread evenly over each stack of bread. Bake until knife inserted 1 inch from center comes out clean, about 1 hour. Let stand 15 minutes before serving. To serve, cut each stack diagonally in half. Makes 8 servings.

Each serving: About 308 calories, 10g protein, 37g carbohydrate, 13g total fat (6g saturated), 184mg cholesterol, 364mg sodium.

SPINACH STRATA

....

This strata is best when assembled the night before, then baked the next day. For a real treat, use fresh mozzarella.

Prep: 15 minutes plus chilling   **Bake: 1 hour**

8 slices firm white bread
4 ounces mozzarella cheese, shredded (1 cup)
1 package (10 ounces) frozen chopped spinach, thawed and squeezed dry
1 tablespoon butter or margarine
6 large eggs
2 cups milk
½ teaspoon salt
¼ teaspoon ground black pepper

1. Lightly grease 8-inch square baking dish. Arrange 4 bread slices in bottom of dish. Sprinkle with ½ cup mozzarella and top with spinach; sprinkle with remaining ½ cup mozzarella. Spread butter on one side of remaining 4 bread slices and arrange, butter side up, over mozzarella.

2. In large bowl, with wire whisk, beat eggs, milk, salt, and pepper until well blended. Slowly pour egg mixture over bread slices; press bread down to absorb egg mixture, spooning egg mixture over any uncoated bread. Cover and refrigerate at least 4 hours or up to overnight.

3. Preheat oven to 350°F. Remove cover and bake strata until golden and knife inserted in center comes out clean, about 1 hour. Let stand 15 minutes before serving. Makes 6 main-dish servings.

Each serving: About 313 calories, 17g protein, 25g carbohydrate, 16g total fat (7g saturated), 244mg cholesterol, 624mg sodium.

STUFFED EGGS

....

Stuffed eggs are make-ahead appetizers that work well with large or small groups.

Prep: 30 minutes   Cook: 10 minutes plus standing

- 6 large eggs
- ¼ cup mayonnaise
- 1 tablespoon milk
- ⅛ teaspoon salt

1. In 3-quart saucepan, place eggs and enough *cold water* to cover by at least 1 inch; heat to boiling over high heat. Immediately remove saucepan from heat and cover tightly; let stand 15 minutes. Pour off hot water and run cold water over eggs to cool. Peel eggs.

2. Slice eggs lengthwise in half. Gently remove yolks and place in medium bowl; with fork, finely mash yolks. Stir in mayonnaise, milk, and salt until evenly blended. Egg-yolk mixture and egg whites can be covered separately and refrigerated up to 24 hours.

3. Place egg whites in jelly-roll pan lined with paper towels (to prevent eggs from rolling). Spoon egg-yolk mixture into pastry bag fitted with star tip or zip-tight plastic bag with one corner cut off. Pipe about 1 tablespoon yolk mixture into each egg-white half, or simply spoon mixture. Cover eggs and refrigerate up to 4 hours. Makes 12 appetizers.

Each appetizer: About 72 calories, 3g protein, 0g carbohydrate, 6g total fat (1g saturated), 109mg cholesterol, 82mg sodium.

BACON-HORSERADISH STUFFED EGGS

Prepare as directed above but add **2 tablespoons crumbled crisp-cooked bacon** and **1 tablespoon bottled white horseradish** to yolk mixture. If not serving right away, sprinkle crumbled bacon on top of stuffed eggs instead of adding to yolk mixture.

Each appetizer: About 80 calories, 4g protein, 1g carbohydrate, 7g total fat (2g saturated), 110mg cholesterol, 102mg sodium.

DRIED TOMATO-CAPER STUFFED EGGS

Prepare as directed (left) but add **1 tablespoon plus 2 teaspoons chopped dried tomatoes packed in oil and herbs, 1 tablespoon plus 2 teaspoons chopped drained capers, and ⅛ teaspoon coarsely ground black pepper** to yolk mixture.

Each appetizer: About 78 calories, 3g protein, 1g carbohydrate, 7g total fat (1g saturated), 109mg cholesterol, 143mg sodium.

LEMON-BASIL STUFFED EGGS

Prepare as directed (left) but add **1 tablespoon chopped fresh basil, ¼ teaspoon freshly grated lemon peel, and ¼ teaspoon coarsely ground black pepper** to yolk mixture.

Each appetizer: About 73 calories, 3g protein, 0g carbohydrate, 6g total fat (1g saturated), 109mg cholesterol, 82mg sodium.

PIMIENTO-STUDDED STUFFED EGGS

Prepare as directed (left) but add **2 tablespoons chopped pimientos, 2 teaspoons Dijon mustard, and ⅛ teaspoon ground red pepper (cayenne)** to yolk mixture.

Each appetizer: About 74 calories, 3g protein, 1g carbohydrate, 6g total fat (1g saturated), 109mg cholesterol, 102mg sodium.

Lemon-Basil Stuffed Eggs

CHEESE

No matter how you slice it, cheese is simply coagulated milk curd. The final product depends on many variables. What kind of milk was used? Cow's is the most common, but many cheeses are made from sheep's or goat's milk. How long was the cheese aged? In general, the older the cheese, the harder the texture. Was any special bacteria, yeast, or mold added to the cheese to give it distinction? Penicillin molds give blue cheeses their unique taste and veined appearance. Brie is treated with a mold that forms an edible rind that cures the cheese from the outside in. Whether you appreciate cheese by itself as an appetizer or dessert course or use it in casseroles, pizzas, salads, paninis, or other dishes, this delicious food delivers a lot of flavor, even in small amounts.

HOW CHEESE IS MADE

Cheese is made by combining milk with a starter: a bacterial culture that curdles the milk to form curds (solids) and whey (liquid). The whey is then drained off. For some fresh cheeses, the curds are served in their soft state (cottage cheese, for example), but for most cheeses, the curds are further coagulated. This is usually accomplished by adding an animal product called rennet. The cheese is then cured by pressing (which removes more whey and makes the cheese harder), cooking, or adding bacterial agents.

HOW CHEESE IS CATEGORIZED

Cheese is often categorized by its texture. *Hard cheeses,* such as Parmigiano-Reggiano and Pecorino-Romano, can be grated. Sliceable cheeses, such as Monterey Jack and Gouda, are considered *semihard. Semisoft cheeses,* such as Camembert and triple-crèmes, are spreadable. *Fresh cheeses,* such as cottage cheese and mascarpone, are soft and usually quite perishable. Blue cheeses and goat cheeses have distinctive flavors that put them in their own separate categories. They can be creamy or crumbly, very sharp or quite mild. *Processed cheese* is made from pasteurized cheese that has been combined with emulsifiers and other ingredients to create a moister, more uniform product. Since processed cheese only has to contain 51 percent actual cheese, its flavor is much milder than that of natural cheese.

BUYING CHEESE

Cheese is a living organism and needs to be treated with respect and a certain amount of care. To buy the best cheese, find a cheese or specialty food store that prides itself on the quality of its merchandise. A cheese seller will be able to recommend cheeses that are ripe and ready to eat, as well as those that should be served at a later date. Avoid cheese that has an ammonia odor. Also, do not buy any hard or semihard cheese with beads of moisture on the surface or with dry, cracked rinds. Semisoft cheese should yield to gentle pressure. Any powdery "bloom" on the rind should be evenly colored and slightly moist.

STORING CHEESE

Store cheese in the refrigerator, tightly wrapped to prevent it from drying out. Leave the original wrapping intact, or rewrap in waxed paper and then in foil. To prolong the life of a cheese, change the wrapping every few days. Strong-smelling cheese should be stored in an airtight container so its aroma doesn't affect other foods in close proximity.

In general, the harder a cheese, the longer it will keep. Soft cheese, especially goat cheese, should be eaten as soon as possible. Semihard cheeses will keep for a few weeks if wrapped tightly. If a cheese (like Cheddar) dries out, grate it and use in cooked dishes. Hard grating cheeses, such as Pecorino-Romano and Parmesan, can be stored for up to several months.

If a hard cheese develops a moldy spot, cut it away; the remaining cheese is fine to eat. Discard any soft cheese that has developed mold, because it could have permeated the cheese.

If absolutely necessary, you can freeze hard or semihard cheese, but when thawed, the cheese will lose moisture and become crumbly. Use it for cooking, not eating. To freeze, wrap the cheese airtight in moisture-proof wrapping and freeze for up to three months.

A CHEESE GLOSSARY

Asiago A sharp cow's milk cheese made in northern Italy since the 16th century. The most readily available version is a domestic hard grating cheese.

Blue cheese An entire category of cheese with blue-green veins that give the cheese a tart, sharp flavor and aroma. American, Canadian, and Danish varieties are simply called "blue cheese." *Danish blue cheese* is especially good in salad dressings. *French Roquefort*, considered the king of blue cheeses, is made with sheep's milk and is crumbly and sharp, with distinct blue veining. *Italian Gorgonzola,* made from cow's milk, has a creamy texture and milder flavor. Young *dolce Gorgonzola* has the softest texture and mildest flavor (although it is still quite tangy), while aged *naturale Gorgonzola* is firmer and more assertive. *British Stilton,* with its inedible thick rind, is another highly regarded cow's milk blue cheese.

Brie Brie is a semisoft cheese with an edible white rind. When purchased, it should have a soft, not runny, consistency.

Camembert A perfectly ripe Camembert has a creamy, runny center and rich buttery flavor. This semisoft cheese has a "bloomed" (velvety looking) edible rind.

Cheddar A semihard cheese that ranges in flavor from mild to extrasharp and in color from ivory to orange. It is named after the British village that specializes in its production, but it has become an American classic.

Edam A mild-flavored Dutch cheese made from partially skimmed cow's milk and shaped into a flattened ball. Edam from Holland is coated with red paraffin and wrapped in red cellophane. Domestic Edam is coated in red paraffin.

Farmer cheese True farmer cheese is a soft fresh curd cheese that is firm enough to slice. It has a mild, tangy flavor.

Feta Depending on its country of origin and the type of milk used, the flavor of feta varies. It is always stored in brine, which imparts an inherent saltiness. European feta cheese is usually made from sheep's milk. *Greek feta* is crumbly, salty, and sharp; *Bulgarian feta* has a more delicate taste and a creamier texture; and *French feta* is milder still. *American feta* is made in the Greek style but is usually made from cow's or goat's milk.

Fontina The classic Fontina d'Aosta, smooth-textured and mildly pungent, is one of the great cheeses of Italy. There are also tasty American, Danish, and Swedish versions.

Goat cheese Sharp, tangy, and brilliant white, this cheese is sometimes referred to by its French name, *chèvre*. It can be young and soft or aged and hard. Some are coated in herbs, spices, or wood ash, wrapped in leaves, or soaked in olive oil. They can be round, button-shaped, or resemble a pyramid; many have rinds. French chèvres are highly revered, but there are excellent American versions.

Gouda Similar in flavor and appearance to Edam but made from cow's milk. Aged Gouda is sharp-tasting and butterscotch in color.

Gruyère See Swiss cheese.

Havarti Danish Havarti is a brick-shaped cheese dotted with tiny holes. It has a mild flavor and soft texture.

Manchego In America, this golden yellow Spanish sheep's milk cheese is available in two stages of ripeness: one-year-old *curado* and two-year-old *añejo*. Some liken its sharp flavor and dry, crumbly texture to fine Cheddar cheese.

Mascarpone This mild clotted cream has a thick, creamy texture. It is best known as a key ingredient in the delectable Italian dessert called tiramisú.

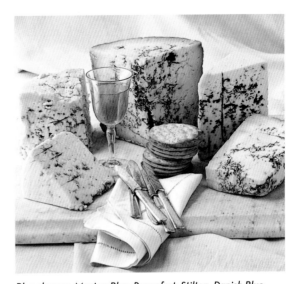

Blue cheeses: Maytag Blue, Roquefort, Stilton, Danish Blue, Gorgonzola

Goat's and sheep's milk cheeses: Classic ash-coated log, buttons, pyramid, ricotta salata, Bûcheron, feta

Monterey Jack An American original developed by Scotsman David Jacks near Monterey, California, in the 1890s. Soft-textured with a mild acidic bite, true Monterey Jack has tiny holes running through it. Jack cheese is sometimes flavored with jalapeño peppers. *Dry Jack* is a very hard, aged cheese that is used primarily for grating.

Mozzarella Mozzarella is one of the best melting cheeses. In southern Italy, it is often made from *bufala* (water buffalo) milk and hand-formed into balls. Domestically, the version found most often is factory-produced from whole or partially skimmed cow's milk. Specialty food stores carry fresh mozzarella that is hand-formed, smoked mozzarella, and imported buffalo milk mozzarella.

Muenster American Muenster is a brick-shaped, paprika-sprinkled cheese with a mild flavor and smooth texture. It is a good melting cheese. There are French, Danish, and German Munsters (note the different spelling), but they are much stronger.

Parmesan There is only one authentic Parmigiano-Reggiano. Protected by Italian law, Parmigiano-Reggiano can be made only in a geographically defined area around Parma, Italy. It is aged for at least fourteen months, and its name is repeatedly stamped on the rind. Whenever possible, buy Parmigiano by the wedge and grate it just before serving.

Port-Salut Formerly made by French Trappist monks, this cheese is now factory-produced. It has a mild flavor, a semisoft texture, and an edible orange-colored rind.

Provolone The somewhat soft, mild provolone found in most supermarkets is the American version. It comes in a variety of shapes, from balls to cylinders, but it is always bound with rope to maintain its form. Italian provolone is often aged until sharp and firm.

Queso blanco A popular cheese in Latino cooking, it is pressed into firm blocks; when sliced and heated, it melts. It is often confused with *queso fresco*, which has a dry texture and does not melt.

Raclette A semisoft cheese from Switzerland with excellent melting qualities.

Ricotta Its name literally means "recooked." The traditional version of this soft, fresh Italian cheese is prepared from the whey collected after making other cheeses. The whey is cooked a second time with coagulants to produce a mild, granular cheese. The ricotta cheese sold in American supermarkets is usually a blend of whey and cow's milk, either partially skimmed or whole.

Ricotta Salata No relation to soft ricotta, this is a pressed, lightly salted Sicilian sheep's milk cheese with a slightly crumbly, firm texture.

Soft-ripened cheeses: Brie, Camembert, Explorateur

Hard (grating) cheeses: Pecorino-Romano, Parmigiano-Reggiano

Romano A hard grating cheese that is often used as a substitute for Parmesan. Romano has a slightly salty, more piquant taste that goes beautifully with the robust tomato sauces and vegetable dishes of southern Italy. Italian *Pecorino-Romano* is made from sheep's milk.

Swiss cheese Americans refer to any cheese with holes as Swiss cheese, but there are distinct types. Generic Swiss cheese is American-made, usually in California or Wisconsin. There are two classic Swiss-made cheeses that are indispensable in fondue: *Gruyère* and *Emmental*. As they age, their characteristic holes are formed by carbon dioxide trapped in the cheese. Gruyère has pea-size holes and a full, rich flavor. The French version is called Comté. Emmental has holes of various shapes and a nutty flavor. *Jarlsberg*, one of the most popular of all imported cheeses, is a Norwegian version of Emmental, but with larger holes and a softer texture.

Taleggio This cow's milk cheese has a soft interior with flavor that can range from tart and salty to rich and buttery. Its reddish brown crust should be dry and uncracked. It is made in the Lombardy region of northern Italy.

Triple-crème cheese A category of cheeses made with cow's milk and enriched with cream, resulting in buttery rich texture and flavor. *Brillat-Savarin, St.-André,* and *Explorateur* are three of the best-known triple-crème cheeses.

BROCCOLI-CHEDDAR PUFF

Serve this golden puff as a side dish or as the star of a holiday brunch.

Prep: 35 minutes   Bake: 40 minutes

- 5   tablespoons butter or margarine
- 6   tablespoons all-purpose flour
- ½   teaspoon salt
- ⅛   teaspoon ground red pepper (cayenne)
- 2¼ cups milk
- 8   ounces sharp Cheddar cheese, shredded (2 cups)
- 2   boxes (10 ounces each) frozen chopped broccoli, thawed and squeezed dry
- 7   large eggs, separated
- 1½ cups coarse soft fresh bread crumbs (about 3 slices firm white bread)

1. In 4-quart sauce pan, melt 4 tablespoons butter over medium-low heat. Stir in flour, salt, and ground red pepper until blended; cook 1 minute, stirring. Gradually stir in milk; cook until mixture boils and thickens, stirring frequently. Stir in Cheddar; cook just until melted. Remove from heat. Stir in broccoli.

2. In small bowl, with fork, lightly beat egg yolks. Stir in about ½ cup cheese sauce. Gradually pour egg-yolk mixture into cheese sauce, stirring rapidly to prevent curdling. Cool slightly.

3. Meanwhile, preheat oven to 325°F. Grease shallow 3½-quart ceramic casserole or 13" by 9" glass baking dish. In microwave-safe small bowl, heat remaining 1 tablespoon butter in microwave oven on High 15 to 20 seconds or until melted, swirling bowl once. Add bread crumbs; stir until well combined.

4. In large bowl, with mixer at high speed, beat egg whites until stiff peaks form when beaters are lifted. With rubber spatula, gently fold one third of whites into cheese mixture. Fold cheese mixture gently back into remaining whites.

5. Pour mixture into prepared casserole. Sprinkle crumb mixture on top. Bake 40 minutes or until top is browned and knife inserted in center comes out clean. Serve immediately. Makes 15 accompaniment servings.

Each serving: About 190 calories, 9g protein, 9g carbohydrate, 13g total fat (7g saturated), 131mg cholesterol, 280mg sodium.

FRESH RICOTTA

···

It's amazingly simple to make fresh ricotta—just three ingredients and less than a half hour required—and it's more delicate than store-bought. Plus, it's only half the price! Use this rich, fluffy cheese for lasagna, cannoli, or simple crostini (with a drizzle of extra-virgin olive oil or topped with chopped fresh herbs). Dieters: See the reduced-fat variation, at left.

Prep: 10 minutes plus standing   Cook: 10 minutes

- 8   cups whole milk
- 1   teaspoon salt
- 3   tablespoons fresh lemon juice

1. Line large strainer with 4 layers cheesecloth and place lined strainer in large bowl; set aside.

2. In heavy-bottom 4-quart saucepan, heat milk and salt to boiling over medium-high heat, stirring occasionally to prevent milk from scorching.

3. Stir in lemon juice; cover and remove from heat. Let stand 5 minutes. With slotted spoon, gently transfer curds from saucepan to lined strainer. Drain 3 minutes. Discard whey in bowl.

4. If not using right away, transfer ricotta to clean bowl, cover, and refrigerate up to 1 week. Makes 15 ounces or about 2 cups.

Each tablespoon: About 25 calories, 2g protein, 0g carbohydrate, 2g total fat (1g saturated), 0g fiber, 8mg cholesterol, 30mg sodium.

Fresh Ricotta

REDUCED-FAT RICOTTA

Substitute **4 cups reduced-fat (2%) milk** for 4 cups whole milk, and follow recipe as above.

Each tablespoon: About 25 calories, 2g protein, 0g carbohydrate, 1.5g total fat (1g saturated), 0g fiber, 6mg cholesterol, 30mg sodium.

Tip: Cheesecloth can be found in the kitchen-supply aisle of supermarkets.

SAVORY RICOTTA CHEESECAKE

···

This basil-scented cheesecake can be served warm or cool with a salad of baby greens or tomatoes and crusty bread.

Prep: 15 minutes   Bake: 1 hour 10 minutes

- 2   garlic cloves, peeled
- 1   cup loosely packed fresh basil leaves
- 1   container (32 ounces) part-skim ricotta cheese
- 1   package (8 ounces) cream cheese
- ⅓   cup freshly grated Parmesan cheese
- 4   large eggs
- 3   tablespoons all-purpose flour
- ¾   teaspoon freshly grated orange peel
- ½   teaspoon salt
- ¼   teaspoon ground black pepper

1. Preheat oven to 350°F. Lightly grease 9-inch springform pan. Place on cookie sheet.

2. In 1-quart saucepan, heat *2 cups water* to boiling over high heat. Add garlic and cook 3 minutes to blanch; drain.

3. In food processor with knife blade attached, process garlic and basil until chopped. Add ricotta, cream cheese, Parmesan, eggs, flour, orange peel, salt, and pepper; puree until smooth and well combined. Pour into prepared pan.

4. Bake until cake is just set and toothpick inserted in center comes out clean, about 1 hour 10 minutes. Cool in pan on wire rack 10 minutes. With small knife, carefully loosen cheesecake from side of pan; remove side of pan. To serve, cut into wedges. Makes 12 first-course servings.

Each serving: About 222 calories, 14g protein, 7g carbohydrate, 15g total fat (9g saturated), 117mg cholesterol, 319mg sodium.

CLASSIC SWISS FONDUE

....

Switzerland's most famous cheese dish. Use a dry, slightly acidic wine, such as sauvignon blanc, or the cheese won't melt smoothly.

Prep: 15 minutes   Cook: 15 minutes

- 1 garlic clove, cut in half
- 1½ cups dry white wine
- 1 tablespoon kirsch or brandy
- 8 ounces Swiss or Emmental cheese, shredded (2 cups)
- 8 ounces Gruyère cheese, shredded (2 cups)
- 3 tablespoons all-purpose flour
- ⅛ teaspoon ground black pepper pinch ground nutmeg
- 1 loaf (16 ounces) French bread, cut into 1-inch cubes

1. Rub inside of fondue pot or heavy nonreactive 2-quart saucepan with garlic; discard garlic. Pour wine into fondue pot. Heat over medium-low heat until very hot but not boiling; stir in kirsch.

2. Meanwhile, in medium bowl, toss Swiss cheese, Gruyère, and flour. Add cheese mixture, one handful at a time, to wine, stirring constantly and vigorously until cheese has melted and mixture is thick and smooth. If mixture separates, increase heat to medium, stirring just until smooth. Stir in pepper and nutmeg.

3. Transfer fondue to table; place over tabletop heater to keep hot, if you like. To eat, spear cubes of French bread onto long-handled fondue forks and dip into cheese mixture. Makes 6 first-course servings.

Each serving: About 567 calories, 29g protein, 45g carbohydrate, 25g total fat (14g saturated), 76mg cholesterol, 689mg sodium.

---

5 IDEAS FOR . . . RICOTTA CHEESE

Italians have known it all along: This fresh, creamy cheese isn't just for lasagna. Take these five fast dishes, some savory, some sweet. They're made with part-skim ricotta—which has 41 percent less fat but no less flavor than the whole-milk variety—and all but one call for a 15- to 16-ounce tub.

PENNE À LA RICOTTA

Cook 1 pound penne pasta; drain, reserving ½ cup cooking water. In bowl, combine ricotta, ½ cup grated Romano cheese, ½ cup chopped fresh basil, and ½ teaspoon each salt and coarsely ground black pepper. Toss with pasta, adding cooking water if needed. Top with 1 pint cherry tomatoes, each cut in half; garnish with basil. Serves 4.

ORANGE-RICOTTA PANCAKES

From 1 navel orange, grate 2 teaspoons peel. Cut off and discard remaining peel and white pith; cut fruit into segments and reserve. In bowl, whisk together ricotta, 4 large eggs, and orange peel. Whisk in ½ cup all-purpose flour and ½ teaspoon baking powder. Spray 12-inch nonstick skillet with nonstick spray; heat on medium 1 minute. Drop batter by ¼ cup into skillet, making 4 to 5 pancakes at a time. Cook 10 to 12 minutes or until golden on both sides. Serve with orange segments and maple syrup. Serves 4.

PUFFY BACON-CHIVE CASSEROLE

Preheat oven to 350°F. Brown 3 slices bacon; drain. Crumble when cool. Separate 5 large eggs, placing yolks in large bowl and whites in medium bowl. Whisk yolks with bacon, ricotta, ¼ cup grated Parmesan, 2 tablespoons snipped chives, and ¼ teaspoon each salt and pepper. Add 2 more egg whites to whites in bowl, and beat on high to stiff peaks. Fold whites into ricotta mixture, one-third at a time, just until blended. Bake in greased shallow 2½-quart baking dish 30 to 35 minutes. Serves 6.

LEMON-RICOTTA FRUIT DIP

In blender, blend 1 cup ricotta with 2 tablespoons chopped candied ginger until smooth. Add ½ cup jarred lemon curd and pulse just until combined. Serve with 1 pound strawberries, hulled, and 4 cups 1-inch cubes angel food cake (about 6 ounces). Makes 1½ cups dip.

EASY CASSATA PARFAITS

Slightly thaw 1 package (10 ounces) frozen cherries. Meanwhile, cut 4 ounces pound cake into 1-inch cubes (2 cups). In bowl, whisk ricotta with ⅓ cup confectioners' sugar. In 4 wine goblets or parfait glasses, layer half of each of the ricotta mixture, cake, and cherries, and sprinkle on 1 tablespoon mini chocolate chips. Repeat layering. Serves 4.

MOZZARELLA IN CARROZZA

··

Mozzarella in carrozza, "mozzarella in a carriage," is usually deep-fried, but we panfry ours. It is served with a buttery anchovy sauce that can be drizzled over each serving, if you like.

Prep: 20 minutes   Cook: 5 minutes

- 8 ounces part-skim mozzarella cheese
- 8 slices firm white bread, crusts removed
- 2 large eggs, well beaten
- ¼ cup milk
- ¼ cup all-purpose flour
- ½ teaspoon salt
- ¼ teaspoon ground black pepper
- ½ cup plain dried bread crumbs
- 3 tablespoons vegetable oil
- 4 tablespoons butter or margarine
- 8 anchovy fillets, drained
- 1 tablespoon chopped fresh parsley
- 1 teaspoon capers, drained
- 1 teaspoon fresh lemon juice

1. Stand mozzarella on its side and cut lengthwise into 4 equal slices. Place 1 slice cheese between 2 slices bread to form sandwich. Repeat with remaining cheese and bread.

2. Preheat oven to 200°F.

3. In pie plate, with wire whisk, beat eggs and milk. On waxed paper, combine flour, salt, and pepper; spread bread crumbs on separate sheet of waxed paper. Dip sandwiches, one at a time, in flour mixture, shaking off excess, then in egg mixture, and finally in bread crumbs, shaking off excess.

4. In nonstick 12-inch skillet, heat oil over medium heat until hot. Add sandwiches; cook until golden brown, about 1½ minutes per side. Cut each sandwich on diagonal in half. Arrange on platter in single layer. Keep warm in oven.

5. In same skillet, melt butter; add anchovies and cook, stirring constantly, 1 minute. Add parsley, capers, and lemon juice; cook 30 seconds longer. Transfer sauce to small bowl. Serve sauce with sandwiches. Makes 8 appetizer servings.

Each serving: About 309 calories, 13g protein, 22g carbohydrate, 19g total fat (8g saturated), 89mg cholesterol, 713mg sodium.

Mozzarella in Carrozza

WELSH RABBIT

....

Whether you call it rarebit or rabbit (perhaps named by an unsuccessful hunter), this is classic comfort food. If you top it with bacon, it becomes Yorkshire rabbit.

Prep: 10 minutes   Cook: 10 minutes

- 2 tablespoons butter or margarine
- ¼ cup all-purpose flour
- 1 cup milk, warmed
- ⅔ cup beer
- 8 ounces sharp Cheddar cheese, shredded (2 cups)
- 1 teaspoon Dijon mustard
- ½ teaspoon Worcestershire sauce
- ⅛ teaspoon ground red pepper (cayenne)
- 9 slices white bread, toasted

1. In 2-quart saucepan, melt butter over medium heat. With wooden spoon, stir in flour. With wire whisk, gradually whisk in warm milk until smooth. Whisk in beer and heat to boiling, whisking constantly. Reduce heat and simmer 1 minute. Stir in Cheddar, mustard, Worcestershire, and ground red pepper; remove from heat. Stir until smooth.

2. Cut toast slices on diagonal in half. Arrange 3 toast halves on each plate and spoon cheese mixture over. Makes 6 main-dish servings.

Each serving: About 342 calories, 14g protein, 26g carbohydrate, 19g total fat (11g saturated), 56mg cholesterol, 521mg sodium.

LACY PARMESAN CRISPS

....

Called frico in Italy, these delicious wafers are simply spoonfuls of grated cheese that are baked and cooled. Reusable nonstick bakeware liners, available at most kitchenware stores and bakery suppliers, yield the best results and are easy to use, but you can use a nonstick cookie sheet instead.

Prep: 20 minutes   Bake: 6 minutes per batch

- 6 ounces Parmesan cheese, coarsely grated (1½ cups)

1. Preheat oven to 375°F. Line large cookie sheet with reusable nonstick bakeware liner. Drop level tablespoons Parmesan 3 inches apart onto cookie sheet; spread to form 2-inch rounds.

2. Bake Parmesan rounds until edges just begin to color, 6 to 7 minutes. Transfer crisps, still on bakeware liner, to wire rack; cool 2 minutes. Transfer to paper towels to drain. Repeat with remaining Parmesan. Makes about 24 crisps.

Each crisp: About 28 calories, 3g protein, 0g carbohydrate, 2g total fat (1g saturated), 5mg cholesterol, 114mg sodium.

CHEDDAR CRISPS

Prepare as directed above but substitute **6 ounces sharp Cheddar cheese,** coarsely shredded (1½ cups) for Parmesan. Bake until bubbling but not browned, 6 to 7 minutes per batch.

Lacy Parmesan Crisps

8

PASTA & PASTA SAUCES

Pasta has become a weeknight favorite for many cooks; it's nutritious, easy to prepare, and delicious. Best of all, pasta is extremely versatile. It can be rich and satisfying when combined with meat, light and luscious when tossed with vegetables or seafood, or positively mouthwatering when layered and baked until golden and bubbling.

We use dried Italian-style pasta for most of our recipes, as it is readily available. For special occasions, homemade or store-bought fresh pasta is an excellent choice. Made with eggs, fresh pasta has a delicate texture that works well with creamy sauces. Dried pasta, made from flour and water, is more economical, lower in fat, and a good match for a wide variety of sauces.

BUYING AND STORING PASTA

For the best taste and texture, buy dried pasta made from durum wheat flour or from semolina flour. Store dried pasta in a cool, dry, dark place for up to one year, but if it is made of whole wheat, store up to six months. Even though clear plastic pasta storage containers are attractive, do not use them. Light destroys riboflavin, a key nutrient in pasta. We recommend buying pasta that comes in cardboard boxes for the same reason.

Store commercially made fresh pasta in the refrigerator for up to one week, or freeze for up to one month. Homemade pasta can be refrigerated for up to three days or frozen for up to one month. For the best results, don't thaw frozen pasta before cooking.

A PASTA GLOSSARY

Long Strands
Bucatini Long, thick tubes resembling hollow spaghetti.
Capellini Also called *capelli d'angelo* or angel hair. Very thin, delicate strands.
Fusilli Long strands resembling a telephone cord but also the name for short spirals.
Spaghetti Italian for "lengths of cord."
Vermicelli Very thin spaghetti.

Flat Ribbons
Egg noodles American-style noodles enriched with egg yolks.
Fettuccine Flat noodles about ¼ inch wide.
Lasagna Very wide flat pasta noodles, also available in a no-boil version.
Linguine Ribbons of pasta that are ⅛ inch wide.
Mafalde Wide ribbons with one long ruffled edge.
Pappardelle Ribbons about 1 inch wide.
Tagliatelle Slightly wider than fettuccine.

Tubular Pastas
Elbow macaroni Small curved tubular pasta.
Mostacciole Tubes about 2 inches long, available smooth and with ridges.
Penne Tubes with diagonally cut ends.
Rigatoni Large tubes with ridges.
Ziti Medium tubes about 1 inch long.

Small Pastas
Acini di pepe Tiny pasta stubs.
Alphabets Tiny letter-shaped pasta.

Penne with Vodka Sauce (recipe page 255)

Ditalini Very short macaroni; also called *tubettini*.

Orzo Although rice-shaped, *orzo* means "barley" in Italian.

Pastina Very, very small pasta flakes.

Miscellaneous Shapes

Cavatelli Small elongated ridged pasta.

Conchiglie Medium shells good for sauce.

Creste di gallo Curly medium-ribbed pasta that resembles a rooster's crest.

Farfalle Italian for "butterflies," also called bow ties.

Gemelli Two short spaghettilike strands that are twisted together.

Manicotti Large tubes of pasta meant for stuffing.

Orecchiette Disks that resemble small ears.

Radiatori Small deeply ribbed pasta resembling little radiators.

Rotini Corkscrew pasta, also called *fusilli* and *rotelle*.

Ruote Wagon wheel–shaped pasta.

Asian Noodles

Cellophane noodles Called bean threads or *mai fun*.

Chinese-style egg noodles Tender whole-wheat strands, similar to egg linguine.

Rice sticks Very thin rice stick noodles, also called *mai fun* or rice vermicelli.

Soba Thin brownish gray noodles made from buckwheat flour.

Udon Long, thick, Japanese wheat noodles.

PERFECT PASTA

Cook the Right Amount of Pasta

Most packages list a 2-ounce serving size, but a more generous main-dish measure is 4 ounces dried pasta or 3 ounces fresh pasta per person. The cooked yield of pasta depends on its shape: Four ounces of tube-shaped pasta, like penne, equals 2½ cups cooked; 4 ounces of long-strand pasta, like spaghetti, equals 2 cups cooked; 4 ounces of egg noodles equals 3 cups cooked.

Cook Pasta in Enough Water

Use at least four quarts of water for each pound of pasta. Cover the pot and bring the water to a rapid boil over high heat. Salt the water, then stir in the pasta.

Be Sure to Salt the Water

Pasta doesn't contain salt, so it needs to be cooked in salted water to be seasoned properly. If you are concerned about the amount of sodium in your diet, rest assured that only 10 percent of the salt in the cooking water is absorbed by the pasta. The basic proportion is 2 teaspoons of salt per pound of pasta.

Stir Frequently

Stirring ensures even cooking and keeps pasta from clumping together and sticking to the bottom of the pot. Do not add oil to the cooking water; it prevents sauce from clinging to the pasta.

Don't Overcook Pasta

The cooking time on pasta packages is only a guide, so start checking for doneness before the suggested time and check often. To test pasta for doneness, remove a piece from the boiling water, rinse it briefly under warm water, and bite into it. When pasta is perfectly cooked, it should be *al dente* ("to the tooth") with no raw flour taste and a tiny chalk white center. After it's drained, pasta will continue to cook from the residual heat and from the hot sauce with which it's tossed. If the pasta is to be baked, undercook it slightly, since it will continue to cook in the oven.

Drain Well and Don't Rinse

Drain the pasta in a colander, shaking to remove excess water. Don't rinse pasta; rinsing cools down pasta and removes both the surface starch that keeps it firm and its essential nutrients. Only lasagna noodles and pasta for salad should be rinsed.

Serve It Hot

When pasta stands, it gets cold and unappetizingly gummy. So call everyone to the table while you're tossing the pasta. To keep it as hot as possible, return the drained pasta to the cooking pot, which will still be warm, and combine it with the sauce there. Or warm the serving bowl and the individual bowls.

Cavatelli

Conchiglie

Manicotti

Rotini

Gemelli

Stelline

Orecchiette

Creste di gallo

Linguine

Ruote

Radiatori

Farfalle

Orzo

MARINARA SAUCE

·····················

This sauce is very versatile—we use it in recipes throughout the book. For a toothsome alternative, stir 8 ounces of sweet or hot Italian-sausage links, cooked and crumbled, into the sauce. Or top each serving with a spoonful of ricotta cheese for a creamy treat.

Prep: 5 minutes   Cook: 30 minutes

- 2 tablespoons olive oil
- 1 small onion, chopped
- 1 garlic clove, finely chopped
- 1 can (28 ounces) plum tomatoes
- 2 tablespoons tomato paste
- 2 tablespoons chopped fresh basil or parsley (optional)
- ½ teaspoon salt

1. In nonreactive 3-quart saucepan, heat oil over medium heat; add onion and garlic and cook, stirring, until onion is tender, about 5 minutes.

2. Stir in tomatoes with their juice, tomato paste, basil if using, and salt. Heat to boiling, breaking up tomatoes with side of spoon. Reduce heat; partially cover and simmer, stirring occasionally, until sauce has thickened slightly, about 20 minutes. Use to coat 1 pound pasta for 4 main-dish servings. Makes 3½ cups.

Each ½ cup: About 67 calories, 1g protein, 7g carbohydrate, 4g total fat (1g saturated), 0mg cholesterol, 388mg sodium.

ARRABBIATA SAUCE

Prepare as directed above, but add **¼ to ½ teaspoon crushed red pepper** with onion and garlic in Step 1. Omit fresh herbs and proceed as directed.

SPAGHETTI ALL'AMATRICIANA

Prepare as directed above, but use **1 tablespoon oil** in Step 1. Add **4 ounces sliced pancetta,** chopped, and cook until crisp before adding **¼ teaspoon crushed red pepper** with onion and garlic. In Step 3, omit tomato paste and basil and proceed as directed. Toss pasta with sauce and ¼ **cup chopped fresh parsley.**

PESTO

·····················

Pesto is the perfect use for all that fresh summer basil. To serve the pesto with pasta, add ¼ cup pasta cooking water. To store pesto, spoon into half-pint containers and top with a few tablespoons of olive oil. Cover and refrigerate up to one week.

Prep: 10 minutes

- 2 cups firmly packed fresh basil leaves
- 1 garlic clove, crushed with garlic press
- 2 tablespoons pine nuts (pignoli) or walnuts
- ¼ cup olive oil
- 1 teaspoon salt
- ¼ teaspoon coarsely ground black pepper
- ½ cup freshly grated Parmesan cheese

In blender or in food processor with knife blade attached, puree basil, garlic, pine nuts, oil, salt, and pepper until smooth. Add Parmesan and blend until combined. Makes about ¾ cup sauce (enough to coat 1 pound pasta).

Each tablespoon: About 66 calories, 2g protein, 1g carbohydrate, 6g total fat (1g saturated), 3mg cholesterol, 256mg sodium.

SAY CHEESE

Look beyond Parmesan and mozzarella—the pasta-topping staples—to these flavorful alternatives:

GRANA PADANO: A cow's-milk cheese similar in flavor and texture to Parmesan.

FONTINA: Rich and nutty cow's-milk cheese, a good substitute for mozzarella (it melts like a dream).

PECORINO: Piquant and full-flavored cheese made of sheep's milk; grate some instead of Parmesan.

FETA: Tangy, salty, and crumbly, this cheese made of sheep's or goat's milk is a good way to add extra zest to citrus-tinged seafood pasta.

RICOTTA SALATA: A sheep's-milk cheese similar to feta, but drier, with a milder, milky flavor; a wonderful addition to dishes accented with fresh tomatoes.

Semihard and hard cheeses last several weeks in the fridge. Cover them with waxed paper, then with plastic wrap or foil. Change the wrapping every few days.

PENNE WITH VODKA SAUCE

(Pictured on page 250)

••••••••••••••••••••••••••••••••••••

This restaurant favorite is a cinch to prepare at home. Don't hesitate to add the vodka. You won't taste it; it just melds the flavors.

Prep: 15 minutes   Cook: 30 minutes

- 1 tablespoon olive oil
- 1 small onion, chopped
- 1 garlic clove, finely chopped
- 1/8 to 1/4 teaspoon crushed red pepper
- 1 can (28 ounces) tomatoes in puree, coarsely chopped
- 3 tablespoons vodka (optional)
- 1/2 teaspoon salt
- 1/2 cup heavy or whipping cream
- 1 cup frozen peas, thawed
- 1 package (16 ounces) penne or rotini
- 1/2 cup loosely packed fresh basil leaves, thinly sliced

1. In nonstick 12-inch skillet, heat oil over medium heat. Add onion and cook until tender, about 5 minutes. Add garlic and crushed red pepper; cook until garlic is golden, about 30 seconds longer. Stir in tomatoes with their puree, vodka if using, and salt; heat to boiling over high heat. Reduce heat and simmer until sauce has thickened, 15 to 20 minutes. Stir in cream and peas; heat to boiling.

2. Meanwhile, in large saucepot, cook pasta as label directs. Drain. In warm serving bowl, toss pasta with sauce and sprinkle with basil. Makes 4 main-dish servings.

Each serving: About 652 calories, 20g protein, 107g carbohydrate, 17g total fat (8g saturated), 41mg cholesterol, 763mg sodium.

LINGUINE WITH RED CLAM SAUCE

••••••••••••••••••••••••••••••••••••

If you wish, substitute two cans (10 ounces each) of whole baby clams plus one-fourth of the clam liquid for the littleneck clams.

Prep: 20 minutes   Cook: 1 hour

- Marinara Sauce (opposite)
- 1/2 cup dry white wine
- 2 dozen littleneck clams, scrubbed (page 214)
- 1 package (16 ounces) linguine
- 1 tablespoon butter or margarine, cut into pieces (optional)
- 1/4 cup chopped fresh parsley

1. Prepare Marinara Sauce.

2. In nonreactive 12-inch skillet, heat wine to boiling over high heat. Add clams; cover and cook until clams open, 5 to 10 minutes, transferring clams to bowl as they open. Discard any clams that have not opened. Strain clam broth through sieve lined with paper towels; reserve 1/4 cup. When cool enough to handle, remove clams from shells and coarsely chop. Discard shells.

3. Meanwhile, in large saucepot, cook pasta as label directs. Drain.

4. In same clean 12-inch skillet, combine marinara sauce, reserved clam broth, and clams; cook over low heat until heated through. In warm serving bowl, toss pasta with sauce and butter, if using. Sprinkle with parsley and serve. Makes 6 main-dish servings.

Each serving: About 429 calories, 20g protein, 67g carbohydrate, 9g total fat (2g saturated), 29mg cholesterol, 582mg sodium.

LINGUINE WITH FRESH TOMATO SAUCE

....

If the ripe summer tomatoes you use taste a bit acidic, simply add 1 teaspoon sugar to the sauce. If using juicy beefsteak tomatoes instead of meaty plum tomatoes, simmer the sauce uncovered for about 20 minutes to allow the excess juices to evaporate.

Prep: 15 minutes   Cook: 30 minutes

- 1 tablespoon olive oil
- 1 small onion, chopped
- 2 pounds ripe plum tomatoes or beefsteak tomatoes, peeled and coarsely chopped
- ½ teaspoon salt
- 3 tablespoons butter, cut into pieces, or olive oil
- 2 tablespoons chopped fresh sage or ½ cup chopped fresh basil
- 1 package (16 ounces) linguine or penne

1. In nonstick 10-inch skillet, heat oil over medium heat. Add onion and cook until tender and golden, about 10 minutes. Add tomatoes with their juice and salt; heat to boiling over high heat. Reduce heat; cover and simmer, stirring and breaking up tomatoes with side of spoon, until sauce has thickened, 15 to 20 minutes. Stir in butter and sage.

2. Meanwhile, in large saucepot, cook pasta as label directs. Drain. In warm serving bowl, toss pasta with sauce. Makes 6 main-dish servings.

Each serving: About 388 calories, 11g protein, 65g carbohydrate, 10g total fat (4g saturated), 16mg cholesterol, 334mg sodium.

SPAGHETTI WITH ROASTED TOMATOES

....

Oven-roasted tomatoes have a sweet, intense flavor that is hard to resist. They make a terrific pasta sauce. If you like, you can use 3 pints of whole grape tomatoes to replace the plum tomatoes; reduce the roasting time to 20 to 30 minutes. No need to peel!

Prep: 10 minutes plus cooling   Roast/Cook: 1 hour

- 2 tablespoons olive oil
- 3 pounds ripe plum tomatoes (16 medium), cut lengthwise in half
- 6 garlic cloves, not peeled
- 1 package (16 ounces) spaghetti or linguine
- ¾ teaspoon salt
- ¼ teaspoon coarsely ground black pepper freshly grated Pecorino-Romano cheese (optional)

1. Preheat oven to 450°F. Brush jelly-roll pan with 1 tablespoon oil. Arrange tomatoes, cut side down, in pan; add garlic. Roast tomatoes and garlic until tomatoes are well browned and garlic has softened, 50 to 60 minutes.

2. When cool enough to handle, peel tomatoes over medium bowl to catch any juices. Place tomatoes in bowl; discard skins. Squeeze garlic to separate pulp from skins. Add garlic to tomatoes.

3. Meanwhile, in large saucepot, cook pasta as label directs. Drain.

4. With back of spoon, crush tomatoes and garlic. Stir in salt, pepper, and remaining 1 tablespoon oil. Serve sauce at room temperature or transfer to saucepan and heat through over low heat. In warm serving bowl, toss pasta with sauce. Serve with Romano, if you like. Makes 4 main-dish servings.

Each serving: About 552 calories, 17g protein, 101g carbohydrate, 10g total fat (1g saturated), 0mg cholesterol, 570mg sodium.

RADIATORI WITH ARUGULA, CHERRY TOMATOES, AND PANCETTA

....

No need to cook the arugula in this easy dish; it quickly wilts when tossed with the hot pasta and sauce.

Prep: 15 minutes   Cook: 25 minutes

- 4 ounces sliced pancetta or bacon, chopped
- 1 garlic clove, crushed with garlic press
- 1 pound cherry tomatoes, cut into quarters
- ½ teaspoon salt
- ¼ teaspoon coarsely ground black pepper
- 1 package (16 ounces) radiatori or rotini
- 2 bunches arugula (10 ounces each), trimmed
- ¼ cup freshly grated Parmesan cheese

1. In nonstick 10-inch skillet, cook pancetta over medium heat until lightly browned. (If cooking bacon, discard all but 1 tablespoon bacon drippings.) Add garlic and cook, stirring, 30 seconds. Add tomatoes, salt, and pepper and cook until tomatoes are warmed through, 1 to 2 minutes longer.

2. Meanwhile, in large saucepot, cook pasta as label directs. Drain. In warm serving bowl, toss pasta with pancetta mixture, arugula, and Parmesan. Makes 4 main-dish servings.

Each serving: About 557 calories, 22g protein, 93g carbohydrate, 11g total fat (4g saturated), 14mg cholesterol, 676mg sodium.

KNOW YOUR PASTA

Choose the right sauce for your pasta. Here are some tried-and-true guidelines:

- Thin pastas, such as capellini and vermicelli, should be dressed with delicate, light sauces that will cling to the skinny strands.
- Fettuccine and linguine are excellent with light meat, vegetable, seafood, cheese, and cream sauces.
- Tubular pastas are great with meat sauces: The nuggets of meat nestle right inside the tubes. Chunky vegetable or olive sauces are also a good match for macaroni-type pastas as well as for baked dishes.
- Tiny pastas are best saved for soups or combined with other ingredients.

PENNE WITH NO-COOK TOMATO SAUCE

....

This sauce is spectacular in summer, when tomatoes are at their peak. Use equal amounts of red and yellow tomatoes for a jewel-like effect.

Prep: 20 minutes plus standing   Cook: 25 minutes

- 2 pounds ripe tomatoes (6 medium), chopped
- 1 cup loosely packed fresh basil leaves, thinly sliced
- 8 ounces fresh mozzarella cheese, cut into ½-inch cubes
- 2 tablespoons olive oil
- 1 tablespoon red wine vinegar
- 1 teaspoon salt
- ¼ teaspoon coarsely ground black pepper
- 1 package (16 ounces) penne or rotini

1. In medium bowl, combine tomatoes, basil, mozzarella, oil, vinegar, salt, and pepper, tossing gently to mix. Let sauce stand at least 15 minutes or up to 1 hour at room temperature to blend flavors.

2. Meanwhile, in large saucepot, cook pasta as label directs. Drain. In warm serving bowl, toss pasta with sauce. Makes 4 main-dish servings.

Each serving: About 698 calories, 27g protein, 99g carbohydrate, 21g total fat (1g saturated), 40mg cholesterol, 749mg sodium.

BOW TIES WITH TOMATOES AND LEMON
Prepare as directed, but omit mozzarella and substitute ¼ **cup loosely packed fresh mint leaves,** chopped, for basil in Step 1. Add **1 teaspoon grated lemon peel** and **1 garlic clove,** crushed with garlic press, to tomato mixture. In Step 2, substitute **1 package (16 ounces) bow ties or ziti** for penne.

FETTUCCINE WITH MUSHROOM SAUCE

....

The combination of dried porcini and fresh shiitake mushrooms gives this sauce a rich, earthy flavor.

Prep: 20 minutes plus standing   Cook: 25 minutes

- ½ cup boiling water
- 1 package (.35 ounce) dried porcini mushrooms
- 2 tablespoons olive oil
- 1 medium onion, chopped
- 2 garlic cloves, finely chopped
- 8 ounces shiitake mushrooms, stems removed and caps thinly sliced
- 12 ounces white mushrooms, trimmed and thinly sliced
- ½ teaspoon salt
- ¼ teaspoon freshly ground black pepper
- 1¼ cups chicken broth
- 1 pound fresh fettuccine
- 2 tablespoons butter, cut into pieces (optional)
- ¼ cup chopped fresh parsley

1. In small bowl, pour boiling water over porcini mushrooms; let stand about 15 minutes. With slotted spoon, remove porcini, reserving liquid. Rinse mushrooms to remove any grit, then chop. Strain mushroom liquid through sieve lined with paper towels; set aside.

2. In 12-inch skillet, heat 1 tablespoon oil over low heat. Add onion and garlic and cook, stirring frequently, until onion is tender. Add shiitake mushrooms; increase heat to medium and cook, stirring, 5 minutes. Add remaining 1 tablespoon oil, white and porcini mushrooms, salt, and pepper; cook until mushrooms are tender, about 7 minutes. Add reserved mushroom liquid and cook, stirring frequently, until liquid has evaporated, about 2 minutes. Add broth and heat to boiling; cook until broth has reduced by one-third.

3. Meanwhile, in large saucepot, cook pasta as label directs. Drain. In warm serving bowl, toss pasta with mushroom sauce, butter if using, and parsley. Makes 6 main-dish servings.

Each serving without butter: About 366 calories, 13g protein, 64g carbohydrate, 6g total fat (1g saturated), 0mg cholesterol, 475mg sodium.

PASTA PRIMAVERA

....

With its lively medley of vegetables this pasta dish is a perfect way to celebrate the arrival of spring and the first asparagus of the season.

Prep: 15 minutes   Cook: 25 minutes

- ½ cup heavy or whipping cream
- 3 tablespoons butter or margarine
- 4 ounces shiitake mushrooms, stems removed and caps thinly sliced
- 2 very small yellow squash or zucchini (4 ounces each), cut into 2" by ¼" matchstick strips
- 4 green onions, thinly sliced
- 1 tablespoon chopped fresh parsley
- 1 package (16 ounces) fettuccine
- 1 pound asparagus, trimmed and cut on diagonal into 1½-inch pieces
- 4 ounces sugar snap peas, strings removed
- ¾ cup freshly grated Parmesan cheese
- ¼ teaspoon salt

1. In 1-quart saucepan, heat cream to boiling and boil 1 minute. Remove from heat and set aside.

2. In nonstick 10-inch skillet, melt butter over medium heat. Add mushrooms and cook, stirring, 1 minute. Add squash and cook, stirring, until vegetables are tender, about 3 minutes. Remove from heat; stir in green onions and parsley. Keep warm.

3. Meanwhile, in large saucepot, cook pasta as label directs. After pasta has cooked 7 minutes, add asparagus and sugar snap peas to pasta water. Cook until pasta and vegetables are tender, 3 to 5 minutes longer. Drain, reserving ½ cup pasta water.

4. In warm bowl, toss pasta and vegetables with reserved pasta water, Parmesan, and salt. Stir in cream and mushroom mixture. Makes 6 main-dish servings.

Each serving: About 491 calories, 18g protein, 64g carbohydrate, 18g total fat (11g saturated), 52mg cholesterol, 462mg sodium.

WHOLE-GRAIN ROTINI WITH ASPARAGUS AND SNAP PEAS

....

Fresh snap peas and asparagus lighten up a pasta dinner (and add plenty of vitamins). Choosing whole-grain pasta helps triple the cholesterol-lowering fiber.

Prep: 10 minutes   Cook: 20 minutes

- 1   package (13¼ ounces) whole-grain rotini or fusilli pasta
- 8   ounces asparagus, ends trimmed, cut into 1-inch pieces
- 1   bag (8 ounces) stringless snap peas
- 1   tablespoon olive oil
- 1   small onion, chopped
- 1   lemon
- ½   cup freshly grated Pecorino-Romano cheese
- ¼   cup loosely packed fresh basil leaves, thinly sliced
- ½   teaspoon salt
- ¼   teaspoon coarsely ground black pepper

1. In large saucepot, cook pasta as label directs, but add asparagus and snap peas when 3 minutes of cooking time remain.

2. Meanwhile, in 10-inch nonstick skillet, heat oil on medium until hot. Add onion and cook 10 to 12 minutes or until tender and browned. From lemon, grate 1 teaspoon peel and squeeze 2 tablespoons juice.

3. Reserve ½ cup pasta cooking water; drain pasta and vegetables. In large serving bowl, toss pasta and vegetables with cooking water, onion, lemon peel and juice, Romano, basil, salt, and pepper. Makes 4 main-dish servings.

Each serving: About 405 calories, 18g protein, 72g carbohydrate, 8g total fat (2g saturated), 9g fiber, 10mg cholesterol, 545mg sodium.

SPAGHETTI WITH GARLIC AND OIL

....

The classic combination of garlic and oil gives this simple pasta its heady flavor. Serve with lots of freshly grated Parmesan or Pecorino-Romano cheese.

Prep: 5 minutes   Cook: 25 minutes

- 1   package (16 ounces) spaghetti or linguine
- ¼   cup olive oil
- 1   large garlic clove, finely chopped
- ⅛   teaspoon crushed red pepper (optional)
- ¾   teaspoon salt
- ¼   teaspoon coarsely ground black pepper
- 2   tablespoons chopped fresh parsley

1. In large saucepot, cook pasta as label directs. Drain, reserving ½ cup cooking water.

2. Meanwhile, in 1-quart saucepan, heat oil over medium heat. Add garlic and cook just until golden, about 1 minute; add crushed red pepper if using, and cook 30 seconds longer. Remove saucepan from heat; stir in salt and black pepper. In warm serving bowl, toss pasta with sauce and parsley, using cooking water to moisten pasta as necessary. Makes 6 main-dish servings.

Each serving: About 362 calories, 10g protein, 57g carbohydrate, 10g total fat (1g saturated), 0mg cholesterol, 361mg sodium.

Whole-Grain Rotini with Asparagus and Snap Peas

GARLICKY BROCCOLI PASTA

Pasta with garlic and broccoli is a time-honored tradition and with good reason: It is absolutely delicious.

Prep: 15 minutes   Cook: 30 minutes

1   package (16 ounces) orecchiette or fusilli
1   bunch broccoli (about 1 pound)
2   tablespoons extra-virgin olive oil
3   garlic cloves, thinly sliced
¼   cup water
½   teaspoon salt
½   cup freshly grated Pecorino-Romano cheese

1. In large saucepot, cook pasta as label directs.

2. Meanwhile, trim broccoli. Coarsely chop stems and florets. You should have about 5 cups broccoli.

3. In nonstick 12-inch skillet, heat oil over medium heat until hot. Add garlic and cook, stirring, until golden, 2 to 3 minutes. Stir in broccoli, water, and salt. Cover and cook, stirring occasionally, until broccoli is tender, 8 to 10 minutes.

4. Drain pasta, reserving ½ cup pasta cooking water. Return pasta to saucepot. Add Romano, broccoli mixture, and reserved cooking water to pasta; toss until well combined. Makes 6 main-dish servings.

Each serving: About 370 calories, 14g protein, 61g carbohydrate, 8g total fat (2g saturated), 7mg cholesterol, 395mg sodium.

WHOLE-WHEAT PASTA WITH GARLICKY GREENS

This delicious, heart-healthy dish makes a great first course, or a light lunch or supper on its own.

Prep: 15 minutes   Cook: 20 minutes

1   large bunch broccoli rabe (1 pound)
1   bunch Swiss chard (½ pound)
1   pound whole-wheat penne or ziti
2   tablespoons extra-virgin olive oil
3   garlic cloves, finely chopped
¼   teaspoon crushed red pepper
½   cup water
½   teaspoon salt
½   cup freshly grated Parmesan

1. Heat large covered saucepot of salted water to boiling over high heat.

2. Meanwhile, trim and discard tough stem ends from broccoli rabe and Swiss chard. Coarsely chop tender stems and leaves. You should have about 20 cups chopped greens.

3. Add pasta to boiling water and cook as label directs. While pasta cooks, in nonstick 12-inch skillet, heat oil over medium heat until hot. Add garlic and crushed red pepper; cook 2 minutes or until garlic is golden, stirring. Stir half of greens, all of water, and salt into garlic in skillet. Increase to medium-high heat; cover and cook 2 to 3 minutes or until greens in skillet wilt. Stir in remaining greens; cover and cook 10 to 12 minutes or until greens are tender, stirring occasionally.

4. Drain pasta, reserving ¼ cup of cooking water. Return pasta to saucepot. Add Parmesan, greens mixture, and reserved cooking water to pasta in saucepot; toss until well combined. Makes about 10 cups or 6 main-dish servings.

Each serving: About 360 calories, 16g protein, 60g carbohydrate, 8g total fat (2g saturated), 8g fiber, 6mg cholesterol, 505mg sodium.

EASY ADD-INS FOR GARLIC AND OIL SAUCE

Spaghetti with Garlic and Oil (opposite) is just the starting point for many delicious possibilities.

• Add 4 to 6 coarsely chopped anchovy fillets in oil, drained (or 1 to 1½ teaspoons anchovy paste), and 2 tablespoons capers, drained, to cooked garlic-oil mixture; reduce heat and stir until anchovies break up, about 30 seconds.

• Add ½ cup Gaeta, Kalamata, or green Sicilian olives, pitted and chopped, to cooked garlic-oil mixture; reduce heat and stir until olives are heated through, about 1 minute.

• Add 2 to 3 ounces crumbled firm goat cheese to tossed pasta; toss again.

• Add ⅓ cup chopped dried tomatoes to pasta with garlic-oil mixture and parsley; toss.

• Substitute 2 to 4 tablespoons chopped fresh basil, oregano, chives, or tarragon for parsley.

PASTA WITH TUNA PUTTANESCA

This tomatoless, no-cook version of puttanesca sauce is simply mouthwatering. The unusual mix of greens, shallots, capers, and lemon hits the spot. For the most authentic Italian flavor, use tuna packed in olive oil.

Prep: 15 minutes   Cook: 25 minutes

- 1 package (16 ounces) rotini or medium shells
- 3 tablespoons capers, drained and chopped
- 3 tablespoons finely chopped shallots
- ½ teaspoon freshly grated lemon peel
- 2 tablespoons red wine vinegar
- 1 tablespoon olive oil
- ½ teaspoon salt
- ¼ teaspoon coarsely ground black pepper
- 1 can (6 ounces) light tuna in olive oil
- 2 bunches watercress (4 to 6 ounces each), tough stems removed
- ½ cup loosely packed fresh basil leaves, chopped

1. In large saucepot, cook pasta as label directs. Drain, reserving ½ cup pasta water.

2. Meanwhile, in large bowl, with fork, mix capers, shallots, lemon peel, vinegar, oil, salt, and pepper until well combined. Add undrained tuna and watercress; toss.

3. In pasta saucepot, toss pasta, basil, tuna mixture, and reserved pasta water. Makes 6 main-dish servings.

Each serving: About 374 calories, 18g protein, 59g carbohydrate, 7g total fat (1g saturated), 11mg cholesterol, 630mg sodium.

LINGUINE WITH WHITE CLAM SAUCE

Start with fresh clams and add a few ingredients to cook up one of the best of all pasta dishes. Don't overcook the clams or they will become tough.

Prep: 15 minutes   Cook: 30 minutes

- ½ cup dry white wine
- 2 dozen littleneck clams, scrubbed (page 214)
- 1 package (16 ounces) linguine or spaghetti
- ¼ cup olive oil
- 1 large garlic clove, finely chopped
- ¼ teaspoon crushed red pepper
- ¼ cup chopped fresh parsley

1. In nonreactive 5-quart Dutch oven, heat wine to boiling over high heat. Add clams; cover and cook until clams open, 5 to 10 minutes, transferring clams to bowl as they open. Discard any clams that have not opened.

2. Strain clam broth through sieve lined with paper towels; set aside. When cool enough to handle, remove clams from shells and coarsely chop. Discard shells.

3. Meanwhile, in large saucepot, cook pasta as label directs. Drain.

4. Add oil, garlic, and crushed red pepper to same clean Dutch oven. Cook over medium heat, stirring occasionally, just until garlic turns golden. Stir in parsley, clams, and clam broth; heat just to simmering. Add pasta to Dutch oven and toss until combined. Makes 6 main-dish servings.

Each serving: About 427 calories, 19g protein, 59g carbohydrate, 11g total fat (1g saturated), 24mg cholesterol, 111mg sodium.

FETTUCCINE ALFREDO

....

Roman restaurateur Alfredo di Lello created this luscious, creamy dish in the early 1900s, and its popularity has never waned. Be sure to use freshly grated Parmesan cheese (preferably Italian Parmigiano-Reggiano) when making this indulgent pasta.

Prep: 10 minutes   Cook: 25 minutes

- 1 package (16 ounces) fettuccine
- 1½ cups heavy or whipping cream
- 1 tablespoon butter or margarine
- ½ teaspoon salt
- ¼ teaspoon coarsely ground black pepper
- ¾ cup freshly grated Parmesan cheese
  chopped fresh parsley

1. In large saucepot, cook pasta as label directs. Drain.

2. Meanwhile, in 2-quart saucepan, heat cream, butter, salt, and pepper to boiling over medium-high heat. Boil until sauce has thickened slightly, 2 to 3 minutes. In warm serving bowl, toss pasta with sauce and Parmesan. Sprinkle with parsley. Makes 6 main-dish servings.

Each serving: About 558 calories, 16g protein, 59g carbohydrate, 29g total fat (17g saturated), 96mg cholesterol, 532mg sodium.

FARFALLE WITH GORGONZOLA SAUCE

....

Farfalle, which means "butterflies" in Italian, are commonly called bow ties. Here, we've combined them with a creamy blue-cheese sauce and a sprinkling of toasted walnuts for fabulous flavor.

Prep: 10 minutes   Cook: 25 minutes

- 1 package (16 ounces) bow ties or penne
- 1 cup half-and-half or light cream
- ¾ cup chicken broth
- 4 ounces Gorgonzola or blue cheese, crumbled
- ¼ teaspoon coarsely ground black pepper
- 1 cup frozen peas, thawed
- ½ cup chopped walnuts, toasted

1. In large saucepot, cook pasta as label directs. Drain.

2. Meanwhile, in 2-quart saucepan, heat half-and-half and broth just to boiling over medium-high heat. Reduce heat to medium; cook 5 minutes. Add Gorgonzola and pepper, stirring constantly until cheese has melted and sauce is smooth. Stir in peas. In warm serving bowl, toss pasta with sauce; sprinkle with walnuts. Makes 6 main-dish servings.

Each serving: About 486 calories, 18g protein, 63g carbohydrate, 18g total fat (8g saturated), 31mg cholesterol, 499mg sodium.

PASTA PERK-UPS

TEST KITCHEN TIP

• Try slivered sun-dried tomatoes to dress up your favorite mac and cheese.

• A tablespoon or two of capers will pump up the flavor of a No-Cook Tomato Sauce (page 257) or embellish a jarred marinara. Add some pitted, chopped olives (and, if your family allows, even a minced anchovy), and you'll be on the way to making your own gutsy Italian-style puttanesca sauce.

• Freshly grated lemon peel, the king of zip, immediately brightens up a creamy seafood sauce.

• Dried mushrooms add rich flavor. You need to rehydrate them before adding them to the pasta: Cover them in boiling water and let soak 15 minutes. With a slotted spoon, remove the mushrooms, but don't discard the liquid! Rinse the mushrooms briefly to remove any grit, then drain them and chop if desired. The flavorful liquid, strained through a paper-towel-lined sieve, can be used to replace some liquid in your recipe. Dried mushrooms keep well in an airtight container in a cool, dry place for up to a year.

PASTA WITH BACON AND PEAS

··

You probably already have most of the ingredients for this dish on hand. The sauce is quickly prepared while the pasta is cooking.

Prep: 10 minutes   **Cook:** 20 minutes

- 1 package (16 ounces) thin spaghetti or vermicelli
- 1 package (10 ounces) frozen peas
- 4 slices bacon
- 1 medium onion, chopped
- 1 container (15 ounces) part-skim ricotta cheese
- ½ cup freshly grated Pecorino-Romano cheese
- ½ teaspoon salt
- ¼ teaspoon coarsely ground black pepper

1. In large saucepot, cook pasta as label directs. After pasta has cooked 6 minutes, add frozen peas to pasta water. Cook until pasta is tender, about 2 minutes longer. Drain, reserving 1 cup pasta water. Return pasta and peas to saucepot.

2. Meanwhile, in 12-inch skillet, cook bacon over medium heat until browned. With tongs, transfer bacon to paper towels to drain. Discard all but 1 tablespoon bacon drippings from skillet. Add onion and cook until tender and golden, about 10 minutes.

3. Add reserved pasta water, onion, ricotta, Romano, salt, and pepper to pasta and peas in saucepot; toss to combine. Crumble in bacon; toss again. Makes 4 main-dish servings.

Each serving: About 738 calories, 37mg protein, 104mg carbohydrate, 19g fat (9g saturated), 51mg cholesterol, 845mg sodium.

SPAGHETTI PIE WITH PROSCIUTTO AND PEAS

··

Pasta makes for a quick and economical meal, and this is a great weeknight change-up. Substitute bacon if prosciutto isn't available.

Prep: 25 minutes   **Bake:** 15 minutes

- 8 ounces thick spaghetti
- 4 large eggs
- 2 large egg whites
- 1 container (15 ounces) part-skim ricotta cheese or Reduced-Fat Ricotta (page 246)
- ¾ cup reduced-fat (2%) milk
- ⅛ teaspoon ground nutmeg
- ¼ teaspoon salt
- ¼ teaspoon ground black pepper
- 1 tablespoon butter or margarine
- 1 bunch green onions, cut into ¼-inch pieces (about 1 cup)
- 1 cup frozen peas
- 6 thin slices prosciutto (about 3 ounces)

1. Preheat oven to 350°F. In large saucepot, cook spaghetti as indicated on label but for 2 minutes less time than directed.

2. Meanwhile, in medium bowl, whisk eggs, egg whites, ricotta, milk, nutmeg, salt, and pepper until blended. Set aside.

In oven-safe nonstick 12-inch skillet, melt butter over medium heat. Add green onions and cook about 5 minutes or until softened. Remove skillet from heat.

3. Drain spaghetti. To green onions in skillet, add spaghetti and frozen peas; toss to combine. Pour egg mixture over pasta and arrange prosciutto slices on top.

4. Place skillet over medium-high heat and cook egg mixture 3 to 5 minutes or until edges just begin to set. Place skillet in oven and bake 15 minutes or until center is set. Slide pie onto large plate to serve. Makes 6 main-dish servings.

Each serving: About 375 calories, 25g protein, 38g carbohydrate, 13g total fat (6g saturated), 2g fiber, 175mg cholesterol, 700mg sodium.

SEAFOOD FRA DIAVOLO

·····················

Packed with shrimp, mussels, and rings of tender squid, this pasta is a seafood lover's dream.

Prep: 25 minutes   Cook: 1 hour

- 8 ounces cleaned squid
- 1 tablespoon olive oil
- 1 large garlic clove, finely chopped
- ¼ teaspoon crushed red pepper
- 1 can (28 ounces) plum tomatoes
- ½ teaspoon salt
- 1 dozen mussels, scrubbed and debearded (page 215)
- 8 ounces medium shrimp, shelled and deveined (page 221)
- 1 package (16 ounces) linguine or spaghetti
- ¼ cup chopped fresh parsley

1. Rinse squid and pat dry with paper towels. Slice squid bodies crosswise into ¼-inch rings. Cut tentacles into several pieces if they are large.

2. In nonreactive 4-quart saucepan, heat oil over medium heat. Add garlic and crushed red pepper; cook just until fragrant, about 30 seconds. Stir in tomatoes with their juice and salt, breaking up tomatoes with side of spoon. Heat to boiling over high heat. Add squid and heat to boiling. Reduce heat; cover and simmer 30 minutes. Remove cover and simmer 15 minutes longer. Increase heat to high. Add mussels; cover and cook 3 minutes. Stir in shrimp; cover and cook until mussels open and shrimp are opaque throughout, about 2 minutes longer. Discard any mussels that have not opened.

3. Meanwhile, in large saucepot, cook pasta as label directs. Drain. In warm serving bowl, toss pasta with seafood mixture and parsley. Makes 6 main-dish servings.

Each serving: About 410 calories, 25g protein, 65g carbohydrate, 5g total fat (1g saturated), 140mg cholesterol, 588mg sodium.

NEAPOLITAN PASTA SAUCE

·····················

This is the kind of old-time pasta sauce that simmers for hours, filling the kitchen with enticing aromas. It makes a big batch, enough to coat about 5 pounds of pasta, so plan to freeze the leftovers. Serve this richly flavored sauce with a sturdy pasta such as rigatoni.

Prep: 15 minutes   Cook: 4 hours 15 minutes

- 2 pounds boneless pork shoulder blade roast (fresh pork butt), trimmed
- 1 garlic clove, thinly sliced
- 1 tablespoon olive oil
- 1 pound sweet Italian-sausage links
- 8 ounces hot Italian-sausage links
- 2 large onions (12 ounces each), finely chopped
- 4 garlic cloves, finely chopped
- 4 cans (28 ounces each) plum tomatoes
- 1 can (28 ounces) tomato puree
- 1 tablespoon sugar
- ½ teaspoon salt

1. With small knife, make several slits in pork shoulder and insert garlic slices. In nonreactive 12-quart saucepot, heat oil over medium heat until very hot. Cook pork and sweet and hot sausages in batches until lightly browned, using slotted spoon to transfer meat to bowl as it is browned.

2. Add onions and chopped garlic to saucepot; cook until onion is tender, about 5 minutes. Add tomatoes with their juice, tomato puree, sugar, and salt; heat to boiling, breaking up tomatoes with side of spoon.

3. Return pork to saucepot. Reduce heat; partially cover and simmer 3 hours. Add sausage and cook until pork is very tender, about 45 minutes longer. Remove pork and cut into bite-size pieces; return to saucepot (keep sausages whole). Use 3 cups sauce to coat 1 pound pasta for 6 main-dish servings. Makes 16 cups.

Each ½ cup: About 139 calories, 9g protein, 5g carbohydrate, 9g total fat (3g saturated), 35mg cholesterol, 318mg sodium.

SPAGHETTI AND MEATBALLS

··

These large meatballs are all cooked at the same time in one skillet. If you prefer smaller meatballs, you'll need to cook them in two skillets or in batches, or simply bake them in a jelly-roll pan at 450°F for 20 minutes. If you like, substitute Leaner Meatballs (page 174).

Prep: 20 minutes   Cook: 1 hour

Marinara Sauce (page 254)

1½ pounds ground meat for meat loaf
    (beef, pork, and/or veal) or ground beef chuck

1 cup fresh bread crumbs (about 2 slices bread)

1 large egg

¼ cup freshly grated Pecorino-Romano or
   Parmesan cheese

¼ cup chopped fresh parsley

1 garlic clove, crushed with garlic press

1 teaspoon salt

¼ teaspoon ground black pepper

2 teaspoons olive oil

1 package (16 ounces) spaghetti

1. Prepare Marinara Sauce.

2. Meanwhile, prepare meatballs: In large bowl, combine ground meat, bread crumbs, egg, Pecorino-Romano, parsley, garlic, salt, and pepper just until blended but not overmixed. Shape into twelve 2-inch meatballs, handling meat as little as possible.

3. In nonstick 10-inch skillet, heat oil over medium heat until hot. Add meatballs and cook, gently turning, until browned and just cooked through, about 20 minutes. Add sauce to meatballs and heat to boiling, stirring to loosen browned bits from bottom of skillet. Reduce heat and simmer while you cook the pasta.

4. In large saucepot, cook pasta as label directs. Drain. In warm serving bowl, gently toss pasta with meatballs and sauce. Makes 6 main-dish servings.

Each serving: About 692 calories, 34g protein, 69g carbohydrate, 30g total fat (10g saturated), 129mg cholesterol, 1,077mg sodium.

CLASSIC BOLOGNESE SAUCE

··

A staple in Bologna, Italy, this tomato-based meat sauce, enriched with cream and mellowed by long simmering, is well worth the time. Freeze leftovers in small batches.

Prep: 10 minutes   Cook: 1 hour 25 minutes

2 tablespoons olive oil

1 medium onion, chopped

1 carrot, peeled and finely chopped

1 stalk celery, finely chopped

1½ pounds ground meat for meat loaf
    (beef, pork, and/or veal) or ground beef chuck

½ cup dry red wine

1 can (28 ounces) plum tomatoes, chopped

2 teaspoons salt

¼ teaspoon ground black pepper

⅛ teaspoon ground nutmeg

¼ cup heavy or whipping cream

1. In nonreactive 5-quart Dutch oven, heat oil over medium heat. Add onion, carrot, and celery and cook, stirring occasionally, until tender, about 10 minutes.

2. Add ground meat and cook, breaking up meat with side of spoon, until no longer pink. Stir in wine and heat to boiling. Stir in tomatoes with their juice, salt, pepper, and nutmeg. Heat to boiling over high heat. Reduce heat and simmer, stirring occasionally, 1 hour.

3. Stir in cream and heat through, stirring constantly. Use 2½ cups sauce to coat 1 pound pasta for 6 main-dish servings. Makes 5 cups.

Each ½ cup: About 210 calories, 13g protein, 6g carbohydrate, 15g fat (6g saturated fat), 1g fiber, 58mg cholesterol, 696mg sodium.

PENNE WITH SAUSAGE

....

This simple dish proves that a pasta sauce doesn't have to cook forever to be flavorful.

Prep: 15 minutes   Cook: 30 minutes

- 8 ounces sweet Italian-sausage links, casings removed
- 2 garlic cloves, finely chopped
- 1 pound mushrooms, trimmed and sliced
- 1 can (28 ounces) plum tomatoes
- 1 teaspoon sugar
- 3/4 teaspoon salt
- 1 package (16 ounces) penne or rotini

1. In 12-inch skillet, cook sausage and garlic over medium-high heat, breaking up sausage with side of spoon, until sausage is browned, about 5 minutes. Add mushrooms and cook over high heat, stirring, until all liquid has evaporated and mushrooms are browned. Stir in tomatoes with their juice, sugar, and salt, breaking up tomatoes with side of spoon; heat to boiling. Reduce heat and simmer until thickened, 5 to 8 minutes.

2. Meanwhile, in large saucepot, cook pasta as label directs. Drain. In warm serving bowl, toss pasta with sauce. Makes 4 main-dish servings.

Each serving: About 690 calories, 27g protein, 100g carbohydrate, 20g total fat (7g saturated), 43mg cholesterol, 1,283mg sodium.

A SIDE OF PASTA–FOUR WAYS

Cook 1 cup orzo or 1 3/4 cups mini bow-tie pasta as label directs. Then make one of these delicious side dishes.

Prep: 10 minutes   Cook: 25 minutes

CONFETTI PASTA

In 10-inch skillet, heat 2 teaspoons olive oil over medium heat. Add 2 carrots, shredded, 1 medium zucchini (8 ounces), shredded, 1 garlic clove, crushed with garlic press, 3/4 teaspoon salt, and 1/4 teaspoon coarsely ground black pepper and cook 5 minutes. Stir in cooked pasta; heat through. Makes 4 accompaniment servings.

Each serving: About 203 calories, 7g protein, 37g carbohydrate, 3g total fat (0g saturated), 0mg cholesterol, 490mg sodium.

PASTA WITH PEAS AND ONION

In 10-inch skillet, heat 2 teaspoons olive oil over medium heat. Add 1 small onion, chopped, and 2 tablespoons water and cook until onion is golden, about 10 minutes. Stir in cooked pasta and 1 cup frozen peas, thawed, and heat through. Makes 4 accompaniment servings.

Each serving: About 216 calories, 8g protein, 39g carbohydrate, 3g total fat (0g saturated), 0mg cholesterol, 81mg sodium.

ORANGE-FENNEL PASTA

In 10-inch skillet, heat 2 teaspoons olive oil over medium heat. Add 1 garlic clove, crushed with garlic press, 3/4 teaspoon salt, and 1/4 teaspoon coarsely ground black pepper and cook 30 seconds. Stir in 1 teaspoon freshly grated orange peel and 1/2 teaspoon fennel seeds, crushed. Stir in cooked pasta and 2 tablespoons chopped fresh parsley; heat through. Makes 4 accompaniment servings.

Each serving: About 181 calories, 6g protein, 32g carbohydrate, 3g total fat (0g saturated), 0mg cholesterol, 477mg sodium.

TUBETTI WITH LEMON AND CREAM

In 2-quart saucepan, combine 1/4 cup plus 2 tablespoons heavy cream, 1/2 teaspoon lemon peel, 1/4 teaspoon salt, and a pinch of pepper; heat to boiling over medium-high heat. Boil 1 minute. Stir in 1 1/2 cups tubetti (7 ounces), cooked as label directs, and 1 tablespoon chopped fresh parsley and cook over medium heat, stirring constantly, 1 minute. Transfer to warm serving bowl and sprinkle with 1 tablespoon chopped fresh parsley. Makes 6 accompaniment servings.

Each serving: About 175 calories, 5g protein, 25g carbohydrate, 6g total fat (3g saturated), 20mg cholesterol, 132mg sodium.

LASAGNA TOSS BOLOGNESE

....

If only lasagna, that perennial family favorite, didn't take two and a half hours to prepare and bake (and that's not counting the 15 minutes it needs once it's out of the oven to settle so it's easier to serve)! Luckily our streamlined version clocks in at just 30 minutes from saucepot to pasta bowl, without losing any of the robust flavors of the original.

Prep: 15 minutes   Cook: 15 minutes

- 1 package (16 ounces) lasagna noodles (see Tip)
- 2 teaspoons olive oil
- 1 pound lean ground beef or meatloaf mix (ground beef, pork, and veal)
- ½ cup dry red wine
- 1 jar (24 ounces) marinara sauce
- ⅓ cup whole milk
- ¾ cup part-skim ricotta cheese or Reduced-Fat Ricotta (page 246)
- ½ cup fresh basil, chopped
- ⅓ cup freshly grated Pecorino-Romano cheese
- ¼ teaspoon coarsely ground black pepper
- ⅓ cup shredded part-skim mozzarella cheese

1. In a large saucepot, cook lasagna noodles as label directs, but increase cooking time by 2 to 3 minutes or until just tender.

2. Meanwhile, in 12-inch skillet, heat oil over medium-high heat. Add meat and cook until no longer pink, breaking it up with spoon, about 3 minutes. (If using meatloaf mix, drain off fat after cooking.) Add wine; cook 2 to 3 minutes or until almost evaporated. Stir in marinara; heat to boiling. Simmer on low 5 minutes.

3. In bowl, stir ricotta with basil, Romano, and pepper; set aside.

4. Drain noodles; return to saucepot. Add meat sauce and mozzarella; toss well. Spoon onto 6 warm plates; top with dollops of ricotta mixture. Makes 6 main-dish servings.

Each serving: About 655 calories, 32g protein, 71g carbohydrate, 26g total fat (10g saturated), 4g fiber, 71mg cholesterol, 800mg sodium.

Tip: Tempted to cook up no-boil lasagna noodles to save time? Don't. They'll break apart when tossed.

LASAGNA TOSS WITH VEGGIES

Prepare recipe (left), but in step 2, in place of meat, use **12 ounces sliced cremini mushrooms** and **1 medium zucchini**, diced; cook 5 minutes. Omit milk. Stir in **1 bag (6 ounces) baby** spinach until wilted. Complete recipe as in steps 3 and 4.

Each serving: About 500 calories, 21g protein, 73g carbohydrate, 13g total fat (4g saturated), 9g fiber, 17mg cholesterol, 800mg sodium.

Lasagna Toss Bolognese

PASTA FOR LASAGNA

When you're shopping for lasagna noodles, you are faced with several options. *Domestic pasta* is on the thick side, whereas *imported pasta* is thinner and more delicate. Choosing one over the other is just a matter of personal preference.

No-boil pasta eliminates the need for boiling the pasta before assembling the lasagna. It has been pre-cooked, then dried: During baking it soaks up liquid from the other ingredients and softens. Follow the instructions on the package for cooking no-boil noodles properly. If you use your own recipe, stir about 1 cup of additional water or tomato juice into your finished sauce so it contains more liquid. Or use your recipe without any changes, but reconstitute the sheets of pasta before using: Let them soak in enough warm water to cover until supple, 5 to 10 minutes, then drain the noodles and assemble the lasagna.

CURLY MAC 'N' CHEESE

Kids will absolutely love the curly corkscrew pasta in this ever-popular supper dish.

Prep: 30 minutes   Bake: 25 minutes

- 1 package (16 ounces) rotini
- 6 cups milk
- 3 tablespoons cornstarch
- ¾ teaspoon salt
- ⅛ teaspoon ground nutmeg
- ½ cup freshly grated Parmesan cheese
- 8 ounces sharp Cheddar cheese, shredded (2 cups)

1. Preheat oven to 375°F. In large saucepot, cook pasta as label directs. Drain.

2. Meanwhile, in 4-quart saucepan, with wire whisk, mix milk, cornstarch, salt, and nutmeg until smooth. Cook over medium heat, whisking frequently, until mixture has thickened slightly and boils. Boil, whisking constantly, 1 minute. Remove pan from heat. Gradually whisk in Parmesan until cheese has melted and sauce is smooth.

3. Spoon pasta into shallow 3½-quart or 13" by 9" baking dish. Pour sauce over pasta and stir to thoroughly mix. Sprinkle Cheddar over top. Bake until Cheddar has melted and mixture is hot and bubbling, about 25 minutes. Makes 8 main-dish servings.

Each serving: About 476 calories, 23g protein, 54g carbohydrate, 18g total fat (11g saturated), 60mg cholesterol, 650mg sodium.

DRESS UP YOUR MAC 'N' CHEESE

 TEST KITCHEN TIP

Here are some delicious cheese and macaroni variations your family is sure to enjoy. Prepare as directed, replacing the Cheddar with:

- 4 ounces fontina and 4 ounces gorgonzola
- 4 ounces goat cheese and 4 ounces Monterey Jack
- 3 ounces sharp Cheddar, 3 ounces Asiago, 3 ounces dry Jack cheese
- 4 ounces sharp white Cheddar, 4 ounces Asiago

NORTHERN-STYLE LASAGNA

This is the classic lasagna of northern Italy: lasagna noodles separated by layers of full-flavored meat sauce, rich béchamel sauce, and a blend of cheeses. Here dried porcini mushrooms add additional flavor.

**Prep: 1 hour 15 minutes plus standing
Bake: 50 minutes**

Meat Sauce

- ½ cup boiling water
- ½ ounce dried porcini mushrooms (about ½ cup)
- 2 tablespoons extra-virgin olive oil
- 3 large garlic cloves, finely chopped
- 2 large carrots, peeled and finely chopped
- 1 large onion (12 ounces), chopped
- 8 ounces lean (90%) ground beef
- 8 ounces ground pork
- 8 ounces ground veal
- ½ cup dry red wine
- 1 can (28 ounces) diced tomatoes
- ½ teaspoon salt

Béchamel Sauce

- 4 tablespoons butter or margarine
- ⅓ cup all-purpose flour
- ½ teaspoon freshly ground black pepper
- ½ teaspoon salt
- ¼ teaspoon ground nutmeg
- 2½ cups milk

Cheese Filling

- 8 ounces Fontina cheese, shredded (2 cups)
- ½ cup freshly grated Parmesan cheese

- 1 package (8 to 9 ounces) no-boil lasagna noodles (6½" by 3½" each)

1. Prepare meat sauce: In small bowl, pour boiling water over porcini mushrooms; let stand 15 minutes.

2. Meanwhile, in 12-inch skillet, heat oil over medium heat until hot. Add garlic, carrots, and onion and cook, stirring occasionally, until vegetables are tender, about 15 minutes. Increase heat to high. Add beef, pork, and veal and cook, breaking up meat with side of spoon, until meat is browned, about 10 minutes.

Northern-Style Lasagna

3. Meanwhile, with slotted spoon, remove porcini, reserving liquid. Rinse mushrooms to remove any grit, then coarsely chop. Strain mushroom liquid through sieve lined with paper towels; set aside.

4. Add wine to meat in skillet and heat to boiling; boil until most of liquid has evaporated, 2 to 3 minutes. Stir in tomatoes with their juice, salt, mushrooms, and reserved soaking liquid; heat to boiling. Reduce heat to medium-low; simmer, uncovered, until sauce thickens slightly, about 20 minutes, stirring occasionally.

5. Preheat oven to 375°F. Meanwhile, prepare béchamel sauce: In nonreactive 2-quart saucepan, melt butter over medium heat. With wire whisk, stir in flour, pepper, salt, and nutmeg and cook 1 minute. Whisking continuously, gradually add milk and heat to boiling. Remove saucepan from heat; set aside.

6. Prepare filling: In small bowl, toss Fontina and Parmesan until well combined.

7. Assemble lasagna: In bottom of 13" by 9" baking dish, evenly spread 1 cup meat sauce. Arrange 4 noodles over sauce, overlapping slightly to fit and making sure they do not touch sides of dish. (If your package of lasagna noodles has only 12 noodles, use 3 noodles per layer and do not overlap them.) Spoon about 1½ cups meat sauce over noodles. Spread about ⅔ cup béchamel sauce over meat sauce and sprinkle with about ½ cup cheese filling. Repeat layering 3 more times with remaining noodles, meat sauce, béchamel sauce, and cheese.

8. Cover lasagna with foil and bake 30 minutes. Remove foil and bake until heated through and cheese is lightly browned, about 20 minutes longer. Let stand 15 minutes for easier serving. Makes 10 main-dish servings.

Each serving: About 460 calories, 29g protein, 34g carbohydrate, 23g total fat (11g saturated), 98mg cholesterol, 933mg sodium.

SAUSAGE-AND-PEPPER BAKED ZITI

....

This new twist on baked ziti will please kids as well as adults. If you like, assemble it up to a day ahead, refrigerate, and bake just before serving.

Prep: 40 minutes plus standing
Bake: 20 minutes

1½ pounds sweet and/or hot Italian-sausage links, cut crosswise into 1-inch-thick pieces

4 garlic cloves, thinly sliced

2 large green, yellow, and/or red peppers, cut into ¼-inch-thick slices

1 jumbo onion (about 1 pound), cut in half, then cut crosswise into ¼-inch-thick slices

1 can (28 ounces) whole tomatoes in puree

1 can (15 ounces) tomato puree

1 teaspoon salt

1 pound ziti or penne pasta

1 package (8 ounces) part-skim mozzarella cheese, cut into ½-inch cubes

½ cup freshly grated Pecorino-Romano cheese

1. Prepare sauce: In deep nonstick 12-inch skillet, cook sausage over medium-high heat, stirring occasionally, until browned on all sides, about 5 minutes.

2. Reduce heat to medium. Discard all but 2 tablespoons sausage drippings from skillet. Add garlic, peppers, and onion to sausage and cook, covered, until vegetables are tender, about 10 minutes, stirring occasionally. Stir in tomatoes with their puree, tomato puree, and salt; heat to boiling over medium heat, breaking up tomatoes with side of spoon. Reduce heat to low; cover and simmer 10 minutes.

3. Meanwhile, preheat oven to 400°F. In large saucepot, cook pasta 2 minutes less than directed on label. Drain pasta; return to saucepot. Add sauce and stir until pasta is evenly coated. Add mozzarella; toss to combine.

4. Transfer pasta mixture to 13" by 9" baking dish and spread evenly; sprinkle with Romano. Bake, uncovered, until hot and bubbling and top is brown, 20 to 25 minutes. Let stand 10 minutes for easier serving. Makes 10 main-dish servings.

Each serving: About 520 calories, 25g protein, 49g carbohydrate, 23g total fat (10g saturated), 65mg cholesterol, 1,190mg sodium.

BAKED RIGATONI AND PEAS

....

This is a terrific dish for a big party. Place one dish on the buffet table, and keep the other warm in the oven. To make a day ahead, prepare through the making of the topping in Step 4. Cover and refrigerate the rigatoni and topping separately. To serve, sprinkle the topping over the rigatoni and bake, allowing for some extra baking time since the rigatoni will be cold.

Prep: 45 minutes   Bake: 30 minutes

14 tablespoons butter or margarine (1¾ sticks)

½ cup all-purpose flour

7 cups milk, warmed

2 cups freshly grated Parmesan cheese

2 teaspoons plus 1 tablespoon salt

2 packages (16 ounces each) rigatoni or ziti

1 bag (20 ounces) frozen peas, thawed

2 cans (14½ ounces each) diced tomatoes

1 cup loosely packed fresh basil leaves, thinly sliced

½ cup plain dried bread crumbs

1. Prepare cheese sauce: In heavy 4-quart saucepan, melt 10 tablespoons butter over low heat. Add flour and cook, stirring, 2 minutes. With wire whisk, gradually whisk in warm milk. Cook over medium heat, stirring constantly with wooden spoon, until sauce has thickened and boils. Reduce heat and simmer, stirring frequently, about 5 minutes. Stir in 1½ cups Parmesan and 2 teaspoons salt. Remove from heat.

2. Meanwhile, in 12-quart saucepot, cook pasta as label directs, adding remaining 1 tablespoon salt to water; drain. Return rigatoni to saucepot.

3. Preheat oven to 350°F. Pour cheese sauce over rigatoni in saucepot, stirring to combine. Stir in peas, tomatoes with their juice, and basil. Spoon pasta mixture into two shallow 3½- to 4-quart casseroles or two 13" by 9" baking dishes.

4. In small saucepan, melt remaining 4 tablespoons butter over low heat. Remove from heat and stir in bread crumbs and remaining ½ cup Parmesan. Sprinkle topping over pasta. Bake until hot and bubbling and topping is golden, 30 to 35 minutes. Makes 20 main-dish servings.

Each serving: About 390 calories, 15g protein, 48g carbohydrate, 15g total fat (9g saturated), 41mg cholesterol, 703mg sodium.

BUTTERNUT SQUASH RAVIOLI

....

Jumbo ravioli filled with squash make an impressive dinner. And our easy cheats cut the prep time by more than an hour: Wonton wrappers, found in most markets, substitute for laboriously homemade pasta, while frozen butternut squash gets dressed up with freshly grated Parmesan.

Prep: 30 minutes   Cook: 15 minutes

- 1 teaspoon olive oil
- 1 small onion (4 to 6 ounces), finely chopped
- 1 package (12 ounces) frozen butternut squash
- ¼ cup freshly grated Parmesan cheese
- 2 tablespoons plain dried bread crumbs
- 1 large egg, lightly beaten
- pinch nutmeg
- ³/₈ teaspoon salt
- ³/₈ teaspoon ground black pepper
- 1 large egg white
- 1 teaspoon water
- 1 package (12 ounces) wonton wrappers (about 50 wrappers)
- 3 tablespoons butter
- 1 tablespoon thinly sliced fresh sage leaves

1. In small nonstick skillet, heat oil on medium 1 minute. Add onion and cook about 12 minutes or until tender and lightly browned, stirring occasionally. Cook squash in microwave as label directs; cool slightly.

2. In medium bowl, combine onion, squash, Parmesan, bread crumbs, whole egg, nutmeg, and ¼ teaspoon each salt and pepper. In small bowl, whisk together egg white and water.

3. Place 1 wonton wrapper on work surface. With pastry brush, brush egg white along edges; place 1 rounded tablespoon squash filling in center of wrapper, keeping filling away from edges. Top with second wrapper; press down firmly around filling to seal ravioli, pushing out any trapped air. Place ravioli on cookie sheet. Repeat with remaining filling and wrappers, using a second cookie sheet so that ravioli do not overlap. Let ravioli dry 30 minutes, turning over halfway through to evenly dry both sides.

Butternut Squash Ravioli

4. Ten minutes before cooking ravioli, heat large saucepot of salted water to boiling on high.

5. Add ravioli to pot; cook 3 to 5 minutes or until tender, stirring gently to separate ravioli.

6. Meanwhile, in 4-quart saucepan, cook butter on medium 3 to 4 minutes or until golden-brown, stirring. Remove from heat; stir in sage and ⅛ teaspoon each salt and pepper.

7. With large slotted spoon, lift out ravioli one at a time; drain, still held in spoon, on paper towels. Transfer ravioli to saucepan with butter; gently stir to coat. Makes 4 main-dish servings.

Each serving: About 455 calories, 15g protein, 66g carbohydrate, 15g total fat (8g saturated), 3g fiber, 89mg cholesterol, 1,025mg sodium.

GNOCCHI

Usually served as a first course, these Italian potato dumplings are perfect with Marinara Sauce (page 254) or Neapolitan Sauce (page 266). Or drizzle with butter, top with Parmesan cheese, and broil just until the cheese has melted.

Prep: 1 hour   Cook: 30 minutes

5   all-purpose potatoes (1½ pounds)
1   teaspoon salt
1½ cups all-purpose flour

1. In 4-quart saucepan, heat potatoes and enough *water* to cover to boiling over high heat. Reduce heat; cover and simmer until potatoes are tender, 20 to 25 minutes. Drain. Cool slightly; peel potatoes.

2. Press warm potatoes through food mill or ricer. With wooden spoon, stir in salt and flour until dough begins to come together. Gently press dough into a ball; divide in half.

3. On floured surface, with floured hands, knead each dough half until smooth. Divide each half into 6 equal pieces. On lightly floured surface, roll one piece of dough at a time into about ¾-inch-thick rope. Cut rope into ¾-inch lengths.

4. Place one piece of dough on inside curve of fork tines, gently pressing on dough with thumb as you roll dough along tines. Allow dough to drop off fork, slightly curling in on itself, forming an oval. One side of gnocchi will have ridges and opposite side will have an indentation. Repeat rolling, cutting, and shaping with remaining dough. (Gnocchi can be made up to 4 hours ahead to this point. Arrange in single layer in floured jelly-roll pan; cover and refrigerate.)

5. In 5-quart saucepot, heat *4 quarts water* to boiling over high heat. Add one third of gnocchi to boiling water. When gnocchi float to surface, cook 30 seconds. With slotted spoon, transfer gnocchi to warm shallow serving bowl. Repeat with remaining gnocchi. Makes 8 first-course servings.

Each serving without sauce: About 160 calories, 4g protein, 35g carbohydrate, 0g total fat, 0mg cholesterol, 295mg sodium.

DRIED FRUIT KUGEL

This heavenly low-fat version of sweet noodle pudding is studded with dried plums. If you prefer an even sweeter dish, use dates.

Prep: 20 minutes   Bake: 35 minutes

8   ounces wide egg noodles
1   container (8 ounces) low-fat (1%) cottage cheese
1   container (8 ounces) reduced-fat sour cream
¼   cup packed brown sugar
1   large egg
⅓   cup water
1   teaspoon vanilla extract
1   cup chopped dried plums (prunes) or dates

1. Preheat oven to 350°F. In medium saucepot, cook noodles as label directs. Drain.

2. In large bowl, with wire whisk, mix cottage cheese, sour cream, brown sugar, egg, water, and vanilla. Add prunes and noodles and toss well. Spoon mixture into 9-inch square baking dish. Bake until golden brown, about 35 minutes. Serve warm or at room temperature. Makes 6 dessert or accompaniment servings.

Each serving: About 347 calories, 14g protein, 56g carbohydrate, 8g total fat (3g saturated), 85mg cholesterol, 229mg sodium.

RICOTTA GNOCCHI WITH BROWNED BUTTER AND SAGE

....

They are also delicious with Marinara Sauce (page 254) and a sprinkling of Parmesan.

Prep: 1 hour   Cook: 17 minutes

- 3 tablespoons butter
- 1 teaspoon chopped fresh sage
- ³/₄ teaspoon salt
- ¹/₄ teaspoon ground black pepper
- 1 container (15 ounces) ricotta cheese
- 6 tablespoons freshly grated Parmesan cheese
- ³/₄ cup chopped fresh parsley
- ³/₄ cup all-purpose flour or as needed

1. Prepare sage butter: In 2-quart saucepan, melt butter over medium heat. Continue to cook, stirring, until butter turns golden brown. (If butter gets too dark, it will be bitter). Remove from heat and stir in sage, ¹/₄ teaspoon salt, and pepper; set aside.

2. In medium bowl, combine ricotta, Parmesan, parsley, and remaining ¹/₂ teaspoon salt. Sprinkle flour over ricotta mixture and, with your hands, work mixture into soft, smooth dough. If dough is sticky, add some flour. Work dough just until flour is incorporated into cheese mixture; do not overwork.

3. Break off piece of dough; on lightly floured surface, roll into ³/₄-inch-thick rope. (If rope doesn't hold together, return to bowl with remaining dough and work in more flour.) Cut dough rope into ³/₄-inch lengths. Place one piece of dough on inside curve of fork tines, gently pressing on dough with thumb as you roll dough along tines. Allow dough to drop off fork, slightly curling in on itself, forming an oval. One side of gnocchi will have ridges and opposite side will have an indentation. Repeat rolling, cutting, and shaping with remaining dough. (Gnocchi can be made up to 4 hours ahead to this point. Arrange in single layer in floured jelly-roll pan; cover and refrigerate.)

4. In 5-quart saucepot, heat *4 quarts water* to boiling over high heat. Add half of gnocchi and cook until gnocchi float to surface, 2 to 3 minutes. With slotted spoon, transfer gnocchi to warm shallow serving bowl. Repeat with remaining gnocchi. To serve, toss gnocchi with sage butter. Makes 8 first-course servings.

Each serving: About 196 calories, 9g protein, 11g carbohydrate, 13g total fat (8g saturated), 42mg cholesterol, 394mg sodium.

Ricotta Gnocchi with Browned Butter and Sage

SPICY SZECHUAN NOODLES

....

Once you cook up these flavorful noodles, you may never order them from take-out again.

Prep: 10 minutes   Cook: 25 minutes

- 1½ pounds ground pork
- 3 garlic cloves, crushed with garlic press
- 3 tablespoons dry sherry
- 3 tablespoons grated, peeled fresh ginger
- 3 tablespoons soy sauce
- ¾ teaspoon crushed red pepper
- 1 can (14 to 14½ ounces) chicken broth, or 1¾ cups Chicken Broth (page 70)
- ¼ cup peanut butter
- 1 tablespoon vegetable oil
- 2 bunches green onions, cut into 2-inch pieces
- 1 package (16 ounces) linguine or thin spaghetti
- 1 tablespoon Asian sesame oil or hot chili oil (optional)

1. In medium bowl, mix pork, garlic, sherry, ginger, soy sauce, and crushed red pepper until blended but not overmixed. In 4-cup measuring cup, with fork, stir broth and peanut butter until well blended.

2. In 12-inch skillet, heat oil over high heat. Add green onions and cook until wilted, 2 to 3 minutes. Transfer onions to another medium bowl. In same skillet, in batches, cook pork, breaking up meat with side of spoon, just until it is no longer pink, 1 to 2 minutes.

3. Return onions to pork mixture in skillet and stir in broth mixture; heat to boiling over high heat. Reduce heat to medium; cook, uncovered, until mixture thickens slightly, 12 to 14 minutes.

4. Meanwhile, in large saucepot, cook pasta as label directs. Drain pasta; return to saucepot. Add sesame oil, if using; toss to coat. Transfer linguine to large serving bowl; top with pork mixture. Makes 6 main-dish servings.

Each serving: About 560 calories, 38g protein, 63g carbohydrate, 16g total fat (4g saturated), 69mg cholesterol, 905mg sodium.

SZECHUAN PEANUT NOODLES

....

Loaded with taste and texture, this quick-and-easy dish is sure to please the peanut butter lovers in your family—adults as well as children. Turn this tasty noodle dish into a hearty main dish by tossing in cooked shrimp or shredded deli roast chicken.

Prep: 15 minutes   Cook: 10 minutes

- 1 package (16 ounces) linguine or spaghetti
- 4 ounces snow peas, strings removed
- 1 small cucumber (6 ounces), peeled, seeded, and cut into 2" by ¼" matchstick strips
  Asian Peanut Sauce (page 506)
- ¼ cup unsalted dry roasted peanuts, coarsely chopped
- 2 green onions, chopped

1. In large saucepot, cook linguine as label directs. Add snow peas during last 1 minute of cooking time. Drain linguini and snow peas and rinse with cold water until cool. Drain well.

2. Remove snow peas and cut into ¼-inch-wide matchstick strips.

3. In large bowl, combine Asian Peanut Sauce and linguine. Add snow peas and cucumber; toss until linguine is coated with sauce. Sprinkle peanuts and green onions on top. Makes 5 main-dish or 8 accompaniment servings.

Each main-dish serving: About 618 calories, 22g protein, 81g carbohydrate, 24g total fat (4g saturated), 0mg cholesterol, 916mg sodium.

PAD THAI

....

Authentic Pad Thai is made with rice noodles (use the ⅛-inch-wide ones) that are available at Asian markets. If you can't find them, use angel hair pasta or linguine (cooked according to the package directions).

Prep: 25 minutes plus soaking noodles
Cook: 5 minutes

1	package (7 to 8 ounces) rice stick noodles (rice vermicelli) or 8 ounces angel hair pasta
¼	cup fresh lime juice
¼	cup Asian fish sauce (nam pla, page 26)
2	tablespoons sugar
1	tablespoon vegetable oil
8	ounces medium shrimp, shelled and deveined (page 221), then cut lengthwise in half
2	garlic cloves, finely chopped
¼	teaspoon crushed red pepper
3	large eggs, lightly beaten
6	ounces bean sprouts (2 cups), rinsed and drained
⅓	cup unsalted roasted peanuts, coarsely chopped
3	green onions, thinly sliced
½	cup loosely packed fresh cilantro leaves lime wedges

1. In large bowl, soak rice stick noodles, if using, in enough *hot water* to cover for 20 minutes. Drain. With kitchen shears, cut noodles into 4-inch lengths. If using angel hair pasta, break in half, cook in large saucepot as label directs, drain, and rinse with cold running water.

2. Meanwhile, in small bowl, combine lime juice, fish sauce, and sugar. Assemble all remaining ingredients and place next to stove.

3. In 12-inch skillet, heat oil over high heat until hot. Add shrimp, garlic, and crushed red pepper; cook, stirring, 1 minute. Add eggs and cook, stirring, until just set, about 20 seconds. Add drained noodles and cook, stirring, 2 minutes. Add fish-sauce mixture, half of bean sprouts, half of peanuts, and half of green onions; cook, stirring, 1 minute.

4. Transfer Pad Thai to warm platter or serving bowl. Top with remaining bean sprouts and sprinkle with remaining peanuts, remaining green onions, and cilantro. Serve with lime wedges. Makes 4 main-dish servings.

Each serving: About 495 calories, 25g protein, 65g carbohydrate, 17g total fat (3g saturated), 235mg cholesterol, 827mg sodium.

Pad Thai

ASIAN NOODLES

Noodles are a worldwide favorite. In Asia, the purported area of their origin, they are consumed for breakfast, lunch, and dinner, and they are simmered in broth, stir-fried with meat and/or vegetables, and deep-fried. They are categorized not by country but by the type of flour—bean, rice, or wheat—from which they are made. Asian noodles are not interchangeable because some require different amounts of presoaking or precooking, and others do not. For the best results, use what your recipe calls for. Asian noodles are available fresh, dried, and frozen at Asian markets, specialty stores, and some well-stocked supermarkets.

9
BEANS, RICE & OTHER GRAINS

BEANS

For many cultures, beans and grains are the major source of protein. Although this low-fat, high-fiber dynamic duo also provides a healthful amount of minerals and vitamins, the protein in beans or grains alone is incomplete. Luckily, the amino acids missing from beans can be found in grains, and vice versa, so when served together, they create a complete protein. Beans or grains can also be served along with small amounts of meat or dairy to complete the protein.

Dry beans encompass a variety of legumes, including split peas and lentils. Since tofu is made from soybeans (actually soy milk), it is included here as well.

Dry beans keep for about one year, but they become less flavorful and drier as time passes, and older beans take longer to cook. Buy them in small quantities and use within six months. Store in an airtight container in a cool, dry place.

Canned beans are a great time-saver because they don't require soaking or cooking. However, they do need to be rinsed under cold water and drained before being used. This quick rinse freshens their flavor and removes some of their sodium. One can of beans (15 to 19 ounces) yields about 2 cups beans once drained.

SOAKING DRY BEANS

Before soaking, always sort through beans to remove tiny stones or debris. Place the beans in a colander and rinse well with cold water. Transfer the beans to a bowl. (Dry beans rehydrate to at least double their size, so use a large bowl.) Add enough cold water to cover by 2 inches. The standard overnight soaking time is really for the cook's convenience. The job is done when the beans have swelled to about double their size, which takes about four hours, but beans can be soaked for up to 24 hours. In hot weather, to prevent the beans from fermenting, refrigerate them while they soak.

When time is of the essence, use this quick-soak technique: Combine the beans and water in a pot and heat to boiling; cook for three minutes. Remove from the heat, cover tightly, and set aside for one hour. Drain and rinse the beans.

COOKING DRY BEANS

There are two reasons to soak dried beans before they're cooked. Soaking returns moisture to the beans and softens them. In so doing, it reduces the cooking time and also allows some of the hard-to-digest complex sugars to dissolve in the water.

There is an enormous range of cooking times for dry beans. Use the directions on the package as a guide, then taste often to check for doneness.

Dry beans should always be cooked in soft water or they will be tough. If you live in an area with hard water, be sure to add a pinch of baking soda to the cooking water. Because water boils at a lower temperature at high altitudes, beans will take longer to cook, so be sure they are well soaked and softened before cooking. Adding salt to beans at the beginning of cooking toughens the skins and increases the cooking time. But beans usually taste better when seasoned early, so we often use a minimal amount of salt when the cooking begins, then add the remainder at the end.

BEAN YIELDS

Although the volume changes with each bean variety, in general, 1 cup dried beans yields about 2 cups cooked beans. Large beans, like limas, yield about 2½ cups, whereas small beans, such as black beans, yield just under 2 cups. Cover leftover cooked beans with some of their cooking liquid in airtight containers; refrigerate for up to five days or freeze for up to six months.

BEANS AND BEAN PRODUCTS GLOSSARY

Black Also called turtle beans. They're the major component of black bean soup and burrito fillings; often mixed with rice for greater nutrition.

Black-eyed peas Beige beans with a black circular "eye," they are also called cowpeas.

Clockwise from left: Black-eyed peas, garbanzo beans, red beans

Fava Also known as broad beans, these flat light-brown beans resemble large limas.

Garbanzo Also called chickpeas, they're best known as the base for hummus.

Great Northern These white beans have a delicate flavor. They can be used in place of other white beans in most recipes.

Lima Also called butter beans, these large oval beans hold their shape well when cooked.

Miso Used in Japanese cooking, this is a salty paste made from fermented soybeans. Several varieties are available: the lighter the color, the milder the flavor.

Navy (pea) Small white beans, also called Yankee beans. They're most often used in baked bean dishes.

Pink Small oval, pinky-beige beans (called *habichuelas rosadas* in Spanish) with a soft creamy texture. Good for chilis, soups, and refried beans.

Pinto Spanish for "speckled," these pale pink beans have reddish brown streaks. They are used in refried beans, soups, and stews.

Red Small red beans that are the main ingredient in red beans and rice. They are also called chili or Mexican red beans.

Red kidney Good all-purpose beans that have a firm, burgundy-colored skin, sweet and pale flesh, and a slightly mealy texture.

Split peas (yellow or green) Dried peas that have been peeled and split in half.

Tofu Made from soy milk that has been coagulated and pressed into cubes. Tofu can be extra-firm, firm, or soft. Silken tofu, sold in aseptic boxes, has not been pressed. Available soft or firm, this tofu is more delicate than the pressed variety.

Clockwise from left: Great Northern beans, white kidney beans, pink beans

White kidney (cannellini) These beans are creamier and milder than the red variety.

KNOW YOUR LENTILS

Protein-packed lentils don't need to be presoaked, and they cook faster than other dried beans.

Black beluga lentils These tiny lentils are named for their caviarlike appearance.

Brown lentils This common variety of lentils has a firm texture and a mild, nutty flavor.

Green lentils Popular in European cooking, they have a firm texture and a nutty, earthy taste.

Red lentils A smaller round variety, they become yellow and soft when cooked; often used in Indian dals.

Small green French lentils (Puy) These tiny plump lentils are considered to have superior flavor. They cook quickly, hold their shape well, and have a nutty taste.

HOPPIN' JOHN

This moist and delicious rice-and-black-eyed-pea mixture is served in the South on New Year's Day for luck: The peas represent coins, ensuring a prosperous year.

Prep: 15 minutes   Cook: 1 hour

- 1 tablespoon vegetable oil
- 2 stalks celery, chopped
- 1 large onion (12 ounces), chopped
- 1 red pepper, chopped
- 2 garlic cloves, finely chopped
- 1 package (16 ounces) dry black-eyed peas, rinsed and picked through
- 1 large smoked ham hock (12 ounces)
- 4 cups water
- 2 cans (14½ ounces each) chicken broth or 3½ cups Chicken Broth (page 70)
- 2 teaspoons salt
- ¼ teaspoon crushed red pepper
- 1 bay leaf
- 2 cups regular long-grain rice

1. In 4-quart saucepan, heat oil over medium heat; add celery, onion, and chopped red pepper. Cook, stirring frequently, until onion is golden, about 10 minutes. Add garlic; cook 2 minutes longer.

2. Add black-eyed peas, ham hock, water, broth, 1 teaspoon salt, crushed red pepper, and bay leaf to celery mixture; heat to boiling over high heat. Reduce heat; cover and simmer, stirring occasionally, until black-eyed peas are tender, about 40 minutes. Discard bay leaf.

3. Prepare rice as label directs, adding remaining 1 teaspoon salt. (Do not add butter or margarine.)

4. In large bowl, combine pea mixture and rice. Makes 14 cups or 18 accompaniment servings.

Each serving: About 188 calories, 9g protein, 33g carbohydrate, 2g total fat (0g saturated), 3mg cholesterol, 549mg sodium.

OLD-FASHIONED BAKED BEANS

An heirloom recipe for not-too-sweet baked beans. This makes a batch big enough for a Fourth-of-July barbecue or a winter potluck party.

Prep: 15 minutes plus soaking beans
Bake: 3 hours 30 minutes

- 2 packages (16 ounces each) dry navy (pea) beans, soaked and drained (page 279)
- 7½ cups water
- 4 slices bacon, cut into 1-inch pieces, or 4 ounces salt pork, finely chopped
- 2 medium onions, chopped
- ½ cup dark molasses
- ⅓ cup packed brown sugar, preferably dark
- 5 teaspoons salt
- 4 teaspoons dry mustard

Preheat oven to 350°F. In 8-quart Dutch oven, combine beans and water; heat to boiling over high heat. Cover and place in oven. Bake 1 hour. Stir in bacon, onions, molasses, brown sugar, salt, and dry mustard. Cover and bake, stirring occasionally, 1 hour. Remove cover and bake until sauce is thickened and coats beans, 1 hour 30 minutes to 2 hours longer. Makes about 11 cups or 14 accompaniment servings.

Each serving: About 312 calories, 15g protein, 54g carbohydrate, 5g total fat (2g saturated), 4mg cholesterol, 895mg sodium.

HAM HOCKS

Ham hocks, a traditional ingredient in Southern cooking, are used to flavor greens and other vegetables. Their delicious smoky flavor makes them a "must" for split pea soup, especially when a ham bone is not available.

The hock, which is the ankle part of a smoked ham, doesn't contain enough meat to be eaten on its own. Smoked ham hocks are found in supermarkets in the refrigerated meat case alongside other pork products, and are usually sold in packages of two or three. Wrap unused hocks in heavy-duty foil and freeze for up to six months.

QUICK "BAKED" BEANS

....

With convenience ingredients and a few pantry staples, you can have authentic-tasting baked beans on the table in only 25 minutes.

Prep: 10 minutes   Cook: 15 minutes

- 2 teaspoons olive oil
- 1 small onion, chopped
- 1 cup ketchup
- ½ cup water
- 3 tablespoons light (mild) molasses
- 1 tablespoon Dijon mustard
- ½ teaspoon Worcestershire sauce
- ¼ teaspoon salt
  pinch ground cloves
- 1 can (15 to 19 ounces) black beans,
  rinsed and drained
- 1 can (15 to 19 ounces) red kidney beans,
  rinsed and drained
- 1 can (15 to 19 ounces) pink beans,
  rinsed and drained
- 1 can (15 to 19 ounces) white beans,
  such as Great Northern, rinsed and drained

1. In 4-quart saucepan, heat oil over medium-low heat. Add onion and cook until tender and golden, 5 to 8 minutes.

2. Stir in ketchup, water, molasses, mustard, Worcestershire, salt, and cloves until blended. Add black, red kidney, pink, and white beans; heat to boiling over high heat. Reduce heat; cover and simmer 5 minutes. Makes about 6 cups or 8 accompaniment servings.

Each serving: About 233 calories, 12g protein, 43g carbohydrate, 2g total fat (0g saturated), 0mg cholesterol, 709mg sodium.

REFRIED BEANS

....

As a Mexican-style side dish, refried beans are hard to beat. Lard is the traditional cooking medium, but we prefer the smoky flavor of bacon.

Prep: 10 minutes   Cook: 22 minutes

- 3 slices bacon, coarsely chopped
- 2 tablespoons water
- 1 medium onion, chopped
- 3 garlic cloves, finely chopped
- 2 cans (15 to 19 ounces each) pinto beans, rinsed
  and drained
- ¾ cup chicken broth

1. In 12-inch skillet, cook bacon with water over medium heat until browned. With slotted spoon, transfer bacon to paper towels to drain.

2. Add onion and garlic to drippings in skillet; cook, stirring frequently, until onion is tender, about 7 minutes. Add beans and ¼ cup broth. With potato masher or wooden spoon, mash beans. Continue cooking beans until liquid has been absorbed, about 3 minutes. Add ¼ cup broth and stir until beans are piping hot and almost all liquid has been absorbed, about 3 minutes. Add remaining ¼ cup broth and heat to boiling. Spoon onto platter and sprinkle with bacon. Makes 4 cups or 4 accompaniment servings.

Each serving: About 241 calories, 11g protein, 25g carbohydrate, 11g total fat (4g saturated), 11mg cholesterol, 661mg sodium.

BAKED BEAN ADD-INS

Here are some easy ways to vary the flavor of baked beans:
- Stir in a few slices of crisp-cooked bacon.
- Add some diced ham or smoked boneless pork chop.
- Add a few drops of hickory liquid smoke.
- Substitute a favorite barbecue sauce for the ketchup.

- Use yellow mustard instead of Dijon.
- Add about 1 tablespoon minced chipotles in adobo.
- Stir in a little chili powder.
- Add some maple syrup or honey.
- Transfer the simmered beans to a shallow baking dish; top with buttered crumbs, and run under the broiler.

10 IDEAS FOR . . . CANNED BEANS

Begin by rinsing and draining 1 to 2 cans of black or red kidney beans (each 15 to 19 ounces).

BLACK BEAN DIP

In food processor, puree 1 can beans with 1 tablespoon fresh lime juice, 1 teaspoon freshly grated lime peel, and 2 teaspoons chipotle pepper sauce. Transfer to small bowl and stir in 1/4 cup chopped cilantro leaves and 2 plum tomatoes, seeded and chopped. Serve with tortilla chips—or for a healthier alternative, try carrot sticks, red pepper strips, or jicama slices. Makes about 2 cups.

BLACK BEAN SALAD

In medium bowl, combine 1 can beans, 1 chopped red pepper, 1 drained can (15 1/4 ounces) corn kernels, 1/3 cup chopped cilantro leaves, and 2 tablespoons ranch dressing. Tastes great alongside grilled chicken or fish. Makes about 3 1/2 cups.

BLACK BEAN SAUTÉ

In 10-inch nonstick skillet, brown 1 small onion, chopped, in 1 teaspoon olive oil. Stir in 1 clove garlic, crushed with press, and cook 1 minute. Stir in 1 can beans and heat through. Remove from heat and stir in 1 to 2 tablespoons chopped pickled jalapeño chiles. This is a good side dish for pork chops. Makes about 1 3/4 cups.

BLACK BEAN SOUP

In 4-quart saucepan, cook 1 cup fresh salsa and a pinch of allspice over medium heat for 3 minutes. Stir in 2 cans beans and 3 cups low-sodium chicken broth; heat to boiling over high heat. Reduce heat and simmer 10 minutes. Use immersion blender or potato masher to coarsely mash beans. Makes about 6 cups.

BLACK BEAN CHILI

In 4-quart saucepan, cook 8 ounces lean ground beef and 1 small onion, chopped, until beef is browned and onion is tender, about 10 minutes. Stir in 2 teaspoons chili powder and cook 1 minute. Stir in 2 cans beans, 1 can (14 1/2 ounces) diced tomatoes with green chiles, and 1 cup water. Heat to boiling over high heat; reduce heat to low and simmer 15 minutes, stirring occasionally. Makes about 5 cups.

VEGETABLE CURRY WITH KIDNEY BEANS

In 4-quart saucepan, heat 4 cups water to boiling. Add 1 package (12 ounces) fresh broccoli/cauliflower-floret mix; cook 4 minutes or just under tender. Drain in colander. Dry saucepan. In same pan, toast 1 teaspoon curry powder on medium 30 seconds. Stir in beans, 1/4 cup chutney, 1/4 cup water, 1 1/2 teaspoons grated fresh ginger, and 1/4 teaspoon salt. Cook 2 minutes. Stir in broccoli mix. Spoon over rice. Serves 4.

AVOCADO AND RED BEAN QUESADILLAS

Divide 4 tablespoons salsa, 1 cup shredded Pepper Jack cheese, beans, and 1 avocado, sliced, on half of each of 4 burrito-size tortillas. Fold in half; press to flatten slightly. Heat 12-inch skillet on medium; add 2 quesadillas to hot pan. Cook 8 minutes or until golden on both sides. Repeat. Serve with salsa. Serves 4.

SUN-DRIED TOMATO AND RED BEAN DIP

In food processor with knife blade attached, finely chop 1/3 cup oil-packed sun-dried tomatoes with 1 tablespoon oil from tomatoes. Add beans, 1/4 cup grated Parmesan, and 2 tablespoons water, and blend until smooth. Add 1/3 cup fresh basil leaves; pulse just until combined. Serve with pita chips. Makes 1 3/4 cups.

RED BEAN FALAFEL

In food processor, pulse beans, 1 egg, 1/3 cup packed fresh parsley, 1/4 cup seasoned dried bread crumbs, 3/4 teaspoon ground cumin, and 1/4 teaspoon each salt and ground black pepper until blended. Place 3 tablespoons crumbs on plate. Shape bean mixture into 8 patties about 2 inches in diameter; coat with crumbs. Spray 12-inch skillet with nonstick spray; heat on medium. Add patties; cook 9 minutes. Serves 4.

MINESTRONE

In 4-quart saucepan, combine kidney beans, 4 cups vegetable broth, 1 can (14 1/2 ounces) diced tomatoes with onion and garlic, and 1/4 teaspoon Italian seasoning; cover and heat to boiling. Stir in 1 bag (16 ounces) frozen Italian vegetables; cover and cook 6 minutes or until tender. Serve with grated Parmesan. Serves 4.

TUSCAN WHITE BEANS WITH SAGE

Leave it to the Italians to give us flawlessly flavored beans. These are perfect with Pork Roast with Fennel and Garlic (page 129).

Prep: 15 minutes plus soaking beans
Bake: 45 minutes

- 1 package (16 ounces) white kidney beans (cannellini), soaked and drained (page 279)
- 3 slices bacon
- 2 small onions, very thinly sliced
- 4 garlic cloves, crushed with side of chef's knife
- 2 sprigs plus 2 teaspoons thinly sliced fresh sage leaves
- 1 bay leaf
- 3 tablespoons olive oil
- 2 teaspoons salt
- ½ teaspoon ground black pepper

1. Preheat oven to 325°F. In 5-quart Dutch oven, combine beans, bacon, onions, garlic, sage sprigs, bay leaf, oil, and enough *water* to cover by 2 inches; heat to boiling over high heat. Cover and place in oven. Bake until beans are tender but still retain their shape, 45 to 60 minutes.

2. Drain beans, reserving cooking liquid. Discard bacon, sage sprigs, and bay leaf. Return beans to pot and stir in sliced sage, salt, pepper, and ½ to 1 cup bean cooking liquid until desired consistency. Spoon into serving bowl and serve hot, warm, or at room temperature. Makes about 6 cups or 8 accompaniment servings.

Each serving: About 263 calories, 14g protein, 37g carbohydrate, 7g total fat (1g saturated), 2mg cholesterol, 617mg sodium.

INDIAN-STYLE LENTILS

Fresh ginger and cumin give lentils an Indian twist, while diced sweet potatoes add flavor and color.

Prep: 20 minutes   Cook: 45 minutes

- 1 tablespoon vegetable oil
- 1 medium onion, chopped
- 1 tablespoon minced, peeled fresh ginger
- 1 large garlic clove, finely chopped
- 1½ teaspoons cumin seeds
- ⅛ teaspoon ground red pepper (cayenne)
- 1 pound sweet potatoes, peeled and cut into ¾-inch pieces (3 cups)
- 1 cup brown lentils, rinsed and picked through
- 1 can (14½ ounces) chicken or vegetable broth or 1¾ cups Chicken Broth (page 70) or Vegetable Broth (page 71)
- 1 cup water
- ¼ teaspoon salt
- 1 container (8 ounces) plain low-fat yogurt
- ¼ cup chopped fresh mint or cilantro

1. In 3-quart saucepan, heat oil over medium heat. Add onion and cook, stirring, until tender, about 5 minutes. Stir in ginger, garlic, cumin seeds, and ground red pepper; cook 30 seconds. Stir in sweet potatoes, lentils, broth, water, and salt; heat to boiling over high heat. Reduce heat; cover and simmer, stirring occasionally, until lentils are just tender, about 30 minutes. Transfer to serving bowl.

2. In small bowl, combine yogurt and mint. Serve with lentils. Makes 6 accompaniment servings.

Each serving: About 234 calories, 13g protein, 38g carbohydrate, 4g total fat (1g saturated), 2mg cholesterol, 421mg sodium.

SLICING FRESH HERBS WITH EASE

Here's the easiest way to slice fresh herbs such as sage and basil. Stack the leaves, then tightly roll them up lengthwise, cigar style. Place on a cutting board and cut crosswise with a large sharp knife into thin or thick slices. This is sometimes referred to as *chiffonade*.

RICE

The USDA divides rice into three categories: long-, medium-, and short-grain. In general, shorter grains contain the most starch. Most Americans are familiar with long-grain white rice, which has had the hull and bran removed. Brown rice retains its bran layer, as do other whole-grain rice varieties that are covered with a black or red bran layer.

Store rice in a cool, dry, insect-free area in its own package. White rice will keep for up to two years; brown rice for up to one year.

COOKING RICE

There's no need to rinse most domestic rice before cooking, as the rice was cleaned before being milled. You should, however, rinse wild rice and imported varieties such as basmati or jasmine, which may be dirty or dusty. Brown rice and sticky (glutinous) rice will cook more quickly if presoaked overnight, but do not soak any other kinds of rice.

There are two methods for cooking rice: immersion and absorption.

Immersion In this method, the rice is boiled like pasta in a large unmeasured amount of salted water until tender, then drained. Unfortunately, the nutrients are also drained away.

Absorption Here the rice is cooked in a measured quantity of liquid, all of which is absorbed, thus conserving the nutrients. The cooking time and amount of liquid depend on the variety of rice.

KNOW YOUR RICE

Long-Grain Rice

Aromatic Some rice varieties become fragrant when cooked. The best-known is basmati, a rice valued for its perfumed scent, delicate taste, and fluffy texture. When cooked, the slender grains swell lengthwise, resulting in thin dry grains perfect for pilafs. Similar fragrant rice varieties include *jasmine* and *popcorn*.

Instant Rice that has been partially or fully cooked, then dehydrated. It cooks quickly.

Parboiled (converted) Rice that has been steamed, pressure treated, and dehydrated; the grains remain firm and separate after cooking.

Regular Slender, polished, elongated white grains that cook into dry grains that separate easily.

Medium-Grain Rice

Arborio The traditional rice for Italian risotto; this plump, roundish medium-grain rice has a high starch content and yields a moist, creamy texture. *Vialone Nano* and *Carnaroli* rice varieties can also be used to make risotto.

Japanese (sushi) Starchy medium-grain rice that clings together after cooking, making it the perfect rice for sushi.

Paella (Valencia) The preferred rice in Spanish and Latino dishes, it cooks up creamy and slightly sticky.

Short-Grain Rice

Sticky Also called glutinous or sweet rice. An opaque white short-grain rice with a slightly sweet taste and a soft, sticky texture.

Brown and Black Rice

Brown The outer hull has been removed, but the nutritious, high-fiber bran layer remains. Brown rice can be long-, medium-, or short-grain. Other varieties include *Wehani,* a new brown rice, and *red rice,* which has a red bran layer.

Black There are many varieties of this hulled rice with its black bran, including *Thai black sticky rice* and *Chinese black rice.*

Wild Rice

Wild rice Not truly a rice but the seed of a water grass. The hand-harvested variety of wild rice, *manohmin,* is gathered the traditional way: in canoes. The rice grains vary in both length and color and have a slightly smoky, earthy flavor and a chewy texture. Commercially cultivated wild rice is uniform in size and color, less expensive than the true wild variety, and available in supermarkets.

OTHER GRAINS

When we cook grains, we are actually using the fruits of grasses, which are called kernels. Whole kernels are also known as berries or groats, while finely cracked groats are called grits. The kernels can be coarsely ground into meal or finely ground into flour.

Each kernel has three components: the bran, the endosperm, and the germ. The bulk of the kernel is the endosperm. The bran is the fiber-rich outer coating of the kernel, and the germ is the seed. Some grains also have an inedible husk, which is always removed. A grain that has the bran, endosperm, and germ intact is called a whole grain. Grains often have their bran and germ removed. These processed grains are often enriched with vitamins to replace some that were lost.

To prevent their oils from turning rancid quickly, store uncooked grains in an airtight container at cool room temperature or in the refrigerator for up to one month, or freeze for up to three months.

COOKING GRAINS

Rinsing Before cooking, whole grains should be washed in cold water to remove any dust, chaff, or natural coatings that could impart a bitter taste. Place the grains in a sieve, then place in a bowl of cold water and swish the sieve back and forth. Lift out the sieve, pour off the water, and repeat until the water looks clear. Give the grains a final rinse, then drain.

Soaking Whole berries and brown rice cook more quickly if presoaked. At least eight or up to 24 hours before cooking, place the rinsed grain berries in a large bowl of cold water and let stand at room temperature. (In hot weather, let stand in the refrigerator.) Drain well before cooking.

Toasting Grains are sometimes toasted (lightly precooked) before using to enhance their aroma and flavor. Millet is toasted to bring out its flavor and texture, and kasha is coated with beaten egg and then toasted to keep the grains separated. In rice pilaf the rice is toasted in the saucepan to firm up the outside layer, making the cooked rice firmer, while in risottos the rice is toasted to seal in the starch. To toast whole grains, place them in a heavy skillet over medium heat. (Add 1 or 2 tablespoons of oil or butter to the pan first, if you wish.) Cook, stirring almost constantly, until the grains are fragrant but not colored, 3 to 5 minutes.

Cooking The rule of thumb when cooking grains is 2 cups of liquid to 1 cup of grain. If the cooking liquid is absorbed before the grain is tender, simply add more hot liquid. Or, if the grain is tender and some liquid remains, simply drain it off. Follow the instructions on the package for exact liquid measurements and estimated cooking times.

As with beans, the outer coating of some whole grains, like whole-wheat berries and amaranth, toughens and prohibits the proper absorption of liquid if salt is present. When in doubt, cook the grains in unsalted water and season when they are almost tender.

COOKING RICE

In all cases, for 1 cup rice, combine the rice, cooking liquid (you can use water, but broth adds flavor), optional salt, and butter or margarine in a 2- to 3-quart saucepan. Heat to boiling. Reduce heat; cover and simmer until done. Do not uncover the saucepan to check on the rice's progress until the last 5 minutes of cooking. When the rice is tender, remove saucepan from heat and let stand, covered, for 5 minutes. This short waiting period ensures a better texture. Fluff the rice with a fork before serving.

RICE VARIETY (1 CUP)	AMOUNT OF LIQUID	COOKING TIME	YIELD
Regular long-grain	1¾ to 2 cups	18 to 20 minutes	3 cups
Medium- or short-grain	1½ to 1¾ cups	18 to 20 minutes	3 cups
Brown	2 to 2½ cups	45 to 50 minutes	3 to 4 cups
Wild	2 to 2½ cups	45 to 60 minutes	2⅔ cups

GRAINS GLOSSARY

Whole grains are the most minimally processed version of grains. All the edible parts that were present when the grain was growing in the field—the bran, the endosperm, and the germ—are intact, through they are often ground up for use in cooking. The majority of the grains that we eat today are refined, a process that strips away many of the nutrients. Whole grains, in contrast, retain their fiber, vitamins, and minerals. Nearly every supermarket now stocks once-obscure grain varieties like quinoa and wheat berries (descriptions follow). Store whole grains in tightly covered containers, and refrigerate them during the warmer months.

Amaranth is a tiny grain native to Central America. It's one of the few whole grains that contain all of the essential amino acids, making it an ideal source of protein. Choose it as a hot cereal, add it to soups as a thickener, or use the flour in pancakes and quick breads.

Buckwheat isn't actually a wheat, but the seed from a plant in the rhubarb family. It's quick-cooking, gluten-free, and a good source of fiber and magnesium. Most familiar to Americans in the form of buckwheat pancakes, it's a grain with global popularity and is found in everything from Japanese soba noodles to Russian porridge.

Bulgur cooks so quickly (in less than 15 minutes) because it has been boiled, dried, and cracked before reaching the market. Perfect for fast side dishes and salads—and the main ingredient in Middle Eastern tabbouleh (page 493), bulgur has a mild flavor that makes it a great starter grain for kids (and husbands) who are picky eaters. A related grain, cracked wheat, is often confused with bulgur. It is actually raw wheat kernels (not boiled and dried ones) that have been cracked to speed the cooking process. Both are available in fine, medium, and coarse textures.

Cornmeal is dried corn kernels that have been ground to a fine, medium, or coarse texture. Stone-ground cornmeal has not been degerminated (had its germ removed).

Couscous is not a grain but actually pellets of semolina pasta. Most couscous is precooked and needs only a soaking in hot liquid to soften it. Serve with a Moroccan-spiced stew, or as an alternative to rice in many dishes.

Farro (or emmer wheat), nicknamed the pharaoh's wheat, was a culinary cornerstone of ancient Egyptian and Roman menus. It gradually fell out of favor because the plant was low-yielding and the grain was difficult to hull. Now grown primarily in Italy, this nutty-flavored grain is undergoing a resurgence as a gourmet food. Try it in soups, or use it as an alternative to Arborio rice in risotto.

Hominy consists of corn kernels that have been first soaked in a lime or lye solution to remove the hulls and germs, then dried. Known as posole in Mexico's Pacific Coast region, hominy is central to a thick, spicy pork (or sometimes chicken) stew by the same name.

Quinoa (pronounced KEEN-wah), grown in the South American Andes since 3,000 BC, is a nutrient-dense grain. Mild and sweet, quinoa needs to be rinsed thoroughly prior to cooking in order to remove its bitter coating. A complete protein, it cooks in less than 15 minutes and can substitute for rice in most dishes.

Rye berries, once cooked, are softer than wheat berries and have a slightly tangy flavor.

Wheat berries are whole kernels of wheat. If processed to remove the bran and the germ, then ground into powder, they would become white flour—but unprocessed, they're a whole grain. Chewy, with a hint of nuttiness, the kernels are versatile add-ins to salads, soups, and side dishes. Wheat berries need at least an hour to cook, although that time can be reduced if they've been soaked overnight.

HOT FLUFFY RICE

....

For drier rice, use only 1¾ cups water; for extra-tender rice, use 2⅓ cups water and cook a bit longer.

Prep: 5 minutes   Cook: 25 minutes

- 2 cups water
- 1 cup regular long-grain rice
- 1 tablespoon butter or margarine (optional)
- 1 teaspoon salt

In 3-quart saucepan, heat water to boiling over high heat. Stir in rice, butter if using, and salt; heat to boiling. Reduce heat; cover and simmer, without stirring or lifting lid, until rice is tender and all liquid has been absorbed, 18 to 20 minutes. Remove from heat and let stand 5 minutes. Fluff rice with fork. Makes about 3 cups or 4 accompaniment servings.

Each serving: About 169 calories, 3g protein, 37g carbohydrate, 0g total fat (0g saturated), 0mg cholesterol, 585mg sodium.

BROWN RICE

Prepare as directed for Hot Fluffy Rice but use **2½ cups water, 1 cup long-grain brown rice,** and **1 teaspoon salt.** Simmer 45 to 50 minutes. Or prepare as label directs. Makes 4 cups or 6 accompaniment servings.

Each serving: About 114 calories, 2g protein, 24g carbohydrate, 1g total fat (0g saturated), 0mg cholesterol, 391mg sodium.

AROMATIC RICE

....

Follow these basic directions to cook up fluffy rice, then add the desired flavoring for one of the options opposite.

Prep: 5 minutes   Cook: 25 minutes

- 1 cup chicken broth
- ¾ cup water
- 1 cup regular long-grain rice
- ¼ teaspoon salt
  seasonings (right)

In 3-quart saucepan, heat broth and water to boiling over high heat. Stir in rice and salt; heat to boiling. Reduce heat; cover and simmer, without stirring or lifting lid, until rice is tender and all liquid has been absorbed,

18 to 20 minutes. Remove from heat and let stand 5 minutes. Fluff rice with fork and add seasoning. Makes about 3 cups or 4 accompaniment servings.

Each serving: About 176 calories, 4g protein, 37g carbohydrate, 1g total fat (0g saturated), 0mg cholesterol, 395mg sodium.

LEMON-PARSLEY RICE

Cook as directed. Stir in **2 tablespoons chopped fresh parsley** and **1 teaspoon freshly grated lemon peel.**

ASIAN RICE

Cook as directed but omit salt. Stir in **2 green onions,** chopped, **2 teaspoons soy sauce,** and **¼ teaspoon Asian sesame oil.**

COCONUT RICE

Cook as directed. Stir in ½ **cup unsweetened coconut milk** (not cream of coconut), ½ **teaspoon freshly grated lime peel,** and **pinch ground red pepper (cayenne).**

LEMON-PARMESAN RICE

Cook as directed. Stir in ¼ **cup freshly grated Parmesan cheese, 1 teaspoon freshly grated lemon peel,** and ¼ **teaspoon ground black pepper.**

PEPPER JACK RICE

Cook as directed. Stir in **2 ounces Monterey Pepper-Jack cheese with jalapeño chiles,** shredded (½ cup), and **3 green onions,** thinly sliced.

GREEN RICE

Cook as directed but after the rice has cooked 15 minutes, stir in **1 package (10 ounces) frozen chopped spinach,** thawed; cover and cook 5 minutes longer. Stir in **2 ounces feta cheese,** finely crumbled (½ cup).

BAKED RICE

....

Here's an alternative to rice cooked on the stove. Substitute chicken or beef broth for the water, if you wish, in which case, delete the salt.

Prep: 5 minutes   Bake: 30 minutes

- 2 cups boiling water
- 1 cup regular long-grain rice
- 1 tablespoon butter or margarine, cut into pieces
- ½ teaspoon salt

Preheat oven to 350°F. Grease shallow 1½-quart casserole or 8-inch square baking dish. In casserole, combine boiling water, rice, butter, and salt. Cover and bake until rice is tender and all liquid has been absorbed, 30 to 35 minutes. Fluff with fork. Makes about 3 cups or 4 accompaniment servings.

Each serving: About 194 calories, 3g protein, 37g carbohydrate, 3g total fat (2g saturated), 8mg cholesterol, 321mg sodium.

CUMIN RICE WITH BLACK BEANS

The time-honored combination of rice and beans is found throughout Latin America and the Caribbean. Serve as a side dish for a juicy grilled steak.

Prep: 10 minutes   Cook: 30 minutes

- 1 tablespoon vegetable oil
- 1 medium onion, finely chopped
- 1 garlic clove, finely chopped
- 2 teaspoons cumin seeds
- 1½ cups regular long-grain rice
- 1 can (14½ ounces) chicken or vegetable broth or 1¾ cups Chicken Broth (page 70) or Vegetable Broth (page 71)
- 1¼ cups water
- ¼ teaspoon salt
- 1 can (15 to 19 ounces) black beans, rinsed and drained
- 2 tablespoons chopped fresh cilantro lime wedges

1. In 3-quart saucepan, heat oil over medium heat. Add onion and cook, stirring, until tender, about 5 minutes. Stir in garlic and cumin seeds; cook, stirring, until fragrant. Add rice and cook, stirring, 1 minute. Add broth, water, and salt; heat to boiling over high heat. Reduce heat; cover and simmer, without stirring or lifting lid, until rice is tender and most of liquid has been absorbed, about 15 minutes.

2. Stir beans into rice. Cover and cook 5 minutes longer. Remove from heat and let stand 5 minutes. Spoon into serving bowl and sprinkle with cilantro. Serve with lime wedges. Makes about 6 cups or 6 accompaniment servings.

Each serving: About 256 calories, 7g protein, 48g carbohydrate, 4g total fat (1g saturated), 0mg cholesterol, 515mg sodium.

JAMBALAYA

A Cajun favorite, jambalaya is a rice dish that has countless variations. Though it can be made with almost any favorite meat, poultry, or shellfish, we are partial to the combination of sausage and shrimp.

Prep: 20 minutes plus cooling   Cook: 55 minutes

- 8 ounces hot Italian-sausage links, pricked with fork
- 1 medium onion, finely chopped
- 1 green pepper, chopped
- 1 stalk celery, chopped
- 1 garlic clove, finely chopped
- ⅛ teaspoon ground red pepper (cayenne)
- 1½ cups regular long-grain rice
- 1 can (14½ ounces) chicken broth or 1¾ cups Chicken Broth (page 70)
- 1¼ cups water
- ¼ teaspoon salt
- ⅛ teaspoon dried thyme
- 1 can (14 to 16 ounces) tomatoes, drained and chopped
- 1 pound medium shrimp, shelled and deveined (page 221)
- 2 green onions, thinly sliced hot pepper sauce (optional)

1. In nonreactive 5-quart Dutch oven, cook sausages over medium heat until browned, about 10 minutes. With slotted spoon, transfer sausages to paper towels to drain. When cool enough to handle, cut sausages into ½-inch pieces.

2. To drippings in Dutch oven, add onion, green pepper, and celery; cook, stirring frequently, until tender, about 10 minutes. Stir in garlic and ground red pepper and cook, stirring, 30 seconds. Add rice and cook, stirring, 1 minute. Stir in sausages, broth, water, salt, and thyme; heat to boiling over high heat. Reduce heat; cover and simmer 15 minutes.

3. Stir in tomatoes; cover and cook 5 minutes. Stir in shrimp; cover and cook until shrimp are opaque throughout, about 5 minutes longer. Transfer to serving bowl and sprinkle with green onions. Serve with hot pepper sauce, if you like. Makes 6 main-dish servings.

Each serving: About 405 calories, 23g protein, 45g carbohydrate, 14g total fat (5g saturated), 122mg cholesterol, 873mg sodium.

PAELLA

....

Every Spanish cook has his or her own version of paella, which may include a wide range of ingredients. The crucial ingredient in every paella is the rice. Opt for a medium-grain rice, such as Spanish Valencia, or a short-grain rice, such as Italian Arborio, for their distinctive texture and the way the grains cling together when cooked. (Long-grain rice, which cooks up fluffy, can be substituted in a pinch.)

Prep: 30 minutes   Cook: 1 hour

1	tablespoon olive oil
1½	pounds skinless, boneless chicken thighs, cut into 2-inch pieces
2	fully cooked chorizo sausages (3 ounces each)
1	medium onion, finely chopped
1	red pepper, finely chopped
2	garlic cloves, finely chopped
¼	teaspoon ground red pepper (cayenne)
½	cup canned tomatoes in puree
½	cup dry white wine
2	cups medium- or short-grain rice
4	ounces green beans, cut into 1-inch pieces
2½	cups water
1	can (14½ ounces) chicken broth or 1¾ cups Chicken Broth (page 70)
1½	teaspoons salt
¼	teaspoon loosely packed saffron threads, crumbled
⅛	teaspoon dried thyme
½	bay leaf
1	pound mussels, scrubbed and debearded (page 215)
12	ounces medium shrimp, shelled and deveined (page 221)
¼	cup chopped fresh parsley
	lemon wedges

1. In deep nonreactive 12-inch skillet, heat oil over medium-high heat until very hot. Add chicken and chorizo; cook until browned, about 10 minutes. With slotted spoon, transfer chicken and chorizo to bowl.

2. Reduce heat to medium. Add onion and chopped red pepper to skillet; cook, stirring frequently, until onion is tender, about 5 minutes. Stir in garlic and ground red pepper; cook, stirring, 30 seconds. Add tomatoes with their puree and wine; cook, breaking up tomatoes with side of spoon, until liquid has evaporated.

3. Stir rice, green beans, water, broth, salt, saffron, thyme, and bay leaf into skillet. Thinly slice chorizo; return chorizo and chicken to skillet. Heat to boiling over high heat. Reduce heat; cover and simmer 20 minutes.

4. Tuck mussels into paella; cover and cook 3 minutes. Tuck shrimp into paella; cover and cook just until mussels have opened and shrimp are opaque throughout, about 3 minutes longer. Remove from heat and let stand 5 minutes. Discard bay leaf and any mussels that have not opened. Sprinkle paella with parsley and serve with lemon wedges. Makes 8 main-dish servings.

Each serving: About 467 calories, 35g protein, 45g carbohydrate, 15g total fat (4g saturated), 146mg cholesterol, 1,110mg sodium.

A PAELLA PRIMER

Paella is known worldwide as a Spanish rice dish that may contain chicken, rabbit, sausage, lobster, shrimp, mussels, or any combination thereof. Originally, however, the word *paella* referred only to the pan in which this dish was cooked, a *paellera*, from the Latin word for frying pan, *patella*. The dish became so popular in Spain that eventually the word came to mean the food itself.

There are likely as many variations of paella as there are cooks who prepare it, though some of the renditions depend upon the region in which the paella is cooked. Among Spanish cooks, however, the one constant in this dish is the rice that is used: Valencia, a short-grain rice that has been harvested in Spain for more than one thousand years.

A paella pan, an inexpensive shallow metal two-handled affair, which ranges in size from about 10 inches to well over several feet across, is the pan of choice, but a deep skillet will do in a pinch.

BULGUR PILAF WITH GARBANZOS AND DRIED APRICOTS

••••••••••••••••••••••••••••

This meatless dish turns grain and beans into a hearty entrée. The amino acids in the bulgur and garbanzos form a complete protein; the apricots reflect the Turkish origins of the preparation.

Prep: 10 minutes   Cook: 20 minutes

- ³⁄₄ cup water
- 1 can (14 to 14¹⁄₂ ounces) vegetable broth or chicken broth, or 1³⁄₄ cups Chicken Broth (page 70)
- 1 cup bulgur
- 1 tablespoon olive oil
- 1 small onion, chopped
- 2 teaspoons curry powder
- 1 clove garlic, crushed with press
- 1 can (15 to 19 ounces) garbanzo beans, rinsed and drained
- ¹⁄₂ cup dried apricots, chopped
- ¹⁄₂ teaspoon salt
- ¹⁄₄ cup loosely packed fresh parsley leaves, chopped

1. In 2-quart covered saucepan, heat water and 1¹⁄₄ cups broth to boiling on high. Stir in bulgur; heat to boiling. Reduce heat to medium-low; cover and simmer 12 to 15 minutes or until liquid is absorbed. Remove saucepan from heat. Uncover and fluff bulgur with fork to separate grains.

Bulgur Pilaf with Garbanzos and Dried Apricots

2. Meanwhile, in 12-inch nonstick skillet, heat oil on medium 1 minute. Add onion and cook 10 minutes, stirring occasionally. Stir in curry powder and garlic; cook 1 minute.

3. Stir in beans, apricots, salt, and remaining ¹⁄₂ cup broth; heat to boiling. Remove from heat; stir in bulgur and parsley. Makes 4 main-dish servings.

Each serving: About 370 calories, 13g protein, 71g carbohydrate, 6g total fat (1g saturated), 15g fiber, 0mg cholesterol, 815mg sodium.

PERSIAN RICE PILAF

••••••••••••••••••••••••••••

Sweet currants and a touch of spice create heavenly fragrant rice. Try this with butterflied leg of lamb or grilled chicken.

Prep: 10 minutes   Cook: 30 minutes

- 1 tablespoon butter or margarine
- 1 small onion, finely chopped
- 1 cup regular long-grain rice
- 1 can (14¹⁄₂ ounces) chicken or vegetable broth or 1³⁄₄ cups Chicken Broth (page 70) or Vegetable Broth (page 71)
- ¹⁄₄ cup water
- ¹⁄₄ cup dried currants
- ¹⁄₈ teaspoon ground black pepper pinch ground cinnamon
- ¹⁄₂ teaspoon freshly grated orange peel
- ¹⁄₄ cup pine nuts (pignoli), toasted
- ¹⁄₄ cup chopped fresh parsley

1. In 2-quart saucepan, melt butter over medium heat. Add onion and cook, stirring, until tender, about 4 minutes. Add rice; cook, stirring, 1 minute. Stir in broth, water, currants, pepper, and cinnamon; heat to boiling. Reduce heat; cover and simmer, without stirring or lifting lid, until rice is tender and all liquid has been absorbed, 18 to 20 minutes.

2. Remove rice from heat; let stand 5 minutes. Add orange peel, fluffing rice with fork until combined. Stir in pine nuts and parsley. Makes 4 cups or 4 accompaniment servings.

Each serving: About 291 calories, 7g protein, 48g carbohydrate, 9g total fat (3g saturated), 8mg cholesterol, 463mg sodium.

BROWN RICE AND VEGETABLE PILAF

Fragrant herbs and a variety of fresh vegetables complement the nutty flavor of brown rice in this tasty and nutritious vegetarian dish. Serve as a hearty accompaniment or main course.

Prep: 15 minutes   Cook: 1 hour 10 minutes

- 1 tablespoon olive or vegetable oil
- 1 medium onion, finely chopped
- 1 stalk celery, finely chopped
- 8 ounces mushrooms, trimmed and sliced
- 1 garlic clove, finely chopped
- 1 cup regular long-grain brown rice
- 2¼ cups water
- 2 carrots, peeled and chopped
- 1¼ teaspoons salt
- teaspoon dried thyme
- ⅛ teaspoon ground black pepper
- pinch dried sage

In 10-inch skillet, heat oil over medium heat. Add onion and celery; cook, stirring frequently, until onion is tender, about 5 minutes. Stir in mushrooms; increase heat to medium-high and cook until mushrooms begin to brown and liquid has evaporated. Stir in garlic. Add rice; cook, stirring, 30 seconds. Stir in water, carrots, salt, thyme, pepper, and sage; heat to boiling. Reduce heat; cover and simmer until rice is tender and all liquid has been absorbed, about 45 minutes. Fluff with fork. Makes about 4½ cups or 6 accompaniment servings.

Each serving: About 167 calories, 4g protein, 31g carbohydrate, 3g total fat (0g saturated), 0mg cholesterol, 503mg sodium.

---

5 IDEAS FOR . . . RICE PILAF

Use original-style pilaf in a 6- to 6½-ounce package.

ASPARAGUS RISOTTO
Prepare pilaf as label directs. Stir in 1 pound thin asparagus, trimmed and cut into 1-inch pieces, and ¾ cup reduced-sodium chicken broth; cover and heat to boiling on high. Reduce heat to low and simmer, covered, 3 to 4 minutes or until asparagus is tender-crisp. Remove from heat; stir in ½ cup crumbled goat cheese (2 ounces), 1 teaspoon grated fresh lemon peel, and 1 tablespoon fresh lemon juice. Serves 4.

FRIED RICE
Prepare pilaf as label directs, except substitute 2 tablespoons reduced-sodium teriyaki sauce for 2 tablespoons of the water. Coat 10-inch skillet with nonstick spray; place over medium heat. Add ½ sliced small red onion and 4 ounces trimmed and halved snow peas; stir-fry 2 to 3 minutes. Transfer to bowl. Remove skillet from heat; spray with nonstick spray and return to medium heat. In cup, lightly beat 2 large eggs; add to skillet and cook, stirring, until scrambled. Fluff rice with fork; stir in vegetables and eggs. Serves 3.

BEAN BURRITOS
Prepare pilaf as label directs. Coat skillet with nonstick spray; place over medium heat. Add 1 can (15 to 19 ounces) pinto or black beans, rinsed and drained, and 1 tablespoon chili powder; cook 2 minutes. Stir in pilaf and ⅓ cup salsa. Spoon about 1 cup filling onto each of 4 warm burrito-size flour tortillas. Roll up and serve with additional salsa. Serves 4.

SPINACH-RICE SALAD
Prepare pilaf as label directs, but do not add butter or oil. Cool 5 minutes. Toss with 1 bag (6 ounces) baby spinach, ½ cup shredded carrots, ½ cup toasted sliced almonds, 2 tablespoons red wine vinegar, and ¼ teaspoon ground black pepper. Serves 4.

CHICKEN AND RICE SOUP
Prepare pilaf as label directs. Stir in 2 cans (14 to 14½ ounces each) reduced-sodium chicken broth, 1 package (10 ounces) frozen peas and carrots, and 2 cups diced cooked chicken; cover and heat to boiling on high. Serves 4.

TOASTED BARLEY AND CHICKEN PILAF

....

A new take on chicken and rice that's filled with fiber, thanks to the whole-grain goodness of barley.

Prep: 10 minutes   Cook: 1 hour 10 minutes

1½ cups pearl barley
3 teaspoons olive oil
4 skinless, boneless chicken thighs (about 1 pound), cut into 1-inch chunks
2 medium carrots, chopped
2 stalks celery, chopped
1 small onion, chopped
1 package (8 ounces) sliced mushrooms
1 can (14 to 14½ ounces) chicken broth or 1¾ cups Chicken Broth (page 70)
2 cups water
½ teaspoon dried thyme
¼ teaspoon ground nutmeg
½ teaspoon salt
¼ teaspoon ground black pepper
   parsley leaves

1. Heat deep 12-inch skillet over medium-high heat until hot. Add barley and cook 4 to 6 minutes or until toasted and fragrant, stirring occasionally. Transfer barley to large bowl.

2. In same skillet, heat 2 teaspoons oil over medium-high heat until hot. Add chicken and cook about 5 minutes or just until it loses its pink color on the outside, stirring occasionally. Transfer chicken to bowl with barley.

3. In same skillet, heat remaining 1 teaspoon oil over medium heat and cook carrots, celery, and onion 7 to 8 minutes or until tender-crisp. Stir in mushrooms and cook about 10 minutes longer or until most of liquid evaporates and vegetables are tender and lightly browned.

4. Return chicken and barley to skillet; stir in broth, water, thyme, nutmeg, salt, and pepper. Heat to boiling over medium-high heat. Reduce heat to low; cover and simmer 30 to 35 minutes or until barley is tender and chicken is no longer pink in center. Serve pilaf garnished with parsley leaves. Makes 8 cups or 4 main-dish servings.

Each serving: About 485 calories, 33g protein, 67g carbohydrate, 10g total fat (2g saturated), 14g fiber, 94mg cholesterol, 865mg sodium.

MUSHROOM-BARLEY PILAF

....

Serve barley instead of rice for a flavorful change.

Prep: 15 minutes   Cook: 55 minutes

1 cup pearl barley
2 tablespoons butter or margarine
1 medium onion, chopped
2 stalks celery, cut into ¼-inch-thick slices
12 ounces mushrooms, trimmed and sliced
1 can (14½ ounces) chicken or vegetable broth or 1¾ cups Chicken Broth (page 70) or Vegetable Broth (page 71)
¾ cup water
½ teaspoon salt
⅛ teaspoon dried thyme
⅛ teaspoon ground black pepper
¼ cup chopped fresh parsley

1. In 3-quart saucepan, toast barley over medium heat, shaking pan occasionally, until barley begins to brown, about 4 minutes. Transfer to bowl.

2. In same saucepan, melt butter over medium heat. Add onion and celery; cook until onion is tender, about 5 minutes. Stir in mushrooms; cook until mushrooms are tender and liquid has evaporated. Stir in toasted barley, broth, water, salt, thyme, and pepper. Heat to boiling over high heat. Reduce heat; cover and simmer until barley is tender, about 30 minutes. Stir in parsley. Makes 4 cups or 6 accompaniment servings.

Each serving: About 187 calories, 6g protein, 32g carbohydrate, 5g total fat (3g saturated), 10mg cholesterol, 536mg sodium.

WILD RICE PILAF WITH DRIED CRANBERRIES

·····································

Sautéed vegetables and dried cranberries add flavor and color to this savory wild- and white-rice mixture.

Prep: 20 minutes   Cook: 45 to 60 minutes

- 1   cup wild rice
- 4   cups water
- ³/₄ cup dried cranberries
- 4   tablespoons butter or margarine
- 3   carrots, peeled and chopped
- 1   stalk celery, chopped
- ½   small fennel bulb (8 ounces), trimmed and chopped
- 1   medium onion, chopped
- 1½ teaspoons chopped fresh thyme or ¼ teaspoon dried thyme
- 2   cups regular long-grain rice
- 1   can (14½ ounces) chicken broth or 1¾ cups Chicken Broth (page 70)
- ³/₄ teaspoon salt
- ¼   teaspoon coarsely ground black pepper

1. Rinse wild rice; drain. In 3-quart saucepan, combine wild rice and 2 cups water; heat to boiling over high heat. Reduce heat; cover and simmer until wild rice is tender and some grains have popped, 45 to 60 minutes. Stir in dried cranberries; heat 1 minute. Drain, if necessary.

2. Meanwhile, in 5-quart Dutch oven, melt butter over medium-high heat. Add carrots, celery, fennel, and onion; cook, stirring occasionally, until vegetables are tender and lightly browned, about 20 minutes. Stir in thyme; cook 1 minute. Transfer vegetables to medium bowl.

3. In same 5-quart Dutch oven, combine white rice, broth, and remaining 2 cups water; heat to boiling over high heat. Reduce heat; cover and simmer, without stirring or lifting lid, until rice is tender and all liquid has been absorbed, 18 to 20 minutes. Stir in salt, pepper, wild-rice mixture, and vegetable mixture; heat through. Makes about 12 cups or 12 accompaniment servings.

Each serving: About 240 calories, 5g protein, 44g carbohydrate, 5g total fat (3g saturated), 10mg cholesterol, 354mg sodium.

LEMONY SHRIMP RISOTTO

(Pictured on page 278)

·····································

We tested this recipe in an 1,100-watt microwave oven. If your microwave has less or more power, you may have to make adjustments in cooking times in order to reach the desired doneness.

Prep: 5 minutes   Cook: 25 minutes

- 2   lemons
- 2   cans (14½ ounces each) chicken broth or 3½ cups Chicken Broth (page 70)
- 1   cup water
- ½   cup dry white wine
- 2   teaspoons butter or margarine
- 2   teaspoons olive oil
- 1   medium shallot, minced (2 tablespoons)
- 2   cups Arborio rice (Italian short-grain rice) or medium-grain rice
- 1   pound medium shrimp, shelled and deveined (page 221), leaving tail part of shell on, if you like
- 1   cup frozen peas
- ³/₄ teaspoon salt
- ¼   teaspoon coarsely ground black pepper

1. From lemons, grate 2 teaspoons peel and squeeze ¼ cup juice. In covered 2-quart saucepan, heat lemon juice, broth, water, and wine to boiling over high heat.

2. Meanwhile, in 3- to 3½-quart microwave-safe casserole, combine butter, oil, and shallot. Cook, uncovered, in microwave oven on High until shallot softens, about 2 minutes. Add rice and stir to coat. Cook on High (100% power) 1 minute.

3. Stir hot broth mixture and lemon peel into rice mixture. Cover casserole with lid or vented plastic wrap and cook on Medium (50% power), stirring once, until most of liquid is absorbed, about 15 minutes.

4. Stir in shrimp, frozen peas, salt, and pepper. Cover and cook on Medium (50% power), stirring once, just until shrimp turn opaque throughout and rice is tender but still firm, 3 to 4 minutes longer. Makes 4 main-dish servings.

Each serving: About 620 calories, 31g protein, 99g carbohydrate, 8g total fat (1g saturated), 4g fiber, 140mg cholesterol, 1,515mg sodium.

RISOTTO MILANESE

••••••••••••••••••••••••••••••••••••••

Saffron-infused Risotto Milanese is the traditional accompaniment to Osso Buco (page 121). It is also delicious as a first course or as a meatless main course when followed by a generous mixed salad.

Prep: 10 minutes   Cook: 35 minutes

3½ cups water
1 can (14½ ounces) chicken broth or
  1¾ cups Chicken Broth (page 70)
2 tablespoons butter or olive oil
1 small onion, finely chopped
2 cups Arborio rice (Italian short-grain rice) or
  medium-grain rice
1 teaspoon salt
½ cup dry white wine
¼ teaspoon loosely packed saffron threads
½ cup freshly grated Parmesan cheese

1. In 2-quart saucepan, heat water and broth to boiling over high heat. Reduce heat to low; cover.

2. Meanwhile, in 4-quart saucepan, melt butter over medium heat. Add onion and cook, stirring occasionally, until tender, about 5 minutes. Add rice and salt and cook, stirring frequently, until rice grains are opaque. Add wine; cook until wine has been absorbed.

3. Add about ½ cup hot broth to rice, stirring until liquid has been absorbed. Continue cooking, adding broth about ½ cup at a time and stirring until most of liquid has been absorbed. After cooking 10 minutes, crumble saffron into rice. Continue cooking, adding remaining broth ½ cup at a time and stirring, until all broth has been absorbed and rice is tender but still firm, about 15 minutes longer (risotto should have a creamy consistency). Remove pot from heat; stir in Parmesan cheese. Makes about 5½ cups or 6 side-dish servings.

Each serving: About 216 calories, 6g protein, 35g carbohydrate, 6g total fat (3g saturated), 13mg cholesterol, 649mg sodium.

GREAT RISOTTOS

─────────────────

RISOTTO PRIMAVERA

Follow Steps 1 through 3 (left); but omit saffron. After cooking 10 minutes, stir 2 cups vegetables (use a combination of shredded carrots, finely diced zucchini, sliced asparagus, and frozen peas) into rice. Follow remaining directions. Stir ½ teaspoon grated lemon peel in with Parmesan cheese. Makes about 6½ cups or 4 main-dish servings.

PORCINI RISOTTO

Prepare risotto (left) but omit saffron. In a small bowl, pour ½ cup boiling water over ½ ounce dried porcini mushrooms (about ½ cup). Let stand 15 minutes. With slotted spoon remove porcini and rinse to remove any grit. Chop porcini. Strain soaking liquid through sieve lined with paper towels set over a small bowl. In Step 1 reduce water to 3¼ cups, and add mushroom liquid. Melt 1 tablespoon butter in 4-quart saucepan and stir in 1 pound trimmed and sliced white mushrooms and ¼ teaspoon salt; cook until mushrooms are tender and liquid has evaporated, about 10 minutes. Stir in chopped porcini and transfer to a bowl. Follow Step 2, using 1 tablespoon butter. Follow Step 3 but after cooking 10 minutes, stir in mushroom mixture. Makes about 7 cups or 4 main-dish servings.

SHRIMP RISOTTO

Prepare risotto (left) but omit saffron and cheese. Shell and devein 1 pound medium shrimp, reserving shells. In Step 1 increase water to 4 cups and add shrimp shells. Heat to boiling; reduce heat and simmer 15 minutes. Strain broth through sieve set over a bowl and measure. If necessary, add enough water to equal 5 cups. Return broth to clean saucepan; heat to boiling. Reduce heat; cover and simmer. In 4-quart saucepan melt 1 tablespoon butter over medium-high heat. Add shrimp and ½ teaspoon salt; cook, stirring, until shrimp are just opaque but not fully cooked, 1½ to 2 minutes. Transfer shrimp to a bowl. Follow Step 2, using 1 tablespoon butter. Follow Step 3. Stir in 1 cup frozen baby peas and shrimp and cook until heated through, 1 to 2 minutes. Stir in ¼ cup chopped parsley. Makes about 8 cups or 4 main-dish servings.

CREMINI MUSHROOM RISOTTO

Prepare Risotto Milanese but in Step 1, use only **1 cup water;** omit saffron. In Step 2, omit oil. In Step 3, while rice cooks, in 12-inch skillet, heat **1 tablespoon oil** on medium. Add **8 ounces sliced cremini mushrooms** and cook 8 minutes or until tender, stirring occasionally. After rice has cooked 8 minutes, stir in mushrooms; cook 8 minutes longer. In Step 4, add **½ teaspoon chopped fresh thyme.** Makes about 5½ cups or 6 side-dish servings.

Each serving: About 365 calories, 11g protein, 64g carbohydrate, 6g total fat (2g saturated), 2g fiber, 4mg cholesterol, 635mg sodium.

MICROWAVE TOMATO RISOTTO

·····································

Tomato, basil, and Parmesan cheese add classic flavor to this traditional Italian rice dish. Our not-so-traditional preparation cuts your time in half.

Prep: 20 minutes   Cook: 18 minutes

- 1 can (14 to 14½ ounces) chicken broth or 1¾ cups Chicken Broth (page 70)
- 2 cups water
- 1 tablespoon butter or margarine
- 1 tablespoon olive oil
- 1 small onion, finely chopped
- 2 cups Arborio or Carnaroli rice (Italian short-grain rice)
- ½ cup loosely packed fresh basil leaves, chopped
- 5 medium ripe tomatoes (2½ pounds)
- 1 small wedge Parmesan cheese
- ¾ teaspoon salt
- ⅛ teaspoon coarsely ground black pepper

1. In 2-quart covered saucepan, heat broth and water to boiling on high.

2. While broth mixture heats, in microwave-safe 3½- to 4-quart bowl, combine butter, oil, and onion. Cook, uncovered, in microwave on High 2 minutes or until onion softens. Add rice and stir to coat; cook on High 1 minute.

3. Stir hot broth mixture and half of basil into rice mixture. Cover bowl with vented plastic wrap; cook in microwave on Medium (50% power) 10 minutes.

4. While rice is cooking, make tomato juice: Grate 3 tomatoes, 1 at a time, using coarse side of box grater and holding tomatoes at stem ends, into medium bowl; discard skins. Cut remaining 2 tomatoes into ½-inch chunks; set aside.

5. Stir 2 cups tomato juice into rice mixture (reserve any remaining juice to add to risotto later). Re-cover bowl with vented plastic wrap, and cook in microwave on Medium 8 minutes or until most of liquid is absorbed. Meanwhile, from wedge of Parmesan, grate enough to equal ¼ cup. (you will use the rest for serving).

6. When rice is cooked, stir in grated Parmesan, salt, pepper, tomato chunks, reserved tomato juice, and remaining basil. Serve with additional grated Parmesan. If you like, use vegetable peeler to make Parmesan shavings for garnish. Makes about 8½ cups or 6 main-dish servings.

Each serving: About 380 calories, 9g protein, 70g carbohydrate, 6g total fat (1g saturated), 4g fiber, 3mg cholesterol, 570mg sodium.

Microwave Tomato Risotto

CHEATER'S RISOTTO MILANESE

....

Classically made, risotto requires laboring over a steamy stove without pause for up to 55 minutes as you stir each ladleful of hot broth into the rice mixture and wait for it to be fully absorbed before adding the next. Our much simpler strategy puts the microwave to work, shaving a whopping 45 minutes off your active time and reducing the constant stirring to just a few strokes.

Prep: 10 minutes   Cook: 20 minutes

  4 cups chicken broth
1¼ cups water
  ½ cup dry white wine
  ¼ teaspoon crushed saffron threads
  1 tablespoon butter or margarine
  1 tablespoon olive oil
  1 small onion, minced
  2 cups Arborio or Carnaroli rice
      (short-grain Italian rice)
  ⅓ cup freshly grated Parmesan cheese plus
      additional for serving
  ⅛ teaspoon salt
  ⅛ teaspoon ground black pepper
      chopped parsley for garnish (optional)

1. In saucepan, heat first 4 ingredients to boiling.

2. Meanwhile, in microwave-safe 4-quart bowl, combine butter, oil, and onion. Cook, uncovered, in microwave on High 2 minutes or until onion softens. Add rice and stir to coat; cook, uncovered, on High 1 minute.

3. Stir hot broth mixture into rice mixture. Cover bowl with vented plastic wrap, and cook in microwave on Medium (50% power) 16 to 18 minutes or until most of liquid is absorbed and rice is tender but still firm, stirring halfway through cooking. Do not overcook; mixture will look loose but will thicken to the proper creamy consistency after cooking.

4. Stir in ⅓ cup Parmesan and salt and pepper. Serve with additional Parmesan. Sprinkle with parsley, if you like. Makes 6 first-course or 4 main-dish servings.

Each serving: About 355 calories, 9g protein, 62g carbohydrate, 6g total fat (2g saturated), 2g fiber, 4mg cholesterol, 620mg sodium.

WARM FARRO SALAD WITH ROASTED VEGETABLES

....

Vegetables become sweeter when roasted, making them the perfect complement to the nutty taste of the farro.

Prep: 25 minutes   Cook: 30 minutes

  2 large carrots, peeled and cut into ½-inch dice
  2 small fennel bulbs, trimmed and cut into 1-inch
      pieces
  1 red onion, halved and sliced through root end
  3 tablespoons olive oil
  1 teaspoon salt
  ¼ teaspoon ground black pepper
  1 bunch radishes, cut into ½-inch dice
  1 tablespoon red wine vinegar
2½ cups water
  1 cup farro
  3 tablespoons fresh lemon juice
  2 teaspoons freshly grated lemon peel
  2 cups lightly packed fresh basil leaves, chopped

1. Preheat oven to 400°F.

2. In large bowl, combine carrots, fennel, red onion, 1 tablespoon oil, ½ teaspoon salt, and ⅛ teaspoon pepper; toss. Turn vegetables onto 15½" by 10½" jelly-roll pan and spread evenly. Roast 20 minutes, stirring once. Stir in radishes and roast until vegetables are tender, about 10 minutes. Stir in vinegar.

3. Meanwhile, in medium saucepan, bring water, farro, and ¼ teaspoon salt to boiling over high heat. Reduce heat to medium-low; cover and simmer until farro is tender and water is absorbed, 25 to 30 minutes.

4. In large bowl, whisk lemon juice, lemon peel, remaining 2 tablespoons oil, ¼ teaspoon salt, and ⅛ teaspoon pepper. Add farro, roasted vegetables, and basil; toss to combine. Serve warm. Makes 6 accompaniment servings.

Each serving: About 215 calories, 6g protein, 34g carbohydrate, 7g total fat (1g saturated), 6g fiber, 0mg cholesterol, 472mg sodium.

BASIC BULGUR

....

Bulgur has a pleasant nutty flavor and takes only minutes to prepare.

Prep: 2 minutes   Cook: 20 minutes

- 1 can (14½ ounces) chicken broth or 1¾ cups Chicken Broth (page 70)
- ¼ cup water
- ¼ teaspoon dried thyme
     pinch ground nutmeg
- 1 cup medium-grind bulgur

In 2-quart saucepan, combine broth, water, thyme, and nutmeg; heat to boiling over high heat. Stir in bulgur. Reduce heat; cover and simmer until all liquid has been absorbed, 10 to 15 minutes. Fluff with fork. Makes 3 cups or 4 accompaniment servings.

Each serving: About 133 calories, 5g protein, 27g carbohydrate, 1g total fat (0g saturated), 0mg cholesterol, 434mg sodium.

BULGUR-BEAN BURGERS

....

These healthy burgers, full of Middle Eastern flavor, will satisfy vegetarians and meat-eaters alike. Black beans make them hearty, so no one will miss the beef.

Prep: 20 minutes   Cook: 20 minutes

- 1 cup water
- ¾ teaspoon salt
- ½ cup bulgur
- 1 can (15 to 19 ounces) reduced-sodium black beans, rinsed, and drained
- 1 container (6 ounces) plain low-fat yogurt
- ¼ teaspoon ground allspice
- ¼ teaspoon ground cinnamon
- ¼ teaspoon ground cumin
- ¼ cup packed fresh mint leaves, chopped
- ½ cup shredded Kirby (pickling) cucumber (about 1 small)
- ⅛ teaspoon ground black pepper
- 4 whole-wheat hamburger buns
- 4 lettuce leaves
- 1 medium tomato, sliced

1. In 1-quart saucepan, heat water and ½ teaspoon salt to boiling over high heat. Stir in bulgur. Reduce heat to low; cover and simmer 10 to 12 minutes or until water is absorbed.

2. Meanwhile, in large bowl, with potato masher or fork, mash beans with 2 tablespoons yogurt until almost smooth. Stir in bulgur, allspice, cinnamon, cumin, and half of mint until combined. With lightly floured hands, shape bean mixture into four 3-inch round patties. Spray both sides of each patty lightly with nonstick cooking spray.

3. Heat nonstick 12-inch skillet over medium heat until hot. Add burgers and cook 8 minutes or until lightly browned and heated through, turning once.

4. While burgers are cooking, prepare yogurt sauce: In small bowl, combine cucumber, remaining yogurt, remaining mint, ¼ teaspoon salt, and pepper. (Makes about 1¼ cups yogurt sauce.)

5. To serve, divide lettuce, tomato slices, and burgers among buns; top with some yogurt sauce. Serve with remaining yogurt sauce. Makes 4 main-dish servings.

Each serving: About 295 calories, 16g protein, 58g carbohydrate, 3g total fat (1g saturated), 13g fiber, 3mg cholesterol, 960mg sodium.

Bulgur-Bean Burgers

QUINOA AND CORN

....

Although unfamiliar to many, quinoa has been a staple grain since the time of the Incas, who called it the "mother grain." It is considered a super grain because it contains more protein—including all eight essential amino acids—than any other grain.

Prep: 10 minutes   Cook: 25 minutes

- 1 cup quinoa
- 1¾ cups water
- ¾ teaspoon salt
- 3 medium ears corn, husks and silk removed
- 1 tablespoon butter or margarine
- 4 green onions, sliced
- ¼ teaspoon ground black pepper
- ½ teaspoon freshly grated lemon peel

1. In sieve, rinse quinoa with cold running water. In 2-quart saucepan, combine water, quinoa, and ½ teaspoon salt; heat to boiling over high heat. Reduce heat; cover and simmer until water has been absorbed, about 15 minutes.

2. Meanwhile, cut corn kernels from cobs. In 10-inch skillet, melt butter over medium-high heat. Add corn, green onions, remaining ¼ teaspoon salt, and pepper. Cook, stirring frequently, until corn is tender-crisp, about 3 minutes. Stir in lemon peel. Add quinoa and cook, stirring, until evenly combined. Makes about 5 cups or 6 accompaniment servings.

Each serving: About 188 calories, 6g protein, 34g carbohydrate, 4g total fat (1g saturated), 5mg cholesterol, 340mg sodium.

WARM QUINOA AND BROCCOLI SALAD WITH CARROT-GINGER DRESSING

....

Quinoa adds a healthy dose of protein to this tasty salad with Asian flavors.

Prep: 12 minutes   Cook: 20 minutes

- 1½ cups quinoa
- 3 cups water
- 3¼ cups plus 3 tablespoons water
- ¾ teaspoon salt
- 1 bag (10 ounces) broccoli florets
- ⅔ cup chopped carrot (about 1 large)
- 3 tablespoons finely chopped peeled fresh ginger
- 3 tablespoons vegetable oil
- 2 tablespoons seasoned rice vinegar
- 2 teaspoons soy sauce
- 2 teaspoons Asian sesame oil

1. In sieve, rinse quinoa with cold running water. In 3-quart saucepan, combine quinoa, water, and ½ teaspoon salt; heat to boiling over high heat. Reduce heat to low; cover and simmer 20 minutes or until water is absorbed. Transfer quinoa to large bowl.

2. Meanwhile, place broccoli and ¼ cup water in microwave-safe medium bowl; cover and cook in microwave oven on High 4 to 5 minutes or until tender-crisp. Drain; add to quinoa in bowl.

3. In blender, combine carrot, ginger, vegetable oil, vinegar, soy sauce, sesame oil, remaining 3 tablespoons water, and ¼ teaspoon salt; blend until pureed. Add to quinoa and broccoli and toss to combine. Serve salad warm or at room temperature. Makes about 6½ cups or 6 accompaniment servings.

Each serving: About 265 calories, 7g protein, 36g carbohydrate, 11g total fat (1g saturated), 4g fiber, 0mg cholesterol, 605mg sodium.

COUSCOUS

Couscous is not a grain but a tiny Moroccan pasta made from semolina flour. Here's a basic recipe and some mouthwatering variations.

Prep: 5 minutes   Cook: 5 minutes

1¼ cups water

¼ cup dark seedless raisins, dried currants, dried cranberries, or dried cherries (optional)

1 tablespoon butter or margarine

¾ teaspoon salt

1 cup couscous (Moroccan pasta)

In 3-quart saucepan, combine water, raisins if using, butter, and salt; heat to boiling over high heat. Stir in couscous. Remove from heat; cover and let stand 5 minutes. Fluff couscous with fork. Makes about 3 cups or 4 accompaniment servings.

Each serving: About 226 calories, 6g protein, 43g carbohydrate, 3g total fat (2g saturated), 8mg cholesterol, 471mg sodium.

LIME COUSCOUS
Prepare couscous as directed but omit raisins and add **1 tablespoon fresh lime juice** and **½ teaspoon freshly grated lime peel** to water.

MOROCCAN COUSCOUS
Prepare couscous as directed but add ¼ **teaspoon ground cinnamon**, ¼ **teaspoon ground turmeric (optional)**, and ¼ **teaspoon ground cumin** to water.

DRIED TOMATO AND
GREEN ONION COUSCOUS
Prepare couscous as directed but omit raisins and add **1 green onion**, sliced, and **5 dried tomato halves**, chopped, to water.

ALMOND COUSCOUS
Prepare couscous as directed but omit raisins and add **a pinch each of ground nutmeg** and **dried thyme** to water. Stir ¼ **cup toasted slivered almonds** into fluffed couscous.

ISRAELI COUSCOUS WITH CURRANTS

Israeli or pearl couscous is a delicious alternative to traditional couscous. This larger, chewier pasta adds a pleasant texture to the dish, and it takes on a hint of nutty flavor when toasted.

Prep: 10 minutes   Cook: 20 minutes

1 bunch green onions

2 tablespoons butter or margarine

3 cups Israeli (pearl) couscous

2 cups water

1 cup chicken broth

¼ teaspoon ground allspice

½ teaspoon salt

¼ teaspoon ground black pepper

¾ cup walnuts, toasted and chopped

½ cup currants

½ cup loosely packed fresh mint leaves, chopped

Israeli Couscous with Currants

1. Cut white and light-green portion of green onions into ½-inch pieces. Thinly slice dark-green portions; reserve dark-green onion slices separate from ½-inch pieces.

2. In 4-quart saucepan, heat butter on medium until melted. Add white and light-green onion pieces, and cook 3 minutes or until beginning to soften. Add couscous and cook 7 to 9 minutes or until most grains are browned, stirring frequently.

3. Add water, broth, allspice, salt, and pepper to couscous; heat to boiling on high. Reduce heat to low; cover and simmer 8 to 10 minutes or until liquid is absorbed and couscous is tender but still slightly chewy.

4. Remove couscous from heat. Stir in toasted walnuts, currants, chopped mint leaves, and reserved sliced green onions. Makes about 6½ cups or 12 accompaniment servings.

Each serving: About 220 calories, 6g protein, 34g carbohydrate, 7g total fat (1g saturated), 3g fiber, 0mg cholesterol, 180mg sodium.

FRUITED MULTIGRAIN PILAF WITH ALMONDS

·····················

Get a double dose of grain goodness (brown rice and bulgur) in this delicious pilaf studded with dried fruit and toasted almonds.

Prep time: 5 minutes
Total time: 40 minutes plus standing

1 teaspoon olive oil
1 medium onion chopped
½ cup instant (10-minute) brown rice
1 can (14½ ounces) chicken broth (about 1³/₄ cups)
½ cup water
½ cup bulgur
½ cup dried fruit bits
½ cup sliced almonds, toasted

1. In 3-quart saucepan, heat oil over medium heat. Add onion and cook until lightly browned, about 4 minutes, stirring. Stir in rice; cook 1 minute. Add broth and water; heat to boiling. Reduce heat to low; cover and simmer 15 minutes.

2. Stir in bulgur; heat to boiling over high heat. Reduce heat to low; cover and simmer until rice and bulgur are tender and liquid is absorbed, 10 to 12 minutes.

3. Remove from heat. Stir in fruit; cover and let stand 5 minutes, then stir in almonds. Makes 6 accompaniment servings.

Each serving: About 180 calories, 5g protein, 28g carbohydrate, 7g total fat (1g saturated), 4g fiber, 0mg cholesterol, 295mg sodium.

WHEAT BERRIES WITH BROWN BUTTER AND PECANS

·····················

Wheat berries have an appealing chewy texture. Combining them with pecans and brown butter brings out the grain's nutty flavor.

Prep: 10 minutes plus overnight to soak
Cook: 1 hour 20 minutes

1 cup wheat berries (whole-grain wheat)
2 tablespoons butter or margarine
1 medium onion, chopped
½ cup pecans, coarsely chopped
½ teaspoon salt
⅛ teaspoon ground black pepper
1 tablespoon water
2 tablespoons chopped fresh parsley

1. In bowl, place wheat berries with enough *water* to cover by 2 inches. Soak overnight. Drain.

2. In 3-quart saucepan, combine wheat berries and *3 cups water*; heat to boiling over high heat. Reduce heat; cover and simmer until wheat berries are tender but still firm to the bite, about 1 hour. Drain.

3. In same clean saucepan, melt butter over medium heat. Add onion and cook, stirring frequently, until tender, about 5 minutes. Stir in pecans, salt, and pepper. Cook, stirring, until pecans are lightly toasted and butter begins to brown, about 3 minutes. Stir in wheat berries and water; heat through. Stir in parsley. Makes about 3½ cups or 6 accompaniment servings.

Each serving: About 212 calories, 5g protein, 27g carbohydrate, 11g total fat (3g saturated), 10mg cholesterol, 233mg sodium.

CREAMY POLENTA

....

Long a popular staple in northern Italy, our method ensures lump-free results.

Prep: 5 minutes   Cook: 30 minutes

- 2 cups cold water
- 1 teaspoon salt
- 1½ cups yellow cornmeal
- 4½ cups boiling water
- ½ cup freshly grated Parmesan cheese
- 4 tablespoons butter or margarine, cut into pieces

1. In 5-quart Dutch oven, combine cold water and salt. With wire whisk, gradually beat in cornmeal until smooth. Whisk in boiling water. Heat to boiling over high heat. Reduce heat to medium-low and cook, stirring frequently with wooden spoon, until mixture is very thick, 20 to 25 minutes.

2. Stir Parmesan and butter into polenta until butter has melted. Serve immediately. Makes 8 accompaniment servings.

Each serving: About 173 calories, 5g protein, 20g carbohydrate, 8g total fat (5g saturated), 20mg cholesterol, 464mg sodium.

BROILED POLENTA WEDGES

Line 13" by 9" baking pan with foil, extending foil over rim. Prepare Creamy Polenta as directed but use only 3½ cups boiling water and cook until mixture is very thick and indentation remains when a spoon is dragged through polenta, 30 to 35 minutes. Stir in Parmesan and butter as directed. Spoon mixture into prepared pan, smoothing top. Refrigerate until very firm, at least 1 hour. Preheat broiler. Lift foil with polenta from baking pan; place on cookie sheet. Cut polenta into 16 triangles; separate triangles. Brush **1 tablespoon melted butter or margarine** on polenta wedges. Broil 5 to 7 inches from heat source until lightly browned and heated through, about 10 minutes.

ROSEMARY POLENTA WEDGES

Prepare Broiled Polenta Wedges as directed but add ½ **teaspoon chopped fresh rosemary** or ¼ **teaspoon dried rosemary,** crumbled, to melted butter.

MICROWAVE POLENTA

In deep 4-quart microwave-safe bowl or casserole, combine **2 cups low-fat milk, 1½ cups cornmeal,** and **1 teaspoon salt** until blended. Stir in **4½ cups boiling water.** Cook in microwave oven on High about 12 to 15 minutes. After first 5 minutes of cooking, with wire whisk, stir vigorously until smooth (mixture will be lumpy at first). Stir two more times during cooking. When polenta is thick and creamy, stir in **4 tablespoons butter,** cut into pieces, and ½ **cup freshly grated Parmesan cheese.**

HAZELNUT-HONEY GRANOLA

....

Eat this granola as a snack, or serve as a breakfast cereal.

Prep: 20 minutes   Bake: 30 minutes

- 3 cups old-fashioned oats, uncooked
- ¾ cup honey
- 4 tablespoons butter or margarine, melted
- 1½ teaspoons vanilla extract
- 1 cup hazelnuts (filberts) and/or whole natural almonds, coarsely chopped
- ½ cup toasted wheat germ
- ½ cup sesame seeds
- 1 cup dried tart cherries (4 ounces) or dark seedless raisins
- ½ cup dried apricots (3 ounces), thinly sliced
- ½ cup golden raisins

1. Preheat oven to 350°F. Divide oats between two jelly-roll pans; bake, stirring twice, until lightly toasted, about 15 minutes.

2. In large bowl, combine honey, melted butter, and vanilla. Add toasted oats, hazelnuts, wheat germ, and sesame seeds, stirring to coat. Spread mixture evenly in same jelly-roll pans.

3. Bake, stirring every 5 minutes, until mixture is dark golden brown, 15 to 20 minutes. Cool granola in pans on wire racks. Transfer granola to bowl and stir in cherries, apricots, and golden raisins. Store in airtight container. Makes about 9 cups.

Each ¼ cup: About 118 calories, 2g protein, 18g carbohydrate, 5g total fat (1g saturated), 3mg cholesterol, 15mg sodium.

PUFFY CHEDDAR GRITS

....

Serve this cheese-filled casserole for brunch along with bacon and sausages or as a side dish for dinner. If you wish, refrigerate the cooked grits overnight and bake them the next morning; just add 20 minutes to the baking time.

Prep: 20 minutes   Bake: 45 minutes

3½ cups milk
2 cups water
2 tablespoons butter or margarine
1 teaspoon salt
1¼ cups quick hominy grits
8 ounces Cheddar cheese, shredded (2 cups)
5 large eggs
1 teaspoon hot pepper sauce
¼ teaspoon ground black pepper

1. Preheat oven to 325°F. Grease shallow 2½-quart casserole. In 4-quart saucepan, combine 1½ cups milk, water, butter, and salt; heat to boiling over medium-high heat. With wire whisk, gradually whisk in grits, beating constantly to prevent lumps. Reduce heat; cover and cook, stirring occasionally with wooden spoon, 5 minutes (grits will be very stiff). Remove from heat; stir in Cheddar.

Spoonbread

2. In medium bowl, with wire whisk, beat eggs, remaining 2 cups milk, hot pepper sauce, and black pepper until blended. Gradually stir egg mixture into grits.

3. Pour grits mixture into prepared casserole. Bake until knife inserted in center comes out clean, about 45 minutes. Makes 8 main-dish servings.

Each serving: About 338 calories, 16g protein, 24g carbohydrate, 20g total fat (11g saturated), 185mg cholesterol, 604mg sodium.

SPOONBREAD

....

Soft enough to eat with a spoon, this Southern classic is a cross between a bread and a soufflé.

Prep: 15 minutes plus standing   Bake: 40 minutes

3 cups milk
½ teaspoon salt
¼ teaspoon ground black pepper
1 cup cornmeal
4 tablespoons butter or margarine, cut into pieces
3 large eggs, separated

1. Preheat oven to 400°F. Generously grease shallow 1½-quart baking dish.

2. In 4-quart saucepan, combine milk, salt, and pepper; heat to boiling over medium-high heat. Remove from heat; with wire whisk, whisk in cornmeal. Add butter, whisking until melted. Let stand 5 minutes.

3. Whisk egg yolks, one at a time, into cornmeal mixture until blended. In medium bowl with mixer at high speed, beat egg whites just until soft peaks form when beaters are lifted. Gently fold beaten egg whites, one-half at a time, into cornmeal mixture just until blended. Pour evenly into prepared baking dish. Bake until spoonbread is set, about 40 minutes. Serve immediately. Makes 8 accompaniment servings.

Each serving: About 203 calories, 7g protein, 18g carbohydrate, 11g total fat (6g saturated), 108mg cholesterol, 272mg sodium.

10
QUICK & EASY WEEKNIGHT MEALS

A balanced, delicious meal does not mean slaving away for hours, which is a good thing in today's busy world. You can have a meal on the table in 30 minutes or less, using some simple steps:

• Have all the tools and cookware that you need out and ready when starting the meal.

• The foods you use can affect how long dinner will take to cook. Choose ingredients that can be purchased partially prepared such as bagged precut vegetables. Take advantage of supermarket convenience foods. Store-bought glazes, rubs, and marinades can add a whole lot of flavor in very little time.

• When a recipe calls for moist heat, turn to your microwave. Salmon steaks, for example, cook more rapidly and are easier to handle than when they're poached on the stovetop. The higher the wattage, the faster food cooks; our recipes were tested in 1,000-watt ovens.

• Have a slow cooker? Before leaving the house for work or errands, load an electric slow cooker with the ingredients for stew or chili. For best results, choose a cooker that has a heating element in the sidewall for even heating, both high and low settings, and a liner or crock that can be removed for cleaning.

UTENSILS

The utensils you use can make all the difference. Here is our list of must-haves:

• heavy 12-inch nonstick skillet with a lid
• paring knife for trimming vegetables and fruits
• chef's knife for fast chopping and slicing
• serrated knife for cutting delicate foods
• kitchen scissors for snipping herbs
• heatproof silicone spatula
• Microplane® grater for grating citrus peel and ginger

GROCERY SHOPPING

When grocery shopping, go to the store with menu concepts for at least several meals. Check your pantry for needed staples before you head out, and stock up on foods that are running low. In the produce aisle, let freshness be your guide.

Good Housekeeping's Favorite Fast Foods:
fresh pasta • couscous • quick-cooking brown rice • marinated or precooked meats and poultry • presliced meats and poultries • spiced blends • salad dressing • packaged salad greens and vegetables • frozen vegetables • flavored cheeses

Faster Food: Favorite Shortcuts

• Take a few minutes to assemble all the ingredients; it saves time in the long run.

• If you're going to need noodles for your dinner, put the water on to boil as soon as you get home.

• Do two tasks at once, but make sure only one requires close attention.

• Use your microwave to precook ingredients that take a long time such as potatoes and squash.

• Cut meat into cubes to speed up cooking time.

• Thinly slice long-cooking vegetables like carrots and parsnips.

STEAK PIZZAIOLA

·······································

Made with ingredients typically found at neighborhood pizzerias, this dish is perfect for a midweek supper. If you like, serve the steak on grilled Italian bread.

Prep: 15 minutes   Cook: 15 minutes

- 2 tablespoons olive oil
- 1 large onion (12 ounces), thinly sliced
- 2 garlic cloves, finely chopped
- 1 large red pepper, thinly sliced
- 1 large yellow pepper, thinly sliced
- 4 ounces mushrooms, trimmed and thickly sliced
- 1 can (15 ounces) crushed tomatoes
- ³/₄ teaspoon salt
- 8 beef minute steaks (2 ounces each)

1. In nonreactive 12-inch skillet, heat 1 tablespoon oil over medium heat. Add onion and garlic and cook, stirring frequently, until onion is tender-crisp, about 2 minutes.

2. Add red and yellow peppers and mushrooms and cook, stirring frequently, until peppers are tender-crisp, about 2 minutes longer.

3. Add tomatoes and ¼ teaspoon salt; cook just until sauce has slightly thickened, about 2 minutes longer. Transfer to medium bowl; keep warm.

4. Wipe skillet with paper towels, then heat remaining 1 tablespoon oil over medium-high heat until very hot. Sprinkle beef with remaining ½ teaspoon salt; cook steaks, in batches, until just cooked through, about 2 minutes per side, transferring steaks to warm platter as they are cooked. Spoon sauce over steaks. Makes 4 main-dish servings.

Each serving: About 355 calories, 26g protein, 14g carbohydrate, 22g total fat (7g saturated), 72mg cholesterol, 668mg sodium.

Steak Pizzaiola

TUSCAN STEAK AND BEANS

·······································

For the most flavor, be sure to purchase steaks with marbling (streaks of internal fat), which will ensure moistness and great taste.

Prep: 5 minutes   Cook: 20 minutes

- 1 teaspoon olive oil
- 2 boneless beef strip (shell) or rib-eye steaks, ³/₄ inch thick (about 10 ounces each)
- ½ teaspoon salt
- ½ teaspoon coarsely ground black pepper
- 1 medium onion, sliced
- ¹/₃ cup balsamic vinegar
- 2 teaspoons chopped fresh rosemary
- 2 tablespoons water
- 1 pint grape or cherry tomatoes
- 1 can (15 to 19 ounces) white kidney beans (cannellini), rinsed and drained fresh rosemary leaves for garnish

1. In 10-inch skillet, heat oil over medium-high heat until very hot. Sprinkle steaks with salt and pepper. Add steaks to skillet and cook, turning once, 8 to 10 minutes for medium-rare or until desired doneness. Transfer steaks to cutting board; keep warm.

2. Reduce heat to medium. Add onion to drippings in skillet and cook, stirring, until browned and tender, about 5 minutes. Add vinegar, chopped rosemary, and water, stirring until browned bits are loosened from bottom of skillet. Stir in tomatoes and beans; cook, stirring occasionally, until heated through, about 2 minutes.

3. Cut steaks into thin slices and serve with tomato-and-bean mixture. Garnish with rosemary leaves. Makes 4 main-dish servings.

Each serving: About 495 calories, 35g protein, 29g carbohydrate, 25g total fat (10g saturated), 76mg cholesterol, 540mg sodium.

2. Spray 15½" by 10½" jelly-roll pan with nonstick cooking spray. Place potatoes in pan and toss with 2 teaspoons oil, ¼ teaspoon salt, and pepper. Roast potatoes in oven 25 minutes or until fork-tender and beginning to brown, stirring once halfway through roasting.

3. Meanwhile, rub steak with tarragon and ¼ teaspoon salt to season both sides. Heat 12-inch cast-iron or other heavy skillet on medium-high. Add 1 teaspoon oil and steak; cook 12 minutes for medium, or until desired doneness, turning over once. Transfer steak to cutting board. To same skillet, add shallot and cook 1 minute, stirring. Add wine and heat to boiling; boil 2 minutes or until reduced to ⅓ cup.

4. Cook spinach in microwave as label directs. Thinly slice steak and serve with wine sauce, potatoes, and spinach. Makes 4 main-dish servings.

Each serving: About 415 calories, 35g protein, 37g carbohydrate, 14g total fat (5g saturated), 9g fiber, 55mg cholesterol, 460mg sodium.

FLANK STEAK WITH RED WINE AND OVEN FRIES

....

Call it French lite: Lean flank steak has all the protein of the high-fat cuts typically used for a bistro-style "steak frites" dinner. It's also rich in iron, zinc, and several key B vitamins. A side of spinach boosts the vitamin and mineral content, especially of folate, vitamin A, and potassium.

Prep: 15 minutes   Cook: 25 minutes

3 medium russet (baking) potatoes (8 ounces each)

3 teaspoons olive oil

½ teaspoon salt

¼ teaspoon coarsely ground black pepper

1¼ pounds beef flank steak, trimmed of fat

½ teaspoon dried tarragon

1 medium shallot, minced

¾ cup dry red wine

1 bag (9 ounces) microwave-in-the-bag baby spinach

1. Preheat oven to 450°F. Cut each unpeeled potato crosswise in half, then cut each half lengthwise into 8 wedges.

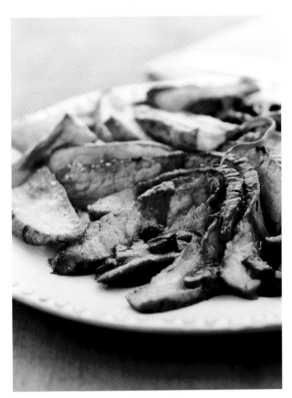

Flank Steak with Red Wine and Oven Fries

CHIPOTLE SKIRT STEAK WITH AVOCADO SALSA

....

Serve this Southwestern winner at your next barbecue.

Prep: 10 minutes plus standing   Grill: 6 minutes

- 1 tablespoon chipotle chile powder
- ³/₄ teaspoon salt
- 1¼ pounds beef skirt steak
- 2 plum tomatoes, coarsely chopped
- 1 ripe medium avocado, pitted and peeled, cut into ½-inch pieces
- ½ cup salsa verde or mild salsa

1. Prepare outdoor grill for direct grilling over medium heat. In cup, with fork, stir chipotle chile powder and salt. Use to rub on steak.

2. Prepare salsa: In medium bowl, stir tomatoes, avocado, and salsa. (Makes 2 cups.)

3. Place steak on grill over medium heat. Cook steak, turning once, 6 to 8 minutes for medium-rare or until desired doneness. Transfer steak to cutting board and let stand 5 minutes to set juices for easier slicing. Cut against the grain into thin slices. Serve with avocado salsa. Makes 4 main-dish servings.

Each serving: About 420 calories, 29g protein, 9g carbohydrate, 30g total fat (10g saturated), 92mg cholesterol, 640mg sodium.

No-Bake Tamale Pie

NO-BAKE TAMALE PIE

....

Making tamale pie is usually a time-consuming job, but our speedy filling is cooked in a skillet and the saucepan topping is replaced by sliced precooked polenta.

Prep: 10 minutes   Cook: 20 minutes

- 4 teaspoons vegetable oil
- 1 small onion, chopped
- 2 garlic cloves, crushed with garlic press
- 1 pound lean (90%) ground beef
- 2 teaspoons chili powder
- 1 teaspoon ground cumin
- ½ teaspoon salt
- 1 log (16 ounces) precooked polenta, cut crosswise into 8 slices
- 1 jar (16 ounces) medium-hot salsa (about 1³/₄ cups)
- 1 cup frozen whole-kernel corn
- ½ cup loosely packed fresh cilantro leaves, chopped

1. In 12-inch skillet, heat 2 teaspoons oil over medium-high heat. Add onion and cook, stirring frequently, until golden, about 3 minutes. Stir in garlic; cook 30 seconds.

2. Stir in ground beef and cook, breaking up meat with side of spoon, until meat is no longer pink, about 5 minutes. Stir in chili powder, cumin, and salt; cook 1 minute, stirring.

3. In nonstick 10-inch skillet, heat remaining 2 teaspoons oil over medium-high heat. Add polenta and cook until golden on both sides and heated through, about 10 minutes.

4. Meanwhile, stir salsa and frozen corn into meat mixture; simmer 3 to 5 minutes to blend flavors. Stir in cilantro.

5. Spoon meat mixture into 9-inch deep-dish pie plate or shallow 1½-quart casserole. Arrange polenta on top. Spoon 2 polenta slices and some chile onto each of 4 dinner plates. Makes 4 main-dish servings.

Each serving: About 425 calories, 32g protein, 38g carbohydrate, 17g total fat (5g saturated), 69mg cholesterol, 1,325mg sodium.

BEEF-STUFFED TOMATOES

Be sure to use the ripest and most flavorful tomatoes you can find for this dish.

Prep: 10 minutes   Cook: 20 minutes

- 1   medium onion, finely chopped
- 1   pound lean (90%) ground beef
- 4   ripe jumbo tomatoes (about 14 ounces each)
- ½   cup uncooked instant white rice or
     ¾ cup cooked rice
- 1¼ teaspoons salt
- 1¼ teaspoons ground black pepper
- 1   cup loosely packed fresh mint leaves

1. In 12-inch skillet, cook onion and ground beef over medium-high heat, breaking up meat with spoon, until meat is browned, about 10 minutes.

2. Meanwhile, cut thin slice from stem end of each tomato; reserve. With spoon, scoop out seeds and pulp from each; reserve. Transfer tomato shells to microwave-safe plate and cook in microwave oven on High just until heated through, about 2 minutes.

3. Chop reserved tomato slices and pulp. Stir tomatoes, rice, salt, and pepper into meat mixture. Cover and cook over medium heat 10 minutes.

4. Meanwhile, chop mint. Stir into meat mixture.

5. Fill tomato shells with hot meat mixture. Makes 4 main-dish servings.

Each serving: About 365 calories, 29g protein, 33g carbohydrate, 15g total fat (5g saturated), 71mg cholesterol, 835mg sodium.

VARIATIONS ON A STUFFED TOMATO

Use our tasty beef-rice mixture to stuff other vegetables. Use one type or a combination, if you like. Substitute the chopped flesh from the vegetables for the tomato pulp.

Zucchini: Halve, seed, and microwave, covered, just until tender, 3 to 5 minutes. Remove all but a ¼-inch wall of flesh.

Baby Eggplant: Halve lengthwise and steam or microwave just until tender. Remove all but a ¼-inch wall of flesh.

PICADILLO

The unusual seasoning of this crowd-pleasing ground-beef stew, a Latino classic, calls for a simple accompaniment of steamed rice and a crisp green salad. To use the mixture as a filling for empanadas or turnovers, cook it until almost all of the liquid has evaporated.

Prep: 10 minutes   Cook: 25 minutes

- 4   teaspoons olive oil
- 1   medium onion, finely chopped
- 4   garlic cloves, finely chopped
- 2   pounds ground beef chuck
- 1   can (15 ounces) crushed tomatoes
- ½   cup pimiento-stuffed olives (salad olives), coarsely chopped
- ⅓   cup dark seedless raisins
- 3   tablespoons tomato paste
- 1   tablespoon red wine vinegar
- 1   teaspoon unsweetened cocoa
- 1   teaspoon ground cumin
- ½   teaspoon salt
- ¼   cup slivered almonds, toasted

1. In 12-inch skillet, heat oil over medium heat. Add onion and garlic and cook, stirring frequently, until onion is tender, about 5 minutes. Stir in ground beef and cook, breaking up meat with side of spoon, until meat is no longer pink, about 5 minutes.

2. Add tomatoes, olives, raisins, tomato paste, vinegar, cocoa, cumin, and salt; stir to combine and heat to boiling. Reduce heat and simmer until slightly thickened, about 5 minutes. Stir in almonds and serve. Makes 6 main-dish servings.

Each serving: About 397 calories, 34g protein, 17g carbohydrate, 23g total fat (7g saturated), 94mg cholesterol, 743mg sodium.

MEATBALL STROGANOFF

··

As an accompaniment to this dish, toss 1 pound green beans, Brussels sprouts, or broccoli florets with 1 tablespoon olive oil and $^1/_4$ teaspoon salt. Spread in jelly-roll pan and roast at 450°F until tender, 15 to 20 minutes.

Prep: 10 minutes   Cook: 20 minutes

- 8   ounces wide egg noodles
- 1   pound lean (90%) ground beef
- 12   saltine crackers, crushed
- 1   small onion, finely chopped
- 1   large egg
- $^1/_4$ teaspoon salt
- 3   tablespoons water
- 1   tablespoon all-purpose flour
- 1   teaspoon paprika
- 1   can (14$^1/_2$ ounces) chicken broth or 1$^3/_4$ cups Chicken Broth (page 70)
- $^1/_2$ cup reduced-fat sour cream

1. In covered 4-quart saucepan, heat *3 quarts salted water* to boiling over high heat. Add noodles and cook as label directs.

2. Meanwhile, in medium bowl, combine beef, saltines, onion, egg, salt, and water just until well blended but not overmixed. Shape mixture into 16 meatballs, handling meat as little as possible.

3. Spray nonstick 12-inch skillet with vegetable cooking spray; heat over medium heat until hot. Add meatballs and cook, turning frequently, until meat is browned and no longer pink in center, about 12 minutes. Transfer meatballs to plate.

4. Stir flour and paprika into drippings in pan; cook, stirring, 30 seconds. Stir in broth and heat to boiling; boil until thickened, about 2 minutes. Reduce heat to low. Stir in sour cream. Return meatballs to pan; heat through.

5. Drain noodles. To serve, spoon meatball mixture over noodles. Makes 4 main-dish servings.

Each serving: About 560 calories, 36g protein, 52g carbohydrate, 22g total fat (9g saturated), 190mg cholesterol, 865mg sodium.

Meatball Stroganoff

EASY BEEF-STUFFED CABBAGE

....

This simple version of the classic dish steams up to look like open flower leaves. Serve it with a cucumber salad.

Prep: 15 minutes   Cook: 20 minutes

- 1   can (28 ounces) diced tomatoes
- 1¼ pounds lean (90%) ground beef
- 1   bag (8.8 ounces) heat-and-serve precooked rice pilaf (do not heat)
- 1   cup loosely packed fresh mint leaves, coarsely chopped
- ¾   teaspoon salt
- ½   teaspoon ground black pepper
- 1   small head green cabbage (about 2 pounds), cored

1. Transfer 1 cup canned tomatoes with some juice to medium bowl. Pour remaining tomatoes with juice into nonstick 12-inch skillet.

2. To tomatoes in bowl, add beef, rice, mint, salt, and pepper; stir until blended.

3. Remove 8 large cabbage leaves from head. Spoon ½ cup meat mixture into center of each leaf; arrange, open side up, in skillet over tomatoes. Cover skillet and cook mixture over medium-high heat until beef loses its pink color throughout, about 20 minutes.

4. To serve, place 2 meat-filled cabbage leaves on each of 4 dinner plates. Spoon tomato sauce over cabbage. Makes 4 main-dish servings.

Each serving: About 405 calories, 34g protein, 28g carbohydrate, 17g total fat (6g saturated), 88mg cholesterol, 1,550mg sodium.

STROGANOFF HISTORY

As one story goes, when a senior member of the affluent Stroganov family could no longer chew chunks of beef, his clever chef thinly shaved the meat, browned, it, then cooked it in sauce. Others believe the dish made its debut at one of the high-class open dinners given by Count Alexander Stroganov of Russia.

VEAL CUTLETS WITH ARUGULA AND TOMATO SALAD

....

This dish is usually prepared with breaded cutlets fried in a large amount of oil. To lighten it up, we sautéed the veal with no coating in just a film of oil. Even without the richness of extra calories, however, this dish is delicious! Try it with turkey or chicken cutlets, too.

Prep: 20 minutes   Cook: 8 minutes

- 1   tablespoon minced shallot
- 1   tablespoon balsamic vinegar
- 1   tablespoon olive oil
- ¾   teaspoon salt
- ½   teaspoon ground black pepper
- 1   pound veal cutlets
- 1   bag (5 ounces) baby arugula or 2 small bunches (3 to 4 ounces each) arugula, tough stems trimmed and leaves coarsely chopped
- 1   cup grape tomatoes, each cut in half
- ½   ounce Parmesan-cheese shavings

1. In large bowl, whisk shallot, vinegar, 2 teaspoons oil, ¼ teaspoon salt, and ¼ teaspoon pepper until blended; set aside.

2. If veal cutlets are large, cut each crosswise in half. If necessary, with meat mallet or with rolling pin, between two sheets of plastic wrap or waxed paper, pound cutlets to even ⅛-inch thickness.

3. In nonstick 12-inch skillet, heat ½ teaspoon oil over medium heat until very hot. Add half of cutlets; sprinkle with ¼ teaspoon salt and ⅛ teaspoon pepper and cook, turning once, until cutlets just lose their pink color throughout, about 2 minutes. Transfer cutlets to warm platter. Repeat with remaining cutlets, remaining ½ teaspoon oil, remaining ¼ teaspoon salt, and remaining ⅛ teaspoon pepper.

4. Add arugula and tomatoes to shallot dressing in bowl and toss until evenly coated. To serve, spoon salad over cutlets on platter and top with Parmesan shavings. Makes 4 main-dish servings.

Each serving: About 225 calories, 31g protein, 5g carbohydrate, 9g total fat (2g saturated), 94mg cholesterol, 585mg sodium.

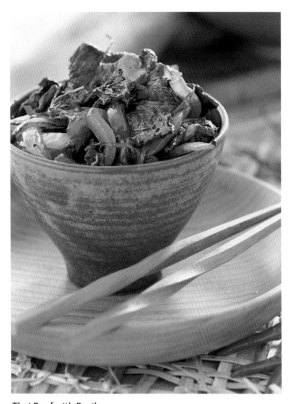

Thai Beef with Basil

1. In medium bowl, combine fish sauce, soy sauce, and brown sugar. Cut round steak lengthwise in half, then cut into ⅛-inch-thick slices across the grain. Add beef to fish-sauce mixture, tossing to coat well; cover and refrigerate beef 30 minutes to marinate.

2. In 12-inch skillet, heat 1 tablespoon oil over high heat until very hot. Add beef mixture and cook, stirring frequently (stir-frying), just until beef is no longer pink, about 1 minute. Transfer beef to clean bowl.

3. Add remaining 1 teaspoon oil to skillet. Add onion and stir-fry until tender-crisp, about 3 minutes. Stir in chiles, garlic, and ginger; cook, stir-frying, 30 seconds.

4. Return beef and any juices to skillet and add basil; heat through. Makes 4 main-dish servings.

Each serving: About 291 calories, 31g protein, 20g carbohydrate, 10g total fat (2g saturated), 65mg cholesterol, 779mg sodium.

THAI BEEF WITH BASIL

Simple and fresh-tasting, this easy but exotic stir-fry is seasoned with fish sauce, one of the basic ingredients of of Thai cooking.

Prep: 15 minutes plus marinating   Cook: 6 minutes

- 3 tablespoons Asian fish sauce (nam pla, page 26)
- 1 tablespoon soy sauce
- 1 tablespoon brown sugar
- 1 beef top round steak (1 pound)
- 1 tablespoon plus 1 teaspoon vegetable oil
- 1 jumbo sweet onion (1 pound), cut into ¼-inch-thick slices
- 3 long red chiles or serrano chiles, seeded and thinly sliced
- 3 garlic cloves, cut into long, thin slices
- 2 teaspoons minced, peeled fresh ginger
- 1 cup loosely packed basil leaves

ORANGE PORK AND ASPARAGUS STIR-FRY

Citrus fruit and grated peel are often used to flavor lean and/or mild-tasting food. Here, pieces of juicy orange, freshly squeezed juice, and grated peel perk up thin slices of lean pork tenderloin that are quickly cooked with fresh asparagus.

Prep: 20 minutes   Cook: 10 minutes

- 2 navel oranges
- 1 teaspoon olive oil
- 1 pork tenderloin (about 12 ounces), trimmed and thinly sliced on diagonal
- ¾ teaspoon salt
- ¼ teaspoon ground black pepper
- 1½ pounds thin asparagus, trimmed and each stalk cut in half
- 1 garlic clove, crushed with garlic press
- ¼ cup water

1. From 1 orange, grate 1 teaspoon peel and squeeze ¼ cup juice. Cut peel and white pith from remaining orange. Cut orange crosswise into ¼-inch-thick slices; cut each slice into quarters.

2. In nonstick 12-inch skillet, heat ½ teaspoon oil over medium heat until very hot. Add half of pork slices and sprinkle with ¼ teaspoon salt and ⅛ teaspoon pepper; cook, stirring frequently (stir-frying), until pork just loses its pink color, about 2 minutes. Transfer pork to plate. Repeat with remaining ½ teaspoon oil, pork, ¼ teaspoon salt, and remaining ⅛ teaspoon pepper. Transfer pork to same plate.

3. To same skillet, add asparagus, garlic, orange peel, remaining ¼ teaspoon salt, and water; cover and cook, stirring occasionally, until asparagus is tender-crisp, about 2 minutes.

4. Return pork and any juices to skillet. Add orange juice and orange pieces; cook, stirring often, until heated through. Makes 4 main-dish servings.

Each serving: About 165 calories, 24g protein, 8g carbohydrate, 4g total fat (1g saturated), 50mg cholesterol, 495mg sodium.

Gingered Pork and Vegetable Stir-fry

GINGERED PORK AND VEGETABLE STIR-FRY

Serve each person ¾ *cup cooked rice, preferably brown, on the side. To make 4 servings, use 1 cup uncooked rice.*

Prep: 15 minutes   Cook: 15 minutes

- 1 pork tenderloin (12 ounces), trimmed and thinly sliced
- 2 tablespoons grated peeled fresh ginger
- 1 cup low-sodium chicken broth
- 2 tablespoons teriyaki sauce
- 2 teaspoons cornstarch
- 2 teaspoons canola oil
- 8 ounces snow peas, strings removed
- 1 medium zucchini (8 ounces), cut lengthwise in half and thinly sliced crosswise
- 3 green onions, cut into 3-inch pieces

1. In medium bowl, toss pork and ginger. In cup, whisk broth, teriyaki sauce, and cornstarch until smooth; set aside.

2. In nonstick 12-inch skillet, heat 1 teaspoon oil over medium heat until hot. Add snow peas, zucchini, and green onions and cook, stirring frequently (stir-frying), until lightly browned and tender-crisp, about 5 minutes. Transfer vegetables to large bowl.

3. In same skillet, heat remaining 1 teaspoon oil; add pork and stir-fry until pork just loses its pink color, about 3 minutes. Transfer to bowl with vegetables.

4. Stir cornstarch mixture; add to skillet and heat to boiling. Boil, stirring constantly, until sauce thickens slightly, about 1 minute. Return pork and vegetables to skillet and stir until coated with sauce; heat through. Makes 4 main-dish servings.

Each serving: About 186 calories, 21g protein, 8g carbohydrate, 8g total fat (1g saturated), 55mg cholesterol, 430mg sodium.

LATIN PORK CHOPS WITH BLACK BEANS

....

Serve with a mixed green salad and steamed white rice.

Prep: 15 minutes   Cook: 15 minutes

- 4 boneless pork loin chops, ³/₄ inch thick (5 ounces each), well trimmed
- ½ teaspoon ground cumin
- ½ teaspoon ground coriander
- ¼ teaspoon dried thyme
- ⅛ teaspoon ground allspice
- ½ teaspoon salt
- 1 teaspoon olive oil
- 1 medium onion, chopped
- 3 garlic cloves, crushed with garlic press
- 1 can (15 to 19 ounces) black beans, rinsed and drained
- ½ cup chicken broth
- 1 tablespoon fresh lime juice
- ¼ teaspoon coarsely ground black pepper
- ¼ cup packed fresh cilantro leaves, chopped fresh orange wedges (optional)

1. Pat pork chops dry with paper towels. In cup, with fork, stir cumin, coriander, thyme, allspice, and ¼ teaspoon salt. Use to rub on pork chops.

2. Spray nonstick 12-inch skillet with vegetable cooking spray; heat over medium heat until hot. Add pork chops and cook 4 minutes; turn pork and cook until lightly browned on the outside and still slightly pink on the inside, 3 to 4 minutes longer. Transfer to platter; cover loosely with foil to keep warm.

3. In same skillet, heat oil over medium heat. Add onion and cook, stirring frequently, until golden, about 5 minutes. Add garlic and cook, stirring, 1 minute longer. Add beans, broth, lime juice, pepper, and remaining ¼ teaspoon salt; heat through.

4. To serve, spoon bean mixture over pork; sprinkle with cilantro. Serve with orange wedges, if you like. Makes 4 main-dish servings.

Each serving: About 340 calories, 42g protein, 25g carbohydrate, 11g total fat (3g saturated), 76mg cholesterol, 760mg sodium.

CRANBERRY-BALSAMIC PORK CHOPS

....

The balsamic vinegar and cranberries are the basis for a rich and tangy sauce that makes this quick preparation anything but ho-hum.

Prep: 15 minutes   Cook: 15 minutes

- 2⅓ cups water
- ³/₄ teaspoon salt
- 1 cup bulgur wheat
- 2 tablespoons chopped fresh parsley
- 1 tablespoon olive oil
- 4 bone-in pork rib chops, ³/₄ inch thick (8 ounces each), trimmed
- ¼ teaspoon ground black pepper
- 1 cup frozen cranberries, thawed
- ¼ cup balsamic vinegar
- 3 tablespoons sugar
- 1 bag (9 ounces) microwave-in-the-bag spinach

1. In 2-quart saucepan, heat 2 cups water and ¼ teaspoon salt to boiling on high. Stir in bulgur; cover and cook on medium-low 10 to 15 minutes, until liquid is absorbed. Stir in parsley.

2. While bulgur cooks, in 12-inch skillet, heat oil on medium until hot. Sprinkle chops with ½ teaspoon salt and pepper. Cook chops in skillet 12 minutes or until browned on both sides and slightly pink in center. Transfer to plate.

3. To same skillet, add cranberries, vinegar, sugar, and ⅓ cup water; heat to boiling, stirring to scrape up brown bits. Add juices from chops on plate; cook 2 minutes to thicken sauce slightly. Cook spinach as label directs.

4. Serve chops with cranberry sauce, bulgur, and spinach. Makes 4 main-dish servings.

Each serving: About 410 calories, 38g protein, 42g carbohydrate, 11g total fat (3g saturated), 13g fiber, 89mg cholesterol, 600mg sodium.

CURRIED PORK WITH OLIVES AND DRIED PLUMS

··

Round out this simple sauté with Almond Couscous (page 302) and some steamed broccoli florets.

Prep: 5 minutes   **Cook: about 20 minutes**

2   pork tenderloins (about 12 ounces each), trimmed
1   tablespoon curry powder
1   can (14½ ounces) low-sodium chicken broth or 1¾ cups Chicken Broth (page 66)
½   cup pitted dried plums (prunes)
¼   cup chopped pimiento-stuffed olives (salad olives)

1. Spray nonstick 10-inch skillet with vegetable cooking spray; heat over medium heat until hot. Meanwhile, rub pork with curry powder.

2. Add pork to skillet and cook 5 to 7 minutes, turning to brown all sides. Add broth, dried plums, and olives; heat to boiling. Partially cover skillet and cook, turning meat occasionally, 10 to 15 minutes longer or until meat thermometer inserted in center of pork reaches 155°F.

3. Transfer pork to cutting board. Slice pork and serve with dried plums, olives, and pan juices. Makes 6 main-dish servings.

Each serving: About 195 calories, 29g protein, 10g carbohydrate, 4g total fat (1g saturated), 68mg cholesterol, 225mg sodium.

---

5 IDEAS FOR . . . FRESH CRANBERRIES

Homemade cranberry sauce will always have a place of honor beside the Thanksgiving turkey. But a bag of these fresh, tart berries can play many other roles in other seasons. Here are five, from an appetizer to dinners and desserts.

GARNET BRUSCHETTA

In microwave-safe 1-quart bowl, combine 1 cup cranberries and 3 tablespoons hot red pepper jelly. Microwave on High 2 minutes or until cranberries begin to pop; cool to room temperature. Spread ¾ cup goat cheese on 24 melba toast rounds; top with cranberry mixture, then sprinkle with 3 tablespoons slivered fresh basil leaves. Serves 6.

RUBY CHICKEN

Coat 12-inch nonstick skillet with nonstick cooking spray; place over medium heat. Add 4 large bone-in skinless chicken thighs (1½ pounds); cook 10 minutes to brown both sides. Add 1½ cups cranberries, ¾ cup pineapple jam, and 1½ teaspoons grated peeled fresh ginger. Cook, covered, 5 minutes until some berries pop. Stir in 3 sliced green onions and ¼ cup water; cook 2 minutes or until thighs are cooked through. Serve with rice. Serves 4.

LINZER WAFFLE SUNDAES

In microwave-safe 2-quart bowl, combine 2 cups cranberries, ⅔ cup packed brown sugar, 2 tablespoons water, and ¼ teaspoon ground cinnamon. Cover loosely with plastic wrap, venting to let steam escape, and microwave on High 3 minutes or until berries begin to pop. Toast 4 frozen Belgian waffles. Divide 1 pint vanilla ice cream onto top of warm waffles, then spoon on cranberry sauce. Serves 4.

TANGY TACO FILLING

In 12-inch nonstick skillet, cook 1 pound lean ground beef on medium 8 minutes or until no longer pink, breaking up meat with side of spoon. Drain off fat. Stir in 1 can (10 ounces) mild enchilada sauce, 1 cup cranberries, and 3 tablespoons ketchup; cook 6 minutes to thicken. Stir in ¼ cup chopped fresh cilantro leaves. Serve with warm tortillas and sour cream. Serves 4.

CRANBERRY COFFEE CAKE

Preheat oven to 400°F. In 9-inch square metal baking pan, melt 5 tablespoons butter or margarine in oven. Spoon 3 tablespoons butter from pan into large bowl; whisk in ¾ cup water, ½ cup sugar, and 2 large eggs. Stir in 2½ cups reduced-fat cake mix just until combined. Top butter remaining in pan with 1 bag (12 ounces) cranberries; sprinkle with ⅔ cup sugar. Spread batter evenly over cranberry mixture in pan. Bake 35 to 40 minutes or until toothpick inserted in center comes out clean. Cool cake in pan 25 minutes, then loosen edges with knife and invert onto plate. Serves 9.

PORK TENDERLOIN WITH ROASTED GRAPES

....

If you have never had roasted grapes, try this! They are absolutely delicious and a perfect match for the pork.

Prep: 5 minutes   Cook: 25 minutes

- 1 teaspoon fennel seeds, crushed
- ½ teaspoon salt
- ½ teaspoon coarsely ground black pepper
- 1 pork tenderloin (1 pound)
- 2 teaspoons extra-virgin olive oil
- 3 cups seedless red and green grapes (about 1 pound)
- ½ cup chicken broth

1. Preheat oven to 475°F. In cup, with fork, stir fennel seeds, salt, and pepper. Use to rub all over pork.

2. In 12-inch skillet with oven-safe handle (if skillet is not oven-safe, wrap handle of skillet with double layer of foil), heat oil over medium-high heat until very hot. Add pork and cook 5 minutes, turning to brown all sides.

3. Add grapes and broth to skillet; heat to boiling. Cover and place in oven. Roast until meat thermometer inserted in center of roast reaches 150°F, 15 to 18 minutes. Internal temperature of meat will rise to 160°F upon standing. Transfer pork to warm platter.

4. Meanwhile, heat grape mixture to boiling over high heat; boil until liquid has thickened slightly, about 1 minute. Slice pork; serve with grapes and pan juices. Makes 4 main-dish servings.

Each serving: About 245 calories, 25g protein, 22g carbohydrate, 7g total fat (2g saturated), 74mg cholesterol, 475mg sodium.

Pork Tenderloin with Roasted Grapes

HAM STEAK WITH APPLE CHUTNEY

··

This freshly made, sweet-and-tangy chutney is perfect with ham steak, but you can also serve it with grilled pork or chicken.

Prep: 10 minutes   Cook: 35 minutes

- 2 teaspoons vegetable oil
- 1 medium onion, chopped
- 2 Golden Delicious apples, peeled, cored, and chopped
- 1 teaspoon minced, peeled fresh ginger
- ¾ cup apple juice
- 1 tablespoon cider vinegar
- ¼ cup golden raisins
- ½ teaspoon freshly grated orange peel
- ¼ teaspoon salt
- 1 fully cooked smoked-ham center slice, 1 inch thick (2 pounds)

1. In nonreactive 2-quart saucepan, heat oil over medium heat. Add onion and cook, stirring occasionally, 5 minutes. Stir in apples and ginger and cook 3 minutes longer. Stir in apple juice, vinegar, raisins, orange peel, and salt; heat to boiling. Reduce heat and simmer 10 minutes. (Makes 2⅔ cups chutney.)

2. Meanwhile, heat 10-inch skillet over medium heat until very hot. Add ham steak and cook until heated through and lightly browned, 8 to 10 minutes per side. Serve with chutney. Makes 6 main-dish servings.

Each serving: About 257 calories, 29g protein, 17g carbohydrate, 8g total fat (2g saturated), 65mg cholesterol, 1,922mg sodium.

HAM STEAK WITH CREAMY CHEESE GRITS

··

For an appetizer, place a bowl of orange and grapefruit sections on the table for everyone to enjoy while the ham and grits cook. Serve this classic combination with toasted pumpernickel-raisin bread from the bakery.

Prep: 5 minutes   Cook: 15 minutes

- 1¼ cups milk
- 1 can (14½ ounces) low-sodium chicken broth or vegetable broth or 1¾ cups Chicken Broth (page 70)
- ¼ teaspoon ground red pepper (cayenne)
- ¼ teaspoon dried thyme
- ¾ cup quick-cooking grits
- 4 ounces Cheddar cheese, shredded (1 cup)
- 1 fully cooked smoked-ham center slice, ½ inch thick (about 1¼ pounds)
- 2 tablespoons light brown sugar green onions for garnish

1. In nonreactive 2-quart saucepan, whisk milk, broth, ground red pepper, and thyme; heat to boiling over high heat. Slowly whisk grits into liquid. Reduce heat to low; cover and simmer, stirring occasionally, until mixture has thickened, 5 to 7 minutes. Remove saucepan from heat and stir in Cheddar.

2. While grits are cooking, prepare ham: Spray nonstick 12-inch skillet with vegetable cooking spray; heat over medium heat until very hot. Pat ham dry with paper towels. Coat both sides of ham with brown sugar. Cook ham, turning once, until glazed and heated through, about 5 minutes. To serve, arrange ham on platter with pan juices and grits. Garnish with green onions. Makes 4 main-dish servings.

Each serving: About 537 calories, 45g protein, 33g carbohydrate, 24g total fat (12g saturated), 122mg cholesterol, 2,499mg sodium.

ITALIAN SAUSAGE AND POTATOES

....

Turn this delicious dish into Italian street-festival fare by omitting the potatoes and dividing the sausage-and-pepper mixture among four split hero rolls.

Prep: 10 minutes   Roast: 30 minutes

- 1 pound sweet and/or hot Italian sausages links, cut crosswise into thirds
- 1 pound small red potatoes, each cut in half
- 1 jumbo onion (about 1 pound), cut into 12 wedges
- 2 red and/or yellow peppers, each cut lengthwise into 8 pieces
- 1 tablespoon olive oil
- ½ teaspoon salt
- ¼ teaspoon ground black pepper

1. Preheat oven to 450°F.

2. In 15½" by 10½" jelly-roll pan, combine sausages, potatoes, onion, peppers, oil, salt, and pepper; toss to coat.

3. Roast sausage mixture, stirring once halfway through roasting, until potatoes are fork-tender and sausages are lightly browned, 30 to 35 minutes. Makes 4 main-dish servings.

Each serving: About 545 calories, 20g protein, 37g carbohydrate, 32g total fat (12g saturated), 80mg cholesterol, 925mg sodium.

---

5 IDEAS FOR . . . INSTANT SPUDS

Just because the label says mashed potatoes doesn't mean these dried flakes can't do a lot more. Here, we've turned the ultimate convenience food into pancakes, a hearty casserole, and even a crusty topping for broiled fish.

POTATO-CRUSTED TILAPIA

Preheat oven to 450°F. Grease wire rack and set it in jelly-roll pan. Measure out ¾ cup potato flakes. In bowl, stir 1 cup tartar sauce, ¼ cup snipped fresh chives, and 2 teaspoons grated fresh lemon peel; reserve ½ cup sauce for serving. Spread each of 4 (6-ounce) tilapia fillets with 2 tablespoons remaining sauce; top each with 3 tablespoons potato flakes. Place fish on rack; bake 8 to 10 minutes or until fish turns opaque and top is golden. Serve with reserved sauce. Serves 4.

PESTO MASHED POTATOES

In 3-quart saucepan, heat 1 can (14 to 14½ ounces) reduced-sodium chicken broth to boiling. Remove from heat; stir in 1¼ cups low-fat (1%) milk and ¼ teaspoon ground black pepper. With spoon, stir in 2 cups potato flakes, then swirl in ¼ cup prepared pesto. Serves 6.

BBQ SHEPHERD'S PIE

Preheat broiler. In broiler-safe 10-inch skillet, cook 1¼ pounds ground beef and 1 medium onion, chopped, on medium-high heat 8 minutes or until beef is no longer pink. Drain off liquid. Stir in 1 can (15 ounces) chili beans, drained, and ¾ cup barbecue sauce. Simmer on low 8 minutes or until reduced slightly. Prepare potato flakes as label directs for 6 servings. Spread potatoes on top of meat mixture. Place skillet in oven and broil 6 minutes or until potatoes brown. Serves 6.

PARMESAN POTATO PANCAKES

In bowl, with fork, beat 2 large eggs with 1 cup water. Stir in ⅔ cup potato flakes, ⅔ cup all-purpose flour, ⅓ cup grated Parmesan cheese, ¼ teaspoon baking powder, and ¼ teaspoon salt; let stand 5 minutes. In 12-inch skillet, heat 1 tablespoon canola oil on medium-high. Drop batter by ¼ cups into hot skillet to make 4 pancakes, and cook 2 minutes per side or until puffed and golden. Transfer to rack on cookie sheet and keep warm in oven. Repeat with remaining potato mixture and 1 tablespoon oil. Makes 8.

POTATO AND GREEN ONION SOUP

In 3-quart saucepan, melt 1 tablespoon butter or margarine on medium. Add 2 bunches sliced green onions and cook 2 minutes or until softened, stirring frequently. Add 1 carton (32 ounces) reduced-sodium chicken broth, 1 cup whole milk, and ¼ teaspoon ground black pepper; heat to boiling on high. Stir in 1¼ cups potato flakes. Puree in batches in blender, with center part of cover removed to allow steam to escape. Serves 4.

CHORIZO AND BEAN BURRITOS

....

For the best results, choose Spanish-style chorizo.

Prep: 20 minutes   Cook: 10 minutes

- $^2/_3$ cup regular long-grain rice
- 2 cans (15 to 16 ounces each) low-sodium pinto beans, not drained
- 1 teaspoon vegetable oil
- 1 small onion, chopped
- 2 teaspoons chili powder
- $^1/_4$ teaspoon ground cumin
- 8 ounces fully cooked chorizo sausage, sliced
- 6 burrito-size (10-inch) flour tortillas, warmed
- 4 ounces Cheddar cheese, shredded (1 cup)
- $^1/_2$ cup packed fresh cilantro
- 1 large ripe tomato, chopped

1. Prepare rice as label directs.

2. In food processor with knife blade attached, process beans with their liquid until coarsely chopped.

3. In nonstick 10-inch skillet, heat oil over medium heat until hot. Add onion and cook, stirring occasionally, until lightly browned, 3 to 4 minutes. Stir in chili powder, cumin, and chorizo; cook 2 minutes. Add beans and cook, stirring frequently, until heated through, about 2 minutes.

SAUSAGES
_____

Sausage is simply ground meat mixed with fat, flavorings, salt, and sometimes filler and preservatives in an edible casing. Here are a few of the most common:

ANDOUILLE CAJUN: A heavily smoked sausage seasoned with garlic, hot peppers, and spices, it is made from pork butt or shank meat.

CHORIZO: Coarsely ground pork that is generously seasoned with chili powder, garlic, and other seasonings. Spanish chorizo is made with smoked pork, and Mexican chorizo is made with fresh pork.

ITALIAN SAUSAGE (SWEET OR HOT): Coarsely ground pork flavored with black pepper and often with fennel seed.

KIELBASA: This Polish favorite comes in many varieties, but the most common is smoked and fully cooked.

---

4. Place tortillas on work surface. Spoon equal amounts of rice, bean mixture, Cheddar, cilantro, and tomato across center of each tortilla. Fold sides of tortilla over filling. Makes 6 main-dish servings.

Each serving: About 730 calories, 32g protein, 89g carbohydrate, 28g total fat (11g saturated), 53mg cholesterol, 940mg sodium.

RED BEANS AND RICE

....

Creole cooks traditionally made this dish on wash day (Monday) because it could simmer unattended all day long. Here's our quick, low-fat version.

Prep: 10 minutes   Cook: 20 minutes

- 1 tablespoon vegetable oil
- 2 stalks celery with leaves, sliced
- 1 medium red onion, coarsely chopped
- 2 garlic cloves, finely chopped
- $^1/_2$ teaspoon dried thyme
- 1 bay leaf
- 2 cans (15 to 19 ounces each) red kidney beans, rinsed and drained
- 1 package (6 ounces) sliced Canadian bacon, cut into thin strips
- 1 cup low-sodium chicken broth
- 5 tablespoons chopped fresh parsley
- 1 teaspoon Worcestershire sauce
- $^1/_8$ to $^1/_4$ teaspoon hot pepper sauce
- 1 cup regular long-grain rice, cooked as label directs

1. Prepare rice as label directs.

2. Meanwhile, in 4-quart saucepan, heat oil over medium heat. Add celery, onion, garlic, thyme, and bay leaf; cook, stirring occasionally, until vegetables are tender and lightly browned, about 10 minutes.

3. Stir in beans, Canadian bacon, broth, 4 tablespoons parsley, Worcestershire, and hot pepper sauce. Cook, stirring occasionally, until heated through. Discard bay leaf.

4. To serve, spoon hot rice into 4 large soup bowls. Top each with bean mixture, and sprinkle with remaining 1 tablespoon parsley. Serve with additional hot pepper sauce, if you like. Makes 4 main-dish servings.

Each serving: About 468 calories, 26g protein, 71g carbohydrate, 8g total fat (2g saturated), 21mg cholesterol, 1,085mg sodium.

ASIAN CHICKEN SALAD

·······································

This fast, easy salad is full of Asian-inspired flavors and lots of crunch thanks to crisp cabbage and radishes.

Prep: 20 minutes   **Cook: 15 minutes**

- 3 limes
- 4 medium skinless, boneless chicken breast halves (1½ pounds)
- 1 bag (16 ounces) frozen shelled edamame (green soybeans)
- ⅓ cup reduced-sodium soy sauce
- ¼ cup loosely packed fresh cilantro leaves, chopped
- 1 tablespoon grated peeled fresh ginger
- 2 teaspoons Asian sesame oil
- 1 pound (½ small head) napa cabbage (Chinese cabbage), sliced
- 1 bunch or 1 bag (6 ounces) radishes, trimmed and thinly sliced

1. Cut 2 limes into thin slices. From remaining lime, squeeze 2 tablespoons juice; set aside.

2. In covered 12-inch skillet, heat half of lime slices and 1 inch water to boiling on high. Add chicken; cover, reduce heat to medium-low and cook 13 to 14 minutes or until chicken loses its pink color throughout. With slotted spoon or tongs, remove chicken from skillet and place in large bowl of ice water; chill 5 minutes. Discard poaching liquid. Drain chicken well; with hands, shred chicken into bite-size pieces.

3. Meanwhile, cook edamame as label directs; drain. Rinse with cold running water to stop cooking and drain again. In large bowl, whisk together soy sauce, cilantro, ginger, sesame oil, and reserved lime juice. Add cabbage, edamame, radishes, and shredded chicken to bowl; toss to combine.

4. To serve, transfer to deep bowls and garnish with remaining lime slices. Makes 6 main-dish servings.

Each serving: About 285 calories, 39g protein, 14g carbohydrate, 8g total fat (1g saturated), 6g fiber, 66mg cholesterol, 560mg sodium.

EASY COBB SALAD

·······································

This California classic has been enjoyed since 1937, when it was created in the Brown Derby restaurant.

Prep: 25 minutes

- 6 slices fully cooked, ready-to-serve bacon
- 2 bags (5 ounces each) mixed baby greens (about 16 cups loosely packed)
- 1 pint red or yellow cherry or grape tomatoes, each cut in half
- 2 cups corn kernels cut from cobs (about 4 ears)
- 2 cups (½-inch cubes) skinless cooked chicken meat (about 10 ounces)
- ½ English (seedless) cucumber, unpeeled, cut into ¼-inch pieces
- 3 ounces blue cheese, crumbled (¾ cup)
- ⅓ cup Tomato Vinaigrette (page 498) or bottled vinaigrette salad dressing

1. Heat bacon in microwave oven as label directs; cool slightly, then coarsely chop.

2. Line deep large platter with baby greens. Arrange cherry tomatoes, corn, chicken, cucumber, blue cheese, and bacon in striped pattern over greens. Serve with Tomato Vinaigrette or favorite dressing. Makes 6 main-dish servings.

Each serving without dressing: About 215 calories, 21g protein, 16g carbohydrate, 10g total fat (4g saturated), 49mg cholesterol, 655mg sodium.

SOUTH OF THE BORDER COBB
Prepare as directed above replacing blue cheese with **queso fresco or mild goat cheese**. Add **2 tablespoons chopped cilantro** to vinaigrette.

MEDITERRANEAN COBB
Prepare as directed above replacing corn with **sliced roasted red peppers**. Substitute **feta** for blue cheese and ½ **cup pitted kalamata olives** for bacon. Add **2 tablespoons chopped fresh mint** to vinaigrette.

BUFFALO CHICKEN SALAD

Chicken tenders make this salad a snap.

Prep: 20 minutes   Cook: 13 minutes

1¼ pounds chicken breast tenders, each cut crosswise in half, then lengthwise in half

¼ teaspoon ground red pepper (cayenne)

¼ teaspoon salt

3 tablespoons cayenne pepper sauce

1 tablespoon butter

1 head (large) Boston lettuce, torn into bite-size pieces

1 cup shredded carrots

2 stalks celery, thinly sliced

½ cup bottled blue cheese salad dressing

1. Preheat oven to 450°F. Spray 15½" by 10½" jelly-roll pan with nonstick cooking spray. Toss chicken with red pepper and salt. Place on prepared pan and bake 10 minutes.

2. Meanwhile, in microwave-safe small bowl, microwave pepper sauce, butter, and 1 tablespoon water on High 30 seconds or until butter is melted. Add sauce to chicken in pan; stir to coat. Bake 2 to 3 minutes longer or until chicken is no longer pink throughout.

3. To serve, arrange lettuce on 4 dinner plates; top with chicken. Sprinkle with carrots and celery and drizzle with dressing. Makes 4 servings.

Each serving: About 360 calories, 35g protein, 7g carbohydrate, 21g total fat (5g saturated), 2g fiber, 96mg cholesterol, 1,085mg sodium.

Buffalo Chicken Salad

CHICKEN CAESAR SALAD

Have a little extra time? Add cherry tomatoes that have been cut in half and sliced cucumbers to greens when tossing. Use your vegetable peeler to make thin shavings of fresh Parmesan cheese to garnish the top of the salad.

Prep: 10 minutes   Cook: 5 minutes

12 ounces chicken-breast tenders

1 tablespoon vegetable oil

¼ teaspoon salt

1 bag (7½ to 10 ounces) regular or reduced-fat Caesar salad kit

1 bag (5 to 6 ounces) baby romaine or baby spinach leaves

2½ ounces carrots, cut into 2" by ¼" matchstick strips (about ¾ cup)

⅛ teaspoon coarsely ground black pepper

1. Heat ridged grill pan or heavy 10-inch skillet over medium-high heat until very hot.

2. Meanwhile, in medium bowl, toss chicken with oil and salt until evenly coated.

3. Add chicken to grill pan and cook, turning once, just until chicken loses its pink color throughout, 4 to 5 minutes.

4. Meanwhile, in large bowl, toss lettuce, dressing, croutons, and Parmesan from Caesar salad kit with romaine and carrots.

5. Add cooked chicken to salad and toss again. Sprinkle with pepper. Makes 4 main-dish servings.

Each serving: About 250 calories, 22g protein, 3g carbohydrate, 14g total fat (2g saturated), 60mg cholesterol, 435mg sodium.

THE ORIGIN OF CAESAR SALAD

During Prohibition, a popular spot for a night out was Caesar's Palace in Tijuana, Mexico. On the evening of July 24, 1924, Caesar Cardini had just about run out of food. He improvised by putting together a salad with what was on hand: romaine lettuce, olive oil, some cheese, and eggs. He then prepared the salad tableside, creating an immediate sensation.

CHICKEN SAUTÉ WITH ARTICHOKES, LEMON, AND MINT

....

One skillet and 30 minutes is all it takes to bring this Greek-inspired sauté to the table.

Prep: 10 minutes   Cook: 20 minutes

- 4 medium skinless, boneless chicken breast halves (1½ pounds)
- ¼ teaspoon salt
- ⅛ teaspoon ground black pepper
- 4 teaspoons olive oil
- 1 package (8 to 10 ounces) frozen artichoke hearts, thawed
- ¾ cup chicken broth
- ¼ cup loosely packed fresh mint leaves, chopped, plus additional for garnish
- 1 tablespoon fresh lemon juice
- ¼ cup crumbled feta cheese

1. Place chicken between 2 sheets plastic wrap. With meat mallet or bottom of skillet, pound chicken to even ½-inch thickness; sprinkle with salt and pepper to season both sides.

2. In 12-inch skillet, heat 2 teaspoons olive oil on medium. Add chicken and cook 12 to 14 minutes or until browned on both sides and chicken has lost its pink color throughout, turning over once. Transfer chicken to shallow serving bowl; cover with foil to keep warm.

3. To same skillet, add remaining 2 teaspoons oil and heat on medium until hot. Add artichokes and cook 3 minutes or until browned, stirring occasionally. Stir in broth and heat to boiling on medium-high; boil 2 to 3 minutes or until liquid is reduced by half. Remove skillet from heat; stir in mint and lemon juice.

4. To serve, spoon artichoke sauce over chicken; top with feta. Garnish with additional chopped mint leaves. Makes 4 main-dish servings.

Each serving: About 285 calories, 43g protein, 7g carbohydrate, 9g total fat (3g saturated), 3g fiber, 107mg cholesterol, 515mg sodium.

CHICKEN AND PESTO STACKS

....

There's a tower's worth of fresh summer flavors in this quick and easy dish. If you have an abundance of basil in your summer garden, make a batch of pesto, freeze it in ice-cube trays, then store the frozen cubes in a plastic bag. In a pinch, though, store-bought is just fine.

Prep: 15 minutes   Cook: 20 minutes

- 3 tablespoons prepared pesto
- 3 tablespoons water
- 1 large sweet onion (12 ounces), cut crosswise into 4 slices
- 2 medium yellow peppers (4 to 6 ounces each), each cut into quarters
- 4 medium skinless, boneless chicken breast halves (1½ pounds)
- ¼ teaspoon salt
- ¼ teaspoon ground black pepper
- 2 teaspoons olive oil
- 4 slices fresh mozzarella (4 ounces)
- 1 medium ripe tomato (8 ounces), cut into 4 slices

1. Preheat broiler. In small bowl, mix pesto with water. Spray 15½" by 10½" jelly-roll pan with nonstick cooking spray. Arrange onion slices on pan; brush onion slices with 2 tablespoons pesto mixture. Place pan in oven 6 inches away from heat source; broil onion 5 minutes. Arrange peppers on pan with onion; broil 12 to 15 minutes longer or until vegetables are tender, turning vegetables over halfway through cooking.

2. Meanwhile, place chicken between 2 sheets plastic wrap; with meat mallet, pound to an even ½-inch thickness; season with salt and pepper.

3. In 12-inch skillet, heat oil on medium until hot. Add chicken and cook 6 to 8 minutes or until browned on both sides, turning over once.

4. Top chicken in pan with mozzarella slices; cover and cook 2 to 3 minutes or until cheese melts and chicken is no longer pink throughout.

5. To serve, on each of 4 dinner plates, place 1 slice onion, 2 slices pepper, 1 slice tomato, and 1 piece chicken and mozzarella; drizzle with remaining pesto mixture. Makes 4 main-dish servings.

Each serving: About 400 calories, 48g protein, 16g carbohydrate, 16g total fat (6g saturated), 3g fiber, 122mg cholesterol, 345mg sodium.

CHICKEN BREASTS WITH SIX QUICK SAUCES

....

A choice of easy sauces makes this recipe one for the file.

Prep: 2 minutes plus making sauce
Cook: 10 minutes

1 teaspoon vegetable oil
4 small skinless, boneless chicken breast halves
   (1 pound)
   choice of sauce (below)

1. In nonstick 12-inch skillet, heat oil over medium heat until very hot. Add chicken and cook until chicken is golden brown and loses its pink color throughout, 4 to 5 minutes per side. Transfer chicken to platter; keep warm.

2. Prepare sauce and spoon over chicken. Makes 4 main-dish servings.

APPLE-CURRY SAUCE

After removing chicken from skillet, add **2 teaspoons vegetable oil** to skillet. Add **1 Golden Delicious apple,** peeled, cored, and chopped, and **1 small onion,** chopped. Cook, stirring, until tender. Stir in **1½ teaspoons curry powder** and **¼ teaspoon salt;** cook, stirring, 1 minute. Stir in **½ cup mango chutney, ½ cup frozen peas,** and **½ cup water.** Heat to boiling; boil 1 minute. Spoon over chicken.

Each serving with chicken: About 352 calories, 34g protein, 38g carbohydrate, 5g total fat (1g saturated), 82mg cholesterol, 596mg sodium.

BLACK BEAN SALSA

After removing chicken from skillet, add **1 can (15 to 19 ounces) black beans,** rinsed and drained, **1 jar (10 ounces) thick-and-chunky salsa, 1 can (8¾ ounces) whole-kernel corn,** drained, **2 tablespoons chopped fresh cilantro,** and **¼ cup water** to skillet. Cook, stirring, until heated through, about 1 minute. Spoon over chicken.

Each serving with chicken: About 282 calories, 38g protein, 22g carbohydrate, 4g total fat (1g saturated), 82mg cholesterol, 1,086mg sodium.

CHINESE GINGER SAUCE

After removing chicken from skillet, reduce heat to medium. Add **1 teaspoon vegetable oil** to skillet. Add **1 red pepper,** thinly sliced, and cook until tender-crisp. Add **½ cup water, 2 tablespoons soy sauce, 2 tablespoons seasoned rice vinegar,** and **1 tablespoon grated, peeled fresh ginger.** Heat to boiling; boil 1 minute. Sprinkle with **2 green onions,** chopped. Spoon over chicken.

Each serving with chicken: About 195 calories, 34g protein, 4g carbohydrate, 4g total fat (1g saturated), 82mg cholesterol, 757mg sodium.

PROVENÇAL SAUCE

After removing chicken from skillet, add **1 teaspoon olive or vegetable oil** to skillet. Add **1 medium onion,** chopped, and cook, stirring, until tender. Stir in **1 can (14½ ounces) Italian-style stewed tomatoes, ½ cup pitted ripe olives,** each cut in half, **1 tablespoon drained capers,** and **¼ cup water.** Cook, stirring, until heated through, about 1 minute. Spoon over chicken.

Each serving with chicken: About 253 calories, 35g protein, 11g carbohydrate, 7g total fat (1g saturated), 82mg cholesterol, 785mg sodium.

CREAMY MUSHROOM SAUCE

After removing chicken from skillet, add **1 teaspoon vegetable oil** to skillet. Add **10 ounces mushrooms,** trimmed and sliced, **1 medium onion,** thinly sliced, and **¾ teaspoon salt.** Cook, stirring, until vegetables are golden brown and tender. Reduce heat to low; stir in **½ cup light sour cream** and **¼ cup water;** heat through (do not boil). Spoon over chicken.

Each serving with chicken: About 260 calories, 37g protein, 9g carbohydrate, 8g total fat (3g saturated), 92mg cholesterol, 548mg sodium.

DIJON SAUCE

After removing chicken from skillet, reduce heat to low. Add ½ **cup half-and-half or light cream, 2 tablespoons Dijon mustard with seeds,** and ¾ **cup seedless red or green grapes,** each cut in half, to skillet. Cook, stirring to blend flavors, until sauce has thickened, about 1 minute. Spoon over chicken.

Each serving with chicken: About 234 calories, 34g protein, 7g carbohydrate, 7g total fat (3g saturated), 93mg cholesterol, 285mg sodium.

CHICKEN WITH SMASHED POTATOES, POTPIE STYLE

·······························

To save time, use half of a 10-ounce bag of shredded carrots. To cut the fat by 6 grams, increase the broth to 1¼ cups and omit the cream.

Prep: 10 minutes   Cook: 20 minutes

- 1½ pounds baby red potatoes, each cut in half
- 1 tablespoon vegetable oil
- 4 medium skinless, boneless chicken breast halves (about 1¼ pounds)
- ½ teaspoon salt
- ¼ teaspoon ground black pepper
- 2 medium carrots, cut into 2" by ¼" matchstick strips (about 1½ cups)
- 1 cup chicken broth
- ¼ cup heavy or whipping cream
- ½ teaspoon dried tarragon, crumbled
- 1 cup tiny frozen peas, thawed
- 1 tablespoon butter or margarine

1. In 5-quart Dutch oven, combine potatoes and enough *water* to cover; heat to boiling over high heat. Reduce heat to medium. Cover and simmer until tender, about 12 minutes.

2. Meanwhile, in 12-inch skillet, heat oil over medium-high heat until very hot. Add chicken and sprinkle with ¼ teaspoon salt and ⅛ teaspoon pepper; cook 6 minutes. Turn chicken and reduce heat to medium; cover and cook until chicken loses its pink color throughout, about 8 minutes longer. Transfer chicken to plate; keep warm.

3. To same skillet, add carrots, broth, cream, and dried tarragon; cover and cook over medium-high heat until carrots are tender, about 5 minutes. Remove skillet from heat and stir in peas.

4. Drain potatoes and return to pot. Coarsely mash potatoes with butter and remaining ¼ teaspoon salt and ⅛ teaspoon pepper.

5. To serve, spoon potatoes onto large platter; top with chicken and spoon vegetable mixture over all. Makes 4 main-dish servings.

Each serving: About 456 calories, 40g protein, 41g carbohydrate, 14g total fat (6g saturated), 110mg cholesterol, 637mg sodium.

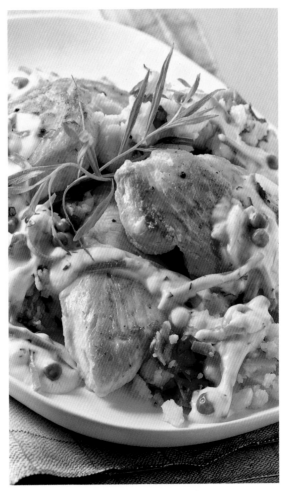

Chicken with Smashed Potatoes, Potpie Style

5 IDEAS FOR . . . BAGGED SLAW

Here, some quick, delicious possibilities.

MOO SHU CHICKEN

In large nonstick skillet, cook 1 package shredded cabbage, ⅓ cup bottled stir-fry sauce, and 4 sliced green onions over medium heat about 4, stirring often. Stir in 2 cups shredded cooked chicken (10 ounces); heat through. Warm 4 (8-inch) flour tortillas and fill with Moo Shu mixture. Makes 4 main-dish servings.

CARIBBEAN PINEAPPLE SALAD

Drain 1 can (20 ounces) pineapple chunks in juice; place in large bowl. Add 1 package shredded cabbage, 2 tablespoons packed brown sugar, 2 tablespoons olive oil, 2 teaspoons grated fresh lime peel, 5 tablespoons fresh lime juice, and ½ teaspoon salt. Toss until well mixed. Makes 6 side-dish servings.

WILTED CABBAGE AND BACON

Chop 3 slices fully cooked bacon and thinly slice 1 small red onion; place in large nonstick skillet and cook over medium heat about 4 minutes, stirring occasionally. Stir in 1 package shredded cabbage, 1 cup shredded carrots, 3 tablespoons cider vinegar, and ½ teaspoon salt; cook until tender-crisp. Makes 6 side-dish servings.

SMOKY TOMATO SOUP

In large microwave-safe bowl, combine ½ package shredded cabbage (4 cups), ¾ cup chopped sweet onion, and 1 tablespoon olive oil. Cover and microwave on High about 4 minutes or until vegetables soften, stirring halfway through. In blender, with center part of cover removed to let steam escape, puree cabbage mixture, 1 can (28 ounces) fire-roasted diced tomatoes, 1 cup water, and 2 teaspoons red wine vinegar. Serve at room temperature or heat in microwave on High 3 minutes to serve hot. Makes 6 first-course servings.

WALDORF SLAW

In large salad bowl, toss 1 package shredded cabbage with 1 cored and chopped Red Delicious apple, 2 stalks chopped celery, ½ cup chopped walnuts, ⅔ cup bottled poppy seed salad dressing, and ½ teaspoon salt. Makes 8 side-dish servings.

BARBECUE CUTLETS WITH CITRUS SLAW

Bring the outdoors in. We doctored bottled barbecue sauce for maximum flavor without firing up the grill and finished with confetti-colored slaw.

Prep: 20 minutes   Cook: 10 minutes

- 1 large navel orange
- 4 medium skinless, boneless chicken breast halves (1½ pounds)
- ¾ cup bottled barbecue sauce
- 1 teaspoon Dijon mustard
- 8 ounces (half 16-ounce bag) shredded cabbage mix for coleslaw
- ¾ fennel bulb (8 ounces), thinly sliced, plus fennel fronds for garnish
- 1 tablespoon white wine vinegar
- ¼ teaspoon salt
- ¼ teaspoon ground black pepper

1. From orange, grate 1½ teaspoons peel. Cut remaining peel and white pith from orange and discard. Holding orange over small bowl to catch juice, cut out segments between membranes; drop segments into bowl. With slotted spoon, transfer segments to cutting board; coarsely chop. Reserve 2 tablespoons orange juice.

2. Place chicken between 2 sheets of plastic wrap; with meat mallet, pound to an even ½-inch thickness.

3. Spray large ridged grill pan with cooking spray and heat over medium-high until hot. Meanwhile, combine ½ cup barbecue sauce, Dijon, and 1 teaspoon orange peel. Generously brush sauce mixture onto chicken.

4. Place chicken on grill pan; cook 4 minutes, turning once. Generously brush chicken with barbecue-sauce mixture; cook 3 to 4 minutes longer or until chicken is no longer pink throughout, turning often and brushing with sauce frequently.

5. Meanwhile, make citrus slaw: In large bowl, mix orange pieces, reserved juice, cabbage mix, fennel bulb, vinegar, salt, pepper, and remaining ½ teaspoon orange peel; toss to combine. (Makes 4½ cups slaw.)

6. Serve slaw with chicken; garnish with fennel fronds. Makes 4 main-dish servings.

Each serving: About 265 calories, 42g protein, 17g carbohydrate, 3g total fat (1g saturated), 4g fiber, 99mg cholesterol, 600mg sodium.

CHICKEN WITH PEARS AND MARSALA

....

To complete the meal, serve with steamed broccoli and rice. Or combine the green vegetable and starch: Cook 1 cup white rice as label directs; stir in 1 cup cooked frozen peas at end.

Prep: 10 minutes   **Cook: 20 minutes**

- 1 teaspoon vegetable oil
- 4 small skinless, boneless chicken breast halves (about 1 pound)
- ¼ teaspoon salt
- ⅛ teaspoon ground black pepper
- 2 ripe Bosc or Anjou pears, peeled, cored, and each cut in quarters
- ¾ cup chicken broth
- ½ cup dry Marsala wine
- 1 tablespoon cornstarch
- 2 teaspoons chopped fresh sage leaves

1. In nonstick 10-inch skillet, heat oil over medium heat until very hot. Add chicken; sprinkle with salt and pepper. Cook, turning once, until chicken loses its pink color throughout, 10 to 12 minutes. Transfer to plate; keep warm.

2. To skillet, add pears and cook until browned on all sides, 3 to 5 minutes.

3. Meanwhile, in small bowl, whisk broth, wine, cornstarch, and sage until smooth.

4. Carefully add broth mixture to skillet. Heat to boiling, stirring, until sauce has thickened slightly, 1 minute. Return chicken with any juices to skillet; heat through. Makes 4 main-dish servings.

Each serving: About 195 calories, 27g protein, 12g carbohydrate, 3g total fat (1g saturated), 66mg cholesterol, 410mg sodium.

PECORINO CHICKEN FINGERS

....

These crispy chicken fingers are the centerpiece of a light and colorful plate with zucchini and marinara dipping sauce on the side.

Prep: 20 minutes   **Cook: 10 minutes**

- 1 cup panko (Japanese-style bread crumbs)
- ⅓ cup freshly grated Pecorino-Romano cheese
- ¼ teaspoon ground red pepper (cayenne)
- ½ teaspoon salt
- 2 large egg whites
- 1 clove garlic, crushed with press
- 1½ pounds chicken tenders
- 3 medium zucchini (8 ounces), cut into ¼-inch-thick half-moons
- 2 tablespoons water
- 1 tablespoon fresh lemon juice
- 1 cup prepared marinara sauce
- ¼ cup loosely packed fresh basil leaves, chopped, plus small whole basil leaves for garnish

1. Preheat oven to 475°F. Place rack in 15½" by 10½" jelly-roll pan; spray pan and rack with cooking spray.

2. On plate, combine panko, Pecorino-Romano, ground red pepper, and ¼ teaspoon salt. Set aside. In pie plate, whisk egg whites and garlic until well mixed.

3. One at a time, dip chicken tenders in egg-white mixture, then into panko mixture to coat evenly; press firmly so crumbs adhere. Arrange chicken on rack in jelly-roll pan; spray chicken lightly with cooking spray.

4. Bake chicken 10 to 12 minutes or until crust is golden brown and chicken is no longer pink throughout.

5. While chicken cooks, in microwave-safe medium bowl, place zucchini and 2 tablespoons water. Cover with vented plastic wrap and cook in microwave on High 5 minutes or until zucchini is just fork-tender. Carefully remove plastic wrap and drain zucchini; stir in lemon juice and ¼ teaspoon salt.

6. Meanwhile, in 1-quart saucepot, heat marinara sauce on medium-low 5 minutes or until hot, stirring occasionally. Remove saucepot from heat and stir in chopped basil. Serve marinara dipping sauce with chicken fingers and zucchini; garnish chicken and dipping sauce with basil leaves. Makes 4 main-dish servings.

Each serving: About 325 calories, 47g protein, 18g carbohydrate, 6g total fat (2g saturated), 106mg cholesterol, 790mg sodium.

TARRAGON CHICKEN WITH GRAPES

Seedless grapes are an unusual but delicious addition to savory dishes. Their mild sweetness complements turkey or chicken cutlets, pork tenderloin, or sausages.

Prep: 15 minutes   Cook: 25 minutes

- 1 cup quick-cooking (10-minute) brown rice
- 4 medium skinless, boneless chicken breast halves (1½ pounds)
- 3 teaspoons chopped fresh tarragon leaves, plus additional sprigs for garnish
- ¼ teaspoon salt
- ¼ teaspoon ground black pepper
- 4 teaspoons olive oil
- 1 small onion, chopped
- ½ cup dry white wine
- 2 cups seedless red grapes
- 1 cup chicken broth

1. Prepare rice as label directs.
2. Meanwhile, place chicken between 2 sheets plastic wrap; with meat mallet, pound to an even ½-inch thickness; season with 2 teaspoons chopped tarragon, salt and pepper.
3. In 12-inch skillet, heat 2 teaspoons oil on medium until hot. Add chicken and cook 12 to 14 minutes or until browned on both sides and chicken loses its pink color throughout, turning over once. Transfer chicken to platter; cover with foil to keep warm.
4. To same skillet, add remaining 2 teaspoons oil and heat on medium until hot. Add onion and cook 6 minutes or until tender, stirring occasionally. Stir in wine and cook on medium-high 1 minute. Add grapes, broth, and remaining 1 teaspoon tarragon and heat to boiling. Cook 5 minutes or until grapes are tender, stirring occasionally.
5. To serve, divide rice evenly among 4 dinner plates; top each with a chicken breast. Spoon grape sauce over chicken; garnish with tarragon sprigs. Makes 4 main-dish servings.

Each serving: About 380 calories, 43g protein, 34g carbohydrate, 8g total fat (1g saturated), 2g fiber, 99mg cholesterol, 420mg sodium.

THAI CHICKEN

Rich coconut-milk sauce infused with seasonings typical of Asian cuisine turns an ordinary chicken dinner into an exotic feast. Serve with jasmine rice.

Prep: 10 minutes   Cook: 20 minutes

- 2 teaspoons vegetable oil
- 4 small skinless, boneless chicken breast halves (about 1 pound)
- ¼ teaspoon salt
- 1 medium lime
- 1 small onion, minced
- 1 tablespoon minced, peeled fresh ginger
- 2 garlic cloves, minced
- ¼ teaspoon crushed red pepper
- ⅓ cup well-stirred unsweetened coconut milk (not cream of coconut)
- 1 tablespoon Asian fish sauce (nam pla, page 26)
- ⅓ cup water
- ¼ cup packed fresh cilantro leaves, chopped

1. In nonstick 12-inch skillet, heat 1 teaspoon oil over medium until very hot. Add chicken; sprinkle with salt and cook 6 minutes. Reduce heat to medium; turn chicken and cook until it loses its pink color throughout, 6 to 8 minutes longer. Transfer chicken to platter; keep warm.
2. Meanwhile, from lime, with vegetable peeler, remove 3 strips peel (2" by 1" each) and squeeze 2 teaspoons juice.
3. In same skillet, heat remaining 1 teaspoon oil over medium heat. Add onion and ginger and cook, stirring occasionally, until onion is tender and golden, about 5 minutes. Add garlic, crushed red pepper, and lime peel; cook, stirring, 30 seconds.
4. Add coconut milk, fish sauce, lime juice, and water to skillet; heat to boiling over medium-high heat.
5. To serve pour sauce over chicken; sprinkle with cilantro. Makes 4 main-dish servings.

Each serving: About 210 calories, 28g protein, 5g carbohydrate, 12g total fat (5g saturated), 66mg cholesterol, 400mg sodium.

SPICY GINGER CHICKEN IN LETTUCE CUPS

· ·

You can use ground turkey or pork in this dish if you prefer, or use a mix of ground meats.

Prep: 15 minutes   Cook: 10 minutes

- 3 tablespoons soy sauce
- 1 tablespoon grated, peeled fresh ginger
- 1 teaspoon sugar
- ⅛ teaspoon crushed red pepper
- 1 garlic clove, crushed with press
- 1 pound ground chicken
- 2 medium stalks celery, chopped
- ½ cup sliced water chestnuts, chopped
- ¼ cup dry-roasted peanuts, coarsely chopped
- 8 to 12 large Boston lettuce leaves

1. In cup, with fork, stir soy sauce, ginger, sugar, crushed red pepper, and garlic; set aside.

2. Spray nonstick 10-inch skillet with vegetable cooking spray; heat over medium heat until hot. Add chicken and cook, breaking up meat with side of spoon, until no longer pink, 4 to 5 minutes.

3. Add celery to chicken in skillet, and cook 2 minutes, stirring occasionally. Add water chestnuts and soy-sauce mixture, cook, stirring constantly, 1 minute to blend flavors. Stir in peanuts.

4. Divide chicken mixture among lettuce leaves. Fold leaves over chicken mixture and eat out of hand. Makes 4 main-dish servings.

Each serving: About 305 calories, 24g protein, 8g carbohydrate, 20g total fat (1g saturated), 66mg cholesterol, 825mg sodium.

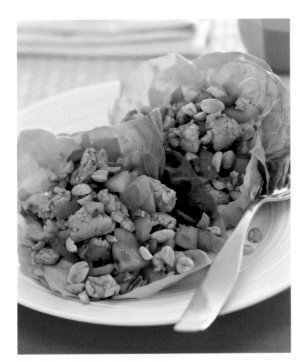

Spicy Ginger Chicken in Lettuce Cups

MAPLE-ROASTED CHICKEN THIGHS WITH SWEET POTATOES

· ·

A mixed-greens salad or green beans with almonds would go nicely with this hearty autumn dish.

Prep: 15 minutes   Roast: 40 minutes

- 4 large bone-in chicken thighs (about 1½ pounds), skin and fat removed
- 2 small sweet potatoes (about 1 pound total), peeled and cut into 1-inch pieces
- 1 small onion, cut into 1-inch pieces
- ½ (16-ounce) bag baby carrots or 8 ounces parsnips, cut into 1-inch pieces
- ¼ cup maple syrup
- 1 teaspoon salt
- ½ teaspoon ground black pepper

1. Preheat oven to 450°F.

2. In jelly-roll pan or large shallow roasting pan, combine chicken, sweet potato, onion, carrots, maple syrup, salt, and pepper; toss to coat.

3. Roast chicken mixture, stirring vegetables once and turning chicken halfway through roasting, until juices run clear when thickest part of thigh is pierced with tip of knife and liquid in pan thickens slightly, 40 to 45 minutes. Makes 4 main-dish servings.

Each serving: About 290 calories, 21g protein, 41g carbohydrate, 4g total fat (1g saturated), 80mg cholesterol, 695mg sodium.

TURKEY CUTLETS WITH CHOPPED SALAD

(Pictured on page 306)

....

Turkey cutlets sautéed until golden, then served over arugula and tomato salad, warm the vegetables just enough to bring out all their flavor.

Prep: 15 minutes   **Cook:** 12 minutes

- 1   green onion, thinly sliced
- 2   tablespoons freshly grated Parmesan cheese
- 4   tablespoons olive oil
- 1   tablespoon red wine vinegar
- ½   teaspoon Dijon mustard
- ¼   teaspoon salt
- ¼   teaspoon coarsely ground black pepper
- 1   pound turkey cutlets
- ⅓   cup seasoned dried bread crumbs
- 1   pound plum tomatoes (4 large), cut into ¾-inch pieces
- 2   small bunches arugula (6 to 8 ounces), coarsely chopped

1. Prepare dressing: In medium bowl, with fork, mix green onion, Parmesan, 2 tablespoons oil, vinegar, mustard, salt, and pepper; set aside.

2. Place turkey cutlets between two sheets of plastic wrap or waxed paper. With meat mallet or rolling pin, pound cutlets to ¼-inch thickness. Coat cutlets with bread crumbs.

3. In 12-inch skillet, heat remaining 2 tablespoons oil over medium-high heat until very hot. Add turkey cutlets, a few at a time, and cook until cutlets are golden brown and lose their pink color throughout, about 2½ minutes per side. Transfer cutlets to warm plate as they are done.

4. Add tomatoes and arugula to reserved dressing; gently toss to mix well. Pile salad on platter and top with turkey cutlets. Makes 4 main-dish servings.

Each serving: About 336 calories, 33g protein, 15g carbohydrate, 16g total fat (3g saturated), 73mg cholesterol, 559mg sodium.

SAUTÉED TURKEY CUTLETS

....

This tender cut is a midweek time-saver: It cooks in just five minutes. Take your pick of the three easy, delicious sauces to spoon over the top.

Prep: 15 minutes plus making sauce
Cook: 15 minutes

- 1   pound turkey cutlets
- ¼   teaspoon salt
- ¼   teaspoon coarsely ground black pepper
- 2   teaspoons olive oil
    choice of sauce (below and opposite)

1. With meat mallet or with rolling pin, between two sheets of plastic wrap or waxed paper, pound turkey cutlets to ¼-inch thickness. Sprinkle cutlets with salt and pepper.

2. In 12-inch skillet, heat oil over medium-high heat until very hot. Add turkey cutlets, a few at a time, and cook until cutlets are golden brown and lose their pink color throughout, about 2 minutes per side, transferring cutlets to platter as they are done. Keep warm while sauce is prepared.

3. In same skillet, prepare one of the sauces. Spoon sauce over turkey cutlets. Makes 4 main-dish servings.

TOMATO-OLIVE SAUCE

To drippings in skillet, add **2 teaspoons olive oil** and **1 small onion,** finely chopped. Cook over medium heat, stirring frequently, until tender, about 5 minutes. Add **1 garlic clove,** finely chopped; cook, stirring, 1 minute. Stir in **1 can (14½ ounces) diced tomatoes with their juice.** Sprinkle with **2 tablespoons coarsely chopped pitted Kalamata olives.** Spoon over turkey cutlets.

Each serving with turkey: About 211 calories, 29g protein, 8g carbohydrate, 7g total fat (1g saturated), 70mg cholesterol, 443mg sodium.

MUSHROOM SAUCE

To drippings in skillet, add **2 teaspoons olive oil** and **1 garlic clove,** crushed with garlic press; cook over medium heat 10 seconds. Add **1 pound mushrooms,** trimmed and sliced, and ¼ **teaspoon dried thyme;** cook, stirring frequently, until mushrooms are golden brown and liquid has evaporated, about 10 minutes. In cup, blend **1 cup chicken broth and 1 teaspoon cornstarch** until smooth. Stir broth mixture into skillet; heat to boiling, stirring. Boil 1 minute.

Each serving with turkey: About 206 calories, 31g protein, 6g carbohydrate, 6g total fat (1g saturated), 70mg cholesterol, 453mg sodium.

CURRY-APRICOT SAUCE

To drippings in skillet, add **2 teaspoons olive oil** and **1 small onion,** chopped; cook over medium heat, stirring occasionally, until onion is tender and golden, 6 to 8 minutes. Increase heat to medium-high. Add **1 teaspoon curry powder** and ½ **teaspoon ground coriander;** cook, stirring, 1 minute. In cup, blend **1 cup chicken broth and 1 teaspoon cornstarch** until smooth. Stir broth mixture and ½ **cup dried apricots,** coarsely chopped, into skillet; heat to boiling, stirring. Boil 1 minute. Spoon over turkey cutlets.

Each serving with turkey: About 259 calories, 36g protein, 13g carbohydrate, 6g total fat (0g saturated), 88mg cholesterol, 465mg sodium.

TYPES OF OLIVE OIL

Supermarkets and specialty food stores carry an array of olive oils from Italy, Spain, Greece, France, and the U.S. The best are cold-pressed, meaning that the oil is extracted through pressure. *Extra-virgin olive oil* is produced by the first pressing of the olives and is considered the finest. *Virgin olive oil* is also a first-press oil but with a higher amount of acidity. *Olive oil* contains a mix of olive oil and virgin or extravirgin olive oil. And *light olive oil* has had some of the flavor removed so it is light (meaning "delicate") in taste.

TURKEY AND WHITE BEAN CHILI

....

We love chili made with ground turkey (or even chicken); it is much lighter—and more healthful—than beef versions but just as flavorful.

Prep: 5 minutes · Cook: 15 minutes

- 1 tablespoon olive oil
- 1 medium onion, chopped
- 1 pound ground turkey
- 2 teaspoons ground coriander
- 2 teaspoons ground cumin
- 2 teaspoons fresh thyme leaves
- 2 cans (15 to 19 ounces each) Great Northern beans, rinsed and drained
- 1 can (4 to 4½ ounces) chopped mild green chiles, not drained
- 1 can (14½ ounces) chicken broth or 1¾ cups Chicken Broth (page 70)
- 2 small ripe tomatoes (about 4 ounces each), coarsely chopped
- 1 lime, cut into wedges

1. In 12-inch skillet, heat oil over medium-high heat. Add onion and cook, stirring frequently, until tender and golden, about 5 minutes. Add turkey and cook, breaking up turkey with side of spoon, until it loses its pink color throughout, about 5 minutes. Stir in coriander, cumin, and thyme; cook, stirring frequently, 1 minute.

2. Meanwhile, in small bowl, mash half of beans.

3. Stir mashed beans, remaining whole beans, chiles with their liquid, and broth into turkey mixture; heat to boiling over medium-high heat. Boil until chili has thickened slightly, about 1 minute. Stir in tomatoes. Serve with lime wedges. Makes 4 main-dish servings.

Each serving: About 495 calories, 35g protein, 49g carbohydrate, 18g total fat (4g saturated), 90mg cholesterol, 1,040 sodium.

ALMOND-CRUSTED TILAPIA

·····················

Appealingly lean and with no fishy taste, mild-mannered tilapia still has plenty of heart-healthy omega-3 fats. (Bonus: It is one of the least mercury-laden fish and is also low in sodium.) Green beans and mushrooms deliver fiber and potassium, while crunchy almonds boast antioxidants.

Prep: 15 minutes   Bake: 15 minutes

- 2 lemons
- 2 tablespoons olive oil
- ½ teaspoon salt
- ¼ teaspoon coarsely ground black pepper
- 4 tilapia fillets (6 ounces each)
- ¼ cup sliced natural almonds (with brown skin still on)
- 1 small onion, chopped
- 1 bag (12 ounces) trimmed fresh green beans
- 1 package (10 ounces) sliced white mushrooms
- 2 tablespoons water

1. Preheat oven to 425°F. From 1 lemon, grate 1 teaspoon peel and squeeze 3 tablespoons juice; cut second lemon into wedges. In cup, mix lemon peel and 1 tablespoon juice, 1 tablespoon oil, ¼ teaspoon salt, and ⅛ teaspoon pepper.

2. Spray 13" by 9" glass baking dish with nonstick spray; place tilapia, dark side down. Drizzle tilapia with lemon mixture; press almonds on top. Bake 15 minutes or until tilapia turns opaque.

3. Meanwhile, in 12-inch skillet, heat remaining 1 tablespoon oil on medium-high 1 minute. Add onion and cook 5 to 6 minutes or until golden, stirring occasionally. Stir in green beans, mushrooms, water, ¼ teaspoon salt, and ⅛ teaspoon pepper. Cook about 6 minutes or until most of liquid evaporates and green beans are tender-crisp. Toss with remaining 2 tablespoons lemon juice. Serve bean mixture and lemon wedges with tilapia. Makes 4 main-dish servings.

Each serving: About 315 calories, 33g protein, 15g carbohydrate, 15g total fat (1g saturated), 5g fiber, 0mg cholesterol, 380mg sodium.

THAI SHRIMP AND ASPARAGUS

·····················

A light and creamy Asian-inspired dish that comes together in minutes.

Prep: 10 minutes   Cook: 12 minutes

- 1 pound shelled and deveined shrimp (page 221)
- 4 teaspoons green curry paste
- 1 tablespoon vegetable oil
- 1 pound asparagus, cut in 2-inch pieces
- 3 tablespoons water
- 2 limes
- 1 can (13½ to 14 ounces) light coconut milk
- 2 tablespoons low-sodium fish sauce (nam pla, page 26)
- 2 packages (8 to 9 ounces each) precooked whole-grain brown rice

1. In medium bowl, toss shrimp with curry paste to coat. In 12-inch skillet, heat oil on medium-high. Add shrimp; cook 3 minutes or just until pink, stirring. Transfer to large bowl.

2. To same skillet, add asparagus and water; cook 4 minutes or until asparagus is tender-crisp and water evaporates, stirring often. From 1 lime, grate 1 teaspoon peel; cut remaining lime into 4 wedges.

3. Add asparagus to shrimp in bowl. To skillet, add coconut milk and lime peel; heat to boiling on high. Reduce heat to medium and cook 5 minutes or until slightly thickened.

4. Return shrimp mixture to skillet. Stir in fish sauce; heat through. Heat rice in microwave as label directs; serve with shrimp and lime wedges. Makes 4 main-dish servings.

Each serving: About 470 calories, 31g protein, 44g carbohydrate, 18g total fat (7g saturated), 3g fiber, 172mg cholesterol, 725mg sodium.

COD LIVORNESE

··

Fish fillets, especially thick ones like cod, may still have a few bones. Before cooking, run your fingers over the flesh, and if you find any strays, use tweezers or needle-nose pliers to remove them.

Prep: 10 minutes   Cook: 20 minutes

2 teaspoons olive oil
1 medium onion, cut lengthwise in half and thinly sliced
2 garlic cloves, crushed with garlic press
⅓ cup dry white wine
1 can (14½ ounces) diced tomatoes
¼ cup pitted Kalamata olives
¼ cup loosely packed fresh parsley leaves, chopped
2 tablespoons drained capers
¼ teaspoon crushed red pepper
4 pieces cod or scrod fillet (about 6 ounces each)
¼ teaspoon salt
1 lemon, cut into wedges

1. In 12-inch skillet, heat oil over medium-high heat. Add onion and cook, stirring occasionally, until lightly browned and tender, about 8 minutes. Stir in garlic; cook, stirring, 30 seconds. Add wine; cook 1 minute. Stir in tomatoes with their juice, olives, parsley, capers, and crushed red pepper; heat to boiling.

2. Arrange cod fillets in single layer over tomato mixture, overlapping as necessary; sprinkle with salt. Cover and cook just until cod turns opaque throughout, 8 to 9 minutes. To serve, squeeze lemon over cod. Makes 4 main-dish servings.

Each serving: About 210 calories, 32g protein, 9g carbohydrate, 5g total fat (1g saturated), 73mg cholesterol, 845mg sodium.

Cod Livornese

ROAST COD WITH BACON, POTATOES, AND KALE

Using frozen chopped kale and frozen mashed potatoes really cuts down on the prep time while still providing the nutrients for a healthy meal.

Prep: 15 minutes   Cook/Roast: 20 minutes

- 1 package (10 ounces) frozen chopped kale
- 1 package (16 ounces) frozen mashed potatoes
- 2 slices bacon, cut crosswise into ½-inch-long pieces
- 1 pound cod or scrod fillet, 1 inch thick, cut into 4 pieces
- ¼ teaspoon salt
- 2 tablespoons cornmeal
- 1 large onion (12 ounces), thinly sliced
- ½ cup chicken broth
- 2 teaspoons cider vinegar

1. In microwave oven, cook kale as label directs; drain. Transfer kale to medium bowl.

2. In microwave oven, heat potatoes as label directs. Add potatoes to bowl with kale and stir until blended. Cover and keep warm.

3. Preheat oven to 450°F. In nonstick 12-inch skillet, cook bacon over medium heat until browned. With slotted spoon, transfer bacon to paper towels to drain. Pour off and discard drippings from skillet.

4. Place cod on waxed paper; sprinkle with salt, then cornmeal, turning to coat.

5. In same skillet, over medium-high heat, cook cod until lightly browned, about 2 minutes per side. Transfer cod to pie plate; place in oven and roast cod until opaque throughout, 8 to 10 minutes.

6. While cod is roasting, to same skillet, add onion. Reduce heat to medium; cover and cook, stirring once, until onion is browned, about 5 minutes. Add broth; cover and cook until onion has wilted, about 4 minutes. Remove from heat; stir in vinegar and bacon.

7. To serve, reheat potato mixture in microwave oven. Divide potato mixture among plates; top with cod, then onion mixture. Makes 4 main-dish servings.

Each serving: About 315 calories, 28g protein, 31g carbohydrate, 9g total fat (4g saturated), 67mg cholesterol, 845mg sodium.

Roast Cod with Bacon, Potatoes, and Kale

ASIAN FLOUNDER BAKE

To toast sesame seeds: Place seeds in a small, dry skillet and cook, stirring, over medium-high heat about one minute until fragrant and golden.

Prep: 10 minutes   Bake: 12 minutes

- ¼ cup reduced-sodium soy sauce
- 2 tablespoons dry sherry
- 1 teaspoon sugar
- 1 teaspoon grated, peeled fresh ginger
- 1 teaspoon Asian sesame oil
- 1 bag (10 ounces) shredded carrots (about 3 cups)
- 1 bag (5 to 6 ounces) baby spinach
- 4 flounder or sole fillets (about 5 ounces each)
- 1 green onion, thinly sliced
- 1 tablespoon sesame seeds, toasted (optional)

1. Preheat oven to 450°F. In small bowl, with fork, stir soy sauce, sherry, sugar, ginger, and sesame oil until blended.

2. In 13" by 9" baking dish, spread carrots evenly. Cover carrots with spinach, then top with flounder. Pour soy-sauce mixture evenly over flounder. Bake until fish turns opaque throughout, 12 to 14 minutes.

3. To serve, sprinkle with green onion and top with sesame seeds, if using. Makes 4 main-dish servings.

Each serving: About 200 calories, 30g protein, 11g carbohydrate, 3g total fat (1g saturated), 68mg cholesterol, 735mg sodium.

HALIBUT WITH BRAISED FENNEL

....

You can substitute other mild white fish for halibut, if you like. Flounder, orange roughy, scrod, and whiting are excellent choices.

Prep: 10 minutes   Cook: 20 minutes

- 2 teaspoons olive oil or vegetable oil
- 1 teaspoon fennel seeds
- 2 medium fennel bulbs (about 1 pound each), trimmed and cut lengthwise into very thin slices
- 3/4 teaspoon salt
- 1/4 teaspoon coarsely ground black pepper
- 1/4 cup balsamic vinegar
- 2 tablespoons water
- 4 halibut steaks, 1 inch thick (about 6 ounces each)

1. In 12-inch skillet, heat oil over medium-high heat. Add fennel seeds; toast, stirring, 1 minute. Add sliced fennel, 1/2 teaspoon salt, and 1/8 teaspoon pepper; cover and cook, stirring occasionally, 5 minutes. Stir in vinegar and water; cover and cook, stirring occasionally, until sauce has thickened and glazes fennel, about 3 minutes.

2. Reduce heat to medium. Arrange halibut in single layer on top of fennel; sprinkle with remaining 1/4 teaspoon salt and remaining 1/8 teaspoon pepper. Cover and cook until halibut turns opaque throughout and flakes easily when tested with a fork, about 10 minutes. Makes 4 main-dish servings.

Each serving: About 270 calories, 38g protein, 14g carbohydrate, 7g total fat (1g saturated), 54mg cholesterol, 615mg sodium.

BALSAMIC VINEGAR

TEST KITCHEN TIP

Authentic balsamic vinegar can only be produced in two areas in Italy: Modena and Reggio Emilia. The bottles' labels must say that the vinegar is Aceto Balsamico Tradizionale as an assurance of quality. This very expensive vinegar is most often used for drizzling—not cooking. Commercial balsamic vinegar from these regions is readily available in the U.S. A well-made commercial balsamic has a delicious rich sweetness with a hint of sourness and a deep brown color; it is ideal for everyday cooking.

ROASTED SCROD WITH TOMATO RELISH

....

A sweet-and-sour relish is just the thing to perk up the simply prepared scrod fillets in this dish.

Prep: 15 minutes   Cook/Roast: 40 minutes

- 1 tablespoon vegetable oil
- 1 small onion, chopped
- 2 tablespoons water
- 1 can (28 ounces) plum tomatoes, drained and each tomato cut into quarters
- 1/4 cup red wine vinegar
- 2 tablespoons brown sugar
- 1/2 teaspoon salt
- 4 pieces scrod fillet (6 ounces each)
- 1/4 teaspoon coarsely ground black pepper

1. Preheat oven to 450°F.

2. In 2-quart saucepan, heat 2 teaspoons oil over medium heat. Add onion and water and cook until onion is tender and golden, about 10 minutes. Stir in tomatoes, vinegar, brown sugar, and 1/4 teaspoon salt; heat to boiling over high heat. Continue cooking over high heat, stirring frequently, until relish has thickened, about 15 minutes.

3. Meanwhile, with tweezers, remove any bones from scrod. Arrange fillets in 9-inch square baking dish; sprinkle with remaining 1 teaspoon oil, pepper, and remaining 1/4 teaspoon salt. Roast scrod until just opaque throughout, 12 to 15 minutes. To serve, transfer fish to platter and spoon tomato relish on top. Makes 4 main-dish servings.

Each serving: About 248 calories, 32g protein, 18g carbohydrate, 5g total fat (1g saturated), 73mg cholesterol, 708mg sodium.

FISH TACOS

Ready-to-use ingredients, such as shredded cabbage mix and bottled salsa, help you get this Mexican-style meal on the table in just 15 minutes.

Prep: 5 minutes   Cook: 10 minutes

- 2 limes
- 4 cups shredded cabbage mix for coleslaw (half 16-ounce bag)
- ½ cup reduced-fat sour cream
- 1 tablespoon olive oil
- 1¼ pounds tilapia fillets
- ¼ teaspoon ground chipotle chile
- ¼ teaspoon salt
- 8 corn tortillas
- 1 cup salsa

1. From limes, grate 2 teaspoons peel and squeeze ¼ cup juice.

2. In large bowl, combine coleslaw mix and lime juice; set aside. In small bowl, stir lime peel into sour cream; set aside.

3. In 12-inch skillet, heat oil on medium-high until hot. On sheet of waxed paper, sprinkle tilapia fillets with chipotle and salt to season both sides. Add fish to skillet and cook 5 to 6 minutes or until it turns opaque throughout, turning over once. Meanwhile, warm tortillas.

4. To serve, cut fillets into 8 pieces. Place 2 pieces tilapia in each tortilla; top with slaw, lime sour cream, and salsa. Makes 4 main-dish servings.

Each serving: About 360 calories, 28g protein, 37g carbohydrate, 12g total fat (3g saturated), 4g fiber, 12mg cholesterol, 790mg sodium.

SALMON WITH GINGERY CABBAGE

Warm spices add exotic flavor—but not burning heat—to a dinner that delivers heart-healthy fish oils, as well as the cancer fighters in the cabbage. Serve with whole-grain rolls.

Prep: 15 minutes   Cook: 25 minutes

- 1 tablespoon olive oil
- 1 small onion, thinly sliced
- 4 pieces salmon fillet (6 ounces each), skin removed
- ½ teaspoon curry powder
- 2 tablespoons Dijon mustard with seeds
- 2 teaspoons water
- 2 teaspoons grated peeled fresh ginger
- ½ teaspoon ground cumin
- 1 bag (16 ounces) shredded cabbage for coleslaw
- ¼ teaspoon salt

1. Preheat oven to 400°F. In 12-inch nonstick skillet, heat olive oil on medium 1 minute. Add onion; cover and cook 8 to 10 minutes or until onion is tender and golden brown, stirring occasionally.

2. Meanwhile, grease 13" by 9" glass baking dish. With tweezers, remove any bones from salmon pieces. Place salmon, rounded sides up, in baking dish. In cup, stir together curry powder, Dijon mustard, and water; use to brush evenly over salmon.

3. Roast salmon, without turning over, 15 minutes or just until opaque throughout.

4. While salmon roasts, add ginger and cumin to onion in skillet, and cook 1 minute, stirring. Add cabbage and salt; cover and cook 11 to 13 minutes or until cabbage is just tender and starts to brown, stirring occasionally.

5. To serve, spoon cabbage mixture onto 4 dinner plates; top with salmon. Makes 4 main-dish servings.

Each serving: About 325 calories, 36g protein, 11g carbohydrate, 15g total fat (2g saturated), 3g fiber, 93mg cholesterol, 295mg sodium.

HEALTHY THREE-BEAN TUNA SALAD

A perfect lunch or light summer supper, this no-cook salad serves up heart-healthy omega-3 fats (the tuna) along with nearly three quarters of a day's worth of cholesterol-lowering fiber (the beans).

Prep: 15 minutes

1 lemon
2 tablespoons extra-virgin olive oil
3 stalks celery, thinly sliced
2 green onions, thinly sliced
¼ teaspoon salt
⅛ teaspoon coarsely ground black pepper
3 cans (15 to 19 ounces each) assorted low-sodium beans such as white kidney beans (cannellini), garbanzo beans, and pink beans, rinsed and drained
2 cans (6 ounces each) chunk light tuna in water, drained and coarsely flaked
4 large Boston lettuce leaves

1. From lemon, grate 1 teaspoon peel and squeeze 2 tablespoons juice.

2. In large bowl, stir together lemon peel and juice, oil, celery, green onions, salt, and pepper. Stir in beans until coated, then gently stir in tuna.

3. Serve bean mixture in lettuce cups. Makes 4 main-dish servings.

Each serving: About 500 calories, 38g protein, 63g carbohydrate, 10g total fat (1g saturated), 16g fiber, 44mg cholesterol, 775mg sodium.

Healthy Three-Bean Tuna Salad

SALMON FILLETS WITH TOMATO JAM

The tartness of orange peel, vinegar, and marinara sauce complement the richness of the salmon. Serve with steamed broccoli and brown rice.

Prep: 10 minutes   **Bake/Cook: 15 minutes**

4 pieces salmon fillets (about 6 ounces each), skin removed
1 tablespoon olive oil
⅛ teaspoon salt
⅛ teaspoon ground black pepper
1 medium onion, chopped
2 large garlic cloves, crushed with garlic press
½ teaspoon dried basil
¼ teaspoon dried oregano
1 tablespoon sugar
¼ cup red wine vinegar
1 cup marinara sauce
½ teaspoon freshly grated orange peel
orange slices

1. Preheat oven to 400°F. Grease 13" by 9" baking dish; set aside.

2. With tweezers, remove any bones from salmon. Arrange salmon in single layer in prepared dish; rub with 1 teaspoon oil and sprinkle with salt and pepper. Bake salmon until it turns opaque throughout and flakes easily when tested with a fork, about 15 minutes.

3. Meanwhile, in nonstick 10-inch skillet, heat remaining 2 teaspoons oil over medium heat. Add onion; cook, stirring occasionally, until lightly browned, about 3 minutes. Stir in garlic, basil, and oregano; cook 20 seconds. Add sugar; cook until sugar begins to caramelize, about 1 minute. Add vinegar and heat to boiling; boil until almost evaporated, about 1 minute. Stir in marinara sauce and orange peel; cook until sauce has a jamlike consistency, about 5 minutes.

4. Serve salmon with tomato jam. Garnish with orange slices. Makes 4 main-dish servings.

Each serving: About 360 calories, 30g protein, 12g carbohydrate, 21g total fat (4g saturated), 80mg cholesterol, 410mg sodium.

BLACK-BEAN AND SWEET-POTATO CHILI

....

This hearty chili is great for cool nights in early fall. Try it with pinto, cannellini, kidney, or pink beans, or use a combination thereof for a colorful entrée.

Prep: 10 minutes   Cook: about 25 minutes

1 tablespoon olive oil

1 medium onion, chopped

2 garlic cloves, chopped

2 medium sweet potatoes (about 12 ounces each), peeled and cut into ½-inch pieces

1 tablespoon chili powder

1 jar (16 ounces) mild salsa (about 1¾ cups)

1 cup water

2 cans (15 to 19 ounces each) low-sodium black beans, not drained

½ cup reduced-fat sour cream

¼ cup loosely packed fresh cilantro leaves, chopped

1. In 4-quart saucepan, heat oil over medium-high heat. Add onion and garlic; cook, stirring occasionally, until soft, about 4 minutes. Stir in sweet potatoes, chili powder, salsa, and water; heat to boiling. Reduce heat to medium-low and cook, stirring occasionally, until potatoes are tender, 12 to 15 minutes. Add beans with their liquid and cook 3 minutes to blend flavors.

2. In small bowl, combine sour cream and cilantro. Serve chili with cilantro cream. Makes about 10 cups or 4 main-dish servings.

Each serving: About 520 calories, 23g protein, 91g carbohydrate, 9g total fat (3g saturated), 12mg cholesterol, 950mg sodium.

MEXICAN PIZZA

....

Here's a spin on a classic dish that everyone loves. This colorful Mexican pizza makes for an easy weeknight dinner or a backyard barbecue.

Prep: 10 minutes   Cook: 8 minutes

½ cup prepared black bean dip

1 large thin pizza crust (10 ounces)

½ cup shredded Mexican cheese blend (2 ounces)

1 to 2 limes

1 ripe avocado, cut into chunks

2 cups shredded romaine lettuce

1 medium tomato, chopped

1. Prepare outdoor grill for covered, direct grilling on medium (or preheat oven to 450°F).

2. Spread black bean dip evenly on crust, leaving ½-inch border; sprinkle with cheese. Place crust on hot grill rack; cover and grill until grill marks appear, 8 to 9 minutes. (Or, place crust on ungreased cookie sheet. Bake 8 to 10 minutes or until cheese melts.)

3. Meanwhile, from limes, grate ¼ teaspoon peel, and squeeze 2 tablespoons juice. Gently stir avocado with 1 tablespoon juice. Toss romaine with peel and remaining juice.

4. Top cooked pizza with romaine mixture and tomato, then with avocado. Makes 4 main-dish servings.

Each serving: About 310 calories, 13g protein, 34g carbohydrate, 15g total fat (4g saturated), 4g fiber, 17mg cholesterol, 520mg sodium.

Mexican Pizza

EASY AS TORTILLA PIE

Reduced-fat ingredients help slim down this Tex-Mex classic; the corn and beans are filling, but low in calories.

Prep: 15 minutes   Bake: 10 minutes

- 1 cup frozen corn kernels
- 2 green onions, thinly sliced
- 1 teaspoon ground cumin
- 1½ cups salsa
- 1 can (15 to 19 ounces) low-sodium black beans, rinsed and drained
- 4 burrito-size flour tortillas (96% fat-free)
- 1 package (8 ounces) reduced-fat (2%) shredded Mexican cheese blend
- 2 tablespoons chopped fresh cilantro leaves

1. Preheat oven to 450°F. Spray large cookie sheet with cooking spray.

2. Spray 12-inch nonstick skillet with cooking spray; place over medium heat. Add frozen corn, green onions, and cumin; cook 3 minutes or until corn thaws. Remove skillet from heat; stir in salsa and beans.

3. Place 1 tortilla on cookie sheet; top with 1 cup bean mixture and ½ cup cheese. Repeat layering, starting with tortilla, twice more, using up bean mixture. Top with remaining tortilla and cheese.

4. Bake pie 10 minutes or until heated through. Carefully transfer pie to cutting board; sprinkle with chopped cilantro. With sharp knife, cut into wedges to serve. Makes 4 main-dish servings.

Each serving: About 440 calories, 26g protein, 58g carbohydrate, 13g total fat (6g saturated), 21g fiber, 41mg cholesterol, 1,105mg sodium.

BLACK BEAN CAKES

Serve these "burgers" on toasted sesame buns with a side of sweet potato fries for a tasty vegetarian entrée. They also make delicious appetizers served on a bed of shredded lettuce.

Prep: 10 minutes   Cook: 7 minutes

- 1 can (15 to 19 ounces) black beans, rinsed and drained
- 2 tablespoons reduced-fat mayonnaise
- ¼ cup chopped fresh cilantro
- 1 tablespoon plain dried bread crumbs
- ½ teaspoon ground cumin
  pinch dried oregano, crumbled
- ¼ teaspoon hot pepper sauce
- 2 tablespoons olive oil
- 2 tablespoons all-purpose flour
- ¼ cup mild or medium salsa
- 8 teaspoons sour cream

1. In large bowl, with potato masher, mash beans and mayonnaise until almost smooth, leaving some lumps. Stir in cilantro, bread crumbs, cumin, oregano, and hot pepper sauce. With lightly floured hands, shape into four 3-inch patties.

2. In 10-inch skillet, heat oil over medium heat. Dust patties with flour, shaking off excess. Cook patties until crusty and lightly browned, about 3 minutes per side, transferring them to plates as they are done.

3. To serve, top each cake with 1 tablespoon salsa and 2 teaspoons sour cream. Makes 4 servings.

Each serving: About 204 calories, 6g protein, 24g carbohydrate, 11g total fat (2g saturated), 6mg cholesterol, 410mg sodium.

JEWELED CINNAMON COUSCOUS

·······················

You can whip up this hearty nonmeat main dish in just ten minutes. If you crave something green, toss in a cup of frozen peas or serve with a crisp salad.

Prep: 10 minutes   Cook: 10 minutes

- 1 tablespoon butter or margarine
- ½ medium red onion, chopped
- 1 package (8 ounces) sliced mushrooms
- 1 can (14½ ounces) low-sodium vegetable broth or 1¾ cups Vegetable Broth (page 71)
- ¼ cup water
- 1 can (15 to 19 ounces) low-sodium garbanzo beans, rinsed and drained
- ½ cup dried cranberries
- ½ cup golden raisins
- ¼ cup dry sherry
- 1 teaspoon salt
- ½ teaspoon ground cinnamon
- ¼ teaspoon ground black pepper
- 1 package (10½ ounces) plain couscous (Moroccan pasta)

1. In deep 12-inch skillet, melt butter over medium-high heat. Add onion and mushrooms; cook, stirring occasionally, 3 minutes.

2. While vegetables are cooking, in 1-quart saucepan, heat broth and water to boiling over high heat.

3. Stir garbanzo beans, cranberries, raisins, sherry, salt, cinnamon, and pepper into mushroom mixture. Remove skillet from heat.

4. Add couscous to skillet; stir in hot broth. Cover and let mixture stand until liquid has been absorbed, about 5 minutes. Fluff with fork before serving. Makes about 8 cups or 4 main-dish servings.

Each serving: About 601 calories, 21g protein, 116g carbohydrate, 6g total fat (2g saturated), 8mg cholesterol, 653mg sodium.

POTATO PANCAKE WITH BROCCOLI AND CHEDDAR

·······················

Meatless doesn't have to be bland, as evidenced by this "cheesy" main dish. It's perfect for those times when a satisfying meatless meal is what you want.

Prep: 5 minutes   Cook: 20 minutes

- 1 tablespoon butter or margarine
- 1 medium onion, chopped
- 1 bag (12 ounces) broccoli flowerets, each cut in half if large
- 1 teaspoon salt
- 2 tablespoons water
- 4 cups refrigerated shredded hash brown potatoes (20 ounces)
- ⅛ teaspoon ground black pepper
- 1 tablespoon vegetable oil
- 4 ounces sharp Cheddar cheese, shredded (1 cup)

1. In nonstick 12-inch skillet, melt butter over medium heat. Add onion and cook, stirring frequently, until golden and tender, about 5 minutes. Stir in broccoli, ¼ teaspoon salt, and water; cover and cook, stirring once, until broccoli is tender, about 3 minutes. Transfer broccoli mixture to medium bowl.

2. In large bowl, combine potatoes, pepper, and remaining ¾ teaspoon salt. In same skillet, heat oil over medium-high heat. Add half the potato mixture, gently patting with rubber spatula to cover bottom of skillet. Leaving 1-inch border, top potatoes with broccoli mixture. Sprinkle Cheddar over broccoli. Cover cheese with remaining potato mixture, patting so that mixture extends to edge of skillet. Cook until golden brown on bottom, about 5 minutes.

3. Place large round platter or cookie sheet upside down over skillet. Grasping platter and skillet firmly together, very carefully and quickly flip skillet over to invert pancake onto platter. Slide pancake back into skillet. Cook until browned, about 5 minutes longer. Cut in quarters. Makes 4 main-dish servings.

Each serving: About 321 calories, 13g protein, 32g carbohydrate, 17g total fat (8g saturated), 37mg cholesterol, 837mg sodium.

Spinach and Jack Cheese Bread Pudding

SPINACH AND JACK CHEESE BREAD PUDDING

....

Rich in eggs and cheese, this easy-to-fix casserole can make a satisfying dinner or a hearty brunch.

Prep: 10 minutes   Cook: 20 minutes

- 6 large eggs
- 2 cups low-fat milk (1%)
- ¼ teaspoon dried thyme
- ¼ teaspoon salt
- ¼ teaspoon coarsely ground black pepper
       pinch ground nutmeg
- 1 package (10 ounces) frozen chopped spinach, thawed and squeezed dry
- 4 ounces Monterey Jack cheese, shredded (1 cup)
- 8 slices firm white bread, torn into ¾-inch pieces

1. Preheat oven to 375°F.

2. In large bowl, with wire whisk, beat eggs, milk, thyme, salt, pepper, and nutmeg until well blended. With rubber spatula, stir in spinach, Monterey Jack, and bread pieces.

3. Pour mixture into 13" by 9" baking dish. Bake bread pudding until browned and puffed and knife inserted in center comes out clean, 20 to 25 minutes.

4. Remove bread pudding from oven; let stand 5 minutes before serving. Makes 6 main-dish servings.

Each serving: About 280 calories, 17g protein, 22g carbohydrate, 13g total fat (6g saturated), 233mg cholesterol, 545mg sodium.

MEXICAN-STYLE BREAD PUDDING

Prepare as directed but substitute **4 ounces Pepper Jack cheese,** shredded, for Monterey Jack cheese and add **4 ounces sliced pepperoni** in Step 2. Serve with your favorite salsa.

11

GRILLING

Whether you cook over a shoebox-size hibachi or in a state-of-the-art gas-powered "kettle," grilling imparts a unique flavor. The intense heat, the smoke, and the pleasure of cooking—and eating—outdoors, all enhance the natural flavor of food.

TYPES OF GRILLS

Charcoal These grills are fueled by charcoal briquettes or natural hardwood charcoal. The simplest is the Japanese-style hibachi, a small cast-iron grill just right for a small patio. For more ambitious grilling, choose a large covered "kettle" grill. Or choose the middle-size uncovered grill, called a brazier.

Gas Gas grills are available with a variety of options, including electric ignition, fuel gauge, extra burners, warming racks, and storage cabinets.

Electric Like gas grills, most electric units have artificial briquettes for authentic smoky flavor. There are large electric grills for the backyard as well as tabletop models.

GRILLING EQUIPMENT

Grill topper If you like seafood and vegetables, you'll want a grill topper: a perforated metal sheet or mesh screen that provides a flat surface.

Grilling basket A good option for delicate or small foods. There are fish-shaped baskets for whole fish as well as square and oblong baskets with handles.

Tongs Better than a fork for turning foods, because they don't pierce the surface and release juices.

Spatula Use a long-handled spatula with a heatproof handle for flipping burgers and moving food on a grill topper.

Skewers Long metal skewers are a must for kabobs. Choose skewers with flat shafts, which prevent the food from slipping around.

Basting brush A heatproof handle and a long shaft are musts. Silicone or natural bristles stand up to the heat better than synthetic ones.

Instant-read thermometer Insert it into the food, and the dial gives you a reading in seconds.

Grilling mitts These are long to protect more of your forearm and well insulated to protect you from the heat.

Water spray bottle The kind used to mist plants; adjust it so it shoots a narrow stream to quash flare-ups.

Brass-bristled scrub brush Use this brush to clean the grill rack.

LIGHTING

Gas and electric grills are easy to light; just follow the manufacturer's directions. A charcoal fire requires a little more work: Spread an even layer of briquettes over the bottom of the firebox, then stack them into a pyramid. Allow 30 to 40 minutes for the coals to burn down to gray ash before cooking. The following will help you get the fire going:

Chimney starter An open-ended metal cylinder with a handle. Place crumpled newspaper in the bottom, top with briquettes, and light the paper through an opening in the bottom.

Peking Chicken Roll-Ups (recipe page 364)

Electric starter A loop-shaped heating element with a handle, this device is placed in a bed of briquettes; plug it in and the briquettes ignite.

Self-starting briquettes These are impregnated with starter fluid. A match will ignite them immediately. Don't add them to a fire that's already hot.

Solid fire starter Place these waxy-looking cubes in the firebox, pile briquettes on top, and light.

FINE-TUNING THE FIRE

Coals are ready when they are about 80 percent ash gray. To test the heat, hold your palm above the coals at cooking height (about 6 inches): If the fire is low (above 200°F), you'll be able to keep your hand there for 5 to 6 seconds. If you can bear the heat for 4 to 5 seconds, the fire is moderate (above 300°F). If you can hold your palm over the fire for just 2 to 3 seconds, the fire is hot (above 375°F).

Tapping the coals will remove their ash cover and make the fire hotter. Pushing the coals together intensifies the heat, whereas spreading them apart decreases it. Opening the vents on a covered grill increases the temperature; partially closing them lowers it.

SAFETY TIPS

• Except for grills intended to be used indoors, always cook in the open air. You're safe under a carport or in the doorway of a garage, but never use a charcoal or gas grill inside.

• Have a bucket of sand or water near the grill in case the fire gets out of hand.

• Never add liquid fire starter to an existing fire, as the stream of fluid could ignite.

• Keep an eye on the grill at all times, especially when children and/or pets are around.

• Don't wear scarves or clothing with loose, billowy sleeves or fringes.

• If the fire flares up or food catches fire, raise the rack and spread the coals apart. If necessary, spray the fire with water.

• If you want to coat the grill rack with nonstick cooking spray, do so while the rack is cold.

MARINADES, RUBS, AND SAUCES

When food is cooked by dry heat, marinating and basting help keep it moist. Although the smoky taste of grilled food is naturally delicious, marinades and dry seasoning rubs can add extra flavor.

Marinades are a classic way to flavor food. Delicate foods, such as seafood and boneless chicken breasts, benefit from 15 minutes of marinating and should not be marinated for more than 30 minutes unless directed in the recipe. Large cuts of beef and pork and bone-in chicken parts should be marinated for at least 1 hour but no more than 24 hours. A marinade can be brushed onto food as it grills, but stop basting 10 minutes before the food is done, or the marinade will not have sufficient time to cook. Discard any leftover marinade.

Seasoning rubs are combinations of spices, dried herbs, salt, and, sometimes, moist ingredients such as mustard, oil, or pureed fresh herbs. The mixture is rubbed onto the food before grilling. Apply the rub 1 or 2 hours ahead for maximum flavor.

Basting sauces, including barbecue sauce, should be thick enough to adhere to food. Sauces containing honey, molasses, or sugar, are likely to burn, so wait until the last 15 minutes of cooking time before brushing them on.

FLAVORING THE FIRE

In addition to seasoning the food you'll be grilling, you can also flavor the fire. This works best in a covered grill.

Grilling woods are sold in chunks or chips to be tossed onto a charcoal fire or gas grill. Chips require about 30 minutes of soaking; larger chunks should be soaked for up to 2 hours. Use oak and mesquite for beef and pork, and hickory for turkey, chicken, and pork. Fruitwoods, such as apple and cherry, are mild enough to use with chicken and seafood. If using chunks of wood, add them to the fire at the beginning; place chips on the coals later on. Whole spices and fresh or dried herbs can be placed directly on a fire if first soaked for 30 minutes.

RED WINE AND ROSEMARY PORTERHOUSE

....

This robust marinade can season a thick, juicy steak in 15 minutes. Marinate for up to one hour for more intense flavor. It's also good on lamb, pork, or poultry. Serve with Lemon-Garlic Potato Packet (page 382) and Crumb-Topped Tomatoes (page 383). For a dry red wine that would work well in this recipe, try a shiraz, merlot, chianti, or cabernet.

Prep: 10 minutes plus marinating   **Grill:** 15 minutes

- ½ cup dry red wine
- 1 tablespoon Worcestershire sauce
- 1 tablespoon tomato paste
- 1 tablespoon Dijon mustard
- 1 tablespoon balsamic vinegar
- 1 tablespoon chopped fresh rosemary
- 1 large garlic clove, crushed with garlic press
- 1 beef porterhouse or T-bone steak, 1½ inches thick (about 1½ pounds)
- 1 lemon, cut into wedges

1. In 13" by 9" baking dish, combine red wine, Worcestershire, tomato paste, mustard, vinegar, rosemary, and garlic.

2. Place steak in marinade, turning to coat both sides. Cover and let stand 15 minutes at room temperature or refrigerate up to 1 hour, turning once.

3. Prepare outdoor grill for direct grilling over medium heat.

4. Remove steak from baking dish; discard marinade. Place steak on grill over medium heat and cook, turning once, 15 to 20 minutes for medium-rare or until desired doneness.

5. Transfer steak to cutting board and let stand 10 minutes to set juices for easier slicing. Cut into thin slices and serve with lemon wedges. Makes 4 main-dish servings.

Each serving: About 395 calories, 32g protein, 1g carbohydrate, 28g total fat (11g saturated), 104mg cholesterol, 125mg sodium.

GRILLING BEEF   To test the internal temperature, insert an instant-read thermometer into the center or thickest part of the meat. If it is ¼ inch thick or less, insert the thermometer horizontally into the meat, halfway in. Always let steak rest approximately 10 minutes before serving or slicing, so the juices have time to redistribute throughout the meat. During the resting time, the internal temperature of the meat will rise about 5 degrees.

CUT	FOR MEDIUM-RARE COOK TO TEMPERATURE	APPROXIMATE COOKING TIME
Steaks (porterhouse, T-bone, sirloin, rib-eye, top round):		
¾" thick	145°F	6–8 minutes
1" thick	145°F	11–14 minutes
Steaks (flank or skirt)	145°F	15–20 minutes
Tenderloin, whole	135°F	30–40 minutes
Burgers, 1" thick	160°F	10–12 minutes

PEPPER-CRUSTED FILET MIGNON

....

These very tender steaks make great company fare, plus they're a snap to cook and can be prepared ahead. Simply coat them with crushed spices as directed, then cover and refrigerate for up to one day until ready to cook.

Prep: 15 minutes plus standing   **Grill: 16 minutes**

- 1 tablespoon whole black peppercorns
- 1 teaspoon whole fennel seeds
- 4 beef tenderloin steaks (filet mignon), each 1 inch thick (about 4 ounces each)
- 3 medium peppers (red, yellow, and/or orange)
- 1 tablespoon minced fresh parsley
- 1 teaspoon olive oil
- ³⁄₄ teaspoon salt

1. Prepare outdoor grill for covered direct grilling over medium-high heat.

2. In mortar with pestle or in zip-tight plastic bag with rolling pin, crush peppercorns and fennel seeds. Use to rub on steaks. Place steaks in 13" by 9" baking dish; cover and refrigerate while grilling the peppers.

3. Cut each pepper lengthwise in half; remove and discard stems and seeds. With hand, flatten each pepper half. Place peppers, skin side down, on grill. Cover grill and cook, without turning, until skins are charred and blistered, 8 to 10 minutes. Transfer peppers to bowl; cover with plate and let steam at room temperature until cool enough to handle, about 15 minutes. If using gas grill, reset temperature to medium.

4. Remove peppers from bowl. Peel skins and discard. Cut peppers lengthwise into ¼-inch-wide strips and return to same bowl. Add parsley, oil, and ¼ teaspoon salt; toss until peppers are evenly coated.

5. Sprinkle steaks with remaining ½ teaspoon salt. Place steaks on grill over medium heat. Cover grill and cook, turning once, 8 to 10 minutes for medium-rare or until desired doneness. Serve steaks topped with peppers. Makes 4 main-dish servings.

Each serving: About 230 calories, 26g protein, 9g carbohydrate, 10g total fat (3g saturated), 71mg cholesterol, 495mg sodium.

FLANK STEAK WITH CHIMICHURRI SAUCE

....

Chimichurri is a thick green herb sauce that is served with grilled meats in Argentina. It can be prepared ahead and refrigerated for up to two days. Bring it to room temperature before serving.

Prep: 15 minutes   **Grill: 12 minutes**

- 1½ cups loosely packed fresh parsley leaves, chopped
- 1½ cups loosely packed fresh cilantro leaves, chopped
- ¼ cup olive oil
- 3 tablespoons red wine vinegar
- 1 garlic clove, crushed with garlic press
- ³⁄₄ teaspoon salt
- ¼ teaspoon ground black pepper
-   pinch crushed red pepper
- ½ teaspoon chili powder
- ½ teaspoon sugar
- ¼ teaspoon ground coriander
- ¼ teaspoon ground cumin
- 1 beef flank steak (1½ pounds)

1. Prepare outdoor grill for direct grilling over medium heat.

2. Meanwhile prepare chimichurri sauce: In small bowl, combine parsley, cilantro, oil, vinegar, garlic, ¼ teaspoon salt, black pepper, and crushed red pepper; set aside.

3. In cup, combine chili powder, sugar, coriander, cumin, and remaining ½ teaspoon salt. Use to rub on flank steak.

4. Place steak on grill and cook about 6 minutes per side for medium-rare or until desired doneness.

5. Transfer steak to cutting board. Holding knife in slanting position, almost parallel to cutting board, slice steak thinly across the grain. Serve with sauce. Makes 4 main-dish servings.

Each serving with 1 tablespoon sauce: About 239 calories, 25g protein, 2g carbohydrate, 14g total fat (5g saturated), 62mg cholesterol, 497mg sodium.

PASTRAMI-SPICED FLANK STEAK

....

Pastrami, a popular New York City deli item, probably came to us via the Romanians, who prepared many of their meats by smoking. Serve ours on sliced rye with a side of coleslaw, deli style!

Prep: 15 minutes plus marinating
Grill: 13 minutes

- 1 tablespoon coriander seeds
- 1 tablespoon paprika
- 1 tablespoon cracked black pepper
- 2 teaspoons ground ginger
- 1½ teaspoons salt
- 1 teaspoon sugar
- ½ teaspoon crushed red pepper
- 3 garlic cloves, crushed with garlic press
- 1 beef flank steak (about 1½ pounds)
- 12 slices rye bread
  deli-style mustard

1. In mortar with pestle or in zip-tight plastic bag with rolling pin, crush coriander seeds. In cup, combine coriander, paprika, black pepper, ginger, salt, sugar, and crushed red pepper.

2. Rub garlic on both sides of steak, then rub with spice mixture. Place steak in large zip-tight plastic bag; seal bag, pressing out as much excess air as possible. Place bag on plate; refrigerate at least 2 hours, or up to 24 hours.

3. Prepare outdoor grill for direct grilling over medium heat.

4. Remove steak from bag. Place steak on grill over medium heat and cook, turning once, 13 to 15 minutes for medium-rare or until desired doneness.

5. Place bread slices on grill over medium heat and toast, without turning, just until grill marks appear on underside of bread.

6. Transfer steak to cutting board. Let stand 10 minutes to set juices for easier slicing. Cut steak across the grain into thin slices and serve with grilled rye bread and mustard. Makes 6 main-dish servings.

Each serving: About 380 calories, 33g protein, 35g carbohydrate, 12g total fat (4g saturated), 47mg cholesterol, 1,015mg sodium.

Pastrami-Spiced Flank Steak

BRISKET WITH CHUNKY BBQ SAUCE

....

A great do-ahead main dish for a summer picnic. You can slow-cook the brisket on the stovetop up to several days ahead. Then, 20 minutes before serving, brush it with sauce and grill until heated through.

Prep: 15 minutes   Cook/Grill: 3 hours 35 minutes

Brisket
- 1 fresh beef brisket (4½ pounds), well trimmed
- 1 medium onion, cut into quarters
- 1 large carrot, peeled and cut into 1½-inch pieces
- 1 bay leaf
- 1 teaspoon whole black peppercorns
- ¼ teaspoon whole allspice

Chunky BBQ Sauce
- 1 tablespoon vegetable oil
- 1 large onion (12 ounces), finely chopped
- 3 garlic cloves, finely chopped
- 2 tablespoons minced, peeled fresh ginger
- 1 teaspoon ground cumin
- 1 can (14½ ounces) tomatoes in puree, chopped
- 1 bottle (12 ounces) chili sauce
- ⅓ cup cider vinegar
- 2 tablespoons light (mild) molasses
- 2 tablespoons brown sugar
- 2 teaspoons dry mustard
- 1 tablespoon cornstarch
- 2 tablespoons water

1. Prepare brisket: In 8-quart Dutch oven, place brisket, onion, carrot, bay leaf, peppercorns, and allspice. Add enough *water* to cover and heat to boiling over high heat. Reduce heat; cover and simmer until meat is tender, about 3 hours.

2. Meanwhile, prepare Chunky BBQ Sauce: In non-stick 12-inch skillet, heat oil over medium heat. Add onion and cook, stirring occasionally, until tender, about 10 minutes. Add garlic and ginger and cook, stirring, 1 minute. Stir in cumin and cook 1 minute longer.

3. Stir in chopped tomatoes with their puree, chili sauce, vinegar, molasses, brown sugar, and dry mustard; heat to boiling over high heat. Reduce heat and simmer, stirring occasionally, 5 minutes.

4. In cup, blend cornstarch and water until smooth. After sauce has simmered 5 minutes, stir in cornstarch mixture. Heat to boiling, stirring; boil 1 minute. Cover and refrigerate sauce if not using right away. Makes about 4 cups.

5. When brisket is done, transfer to large platter. If not serving right away, cover and refrigerate until ready to serve.

6. Prepare outdoor grill for covered direct grilling over medium heat. Place brisket on grill, cover and cook 10 minutes. Turn brisket and cook 5 minutes longer. Spoon 1 cup barbecue sauce on top of brisket and cook until brisket is heated through, about 5 minutes longer. (Do not turn brisket after topping with sauce.)

7. Transfer brisket to cutting board. To serve, reheat remaining sauce in small saucepan on grill or stovetop. Slice brisket thinly across the grain and serve with sauce. Makes 12 main-dish servings.

Each serving: About 241 calories, 26g protein, 6g carbohydrate, 11g total fat (4g saturated), 81mg cholesterol, 174mg sodium.

Each ¼ cup sauce: About 61 calories, 1g protein, 13g carbohydrate, 1g total fat (0g saturated), 0mg cholesterol, 328mg sodium.

SPICE-RUBBED BEEF TENDERLOIN

....

You can grill the meat right after seasoning it, or refrigerate it for up to 24 hours for even more flavor.

Prep: 5 minutes   Grill: 30 minutes

- 1 tablespoon fennel seeds, crushed
- 2 teaspoons salt
- ½ teaspoon ground ginger
- ½ teaspoon crushed red pepper
- 1 center-cut beef tenderloin roast (2½ pounds), trimmed and tied

1. Prepare outdoor grill for direct grilling over medium heat.

2. In cup, combine fennel seeds, salt, ginger, and crushed red pepper. Use to rub on beef tenderloin.

3. Place tenderloin on grill and cook, turning occasionally, until meat thermometer inserted in center of meat reaches 140°F, 30 to 40 minutes. Internal temperature of meat will rise to 145°F (medium) upon standing. Or cook until desired doneness. Transfer roast to cutting board and let stand 10 minutes to set juices for easier slicing. Cut into thin slices and serve. Makes 8 main-dish servings.

Each serving: About 177 calories, 22g protein, 1g carbohydrates, 9g total fat (3g saturated), 65mg cholesterol, 631mg sodium.

KOREAN STEAK

....

Set out bowls of crisp romaine lettuce, rice, green onions, and sesame seeds and let each person assemble his or her own package.

Prep: 40 minutes plus marinating
Grill: 14 minutes

- ½ cup reduced-sodium soy sauce
- 2 tablespoons sugar
- 2 tablespoons minced, peeled fresh ginger
- 2 tablespoons seasoned rice vinegar
- 1 tablespoon Asian sesame oil
- ¼ teaspoons ground red pepper (cayenne)
- 3 garlic cloves, pressed
- 1½ pounds beef top round or sirloin steak, 1 inch thick
- 1 cup regular long-grain rice
- 3 green onions, thinly sliced
- 1 tablespoon sesame seeds, toasted
- 1 head romaine lettuce, separated into leaves

Korean Steak

1. In large zip-tight plastic bag, combine soy sauce, sugar, ginger, vinegar, sesame oil, ground red pepper, and garlic; add steak, turning to coat. Seal bag, pressing out excess air. Place on plate; refrigerate steak 1 to 4 hours to marinate, turning once.

2. Prepare outdoor grill for direct grilling over medium heat.

3. Just before grilling steak, prepare rice as label directs; keep warm.

4. Remove steak from bag; reserve marinade. Place steak on hot grill rack over medium heat and grill, turning once, 14 to 15 minutes for medium-rare or until desired doneness. Transfer steak to cutting board; let stand 10 minutes to allow juices to set for easier slicing.

5. In 1-quart saucepan, heat reserved marinade and ¼ *cup water* to boiling over high heat; boil 2 minutes.

6. To serve, thinly slice steak. Let each person place some steak slices, rice, green onions, and sesame seeds on a lettuce leaf, then drizzle with some cooked marinade. Fold side of lettuce leaf over filling to form a packet to eat like a sandwich. Makes 6 servings.

Each serving: About 370 calories, 30g protein, 35g carbohydrate, 11g total fat (3g saturated), 69mg cholesterol, 960mg sodium.

A SOY SAUCE PRIMER

One of the oldest condiments known, soy sauce originated in China over 2,500 years ago. But it wasn't until the sixth century, when Buddhism and its meatless principles were embraced, that it began to be used in Japan. The strict vegetarian diet meant giving up traditional meat- and fish-based seasonings. Luckily, a Japanese priest who had studied in China began making a seasoning from fermented soybeans—soy sauce in Japan. After some time, wheat was added to give the sauce a more balanced flavor.

Supermarkets carry two types of soy sauce:

REGULAR SOY SAUCE, which is brewed from wheat, soybeans, water, and salt, is aged for several months to develop its flavor.

REDUCED-SODIUM SOY SAUCE is brewed the same way as regular but contains about 40 percent less sodium.

Grab a bottle of your favorite brand and whip up these five new winners.

1. CHEDDAR SPREAD: Cut 8 ounces extra-sharp Cheddar cheese into 1-inch cubes. In food processor with knife blade attached, pulse Cheddar until crumbly. Add ½ cup barbecue sauce, ¼ cup reduced-fat sour cream, 1 tablespoon Dijon mustard, and 1½ teaspoons chipotle hot sauce. Process 1 minute or until smooth. Spoon into serving bowl. If not serving spread right away, cover and refrigerate up to 1 week. Serve with crackers. Makes 1¾ cups.

2. APPLE-CABBAGE SLAW: In large bowl, whisk together ⅓ cup barbecue sauce, ⅓ cup reduced-fat sour cream, 3 tablespoons fresh lemon juice, and ½ teaspoon salt. Add 1 bag (16 ounces) shredded cabbage and 1 Red Delicious apple cut into matchstick-thin strips; toss to combine. Serves 6.

3. SOUTHWESTERN BURGERS: In large bowl, mix 1¼ pounds lean ground beef, ¼ cup barbecue sauce, 2 chopped green onions, 1 tablespoon chopped jalapeño chile, and ½ teaspoon salt just until combined. Shape into four (4-inch) burgers. Place burgers on hot grill grate, and cook on medium 4 minutes. Turn burgers over; brush with ¼ cup barbecue sauce; cook 4 to 6 minutes longer for medium or until desired doneness. Place on grilled buns. Serves 4.

4. SKILLET BBQ BEANS: In 12-inch skillet, cook 3 slices bacon, chopped, on medium 4 minutes. Add ½ large sweet onion, chopped, and cook 8 minutes or until onion is tender and lightly browned. Add 2 cans (15 to 19 ounces each) rinsed and drained pinto or pink beans, ¾ cup barbecue sauce, ¼ cup water, and 1 tablespoon spicy brown mustard. Simmer, uncovered, on medium-low 5 minutes. Serves 4.

5. ZESTY GRILLED CORN: In small bowl, stir together ½ cup barbecue sauce, 2 tablespoons snipped fresh chives, ½ teaspoon Chinese five-spice powder, ½ teaspoon grated fresh orange peel, and ¼ teaspoon salt. Place 6 husked ears of corn on hot grill grate and cook on medium 6 to 7 minutes or until lightly charred all over. Brush corn with sauce mixture; grill 2 minutes, turning often. Serves 6.

THE PERFECT BURGER

- For juiciness and flavor, use relatively lean meat but not the very leanest. You need to have a little fat for great burgers.
- Don't overmix when combining meat and other ingredients, and don't squeeze or compress the mixture when shaping patties or you'll end up with dry, tough burgers.
- To prevent sticking, get the grill good and hot before putting on the burgers.
- Never flatten or score burgers with a spatula as they cook or you'll lose precious juices.
- For safety's sake, cook thoroughly, until just a trace of pink remains in the center (160°F). Burgers don't have to be well done, but they should not be rare.
- Keep ground beef refrigerated up to two days in its supermarket wrap. For longer storage, rewrap in freezer wrap and freeze; use within three months.

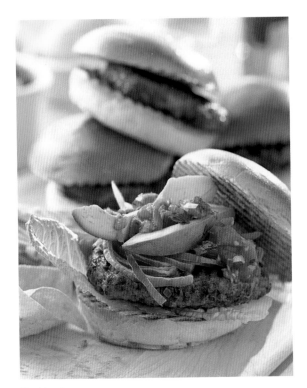

Tex-Mex Burgers

CLASSIC HAMBURGERS

....

What could be more satisfying than a classic burger? Here's the way to do it right.

Prep: 5 minutes   Grill: 8 minutes

1¼ pounds ground beef chuck
½ teaspoon salt
¼ teaspoon ground black pepper

1. Prepare outdoor grill for direct grilling over medium-high heat.

2. Shape ground beef into 4 patties, each ¾ inch thick, handling meat as little as possible. Sprinkle patties with salt and pepper.

3. Place patties on grill rack and cook about 4 minutes per side for medium or until desired doneness. Makes 4 burgers.

Each burger: About 243 calories, 29g protein, 0g carbohydrate, 14g total fat (6g saturated), 88mg cholesterol, 391mg sodium.

CLASSIC CHEESEBURGERS
Prepare as directed but during last 2 minutes of grilling top each burger with **1 ounce sliced Cheddar or Swiss cheese.** Cover grill to melt cheese.

GRILLED HAMBURGERS

TEX-MEX BURGERS
Before shaping into patties, combine 2 tablespoons finely chopped onion, 2 tablespoons bottled salsa, 1 teaspoon salt, and 1 teaspoon chili powder with ground beef just until well blended but not overmixed. Grill or panfry as directed.

Each burger: About 249 calories, 29g protein, 1g carbohydrate, 14g total fat (6g saturated), 88mg cholesterol, 771mg sodium.

TERIYAKI BURGERS
Before shaping into patties, combine ¼ cup chopped green onions, 2 tablespoons soy sauce, 1 tablespoon brown sugar, and ¼ teaspoon ground red pepper (cayenne) with ground beef just until well blended but not overmixed. Grill or panfry as directed, but during last 2 minutes of cooking, brush burgers on each side with a mixture of 2 tablespoons apple jelly, 2 teaspoons minced, peeled fresh ginger, and 1 teaspoon soy sauce.

Each burger: About 290 calories, 29g protein, 12g carbohydrate, 14g total fat (6g saturated), 88mg cholesterol, 708mg sodium.

GREEK BURGERS
Before shaping into patties, combine ¼ cup chopped fresh parsley, 1 teaspoon dried mint, crumbled, 1 teaspoon salt, and ¼ teaspoon ground black pepper with ground beef just until well blended but not overmixed. Grill or panfry as directed.

Each burger: About 245 calories, 29g protein, 0g carbohydrate, 14g total fat (6g saturated), 88mg cholesterol, 686mg sodium.

ROQUEFORT BURGERS
Before shaping into patties, combine 1 tablespoon Worcestershire sauce and ½ teaspoon coarsely ground black pepper with ground beef just until well blended but not overmixed. Shape mixture into 4 balls. Make indentation in center of each ball; place ½ ounce crumbled Roquefort or blue cheese into each indentation. Shape ground-beef mixture around cheese; flatten each into ¾-inch-thick patty. Grill or panfry as directed.

Each burger: About 299 calories, 32g protein, 1g carbohydrate, 19g total fat (8g saturated), 101mg cholesterol, 399mg sodium.

GRILLED PORTOBELLO BURGERS

....

With their rich flavor and meaty texture, porto-bello mushrooms are a satisfying substitute for real burgers—and the swap saves you almost 16 grams of fat, 76 milligrams of cholesterol, and 200-plus calories.

Prep: 10 minutes   Grill: 10 minutes

- 2 packages (6 ounces each) portobello mushroom caps (4 large)
- 3 tablespoons bottled balsamic vinaigrette
- ⅓ cup light mayonnaise
- ¼ cup drained jarred roasted red peppers
- 4 whole-wheat hamburger buns, split
- 1 large ripe tomato (10 to 12 ounces), thinly sliced
- 4 Boston lettuce leaves
- 2 large carrots, sliced diagonally

1. Heat ridged grill pan on medium-high until hot. Place mushrooms, stem sides down, in pan. Brush with half of vinaigrette and grill 5 minutes. Turn mushrooms over; brush with remaining vinaigrette and grill 5 to 8 minutes longer or until very tender.

2. Meanwhile, place mayonnaise and red peppers in blender. Pulse until red peppers are chopped but not pureed, turning off blender and scraping down sides several times. Toast hamburger buns.

3. To serve, spread red pepper mayonnaise on cut sides of bottom buns. Place mushrooms on the buns and top with tomato slices, lettuce, then bun tops. Serve carrot slices with burgers. Makes 4 main-dish servings.

Each serving: About 270 calories, 8g protein, 33g carbohydrate, 12g total fat (2g saturated), 5g fiber, 7mg cholesterol, 590mg sodium.

STUFFED VEAL CHOPS

....

Thick, juicy veal chops, stuffed with a mixture of creamy cheese, roasted peppers, and basil, sit atop a bed of spicy greens. The combination of warm chops and cool greens is a real winner. Use a small paring knife to cut the pocket so that it is deep but not wide.

Prep: 15 minutes   Grill: 10 minutes

- ¼ cup roasted red peppers (one-third 7-ounce jar), drained and chopped
- 3 tablespoons chopped fresh basil
- 4 veal rib chops, each 1 inch thick (about 10 ounces each)
- 2 ounces Fontina cheese, sliced
- ½ plus ⅛ teaspoon salt
- ½ plus ⅛ teaspoon coarsely ground black pepper
- 1 tablespoon olive oil
- 1 tablespoon balsamic vinegar
- ½ teaspoon Dijon mustard
- 4 ounces arugula, watercress, or baby spinach, tough stems removed

1. Prepare outdoor grill for direct grilling over medium-high heat.

2. In small bowl, mix roasted red peppers and 2 tablespoons chopped basil.

3. Pat veal dry with paper towels. Holding knife parallel to surface, cut a horizontal pocket in each chop. Tuck cheese slices into pocket of each chop, then stuff each with one-fourth of red-pepper mixture. Sprinkle chops with ½ teaspoon salt and ½ teaspoon pepper.

4. Place chops on grill and cook, turning once, until chops are lightly browned on both sides and just lose their pink color throughout, 10 to 12 minutes.

5. Meanwhile, in medium bowl, with wire whisk, mix oil, vinegar, remaining 1 tablespoon basil, mustard, remaining ⅛ teaspoon salt, and remaining ⅛ teaspoon pepper until blended. Add arugula to dressing bowl; toss until evenly coated.

6. To serve, spoon arugula mixture onto platter; arrange chops on top. Makes 4 servings.

Each serving: About 440 calories, 40g protein, 2g carbohydrate, 29g total fat (11g saturated), 181mg cholesterol, 655mg sodium.

GRILLING PORK

CUT	COOK TO TEMPERATURE	COOKING TIME
Chops (rib or loin), 1" thick	150°F	10–12 minutes
Tenderloin, whole	150°F	13–23 minutes
Tenderloin steaks, ¼" thick	150°F	5–6 minutes

PORK TENDERLOIN CUTLETS WITH PLUM GLAZE

Serve with ginger iced tea and scallion pancakes.

Prep: 10 minutes   Grill: 6 minutes

- 1   pork tenderloin (1 pound), trimmed
- ¾   teaspoon salt
- ¼   teaspoon coarsely ground black pepper
- ½   cup plum jam or preserves
- 1   tablespoon brown sugar
- 1   tablespoon grated, peeled fresh ginger
- 2   garlic cloves, crushed with garlic press
- 1   tablespoon fresh lemon juice
- ½   teaspoon ground cinnamon
- 4   large plums (1 pound), each pitted and cut in half

1. Prepare outdoor grill for direct grilling over medium heat.

2. Using sharp knife, cut tenderloin lengthwise almost in half, being careful not to cut all the way through. Open and spread flat like a book. Place tenderloin between two sheets of plastic wrap or waxed paper. With meat mallet or rolling pin, pound meat to ¼-inch thickness. Cut crosswise into 4 equal pieces; sprinkle cutlets with salt and pepper.

3. In small bowl, combine plum jam, brown sugar, ginger, garlic, lemon juice, and cinnamon. Brush one side of each cutlet and cut side of each plum half with plum glaze. Place cutlets and plums on grill, glaze side down, and cook 3 minutes. Brush cutlets and plums with remaining plum glaze; turn pork and plums over and cook until cutlets are lightly browned on both sides and just

lose their pink color throughout and plums are hot, about 3 minutes longer. Makes 4 main-dish servings.

Each serving: About 333 calories, 27g protein, 44g carbohydrate, 6g total fat (2g saturated), 80mg cholesterol, 509mg sodium.

PORK MEDALLIONS WITH MELON SALSA AND GRILLED LIMES

Melon salsa makes a luscious summer topper.

Total time 30 minutes

Prep: 20 minutes   Grill: 8 minutes

- 1   whole pork tenderloin (1¼ pounds), trimmed
- 4   to 5 limes
- 1   tablespoon olive oil
- ½   cup loosely packed fresh cilantro leaves, chopped
- ¼   teaspoon salt
- ⅛   teaspoon coarsely ground black pepper
- 2   cups chopped cantaloupe
- 1   cup chopped honeydew melon
- 1   jalapeño chile, minced

1. Prepare outdoor grill for direct grilling on medium heat.

2. Cut pork tenderloin crosswise into 8 equal pieces. With palm of hand, firmly press on cut side of each piece to flatten to about 1-inch-thick medallion.

3. Cut 2 limes in half; reserve for grilling. From remaining limes, grate 1 teaspoon peel and squeeze ¼ cup juice. In medium bowl, combine oil, ½ teaspoon lime peel, half of cilantro, ⅛ teaspoon salt, and pepper. Add pork medallions to bowl; toss to coat.

4. Place pork on hot grill grate and cook 4 minutes. Turn pork over. Add lime halves, cut sides down, to grill; cook 3 to 4 minutes or until lightly browned and warm. Cook pork 4 to 5 minutes longer or until browned on the outside and still slightly pink in the center.

5. In medium bowl, combine melons, jalapeño, lime juice, ⅛ teaspoon salt, and remaining cilantro and lime peel. (Makes about 3 cups salsa.) Serve pork with melon salsa and grilled limes. Makes 4 main-dish servings.

Each serving: About 240 calories, 31g protein, 17g carbohydrate, 8g total fat (2g saturated), 2g fiber, 78mg cholesterol, 225mg sodium.

BASIC GRILLED PORK TENDERLOINS

Lean, tasty pork tenderloins are perfect for grilling.

Prep: 15 minutes plus marinating
Grill: 16 minutes

1 pork tenderloin (about 1 pound)
   choice of dry spice rub (below)

1. Prepare outdoor grill for covered direct grilling over medium heat.

2. In cup, combine rub ingredients; use to rub on tenderloins.

3. Place tenderloins on grill, cover and cook, turning tenderloins once, until browned on the outside and still slightly pink in the center, 16 to 20 minutes. Meat thermometer inserted in thickest part of tenderloin should register 150°F.

4. Transfer tenderloin to cutting board; cover and let rest 5 minutes. Thinly slice. Makes 8 main-dish servings.

Each serving: About 177 calories, 26g protein, 0g carbohydrate, 7g total fat (2g saturated), 77mg cholesterol, 48mg sodium.

DRY SPICE RUBS

CURRY RUB
Combine 2 tablespoons brown sugar, 1 tablespoon curry powder, ½ teaspoon salt, and ¼ teaspoon ground black pepper.

SOUTHWESTERN RUB
Combine 2 teaspoons chili powder, ½ teaspoon salt, ¼ teaspoon ground cumin, ¼ teaspoon ground coriander, ¼ teaspoon ground red pepper (cayenne), and ¼ teaspoon ground black pepper.

MIDDLE EASTERN RUB
Combine 1 tablespoon dried mint, crumbled, 1 teaspoon ground cumin, ½ teaspoon salt, and ¼ teaspoon ground black pepper.

HERBES DE PROVENCE RUB
Combine 1½ teaspoons dried thyme, crumbled, 1 teaspoon dried rosemary, crumbled, ½ teaspoon dried marjoram, crumbled, ½ teaspoon salt, and ¼ teaspoon ground black pepper.

JERK PORK TENDERLOINS

From Jamaica, jerk seasoning uses lots of allspice, which is native to the island. Combined with thyme, bay leaves, and hot chiles, it makes a unique and delicious rub for pork, chicken, and fish.

Prep: 15 minutes plus marinating
Grill: 23 minutes

1 bunch green onions, cut into 1-inch pieces
3 bay leaves, broken into pieces
3 garlic cloves, peeled
2 jalapeño chiles, seeded and coarsely chopped
2 tablespoons distilled white vinegar
1 tablespoon dried thyme
2 teaspoons ground allspice
1 teaspoon salt
½ teaspoon coarsely ground black pepper
2 whole pork tenderloins (1 pound each)
2 small or 1 large ripe pineapple

1. In food processor with knife blade attached, puree green onions, bay leaves, garlic, jalapeños, vinegar, thyme, allspice, salt, and pepper until thick paste is formed. Use to rub on tenderloins. Place pork on large plate; cover and refrigerate 1 hour or overnight.

2. Prepare outdoor grill for covered direct grilling over medium heat.

3. Meanwhile, with sharp knife, cut pineapples lengthwise through crown to stem end into a total of 8 wedges, leaving on leafy crown.

4. Place tenderloins on grill, cover and cook, turning tenderloins once, until browned on outside and still slightly pink in center, 18 to 22 minutes. Meat thermometer inserted in thickest part of tenderloin should register 150°F. Transfer tenderloin to cutting board; cover and let stand 5 minutes.

5. Meanwhile, add pineapple wedges, cut sides down, to same grill rack; cook, turning once, until golden brown and heated through, 5 to 8 minutes.

6. Transfer pineapple to platter. Cut tenderloin into thin slices. Serve with pineapple wedges. Makes 8 main-dish servings.

Each serving: About 205 calories, 27g protein, 10g carbohydrate, 6g total fat (2g saturated), 78mg cholesterol, 340mg sodium.

TERIYAKI PORK CHOPS WITH GRILLED PINEAPPLE SLICES

Many fruits go well with pork, but pineapple tops the list. Before grilling, the pork chops are marinated in a Polynesian-style mixture that deliciously complements the pineapple.

Prep: 15 minutes plus marinating
Grill: 20 minutes

- ⅓ cup soy sauce
- 2 tablespoons plus ¼ cup packed brown sugar
- 2 green onions, chopped
- 2 tablespoons grated, peeled fresh ginger
- 4 pork loin chops, ¾ inch thick (6 to 8 ounces each)
- 1 small pineapple

1. Prepare outdoor grill for direct grilling over medium heat.

2. In 13" by 9" baking dish, combine soy sauce, 2 tablespoons brown sugar, green onions, and ginger. Add chops, turning to coat. Let stand 20 minutes at room temperature to marinate.

3. Meanwhile, cut off crown and stem end from pineapple. Stand pineapple upright and cut off rind and eyes. Then place pineapple on its side and cut crosswise into ½-inch-thick slices. Sprinkle pineapple slices with remaining ¼ cup brown sugar.

4. Place pineapple on grill and cook, turning slices occasionally, until browned on both sides, 15 to 20 minutes. After pineapple has cooked 10 minutes, place chops on grill and cook, turning occasionally and brushing with remaining teriyaki mixture halfway through cooking, until chops are browned on both sides and juices run clear when center is pierced with tip of knife, about 10 minutes. Serve chops with grilled pineapple slices. Makes 4 main-dish servings.

Each serving: About 399 calories, 30g protein, 48g carbohydrate, 11g total fat (4g saturated), 78mg cholesterol, 1,433mg sodium.

HERBED PORK CHOPS

For a delicious and interesting change of pace, fennel seeds, with their subtle licoricelike flavor, perk up the pork chops. Crushing the seeds just before using them maximizes their flavor and fragrance.

Prep: 15 minutes   Grill: 11 minutes

- 1 tablespoon chopped fresh rosemary leaves
- 2 teaspoons fennel seeds, crushed
- ¾ teaspoon salt
- ⅛ teaspoon ground black pepper
- 4 bone-in pork loin or rib chops, ¾ inch thick (about 6 ounces each)
- 1 pound plum tomatoes, each cut lengthwise in half
- 1 tablespoon extra-virgin olive oil
- 2 tablespoons chopped fresh parsley leaves
- 1 teaspoon grated fresh lemon peel
- 1 garlic clove, crushed with press

1. Prepare outdoor grill for covered direct grilling over medium heat.

2. Meanwhile, in cup, combine rosemary, fennel seeds, ½ teaspoon salt, and pepper. Use to rub on pork chops.

3. In medium bowl, combine tomatoes, oil, and remaining salt; set aside.

4. Place pork chops on grill, cover and cook chops 5 minutes. Turn chops and arrange on one side of grill. Place tomatoes, cut sides down, on other side of grill; set bowl aside. Cover grill and cook pork chops until browned on outside and still slightly pink on inside, 4 to 5 minutes; cook tomatoes until evenly charred on both sides, 6 to 7 minutes.

5. Transfer chops to platter and tomatoes to cutting board. Cool tomatoes slightly, then cut into large pieces. Return tomatoes and their juices to reserved bowl; stir in parsley, lemon peel, and garlic. Serve chops with tomato salad. Makes 4 main-dish servings.

Each serving: About 315 calories, 28g protein, 6g carbohydrate, 19g total fat (6g saturated), 88mg cholesterol, 520mg sodium.

BARBECUED PORK SPARERIBS

·······························

Plain spareribs? Of course not! It's the sauces that make these special. Here are three of our favorites.

Prep: 1 hour 20 minutes **Grill: 20 minutes**

4 pounds pork spareribs, cut into 1- or 2-rib portions
choice of sauce (below and right)

1. Early in day or one day ahead, precook spareribs: In 8-quart Dutch oven, place ribs. Add enough *water* to cover and heat to boiling over high heat. Reduce heat; cover and simmer until spareribs are tender, about 1 hour. Transfer spareribs to platter; cover and refrigerate.

2. Prepare outdoor grill for direct grilling over medium heat.

3. Meanwhile, prepare desired barbecue sauce.

4. To grill: Place cooked spareribs on grill and cook, turning ribs frequently and brushing with barbecue sauce often, until heated through, about 20 minutes. Makes 8 main-dish servings.

BALSAMIC-ROSEMARY SAUCE

In 1-quart saucepan, combine **⅔ cup balsamic vinegar, 2 tablespoons brown sugar, 1 teaspoon salt,** and **½ teaspoon ground black pepper** and heat to boiling over medium heat. Cook until sauce has reduced to ⅓ cup, about 15 minutes. Stir in **1 teaspoon dried rosemary,** crumbled.

Each serving with Balsamic-Rosemary Sauce: About 368 calories, 26g protein, 4g carbohydrate, 27g total fat (10g saturated), 107mg cholesterol, 376mg sodium.

ORANGE-DIJON SAUCE

In cup, combine **1 cup sweet orange marmalade, ¼ cup Dijon mustard, ¼ cup packed brown sugar, 1 teaspoon freshly grated orange peel,** and **1½ teaspoons salt.**

Each serving with Orange-Dijon Sauce: About 483 calories, 26g protein, 33g carbohydrate, 27g total fat (10g saturated), 107mg cholesterol, 723mg sodium.

ASIAN BARBECUE SAUCE

In 1-quart saucepan, heat **1 tablespoon vegetable oil** over medium heat; add **2 green onions,** finely chopped, and cook until tender, about 5 minutes. Add **2 teaspoons grated, peeled fresh ginger** and **1 garlic clove** crushed with garlic press; cook, stirring frequently, 1 minute longer. Stir in **⅔ cup packed brown sugar, ¼ cup soy sauce, ¼ cup dry sherry, 1 tablespoon cornstarch,** and **½ teaspoon salt.** Heat to boiling over medium-high heat, stirring, until mixture has thickened and boils. Remove from heat; stir in **1 teaspoon Asian sesame oil.**

Each serving with Asian Barbecue Sauce: About 453 calories, 26g protein, 20g carbohydrate, 29g total fat (10g saturated), 107mg cholesterol, 750mg sodium.

PORK RIBS GLOSSARY

TEST KITCHEN TIP

Nothing says summer more than pork ribs on the grill. There are several types of ribs you are likely to find at your local supermarket.

SPARERIBS: A rack, made up of the 13 ribs from the belly of a pig, weighs around 2 to 3 pounds, with lots of meat at the wider end. It will feed from two to three people.

BABY BACK RIBS: These are pork chop bones from the upper portion of the rib section of the loin with the boneless meat removed. Baby back ribs are not, as one might think, from baby pigs. These ribs have much less meat on them than spareribs, as the meat is cut very close to the bone. One rack will feed one or two people. With their smaill size, they make great cocktail food.

COUNTRY-STYLE RIBS: These ribs are actually loin pork chops that have been split. These meaty, slightly fatty ribs are delicious grilled or braised. They are sold bone-in and boneless.

PLUM-GOOD BABY BACK RIBS

....

Licorice-flavored star anise—one of the spices in Chinese five-spice powder—gives these ribs their distinctive appeal. The ribs can be cooked in the seasoned liquid up to two days ahead, then cooled, covered, and refrigerated. Remove the ribs from the refrigerator while the grill heats, then proceed with the recipe.

Prep: 1 hour   Grill: 15 minutes

- 4 racks pork baby back ribs (about 1 pound each)
- 12 whole black peppercorns
- 2 bay leaves
- 10 whole star anise
- 2 cinnamon sticks (each 3 inches long)
- ¼ cup soy sauce
- 1 jar (12 ounces) plum jam (1 cup)
- 1 tablespoon grated, peeled fresh ginger
- 1 garlic clove, crushed with garlic press

1. In 8-quart saucepot, combine ribs, peppercorns, bay leaves, 4 star anise, and 1 cinnamon stick. Add enough *water* to cover and heat to boiling over high heat. Reduce heat to low; cover and simmer until ribs are fork-tender, 50 minutes to 1 hour. Transfer ribs to platter. If not serving right away, cover and refrigerate until ready to serve.

2. Prepare glaze: In 1-quart saucepan, heat soy sauce, remaining 6 star anise, and remaining cinnamon stick to boiling over high heat. Reduce heat to low; cover and simmer 5 minutes. Remove from heat; let stand, covered, 5 minutes. Strain mixture into bowl; discard star anise and cinnamon. Stir in plum jam, ginger, and garlic.

3. Prepare outdoor grill for direct grilling over medium heat.

4. Place ribs on grill and cook, turning once, until browned, about 10 minutes. Brush ribs with some glaze and grill, brushing with remaining glaze and turning frequently, 5 to 10 minutes longer. Makes 6 main-dish servings.

Each serving: About 690 calories, 37g protein, 38g carbohydrate, 43g total fat (16g saturated), 172mg cholesterol, 860mg sodium.

SAUSAGE-AND-PEPPER GRILL

....

For hearty sandwiches reminiscent of those found at Italian street fairs, grill Italian hero rolls, split them open, and top with this sausage, pepper, and onion mixture. If you prefer, toss the grilled sausages and vegetables with cooked ziti, add grated Parmesan cheese, and serve.

Prep: 15 minutes   Grill: 15 minutes

- ⅓ cup balsamic vinegar
- 1 teaspoon brown sugar
- ½ teaspoon salt
- ¼ teaspoon coarsely ground black pepper
- 2 medium red peppers, cut into 1½-inch-wide strips
- 2 medium green peppers, cut into 1½-inch-wide strips
- 2 large red onions (about 8 ounces each), each cut into 6 wedges
- 1 tablespoon olive oil
- ¾ pound sweet Italian sausage links
- ¾ pound hot Italian sausage links

1. Prepare outdoor grill for direct grilling over medium heat.

2. In cup, with fork, mix vinegar, brown sugar, salt, and black pepper. In large bowl, toss red and green peppers and onions with oil until evenly coated.

3. Place sausages and vegetables on grill. Cook sausages, turning occasionally, until golden brown and cooked through, 15 to 20 minutes. Cook vegetables, turning occasionally and brushing with some balsamic mixture during last 3 minutes of cooking, until tender, about 15 minutes. Transfer vegetables and sausages to platter as they finish cooking.

4. To serve, cut sausages diagonally into 2-inch-thick slices. Drizzle remaining balsamic mixture over vegetables. Makes 4 main-dish servings.

Each serving: About 500 calories, 27g protein, 19g carbohydrate, 36g total fat (12g saturated), 97mg cholesterol, 1,450mg sodium.

SOUTHWESTERN HAM STEAK

··

Serve with one of our fresh salsas (pages 506–508).

Prep: 5 minutes   Grill: 8 minutes

- 2 teaspoons chili powder
- ½ teaspoon ground cumin
- ¼ teaspoon ground coriander
- ¼ teaspoon ground red pepper (cayenne)
- ¼ teaspoon sugar
- 1 fully cooked smoked ham center slice, ½ inch thick (1¼ pounds)

1. Prepare outdoor grill for direct grilling over medium heat.

2. In small bowl, combine chili powder, cumin, coriander, ground red pepper, and sugar. Use to rub on ham steak.

3. Place ham steak on grill and cook until heated through and lightly browned, about 4 minutes per side. Makes 4 main-dish servings.

Each serving: About 171 calories, 27g protein, 1g carbohydrate, 6g total fat (2g saturated), 61mg cholesterol, 1,727mg sodium.

GRILLED LAMB CHOPS WITH SPICE RUB

··

Grilling chops that have been seasoned with a rub is the easiest way to guarantee lots of flavor.

Prep: 5 minutes   Grill: 10 minutes

- 4 lamb shoulder chops, ¾ inch thick (8 ounces each)
  choice of dry spice rub (page 356)

1. Prepare outdoor grill for direct grilling over medium heat.

2. In small bowl, combine rub ingredients; use to rub on lamb chops.

3. Place chops on grill and cook about 5 minutes per side for medium-rare or until desired doneness. Makes 4 main-dish servings.

Each serving: About 454 calories, 57g protein, 2g carbohydrate, 22g total fat (8g saturated), 196mg cholesterol, 470mg sodium.

AROMATIC LEG OF LAMB

··

Once your butcher has boned out a leg of lamb for you, ask for the lamb bone. Use it to cook up some flavorful lamb broth for an especially tasty stew or hearty soup.

Prep: 20 minutes   Grill: 15 minutes

- 3 pounds butterflied boneless lamb leg, trimmed
- 3 garlic cloves, each cut in half and crushed with side of chef's knife
- 1 tablespoon olive oil
- 2 teaspoons fennel seeds, crushed
- 2 teaspoons cumin seeds, crushed
- 2 teaspoons coriander seeds, crushed
- 1½ teaspoons salt
  lemon wedges

1. Prepare outdoor grill for covered direct grilling over medium heat. Rub both sides of lamb with cut sides of garlic cloves; discard garlic.

2. In small bowl, combine oil, fennel seeds, cumin seeds, coriander seeds, and salt. Use to rub on lamb.

3. Place lamb on grill, cover and cook, turning lamb occasionally, 15 to 25 minutes for medium-rare or until desired doneness. Thickness of butterflied lamb will vary throughout; cut off sections of lamb as they are done and place on cutting board. Let stand 10 minutes to set juices for easier slicing. Cut into thin slices and serve lamb with lemon wedges. Makes 8 main-dish servings.

Each serving: About 265 calories, 36g protein, 1g carbohydrate, 12g total fat (4g saturated), 114mg cholesterol, 525mg sodium.

SPICES

Spices come from the bark, buds, fruit, roots, seeds, or stems of plants and trees, unlike herbs, which come from the leafy parts of plants. Spices have always been used for flavoring food and drinks as well as for medicinal and ceremonial purposes. The most common spices are allspice, anise, caraway, celery seed, chili powder, cinnamon, coriander, cumin, fennel, juniper, mustard, and pepper.

BUTTERFLIED LEG OF LAMB
WITH MINT PESTO

···

Why can't leg of lamb be summer fare? Our juicy chargrilled roast is butterflied to take it out of the oven and onto the grill. Check thinner portions of the butterflied meat early for doneness; cut off those sections as they are cooked and place them on a cutting board, covered with foil, to keep warm.

Prep: 15 minutes plus marinating and standing
Grill: 20 minutes

4½ cups loosely packed fresh mint leaves
 2 cloves garlic, crushed with press
 ½ cup water
 ⅓ cup olive oil
 1 teaspoon salt
 1 teaspoon coarsely ground black pepper
 4 pounds butterflied boneless lamb leg, trimmed
 ¾ cup blanched almonds

1. In food processor with knife blade attached, pulse mint leaves, garlic, water, oil, salt, and pepper until well blended.

2. Place lamb in 13" by 9" glass baking dish. Remove ¼ cup mint mixture from food processor; spread on lamb to coat both sides. Cover and refrigerate at least 1 hour or up to 6 hours.

3. Meanwhile, add almonds to mint mixture remaining in food processor and pulse until almonds are finely chopped. Spoon pesto into serving bowl; cover and refrigerate until ready to serve.

4. Remove lamb from refrigerator about 15 minutes before cooking. Prepare outdoor grill for covered, direct grilling on medium.

5. Place lamb on hot grill grate; cover and cook 20 to 35 minutes (depending on thickness) for medium-rare, turning lamb over once halfway through cooking and removing pieces to cutting board as they are done. When remaining lamb is done, transfer to same cutting board and let stand 10 minutes to set juices for easier slicing. Serve lamb with mint pesto. Makes 12 main-dish servings.

Each serving: About 380 calories, 32g protein, 5g carbohydrate, 26g total fat (8g saturated), 4g fiber, 99mg cholesterol, 270mg sodium.

ROSEMARY LAMB KABOBS

···

The fresh, clean flavors of orange and rosemary are wonderful with lamb. Serve alongside skewers of grilled cherry tomatoes and a bowl of yellow rice.

Prep: 30 minutes plus marinating
Grill: 10 minutes

 3 oranges
 1 tablespoon olive oil
 1 tablespoon chopped fresh rosemary
    or 1½ teaspoons dried rosemary, crumbled
 2 garlic cloves, each cut in half
 ¼ teaspoon salt
 ¼ teaspoon ground red pepper (cayenne)
 1 pound boneless lamb leg, cut into 1½-inch pieces
 8 metal skewers
 1 red pepper, cut into 1½-inch squares
 1 yellow pepper, cut into 1½-inch squares
 1 orange pepper, cut into 1½-inch squares
 1 pint cherry tomatoes
 6 green onions, cut into 2-inch pieces
10 ounces small mushrooms, trimmed

1. Prepare outdoor grill for direct grilling over medium heat.

2. Meanwhile, from oranges, grate 1 teaspoon peel and squeeze 1 cup juice. In large bowl, combine orange peel and juice, oil, rosemary, garlic, salt, and ground red pepper. Add lamb, turning to coat, and let stand, stirring occasionally, 10 minutes at room temperature.

3. Thread lamb onto 4 metal skewers and thread vegetables onto remaining 4 skewers, alternating vegetables. Place skewers on grill. Cook lamb and vegetables, turning once, 10 to 12 minutes for medium-rare or until desired doneness. Transfer to platter. Makes 4 main-dish servings.

Each serving: About 245 calories, 28g protein, 12g carbohydrate, 10g total fat (3g saturated), 81mg cholesterol, 118mg sodium.

ALL-AMERICAN BARBECUED CHICKEN

························

Our traditional-style barbecue sauce is perfect with grilled chicken, beef, or spareribs. We like to remove the skin from the chicken; it reduces the chance of flare-ups.

Prep: 1 hour   Grill: 40 minutes

- 2   tablespoons olive oil
- 1   large onion (12 ounces), chopped
- 2   cans (15 ounces each) tomato sauce
- 1   cup red wine vinegar
- ½   cup light (mild) molasses
- ¼   cup Worcestershire sauce
- ⅓   cup packed brown sugar
- ¾   teaspoon ground red pepper (cayenne)
- 2   chickens (3½ pounds each), each cut into quarters, skin removed from all but wings, if desired

1. In nonstick 10-inch skillet, heat oil over medium heat. Add onion and cook until tender, about 5 minutes. Stir in tomato sauce, vinegar, molasses, Worcestershire, brown sugar, and ground red pepper; heat to boiling over high heat. Reduce heat to medium-low and cook, stirring occasionally, until sauce has thickened slightly, about 45 minutes. (Makes about 3½ cups sauce.) If not using sauce right away, cover and refrigerate to use within 2 weeks.

2. Prepare outdoor grill for covered direct grilling over medium heat.

3. Reserve 1½ cups sauce to serve with chicken. Place chicken on grill; cover and cook turning once, 20 to 25 minutes. Generously brush chicken with some of remaining barbecue sauce and cook, brushing frequently with sauce and turning chicken often, until juices run clear when thickest part of chicken is pierced with tip of knife, about 20 minutes longer. Serve with reserved sauce. Makes 8 main-dish servings.

Each serving without additional sauce, without skin: About 370 calories, 42g protein, 21g carbohydrate, 13g total fat (3g saturated), 127mg cholesterol, 543mg sodium.

Each ¼ cup sauce: About 160 calories, 1g protein, 20g carbohydrate, 2g total fat (0g saturated), 0mg cholesterol, 422mg sodium.

GINGER-GRILLED CHICKEN FOR A CROWD

························

When you have a crowd to feed at a backyard bash, try this honey-and-ginger party pleaser.

**Prep: 10 minutes plus overnight to marinate
Grill/Broil: 35 minutes**

- 1¼   cups soy sauce
- ¾   cup honey
- ¼   cup fresh lemon juice
- 2   tablespoons vegetable oil
- 2   tablespoons minced, peeled fresh ginger
- 2   garlic cloves, crushed with garlic press
- 3   chickens (3 pounds each), each cut into quarters

1. In small bowl, combine soy sauce, honey, lemon juice, oil, ginger, and garlic until well blended. Divide chicken and marinade among three zip-tight plastic bags, turning chicken to coat; place in 15" by 9" baking dish. Seal bags, pressing out as much air as possible. Refrigerate chicken overnight to marinate.

2. Prepare outdoor grill for covered direct grilling over medium heat. Alternatively, preheat broiler.

3. Remove chicken from marinade; discard marinade. To grill, place chicken on grill, cover and cook until golden brown, about 5 minutes per side. Move chicken to perimeter of grill (where it is cooler); cover and cook until juices run clear when thickest part of chicken is pierced with tip of knife, about 25 minutes longer.

To broil in oven: Marinate chicken as in Step 1. Preheat broiler. Place chicken, skin side down, on rack in large broiling pan. (Chicken may have to be broiled in batches.) Place pan in broiler 8 to 10 inches from heat source. Broil chicken until golden brown, about 20 minutes. Turn chicken skin side up; broil, brushing occasionally with marinade, until juices run clear when thickest part of chicken is pierced with tip of knife, about 20 minutes longer. Makes 12 main-dish servings.

Each serving: About 410 calories, 42g protein, 10g carbohydrate, 22g total fat (6g saturated), 132mg cholesterol, 988mg sodium.

GRILLING POULTRY

Different chicken parts require different amounts of time on the grill, but it is nice to be able to remove all of the chicken from the grill at the same time so it is equally hot. Here's an easy way to accomplish this: When grilling a cut-up chicken, put the legs on the grill first. After 5 minutes, place the breasts on the grill. After another 10 minutes, put the thighs on to cook.

CUT	COOK TO TEMPERATURE	APPROXIMATE COOKING TIME
Legs, bone-in	170°F	35–40 minutes
Thighs, bone-in	170°F	12–15 minutes
Thighs, boneless	170°F	10–12 minutes
Breasts, bone-in	165°F	30–35 minutes
Breasts, boneless	160°F	10–12 minutes
Cornish game hens, halved	170°F	35–45 minutes

BEER-CAN CHICKEN

Your favorite brew keeps this chicken moist and juicy. If you're using a charcoal grill, add ten charcoal briquettes per side if cooking time is more than 1 hour.

Prep: 15 minutes plus standing   Grill: 1 hour

- 3 tablespoons paprika
- 1 tablespoon sugar
- 1 tablespoon salt
- 2 teaspoons coarsely ground black pepper
- 1 teaspoon onion powder
- 1 teaspoon garlic powder
- 1 teaspoon ground red pepper (cayenne)
- 2 whole chickens (about 3½ pounds each)
- 2 cans (12 ounces each) beer

1. Prepare charcoal fire for covered indirect-heat grilling with drip pan as manufacturer directs or preheat gas grill for covered indirect grilling over medium heat.

2. In cup, combine paprika, sugar, salt, black pepper, onion powder, garlic powder, and ground red pepper.

3. Remove giblets and necks from chickens. Rinse chickens inside and out with cold running water and drain well; pat dry with paper towels. Sprinkle 1 tablespoon spice mixture inside cavity of each chicken. Rub remaining spice mixture all over chickens.

4. Wipe beer cans clean. Open cans; pour ½ cup beer out of each can and reserve for another use. With church key, make four more holes in top of each can. With partially filled can on flat surface, hold 1 chicken upright, with opening of body cavity down, and slide chicken over top of beer can so can fits inside cavity. Repeat with remaining chicken and can.

5. With large spatula, transfer chickens to center of grill rack, keeping cans upright. (If using charcoal, place chickens over drip pan.) Spread chicken legs to balance chickens on rack. Cover grill and cook chickens until juices run clear when thickest part of thigh is pierced with tip of knife, 1 hour to 1 hour 15 minutes.

6. With tongs and barbecue mitts, remove chickens and cans from grill, being careful not to spill beer. Let chickens stand 10 minutes before lifting from cans. Transfer chickens to large platter or cutting board; discard beer. Makes 8 main-dish servings.

Each serving: About 350 calories, 39g protein, 4g carbohydrate, 19g total fat (5g saturated), 152mg cholesterol, 985mg sodium.

GRILLED CHICKEN BREASTS SALTIMBOCCA

·······································

In Italian, saltimbocca means "jump in your mouth" and these prosciutto-and-sage–topped chicken breasts will do just that. One note of caution: Don't slice the prosciutto paper-thin or it could burn.

Prep: 10 minutes   Grill: 10 minutes

- 4 medium skinless, boneless chicken breast halves (1¼ pounds)
- ⅛ teaspoon salt
- ⅛ teaspoon ground black pepper
- 12 fresh sage leaves
- 4 large slices prosciutto (4 ounces)

1. Prepare outdoor grill for covered direct grilling over medium heat.

2. Sprinkle chicken with salt and pepper. Place 3 sage leaves on each breast half. Place 1 prosciutto slice on top of each breast half, tucking in edges if necessary; secure with toothpicks.

3. Place chicken, prosciutto side down, on grill, cover and cook 5 to 6 minutes. Turn and grill until chicken loses its pink color throughout, 5 to 6 minutes longer. Makes 4 main-dish servings.

Each serving: About 223 calories, 41g protein, 0g carbohydrate, 6g total fat (1g saturated), 105mg cholesterol, 690mg sodium.

Grilled Chicken Breasts Saltimbocca

PEKING CHICKEN ROLL-UPS

(Pictured on page 344)

·······································

The traditional Chinese recipe for duck is quite labor-intensive and takes several days to make. Our version, prepared in minutes, is made with grilled boneless chicken thighs and served in flour tortillas with hoisin sauce.

Prep: 25 minutes   Grill: 10 minutes

- 8 (8-inch) flour tortillas
- 2 tablespoons honey
- 2 tablespoons soy sauce
- 1 tablespoon grated, peeled fresh ginger
- ⅛ teaspoon ground red pepper (cayenne)
- 2 garlic cloves, crushed with garlic press
- 6 skinless, boneless chicken thighs (about 1¼ pounds)
- 1 teaspoon vegetable oil
- ¼ cup hoisin sauce
- ½ English (seedless) cucumber, cut into 2" by ¼" matchstick strips
- 2 green onions, thinly sliced

1. Prepare outdoor grill for direct grilling over medium-high heat.

2. Stack tortillas and wrap in foil. In small bowl, mix honey, soy sauce, ginger, ground red pepper, and garlic until blended. Set aside tortillas and honey mixture.

3. Coat chicken with oil and place on grill and cook, turning once, 5 minutes. Brush chicken all over with honey mixture and cook, turning once, until juices run clear when thickest part of thigh is pierced with tip of knife, 5 to 7 minutes longer.

4. While chicken is cooking, place foil-wrapped tortillas on same grill rack and heat until warm, 3 to 5 minutes.

5. Transfer chicken to cutting board and cut into thin slices. Spread hoisin sauce on one side of each tortilla. Top each with chicken, cucumber, and green onions; roll up to serve. Makes 4 main-dish servings.

Each serving: About 400 calories, 27g protein, 50g carbohydrate, 10g total fat (3g saturated), 75mg cholesterol, 1,255mg sodium.

CITRUS-SAGE CHICKEN

....

Sage makes an excellent addition to a garden or window box. It doesn't require much attention, and it grows more lush and beautiful each year. At summer's end, harvest some of the leaves and hang them upside down in bunches in a cool, dark place to dry.

**Prep: 25 minutes plus marinating
Grill: 30 minutes**

- 2 large oranges
- 2 large lemons
- ¼ cup chopped fresh sage plus additional whole leaves
  for garnish
- 2 tablespoons olive oil
- 2 teaspoons salt
- ¾ teaspoon coarsely ground black pepper
- 2 chickens (3½ pounds each), each cut into 8 pieces and skin removed from all but wings

1. From oranges, grate 1 tablespoon peel and squeeze 3 tablespoons juice. From lemons, grate 1 tablespoon peel and squeeze 3 tablespoons juice.

2. In large bowl, with wire whisk, combine orange and lemon peels and juices, chopped sage, oil, salt, and pepper. Add chicken, turning to coat. Cover and refrigerate chicken 2 hours to marinate, turning three or four times.

3. Prepare outdoor grill for covered direct grilling over medium heat.

4. Place chicken, meat side down, on grill; cover and cook 20 minutes. Turn chicken and cook until juices run clear when thickest part of chicken is pierced with tip of knife, 10 to 15 minutes longer.

5. To serve, arrange chicken on warm platter; garnish with sage leaves. Makes 8 main-dish servings.

Each serving: About 307 calories, 41g protein, 2g carbohydrate, 14g total fat (3g saturated), 127mg cholesterol, 705mg sodium.

MOJITO-RUBBED CHICKEN WITH GRILLED PINEAPPLE

....

Bring a taste of the tropics to your barbecue with a refreshingly mint-flavored chicken paired with smoky-sweet grilled pineapple rings.

Prep: 20 minutes   Grill: 10 minutes

- 4 medium skinless, boneless chicken breast halves (1½ pounds)
- 2 limes
- 1 tablespoon olive oil
- 1 medium pineapple (3½ pounds), peeled and cut into ½-inch-thick slices
- ¼ cup loosely packed fresh mint leaves, chopped
- ½ teaspoon salt
- ¼ teaspoon ground black pepper

1. Prepare outdoor grill for direct grilling on medium, or preheat large ridged grill pan on medium.

2. Meanwhile, place chicken breast halves between 2 sheets plastic wrap; with meat mallet, pound to an even ½-inch thickness.

3. From 1 lime, grate 1 teaspoon peel and squeeze 2 tablespoons juice. Cut remaining lime into 4 wedges; set aside. In small bowl, combine oil, lime peel, and juice. Lightly brush pineapple on both sides with lime mixture; set aside remaining lime mixture in bowl. Place pineapple slices on hot grill rack and cook 10 minutes or until browned on both sides, turning over once.

4. Stir mint into remaining lime mixture and pat onto both sides of chicken. Sprinkle chicken with salt and pepper to season both sides. Place chicken on hot grill rack and cook 5 minutes or until chicken is browned on both sides and no longer pink throughout, turning over once. Serve chicken with pineapple and lime wedges. Makes 4 main-dish servings.

Each serving: About 320 calories, 40g protein, 27g carbohydrate, 6g total fat (1g saturated), 3g fiber, 99mg cholesterol, 385mg sodium.

Tip: To round out your meal, serve with steamed broccolini spears.

TANDOORI-STYLE GRILLED CHICKEN

....

A yogurt marinade seasoned with aromatic Indian spices keeps skinless chicken moist and succulent and provides lots of flavor without extra fat.

Prep: 10 minutes plus marinating   Grill: 20 minutes

- 1 tablespoon paprika, preferably sweet Hungarian
- ½ teaspoon ground cinnamon
- ½ teaspoon ground coriander
- ½ teaspoon ground cumin
- ¼ teaspoon ground cardamom
- 1 cup (8 ounces) plain low-fat yogurt
- 2 tablespoons fresh lemon juice
- 1 tablespoon olive oil
- ½ small onion, cut into quarters
- 2 garlic cloves
- 1 tablespoon sliced pickled jalapeño chile or diced fresh jalapeño chile with seeds
- 1 tablespoon sliced, peeled fresh ginger
- ½ teaspoon salt
- 1 chicken (3½ pounds), cut into 8 pieces and skin removed from all but wings
  lemon wedges (optional)

1. In 6-inch skillet, heat paprika, cinnamon, coriander, cumin, and cardamom over low heat until very fragrant, about 3 minutes. Transfer spices to blender. Add yogurt, lemon juice, oil, onion, garlic, jalapeño, ginger, and salt; puree until smooth.

2. Make several ¼-inch-deep slashes in each chicken piece. Place chicken in zip-tight plastic bag, pour in yogurt mixture, and turn chicken to coat. Seal bag, pressing out as much air as possible. Refrigerate chicken 1 to 3 hours to marinate, turning once or twice.

3. Lightly grease grill rack. Prepare outdoor grill for covered direct grilling over medium heat.

4. Place chicken on grill over medium heat, cover and cook, turning chicken every 5 minutes, until juices run clear when thickest part of chicken is pierced with tip of knife, 20 to 25 minutes. Transfer to warm platter and serve with lemon wedges, if desired. Makes 4 main-dish servings.

Each serving: About 301 calories, 44g protein, 7g carbohydrate, 10g total fat (2g saturated), 136mg cholesterol, 466mg sodium.

GRILLED CHICKEN BREASTS

Prepare outdoor grill for direct grilling over medium heat. Place 4 medium skinless, boneless chicken breast halves (1¼ pounds) between sheets of plastic wrap and pound thick portion so the breasts are an even thickness. In medium bowl, toss chicken with 1 tablespoon olive oil, ¼ teaspoon salt, and ¼ teaspoon freshly ground pepper.

Oil grill rack and place chicken on grill; cook 5 minutes, turning once and cooking 4 to 5 minutes longer, or until juices run clear when chicken is pierced with tip of knife. Makes 4 main-dish servings.

GRILLED CHICKEN BREASTS WITH LEMON AND ROSEMARY

Prepare grill and pound chicken breasts. From 2 lemons, grate 2 teaspoons peel, and squeeze 3 tablespoons juice. In bowl, combine lemon peel, lemon juice, 1 tablespoon chopped fresh rosemary, 1 finely chopped garlic clove, ½ teaspoon salt, and ¼ teaspoon freshly ground pepper. Add chicken breasts to bowl, turning to coat. Grill as directed above, brushing with remaining mixture.

GRILLED CHICKEN BREASTS WITH CUMIN, CORIANDER, AND LIME

Prepare grill and pound chicken breasts. In bowl, whisk 3 tablespoons fresh lime juice, 2 tablespoons olive oil, 1 teaspoon ground cumin, 1 teaspoon ground coriander, 1 teaspoon sugar, 1 teaspoon salt, and ⅛ teaspoon ground red pepper (cayenne). Add chicken, turning to coat. Grill as directed above, brushing with remaining lime mixture halfway through cooking.

GRILLED CHICKEN BREASTS WITH TOMATO-OLIVE RELISH

In small bowl, combine 2 medium tomatoes, chopped, ¼ cup coarsely chopped pitted Kalamata olives, 2 tablespoons finely chopped red onion, 2 tablespoons drained capers, 1 teaspoon olive oil, and 1 teaspoon red wine vinegar. Prepare chicken as directed above. Serve chicken topped with tomato mixture.

COFFEE-SPICE CHICKEN AND FRUIT-BASIL SALSA

A jerk-style seasoning of Jamaican allspice and java gives this Caribbean chicken its caffeinated kick. Balancing the heat: a cooling summer salsa of just-picked nectarines and juicy watermelon.

Prep: 20 minutes   Grill: 8 minutes

- 1 (4-pound) piece seedless watermelon, cut into ½-inch chunks (3 cups)
- 1 large ripe nectarine, pitted and cut into ½-inch chunks
- 3 tablespoons finely chopped red onion
- 1 tablespoon fresh lemon juice
- 2 tablespoons instant coffee
- 1 tablespoon grated, peeled fresh ginger
- 1 tablespoon olive oil
- 1¼ teaspoons ground allspice
- ¾ teaspoon salt
- 8 skinless, boneless chicken breast halves (3 pounds)
- ½ cup packed fresh basil leaves, coarsely chopped

1. In medium bowl, combine watermelon, nectarine, red onion, and lemon juice. Cover and refrigerate while preparing chicken. (Makes 4 cups.)

2. Prepare outdoor grill for covered direct grilling over medium heat.

3. In large bowl, with spoon or fingers, press coffee to pulverize. Add ginger, oil, allspice, and ½ teaspoon salt; stir to combine. Add chicken and toss to evenly coat with spice mixture (you may need to pat spice mixture onto chicken with fingers).

4. Place chicken breasts on hot grill grate. Cover and cook 8 to 10 minutes or until juices run clear when thickest part of chicken is pierced with tip of knife, turning once. Transfer chicken to cutting board and let rest 5 minutes. Meanwhile, stir basil and ¼ teaspoon salt into salsa. Slice chicken crosswise and serve with salsa. Makes 8 main-dish servings.

Each serving: About 235 calories, 40g protein, 8g carbohydrate, 4g total fat (1g saturated), 1g fiber, 99mg cholesterol, 310mg sodium.

Coffee-Spice Chicken and Fruit-Basil Salsa

Curried Chicken with Mango and Cantaloupe Slaw

CURRIED CHICKEN WITH MANGO AND CANTALOUPE SLAW

....

Here, curry, crystallized ginger, and crushed red pepper bring out the full sweet flavor of fresh fruit.

Prep: 25 minutes plus marinating   Grill: 10 minutes

- 1 to 2 limes
- 1 container (6 ounces) plain low-fat yogurt
- ³/₄ teaspoon curry powder
- ¹/₄ cup chopped crystallized ginger
- 1 teaspoon salt
- ¹/₄ teaspoon crushed red pepper
- 4 medium skinless, boneless chicken breast halves (about 1¹/₄ pounds)
- ¹/₂ small cantaloupe, rind removed, cut into julienne strips (2 cups)
- 1 large mango, peeled and cut into julienne strips (2 cups)
- ¹/₂ cup loosely packed fresh cilantro leaves, chopped
- 1 head Boston lettuce
  lime wedges (optional)

1. Prepare outdoor grill for covered direct grilling over medium heat.

2. From limes, grate ¹/₂ teaspoon peel and squeeze 2 tablespoons juice. In large bowl, combine 1 tablespoon lime juice and ¹/₄ teaspoon lime peel with yogurt, curry powder, 2 tablespoons ginger, ³/₄ teaspoon salt, and ¹/₈ teaspoon crushed red pepper and whisk until blended. Add chicken, turning to coat with marinade. Cover and let stand 15 minutes at room temperature or 30 minutes in refrigerator, turning occasionally.

3. Prepare slaw: In medium bowl, with rubber spatula, gently stir cantaloupe and mango with cilantro, remaining 2 tablespoons ginger, 1 tablespoon lime juice, ¹/₄ teaspoon lime peel, ¹/₄ teaspoon salt, and ¹/₈ teaspoon crushed red pepper; set aside. (Makes about 4 cups.)

4. Grease grill rack. Remove chicken from marinade; discard marinade. Place chicken on grill. Cover and cook chicken, turning once, until juices run clear when thickest part of breast is pierced with tip of knife, 10 to 12 minutes. Transfer chicken to cutting board; cool slightly to set juices for easier slicing, then cut into long, thin slices.

5. To serve, divide lettuce leaves among 4 dinner plates; top with chicken and slaw. Serve with lime wedges, if you like. Makes 4 main-dish servings.

Each serving chicken with lettuce: About 205 calories, 34g protein, 5g carbohydrate, 4g total fat (1g saturated), 92mg cholesterol, 330mg sodium.

Each ½ cup slaw: About 50 calories, 1g protein, 13g carbohydrate, 0g total fat, 0mg cholesterol, 150mg sodium.

THAI CHICKEN SATÉ

Chicken marinated in curried coconut milk is teamed with pickled cucumbers and creamy peanut sauce.

Prep: 45 minutes   Grill: 5 minutes

- 1 English (seedless) cucumber, cut crosswise into thin slices
- 1½ teaspoons salt
- 1 tablespoon Thai green curry paste
- ¼ cup plus ⅓ cup well-stirred unsweetened coconut milk (not cream of coconut)
- 4 medium skinless, boneless chicken breast halves (about 1¼ pounds), each cut diagonally into 6 strips
- ¼ cup creamy peanut butter
- 2 teaspoons soy sauce
- 1 teaspoon packed dark brown sugar
- ⅛ teaspoon ground red pepper (cayenne)
- 1 tablespoon hot water
- 1¼ cups rice vinegar
- 3 tablespoons granulated sugar
- 2 medium shallots, thinly sliced
- 1 jalapeño chile, seeded and minced
- 12 (12-inch) metal skewers

1. In medium bowl, toss cucumber with salt; let stand 30 minutes at room temperature.

2. In another bowl, stir curry paste and ¼ cup coconut milk until blended. Add chicken and turn to coat. Let stand 15 minutes at room temperature, stirring occasionally.

3. Prepare outdoor grill for covered direct grilling over medium heat.

4. Meanwhile, prepare peanut sauce: In small bowl, with wire whisk, mix peanut butter, soy sauce, brown sugar, ground red pepper, remaining ⅓ cup coconut milk, and hot water until blended and smooth. Transfer sauce to serving bowl. (Makes about ⅔ cup.)

5. Drain cucumber, discarding liquid in bowl. Pat cucumber dry with paper towels. Return cucumber to bowl. Add vinegar, granulated sugar, shallots, and jalapeño; toss to combine. Cover and refrigerate until ready to serve.

6. Thread 2 chicken strips, accordion-style, on each of 12 metal skewers; discard marinade. Place skewers on grill, cover grill and cook, turning skewers once, just until chicken loses its pink color throughout, 5 to 8 minutes. Makes 4 main-dish servings.

7. Arrange skewers on platter. Serve with peanut sauce and cucumbers.

Each serving without peanut sauce: About 260 calories, 34g protein, 15g carbohydrate, 6g total fat (3g saturated), 90mg cholesterol, 525mg sodium.

CHICKEN AND BEEF SATÉ

Here's another tasty recipe for this great party dish: Cut 1 pound skinless, boneless chicken breast halves lengthwise into ¾-inch-wide strips; place in bowl. Holding knife almost parallel to work surface, slice 1 (1-inch-thick) boneless beef top sirloin steak (about 1¼ pounds) crosswise into thin strips; place in separate bowl.

From 2 large limes, grate 2 teaspoons peel and squeeze 2 tablespoons juice. In small bowl, mix lime peel and juice, ¼ cup soy sauce, 1 tablespoon grated, peeled fresh ginger, 2 teaspoons sugar, and 2 garlic cloves, crushed with garlic press. Pour half of sauce over chicken and half over beef; stir to coat. Refrigerate 30 minutes.

Prepare outdoor grill for direct grilling over medium heat. Separately thread chicken strips and beef strips, accordian-style, onto metal skewers. Place skewers on hot grill rack and grill, turning once, until just cooked through, 3 to 7 minutes. Serve with peanut sauce, if desired (see Thai Chicken Saté, left).

SUMMER SQUASH AND CHICKEN

....

For this easy summer supper, simply toss the sliced squash on the grill along with the marinated chicken. You can use either zucchini or yellow squash alone, or a combination of the two.

Prep: 15 minutes plus marinating
Grill: 10 minutes

- 1 lemon
- 1 tablespoon olive oil
- ½ teaspoon salt
- ¼ teaspoon coarsely ground black pepper
- 4 medium skinless, boneless chicken thighs (about 1¼ pounds)
- 4 medium yellow summer squash and/or zucchini (about 6 ounces each), each cut lengthwise into 4 wedges
- ¼ cup snipped fresh chives

1. Prepare outdoor grill for covered direct grilling over medium heat.

2. From lemon, grate 1 tablespoon peel and squeeze 3 tablespoons juice. In medium bowl, combine lemon peel and juice, oil, salt, and pepper and whisk until blended. Transfer 2 tablespoons marinade to cup and set aside.

3. Add chicken thighs to bowl with marinade; turn to evenly coat. Cover and let stand 15 minutes at room temperature or 30 minutes in the refrigerator.

4. Remove chicken from marinade; discard marinade. Place chicken and squash on grill, cover and cook, turning chicken and squash once, until juices run clear when thickest part of thigh is pierced with tip of knife and squash is tender and browned, 10 to 12 minutes, transferring pieces to platter as they are done.

5. Transfer chicken and squash to cutting board. Cut chicken into 1-inch-wide strips; cut each squash wedge crosswise in half.

6. To serve, on large platter, toss squash with reserved marinade, then toss with chicken and sprinkle with chives. Makes 4 main-dish servings.

Each serving: About 255 calories, 29g protein, 8g carbohydrate, 8g total fat (3g saturated), 101mg cholesterol, 240mg sodium.

Summer Squash and Chicken

CHARCOAL-GRILLED WHOLE TURKEY

....

Grilled turkey has become so popular that some cooks serve it for Thanksgiving, but keep in mind that a 12-pound bird is the largest that comfortably fits on a grill. Don't be concerned about the pink color of the meat under the skin—it's caused by the smoke.

Prep: 15 minutes
Grill: 2 hours 15 minutes to 3 hours

- 1 turkey (12 pounds)
- 2 tablespoons vegetable oil
- 2 teaspoons dried sage
- 2 teaspoons dried thyme
- 2 teaspoons salt
- ½ teaspoon ground black pepper

1. Prepare grill: In bottom of covered charcoal grill, with vents open and grill uncovered, ignite 60 charcoal briquettes (not self-starting). Allow to burn until all coals are covered with thin coat of gray ash, about 30 minutes. With tongs, move hot briquettes to two op-posite sides of grill and arrange in two piles. Place sturdy disposable foil pan (13" by 9" by 2") in center of grill between piles of coals to catch drips.

2. Remove giblets and neck from turkey; reserve for another use. Rinse turkey inside and out with cold run-ning water and drain well; pat dry with paper towels.

3. Fasten neck skin to turkey back with skewers. Tie legs and tail together with string. Secure wings to body with string, if desired. In cup, combine oil, sage, thyme, salt, and pepper; use to rub on outside of turkey.

4. Place turkey, breast side up, on rack over foil pan. Cover grill and cook 2 hours 15 minutes to 3 hours, adding 8 or 9 briquettes to each side of grill every hour to maintain grill temperature of 325°F on oven or grill thermometer. Turkey is done when temperature on meat thermometer inserted in thickest part of thigh reaches 175° to 180°F and juices run clear when thick-est part of thigh is pierced with tip of knife.

5. When turkey is done, transfer to warm platter; let stand 15 minutes to set juices for easier carving. Skim and discard fat from drippings in bottom of pan; serve drippings with turkey. Makes 12 main-dish servings.

Each serving: About 524 calories, 73g protein, 0g carbohydrate, 23g total fat (7g saturated), 212mg cholesterol, 575mg sodium.

SPICED GRILLED TURKEY BREAST

....

Soaking a whole turkey breast overnight in a spiced salt solution (brine) produces exceptionally tender and flavorful meat. You can also brine a whole chicken before roasting. Serve with Peach Salsa.

**Prep: 35 minutes plus brining and standing
Grill: 25 minutes**

Spiced Turkey
- ¼ cup sugar
- ¼ cup kosher salt
- 2 tablespoons cracked black pepper
- 2 tablespoons ground ginger
- 1 tablespoon ground cinnamon
- 1 whole boneless turkey breast (about 4 pounds), skin removed and breast cut in half
- 4 garlic cloves, crushed with side of chef's knife

Honey Glaze
- 2 tablespoons honey
- 2 tablespoons Dijon mustard
- 1 chipotle chile in adobo, minced
- 1 teaspoon balsamic vinegar
  Peach Salsa (optional, page 508)

1. Prepare brine solution: In 2-quart saucepan, heat sugar, salt, pepper, ginger, cinnamon, and *1 cup water* to boiling over high heat. Reduce heat to low; simmer 2 minutes. Remove from heat; stir in *3 cups ice water*.

2. Place turkey breast in large zip-tight plastic bag; add brine and garlic. Seal bag, pressing out excess air. Place bag in bowl and refrigerate breast, turning occa-sionally, 24 hours.

3. Prepare outdoor grill for covered direct grilling over medium heat.

4. Meanwhile, prepare glaze: In small bowl, stir honey, mustard, chipotle, and vinegar until blended; set aside.

5. Remove turkey from bag; discard brine and gar-lic. With paper towels, pat turkey dry and brush off most of pepper. With long-handled basting brush, oil grill rack. Place turkey on grill, cover and cook turkey, turning once, 20 minutes. Brush turkey with glaze and cook, basting and turning frequently, until temperature on meat thermometer inserted into thickest part of breast reaches 165°F, 5 to 10 minutes longer (depend-ing on thickness of breast). Internal temperature will rise 5°F upon standing. Transfer turkey to cutting board and let rest 10 minutes to set juices for easier slicing.

6. While turkey rests, prepare Peach Salsa if desired.

7. Serve turkey hot, or cover and refrigerate to serve cold. Accompany with salsa. Makes 12 main-dish servings.

Each serving: About 170 calories, 34g protein, 4g carbohydrate, 1g total fat (0g saturated), 94mg cholesterol, 555mg sodium.

PORTUGUESE MIXED GRILL

This dish, with its vinegar marinade and use of chorizo sausage, is a good example of typical Portuguese cooking. The Portuguese use vinegar marinades to tenderize tough cuts of meat and poultry. Our chicken rarely needs tenderizing, but we like the zesty flavor.

Prep: 30 minutes plus marinating
Grill: 25 minutes

¼ cup red wine vinegar
2 tablespoons olive oil
2 tablespoons chopped fresh oregano
   or 1 teaspoon dried oregano
1 teaspoon salt
½ teaspoon coarsely ground black pepper
8 medium bone-in skinless chicken thighs
   (1¾ pounds), fat removed
3 medium red onions, each cut into 6 wedges
3 long metal skewers
12 ounces fully cooked chorizo sausage links,
   each cut crosswise in half
⅔ cup assorted olives such as Kalamata, cracked
   green, and picholine

1. Prepare outdoor grill for direct grilling over medium heat.

2. In bowl, combine vinegar, 1 tablespoon oil, 1 tablespoon oregano, salt, and pepper. Add chicken, turning to coat. Cover and refrigerate 30 minutes to marinate, no longer.

3. Thread onion wedges onto each metal skewer. Place onion skewers on grill; brush with remaining 1 tablespoon oil and grill 5 minutes.

4. Place chicken on grill and cook, turning onions and chicken once, until onions are tender and juices run clear when thickest part of chicken is pierced with tip of knife, about 20 minutes longer.

5. About 10 minutes before onions and chicken are done, place chorizo pieces on grill and cook, turning occasionally, until lightly browned and heated through.

6. To serve, remove onion wedges from skewers and arrange on warm platter with chicken and chorizo. Scatter olives on top and sprinkle with remaining 1 tablespoon oregano. Makes 6 main-dish servings.

Each serving: About 482 calories, 34g protein, 11g carbohydrate, 33g total fat (10g saturated), 130mg cholesterol, 1,495mg sodium.

Portuguese Mixed Grill

PEPPERCORNS

Pepper has been used to flavor foods for hundreds of years. Peppercorn berries grow in clusters on a plant that is native to India and Indonesia. Whether peppercorns end up being black, white, or green depends upon how they are processed. **Black peppercorns** are picked when the berries are not quite ripe, then dried until shriveled and brownish black. **White peppercorns** are picked ripe, then skinned and dried. They are smaller and milder than black peppercorns. **Green peppercorns** are soft, underripe berries and are usually processed in brine. They have a fresh, mild flavor. Whole black and white peppercorns can be stored in a cool, dark place for up to a year.

GRILLED CAESAR SALAD

Grilling romaine, or other sturdy greens that grow in a head (like endive, radicchio, or chicory), transforms it into a totally different vegetable with a rich "meaty" taste that can add instant flavor to any salad.

Prep: 10 minutes   Grill: 7 minutes

- 2 tablespoons olive oil
- 4 ounces Italian bread, cut into ½-inch-thick slices
- ¼ cup light mayonnaise
- ¼ cup freshly grated Parmesan cheese
- 3 tablespoons fresh lemon juice (from 1 lemon)
- 1 teaspoon anchovy paste or 2 anchovy fillets, mashed
- ¼ teaspoon coarsely ground black pepper
- 1 clove garlic, cut in half
- 1 package (18 to 22 ounces) hearts of romaine, each head cut lengthwise in half

1. Prepare outdoor grill for direct grilling over medium heat.

2. Prepare croutons: Use 1 tablespoon oil to lightly brush bread slices on both sides. Place bread on hot grill grate and cook 2 to 3 minutes or until toasted, turning slices over once. Transfer to plate; cool until easy to handle.

3. Meanwhile, prepare dressing: In small bowl, whisk together mayonnaise, Parmesan, lemon juice, anchovy paste, pepper, and remaining 1 tablespoon oil.

4. When bread is cool, lightly rub both sides of each slice with cut side of garlic clove. Cut bread into ½-inch cubes.

5. Place romaine halves on hot grill grate, and cook 4 to 5 minutes or until lightly browned and wilted, turning over once. Transfer romaine to 4 salad plates; drizzle with dressing and sprinkle with croutons to serve. Makes 4 side-dish servings.

Each serving: About 245 calories, 7g protein, 20g carbohydrate, 14g total fat (3g saturated), 3g fiber, 10mg cholesterol, 420mg sodium.

SCALLOP AND CHERRY TOMATO SKEWERS

Fresh lemon and Dijon mustard give these scallop and cherry tomato skewers their spicy, tart flavor.

Prep: 10 minutes   Grill: 12 minutes

- 8 (8-inch) bamboo skewers
- 1 lemon
- 2 tablespoons olive oil
- 2 tablespoons Dijon mustard
- ⅛ teaspoon salt
- 24 cherry tomatoes
- 16 large sea scallops (1¼ pounds)

1. Soak skewers in hot water at least 30 minutes.

2. Meanwhile, from lemon, grate 1½ teaspoons peel and squeeze 1 tablespoon juice. In small bowl, whisk lemon peel and juice, oil, Dijon, and salt until blended; set aside.

3. Thread 3 tomatoes and 2 scallops alternately on each skewer, beginning and ending with tomatoes. Then, to prevent exposed parts of skewer from charring, wrap a few inches of each end in foil.

4. Preheat outdoor grill for direct grilling over medium heat.

5. Brush scallops and tomatoes with half of Dijon mixture; place on hot grill grate. Cook 7 to 9 minutes, turning several times. Brush with remaining Dijon mixture, and cook 5 minutes longer or until scallops just turn opaque throughout. Makes 4 main-dish servings.

Each serving: About 215 calories, 25g protein, 9g carbohydrate, 9g total fat (1g saturated), 1g fiber, 47mg cholesterol, 355mg sodium.

Scallop and Cherry Tomato Skewers

GRILLED WHOLE SEA BASS WITH LEMON AND HERBS

....

The firm white flesh of sea bass holds up well on the grill. If you can't get whole sea bass, substitute red snapper or striped bass.

Prep: 5 minutes   Grill: 16 minutes

- 2 whole sea bass (1½ pounds each), cleaned and scaled
- 1½ teaspoons salt
- 4 thin lemon slices, each cut in half
- 8 oregano or rosemary sprigs
- 1 tablespoon olive oil

1. Prepare outdoor grill for covered direct grilling over medium heat.

2. Rinse bass inside and out with cold running water; pat dry with paper towels. Make three diagonal slashes on each side of fish, cutting almost to bone. Sprinkle fish inside and out with salt. Place lemon slices and oregano sprigs in fish cavities. Rub oil all over bass.

3. Place bass on grill, cover and cook until just opaque when knife is inserted at backbone, about 8 minutes per side.

4. To serve, slide cake server under front section of top fillet of each fish and lift off fillet; transfer to platter. Slide server under backbone and lift it away from bottom fillet; discard. Slide cake server between bottom fillet and skin and transfer fillet to platter. Makes 4 main-dish servings.

Each serving: About 162 calories, 25g protein, 1g carbohydrate, 6g total fat (1g saturated), 54mg cholesterol, 673mg sodium.

SALMON WITH MUSTARD-DILL SAUCE

....

We brought the flavors of Swedish gravlax to the grill. Traditional gravlax is made by marinating raw salmon in a savory mixture of fresh dill, sugar, and salt, then serving it with a sweet mustard sauce.

Prep: 15 minutes   Grill: 8 minutes

Grilled Salmon

- 2 tablespoons sugar
- 1 tablespoon chopped fresh dill
- 2 tablespoons white wine vinegar
- ¾ teaspoon salt
- ¼ teaspoon coarsely ground black pepper
- 4 salmon steaks, each ¾ inch thick (about 6 ounces each)

Mustard-Dill Sauce

- 3 tablespoons chopped fresh dill
- 3 tablespoons Dijon mustard
- 3 tablespoons light mayonnaise
- 2 teaspoons sugar
- 4 teaspoons white wine vinegar
- ¼ teaspoon coarsely ground black pepper

1. Prepare outdoor grill for direct grilling over medium heat.

2. Prepare salmon: In medium bowl, mix sugar, dill, vinegar, salt, and pepper.

3. With tweezers, remove small bones from salmon; add salmon steaks to bowl with sugar mixture, turning each to coat. Let stand at room temperature 10 minutes.

4. Meanwhile, prepare sauce: In small bowl, mix dill, mustard, mayonnaise, sugar, vinegar, and pepper.

5. Place salmon on grill and cook, turning once, until just opaque throughout, 8 to 9 minutes. Serve with mustard sauce. Makes 4 main-dish servings.

Each serving: About 270 calories, 30g protein, 13g carbohydrate, 11g total fat (1g saturated), 80mg cholesterol, 850mg sodium.

GLAZED SALMON WITH WATERMELON SALSA

···

We love blending sweet and spicy flavors, so we added a jalapeño chile to the fruit salsa—with delicious results.

Prep: 20 minutes   Grill: 9 minutes

Watermelon Salsa

- 1 lime
- 4 cups (½-inch cubes) seedless watermelon (from about 2½-pound piece)
- ¼ cup loosely packed fresh mint leaves, chopped
- 2 tablespoons chopped green onions
- 1 small jalapeño chile, seeded and finely chopped (1 tablespoon)

Glazed Salmon

- ¼ cup hoisin sauce
- ½ teaspoon Chinese five-spice powder
- 4 salmon steaks, 1 inch thick (about 6 ounces each)

1. Prepare outdoor grill for covered direct grilling over medium heat.

2. Meanwhile, prepare salsa: From lime, grate 1 teaspoon peel and squeeze 1 tablespoon juice. In serving bowl, toss lime peel and juice with watermelon, mint, green onions, and jalapeño. (Makes about 3⅔ cups.)

3. In cup, stir hoisin sauce and five-spice powder.

4. Place salmon on grill over medium heat. Brush salmon with half of hoisin mixture. Cover grill and cook salmon 3 minutes. Turn salmon over and brush with remaining hoisin mixture. Cover grill and cook 3 minutes. Turn salmon over again and cook until just opaque throughout, about 3 minutes longer. Serve salmon with salsa. Makes 4 main-dish servings.

Each serving: About 345 calories, 30g protein, 18g carbohydrate, 17g total fat (3g saturated), 81mg cholesterol, 260mg sodium.

Glazed Salmon with Watermelon Salsa

GRILLED SPICED SALMON STEAKS

···

Spice rubs are excellent with fresh fish that is not delicately flavored, like salmon.

Prep: 5 minutes   Grill: 8 minutes

- 1 tablespoon chili powder
- 2 teaspoons brown sugar
- 1 teaspoon ground cumin
- 1 teaspoon dried thyme
- 1 teaspoon salt
- 2 teaspoons olive oil
- 4 salmon steaks, ¾ inch thick (8 ounces each)
  lemon wedges

1. Prepare outdoor grill for covered direct grilling over medium heat. In cup, combine chili powder, brown sugar, cumin, thyme, salt, and oil. Use to rub on both sides of salmon steaks.

2. Place salmon on grill, cover and cook until just opaque throughout, about 4 minutes per side. Serve with lemon wedges. Makes 4 main-dish servings.

Each serving: About 403 calories, 40g protein, 4g carbohydrate, 24g total fat (5g saturated), 118mg cholesterol, 721mg sodium.

MISO-GLAZED SALMON WITH EDAMAME SALAD

··

Japanese flavors predominate in this healthy meal.

Prep: 30 minutes   Grill: 10 minutes

Edamame Salad

- 1 bag (16 ounces) frozen shelled edamame (green soybeans) or frozen baby lima beans
- ¼ cup seasoned rice vinegar
- 1 tablespoon vegetable oil
- 1 teaspoon sugar
- ¾ teaspoon salt
- ⅛ teaspoon ground black pepper
- 1 bunch radishes (8 ounces), each cut in half and thinly sliced
- 1 cup loosely packed fresh cilantro leaves, chopped

Miso-Glazed Salmon

- 2 tablespoons red miso
- 1 green onion, minced
- 1 tablespoon grated, peeled fresh ginger
- 1 teaspoon brown sugar
- ⅛ teaspoon ground red pepper (cayenne)
- 1 salmon fillet (1½ pounds), with skin

1. Prepare outdoor grill for direct grilling over medium-low heat.

2. Prepare salad: Cook edamame as label directs; drain. Rinse edamame with cold running water to stop cooking and drain again.

3. In medium bowl, whisk vinegar, oil, sugar, salt, and pepper until blended. Add edamame, radishes, and cilantro and toss until evenly coated. Cover and refrigerate salad up to 1 day if not serving right away. (Makes about 4 cups.)

4. Prepare salmon: In small bowl, with spoon, mix miso, green onion, ginger, brown sugar, and ground red pepper. Use to rub on flesh side of salmon.

5. Place salmon, skin side down, on grill and cook until just opaque throughout, 10 to 12 minutes. Serve with edamame salad. Makes 4 main-dish servings.

Each serving salmon: About 280 calories, 29g protein, 3g carbohydrate, 16g total fat (3g saturated), 80mg cholesterol, 450mg sodium.

Each 1 cup salad: About 220 calories, 16g protein, 23g carbohydrate, 8g total fat (0g saturated), 0mg cholesterol, 1,020mg sodium.

Miso-Glazed Salmon with Edamame Salad

SALMON WITH DILL AND CAPER SAUCE

···

Salmon and dill are a classic Scandinavian combination. Here, the saltiness of the anchovy paste and capers pairs beautifully with the bright, fresh flavors of the dill and lemon juice.

Prep: 10 minutes   Grill: 10 minutes

- ¼ cup drained capers, chopped
- 2 tablespoons chopped fresh dill
- 2 tablespoons fresh lemon juice
- 2 teaspoons sugar
- 2 teaspoons anchovy paste
- 1 salmon fillet (2 pounds), with skin
- ¼ teaspoon salt
  lemon wedges

1. Prepare outdoor grill for direct grilling over medium heat.

2. In small bowl, mix capers, dill, lemon juice, sugar, and anchovy paste.

3. With tweezers, remove any bones from salmon; sprinkle with salt. Place salmon in lightly oiled fish basket. Brush all of caper sauce on flesh side only.

4. Place fish basket on grill. Cook salmon, turning once, until just opaque throughout, about 10 minutes. Serve with lemon wedges. Makes 8 main-dish servings.

Each serving: About 210 calories, 22g protein, 2g carbohydrate, 12g total fat (2g saturated), 64mg cholesterol, 395mg sodium.

Tip: Anchovy paste is available in tubes in the dairy section of many supermarkets. If you can't find anchovy paste, substitute two anchovy fillets. Mash the fillets with the flat side of a knife until they're the consistency of a smooth paste.

SWEET AND SMOKY SALMON KABOBS

···

This healthy main dish couldn't be easier: Just toss salmon chunks and zucchini slices in a bowl of brown sugar and spices and thread them onto skewers.

Prep: 20 minutes   Grill: 9 minutes

- 12 (10-inch) metal or bamboo skewers
- 2 tablespoons packed dark brown sugar
- 1½ teaspoons smoked paprika
- 1 teaspoon chili powder
- ½ teaspoon ground red pepper (cayenne)
- ¾ teaspoon salt
- ½ teaspoon ground black pepper
- 2¼ pounds skinless salmon fillet, cut into 1½-inch chunks
- 2 medium zucchini (8 ounces each), cut into ¼-inch-thick slices

1. If using bamboo skewers, soak skewers in hot water at least 30 minutes. Prepare outdoor grill for direct grilling on medium.

2. In large bowl, combine sugar, paprika, chili powder, red pepper, salt, and black pepper. Rub mixture between fingers to break up any lumps of sugar. Add salmon and zucchini and toss to evenly coat with spice mixture.

3. Thread zucchini slices, 2 at a time and alternating with salmon, onto skewers. Place on hot grill grate and cook 9 to 11 minutes or until salmon turns opaque throughout, turning occasionally. Makes 8 main-dish servings.

Each serving: About 205 calories, 26g protein, 6g carbohydrate, 8g total fat (1g saturated), 1g fiber, 70mg cholesterol, 280mg sodium.

SWORDFISH KABOBS

....

This is the method of choice for preparing swordfish along the coasts of Turkey. Serve it with steamed rice.

Prep: 25 minutes plus marinating
Grill: 5 minutes

- 1 pound boneless swordfish steak, 1 inch thick
- ½ cup chicken or vegetable broth
- 3 tablespoons fresh lemon juice
- 1 tablespoon olive oil
- 1 very small onion, thinly sliced
- 2 garlic cloves, thinly sliced
- 14 large bay leaves
- ½ teaspoon salt
- ½ teaspoon paprika
- ¼ teaspoon ground coriander
- ⅛ teaspoon ground black pepper
- 12 (7-inch) bamboo skewers
- 12 thin lemon slices, seeded and each cut in half
- 1 tablespoon chopped fresh parsley

1. Remove skin from swordfish and discard. Cut fish into 1-inch cubes.

2. In medium bowl, combine broth, lemon juice, oil, onion, garlic, 2 bay leaves, salt, paprika, coriander, and pepper. Add swordfish and toss to coat. Cover and refrigerate fish 3 hours to marinate, tossing occasionally.

3. Meanwhile, soak remaining 12 bay leaves and bamboo skewers 1 hour in enough *boiling water* to cover. Drain. With kitchen shears, snip each bay leaf crosswise in half.

4. Prepare outdoor grill for covered direct grilling over medium-high heat.

5. Remove swordfish from marinade, reserving marinade. Thread each skewer as follows: ½ bay leaf, 1 swordfish cube, ½ lemon slice, 1 swordfish cube; then repeat once, gently pressing bay leaves, lemon slices, and fish together.

6. Place kabobs on grill, cover and cook, turning kabobs and brushing with marinade during first half of cooking, until fish is just opaque throughout, 5 to 8 minutes.

7. Meanwhile, strain remaining marinade into small saucepan and heat to boiling; boil 3 minutes. Arrange kabobs on platter, drizzle with hot marinade, and sprinkle with parsley. Makes 4 main-dish servings.

Each serving: About 189 calories, 22g protein, 7g carbohydrate, 8g total fat (2g saturated), 42mg cholesterol, 514mg sodium.

GREEK-STYLE GRILLED HALIBUT

....

Greek cooks have long favored the clean, simple flavors of fresh lemon and oregano with fish. One bite of this, and you'll understand why.

Prep: 10 minutes plus marinating
Grill: 6 minutes

- 1 lemon
- 3 tablespoons olive oil
- 2 garlic cloves, finely chopped
- 2 teaspoons chopped fresh oregano
- ½ teaspoon salt
- 4 halibut steaks, ¾ inch thick (6 ounces each)

1. From lemon, grate 1 teaspoon peel and squeeze 2 tablespoons juice. In large bowl, with wire whisk, whisk lemon peel and juice, oil, garlic, oregano, and salt until mixed. Add halibut steaks, turning each to coat. Cover and refrigerate 1 hour to marinate, turning once or twice.

2. Meanwhile, prepare outdoor grill for covered direct grilling over medium heat.

3. Remove halibut from marinade. Place halibut on grill, cover and cook, brushing with marinade during first half of grilling, until halibut is just opaque throughout, 3 to 4 minutes per side; discard remaining marinade. Makes 4 main-dish servings.

Each serving: About 199 calories, 29g protein, 1g carbohydrate, 8g total fat (1g saturated), 44mg cholesterol, 218mg sodium.

SWORDFISH WITH BALSAMIC GLAZE

....

Balsamic vinegar blended with brown sugar and reduced to a syrup makes a rich, winelike glaze that is perfect with meaty swordfish. For a delicious variation, serve the fish atop a salad.

Prep: 15 minutes   Grill: 7 minutes

- 2 teaspoons olive oil
- ¼ cup finely chopped shallots
- ½ cup balsamic vinegar
- 2 teaspoons brown sugar
- 2 teaspoons tomato paste
- ¼ teaspoon dried thyme
- ¼ teaspoon salt
- ¼ teaspoon ground black pepper
- 4 swordfish steaks, 1 inch thick (6 ounces each)

1. Prepare outdoor grill for direct grilling over medium-high heat.

2. In 10-inch skillet, heat oil over medium-low heat. Add shallots and cook, stirring occasionally, until tender, about 4 minutes. Add vinegar and brown sugar; heat to boiling over high heat. Boil until liquid has thickened and is syrupy, about 5 minutes. Remove from heat and stir in tomato paste until blended.

3. Sprinkle thyme, salt, and pepper on swordfish. Place fish on grill and cook 4 minutes. Turn swordfish steaks and brush each with glaze; cook until just opaque throughout, 3 to 4 minutes longer. Makes 4 main-dish servings.

Each serving: About 226 calories, 30g protein, 5g carbohydrate, 8g total fat (2g saturated), 59mg cholesterol, 305mg sodium.

BALSAMIC-GLAZED SWORDFISH WITH GREENS

Prepare fish as directed above. In large bowl, whisk together **2 tablespoons balsamic vinegar, 2 tablespoons extra-virgin olive oil,** and **⅛ teaspoon salt.** Add **2 cups each washed, dried, and torn Bibb and Boston lettuce** and **2 cups sliced Belgian endive;** toss to coat. Arrange greens on dinner plates; top with fish.

Each serving: About 299 calories, 31g protein, 8g carbohydrate, 16g total fat (3g saturated), 59mg cholesterol, 388mg sodium.

SKEWERED SHRIMP

....

Seafood doesn't get any speedier than these crowd-pleasing kabobs: Just quick-toss the shrimp in a lemon-dill mixture, alternate with grape tomatoes, and grill.

Prep: 30 minutes   Grill: 4 minutes

- 15 (10-inch) metal or bamboo skewers
- 3 lemons
- 2 tablespoons olive oil
- 1 large clove garlic, crushed with press
- 4 tablespoons chopped fresh dill plus additional sprigs for garnish
- ½ teaspoon salt
- ¼ teaspoon ground black pepper
- 2¼ pounds peeled and deveined large shrimp
- 1 pint grape tomatoes

1. If using bamboo skewers, soak skewers in hot water at least 30 minutes. Prepare outdoor grill for direct grilling on medium.

2. From lemons, cut 1 into 8 wedges and set aside for garnish; from remaining lemons, grate 4 teaspoons peel and squeeze 2 tablespoons juice. In large bowl, with wire whisk or fork, whisk lemon peel and juice, olive oil, garlic, 3 tablespoons chopped dill, salt, and pepper until blended. Add shrimp; toss to coat.

3. Thread shrimp and tomatoes alternately on skewers. Place on hot grill grate and cook 4 to 5 minutes or until shrimp are opaque throughout and tomatoes are slightly charred, turning skewers occasionally.

4. To serve, transfer skewers to platter; sprinkle with remaining 1 tablespoon dill. Garnish platter with lemon wedges and dill sprigs. Makes 8 main-dish servings.

Each serving: About 175 calories, 26g protein, 4g carbohydrate, 6g total fat (1g saturated), 1g fiber, 194mg cholesterol, 340mg sodium.

SHRIMP SONOMA

Some of the sweetest dried tomatoes we've tried come from the Sonoma Valley in California. Choose dried tomatoes that are plump rather than dry and leathery. Serve shrimp on a bed of couscous seasoned with extra-virgin olive oil.

Prep: 25 minutes   Grill: 8 minutes

- 1   ounce dried tomatoes without salt
- 1   cup boiling water
- 1½ pounds large shrimp
- 2   tablespoons fresh lemon juice
- 2   tablespoons olive oil
- ½   teaspoon salt
- ½   teaspoon crushed red pepper
- 4   (12-inch) metal skewers

1. Place dried tomatoes in small bowl. Pour boiling water over tomatoes; let stand while preparing shrimp.

2. Meanwhile, pull off legs from shrimp. Insert tip of kitchen shears under shell of each shrimp and snip along back to tail, cutting about ¼ inch deep to expose dark vein. Leaving shell on, rinse shrimp to remove vein; pat dry with paper towels. Place shrimp in bowl.

3. Prepare outdoor grill for direct grilling over medium heat. Drain dried tomatoes, reserving ¼ cup soaking liquid.

4. In blender or in food processor with knife blade attached, puree tomatoes, reserved soaking liquid, lemon juice, oil, salt, and crushed red pepper until smooth. Pour mixture over shrimp; toss until shrimp are evenly coated.

5. Thread shrimp onto metal skewers. Place skewers on grill. Cook shrimp, turning skewers occasionally and basting with any remaining dried tomato mixture, until just opaque throughout, 8 to 10 minutes. Makes 6 main-dish servings.

Each serving: About 140 calories, 20g protein, 3g carbohydrate, 5g total fat (1g saturated), 140mg cholesterol, 290mg sodium.

Shrimp Sonoma

CAJUN SHRIMP WITH RÉMOULADE SAUCE

This dish takes only four minutes on the fire! To streamline preparation, we added fresh lemon peel to store-bought Cajun seasoning (a blend of garlic, onion, chiles, peppers, and herbs). Seasoning mixes vary among manufacturers, especially with regard to salt content. Add salt to taste if necessary.

Prep: 25 minutes   Grill: 3 minutes

Rémoulade Sauce
- ½ cup light mayonnaise
- 2 tablespoons ketchup
- 2 tablespoons minced celery
- 1 tablespoon Dijon mustard with seeds
- 1 tablespoon minced fresh parsley
- 2 teaspoons fresh lemon juice
- ½ teaspoon Cajun seasoning
- 1 green onion, minced

Cajun Shrimp
- 1 tablespoon Cajun seasoning
- 1 tablespoon olive oil
- 2 teaspoons fresh lemon peel
- 1¼ pounds large shrimp, shelled and deveined, leaving tail part of shell on, if you like (page 221)
  lemon wedges

1. Prepare outdoor grill for direct grilling over medium-high heat.

2. Meanwhile, prepare sauce: In small bowl, mix mayonnaise, ketchup, celery, mustard, parsley, lemon juice, Cajun seasoning, and green onion. Cover and re-frigerate up to 3 days if not serving right away. Makes about 1 cup.

3. Prepare shrimp: In medium bowl, mix Cajun seasoning, oil, and lemon peel. Add shrimp to spice mixture and toss until evenly coated.

4. Place shrimp on grill and cook, turning once, until just opaque throughout, 3 to 4 minutes.

5. Transfer shrimp to platter; serve with Rémoulade Sauce and lemon wedges. Makes 4 main-dish servings.

Each serving shrimp: About 155 calories, 24g protein, 2g carbohydrate, 5g total fat (1g saturated), 175mg cholesterol, 575mg sodium.

Each 1 tablespoon sauce: About 30 calories, 0g protein, 2g carbohydrate, 3g total fat (1g saturated), 3mg cholesterol, 95mg sodium.

GRILLED SHRIMP

Be sure to buy the freshest and most flavorful shrimp you can find for this simple preparation.

**Prep: 10 minutes plus marinating
Grill: 5 minutes**

- 1 lemon
- 1 tablespoon olive oil
- ¼ teaspoon salt
- ⅛ teaspoon freshly ground pepper
- 1 pound large shrimp, shelled and deveined, leaving tail part of shell on, if desired (page 221)
- 4 long metal skewers

1. Prepare outdoor grill for direct grilling over medium-high heat.

2. From lemon, grate ½ teaspoon peel and squeeze 1 tablespoon juice. In large bowl, whisk lemon peel and juice, oil, salt, and pepper. Add shrimp and toss to coat; let stand 10 minutes to marinate.

3. Thread shrimp on skewers. Place skewers on grill and cook, turning skewers occasionally, until shrimp are just opaque throughout, about 4 minutes. Makes 4 main-dish servings.

Each serving: About 129 calories, 19g protein, 1g carbohydrate, 5g total fat (1g saturated), 140mg cholesterol, 282mg sodium.

LEMON-GARLIC POTATO PACKET

....

Whole cloves of garlic grill up butter-soft along with the potatoes. If you like, once the potatoes and garlic are cooked (and while they're still warm), toss them with your favorite vinaigrette for a grilled potato salad.

Prep: 15 minutes   Grill: 30 minutes

2½ pounds red potatoes, not peeled and cut into 1-inch chunks
12 garlic cloves, peeled
2 tablespoons olive oil
1½ teaspoons freshly grated lemon peel
1 teaspoon salt
¼ teaspoon coarsely ground black pepper

1. Prepare outdoor grill for covered direct grilling over medium heat.

2. In large bowl, toss potatoes, garlic, oil, lemon peel, salt, and pepper until potatoes are evenly coated.

3. Layer two 30" by 18" sheets heavy-duty foil to make double-thick sheet. Place potato mixture in center of stacked foil. Bring short ends of foil up and over potatoes; fold several times to seal. Fold remaining sides of foil several times to seal in juices.

4. Place packet on grill, cover and cook, turning packet once halfway through grilling, until potatoes are fork-tender, 30 minutes.

5. Before serving, with kitchen shears, cut an X in top of foil packet to let steam escape, then carefully pull back foil to open. Makes 8 accompaniment servings.

Each serving: About 140 calories, 3g protein, 25g carbohydrate, 4g total fat (1g saturated), 0mg cholesterol, 275mg sodium.

SHALLOT-AND-HERB POTATO PACKET

Prepare as directed but omit garlic. Add **2 medium shallots,** thinly sliced, and **2 teaspoons minced fresh thyme or ½ teaspoon dried thyme.** Wrap and grill as directed. Sprinkle with ⅓ **cup chopped fresh parsley** before serving.

Each serving: About 140 calories, 3g protein, 25g carbohydrate, 4g total fat (1g saturated), 0mg cholesterol, 280mg sodium.

GRILLED VEGETABLE STACKS

....

Perfect buffet fare, these colorful vegetable "napoleons" can be served hot, warm, or at room temperature. If you like, grate some Parmesan cheese over each stack before serving or set out in a bowl for self-serve.

Prep: 20 minutes   Grill: 8 minutes

wooden toothpicks or bamboo skewers
1 medium red onion, cut into ½-inch-thick slices
2 medium zucchini and/or yellow summer squashes, cut diagonally into ½-inch-thick slices
1 large yellow or red pepper, cut lengthwise into quarters
1 medium eggplant, cut diagonally into eight ½-inch-thick slices
3 tablespoons olive oil
½ cup balsamic vinegar
½ teaspoon crushed red pepper
½ teaspoon salt
4 plum tomatoes, each cut lengthwise in half
8 large basil leaves
¾ pound fresh mozzarella cheese, thinly sliced basil sprigs for garnish

1. Prepare outdoor grill for covered direct grilling over medium heat.

2. Soak toothpicks in water for 10 minutes. Insert 2 toothpicks horizontally through center of each onion slice to hold rings together.

3. In large bowl, toss onion, zucchini, yellow pepper, and eggplant with oil; set aside.

4. In microwave-safe 2-cup liquid measuring cup, combine vinegar, crushed red pepper, and salt. Heat vinegar mixture in microwave oven on High 2 to 3 minutes or until reduced to ¼ cup.

5. Place onion, zucchini, yellow pepper, and eggplant on grill rack. Place tomatoes, cut sides down, on same rack. Cover grill and cook vegetables until grill marks appear and they begin to soften, 4 to 5 minutes. Turn vegetables; brush with vinegar mixture. Cook, covered, until tender, 4 to 8 minutes longer, transferring vegetables to platter as they are done.

6. Assemble vegetable stacks: Remove toothpicks from onion slices. In center of each of 4 dinner plates, place 1 eggplant slice. Top each with one-fourth of onion, zucchini, yellow pepper, tomatoes, basil, and mozzarella to make 4 equal stacks. Top stacks with eggplant slice. Drizzle any juices over and around stacks. Garnish with basil sprigs. Makes 4 main-dish servings.

Each serving: About 445 calories, 19g protein, 29g carbohydrate, 29g total fat (13g saturated), 66mg cholesterol, 370mg sodium.

CRUMB-TOPPED TOMATOES
....

You can't get the bread crumbs crusty on the grill, so brown them ahead of time in a skillet. The crumbs may be prepared up to a day ahead and refrigerated. These tomatoes would be perfect as an accompaniment to Greek-Style Grilled Halibut (page 378) or Red Wine and Rosemary Porterhouse (page 347).

Prep: 15 minutes   Grill: 8 minutes

- 2 tablespoons butter or margarine
- 1 cup fresh bread crumbs (about 2 slices firm white bread)
- 1 garlic clove, crushed with garlic press
- 2 tablespoons chopped fresh parsley
- ½ teaspoon salt
- ½ teaspoon coarsely ground black pepper
- 8 large ripe plum tomatoes

1. Prepare outdoor grill for direct grilling over medium heat.

2. In 10-inch skillet, melt butter over low heat. Add bread crumbs and cook, stirring, until lightly browned. Stir in garlic; cook 30 seconds. Remove skillet from heat; stir in parsley, salt, and pepper.

3. Cut each tomato horizontally in half. Top each tomato half with some crumb mixture. Place tomatoes on grill and cook until hot but not mushy, 8 to 10 minutes. Makes 8 accompaniment servings.

Each serving: About 40 calories, 1g protein, 3g carbohydrate, 3g total fat (2g saturated), 8mg cholesterol, 191mg sodium.

GRILLED PIZZA
....

Quick-rise yeast gets mixed right in with the flour and salt and needs no proofing. Grilling pizza gives it a smoky flavor not unlike that from a wood-burning oven. If you like, grill onions, peppers, and sausages and let guests personalize their own pizzas.

**Prep: 15 minutes plus dough resting
Grill: 5 minutes**

- 2 cups all-purpose flour
- 1 package quick-rise yeast
- ¾ teaspoon salt
- ¾ cup hot water (120°F to 130°F)
- 2 teaspoons plus 2 tablespoons olive oil
- 8 ounces fresh mozzarella cheese, thinly sliced
- 12 fresh basil leaves
- 2 small ripe tomatoes, thinly sliced
    salt
    coarsely ground black pepper

1. Prepare outdoor grill for direct grilling over medium heat.

2. In large bowl, combine flour, yeast, and salt. Stir in hot water and 2 teaspoons oil until blended and dough comes away from side of bowl. Turn onto lightly floured surface; knead until smooth and elastic, about 5 minutes.

3. Shape pizza dough into two 10-inch rounds or four 6-inch rounds (do not form rims). Cover with greased plastic wrap; let rest 15 minutes.

4. Place dough rounds on grill over medium heat and grill until underside of dough turns golden and grill marks appear, 2 to 5 minutes. With tongs, turn rounds over. Brush lightly with some remaining oil. Top with mozzarella, basil, and tomato slices. Grill until cheese begins to melt, 3 to 5 minutes longer. Drizzle with remaining olive oil and sprinkle with salt and pepper. Makes 12 appetizer servings.

Each serving: About 170 calories, 7g protein, 17g carbohydrate, 8g total fat (3g saturated), 17mg cholesterol, 225mg sodium.

GUIDE TO GRILLED VEGETABLES

Preheat grill to medium-high.

VEGETABLE (4 SERVINGS)	PREPARATION	SEASONING	GRILLING TIME
8 ears corn	Soak 15 minutes, then remove silk (leave husks on).	Brush with 1 tablespoon oil.	45 minutes
	Remove husks and silk.		20 minutes, turning occasionally
1½-pound eggplant	Cut crosswise into ½-inch-thick slices.	Brush with ¼ cup oil.	11 to 13 minutes per side
4 heads endive	Cut lengthwise in half.	Brush with 1 tablespoon oil.	10 to 12 minutes per side
2 medium fennel bulbs (1 pound each)	Cut lengthwise into ¼-inch-thick slices.	Brush with 4 teaspoons oil.	6 to 8 minutes per side
6 medium leeks	Remove dark green tops; blanch and cut lengthwise in half.	Toss with 1 tablespoon oil.	11 to 13 minutes per side
8 ounces large white mushrooms	Trim and thread onto skewers.	Brush with 2 teaspoons oil.	20 minutes, turning several times
4 large portobello mushrooms (about 1 pound)	Remove stems.	Brush with 4 teaspoons oil.	15 minutes per side
4 medium red or white onions	Cut crosswise into ½-inch-thick slices; secure with toothpicks.	Brush with 4 teaspoons oil.	12 to 14 minutes per side
2 bunches small green onions	Trim.	Toss with 4 teaspoons oil.	2 to 4 minutes, turning several times
4 red, green, or yellow peppers	Cut lengthwise into quarters.		10 to 12 minutes per side
2 heads radicchio (12 ounces each)	Cut lengthwise into quarters.	Brush with 2 tablespoons oil.	5 minutes per side
4 medium yellow squash or zucchini	Cut lengthwise into ¼-inch-thick slices.	Brush with 4 teaspoons oil.	5 minutes per side
4 medium tomatoes (8 ounces each)	Cut crosswise in half.	Brush cut sides with 2 tablespoons oil.	14 to 17 minutes per side
1 pint cherry tomatoes	Thread onto skewers.	Brush with 2 teaspoons oil.	5 to 7 minutes, turning several times

GRILLED SWEET POTATOES

For a deliciously unexpected side dish, we steam and slice sweet potatoes and then give them a turn on the grill to develop a smoky, crispy crust.

Prep: 5 minutes   Cook/Grill: 25 minutes

- 2½ pounds sweet potatoes (5 medium)
- 1 tablespoon olive oil
- ¼ teaspoon salt
- ¼ teaspoon coarsely ground black pepper
  Chopped parsley for garnish

1. Prepare outdoor grill for covered, direct grilling on medium.

2. In 5- to 6-quart saucepot or Dutch oven, place collapsible steamer basket and *1 inch water*. Cover saucepot; heat water to boiling on high on range top.

3. Peel sweet potatoes, if you like, and cut into ½-inch-thick diagonal slices. Places potato slices in steamer basket; reduce heat to low. Cover saucepot and simmer 12 to 15 minutes or until potatoes are just fork-tender; do not overcook. (Potatoes can be steamed a day ahead and refrigerated until ready to grill.)

4. Transfer potato slices to jelly-roll pan; brush with olive oil and sprinkle with salt and pepper to season both sides.

5. Place potato slices on hot grill grate. Cover grill and cook potatoes 10 to 12 minutes or until lightly charred and tender, turning slices over once with large metal spatula.

6. Transfer potatoes to serving bowl; garnish with parsley. Makes 4 accompaniment servings.

Each serving: About 245 calories, 3g protein, 50g carbohydrates, 4g total fat (1g saturated), 6g fiber, 0mg cholesterol, 170mg sodium.

GRILLED PEACH MELBA

This classic dessert of poached peaches was created in the late 1800s in honor of a famous opera singer. Our updated version moves the peaches outdoors and onto the grill, a delightful and delicious way to prepare summer fruits.

Prep: 4 minutes   Grill: 5 minutes

- 2 large ripe peaches, each cut in half and pits discarded
- ½ pint raspberries
- 1 tablespoon sugar
- 1½ cups vanilla ice cream

1. Prepare outdoor grill for direct grilling on medium.

2. Place peach halves on hot grill grate and cook 5 to 6 minutes or until lightly charred and tender, turning over once.

3. Meanwhile, prepare sauce: In bowl, with fork, mash half the raspberries with sugar. Stir in remaining raspberries.

4. To serve, place a peach half in each of 4 dessert bowls; top with ice cream and raspberry sauce. Makes 4 servings.

Each serving: About 160 calories, 2g protein, 22g carbohydrate, 8g total fat (5g saturated), 3g fiber, 26mg cholesterol, 25mg sodium.

Grilled Peach Melba

12
VEGETABLES

In kitchens across America, cooks are preparing lighter meals and are looking for ways to serve more vegetables as part of a well-balanced, healthful diet. Vegetables that were once considered exotic are now everyday fare. What was old is new again, as farmers' markets offer intriguing and delicious heirloom varieties. And all sorts of vegetables are being tossed onto the grill (see Guide to Grilled Vegetables, page 384).

Vegetables are often grouped according to their family: onions, leafy greens, cruciferous (cabbage, broccoli, and cauliflower), fruits that aren't sweet and are therefore treated like vegetables (eggplants, peppers, and tomatoes), roots (carrots, turnips, and the like), stalks (asparagus and celery), tubers (starchy potatoes and sweet potatoes), and mushrooms. For easy reference, we present our recipes alphabetically by vegetable name.

BUYING AND STORING VEGETABLES

When buying vegetables, appearance is usually the best indication of freshness. Avoid bruised vegetables or those with soft spots. Leafy tops should be crisp and fresh looking. Prepackaged vegetables in bags aren't always a good choice because you can't inspect them thoroughly. Some vegetables are covered with a thin edible wax coating that seals in their moisture and gives them a fake sheen.

If you prefer to buy organic produce, it is available at natural-food stores and at most supermarkets. These vegetables and fruits have been grown without the use of synthetic fertilizers or pesticides.

Refrigeration is the key to keeping most vegetables in prime condition. Store them in the coolest part of the refrigerator or in the crisper drawer. Don't store vegetables in zip-tight plastic bags, as the condensation that forms encourages rapid decay. The exception is leafy greens. Store them, loosely wrapped in paper towels, in a plastic bag, pressing out all the air. Mushrooms should be kept in a brown paper bag in the refrigerator, but store potatoes, onions, garlic, and winter squash in a dark, well-ventilated place at cool room temperature.

PREPARING VEGETABLES

Wash vegetables briefly under cold running water just before using. If necessary, a gentle scrub with a soft vegetable brush will remove any surface dirt. When washing leafy greens, swish them around in a large bowl of cool water, changing the water several times. Cut or peel vegetables as close to serving time as possible. Once the skin on vegetables is broken, they begin to lose valuable nutrients. Some vegetables, such as artichokes, discolor when their cut surfaces are exposed to air. To prevent this, rub the cut surfaces with the cut side of a lemon half.

Not all vegetables require peeling, but you may want to peel certain types if their peel is tough or unpleasant tasting. It is important to remove as thin a layer of peel as possible; a vegetable peeler is the best choice. Vegetables should be cut into uniform pieces to ensure even cooking. If you are making soup or preparing a recipe for which evenly cut pieces aren't important, use a food processor to save time.

Savory Tomato Tart (recipe page 440)

ARTICHOKES

Availability
Year-round

Peak Season
March, April, and May

Buying Tips
Buy compact, plump artichokes that are heavy for their size. The leaves should be thick, tightly closed, and evenly colored. Don't worry about brown spots or streaks; they are usually caused by frost. Avoid artichokes with dry, spreading, or hard-tipped leaves. An artichoke's size depends on where it grows on the plant. *Baby artichokes,* which are entirely edible, grow near the base between the leaves and the stalk, while larger ones grow higher up on the stalk.

To Store
Refrigerate in the crisper drawer up to three days.

To Prepare
Rinse the artichokes. Bend back the outer green leaves from around the base of an artichoke and snap them off. With kitchen shears, trim the thorny tops from the remaining outer leaves, rubbing all the cut surfaces with a lemon half to prevent browning. Lay the artichoke on its side and cut off the stem level with the bottom of the artichoke. Cut 1 inch off the top of the artichoke, then place in a bowl containing cold water and the juice of the remaining lemon half. Repeat with the remaining artichokes.

To Cook
Artichokes are often steamed or boiled, then served with a dip such as lemon butter. To steam artichokes, in a nonreactive 5-quart saucepot, heat 1 inch of water and 1 tablespoon lemon juice to boiling over high heat. Stand the artichokes in the boiling water. Reduce heat; cover and simmer until a knife inserted in bottom of an artichoke goes in easily, 30 to 40 minutes. Drain and cool. Cooked artichokes can also be stuffed and baked (remove the center leaves and choke).

To Eat
With your fingers, starting at the bottom, pluck off the leaves one by one until you reach leaves that are too thin to eat. Dip the base of each leaf in a dip or sauce, if using, then pull the leaf through your teeth, scraping off the pulp. Place the discarded leaves in a pile on your plate. Pull out all the remaining thin leaves from the artichoke to reveal the fuzzy choke. With the tip of a teaspoon, scrape out the choke and discard. Cut the solid heart into chunks and enjoy.

BRAISED BABY ARTICHOKES WITH OLIVES

Cook baby artichokes the way Italians do: with garlic and olives.

Prep: 20 minutes   Cook: 15 minutes

- 2 pounds baby artichokes (about 16)
- 1 lemon, cut in half
- ¼ cup olive oil
- 3 garlic cloves, thinly sliced
- 1 cup water
- ½ teaspoon salt
- ½ teaspoon coarsely ground black pepper
- ⅓ cup oil-cured olives, pitted and coarsely chopped

1. Trim artichokes: Bend back outer green leaves and snap them off at base until remaining leaves are green on top and yellow at bottom. Cut off stem, level with bottom of artichoke. Cut off top half of each artichoke and discard. Rub cut surfaces with lemon half to prevent browning. Cut each artichoke lengthwise in half or into quarters if large, dropping them into bowl of cold water and juice of remaining lemon half.

2. In 12-inch skillet, heat *1 inch water* to boiling over high heat. Drain artichokes and add to skillet; cook 5 minutes, then drain. Wipe skillet dry with paper towels.

3. In same skillet, heat oil over medium-high heat. Add garlic and cook, stirring, until golden. Add artichokes; cook, turning once, until lightly browned, about 2 minutes. Stir in water, salt, and pepper; cover and cook until knife inserted in bottom of artichoke goes in easily, about 5 minutes longer. Stir in olives and heat through. Makes 8 first-course servings.

Each serving: About 103 calories, 2g protein, 6g carbohydrate, 9g total fat (1g saturated), 0mg cholesterol, 383mg sodium.

BAKED ARTICHOKES WITH PARMESAN STUFFING

∙∙∙

If serving as a first course, use six small artichokes.

Prep: 1 hour   Bake: 15 minutes

- 4 large artichokes
- 1 lemon, cut in half
- 2 tablespoons fresh lemon juice
- 4 slices firm white bread, coarsely grated (lower right)
- 2 tablespoons olive oil
- 2 large garlic cloves, finely chopped
- 4 anchovy fillets, chopped
- ½ cup pine nuts (pignoli), lightly toasted (page 692), or walnuts, toasted and chopped
- ⅓ cup freshly grated Parmesan cheese
- 2 tablespoons chopped fresh parsley
- ¼ teaspoon salt
- ¾ cup chicken broth

1. Trim artichokes: From around base of artichoke, bend back outer green leaves and snap off. With kitchen shears, trim thorny tops from outer leaves, rubbing all cut surfaces with lemon half to prevent browning. Lay artichoke on its side and cut off stem, level with bottom of artichoke. Peel stem; place in bowl of cold water and juice of remaining lemon half. Cut 1 inch off top of artichoke; add artichoke to lemon water. Repeat with remaining artichokes and stems.

2. In nonreactive 5-quart saucepot, heat *1 inch water* and 1 tablespoon lemon juice to boiling over high heat. Stand artichokes in boiling water; add stems and heat to boiling. Reduce heat; cover and simmer until knife inserted in bottom of artichoke goes in easily, 30 to 40 minutes. Drain. When cool enough to handle, pull out prickly center leaves from each artichoke and, with teaspoon, scrape out fuzzy choke (without cutting into the heart) and discard. Finely chop stems.

3. Meanwhile, preheat oven to 400°F. Spread grated bread in jelly-roll pan. Place in oven and toast, stirring once, until golden, about 5 minutes.

4. In 1-quart saucepan, heat oil over medium heat. Add garlic and cook, stirring, 1 minute. Add anchovies and cook, stirring, until garlic is golden and anchovies have almost dissolved.

5. In medium bowl, combine toasted bread, pine nuts, Parmesan, parsley, chopped artichoke stems, garlic mixture, salt, ¼ cup broth, and remaining 1 tablespoon lemon juice.

6. Pour remaining ½ cup broth into 13" by 9" baking dish; stand artichokes in dish. Spoon bread mixture between artichoke leaves and into center cavities. Bake until stuffing is golden and artichokes are heated through, 15 to 20 minutes. Makes 4 main-dish servings.

Each serving: About 359 calories, 17g protein, 35g carbohydrate, 20g total fat (4g saturated), 9mg cholesterol, 934mg sodium.

GRATING FRESH BREAD CRUMBS

Grate firm day-old Italian or French bread on the large holes of a box grater. Or process the bread in a food processor with the knife blade attached to form coarse crumbs. One slice of bread yields about ½ cup crumbs.

ASPARAGUS

Availability
Almost year-round

Peak Season
March, April, and May

Buying Tips
Look for bright green, firm, crisp stalks with compact tips and no trace of brown or rust. Buy evenly sized stalks for uniform cooking. White asparagus, imported from Europe, is an expensive delicacy.

To Store
Asparagus is very perishable. Stand the stalks in ½ inch of cold water in a container. Refrigerate up to two days.

To Prepare
Hold the base of each asparagus spear in one hand and bend back the stalk; the end will break off at the spot where the stalk becomes too tough to eat. Discard the tough portion. Rinse well to remove any sand. Some cooks like to peel asparagus, but this is a matter of personal choice. Leave asparagus whole or cut diagonally into 1- to 2-inch pieces.

To Cook
Asparagus can be boiled, steamed, stir-fried, roasted, or grilled. Serve hot, room temperature, or cold. To boil, in a 12-inch skillet, heat 1 inch of water to boiling over high heat. Add asparagus and ½ teaspoon salt; heat to boiling. Reduce heat to medium-high and cook, uncovered, until barely tender, 5 to 10 minutes (depending on the thickness of asparagus); drain. If serving cold, rinse under cold running water to stop cooking; drain again.

ROASTED ASPARAGUS

Easy and tasty, oven-roasting is sure to become a favorite way to enjoy this vegetable.

Prep: 12 minutes   Roast: 20 minutes

- 2 pounds asparagus, trimmed
- 1 tablespoon olive oil
- ½ teaspoon salt
- ¼ teaspoon coarsely ground black pepper
  freshly grated lemon peel (optional)
  lemon wedges

1. Preheat oven to 450°F.

2. In large roasting pan (17" by 11½"), toss asparagus, oil, salt, and pepper until coated.

3. Roast asparagus, shaking pan occasionally, until tender and lightly browned, about 20 minutes. Sprinkle with grated lemon peel, if you like, and serve with lemon wedges. Makes 6 accompaniment servings.

Each serving: About 47 calories, 4g protein, 5g carbohydrate, 3g total fat (0g saturated), 0mg cholesterol, 195mg sodium.

SESAME STIR-FRIED ASPARAGUS

Thin asparagus is the ideal candidate for stir-frying.

Prep: 15 minutes   Cook: 5 minutes

- 1 tablespoon vegetable oil
- ½ teaspoon Asian sesame oil
- 1 pound thin asparagus, trimmed and cut on diagonal into 1-inch pieces
- ¼ teaspoon salt
- 1 tablespoon sesame seeds, toasted

In 10-inch skillet, heat vegetable and sesame oils over high heat until hot. Add asparagus and sprinkle with salt; cook, stirring frequently (stir-frying), until tender-crisp, about 5 minutes. Transfer to serving bowl and sprinkle with toasted sesame seeds. Makes 4 accompaniment servings.

Each serving: About 68 calories, 3g protein, 4g carbohydrate, 5g total fat (1g saturated), 0mg cholesterol, 145mg sodium.

AVOCADOS

Availability
Year-round, but less plentiful in early winter

Buying Tips
The avocado is really a fruit, but because it isn't sweet, we treat it like a vegetable. Avoca-

dos must be ripened until they yield to gentle pressure, or they will be flavorless. Buy avocados that are heavy for their size and free of bruises and soft spots. Don't buy very soft avocados; they are overripe. The most common avocado is the *Hass* variety: It has thick pebbled skin that turns dark purple when ripe. The *Fuerte* (also called Florida) avocado is somewhat larger than the Hass and has shiny green skin that doesn't change color when ripe.

To Store
Ripen firm avocados at room temperature. To speed up ripening, place in a closed paper bag (this traps the gases given off by the avocado). Refrigerate ripe avocados up to three or four days.

To Prepare
Cut the avocado lengthwise in half, cutting around the seed. Twist the two halves to separate. To remove the seed, give it a whack with the blade of a knife so it is slightly embedded in the seed. Twist and lift out. With your fingers, gently peel away the skin from the avocado and discard. Slice or cut up the avocado. Avocado flesh darkens quickly when exposed to air; toss with lemon or lime juice to discourage discoloration, or press plastic wrap onto the cut surfaces. Avocados lose their flavor when cooked, so they are almost always served raw in salads and sandwiches or in dips.

BEANS, GREEN AND WAX

Availability
Year-round

Peak Season
June, July, and August

Buying Tips
The term *bean* refers to an enormous category of plants with edible seeds, but in some cases the pods are also edible. When buying fresh

green beans or wax beans, look for crisp, firm pods without any brown spots. You can use the old-fashioned test of breaking a bean in half; it should snap, and beads of moisture should appear at the break. Look for uniformly green or yellow beans. *Purple wax beans* turn green when cooked. Small, thin *haricots verts* aren't as firm as regular green beans, so they cook quickly. Flat *Italian (Romano)* beans are larger and take a bit longer to cook.

To Store
Refrigerate fresh beans in the crisper drawer up to two or three days.

To Prepare
Rinse the beans under cold running water. Snap off or trim the ends. Leave the beans whole or cut into bite-size pieces.

To Cook

Green and wax beans are most often steamed or boiled, but they can also be roasted or stir-fried. To steam, in a 12-inch skillet, heat 1 inch of water and 1 teaspoon salt to boiling over medium-high heat. Add beans; cover and cook until tender-crisp, 5 to 10 minutes; drain.

ROASTED GREEN BEANS WITH DILL VINAIGRETTE

....

Instead of steaming green beans, roast them. Toss the beans in the quick and tasty vinaigrette dressing, and serve warm.

Prep: 20 minutes   Roast: 20 to 30 minutes

- 2 pounds green beans, trimmed
- 3 tablespoons olive oil
- ¾ teaspoon salt
- 2 tablespoons white wine vinegar
- 1½ teaspoons Dijon mustard
- ½ teaspoon sugar
- ½ teaspoon coarsely ground black pepper
- 2 tablespoons chopped fresh dill

1. Preheat oven to 450°F. In large roasting pan (17" by 11½"), toss green beans, 1 tablespoon oil, and ½ teaspoon salt until coated. Roast, stirring twice, until tender and lightly browned, 20 to 30 minutes.

2. Meanwhile, prepare vinaigrette: In small bowl, with wire whisk, mix vinegar, mustard, sugar, remaining ¼ teaspoon salt, and pepper until blended. In thin, steady stream, whisk in remaining 2 tablespoons oil until blended; stir in dill.

3. When green beans are done, transfer to serving bowl. Drizzle vinaigrette over green beans; toss until coated. Makes 8 accompaniment servings.

Each serving: About 79 calories, 2g protein, 8g carbohydrate, 5g total fat (1g saturated), 0mg cholesterol, 247mg sodium.

GREEN BEANS WITH HAZELNUTS

....

Green beans are always popular at large holiday get-togethers. Here's a special way to serve them: with a hint of lemon and lots of crunchy toasted nuts.

Prep: 20 minutes   Cook: 15 minutes

- 1½ teaspoons salt
- 2 pounds green beans, trimmed
- 2 tablespoons butter or margarine
- ½ cup hazelnuts (filberts), toasted and skinned (page 692), chopped
- 1 teaspoon freshly grated lemon peel
- ¼ teaspoon ground black pepper

1. In 12-inch skillet, heat *1 inch water* and 1 teaspoon salt to boiling over high heat. Add green beans and heat to boiling. Cover and cook until tender-crisp, 6 to 8 minutes. Drain; wipe skillet dry with paper towels.

2. In same skillet, melt butter over medium heat. Add hazelnuts and cook, stirring, until butter just begins to brown, about 3 minutes. Add green beans, lemon peel, remaining ½ teaspoon salt, and pepper. Cook, stirring, until heated through, about 5 minutes. Makes 8 accompaniment servings.

Each serving: About 143 calories, 3g protein, 9g carbohydrate, 12g total fat (4g saturated), 16mg cholesterol, 356mg sodium.

GREEN BEANS AMANDINE
Prepare as directed above but substitute ⅔ cup slivered **almonds,** toasted, for hazelnuts.

LEMONY GREEN BEANS
Prepare as directed above but omit hazelnuts in Step 2. Instead, add ¼ **teaspoon ground coriander,** ¼ **cup chopped fresh mint, 1 tablespoon fresh lemon juice,** and ½ **teaspoon lemon peel.** Toss until beans are evenly coated.

BEETS

Availability
Year-round

Peak Season
June through October

Buying Tips
Choose smooth, deeply colored beets without ridges and blemishes; soft spots indicate decay. Buy evenly sized beets for uniform cooking. The green tops, if attached, should be fresh-looking. (They can be cooked separately like other greens; see Stir-Frying 101, page 410.) In addition to the familiar crimson-colored beets, *golden beets* and *striped beets* are often available at specialty food stores and farmers' markets.

To Store
If the tops are attached, trim them, leaving about 1 inch of stem attached (this prevents the beets from "bleeding" and losing color). Place the tops and beets in separate plastic bags. Refrigerate in the crisper drawer: beets up to one week, tops up to two days (they wilt quickly).

To Prepare
Wash beet tops under cool running water to remove any hidden grit. Scrub beets well under cold running water.

To Cook
Beets can be boiled, but roasting enhances their natural sweetness. Cook beets unpeeled and uncut to retain their color.

HOW TO AVOID BEET STAINS

Here is a simple way to protect your hands from beet stains. Before trimming raw beets or before removing the skins from and cutting up cooked beets, slip on a pair of rubber kitchen gloves or disposable surgical gloves. They will keep your hands from turning an unsightly pink.

ROASTED BEETS AND ONIONS

....

An easy sweet-and-sour skillet sauce transforms roasted beets and red onions into a luscious side dish.

Prep: 20 minutes plus cooling
Roast/Cook: 1 hour 40 minutes

- 2 bunches beets with tops (2 pounds)
- 3 small red onions (1 pound), not peeled
- 2 tablespoons extra-virgin olive oil
- ⅓ cup chicken broth
- ¼ cup balsamic vinegar
- 1 teaspoon brown sugar
- 1 teaspoon fresh thyme
- ¼ teaspoon salt
- ¼ teaspoon coarsely ground black pepper
- 1 tablespoon chopped fresh parsley

1. Preheat oven to 400°F.

2. Trim all but 1 inch of top stems from beets. Place beets and onions in oven-safe 10-inch skillet (if skillet is not oven-safe, wrap handle with double layer of foil) or in 13" by 9" baking pan; drizzle with oil. Roast, shaking skillet occasionally, until onions have softened and beets are tender, about 1 hour 30 minutes, transferring vegetables to plate as they are done.

3. In same skillet, combine broth, vinegar, brown sugar, and thyme; heat to boiling over medium-high heat. Boil, stirring and scraping bottom of skillet, until vinegar mixture is dark brown and syrupy and has reduced to about ¼ cup, 5 to 7 minutes. Stir in salt and pepper. Remove from heat.

4. When cool enough to handle, peel beets and onions. Cut beets into ¼-inch-wide matchstick strips and onions into thin rounds; place in serving bowl. Pour vinegar mixture over vegetables and toss until coated. Sprinkle with parsley. Makes 6 accompaniment servings.

Each serving: About 103 calories, 2g protein, 14g carbohydrate, 5g total fat (1g saturated), 0mg cholesterol, 203mg sodium.

BOK CHOY

Availability
Year-round

Buying Tips
Look for bok choy in Asian markets and large super-markets. Select heads that have crisp white stalks and bright green leaves, which may be slightly wilted. Avoid bok choy that has any brown spots.

To Store
Refrigerate in the the crisper drawer up to three days.

To Prepare
Separate the stalks from their leafy tops; cut both into ½-inch-thick slices.

To Cook
Bok choy is almost always stir-fried with Asian season-ings to enhance its mild flavor. Cook the stalks first, then add the tender tops at the end.

BROCCOFLOWER

Availability
October through February

Buying Tips
Even though its fluorescent-green color is reminiscent of broccoli, broccoflower is more closely related to cauli-flower. Look for firm heads with tightly packed flowerets and no browning. The leaves should look crisp.

To Store
Place in a plastic bag with a few holes poked in it. Re-frigerate in the crisper drawer up to two days.

To Prepare
Discard the leaves; cut into bite-size flowerets or keep whole.

To Cook
Cook like cauliflower (boil, steam, or roast). When cooked, broccoflower turns deep green.

BROCCOLI

Availability
Year-round

Peak Season
October through February

Buying Tips
Look for firm stalks with tightly closed dark green flowerets. Avoid stalks with yellowing or blooming flowerets. *Purple broccoli* turns dark green when cooked.

To Store
Place in a plastic bag with a few holes poked in it. Re-frigerate in the crisper drawer up to two days.

To Prepare
Remove the large leaves and trim the ends of the stalks if woody. Cut the broccoli tops into 2-inch flowerets. Peel the stalks and cut into ¼- to ½-inch-thick slices.

To Cook
Broccoli can be stir-fried, steamed, or boiled. To cook, in a skillet, heat 1 inch of water to boiling over high heat; add broccoli stalks and heat to boiling. Cook 1 minute. Add flowerets and heat to boiling. Reduce heat to medium-low; cover and cook until broccoli is tender-crisp, about 5 minutes. Drain.

BROCCOLI RABE

Availability
Year-round

Buying Tips
This slightly bitter green is also called *broccoli raab, broccoli rape*, and *broccoli di rape*. The leaves should be perky, with thin green stalks and small, tight bud clus-ters. Avoid stalks with yellowish leaves.

To Store

Place in a plastic bag with a few holes poked in it. Refrigerate in the crisper drawer up to two days.

To Prepare

Trim stems and discard any tough leaves. Wash in several changes of cold water to remove any grit.

To Cook

Broccoli rabe is cooked like other leafy greens. In a large skillet, heat ½ inch of water to boiling; add broccoli rabe and heat to boiling. Reduce heat to medium-high and cook until stems are almost tender, about 5 minutes; drain well. Wipe skillet dry. In same skillet, cook some chopped garlic in olive oil until golden. Stir in broccoli rabe; cook, stirring, until heated through. Season with salt and pepper.

BROCCOLI RABE WITH GARBANZO BEANS

For a quick and flavorful weeknight supper, toss these tasty bitter greens with a hearty pasta, such as penne, rotelle, or bow ties, and sprinkle with Parmesan cheese.

Prep: 10 minutes   Cook: 18 minutes

- 2   bunches broccoli rabe (1¼ pounds each), trimmed
- 2½ teaspoons salt
- 2   tablespoons olive oil
- 3   garlic cloves, crushed with side of chef's knife
- ¼   teaspoon crushed red pepper
- 1   can (15 to 19 ounces) garbanzo beans, rinsed and drained

1. In 8-quart saucepot, heat *4 quarts water* to boiling over high heat. Add broccoli rabe and 2 teaspoons salt; heat to boiling. Cook until thickest part of stems is tender, about 3 minutes. Drain, reserving ¼ cup cooking water. Cool slightly, then cut into 1½-inch pieces.

2. Wipe saucepot dry with paper towels; add oil and heat over medium heat. Add garlic and cook, stirring, until golden. Add crushed red pepper and cook 15 seconds. Add broccoli rabe, garbanzo beans, reserved cooking water, and remaining ½ teaspoon salt. Cook, stirring, until heated through, about 3 minutes. Makes 8 accompaniment servings.

Each serving: About 93 calories, 5g protein, 10g carbohydrate, 4g total fat (0g saturated), 0mg cholesterol, 378mg sodium.

BRUSSELS SPROUTS

Availability

Year-round, except June and July

Peak Season

October through January

Buying Tips

Purchase firm, bright green sprouts with tight outer leaves. Avoid soft sprouts or any with black spots. Brussels sprouts are usually available in 10-ounce boxes, but sometimes they are sold still attached to their long stalks.

To Store

Refrigerate in the crisper drawer up to two days.

To Prepare

Trim off any yellow or wilted leaves, and trim the stem end. Cut a shallow X in the stem end to shorten the cooking time. Rinse well under cold running water.

To Cook

Brussels sprouts are usually boiled, but for a delicious change of pace, thinly slice and sauté until tender. For steamed Brussels sprouts with the freshest flavor, cook the sprouts just until tender-crisp; long cooking brings out their strong flavor and an unappealing sulfurous aroma. In a large saucepan, heat 1 inch of water to boiling over high heat; add Brussels sprouts and heat to boiling. Reduce heat to medium-high. Cover and cook until tender-crisp, about 10 minutes (or a little longer if you prefer very tender sprouts); drain.

BRUSSELS SPROUTS WITH BACON

··

For many families, Brussels sprouts are a given at the Thanksgiving table. If you wish, prepare ahead through Step 2; then finish cooking at the last minute.

Prep: 15 minutes   Cook: 25 minutes

3   containers (10 ounces each) Brussels sprouts, trimmed and cut lengthwise in half
6   slices bacon
1   tablespoon olive oil
2   garlic cloves, finely chopped
½   teaspoon salt
¼   teaspoon coarsely ground black pepper
¼   cup pine nuts (pignoli), toasted (page 692)

1. In 4-quart saucepan, heat *2 quarts water* to boiling over high heat. Add Brussels sprouts and heat to boiling. Cook until tender-crisp, about 5 minutes; drain.

2. In 12-inch skillet, cook bacon over medium heat until browned. With tongs, transfer bacon to paper towels to drain; crumble.

3. Discard all but 1 tablespoon bacon drippings from skillet. Add oil and heat over medium-high heat. Add Brussels sprouts, garlic, salt, and pepper. Cook, stirring frequently, until Brussels sprouts are lightly browned, about 5 minutes. To serve, sprinkle with pine nuts and bacon. Makes 10 accompaniment servings.

Each serving: About 96 calories, 5g protein, 8g carbohydrate, 6g total fat (1g saturated), 4mg cholesterol, 202mg sodium.

BRUSSELS SPROUTS WITH BACON AND CHESTNUTS

Prepare as directed but substitute **Roasted Chestnuts** (page 403) for pine nuts. Cut chestnuts into quarters; add to Brussels sprouts with garlic, salt, and pepper.

NAPA OR CHINESE CABBAGE

Availability
Year-round

Buying Tips
Although *Chinese cabbage* is cylindrical and *napa cabbage* is roundish, they can be used interchangeably in most recipes. Look for crisp, fresh-looking cabbage, free from blemishes. Tiny brown freckles are to be expected.

To Store
Place in a plastic bag with a few holes poked in it. Refrigerate in the crisper drawer up to three days.

To Prepare
Remove any wilted leaves and cut cabbage lengthwise in half or into quarters. Rinse well. Cut out most of the core and thinly slice or prepare as directed.

GREEN AND RED CABBAGE

Availability
Year-round

Buying Tips
Buy heavy, firm, blemish-free heads with tightly packed crinkly leaves; the outer leaves of summer-harvested cabbage will be loosely packed and should be crisp and brightly colored. *Savoy* cabbage is considered the best-tasting green variety.

To Store
Place in a plastic bag with a few holes poked in it. Refrigerate in the crisper drawer up to one week.

To Prepare
Discard any tough outer leaves. Cut the head into wedges and cut away most of the tough core from each wedge, leaving just enough to hold the cabbage together. With a large knife, thinly slice, or shred in a food processor with the knife blade attached.

To Cook

Cabbage can be boiled, stir-fried, sautéed, braised, or served raw. To retain the color of red cabbage, add a little vinegar or lemon juice while it is cooking.

BRAISED SWEET-AND-SOUR RED CABBAGE

....

Not your usual sweet-and-sour treatment: For sweet, we use fresh pear, apple juice, and brown sugar; for sour, cider vinegar. Then we add a hint of allspice for balance.

Prep: 20 minutes   Cook: 1 hour 30 minutes

- 3 tablespoons vegetable oil
- 2 medium onions, chopped
- 1 pear, peeled, cored, and chopped
- 2 medium heads red cabbage (2 pounds each), cut into quarters, cored, and thinly sliced
- 1 can (14½ ounces) beef broth or 1¾ cups Brown Beef Stock (page 71)
- 1 cup apple juice
- ⅓ cup cider vinegar
- ¼ cup packed brown sugar
- 2 small bay leaves
- ¾ teaspoon salt
- ¼ teaspoon coarsely ground black pepper
- ⅛ teaspoon ground allspice

1. In nonreactive 8-quart saucepot, heat oil over medium heat. Add onions and pear; cook, stirring frequently, until tender, 10 minutes.

2. Stir in cabbage, broth, apple juice, vinegar, brown sugar, bay leaves, salt, pepper, and allspice; heat to boiling over high heat. Reduce heat; cover and simmer, stirring occasionally, until cabbage is very tender, about 1 hour. Remove cover and cook over medium-high heat, stirring occasionally, until most of liquid has evaporated, about 15 minutes longer. Remove and discard bay leaves. Makes 10 accompaniment servings.

Each serving: About 136 calories, 3g protein, 23g carbohydrate, 5g total fat (1g saturated), 1mg cholesterol, 335mg sodium.

BRAISED CABBAGE WITH GINGER AND CUMIN

....

Adding fresh ginger and cumin—spices typical of Indian cuisine—to braised cabbage turns an ordinary vegetable into an exotic taste experience.

Prep: 10 minutes   Cook: 20 minutes

- 1 tablespoon butter or margarine
- 1 tablespoon vegetable oil
- 1 medium onion, chopped
- 2 tablespoons minced, peeled fresh ginger
- 2 garlic cloves, finely chopped
- 1 medium head green cabbage (2 pounds), cut into quarters, cored, and very thinly sliced
- ½ teaspoon cumin seeds, crushed
- ½ teaspoon salt
- 1 cup water

In 12-inch skillet, melt butter with oil over medium heat. Add onion and cook until tender, about 5 minutes. Stir in ginger and garlic; cook, stirring, 30 seconds. Stir in cabbage, cumin seeds, and salt; increase heat to medium-high and cook, stirring frequently, until cabbage begins to wilt, about 5 minutes (do not let garlic burn). Add water and cook, stirring occasionally, until cabbage is very tender and water has evaporated, about 10 minutes. Makes 6 accompaniment servings.

Each serving: About 80 calories, 2g protein, 10g carbohydrate, 4g total fat (1g saturated), 5mg cholesterol, 236mg sodium.

THE VINEGAR CONNECTION

TEST KITCHEN TIP

Recipes for cooked cabbage often include a bit of vinegar. Here's why: If cut cabbage is exposed to even slightly alkaline conditions, such as hard water, the cabbage will turn blue. Adding a small amount of acid (fruit or fruit juice, vinegar, or wine) will prevent this from happening.

CARDOON

Availability
October through February

Buying Tips
Also called *cardoni*. Look for cardoons in Italian markets, especially around Christmas. Buy large, thick, ivory-colored stalks with prickly leaves.

To Store
Refrigerate in the crisper drawer up to five days.

To Prepare
Cardoons discolor when their cut surfaces are exposed to air. To discourage browning, rub the cut surfaces with lemon halves (but even if the surfaces brown, they will turn grayish white when cooked). Separate the stalks, discarding the tough outer ones. Using a vegetable peeler, remove the outer strings.

To Cook
Cardoons are always eaten cooked. In a medium saucepan, heat 1 inch of water to boiling over high heat; add cardoons and return to boiling. Reduce heat to medium-high and cook until tender, about 20 minutes; drain.

CARROTS

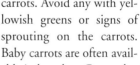

Availability
Year-round

Buying Tips
Buy firm brightly colored carrots. Avoid any with yellowish greens or signs of sprouting on the carrots. Baby carrots are often available in bunches. Cut or shredded carrots, sold in plastic bags, should show no sign of moisture.

To Store
Cut off the greens, leaving about 2 inches of stem. Place in a plastic bag. Refrigerate in the crisper drawer up to five days.

To Prepare
Scrub under cold running water or peel. Leave carrots whole or slice, shred, or cut them into pieces.

To Cook
No longer are carrots simply boiled: They are glazed, candied, stir-fried, roasted, shredded, or served as slaw. To serve them the old-fashioned way, in a saucepan, heat 1 inch of water to boiling over high heat; add carrots and heat to boiling. Reduce heat to medium-high; cover and cook until tender-crisp, whole carrots about 15 minutes, cut-up carrots, 5 to 10 minutes.

CANDIED CARROTS

....

These delicately sweetened carrots are sure to please children and adults alike.

Prep: 15 minutes   Cook: 25 minutes

- 1 bag (16 ounces) carrots, peeled
- 1 lemon
- 2 tablespoons butter or margarine
- 3 tablespoons brown sugar

1. Cut each carrot crosswise in half. Cut thick portion lengthwise in half. In 4-quart saucepan, heat *1 inch water* to boiling over medium heat. Add carrots and heat to boiling. Cover and simmer until tender, about 15 minutes. Drain and return to saucepan.

2. Meanwhile, from lemon, grate ½ teaspoon peel and squeeze 1 teaspoon juice.

3. Add butter, brown sugar, and lemon juice to carrots; cook over medium heat, stirring gently, until sugar has dissolved and carrots are glazed, about 5 minutes.

4. Stir in peel. Makes 4 accompaniment servings.

Each serving: About 133 calories, 1g protein, 20g carbohydrate, 6g total fat (4g saturated), 16mg cholesterol, 98mg sodium.

GINGER CANDIED CARROTS
Prepare as directed above but add **1 teaspoon grated, peeled fresh ginger** with butter.

CANDIED PARSNIPS
Prepare as directed above but substitute **1 pound parsnips,** peeled, for carrots.

BALSAMIC-GLAZED BABY CARROTS

This recipe is perfect for a family dinner or a large dinner party. The balsamic glaze adds a flavor burst to everyday carrots.

Prep: 15 minutes   Roast: 31 minutes

- 2 pounds trimmed baby carrots or medium carrots
- 1 tablespoon olive oil
- ¼ teaspoon salt
- ⅛ teaspoon ground black pepper
- 2 tablespoons white or traditional balsamic vinegar
- 1 tablespoon sugar

1. Preheat oven to 400°F. With vegetable brush, scrub carrots and rinse under cold water. Pat dry with paper towels. Trim baby carrots, leaving 1 inch green stem on, if you like; cut medium carrots into quarters lengthwise, then in half crosswise.

2. In 15½" by 10½" jelly-roll pan, toss carrots with olive oil, salt, and pepper. Roast 25 minutes. Stir in vinegar and sugar until carrots are coated. Roast 6 to 8 minutes longer or until carrots are tender and sugar has dissolved. Makes 8 side-dish servings.

Each serving: About 65 calories, 1g protein, 11g carbohydrate, 2g total fat (0g saturated), 2g fiber, 0mg cholesterol, 110mg sodium.

Tip: In springtime, bunches of fresh baby carrots should be readily available at supermarkets and farmers' markets. If not, use two pounds medium carrots, quartered lengthwise then halved crosswise. For this recipe, we don't recommend using prepackaged "baby" carrots; they require a much longer roasting time, and we've found they don't caramelize as well.

SHREDDED CARROTS

This is the fastest way to cook carrots and also one of the best. Add a pinch each of cloves and ginger for a spicier dish, if you like.

Prep: 5 minutes   Cook: 5 minutes

- 4 carrots, peeled and shredded (2 cups)
- 2 tablespoons water
- 2 tablespoons butter or margarine
- 1 teaspoon sugar
- ½ teaspoon salt

In small saucepan, combine carrots, water, butter, sugar, and salt; heat to boiling over high heat. Reduce heat; cover and simmer, stirring occasionally, until carrots are tender, 3 to 4 minutes. Makes 4 accompaniment servings.

Each serving: About 78 calories, 1g protein, 7g carbohydrate, 6g total fat (4g saturated), 16mg cholesterol, 367mg sodium.

CAULIFLOWER

Availability
Year-round

Peak Season
October through January

Buying Tips
Heads should be firm and creamy white with granular-looking flowerets. The leaves should be fresh-looking. Do not buy heads with brown spots or flowering buds. *Purple* or *green cauliflower* occasionally shows up at farmers' markets.

To Store
Place in a plastic bag with a few holes poked in it. Refrigerate in the crisper drawer up to five days.

To Prepare
Remove the leaves and cut out the core. Separate the head into flowerets or leave whole. Rinse under cold running water.

To Cook

Cauliflower is frequently steamed, but it's also delicious roasted (see below). To steam, in a large saucepan, heat 1 inch of water to boiling over high heat; add cauliflower and heat to boiling. Reduce heat to medium-high. Cover and cook whole cauliflower until tender, 10 to 15 minutes, or flowerets until tender-crisp, about 5 minutes; drain well.

ROASTED CAULIFLOWER

Roasting cauliflower until it caramelizes turns its starch to sugar and gives it a delicious nutty flavor.

Prep: 10 minutes   Roast: 23 minutes

1   medium head cauliflower (2 pounds), cut into 1½-inch flowerets
1   tablespoon olive oil
½   teaspoon salt
¼   teaspoon coarsely ground black pepper
2   tablespoons chopped fresh parsley
1   garlic clove, finely chopped

1. Preheat oven to 450°F. In jelly-roll pan, toss cauliflower, oil, salt, and pepper until evenly coated. Roast until cauliflower is tender, about 20 minutes, stirring halfway through roasting.

2. In small cup, combine parsley and garlic. Sprinkle over cauliflower and stir to mix evenly. Roast 3 minutes longer. Spoon into serving dish. Makes 6 accompaniment servings.

Each serving: About 35 calories, 1g protein, 3g carbohydrate, 2g total fat (0g saturated), 0mg cholesterol, 202mg sodium.

CURRY-ROASTED CAULIFLOWER

Prepare as directed above but substitute **2 tablespoons chopped fresh cilantro** for parsley and add **1 teaspoon curry powder** to garlic mixture.

CAULIFLOWER WITH GOLDEN RAISINS AND PINE NUTS

In Sicily, anchovies are used as a seasoning. If you prefer, omit the anchovy paste, and add a little more salt.

Prep: 20 minutes   Cook: 18 minutes

1   large head cauliflower (2½ pounds), cut into 1½-inch flowerets
2¼   teaspoons salt
2   tablespoons olive oil
2   garlic cloves, crushed with side of chef's knife
1   teaspoon anchovy paste (optional)
¼   teaspoon crushed red pepper
¼   cup golden raisins
2   tablespoons pine nuts (pignoli), lightly toasted (page 692)
1   tablespoon chopped fresh parsley

1. In 5-quart Dutch oven, heat *2 quarts water* to boiling over high heat. Add cauliflower and 2 teaspoons salt; heat to boiling. Cook until tender, 5 to 7 minutes; drain. Wipe Dutch oven dry.

2. In same Dutch oven, heat oil over medium heat. Add garlic and cook, stirring, until golden. Add anchovy paste, if using, and crushed red pepper; cook 15 seconds. Add cauliflower, raisins, pine nuts, and remaining ¼ teaspoon salt; cook, stirring, until heated through, about 2 minutes. To serve, sprinkle with parsley. Makes 6 accompaniment servings.

Each serving: About 93 calories, 2g protein, 9g carbohydrate, 6g total fat (1g saturated), 0mg cholesterol, 401mg sodium.

PINE NUTS

TEST KITCHEN TIP

These tasty little nuts are the seeds of a particular variety of pine tree and have been cultivated for over 6,000 years. They contain about 31 grams of protein per 100 grams, the highest amount of any nut or seed. Pine nuts are called *piñones* in Spanish and *pignoli* in Italian.

CELERY

Availability
Year-round

Buying Tips
Choose a compact bunch of light-colored, crisp stalks with fresh-looking leaves. (Thin, dark-colored stalks can be bitter and stringy.)

To Store
Refrigerate in the crisper drawer up to five days.

To Prepare
Remove the leaves (use in soups or stews) and trim the root end. Rinse the stalks under cold running water. Use the outer stalks for cooking or cut up for salads. Serve the tender inner stalks raw in salads or with dips.

To Cook
To braise as a side dish, cut stalks into 4- to 6-inch pieces and place in shallow baking dish. Add enough chicken broth to come halfway up celery; sprinkle with pepper. Bake at 375°F, basting frequently, until very tender, about 30 minutes.

CELERY ROOT (CELERIAC)

Availability
Year-round

Peak Season
October through March

Buying Tips
Choose firm, small (less than 4 inches in diameter) celery root knobs that are well shaped (the smoother the knob, the easier it is to peel). If only large celery root is available, remove the center if soft and woody.

To Store
Refrigerate in the crisper drawer up to five days.

To Prepare
Scrub under cold running water. Use a small knife to cut away the peel and root end. Cut as directed. The flesh of celery root discolors when exposed to air. If preparing ahead, place the cut celery root in a bowl containing 4 cups cold water and 2 tablespoons lemon juice or vinegar; set aside until ready to cook. Drain well.

To Cook
Celery root can be served raw (as a salad), boiled, mashed (alone or with potatoes), or braised.

CELERY ROOT RÉMOULADE

Although rémoulade is usually paired with cold seafood salads, it is also excellent served as a dip for raw vegetables. Our version, which contains crunchy strips of celery root, can stand alone.

Prep: 25 minutes plus chilling

- 2 tablespoons fresh lemon juice
- 1½ pounds celery root (celeriac), trimmed and peeled
- ½ cup mayonnaise
- 2 tablespoons Dijon mustard
- 1 tablespoon chopped fresh parsley
- ¼ teaspoon ground black pepper

1. Pour lemon juice into large bowl. With adjustable-blade slicer or very sharp knife, cut celery root into ⅛-inch-thick matchstick strips. Immediately place celery root in lemon juice as it is cut, tossing to coat completely to prevent celery root from browning.

2. In small bowl, combine mayonnaise, mustard, parsley, and pepper. Add to celery root and toss to coat. Cover and refrigerate at least 1 hour to blend flavors or up to overnight. Makes 6 accompaniment servings.

Each serving: About 176 calories, 2g protein, 10g carbohydrate, 15g total fat (2g saturated), 11mg cholesterol, 322mg sodium.

TWICE-BAKED
CELERY ROOT POTATOES

....

An easy self-service option for the holiday buffet table.

Prep: 30 minutes   Cook/Bake: 1 hour 10 minutes

  6 medium russet (baking) potatoes (8 ounces each)
  1 pound celery root, peeled and cut into 1-inch chunks
  ½ cup milk
  4 tablespoons butter or margarine
  ¾ teaspoon salt
  ¼ teaspoon ground black pepper
  ½ cup freshly grated Parmesan cheese
     chopped parsley for garnish

1. Preheat oven to 450°F. Place potatoes in oven, directly on rack, and bake 45 to 50 minutes or until tender when pierced with knife. Remove potatoes from oven and set aside until cool enough to handle. Reset oven temperature to 400°F.

2. Meanwhile, in 3-quart saucepan, place celery root and enough *water* to cover; heat to boiling on high. Reduce heat to low; cover and simmer 15 minutes or until celery root is tender. Drain.

3. In food processor with knife blade attached, blend celery root with milk, butter, salt, and pepper until pureed. Transfer puree to large bowl.

4. When potatoes are cool enough to handle, cut ¼-inch slice from the narrow ends of each potato, then cut each potato crosswise in half. Stand potato halves on narrow ends. With spoon, scoop potato from skins into bowl with celery root puree, leaving about ¼-inch of potato with skin and being careful not to break through bottom of potato. Reserve potato-skin cups. With potato masher, mash potato with celery root mixture until almost smooth. Stir in Parmesan.

5. Spray 15½" by 10½" jelly-roll pan with nonstick cooking spray. Spoon potato mixture into potato-skin cups, mounding slightly. Place cups in prepared pan. Bake 25 minutes or until heated through and lightly browned. (If not baking right away, cover and refrigerate filled potatoes overnight; bake 35 to 40 minutes.) Sprinkle with parsley to serve. Makes 12 side-dish servings.

Each serving: About 160 calories, 4g protein, 25g carbohydrate, 5g total fat (2g saturated), 2g fiber, 4mg cholesterol, 290mg sodium.

CHAYOTE

Availability
Year-round

Buying Tips
Also called *mirliton* and *christo-phene*, this ridged, pear-shaped dark green squash tastes like summer squash. When buying, choose firm chayote.

To Store
Refrigerate in the crisper drawer up to one week.

To Prepare
Small chayotes have thin skins that do not require peeling. Otherwise, remove the peel with a vegetable peeler or knife. Cut in half and discard the hard central seed; cut as directed.

To Cook
Chayote can be steamed, sautéed, or braised just like summer squash. To roast, brush the cut sides of chayote halves with some fruity olive oil and bake in a preheated 375°F oven until tender, 30 to 40 minutes.

CHESTNUTS

Availability
November through January, but most plentiful in November

Buying Tips
Chestnuts are always imported (usually from Italy), so buy them from a store with good turnover to ensure freshness. Buy chestnuts with firm, shiny shells; avoid any with tiny holes. Vacuum-packed chestnuts are acceptable in stuffings, but canned chestnuts don't have much flavor. One pound of fresh chestnuts yields about 2 cups peeled.

To Store
Refrigerate in a brown paper bag up to two weeks.

To Prepare
Chestnuts are always cooked and peeled before eating. The recipe opposite is the traditional method.

ROASTED CHESTNUTS

······························

Chestnuts can be presented in many guises: in almost any stuffing, added to your favorite vegetable medley, or pureed with sugar and vanilla and served with whipped cream for a special dessert.

Prep: 30 minutes   Roast: 20 minutes

1 **pound fresh chestnuts**

1. Preheat oven to 400°F. With sharp knife, cut an X in flat side of shell of each chestnut. Place in jelly-roll pan and roast chestnuts until shells open, about 20 minutes.

2. Cover chestnuts with a clean kitchen towel. When cool enough to handle, with paring knife, peel hot chestnuts, keeping unpeeled chestnuts warm for easier peeling. Makes 2 cups.

Each ½ cup: About 179 calories, 2g protein, 38g carbohydrate, 2g total fat (0g saturated), 0mg cholesterol, 3mg sodium.

CHICORY

Availability
Year-round

Buying Tips
Chicory is sometimes called *curly endive*. Buy heads with curly, spiky, fresh-looking leaves that have dark green tops and pale green ribs.

To Store
Wrap loosely in paper towels and place in a plastic bag. Refrigerate in the crisper drawer up to five days.

To Prepare
Trim the stems. Wash leaves well in several changes of cold water to remove grit. Tear into bite-size pieces.

To Cook
Serve raw in salads combined with sweet-tasting greens, or cook like other bitter greens (page 409).

CORN

Availability
Year-round

Peak Season
July through September

Buying Tips
Buy ears that are firm and well shaped under

fresh-looking husks with shiny, moist silk. (Unshucked corn stays fresh longer.) Pick ears that look plump, with kernels running to the tops of the ears. Tiny kernels indicate immaturity, but very large deep yellow kernels can be chewy. The fresher the corn, the sweeter the kernels: With age, the sugar in corn converts to starch. Frozen and canned corn kernels are good substitutes for fresh. Canned baby corn is used in Asian stir-fries. One medium ear of corn yields about ½ cup corn kernels.

To Store
Cook and eat corn as soon as possible after picking. If you must, refrigerate in the crisper drawer up to one or two days.

To Prepare
Shuck the corn and remove the silk just before cooking. (An exception is corn grilled with the husks intact.) To remove the kernels, trim the tip so you can stand the ear on end, then slice down to cut off the kernels, cutting close to the cob.

To Cook

Corn is one of the most versatile vegetables. Sauté the kernels alone or with other vegetables; stir into puddings, fritters, or other batters; or roast, microwave, or boil on the cob. To boil, in a large saucepot, heat 3 inches of water to boiling over high heat; add shucked corn and heat to boiling. Do not add salt; it toughens corn. Reduce heat to low. Cover and simmer 5 minutes; drain.

CREAMY CORN PUDDING

This savory pudding goes exceptionally well with baked ham. Perfect for a late summer feast.

Prep: 30 minutes   Bake: 1 hour 15 minutes

- 2 tablespoons butter or margarine
- 1 small onion, chopped
- ¼ cup all-purpose flour
- 2 cups half-and-half or light cream, warmed
- 1 cup milk, warmed
- 2 cups corn kernels cut from cobs (4 ears)
- 1 teaspoon salt
- ¼ teaspoon coarsely ground black pepper
- 4 large eggs

1. Preheat oven to 325°F. In 2-quart saucepan, melt butter over medium heat. Add onion and cook, stirring frequently, until tender and golden, about 10 minutes. Add flour and cook, stirring, 1 minute. With wire whisk, gradually whisk in warm half-and-half and warm milk; heat to boiling, whisking constantly. Reduce heat and simmer, stirring occasionally, until sauce has thickened and boils, about 5 minutes. Remove from heat; stir in corn, salt, and pepper.

2. In 2-quart casserole, with wire whisk, beat eggs lightly. Slowly add corn mixture, beating constantly.

3. Set casserole in 13" by 9" baking pan; place pan on oven rack. Pour enough *boiling water* into pan to come halfway up sides of casserole. Bake until knife inserted in center comes out clean, about 1 hour 15 minutes. Makes 10 accompaniment servings.

Each serving: About 168 calories, 6g protein, 13g carbohydrate, 11g total fat (6g saturated), 112mg cholesterol, 315mg sodium.

SAUTÉED FRESH CORN

While this is a fine way to cook raw corn, it's also a very clever way to heat up kernels cut from leftover corn on the cob.

Prep: 15 minutes   Cook: 5 minutes

- 2 tablespoons butter or margarine
- 4 cups corn kernels cut from cobs (about 6 ears)
- ½ teaspoon salt
- ¼ teaspoon coarsely ground black pepper
- ¼ cup snipped fresh chives or thinly sliced green onions

In 10-inch skillet, melt butter over medium-high heat. Add corn, salt, and pepper and cook, stirring frequently, until tender, about 4 minutes. Remove from heat and stir in chives. Makes 4 accompaniment servings.

Each serving: About 238 calories, 7g protein, 41g carbohydrate, 8g total fat (4g saturated), 16mg cholesterol, 381mg sodium.

CUCUMBERS

Availability
Year-round

Peak Season
June through September

Buying Tips
Pick firm, uniformly slender cucumbers. Overmature cucumbers, which are generally seedy, are dull or yellowish and have an overgrown, puffy look. Smaller varieties, such as *Kirbys*, are preferred for pickling. *English* (seedless) cucumbers are long and slender and have very small seeds that do not have to be removed.

To Store
Refrigerate in the crisper drawer up to one week.

To Prepare

Rinse cukes under cold running water; scrub Kirbys with a vegetable brush. If the skin is tender and unwaxed (Kirbys and seedless varieties), cucumbers do not have to be peeled. Simply trim the ends and cut the cucumber as desired. To remove the seeds, cut the cucumber lengthwise in half and scoop out the seeds with a spoon.

To Cook

Cucumbers are well known as a salad ingredient, but they can also be sautéed alone or with other vegetables. When cooked, they have a mild squashlike flavor.

EGGPLANT

Availability
Year-round

Peak Season
July through October

Buying Tips
Eggplant should be firm and shiny with a bright green cap and no scars, cuts, or bruises. It should feel heavy for its size. Varieties include the familiar plump oval dark purple *Mediterranean*, the slender light purple *Japanese*, and the round green *Thai* eggplant.

To Store
Refrigerate in the crisper drawer up to one week.

To Prepare
Rinse under cold running water. Do not peel eggplant unless the skin seems tough. Some recipes call for salting eggplant, which draws out the water and any bitter juices. Slice or cut eggplant as desired just before cooking; it discolors quickly.

To Cook
Braise, grill, bake, sauté, or roast eggplant. It is often combined with tomato, zucchini, or roasted peppers.

CAPONATA

....

Caponata (which gets its name from the capers that accent it) has an intriguing sweet-and-sour flavor. Serve it as part of a cold antipasto, spread it on bruschetta, or offer it as a first course.

Prep: 30 minutes plus cooling
Roast/Cook: 55 minutes

- 2 small eggplants (1 pound each), ends trimmed, cut into ³/₄-inch pieces
- ½ cup extra-virgin olive oil
- ¼ teaspoon salt
- 3 small red onions, thinly sliced
- 1½ pounds ripe tomatoes (4 medium), peeled and seeded (page 440), chopped
- 1 cup olives, such as Gaeta, green Sicilian, or Kalamata, pitted and chopped
- 3 tablespoons capers, drained
- 3 tablespoons golden raisins
- ¼ teaspoon coarsely ground black pepper
- 4 stalks celery with leaves, thinly sliced
- ⅓ cup red wine vinegar
- 2 teaspoons sugar
- ¼ cup chopped fresh flat-leaf parsley

1. Preheat oven to 450°F. In two jelly-roll pans, place eggplant, dividing evenly. Drizzle with ¼ cup oil and sprinkle with salt; toss to coat. Roast eggplant 10 minutes; stir, then roast until browned, about 10 minutes longer.

2. Meanwhile, in nonstick 12-inch skillet, heat remaining ¼ cup oil over medium heat. Add onions and cook, stirring, until tender and golden, about 10 minutes. Add tomatoes, olives, capers, raisins, and pepper. Reduce heat; cover and simmer 15 minutes.

3. Add eggplant and celery to skillet and cook, uncovered, over medium heat, stirring frequently, until celery is just tender, 8 to 10 minutes. Stir in vinegar and sugar and cook 1 minute longer. Cool to room temperature, or cover and refrigerate up to overnight. To serve, sprinkle with parsley. Makes about 5 cups.

Each ¼ cup: About 106 calories, 1g protein, 9g carbohydrate, 8g total fat (1g saturated), 0mg cholesterol, 336mg sodium.

ROASTED EGGPLANT PARMESAN

....

Eggplant Parmesan usually involves lots of frying, but for our version, the eggplant is roasted, requiring much less oil and much less time.

Prep: 35 minutes plus cooling
Roast/Cook: 55 minutes

- 2 small eggplants (1¼ pounds each), ends trimmed, cut into ½-inch-thick slices
- ¼ cup olive oil
- ½ teaspoon salt
- 1 can (28 ounces) plum tomatoes, drained and chopped
- ¼ teaspoon ground black pepper
- ⅓ cup chopped fresh parsley
- 4 ounces mozzarella cheese, shredded (1 cup)
- ½ cup freshly grated Parmesan cheese

1. Preheat oven to 450°F. Place eggplant slices on two large cookie sheets. Brush oil on both sides and sprinkle with ¼ teaspoon salt. Roast 15 minutes; turn slices and roast until browned and tender, 20 to 25 minutes longer.

2. Meanwhile, in nonstick 12-inch skillet, combine tomatoes, remaining ¼ teaspoon salt, and pepper; heat to boiling over medium heat. Reduce heat to low; cook, stirring occasionally, until tomatoes have thickened, about 20 minutes. Stir in parsley.

3. Turn oven control to 400°F. In shallow 2½-quart casserole, layer half of eggplant and top with half of tomato sauce; sprinkle with half of mozzarella. Repeat layers; top with grated Parmesan.

4. Cover loosely with foil. Bake until bubbling, about 10 minutes. Remove casserole from oven and let stand at least 10 minutes before serving. Serve hot or at room temperature. Makes 6 main-dish servings.

Each serving: About 248 calories, 11g protein, 19g carbohydrate, 16g total fat (5g saturated), 21mg cholesterol, 693mg sodium.

BELGIAN ENDIVE

Availability
Year-round

Peak Season
September through May

Buying Tips
Choose small compact heads with white leaves and pale yellow or deep red tips. Avoid wilted, brown-tipped, or green outer leaves or totally pale green heads. (Belgian endive is grown in the dark; light turns the leaves green and bitter.)

To Store
Wrap in paper towels. Refrigerate in the crisper drawer up to one week.

To Prepare
Trim away any bruised leaves. Rinse briefly under cold running water; Belgian endive is usually quite clean. If using for salad, cut out the tough inner core.

To Cook
Serve Belgian endive raw in salads, with dips, or braise.

BUTTER-BRAISED BELGIAN ENDIVE

....

This meltingly tender endive is deliciously luxurious.

Prep: 5 minutes   Cook: 20 minutes

- 4 tablespoons butter or margarine
- ½ teaspoon sugar
- ¼ teaspoon salt
- 6 large heads Belgian endive, each halved lengthwise

In 12-inch skillet, melt butter with sugar and salt over medium-low heat. Arrange endive in skillet in one layer. Cover and cook, turning occasionally, until tender and lightly browned, about 15 minutes. Remove cover; cook until half of liquid has evaporated, about 5 minutes longer. Makes 6 accompaniment servings.

Each serving: About 79 calories, 1g protein, 2g carbohydrate, 8g total fat (5g saturated), 21mg cholesterol, 178mg sodium.

ESCAROLE

Availability
Year-round

Peak of Season
October through April

Buying Tips
Like chicory and Belgian endive, escarole's bitterness is its attraction. Look for broad heads of escarole with dark green leaves. If the leaves have white ribs, it indicates that the heads were blanched during cultivation, which is similar to the technique used to keep endive white.

To Store
Refrigerate in open plastic bag up to five days.

To Prepare
Trim stems. Wash well in several changes of cool water to remove any grit. Tear into bite-size pieces.

To Cook
Serve raw in salad combined with sweet-tasting greens, or cook like other bitter greens (See Stir-Frying 101 on page 410).

FENNEL

Availability
September through April

Buying Tips
Fennel is also called *finocchio*. Buy firm, compact, unblemished bulbs. The fronds, if attached, should be bright green and sprightly.

To Store
Refrigerate in the crisper drawer up to three days.

To Prepare
Trim off the fronds, if attached. Rinse fennel under cold running water. Trim the root end and remove the stalks. Cut the bulb lengthwise into wedges or slices; trim the central core.

To Cook
The mild licorice flavor and celerylike texture of fennel is accentuated by roasting. Layer with potatoes in a gratin, or braise.

OVEN-BRAISED FENNEL WITH PARMESAN CRUST

·······················

Fennel, with its subtle licorice flavor, takes nicely to being braised. The Parmesan–bread crumb topping is a classic way to finish the dish.

Prep: 15 minutes   Bake: 45 minutes

- 3 medium fennel bulbs (about 1¼ pounds each)
- 1 cup chicken broth, heated
- ½ teaspoon salt
- ¼ teaspoon ground black pepper
- ¾ cup plain dried bread crumbs
- ¾ cup freshly grated Parmesan cheese
- 3 tablespoons extra-virgin olive oil

1. Preheat oven to 400°F. Trim root ends and remove stalks from fennel bulbs. Cut each fennel bulb lengthwise in half. Cut each half into 6 wedges. Arrange wedges in 13" by 9" baking dish.

2. Pour hot broth over fennel; sprinkle with salt and pepper. Cover tightly with foil and bake 30 minutes.

3. In small bowl, combine bread crumbs, Parmesan, and oil.

4. Remove foil from baking dish. Sprinkle bread-crumb mixture over fennel. Bake, uncovered, until top browns and fennel is tender, 15 minutes longer. Makes 8 accompaniment servings.

Each serving: About 170 calories, 7g protein, 19g carbohydrate, 8g total fat (2g saturated), 5g fiber, 6mg cholesterol, 575mg sodium.

GARLIC

Availability
Year-round

Buying Tips
A garlic head should be firm, heavy for its size, and enclosed in dry, papery layers. Do not buy heads that have soft spots or are sprouting. Store-bought chopped garlic is a nice convenience, but nothing beats the flavor of freshly chopped garlic.

To Store
Store at cool room temperature in a well-ventilated area; it will keep for several months. Do not refrigerate.

To Prepare
Separate the garlic cloves from the head as needed. To peel, place a clove on the work surface and place the flat side of a large knife on top. Press down on the knife to lightly crush the garlic; remove the peel.

To Cook
Garlic is an indispensable seasoning, enhancing everything from soups to sauces. It is often used raw. Whole peeled garlic cloves can also be cooked in oil until golden and then removed, once their flavor has permeated the oil. When cooking garlic, take care not to let it brown, or it could turn bitter. Roasting a whole head of garlic (right) mellows its flavor.

ROASTED GARLIC

When garlic is roasted, it turns into a soft, spreadable paste with a tantalizingly sweet, mellow flavor. Try it the classic way: spread on grilled or toasted country-style bread. Or toss some of the garlic with cooked vegetables or hot pasta. Tightly covered, the paste will keep for a week in the refrigerator.

Prep: 10 minutes plus cooling   Roast: 1 hour

- 4 heads garlic
- 2 tablespoons extra-virgin olive oil
- ⅛ teaspoon salt
- ⅛ teaspoon coarsely ground black pepper
- 4 thyme sprigs

1. Preheat oven to 350°F. Remove any loose papery skin from garlic, leaving heads intact. Place garlic on sheet of heavy-duty foil; drizzle with oil and sprinkle with salt and pepper. Place 1 thyme sprig on top of each head.

2. Loosely wrap foil around garlic, folding foil edges securely to keep in oil. Roast until garlic has softened, about 1 hour. Transfer packet to plate. Open carefully and discard foil and herb sprigs.

3. When cool enough to handle, separate garlic into cloves. Squeeze soft garlic from each clove into small bowl and stir until smooth. Makes about 1¼ cups.

Each tablespoon: About 25 calories, 1g protein, 3g carbohydrate, 1g total fat (0g saturated), 0mg cholesterol, 16mg sodium.

ROASTED GARLIC—TASTY AND VERSATILE

Here are some flavorful ways to enjoy roasted garlic:

- Mash roasted garlic with softened unsalted butter. Pack into a small crock and serve as a spread for sliced bread.
- When mashing potatoes, toss in some roasted garlic cloves.
- Whisk roasted garlic into the pan juices after roasting a chicken. Add a squeeze of fresh lemon juice, and you have a fabulous sauce.
- Whisk some roasted garlic into homemade or canned minestrone soup for rich flavor.

- Add roasted garlic to your favorite salad dressing, pesto, or stuffing.
- Dot a homemade pizza or focaccia with bits of roasted garlic for extra flavor.
- After steaming green beans, heat oil in a skillet and sauté some halved cherry tomatoes and roasted garlic. Add the beans, season with salt and pepper, and toss until heated through.
- When making quesadillas, spread a thin layer of mashed roasted garlic over half of each tortilla. Top as desired, then fold each tortilla in half and pan-fry.

GREENS

Availability
Year-round

Buying Tips
Buy clean, crisp (or tender) leaves, free of decay and dirt. Coarse stems or bruised, dried, or yellowing leaves indicate poor quality. Some greens are quite strongly flavored, even spicy. Popular greens for cooking include the following:

Collard greens Wide dark green leaves with thick stems and a pronounced spiciness.

Dandelion greens Spiky green leaves with a slight lemon flavor. Sometimes served raw in salads.

Kale Curly dark green leaves with a mildly bitter taste. Some purple or variegated kales are grown as ornamentals, but they are edible and have a milder flavor than regular kale. Varieties include *Tuscan kale* and *black kale (cavolo nero)*.

Mustard greens Spicy and bitter, with large coarse leaves.

Swiss chard Delicately flavored greens with wide curly leaves. The stems are edible and should be cut off and prepared separately. *Red Swiss chard* has thin red stems and veins.

Also see beet greens (page 393), bok choy (page 394), broccoli rabe (page 394), chicory (page 403), escarole (page 407), napa or Chinese cabbage (page 396), and spinach (page 431).

To Store
Wrap loosely in paper towels and place in a plastic bag. Refrigerate in the crisper drawer up to two days.

To Prepare
Rinse in several changes of cool water to remove all the grit. Drain but do not shake dry. Trim tough stems or ribs. Leave whole, or stack and cut into ½- to 1-inch-wide slices.

To Cook
See Stir-Frying 101, page 410.

SOUTHERN-STYLE GREENS
....

This classic recipe makes a big batch, but it can easily be halved. Be traditional and do what Southerners do: drink the flavorful cooking liquid (pot liquor) or dunk chunks of corn bread into it.

Prep: 30 minutes   Cook: 1 hour 15 minutes

  5 pounds assorted greens, such as kale, collard greens, and mustard greens

1½ pounds smoked ham hocks

  1 medium onion, quartered

  8 cups water

  1 teaspoon salt

     hot pepper sauce

1. Trim and discard stems and tough ribs from greens; rinse well with cool running water. Cut into ½-inch pieces.

2. In 8-quart saucepot, combine ham hocks, onion, water, and salt; heat to boiling over high heat. Add greens in batches, stirring to wilt. Return to boiling. Reduce heat; cover and simmer until very tender, about 1 hour. Discard ham hocks. Serve with hot pepper sauce. Makes 10 accompaniment servings.

Each serving: About 82 calories, 5g protein, 13g carbohydrate, 3g total fat (1g saturated), 2mg cholesterol, 560mg sodium.

STIR-FRYING 101

One of the best ways to serve nutritious greens is to stir-fry them, which cooks them just enough to mellow their flavor but retains their bright color. Tough, bitter greens, such as broccoli rabe and collard greens, should be blanched first to tenderize them and to remove some of their bitterness.

PREPARATION

Discard discolored leaves and trim thick stem ends; slice or tear leaves, if necessary. To blanch (if recommended), add greens to *6 quarts boiling water*; cook, uncovered, as directed (begin timing as soon as greens are added), then drain. Now you're ready to let things sizzle.

STIR-FRYING

In 12-inch skillet or wok, heat 1 tablespoon olive oil over high heat until hot. Add 2 garlic cloves, crushed with flat side of chef's knife. Cook, stirring frequently (stir-frying), until golden. Add ⅛ teaspoon salt and stir-fry as directed below. Discard garlic, if desired.

TYPE OF GREENS (1 POUND)	PREPARATION	BLANCH	STIR-FRY
Beet greens	Wash.	No	5 minutes
Bok choy (pak choi, pak choy, Chinese mustard cabbage)	Wash and thinly slice stems. Cut leaves into 1-inch-wide slices.	No	5 minutes
Broccoli rabe (rape, rapini, broccoli di rape)	Wash; trim stems.	5 minutes	5 minutes
Chicory (curly endive)	Wash; tear leaves into bite-size pieces.	No	5 minutes
Collard greens	Wash. Discard stems; cut leaves into 1-inch pieces.	3 minutes	5 minutes
Dandelion greens	Wash.	3 minutes	5 minutes
Escarole (broad-leaf endive)	Wash; tear leaves.	No	5 minutes
Kale, dinosaur kale (lacinato kale, Tuscan kale, black kale)	Wash; discard stems and center ribs. Cut leaves into 1-inch-wide slices.	5 minutes	5 minutes
Mustard greens	Wash.	5 minutes	5 minutes
Napa or Chinese cabbage, celery cabbage	Wash and thinly slice.	No	3 minutes
Spinach	Wash thoroughly.	No	3 minutes
Swiss chard	Wash and thinly slice stems. Cut leaves into 1-inch-wide slices.	No	3 minutes
Watercress	Wash.	No	3 minutes

JICAMA

Availability
Year-round

Buying Tips
Turnip-shaped jicama has thin brown skin and white flesh. It tastes like water chestnuts and ranges in size from one to six pounds. Choose smaller jicama to avoid any woodiness.

To Store
Refrigerate in the crisper drawer up to two weeks.

To Prepare
Scrub under cold running water. Peel and slice to serve raw in salads or with dips, or cut into bite-size pieces; substitute for water chestnuts in stir-fries.

KOHLRABI

Availability
Year-round

Peak Season
May and June

Buying Tips
Bulbs should be pale green or purple, smooth and un-blemished, with fresh-looking tops and tender skin.

To Store
Discard leafy tops. Refrigerate bulbs in the crisper drawer up to one week.

To Prepare
Cut off the stems, then peel the bulb with a vegetable peeler or small knife, being sure to remove the fibrous layer just under the skin. Slice, quarter, shred, or cut into matchstick strips.

To Cook
Kohlrabi can be served raw in salads, sautéed, or simmered. In a medium saucepan, heat 1 inch of water to boiling over high heat; add sliced kohlrabi and heat to boiling. Reduce heat to medium-low; cover and cook until tender, 15 to 30 minutes; drain. Toss with butter.

LEEKS

Availability
Year-round

Peak Season
April through September

Buying Tips
Buy leeks that are straight, with firm white roots and leafy green tops. Avoid leeks with wilted or yellowish tops or cracked roots.

To Store
Refrigerate in the crisper drawer up to three days.

To Prepare
Cut off the roots and trim the dark green tops, leaving about 1 inch of the pale green area. Leeks have sand hidden between their layers and should be washed carefully. Cut the leeks lengthwise, almost halfway through, leaving 2 to 3 inches of the root ends uncut. Rinse the leeks in a large bowl of cold water, swishing to remove all the sand. Or chop the trimmed leeks and swish in a bowl of cold water. With a slotted spoon, transfer to a colander to drain.

BRAISED LEEKS

Chopped leeks braised with a bit of butter make a divine side dish for mild-flavored fish.

Prep: 10 minutes   Cook: 15 minutes

- 1 bunch leeks (about 1½ pounds)
- 1 tablespoon butter or margarine
- ⅛ teaspoon salt
- ¼ cup water

1. Cut off roots and trim dark green tops from leeks; cut each leek lengthwise in half, then crosswise into ½-inch-thick slices. Rinse leeks in large bowl of cold water, swishing to remove sand. Transfer to colander to drain, leaving sand in bottom of bowl.

(continued)

Leeks Vinaigrette

2. In 2-quart saucepan, combine leeks, butter, salt, and water; heat to boiling over high heat. Reduce heat; cover and simmer until just tender, about 5 minutes. Remove cover; cook until water has evaporated, about 5 minutes longer. Makes 4 accompaniment servings.

Each serving: About 68 calories, 1g protein, 10g carbohydrate, 3g total fat (2g saturated), 8mg cholesterol, 116mg sodium.

LEEKS VINAIGRETTE

·······································

If you can find only large leeks, use just four. Cook them until tender (they'll take a bit longer), then cut lengthwise in half to serve.

Prep: 25 minutes   Cook: 10 minutes

  8 slender leeks (2½ pounds)
2⅛ teaspoons salt
  1 tablespoon red wine vinegar
  1 teaspoon Dijon mustard
     pinch ground black pepper
  2 tablespoons olive oil
  1 tablespoon chopped fresh parsley

1. In 5-quart Dutch oven, heat *3 quarts water* to boiling over high heat. Meanwhile, cut off roots from leeks and trim leeks to 6 inches; discard green tops. Beginning at green end, make 4-inch-long slit in each leek, cutting almost halfway through, leaving 2 inches of root end uncut. Rinse leeks in large bowl of cold water, swishing to remove sand. Transfer to colander to drain, leaving sand in bottom of bowl.

2. Add leeks and 2 teaspoons salt to boiling water in Dutch oven; cook until tender, about 10 minutes. Transfer leeks to colander; rinse with cold running water. Drain; pat dry.

3. Prepare vinaigrette: In small bowl, with wire whisk, mix vinegar, mustard, remaining ⅛ teaspoon salt, and pepper until blended. In thin, steady stream, whisk in oil until blended, then whisk in parsley.

4. Arrange leeks on serving platter in single layer. Spoon vinaigrette over. Makes 4 first-course servings.

Each serving: About 146 calories, 2g protein, 20g carbohydrate, 7g total fat (1g saturated), 0mg cholesterol, 424mg sodium.

MUSHROOMS

Availability
Year-round

Buying Tips
Mushrooms generally fall into three categories: *common*, *wild*, and *exotic*. Common mushrooms are the familiar *white button* variety. Wild mushrooms are foraged from forests and are strictly seasonal: They include the

chanterelle, morel, and *porcini.* Exotic mushrooms are sometimes called wild mushrooms, but they are really just unusual cultivated varieties. Some exotic mushrooms include *shiitake* (meaty-tasting and often used in stir-fries), *oyster* (mild-flavored and smooth-textured), *enoki* (long thin white stems with tiny caps), *portobello* (very large with somewhat flat caps and a rich meaty flavor), and *cremini* (small portobellos with dark brown caps). Buy firm mushrooms with tightly closed gills (dark undersides). Mushrooms should never be withered, wrinkled, or show any sign of moisture.

To Store

Place mushrooms (unwashed) in a brown paper bag. Refrigerate up to three days.

To Prepare

Do not peel mushrooms. Rinse them briefly under cold running water and drain well on paper towels. The tough stems of shiitake mushrooms must be removed; trim the stem ends of other varieties. Leave mushrooms whole or prepare as the recipe directs.

SAUTÉED MIXED MUSHROOMS

This classic French preparation brings out the meaty texture and earthy flavor of mushrooms. Use just one variety, if you prefer.

Prep: 15 minutes   Cook: 10 minutes

2 tablespoons butter or margarine
¼ cup minced shallots
8 ounces white mushrooms, trimmed and quartered
4 ounces shiitake mushrooms, stems removed and caps cut into 1-inch-thick slices
4 ounces oyster mushrooms, cut in half if large
¼ teaspoon salt
⅛ teaspoon ground black pepper
⅛ teaspoon dried thyme
1 small garlic clove, finely chopped
1 tablespoon chopped fresh parsley

In 12-inch skillet, melt butter over medium-high heat. Add shallots and cook, stirring, 1 minute. Stir in white, shiitake, and oyster mushrooms. Sprinkle with salt, pepper, and thyme and cook, stirring frequently, until mushrooms are tender and liquid has evaporated, about 8 minutes. Stir in garlic and parsley and cook 1 minute longer. Makes 4 accompaniment servings.

Each serving: About 86 calories, 3g protein, 7g carbohydrate, 6g total fat (4g saturated), 16mg cholesterol, 207mg sodium.

LEMON-MARINATED MUSHROOMS

A generous addition of shallots and a hit of fresh lemon juice bring out the flavor of the mushrooms.

Prep: 15 minutes plus standing

1 pound small mushrooms, trimmed and cut into quarters
¼ cup minced shallots
¼ cup chopped fresh parsley
5 tablespoons olive oil
1 tablespoon plus 1 teaspoon fresh lemon juice
½ teaspoon salt
¼ teaspoon ground black pepper

In large bowl, combine mushrooms, shallots, parsley, oil, lemon juice, salt, and pepper until mixed. Let stand at room temperature 1 hour, stirring occasionally. Serve, or refrigerate up to 6 hours. Makes 6 accompaniment servings.

Each serving: About 124 calories, 2g protein, 5g carbohydrate, 12g total fat (2g saturated), 0mg cholesterol, 198mg sodium.

MUSHROOM MEASUREMENTS

One pound of fresh white mushrooms equals approximately:

12 large (stuffing) mushrooms

20 medium mushrooms

30 to 40 small mushrooms

5 cups sliced mushrooms

2 cups cooked sliced mushrooms

½ cup cooked finely chopped mushrooms

OKRA

Availability
Year-round

Peak Season
July through September

Buying Tips
Buy tender, young pods less than 4½ inches long, without any brown spots.

To Store
Place in a brown paper bag. Refrigerate in the crisper drawer up to two days.

To Prepare
Rinse okra under cold running water and cut off the stem ends. Leave whole or slice.

FRIED OKRA

....

In this down-home favorite, okra gets a classic cornmeal coating. If pods are small, there is no need to cut them.

Prep: 15 minutes   Cook: 3 minutes per batch

  1 large egg
  12 ounces okra, cut crosswise into 1-inch pieces
  ½ cup cornmeal
  ½ teaspoon salt
  ⅛ teaspoon ground red pepper (cayenne)
     vegetable oil for frying

  1. In medium bowl, lightly beat egg; add okra and toss to coat. On waxed paper, combine cornmeal, salt, and ground red pepper. Add okra and toss to coat.

  2. Meanwhile, in heavy 10-inch skillet, heat ¼ inch oil over medium-high heat until hot. In small batches, fry okra until golden, 2 to 3 minutes. With slotted spoon, transfer to paper towels to drain. Makes 4 accompaniment servings.

Each serving: About 205 calories, 5g protein, 20g carbohydrate, 12g total fat (2g saturated), 53mg cholesterol, 313mg sodium.

ONIONS

Availability
Year-round

Buying Tips
Onions should be firm and clean, with dry, papery skin. Do not buy onions that have sprouted. Yellow *cooking onions* (also called *Spanish* onions) range from small to very large and have a sharp flavor that sweetens and mellows when cooked. *Red onions* have a stronger flavor than yellow onions, and although some people like to cook with them, they are probably best when sliced and served raw in salads. *White onions* are quite mild; they are the preferred cooking onion of many Latino cooks. *Sweet onions,* often named for the location of their harvest, are the ultimate salad onion: *Maui, Walla Walla,* and *Vidalia* are three of the most well known. Most are available in the late spring. *Small white onions* are often called *boiling onions;* they are braised until tender and often mixed with cream sauce. *Pearl onions* are smaller than boiling onions and can be red, white, or yellow.

To Store
Store onions in a cool (60°F or below) dark place (or in the refrigerator) in a container with good air circulation for up to several weeks.

To Prepare
To peel cooking, red, and sweet onions, trim the root and blossom ends, cutting off as little flesh as possible. With a small knife, peel off all the skin, along with the first layer of onion and the slippery membrane. To loosen the skins of small white boiling or pearl onions to make them easier to peel, in a large saucepan, heat 2 inches of water to boiling. Add onions and cook for 1 minute. Drain and rinse under cold running water.

CARAMELIZED ONIONS

....

Sweet glazed onions are perfect with a holiday roast.

Prep: 15 minutes   Cook: 35 minutes

- 2 pounds small white onions
- 3 tablespoons butter or margarine
- 2 tablespoons sugar
- ½ teaspoon salt

1. Peel onions, leaving a little bit of the root end attached to help onions hold their shape.

2. In 12-inch skillet, combine onions and *3 cups water;* heat to boiling over high heat. Reduce heat; cover and simmer until tender, 10 to 15 minutes. Drain well.

3. In same skillet, melt butter over medium heat. Add onions, sugar, and salt; cook, shaking skillet occasionally, until onions have browned, about 15 minutes. Makes 10 accompaniment servings.

Each serving: About 71 calories, 1g protein, 10g carbohydrate, 4g total fat (2g saturated), 9mg cholesterol, 159mg sodium.

CARAMELIZED ONIONS WITH RAISINS
Prepare as directed above but add ½ **cup golden raisins** at end of cooking; heat through.

CARAMELIZED SHALLOTS
Prepare as directed but substitute **shallots** for onions.

CREAMED PEARL ONIONS

....

A traditional Thanksgiving side dish that is great year-round. For a classic look, be sure to use white—not purple—onions.

Prep: 20 minutes   Cook: 20 minutes

- 2 baskets (10 ounces each) pearl onions
- 3 tablespoons butter or margarine
- 3 tablespoons all-purpose flour
- 2 cups milk, warmed
- ¼ teaspoon salt
- ⅛ teaspoon ground black pepper
     pinch ground nutmeg

1. In 10-inch skillet, heat *1 inch water* to boiling over high heat. Add onions; heat to boiling. Reduce heat; cover and simmer until tender, 10 to 15 minutes. Drain.

2. When cool enough to handle, peel onions, leaving a little of root end attached to help onions hold their shape.

3. Meanwhile, prepare white sauce: In heavy 2-quart saucepan, melt butter over low heat. Add flour and cook, stirring, 1 minute. With wire whisk, gradually whisk in warm milk. Cook over medium heat, stirring constantly with wooden spoon, until sauce has thickened and boils. Reduce heat and simmer, stirring frequently, 3 minutes. Stir in salt, pepper, and nutmeg; remove from heat.

4. Return onions to skillet. Add white sauce and cook, stirring, until heated through. Makes 10 accompaniment servings.

Each serving: About 87 calories, 2g protein, 8g carbohydrate, 5g total fat (3g saturated), 16mg cholesterol, 121mg sodium.

CREAMED ONIONS AND PEAS
Prepare as directed above but add **1 package (10 ounces) frozen peas,** thawed, to onions with sauce.

GREEN ONIONS, SCALLIONS, RAMPS, AND SHALLOTS

Availability
Green onions, scallions, and shallots, year-round; ramps, late March, April, and May

Buying Tips
Green onions are the shoots of any onion before the bulb has formed. *Scallions* are the shoots of white onions, although in some parts of the United States, the word *scallion* is used to mean any green onion. *Ramps* are tender wild onions that shoot up in the forests of West Virginia; they are very strong and should be used judiciously. *Shallots* are made up of bulbs containing two or three cloves each (similar to garlic). They have a complex flavor and are an integral part of French cooking.

SAUTÉED GREEN ONIONS

Try these as a light side dish or as a topping for fish.

Prep: 15 minutes   Cook: 8 minutes

- 1   tablespoon vegetable oil
- 5   bunches green onions, cut into 2-inch pieces (2½ cups)
- ½   teaspoon freshly grated lemon peel
- ¼   teaspoon salt
- ⅛   teaspoon coarsely ground black pepper
- ½   cup water

In 12-inch skillet, heat oil over medium-high heat. Add green onions, lemon peel, salt, and pepper and cook, stirring frequently, 2 minutes. Add water and cook, stirring, until green onions are tender and lightly browned and liquid has evaporated, 5 to 7 minutes longer. Makes 4 accompaniment servings.

Each serving: About 52 calories, 1g protein, 5g carbohydrate, 4g total fat (0g saturated), 0mg cholesterol, 154mg sodium.

PARSNIPS

Availability
Year-round, but less plentiful in April, May, and September

Buying Tips
Look for smooth, firm, well-shaped medium parsnips. Avoid large coarse roots and gray or soft spots.

To Store
Place in a plastic bag with a few holes poked in it. Refrigerate in the crisper drawer up to two weeks.

To Prepare
Scrub under cold running water. Trim the ends and peel. Leave whole, slice, cut lengthwise in half, or cut into quarters.

PURÉED PARSNIPS

When puréed, parsnips may look like mashed potatoes, but that's where the similarity ends. They are one of the sweetest of all the root vegetables.

Prep: 15 minutes   Cook: 15 minutes

- 2½   pounds parsnips, peeled and cut into 1-inch pieces
- 1   cup milk, warmed
- 4   tablespoons butter or margarine, softened
- 1   teaspoon salt
- 2   tablespoons chopped fresh parsley (optional)

1. In 4-quart saucepan, combine parsnips and enough *water* to cover; heat to boiling over high heat. Reduce heat; cover and simmer until tender, about 15 minutes. Drain.

2. In food processor with knife blade attached, combine parsnips, warm milk, butter, and salt and puree until smooth. Serve hot, sprinkled with parsley, if desired. Makes 8 accompaniment servings.

Each serving: About 166 calories, 3g protein, 23g carbohydrate, 7g total fat (4g saturated), 20mg cholesterol, 377mg sodium.

PEAS

Availability
Year-round

Peak Season
April, May, and June

Buying Tips
The majority of peas are frozen or canned, so relatively few fresh peas ever make it to market. Frozen peas are a very good, reliable product, and we use them often in our recipes. When buying fresh peas, look for shiny light green pods that feel heavy, indicating they are full of plump medium peas. Large overmature peas tend to be starchy. *Petit pois* are small baby peas. One pound of peas in the pod yields about 1 cup shelled peas.

To Store
Place peas in their pods in a plastic bag. Refrigerate in the crisper drawer up to two days.

To Prepare
Remove the stem and string from each pod. Run your thumb along the length of the "seam" to open the pod and release the peas.

To Cook
To cook fresh peas, in a saucepan, heat 1 inch of water and 1 teaspoon salt to boiling over high heat; add peas and heat to boiling. Reduce heat to medium-high; cover saucepan and cook just until tender, 3 to 5 minutes; drain.

PEAS WITH GREEN ONIONS AND MINT

....

Fresh mint is a very good match for peas; the green onions add an extra touch of flavor.

Prep: 10 minutes   Cook: 6 minutes

2 tablespoons butter or margarine
½ cup chopped green onions
1 bag (20 ounces) frozen peas, thawed
½ teaspoon salt
¼ teaspoon coarsely ground black pepper
¼ cup chopped fresh mint

1. In 10-inch skillet, melt butter over medium heat. Add green onions and cook, stirring frequently, until tender, about 2 minutes. Stir in peas, salt, and pepper and cook, stirring frequently, until heated through, about 3 minutes longer.

2. Remove skillet from heat; stir in mint. Makes 6 accompaniment servings.

Each serving: About 111 calories, 5g protein, 14g carbohydrate, 4g total fat (2g saturated), 10mg cholesterol, 340mg sodium.

SNOW PEAS AND SUGAR SNAP PEAS

Availability
Snow peas, year-round; sugar snap peas, May through August

Buying Tips
Snow peas (also called *Chinese pea pods*) should have fresh-looking, flat, bright green pods; the pods are so tender that they are eaten. *Sugar snap peas*, a variety of snow peas, should look plump, bright green, and crisp. Avoid wilted, mottled, or brown-tipped pods. The peas resemble regular green peas, but the pod is always eaten along with the peas.

To Store
Place in a plastic bag. Refrigerate in the crisper drawer up to two days.

To Prepare
Rinse under cold running water. Remove the stem and the string from each pod; do not shell.

MIXED PEA POD STIR-FRY

···

This sweet and tender-crisp medley celebrates the glorious flavor of fresh green vegetables.

Prep: 15 minutes   Cook: 10 minutes

1 teaspoon salt
8 ounces green beans, trimmed
2 teaspoons vegetable oil
4 ounces snow peas, trimmed and strings removed
4 ounces sugar snap peas, trimmed and strings removed
1 garlic clove, finely chopped
1 tablespoon soy sauce

1. In 12-inch skillet, combine *4 cups water* and salt; heat to boiling over high heat. Add green beans and cook 3 minutes. Drain; wipe skillet with paper towels.

2. In same skillet, heat oil over high heat. Add green beans and cook, stirring frequently (stir-frying), until they begin to brown, 2 to 3 minutes Add snow peas, sugar snap peas, and garlic; stir-fry until snow peas and sugar snap peas are tender-crisp, about 1 minute longer. Stir in soy sauce and remove from heat. Makes 4 accompaniment servings.

Each serving: About 63 calories, 3g protein, 8g carbohydrate, 2g total fat (0g saturated), 0mg cholesterol, 844mg sodium.

Mixed Pea Pod Stir-Fry

PEPPERS, HOT

Availability
Year-round

Buying Tips
Purchase peppers that will provide the desired amount of heat to fit the recipe and to suit your taste. Depending on the variety of pepper, the degree of heat can range from relatively mild to fiery hot. *Anaheim peppers* are long and tapering, usually green, and among the mildest. *Poblano peppers* are large tapered dark green peppers that are moderately hot and are usually stuffed. The ever-popular *jalapeño pepper* is the workhorse of the well-spiced kitchen. It can be dark green or red and is often quite hot. Long curved *cayenne peppers* can be green or red and are a staple of Indian cooking. *Serrano peppers* are thin and small, with tapered tips, and are hotter still. The hottest of them all are the *habanero* and *Scotch bonnets*: Yellow, red, orange, or green, they resemble deflated little bells, 1 to 2 inches in diameter. They have a distinctive vegetablelike flavor that manages to hold its own even through the incendiary heat.

To Store
Refrigerate in the crisper drawer up to one week.

To Prepare
Hot peppers contain capsaicin, a colorless substance that can seriously irritate your skin and eyes. Wear rubber gloves while preparing hot peppers, and avoid touching your face, eyes, or other areas with delicate skin. Wash the gloves and your hands thoroughly with hot soapy water after handling hot peppers.

Remove the stems, seeds, and membranes (ribs) from the peppers. (Most of the heat is in the membranes and seeds; don't remove them if you prefer more heat.) Rinse the peppers under cold running water. Roast and peel Anaheim or poblano peppers (see Roasted Peppers Master Recipe, opposite) before using in recipes.

PEPPERS, SWEET

Availability
Year-round

Buying Tips
Buy peppers that are firm, shiny, and thick-fleshed. Avoid wilted or flabby peppers with cuts or soft spots. *Red peppers* are mature (ripe) *green peppers*, but *yellow* and *purple peppers* are different varieties. Long pale green *Italian frying peppers* are mild flavored and a good substitute for green peppers. *Pimientos* are mild thick-fleshed red peppers that are almost always canned.

To Store
Refrigerate in the crisper drawer up to one week.

To Prepare
Rinse peppers under cold running water. Trim the stem end and remove the seeds and white membranes (ribs). Use peppers whole, cut in half to stuff, chopped, or cut into strips, rings, or matchstick strips.

ROASTED PEPPERS WITH FRESH BASIL

···

These colorful peppers are very versatile. Consider topping them with any of the following items, or a combination: chopped fresh herbs; drained capers; anchovy fillets, drained and chopped; minced garlic; crushed red pepper; chopped pitted olives, such as Kalamata or Gaeta; crumbled feta cheese; or sliced fresh mozzarella cheese.

Prep: 35 minutes

- 2 large red peppers, roasted (left)
- 2 large yellow peppers, roasted (left)
- 1 tablespoon extra-virgin olive oil
- ¼ teaspoon salt or to taste
- ⅛ teaspoon ground black pepper
- 3 large fresh basil leaves, thinly sliced

1. Cut peppers lengthwise into ½-inch-wide strips. Pat dry with paper towels.

2. Place pepper strips on serving platter; drizzle with oil and sprinkle with salt and black pepper. To serve, top with basil leaves, or cover and refrigerate up to overnight. Makes 6 appetizer servings.

Each serving without additional toppings: About 38 calories, 1g protein, 4g carbohydrate, 2g total fat (0g saturated), 0mg cholesterol, 97mg sodium.

ROASTED PEPPERS MASTER RECIPE

1. Preheat broiler. Line broiling pan with foil. Cut each pepper lengthwise in half; remove and discard stems and seeds. Arrange peppers, cut side down, in prepared broiling pan. Place pan in broiler, 5 to 6 inches from heat source. Broil, without turning, until skin is charred and blistered, 8 to 10 minutes.

2. Wrap peppers in foil and allow to steam at room temperature 15 minutes or until cool enough to handle.

3. Remove peppers from foil. Peel skin and discard. If not using right away, place in airtight container and refrigerate up to 3 days or freeze up to 3 months.

5 IDEAS FOR . . . ROASTED RED PEPPERS

Add an instant taste of summer to savory winter dishes with a peck of bright peppers. When you can't—or don't have time to—grill them yourself, grab a 12-ounce jar off the pantry shelf, drain well, and chop, and try them in one of these quick recipes. Each idea below uses 1 jar's worth of peppers.

ROASTED CAULIFLOWER

Preheat oven to 450°F. On foil-lined 15½" by 10½" jelly-roll pan, place 1 head cauliflower, cut into small florets. Drizzle with 2 tablespoons olive oil, and sprinkle with 2 teaspoons chopped fresh rosemary leaves; toss to coat. Spread in single layer, and roast 20 minutes or until cauliflower is browned and tender, stirring once. Add red peppers to cauliflower in pan; toss to combine, then spread evenly. Sprinkle with ½ cup freshly grated Parmesan cheese, and roast 5 minutes longer or until cheese melts. Serves 6.

PEPPER AND EGG SANDWICHES

Spray 12-inch nonstick skillet with nonstick spray; then heat on medium 1 minute. Chop 1 large sweet onion, and cook, covered, 10 minutes or until lightly browned, stirring occasionally. Meanwhile, in bowl, whisk together 8 large eggs, ½ teaspoon salt, and ¼ teaspoon ground black pepper. Add red peppers to onion in skillet. Pour eggs over vegetables; cover and cook 8 minutes or until almost set, stirring occasionally. Sprinkle with 4 ounces shredded provolone cheese (1 cup); cover and cook 2 minutes or until cheese melts. Spoon egg mixture into 4 (6-inch) hero rolls, split. Serves 4.

ARTICHOKE DIP

From 1 lemon, grate 1 teaspoon peel and squeeze 2 tablespoons juice. In bowl, stir lemon peel and juice with 1 tub (8 ounces) vegetable-flavored cream cheese spread, ½ cup chopped fresh basil leaves, and ½ teaspoon ground black pepper until combined. Stir in 1 can (14 ounces) artichoke hearts, well drained and chopped, and red peppers. Serve with vegetable sticks. Makes 3 cups.

PASTA PUTTANESCA

In saucepot, cook 1 pound farfalle pasta as label directs. Meanwhile, in 2-quart saucepan, heat 2 cups jarred tomato-basil sauce, red peppers, ⅓ cup chopped Kalamata olives, ¼ cup chopped fresh parsley leaves, and ½ teaspoon ground black pepper to boiling on medium-high. Simmer on low 4 minutes. Drain farfalle; return to saucepot. Pour sauce over pasta and toss well. Serves 6.

CHICKEN MARSALA

In 12-inch skillet, heat 2 teaspoons canola oil on medium until hot. Add 1 pound chicken-breast tenders, each cut crosswise in half, and cook 6 minutes or until golden on all sides. Add red peppers, ¼ cup Marsala wine, 4 sliced green onions, ¼ teaspoon salt, and ⅛ teaspoon ground black pepper. Increase heat to medium high, and cook, stirring occasionally, 3 to 4 minutes or until liquid is slightly reduced and chicken is no longer pink inside. Serve with brown rice. Serves 4.

PLANTAINS

Availability
Year-round

Buying Tips
Plantains are related to the banana but they aren't as sweet. Unripe green plantains are very hard and starchy and are usually boiled. Ripe yellow plantains have a mild bananalike flavor. Very ripe plantains have dark brown to black skin and are slightly sweet.

To Store
Store plantains at room temperature, but refrigerate if they are very ripe.

To Prepare
Cut plantains crosswise into three or four pieces. Score the peel along the ridges, down to the flesh. Pull the peel away from the flesh and cut into pieces as directed.

GOLDEN SAUTÉED PLANTAINS

These are a great change of pace when you want an unusual side dish. Try them with roast pork or ham. If you can't find plantains, substitute very green unripe bananas; the cooking time may be slightly shorter.

Prep: 10 minutes   Cook: 20 minutes

- 4   tablespoons butter or margarine
- 4   very ripe plantains (2¼ pounds), peeled and cut on diagonal into ½-inch-thick slices
- ½   teaspoon salt or 1 tablespoon brown sugar

1. In 12-inch skillet, melt 2 tablespoons butter over medium-high heat. Add half of plantains and cook until lightly browned, about 5 minutes per side. Transfer to warm platter; sprinkle lightly with half of salt or brown sugar. Keep warm.

2. Repeat with remaining plantains, butter, and salt or brown sugar. Makes 8 accompaniment servings.

Each serving: About 152 calories, 1g protein, 26g carbohydrate, 6g total fat (4g saturated), 16mg cholesterol, 207mg sodium.

POTATOES

Availability
Year-round

Peak Season
October through December; new potatoes, April through June

Buying Tips
Buy potatoes that are well shaped and firm, without any blemishes or sprouts. Large cuts or bruises only mean you will have a lot of waste when peeling. Avoid potatoes with a greenish cast. Potatoes are categorized by the amount of starch in the flesh. *Baking potatoes,* such as russet, Idaho, and Burbank, are quite starchy: when baked, their flesh becomes fluffy and dry. *Waxy potatoes,* such as the red-skinned variety, hold their shape after cooking and are preferred for salads and boiling. When time is short, don't bother to peel them. *All-purpose potatoes,* such as Yukon Gold, have the qualities of both varieties and are, therefore, quite versatile. Not all small potatoes are new potatoes. True *new potatoes* are baby potatoes that have been harvested before they are fully grown; they are a seasonal delicacy worth waiting for.

To Store
Store in a cool (45° to 50°F) dark place with good air circulation, up to several weeks (don't refrigerate). In warmer weather, potatoes will keep up to one week.

To Prepare
If recipe directs, peel the potatoes and remove any "eyes" with the end of the vegetable peeler or the tip of a small knife. If there are any green areas, cut them away. The green is chlorophyll, which is harmless on its own, but can signal the presence of solanine, a plant poison that can be toxic if consumed in very large amounts, such as a 10-pound bag of spuds. Otherwise, scrub the potatoes with a vegetable brush under cold running water.

BASIC MASHED POTATOES

....

Here is our recipe for fluffy potatoes, plus five easy variations. To achieve a perfectly smooth texture, use a ricer or food mill.

Prep: 25 minutes   Cook: 30 minutes

- 3 pounds all-purpose potatoes (9 medium), peeled and cut into 1-inch pieces
- 4 tablespoons butter or margarine, cut into pieces
- 1½ teaspoons salt
- 1 cup milk, warmed

1. In 4-quart saucepan, combine potatoes and enough *water* to cover; heat to boiling over high heat. Reduce heat; cover and simmer until tender, about 15 minutes. Drain.

2. Return potatoes to saucepan. Mash potatoes with butter and salt. Gradually add warm milk; continue to mash until smooth and well blended. Keep warm. Makes 8 accompaniment servings.

Each serving: About 204 calories, 4g protein, 32g carbohydrate, 7g total fat (4g saturated), 20mg cholesterol, 516mg sodium.

MASHED POTATOES WITH GARLIC AND LEMON

Prepare as directed above in Step 1. Meanwhile, with garlic press, press **2 garlic cloves** into 1-quart saucepan with butter and salt. Cook, stirring, over low heat until butter has melted and garlic is golden, 2 to 3 minutes. Add garlic mixture to mashed potatoes with milk; mash. Stir in **2 tablespoons finely chopped parsley** and **1 teaspoon freshly grated lemon peel**.

MASHED POTATOES WITH HORSERADISH

Prepare as directed (above) but add **2 tablespoons bottled white horseradish** with milk.

MASHED POTATOES WITH PARSNIPS

Prepare as directed (above) but substitute **1 pound parsnips,** peeled and cut into 1-inch pieces, for 1 pound potatoes and use only **¾ cup milk.**

LOWFAT-MASHED POTATOES

Prepare as directed (above) but use Yukon Gold potatoes. Omit butter and substitute **3 tablespoons olive oil;** use only **1 teaspoon salt** and use **low-fat (1%) milk.**

MASHED POTATOES WITH CARAMELIZED ONIONS

Prepare as directed (left) in Step 1. Meanwhile, heat **¼ cup olive oil** in 12-inch skillet over medium heat. Add **4 large red onions** (about 3 pounds), thinly sliced, and **¼ teaspoon salt.** Cook, stirring occasionally, until very tender and deep golden brown, about 30 minutes. In Step 2, omit butter and use only **½ cup milk;** coarsely mash potatoes. Stir all but 3 tablespoons caramelized onions into potatoes; heat through. Top with remaining caramelized onions.

LIGHT MASHED POTATOES

....

Fat-free half-and-half gives these potatoes the same silky texture you'd get with heavy cream but without the fat and cholesterol.

Prep: 10 minutes   Cook: 8 minutes

- 2 pounds Yukon Gold potatoes, peeled and cut into 1-inch pieces
- 1 tablespoon butter or margarine
- ¾ teaspoon salt
- ½ cup fat-free half-and-half, warmed
- ¼ teaspoon coarsely ground black pepper

1. In 4-quart saucepan, combine potatoes and enough *water* to cover; heat to boiling on high. Reduce heat to low; cover and simmer 8 to 10 minutes or until potatoes are fork-tender. Reserve ½ cup cooking water; drain potatoes.

2. Return potatoes to saucepan. Mash with butter and salt. Gradually add warm half-and-half, continuing to mash potatoes until smooth and well blended; add reserved cooking water if necessary. Transfer to serving dish and sprinkle with pepper. Makes about 4½ cups or 6 side-dish servings.

Each serving: About 145 calories, 3g protein, 29g carbohydrate, 2g total fat (0g saturated), 2g fiber, 0mg cholesterol, 345mg sodium.

ACCORDION POTATOES

....

Bake this festive dish in the same oven with a holiday ham or Sunday roast. Cut whole potatoes almost all the way through in a series of close vertical slices so they fan out as they cook. Choose potatoes that weigh no more than 6 ounces each; they won't cook in time if too large.

Prep: 20 minutes   Bake/Broil: 1 hour 22 minutes

- 8 medium red potatoes (about 6 ounces each)
- 32 (3-inch) thyme sprigs
- 4 tablespoons butter or margarine, melted
- ½ teaspoon salt
- ½ teaspoon coarsely ground black pepper
- 1 tablespoon chopped fresh parsley
- 1 tablespoon snipped fresh chives

1. Preheat oven to 325°F and grease 13" by 9" baking pan.

2. Set 1 potato on cutting board. With large knife, starting at one end of potato, cut a series of vertical slices about ⅛ inch apart, making sure not to cut all the way through (see photo, right). Repeat with remaining potatoes.

3. Insert a thyme sprig into 4 of the cuts in each potato. Arrange potatoes in prepared pan, cut side up; drizzle butter over the tops. Sprinkle potatoes with salt and pepper; cover baking pan tightly with foil.

4. Place pan in oven on lowest oven rack and bake potatoes 1 hour and 15 minutes or until fork-tender. Remove pan from oven and remove foil.

5. Turn oven control to broil. Place pan with potatoes on rack in broiler at closest position to heat source. Broil until browned on top, 5 to 7 minutes. Sprinkle with parsley and chives. Makes 8 accompaniment servings.

Each serving: About 206 calories, 3g protein, 35g carbohydrate, 16g total fat (4g saturated) 16mg cholesterol, 219mg sodium.

Accordion Potatoes

BABY POTATOES WITH ROSEMARY

....

For the best golden brown potatoes, roast them with olive oil and herbs in a hot oven. Instead of baby potatoes, you can also use larger potatoes cut into bite-size pieces.

Prep: 20 minutes   Roast: 30 to 40 minutes

- 5 pounds assorted small potatoes, such as red, white, purple, or golden, cut in half
- ¼ cup olive oil
- 2 tablespoons chopped fresh rosemary or thyme or 1 teaspoon dried rosemary or thyme
- 1½ teaspoons salt
- ½ teaspoon coarsely ground black pepper

Preheat oven to 425°F. In large roasting pan (17" by 11½"), toss potatoes, oil, rosemary, salt, and pepper to coat. Roast potatoes, turning occasionally, until golden and tender, 30 to 40 minutes. Makes 10 accompaniment servings.

Each serving: About 232 calories, 4g protein, 41g carbohydrate, 6g total fat (1g saturated), 0mg cholesterol, 366mg sodium.

HERBED ROASTED POTATOES

....

Potato chunks tossed with parsley and butter cook into tender morsels when wrapped in foil.

Prep: 15 minutes   Bake: 30 minutes

2   tablespoons butter or margarine
1   tablespoon chopped fresh parsley
½   teaspoon freshly grated lemon peel
½   teaspoon salt
⅛   teaspoon coarsely ground black pepper
1½ pounds small red potatoes, cut in half

1. Preheat oven to 450°F. In 3-quart saucepan, melt butter with parsley, lemon peel, salt, and pepper over medium-low heat. Remove saucepan from heat; add potatoes and toss well to coat.

2. Place potato mixture in center of 24" by 18" sheet of heavy-duty foil. Fold edges over and pinch to seal tightly.

3. Place package in jelly-roll pan and bake until potatoes are tender when they are pierced (through foil) with knife, about 30 minutes. Makes 6 accompaniment servings.

Each serving: About 126 calories, 2g protein, 20g carbohydrate, 4g total fat (2g saturated), 10mg cholesterol, 241mg sodium.

OVEN FRIES

....

A quick way to make crispy "fries" without frying. Just don't crowd them in the pan, or they won't crisp.

Prep: 10 minutes   Bake: 45 minutes

3   medium baking potatoes or sweet potatoes
    (8 ounces each), not peeled
1   tablespoon vegetable oil
½   teaspoon salt
⅛   teaspoon ground black pepper

1. Preheat oven to 425°F. Cut each potato lengthwise into quarters, then cut each quarter lengthwise into 3 wedges.

2. In jelly-roll pan, toss potatoes, oil, salt, and pepper to coat. Bake, turning occasionally, until tender, about 45 minutes. Makes 4 accompaniment servings.

Each serving: About 156 calories, 4g protein, 28g carbohydrate, 4g total fat (0g saturated), 0mg cholesterol, 301mg sodium.

BAKED POTATOES

....

Utterly simple and always satisfying.

Prep: 5 minutes   Bake: 45 minutes

6   medium baking potatoes (8 ounces each), not
    peeled
    choice of toppings: sour cream, butter or
    margarine, shredded Cheddar cheese, snipped
    fresh chives, crumbled cooked bacon (optional)

Preheat oven to 450°F. Wash potatoes and dry with paper towels; pierce with fork. Place directly on oven rack and bake until tender, about 45 minutes. If desired, slash top of potatoes; serve with choice of toppings. Makes 6 accompaniment servings.

Each serving without topping: About 166 calories, 3g protein, 38g carbohydrate, 0g total fat (0g saturated), 0mg cholesterol, 12mg sodium.

TWICE-BAKED POTATOES

Bake potatoes as directed. Cut them lengthwise in half. Scoop potato flesh into bowl; reserve shells. Mash potatoes with **4 tablespoons butter or margarine,** cut into pieces. Stir in **2 cups ricotta or cottage cheese, 1 cup shredded sharp Cheddar cheese,** ½ **teaspoon salt,** and ¼ **teaspoon coarsely ground black pepper.** Spoon into reserved potato shells, mounding slightly. Place in jelly-roll pan; sprinkle with ½ **cup shredded sharp Cheddar cheese.** Bake in 450°F oven 10 minutes longer. Makes 12 servings.

Each serving: About 245 calories, 10g protein, 21g carbohydrate, 14g total fat (9g saturated), 46mg cholesterol, 263mg sodium.

SCALLOPED POTATOES

....

Elegant and easy scalloped potatoes make a great family or company dish. For a variation, 30 minutes before the potatoes are done, generously sprinkle with shredded Gruyère cheese—a classic French treatment.

Prep: 30 minutes   Bake: 1 hour 30 minutes

- 3 tablespoons butter or margarine
- 1 small onion, chopped
- 3 tablespoons all-purpose flour
- 1½ cups milk, warmed
- 1 teaspoon salt
- ⅛ teaspoon ground black pepper
- 2 pounds all-purpose potatoes (6 medium), peeled and thinly sliced

1. Preheat oven to 375°F. In heavy 2-quart saucepan, melt butter over low heat. Add onion and cook until tender, about 5 minutes. Add flour and cook, stirring, 1 minute. With wire whisk, gradually whisk in warm milk. Cook over medium heat, stirring constantly with wooden spoon, until sauce has thickened and boils. Reduce heat and simmer, stirring frequently, 1 minute. Stir in salt and pepper; remove from heat.

2. Grease 9-inch square baking dish or shallow 2-quart casserole. Arrange half of potatoes in single layer in prepared dish; pour half of sauce on top. Repeat layers. Cover and bake 1 hour. Remove cover and bake until potatoes are tender and top is golden, about 30 minutes longer. Makes 6 accompaniment servings.

Each serving: About 199 calories, 5g protein, 28g carbohydrate, 8g total fat (5g saturated), 24mg cholesterol, 484mg sodium.

POTATOES ANNA

....

This potato cake gets its distinctive appearance from weighting the concentric circles of layered sliced potatoes during baking so they stick together. A nonstick skillet makes unmolding a snap.

Prep: 25 minutes   Cook/Bake: 45 minutes

- 4 medium baking potatoes (8 ounces each)
- 3 tablespoons butter or margarine
- ½ teaspoon salt
- ⅛ teaspoon ground black pepper

1. Preheat oven to 425°F. Peel potatoes and cut into paper-thin slices. In oven-safe 10-inch skillet (if skillet is not oven-safe, wrap handle with double layer of foil), melt butter over low heat. Remove skillet from heat. Beginning at outside edge of skillet, arrange one layer of potatoes in circles of slightly overlapping slices. Sprinkle with some salt and pepper. Continue layering potatoes in concentric circles to make two or three more layers, sprinkling each layer with salt and pepper.

2. Lightly grease sheet of foil; place foil, greased side down, on top of potatoes. Place heavy 10-inch skillet on top of foil to weight down potatoes and cook over medium-high heat until underside is lightly browned, 5 to 10 minutes.

3. Place skillet in oven and bake 15 minutes. Uncover and bake until potatoes are tender, about 10 minutes more. Invert skillet onto serving plate. To serve, cut potato cake into wedges. Makes 8 accompaniment servings.

Each serving: About 110 calories, 2g protein, 15g carbohydrate, 5g total fat (3g saturated), 12mg cholesterol, 194mg sodium.

PARMESAN POTATOES

....

Melted Parmesan cheese makes these roasted red potatoes absolutely irresistible.

Prep: 10 minutes   Bake: 30 minutes

- 4 medium red potatoes (5 ounces each)
- ½ cup freshly grated Parmesan cheese
- 1 tablespoon butter or margarine, melted
- ¼ teaspoon coarsely ground black pepper

1. Preheat oven to 450°F. Line jelly-roll pan with foil; lightly grease foil. Cut potatoes lengthwise in half and place, cut side down, on foil. Bake until tender, about 25 minutes.

2. Spread Parmesan on waxed paper. Turn potatoes. Brush cut side of each potato with melted butter, then dip in Parmesan. Return potatoes, Parmesan side up, to jelly-roll pan. Sprinkle with pepper. Bake until Parmesan melts, 5 to 7 minutes longer. Makes 4 accompaniment servings.

Each serving: About 196 calories, 8g protein, 26g carbohydrate, 7g total fat (4g saturated), 17mg cholesterol, 267mg sodium.

POTATO LATKES

....

These potatoes, a must for Hanukkah, are best enjoyed right out of the skillet, but they can be kept warm in a 250°F oven until ready to serve. If you are preparing a large batch several hours ahead, to reheat them, place on a rack set over a cookie sheet in a 375°F oven for about 10 minutes or until piping hot.

Prep: 35 minutes
Cook: 8 to 10 minutes per batch

2½ pounds baking potatoes (4 large), peeled
1 medium onion, peeled
1 large egg
2 tablespoons matzoh meal or all-purpose flour
1 tablespoon chopped fresh parsley or dill
1 tablespoon fresh lemon juice
½ teaspoon baking powder
½ teaspoon salt
¼ teaspoon coarsely ground black pepper
¾ cup vegetable oil for frying
    applesauce or sour cream

1. In food processor with shredding blade attached, or with coarse side of box grater, shred potatoes and onion. Place in colander. With hands, squeeze to press out as much liquid as possible. Place potato mixture in large bowl; stir in egg, matzoh meal, parsley, lemon juice, baking powder, salt, and pepper.

2. Preheat oven to 250°F. In 12-inch skillet, heat 3 tablespoons oil over medium heat until hot. Drop potato mixture by scant ¼ cups into hot oil to make 5 latkes. With back of spoon, flatten each latke into 3-inch round. Cook until underside is golden, 4 to 5 minutes. With slotted spatula, turn latkes and cook until second side is golden brown and crisp, 4 to 5 minutes longer. Transfer latkes to paper towel–lined cookie sheet to drain; keep warm in oven.

3. Repeat with remaining potato mixture, stirring the mixture before each batch and using 3 tablespoons more oil for each new batch. Serve latkes hot with applesauce or sour cream. Makes about 20 latkes or 10 accompaniment servings.

Each latke without applesauce or sour cream: About 208 calories, 3g protein, 18g carbohydrate, 14g total fat (2g saturated), 21mg cholesterol, 152mg sodium.

"LEFTOVER" MASHED-POTATO PANCAKES

....

These pancakes are a great "second act" for leftover mashed potatoes. In fact, plan to make extra so you can enjoy this easy dish the following day.

Prep: 10 minutes   Cook: 6 minutes

1½ cups cold or room-temperature mashed potatoes
2 tablespoons plain dried bread crumbs
1 tablespoon freshly grated Parmesan cheese
1 tablespoon butter or margarine

1. With hands, shape potatoes into eight 2-inch patties. On waxed paper, combine bread crumbs and Parmesan. Coat patties with bread-crumb mixture, patting crumbs to cover.

2. In nonstick 10-inch skillet, melt butter over medium heat. Add patties and cook until golden and heated through, 2 to 3 minutes per side. Makes 4 accompaniment servings.

Each serving: About 129 calories, 3g protein, 16g carbohydrate, 7g total fat (3g saturated), 11mg cholesterol, 319mg sodium.

POTATO AND
ROOT VEGETABLE GRATIN

··

This hearty side can also be served as a satisfying main dish.

Prep: 20 minutes plus standing
Bake: 1 hour 10 minutes

- ³/₄ cup chicken broth
- 2 tablespoons butter or margarine
- 3 medium russet (baking) potatoes (8 ounces each), peeled and thinly sliced
- 1 pound celery root (1 large or 2 small), trimmed, peeled, quartered, and thinly sliced
- 6 medium parsnips (1 pound), peeled and thinly sliced
- 1¼ teaspoons salt
- ½ teaspoon ground black pepper
- 1 cup heavy or whipping cream
- 2 tablespoons snipped fresh chives

1. Preheat oven to 400°F. In shallow 3½- to 4-quart baking pan or shallow casserole, combine broth and butter; place in oven while oven preheats to melt butter, about 5 minutes.

2. Meanwhile, in large bowl, toss potatoes, celery root, and parsnips with salt and pepper until well mixed.

3. Remove baking pan from oven. Add broth mixture to vegetables and stir to coat. Spoon vegetable mixture into same baking pan; cover with foil and bake 40 minutes.

4. Remove pan from oven. In 1-cup liquid measuring cup, heat cream in microwave on High 45 seconds to warm. Pour cream evenly over vegetables.

5. Return baking pan to oven and bake vegetables, uncovered, 30 to 35 minutes longer or until top is golden and vegetables are fork-tender. Let stand 10 minutes before serving. Sprinkle with chives to serve. Makes 16 side-dish servings.

Each serving: About 145 calories, 2g protein, 19g carbohydrate, 7g total fat (4g saturated), 3g fiber, 21mg cholesterol, 255mg sodium.

Potato and Root Vegetable Gratin

PUMPKIN

Availability
September through December

Peak Season
October

Buying Tips
Buy firm, bright-colored pumpkins, free from cuts or nicks. *Mini pumpkins* have a rich, sweet flavor. Other cooking pumpkins include *sugar, cheese,* and *pie pumpkins.* They are often cooked and used for pie filling, but canned solid-pack pumpkin is a very convenient, high-quality product. *Jack-o'-lantern pumpkins* have stringy, watery flesh and are best reserved for Halloween decorations.

To Store

Store pumpkins in a cool dry place up to one month.

To Prepare

Cut pumpkin in half or into quarters; remove seeds and scrape out stringy portions. Cut into large pieces.

To Cook

To steam, in a saucepot, heat 1 inch of water to boiling over high heat; add pumpkin pieces and heat to boiling. Reduce heat to medium-high; cover and cook until tender, 25 to 30 minutes. Drain, cool, and peel. If desired, mash with butter, brown sugar, and cinnamon. Or, if using for pie filling, puree in a blender or food processor with knife blade attached. Do not add other ingredients. Place in a paper towel–lined sieve set over a bowl and let drain to remove excess liquid; puree should have the same thickness as solid-pack canned pumpkin. One pound of uncooked pumpkin yields about 1 cup puree.

RADISHES

Availability
Year-round

Peak Season
Round radishes, April and May; Asian varieties, October

Buying Tips
Radishes should be uniformly shaped, free from blemishes, firm, and bright red (or white, if icicle radishes).

To Store
If not serving within one day, remove leaves and place radishes in a plastic bag. Refrigerate up to one week.

To Prepare
Trim the radish roots and tops, if necessary. Rinse well under cold running water. If using as a garnish or in a relish tray, cut as desired and store in ice water in the refrigerator.

To Cook
Radishes can be sautéed in butter and served as a side dish; their flavor will be reminiscent of turnips.

WHAT ELSE CAN IT DO? VEGETABLE PEELER

Don't underestimate this simple, swivel-bladed tool. For many kitchen tasks, it's handier than a knife (and because the sharp edges face inward, it's safer, too). To expand its repertoire:

• Create elegant chocolate curls or coconut shavings to garnish cakes and other desserts.

• Shave cheese. Make wisps of Parmesan or Romano cheese to garnish your Caesar salad. Thinly slice semi-hard cheeses, like Cheddar or Gouda, for grilled-cheese sandwiches and panini.

• Don't stop at the peel. Shave zucchini or carrots lengthwise; sauté the ribbons in a bit of butter until tender for a yummy side dish.

RUTABAGAS

Availability
Year-round

Peak Season
October through March

Buying Tips
Also called *yellow turnip, wax turnip*, and *Swede*. Rutabagas should be large, heavy, and without any decay or soft spots. Extremely large ones should be passed over, however. Rutabagas are usually coated with a thick protective wax, which isn't a problem, because they are always peeled.

To Store
Store at cool room temperature or in the refrigerator in the crisper drawer up to one month.

To Prepare
Cut rutabaga into quarters; peel using a small knife.

MASHED RUTABAGAS WITH BROWN BUTTER

....

Mashed rutabagas have a silken texture and a slightly sweet flavor. If using older rutabagas, they will take longer to cook.

Prep: 10 minutes   Cook: 30 minutes

- 2 rutabagas (1¼ pounds each)
- 1¾ teaspoons salt
- 4 tablespoons butter or margarine
- ½ teaspoon sugar
- ¼ cup milk, warmed

1. Cut each rutabaga into quarters; peel, then cut into 1-inch pieces. In 4-quart saucepan, combine rutabagas, enough *water* to cover, and 1 teaspoon salt; heat to boiling over high heat. Reduce heat to medium; cover and cook until tender, about 15 minutes. Drain.

2. In food processor with knife blade attached, combine rutabagas, 2 tablespoons butter, sugar, and remaining ¾ teaspoon salt, and puree until smooth, occasionally scraping down side with rubber spatula. With processor running, gradually add warm milk until blended.

3. In small saucepan over medium heat, melt remaining 2 tablespoons butter; cook, stirring, until golden brown (do not let burn).

4. To serve, spoon rutabaga puree into warmed bowl and pour brown butter over. Makes 12 accompaniment servings.

Each serving: About 67 calories, 1g protein, 7g carbohydrate, 4g total fat (3g saturated), 11mg cholesterol, 299mg sodium.

SALSIFY

Availability
Year-round

Peak Season
October through March

Buying Tips
There are two types: a light brown, slender, parsnip-shaped root that is sometimes referred to as "true" salsify and a brownish-black-skinned variety that is much larger and more regularly shaped. They are interchangeable in most recipes.

To Store
Place in a plastic bag. Refrigerate up to one week.

To Prepare
Scrub salsify under cold running water; cut off the tops. Peel and cut as directed. Salsify discolors easily; place peeled pieces into a bowl containing 8 cups of water and 1 tablespoon of lemon juice.

To Cook
Cut the salsify into 1-inch pieces. In a 3-quart saucepan, combine the salsify, 2 quarts water, 1 tablespoon fresh lemon juice, and 1 teaspoon salt. Heat to boiling over high heat. Boil until tender, 10 to 15 minutes. Drain and return the salsify to the saucepan. Add 1 tablespoon butter, ¼ teaspoon salt, and pinch of ground black pepper; cook, stirring frequently, until the butter begins to brown, about 2 minutes. Transfer to a serving dish and sprinkle with parsley.

SPINACH

Availability
Year-round

Peak Season
September through October,
March through April

Buying Tips
Buy spinach with bright
green leaves. Avoid spinach
that is yellowish or wilted. Packaged *curly spinach* is
more strongly flavored than *loose-leaf spinach*. Curly
spinach is better for cooking than delicate flat-leaf
spinach. *Baby spinach*, available in bags, has very tender,
edible stems. Frozen spinach is a very handy and excel-
lent-quality convenience product.

To Store
Place unwashed in a plastic bag. Refrigerate up to two
days.

To Prepare
Trim tough stems. Wash spinach well in several changes
of cool water, swishing to remove all the grit. Transfer to
a colander to drain. To use spinach raw, dry in a salad
spinner or pat dry with paper towels.

SPINACH BASICS:
STEAMING AND SAUTÉING

Steaming and sautéing are the
easiest ways to prepare this nutritious green. For 4 accompaniment
servings, trim and wash two 10-ounce bags or 2
pounds of loose spinach. To steam the spinach, bring
¼ cup water to boiling in a 12-inch skillet. Add the
spinach; cover and cook until wilted, about 3 minutes.
To sauté the spinach, heat 1 tablespoon oil and 1 or
2 cloves peeled garlic in 12-inch skillet. Cook until
garlic begins to color. Add spinach and cover; cook 1
minute. Uncover; stir until spinach is wilted and water
is evaporated.

CREAMED SPINACH

*Parsley adds fresh flavor to frozen spinach, while cream
cheese and sour cream add richness and a delicate tang.*

Prep: 20 minutes   Cook: 15 minutes

- 2 tablespoons butter or margarine
- 3 large shallots, finely chopped (about ¾ cup)
- 2 tablespoons all-purpose flour
- ½ cup milk
- ¾ teaspoon salt
- ¼ teaspoon coarsely ground black pepper
- ⅛ teaspoon ground nutmeg
- 1 small package (3 ounces) cream cheese, softened
     and cut into pieces
- 3 packages (10 ounces each) frozen chopped spinach,
     thawed and squeezed dry
- 1 cup loosely packed fresh parsley leaves
- ¼ cup sour cream

1. In 4-quart saucepan, melt butter over medium-
low heat. Add shallots and cook, stirring frequently,
until tender, about 3 minutes. Add flour and cook, stirring, 1 minute. With wire whisk, gradually whisk in
milk; heat to boiling, whisking constantly. Reduce heat
and simmer, stirring occasionally with wooden spoon,
until sauce has thickened and boils, about 2 minutes.
Stir in salt, pepper, and nutmeg.

2. Remove from heat; stir in cream cheese until
smooth. Stir in spinach, parsley, and sour cream; heat
through, stirring frequently (do not boil). Makes 6
accompaniment servings.

Each serving: About 180 calories, 7g protein, 14g carbohydrate,
12g total fat (7g saturated), 33mg cholesterol, 500mg sodium.

INDIAN-STYLE CREAMED SPINACH

Cook shallots as directed above but stir in **2½ teaspoons minced, peeled fresh ginger, 2 garlic cloves,
finely chopped, ¾ teaspoon each ground coriander
and cumin,** and **⅛ teaspoon ground red pepper
(cayenne).** Cook, stirring, 1 minute. Omit flour, milk,
nutmeg, and cream cheese. Stir in spinach and **¼ cup
heavy cream** and heat through. Stir in sour cream.

Each serving: About 122 calories, 4g protein, 9g carbohydrate,
9g total fat (5g saturated), 28mg cholesterol, 415mg sodium.

SAUTÉED SPINACH WITH GARLIC AND LEMON

....

This lemon-kissed sautéed spinach is packed with folate, iron, calcium, and vitamins A and C—and is so flavor-filled that it's a perfect accompaniment to grilled meat, chicken, or fish.

Prep: 5 minutes   Cook: 6 minutes

- 1   tablespoon olive oil
- 2   cloves garlic, crushed with side of chef's knife
- 2   bags (10 ounces each) spinach, rinsed
- 1   tablespoon lemon juice
- ¼   teaspoon salt

1. In 5- to 6-quart saucepot, heat oil on medium-high until hot. Add garlic and cook 1 minute or until golden, stirring.

2. Add spinach, with water clinging to leaves, in 2 to 3 batches; cook 2 minutes or until all spinach fits in saucepot. Cover and cook 2 to 3 minutes longer or just until spinach wilts, stirring once. Remove from heat. Stir in lemon juice and salt. Makes 4 side-dish servings.

Each serving: About 45 calories, 4g protein, 1g carbohydrate, 4g total fat (1g saturated), 12g fiber, 0mg cholesterol, 305mg sodium.

EGGPLANT AND SPINACH STACKS

....

Thick slices of roasted eggplant are layered with spinach, zucchini, and cheese for a pretty presentation.

Prep: 25 minutes   Roast: 25 minutes

- 1   medium eggplant (1½ to 2 pounds)
- 1   tablespoon plus 3 teaspoons olive oil
- 1   teaspoon salt
- 2   garlic cloves, crushed with garlic press
- ⅛   teaspoon crushed red pepper
- 1   small zucchini (6 ounces), coarsely shredded
- 1   bag (6 ounces) baby spinach leaves
- 1   cup part-skim ricotta cheese
- ¼   cup freshly grated Parmesan cheese
- 2   ripe plum tomatoes, seeded and cut into paper-thin strips
- ⅛   teaspoon cracked black pepper
     fresh thyme leaves for garnish

1. Preheat oven to 450°F. Cut ends from eggplant and discard. Cut crosswise into 8 rounds of equal thickness. Brush cut sides of eggplant slices with 1 tablespoon plus 2 teaspoons oil. Sprinkle slices with ½ teaspoon salt and place in 15½" by 10½" jelly-roll pan. Roast eggplant slices until tender and golden, 20 to 25 minutes, carefully turning slices over halfway through cooking.

2. Meanwhile, in nonstick 12-inch skillet, heat remaining 1 teaspoon oil over medium heat until hot. Add garlic and crushed red pepper, and cook 30 seconds, stirring. Add zucchini and ¼ teaspoon salt, and cook 2 minutes, stirring. Gradually add spinach to skillet, stirring until wilted and water has evaporated, about 3 minutes; set aside.

3. In small bowl, mix ricotta, Parmesan, and remaining ¼ teaspoon salt until blended.

4. Remove pan with eggplant from oven. Mound spinach mixture on 4 of the larger eggplant slices in pan; top with remaining eggplant slices. Mound equal amounts of cheese mixture on each eggplant stack. Return to oven; heat through, about 5 minutes (cheese will melt over side of stacks). With wide metal spatula, transfer stacks to 4 dinner plates; top with tomato slices, sprinkle with black pepper, and garnish with thyme leaves. Makes 4 main-dish servings.

Each serving: About 230 calories, 13g protein, 17g carbohydrate, 14g total fat (5g saturated), 6g fiber, 23mg cholesterol, 795mg sodium.

Sautéed Spinach with Garlic and Lemon

SQUASH, SUMMER

Availability
Year-round

Peak Season
June through August

Buying Tips
Summer squash are picked while very young, before their skins have had time to mature and harden. *Zucchini* is the most common summer squash; some farmers' markets carry *yellow zucchini*. *Crookneck* squash is another popular summer squash. *Pattypan* squash is round and squat with firm flesh. If squash is allowed to mature, the skin will harden and must be removed before cooking. Buy thin-skinned, shiny squash without blemishes or soft spots.

To Store
Refrigerate in the crisper drawer up to three days.

To Prepare
Scrub gently under cold running water. Trim both ends. Do not remove the seeds or skin unless the squash is mature.

ZUCCHINI RIBBONS WITH MINT
·······································

Making long paper-thin strips of zucchini is an out-of-the-ordinary way to prepare it. If you don't have fresh mint, use basil or parsley instead.

Prep: 10 minutes   Cook: 4 minutes

- 4 small zucchini (4 ounces each) or 2 medium zucchini (8 ounces each)
- 1 tablespoon olive oil
- 2 garlic cloves, crushed with side of chef's knife
- ½ teaspoon salt
- 2 tablespoons chopped fresh mint

1. Trim ends from zucchini. With vegetable peeler, peel long thin ribbons from each zucchini.

2. In 12-inch skillet, heat oil over medium heat. Add garlic and cook, stirring, until golden; discard. Increase heat to high. Add zucchini and salt and cook, stirring, just until zucchini wilts, about 2 minutes. Remove from heat and stir in mint. Makes 4 accompaniment servings.

Each serving: About 49 calories, 1g protein, 4g carbohydrate, 4g total fat (0g saturated), 0mg cholesterol, 294mg sodium.

PARMESAN-BROILED SQUASH
·······································

Sure to please kids and grown-ups alike, this quick dish can be made with zucchini, yellow squash, or both.

Prep: 10 minutes   Broil: 7 minutes

- 2 medium zucchini or yellow squash (8 ounces each), each cut crosswise in half, then lengthwise into ½-inch-thick slices
- 1 teaspoon olive oil
- ⅛ teaspoon salt
- ⅛ teaspoon ground black pepper
- ¼ cup freshly grated Parmesan cheese

1. Preheat broiler. In broiling pan without rack, toss zucchini and oil to coat; arrange in single layer and sprinkle with salt and pepper.

2. Place pan in broiler, 5 inches from heat source. Broil until zucchini is tender and begins to brown, 3 to 5 minutes per side. Sprinkle evenly with Parmesan and broil until bubbling, 30 to 60 seconds longer. Makes 4 accompaniment servings.

Each serving: About 54 calories, 4g protein, 4g carbohydrate, 3g total fat (1g saturated), 5mg cholesterol, 190mg sodium.

SQUASH, WINTER

Availability
Year-round, but less plentiful April through July

Peak Season
October through January

Buying Tips
Unlike summer squash, the skin of winter squash is thick and inedible, and the seeds are rarely eaten (except for pumpkin). *Butternut* squash

resembles an elongated pear and has orange-colored flesh. The skin can be removed with a vegetable peeler. *Buttercup* is similar, but turban-shaped with very hard skin. *Acorn* squash has ridges that makes peeling difficult, so it isn't peeled. It has delicious flesh that is enhanced by sweet flavors, such as brown sugar and maple syrup. *Spaghetti squash* has unusual flesh: It separates into pastalike strands when scraped out of the cooked shell. *Delicata* squash has beautiful markings on its skin and its taste is reminiscent of sweet potatoes. *Sweet Dumpling* squash is closely related to Delicata but is round. *Hubbard* squash is very large and has hard, dry, sweet flesh. Buy winter squash with thick, hard skin; tender (softish) skin indicates immaturity and poor quality. Harmless bumpy "warts" appear on some varieties.

To Store
Refrigerate or store at cool room temperature up to two weeks.

To Prepare
Rinse under cold running water. Cut in half, or as directed. Scoop out and discard the seeds and stringy portion.

MAPLE BUTTERNUT SQUASH

••

We've added a generous amount of maple syrup to liven up the flavor of this puree.

Prep: 20 minutes   Cook: 20 minutes

2 medium butternut squash (2 pounds each)
½ cup maple or maple-flavored syrup
4 tablespoons butter or margarine, cut into pieces
½ teaspoon salt
¼ teaspoon ground black pepper

1. Cut each squash lengthwise in half; discard seeds. With vegetable peeler, remove peel, then cut squash crosswise into 1-inch-thick slices.

2. In 5-quart saucepot, heat *1 inch water* to boiling over high heat; add squash. Reduce heat; cover and simmer until tender, about 15 minutes. Drain.

3. In large bowl, combine squash, maple syrup, butter, salt, and pepper. With mixer at low speed, beat until smooth. Spoon puree into serving bowl. Makes 10 accompaniment servings.

Each serving: About 151 calories, 2g protein, 28g carbohydrate, 5g total fat (3g saturated), 12mg cholesterol, 170mg sodium.

BAKED ACORN SQUASH

••

To ensure that the squash sits flat, trim about ¼ inch off the bottom of each half.

Prep: 10 minutes   Bake: 35 minutes

2 small acorn squash or other winter squash (1 pound each), each cut lengthwise in half and seeded
2 tablespoons butter or margarine, cut into pieces
¼ cup packed brown sugar

Preheat oven to 350°F. Grease 13" by 9" baking dish. Place squash, cut side down, in baking pan; bake 30 minutes. Turn cut side up. Place one-fourth of butter and brown sugar in each cavity. Bake until squash is tender and butter and brown sugar have melted, about 5 minutes longer. Makes 4 accompaniment servings.

Each serving: About 181 calories, 1g protein, 31g carbohydrate, 7g total fat (4g saturated), 16mg cholesterol, 69mg sodium.

SPAGHETTI SQUASH WITH TOMATOES

····································

We love the flavor of oven-roasted spaghetti squash, but if you're in a hurry, you can use your microwave.

Prep: 10 minutes   **Cook/Bake:** 1 hour

- 1 medium spaghetti squash (2½ pounds), cut lengthwise in half and seeded
- 3 tablespoons butter or margarine
- 1 garlic clove, finely chopped
- 1 can (28 ounces) diced tomatoes, drained
- ½ teaspoon salt
- ¼ teaspoon ground black pepper
- 2 tablespoons chopped fresh parsley

1. Preheat oven to 400°F. Place squash, cut side down, in jelly-roll pan; pour *¼ inch water* into pan. Bake 45 minutes. Turn squash cut side up, and bake until very tender, about 15 minutes longer.

2. Meanwhile, in nonstick 12-inch skillet, melt 2 tablespoons butter over medium heat. Add garlic and cook, stirring, 1 minute. Stir in tomatoes, ¼ teaspoon salt, and ⅛ teaspoon pepper and cook, stirring, until flavors blend, about 5 minutes. Remove from heat and stir in parsley.

3. Using two forks, scrape out pulp from squash in long strands and place on serving platter. Add remaining 1 tablespoon butter, remaining ¼ teaspoon salt, and remaining ⅛ teaspoon pepper and toss to mix. Spoon tomato sauce over squash. Serve hot. Makes 6 accompaniment servings.

Each serving: About 127 calories, 2g protein, 16g carbohydrate, 7g total fat (4g saturated), 16mg cholesterol, 493mg sodium.

SWEET AND SMOKY SPAGHETTI SQUASH

Prepare as directed in Step 1 (left). Omit butter, garlic, tomatoes, salt, pepper, and parsley. In microwave-safe bowl, microwave **3 slices bacon,** chopped, and **1 onion,** chopped, on High, stirring once, until bacon is browned, about 4 minutes. Using 2 forks, scrape squash pulp onto serving platter. Add bacon mixture, **3 tablespoons maple or maple-flavored syrup,** and ⅛ **teaspoon ground black pepper** and toss to mix.

SOUTHWESTERN SPAGHETTI SQUASH

Prepare as directed in Step 1 (left). Omit butter, garlic, tomatoes, salt, pepper, and parsley. Using 2 forks, scrape squash pulp onto serving platter. Add ¾ **cup mild salsa** and toss to mix. Sprinkle with **crushed tortilla chips.**

ASIAN SPAGHETTI SQUASH

Prepare as directed in Step 1 (left). Omit butter, garlic, tomatoes, salt, pepper, and parsley. Using 2 forks, scrape squash pulp onto serving platter. Add ¼ **cup soy sauce, 1 tablespoon grated, peeled fresh ginger,** and **1 teaspoon Asian sesame oil** and toss to mix.

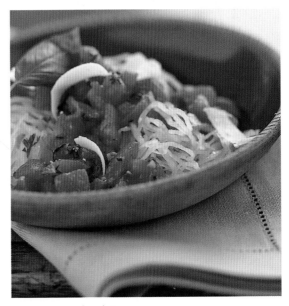

Spaghetti Squash with Tomatoes

ROASTING VEGETABLES 101

Roasting vegetables in the oven produces a rich caramelized flavor and a beautifully browned exterior.

To roast, preheat oven to 450°F. In large bowl, toss 2 pounds of vegetables with 1 tablespoon olive oil, ½ teaspoon salt, and ¼ teaspoon pepper until coated. Spread vegetables in one layer in a shallow 15½" by 10½" roasting pan. Roast until tender and lightly browned, stirring once or twice during cooking. You can roast different vegetables together as long as their cooking times are similar. If using a larger amount of vegetables, divide them between two pans. Overcrowding the vegetables will cause them to steam instead of roast. Rotate pans between upper and lower oven racks halfway through cooking.

SEASONINGS

If desired, you can add other flavorings to the vegetables. Fresh or dried herbs are a wonderful addition to any roasted vegetable. Toss hearty herbs like rosemary, sage, or thyme with the vegetables before they roast, but save more tender herbs like dill, parsley, mint, or oregano for sprinkling on at or near the end of cooking. Roast strips of orange or lemon peel along with the vegetables, or sprinkle on freshly grated peel right after they come out of the oven.

VEGETABLES	HOW TO CUT	ROAST TIME (450°F)	SEASONINGS
Beets 2 lbs. not including tops (about 10 small)	Whole, unpeeled, pricked with fork	1 hour	Peel, quarter, and sprinkle with salt, pepper, and 1 tsp. freshly grated orange peel after roasting
Carrots 2 lbs.	1-inch pieces	30 to 40 minutes	Toss with ½ tsp. pumpkin pie spice before roasting.
Potatoes 2 lbs. unpeeled	2-inch pieces	45 minutes	Toss with 1 tbsp. chopped fresh thyme or 1 tsp. dried thyme before roasting.
Cauliflower 1 medium head (1½ lbs.)	1½-inch flowerets	20 to 30 minutes	Sprinkle with 2 tbsp. chopped fresh parsley after roasting.
Onions 2 jumbo (1 lb. each)	Each cut into 12 wedges	20 to 30 minutes	Brush with mixture of 1 tbsp. brown sugar, 1 tsp. cider vinegar; roast 5 minutes more.
Fennel 2 large bulbs (1 lb. each)	Trimmed and each cut into 12 wedges	35 to 40 minutes	Sprinkle with freshly grated orange peel 2 large bulbs (1 lb. each)
Sweet Potatoes (or Winter Squash) 2 lbs.	Peeled and cut into 1-inch chunks	30 minutes	Toss with 2 tbsp. chopped fresh rosemary before roasting.
Sunchokes 2 lbs.	Whole, pricked with fork	20 to 30 minutes	Sprinkle with 2 tbsp. chopped fresh chives after roasting.
Eggplant 2 medium (1 lb. each)	½-inch-thick slices	20 to 25 minutes	Drizzle with 1 tbsp. extra-virgin olive oil after roasting.
Sweet Peppers 2 lbs.	1-inch-wide strips	30 minutes	Sprinkle with 3 large fresh basil leaves, thinly sliced, after roasting.
Asparagus 2 lbs.	Trimmed	10 to 15 minutes	Sprinkle with freshly grated lemon peel after roasting.
Green Beans 2 lbs.	Trimmed	20 to 30 minutes	Toss with favorite vinaigrette.

SUNCHOKES

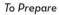

Availability
Year-round

Peak Season
September through March

Buying Tips
Also called *Jerusalem artichokes*. Buy firm, irregularly shaped sunchokes that are free from mold.

To Store
Place in a plastic bag with a few holes poked in it. Refrigerate in the crisper drawer up to two weeks.

To Prepare
Scrub under cold running water. Peel and drop into cold water to prevent discoloration.

SWEET POTATOES

Availability
Year-round

Peak Season
October through January

Buying Tips
There are many varieties of sweet potatoes. What most Americans are familiar with is a rather sweet, moist, orange-fleshed potato with very dark skin. When this variety was introduced in the 1930s, it was marketed as a Louisiana "yam," though it's not a yam at all. To make matters more confusing, in the rest of the world, sweet potatoes have rather dry, slightly sweet, white or yellow flesh. Look for sweet potatoes that feel heavy for their size and have no bruises, soft spots, or sign of sprouting. Handle them gently; they bruise easily.

To Store
Sweet potatoes are quite perishable. Store in a cool dark place up to one week. Do not refrigerate.

To Prepare
Scrub under cold running water.

To Cook
Sweet potatoes are often treated like their savory (white) cousins and mashed, sautéed, fried, or turned into pancakes. To bake, preheat oven to 450°F and bake on a cookie sheet until tender, 45 minutes to 1 hour.

CANDIED SWEET POTATOES

If you wish, sprinkle with toasted sliced almonds (page 692), chopped walnuts, or chopped pecans before serving. Or top with tiny marshmallows and broil until lightly browned.

Prep: 25 minutes   Cook/Bake: 1 hour 20 minutes

- 4   large sweet potatoes (12 ounces each), each peeled, cut crosswise in half, and each half cut lengthwise into 4 wedges
- 2½ teaspoons salt
- ⅓   cup packed brown sugar
- 3   tablespoons butter or margarine, cut into pieces
- ⅛   teaspoon ground red pepper (cayenne)
- 2   tablespoons dry sherry (optional)

1. Preheat oven to 375°F. In 5-quart Dutch oven, combine sweet potatoes, enough *water* to cover, and 2 teaspoons salt; heat to boiling over high heat. Boil until tender, about 10 minutes. Drain.

2. Meanwhile, in nonstick 10-inch skillet, combine brown sugar, butter, remaining ½ teaspoon salt, and ground red pepper; heat over medium heat, stirring, until butter melts, about 1 minute. Stir in sherry, if using. Cook, stirring occasionally, 2 minutes longer.

3. Transfer potatoes to shallow 13" by 9" baking dish and top with brown-sugar mixture. Cover with foil and bake 30 minutes, stirring halfway through baking. Remove foil and bake until syrup is dark and very thick, 30 to 40 minutes longer, stirring halfway through. Makes 8 accompaniment servings.

Each serving: About 201 calories, 2g protein, 39g carbohydrate, 5g total fat (3g saturated), 12mg cholesterol, 499mg sodium.

MAPLE-CRANBERRY
SWEET POTATOES

·····································

This is a pretty and delicious addition to the holiday buffet; a welcome change from the expected casserole.

Prep: 10 minutes plus cooling
Cook/Bake: 50 minutes

5	medium sweet potatoes (4 pounds), peeled
1½	teaspoons salt
1	cup pure maple syrup
1½	cups cranberries (half 12-ounce bag)
3	tablespoons butter (do not use margarine)

1. In covered 6-quart saucepot, heat whole sweet potatoes with 1 teaspoon salt and enough *water* to cover to boiling on high. Reduce heat to low; simmer, covered, about 30 minutes or just until potatoes are fork-tender. Drain. Set aside until cool enough to handle.

2. Meanwhile, in 1-quart saucepan, heat maple syrup to boiling on high. Reduce heat to medium, and boil gently 10 to 15 minutes or until reduced to ½ cup. Stir in cranberries, butter, and ½ teaspoon salt, and cook just until cranberries pop, about 5 minutes longer.

3. Preheat oven to 400°F. Cut cooled sweet potatoes crosswise into 1-inch-thick slices and arrange in shallow 3-quart ceramic or glass baking dish, overlapping slices if necessary.

4. Spoon maple-cranberry syrup evenly over potatoes. Bake, uncovered, 20 minutes or until hot. Makes 10 side-dish servings.

Each serving: About 260 calories, 2g protein, 55g carbohydrate, 4g total fat (2g saturated), 5g fiber, 9mg cholesterol, 230mg sodium.

Tip: You can prepare the sweet potatoes (even arrange them in a casserole) and the syrup up to 1 day ahead and refrigerate them separately. Allow both to come to room temperature before baking. Select sweet potatoes of the same size so they cook evenly.

HEALTHY GINGER-ALMOND SWEET POTATOES

Prepare sweet potatoes as above in step 1. In step 2, instead of maple-cranberry syrup, prepare ginger syrup: In 1-quart saucepan, melt 1 tablespoon butter or margarine over medium heat. Add 2 teaspoons **grated peeled fresh ginger;** cook 1 minute, stirring. Stir in ½

Maple-Cranberry Sweet Potatoes

cup apricot preserves, ¼ cup orange juice, and **½ teaspoon salt;** heat to boiling, stirring. Complete recipe as in steps 3 and 4, spooning ginger syrup over potatoes and sprinkling with ½ **cup toasted sliced natural almonds** (with brown skin still on) before baking.

Each serving: About 230 calories, 4g protein, 45g carbohydrate, 4g total fat (1g saturated), 5g fiber, 0mg cholesterol, 210mg sodium.

BUTTERSCOTCH-SPICE SWEET POTATOES

Prepare sweet potatoes as above in step 1. In step 2, instead of maple-cranberry syrup, prepare butterscotch-spice syrup: In 1-quart saucepan, heat ½ **cup packed brown sugar, 3 tablespoons butter** (do not use margarine), **2 tablespoons water, 1 teaspoon pumpkin pie spice, ¼ teaspoon salt,** and **⅛ teaspoon ground red pepper (cayenne)** to boiling, stirring until smooth; remove from heat. Complete recipe as in steps 3 and 4, spooning butterscotch-spice syrup over potatoes before baking.

Each serving: About 210 calories, 2g protein, 43g carbohydrate, 4g total fat (2g saturated), 4g fiber, 10mg cholesterol, 175mg sodium.

PRALINE SWEET POTATOES

....

These sweet potatoes are great for a crowd. You may prepare the praline up to one week ahead and the sweet potatoes one day ahead. When ready to serve, spread the potatoes in a 9-inch square baking dish. Cover with foil and reheat in a 350°F oven for 45 minutes; remove foil and bake 15 minutes longer, or until heated through. Sprinkle with the praline and serve.

Prep: 30 minutes   Cook: 40 minutes

5	pounds sweet potatoes (8 medium), peeled and cut crosswise into thirds
¼	cup sugar
¼	cup water
1	cup chopped pecans (4 ounces)
5	tablespoons butter or margarine
½	cup milk
1¼	teaspoons salt

1. In 8-quart saucepot, combine sweet potatoes and enough *water* to cover; heat to boiling over high heat. Reduce heat; cover and simmer until tender, about 25 minutes. Drain; return potatoes to saucepot.

2. Meanwhile, prepare praline: Grease cookie sheet. In 1-quart saucepan, combine sugar and water; heat over low heat, stirring gently, until sugar has dissolved, about 1 minute. Increase heat to medium-high and boil rapidly, without stirring, until syrup has turned light golden brown, about 7 minutes. Working quickly, stir in pecans and 1 tablespoon butter until combined and butter melts. Spread pecan mixture in thin layer on cookie sheet; cool.

3. To sweet potatoes in saucepot, add milk, remaining 4 tablespoons butter, and salt. With mixer at low speed, beat sweet potatoes until smooth, frequently scraping down side with rubber spatula. Increase speed to medium; beat until fluffy, about 2 minutes longer.

4. To serve, spoon potatoes into large bowl. Break praline into small pieces and sprinkle on top. Makes 12 accompaniment servings.

Each serving: About 329 calories, 4g protein, 47g carbohydrate, 15g total fat (5g saturated), 17mg cholesterol, 376mg sodium.

TOMATOES

Availability
Year-round

Peak Season
July through September

Buying Tips
Buy firm, plump, unblemished tomatoes. Size is not an indication of quality or flavor. Not so very long ago, only red tomatoes could be found in markets, but now there are orange, yellow, purple, green, and even striped varieties. Most tomatoes are picked unripe and allowed to ripen during shipping and storage. Vine-ripened tomatoes, usually locally grown and available midsummer to early autumn, are picked as close to their flavorful peak as possible and have superior flavor.

Tomatoes are categorized by their shape. Round tomatoes range from the small *cherry tomatoes* to the large *beefsteak* variety. They are especially juicy and excellent in salads. *Plum tomatoes* are oval and have meatier flesh. *Roma tomatoes* are a popular West Coast plum tomato. They are best cooked into sauces. *Green tomatoes* have not been allowed to ripen; they have a nice lemonlike flavor.

To Store
Refrigeration dulls the flavor of tomatoes; only overripe tomatoes should be refrigerated. Store tomatoes, stem side up, at cool room temperature, out of direct sunlight, up to three or four days. As tomatoes ripen, their color deepens, but the amount of natural sugar remains the same.

To Prepare

Tomatoes do not usually have to be peeled before use. But if you wish to peel them, here's how: With a sharp knife, cut a small shallow X in the bottom of each tomato. Lower the tomatoes into a saucepot of boiling water for 1 minute. Remove with a slotted spoon and plunge into very cold water; drain and gently remove the skin with a knife. To seed tomatoes, cut them crosswise in half and gently squeeze to remove the seeds.

CHERRY TOMATO GRATIN

Try using a pint each of red and yellow cherry tomatoes, or substitute grape tomatoes. Either way, this recipe is sure to be a winner.

Prep: 10 minutes   Bake: 20 minutes

- ¼ cup plain dried bread crumbs
- ¼ cup freshly grated Parmesan cheese
- 1 garlic clove, crushed with garlic press
- ¼ teaspoon coarsely ground black pepper
- 1 tablespoon olive oil
- 2 pints ripe cherry or grape tomatoes
- 2 tablespoons chopped fresh parsley

1. Preheat oven to 425°F. In small bowl, combine bread crumbs, Parmesan, garlic, pepper, and oil until blended.

2. Place cherry tomatoes in shallow 1½-quart casserole or 9-inch deep-dish pie plate. Top with breadcrumb mixture and sprinkle with parsley. Bake until heated through and crumbs have browned, about 20 minutes. Makes 6 accompaniment servings.

Each serving: About 72 calories, 3g protein, 7g carbohydrate, 4g total fat (1g saturated), 3mg cholesterol, 121mg sodium.

SAVORY TOMATO TART

(Pictured on page 386)

A show-stopping main dish. For the most color, include the yellow tomato, but it's equally delicious made with all red tomatoes.

Prep: 45 minutes   Bake/Broil: 31 minutes

Pastry for 11-Inch Tart (page 658)
- 1 tablespoon olive oil
- 3 medium onions, thinly sliced
- ½ teaspoon salt
- 1 package (3½ ounces) goat cheese
- 2 ripe medium red tomatoes (8 ounces each), cored and cut into ¼-inch-thick slices
- 1 ripe medium yellow tomato (8 ounces), cored and cut into ¼-inch-thick slices
- ½ teaspoon coarsely ground black pepper
- ¼ cup Kalamata olives, pitted and chopped

1. Preheat oven to 425°F. Prepare dough for 11-inch tart and use to line tart pan as directed. Line tart shell with foil; fill with pie weights or dry beans. Bake 15 minutes. Remove foil with weights and bake until golden, 5 to 10 minutes longer. If shell puffs up during baking, gently press it down with back of spoon.

2. Meanwhile, in nonstick 12-inch skillet, heat oil over medium heat. Add onions and ¼ teaspoon salt; cook, stirring frequently, until very tender, about 20 minutes.

3. Turn oven control to broil. Spread onions over bottom of tart shell and crumble half of goat cheese on top. Arrange red and yellow tomato slices, alternating colors, in concentric circles over onion-cheese mixture. Sprinkle with remaining ¼ teaspoon salt and the pepper. Crumble remaining goat cheese on top of tart.

4. Place tart on rack in broiling pan. Place pan in broiler about 7 inches from heat source. Broil until cheese has melted and tomatoes are heated through, 6 to 8 minutes. Sprinkle with olives. Carefully remove side of tart pan. Serve hot or at room temperature. Makes 6 main-dish servings.

Each serving: About 420 calories, 8g protein, 33g carbohydrate, 29g total fat (15g saturated), 54mg cholesterol, 753mg sodium.

TOMATO-PHYLLO TARTS

···

Store-bought phyllo dough makes for an easy, elegant presentation. The shells can be prepared and baked up to 24 hours ahead, then stored, unfilled, in a tightly sealed container.

Prep: 20 minutes plus cooling   Cook: 12 minutes

- 8 sheets (16" by 12" each) fresh or frozen (thawed) phyllo dough
- 3 tablespoons melted butter or margarine
- ⅓ cup reduced-fat cream cheese or Neufchâtel cheese, softened
- ¼ cup crumbled feta cheese (1 ounce)
- ¼ teaspoon dried oregano
- 3 medium ripe tomatoes (1 pound), cut into 1-inch chunks
- 1 small kirby cucumber (4 ounces), not peeled, cut into ½-inch chunks
- ¼ cup Kalamata olives, pitted and coarsely chopped
- 1 tablespoon extra-virgin olive oil chopped fresh basil for garnish (optional)

1. Preheat oven to 375°F.

2. On work surface, place 1 sheet phyllo; lightly brush with some butter. Place second phyllo sheet on top; lightly brush with some butter. Cut layered phyllo crosswise in half into 2 rectangles. Place 1 rectangle over the other, rotating it so that points of second rectangle are angled slightly away from points of first. Set 6-ounce custard cup or ramekin, right side up, in center of phyllo stack, and gather phyllo up around custard cup to form phyllo shell. Place phyllo shell with cup in 15½" by 10½" jelly-roll pan. Repeat with remaining phyllo and butter to make 4 shells in all.

3. Bake phyllo shells 12 to 15 minutes or until golden. Cool in pan on wire rack 15 minutes; remove cups from shells. Cool shells completely, about 45 minutes.

4. Meanwhile, in medium bowl, stir cream cheese, feta, and oregano until smooth and spreadable. Cover and refrigerate if not using right away.

5. To serve, in large bowl, gently stir tomatoes, cucumber, and olives with oil to coat. Spread scant 2 tablespoons cheese mixture in bottom of each phyllo shell. Spoon vegetable mixture over cheese mixture. Sprinkle with basil, if you like. Makes 4 main-dish servings.

Each serving: About 325 calories, 7g protein, 28g carbohydrate, 22g total fat (10g saturated), 3g fiber, 44mg cholesterol, 540mg sodium.

FRIED GREEN TOMATOES

···

Here's a classic Southern way to fry up green tomatoes. Serve as a side dish or use them in BLT sandwiches for a refreshing change of pace.

Prep: 20 minutes   Cook: 3 minutes per batch

- 6 slices bacon
- 1 large egg white
- ¼ teaspoon salt
- ½ cup cornmeal
- ¼ teaspoon coarsely ground black pepper
- 3 medium green tomatoes (1 pound), cut into scant ½-inch-thick slices

1. In 12-inch skillet, cook bacon over medium heat until browned. With tongs, transfer bacon to paper towels to drain; crumble. Set aside skillet with bacon drippings.

2. In pie plate, beat egg white and salt. On waxed paper, combine cornmeal and pepper. Dip tomatoes in egg mixture to coat both sides, then dip into cornmeal mixture, pressing so mixture adheres. Place on waxed paper.

3. Heat bacon drippings in skillet over medium-high heat. In batches, cook tomatoes until golden brown, about 1½ minutes per side, transferring to paper towels to drain.

4. Transfer tomatoes to platter and top with bacon. Makes 6 accompaniment servings.

Each serving: About 189 calories, 4g protein, 13g carbohydrate, 13g total fat (5g saturated), 15mg cholesterol, 270mg sodium.

SKILLET CHERRY TOMATOES

From start to finish, this cherry tomato side dish takes less than ten minutes.

Prep: 5 minutes   Cook: 3 minutes

- 1 tablespoon butter or margarine
- 1 pint ripe cherry or grape tomatoes
- ⅛ teaspoon salt
  chopped fresh parsley or basil

In 10-inch skillet, melt butter over medium-high heat. Add cherry tomatoes and salt and cook, shaking skillet frequently, just until heated through and skins split, about 2 minutes. Sprinkle with parsley. Makes 4 accompaniment servings.

Each serving: About 36 calories, 0g protein, 2g carbohydrate, 3g total fat (2g saturated), 8mg cholesterol, 107mg sodium.

SKILLET CHERRY TOMATOES WITH GARLIC

Prepare as directed above but add **1 garlic clove,** finely chopped, to skillet with butter.

GREEN TOMATO STACKS WITH LEMON-CHIVE MAYONNAISE

Fried green tomatoes are the basis for this delicious stack of summer. Combine them with juicy red tomatoes, Canadian bacon, and top with a chive-and-lemon-spiked light mayonnaise. Delish!

Prep: 15 minutes   Cook: 8 minutes

- 1 large egg white
- ⅓ cup cornmeal
- ½ teaspoon coarsely ground black pepper
- ¼ teaspoon salt
- 2 medium green tomatoes (6 ounces each), cut into 4 slices apiece
- 2 medium ripe red tomatoes (8 ounces each), cut into 4 slices apiece
- 3 tablespoons olive oil
- 1 lemon
- ⅓ cup light mayonnaise
- 2 tablespoons snipped fresh chives
- 8 slices Canadian bacon

1. In pie plate, with fork, beat egg white. On waxed paper, combine cornmeal and ¼ teaspoon coarsely ground black pepper. Use salt to sprinkle on green and red tomato slices. Dip green tomato slices in beaten egg white to coat, then dip into cornmeal mixture to coat both sides well. Place coated slices on waxed paper.

2. In 12-inch skillet, heat half of oil on medium-high until hot. Add half of green tomato slices, and cook 4 to 5 minutes or until golden-brown on both sides and heated through, turning slices over once and turning heat down to medium if tomatoes brown too quickly. Transfer cooked green tomatoes to plate. Repeat with remaining oil and green tomatoes.

3. Meanwhile, from lemon, grate 1 teaspoon peel and squeeze 2 tablespoons juice. In small bowl, mix lemon peel and juice with mayonnaise, chives, and ¼ teaspoon coarsely ground black pepper; set aside.

4. To same skillet, add Canadian bacon and cook on medium-high 2 to 3 minutes or until lightly browned on both sides and heated through, turning slices over once.

5. To serve, on each of 4 dinner plates, alternately stack slices of red and green tomatoes and Canadian bacon; drizzle with lemon-chive mayonnaise. Makes 4 main-dish servings.

Each serving: About 260 calories, 10g protein, 15g carbohydrate, 19g total fat (4g saturated), 3g fiber, 26mg cholesterol, 820mg sodium.

OVEN-DRIED TOMATOES

Preheat oven to 250°F. Peel 12 plum tomatoes (3 pounds; see page 440). Cut each lengthwise in half; scoop out seeds with small spoon. In large bowl, toss tomatoes with 2 tablespoons extra-virgin olive oil, ½ teaspoon dried basil, ½ teaspoon dried thyme, ½ teaspoon salt, and ¼ teaspoon coarsely ground black pepper. Arrange tomatoes, cut side down, on wire rack set over cookie sheet. Bake until tomatoes are shriveled and partially dried, about 5½ hours. Cool completely, then transfer to a zip-tight plastic bag. Refrigerate up to 2 months, or freeze up to 6 months. Makes 24 tomato halves.

BROILED PARMESAN TOMATOES

....

These warm and juicy tomatoes are a guaranteed hit.

Prep: 10 minutes   Broil: 3 minutes

1   tablespoon butter or margarine
1   garlic clove, finely chopped
¼   cup freshly grated Parmesan cheese
4   small ripe plum tomatoes (3 ounces each),
     each cut lengthwise in half

1. Preheat broiler. In 1-quart saucepan, melt butter over low heat. Add garlic and cook, stirring, until golden; remove from heat.

2. Spread Parmesan on waxed paper. Dip cut side of each tomato in melted-butter mixture, then in Parmesan; place, cheese side up, on rack in broiling pan. Sprinkle any remaining Parmesan on top; drizzle with any remaining butter mixture.

3. Place pan in broiler at closest position to heat source. Broil until Parmesan is golden, 3 to 4 minutes. Makes 4 accompaniment servings.

Each serving: About 72 calories, 3g protein, 4g carbohydrate, 5g total fat (3g saturated), 13mg cholesterol, 151mg sodium.

PEPPERED HONEY TURNIPS

....

The honey added to these turnips helps to bring out their full flavor by caramelizing them.

Prep: 15 minutes   Cook: 25 minutes

½   cup chicken broth
¼   cup white wine
2   tablespoons butter or margarine
1   teaspoon salt
½   teaspoon coarsely ground black pepper
3   pounds small turnips, peeled and each cut into
     8 wedges
¼   cup honey

1. In 12-inch skillet, heat broth, wine, butter, salt, and pepper to boiling over medium-high heat.

2. Add turnips and cook, stirring occasionally, until most of liquid has evaporated, 10 to 12 minutes. Stir in honey; cook, stirring frequently, until turnips are very tender and browned, 13 to 15 minutes longer. Makes 12 accompaniment servings.

Each serving: About 66 calories, 1g protein, 12g carbohydrate, 2g total fat (1g saturated), 5mg cholesterol, 315mg sodium.

TURNIPS

Availability
Year-round

Peak Season
October through March

Buying Tips
Buy firm, unblemished turnips with fresh green tops, if attached. (Turnip greens can be cooked separately, just like beet greens. See Stir-Frying 101, page 410.)

To Store
Refrigerate the tops and turnips separately in plastic bags in the crisper drawer. Store turnips up to one week and the tops up to two days.

To Prepare
Rinse turnips under cold running water; peel. Leave whole, slice, or cut into pieces. Cook the turnips and the tops as directed in recipe.

FOUR-INGREDIENT CANDIED TURNIPS

In 12-inch skillet, combine 1½ pounds turnips, peeled and cut into 1-inch wedges, enough water to cover, and 1 teaspoon salt; heat to boiling over high heat. Reduce heat and simmer until tender, 7 to 10 minutes. Drain; wipe skillet dry.

In same skillet, melt 2 tablespoons butter or margarine over high heat. Add ⅓ cup sugar and cook, stirring, until sugar has turned amber, about 2 minutes. Add turnips and cook, stirring frequently, until well coated and golden, about 5 minutes. Makes 6 accompaniment servings.

VEGETABLE COMBINATIONS

ROOT VEGETABLE GRATIN

....

A gratin is any dish that is topped with either cheese or bread crumbs and then heated until browned. Ours, made with a combination of root vegetables and topped with Gruyère, is a delicious example.

Prep: 25 minutes plus standing
Bake: 1 hour 10 minutes

- ½ cup chicken broth
- 2 tablespoons butter or margarine
- 1½ pounds baking potatoes (about 3 medium), peeled and thinly sliced
- 1½ pounds sweet potatoes (about 3 small), peeled and thinly sliced
- 1 pound celery root (celeriac), trimmed, peeled, and thinly sliced
- 1 pound parsnips, peeled and thinly sliced
- 1¼ teaspoons salt
- ½ teaspoon black pepper
- ⅔ cup heavy or whipping cream
- 6 ounces Gruyère cheese, shredded (1½ cups)

1. Preheat oven to 400°F. In 13" by 9" baking dish, combine broth and butter; place in oven to melt butter.

2. Meanwhile, in large bowl, toss baking and sweet potatoes, celery root, and parsnips with salt and pepper until well mixed.

3. Remove baking dish from oven; add vegetables and stir to coat with broth mixture. Cover dish with foil and bake vegetables 40 minutes.

4. Remove dish from oven. In 1-cup liquid measuring cup, heat cream in microwave oven on High, 45 seconds. Pour cream evenly over vegetables; sprinkle with Gruyère. Bake, uncovered, until top is golden and vegetables are fork-tender, about 30 minutes longer. Let stand 10 minutes before serving. Makes 12 accompaniment servings.

Each serving: About 218 calories, 6g protein, 23g carbohydrate, 12g total fat (7g saturated) 39mg cholesterol, 383mg sodium.

CIAMBOTTA

....

You can vary the vegetables depending on what you have on hand and the flavors you prefer.

Prep: 30 minutes   Cook: 30 minutes

- 3 tablespoons olive oil
- 1 medium onion, chopped
- 2 garlic cloves, finely chopped
- 2 red peppers, cut into 1-inch pieces
- 1½ pounds zucchini (3 medium), cut lengthwise in half, then crosswise into ½-inch-thick pieces
- 1½ pounds ripe tomatoes, peeled and seeded (see page 440), chopped
- ¾ teaspoon salt
- ⅓ cup chopped fresh basil

1. In nonreactive 12-inch skillet, heat 2 tablespoons oil over medium heat. Add onion and garlic and cook, stirring frequently, until onion is tender, about 5 minutes. Add red peppers and cook, stirring frequently, until red peppers are tender-crisp, about 5 minutes longer.

2. Add remaining 1 tablespoon oil and zucchini; cook, stirring, until zucchini is tender-crisp, about 5 minutes. Add tomatoes and salt; heat to boiling. Reduce heat; cover and simmer until vegetables are very tender, about 10 minutes. Stir in basil. Makes 6 accompaniment servings.

Each serving: About 117 calories, 3g protein, 13g carbohydrate, 7g total fat (1g saturated), 0mg cholesterol, 305mg sodium.

MASHED ROOT VEGETABLES

....

Use just one of your favorite root vegetables or a combination of them for mashing with the potatoes.

Prep: 15 minutes   Cook: 25 minutes

- 2 pounds root vegetables, such as carrots, celery root, parsnips, white turnips, or rutabaga, peeled and cut into 1-inch pieces (5 cups)
- 1 pound all-purpose potatoes (3 medium), peeled and cut into 1-inch pieces
- 2½ teaspoons salt
- 3 tablespoons butter or margarine, cut into pieces
- ¼ teaspoon ground black pepper
  pinch ground nutmeg

1. In 4-quart saucepan, combine root vegetables, potatoes, enough *water* to cover, and 2 teaspoons salt; heat to boiling over high heat. Reduce heat; cover and simmer until vegetables are tender, about 15 minutes. Drain.

2. Return vegetables to saucepan. Add butter, remaining ½ teaspoon salt, pepper, and nutmeg; mash until smooth and well blended. Makes 8 accompaniment servings.

Each serving: About 118 calories, 2g protein, 18g carbohydrate, 5g total fat (3g saturated), 12mg cholesterol, 534mg sodium.

SUCCOTASH

We've added bacon to the traditional combo of corn and lima beans, two staples of Native American cooking. As a matter of fact, the name succotash *comes from the Narraganset word for "ear of corn."*

Prep: 10 minutes   Cook: 25 minutes

- 5 slices bacon
- 3 stalks celery, cut into ¼-inch-thick slices
- 1 medium onion, chopped
- 2 cans (15¼ to 16 ounces each) whole-kernel corn, drained
- 2 packages (10 ounces each) frozen baby lima beans
- ½ cup chicken broth
- ¾ teaspoon salt
- ¼ teaspoon coarsely ground black pepper
- 2 tablespoons chopped fresh parsley

1. In 12-inch skillet, cook bacon over medium-low heat until browned. With tongs, transfer to paper towels to drain; crumble.

2. Discard all but 2 tablespoons bacon drippings from skillet. Add celery and onion and cook over medium heat, stirring frequently, until vegetables are tender and golden, about 15 minutes. Stir in corn, lima beans, broth, salt, and pepper; heat to boiling over high heat. Reduce heat; cover and simmer until heated through, 5 to 10 minutes longer. Stir in parsley and sprinkle with bacon. Makes 10 accompaniment servings.

Each serving: About 171 calories, 7g protein, 27g carbohydrate, 5g total fat (1g saturated), 5mg cholesterol, 458mg sodium.

RATATOUILLE

This Provençal classic is very flexible: Serve it hot or cold, or as a first course, salad, or a side dish to accompany meat, poultry, or fish.

Prep: 20 minutes   Cook: 1 hour

- 2 tablespoons olive oil
- 1 medium onion, chopped
- 1 small eggplant (1 pound), ends trimmed, cut into 1-inch pieces
- ¾ teaspoon salt
- ¼ teaspoon ground black pepper
- 1 yellow or red pepper, cut into 1-inch pieces
- 1 medium zucchini (8 ounces), cut into 1-inch pieces
- 2 large garlic cloves, finely chopped
- 1 can (28 ounces) tomatoes, chopped
- ⅛ teaspoon dried thyme
- ¼ cup chopped fresh basil or parsley

In nonreactive 5-quart saucepot, heat oil over medium heat. Add onion; cook, stirring frequently, until tender and golden, about 10 minutes. Add eggplant, salt, and black pepper; cook, stirring frequently, until eggplant begins to brown, about 10 minutes. Stir in yellow pepper, zucchini, and garlic; cook, stirring, 1 minute. Stir in tomatoes with their juice and thyme; heat to boiling. Reduce heat; cover and simmer until eggplant is tender, about 30 minutes. Remove from heat; stir in basil. Makes 8 accompaniment servings.

Each serving: About 81 calories, 2g protein, 12g carbohydrate, 4g total fat (0g saturated), 0mg cholesterol, 384mg sodium.

13
FRUIT

Vitamin-packed, fiber-rich fruits are important components of a well-balanced diet: The USDA recommends two to four servings per day. There are many delicious ways to meet this goal. Enjoy a refreshing fruit salad for lunch, or top a green salad with orange or grapefruit sections. Serve juicy grapes or figs with cheese as a snack or dessert, or slip sliced fruit into a meat sandwich (try sliced peaches with baked ham and Dijon mustard). Toss dried apricots or prunes into braised chicken dishes and beef or lamb stews, or eat ripe fruit out of hand and savor every sweet bite.

BUYING AND STORING FRUIT

Over the years, more and more imported fruit (from Central America, South America, and New Zealand) has appeared in stores, making otherwise out-of-season fruit available. But practically every fruit has a season when it is at its flavorful peak and most reasonable price. Whenever you can, buy fruits in season from local farmers' markets; you will be rewarded with the most delicious produce possible.

Some fruits, such as apples, cherries, citrus fruits, pomegranates, and rhubarb, are purchased fully ripe and can be enjoyed immediately. Other fruits, especially those that have been shipped long distances, need further ripening. These include apricots, nectarines, peaches, pears, and plums. To ripen these fruits, place them in a closed paper (not plastic) bag or fruit-ripening bowl, and leave at room temperature for a few days. Some fruits, such as bananas, kiwifruit, mangoes, melons, papayas, and persimmons, ripen best at room temperature, away from direct sunlight. Refrigerate all ripened fruits to keep them from becoming overripe.

PREPARING FRUIT

All fruits with edible skins should be rinsed well before eating to remove any residual pesticides and surface bacteria. Some fruits, such as apples, are often covered with an edible wax coating to give them an attractive shine. Peel waxed fruit before eating, if you wish.

Nothing beats the flavor of fresh seasonal fruit, but canned fruit is a good pantry staple for a quick lunch or dessert. Some canned fruits are better than others; we are especially fond of pears and apricots. Keep in mind that fruits canned in light syrup have a fresher flavor than those in heavy syrup.

In this chapter, we offer tempting recipes that are easy and delicious for just about every fruit you will find in your supermarket, local produce market, or farmers' market. You'll learn how to choose each fruit, how to store it at home, how long it will keep, and the best way to prepare the fruit for eating out of hand or for cooking. Additional fruit recipes can be found in the Desserts chapter (page 596) and throughout the book.

APPLES

Availability
Year-round

Peak Season
October through March

Buying Tips
Buy firm, crisp apples that are free of brown bruise spots. Apples range in color from yellow to bright green to deep red.

Choose a variety that will work well in your recipe. Use cooking apples for baking and pies. Some apples fall apart when cooked, so they make great applesauce.

Cortland A fine all-purpose apple, this large, round apple remains firm when baked. Cortland is good for fruit salads because the raw slices do not discolor.

Gala This New Zealand import is a cross between Kidd's Orange Red and Golden Delicious. Sweet, crisp, and juicy with red-streaked yellow skin, it is good for cooking.

Golden Delicious Another good all-purpose apple with yellow-gold skin and a sweet flavor. Excellent for eating out of hand, pies, applesauce, and salads.

Granny Smith Very crisp and slightly acidic, this green-skinned apple is named for its original cultivator, an Australian grandmother. Its slices hold their shape well during baking, so it's a good choice for pies.

Jonagold A crisp, yellow-fleshed apple that works well in pies, cobblers, and applesauce.

Macoun A cross between the McIntosh and Jersey Black, it has fragrant white flesh and is a good all-purpose apple.

McIntosh Round and juicy, this apple's flesh softens when cooked. Best for applesauce, eating out of hand, or in combination with firmer apples in pies.

Newtown Pippin A somewhat small apple with tart, firm flesh. Great in pies.

Red Delicious The most familiar red-skinned apple; best for eating out of hand.

Rome Beauty A large, aromatic apple that is excellent for baking whole.

Winesap A crisp pie apple with winelike juice.

To Store
Store apples in the crisper drawer in the refrigerator and use within two weeks.

To Prepare
Rinse apples and core. If the apples (except for Golden Delicious or Cortland) are to be peeled or sliced, sprinkle with lemon juice, vinegar, or a little vinaigrette (depending on their use) to prevent browning.

THE FASTEST BAKED APPLE

Our microwaved apples are ready in minutes. With a generous dollop of plain or vanilla yogurt, they make a nutritious breakfast or dessert.

Prep: 10 minutes   Microwave: 9 minutes

Remove cores from 4 large cooking apples (10 ounces each), such as Romes, but don't cut through to bottom. Peel one-third of way down. Stand apples in small individual bowls or 8-inch square baking dish. Spoon 1 teaspoon butter and 1 tablespoon brown sugar into cavity of each apple. Cover and cook on medium-high (70% power) until tender, about 9 minutes, turning halfway through. Cover and let stand 5 minutes.

Each apple: About 234 calories, 0g protein, 52g carbohydrate, 5g total fat (3g saturated), 10mg cholesterol, 44mg sodium.

MCINTOSH APPLESAUCE

Cooking the apples with the cores and peels adds flavor and body to applesauce, and pressing the mixture through a sieve makes it silky smooth. If the apples you use are red-skinned, the sauce will turn a lovely pink.

Prep: 15 minutes   Cook: 15 minutes

- 1½ pounds McIntosh or other cooking apples (6 small), preferably McIntosh
- ¼ cup water
- ⅓ cup sugar or more to taste
- 1 teaspoon fresh lemon juice

1. Cut apples into quarters but do not peel or remove cores. In 4-quart saucepan, combine apples and water; heat to boiling over high heat. Reduce heat; cover and simmer, stirring occasionally, until very tender, 10 to 15 minutes. Stir in sugar and lemon juice.

2. Press apple mixture through sieve or food mill set over large bowl; discard skins and seeds. Taste and add more sugar, if desired. Serve warm, or cover and refrigerate to serve chilled. Makes about 3½ cups.

Each ½ cup: About 84 calories, 0g protein, 22g carbohydrate, 0g total fat (0g saturated), 0mg cholesterol, 0mg sodium.

GINGER APPLESAUCE

Prepare as directed above but add **1½ teaspoons grated, peeled fresh ginger** to apples.

LEMON APPLESAUCE

Prepare as directed but add **2 strips (2" by 1" each) lemon peel** to apples.

SPICED APPLESAUCE

Prepare as directed above but add **1 cinnamon stick (3 inches)** and **3 whole cloves** to apples. Remove and discard cinnamon stick before straining.

HORSERADISH APPLESAUCE

Prepare as directed above but after straining, stir **2 tablespoons bottled white horseradish** into applesauce. (Serve with pork.)

CRANBERRY APPLESAUCE

Prepare as directed (above) but increase sugar to ½ **cup** and add 1½ **cups fresh or frozen cranberries** to apples.

VERMONT BAKED APPLES

Choose a sweet apple that holds its shape when baked, such as Rome Beauty or Cortland. If you like, serve with whipped cream.

Prep: 10 minutes   Bake: 1 hour

- 6 large cooking apples (7 to 8 ounces each)
- 3 tablespoons butter or margarine
- 1 cup maple syrup or maple-flavored syrup

1. Preheat oven to 350°F. Remove apple cores; beginning at stem end, peel apples one-third of way down. Stand apples in shallow 13" by 9" baking dish. Place 1½ teaspoons butter into cavity of each apple. Pour maple syrup over and around apples.

2. Bake apples, basting occasionally with syrup in baking dish, until tender, about 1 hour. Serve hot, or cover and refrigerate to serve chilled. Makes 6 servings.

Each serving: About 288 calories, 0g protein, 61g carbohydrate, 6g total fat (4g saturated), 16mg cholesterol, 63mg sodium.

Vermont Baked Apples

APRICOTS

Availability
June and July

Buying Tips
Select plump, juicy-looking, orange-yellow fruit; ripe apricots will yield to gentle pressure.

To Store
Handle carefully; apricots bruise easily. Ripen at room temperature, then refrigerate for up to three days.

To Prepare
Wash apricots and cut in half to remove the pit; peel if desired. If the apricots are not to be eaten immediately, sprinkle with lemon juice to prevent browning.

BANANAS

Availability
Year-round

Buying Tips
Yellow bananas are supermarket staples, but red and small yellow bananas are also available in some areas. Plantains (page 420) are considered cooking bananas because they are not sweet.

If you want to eat bananas right away, buy solid yellow bananas with some brown flecks. Bananas that are somewhat green will ripen within a few days at room temperature. To hasten ripening, store in a closed paper bag at room temperature.

To Store
After bananas ripen, they can be refrigerated for two or three days. (The skins will darken, but the fruit inside will remain ripe and fresh.) For longer storage, mash the fruit with a little lemon juice, pack into freezer containers (leaving ½-inch headspace), and freeze. Thaw in the refrigerator before using.

To Prepare
Peel and slice or cut bananas up, depending on their use. If they are not to be eaten immediately, sprinkle with a little lemon juice to prevent browning.

FLAMBÉED BANANAS

For our version of this classic dessert, we have added a touch of fresh lemon juice to balance the sweetness of the bananas.

Prep: 5 minutes   Cook: 8 minutes

- 3 tablespoons butter or margarine
- ³/₄ cup packed brown sugar
- 1 tablespoon fresh lemon juice
- 4 ripe medium bananas, each peeled, cut crosswise in half, and then lengthwise in half
- ¹/₃ cup dark Jamaican rum
  vanilla ice cream (optional)

1. In 12-inch skillet, melt butter over medium heat. Stir in brown sugar and lemon juice. Place bananas in single layer in skillet; cook until just slightly softened, about 2 minutes per side. Reduce heat to low.

2. In 1-quart saucepan, heat rum over low heat. With long match, carefully ignite rum; pour over bananas in skillet. Spoon pan juices over bananas until flames die. Serve warm, with ice cream, if you like. Makes 8 servings.

Each serving: About 179 calories, 1g protein, 34g carbohydrate, 5g total fat (3g saturated), 12mg cholesterol, 53mg sodium.

BERRIES

Availability
Year-round, depending on variety

Peak Season
June through October

Buying Tips
Berries should be plump, uniformly colored, and free of stems and leaves. Avoid bruised berries and cartons that are stained with berry juice. Beware of moldy berries and don't be tempted by the dewy-looking water-sprayed berries at the market; the moisture will only accelerate the decaying of the berries.

Blackberries For the best flavor, buy deeply colored berries. Choose large maroon *boysenberries* for their rich, tart taste; deep red *loganberries,* which are long and tangy; medium to large purple *marionberries,* which have small seeds and an intense flavor; and large black *olallieberries,* whose flavor ranges from sweet to tart.

Blueberries The silvery "bloom" on this berry is a natural protective coating and a sign of freshness. Only buy berries that still have their bloom. Blueberries range in color from purplish blue to almost black. Wild blueberries, also called *lowbush berries,* are pea-sized and quite tart; they hold their shape well in baked goods. Look for cultivated berries June through August; wild berries, most easily found along the coasts, in August and September. Refrigerate in their baskets for up to ten days.

Currants Currants are red, white, and black. *Red* and *white currants,* found in farmers' markets in July and August, are sweet enough to eat out of hand and are often used in summer puddings. *Black currants* are made into liqueurs, syrups, and jams.

Dewberries Dewberries resemble blackberries in appearance and flavor, but they grow on trailing ground-running vines.

Gooseberries Ranging in color from green (the most common) to amber to red, tart gooseberries are usually cooked into jams, sauces, or pies. The *Chinese (Cape) gooseberry* is an entirely different species that is covered with a balloonlike papery husk (peel the shell back for a dramatic-looking dessert garnish). Gooseberries are available in June and July. You'll most likely find them in farmers' markets.

Raspberries Red raspberries are the most common, but also look for sweet apricot-colored berries and sweet-tart black raspberries in produce or farmers' markets. If red raspberries have darkened to a dusky shade, they are past their prime. There are two peak seasons: June and July and September and October.

Strawberries Choose bright red berries with fresh green stems still attached: Pale or yellowish white strawberries are unripe and sour. Strawberries do not ripen after they are picked. Local strawberries are available from April to July, but strawberries are found year-round.

To Store
Berries are very perishable and can deteriorate within twenty-four hours of purchase. You can store them in their baskets for a brief period, but to keep them for more than two days, place the (unwashed) berries in a paper towel–lined jelly-roll or baking pan, cover loosely with paper towels, and refrigerate.

To freeze berries, wash and drain, then spread in a single layer in a jelly-roll pan and place in the freezer. Once they're frozen, transfer to a heavy-duty zip-tight plastic bag and freeze for up to one year. Do not thaw or rinse frozen berries before using. Extend the cooking time ten to fifteen minutes for berry pies and five to ten minutes for muffins and quick breads.

To Prepare
Rinse fresh berries just before serving. Remove hulls from strawberries (with a huller or small knife) and any stems from the other berry varieties; drain well.

RASPBERRY-LEMONADE GRANITA

Be sure to use a metal baking pan, not a glass baking dish, when making granita; it will freeze more efficiently. For a variation, layer the granita in wineglasses with fresh raspberries and top each with an emerald-green mint sprig just before serving.

Prep: 20 minutes plus freezing

- 2 to 3 lemons
- ³/₄ cup sugar
- 3 cups water
- 1 pint raspberries

1. From lemons, grate 1 teaspoon peel and squeeze ¼ cup juice.

2. In 1-quart saucepan, heat sugar, lemon peel, and 1½ cups water to boiling over high heat, stirring to dissolve sugar. Remove saucepan from heat; stir in raspberries. Cool sugar syrup to room temperature.

3. In food processor with knife blade attached, blend mixture until pureed. With back of spoon, press puree through sieve into bowl; discard seeds. Stir in lemon juice and remaining 1½ cups water. Pour into 13" by 9" metal baking pan.

4. Cover and freeze mixture about 1½ hours or until frozen around the edges. With fork, scrape ice, mixing it from the edge to the center. Repeat process about every 30 minutes or until mixture turns into ice shards, about 1½ hours.

5. Serve granita right away, spooning shards into chilled dessert dishes or wine goblets. Or, cover and freeze up to 1 month. To serve, let stand about 5 minutes at room temperature to soften slightly. Makes about 8 cups or 16 servings.

Each serving: About 45 calories, 0g protein, 11g carbohydrate, 0g total fat, 0mg cholesterol, 0mg sodium.

FRESH FRUIT WITH RASPBERRY-LIME DIPPING SAUCE

(Pictured on page 446)

Greek-style yogurt has the rich texture of sour cream, making it perfect for sauces.

Prep: 20 minutes

- 1 cup raspberries
- 1 lime
- 1½ cups reduced-fat (2%) Greek (strained) yogurt
- ¼ cup packed light brown sugar
  assorted fresh fruit for dipping, such as strawberries, grapes, cut-up melon, banana or kiwifruit slices, and plum, peach, nectarine, pear, and/or apricot wedges

1. Place raspberries in sieve set over bowl. With back of spoon, mash and press raspberries through sieve into bowl; discard seeds. From lime, grate 1 teaspoon peel and squeeze 1 tablespoon juice.

2. Add lime peel and juice, yogurt, and brown sugar to raspberry puree and stir to combine. If not serving right away, cover and refrigerate up to 1 day.

3. To serve, spoon sauce into serving bowl and place on large platter. Arrange fruit on same platter. Makes about 2 cups sauce or enough for 8 servings.

Each ¼ cup sauce: About 55 calories, 3g protein, 10g carbohydrate, 1g total fat (1g saturated), 2mg cholesterol, 15mg sodium.

GREEK YOGURT

TEST KITCHEN TIP Greek yogurt has recently gained in popularity in the U.S. It has a texture similar to that of sour cream but with the added health benefit of live bacteria, including *Lactobacillus bulgaricus* and *Streptococcus thermophilus*. The yogurt is strained to remove the whey (milky liquid), which is how it gets its thick and creamy texture. Imported Greek yogurt is available in large supermarkets and in health-food stores in full-fat, light, 2%, and 0% fat versions. Unlike sour cream, Greek yogurt can be heated to high temperatures without curdling.

CACTUS PEARS

Availability
October through May

Peak Season
October and November

Buying Tips
Look for brightly colored cactus pears (also called *prickly pears*) minus their sharp spines (to be safe, pick up the fruit with a paper bag to protect your hands). When ripe, cactus pears yield to gentle pressure. Avoid shriveled or dried-out fruit.

To Store
Keep cactus pears at room temperature and use within two or three days.

To Prepare
Wearing rubber gloves or using a paper bag to protect your hands, peel a ripened cactus pear as you would an apple, being sure to cut away spines. Slice for salads, or eat out of hand with a squeeze of lime or lemon juice.

CHERIMOYAS

Availability
November through May

Buying Tips
Pick large, uniformly green cherimoyas (custard apples) without bruises or black-ened skin. Because ripe cherimoyas are very fragile, it is best to choose firm fruit and ripen at home. When ripe, cherimoyas yield to gentle pressure.

To Store
Ripen at room temperature, then refrigerate and use within one or two days.

To Prepare
Wash, then cut lengthwise in half or into quarters. Serve as you would melon wedges. Discard the seeds when eating.

CHERRIES

Availability
Sweet cherries, May through July; tart (sour) cherries, late June to mid-July

Buying Tips
Look for plump, brightly colored cherries with fresh-looking stems still attached; stemless cherries are prone to mold. Avoid fruit that is soft, bruised, or moldy.

Sweet cherries, such as dark red *Bing* or golden *Rainier* (*Royal Anne*) varieties, make delicious summer eating. Fresh *tart* (*sour*) cherries, which can be found in farmers' markets, at roadside stands, and at some supermarkets are excellent in pies.

To Prepare
Wash and remove stems just before using. To use in desserts and salads, remove the pits.

CHERRY BRUSCHETTA

Serve this special bruschetta for afternoon tea or as part of a brunch menu.

Prep: 15 minutes plus standing

- ¾ pound dark, sweet fresh cherries, pitted and cut in half
- 1 tablespoon sugar
- 1 teaspoon fresh lemon juice
- 4 large slices rustic bread, about ¾ inch thick
- ½ cup Neufchâtel or mascarpone cheese or Greek (strained) yogurt

1. In medium bowl, toss cherries, sugar, and lemon juice. Let stand 15 minutes to allow juices to run.

2. Lightly toast bread; cool slightly. Spread bread with Neufchâtel. Cut slices in half; arrange on platter. Spoon cherries with juices on top. Makes 4 servings.

Each serving: About 255 calories, 7g protein, 38g carbohydrate, 9g total fat (5g saturated), 21mg cholesterol, 370mg sodium.

COCONUTS

Availability
Year-round

Peak Season
October through December

Buying Tips
Choose a coconut that is heavy for its size and sounds full of liquid when shaken. Avoid coconuts with moldy or wet eyes (the three indentations at one end).

To Store
Refrigerate and use whole coconut within one week. Shredded fresh coconut will keep in the refrigerator for one or two days.

To Prepare
Pierce two of the eyes using a clean screwdriver or an ice pick and hammer; drain the liquid (or strain and reserve for another use). Bake the coconut in a pre-heated 350°F oven for 15 minutes. Remove it from the oven and wrap in a kitchen towel. With the hammer, hit the coconut to break it into large pieces. With a knife, pry the coconut meat from the shell.

To shred With a vegetable peeler, remove the brown outer skin from the meat. Shred the meat on the coarse side of a box grater or in a food processor fitted with the fine shredding blade. One 1½-pound coconut yields 4 to 5 cups of shredded coconut.

To toast Preheat the oven to 350°F. Evenly spread the shredded coconut in a jelly-roll pan. Bake until delicately browned, 20 to 30 minutes, stirring occasionally to toast evenly.

CRANBERRIES

Availability
September through mid-December

Buying Tips
Berries should be plump and firm, from light to dark red, with a glossy sheen. Avoid shriveled, discolored, or moist berries.

To Store
Refrigerate and use within two weeks. To freeze, place cranberries in the freezer in their original bag.

To Prepare
Rinse the cranberries and remove any stems; discard any shriveled fruit and drain well. To use, do not thaw frozen cranberries, just rinse with cold water and drain.

DATES

Availability
Year-round

Buying Tips
The intensely sweet and moist *Deglet Noor* and *Medjool* dates are the most common. Choose dates that are shiny, plump, and rich golden brown. They are sold with and without pits and packaged or loose.

To Store
Wrap dates tightly in plastic wrap and refrigerate for up to several weeks.

To Prepare
Remove pits, if necessary.

FIGS

Availability
June through November

Buying Tips
Varieties range in color from greenish yellow (*Kadota*) to green (*Calimyrna*) to dark purple (*Black Mission*). Buy slightly firm fruit that yields to gentle pressure. Avoid bruised or very soft fruit, or fruit with a sour odor.

To Store
Figs are very perishable; refrigerate them and use within two days.

To Prepare
Wash figs and remove any stems.

To Serve

Eat figs out of hand, serve them as a first course topped with thinly sliced prosciutto, alongside a salad of mixed greens, or for dessert with a soft, mild cheese.

STUFFED FRESH FIGS

....

In addition to being delicious, figs are a good source of iron, calcium, and phosphorus. In this recipe, the figs are filled with a honey-sweetened ricotta-almond mixture for a lovely dessert. Use any variety of green or black figs.

Prep: 25 minutes

19 fresh ripe small figs (about 1¼ pounds)
¼ cup honey
½ cup part-skim ricotta cheese
¼ cup natural almonds, toasted and chopped

1. On plate, with fork, mash the ripest fig with honey; set aside.

2. With sharp knife, trim stems from remaining figs, then cut a deep X in the top of each, making sure not to cut all the way through to the bottom. With fingertips, gently spread each fig apart to make "petals."

3. In small bowl, combine ricotta and almonds. With back of spoon, press mashed fig mixture through sieve into 1-cup measure.

4. To serve, spoon ricotta mixture into figs. Arrange on platter. Drizzle with fig honey. Makes 6 servings.

Each serving: About 170 calories, 4g protein, 32g carbohydrate, 4g total fat (1g saturated), 4g fiber, 6mg cholesterol, 25mg sodium.

5-MINUTE FRUIT DESSERTS
————————————

NO-COOK RASPBERRY ROMANOFF

In blender, combine 1 cup vanilla ice cream, ½ cup fresh raspberries, ½ cup sour cream, and 2 tablespoons orange-flavor liqueur or orange juice and blend until smooth. Spoon into champagne flutes or parfait glasses and top with additional raspberries.

SANGRIA-STEEPED BERRIES

In medium bowl, combine 1 cup dry red wine, ¼ cup orange-flavor liqueur or orange juice, 2 tablespoons sugar, 1 teaspoon grated fresh lemon peel, and ½ teaspoon grated fresh orange peel. Add 4 cups assorted fresh berries, such as blackberries, blueberries, raspberries, and sliced strawberries. Cover and refrigerate 30 minutes or up to 4 hours to blend flavors.

HONEY-DIPPED FIGS WITH YOGURT

Top individual dessert dishes of plain yogurt with figs that have been brushed with honey and coated with finely chopped walnuts.

GINGERED CREAM AND GRAPES

Serve halved red and green seedless grapes with a dollop of sour cream topped with coarsely chopped crystallized ginger or preserved ginger in syrup.

HONEYDEW FRAPPÉ

In blender, combine 4 cups cut-up ripe honeydew melon (about 2 pounds), 2 tablespoons fresh lime juice, ¼ cup loosely packed fresh mint leaves, and 1 to 2 tablespoons sugar (depending on sweetness of melon) and blend until smooth. Add 3 cups ice cubes and blend until thick and frothy.

MINT MELON CUPS

Toss 1-inch chunks of honeydew and cantaloupe with fresh lime juice and honey. Spoon into wineglasses and garnish with a twist of lime peel.

BROILED AMARETTI PLUMS

Place fresh plum halves, cut side up, in ungreased broiler-safe pan. Sprinkle with crushed amaretti (almond-flavored) cookies and broil just until crumbs have lightly browned and plums are tender. Great with peeled peaches, too.

GRAPEFRUIT

Availability
Year-round

Peak Season
January through April

Buying Tips
Grapefruit can have seeds or be seedless; they can be pink-, red-, or white-fleshed. Select well-shaped firm fruit that is heavy for its size. Brownish discolorations on the skin usually do not affect the eating quality. Avoid fruit that is soft or discolored at the stem end.

Pummelo (also called *pomelo* or *Chinese grapefruit*) looks like an overgrown grapefruit but is sweeter and firmer. Because it is seedy, it should be peeled, seeded, and sectioned like an orange (page 461) before eating.

To Store
Refrigerate grapefruit and use within one to two weeks.

To Prepare
Cut the fruit crosswise in half. With a knife, cut out the sections from between the membranes; leave the sections in place if serving the fruit in the shell. Remove any seeds.

BROILED GRAPEFRUIT

Serve this warm-and-juicy treat at breakfast or as a healthful dessert. Instead of sugar, spoon on one tablespoon of honey or orange marmalade.

Prep: 10 minutes   Broil: 10 minutes

1 medium ruby red or pink grapefruit, cut in half
1 tablespoon brown sugar
1 tablespoon butter or margarine, cut into pieces

1. Preheat broiler. Section grapefruit; remove seeds.
2. Line broiling pan with foil. Place grapefruit halves in pan, sprinkle with brown sugar, then dot with butter. Place pan in broiler, about 5 inches from heat source. Broil until golden on top and heated through, about 10 minutes. Serve hot. Makes 2 servings.

Each serving: About 115 calories, 1g protein, 16g carbohydrate, 6g total fat (4g saturated), 16mg cholesterol, 61mg sodium.

GRAPES

Availability
Year-round, depending on variety

Buying Tips
Grapes bunches should be plump and fresh-looking, with individual grapes firmly attached to their stems. Avoid dry, brittle stems, shriveled grapes, or fruit that is leaking moisture.

Table grapes, which are for eating rather than wine-making (although a few varieties do double duty), are categorized as seedless or with seeds. Seedless grapes, derived from European varieties, include *Thompson, Perlette, Flame,* and *Ruby Seedless.* Grapes with seeds usually are indigenous American varieties and have a distinct musky flavor. Lambruscas, such as the purple *Concord,* pale red *Delaware,* and red-purple *Catawba,* are prized for their pectin-rich juice and make fine jellies. Muscadine grapes, which include the sweet-juiced southern *Scuppernong,* are also great for jellies.

To Store
Refrigerate grapes in their perforated plastic bags, if supplied, and use within one week.

To Prepare
Rinse grapes well and dry with paper towels.

GRAPES WITH SOUR CREAM

Even if you are pressed for time, you can make this easy, delicious treat.

Prep: 10 minutes

2   cups seedless grapes
¼   cup sour cream
1   tablespoon brown sugar

In small bowl, gently stir grapes, sour cream, and brown sugar until well combined. Cover and refrigerate until ready to serve. Makes 4 servings.

Each serving: About 100 calories, 1g protein, 18g carbohydrate, 3g total fat (2g saturated), 6mg cholesterol, 11mg sodium.

GUAVAS

Availability
September through
November

Buying Tips
Depending on the variety, guavas have green to yellowish red skin. Ripe guavas yield to gentle pressure. As with other tropical fruits, it is best to buy firm, uncracked guavas and ripen them at home.

To Store
Ripen fruit at room temperature in a brown paper bag. Refrigerate guavas after ripening and use within two or three days.

To Prepare
Wash guavas and remove the skin. Cut large guavas into pieces for eating out of hand. The tiny seeds are edible but can be cut out before serving, if you wish.

KIWIFRUIT

Availability
Year-round

Buying Tips
Kiwifruit should be slightly
firm with very fuzzy skin. When fully ripe, they yield to gentle pressure.

To Store
Ripen kiwifruit at room temperature; refrigerate after ripening and use within one or two days. Firm, unripened, unwashed kiwifruit can be stored in a plastic bag in the refrigerator for up to several months.

To Prepare
With a sharp knife, peel off the skin, then cut into wedges or slices. Or cut unpeeled fruit crosswise in half and scoop out the pulp with a spoon.

KUMQUATS

Availability
November through April

Peak Season
November through
December

Buying Tips
Buy firm, glossy, bright orange kumquats. They are often sold with some stems and leaves still attached. Avoid soft, blemished, or shriveled fruit.

To Store
Keep kumquats at room temperature for up to two days, or refrigerate and use within two weeks.

To Prepare
Wash the fruit and remove the stems, then cut in half to remove the seeds.

To Serve
Eat the entire fruit, peel and all. Add cut-up kumquats to fruit salads or leave them whole as a garnish.

LEMONS AND LIMES

Availability
Year-round

Buying Tips
The fruits should be firm, brightly colored, and heavy for their size. Pale or greenish yellow lemons usually indicate fruit that is more acidic. Limes should be glossy-skinned; irregular purplish brown marks on the skin do not affect the quality. Avoid soft, shriveled, or hard-skinned fruits.

In addition to the familiar supermarket varieties, two fragrant, distinctively flavored varieties can sometimes be found in well-stocked produce markets. Thin-skinned *Meyer* lemons, more aromatic and sweeter than regular lemons, are favored by West Coast cooks. Small tart *key* limes (also known as *West Indian, bartender,* or *Mexican* limes) are so highly regarded that a pie was created for them. If you can't find fresh key limes, excellent bottled key lime juice is available.

To Store

Keep lemons and limes at room temperature for up to a few days, or refrigerate and use within two weeks.

To Prepare

When grating lemon or lime peel, be sure to grate only the zest (the thin colored part of the peel). The white pith underneath is very bitter. To get the most juice out of lemons or limes, press down on them while rolling them back and forth, or place them in hot tap water for several minutes.

LOQUATS

Availability
April through early May

Buying Tips
Look for fruit with deep orange-yellow skin that yields to gentle pressure.

To Store
Refrigerate loquats and use within two or three days.

To Prepare
For eating out of hand, pull off the peel, cut in half, and remove the large central seeds, or cut up to use in salads.

LYCHEES

Availability
Late May through July

Buying Tips
Lychees are usually found in Asian markets. They have a bumpy, deep reddish brown shell that protects their slightly translucent soft white flesh. Choose blemish-free fruit.

To Store
Refrigerate lychees and use within one or two days.

To Prepare
With your thumb, beginning at the stem, pull off the skin as you would that of an orange; remove the seed (which clings tightly to the fruit). Eat lychees out of hand, or use in salads.

CUTTING A MANGO

With a sharp knife, cut a lengthwise slice from each side of the long flat seed, as close to the seed as possible. Peel seed section; cut off as much flesh as you can; discard seed.

Cut the mango pieces lengthwise into thick wedges. Use a sharp, thin knife to remove the peel from each wedge, cutting close to the peel.

For eating mango out of hand, score the flesh of each piece without cutting through the skin, and gently press on the skin to separate sections for eating.

MANGOES

Availability
Year-round

Peak Season
May through August

Buying Tips
Purchase plump fruit with a fresh, sweet aroma. Some varieties are speckled, but tiny black spots indicate very ripe fruit. Ripe mangoes yield to gentle pressure. Avoid oversoft, shriveled, or bruised fruit.

To Store
Let mangoes ripen at room temperature, then refrigerate and use within two or three days.

BLUEBERRY-MANGO COMPOTE

....

This lively dessert is a celebration of contrasts—appetizing primary colors and sweet versus acidic flavors—each balancing the other for a sweet, refreshing flavor.

Prep: 15 minutes

- 1 tablespoon dark Jamaican rum
- 1 tablespoon fresh lime juice
- 1 tablespoon sugar
- 2 large ripe mangoes, peeled and cut into ³/₄-inch pieces
- 1 pint blueberries

In medium bowl, combine rum, lime juice, and sugar. Add mangoes and blueberries; toss to coat. Cover and refrigerate if not serving right away. Makes 6 servings.

Each serving: About 97 calories, 1g protein, 24g carbohydrate, 0g total fat (0g saturated), 0mg cholesterol, 5mg sodium.

MELONS

Availability
April through December, depending on variety

Buying Tips
Summer melons have a netted rind and thrive in hot climates. Winter melons, which are typically oblong in shape and can be grown in temperate climates, take longer to mature on the vine and appear later in produce markets.

Buy fully ripened melons for the most flavor and sweetness. (Only winter melons ripen after picking.) Melons should feel heavy for their size and exude a fruity aroma from the smooth (blossom) end. Avoid bruised or cracked melons or those with soft or damp spots. (See Watermelons, page 471.)

Canary This winter melon is oval in shape and has a bright yellow rind. When ripe, it gives off a rich aroma. The sweet flesh tastes similar to honeydew. Look for canary melons from mid-June to mid-September.

Cantaloupe Available June through September, this luscious melon has golden or greenish beige skin covered with thick netting. The scar at the stem end should be smooth, without any stem remaining. When ripe, cantaloupe has a sweet aroma and salmon-colored flesh. It should feel tender but not mushy at the blossom end.

Casaba Chartreuse-yellow casaba is round with a point at one end. It has deep lengthwise furrows and cream-colored flesh. When ripe, the rind is a rich yellow (but the stem end may remain light green), and the blossom end will yield to gentle pressure.

Cranshaw (Crenshaw) Globe-shaped, with shallow furrows and a point at the stem end, this winter melon has a gold-green rind that turns completely gold when the melon is ripe. The pink flesh has a rich aroma, and the blossom end yields to gentle pressure. These melons are at their peak from July through October.

Honeydew, Honeyball These melons are similar except that the honeyball is smaller. The rind is cream-colored and covered with patches of netting. When the melon is ripe, the skin should feel velvety and the rind should give slightly. Look for honeyballs from July through November; honeydews year-round.

Although the flesh of the honeydew is usually green, there are several varieties that differ: These include the *Golden Honeydew*, the *Orange Honeydew*, and the *Temptation Honeydew*.

Persian Resembling a large cantaloupe but with finer netting, the Persian melon has a dark green background that turns lighter green when ripe. The skin will yield to gentle pressure when ripe. The orange-pink flesh has a distinctive aroma. Persian melons are available from June through November.

Santa Claus Available in December, this melon is large and oblong with yellow-green flesh and a lightly netted, green-gold rind that turns yellow when the melon is ripe. The blossom end will yield to gentle pressure.

To Store

Let melon ripen at room temperature, then refrigerate and use within two or three days. Keep the melon well wrapped after cutting to prevent it from absorbing odors from other foods.

NECTARINES

Availability
May through September

Peak Season
June through August

Buying Tips
Buy plump, richly colored, smooth-skinned fruit. The color should be deep reddish to yellowish. Slightly firm nectarines ripen well at room temperature. Avoid hard, soft, or shriveled nectarines or any with a large proportion of green skin.

To Store
Let nectarines ripen at room temperature, then refrigerate and use within two or three days.

To Prepare
Wash the fruit, cut in half along the seam line, and remove the pit. Nectarine skin is quite thin, so it does not need to be peeled. To prevent browning, sprinkle with lemon juice.

NECTARINES IN RED WINE

....

Top each serving with a dollop of sweetened sour cream or crème fraîche or with a scoop of strawberry or raspberry sorbet.

Prep: 10 minutes plus chilling

- 2 cups fruity red wine, such as Beaujolais, Shiraz, or Merlot
- 2/3 cup sugar
- 2 1/2 pounds ripe nectarines (about 6 large), pitted and cut into 1/2-inch-thick wedges

In large bowl, stir wine and sugar until sugar dissolves. Add nectarines; cover and refrigerate at least 4 hours or up to 1 day to allow flavors to blend. Serve nectarines with wine in goblets or dessert bowls. Makes about 7 cups or 6 servings.

Each serving: About 225 calories, 2g protein, 43g carbohydrate, 1g total fat (0g saturated), 3g fiber, 0mg cholesterol, 5mg sodium.

ORANGES

Availability
Year-round

Peak Season
December through April

Buying Tips
Eating oranges, such as *Temple* and *navel,* are easily peeled and segmented. Other orange varieties, such as *Valencia, Pineapple,* and *Hamlin,* are valued for their abundant juice. Some specialty markets carry sweet, maroon-fleshed *Moro (blood)* oranges from late winter through early spring. *Bitter oranges* (also called *Seville* or *sour* oranges), which are used in Latino cooking and marmalades, have very thick skins and tart juice.

Oranges should be firm and heavy for their size. A slight greenish color or russeting on the skin does not affect the quality.

To Store
Keep at room temperature for a few days, or refrigerate and use within two weeks.

To Prepare
Peel oranges and separate into segments; slice or cut into pieces. When grating orange peel, be sure to grate only the zest (the thin colored part of the peel). The white pith underneath is very bitter.

CANDIED FRUITS

TEST KITCHEN TIP

Candied fruits (fruits that have been preserved in sugar) are indispensable in many holiday recipes. They are sometimes crystallized (coated with granulated sugar) or glacéed (dipped into a glossy syrup). For the highest-quality candied fruits, shop at a store that specializes in European ingredients.

Most candied fruit is simply sweetened and artificially colored. Examples include cherries, citrus peel, pineapple, oranges, and apricots. A few edibles are cultivated almost exclusively so they can be candied. Citron is a large citrus fruit with thick skin; when candied it turns dull green. It is used in fruit cakes.

PREPARING CITRUS FRUITS

Using a vegetable peeler, remove the colored part of the citrus peel in strips. (Do not remove the bitter white pith.)

If directed, cut the citrus peel into thin slivers.

Cut a slice off the top and bottom of the fruit to steady it. Stand fruit upright on cutting board and cut off peel and white pith, turning the fruit as you cut.

Holding the fruit over a bowl to catch the juices, cut between the membranes to release the sections.

ORANGES WITH CARAMEL

....

When these caramel-drizzled orange rounds are refrigerated, the caramel is transformed into a luscious golden syrup. Serve as a light and elegant finale to a rich meal.

Prep: 30 minutes plus chilling   Cook: 10 minutes

- 6   large navel oranges
- 2   tablespoons brandy (optional)
- 1   cup sugar

1. From oranges, with vegetable peeler, remove 6 strips (3" by ¾" each) peel. Cut strips lengthwise into slivers.

2. Cut remaining peel and white pith from oranges. Slice oranges into ¼-inch-thick rounds and place on deep platter, overlapping slices slightly. Sprinkle with brandy, if desired, and orange peel slivers.

3. In 1½-quart saucepan, cook sugar over medium heat, stirring to dissolve any lumps, until sugar has melted and turned deep amber. Drizzle caramel over orange slices. Cover and refrigerate until caramel melts, about 2 hours. Makes 6 servings.

Each serving: About 208 calories, 2g protein, 53g carbohydrate, 0g total fat (0g saturated), 0mg cholesterol, 2mg sodium.

Oranges with Caramel

ORANGES WITH CARAMEL

Cook the sugar over medium heat until melted, stirring constantly to dissolve any lumps.

Continue cooking until the syrup turns dark amber.

Carefully drizzle the caramel over the orange slices.

AMBROSIA

·······································

Some ambrosias have gotten away from the pure simplicity of the original recipe—not ours.

Prep: 50 minutes   Bake: 15 minutes

1 fresh coconut
1 ripe pineapple
6 large navel oranges

1. Preheat oven to 350°F. Prepare coconut: Using hammer and screwdriver or large nail, puncture two of the three eyes (indentations) in coconut. Drain liquid. Bake coconut 15 minutes. Remove from oven and wrap in kitchen towel. With hammer, hit coconut to break it into large pieces. With knife, pry coconut meat from shell. With vegetable peeler, peel brown outer skin from coconut meat. With vegetable peeler or on large holes of grater, shred 1 cup coconut. (Wrap and refrigerate remaining coconut up to 2 days for another use.)

2. Prepare pineapple: Cut crown and stem end from pineapple. Stand pineapple on cutting board, cut off rind, and remove eyes. Cut pineapple lengthwise into quarters. Cut out core. Cut quarters lengthwise in half, then crosswise into pieces. Place in large bowl.

3. Prepare oranges: Cut ends off oranges; stand on cutting board and cut off peel and white pith. Holding oranges over bowl with pineapple, cut sections from between membranes, allowing sections to drop into bowl. Squeeze juice from membranes into bowl.

4. Add shredded coconut to bowl and toss gently to combine. Makes 10 servings.

Each serving: About 120 calories, 2g protein, 24g carbohydrate, 3g total fat (2g saturated), 0mg cholesterol, 3mg sodium.

PAPAYAS

Availability
Year-round

Buying Tips
Pick evenly colored gold-yellow fruit. Papayas are sometimes speckled with a few black spots; they do not affect the flavor or quality. The fruit should yield to gentle pressure. Fruit that is too hard will never fully ripen. Avoid oversoft, shriveled, or bruised fruit.

To Store
Ripen papayas at room temperature, then refrigerate and use within three or four days.

To Prepare
Cut papayas lengthwise in half and scoop out the black, peppery seeds. Peel and slice or simply cut up.

PASSION FRUIT

Availability
February through July

Buying Tips
Ripe passion fruit isn't very pretty (the skin is wrinkled and puckered), but the prize is the highly perfumed flesh inside. The skin is usually purple but may be yellow-gold.

To Store
Refrigerate ripe fruit and use within three days.

To Prepare
Cut the fruit crosswise in half and with a spoon, scoop out the pulp and seeds. If desired, strain the pulp through a fine sieve to remove the tiny edible seeds, pressing hard to extract all the juices. One passion fruit yields about 2 tablespoons pulp.

TEST KITCHEN TIP

Dried fruits are great for snacking and stirring into cookies, muffins, and cakes. Sulfur dioxide is often used to preserve and enhance their color. If you have a sulfite allergy, look for sulfur-free dried fruits (they won't have the same bright color) at supermarkets and natural-food stores. Store in an airtight container in a dark, dry place at room temperature for up to one year.

DRIED APPLES: Dried apple rings are often added to fruit compotes. Health-food store varieties are usually firmer and more flavorful than the packaged supermarket variety.

DRIED APRICOTS: Two types of dried apricots are sold in supermarkets and other food stores: apricot halves from California, which are deep orange and very flavorful, and smaller whole apricots from Turkey, which are pale orange and tart rather than sweet.

DRIED BANANAS: Sold in strips, dried bananas can be cut up and used much like dried figs in cakes and muffins. Crisp banana chips are eaten as a snack, not used for cooking.

DRIED BLUEBERRIES: These berries sometimes lose a bit of flavor in the drying process, but they are a nice addition to muffins, scones, and quick breads. It's easy to dry your own: Spread blueberries in a single layer in a jelly-roll pan and place in a 200°F oven. Bake until leathery and all of the moisture has been removed, at least 5 hours. The drying time will depend on the size of the berries.

DRIED CHERRIES: Available tart or sweet. Dried sweet cherries are a delicious snack; dried tart cherries are excellent in baked goods. Dried cherries (sweet or tart) make a healthful and flavorful addition to homemade or store-bought granola and dried fruit compote.

DRIED CRANBERRIES: Most popularly sold under the Craisins brand, they are sprayed with sugar syrup, which tames their characteristic tartness. Use them instead of raisins in oatmeal cookies and in bar cookies.

DRIED DATES: Use dried dates in small amounts because they are very sweet. They are also very sticky; cut them up with oiled kitchen scissors. Prechopped dates are very convenient but not as tasty.

DRIED FIGS: Two types of figs are grown in the San Joaquin Valley in California: Mission and Calimyrna. Unlike other fruit trees, fig trees have no blossoms. The tiny flowers develop inside the figs and become crunchy seeds. Mission figs are small and black, while Calimyrnas are light golden and have a slightly nutty flavor. Choose dried figs that are plump and moist looking. Stuff them with herbed goat cheese or poach them in red wine just like fresh pears. Dried figs can be frozen for up to one year.

DRIED PEACHES AND PEARS: Though mostly appreciated as an out-of-hand snack, these fruits can be turned into a lovely fruit compote when cooked up with dried plums, raisins, and sliced fresh lemon. Snipped into small pieces with oiled kitchen scissors, they can be added to quick breads, scones, or muffins for a nice flavor variation.

DRIED PLUMS: Formerly known as prunes, dried plums are sold pitted and unpitted. They are a quick source of energy and a good source of potassium, iron, and vitamins A and C. Organic dried plums, found in some supermarkets and in health-food stores, are very tasty and have a pleasant chewy texture.

RAISINS: Grapes have been sun-dried into raisins since 1490 bc, but it is believed that it wasn't until 1873 that California produced its first raisin crop. Even today raisins are made from sun-dried grapes. For optimum freshness, store raisins in an airtight container in the refrigerator or in a cool area in your kitchen. They also freeze well for up to one year and are quickly thawed at room temperature. To plump raisins, cover them with very hot tap water and soak for 3 to 5 minutes, then drain.

GOLDEN RAISINS: Good in baking, these are seedless Thompson grapes that have been treated with sulfur dioxide to retain their light color.

CURRANTS: Also known as Zante currants, these are dried seedless grapes, totally unrelated to fresh currants. The name is derived from the grape variety's place of origin: Corinth, Greece.

PEACHES

Availability
May through September

Buying Tips
Peaches are classified as *freestone,* which means the fruit easily separates from the pit, or *clingstone,* where the fruit clings tightly to the pit.

Tree-ripened peaches have a sweet, fruity aroma, yield to gentle pressure, and have the best flavor. Under ripe peaches will soften at room temperature but will not get sweeter than they were when purchased. Avoid green, shriveled, or bruised fruit.

To Store
Refrigerate ripe peaches and use within five days.

To Prepare
Peel the fruit, cut in half along the seam line, and remove the pit. To peel, dip whole peaches into rapidly boiling water for about 15 seconds, then plunge into a bowl of cold water; slip off the skins. Some peaches are almost impossible to peel this way, though; simply use a vegetable peeler. To prevent browning, sprinkle peeled fruit with lemon juice.

PEARS

Availability
Year-round

Buying Tips
Pears are picked unripe, then ripen during shipping and storage. Select well-shaped, fairly firm fruit; the color depends on the variety. Avoid shriveled, discolored, cut, or bruised fruit.

For cooking, *Bartlett, Anjou,* or *Bosc* pears are good choices. The elegant shape of the Bosc pear makes it especially appealing for poaching. Delicious eating pears include the *Comice, Seckel, Winter Nelis,* and *Kieffer* varieties. The *Asian* pear, a crisp and not very sweet relative of the common pear, is perfect for green salads or for use in combination with other fruits.

To Store
Knowing when a particular pear is ripe depends on the variety. Bartletts go from green to soft yellow; greenish brown Boscs turn the color of milk chocolate; and Anjous yield to gentle pressure. Let firm pears ripen at room temperature in a brown paper bag for a few days (it may even take up to a week), then refrigerate and use within three to five days. Never refrigerate pears in an airtight plastic bag; the centers will turn dark brown. Store pears away from strong-smelling foods, because they absorb odors easily. To prevent peeled or cut-up pears from browning, sprinkle with lemon juice.

To Prepare
Peel pears, if desired. Cut the fruit lengthwise in half and remove the core (use a small melon baller) and stem, if desired.

ROASTED PEARS WITH MARSALA

Roasting pears at high heat intensifies their flavor, and the Marsala adds a sweet nuttiness. If you have some Ruby port on hand, use that instead.

Prep: 25 minutes   Bake: 40 minutes

- 1 lemon
- 8 ripe medium Bosc pears with stems
- 2 teaspoons plus ⅓ cup sugar
- ½ cup sweet Marsala wine
- ⅓ cup water
- 2 tablespoons butter or margarine, melted

1. Preheat oven to 450°F. From lemon, with vegetable peeler, remove peel in strips (2½" by ½" each); squeeze juice.

2. With melon baller or small knife, remove cores from pears by cutting through blossom end (bottom) of unpeeled pears (do not remove stems). With pastry brush, brush cavity of each pear with lemon juice, then sprinkle each cavity with ¼ teaspoon sugar.

3. In shallow 1½- to 2-quart baking dish, combine lemon peel, wine, and water. Place remaining ⅓ cup sugar on waxed paper. With pastry brush, brush pears with melted butter, then roll in sugar to coat. Stand pears upright in baking dish. Sprinkle any remaining sugar into baking dish.

4. Bake pears, basting occasionally with syrup in dish, until tender, 40 to 45 minutes.

5. Cool slightly to serve warm, or cool completely and cover and refrigerate up to 1 day. Reheat to serve warm, if you like. Makes 8 servings.

Each serving: About 201 calories, 1g protein, 45g carbohydrate, 4g total fat (2g saturated), 8mg cholesterol, 31mg sodium.

ZINFANDEL-POACHED PEARS

Poaching is an easy way to cook the pears and to create a luscious, fat-free ruby-red syrup at the same time.

Prep: 20 minutes plus chilling   Cook: 45 minutes

- 1 bottle (750 ml) red zinfandel wine (about 3 cups)
- 2 cups cranberry-juice cocktail
- 1¼ cups sugar
- 1 cinnamon stick (3 inches)
- 2 whole cloves
- ½ teaspoon whole black peppercorns
- 8 ripe medium Bosc pears with stems

1. In nonreactive 5-quart Dutch oven, combine wine, cranberry-juice cocktail, sugar, cinnamon, cloves, and peppercorns; heat just to boiling over high heat, stirring occasionally, until sugar has dissolved.

2. Meanwhile, peel pears, leaving stems on. With melon baller or small knife, remove cores by cutting through blossom end (bottom).

3. Place pears in wine mixture; heat to boiling. Reduce heat; cover and simmer, turning pears occasionally, until tender but not soft, 15 to 25 minutes.

4. With slotted spoon, carefully transfer pears to platter. Strain wine mixture through sieve into bowl; pour back into Dutch oven. Heat to boiling over high heat. Cook, uncovered, until liquid has reduced to 1½ cups, 15 to 30 minutes.

5. Cover pears and syrup separately and refrigerate until well chilled, at least 6 hours. To serve, spoon syrup over pears. Makes 8 servings.

Each serving: About 352 calories, 1g protein, 76g carbohydrate, 1g total fat (0g saturated), 0mg cholesterol, 6mg sodium.

QUICK PEAR DESSERTS

CHOCOLATE PEARS
Microwave cored whole pears, covered, until tender; spoon hot fudge sauce over each.

PEAR AND DRIED-CHERRY RICE PUDDING
Cook diced pears in nonstick skillet until tender. Stir into deli rice pudding along with some dried cherries.

PEAR SMOOTHIES
Peel very ripe pears; coarsely chop. Whirl in blender with milk, yogurt, honey, and ice until smooth.

PERSIMMONS

Availability
October through February

Buying Tips
The most common persimmon is the *Hachiya*. It is deep orange, heart-shaped, and eaten raw or cooked. This persimmon must be ripened until very soft and almost translucent before using, or it will be inedibly tannic. *Fuyu* persimmons are pale orange and squat with a light bloom covering the skin. They are preferred for salads and are firm even when ripe.

Buy slightly firm, plump fruit with smooth, unbroken skin and the stem cap still attached; ripen at home. If you buy soft-ripe fruit, transport it very carefully and use the same day. Avoid purchasing bruised or cracked fruit.

To Store
Ripen Hachiya persimmons at room temperature in a closed brown paper bag until very soft. Refrigerate and use within one or two days. Hachiya pulp freezes very well in an airtight container for up to two months.

To Prepare
Remove the stem cap. To use Hachiya pulp, cut persimmon in half and, with a spoon, scoop out the soft flesh; discard the seeds. Puree in a blender or food processor, or press through a fine sieve. To enjoy Fuyu persimmons, simply peel and slice.

PINEAPPLES

Availability
Year round

Buying Tips
A pineapple's color depends on the variety: It can range from deep yellow to reddish brown to green. Pineapple is always picked ripe: It does not get sweeter with time, it only softens. Pick a pineapple that is slightly soft with a deep sweet fragrance. The leaves should be firm and green. Avoid fruit with soft spots or dark areas.

To Store
If you like, chill pineapples before serving.

To Prepare
For rings or chunks, cut off the crown and stem end. Stand the pineapple upright and slice off the rind and eyes. Place the fruit on its side and cut crosswise into ¼- to 1-inch-thick slices. Core the pineapple with a pineapple corer or knife and cut into chunks, if desired. For wedges, with a long serrated knife, cut fruit lengthwise in half, then into quarters, cutting from the crown to the stem. Slice off the core by cutting along the top of the wedges, then slide a knife between the rind and flesh, keeping the knife close to the rind. Leave the flesh in the shell and cut each wedge into ¼- to ½-inch-thick slices.

PLUMS

Availability
June through September

Buying Tips
A plum's sweetness does not increase after it is picked, so purchase ripe fruit. Color is determined by the variety. Ripe plums should be plump and evenly colored and yield to gentle pressure. If the powdery bloom is still on the skin, it's a sign they haven't been overhandled. Avoid hard, shriveled, or cracked plums.

Greengage A round, very sweet, perfumed fruit with greenish yellow skin. *Damson* and *Mirabelle* plums are members of the same family.

Italian prune plums These are purplish black, oval, freestone plums. Because the flesh is somewhat dry, this plum is best cooked or dried. Look for them from late summer through early autumn.

Santa Rosa One of the most popular plum varieties. Grown primarily in California, this excellent all-purpose plum has juicy, sweet-tart flesh. *Friar* and *Queen Anne* plums are related to the Santa Rosa and have similar qualities.

Wild plums Although the name varies depending on the locale (from the *Sierra* plum in the West to the *beach* plum along the Atlantic Coast), these small plums grow in bunches and are used to make jams and jellies.

To Store
Refrigerate ripe plums and use within five days.

To Prepare
Wash plums, then cut into each center to remove the pit, if desired. For serving, slice or cut up the fruit, with or without the skin. When cooked, the amount of sugar needed will depend on the variety.

ROASTED ALMOND-CRUSTED PLUMS

This quick and easy fruit crisp is perfect served warm with a scoop of vanilla ice cream.

Prep: 15 minutes   Bake: 25 minutes

- 6 large ripe plums (4 to 5 ounces each), each cut in half and pitted
- 3 tablespoons butter or margarine, softened
- ⅓ cup packed brown sugar
- ¼ cup all-purpose flour
- ⅓ cup sliced natural almonds

1. Preheat oven to 425°F. In shallow baking dish, arrange plums, cut side up, close together in one layer.

2. In medium bowl, beat butter and brown sugar until smooth. Stir in flour until blended. Stir in almonds. Sprinkle mixture evenly over plums. Bake until plums are tender, 25 to 35 minutes. Makes 6 servings.

Each serving: About 204 calories, 2g protein, 31g carbohydrate, 9g total fat (4g saturated), 16mg cholesterol, 64mg sodium.

POMEGRANATES

Availability
September through December but most plentiful in October

Buying Tips
Select fresh-looking fruit that is heavy for its size. Avoid shriveled fruit or any with broken peel or soft spots.

To Prepare
To eat out of hand, with a sharp knife held one inch from, and parallel to, the blossom end, make a shallow cut all around. With your fingers, pull off the top. Score the fruit (only cutting through the peel) into six wedges. Break the wedges apart.

To remove the seeds (which are very juicy and stain), immerse the wedges in a bowl of cold water; gently separate the seeds from the pith and peel, and let the seeds sink to the bottom of the bowl. Pomegranate seeds can be frozen in an airtight container for up to three months; rinse with cold water before serving.

To extract the juice, puree the seeds in a blender, then strain through a paper towel–lined sieve. (A medium pomegranate yields about ½ cup juice.)

To Serve
Use the juice in fruit drinks. Eat the seeds out of hand, add to fruit salads, or sprinkle on as a garnish.

POMEGRANATE POINTERS

TEST KITCHEN TIP

Garnet-colored pomegranate seeds add a splash of color to foods. Sprinkle on Mixed Greens with Pears and Pecans (page 475), Citrus Salad with Sherry Dressing (page 475), or Curry-Grape Chicken Salad (page 496). Pomegranate juice has a tangy citruslike flavor that can substitute for some or all of the lime or lemon juice in your favorite pork or chicken marinades. It also adds a delicious zip to margaritas.

QUINCES

Availability
October and November

Buying Tips
Quinces are never eaten raw. Their hard flesh, tart flavor, and abundance of pectin, however, make them popular for jams and jellies. Buy fruit that is golden yellow with fuzzy skin. Depending on the variety, the fruit will be either round or pear-shaped. Avoid small, knotty, or bruised fruit.

To Store
Store for up to a few days at room temperature or refrigerate in a perforated plastic bag for up to two weeks.

To Prepare
First peel the fruit. Using a heavy knife, cut the fruit in half, remove all the seeds and every bit of core, and slice. In a saucepan, place the slices in 1 inch of boiling water over medium-high heat. Return to boiling. Reduce heat; cover and simmer until tender and deep gold or rose-colored (the cooking time depends on the size of the slices). Add sugar to taste. (The cooked fruit will remain firm even when tender.)

To Serve
The cooked fruit can be served as a sauce or dessert or used in puddings, pies, and tarts.

RHUBARB

Availability
April and May

Buying Tips
The stalks should be firm, crisp, and fairly thick. Rhubarb can range in color from pale pink to deep red. Avoid flabby stalks.

To Store
Refrigerate rhubarb and use within three to five days.

To Prepare
Wash and trim the stalks, then cut off and discard any leaves (which are toxic and should not be eaten).

TANGERINES, TANGELOS, AND OTHER MANDARIN ORANGES

Availability
November through May

Buying Tips
Tangerines, tangelos, clementines, satsumas, and *ugli fruit* are all members of the mandarin orange family. They are sweet and have loose-fitting, easy-to-peel skin and segments that come apart easily. No matter what type you purchase, buy fruit that is heavy for its size. Some popular varieties (with their seasons) include:

Tangerine Named for the city of Tangiers. Look for fruits with deep orange-red skin. They are in season from November through May.

Tangelo A cross between the tangerine and grapefruit, this fruit has a mild flavor and few seeds. The season runs from November through April.

Clementine Look for these sweet, seedless, compact mandarins from October through February.

Satsuma A super-juicy, virtually seedless favorite that's easy to peel and separate into segments. Available from mid-October through December.

RHUBARB-APPLE CRUMBLE
————————————————

Preheat the oven to 375°F. In large bowl, combine ⅓ cup granulated sugar and 1 tablespoon cornstarch. Add 1¼ pounds rhubarb, cut into ½-inch pieces (4 cups) and 1¼ pounds Golden Delicious apples (3 medium), peeled, cored, and cut into 1-inch pieces; toss to coat. Spoon into 11" by 7" baking dish. In medium bowl, with fingertips, mix ½ cup packed brown sugar, 2 tablespoons butter or margarine, and ¼ teaspoon cinnamon until blended. Stir in ⅓ cup old-fashioned or quick-cooking oats and ¼ cup all-purpose flour until combined; sprinkle over fruit. Bake until filling is bubbling and topping has evenly browned, about 45 minutes. Makes 6 servings.

Ugli fruit This looks like a large greenish grapefruit (and has similar flesh) but is a bit sweeter. Dark spots on the skin are harmless, but don't buy fruit with a dried-out stem end. The season runs from December through May.

WATERMELONS

Availability
May through September

Buying Tips
Watermelons come in two sizes: icebox (around 8 pounds) and large (up to 20 pounds). The flesh can be red, the classic color, or
yellow, and some varieties are seedless. Watermelons should be firm and symmetrically shaped, either oblong or round, depending on the variety. The side of the melon that touched the soil should be yellowish or cream-colored, not pale green or white. The rind should have a velvety bloom, giving it a dull, not shiny, appearance.

To test a whole melon for ripeness, slap the side of the melon with the open palm of your hand; the sound should be deep and resonant. A dull thud indicates an underripe melon, and a hollow sounds means it is overripe and mushy.

Cut watermelon should have firm, deep-red flesh with dark brown or black seeds. Avoid melons with white streaks running through the flesh.

To Store
Refrigerate whole watermelon and use within one week. After cutting, cover the cut surface with waxed paper; use within one or two days.

To Serve
For wedges, with a large knife, cut the whole melon in half from stem to blossom end. Cut each piece lengthwise in half and cut crosswise into slices of desired thickness. Or, cut the melon flesh into bite-size chunks and discard the rind.

WATERMELON BOWL
....

For a great presentation, serve this colorful mixture of sweet summer fruits and minty syrup in the hollowed-out watermelon. It makes a very large amount, so it's just right for casual summer get-togethers.

Prep: 1 hour plus chilling   Cook: 10 minutes

1½ cups water
1 cup sugar
1½ cups loosely packed fresh mint leaves and stems, chopped
3 tablespoons fresh lime juice
1 large watermelon (20 pounds), cut lengthwise in half
1 small ripe cantaloupe, cut crosswise in half
6 large ripe plums (about 1½ pounds)
4 large ripe nectarines (about 2 pounds)
1 pound seedless green grapes

1. In 2-quart saucepan, combine water and sugar; heat to boiling over medium heat, stirring occasionally, until sugar has dissolved. Cook 5 minutes. Stir in mint and lime juice and refrigerate until well chilled.

2. Meanwhile, cut watermelon flesh into bite-size pieces; discard seeds. Cut cantaloupe flesh into bite-size pieces. Cut plums and nectarines into wedges; discard pits. Combine cut-up fruit with grapes in very large bowl or in shell of watermelon. Hold sieve over fruit and pour chilled syrup through. Gently toss to mix well. Cover and refrigerate about 2 hours to blend flavors, stirring occasionally. Makes about 32 cups.

Each cup: About 111 calories, 2g protein, 26g carbohydrate, 1g total fat (0g saturated), 0mg cholesterol, 7mg sodium.

ANISE FRUIT BOWL
Prepare as directed above but substitute **2 tablespoons anise seeds** for mint.

14
····

SALADS & SALAD DRESSINGS

Salad, in its most familiar guise, is a cool, crisp, refreshing collection of greens tossed with a piquant dressing. The possibilities, however, don't end there. A salad can be created from a seemingly endless array of ingredients, each contributing different flavors and textures and sometimes even dictating different serving temperatures. Whether prepared with beans or bread, with grains or greens, or served chilled or warm, a salad is always welcome. It can also play a variety of roles. A salad can be an appetite-teasing first course or a tempting side dish, especially at summer barbecues and picnics, but, bolstered with meat, chicken, or seafood, a salad can also serve as a satisfying but light main dish for warm-weather meals.

BUYING, PREPARING, AND STORING SALAD GREENS

Choose crisp-looking greens with no bruised, yellowing, or brown-tipped leaves. Iceberg lettuce should be heavy for its size and feel firm when squeezed.

As soon as you get it home, wash, dry, and store the lettuce leaves. This will keep the greens fresh longer and provide a few days' worth of salad ready to be put together when you are. Even prewashed greens should be washed and dried to refresh them and to rinse off any bacteria from the surface of the leaves.

No one wants a gritty salad, so wash greens well. Separate the leaves, submerge them in a sinkful or large bowl of cold water, and gently agitate the greens to loosen the dirt. Lift the greens from the water, leaving the grit to sink to the bottom. Curly-leafed greens, as well as spinach and arugula, are especially sandy, and dirt often gets trapped in the crevices of the leaves. Wash these in cool water (the slightly warmer temperature loosens dirt better than cold water), and, if necessary, give the greens a second washing.

Dry salad greens thoroughly before using or storing. Not only do wet greens dilute the dressing and make for a less flavorful, soggy salad, but they won't keep well either. A salad spinner provides an efficient way to dry greens, but you can also pat greens dry with paper towels or clean kitchen towels. If you are washing spinach, arugula, or watercress, remove their tough stems after rinsing.

To store, wrap the rinsed and dried greens in a clean kitchen towel (or in a few paper towels), place in a plastic bag (pressing out all the excess air), and store in the vegetable crisper drawer of the refrigerator. Tender leaf lettuce will keep for two to three days; iceberg and other sturdy lettuces will keep for up to five days. Very delicate greens, such as arugula or watercress, will keep for only a day or so.

A GLOSSARY OF GREENS

Salad greens fall into either of two basic categories: delicate and tender or assertive and slightly bitter. Tender greens, such as lettuce, are served alone or combined with other vegetables. There are four types of lettuce: crisphead (iceberg) varieties are crisp and mild-flavored and stand up well to thicker dressings; butterhead (Bibb, Boston) is sweet-tasting and delicate and should be served with an appropriately light-bodied dressing; loose-leaf (oak leaf) is tender but has a slightly stronger flavor than butterhead; long-leaf (romaine) has long, firm, crisp leaves and is another candidate for rich, thick dressings.

Stronger-flavored greens (including members of the chicory family) are usually combined with sweeter lettuces for a well-balanced salad. Flavorwise, their mild bitterness contrasts nicely with the natural sweetness of the lettuces, but greens such as radicchio and Belgian endive are also invaluable as color elements in the salad palette.

Here are the basic characteristics of the different greens to help you make the right choice at the market.

Arugula Peppery arugula is also known as rugula or rocket. The older and larger the leaves, the more assertive the flavor. The leaves can be very gritty, so rinse them thoroughly.

Baby greens Available in bags or in bulk at many supermarkets, this combination of very young, tender salad greens is an Americanization of the French salad mix known as mesclun (see right).

Belgian endive A member of the chicory family, Belgian endive is appreciated for its crisp texture and slightly bitter flavor. The leaves should be very white, graduating to pale yellow tips.

Bibb lettuce Also called limestone lettuce, has cup-shaped leaves and is best with mild vinaigrettes.

Boston lettuce A loose-leaf lettuce with tender floppy leaves, it is sometimes called butterhead lettuce.

Chicory Although chicory is an entire family of mildly bitter greens, Americans use the term to identify a dark green variety with fringed leaves. It is also known as curly endive.

Chinese cabbage A tightly formed head of white leaves with wide stalks.

Dandelion Tart greens that make a pungent addition to a salad. Some cooks gather the wild variety in the spring.

Escarole Sharp-tasting escarole should have curly leaves with firm stems that snap easily.

Frisée A delicate, pale green variety of chicory with curly, almost spiky leaves.

Iceberg lettuce A lettuce that is best appreciated for its refreshing crisp texture rather than for its mild flavor. Cut out the core before rinsing the leaves.

Mâche Also called lamb's lettuce, this green has a nutty taste and tiny tender leaves. Use within one day; it wilts easily.

Mesclun From the Provençal word for "mixture," true mesclun is made up of wild baby greens from the hillsides of southern France, and often includes herbs and edible flowers. Here, it is commonly a mix of sweet lettuces and bitter greens such as arugula, dandelion, frisée, mizuna, oak leaf, mâche, sorrel, and radicchio.

Mizuna A small, feathery, delicately flavored green of Japanese origin.

Napa cabbage Very similar to, and interchangeable with, Chinese cabbage, but shorter and rounder.

Oak leaf A variety of Boston lettuce with ruffled leaves. Green oak leaf is uniformly green, whereas red oak leaf has dark red tips.

Radicchio The most common radicchio is round with white-veined ruby-red leaves. Radicchio di Treviso has long, narrow red leaves that form a tapered head.

Radish sprouts Innocent-looking sprouts with tiny clover-shaped heads that pack a peppery punch.

Romaine Its long, crisp, dark green leaves and slightly nutty flavor make romaine the preferred lettuce for Caesar salad.

Spinach Whether dark green and crinkled or flat, spinach needs to be washed thoroughly to remove all the grit. Baby spinach has very tender edible stems.

Watercress Watercress adds crisp texture and a mildly spicy flavor to salads. It is very perishable, so use within one or two days of purchase.

MIXED GREENS WITH
PEARS AND PECANS

Sweet ripe pears and crunchy buttery pecans make this an irresistible holiday salad.

Prep: 45 minutes

- 3 tablespoons red wine vinegar
- 2 teaspoons Dijon mustard
- ½ teaspoon salt
- ½ teaspoon coarsely ground black pepper
- ⅓ cup olive oil
- 3 ripe medium pears, each peeled, cored, and cut into 16 wedges
- 1 wedge Parmesan cheese (4 ounces)
- 2 small heads radicchio, cored and torn into large pieces
- 2 small heads Belgian endive, separated into leaves
- 2 small bunches arugula (4 ounces each), tough stems trimmed, or 2 bags (5 ounces each) arugula
- ½ cup pecans, toasted (page 692) and coarsely chopped

1. Prepare dressing: In very large bowl, with wire whisk, mix vinegar, mustard, salt, and pepper. In thin, steady stream, whisk in oil until blended. Add pears, tossing to coat.

2. With vegetable peeler, remove enough shavings from wedge of Parmesan to measure 1 cup, loosely packed.

3. Add radicchio, endive, and arugula to pears; toss until mixed and coated with dressing. Top salad with Parmesan shavings and sprinkle with pecans. Makes 10 first-course servings.

Each serving: About 166 calories, 4g protein, 11g carbohydrate, 13g total fat (2g saturated), 4mg cholesterol, 244mg sodium.

CITRUS SALAD WITH
SHERRY DRESSING

Spicy watercress is the perfect complement for this combination of tart apples, sweet oranges, and tangy grapefruit.

Prep: 30 minutes

- 2 tablespoons dry sherry
- 1 tablespoon red wine vinegar
- 1 teaspoon Dijon mustard
- ¼ teaspoon salt
- ⅛ teaspoon coarsely ground black pepper
- 2 tablespoons olive oil
- 1 large Granny Smith apple, cored and cut into paper-thin slices
- 2 large navel oranges
- 1 large pink grapefruit
- 1 bunch watercress (4 ounces), tough stems trimmed

1. Prepare dressing: In large bowl, with wire whisk, mix sherry, vinegar, mustard, salt, and pepper. In thin, steady stream, whisk in oil until blended.

2. Add apple slices to dressing in bowl and toss to coat. Cut peel and white pith from oranges and grapefruit. Holding oranges and grapefruit over small bowl to catch juice, cut sections from between membranes. (If you like, squeeze juice from membranes and reserve for another use.) Add orange and grapefruit sections to dressing in bowl; toss to coat.

3. Arrange watercress on platter. Spoon fruit mixture and dressing over watercress. Makes 6 accompaniment servings.

Each serving: About 109 calories, 2g protein, 16g carbohydrate, 5g total fat (1g saturated), 0mg cholesterol, 127mg sodium.

FRISÉE SALAD WITH WARM BACON VINAIGRETTE

························

If you don't find frisée in your grocery store, this salad works well with curly endive, frisée's less delicate cousin (also called chicory). Trim away the outer leaves and use only the pale center leaves for the salad.

Prep: 20 minutes   Bake: 10 minutes

- 2 tablespoons olive oil
- ¼ teaspoon salt
- 4 ounces country-style bread or French bread, cut into ½-inch cubes
- 4 slices thick-sliced bacon, cut into ½-inch pieces
- 2 tablespoons red wine vinegar
- 1 tablespoon Dijon mustard
- ⅛ teaspoon coarsely ground black pepper
- 1 pound frisée, ends trimmed
- 6 large eggs, poached (optional)

1. Preheat oven to 400°F. In large serving bowl, combine oil and salt. Add bread cubes to oil mixture and toss to coat. Transfer bread to jelly-roll pan and bake, stirring once, until golden brown and crisp, about 10 minutes. Cool in pan on wire rack.

2. Meanwhile, in 2-quart saucepan, cook bacon over medium heat, stirring frequently, until browned, about 8 minutes. Remove saucepan from heat. With slotted spoon, transfer bacon to paper towels to drain. Discard all but 3 tablespoons bacon drippings from saucepan.

3. With wire whisk, mix vinegar, mustard, pepper, and *2 tablespoons water* into bacon drippings in saucepan.

4. To serve, in same serving bowl, tear frisée into bite-size pieces. Toss frisée with warm bacon vinaigrette until coated. Arrange frisée on 6 dinner plates. Top each with croutons, bacon, and a poached egg, if you like. Makes 6 first-course servings.

Each serving without egg: About 210 calories, 6g protein, 13g carbohydrate, 15g total fat (4g saturated), 13mg cholesterol, 425mg sodium.

Each serving with egg: About 285 calories, 12g protein, 14g carbohydrate, 20g total fat (6g saturated), 224mg cholesterol, 565mg sodium.

WARM ARUGULA AND MUSHROOM SALAD

························

Peppery arugula leaves are coated with a warm mushroom dressing infused with rosemary, then topped with Parmesan cheese shavings.

Prep: 25 minutes   Cook: 12 to 14 minutes

- ¼ cup chicken broth
- 3 tablespoons olive oil
- 2 tablespoons balsamic vinegar
- 2 tablespoons dry vermouth
- ½ teaspoon sugar
- ½ teaspoon salt
- ½ teaspoon coarsely ground black pepper
- 3 small bunches arugula (4 ounces each), tough stems trimmed, or 3 bags (5 ounces each) arugula
- 1 wedge Parmesan cheese (4 ounces)
- 3 garlic cloves, crushed with side of chef's knife
- 8 ounces shiitake mushrooms, stems removed and caps cut into quarters
- 8 ounces white mushrooms, trimmed and sliced
- 1 teaspoon chopped fresh rosemary or ¼ teaspoon dried rosemary, crumbled

1. In small bowl, mix broth, 2 tablespoons oil, vinegar, vermouth, sugar, salt, and pepper. Arrange arugula on large serving platter.

2. With vegetable peeler, remove enough shavings from wedge of Parmesan to measure 1 cup, loosely packed.

3. In nonstick 12-inch skillet, heat remaining 1 tablespoon oil over medium heat. Add garlic and cook, stirring, just until golden. Increase heat to medium-high. Add shiitake and white mushrooms and rosemary; cook, stirring frequently, until mushrooms are browned and liquid has evaporated, 8 to 10 minutes; discard garlic, if you like.

4. Add broth mixture to skillet; cook, stirring, 30 seconds. Immediately spoon mushrooms and pan juices over arugula; top with Parmesan shavings. Makes 4 first-course servings.

Each serving: About 197 calories, 9g protein, 8g carbohydrate, 14g total fat (4g saturated), 10mg cholesterol, 596mg sodium.

WARM GOAT CHEESE SALAD

If you like, coat the goat cheese with the bread crumbs early in the day, then refrigerate for last-minute baking.

Prep: 15 minutes   Bake: 8 minutes

- ¼ cup plain dried bread crumbs
- 1 tablespoon chopped fresh parsley
- 1 tablespoon olive oil
- ¼ teaspoon coarsely ground black pepper
- 1 log (5 to 6 ounces) mild goat cheese
- 8 ounces mixed baby salad greens
- 3 tablespoons Classic French Vinaigrette (page 498)

1. Preheat oven to 425°F. In small bowl, stir bread crumbs, parsley, oil, and pepper until well blended. Slice goat cheese crosswise into 6 equal disks. Place on waxed paper; use bread-crumb mixture to coat cheese disks, patting crumbs to cover evenly.

2. Place crumb-coated cheese disks on cookie sheet and bake until crumbs are golden, 8 to 10 minutes.

3. Meanwhile, in large bowl, toss salad greens with dressing to coat. Divide greens among 6 salad plates and top each serving with a warm goat-cheese disk. Makes 6 first-course servings.

Each serving: About 178 calories, 7g protein, 5g carbohydrate, 15g total fat (6g saturated), 20mg cholesterol, 264mg sodium.

HEALTHY CAESAR SALAD

It's hard to believe a salad could use an overhaul, but in the case of the notoriously high-calorie Caesar, there's room for improvement. We coated the croutons with cooking spray instead of olive oil, then replaced egg yolk with light mayonnaise to keep the classic dressing's creamy texture—without the classic guilt. Now 100 calories and 9 grams of fat slimmer, this crisper is ready for its reveal.

Prep: 15 minutes   Bake: 10 minutes

- 4 ounces Italian bread
- 1 clove garlic, cut in half
  nonstick olive oil cooking spray
- ¼ cup light mayonnaise
- ¼ cup freshly grated Parmesan cheese
- 3 tablespoons fresh lemon juice
- 1 tablespoon olive oil
- 1 teaspoon anchovy paste
- ½ teaspoon coarsely ground black pepper
- 1 package (18 ounces) hearts of romaine lettuce, torn into bite-size pieces

1. Preheat oven to 400°F.

2. Cut bread into ½-inch-thick slices. Rub bread slices, on both sides, with cut sides of garlic. Cut bread into ½-inch cubes; place in jelly-roll pan. Spray bread liberally with cooking spray. Bake 10 minutes or until golden-brown and crisp. Cool croutons in pan.

3. Meanwhile, in large salad bowl, with wire whisk, mix together mayonnaise, Parmesan, lemon juice, olive oil, anchovy paste, and pepper.

4. Add lettuce and croutons to dressing in bowl; toss to coat. Makes 6 first-course servings.

Each serving: About 140 calories, 4g protein, 13g carbohydrate, 8g total fat (2g saturated), 2g fiber, 7mg cholesterol, 280mg sodium.

Healthy Caesar Salad

GREENS WITH GOAT CHEESE AND TANGERINE VINAIGRETTE

·······························

Savory goat cheese is the perfect companion to our sweet and tangy citrus vinaigrette. For variety and an extra burst of color, try dried cranberries or cherries instead of raisins.

Prep: 15 minutes

- 2 tangerines
- 2 teaspoons cider vinegar
- ½ teaspoon Dijon mustard
- ¼ teaspoon salt
- ⅛ teaspoon ground black pepper
- 2 tablespoons olive oil
- 1 tablespoon chopped fresh chives
- 8 cups loosely packed mixed baby greens, such as romaine, arugula, and spinach (about 5 ounces)
- ½ cup (2 ounces) crumbled goat cheese
- ¼ cup golden raisins

1. From tangerines, grate 1 teaspoon peel; place in small bowl. Cut remaining peel and pith from fruit. Holding tangerines, 1 at a time, over another small bowl, cut on either side of membranes to remove each segment, allowing fruit and juice to drop into bowl.

Greens with Goat Cheese and Tangerine Vinaigrette

Squeeze 3 tablespoons juice from membranes; add to bowl with peel. Whisk in vinegar, mustard, salt, and pepper until mixed. In thin, steady stream, whisk in oil until vinaigrette is blended. Stir in tangerine segments and chives.

2. Place greens on 4 salad plates; sprinkle each with goat cheese and raisins. Drizzle with vinaigrette. Makes 4 accompaniment servings.

Each serving: About 165 calories, 3g protein, 15g carbohydrate, 10g total fat (3g saturated), 2g fiber, 10mg cholesterol, 335mg sodium.

CHOPPED SALAD

·······························

A chopped salad can be prepared from your favorite salad ingredients. Here's a classic combination. If you have a mezzaluna—a chopper with a crescent blade— it will make preparation a breeze.

Prep: 25 minutes

- 1 large head romaine lettuce (1¼ pounds), chopped into ½-inch pieces
- 1 bunch watercress (4 ounces), tough stems trimmed, coarsely chopped
- 1¼ pounds ripe tomatoes (2 large), cut into ½-inch pieces
- 1 medium cucumber (8 ounces), peeled, seeded, and cut into ½-inch pieces
- 1 cup radishes, cut into quarters
- ¼ cup Classic French Vinaigrette (page 498) or dressing of choice

In large bowl, combine romaine, watercress, tomatoes, cucumber, radishes, and dressing; toss to coat. Makes 8 accompaniment servings.

Each serving: About 67 calories, 2g protein, 5g carbohydrate, 5g total fat (1g saturated), 0mg cholesterol, 109mg sodium.

BORDER TOWN TACO SALAD

....

Just fifteen minutes from here to the border—and our lightened-up version of this family-restaurant staple.

Prep: 15 minutes   Cook: 8 minutes

- 1 pound lean (90%) ground beef or ground chicken
- 1½ teaspoons chili powder
- ¾ cup salsa
- 1 bag (10 ounces) chopped romaine lettuce
- 2 cups baked tortilla chips
- ⅓ cup shredded reduced-fat Mexican cheese blend
- 1 medium ripe avocado, pitted and cut into ½-inch chunks
- ¼ cup reduced-fat sour cream

1. In 12-inch skillet, cook ground beef on medium 4 to 5 minutes or until beef begins to brown, breaking up meat with spatula as it cooks. Stir in chili powder, and cook 1 minute longer. Add ½ cup salsa and cook 3 to 4 minutes to heat through.

2. Divide lettuce among 4 serving plates. Top each with beef mixture, tortilla chips, cheese, avocado, sour cream, and remaining salsa. Makes 4 main-dish servings.

Each serving: About 405 calories, 28g protein, 21g carbohydrate, 23g total fat (8g saturated), 6g fiber, 86mg cholesterol, 425mg sodium.

Border Town Taco Salad

SALAD IN A SNAP

Pair a quick salad with everything from pasta to pork chops and dinner is served! It all starts with a simple vinaigrette.

BASIC VINAIGRETTE

In a small bowl, whisk together 3 tablespoons vinegar, ½ teaspoon Dijon mustard, and a pinch each of salt and pepper, then slowly drizzle in ¼ cup olive oil, whisking until the mixture emulsifies. Change the flavor by using a different vinegar, such as balsamic, sherry, or tarragon, or experiment with your own favorites.

BABY ROMAINE WITH FENNEL AND CITRUS

Toss together one 5-ounce bag baby romaine, 1 cup thinly sliced fennel, 1 cup jarred citrus segments, ½ cup rinsed and drained chickpeas, and 6 thinly sliced radishes. Dressing tip: Use lemon juice or a combination of lemon and lime juice instead of vinegar.

GREEK SALAD WITH FETA AND OLIVES

Toss together one 5-ounce bag spring mix with herbs, 1 cup grape tomatoes, 1 seedless cucumber cut into ½-inch chunks, and ½ cup pitted Kalamata olives. Top with ¼ cup crumbled goat or feta cheese. Dressing tip: Use tarragon or white wine vinegar.

CARROT COLESLAW WITH DRIED CHERRIES AND ALMONDS

Toss together one 10-ounce bag shredded carrots, 1 large red pepper cut into ¼-inch-wide strips, ½ cup dried cherries, and ½ cup toasted slivered almonds. Dressing tip: Use seasoned rice vinegar and add a teaspoon of toasted sesame oil.

APPLE COLESLAW WITH GOLDEN RAISINS AND PECANS

Toss together one 16-ounce bag coleslaw mix, 1 Granny Smith apple cored and cut into ½-inch chunks, ½ cup golden raisins, and ½ cup chopped pecans. Dressing tip: Whisk 1 tablespoon light mayonnaise into basic vinaigrette.

SPINACH AND ENDIVE WITH PEARS AND WALNUTS

Toss together one 6-ounce bag baby spinach, 2 heads sliced Belgian endive, 1 cored and thinly sliced Bosc pear, and ½ cup toasted walnut pieces. Dressing tip: Use raspberry vinegar.

WALDORF SALAD

Serve this chunky salad alongside your favorite grilled chicken for a sweet and savory meal.

Prep: 30 minutes

- ⅓ cup mayonnaise
- ¼ cup sour cream
- 1 tablespoon fresh lemon juice
- 1 teaspoon honey
- ¼ teaspoon salt
- 2 red apples, such as Braeburn, Cortland, or Red Delicious, each cored, cut into 8 wedges, then crosswise into ¼-inch pieces
- 1 Granny Smith apple, cored, cut into 8 wedges, then crosswise into ¼-inch pieces
- 2 stalks celery, each cut lengthwise in half, then thinly sliced (½ cup)
- ½ cup walnuts, toasted (page 692) and coarsely chopped
- ⅓ cup dark seedless raisins

Prepare dressing: In medium bowl, with wire whisk, mix mayonnaise, sour cream, lemon juice, honey, and salt until blended. Add red and Granny Smith apples, celery, walnuts, and raisins to dressing in bowl and toss until mixed and coated with dressing. Makes 8 accompaniment servings.

Each serving: About 181 calories, 2g protein, 16g carbohydrate, 14g total fat (2g saturated), 9mg cholesterol, 135mg sodium.

MOZZARELLA AND TOMATO SALAD

For this simple combination to be at its best, use only fresh mozzarella and vine-ripened summer tomatoes.

Prep: 15 minutes

- 2 ripe medium tomatoes (8 ounces each), thinly sliced
- 10 ounces fresh mozzarella, thinly sliced
- 2 tablespoons extra-virgin olive oil
- ¼ teaspoon salt
- ¼ teaspoon ground black pepper
- 2 tablespoons thinly sliced fresh basil leaves

On large platter, arrange tomatoes and mozzarella in overlapping rows. Drizzle with oil and sprinkle with salt and pepper. Top with basil. Makes 4 accompaniment servings.

Each serving: About 285 calories, 14g protein, 8g carbohydrate, 22g total fat (1g saturated), 50mg cholesterol, 203mg sodium.

THREE-BEAN SALAD

If you can't find wax beans, simply double the amount of green beans called for.

Prep: 25 minutes plus chilling   Cook: 13 minutes

- 8 ounces green beans, trimmed and cut into 1-inch pieces (2 cups)
- 8 ounces wax beans, trimmed and cut into 1-inch pieces (2 cups)
- 1½ teaspoons salt
- 3 tablespoons olive or vegetable oil
- 3 tablespoons cider vinegar
- 2 tablespoons sugar
- 1 can (15 to 19 ounces) red kidney beans, rinsed and drained
- ¼ cup chopped onion

1. In 4-quart saucepan, heat *3 inches water* to boiling over high heat. Add green and wax beans and ½ teaspoon salt; heat to boiling. Cook until tender-crisp, 6 to 8 minutes. Drain. Rinse beans with cold running water to cool slightly; drain.

2. Meanwhile, prepare dressing: In large bowl, with wire whisk, mix oil, vinegar, sugar, and remaining 1 teaspoon salt until well blended. Add green and wax beans, kidney beans, and onion; toss until mixed and coated with dressing. Cover and refrigerate salad at least 2 hours to blend flavors or up to 24 hours. Makes 8 accompaniment servings.

Each serving: About 118 calories, 4g protein, 14g carbohydrate, 5g total fat (1g saturated), 0mg cholesterol, 441mg sodium.

GREEK PEASANT SALAD

....

Serve this cool Mediterranean-style dish alongside grilled chicken, fish, or pork, or on its own with crusty bread.

Prep: 25 minutes

- 4 kirby cucumbers (about 1 pound), not peeled
- 2 tablespoons fresh lemon juice
- 1 tablespoon olive oil
- ¼ teaspoon salt
- ⅛ teaspoon ground black pepper
- 2 pounds ripe red and/or yellow tomatoes (about 6 medium), cut into 1-inch chunks
- ½ cup loosely packed fresh mint leaves, chopped
- ⅓ cup Kalamata olives, pitted and coarsely chopped
- ¼ cup loosely packed fresh dill, chopped
- 2 ounces feta cheese, crumbled (½ cup)

1. With vegetable peeler, remove 3 or 4 evenly spaced lengthwise strips of peel from each cucumber. Cut each cucumber lengthwise into quarters, then crosswise into ½-inch pieces.

Greek Peasant Salad

2. In large bowl, with wire whisk, mix lemon juice, oil, salt, and pepper. Add cucumbers, tomatoes, mint, olives, and dill, and toss until evenly mixed and coated with dressing. Top with feta. Makes about 6½ cups or 6 accompaniment servings.

Each serving: About 100 calories, 3g protein, 11g carbohydrate, 6g total fat (2g saturated), 8mg cholesterol, 280mg sodium.

SUMMER CORN SALAD

....

We've created this colorful salad from a mélange of farmstand-fresh summer vegetables.

Prep: 30 minutes   Cook: 10 minutes

- 12 medium ears corn, husks and silk removed
- 12 ounces green beans, trimmed and cut into ¼-inch pieces
- ½ cup cider vinegar
- ¼ cup olive oil
- ¼ cup chopped fresh parsley
- 1 teaspoon salt
- ½ teaspoon coarsely ground black pepper
- 1 red pepper, finely chopped
- 1 small sweet onion, such as Vidalia or Walla Walla, finely chopped

1. In 8-quart saucepot, heat *2 inches water* to boiling over high heat; add corn. Return to boiling. Reduce heat; cover and simmer 5 minutes. Drain. When cool enough to handle, cut kernels from cobs.

2. Meanwhile, in 2-quart saucepan, heat *1 inch water* to boiling over high heat; add green beans and return to boiling. Reduce heat; simmer until tender-crisp, 3 to 5 minutes. Drain green beans. Rinse with cold running water; drain.

3. Prepare dressing: In large bowl, with wire whisk, mix vinegar, oil, parsley, salt, and black pepper until thoroughly blended.

4. Add corn, green beans, red pepper, and onion to dressing in bowl; toss to coat. If not serving immediately, cover and refrigerate up to 2 hours. Makes 12 accompaniment servings.

Each serving: About 179 calories, 5g protein, 31g carbohydrate, 6g total fat (1g saturated), 0mg cholesterol, 219mg sodium.

CORN AND BARLEY SALAD

....

In the height of summer, corn is so fresh and sweet you can eat it raw, which is how we use it in this salad. Edamame and barley add protein and fiber.

Prep: 20 minutes plus chilling   Cook: 30 minutes

- 2 cups water
- 1 cup pearl barley
- ³/₄ teaspoon salt
- 6 ears corn (husks and silks removed)
- ¹/₃ cup rice vinegar
- 2 tablespoons olive oil
- ¹/₂ teaspoon ground black pepper
- 1¹/₂ cups frozen shelled edamame (green soybeans), thawed
- ¹/₂ cup packed fresh mint leaves, chopped, plus additional sprigs for garnish

1. In covered 2-quart saucepan, heat water to boiling on high. Stir in barley and ¹/₂ teaspoon salt; heat to boiling. Reduce heat to low; cover and simmer 30 to 35 minutes or until barley is tender and liquid is absorbed.

2. Meanwhile, with sharp knife, carefully cut corn kernels from cobs; discard cobs. In large bowl, with wire whisk or fork, whisk vinegar, oil, ¹/₄ teaspoon salt, and pepper until blended; stir in warm barley, corn kernels, edamame, and chopped mint. Cover salad and refrigerate at least 1 hour or up to 8 hours. To serve, garnish with mint sprigs. Makes 8 cups or 12 servings.

Each serving: About 155 calories, 6g protein, 25g carbohydrate, 5g total fat (1g saturated), 5g fiber, 0mg cholesterol, 160mg sodium.

Bloody Mary Tomato Salad

BLOODY MARY TOMATO SALAD

....

This fresh salad combines the spicy flavors of the cocktail—lemon juice, Worcestershire sauce, and hot pepper sauce—with tomatoes and celery for delicious results. Be sure to leave enough time to chill the salad before serving.

Prep: 15 minutes plus chilling

- 2 tablespoons prepared horseradish
- 2 tablespoons olive oil
- 2 tablespoons vodka (optional)
- 1 tablespoon fresh lemon juice
- 1¹/₂ teaspoons hot pepper sauce
- 1 teaspoon Worcestershire sauce
- ¹/₂ teaspoon salt
- ¹/₂ teaspoon ground black pepper
- 3 pints grape or cherry tomatoes, each cut in half
- 4 stalks celery, cut into 1/4-inch-thick diagonal slices, leaves reserved for garnish

1. In large bowl, whisk horseradish, oil, vodka (if using), lemon juice, pepper sauce, Worcestershire, salt, and pepper until blended. Add tomatoes and celery; toss to combine. Cover and refrigerate 2 hours.

2. To serve, toss salad again to coat with dressing and garnish with celery leaves. Makes 8 side-dish servings.

Each serving: About 65 calories, 1g protein, 7g carbohydrate, 4g total fat (1g saturated), 2g fiber, 0mg cholesterol, 190mg sodium.

MUSHROOM SALAD

....

Marinate fresh mushrooms to serve over a selection of baby greens for an elegant, flavorful side salad.

Prep: 30 minutes plus marinating

- 1 to 2 lemons
- 4 tablespoons olive oil
- 2 cloves garlic, each cut in half
- ½ teaspoon salt
- ¼ teaspoon ground black pepper
- 2 pounds white mushrooms, trimmed and cut into quarters
- ½ cup loosely packed fresh parsley, chopped
- 3 tablespoons snipped chives plus additional for garnish
- 1 bag (5 ounces) baby arugula
- 1 bag (5 ounces) mixed baby greens
  thinly shaved Pecorino-Romano cheese for garnish

1. From lemons, grate ½ teaspoon peel and squeeze ⅓ cup juice. In 4-quart saucepan, heat lemon peel and juice, 3 tablespoons oil, garlic, salt, and pepper to boiling on high. Reduce heat to medium and simmer 30 seconds.

2. Stir in mushrooms, parsley, and chives. Transfer to large zip-tight plastic bag. Seal bag, pressing out excess air. Place bag in bowl and refrigerate 6 hours or overnight.

3. Place sieve over large bowl; drain mushrooms over bowl (do not discard drained marinade). Discard garlic cloves; set mushrooms aside. Add remaining 1 tablespoon oil to marinade in bowl; whisk until blended. Add arugula and mixed greens; toss to combine.

4. Serve mushrooms on greens. Garnish with additional snipped chives and Romano shavings. Makes 12 side-dish servings.

Each serving: About 65 calories, 3g protein, 5g carbohydrate, 5g total fat (1g saturated), 1g fiber, 0mg cholesterol, 105mg sodium.

CANTALOUPE AND CUCUMBER SALAD

....

When summer produce is at its peak, delicious salads can be made from the right combinations of fruits and veggies. Here, juicy, ripe cantaloupes and crunchy English cucumbers make a tempting pair.

Prep: 20 minutes

- ¼ cup fresh lime juice
- ¼ teaspoon salt
- ⅛ teaspoon ground black pepper
- 1 large English (seedless) cucumber (1 pound), peeled in alternating strips and coarsely chopped
- 2 ripe cantaloupes, coarsely chopped
- 3 green onions, thinly sliced
- ½ cup loosely packed fresh cilantro leaves, chopped

In large bowl, whisk lime juice, salt, and pepper until blended. Add cucumber, cantaloupe, green onions, and cilantro; toss to coat. Makes 8½ cups or 10 servings.

Each serving: About 45 calories, 2g protein, 11g carbohydrate, 0g total fat, 1g fiber, 0mg cholesterol, 70mg sodium.

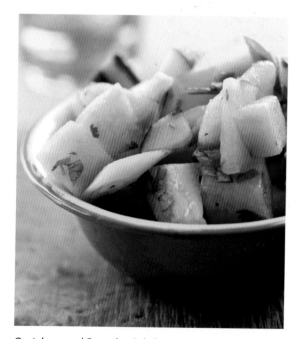

Cantaloupe and Cucumber Salad

SPICED WATERMELON AND TOMATO SALAD

∙∙∙∙∙∙∙∙∙∙∙∙∙∙∙∙∙∙∙∙∙∙∙∙∙∙∙∙∙∙∙∙∙

The combination of watermelon and tomato makes a surprisingly tasty and refreshing salad. Seedless watermelon makes preparation easy. Choose one that is heavy for its size and makes a thud when tapped.

Prep: 20 minutes

- 3 ripe medium tomatoes (about 1 pound), cut into 3/4-inch pieces
- 1/4 cup fresh lime juice (2 to 3 limes)
- 1/2 teaspoon salt
- 1 piece watermelon (about 2 1/2 pounds with rind)
- 2 tablespoons chopped fresh cilantro leaves
- 1/2 teaspoon ground cumin
- 1/2 teaspoon ground coriander
- 1/8 teaspoon ground red pepper (cayenne)

1. In large bowl, toss tomatoes with lime juice and salt; set aside.

2. Cut rind from watermelon; discard rind. Cut flesh into 1/2-inch pieces to equal 4 cups; discard seeds.

3. Add watermelon, cilantro, cumin, coriander, and ground red pepper to tomato mixture; toss well to combine. Serve at room temperature or cover and refrigerate to serve later. Makes about 6 cups or 10 accompaniment servings.

Each serving: About 30 calories, 1g protein, 7g carbohydrate, 0g total fat, 0mg cholesterol, 120mg sodium.

KIRBY CUCUMBER SALAD

∙∙∙∙∙∙∙∙∙∙∙∙∙∙∙∙∙∙∙∙∙∙∙∙∙∙∙∙∙∙∙∙∙

The unwaxed skin of kirby (pickling) cucumbers doesn't need to be peeled. If you can't find them, buy regular cucumbers and remove half the peel in strips, creating stripes.

Prep: 30 minutes plus standing and chilling

- 4 pounds kirby cucumbers, not peeled, thinly sliced
- 1 tablespoon salt
- 3/4 cup distilled white vinegar
- 2 tablespoons sugar
- 2 tablespoons chopped fresh dill

1. In colander set over large bowl, toss cucumber slices and salt; let stand 30 minutes at room temperature. Discard liquid in bowl. Pat cucumbers dry with paper towels.

2. In same clean bowl, combine vinegar, sugar, and dill. Add cucumber slices and toss to coat. Cover and refrigerate, stirring occasionally, at least 1 hour to blend flavors or up to 4 hours. Makes 12 accompaniment servings.

Each serving: About 30 calories, 1g protein, 7g carbohydrate, 0g total fat, (0g saturated), 0mg cholesterol, 149mg sodium.

CREAMY CUCUMBER AND DILL SALAD

∙∙∙∙∙∙∙∙∙∙∙∙∙∙∙∙∙∙∙∙∙∙∙∙∙∙∙∙∙∙∙∙∙

On hot summer days, serve these thinly sliced cucumbers as a cool side dish with grilled salmon.

Prep: 15 minutes plus standing and chilling

- 2 English (seedless) cucumbers, not peeled, thinly sliced
- 2 teaspoons salt
- 1/2 cup sour cream
- 2 tablespoons chopped fresh dill
- 2 teaspoons chopped fresh mint
- 1 teaspoon distilled white vinegar
- 1/8 teaspoon ground black pepper

1. In colander set over large bowl, toss cucumbers and salt; let stand 30 minutes at room temperature to drain. Discard liquid in bowl. Pat cucumbers dry with paper towels.

2. In same clean bowl, combine sour cream, dill, mint, vinegar, and pepper. Add cucumbers, stirring to coat. Cover and refrigerate at least 1 hour to blend flavors or up to 4 hours. Makes 6 accompaniment servings.

Each serving: About 60 calories, 2g protein, 5g carbohydrate, 4g total fat (3g saturated), 8mg cholesterol, 203mg sodium.

COLESLAW WITH VINAIGRETTE

··

Flavored with caraway seeds, this tasty coleslaw is best when thoroughly chilled.

Prep: 20 minutes plus chilling

- 2 tablespoons olive or vegetable oil
- 2 tablespoons red wine vinegar
- 1 tablespoon sugar
- 1 teaspoon salt
- ½ teaspoon caraway seeds or ¼ teaspoon celery seeds, crushed
- 1 small head green cabbage (1½ pounds), quartered, cored, and thinly sliced, tough ribs discarded (6 cups)
- 1 large red pepper, cut into 2" by ¼" matchstick strips

Prepare dressing: In large bowl, with wire whisk, mix oil, vinegar, sugar, salt, and caraway seeds until blended. Add cabbage and red pepper; toss to coat well. Cover and refrigerate at least 1 hour to blend flavors or up to 6 hours. Makes 6 accompaniment servings.

Each serving: About 75 calories, 1g protein, 8g carbohydrate, 5g total fat (1g saturated), 0mg cholesterol, 405mg sodium.

ASIAN COLESLAW

··

Plan ahead: Prepare all the vegetables for the coleslaw, cover and refrigerate for up to 6 hours. Combine the dressing ingredients in a jar, cover tightly, and store at room temperature. When ready to serve, shake the dressing and toss with the vegetables.

Prep: 35 minutes

- ⅓ cup seasoned rice vinegar
- 2 tablespoons vegetable oil
- 2 teaspoons Asian sesame oil
- ¾ teaspoon salt
- 1 medium head savoy cabbage (2½ pounds), quartered, cored, and thinly sliced, tough ribs discarded
- 1 bag (16 ounces) carrots, peeled and shredded
- ½ cup chopped fresh cilantro
- 4 green onions, thinly sliced

1. Prepare dressing: In large bowl, with wire whisk, mix vinegar, vegetable and sesame oils, and salt until blended.

2. Add cabbage, carrots, cilantro, and green onions to dressing in bowl; toss until mixed and coated with dressing. If not serving right away, cover and refrigerate up to 2 hours. Makes 12 accompaniment servings.

Each serving: About 69 calories, 2g protein, 10g carbohydrate, 3g total fat (0g saturated), 0mg cholesterol, 310mg sodium.

LIGHT AND LEMONY SLAW

··

A crisp complement to any barbecue and lower in fat than the typical deli slaw. Its subtle sweetness is also a nice change of pace.

Prep: 25 minutes

- 2 lemons
- ½ cup light mayonnaise
- ¼ cup reduced-fat sour cream
- 1 tablespoon sugar
- 1 teaspoon salt
- ½ teaspoon coarsely ground black pepper
- ¼ teaspoon celery seeds, crushed
- 1 large head green cabbage (3 pounds), quartered, cored, and thinly sliced, tough ribs discarded (12 cups)
- 4 carrots, peeled and shredded

1. From lemons, grate 1 teaspoon peel and squeeze ¼ cup juice. In large bowl, with wire whisk, mix lemon peel and juice, mayonnaise, sour cream, sugar, salt, pepper, and celery seeds until blended.

2. Add cabbage and carrots to dressing in bowl; toss to coat. Serve at room temperature, or cover and refrigerate up to 4 hours. Makes 12 accompaniment servings.

Each serving: About 80 calories, 2g protein, 10g carbohydrate, 4g total fat (1g saturated), 5mg cholesterol, 298mg sodium.

RED POTATO SALAD

In France, potato salad is prepared with a shallot vinaigrette and the freshest, smallest red potatoes available. A bit of crumbled bacon sprinkled over the top is a delicious counterpoint that brings out the sweetness of the potatoes.

Prep: 25 minutes plus cooling   Cook: 30 minutes

- 4 pounds small red potatoes, not peeled, cut into quarters or eighths if large
- 3½ teaspoons salt
- 4 slices bacon
- 3 large shallots, chopped (¾ cup)
- ⅓ cup cider vinegar
- ¼ cup olive oil
- 2 teaspoons sugar
- 2 teaspoons Dijon mustard
- ¼ teaspoon coarsely ground black pepper
- 2 green onions, chopped

1. In 5-quart saucepot, combine potatoes, enough *water* to cover, and 2 teaspoons salt; heat to boiling over high heat. Reduce heat; cover and simmer until tender, 10 to 12 minutes.

2. Meanwhile, in 10-inch skillet, cook bacon over medium-low heat until browned. With slotted spoon, transfer to paper towels to drain; crumble.

3. Discard all but 1 teaspoon bacon drippings from skillet. Reduce heat to low. Add shallots and cook, stirring, until tender, about 5 minutes. Remove from heat.

4. Prepare dressing: In large bowl, with wire whisk, mix shallots, vinegar, oil, sugar, mustard, remaining 1½ teaspoons salt, and pepper until blended.

5. Drain potatoes. Add hot potatoes to dressing in bowl. With rubber spatula, stir gently until potatoes absorb dressing. Let potatoes cool 30 minutes at room temperature, stirring occasionally. Stir in green onions.

6. If not serving right away, cover and refrigerate up to 4 hours. If chilled, let stand 30 minutes at room temperature before serving. To serve, sprinkle with crumbled bacon. Makes 12 accompaniment servings.

Each serving: About 185 calories, 4g protein, 29g carbohydrate, 6g total fat (1g saturated), 2mg cholesterol, 456mg sodium.

DILLED RED POTATOES WITH MINT

Prepare potatoes as directed in Step 1 (left); drain. Omit bacon, shallots, vinegar, sugar, and mustard. In large bowl, mix olive oil, remaining 1½ teaspoons salt, and pepper. Add **6 green onions**, chopped, **⅓ cup chopped fresh dill**, and **¼ cup chopped fresh mint**. Add hot potatoes to herb mixture in bowl and toss until mixed. Makes 8 accompaniment servings.

Each serving: About 124 calories, 2g protein, 21g carbohydrate, 4g total fat (0g saturated), 0mg cholesterol, 301mg sodium.

CREAMY POTATO SALAD

As familiar as this classic recipe may be, it is always welcome. For a variation, add ¼ cup chopped smoked ham or 2 coarsely chopped hard-cooked eggs.

Prep: 20 minutes   Cook: 35 minutes

- 3 pounds all-purpose potatoes (9 medium), not peeled
- ½ cup mayonnaise
- ½ cup milk
- 2 tablespoons distilled white vinegar
- 2 tablespoons chopped green onion
- 1 teaspoon sugar
- 1 teaspoon salt
- ¼ teaspoon coarsely ground black pepper
- 2 large stalks celery, thinly sliced

1. In 4-quart saucepan, combine potatoes and enough *water* to cover; heat to boiling over high heat. Reduce heat; cover and simmer until tender, 25 to 30 minutes. Drain. When cool enough to handle, peel potatoes and cut into ¾-inch cubes.

2. Meanwhile, prepare dressing: In large bowl, with wire whisk, mix mayonnaise, milk, vinegar, green onion, sugar, salt, and pepper until blended. Add potatoes and celery to dressing; toss to coat. If not serving right away, cover and refrigerate up to 4 hours. Makes 10 accompaniment servings.

Each serving: About 198 calories, 3g protein, 27g carbohydrate, 9g total fat (2g saturated), 8mg cholesterol, 315mg sodium.

TWO-POTATO SALAD

Tossing warm potatoes with dressing is a traditional French technique; it enables the potatoes to soak up all the flavor.

Prep: 15 minutes plus cooling   Cook: 15 minutes

- 2 pounds red potatoes (about 8 medium), cut into 1-inch chunks
- 1 pound sweet potatoes (2 small), peeled and cut into 1-inch chunks
- ¼ cup red wine vinegar
- 1 tablespoon spicy brown mustard
- 1¼ teaspoons salt
- ½ teaspoon coarsely ground black pepper
- ½ cup mayonnaise
- ¼ cup milk
- 2 medium celery stalks, chopped
- 1 small red onion, minced
- ⅓ cup loosely packed fresh flat-leaf parsley leaves, chopped

1. In 5- to 6-quart saucepot, place red potatoes and enough *water* to cover by 1 inch; heat to boiling over high heat. Reduce heat to low and simmer 2 minutes. Stir in sweet potatoes; heat to boiling over high heat. Reduce heat to low; cover and simmer until potatoes are just fork-tender, 8 to 10 minutes.

2. Meanwhile, prepare dressing. In large bowl, with wire whisk, mix vinegar, mustard, salt, and pepper.

3. Drain potatoes. Add hot potatoes to dressing in bowl; gently stir with rubber spatula until evenly coated. Let stand until cool.

4. In small bowl, whisk mayonnaise and milk until smooth. Add mayonnaise mixture, celery, onion, and parsley to potato mixture; gently stir with rubber spatula until potatoes are well coated. Serve while still warm, or cover and refrigerate until ready to serve. Makes 14 accompaniment servings.

Each serving: About 150 calories, 2g protein, 21g carbohydrate, 7g total fat (1g saturated), 5mg cholesterol, 280mg sodium.

HEALTHY POTATO SALAD

Our healthy take on a favorite recipe now is our new favorite recipe. This slimmed-down salad (minus 50 calories and 7 fat grams per serving) has just the right level of tangy flavor and no gloppiness. Plus, it was a cinch to overhaul.

Prep: 20 minutes plus chilling   Cook: 10 minutes

- 3 pounds Yukon Gold potatoes, peeled and cut into 1-inch chunks
- 1¼ teaspoons salt
- ¾ cup buttermilk
- ¼ cup light mayonnaise
- 2 tablespoons snipped fresh dill
- 2 tablespoons cider vinegar
- 1 tablespoon Dijon mustard
- 2 green onions, thinly sliced
- ¼ teaspoon coarsely ground black pepper

1. In 4-quart saucepan, combine potatoes, 1 teaspoon salt, and enough *water* to cover; heat to boiling on high. Reduce heat to medium-low; cover and simmer 10 minutes or until potatoes are just fork-tender.

2. Meanwhile, in large bowl, whisk buttermilk with mayonnaise, dill, vinegar, Dijon, green onions, ¼ teaspoon salt, and pepper.

3. Drain potatoes well. Toss hot potatoes with buttermilk mixture until coated. (Mixture will look very loose before chilling.) Cover and refrigerate potato salad at least 2 hours or overnight to blend flavors and chill, stirring gently after 1 hour. Makes about 6 cups or 10 side-dish servings.

Each serving: About 150 calories, 3g protein, 29g carbohydrate, 2g total fat (0.5g saturated), 2g fiber, 3mg cholesterol, 200mg sodium.

WHITE AND WILD RICE SALAD

·············

When people hear the word salad, *they don't usually think of grains. This festive combination of white and wild rice tossed with cranberries, grapes, and toasted pecans is perfect for a holiday buffet.*

**Prep: 25 minutes plus cooling
Cook: 50 to 60 minutes**

½ cup wild rice
1½ teaspoons salt
¾ cup regular long-grain rice
⅓ cup dried cranberries or currants
2 tablespoons olive oil
2 tablespoons red wine vinegar
½ teaspoon freshly grated orange peel
¼ teaspoon ground black pepper
2 cups seedless red grapes, cut in half
2 stalks celery, thinly sliced (1 cup)
2 tablespoons chopped fresh parsley
½ cup pecans, toasted (page 692) and coarsely chopped

1. Cook wild rice as label directs, using ½ teaspoon salt. Cook white rice as label directs, using ¼ teaspoon salt. Set aside.

2. In small bowl, combine cranberries with just enough *boiling water* to cover; let stand 5 minutes to soften. Drain.

3. Meanwhile, prepare dressing: In large bowl, with wire whisk, mix oil, vinegar, orange peel, remaining ¾ teaspoon salt, and pepper until blended. Add wild and white rice and cranberries; toss to coat. Let cool 30 minutes, tossing several times.

4. Add grapes, celery, and parsley to rice mixture; toss until thoroughly mixed and coated with dressing. Transfer to serving bowl. Sprinkle with pecans. Makes 8 accompaniment servings.

Each serving: About 220 calories, 4g protein, 34g carbohydrate, 8g total fat (1g saturated), 0mg cholesterol, 452mg sodium.

MEDITERRANEAN RICE SALAD

·············

For extra color and flavor, add some ripe, juicy chopped tomatoes to this fresh-tasting salad.

Prep: 25 minutes plus cooling   Cook: 30 minutes

2 cups water
1 cup regular long-grain rice
3 garlic cloves, finely chopped
1¼ teaspoons salt
3 tablespoons olive oil
1 small red onion, chopped
1 red pepper, chopped
1 medium zucchini (8 ounces), cut lengthwise into quarters, then crosswise into ½-inch-thick pieces
2 tablespoons fresh lemon juice
⅓ cup Kalamata olives, pitted and coarsely chopped

1. In 2-quart saucepan, heat water to boiling over high heat. Add rice, garlic, and ½ teaspoon salt. Reduce heat; cover and simmer until rice is tender, about 17 minutes.

2. Meanwhile, in 10-inch skillet, heat 1 tablespoon oil over medium heat. Add onion and cook, stirring, 2 minutes. Add red pepper, zucchini, and ¼ teaspoon salt and cook, stirring occasionally, until tender-crisp, about 4 minutes.

3. Prepare dressing: In large bowl, with wire whisk, mix lemon juice, remaining 2 tablespoons oil, and remaining ½ teaspoon salt until blended. Add rice, vegetable mixture, and olives; toss until mixed and coated with dressing. Cool to room temperature. Serve at room temperature, or cover and refrigerate up to 2 hours. Makes 6 accompaniment servings.

Each serving: About 214 calories, 3g protein, 30g carbohydrate, 9g total fat (1g saturated), 0mg cholesterol, 623mg sodium.

BARLEY SALAD WITH NECTARINES

Barley is another grain that makes a flavorful salad. You can use mangoes or peaches instead of the nectarines, if you prefer.

Prep: 30 minutes   Cook: 55 minutes

- 1 package (16 ounces) pearl barley
- 2³/₄ teaspoons salt
- 4 limes
- ¹/₃ cup olive oil
- 1 tablespoon sugar
- ³/₄ teaspoon coarsely ground black pepper
- 1¹/₂ pounds nectarines (4 medium), cut into ¹/₂-inch pieces
- 1 pound ripe tomatoes (2 large), halved, seeded, and cut into ¹/₂-inch pieces
- 4 green onions, thinly sliced
- ¹/₂ cup chopped fresh mint

1. In 4-quart saucepan, heat *6 cups water* to boiling over high heat. Add barley and 1¹/₂ teaspoons salt; heat to boiling. Reduce heat; cover and simmer until barley is tender and liquid has been absorbed, about 45 minutes. (Barley will have a creamy consistency.)

2. Meanwhile, from limes, grate 1 tablespoon peel and squeeze ¹/₂ cup juice. Prepare dressing: In large bowl, with wire whisk, mix lime peel and juice, oil, sugar, pepper, and remaining 1¹/₄ teaspoons salt until blended.

3. Rinse barley with cold running water; drain. Add barley, nectarines, tomatoes, green onions, and mint to dressing in bowl; stir gently until mixed and coated with dressing. If not serving right away, cover and refrigerate up to 1 hour. Makes 16 accompaniment servings.

Each serving: About 172 calories, 4g protein, 30g carbohydrate, 5g total fat (1g saturated), 0mg cholesterol, 333mg sodium.

TUBETTI MACARONI SALAD

Carrots and celery add crunch to this tangy salad. If, after chilling, the salad seems a little dry, stir in a tablespoon or two of milk.

Prep: 25 minutes   Cook: 25 minutes

- 1 package (16 ounces) tubetti or ditalini pasta
- 2³/₄ teaspoons salt
- 4 carrots, peeled and cut into 2" by ¹/₄" matchstick strips
- 1 to 2 lemons
- ²/₃ cup light mayonnaise
- ¹/₃ cup milk
- 2 stalks celery, cut into 2" by ¹/₄" matchstick strips
- 2 green onions, thinly sliced

1. In large saucepot, cook pasta as label directs, using 2 teaspoons salt. After pasta has cooked 10 minutes, add carrots to pasta water and cook until carrots are just tender-crisp and pasta is done, 1 to 2 minutes longer.

2. Meanwhile, from lemons, grate 1 teaspoon peel and squeeze 3 tablespoons juice. Prepare dressing: In large bowl, with wire whisk, mix mayonnaise, milk, lemon peel and juice, and remaining ³/₄ teaspoon salt until blended.

3. Drain pasta and carrots and add to dressing in bowl along with celery and green onions; toss until mixed and coated with dressing. Serve at room temperature, or cover and refrigerate up to 4 hours. Makes 12 accompaniment servings.

Each serving: About 202 calories, 5g protein, 33g carbohydrate, 5g total fat (1g saturated), 5mg cholesterol, 463mg sodium.

MACARONI SALAD

Though popularized in the 1950s in school cafeterias across America, this creamy crowd-pleaser has been around since at least 1917. One of the first printed recipes appeared in Mrs. Allen's Cook Book, which was written by Ida Bailey Allen. The salad contained four simple ingredients—macaroni, celery, stuffed olives, and mayonnaise—and was served chilled on a bed of lettuce.

COBB SALAD

....

The California classic is a composed salad in which the ingredients are artfully arranged rather than tossed. Make one large salad or, if you prefer, arrange on individual serving plates.

Prep: 25 minutes   Broil/Cook: 8 minutes

- 12 ounces skinless, boneless chicken-breast halves
- ¼ teaspoon salt
- ⅛ teaspoon ground black pepper
- 6 slices bacon, coarsely chopped
- 1 large head iceberg lettuce, thinly sliced (12 cups)
- 3 large hard-cooked eggs, peeled and coarsely chopped
- 1 large ripe tomato (10 ounces), cut into ½-inch pieces
- 1 ripe avocado, pitted, peeled, and cut into ½-inch pieces
- 3 ounces Roquefort cheese, crumbled (¾ cup) Classic French Vinaigrette (page 498)

1. Preheat broiler. Place chicken on rack in broiling pan and sprinkle with salt and pepper. Place pan 6 inches from heat source. Broil until chicken loses its pink color throughout, about 4 minutes per side. When chicken is cool enough to handle, cut into ½-inch pieces.

2. Meanwhile, in 10-inch skillet, cook bacon over medium heat until browned. With slotted spoon, transfer bacon to paper towels to drain.

3. Line large platter with iceburg lettuce. Arrange eggs, tomato, avocado, Roquefort, chicken, and bacon in striped pattern over lettuce. Pass dressing separately. Makes 6 main-dish servings.

Each serving (without dressing): About 272 calories, 24g protein, 9g carbohydrate, 16g total fat (6g saturated), 157mg cholesterol, 537mg sodium.

BLUE CHEESE

TEST KITCHEN TIP

Cheeses in this category have been injected with the spores of special molds so that they develop blue or blue-green veins or spotting. Most blue cheeses are strongly flavored and have a soft, crumbly texture. Some can be easily sliced, but most are best spread or crumbled.

DANISH BLUE: A cow's milk cheese with a creamy, moist texture and uncomplicated flavor.

GORGONZOLA: An ivory-colored cow's milk cheese from Italy with a deliciously complex flavor and a creamy texture. There are two kinds of gorgonzola: *dolce*, which is milder, and *naturale*, which is more pungent.

MAYTAG BLUE: An American-made blue cow's milk with a pleasantly bold flavor and creamy texture.

ROQUEFORT: Known by many as the "king of cheeses," it is one of the oldest and most famous cheeses in the world. It is made from sheep's milk and is aged for at least three months in the limestone caverns of Mount Combalou near the town of Roquefort in France. It has a moist, crumbly texture, assertive flavor, and is somewhat salty.

STILTON: A cow's milk cheese from England with a firm yet creamy texture and bold flavor.

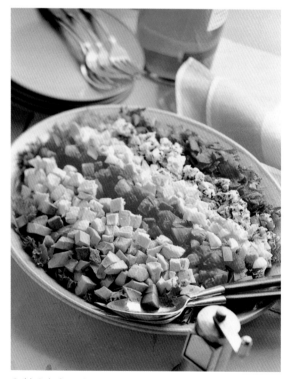

Cobb Salad

NIÇOISE SALAD

(Pictured on page 472)

As the story goes, the first Niçoise salad was created in eighteenth-century France, and it's been a hit ever since.

Prep: 35 minutes   Cook: 25 minutes

- 1 tablespoon white wine vinegar
- 1 tablespoon fresh lemon juice
- 1 tablespoon minced shallot
- 1 teaspoon Dijon mustard
- 1 teaspoon anchovy paste
- 1/4 teaspoon sugar
- 1/4 teaspoon coarsely ground black pepper
- 3 tablespoons extra-virgin olive oil
- 1 pound medium red potatoes, not peeled, cut into 1/4-inch-thick slices
- 8 ounces French green beans (haricots verts) or regular green beans, trimmed
- 1 head Boston lettuce, leaves separated
- 12 cherry tomatoes, each cut in half
- 1 can (12 ounces) solid white tuna in water, drained and flaked
- 2 large hard-cooked eggs, peeled and each cut into quarters
- 1/2 cup Niçoise olives

1. Prepare dressing: In small bowl, with wire whisk, mix vinegar, lemon juice, shallot, mustard, anchovy paste, sugar, and pepper until blended. In thin, steady stream, whisk in oil until blended.

2. In 3-quart saucepan, combine potatoes and enough *water* to cover; heat to boiling over high heat. Reduce heat; cover and simmer until tender, about 10 minutes. Drain.

3. Meanwhile, in 10-inch skillet, heat *1 inch water* to boiling over high heat. Add green beans; heat to boiling. Reduce heat to low and cook until tender-crisp, 6 to 8 minutes. Drain; rinse with cold running water. Drain.

4. To serve, pour half of dressing into medium bowl. Add lettuce leaves and toss to coat. Line large platter with dressed lettuce leaves. Arrange potatoes, green beans, cherry tomatoes, tuna, eggs, and olives in separate piles on lettuce. Drizzle remaining dressing over salad. Makes 4 main-dish servings.

Each serving: About 440 calories, 30g protein, 30g carbohydrate, 23g total fat (4g saturated), 140mg cholesterol, 716mg sodium.

ITALIAN SEAFOOD SALAD

Italians often serve this salad on Christmas Eve, but why not enjoy it throughout the year?

Prep: 50 minutes plus chilling   Cook: 15 minutes

- 1 pound sea scallops
- 2 pounds cleaned squid
- 1 small lemon, thinly sliced
- 2 pounds large shrimp, shelled and deveined (page 221)
- 2/3 cup fresh lemon juice (4 lemons)
- 1/2 cup olive oil
- 1 small garlic clove, minced
- 1/2 teaspoon salt
- 1/2 teaspoon coarsely ground black pepper
- 4 large stalks celery, cut into 1/2-inch pieces
- 1/2 cup Gaeta or Niçoise olives (optional)
- 1/4 cup loosely packed fresh parsley leaves

1. Pull tough crescent-shaped muscle from side of each scallop; discard. Rinse squid; slice bodies crosswise into 3/4-inch-thick rings. Cut tentacles into several pieces if large. In 5-quart saucepot, combine *2 1/2 inches water* and lemon slices; heat to boiling over high heat. Add shrimp. Reduce heat to medium; cook until shrimp are opaque throughout, 1 to 2 minutes. With slotted spoon, transfer shrimp to colander to drain; transfer to large bowl.

2. To boiling water in saucepot, add scallops; cook just until opaque throughout, 2 to 3 minutes. With slotted spoon, transfer to colander to drain; add to shrimp in bowl.

3. To boiling water in saucepot, add squid; cook until tender and opaque, 30 seconds to 1 minute. Drain in colander; add to shrimp and scallops in bowl.

4. Prepare dressing: In small bowl, with wire whisk, mix lemon juice, oil, garlic, salt, and pepper until blended. Add celery, olives if using, and parsley to seafood in bowl; toss to mix. Add dressing and toss until salad is mixed and coated with dressing. Cover and refrigerate salad at least 3 hours to blend flavors or up to 8 hours. Makes 12 first-course servings.

Each serving: About 255 calories, 31g protein, 6g carbohydrate, 11g total fat (2g saturated), 282mg cholesterol, 200mg sodium.

WARM LENTIL SALAD WITH SHRIMP, APPLES, AND MINT

······················

This heart-healthy salad is chock-full of fiber, thanks to crisp Golden Delicious apples and a nutty lentil base.

Prep: 20 minutes   Cook: 8 minutes

- 3 tablespoons olive oil
- 3 tablespoons cider vinegar
- 1½ teaspoons salt
- ¼ teaspoon coarsely ground black pepper
- 1 pound fresh or frozen (thawed) shelled and deveined medium shrimp
- 1 cup lentils, rinsed and picked through
- 6 cups water
- 1 small onion, chopped
- ½ cup loosely packed fresh mint leaves, chopped
- 1 Golden Delicious apple, not peeled, cored and cut into ½-inch chunks
- 1 stalk celery, thinly sliced

1. In small bowl, whisk together oil, vinegar, salt, and pepper. Spoon 2 tablespoons dressing into medium bowl. Add shrimp; toss to coat.

2. In 4-quart saucepan, combine lentils, water, onion, and 2 tablespoons mint; heat to boiling on high. Reduce heat to low; cover and simmer 12 to 15 minutes or until lentils are tender but still hold their shape. Drain well.

3. Meanwhile, heat 12-inch skillet on medium-high until hot. Add shrimp and cook 4 to 5 minutes or until shrimp turn opaque. Remove from heat; stir in 1 tablespoon mint.

4. Stir shrimp, apple, celery, and remaining mint and dressing into lentils. Makes 4 main-dish servings.

Each serving: About 410 calories, 37g protein, 37g carbohydrate, 13g total fat (2g saturated), 17g fiber, 172mg cholesterol, 475mg sodium.

Warm Lentil Salad with Shrimp, Apples, and Mint

TOMATO AND MINT TABBOULEH

....

Tabbouleh, the popular bulgur wheat and vegetable salad, offers one of the best ways to enjoy tomatoes, cucumbers, and fresh herbs.

Prep: 20 minutes plus standing and chilling

1½ cups medium-grain bulgur wheat

¼ cup fresh lemon juice (2 to 3 lemons)

1½ cups boiling water

1 pound ripe tomatoes (3 medium), cut into ½-inch pieces

1 medium cucumber (8 ounces), peeled and cut into ½-inch pieces

3 green onions, chopped

¾ cup loosely packed fresh flat-leaf parsley leaves, chopped

½ cup loosely packed fresh mint leaves, chopped

1 tablespoon olive oil

¾ teaspoon salt

¼ teaspoon coarsely ground black pepper

1. In medium bowl, combine bulgur, lemon juice, and boiling water, stirring to mix. Let stand until liquid has been absorbed, about 30 minutes.

2. To bulgur mixture, add tomatoes, cucumber, green onions, parsley, mint, oil, salt, and pepper, stirring to mix. Cover and refrigerate at least 1 hour to blend flavors or up to 4 hours. Makes 12 accompaniment servings.

Each serving: About 87 calories, 3g protein, 17g carbohydrate, 2g total fat (0g saturated), 0mg cholesterol, 157mg sodium.

TABBOULEH

TEST KITCHEN TIP

Also spelled tabouli and tabouleh, this Lebanese bulgur-based salad is often served as part of a meze (spread of appetizers). Its primary ingredients are bulgur, lots of fresh chopped parsley and mint, chunks of tomato, green onions, and a fresh lemon dressing. Some tabboulehs are flavored with crushed red pepper or fresh chiles, while others contain a hint of cinnamon or allspice.

SOPRESSATA AND ROMA BEAN SALAD WITH PECORINO

....

Slightly sweeter than green beans, broad beans are the oldest beans in existence. Look for those that are pale green, soft, and tender. These beans are best eaten within a few days of purchase.

Prep: 10 minutes   Cook: 12 minutes

1¼ pounds Roma (broad) beans or green beans, trimmed

1 lemon

2 tablespoons extra-virgin olive oil

¼ teaspoon salt

⅛ teaspoon coarsely ground black pepper

4 ounces thinly sliced sopressata or Genoa salami, cut into ½-inch-wide strips

2 small bunches arugula (4 ounces each), tough stems trimmed, or 2 bags (5 ounces each) arugula

1 wedge Pecorino-Romano cheese (about 2 ounces)

1. If Roma beans are very long, cut crosswise into 2½-inch pieces. In 12-inch skillet, heat *1 inch water* to boiling over high heat. Add beans; heat to boiling. Reduce heat to low; simmer until beans are tender-crisp, 6 to 8 minutes. Drain beans. Rinse with cold running water to stop cooking; drain.

2. Meanwhile, from lemon, grate ½ teaspoon peel and squeeze 2 tablespoons juice. In large bowl, with wire whisk, mix lemon peel and juice, oil, salt, and pepper.

3. Add beans, sopressata, and arugula to dressing in bowl; toss to coat.

4. To serve, spoon salad onto serving platter. With vegetable peeler, shave thin strips from wedge of Pecorino onto salad. Makes 4 main-dish servings.

Each serving: About 280 calories, 14g protein, 14g carbohydrate, 21g total fat (7g saturated), 41mg cholesterol, 845mg sodium.

PANZANELLA SALAD

We flavored our version of this classic Italian bread salad with pancetta and arugula.

Prep: 25 minutes   Cook: 15 minutes

- 4 ounces pancetta or 4 slices thick-sliced bacon, cut into ¼-inch pieces
- ½ small loaf peasant bread, cut into ½-inch cubes (about 4 cups)
- 3 tablespoons red wine vinegar
- 2 tablespoons extra-virgin olive oil
- 1 medium shallot, minced (¼ cup)
- ¾ teaspoon salt
- ½ teaspoon sugar
- ¼ teaspoon ground black pepper
- 2 pounds ripe tomatoes (about 6 medium), cut into 1-inch pieces
- 2 small bunches arugula (about 4 ounces each), tough stems trimmed, or 2 bags (5 ounces each) arugula

1. In nonstick 12-inch skillet, cook pancetta over medium heat until lightly browned. With slotted spoon, transfer to paper towels to drain.

2. To pancetta drippings in skillet, add bread cubes and cook, stirring frequently, until lightly browned, 2 to 3 minutes.

3. Meanwhile, prepare dressing: In large bowl, with fork, mix vinegar, oil, shallot, salt, sugar, and pepper until blended.

4. Add tomatoes, arugula, bread cubes, and pancetta to dressing in bowl; toss to combine. Makes 4 main-dish servings.

Each serving: About 300 calories, 9g protein, 29g carbohydrate, 17g total fat (5g saturated), 11mg cholesterol, 735mg sodium.

---

5 IDEAS FOR . . . ITALIAN DRESSING

Ready to use up that family-size bottle that has languished in your fridge for six months?

HERBED PORK CHOPS

In blender, puree ¾ cup dressing, 1 cup packed fresh parsley, and 2 cloves garlic. Reserve ½ cup sauce for serving; place remainder in self-sealing plastic bag with 4 (¾-inch-thick) boneless pork loin chops (1¼ pounds). Seal bag, pressing out air; let stand 20 minutes. Meanwhile, heat ridged grill pan on medium high until very hot. Place chops in pan and cook 4 to 5 minutes per side until still slightly pink in the center. Serve chops with reserved sauce. Serves 4.

MARMALADE CHICKEN

Preheat oven to 400°F. Place 8 bone-in pieces chicken (4 pounds) on foil-lined jelly-roll pan; roast 20 minutes. In bowl, whisk ½ cup orange marmalade with ⅓ cup dressing and 2 teaspoons crushed fennel seeds. Spoon half of marmalade mixture over chicken; roast 20 minutes longer, spooning on remaining mixture after 10 minutes. Transfer chicken to platter. Skim and discard fat from pan juices; serve juices with chicken. Serves 4.

POTATO AND GREEN BEAN SALAD

Peel 1½ pounds Yukon Gold potatoes; cut into 1-inch chunks. In saucepan, heat potatoes and enough water to cover to boiling over high heat. Reduce heat; cook 5 minutes. Add ¾ pound trimmed green beans, cut into 1½-inch pieces; cook 4 minutes longer or until potatoes and beans are tender. Drain vegetables well; place in bowl with ⅓ cup dressing and 3 slices chopped cooked bacon and toss to coat. Serves 8.

ZUCCHINI AND PEPPER MEDLEY

Slice ½ sweet onion and place in microwave-safe large bowl. Cover and microwave on High 2 minutes. Add 2 medium zucchini (sliced into half rounds), 1 yellow pepper (cut into 2-inch-long strips), ¼ cup dressing, and ¼ teaspoon salt. Microwave, covered, 7 to 9 minutes or until vegetables are tender-crisp. Serves 4.

CREAMY BASIL DIP

In blender or food processor, blend 1 cup drained canned white beans, 1 cup packed fresh basil, ¼ cup dressing, and 1 tablespoon fresh lemon juice until smooth. Serve with vegetable sticks. Makes 1½ cups.

THAI BEEF SALAD

Thinly sliced carrots and red pepper add color and crunch to this tangy, herb-packed salad. Roast beef from the deli makes it especially easy to prepare. You could also use grilled flank steak, cooked shrimp, or rotisserie chicken.

Prep: 30 minutes

Thai Dressing

- ¼ cup seasoned rice vinegar
- ¼ cup fresh lime juice (2 to 3 limes)
- 3 tablespoons vegetable oil
- 2 tablespoons grated, peeled fresh ginger
- 1 tablespoon Asian fish sauce (nam pla, see Fish Sauce page 26)
- ⅛ teaspoon ground red pepper (cayenne)

Salad

- 8 ounces thinly sliced deli roast beef, cut into ½-inch-wide strips
- 2 medium carrots, cut into 2" by ¼" matchstick strips
- 1 small red pepper, cut into 2" by ¼" matchstick strips
- 2 green onions, thinly sliced diagonally
- 1 large head Boston lettuce (10 ounces)
- 1½ cups loosely packed fresh cilantro leaves
- 1½ cups loosely packed fresh basil leaves
- 1½ cups loosely packed fresh mint leaves

1. Prepare dressing: In large bowl, with wire whisk, mix vinegar, lime juice, oil, ginger, fish sauce, and ground red pepper.

2. Prepare salad: Add roast beef, carrots, red pepper, and green onions to dressing in bowl; toss to coat.

3. To serve, separate 4 large leaves from head of lettuce and reserve. Tear remaining lettuce into bite-size pieces. Add torn lettuce, cilantro, basil, and mint to bowl with beef; toss again. Place 1 reserved lettuce leaf on each of 4 dinner plates; fill with salad mixture. Makes 4 main-dish servings.

Each serving: About 275 calories, 19g protein, 17g carbohydrate, 15g total fat (2g saturated), 46mg cholesterol, 880mg sodium.

CLASSIC EGG SALAD

The perfect egg salad, like other old-fashioned dishes, is a matter of individual taste. Our recipe leaves room for lots of creativity (see the variations below).

Prep: 10 minutes   Cook: 10 minutes plus standing

- 6 large eggs
- ¼ cup mayonnaise
- 1½ teaspoons Dijon or spicy brown mustard
- ¼ teaspoon salt

1. In 3-quart saucepan, place eggs and enough *cold water* to cover by at least 1 inch; heat to boiling over high heat. Immediately remove saucepan from heat and cover tightly; let stand 15 minutes. Pour off hot water and run cold water over eggs to cool. Peel eggs.

2. Coarsely chop eggs and transfer to medium bowl. Add mayonnaise, mustard, and salt and stir to combine. If not serving right away, cover and refrigerate up to 4 hours. Makes 2 cups or 4 main-dish servings.

Each serving: About 217 calories, 10g protein, 1g carbohydrate, 19g total fat (4g saturated), 327mg cholesterol, 359mg sodium.

CURRIED EGG SALAD

Prepare as directed but add **4 teaspoons chopped mango chutney** and **½ teaspoon curry powder** to egg mixture.

CAESAR-STYLE EGG SALAD

Prepare as directed but use only **⅛ teaspoon salt.** Add **2 tablespoons freshly grated Parmesan cheese** and **1 teaspoon anchovy paste** to egg mixture.

MEXICAN-STYLE EGG SALAD

Prepare as directed but add **⅓ cup chopped fresh cilantro** and **½ teaspoon hot pepper sauce** to egg mixture.

DELI-STYLE EGG SALAD

Prepare as directed but add **¼ cup chopped celery** and **¼ cup chopped red onion** to egg mixture.

BEST CHICKEN SALAD

Plain or fancy, chicken salad is always a treat. Here's a basic recipe plus three of our favorite ways to make it extra special. If you don't want to poach a whole chicken, substitute 3 cups of coarsely chopped deli-roasted chicken or leftover turkey.

Prep: 20 minutes plus cooling   Cook: 1 hour

- 1 chicken (3 pounds)
- 1½ teaspoons salt
- 3 stalks celery, finely chopped
- ¼ cup mayonnaise
- 2 teaspoons fresh lemon juice
- ¼ teaspoon ground black pepper

1. In 4-quart saucepan, combine chicken, 1 teaspoon salt, and enough *water* to cover; heat to boiling over high heat. Reduce heat; cover and simmer gently until chicken loses its pink color throughout, about 45 minutes. Let stand 30 minutes; drain (reserve broth for another use). When chicken is cool enough to handle, discard skin and bones; cut meat into bite-size pieces.

2. In large bowl, combine celery, mayonnaise, lemon juice, remaining ½ teaspoon salt, and pepper; stir until blended. Add chicken and toss to coat. Makes 4 main-dish servings.

Each serving: About 337 calories, 36g protein, 2g carbohydrate, 20g total fat (4g saturated), 117mg cholesterol, 779mg sodium.

BASIL AND DRIED TOMATO CHICKEN SALAD
Prepare as directed but add ¼ **cup chopped fresh basil** and **2 tablespoons finely chopped oil-packed dried tomatoes,** drained, to mayonnaise mixture.

CURRY-GRAPE CHICKEN SALAD
Prepare as directed but add **2 cups red or green seedless grapes,** cut in half, **1 teaspoon curry powder,** and **1 teaspoon honey** to mayonnaise mixture.

LEMON-PEPPER CHICKEN SALAD
Prepare as directed but use **1 tablespoon fresh lemon juice** and ½ **teaspoon black pepper,** coarsely ground; add ½ **teaspoon freshly grated lemon peel** to mayonnaise mixture.

CLASSIC TUNA SALAD

There are other ways to serve tuna salad besides between two slices of bread. Have fun personalizing your salad ingredients, then serve as an open-faced tuna melt or on a bed of crispy greens.

Prep: 10 minutes

- 1 can (6 ounces) solid white tuna in water, drained and broken into pieces
- 2 stalks celery, finely chopped
- 3 tablespoons mayonnaise
- 2 teaspoons fresh lemon juice
- ¼ teaspoon ground black pepper

In small bowl, combine tuna, celery, mayonnaise, lemon juice, and pepper, flaking tuna with fork. If not serving right away, cover and refrigerate up to 4 hours. Makes 1⅓ cups or 2 main-dish servings.

Each serving: About 264 calories, 22g protein, 3g carbohydrate, 18g total fat (3g saturated), 45mg cholesterol, 462mg sodium.

CURRIED TUNA SALAD
Prepare as directed but substitute ½ **Granny Smith apple,** finely chopped, for celery, and add **1 teaspoon curry powder** to tuna mixture.

MEXICAN-STYLE TUNA SALAD
Prepare as directed but add **2 tablespoons chopped fresh cilantro** and **1 pickled jalapeño chile,** finely chopped, to tuna mixture.

MEDITERRANEAN TUNA SALAD
Prepare as directed but omit celery and mayonnaise, and increase lemon juice to 2 tablespoons. Rinse and drain **1 can (15 to 19 ounces) white kidney beans (cannellini).** In large bowl, mash 1 cup beans. Stir in ½ **cup chopped fresh basil, 3 tablespoons minced red onion, 3 tablespoons capers,** drained and chopped, **2 tablespoons olive oil, lemon juice,** and **pepper.** Add tuna and remaining beans; toss to combine. Makes 4 main-dish servings.

CRANBERRY PORT-WINE MOLD

....

A side dish for grown-ups, this jewel-like mold is luscious with a beef rib roast or roast turkey.

Prep: 20 minutes plus chilling   Cook: 15 minutes

- 1 lemon
- 3 cups cranberry-juice cocktail
- 1¼ cups sugar
- 4 whole allspice berries
- 1 cinnamon stick (3 inches), broken in half
- 2 envelopes unflavored gelatin
- 1 cup port wine
  pinch salt
  kumquats, lemon leaves, and frosted cranberries for garnish (optional)

1. From lemon, with vegetable peeler or sharp paring knife, remove 4 strips peel (3" by ¾" each); squeeze 3 tablespoons juice.

2. In nonreactive 2-quart saucepan, heat cranberry juice, sugar, allspice, cinnamon stick, and lemon peel to boiling over high heat; boil 10 minutes.

3. Meanwhile, in small bowl, evenly sprinkle gelatin over port wine; let stand 2 minutes to soften gelatin.

4. With slotted spoon, remove lemon peel and whole spices from cranberry juice and discard. Stir in gelatin mixture and cook over low heat, stirring frequently, until gelatin has completely dissolved, 1 to 2 minutes. Stir in lemon juice and salt.

5. Pour gelatin mixture into 5- to 6-cup decorative mold. Cover with plastic wrap and refrigerate 6 hours or overnight until firm.

6. To unmold, dip pan in large bowl of hot water for 10 seconds and invert onto large round platter. Garnish as desired. Cover and refrigerate up to 2 hours before serving. Makes 8 accompaniment servings.

Each serving: About 225 calories, 2g protein, 48g carbohydrate, 0g total fat, 0mg cholesterol, 25mg sodium.

Cranberry Port-Wine Mold

SALAD DRESSINGS

TOMATO VINAIGRETTE

....

For this salad dressing, a ripe tomato is de rigueur. It's perfect spooned over sliced tomatoes and feta cheese, spinach salad, or mixed greens.

Prep: 15 minutes

- 1 small tomato (4 ounces), peeled and coarsely chopped
- 1 small shallot, cut in half
- 2 tablespoons olive oil
- 1 tablespoon red wine vinegar
- 1 tablespoon balsamic vinegar
- 2 teaspoons Dijon mustard with seeds
- 1 teaspoon chopped fresh oregano
- 1 teaspoon sugar
- ¼ teaspoon salt
- ¼ teaspoon ground black pepper

In blender, combine tomato, shallot, oil, red wine and balsamic vinegars, mustard, oregano, sugar, salt, and pepper; puree just until smooth. Transfer to small bowl or jar. Cover and refrigerate up to 1 day. Makes about 1 cup.

Each tablespoon: About 19 calories, 0g protein, 1g carbohydrate, 2g total fat (0g saturated), 0mg cholesterol, 51mg sodium.

CLASSIC FRENCH VINAIGRETTE

....

Dijon mustard gives this vinaigrette smoothness and just the right amount of zing.

Prep: 5 minutes

- ¼ cup red wine vinegar
- 1 tablespoon Dijon mustard
- ¾ teaspoon salt
- ½ teaspoon coarsely ground black pepper
- ½ cup olive oil

In medium bowl, with wire whisk, mix vinegar, mustard, salt, and pepper until blended. In thin, steady stream, whisk in oil until blended. Cover and refrigerate up to 1 week. Makes about ¾ cup.

Each tablespoon: About 82 calories, 0g protein, 0g carbohydrate, 9g total fat (1g saturated), 0mg cholesterol, 175mg sodium.

BLUE CHEESE VINAIGRETTE

Prepare as directed but add **2 ounces blue cheese, crumbled** (½ cup). Cover and refrigerate up to 2 days. Makes about 1 cup.

MUSTARD-SHALLOT VINAIGRETTE

Prepare as directed but add **1 tablespoon minced shallot.** Cover and refrigerate up to 1 day. Makes about ¾ cup.

BALSAMIC VINAIGRETTE

Prepare as directed but replace red wine vinegar with **balsamic vinegar** and reduce mustard to 1 teaspoon.

CREAMY BLUE CHEESE DRESSING

....

This versatile dressing can be served on mixed greens, lettuce and tomato wedges, chilled cooked vegetables, cold sliced roast beef, or even hard-cooked eggs.

Prep: 10 minutes

- 4 ounces blue cheese, crumbled (1 cup)
- 3 tablespoons half-and-half or light cream
- ½ cup reduced-fat mayonnaise
- 2 tablespoons white wine vinegar
- 1 teaspoon Dijon mustard
- ⅛ teaspoon salt
- ⅛ teaspoon ground black pepper

In small bowl, with fork, mash cheese with half-and-half until creamy; add mayonnaise, vinegar, mustard, salt, and pepper. With wire whisk, beat until well mixed. Cover and refrigerate up to 3 days. Makes about 1 cup.

Each tablespoon: About 55 calories, 2g protein, 1g carbohydrate, 5g total fat (2g saturated fat), 9mg cholesterol, 178mg sodium.

HONEY-LIME VINAIGRETTE

Try this sweet and tangy fat-free dressing on sliced cucumbers or your favorite greens.

Prep: 5 minutes

- ⅓ cup fresh lime juice (2 to 3 limes)
- 4 teaspoons honey
- 1 tablespoon rice vinegar
- ⅛ teaspoon salt

In small bowl, with wire whisk, mix lime juice, honey, vinegar, and salt until blended. Cover and refrigerate up to 3 days. Makes about ½ cup.

Each tablespoon: About 13 calories, 0g protein, 4g carbohydrate, 0g total fat (0g saturated), 0mg cholesterol, 37mg sodium.

RANCH DRESSING

Buttermilk gives ranch dressing its characteristic tang and creaminess. Use the large holes on a box grater to grate the onion.

Prep: 10 minutes

- ½ cup buttermilk
- ⅓ cup mayonnaise
- 1 tablespoon chopped fresh parsley
- ½ teaspoon grated onion
- ¼ teaspoon salt
- ¼ teaspoon ground black pepper
- 1 garlic clove, cut in half

In small bowl, with wire whisk, mix buttermilk, mayonnaise, parsley, onion, salt, and pepper until blended; stir in garlic. Cover and refrigerate up to 3 days. Remove garlic before serving. Makes about ¾ cup.

Each tablespoon: About 48 calories, 0g protein, 1g carbohydrate, 5g total fat (1g saturated), 4mg cholesterol, 93mg sodium.

TAHINI DRESSING

Try this sesame-paste dressing on sautéed or broiled chicken or vegetables, as well as on salads.

Prep: 10 minutes

- ⅓ cup tahini (sesame seed paste)
- 2 tablespoons fresh lemon juice
- 4 teaspoons soy sauce
- 1 tablespoon honey (optional)
- ½ small garlic clove, minced
- ½ teaspoon ground black pepper

In small bowl, with wire whisk, mix tahini, lemon juice, soy sauce, honey if using, garlic, and pepper until smooth. Cover and refrigerate up to 2 days. Makes about ¾ cup.

Each tablespoon: About 41 calories, 1g protein, 2g carbohydrate, 4g total fat (0g saturated), 0mg cholesterol, 122mg sodium.

JAPANESE MISO VINAIGRETTE

Miso comes in different colors and flavor variances, but any one will make a tasty dressing.

Prep: 10 minutes

- 2 tablespoons miso (fermented soybean paste)
- ½ cup rice vinegar
- ¼ cup olive oil
- 1 tablespoon minced, peeled fresh ginger
- 1 tablespoon sugar

In small bowl, with wire whisk, stir miso into vinegar until smooth. In blender, combine miso mixture, oil, ginger, and sugar; puree until smooth. Transfer to small bowl or jar. Cover and refrigerate up to 3 days. Makes about 1 cup.

Each tablespoon: About 38 calories, 0g protein, 1g carbohydrate, 4g total fat (0g saturated), 0mg cholesterol, 78mg sodium.

15

SAUCES, SALSAS & CONDIMENTS

In fashion, a beautiful necklace can turn a simple black dress into an exquisite outfit. And in cooking, a fine sauce can turn simple food into something fabulous.

Sauces are typically described as liquid or semi-liquid accompaniments to main courses or desserts. Most of the classic sauces are French, with the base sauces called mother sauces. Different ingredients are added to these mother sauces to make an almost endless number of variations. For example, when béchamel (white sauce) has Gruyère cheese added, it becomes Mornay sauce. Many of the traditional sauces are cooked, and most depend on butter and homemade stock for body and flavor.

But these days, the French dominance over the saucepot no longer exists. Today's sauces come from all around the world; many aren't cooked at all and don't contain any stock or butter. Salsa, that sprightly chile-kissed sauce from south of the border, can be made with vegetables or fruits and served with everything from grilled fish to tortilla chips. And some sauces, such as the Italian *salmoriglio* and the Argentinean *chimichurri*, are based on olive oil and a combination of fragrant fresh herbs. These sauces are ideal for simple grilled fish, poultry, pork, or beef. In fact, chimichurri is the classic accompaniment to grilled steak in Argentina.

Classic French butter sauces, such as hollandaise, béarnaise, and beurre blanc, are meant to be served warm. They cannot be reheated, or they will curdle. So keep them at serving temperature the way they do in restaurants. To hold a butter sauce warm for up to 20 minutes, place the bowl of sauce in a skillet of very hot—not simmering—water. Whisk well before serving to dissolve any thin skin that may have formed. To hold for up to one hour, transfer the sauce, as soon as it is prepared, to a wide-mouthed vacuum bottle (rinse the bottle first with hot water to warm it) and seal. When ready to serve, transfer the sauce to a serving dish.

Sometimes a thick sweet-and-tangy condiment is the preferred way to accent a main course. Intricately seasoned but easy to make Indian-inspired fruit chutneys are excellent with grilled meats. In this chapter, you'll also find an assortment of tasty condiments, perfect accompaniments for the holiday turkey, a favorite sandwich, or your grilled London broil.

Dessert sauces are for those times when you want to gild the lily. A piece of chocolate cake can be wonderful, but when served in a pool of jewel-colored raspberry sauce, it becomes sublime. These sauces are also delicious served over ice cream or spooned over waffles for a special breakfast treat.

Peach Salsa, Tomato Salsa, and Tomatillo Salsa
(recipes pages 507–508)

WHITE SAUCE (BÉCHAMEL)

....

This classic sauce is the foundation for many popular dishes, including moussaka and macaroni and cheese.

Prep: 2 minutes   Cook: 15 minutes

- 2 tablespoons butter or margarine
- 2 tablespoons all-purpose flour
- 1 cup milk, warmed
- ½ teaspoon salt
  pinch ground nutmeg

In heavy 1-quart saucepan, melt butter over low heat. Add flour and cook, stirring, 1 minute. With wire whisk, gradually whisk in warm milk. Cook over

medium heat, stirring constantly with wooden spoon, until sauce has thickened and boils. Reduce heat and simmer, stirring frequently, 5 minutes. Remove from heat and stir in salt and nutmeg. Makes about 1 cup.

Each tablespoon: About 26 calories, 1g protein, 1g carbohydrate, 2g total fat (1g saturated), 6mg cholesterol, 94mg sodium.

CHEESE SAUCE

Prepare sauce as directed above. Remove saucepan from heat. Add **4 ounces sharp Cheddar cheese,** shredded (1 cup); stir until cheese has melted and sauce is smooth. Makes about 1¼ cups.

Each tablespoon: About 54 calories, 2g protein, 2g carbohydrate, 4g total fat (3g saturated), 13mg cholesterol, 138mg sodium.

MORNAY SAUCE

Prepare sauce as directed above. Remove saucepan from heat. Add **2 ounces Gruyère cheese,** shredded (½ cup); stir until cheese has melted and sauce is smooth. Makes about 1 cup.

Each tablespoon: About 40 calories, 2g protein, 1g carbohydrate, 3g total fat (2g saturated), 10mg cholesterol, 106mg sodium.

HOLLANDAISE SAUCE

....

An irresistible velvety sauce that's easier to make than you would expect. The traditional recipe uses undercooked eggs, but our updated version cooks them long enough to make them safe to eat.

Prep: 5 minutes   Cook: 10 minutes

- 3 large egg yolks
- ¼ cup water
- 2 tablespoons fresh lemon juice
- ½ cup cold butter (1 stick), cut into 8 pieces
  (do not use margarine)
- ¼ teaspoon salt

1. In heavy nonreactive 1-quart saucepan, with wire whisk, mix egg yolks, water, and lemon juice until well blended. Cook over medium-low heat, stirring constantly with wooden spoon or heat-safe rubber spatula, until egg-yolk mixture just begins to bubble at edge, 6 to 8 minutes.

2. Reduce heat to low. With wire whisk, whisk in butter, one piece at a time, until each addition is incorporated and sauce has thickened. Remove from heat and stir in salt. Strain through sieve, if you like. Makes scant 1 cup.

Each tablespoon: About 62 calories, 1g protein, 0g carbohydrate, 7g total fat (4g saturated), 55mg cholesterol, 96mg sodium.

CAPER SAUCE

Prepare as directed, above, but stir **1 tablespoon drained capers** into the sauce. Serve with fish or chicken.

MALTESE SAUCE

Prepare as directed, above, but substitute **orange juice** for the lemon juice and add **1½ teaspoons grated orange peel** to the sauce after straining. Pair this with asparagus.

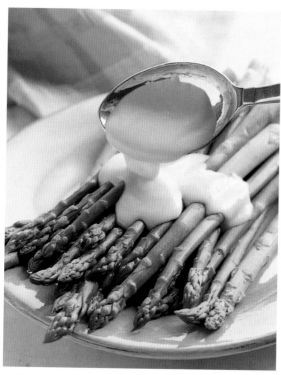
Hollandaise Sauce

1. In nonreactive 1-quart saucepan, combine vinegar, wine, and shallots; heat to boiling over high heat. Boil until liquid has reduced to ¼ cup, about 7 minutes. With back of spoon, press mixture through fine sieve into medium bowl or top of double boiler.

2. With wire whisk, beat egg yolks, water, and pepper into vinegar mixture. Set bowl over saucepan of simmering water. Cook, whisking constantly, until egg-yolk mixture bubbles around edge and has thickened, about 10 minutes.

3. Reduce heat to very low. With wire whisk, whisk in butter, one piece at a time, until each addition is incorporated and sauce has thickened. Remove from heat and stir in tarragon and salt. Makes 1 cup.

Each tablespoon: About 68 calories, 1g protein, 1g carbohydrate, 7g total fat (4g saturated), 55mg cholesterol, 60mg sodium.

BÉARNAISE SAUCE

* *

A rich yet tangy topping for steak, grilled chicken, vegetables, or poached eggs. If you don't have tarragon vinegar, use white wine vinegar and toss in an extra tablespoon of fresh tarragon.

Prep: 5 minutes   Cook: 30 minutes

- ½ cup tarragon vinegar
- ⅓ cup dry white wine
- 2 shallots, finely chopped
- 3 large egg yolks
- ¼ cup water
  pinch ground black pepper
- ½ cup cold butter (1 stick), cut into 8 pieces (do not use margarine)
- 1 tablespoon chopped fresh tarragon
- ¼ teaspoon salt

SAUCE RÉMOULADE

* *

This rich flavorful sauce is excellent with chilled shellfish or cooked vegetables. You can also spice it up Cajun style: Omit the tarragon and Dijon, and heat it up with some Creole mustard and ground red pepper.

Prep: 20 minutes

- ⅓ cup mayonnaise
- 2 tablespoons sour cream
- 3 tablespoons finely chopped dill pickle
- 1 tablespoon chopped fresh parsley
- ¾ teaspoon chopped fresh tarragon or ¼ teaspoon dried tarragon
- ½ teaspoon chopped fresh chives
- 1 anchovy fillet, finely chopped
- 1 teaspoon capers, drained and chopped
- 1 teaspoon Dijon mustard

In small bowl, combine mayonnaise, sour cream, pickle, parsley, tarragon, chives, anchovy, capers, and mustard until well blended. Serve, or cover and refrigerate up to 1 day. Makes about ⅔ cup.

Each tablespoon: About 61 calories, 0g protein, 0g carbohydrate, 6g total fat (1g saturated), 6mg cholesterol, 143mg sodium.

FLAVORED BUTTERS

Flavored butters are ideal for dressing up panfried or grilled steak or fish when unexpected company drops by. Here are a few favorites, but you can stir in just about any flavoring that strikes your fancy. For strong-flavored ingredients like horseradish or capers, start with about 2 tablespoons per stick of butter. You can add up to ¼ cup of ingredients total; just be sure to drain wet items well. Prepare ahead—these take just 10 minutes—and freeze to eliminate last-minute fussing.

In medium bowl, beat ½ cup butter or margarine (1 stick), softened, with wooden spoon until creamy. Beat in your choice of flavor ingredients (right); blend well. Transfer flavored butter to waxed paper and shape into log about 6 inches long; wrap, twisting ends of waxed paper to seal. Overwrap in plastic or foil before chilling or freezing. Flavored butters can be refrigerated up to 2 days or frozen up to 1 month. To serve, cut into ½-inch-thick slices. Makes 12 servings each.

MAÎTRE D'HÔTEL BUTTER

Very versatile; use on beef, veal, chicken, pork, and fish.

- 2 tablespoons chopped fresh parsley
- ¼ teaspoon freshly grated lemon peel
- 1 tablespoon fresh lemon juice

OLIVE BUTTER

Best on fish and chicken.

- ⅓ cup Kalamata olives, pitted and finely chopped
- 1 tablespoon chopped fresh parsley

GINGER-CILANTRO BUTTER

Good on chicken and fish.

- 2 tablespoons finely chopped fresh cilantro
- 2 teaspoons fresh lime juice
- ½ teaspoon grated, peeled fresh ginger

CAPER BUTTER

Good on beef, veal, pork, fish, and chicken.

- 2 tablespoons capers, drained and chopped
- 1 tablespoon chopped fresh parsley
- ½ teaspoon freshly grated lemon peel

TARTAR SAUCE

Serve this tasty sauce with Crab Cakes (page 47), shrimp, and baked, broiled, or fried fish.

Prep: 15 minutes

- ½ cup mayonnaise
- ¼ cup finely chopped dill pickle
- 1 tablespoon chopped fresh parsley
- 2 teaspoons milk
- 2 teaspoons distilled white vinegar
- ½ teaspoon finely chopped onion
- ½ teaspoon Dijon mustard

In small bowl, combine mayonnaise, pickle, parsley, milk, vinegar, onion, and mustard until well blended. Serve, or cover and refrigerate up to 2 days. Makes about ¾ cup.

Each tablespoon: About 68 calories, 0g protein, 0g carbohydrate, 7g total fat (1g saturated), 6mg cholesterol, 125mg sodium.

CILANTRO SAUCE

As with many fresh herb-based sauces, this one is perfect with beef tenderloin, cold roast turkey, or poached salmon.

Prep: 10 minutes

- 1 cup tightly packed fresh cilantro leaves
- ¾ cup light mayonnaise
- ¾ cup reduced-fat sour cream
- 2 teaspoons fresh lime juice
- ¼ teaspoon hot pepper sauce

In blender or in food processor with knife blade attached, puree cilantro, mayonnaise, sour cream, lime juice, and hot pepper sauce until smooth. Serve, or cover and refrigerate up to 1 day. Makes 1⅔ cups.

Each tablespoon: About 35 calories, 1g protein, 1g carbohydrate, 3g total fat (1g saturated), 5mg cholesterol, 59mg sodium.

SALMORIGLIO SAUCE

If you have oregano growing in your garden, chop enough to equal 1 tablespoon and use instead of dried oregano.

Prep: 10 minutes plus standing

- ¼ cup fresh lemon juice (1 to 2 lemons)
- 1 garlic clove, crushed with side of chef's knife
- 1 teaspoon dried oregano, crumbled
- ¼ teaspoon salt
- ¼ teaspoon coarsely ground black pepper
- ⅓ cup extra-virgin olive oil

1. In medium bowl, combine lemon juice, garlic, oregano, salt, and pepper. Let stand 30 minutes.

2. With wire whisk, in thin, steady stream, whisk in oil until blended. Serve, or let stand up to 4 hours at room temperature. Whisk just before serving. Makes scant ⅔ cup.

Each tablespoon: About 66 calories, 0g protein, 1g carbohydrate, 7g total fat (1g saturated), 0mg cholesterol, 57mg sodium.

CHIMICHURRI SAUCE

This Argentinean herb vinaigrette is the sauce served at Buenos Aires steak houses. Drizzle it on sandwiches, or serve with grilled or roasted meats.

Prep: 20 minutes

- 1 large garlic clove, minced
- ½ teaspoon salt
- 1½ cups loosely packed fresh parsley leaves, chopped
- 1 cup loosely packed fresh cilantro leaves, chopped
- ¾ cup olive oil
- 2 tablespoons red wine vinegar
- ½ teaspoon crushed red pepper

1. With side of chef's knife, mash garlic and salt to a smooth paste.

2. In small bowl, combine garlic mixture, parsley, cilantro, oil, vinegar, and crushed red pepper until well blended. Serve, or cover and refrigerate up to 4 hours. Makes about 1 cup.

Each tablespoon: About 93 calories, 0g protein, 1g carbohydrate, 10g total fat (1g saturated), 0mg cholesterol, 76mg sodium.

SALSA VERDE (GREEN SAUCE)

Especially good with fish, this uncooked bright green Italian sauce goes with almost any savory food.

Prep: 20 minutes

- 1 large garlic clove, minced
- ¼ teaspoon salt
- 2 cups tightly packed fresh flat-leaf parsley leaves
- 8 anchovy fillets, drained and finely chopped (optional)
- 3 tablespoons capers, drained
- 1 teaspoon Dijon mustard
- ⅛ teaspoon ground black pepper
- ½ cup olive oil
- 3 tablespoons fresh lemon juice (1 lemon)

1. With side of chef's knife, mash garlic and salt to a smooth paste.

2. In blender or in food processor with knife blade attached, puree parsley, anchovies if using, capers, mustard, pepper, oil, lemon juice, and garlic mixture, until almost smooth. Serve, or cover and refrigerate up to 4 hours. Makes about 1 cup.

Each tablespoon: About 69 calories, 1g protein, 2g carbohydrate, 7g total fat (1g saturated), 0mg cholesterol, 123mg sodium.

GARLIC GLOSSARY

AMERICAN: This variety is white-skinned and strongly flavored.

ITALIAN: A variety with purplish skin; it is slightly milder than white-skinned garlic.

MEXICAN: Similar to Italian, it has purplish skin and a slightly milder taste than American garlic.

ELEPHANT: Not a true garlic but a member of the leek family, it has a relatively tame garlic flavor. With a bulb the size of a grapefruit, it is sometimes sold by the clove.

GARLIC SHOOTS: These green shoots, which resemble chives, are the stems of an immature garlic plant. They have a mild garlic flavor and can be used raw or cooked.

GREEN GARLIC: Garlic that is harvested just before it begins to form cloves.

ASIAN PEANUT SAUCE

....

Toss with linguine, along with slivers of green onion, thin strips of red bell peppers, and half-moon slices of seedless cucumber for a tasty summertime side dish.

Prep: 10 minutes

- ½ cup creamy peanut butter
- ½ cup water
- ¼ cup soy sauce
- 1 tablespoon grated, peeled fresh ginger
- 2 tablespoons distilled white vinegar
- 2 tablespoons Asian sesame oil
- 1 tablespoon packed brown sugar
- ¼ teaspoon hot pepper sauce

In a blender or food processor with knife blade attached, combine peanut butter, water, soy sauce, ginger, vinegar, sesame oil, brown sugar, and hot pepper sauce; puree until smooth. Serve, or cover and refrigerate up to 1 day. Makes 1½ cups.

Each tablespoon: About 47 calories, 2g protein, 2g carbohydrate, 4g total fat (1g saturated), 0mg cholesterol, 189mg sodium.

SWEET CORN SALSA

....

This deftly seasoned salsa tastes equally delicious made with frozen corn kernels or with fresh. It keeps well in the refrigerator.

Prep: 20 minutes plus chilling   Cook: 10 minutes

- 8 ears corn, husks and silk removed, or 1 bag (20 ounces) frozen whole-kernel corn, thawed
- 3 tablespoons fresh lime juice (about 2 limes)
- 2 tablespoons olive oil
- ¾ teaspoon ground cumin
- ¾ teaspoon ground coriander
- ¾ teaspoon salt
- ½ teaspoon chili powder
- 1 large red pepper, finely chopped

1. If using fresh corn, with sharp knife, cut kernels from cobs. Heat 6-quart saucepot of *water* to boiling over high heat. Add corn kernels and heat to boiling; boil 30 seconds. Drain. Rinse with cold running water and drain.

2. In medium bowl, whisk lime juice, oil, cumin, coriander, salt, and chili powder until blended. Add corn and red pepper; toss until mixed and coated with dressing. Cover and refrigerate until well chilled, about 2 hours or up to 2 weeks. Makes about 5 cups.

Each ¼ cup: About 41 calories, 1g protein, 6g carbohydrate, 2g total fat (0g saturated), 0mg cholesterol, 93mg sodium.

OLIVE AND LEMON SALSA

....

The sweet citrus flavor of oranges and lemons is the perfect foil for the salty olives in this sauce.

Prep: 15 minutes

- 2 small navel oranges
- 2 lemons
- ¼ cup coarsely chopped pimiento-stuffed olives (salad olives)
- 2 tablespoons chopped shallots
- 2 tablespoons chopped fresh parsley
- ½ teaspoon sugar
- ¼ teaspoon coarsely ground black pepper

1. Cut peel and white pith from oranges and lemons. Cut fruit into ¼-inch-thick slices; discard seeds. Cut slices into ½-inch pieces.

2. In small bowl, gently stir orange and lemon pieces, olives, shallots, parsley, sugar, and pepper until well mixed. Serve, or cover and refrigerate up to 1 day. Makes about 2 cups.

Each ¼ cup: About 28 calories, 1g protein, 7g carbohydrate, 1g total fat (0g saturated), 0mg cholesterol, 104mg sodium.

GINGER

Ginger is not a root—though it is often called gingerroot—but a rhizome (underground stem). It is widely used in Asian dishes as an essential aromatic ingredient. Its flavor is a combination of spicy and slightly sweet. Peeled and chopped, or grated, sliced and pounded, it adds loads of flavor. Ginger is also available crystallized, ground, and pickled.

TOMATO SALSA

(Pictured on page 500)

....

As a topping for burgers, this flavor-packed salsa is stiff competition for plain old ketchup.

Prep: 20 minutes plus chilling

- 1 large lime
- 1½ pounds ripe tomatoes (3 large), chopped
- ½ small red onion, finely chopped
- 1 small jalapeño chile, seeded and minced
- 2 tablespoons chopped fresh cilantro
- ¾ teaspoon salt
- ¼ teaspoon coarsely ground black pepper

From lime, grate ½ teaspoon peel and squeeze 2 tablespoons juice. In medium bowl, gently stir lime peel and juice, tomatoes, onion, jalapeño, cilantro, salt, and pepper until well mixed. Cover and refrigerate at least 1 hour or up to 2 days. Makes about 3 cups.

Each ¼ cup: About 15 calories, 1g protein, 3g carbohydrate, 0g total fat (0g saturated), 0mg cholesterol, 151mg sodium.

TOMATILLO SALSA

(Pictured on page 500)

....

The tomatillo, also called a Mexican green tomato, is actually related to the gooseberry. It has an acidic fruity flavor that is great with grilled meats and fish.

Prep: 25 minutes plus chilling

- 1 pound fresh tomatillos (about 10 medium), husked, washed well, and cut into quarters
- ¾ cup loosely packed fresh cilantro leaves, chopped
- ¼ cup finely chopped onion
- 1 or 2 serrano or jalapeño chiles, seeded and minced
- 1 garlic clove, minced
- 1 tablespoon olive oil
- 1 teaspoon sugar
- ½ teaspoon salt

1. In food processor with knife blade attached, coarsely chop tomatillos.

2. In medium bowl, gently stir tomatillos, cilantro, onion, serranos, garlic, oil, sugar, and salt until well mixed. Cover and refrigerate at least 1 hour to blend flavors or up to 3 days. Makes about 2 cups.

Each ¼ cup: About 34 calories, 1g protein, 3g carbohydrate, 2g total fat (0g saturated), 0mg cholesterol, 146mg sodium.

ORANGE-FENNEL SALSA

....

Not your usual tomato-based salsa, this is sweet, spicy, and aromatic. It is excellent with grilled fish or pork.

Prep: 20 minutes

- 3 small navel oranges
- 1 large fennel bulb (1½ pounds), trimmed and chopped
- ½ small red onion, thinly sliced
- ¼ cup chopped fresh cilantro leaves
- 1 jalapeño chile, seeded and minced
- ¼ teaspoon salt

1. Cut peel and white pith from oranges. Holding oranges over medium bowl to catch juice, cut sections from between membranes, allowing sections to drop into bowl.

2. Add fennel, onion, cilantro, jalapeño, and salt; gently stir until well mixed. Serve, or cover and refrigerate up to 1 day. Makes about 3 cups.

Each ¼ cup: About 24 calories, 1g protein, 5g carbohydrate, 0g total fat (0g saturated), 0mg cholesterol, 94mg sodium.

SEEDING CHILES

TEST KITCHEN TIP

Recipes usually call for seeding chiles, which tones down the heat. To avoid irritation, wear surgical or rubber gloves and do not touch your eyes. To seed a chile, using a small knife, cut the chile lengthwise in half, then cut out the membranes (which hold a lot of heat) and seeds; discard. Cut off and discard the stem and mince or cut up chile as directed.

PEACH SALSA

(Pictured on page 500)

....

For the best flavor, wait until it is the height of peach season to make this salsa. Spoon it over grilled chicken breasts or pork chops.

Prep: 30 minutes plus chilling

- 1¾ pounds ripe peaches (5 medium), peeled, pitted, and chopped
- 2 tablespoons finely chopped red onion
- 1 tablespoon chopped fresh mint
- 1 teaspoon seeded, minced jalapeño chile
- 1 tablespoon fresh lime juice
- ⅛ teaspoon salt

In medium bowl, gently stir peaches, onion, mint, jalapeño, lime juice, and salt until well mixed. Cover and refrigerate 1 hour to blend flavors or up to 2 days. Makes about 3 cups.

Each ¼ cup: About 23 calories, 0g protein, 6g carbohydrate, 0g total fat (0g saturated), 0mg cholesterol, 25mg sodium.

PLUM SALSA

Prepare as directed above but substitute **1½ pounds ripe plums,** pitted and chopped, for peaches. Use only **1 tablespoon red onion,** finely chopped. Omit mint, jalapeño, and lime juice. Add **2 tablespoons balsamic vinegar** and **1 tablespoon chopped fresh basil** with salt.

Each ¼ cup: About 30 calories, 0g protein, 7g carbohydrate, 0g total fat (0g saturated), 0mg cholesterol, 25mg sodium.

WATERMELON SALSA

Prepare as directed above but substitute **2½ pounds watermelon,** seeded and chopped, for peaches. Use only **1 tablespoon red onion,** finely chopped. Omit mint. Add **2 teaspoons seeded and minced jalapeño chile,** and **2 tablespoons fresh lime juice** with salt.

Each ¼ cup: About 17 calories, 0g protein, 4g carbohydrate, 0g total fat (0g saturated), 0mg cholesterol, 26mg sodium.

NO-COOK KIRBY AND CARROT PICKLES

....

Kirbys are thin-skinned small cucumbers that make the best pickles.

Prep: 10 minutes plus chilling

- 1 garlic clove, cut in half
- ½ cup distilled white vinegar
- ½ cup sugar
- ¾ teaspoon salt
- 5 small kirby (pickling) cucumbers (about 3 ounces each), unpeeled and cut crosswise into ¼-inch-thick slices
- 2 large carrots, peeled and cut crosswise into ¼-inch-thick slices

1. In large zip-tight plastic bag, combine all ingredients; seal bag, pressing out excess air. Shake to mix ingredients. Place bag on plate; refrigerate overnight, turning bag occasionally.

2. To serve, drain pickles or, if you like, spoon pickles with their liquid into jars with tight-fitting lids and refrigerate up to 1 week. Makes about 3½ cups.

Each ¼ cup, drained: About 15 calories, 0g protein, 3g carbohydrate, 0g total fat, 0mg cholesterol, 90mg sodium.

NO-COOK CRANBERRY-ORANGE RELISH

....

A classic holiday recipe that's truly no-fuss.

Prep: 15 minutes plus chilling

- 1 bag (12 ounces) cranberries, picked over and rinsed
- 1 medium orange, cut into pieces, seeds discarded
- ⅔ cup sugar

In food processor with knife blade attached, combine cranberries, orange, and sugar; pulse until coarsely chopped. Transfer to bowl. Cover and refrigerate until well chilled, about 2 hours or up to 2 days. Makes about 3 cups.

Each ¼ cup: About 62 calories, 0g protein, 17g carbohydrate, 0g total fat (0g saturated), 0mg cholesterol, 1mg sodium.

SOUTHWESTERN-STYLE CRANBERRY RELISH

....

A finely chopped jalapeño pepper adds lots of unexpected, delicious heat to cranberries. This relish is the perfect accompaniment for a smoky grilled turkey at Thanksgiving.

Prep: 10 minutes plus chilling   **Cook: 15 minutes**

- 1 lemon
- 1 bag (12 ounces) cranberries, picked over and rinsed
- 1 pickled jalapeño chile, finely chopped
- ½ cup honey
- ¼ cup cider vinegar
- 1 teaspoon mustard seeds
- ½ teaspoon salt
- ½ teaspoon ground black pepper

1. From lemon, with vegetable peeler, remove peel in 1-inch-wide strips. Cut strips crosswise into slivers.

2. In nonreactive 2-quart saucepan, combine cranberries, lemon peel, pickled jalapeño, honey, vinegar, mustard seeds, salt, and pepper; heat to boiling over high heat. Reduce heat; simmer, stirring occasionally, until most cranberries have popped and mixture has thickened slightly, about 10 minutes.

3. Cover and refrigerate until well chilled, about 3 hours or up to 4 days. Makes about 2 cups.

Each ¼ cup: About 90 calories, 0g protein, 24g carbohydrate, 0g total fat, 0mg cholesterol, 174mg sodium.

CRANBERRY-FIG CHUTNEY

....

This sweet-tart condiment will stand up to any spicy food, especially Indian, but it will also perk up less highly seasoned dishes.

Prep: 15 minutes plus chilling   **Cook: 35 minutes**

- 1 bag (12 ounces) cranberries, picked over and rinsed
- 1 package (8 ounces) dried Calimyrna figs, stemmed and sliced
- 1 cup packed brown sugar
- 1 cup water
- ⅓ cup red wine vinegar
- 1 small onion, chopped
- ½ small lemon, chopped, seeds discarded
- 2 tablespoons minced, peeled fresh ginger
- ½ teaspoon salt
- ¼ teaspoon coarsely ground black pepper

1. In nonreactive 3-quart saucepan, combine cranberries, figs, brown sugar, water, vinegar, onion, lemon, ginger, salt, and pepper; heat to boiling over high heat, stirring occasionally. Reduce heat and simmer, stirring occasionally, 30 minutes.

2. Cover and refrigerate until well chilled, about 4 hours or up to 2 days. Makes about 4 cups.

Each ¼ cup: About 103 calories, 1g protein, 27g carbohydrate, 0g total fat (0g saturated), 0mg cholesterol, 80mg sodium.

TASTY WAYS TO SERVE OUR CRANBERRY-FIG CHUTNEY

- Puree in a blender until smooth and use as a glaze for roast ham or chicken.

- Stir in a little Dijon mustard and use as a dipping sauce for shish kebabs or mini frankfurters.

- Swirl into softened cream cheese or goat cheese and serve with crackers or apple slices.

- Stir into mayonnaise for a delicious spread for ham or turkey sandwiches.

- Serve as an accompaniment for grilled Cheddar cheese sandwiches.

Hot Fudge Sauce

HOT FUDGE SAUCE

....

Use this rich sauce as a topping for ice cream or other desserts. Unsweetened cocoa powder makes it quick and easy to prepare.

Prep: 5 minutes   Cook: 5 minutes

- ³/₄ cup sugar
- ¹/₂ cup unsweetened cocoa
- ¹/₂ cup heavy or whipping cream
- 4 tablespoons butter or margarine, cut into pieces
- 1 teaspoon vanilla extract

In heavy 1-quart saucepan, combine sugar, cocoa, cream, and butter; heat to boiling over high heat, stirring frequently. Remove saucepan from heat; stir in vanilla. Serve warm, or cool completely, then cover and refrigerate up to 2 weeks. Gently reheat before using. Makes about 1¼ cups.

Each tablespoon: About 75 calories, 1g protein, 9g carbohydrate, 5g total fat (3g saturated), 14mg cholesterol, 26mg sodium.

BUTTERSCOTCH SAUCE

....

This old-fashioned favorite can be depended on to liven up a simple scoop of ice cream, but it's also wonderful with apple pie.

Prep: 5 minutes   Cook: 5 minutes

- 1 cup packed brown sugar
- ¹/₂ cup heavy or whipping cream
- ¹/₃ cup light corn syrup
- 2 tablespoons butter or margarine
- 1 teaspoon distilled white vinegar
- ¹/₈ teaspoon salt
- 1 teaspoon vanilla extract

In heavy 3-quart saucepan, combine brown sugar, cream, corn syrup, butter, vinegar, and salt; heat to boiling over high heat, stirring occasionally. Reduce heat and simmer 2 minutes. Remove saucepan from heat; stir in vanilla. Serve warm, or cover and refrigerate up to 1 week. Makes 1¹/₃ cups.

Each tablespoon: About 84 calories, 0g protein, 14g carbohydrate, 3g total fat (2g saturated), 11mg cholesterol, 38mg sodium.

HARD SAUCE

....

The essential companion to any warm steamed pudding—especially Christmas plum pudding.

Prep: 10 minutes

- 1 cup butter (2 sticks), softened (do not use margarine)
- 2 cups confectioners' sugar
- ¹/₄ cup dark rum or brandy
- 1 teaspoon vanilla extract

1. In small bowl, with mixer at medium speed, beat butter until creamy. Reduce speed to low and gradually beat in confectioners' sugar until light and fluffy. Beat in rum and vanilla.

2. Serve, or transfer to airtight container and refrigerate up to 1 month. Let stand at room temperature until soft enough to spread, about 30 minutes. Makes about 2 cups.

Each tablespoon: About 84 calories, 0g protein, 7g carbohydrate, 6g total fat (4g saturated), 16mg cholesterol, 59mg sodium.

CUSTARD SAUCE

This classic dessert sauce, also known as crème anglaise, *goes beautifully with pies, tarts, simple cakes, and fruit. If you like, substitute 1 tablespoon of your favorite liqueur or brandy for the vanilla.*

Prep: 5 minutes   Cook: 15 minutes

1¼ cups milk
  4 large egg yolks
 ¼ cup sugar
  1 teaspoon vanilla extract

1. In heavy 2-quart saucepan, heat milk to boiling over high heat.

2. Meanwhile, in medium bowl, with wire whisk, mix egg yolks and sugar until well blended. In thin, steady stream, whisk about ¼ cup hot milk into egg-yolk mixture. Gradually whisk remaining hot milk into egg-yolk mixture. Return mixture to saucepan; cook over medium heat, stirring constantly with wooden spoon, just until mixture has thickened slightly and coats back of spoon. Do not boil, or sauce will curdle.

3. Remove saucepan from heat; strain custard through sieve into clean bowl. Stir in vanilla. Serve warm, or cover and refrigerate up to 1 day. Makes about 1½ cups.

Each tablespoon: About 26 calories, 1g protein, 3g carbohydrate, 1g total fat (1g saturated), 37mg cholesterol, 7mg sodium.

SWEETENED WHIPPED CREAM

Feel free to flavor the cream with vanilla or with one of the other tasty suggestions.

Prep: 10 minutes

1 cup heavy or whipping cream (preferably not ultrapasteurized), well chilled
1 to 2 tablespoons sugar
1 teaspoon vanilla extract, ⅛ teaspoon almond extract, or 1 tablespoon brandy, rum, or orange-flavored liqueur

1. Chill medium bowl and beaters 20 minutes.

2. In chilled bowl, with mixer at medium speed, beat cream, sugar to taste, and vanilla or other flavoring until soft, fluffy peaks form. Do not overbeat, or cream will separate. Makes about 2 cups.

Each tablespoon: About 28 calories, 0g protein, 1g carbohydrate, 3g total fat (2g saturated), 10mg cholesterol, 3mg sodium.

BEST BERRY SAUCE

The versatility of this fresh berry sauce cannot be exaggerated. Use a single variety of berry or your favorite combination. The acidity of the berries complements the sweetness of many desserts, such as vanilla ice cream and pound cake.

Prep: 5 minutes   Cook: 5 minutes

3 cups fresh berries (blueberries, hulled, sliced strawberries, raspberries)
½ to ¾ cup confectioners' sugar
3 tablespoons water
1 to 2 teaspoons fresh lemon or lime juice

1. In nonreactive 2-quart saucepan, combine berries, ½ cup confectioners' sugar, and water. Cook over medium heat, stirring occasionally, until berries have softened and sauce has thickened slightly, 5 to 8 minutes.

2. Remove saucepan from heat; stir in 1 teaspoon lemon juice. Taste, and stir in additional sugar and lemon juice, if desired. Serve warm, or cover and refrigerate up to 1 day. Reheat to serve, if you like. Makes about 2 cups.

Each tablespoon: About 17 calories, 0g protein, 4g carbohydrate, 0g total fat (0g saturated), 0mg cholesterol, 1mg sodium.

16

CANNING & FREEZING

Before refrigeration, cooks fought a constant battle against spoilage, working hard to put up enough food to feed their families until the next harvest. Now putting up food is as easy as wrapping and freezing it. In this chapter, we concentrate on the most popular modern methods of food preservation: canning and freezing. And we offer a number of small-batch recipes that use less produce to take into account the needs of urban cooks and smaller families who want to enjoy healthful homemade canned goods. Also included are recipes for freezer jams, which are not processed in boiling water baths, but instead, simply stored in the freezer.

KEEPING THE COLOR BRIGHT

Some fruit will turn brown if left untreated after it's been cut or peeled. Whether you're canning or freezing, you may want to treat such fruit (like peaches and bananas) to keep their color bright. One way is to treat the cut fruit with an ascorbic acid solution prepared from a commercial mix, which is available in most supermarkets during canning season, as well as in drugstores. Ascorbic acid can also be added to the sugar syrup or mixed with a little water and sprinkled over the fruit. Or, in a large bowl, combine 4 quarts water, 2 tablespoons salt, and 2 tablespoons cider or white vinegar. Drop the peeled or cut fruit into the solution as soon as the fruit is prepared; let stand a few minutes, then remove and rinse well. Drain on paper towels.

CANNING

Today, most people process fruits and vegetables because they enjoy it, not because they have to. (Processing means heating food in canning jars at high temperatures for periods long enough to kill spoilage-causing microorganisms and enzymes that would alter the food's flavor, texture, and color.) The fruits and vegetables for homemade pickles, jams, preserves, and jellies can come from an urban farmers' market or the garden out back. Making homemade canned goods is a satisfying pleasure, and nothing produced commercially can equal the quality or flavor.

EQUIPMENT FOR CANNING FRUITS AND TOMATOES

Boiling water bath canning pot: If you plan on doing a lot of canning, you may want to purchase a canning pot. It comes with a basket to hold the jars and a tight-fitting lid. However, any large stockpot will do, as long as it is deep enough that the pot's rim is 3 to 4 inches above the tops of the jars (as they sit on the wire basket or rack) and large enough that the jars don't touch each other. Instead of a wire canning basket, you can use any sturdy heatproof rack that will fit in the pot; round wire cooling racks work well. If your improvised rack needs a little extra support to hold heavy jars, place several metal jar bands underneath the center of the rack.

Jars: Tempered glass canning jars, sometimes called Mason jars, are the only recommended jars for home canning. Their special two-piece lids ensure a vacuum-tight seal that discourages spoilage. Also, the specially treated glass will keep them from cracking when they're subjected to extreme temperatures. If you plan to put your jars in the freezer, buy the ones with straight or tapered sides; jars with "shoulders" don't work in the freezer.

Jars range in size from four ounces to half a gallon. Use the size recommended in the recipe, especially for hot water bath canning; if you use larger jars than recommended, the heat that kills harmful microorganisms may not penetrate all the way through the food or preserves may not set up properly. Wide-mouthed jars are easier to fill than narrow ones. The jars are reusable, but check them carefully beforehand for any signs of wear, like cracks or chips.

Caps: The most common cap is made of two pieces: a flat lid with a rubberlike sealing compound on the underside and a metal screw band that holds the lid in place during processing. You must use new lids each time you can food. Undamaged screw bands, however, can be reused.

Utensils for canning: A wide-mouthed funnel for transferring the food to the jars and a jar lifter to grip the jars so they can be easily lifted in and out of the boiling water aren't essential but facilitate the canning process. To remove air bubbles, use a narrow rubber spatula (a metal spatula or knife could chip the glass).

CANNING STEPS

For best results, read these steps all the way through before you begin.

1. Prepare jars and lids for processing. Check the jars to be sure there are no chips or cracks. Wash the jars, lids, and screw bands in hot soapy water; rinse. The jars must be heated before canning to prevent breakage. Submerge them in enough cool water to cover; heat to boiling. Remove the pot from the heat and cover it. Leave the jars in the hot water for at least 10 minutes. Place the lids and bands in a saucepan with enough water to cover; bring to a simmer (180°F). Remove the pan from the heat, cover it, and keep hot until ready to use. Remove the jars and lids, one at a time, as needed.

2. Prep fruit/tomatoes and pack jars. Fruit and tomatoes can be packed into the hot jars raw (cold pack) or slightly cooked (hot pack). In both methods, the fruit is covered with boiling hot liquid—water, juice, or sugar syrup. See the chart on pages 524–525 for the best methods for the fruit you intend to can.

SUGAR SYRUP AND OTHER LIQUIDS FOR CANNING AND FREEZING

Fruit can be canned or frozen in syrup, fruit juice, or water. Sugar adds flavor and helps retain the color, but it is not needed to prevent spoilage. The sweetness of your fruit will determine whether you want a light or heavy syrup, but we give you recommendations in our charts.

If you want to make your own fruit juice for preserving, prepare it just before packing the fruit or making the sugar syrup. Place ripe, juicy fruit in a large nonreactive saucepan. With a potato masher or large spoon, crush the fruit well. Over low heat, stirring frequently, heat to simmering. Strain the juice through a double layer of cheesecloth; discard the fruit pulp.

To make sugar syrup, in a medium nonreactive saucepan, heat water or fruit juice and sugar over high heat, stirring until the sugar has dissolved. If directed, stir in ascorbic acid. Reduce the heat to low; keep it hot (do not boil) for canning; cool, then chill it for freezing.

LIGHT SUGAR SYRUP

4 cups water or juice and 1⅓ cups sugar.
Yields 4½ cups.

MEDIUM SUGAR SYRUP

4 cups water or juice and 2 cups sugar.
Yields 5 cups.

HEAVY SUGAR SYRUP

4 cups water or juice and 4 cups sugar.
Yields 6 cups.

Cold pack: Prep the fruit as indicated in the chart. Firmly pack the unheated raw fruit into hot jars, then fill with boiling liquid to within ½ inch of the rim. You will need ½ to 1½ cups of liquid for every 4 cups of fruit.

Hot pack: Heat the fruit to boiling in the liquid of your choice, or simmer it in its own juices. Cooking makes food more pliable and easier to pack, so you will need fewer jars. Pack the hot food loosely into hot jars and fill with boiling liquid to within ½ inch of the rim.

For both cold and hot pack: Headspace is important: If a jar has too little, the food may swell and force itself under the lid, breaking the seal. Too much headspace and the food at the top of the jar could discolor.

After filling each jar, with cold or hot food, run a narrow rubber spatula between food and side of jar to remove any air bubbles.

Using a clean, damp cloth, thoroughly wipe the jar rims and threads to remove any drips of food or liquid. Cover with the hot lids. Screw on the bands just until tightened; do not force.

3. *Process jars.* The filled jars must be processed in a boiling water bath immediately after packing to maintain the proper temperature. The processing time will vary according to the type of fruit, the method of packing, and the size of the jars.

Place the basket or a rack in the canning pot. Fill the pot halfway with hot water; heat it to simmering over high heat. In another pot or kettle, heat additional water to boiling. Carefully place the filled jars in the basket far enough apart so the water can circulate freely around them. The water level should be 1 to 2 inches above the tops of the jars; add boiling water if needed.

Cover the canner and heat the water to boiling. Start timing as soon as the water comes to a full boil; check often. Reduce the heat to maintain a gentle boil for the time indicated in the recipe. If necessary, add boiling water to keep the jars properly covered.

Once you've processed the jars the required time, turn off the heat, remove the lid, and let the jars sit in the hot water for 5 minutes.

4. *Cool jars.* In a draft-free place, line the counter surface with folded kitchen towels (contact with a cold, hard surface could break the

jars). With a jar lifter, remove the jars from the pot and place them on the towels, allowing 1 to 2 inches between them for air circulation. (If any liquid has boiled out of the jars, do not open them to add more.) Cool to room temperature, at least 12 hours or up to 24 hours.

5. *Test jars for airtight seal.* When the jars are cool, check the seals. The lid should be slightly concave (indented), not flat or bulging. Also, if you hit the top of the lid of a properly sealed jar with a teaspoon, you will be rewarded with a high-

pitched ringing sound. If you get a dull thud, you don't have a proper seal. Any food in a jar that hasn't sealed properly needs to be refrigerated and eaten within several days or reheated and processed in a newly sterilized jar with a new lid.

6. *Store jars properly.* Wipe the jars with a clean damp cloth to remove any food residue and label them, including the date of processing. Store the jars in a cool, dark place, preferably between 50° and 70°F. Under ideal conditions, home-processed foods will keep for about a year; after that, changes in the flavor, color, and texture will affect the quality.

SAFETY IN THE PANTRY

Before eating canned food, check the jar carefully for signs of spoilage. Do not taste or use any canned food if the lid is loose; there are gas bubbles; there is spurting liquid; the contents are moldy, slimy, or uncharacteristically soft or mushy; the color is unnatural; there is sediment at the bottom of the jar; or the food smells unpleasant.

If you reject the contents of a jar, destroy the food in such a way that it cannot be accidentally eaten by children or pets. Be sure to wear heavy plastic gloves when you handle it, as botulinum toxins can be fatal when ingested or absorbed through the skin. Afterward, thoroughly wash any surface that may have come in contact with the spoiled food using a chlorine solution, and discard any kitchen sponges used during cleanup.

MAKING JAM, JELLY, AND OTHER FRUIT SPREADS

If you have a large quantity of fruit and the inclination to do so, make a big batch of jam. And remember, you don't always have to pull out the canning pot for water bath processing. Excellent jams can be prepared for storage right in your freezer (see page 526 for recipes).

The equipment you'll need, if you're canning, will be the same as for canning fruit, with the addition of a broad 8-quart Dutch oven for preparing large-batch recipes and a 12-inch skillet for small-batch skillet jams. Don't use unlined aluminum pots or skillets, as they can react with the acid in fruit and affect the flavor and color.

When preparing the fruit, don't puree it or it won't set. Cook as directed.

Some recipes use commercial pectin to set mixtures properly. Pectin is a naturally occurring substance found in varying amounts in fruits; underripe fruit contains more pectin than fully ripe fruit. Commercial pectin comes in powdered and liquid forms: They are not interchangeable.

If the recipe calls for the fruit to come to a "rolling boil," heat it until the mixture forms bubbles all across its surface that cannot be stirred down.

Skim off the foam. To do this, remove the pan from the heat. Use a large metal spoon to skim the foam from the surface.

Once you've cooked the jam, jelly, or fruit spread as directed, spoon it into hot jars prepared as instructed on page 514. For freezer jams, pack the jam into containers to ½ inch from the tops; cover tightly. Freeze. For processed spreads, preferably using a wide-

mouthed funnel, fill and close the jars one at a time. For jellies, fill the jars to ⅛ inch from the tops; for jams, ¼ inch from the tops. Wipe the rims of the jars with a clean, damp cloth. Place the lids on top, then screw on the bands.

Process, cool, test, and store the jars as instructed on page 515.

FREEZING

Freezing is a great way to preserve fruits and vegetables. (For information on freezing meats, poultry, and seafood, see the Storing sections of their respective chapters.) Freezing maintains the natural color and flavor of food better than other methods of preservation. For the best flavor and texture, all home-frozen fruits and vegetables should be used within nine months.

STORE IT RIGHT

Frozen food must be stored properly to prevent "freezer burn" (a tough, dry surface that forms when food is exposed to the air in the freezer). It is best to use storage materials designed specifically for the freezer. For long-term freezer storage (more than a month), use tempered glass jars suitable for canning and freezing, plastic freezer-safe containers, waxed cardboard cartons, foil containers, or heavy-duty ziptight plastic bags. Use waterproof markers for writing on labels or freezer tape.

FREEZING SUCCESS

• Chill foods and liquids before packing.
• Wipe edges of containers or jar rims clean.
• When wrapping food in freezer wrap or using plastic bags, press out as much air as possible before sealing.
• Label each package with the name of the food and the date packed.
• Put only as much unfrozen food into your freezer as will freeze within twenty-four hours. (The rule of thumb is 2 to 3 pounds of food for each cubic foot of freezer space.) Overloading slows the freezing process and raises the temperature of the freezer, which affects the quality of the food already inside. Check the manufacturer's instructions to see how much unfrozen food you can place in the freezer at one time.
• Place the unfrozen packages against the freezing plates or coils, leaving enough space between them for the air to circulate. Freeze foods at 0°F or lower. After the packages are frozen, you can store them close together.

FREEZING FRUIT

There are three ways to freeze fruit: in syrup, in sugar, and dry pack (with nothing added). While some fruits can be frozen without sweetening, most have better flavor and texture if packed with sugar or in syrup. The chart Freezing Fruit (pages 518–520) lists the fruits that freeze well and the best methods for preparing them.

Packing Fruit for Freezing

• To pack fruit in syrup, first prepare and completely chill the sugar syrup you intend to use (page 514). Each pint container usually takes ½ to ⅔ cup syrup. If directed to do so, add ascorbic acid to the cold syrup just before using it, taking care not to beat in any air bubbles. Pour about ½ cup of the syrup into the container, fill the container with fruit, and add enough syrup to cover the fruit, leaving the proper amount of headspace (see below). Press the fruit down under the syrup and hold it in place with a small piece of crumpled foil; remove foil. Close and seal the container.

HEADSPACE WHEN FREEZING PRODUCE IN LIQUID OR SUGAR

How much headspace you need to leave will depend on the size of the jar and the size of the opening:

Pint jar with wide top: ½ inch
Pint jar with narrow top: ¾ inch
Quart jar with wide top: 1 inch
Quart jar with narrow top: 1½ inch

• To pack fruit in sugar, cut the fruit into a bowl and, if directed to do so, dissolve ascorbic acid in a small amount of water and sprinkle it over the fruit. Then sprinkle with the amount of sugar specified. With a rubber spatula, gently mix the fruit and sugar until the fruit releases its juices and the sugar has dissolved. Transfer the mixture to containers or jars, then close and seal, leaving headspace as directed above.

• To dry-pack fruit, place the prepared fruit in a container or jar. If necessary, sprinkle dissolved ascorbic acid over the fruit and mix well just before packing. Close and seal, leaving a ½-inch headspace.

• Tray-freezing before dry-packing is a great way to freeze fruit for use in baking or smoothies. It also prevents the fruit from sticking together. To do it, spread the fruit in a single layer, without touching, in a jelly-roll pan. Freeze until hard, 1 to 2 hours. Pack into heavy-duty zip-tight plastic bags, pressing out all the air.

To Thaw and Use Frozen Fruit

• Thaw fruit in its sealed container in the refrigerator or in a pan of cold water on the counter.

• To serve the fruit uncooked, serve it as soon as it has thawed (while a few ice crystals remain).

• To serve the fruit cooked, thaw it just until the pieces can be separated. Add sugar to taste, keeping in mind whether or not the fruit was already sweetened; if needed, add 1 to 2 tablespoons water.

FREEZING VEGETABLES

Vegetables you intend to freeze should be fresh and at their peak of ripeness. Wash and drain them thoroughly. Sort them according to size, unless you plan to cut them up. Prepare each vegetable as directed in the Freezing Vegetables chart (pages 521–523).

Step 1: Blanching

Blanching vegetables before freezing is an essential step for some produce. Carefully follow the blanching time for each vegetable, because underblanching stimulates enzyme activity and is worse than no blanching at all.

Fill an 8-quart saucepot halfway with water and bring it to a full boil over high heat. Do not add salt unless this is specified in the chart. Place a small amount of vegetables (about 4 cups) in a wire basket or strainer so they can be lowered into and removed from the water at the same time. Completely immerse the basket in the boiling water; cover the pot and start timing immediately, without waiting for the water to boil.

Meanwhile, fill a large bowl halfway with cold water; add one tray of ice cubes. As soon as the blanching time is up, lift out the vegetables and plunge them into the iced water to stop the cooking and to cool them quickly. Stir several times; the cooling time should not exceed the blanching time. Drain thoroughly. The blanching water may be reused (return it to a full boil); the cooling water must be replenished with ice cubes for each batch of vegetables.

Step 2: Packing

Pack vegetables without liquid into freezer-safe containers with the headspace specified in the chart (page 517), or into heavy-duty zip-tight plastic bags, pressing out all the air. Seal, label, and freeze.

Cooking Frozen Vegetables

Since blanching partially cooks the vegetables, the cooking time will be shorter than for fresh vegetables. Most can be cooked without being thawed first, although leafy vegetables, such as spinach, cook more evenly if thawed just enough to separate the leaves. Corn on the cob should also be partially thawed so the cobs can heat through in the same time it takes to cook the kernels.

Try to cook frozen vegetables in as little water as possible, as some nutrients are water soluble. Usually ½ cup water is enough to cook a pint of vegetables. For corn on the cob, use 2 to 3 inches of water. Salt the water lightly, if desired.

In a 2-quart saucepan over high heat, heat the water to boiling. Add the frozen vegetables and heat again to boiling, separating the pieces with a fork. Reduce the heat to medium and cover. Simmer just until the vegetables are tender. Drain, season as desired, and serve.

PREP, PACK, FREEZE: FRUIT

BEFORE BEGINNING, READ PACKING FRUIT FOR FREEZING, PAGE 517.

HOW TO PREPARE	HOW TO PACK	IN SYRUP	DRY PACK
Applesauce Make according to your favorite recipe. Cool; pack into containers or jars, leaving ½" headspace.			
Apricots Rinse; peel if desired. Leave whole or cut in half and remove pits. If not peeled, heat in boiling water 30 seconds to prevent skin from toughening during freezing.	Use light, medium, or heavy syrup. Add ¾ teaspoon ascorbic acid to each 4 cups syrup. Pack fruit in containers; cover with cold syrup.	Sprinkle fruit with ¼ teaspoon ascorbic acid mixed with 3 tablespoons water for each 4 cups fruit. Add ½ cup sugar; stir until dissolved. Pack fruit in containers, pressing down till covered with juice.	Pack in containers, leaving ½" headspace, or tray-freeze (page 517).
Bananas Mash firm, ripe bananas with a little lemon juice. Thawed mixture may discolor but is excellent for baked goods.			

PREP, PACK, FREEZE: FRUIT

BEFORE BEGINNING, READ PACKING FRUIT FOR FREEZING, PAGE 517.

HOW TO PREPARE	HOW TO PACK	IN SYRUP	DRY PACK
Blackberries/Dewberries/ Raspberries Remove any stems or leaves. Rinse carefully, removing less-than-perfect berries.	Pack berries in containers; cover with cold medium or heavy syrup.	Mix each 4 cups berries with ¾ cup sugar. Pack in containers.	Pack in containers, leaving ½" headspace, or tray-freeze (page 517).
Blueberries/Huckleberries Remove stems. Don't rinse; makes skins tough in freezer.			Pack in containers, leaving ½" headspace, or tray-freeze (page 517). Rinse before using.
Cherries, sweet Rinse; remove stems and pits.	Use medium or heavy syrup. Add ½ teaspoon ascorbic acid to each 4 cups syrup. Pack in containers; cover with cold syrup.		Pack in containers, leaving ½" headspace, or tray-freeze (page 517).
Cherries, tart (sour) Rinse; remove stems and pits.	Pack in containers; cover with cold heavy syrup.	Mix each 4 cups cherries with 1 cup sugar until dissolved. Pack into containers.	See Cherries, sweet.
Cranberries			Leave in original bags; freeze. Rinse before using.
Gooseberries Remove blossom ends. Rinse and drain.	Pack in containers; cover with cold heavy syrup.		Pack in containers, leaving ½" headspace, or tray-freeze (page 517). (Preferred method for berries to be used in pies.)
Figs Rinse; peel, if desired.	Use medium or heavy syrup. Add ¾ teaspoon ascorbic acid to each 4 cups syrup. Pack in containers; cover with cold syrup.		Sprinkle each 4 cups figs with ¾ teaspoon ascorbic acid dissolved in 3 tablespoons water. Pack in containers, leaving ½" headspace, or tray-freeze (page 517).

PREP, PACK, FREEZE: FRUIT

BEFORE BEGINNING, READ PACKING FRUIT FOR FREEZING, PAGE 517.

HOW TO PREPARE	IN SYRUP	IN SUGAR	DRY PACK
Mangoes Peel ripe mangoes; cut flesh away from seed and cut into chunks or slices.	Pack in containers; cover with cold medium syrup.		Tray-freeze (page 517).
Melons (cantaloupe, Crenshaw, watermelon) Cut in half; remove seeds and rind. Cut into slices, cubes, or balls.	Pack in containers; cover with cold medium syrup.		Pack in containers; leave ½" headspace.
Peaches Peel firm but ripe peaches. Pit and slice, if desired.	Pack as for Apricots.	Pack as for Apricots, using ⅔ cup sugar for each 4 cups fruit.	Pack in containers, leaving ½" headspace, or tray-freeze (page 517) peach slices.
Plums Wash; leave whole or cut in half or quarters. Remove pits.	Use medium or heavy syrup. Add ½ teaspoon ascorbic acid to each 4 cups syrup. Pack in containers; cover with cold syrup.		Pack in containers, leaving ½" headspace, or tray-freeze (page 517).
Rhubarb Trim crisp, well-colored rhubarb stalks. Cut into 1" to 2" pieces. If desired, blanch in boiling water 1 minute. (Blanching preserves color and flavor.)	Pack tightly in containers with cold medium or heavy syrup.		Pack tightly in containers; leave ½" headspace.
Strawberries Rinse; hull.	Pack in containers; cover with cold light, medium, or heavy syrup.	Mix each 4 cups berries with ¾ cup sugar; let stand until sugar has dissolved. Can also slice or crush berries. Pack in containers.	Pack in containers, leaving ½" headspace, or tray-freeze (page 517).

PREP, BLANCH, FREEZE: VEGETABLES

BEFORE BEGINNING, SEE PACKING VEGETABLES FOR FREEZING, PAGE 518.

HOW TO PREPARE	BLANCHING TIME (FOR 4 QUARTS OF WATER)		SPECIAL INSTRUCTIONS
Asparagus Break off tough ends of spears and remove "scales"; rinse. Cut into lengths to fit package or 2" pieces.	Large spears Medium spears Small spears	4 minutes 3 minutes 2 minutes	Pack spears alternating tips and stem ends; leave no headspace.
Basil Puree ¼ cup packed leaves with 1 tablespoon oil; freeze in ice cube trays. Do not freeze whole basil leaves.			Remove cubes from trays; transfer to zip-tight plastic bags. Add cubes to soups or stews.
Beans, green or wax Rinse; trim ends. Leave whole, slice lengthwise for French-cut, or cut into 2" pieces.		3 minutes	Pack in containers; leave ½" headspace.
Beans, butter, lima, or pinto Rinse then shell.	Large Medium Small	4 minutes 3 minutes 2 minutes	Pack in containers; leave ½" headspace.
Beets Select beets no larger than 3". Trim tops (leave on ½" to prevent bleeding). Cook in boiling water until tender. Drain, cool, and peel. Leave whole, slice, or cube.			Pack in containers; leave ½" headspace.
Broccoli Rinse. Cut into stalks with flowerets no larger than 1½" across. Soak in brine (4 teaspoons salt in 1 gallon water) to remove bugs. Drain.		3 minutes	Pack in containers; leave no headspace.
Brussels sprouts Trim outer leaves and root ends. Sort by size.	Large Medium Small	5 minutes 4 minutes 3 minutes	Pack in containers; leave no headspace.

PREP, BLANCH, FREEZE: VEGETABLES

BEFORE BEGINNING, SEE PACKING VEGETABLES FOR FREEZING, PAGE 518.

HOW TO PREPARE	BLANCHING TIME (FOR 4 QUARTS OF WATER)		SPECIAL INSTRUCTIONS
Carrots Peel. Leave small carrots whole; cut larger carrots lengthwise into strips, slices, or cubes.	Whole Strips, slices, or cubes	5 minutes 2 minutes	Pack in containers; leave ½" headspace.
Cauliflower Separate into 1" flowerets. Treat as for broccoli.	Add 4 teaspoons salt to blanching water.	3 minutes	Pack in containers; leave no headspace.
Corn, whole-kernel or cream-style Remove husks and silk.		4 minutes	Drain; cool. For whole-kernel corn, cut kernels from cob at about ⅔ depth of kernels. For cream-style, cut off kernels were they meet cob; scrape off pulp. Pack in containers; leave ½" headspace.
Corn, on the cob Remove husks and silk. Sort ears by size.	Large (over 1½" diameter) Medium (1¼" to 1½") Small (under 1¼")	11 minutes 9 minutes 7 minutes	Pack in zip-tight plastic bags.
Greens **(beet or turnip tops, collards, kale, mustard greens, spinach, Swiss chard)** Trim tough ribs and stems. Rinse well to remove all grit. Cut into pieces as desired.	Collards Other greens	3 minutes 2 minutes	Pack in containers; leave ½" headspace.
Herbs Rinse; drain and pat dry. For mint, oregano, parsley, and sage, remove leaves from stems. For chervil, dill, marjoram, rosemary, savory, tarragon, and thyme, keep leaves on their stems.			Wrap sprigs or leaves in foil, then place in zip-tight plastic bags. Use frozen herbs in cooked dishes.

PREP, BLANCH, FREEZE: VEGETABLES

BEFORE BEGINNING, SEE PACKING VEGETABLES FOR FREEZING, PAGE 518.

HOW TO PREPARE	BLANCHING TIME (FOR 4 QUARTS OF WATER)		SPECIAL INSTRUCTIONS
Okra Remove stems without cutting into pods. Blanch; drain and cool. Leave whole or slice.	Large Small (under 4")	5 minutes 3 minutes	Pack in containers; leave ½" headspace.
Pea pods, Chinese (snow peas), snap peas Rinse; remove stems and strings from pea pods.	Small	1½ minutes	Pack in containers; leave ½" headspace.
Peas, green Rinse, then shell.		1½ minutes	Pack in containers; leave ½" headspace.
Squash, summer (zucchini, yellow crookneck) Do not peel; cut into ½"-thick slices or grate (good for use in baking).	Slices Grated	3 minutes 1 to 2 minutes, until translucent (Blanch grated squash in small batches.)	Pack in containers; leave ½" headspace. Drain grated squash before using.
Squash, winter (acorn, banana, butternut, Delicious, Hubbard) Cut into large chunks; peel. Remove seeds and stringy portion. Cook in boiling water, steam, or roast until tender. Mash; let cool.			Pack in containers; leave ½" headspace.
Tomatoes **Raw:** Plunge into boiling water 30 seconds to loosen skin. Peel and cut out stem ends. Freeze whole or in pieces. **Stewed:** Cut into quarters. Cook until tender, 10 to 20 minutes; cool.			**Raw:** Pack in containers; leave 1" headspace. **Stewed:** See headspace chart on page 517.

CANNING FRUITS AND TOMATOES IN A BOILING WATER BATH

THESE BOILING TIMES ARE BASED ON AN ALTITUDE OF 1 TO 1,000 FEET ABOVE SEA LEVEL.

HOW TO PREPARE	HOW TO PACK	MINUTES TO PROCESS	
		PINTS	QUARTS
Applesauce Make applesauce, using your favorite recipe.	**Hot pack:** Heat to boiling. Pour bubbling applesauce into hot jars; leave 1/2" headspace. Adjust caps.	20 minutes	20 minutes
Apricots Peel apricots, if you like. To peel, plunge fruit into boiling water for 30 seconds; transfer to cold water to help loosen skins. Cut in half; remove pits. Slice, if desired. Treat to prevent darkening (page 513).	**Hot pack:** Heat apricots in water, juice, or light or medium syrup to boiling. Pack fruit in hot jars in layers. Cover with boiling liquid; leave 1/2" headspace. Adjust caps.	20 minutes	25 minutes
Berries Wash berries; drain. Remove stems. (Use sugar syrup appropriate for sweetness of your berries.)	**Cold pack:** Pack berries in hot jars; gently shake to pack tightly. Cover with boiling water, juice, or syrup; leave 1/2" headspace. Adjust caps. **Hot pack:** Cook berries in boiling water for 30 seconds; drain. Pack in hot jars. Cover with boiling liquid; leave 1/2" headspace. Adjust caps.	15 minutes 15 minutes	20 minutes 15 minutes
Cherries Rinse, then remove stems; pit, if desired. If pitted, treat to prevent darkening (page 513). If unpitted, prick cherries to prevent splitting.	**Cold pack:** Pour 1/2 cup boiling water, juice, or light or medium sugar syrup for sweet cherries or medium or heavy sugar syrup for sour cherries into each hot jar. Fill jar with cherries; shake to pack down. Cover with boiling liquid; leave 1/2" headspace. Adjust caps. **Hot pack:** In saucepot, add 1/2 cup liquid for each 4 cups cherries. Cover; heat to boiling. Pack cherries in hot jars. Cover with boiling liquid; leave 1/2" headspace. Adjust caps.	25 minutes 15 minutes	25 minutes 20 minutes
Figs Rinse; drain. In saucepot, cover figs with water and heat to boiling; boil 2 minutes. Drain.	**Hot pack:** In saucepot, in light syrup, heat figs to boiling; boil 5 minutes. Add bottled lemon juice per Tomatoes, opposite page. Pack hot jars with figs. Cover with boiling syrup; leave 1/2" headspace. Adjust caps.	45 minutes	50 minutes

CANNING FRUITS AND TOMATOES IN A BOILING WATER BATH

THESE BOILING TIMES ARE BASED ON AN ALTITUDE OF 1 TO 1,000 FEET ABOVE SEA LEVEL.

HOW TO PREPARE	HOW TO PACK	MINUTES TO PROCESS	
		PINTS	QUARTS
Peaches Peel peaches (see Apricots); cut in half. Remove pits. Scrape red fibers from cavities. Slice, if desired. Treat to prevent darkening (page 513).	**Hot pack:** Heat peaches in water, juice, or medium or heavy syrup to boiling. Pack as for Apricots, in layers, cut side down.	20 minutes	25 minutes
Pears Cut pears in half or into quarters; core and peel. Treat to prevent darkening (page 513).	**Hot pack:** In saucepot, in water, juice, or light or medium syrup, heat pears to boiling; boil 5 minutes. Pack in hot jars. Cover with boiling liquid; leave 1/2" headspace. Adjust caps.	20 minutes	25 minutes
Plums Use firm, meaty varieties, not very juicy ones. Wash; prick skins if left whole to prevent bursting. For Italian prune plums and other freestone varieties, cut in half and remove pits, if desired.	**Hot pack:** In saucepot, in water or medium syrup, heat plums to boiling; boil 2 minutes. Remove pot from heat. Cover; let stand 20 to 30 minutes. Pack plums in hot jars. Cover with boiling liquid; leave 1/2" headspace. Adjust caps.	20 minutes	25 minutes
Rhubarb, stewed Cut stewed rhubarb stalks into 1/2" to 1" pieces.	**Hot pack:** In saucepot, combine 1/2 cup sugar for each 4 cups rhubarb; mix well. Let stand till juices appear. Heat mixture to boiling. Immediately pack in hot jars; leave 1/2" headspace (add boiling water to cover rhubarb if needed). Adjust caps.	15 minutes	15 minutes
Tomatoes Use only firm-ripe—not overripe—tomatoes (tomatoes lose their acidity as they mature). Plunge into boiling water 30 seconds to loosen skins. Transfer to cold water; drain. Peel and cut out stem ends. Leave whole or cut in half or into quarters for cold pack; quarter for crushed tomatoes (hot pack).	**Cold pack:** To each quart jar, add 2 tablespoons bottled lemon juice; to each pint jar, add 1 tablespoon. Add salt, if desired, 1 teaspoon per quart or 1/2 teaspoon per pint. Pack hot jars with raw tomatoes, pressing down on them till all the spaces are filled with juices. Leave 1/2" headspace. Adjust caps.	85 minutes	85 minutes
	Hot pack: In saucepot, crush one quarter of the tomatoes with a wooden spoon. Heat crushed tomatoes to boiling, stirring. Add remaining tomatoes (without crushing) and heat to boiling; boil 5 minutes. Add lemon juice and salt, and pack in jars per cold pack, above. Adjust caps.	35 minutes	45 minutes

SKILLET JAMS

Prepare jars and lids (page 514). If using blackberries and/or raspberries, press ½ cup crushed berries through a sieve to remove seeds, if you like. In heavy nonstick skillet, combine desired fruit and indicated amount of pectin and butter. Heat to boiling over high heat, stirring constantly. Stir in sugar and heat to boiling, stirring constantly; boil 1 minute or, for apricots, boil until softened, 2 to 3 minutes. Remove skillet from heat. Quickly ladle hot jam into hot jars. Wipe jar rims and threads clean; cover with lids. Refrigerate until set, about 6 hours. Refrigerate up to 3 weeks. Each recipe makes two 8-ounce jars.

JAM	FRUIT MIXTURE	POWDERED FRUIT PECTIN	BUTTER OR MARGARINE	SUGAR
Blackberry-Blueberry Skillet Jam	2 cups each blackberries and blueberries, crushed	2 tablespoons	½ teaspoon	¾ cup
Three-Berry Skillet Jam (pictured on page 512)	1 cup each blackberries, raspberries, and sliced strawberries, crushed	4 teaspoons	½ teaspoon	1 cup
Strawberry Skillet Jam	2 cups sliced strawberries, crushed	4 teaspoons	½ teaspoon	1 cup
Raspberry Skillet Jam	3 cups raspberries, crushed	4 teaspoons	½ teaspoon	1½ cups
Blueberry Skillet Jam	2 cups blueberries, crushed	2 tablespoons	½ teaspoon	1 cup
Peach Skillet Jam	1 pound peaches, peeled, pitted, and mashed with 2 teaspoons fresh lemon juice	2 tablespoons	½ teaspoon	1 cup
Apricot Skillet Jam	1 pound apricots, pitted and finely chopped, tossed with 2 tablespoons fresh lemon juice	2 tablespoons	none	1 cup

FREEZER STRAWBERRY JAM

Jewel-like freezer jam is especially fresh-tasting. Peak-of-the-season farmstand strawberries work best.

Prep: 35 minutes plus overnight to stand
Cook: 8 minutes

- 5 half-pint freezer-safe containers with tight-fitting lids
- 1 quart fully ripe strawberries, hulled
- 4 cups sugar
- 2 tablespoons fresh lemon juice
- ¾ cup water
- 1 package (1¾ ounces) powdered fruit pectin

1. Prepare containers and lids (page 514).

2. In large bowl, thoroughly crush enough strawberries to equal 2 cups. Stir in sugar and lemon juice until thoroughly mixed; let stand 10 minutes.

3. In 1-quart saucepan, combine water and pectin and heat to boiling over high heat. Boil, stirring constantly, 1 minute. Stir pectin mixture into fruit until sugar has dissolved and mixture is no longer grainy, 3 to 4 minutes. A few sugar crystals will remain.

4. Quickly ladle jam into containers to within ½ inch of tops. Wipe container rims clean; cover with lids.

5. Let stand at room temperature until set, about 24 hours. Refrigerate up to 3 weeks, or freeze up to 1 year. To use, place frozen jam in refrigerator until thawed, about 4 hours. Makes five 8-ounce containers.

Each tablespoon: About 43 calories, 0g protein, 11g carbohydrate, 0g total fat (0g saturated), 0mg cholesterol, 1mg sodium.

FREEZER RASPBERRY JAM

For this quick way to prepare ruby red raspberry jam, thoroughly crush **2 pints fully ripe raspberries** instead of strawberries. If you like, press half of crushed berries through sieve into bowl to remove seeds; discard seeds. Combine with whole berries. Stir in sugar until thoroughly mixed; let stand 10 minutes.

Substitute **1 pouch (3 ounces) liquid fruit pectin** for powdered pectin. In small bowl, combine pectin and lemon juice. Stir pectin mixture into fruit until sugar has dissolved and continue with recipe as directed. Makes 4 half-pint freezer-safe containers of jam.

Each tablespoon: About 52 calories, 0g protein, 13g carbohydrate, 0g total fat (0g saturated), 0mg cholesterol, 0mg sodium.

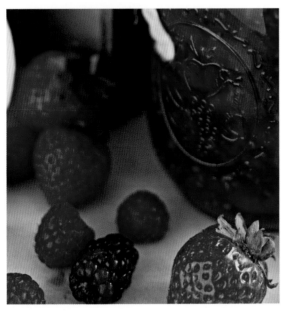

Freezer Jam

ALL-SEASON APPLE JELLY

··

Try this delicious apple jelly or one of the variations to brighten up your morning toast or glaze a ham or pork roast.

Prep: 5 minutes plus preparing jars and lids
Cook: 15 minutes plus processing

4 half-pint canning jars and lids
4 cups apple juice
1 package (1¾ ounces) powdered fruit pectin
5 cups sugar

1. Prepare jars and lids (page 514). Fill canner halfway with *water;* cover and heat to simmering over high heat.

2. Meanwhile, in nonreactive 5-quart Dutch oven, combine apple juice and pectin. Heat to boiling over high heat, stirring constantly; immediately stir in sugar. Cook, stirring constantly, until mixture comes to rolling boil; boil 1 minute. Remove from heat. With spoon, skim off any foam.

3. Quickly ladle hot jelly into hot jars to within ¼ inch of tops. Wipe jar rims and threads clean; cover quickly with lids and screw bands on securely but not too tightly. Process in boiling water bath (page 515) 10 minutes; cool jars and test for airtight seal (page 515). Makes four 8-ounce jars.

Each tablespoon: About 70 calories, 0g protein, 18g carbohydrate, 0g total fat (0g saturated), 0mg cholesterol, 2mg sodium.

APPLE-CIDER JELLY

Prepare as directed but substitute **4 cups apple cider** for apple juice.

SPICED APPLE JELLY

With vegetable peeler, remove peel from **1 large navel orange.** With string, tie **12 cloves, 2 cinnamon sticks** (3 inches each), and **orange peel** in double thickness of cheesecloth. Prepare jelly as directed. Add spice bag to pot with apple juice and pectin. Before ladling jelly, discard spice bag.

GRAPE JELLY

Prepare as directed but substitute **2 cups unsweetened grape juice** and **1 cup water** for apple juice; use only **3½ cups sugar. **Makes three 8-ounce jars.

Strawberry Jam

STRAWBERRY JAM

···

Here's an old-fashioned way to make a large batch of thick and delicious jam.

Prep: 25 minutes plus preparing jars and lids
Cook: 20 minutes plus processing

- 8 half-pint canning jars and lids
- 2 quarts fully ripe strawberries, hulled
- 6 cups sugar
- ¼ cup fresh lemon juice
- 1 pouch (3 ounces) liquid fruit pectin

1. Prepare jars and lids (page 514). Fill canner halfway with *water;* cover and heat to simmering over high heat.

2. Meanwhile, in large bowl, crush enough strawberries to equal 4 cups, leaving berries slightly chunky.

3. In heavy nonreactive 8-quart saucepot, combine strawberries, sugar, and lemon juice; heat to boiling over high heat, stirring constantly. Boil rapidly 1 minute, stirring constantly; stir in pectin. Cook until mixture comes to rolling boil; boil 1 minute. Remove from heat. With spoon, skim off any foam.

4. Quickly ladle hot jam into hot jars to within ¼ inch of tops. Wipe jar rims and threads clean; cover quickly with lids and screw bands on securely but not too tightly. Process in boiling water bath (page 515) 10 minutes; cool jars and test for airtight seal (page 515). Makes eight 8-ounce jars.

Each tablespoon: About 39 calories, 0g protein, 10g carbohydrate, 0g total fat (0g saturated), 0mg cholesterol, 0mg sodium.

JALAPEÑO PEPPER JELLY
....

This sweet and spicy jelly is a great accompaniment to meat and chicken dishes, or dollop onto crackers that are spread with cream cheese for a flavor-packed appetizer.

Prep: 20 minutes plus preparing jars and lids
Cook: 25 minutes plus processing

- 6 half-pint canning jars and lids
- 8 large green peppers, each cut into quarters
- 6 jalapeño chiles or hot red chiles, seeded
- 6 cups sugar
- ½ cup distilled white vinegar
- 1 package (6 ounces) liquid fruit pectin
- 4 drops green food coloring (optional)

1. Prepare jars and lids (page 514). Fill canner halfway with *water.* Cover; heat to simmering over high heat.

2. Meanwhile, in blender or in food processor with knife blade attached, process green peppers and jalapeños until very finely chopped. Transfer pepper mixture to sieve set over large bowl. With spoon, press pepper mixture until all liquid is removed. (There should be about 2 cups liquid.) Discard peppers.

3. In nonreactive 8-quart saucepot, combine sugar, pepper liquid, and vinegar; heat to boiling over high heat. Boil 10 minutes. Stir in pectin and food coloring, if using. Cook, stirring constantly, until mixture comes to rolling boil; boil 1 minute. Remove from heat. With spoon, skim off any foam.

4. Quickly ladle hot jelly into hot jars to within ¼ inch of tops. Wipe jar rims and threads clean; cover quickly with lids and screw bands on securely but not too tightly. Process jars in boiling water bath (page 515) 10 minutes; cool jars and test for airtight seal (page 515). Makes six 8-ounce jars.

Each tablespoon: About 50 calories, 0g protein, 13g carbohydrate, 0g total fat (0g saturated), 0mg cholesterol, 0mg sodium.

SWEET CHERRY JAM
....

Who can resist homemade cherry jam? Take the time to find perfectly ripe fruit for the best results.

Prep: 45 minutes plus preparing jars and lids
Cook: 20 minutes plus processing

- 5 half-pint canning jars and lids
- 2 pounds dark sweet cherries
- 5 cups sugar
- ¼ cup fresh lemon juice
- 1 pouch (3 ounces) liquid fruit pectin

1. Prepare jars and lids (page 514). Fill canner halfway with *water.* Cover; heat to simmering over high heat.

2. Meanwhile, remove pits from cherries; finely chop enough cherries to equal 3 cups.

3. In heavy nonreactive 8-quart saucepot, combine cherries, sugar, and lemon juice; heat to boiling over high heat, stirring constantly; stir in pectin. Cook until mixture comes to rolling boil; boil 1 minute. Remove from heat. With spoon, skim off any foam.

4. Quickly ladle hot jam into hot jars to within ¼ inch of tops. Wipe jar rims and threads clean; cover quickly with lids and screw bands on securely but not too tightly. Process in boiling water bath (page 515) 10 minutes; cool jars and test for airtight seal (page 515). Makes five 8-ounce jars.

Each tablespoon: About 56 calories, 0g protein, 14g carbohydrate, 0g total fat (0g saturated), 0mg cholesterol, 0mg sodium.

TART CHERRY JAM

Prepare as directed but substitute **2 pounds tart cherries** for sweet cherries, use only **4½ cups sugar,** and omit lemon juice. Remove pits from cherries and finely chop enough cherries to equal about 2½ cups. Makes three 8-ounce jars.

Each tablespoon: About 98 calories, 0g protein, 25g carbohydrate, 0g total fat (0g saturated), 0mg cholesterol, 1mg sodium.

PEAR MARMALADE

·····················

Here, pears are combined with thinly sliced orange peel, fresh ginger, and a touch of allspice to make an unusually delectable marmalade. Use any variety of pear you like.

**Prep: 30 minutes plus preparing jars and lids
Cook: 1 hour plus processing**

3 large oranges
6 pounds pears (12 large), peeled, cored, and coarsely chopped (12 cups)
2 tablespoons minced, peeled fresh ginger
4 cups sugar
⅓ cup fresh lemon juice
½ teaspoon ground allspice
7 half-pint canning jars and lids

1. From oranges, with vegetable peeler, remove peel along with some white pith. Cut enough peel into 2" by ⅛" strips to equal ¾ cup. Coarsely chop enough oranges to equal 1½ cups; discard seeds.

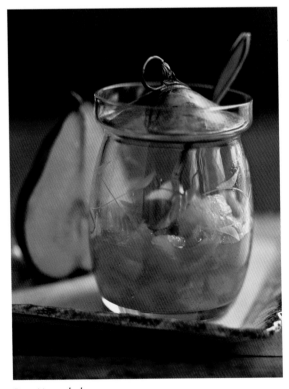

Pear Marmalade

2. In heavy nonreactive 8-quart saucepot, combine pears, oranges and peel, ginger, sugar, lemon juice, and allspice; heat to boiling over high heat, stirring frequently. Reduce heat to medium-high; cook, stirring frequently, until mixture is very thick, about 45 minutes. With spoon, skim off any foam.

3. Meanwhile, prepare jars and lids (page 514). Fill canner halfway with *water;* cover and heat to simmering over high heat.

4. Quickly ladle simmering marmalade into hot jars to within ¼ inch of tops. (Keep marmalade simmering while filling jars.) Wipe jar rims and threads clean; cover quickly with lids and screw bands on securely but not too tightly. Process in boiling water bath (page 515) 15 minutes; cool jars and test for airtight seal (page 515). Makes seven 8-ounce jars.

Each tablespoon: About 43 calories, 0g protein, 11g carbohydrate, 0g total fat (0g saturated), 0mg cholesterol, 0mg sodium.

PEACH BUTTER

·····················

An exquisitely delicious spread that has the rich flavor of ripe peaches and just a touch of cinnamon.

**Prep: 30 minutes plus preparing jars and lids
Cook: 1 hour 30 minutes plus processing**

6 pounds ripe peaches (18 to 20 medium), peeled, pitted, and cut into quarters
2½ cups sugar
½ teaspoon ground cinnamon
4 half-pint canning jars and lids

1. In heavy nonreactive 8-quart saucepot, cook peaches over medium heat, stirring, until very soft, about 20 minutes. Remove from heat. In batches, in blender with center part of cover removed to let steam escape, or in food processor with knife blade attached, puree peaches until smooth.

2. Return peach puree to clean saucepot; stir in sugar and cinnamon. Heat peach mixture to boiling over high heat. Reduce heat to medium-low; cook, stirring frequently, until puree has thickened and mixture mounds when dropped from spoon, about 1 hour.

3. Meanwhile, prepare jars and lids (page 514). Fill canner halfway with *water;* cover and heat to simmering over high heat.

4. Quickly ladle simmering peach butter into hot jars to within ¼ inch of tops. (Keep mixture simmering while filling jars.) Wipe jar rims and threads clean; cover quickly with lids and screw bands on securely but not too tightly. Process in boiling water bath (page 515) 10 minutes; cool jars and test for airtight seal (page 515). Makes four 8-ounce jars.

Each tablespoon: About 44 calories, 0g protein, 11g carbohydrate, 0g total fat (0g saturated), 0mg cholesterol, 0mg sodium.

BLUSHING APPLE BUTTER

Cranberries tint this apple butter pink. Plan ahead: Make a batch to give as gifts during the holidays.

**Prep: 30 minutes plus preparing jars and lids
Cook: 1 hour 30 minutes**

2	lemons
3¾	pounds Granny Smith apples (8 large), peeled, cored, and thinly sliced
1	cup cranberries
1½	cups apple cider or apple juice
1½	cups sugar
5	half-pint jars with tight-fitting lids

1. From lemons, with vegetable peeler, remove 3 strips (3" by 1" each) peel; squeeze 3 tablespoons juice. In heavy nonreactive 5-quart Dutch oven, combine apples, cranberries, lemon peel and juice, and apple cider; heat to boiling over high heat. Reduce heat; simmer, stirring occasionally, until apples are very soft, about 10 minutes.

2. Stir in sugar; heat to boiling over high heat. Reduce heat to medium; partially cover and cook, stirring occasionally, until apple butter is very thick, about 1 hour. (Mixture may sputter and splash, so be careful when stirring.)

Blushing Apple Butter

3. Meanwhile, prepare jars and lids (page 514). Fill canner halfway with *water;* cover and heat to simmering over high heat. In batches, in blender with center part of cover removed to let steam escape, or in food processor with knife blade attached, puree apple butter until smooth.

4. Ladle hot apple butter into clean jars to within ¼ inch of tops. Wipe jar rims and threads clean. Cover quickly and screw bands on securely but not too tightly. Process in boiling water bath (page 515) 10 minutes; cool jars and test for airtight seal (page 515). Makes five 8-ounce jars.

Each tablespoon: About 31 calories, 0g protein, 8g carbohydrate, 0g total fat (0g saturated), 0mg cholesterol, 0mg sodium.

WATERMELON-RIND PICKLES

....

These pickles look especially nice, because a little of the red flesh is left on the rind.

Prep: 30 minutes plus overnight to refrigerate and preparing jars and lids

Cook: 1 hour 40 minutes plus processing

rind from 1 medium watermelon (10 pounds)
½ cup kosher, canning, or pickling salt
6 cinnamon sticks (3 inches each)
2 teaspoons whole cloves
4 cups sugar
2 cups distilled white vinegar
2 cups water
5 one-pint canning jars and lids

1. Trim and discard outer dark green skin from watermelon rind. Cut enough rind into 1-inch pieces to equal 14 cups, leaving about ⅛-inch red flesh. In very large bowl, combine salt and *6 cups water,* stirring until salt has dissolved; add watermelon rind. If necessary, add enough *water* to cover. Cover and refrigerate overnight.

2. Next day, pour rind mixture into colander to drain. Rinse with cold running water; drain. In heavy nonreactive 8-quart saucepot, combine rind and enough *water* to cover; heat to boiling over high heat. Reduce heat and simmer 20 minutes; drain and return to pot.

3. With string, tie cinnamon sticks and cloves in double thickness of cheesecloth. Add sugar, vinegar, water, and spice bag to saucepot. Heat to boiling over high heat. Reduce heat; cover and simmer, stirring frequently, 45 minutes.

4. Meanwhile, prepare the jars and lids (page 514). Fill canner halfway with *water;* cover and heat to simmering over high heat.

Watermelon-Rind Pickles

5. Discard spice bag. Spoon hot pickle mixture into hot jars to within ½ inch of tops. Immediately ladle simmering syrup into hot jars to within ¼ inch of top, making sure rind is completely covered with syrup. (Keep syrup simmering while filling jars.) Wipe jar rims and threads clean; cover quickly with lids and screw bands on securely but not too tightly. Process in boiling water bath (page 515) 10 minutes; cool the jars and test for airtight seal (page 515). Makes five 16-ounce jars.

Each ¼ cup: About 84 calories, 0g protein, 22g carbohydrate, 0g total fat (0g saturated), 0mg cholesterol, 177mg sodium.

HOME-STYLE CHUTNEY

···

This chutney gets its full flavor from a tempting mix of fruits and vegetables; it is a fine accompaniment to grilled lamb.

Prep: 40 minutes plus preparing jars and lids
Cook: 2 hours 15 minutes plus processing

- 2 to 3 medium oranges
- 3 pounds ripe nectarines (6 large), pitted and cut into wedges
- 1½ pounds Granny Smith apples (3 large), peeled, cored, and cut into ½-inch pieces
- 1 pound firm-ripe tomatoes (3 medium), cut into ½-inch pieces
- 3 medium onions, cut into ½-inch pieces
- 3 tablespoons minced, peeled fresh ginger
- 1 package (16 ounces) light brown sugar
- 2¼ cups distilled white vinegar
- 2 teaspoons dry mustard
- 1 teaspoon salt
- ¼ teaspoon ground red pepper (cayenne)
- 1 cup dark seedless raisins
- 6 half-pint canning jars and lids

1. From oranges, grate 2 tablespoons peel and squeeze ⅔ cup juice. In nonreactive 5-quart Dutch oven, combine nectarines, apples, tomatoes, onions, ginger, orange peel and juice, brown sugar, vinegar, mustard, salt, and ground red pepper. Heat to boiling over high heat, stirring frequently. Reduce heat and simmer 1 hour. Add raisins; cook, stirring frequently, until mixture is very thick, about 45 minutes.

2. Meanwhile, prepare the jars and lids (page 514). Fill canner halfway with *water;* cover and heat to simmering over high heat.

3. Ladle simmering chutney into hot jars to within ¼ inch of tops. (Keep chutney simmering while filling jars.) Wipe jar rims and threads clean; cover quickly with lids and screw bands on securely but not too tightly. Process in boiling water bath (page 515) 10 minutes; cool jars and test for airtight seal (page 515). Makes six 8-ounce jars.

Each tablespoon: About 34 calories, 0g protein, 9g carbohydrate, 0g total fat (0g saturated), 0mg cholesterol, 27mg sodium.

BREAD-AND-BUTTER PICKLES

···

Take a jar of these sweet pickles to your next family barbecue. Use absolutely fresh kirby cucumbers from a farmers' market or farm stand for the best results.

Prep: 20 minutes plus standing and preparing jars and lids
Cook: 45 minutes plus processing

- 4 pounds very firm unwaxed cucumbers (4 to 6 inches long), cut into ¼-inch-thick slices
- 3 large onions, thinly sliced
- ½ cup kosher, canning, or pickling salt
- 8 cups ice cubes (3 trays)
- 5 cups sugar
- 5 cups cider vinegar
- 1 teaspoon ground turmeric
- 1½ teaspoons celery seeds
- 1½ teaspoons mustard seeds
- 6 one-pint canning jars and lids

1. In 8-quart enamel, stainless steel, or glass container, combine cucumbers, onions, salt, and enough *cold water* to cover. Stir until salt has dissolved; stir in ice. Cover and let stand in cool place 3 hours. Drain vegetables and rinse with cold running water; drain.

2. In nonreactive 8-quart saucepot, combine sugar, vinegar, turmeric, celery seeds, and mustard seeds; heat to boiling over high heat. Reduce heat; simmer, stirring, 30 minutes.

3. Meanwhile, prepare the jars and lids (page 514). Fill canner halfway with *water;* cover and heat to simmering over high heat.

4. Add cucumbers and onions to pot; heat to boiling. Spoon hot vegetables into hot jars to within ½ inch of tops. Immediately ladle simmering syrup over vegetables to within ¼ inch from tops, making sure vegetables are completely covered with syrup. (Keep syrup simmering while filling jars.) Wipe jar rims and threads clean; cover quickly with lids and screw bands on securely but not too tightly. Process in boiling water bath (page 515) 10 minutes; cool jars and test for airtight seal (page 515). Makes six 16-ounce jars.

Each ¼ cup: About 95 calories, 0g protein, 25g carbohydrate, 0g total fat (0g saturated), 0mg cholesterol, 292mg sodium.

PEPPERY DILLED BEANS

These tangy green beans have great dill flavor. They look their best when tightly packed into the jars.

Prep: 45 minutes plus preparing jars and lids
Cook: 10 minutes plus processing

2½ pounds green beans
6 half-pint canning jars and lids
2½ cups distilled white vinegar
2 cups water
¼ cup kosher, canning, or pickling salt
1 garlic clove, peeled
6 dill sprigs
¾ teaspoon crushed red pepper

1. Trim green beans to ¼ inch shorter than height of glass canning jars.

2. Prepare jars and lids (page 514). Fill canner halfway with *water*. Cover canner and heat to simmering over high heat.

3. In nonreactive 2-quart saucepan, combine vinegar, water, salt, and garlic; heat to boiling over high heat. In each hot jar, place 1 dill sprig and ⅛ teaspoon crushed red pepper. Pack green beans tightly into jars. Discard garlic and immediately ladle in simmering liquid to within ¼ inch of tops. (Keep liquid simmering while filling jars.) Wipe jar rims and threads clean; cover quickly with lids and screw bands on securely but not too tightly. Process jars in boiling water bath (page 515) 10 minutes; cool and test for airtight seal (page 515). Makes six 8-ounce jars, 6 servings each.

Each serving: About 9 calories, 0g protein, 2g carbohydrate, 0g total fat (0g saturated), 0mg cholesterol, 583mg sodium.

CORN RELISH

Jars of colorful corn relish are pretty enough to share with friends.

Prep: 40 minutes plus preparing jars and lids
Cook: 35 minutes plus processing

5 one-pint canning jars and lids
12 ears corn, husks and silk removed
2 green peppers, finely chopped (1½ cups)
2 red peppers, finely chopped (1½ cups)
1 pound firm-ripe medium tomatoes, chopped (1½ cups)
2 medium onions, chopped (1 cup)
1½ cups sugar
3 cups cider vinegar
4 teaspoons kosher, canning, or pickling salt
1 teaspoon celery seeds
1 teaspoon dry mustard
1 teaspoon ground turmeric

1. Prepare jars and lids for canning (page 514). Fill canner halfway with *water*. Cover canner and heat to simmering over high heat.

2. With sharp knife, cut 8 cups kernels from corncobs.

3. In nonreactive 5-quart Dutch oven, combine corn, green and red peppers, tomatoes, onions, sugar, vinegar, salt, celery seeds, dry mustard, and turmeric; heat to boiling over high heat. Reduce heat; simmer, stirring, 20 minutes.

4. Ladle simmering relish into hot jars to within ¼ inch of tops. (Keep relish simmering while filling jars.) Wipe jar rims and threads clean; cover quickly with lids and screw bands on securely but not too tightly. Process in boiling water bath (page 515) 15 minutes; cool jars and test for airtight seal (page 515). Makes five 16-ounce jars.

Each tablespoon: About 16 calories, 0g protein, 4g carbohydrate, 0g total fat (0g saturated), 0mg cholesterol, 60mg sodium.

GIARDINIERA

....

Usually served as part of an Italian antipasto. If you like, combine it with some peperoncini and oil-cured black olives.

Prep: 1 hour plus preparing jars and lids
Cook: 20 minutes plus processing

- 5 one-pint canning jars and lids
- 1 small head cauliflower (1½ pounds), cut into small flowerets (3 cups)
- 2 large red peppers, cut into 1-inch pieces
- 5 large carrots, peeled and thickly sliced (2 cups)
- 4 large stalks celery, thickly sliced (2 cups)
- 1 jar (5 ounces) green olives, drained
- 1 cup sugar
- 4½ cups distilled white vinegar
- 1½ cups water
- 2 tablespoons kosher, canning, or pickling salt
- ½ teaspoon mustard seeds
- ¼ teaspoon crushed red pepper

1. Prepare jars and lids (page 514). Fill canner halfway with *water;* cover canner and heat to simmering over high heat.

2. In large bowl, combine cauliflower, red peppers, carrots, celery, and olives. In nonreactive 4-quart saucepan, combine sugar, vinegar, water, and salt; heat to boiling over high heat, stirring occasionally. Reduce heat to low.

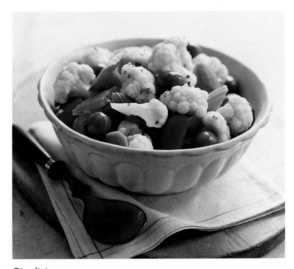

Giardiniera

3. In each hot jar, place some mustard seeds and crushed red pepper; pack vegetables tightly into hot jars to within ½ inch of tops. Immediately ladle simmering syrup over vegetables to within ¼ inch of tops, making sure vegetables are completely covered with syrup. (Keep syrup simmering while filling jars.) Wipe jar rims and threads clean; cover quickly with lids and screw bands on securely but not too tightly. Process in boiling water bath (page 515) 20 minutes; cool jars and test for airtight seal (page 515). Makes five 16-ounce jars.

Each ¼ cup: About 34 calories, 0g protein, 8g carbohydrate, 0g total fat (0g saturated), 0mg cholesterol, 443mg sodium.

PICKLED OKRA

....

Tender okra pods preserved with dill, garlic, and crushed red pepper are an old-time Southern favorite.

Prep: 20 minutes plus preparing jars and lids
Cook: 20 minutes plus processing

- 8 half-pint canning jars and lids
- 3½ cups distilled white vinegar
- 2 cups water
- ¼ cup kosher, canning, or pickling salt
- 8 garlic cloves, peeled
- 8 dill sprigs
- 2 teaspoons crushed red pepper
- 1¼ pounds small firm okra, stems trimmed

1. Prepare jars and lids (page 514). Fill canner halfway with *water;* cover and heat to simmering over high heat.

2. In nonreactive 2-quart saucepan, combine vinegar, water, and salt; heat to boiling over high heat.

3. In each hot jar, place 1 garlic clove, 1 dill sprig, and ¼ teaspoon crushed red pepper. Tightly pack okra, stem end up, into hot jars. Immediately ladle simmering liquid over okra to within ¼ inch of tops, making sure okra is completely covered with liquid. (Keep liquid simmering while filling jars.) Wipe jar rims and threads clean; cover with lids and screw bands on securely but not too tightly. Process in boiling water bath (page 515) 10 minutes; cool jars and test for airtight seal (page 515). Makes eight 8-ounce jars, 4 servings each.

Each serving: About 11 calories, 0g protein, 3g carbohydrate, 0g total fat (0g saturated), 0mg cholesterol, 874mg sodium.

17
....
HOLIDAY CELEBRATIONS

Holiday meals are a time to think big. A juicy turkey, holiday roast beef, succulent ham, or spring leg of lamb are all suitably grand centerpieces; the choice often depends on your family traditions. Then make that sideboard groan with an array of accompaniments, from potato casseroles and stuffings to favorite recipes for green beans, Brussels sprouts, and relishes—and don't forget the gravy! After everyone has had time to rest and digest, out come the desserts: festive cookies, puddings, pies, and cakes made from recipes handed down for generations or promising new sweets that may be brought back next year if they prove popular enough.

On the pages that follow, you'll find special-occasion menus, recipes, tips, and shortcuts to help it all go smoothly. (The menus feature recipes that are all in this book, either within this chapter or cross-referenced with page numbers for easy access.) We share suggestions for instant appetizers and teach you how to roast a turkey that's moist on the inside and crispy on the outside. We also offer recipes and guidance on storing and using all those yummy leftovers. But don't expect perfection: first and foremost, holiday celebrations are about bringing family and friends together for good times. As the host you should enjoy yourself, too.

TIMING

Until you host a holiday meal yourself, you don't truly appreciate the days or even weeks of planning and preparation required. Think of hosting a holiday party as being akin to conducting an orchestra. You want each section to be in tune and for the whole to be harmonious. When planning your menu, plot a variety of colors, textures, and flavors. All sorts of puréed side dishes can be monotonous. If you're serving mashed potatoes with your roast, add a bit of crunch with green beans or broccoli. A stewy entrée pairs with polenta or another soft and creamy side to sop up juices.

Here, some of our favorite tips and shortcuts to help make your entertaining easier.

Checklist, please. Start with a menu and a list of every dish you'll be serving, including bread and drinks. Review recipes and note what you can do ahead. The day before the big dinner, set out serving pieces and utensils (label with Post-it notes to remind yourself which piece goes with which food). For additional tips on planning a party, see Think Ahead, page 19.

Zip It! Side dishes like green beans and sweet potatoes can be made ahead and reheated on the stovetop. Store cut-up veggies in self-sealing plastic bags; you'll fit the foods into small spaces in the fridge.

Stuffing for roast turkey or chickens can be prepared a couple of days in advance; just don't combine the bread with the eggs or sautéed vegetables until you're ready to bake the stuffing.

Gravy Master. To avoid last-minute panic and lumpy gravy, make the base ahead. Into a medium saucepan, measure 1 cup cornstarch or 2 tablespoons flour for every cup of broth (use homemade or select a good-quality low-sodium beef, veal, or chicken broth). Stir 1 cup of the broth into the starch until smooth. Add remaining broth and bring to a boil, stirring often. Boil 1 minute for cornstarch, 3 minutes for flour. Cover and refrigerate for up to 2 days.

While the holiday roast or turkey rests before carving, skim the fat from roasting-pan drippings (leave some to flavor the gravy). Add the gravy base to the roasting pan and boil, scraping up any brown bits. Strain the liquid into a saucepan; reheat and serve.

Beef Tenderloin with White Wine Sauce (recipe page 552)

Low and Slow. Mashed potatoes don't taste the same after they've been refrigerated. Make them in the morning and keep them hot in a slow cooker.

Sweet Finales. Most desserts can be made a day or two ahead; remove them from the refrigerator an hour before serving. Reheat pies in a 350°F oven for 15 minutes.

Heat Up the Plates. If you have oven space, warm the serving plates there. Otherwise, run them under the hottest water available and quickly dry them.

Set a Dazzling Table. A special meal deserves a special table setting. These are the occasions to pull out your china and that stunning crystal you never use. See Setting a Proper Table, page 20, for guidance. If you plan to let guests serve themselves, Buffet Basics, page 19, will help.

Wine and Dine. Reisling and Zinfandel pair well with a turkey dinner. Look for drier Rieslings or spicy, fruity Zinfandels. For advice on wine selection, see Know Your Wines, page 20.

Sit Back, Relax, and Enjoy Your Guests. We've heard of a tradition we think all households should institute. Those who cook, don't clean up.

REMEMBER, IT'S JUST A TURKEY

Whether you're a first-timer or a seasoned holiday cook, the following tips will help you prepare and roast the holiday bird with confidence.

WHAT TO BUY

• Frozen turkeys are widely available and often on sale during the holidays. Some are prebasted to enhance juiciness. You can buy them well in advance of Thanksgiving or Christmas, but you'll need to allow enough time for them to thaw before you put them in the oven (see How to Thaw, opposite).

• Fresh turkeys are preferred by many people but are usually more expensive, have a shorter shelf life, and may need to be special-ordered. Don't buy one more than two days ahead of the big day.

• Kosher turkeys are available fresh and frozen. They're salted as part of the koshering process, so no additional salt is needed in their preparation. This process makes the meat very tender and juicy, similar to the results you'd get from a brined bird.

Roast Turkey

HOW MUCH TO BUY

Estimate 1 pound uncooked turkey per person to ensure enough meat for Thanksgiving or Christmas dinner and for sandwiches later on. For quantities for stuffing, mashed potatoes, and other essential holiday dishes, see How Much Do I Need?, below.

HOW TO THAW

The best way: Place frozen turkey (still in packaging) in a shallow pan on the bottom shelf of the refrigerator. Allow 24 hours thawing time for every 4 to 5 pounds. A thawed bird can keep up to 4 days in the fridge.

(continued)

HOW MUCH DO I NEED?

Cooking for a crowd can be complicated—the prep takes longer and there are more (and bigger) pots to watch. But first comes the essential step: doing the math. Maybe you know how much stuffing to make for eight people, but how much for 20?

Our at-a-glance guidelines for 11 holiday basics shows the minimum amount you'll need to buy whether you're entertaining eight or 24 or various numbers in between.

DISH	SERVINGS					
	8	**10**	**12**	**16**	**20**	**24**
Turkey	8 pounds	10 pounds	12 pounds	16 pounds	20 pounds	24 pounds
Stuffing (dry mix)	8 ounces	10 ounces	12 ounces	16 ounces	20 ounces	24 ounces
Potatoes	3 pounds (6 large)	3½ pounds (7 large)	4½ pounds (9 large)	6 pounds (12 large)	7½ pounds (15 large)	9 pounds (18 large)
Butternut squash	3½ pounds (2 small)	4 pounds (2 medium)	5 pounds (2 large)	6¾ pounds (3 medium)	8 pounds (4 medium)	10 pounds (4 large)
Brussels sprouts (10-ounce container)	2 containers	3 containers	3 containers	4 containers	5 containers	6 containers
Green beans	2 pounds	2½ pounds	3 pounds	4 pounds	5 pounds	6 pounds
Sweet potatoes	3 pounds (3 large)	3¾ pounds (4 large)	4½ pounds (5 large)	6 pounds (6 large)	7½ pounds (8 large)	9 pounds (9 large)
Pearl onions (10-ounce container)	2 containers	2 containers	3 containers	3 containers	4 containers	4 containers
Cranberry sauce (16-ounce can)	2 cans	2 cans	3 cans	3 cans	4 cans	4 cans
Creamed spinach (frozen, 10-ounce package)	3 packages	4 packages	4 packages	6 packages	8 packages	8 packages
Pie (9" to 9½" pie)	1 to 2 pies	2 pies	2 pies	2 to 3 pies	3 pies	3 to 4 pies

DEEP-FRIED TURKEY

 We'll let you in on a little Southern secret: Immersing a turkey in a hot vat of oil produces a supermoist and juicy treat with a crackling, not greasy, mahogany-colored skin in record time—about 3 to 5 minutes per pound (as opposed to the usual 20 minutes).

This unorthodox method of cooking requires a special liquid propane-powered fryer (available with baskets and/or hooks to lower and raise the bird in and out of the fat) and a whole lot of oil—approximately 5 gallons for a 15 pounder. Do this outside—never indoors—and proceed with caution: Make sure your fryer is set on solid ground; wear protective gloves as you work; keep children and pets far away; and cook to a safe temperature, until a thermometer inserted into the thigh of the bird reads 180°F.

TOP SANDWICH IDEAS
FOR COLD TURKEY

Everyone looks forward to leftover turkey sandwiches, that is, until they've had one too many. To jazz things up, stack your sliced white meat with the following items:
• Sautéed onions and cranberry sauce on toasted walnut-raisin bread
• Coleslaw and tomato slices on multigrain bread
• Thinly sliced ham, American cheese, and mustard on white bread; brown in a buttered skillet until golden
• Jarred roasted red peppers and prepared pesto on Italian bread
• Mango chutney and Brie on a French baguette or sourdough roll
• Potato salad and horseradish on pumpernickel
• Cheddar cheese and pickles on a sesame-seed bun
• Thousand Island dressing, sauerkraut, and Swiss cheese on rye; cook in an oiled skillet until golden
• Blue cheese dressing and apple slices on toasted pecan bread
• Jalapeño-pepper Monterey-Jack and salsa between flour tortillas; panfry quesadilla-style in a nonstick skillet until cheese melts

Last-minute solution: Place a still-wrapped turkey in a large cooler or bowl and submerge in cold water. Allow 30 minutes of thawing time per pound and change the water every 30 minutes. Cook turkey immediately.

HOW TO STUFF

The best way: Bake stuffing separately in a shallow casserole in the oven alongside the turkey. If you prefer to stuff the bird, follow these guidelines:
• Make sure the turkey is fully thawed.
• Mix ingredients just before using and pack stuffing loosely into the cavity to allow room for expansion.
• Roast the turkey about 30 minutes longer than an unstuffed one.
• Check that the internal temperature of the stuffing reaches 165°F.

HOW TO ROAST

• Place the turkey (breast side up) on a rack in a large roasting pan in an oven preheated to 325°F. If you don't have a rack, place 2 or 3 large carrots crosswise underneath the bird to ensure good heat circulation.
• For moist meat, cover with foil from the start—but remove foil during the last hour of roasting for browner, crispier skin.
• Basting with pan juices isn't necessary, but it will help with browning after the foil is removed.
• Roast turkey 3 to 3¾ hours for a 12- to 14-pounder. (That's around 15 to 17 minutes per pound for an unstuffed bird.)
• Use an instant-read meat thermometer to test doneness. Turkey should be taken out of the oven when the thickest part of the thigh (next to but not touching the bone) reaches 175°F and the breast reaches 165°F. Keep in mind that the temperature will rise 5° to 10°F upon standing.
• If the turkey is fully cooked earlier than expected, wrap the entire bird and pan with foil and place a large bath towel on top to keep it hot and moist for 1 hour.
• Never leave at room temperature longer than 2 hours.

WHEN IN DOUBT

Having a turkey meltdown? Try these phone numbers and Web sites for help.
• Butterball Turkey Talk-Line . . . 800-288-8372
  November 1 to December 29
  butterball.com (with links to Butterball's Facebook page and Twitter account)
• Reynolds Turkey Tips Hot Line . . . 800-745-4000
  November 1 to December 31
  reynoldskitchen.com
• USDA Meat & Poultry Hot Line . . . 800-674-6854
  fsis.usda.gov

SAFELY STORING TURKEY LEFTOVERS

The pie has been served, the table is cleared, the dishes await. If you're tempted to curl up in front of a good movie and leave cleanup for the rest of the gang, at least put the turkey away first.

"Store it within two hours of serving. Bacteria grow rapidly at room temperature, and refrigeration will not eliminate microorganisms that have already grown," says Sandy Kuzmich, Ph.D., the Good Housekeeping Institute's Chemistry Director.

Leftover turkey can be stored in the refrigerator for 3 to 4 days. In the freezer it will keep for 4 months (plain) or 6 months (in broth or gravy). Here are some additional pointers for safe stowaways:
• Take all meat off the carcass and store in serving-size packets or shallow containers. The smaller the portion, the faster you can thoroughly defrost and reheat it. (To refrigerate in packets, wrap meat in plastic wrap or foil and place in self-sealing plastic bags. To freeze, use the same procedure but with freezer-weight bags.)
• To thaw leftover turkey, place it in the refrigerator overnight. To warm, stir in hot grazy just to heat through. Or stir frozen turkey shreds or small pieces directly into soups at the last minute; cook just until hot.

For tips on freezing, thawing, and using other types of leftovers, see Canning and Freezing, pages 512–535.

MENUS

TRADITIONAL THANKSGIVING

Butternut-Apple Soup (p. 52)
Traditional Roast Turkey with Giblet Gravy (p. 176)
Northwest Fruit Stuffing (p. 188)
Brussels Sprouts with Bacon (p. 396)
Double recipe of Ginger Candied Carrots (p. 398)
Green Beans with Hazelnuts (p. 392)
Pumpkin Cheesecake (p. 648)
Pecan Pie (p. 666)
No-Cook Cranberry-Orange Relish (p. 508)

POTLUCK THANKSGIVING

Host makes Traditional Turkey with Giblet Gravy (p. 176)
Easy Spicy Cheese Straws (p. 43)
Hot Crabmeat Spread (p. 35)
Spicy Curried Carrot Soup (p. 52)
Double recipe of Basic Mashed Potatoes (p. 422)
Lemony Green Beans (p. 392)
Brussels Sprouts with Bacon and Chestnuts (p. 396)
Creamed Pearl Onions and Peas (p. 415)
Candied Sweet Potatoes (p. 437)
Country Sausage and Corn Bread Stuffing (p. 18)
Chestnut and Apple Stuffing (p. 187)
Apple Crumb Squares (p. 668)
Pilgrim Pumpkin Pie (p. 665)
Chocolate Pecan Pie (p. 667)

THANKSGIVING FOR FOUR

Quick Cream of Broccoli Soup (p. 54)
Apple and Thyme Roast Chicken (p. 154)
Mashed Potatoes with Parsnips (p. 422)
Steamed Green Beans with Maître d'Hôtel Butter (p. 504)
Moist Bread Stuffing (p. 189)
Pilgrim Pumpkin Pie (p. 665)

DAY AFTER THANKSGIVING IDEAS

Turkey Soup (p. 68)
Turkey Potpie with Cornmeal Crust (p. 181)
Old-Fashioned Creamed Turkey (p. 182)

ROASTED RED AND GREEN PEPPER QUESADILLAS

Not just for southwestern Santas, your holiday revelers will love our festive take on this spicy snack.

Prep: 45 minutes   **Roast/brown:** 30 minutes

4 poblano peppers (12 ounces)

2 large red peppers (8 to 10 ounces each)

1 large onion (10 to 12 ounces), cut into ¼-inch pieces

1 pint grape tomatoes

1 teaspoon vegetable oil

16 soft-taco-size (8-inch) flour tortillas

4 cups shredded Monterey jack cheese (1 pound)

½ cup packed fresh cilantro leaves, chopped

5 ripe avocados (2 pounds)

3 tablespoons fresh lime juice

½ teaspoon salt

1. Arrange oven rack 5 inches from heat source. Preheat broiler. In broiling pan lined with foil, arrange poblanos and red peppers in single layer. Broil 15 to 20 minutes or until blackened all over, turning occasionally to evenly blacken. Wrap peppers in foil; let cool. In 15½" by 10½" jelly-roll pan, toss onion and tomatoes with oil until coated; arrange in single layer. Broil 12 to 15 minutes or until onion is brown and tomatoes begin to burst, stirring once. Remove from broiler and cool in pan. Reset oven control to 200°F. Remove peppers from foil; peel off skin and discard. Remove and discard stems and seeds; finely chop peppers.

2. Prepare quesadillas: On large work surface, arrange 8 tortillas in single layer. Divide Monterey jack, cilantro, and chopped peppers among tortillas. Top with remaining tortillas.

3. Heat 10-inch skillet on medium until hot. Place one assembled quesadilla in skillet and cook 1 to 3 minutes or until bottom browns. Carefully turn and cook 1 to 3 minutes or until bottom browns. Transfer to clean large cookie sheet and place in warm oven. Repeat until all quesadillas are cooked.

4. Prepare guacamole: Cut avocados in half. Remove and discard seeds and peel, then transfer to large serving bowl. Add lime juice, onion and tomatoes, and salt. Using potato masher or fork, mash until almost smooth with a few chunks remaining. (Makes 5 cups.)

5. Cut each quesadilla into 6 wedges and serve with guacamole on the side. Makes 48 appetizers.

Each wedge: About 120 calories, 4g protein, 12g carbohydrate, 7g total fat (2g saturated), 1g fiber, 10mg cholesterol, 200mg sodium.

Tip: Check your local big-box store for 5-pound bags of avocados at a fraction of the usual price. You can roast the peppers and the onion and tomatoes up to two days ahead. Just follow the directions in step 1, then wrap and refrigerate each vegetable separately. If you have two skillets, it will speed things up—you can cook the quesadillas two at a time.

Roasted Red and Green Pepper Quesadillas

POMEGRANATE MARGARITAS

Fill your punchbowl with this jewel-toned version of the classic cocktail. Use pomegranate seeds and lime wedges for garnish and no one will miss the salt!

Prep: 5 minutes

- 1 can (12 ounces) frozen limeade concentrate, thawed
- 2 cups water
- 3½ cups gold tequila
- 2 cups pomegranate juice
- 1 cup triple sec
- 5 limes
  ice cubes for serving
- 1 cup fresh pomegranate seeds (from 1 pomegranate)

1. In large bowl, combine limeade and water until well blended. Stir in tequila, pomegranate juice, and triple sec. Ladle into large pitcher. Cut each lime crosswise into ¼-inch-thick wheels; cut a slit in each wheel, from center to edge. To serve, place ice cubes and a few pomegranate seeds in each glass, set a lime wheel on rim, and fill with mixture. Makes 10½ cups or 18 servings.

Each serving: About 210 calories, 0g protein, 23g carbohydrate, 0g total fat, 1g fiber, 0mg cholesterol, 2mg sodium.

Tip: A budget-friendly can of concentrate contributes intense lime flavor. Mix and refrigerate the margarita mixture up to a day ahead.

VIRGIN POMEGRANATE MARGARITAS
Substitute **2 cups lemon-lime seltzer** for tequila and triple sec. **Substitute pomegranate-cranberry juice for** pomegranate juice. Proceed as above. Makes 8½ cups.

Each serving: About 70 calories, 0g protein, 18g carbohydrate, 0g total fat, 1g fiber, 0mg cholesterol, 10mg sodium.

JICAMA AND ORANGE SALAD

This refreshing salad takes advantage of low-cost, in-season oranges and jicama.

Prep: 45 minutes

- 1 large jicama (2 pounds)
- 1 English (seedless) cucumber
- 4 medium navel oranges (2¼ pounds)
- 3 to 4 limes
- 1 cup packed fresh cilantro leaves, coarsely chopped
- 1 tablespoon vegetable oil
- ⅛ teaspoon ground red pepper (cayenne)
- ¼ teaspoon salt

1. Using sharp knife, trim top and bottom of jicama and generously peel tough brown skin. Cut jicama into matchstick-size pieces; you should have about 8 cups. Peel cucumber in alternating strips; cut in half lengthwise, then into ¼-inch-thick half-moons.

2. With knife, cut peel and white pith from oranges and discard. Working one at a time, hold each orange over large bowl to catch juice, cut out segments between membranes, and drop segments into bowl. Squeeze membranes to extract extra juice. From limes, grate 2 teaspoons peel and squeeze 5 tablespoons juice.

3. To bowl with oranges, add jicama, cucumber, lime peel and juice, cilantro, oil, ground red pepper, and salt. Toss well. Serve immediately or refrigerate up to 4 hours. Makes 20 first-course servings.

Each serving: About 40 calories, 1g protein, 8g carbohydrate, 1g total fat (0g saturated), 3g fiber, 0mg cholesterol, 35mg sodium.

MENU

DESSERT BUFFET

Raspberry-Banana Trifle (p. 601)

Double recipe of Chocolate Fondue with Fruit (p. 609)

Apple-Walnut Bundt Cake (p. 636)

Margarita Cheesecake (p. 648)

Cranberry-Almond Tart (p. 679)

Autumn Fruit Compote (p. 622)

Almond Crescents (p. 692)

Praline-Iced Brownies (p. 683)

MENU
CHRISTMAS DINNER

Roasted-Beet and Pistachio Salad (below)
Beef Rib Roast with Creamy Horseradish (p. 99)
Wild Mushrooms and Peas (p. 546)
Creamy Potato Gratin (p. 546)
Praline Cream Puff Wreath (p. 614)

ROASTED-BEET AND PISTACHIO SALAD

Roasting the beets adds to their natural sweetness.

Prep: 20 minutes plus cooling   Bake: 1 hour

- 6 medium beets (4 ounces each)
- ½ cup shelled unsalted pistachios
- 3 tablespoons balsamic vinegar
- 2 teaspoons Dijon mustard
- ¼ teaspoon salt
- ¼ teaspoon ground black pepper
- ⅓ cup olive oil
- 3 bags (4 ounces each) baby greens and herbs mix
- ¼ cup crumbled blue cheese
- ¼ cup packed fresh mint leaves, torn

1. Preheat oven to 400°F. Arrange beets in single layer on large sheet of foil and wrap tightly. Place in shallow baking pan and bake 1 hour or until tender when pierced with tip of knife. While beets are cooking, in small baking pan, spread pistachios in single layer. Bake alongside beets 4 minutes or until golden and toasted. Cool nuts in pan. When beets are done, unwrap and let sit until cool enough to handle; peel and cut into ½-inch chunks.

2. Prepare dressing: In small bowl, with fork or wire whisk, mix vinegar, mustard, salt, and pepper until blended. Whisk in oil until blended.

3. In medium bowl, combine beets and 2 tablespoons dressing. In large serving bowl, toss greens with remaining dressing until coated. Top with blue cheese, pistachios, beets, and mint. Makes 12 side-dish servings.

Each serving: About 115 calories, 3g protein, 6g carbohydrate, 9g total fat (2g saturated), 2g fiber, 2mg cholesterol, 120mg sodium.

THE PERFECT CHEESE PLATTER

A thoughtful selection of cheeses can be the cornerstone of a cocktail party or set the stage for the feast to come. You'll need 3 to 4 ounces of cheese per guest.

WHAT TO BUY

Fresh: Uncooked, unripened cheeses (such as ricotta and cream cheese) are moist and mild and have a slight tartness. Some of our favorites are sweet mascarpone and fresh goat cheeses like tangy Montrachet.

Soft-Ripened: With their white and bloomy rind, soft and buttery cheese like Brie and Camembert ripen from the outside in. For a real treat, serve a decadent triple-cream like Brillat-Savarin or Pierre Robert.

Washed Rind: The surfaces of these cheeses have been washed with brine or liquor. The orange-hued rind smells strong, but the interior is creamy and mellow. Wonderful choices include Taleggio, Limburger, and French Munster.

Firm: Almost all moisture has been pressed out of these flavorful, aged cheeses. Start with an American classic like Vermont or Wisconsin Cheddar. Then sample caramel-like aged Gouda, Emmenthaler, authentic Parmigiano-Reggiano, and aged Pecorino.

Blue: Salty and piquant, these cheeses go best with a full-bodied red wine. Roquefort, Stilton, and Gorgonzola are all flavorful picks.

HOW TO SERVE AND STORE

- Always bring cheese to room temperature in original wrapping before serving.
- Set out selections on a board or platter with a separate cutting utensil for each cheese.
- Don't put strong cheeses next to mild ones; the heavy scent will overpower the lighter one. When tasting, go from the mildest to the strongest cheese.
- Pair cheeses with crusty breads, stoned wheat or water crackers, cured meats like proscuitto or salami, fruit (dried or fresh), olives, nuts, and chutneys.
- Semihard and hard cheeses can last up to a week in plastic wrap in the fridge. After that, rewrap in parchment or waxed paper so cheese can "breathe." For long-term storage, place parchment-wrapped cheese in a plastic container.

WILD MUSHROOMS AND PEAS

We stretch the mushroom flavor by adding inexpensive white mushrooms to our mix of oysters and shiitakes.

Prep: 15 minutes   Cook: 25 minutes

- 2 packages (10 ounces each) sliced white mushrooms
- 8 ounces shiitake mushrooms, stems discarded, caps cut into ½-inch-thick slices
- 8 ounces oyster mushrooms, tough ends trimmed and mushrooms separated into lobes
- ½ cup water
- 2 tablespoons butter or margarine
- 4 green onions
- 1 package (16 ounces) frozen peas
- 1 tablespoon lower-sodium soy sauce
- ¼ teaspoon salt
- ½ teaspoon ground black pepper

Wild Mushrooms and Peas

1. In 12-inch skillet, combine mushrooms, water, and 1 tablespoon butter. Cover and cook on medium 10 minutes. Uncover and cook 15 minutes or until mushrooms are tender and browned, stirring occasionally.

2. Meanwhile, finely chop white and pale green parts of green onions; thinly slice dark green tops and set aside. Stir chopped green onions and peas into mushroom mixture. Cook 2 to 3 minutes or until peas are heated through and liquid in pan returns to boiling, stirring occasionally. Stir in soy sauce, salt, and pepper. Add remaining 1 tablespoon butter, stirring until melted. Remove pan from heat and stir in reserved green onions; transfer to serving bowl. Makes 12 side-dish servings.

Each serving: About 80 calories, 5g protein, 11g carbohydrate, 3g total fat (0g saturated), 3g fiber, 0mg cholesterol, 175mg sodium.

Tip: You can clean and sauté the mushrooms the day before, then keep them, covered, in the refrigerator. Rewarm them in the skillet over medium heat before stirring in the chopped green onions and peas.

CREAMY POTATO GRATIN

This classic French dish gains extra richness when subtle hints of garlic flavor are added.

Prep: 25 minutes   Cook/Bake: 40 minutes

- 3 cloves garlic, each cut in half
- 3 tablespoons butter or margarine
- 3 pounds Yukon Gold potatoes, peeled and scrubbed
- 3 cups milk
- ⅛ teaspoon ground nutmeg
- 1 teaspoon salt
- ½ teaspoon ground black pepper

1. Preheat oven to 425°F. Rub half of 1 clove garlic all over inside of 3-quart shallow glass or ceramic baking dish; discard garlic piece. Rub ½ tablespoon butter all over dish; cut remaining butter into small pieces and reserve.

Creamy Potato Gratin

2. With adjustable-blade slicer or sharp knife, cut potatoes into ⅛-inch-thick slices. In 12-inch skillet, combine potatoes, milk, and remaining garlic. Heat to boiling on medium, stirring occasionally. Reduce heat to medium-low and simmer 3 minutes. Stir in nutmeg, salt, and pepper. Remove and discard garlic cloves. Carefully transfer potato mixture to prepared baking dish, spreading evenly. Top with reserved butter pieces.

3. Bake gratin 30 minutes or until golden brown with some darker brown spots; potatoes should be tender when pierced with tip of knife. Cool on wire rack 10 minutes before serving. Makes 12 side-dish servings.

Each serving: About 160 calories, 4g protein, 26g carbohydrate, 5g total fat (2g saturated), 2g fiber, 8mg cholesterol, 265mg sodium.

INSTANT APPETIZERS

When unexpected guests stop by, these tasty morsels can be whipped up in minutes. Uncork the wine or mix up some cocktails and let the festivities begin.

LITTLE LATKES: Heat frozen mini potato pancakes; top with dollops of sour cream and sliced green onion.

TOASTED ALMONDS: Spread whole natural nuts in a single layer on a cookie sheet; sprinkle with salt if you like. Bake at 350°F for about 10 minutes or until lightly browned and fragrant, stirring occasionally. Serve in a pretty bowl.

GREEK PLATTER: Arrange baby carrots, celery sticks, toasted pita wedges, and assorted olives around store-bought hummus.

GOURMET GRILLED CHEESE: In a skillet, prepare grilled Cheddar cheese sandwiches on raisin-nut or thick country bread. Cut each sandwich into eighths and serve with jarred chutney.

WINTER'S NIGHT GOAT CHEESE: Coat a log of plain goat cheese with cracked black pepper and sprinkle with chopped roasted red peppers from a jar. Drizzle with extra virgin olive oil and serve with toasted, sliced French bread or water crackers.

STUFFED CELERY: Toast chopped walnuts in a skillet for 2 minutes, until fragrant, shaking pan often. Mix crumbled blue cheese and cream cheese until smooth. Spoon into celery sticks and sprinkle with nuts.

HOT POPCORN: Toss microwaved popcorn with Cajun seasoning mix or grated Parmesan cheese and ground red pepper (cayenne).

MEXICAN DIP: In a glass pie plate, layer store-bought bean dip, jarred salsa, sour cream, shredded Cheddar cheese, and sliced green onion. Serve with tortilla chips at room temperature or warm (microwave, lightly covered, on High for 1 minute).

QUICK PINWHEELS: Spread large plain or flavored flour tortillas with cream cheese and sprinkle with chopped pimiento-stuffed olives or sun-dried tomatoes. Roll up and slice crosswise into rounds.

> **MENU**
>
> **CHRISTMAS BRUNCH**
> _____
>
> Blood Orange Mimosas (opposite)
> Green-Apple Salad with Endive and Radicchio (below)
> Overnight Savory French Toast (right)
> Smoked Salmon Spread and Bagels (opposite)
> Cinnamon Crumb Cake (p. 550)

GREEN-APPLE SALAD WITH ENDIVE AND RADICCHIO

···

Crisp and refreshing, this salad also combines the colors of the season.

Prep: 15 minutes

- 1 tablespoon finely chopped shallot
- ¼ cup fresh lemon juice
- 2 large heads Belgian endive, cut diagonally into 1-inch pieces
- 1 Granny Smith apple, cored and very thinly sliced
- 1 head Boston lettuce, torn into bite-size pieces
- 1 head radicchio, thinly sliced
- 2 tablespoons olive oil
- ¼ teaspoon salt
- ¼ teaspoon ground black pepper

1. In small bowl, combine shallot and lemon juice. Set aside.

2. In large serving bowl, combine endive, apple, lettuce, and radicchio; toss with oil, salt, and pepper until evenly coated. Add shallot mixture and toss again. Serve immediately. Makes 8 first-course servings.

Each serving: About 60 calories, 1g protein, 7g carbohydrate, 4g total fat (1g saturated), 2g fiber, 0mg cholesterol, 80mg sodium.

Tip: You can clean and prepare the lettuce and radicchio up to a day ahead. Refrigerate them, wrapped in damp paper towels, in a zip-tight plastic bag.

OVERNIGHT SAVORY FRENCH TOAST

···

A sophisticated take on everyone's favorite brunch fare.

Prep: 25 minutes plus chilling and standing
Bake: 50 minutes

- 6 large eggs
- 2 cups milk
- 1 tablespoon Dijon mustard
- ¼ teaspoon salt
- ¼ teaspoon ground black pepper
- ¼ cup snipped chives plus additional for garnish
- 1 loaf (9 ounces) French bread (preferably day-old), cut into ¼-inch-thick slices
- 3 cups shredded Gruyère cheese (6 ounces)

1. Grease shallow 1½-quart ceramic baking dish. In medium bowl, with wire whisk, beat eggs, milk, Dijon, salt, and pepper until well blended. Stir in chives.

2. Arrange half of bread in prepared baking dish, overlapping slices to fit. Pour half of egg mixture over bread and sprinkle with 2 cups Gruyère. Cover with remaining bread, overlapping slices. Pour remaining egg mixture over bread; gently press down to help bread absorb egg mixture. Sprinkle with remaining 1 cup Gruyère. Cover and refrigerate overnight.

3. Preheat oven to 350°F. Bake French toast 50 to 60 minutes or until puffed and golden and tip of knife inserted in center comes out clean. Cover top during last 15 minutes if browning occurs too quickly. Let stand 10 minutes to set custard before serving. Garnish with snipped chives. Makes 8 main-dish servings.

Each serving: About 355 calories, 22g protein, 20g carbohydrate, 20g total fat (11g saturated), 1g fiber, 214mg cholesterol, 495mg sodium.

Tip: Look for discounted day-old French bread in your market or bakery.

SMOKED SALMON SPREAD AND BAGELS

....

Buying enough sliced smoked salmon to top bagel appetizers can be expensive. Instead, stretch your dollars and treat your guests to this flavorful spread. It delivers the big flavor of smoked salmon without the big bucks. You can prepare the salmon spread up to 1 day ahead; just keep it covered in the refrigerator.

Prep: 15 minutes plus chilling   Toast: 10 minutes

- 4 ounces reduced-fat cream cheese (Neufchâtel), softened
- 1 container (8 ounces) reduced-fat sour cream
- 4 ounces smoked salmon, chopped
- 2 tablespoons fresh dill, chopped
- 1 tablespoon capers, drained and chopped
- ¼ teaspoon salt
- ¼ teaspoon ground black pepper
- 1 lemon
- 2 bagels, preferably sesame seed and poppy seed
- ½ small red onion, thinly sliced
- ½ English (seedless) cucumber, thinly sliced
- 4 red radishes, thinly sliced

1. Prepare smoked salmon spread: In large bowl, stir cream cheese until light and fluffy. Fold in sour cream, salmon, dill, capers, salt, and pepper. From lemon, grate 1 teaspoon peel and squeeze 1 teaspoon juice; stir juice and peel into spread. Transfer to serving bowl. Cover and refrigerate at least 1 hour and up to overnight.

2. Preheat oven to 375°F. Cut bagels in half to form four C shapes. Hold bagel halves cut-side-down and slice each lengthwise into four pieces, to form 16 flat C shapes. Cut each in half crosswise to form 32 pieces.

3. On large cookie sheet, arrange bagel pieces in single layer; bake 8 to 10 minutes or until golden and crisp. Transfer to wire rack to cool completely.

4. Serve bagel toasts with smoked salmon spread and red onion, cucumber, and radishes for topping. Makes 32 toasts.

Each toast: About 35 calories, 2g protein, 3g carbohydrate, 2g total fat (1g saturated), 0g fiber, 6mg cholesterol, 140mg sodium.

Blood Orange Mimosas

BLOOD ORANGE MIMOSAS

....

Good-quality Prosecco—an Italian sparkling wine— is a great stand-in for pricey champagne.

Prep: 3 minutes

- 2 cups fresh blood orange juice, well chilled
- 1 bottle (750ml) dry Prosecco or other dry sparkling wine, well chilled
   Fresh blood orange slices for garnish (optional)

Into each of 8 champagne flutes, pour ¼ cup juice. Top off each glass with Prosecco, and, if you like, a slice of blood orange. Makes 8 servings.

Each serving: About 95 calories, 1g protein, 9g carbohydrate, 0g total fat, 0g fiber, 0mg cholesterol, 0mg sodium.

CINNAMON CRUMB CAKE

·····································

Whether your beverage of choice is coffee or hot cocoa, this delicious cake provides the perfect accompaniment.

Prep: 25 minutes plus cooling   Bake: 40 minutes

Crumb Topping
- ½ cup pecans, toasted and chopped
- ⅓ cup packed dark brown sugar
- ¼ cup all-purpose flour
- ½ teaspoon ground cinnamon
- 2 tablespoons butter or margarine, softened

Cake
- 1½ cups all-purpose flour
- 1 teaspoon baking powder
- ¼ teaspoon baking soda
- ¼ teaspoon salt
- ¾ cup granulated sugar
- 4 tablespoons butter or margarine
- 1 teaspoon vanilla extract
- 2 large eggs
- ⅔ cup sour cream

Cinnamon Crumb Cake

1. Prepare crumb topping: In small bowl, mix pecans, brown sugar, flour, and cinnamon until well blended. With fingertips, work in butter until mixture resembles marbles. Set aside.

2. Prepare cake: Preheat oven to 350°F. Grease 9-inch springform pan; dust with flour. On sheet of waxed paper, combine flour, baking powder, baking soda, and salt.

3. In large bowl, with mixer on medium speed, beat granulated sugar, butter, and vanilla 5 to 6 minutes or until fluffy, occasionally scraping bowl with rubber spatula. Reduce speed to low; add eggs, one at a time, beating well after each addition.

4. With mixer on low speed, add flour mixture alternately with sour cream, beginning and ending with flour mixture, scraping bowl occasionally, until batter is smooth.

5. Pour batter into prepared pan. Sprinkle with crumb topping and gently press into batter. Bake 40 to 45 minutes, until toothpick inserted in center of cake comes out clean. To serve warm: Cool cake in pan on wire rack 15 minutes. With small metal spatula, loosen cake from side of pan and remove, then cool an additional 30 minutes. To serve later: Cool cake completely in pan. Makes 10 servings.

Each serving: About 300 calories, 5g protein, 37g carbohydrate, 15g total fat (7g saturated), 1g fiber, 68mg cholesterol, 225mg sodium.

Tip: Bake and freeze the cake, tightly wrapped, for up to 1 month before you serve it.

MENU

SOUTHERN CHRISTMAS

Tomato and Onion Glazed Ham (p. 128)
Buttermilk Biscuits (p. 559)
Creamy Corn Pudding (p. 404)
Candied Carrots (p. 398)
Southern-Style Greens (p. 409)
Cranberry-Fig Chutney (p. 509)
Oranges with Caramel (p. 462)
Coconut Cake (Golden Butter Cake, p. 632,
with Fluffy White Frosting, p. 652,
sprinkled with shredded coconut)

MENU

HANUKKAH

Potato Latkes (p. 427)
Cranberry Applesauce (p. 449)
Tarragon-Roasted Salmon with Caper Sauce (p. 194)
Citrus Salad with Sherry Dressing (p. 475)
Green Beans Amandine (p. 392)
Sufganiyot (below)

SUFGANIYOT

Jelly doughnuts, called "sufganiyot" in Israel, are a popular Hanukkah treat. Although fried foods are often associated with this holiday, we bake these doughnuts for a lighter version.

Prep: 30 minutes plus dough rising and cooling
Bake: 12 minutes per batch

- 3 cups all-purpose flour
- ¼ cup granulated sugar
- 5 teaspoons rapid-rise yeast (2 packages)
- 1 teaspoon ground cinnamon
- 1 teaspoon salt
- ¼ cup vegetable oil
- ¾ cup warm whole milk (120 to 130°F), plus extra for brushing
- 2 large eggs, at room temperature
- 1 cup sour cherry or other jam
- 2 tablespoons confectioners' sugar

1. In electric stand mixer bowl, combine flour, granulated sugar, yeast, cinnamon, and salt. With paddle attachment of stand mixer, mix on low 15 seconds or until combined. Add oil and milk; beat on medium-low speed 3 to 5 minutes or until well combined. Add eggs, one at a time; beat 10 minutes or until dough is elastic, occasionally scraping sides of bowl.

2. Meanwhile, lightly oil large bowl. Transfer dough to prepared bowl; cover loosely with plastic wrap. Let rise 40 minutes or until doubled in bulk.

3. Lightly grease three cookie sheets. Gently punch down dough, folding it onto itself. On lightly oiled work surface, gently roll dough into 16-inch log; cut log crosswise into 1-inch pieces. Shape each piece into ball; transfer to prepared cookie sheets, 3 inches apart. Cover loosely with lightly oiled plastic wrap; let rise 20 to 30 minutes or until slightly puffed. (May be made up to 1 day ahead up to this point. Refrigerate, loosely covered. Bring to room temperature before baking.)

4. Preheat oven to 350°F. Brush tops of dough with milk. Bake, one sheet at a time, 12 to 15 minutes or until pale golden. Cool on sheets on wire racks 5 minutes.

5. Cut off corner of self-sealing plastic bag to make ¼-inch-diameter hole; fit with ¼- to ½-inch plain piping tip, and fill bag with jam. Slide paring knife horizontally into one side of each doughnut and, using sawing motion, carefully cut pocket in pastry. Fit piping tip into hole, and pipe jam into it until filled. Repeat. Dust doughnuts with confectioners' sugar to serve. Makes 16 doughnuts.

Each doughnut: About 215 calories, 4g protein, 37g carbohydrate, 6g total fat (1g saturated), 1g fiber, 28mg cholesterol, 165mg sodium.

Sufganiyot

HERBED GOUGÈRES

These rich herb-flecked cheese puffs are sure to be a hit.

Prep: 50 minutes   Bake: 20 minutes

1	cup water
6	tablespoons butter or margarine, cut into tablespoons
¼	teaspoon salt
	pinch ground red pepper (cayenne)
1	cup all-purpose flour
4	large eggs
6	ounces Gruyère cheese, shredded (2 cups)
¼	cup fresh flat-leaf parsley leaves, finely chopped
2	tablespoons finely chopped fresh chives
1	teaspoon freshly grated lemon peel

1. Preheat oven to 400°F. Line two large cookie sheets with parchment paper.

2. In 3-quart saucepan, heat water, butter, salt, and ground red pepper to boiling on medium. Remove from heat. With wooden spoon, vigorously stir in flour all at once until mixture forms ball and pulls away from side of pan.

3. Add eggs, one at a time, beating well after each addition, until batter is smooth and satiny. Stir in cheese, parsley, chives, and lemon peel until well mixed. Drop batter by rounded teaspoons, about 1½ inches apart, onto prepared cookie sheets.

4. Bake 20 to 25 minutes or until puffed and golden brown, rotating sheets between upper and lower racks halfway through baking. Cool slightly on sheets on wire racks, 3 to 5 minutes. Serve warm. To make ahead, cool completely, then transfer to airtight containers and freeze up to 1 month. Transfer from freezer to cookie sheets; reheat in 350°F oven 10 minutes or until warm. Makes 58 gougères.

Each serving (4 gougères): About 140 calories, 6g protein, 7g carbohydrate, 10g total fat (7g saturated), 0g fiber, 84mg cholesterol, 160mg sodium.

BEEF TENDERLOIN WITH WHITE WINE SAUCE

(Pictured on page 536)

White wine with beef? Absolutely! This tarragon-scented sauce is lighter than the typical red-wine reduction, but it makes an oh-so-flavorful accompaniment to the meat.

Prep: 45 minutes plus resting   Roast: 50 minutes

3	large shallots, finely chopped (1¼ cups)
4	tablespoons packed fresh tarragon leaves, finely chopped, plus additional for garnish
2	tablespoons olive oil
1½	teaspoons salt
2	teaspoons coarsely ground black pepper
1	whole beef tenderloin (5 pounds), trimmed and tied
2	tablespoons white wine vinegar
1	cup dry white wine
2	tablespoons butter or margarine
	Rosemary sprigs and bay leaves for garnish

1. Preheat oven to 425°F. In small bowl, combine half of shallots, 2 tablespoons chopped tarragon, 1 tablespoon oil, salt, and pepper. Rub all over tenderloin. Place tenderloin, smooth side up, on rack in large roasting pan (17" by 13½").

2. Roast tenderloin 45 to 50 minutes or until instant-read thermometer inserted in center reaches 135°F. Internal temperature of meat will rise 5° to 10°F (medium-rare) upon standing. Or, roast to desired doneness. Transfer to serving platter and tent loosely with foil. Let stand 15 to 20 minutes to set juices for easier slicing.

Prep: 30 minutes plus cooling   Bake: 40 minutes

- 1 cup hazelnuts (4 ounces, filberts)
- 1¼ cups sugar
- 8 squares (8 ounces) semisweet chocolate, chopped
- 4 tablespoons butter or margarine
- 5 large eggs
- ¾ cup heavy or whipping cream

1. Preheat oven to 350°F. Lightly grease 9-inch springform pan. Line bottom with waxed or parchment paper; grease paper.

2. Place hazelnuts in 15½" by 10½" jelly-roll pan. Bake 10 to 15 minutes or until toasted and fragrant, shaking pan occasionally. Remove pan from oven. Wrap hot hazelnuts in clean kitchen towel; with hands, roll hazelnuts back and forth until as much skin as possible rubs off. Cool nuts completely.

3. In food processor with knife blade attached, place ¾ cup nuts and ¼ cup sugar; pulse until finely ground. With chef's knife, roughly chop remaining nuts; set aside.

4. In 3-quart saucepan, melt chocolate and butter on medium-low, stirring occasionally. Meanwhile, in large bowl, with mixer on medium-high speed, beat eggs and ½ cup sugar 7 minutes or until tripled in volume. With rubber spatula, fold in chocolate mixture, then fold in ground-nut mixture. Pour batter into prepared pan and bake 35 minutes or until top is dry and cracked and toothpick inserted in center comes out slightly wet. Cool in pan on wire rack 10 minutes. Remove side of pan and cool 30 minutes longer on wire rack.

5. Meanwhile, prepare praline: Line 9-inch cake pan with foil. In pan, spread reserved chopped hazelnuts in single layer. In 12-inch skillet, spread remaining ½ cup sugar in even layer. Cook on medium-high 3 to 5 minutes or until sugar is melted and golden amber, swirling sugar in pan to cook evenly. (Do not stir.) Immediately drizzle melted sugar over nuts in pan to coat evenly. Cool praline completely in pan. When cool and hardened, break into 12 large pieces. While praline cools, in large bowl, with mixer on medium speed, beat cream until soft peaks form, 3 to 5 minutes.

6. To serve, cut cake and divide slices among serving plates. Top each slice with a dollop of whipped cream and piece of hazelnut praline. Makes 12 servings.

Each serving: About 360 calories, 6g protein, 33g carbohydrate, 25g total fat (11g saturated), 2g fiber, 120mg cholesterol, 75mg sodium.

---

3. Meanwhile, prepare sauce: Place roasting pan over 2 burners on top of range on medium and add remaining 1 tablespoon oil and remaining shallots. Cook 1 to 2 minutes or until tender, stirring. Add vinegar and cook 1 to 2 minutes or until reduced by half, stirring and scraping pan to loosen any browned bits. Add wine, bring to a simmer and cook 4 to 5 minutes or until reduced by half, stirring and scraping pan. Remove from heat; stir in butter until melted. Carefully pour sauce through fine-mesh strainer into gravy boat. Stir in remaining 2 tablespoons tarragon and any accumulated beef juices on platter. (Makes about ¾ cup sauce.)

4. Remove and discard string from tenderloin. Garnish platter with rosemary sprigs and bay leaves; sprinkle tenderloin with additional chopped tarragon. To serve, cut tenderloin into slices and serve with sauce. Makes 12 main-dish servings.

FLOURLESS CHOCOLATE
HAZELNUT CAKE

In 1984, a gooey gâteau au chocolat *kicked off* Good Housekeeping's *long-running love affair with flour-free cakes. This recipe is almost identical to that first fudgy forerunner—five eggs provide the leavening, and there's a trufflelike creaminess to the texture. But there is one noteworthy change: Toasted hazelnuts are folded into the batter, adding a delectable depth of flavor.*

MENU

ROSH HASHANA

Roasted Red Pepper Dip with vegetable crudités (p. 30)
Brisket with Mushrooms (p. 102)
Potato Kugel (below)
Double recipe of Candied Carrots and Parsnips (p. 398)
Coleslaw with Vinaigrette (p. 485)
Honey Cake (below)
Apple wedges for dipping in honey

4. Divide batter between prepared pans. Bake 45 to 55 minutes, until tops spring back when lightly touched and a toothpick inserted in center of loaves come out clean (tops may be a bit sticky). With small knife, loosen loaves from sides of pans; invert loaves onto wire racks. Turn loaves right side up and cool completely. Makes 2 loaves, 12 slices each.

Each slice: About 160 calories, 3g protein, 31g carbohydrate, 4g total fat (1g saturated), 0.5g fiber, 35mg cholesterol, 165mg sodium.

HONEY CAKE

Dark and glossy but not terribly rich, this cake is traditionally enjoyed during the Jewish New Year, when honey is eaten as a symbolic "sweetener" of the coming year. You might like to decorate the top (before baking) with a few whole blanched almonds.

Prep: 15 minutes   Bake: 45 minutes

- 3 cups all-purpose flour
- 2½ teaspoons baking powder
- 1 teaspoon baking soda
- ½ teaspoon salt
- ½ teaspoon ground cloves
- ¼ teaspoon ground allspice
- 1 cup honey
- ¾ cup packed light brown sugar
- ¾ cup vegetable oil
- 2 tablespoons whiskey
- 2 teaspoons freshly grated lemon peel
- 3 large eggs
- 1 large egg yolk

1. Preheat oven to 325°F. Grease two 8½" by 4½" metal loaf pans.

2. In medium bowl, stir together flour, baking powder, baking soda, salt, cloves, and allspice.

3. In large bowl, with mixer at medium speed, beat honey, brown sugar, coffee, oil, whiskey, and lemon peel until light and creamy. Beat in eggs and egg yolk, one at a time, beating well after each addition. Reduce speed to low. Beat in flour mixture just until combined.

POTATO KUGEL

This traditional savory pudding is as comforting as can be.

Prep: 25 minutes plus cooling
Cook/Bake: 1 hour 10 minutes

- 4 tablespoons olive oil
- 1 large onion (10 to 12 ounces), finely chopped
- 3 large eggs
- 1 large egg white
- ¼ cup packed fresh flat-leaf parsley leaves, finely chopped
- 1 teaspoon salt
- ¼ teaspoon ground black pepper
- 1 teaspoon fresh thyme leaves, chopped, plus additional sprigs for garnish
- 3 pounds all-purpose potatoes

Potato Kugel

1. Preheat oven to 400°F. Brush shallow 2-quart ceramic or glass baking dish with 1 tablespoon oil.

2. In 12-inch skillet, heat 1 tablespoon oil on medium until hot. Add onion and cook 9 minutes or until golden brown and tender, stirring occasionally. Meanwhile, in large bowl, combine eggs, egg white, parsley, salt, and pepper until eggs are blended. Add thyme to skillet and cook 1 minute, stirring. Remove from heat.

3. Working quickly, peel potatoes and grate in food processor with grating attachment or using large holes of box grater. Add potatoes to egg mixture as you grate to prevent oxidation, then add onions. Stir until well blended. Transfer to prepared dish and spread in even layer. Brush top with remaining 2 tablespoons oil.

4. Bake 1 hour to 1 hour 10 minutes or until browned on top and knife pierces easily through potato mixture. Cool in pan 10 to 15 minutes. Garnish with thyme sprigs; serve warm. To make ahead, cool completely, cover with foil, and refrigerate up to overnight. Reheat, covered, in 400°F oven 30 minutes or until warm. Makes 8 side-dish servings.

Each serving: About 210 calories, 6g protein, 28g carbohydrate, 9g total fat (2g saturated), 3g fiber, 80mg cholesterol, 330mg sodium.

Radishes with Pea Puree

MENU
EASTER DINNER

Eggs Stuffed with Smoked Salmon and Cucumber (p. 39)
Radishes with Pea Puree (below)
Pineapple-Glazed Ham (p. 128)
Roasted Asparagus (p. 390)
Double recipe of Scalloped Potatoes (p. 426)
Deluxe Carrot Cake (p. 637)
Lemon-Ricotta Cheesecake (p. 646)

RADISHES WITH PEA PUREE

Crisp radish slices topped with dollops of sweet pea puree welcome springtime with style.

Prep: 30 minutes   Cook: 6 minutes

- 13 large radishes (about 1 pound), trimmed and cut into scant ¼-inch-thick rounds
- ⅝ teaspoon salt
- 2 sprigs fresh tarragon
- 3 tablespoons extra-virgin olive oil
- 1 clove garlic, crushed with press
- 1 package (10 ounces) frozen peas
- pea shoots or mint leaves, for garnish

1. On work surface covered with paper towels, arrange radish rounds in single layer. Sprinkle with ? teaspoon salt. Let stand 10 minutes on paper towels.

2. Meanwhile, finely chop leaves of 1 tarragon sprig. Set aside. In 2-quart saucepan, combine oil, garlic, and remaining (unchopped) tarragon sprig. Cook on medium 2 to 3 minutes or until mixture is fragrant and garlic is golden. Stir in peas and cook 4 to 5 minutes longer or until peas are just tender, stirring occasionally. Discard tarragon sprig. Transfer pea mixture to food processor. Add reserved chopped tarragon and remaining ⅛ teaspoon salt and puree until very smooth, scraping down sides and bottom of bowl occasionally.

3. With paper towels, blot radish rounds dry. Place about 1 teaspoon pea puree on each radish round. Garnish with pea shoots. Makes 60 rounds.

Each serving (6 rounds): About 65 calories, 2g protein, 5g carbohydrate, 4g total fat (1g saturated), 0mg cholesterol, 130mg sodium.

18
····
QUICK BREADS

As their name implies, quick breads are faster to prepare than their yeast-leavened "cousins." Thanks to fast-acting leavening agents, these simple breads don't require a rising period. Just mix them up and pop them into the oven. Favorite breads from this wide-ranging category include biscuits, muffins, coffee cakes, popovers, pancakes, and waffles.

RISING TO THE OCCASION

Most quick breads rely on chemical leavenings, such as baking powder or baking soda, to make them rise.

Baking soda is an alkali that forms carbon dioxide gas bubbles when combined with an acidic ingredient, such as buttermilk, yogurt, chocolate, brown sugar, or molasses. Store baking soda in an airtight container in a cool, dry place for up to one year.

Baking powder is a combination of baking soda and a dry acid, such as cream of tartar. Most commercial baking powders are double-acting: They start to produce gas bubbles as soon as they are moistened, then release more when heated in the oven. Baking powder can stay potent for up to six months if stored airtight in a cool, dry place.

Buttermilk was originally the liquid left over from churning butter, but it is now made from milk to which bacterial cultures have been added. It is a favorite baking ingredient; its acidity balances sugar's sweetness, and it reacts with baking soda to give baked goods a fine crumb. It's a good ingredient to have on hand in your refrigerator. Dehydrated buttermilk powder is also available. Reconstitute it according to the package directions. In a pinch, a good substitute for buttermilk is sour cream (not reduced-fat) or plain low-fat yogurt blended with an equal amount of whole milk. You can also use soured milk: Place 1 tablespoon fresh lemon juice or distilled white vinegar in a glass measuring cup, then pour in enough whole milk to equal 1 cup. Stir and let stand for five minutes to thicken.

MIXING IT RIGHT

Always mix quick breads with a light hand. Simply combine the dry ingredients, add the liquids, and stir. Before starting, be sure your baking powder or baking soda is active. To test soda or powder, stir 1 teaspoon into 1 cup of boiling water; it should bubble and foam vigorously. All-purpose flour makes tender quick breads. Except for recipes in which chilled butter or margarine is cut into the flour mixture, batters are easier to mix and bake better if all the ingredients are at room temperature. After adding the liquids to the flour mixture, stir just until the batter is blended. If any lumps remain, they will disappear during baking. Overmixing will cause the bread to be tough, dense, and full of tunnels. Biscuit dough is usually kneaded just a few times to blend the mixture together. Lastly, quick breads should be baked as soon as the batter is mixed, while the leavening still has its rising power.

Buttermilk Pancakes (recipe page 570)

BAKING SUCCESS

Bake quick breads in the center of the oven. And if baking two loaves at once, be sure there is enough space between them so the air can circulate freely.

Always use the correct size pan. Loaf pans come in two standard sizes, 8½" by 4½" and 9" by 5". The larger pans holds 2 cups more than the smaller one! Fill loaf pans about two-thirds full. Smooth the top with a rubber spatula so the bread bakes uniformly. Don't be concerned if a lengthwise crack appears along the top during baking; it's very typical.

Muffin pans come in various sizes. Standard muffin-pan cups are about 2½" by 1¼", with 12 cups to the pan. There are also giant (4" by 2") and mini (1⅞" by ¾") muffin-pan cups. Regardless of their size, fill muffin-pan cups two-thirds to three-quarters full (to allow room for rising). Fill any empty cups with water to prevent the pan from warping during baking.

To test quick breads for doneness, use the toothpick test: Insert a wooden toothpick into the center of the bread. It should come out clean without any moist crumbs clinging. If it does not, bake the bread a few minutes longer, then test again. The bread might be done even if the crack in the top looks moist.

COOLING, STORING, AND REHEATING QUICK BREADS

Immediately remove baked biscuits, scones, and muffins from their cookie sheets or pans to prevent them from sticking. Most fruit-filled quick breads should be cooled in their pans for ten minutes to allow them to set. Invert them onto wire racks, then turn right side up to cool completely.

In general, the richer the batter (those containing eggs, butter, or fruit), the longer the baked bread will stay moist. Dense fruit breads are even better if made a day ahead so their flavors can blend. They'll also be firmer and easier to slice. Most muffins, biscuits, scones, and corn breads are best eaten the day they are made, otherwise freeze to serve later.

To store fruit breads and muffins at room temperature, first cool them completely. Wrap them in plastic wrap and then in foil; they will keep for up to three days. To freeze fruit breads, wrap them tightly in plastic wrap and then in heavy-duty foil, pressing out the air. Freeze for up to three months. Smaller items like muffins and biscuits can be frozen for up to one month. Thaw them, still wrapped, at room temperature.

Waffles can be frozen, too. Cook them until lightly browned, then cool completely on wire racks. Place them on cookie sheets and freeze until firm, then seal in heavy-duty zip-tight plastic bags and return to the freezer. To reheat, toast the frozen waffles until golden.

To warm fruit breads, wrap in foil, and heat at 400°F. Muffins, scones, and biscuits will take about ten minutes, while loaves and coffee cakes will take about twenty minutes. Muffins also warm well in a microwave oven. Loosely wrap each muffin in a paper towel and microwave on High for about ten seconds. Be careful, though: If the muffins have sugary add-ins, such as chocolate chips or jam, they could get very hot, and if baked goods are reheated too long, they become tough.

REMOVING MUFFINS FROM PAN

Run a small metal spatula or knife around the inside of the muffin-pan cups. Turn the pan on its side and rap it on the counter to remove the muffins.

BAKING POWDER BISCUITS

···

To cut out biscuits, press the cutter straight down. If you twist it, the biscuits may rise unevenly.

Prep: 15 minutes   Bake: 12 minutes

- 2 cups all-purpose flour
- 1 tablespoon baking powder
- ½ teaspoon salt
- ¼ cup vegetable shortening
- ¾ cup milk

1. Preheat oven to 450°F. In large bowl, with wire whisk, stir flour, baking powder, and salt. With pastry blender or two knives used scissor-fashion, cut in shortening until mixture resembles coarse crumbs. Stir in milk, stirring just until mixture forms soft dough that leaves side of bowl.

2. Turn dough onto lightly floured surface; knead 6 to 8 times, just until smooth. With floured rolling pin, roll dough ½ inch thick for high, fluffy biscuits or ¼ inch thick for thin, crusty biscuits.

3. With floured 2-inch biscuit cutter, cut out rounds, without twisting cutter. Arrange biscuits on ungreased cookie sheet, 1 inch apart for crusty biscuits or nearly touching for soft-sided biscuits.

4. Press trimmings together; reroll and cut out more biscuits. Bake until golden, 12 to 15 minutes. Serve warm. Makes about 18 tall or 36 thin biscuits.

Each tall biscuit: About 86 calories, 2g protein, 12g carbohydrate, 3g total fat (1g saturated), 1mg cholesterol, 151mg sodium.

BUTTERMILK BISCUITS

Prepare as directed above but substitute ¾ **cup buttermilk** for milk and use only **2½ teaspoons baking powder;** add **½ teaspoon baking soda** to flour mixture. Makes about 18 biscuits.

DROP BISCUITS

Prepare as directed above but use **1 cup milk.** Stir dough just until ingredients are blended. Drop heaping tablespoons of mixture, 1 inch apart, on ungreased cookie sheet. Makes about 20 biscuits.

DILL-PEPPER BUTTERMILK BISCUITS

···

The savory combination of dill and black pepper gives these biscuits a sophisticated flavor that makes them a perfect accompaniment to salads, soups, or stews.

Prep: 20 minutes   Bake: 12 minutes

- 2 cups all-purpose flour
- 2½ teaspoons baking powder
- ½ teaspoon baking soda
- ½ teaspoon freshly ground black pepper
- ¼ teaspoon salt
- ¼ cup vegetable shortening
- ¾ cup buttermilk
- 3 tablespoons chopped fresh dill

1. Preheat oven to 450°F. In large bowl, combine flour, baking powder, baking soda, pepper, and salt. With pastry blender or two knives used scissor-fashion, cut in vegetable shortening until mixture resembles coarse crumbs. In cup, combine buttermilk and dill; stir into flour mixture just until mixture forms soft dough that leaves side of bowl.

2. Turn dough onto lightly floured surface; knead 6 to 8 times or just until smooth. With floured rolling pin, roll dough ¼ inch thick.

3. With floured 2-inch biscuit cutter, cut out rounds without twisting cutter. Arrange biscuits on ungreased cookie sheet, 1 inch apart.

4. Press trimmings together; reroll and cut out additional biscuits. Bake 12 to 14 minutes or until golden. Serve warm. Makes 18 biscuits.

Each biscuit: About 80 calories, 2g protein, 11g carbohydrate, 3g total fat (1g saturated), 0g fiber, 0mg cholesterol, 135mg sodium.

SCONES

···

A traditional Scottish quick bread, scones are welcome as a treat for breakfast or as an afternoon snack with tea. For currant scones, stir 1 cup dried currants into the dry ingredients before adding the milk mixture.

Prep: 15 minutes   Bake: 22 minutes

- 2   cups all-purpose flour
- 2   tablespoons plus 2 teaspoons sugar
- 2½ teaspoons baking powder
- ¼   teaspoon salt
- ½   cup cold butter or margarine (1 stick), cut into pieces
- ¾   cup milk
- 1   large egg, separated

1. Preheat oven to 375°F. In large bowl, with wire whisk, stir flour, 2 tablespoons sugar, baking powder, and salt. With pastry blender or two knives used scissor-fashion, cut in butter until mixture resembles coarse crumbs.

2. In 1-cup measuring cup, with fork, mix milk and egg yolk until blended. Make well in center of flour mixture and pour in milk mixture. Stir just until combined.

3. Turn dough onto lightly floured surface and knead 5 to 6 times, just until smooth. With lightly floured hands, pat into 7½-inch round. Transfer to ungreased cookie sheet.

4. With lightly floured knife, cut dough into 8 wedges (do not separate wedges). In small cup, lightly beat egg white. Brush scones with egg white and sprinkle with remaining 2 teaspoons sugar. Bake until golden brown, 22 to 25 minutes. Separate wedges. Serve warm, or cool on wire rack to serve later. Makes 8 scones.

Each scone: About 259 calories, 5g protein, 30g carbohydrate, 13g total fat (8g saturated), 61mg cholesterol, 361mg sodium.

BUTTERMILK SCONES

Prepare as directed (left) but use only **2 teaspoons baking powder.** Add ½ **teaspoon baking soda** to flour mixture. Substitute ¾ **cup buttermilk** for milk.

RICH SCONES

Prepare as directed (left) but preheat oven to 400°F. Use **3½ cups all-purpose flour, ½ cup sugar, 2 tablespoons baking powder, ½ teaspoon salt,** and **6 tablespoons butter or margarine.** Substitute **1 cup half-and-half or light cream** for milk and blend with **2 eggs.** Turn dough onto greased large cookie sheet (dough will be sticky), and with lightly floured hands, pat dough into 9-inch round. Brush with **1 table-spoon half-and-half or light cream** and sprinkle with **1 tablespoon sugar.** With floured knife, cut dough into 8 wedges (do not separate). Bake until golden, 15 to 20 minutes.

Each scone: About 390 calories, 8g protein, 58g carbohydrate, 14g total fat (8g saturated), 88mg cholesterol, 628mg sodium.

LEMON-WALNUT SCONES

Prepare as directed above for Rich Scones but add **1 tea-spoon freshly grated lemon peel** to flour mixture; add **1 cup chopped walnuts (4 ounces)** with half-and-half mixture.

Rich Scones

OATMEAL SCONUTS

If your kids turn their noses up at anything made with whole-wheat flour, you may be looking for ways to get other whole grains into their diets. Try sconuts—a riff on that traditional breakfast favorite, scones, with a touch of donut added. They've been pumped full of oats and given a hit of nutmeg. Leftovers can be frozen for up to a month (to warm them, microwave them for about 20 seconds).

Prep: 10 minutes   Bake: 15 minutes

- 2 cups old-fashioned oats, uncooked
- 2 cups all-purpose flour
- ½ cup brown sugar
- 2½ teaspoons baking powder
- ½ teaspoon baking soda
- ½ teaspoon salt
- ¼ teaspoon ground nutmeg
- ½ cup butter (1 stick), cut into pieces (do not use margarine)
- ¾ cup buttermilk
- 1 large egg
- cinnamon sugar

1. Heat oven to 425°F.

2. In food processor, combine oats, flour, sugar, baking powder, baking soda, salt, and nutmeg; pulse to blend. Add butter; pulse until coarse crumbs form.

3. In cup, beat buttermilk and egg. With processor running, add egg mixture to dry ingredients and pulse until a dough forms.

4. Scoop dough by ¼ cups onto cookie sheet. Flatten each mound into a 2½-inch round. Sprinkle with cinnamon sugar. Bake 15 to 17 minutes or until golden on bottoms. Makes 13 sconuts.

Each scout: About 235 calories, 5g protein, 34g carbohydrate, 9g total fat (5g saturated), 2g fiber, 37mg cholesterol, 315mg sodium.

POPOVERS

Popovers are crispy on the outside and hollow on the inside. Serve them fresh from the oven or make them ahead and reheat in a 400°F oven for 15 minutes.

Prep: 10 minutes   Bake: 1 hour

- 3 large eggs
- 1 cup milk
- 3 tablespoons butter or margarine, melted
- 1 cup all-purpose flour
- ½ teaspoon salt

1. Preheat oven to 375°F. Generously grease eight 6-ounce custard cups or twelve 2½" by 1¼" muffin-pan cups with butter or vegetable oil. Place custard cups in jelly-roll pan for easier handling.

2. In blender, combine eggs, milk, melted butter, flour, and salt; blend until smooth.

3. Pour about ⅓ cup batter into each prepared custard cup, or fill muffin-pan cups half full. Bake 50 minutes, then, with tip of knife, quickly cut small slit in top of each popover to release steam; bake 10 minutes longer. Immediately remove popovers from cups, loosening with spatula if necessary. Serve hot. Makes 8 medium or 12 small popovers.

Each medium popover: About 159 calories, 5g protein, 14g carbohydrate, 9g total fat (5g saturated), 101mg cholesterol, 247mg sodium.

GIANT POPOVERS

Generously grease six deep 8-ounce ceramic custard cups; place in jelly-roll pan. Prepare popovers as directed above but use **6 eggs, 2 cups milk, 6 tablespoons butter or margarine,** melted, **2 cups flour,** and **1 teaspoon salt.** Bake 1 hour before cutting slit in top of popovers. Makes 6 giant popovers.

Each popover: About 394 calories, 13g protein, 36g carbohydrate, 22g total fat (12g saturated), 260mg cholesterol, 629mg sodium.

BASIC MUFFINS

Easy, buttery muffins are a snap to prepare. To make chocolate chip muffins, stir 3/4 cup chocolate chips into the batter before baking. For orange muffins, add 1 teaspoon freshly grated orange peel to the dry ingredients.

Prep: 10 minutes **Bake: 20 minutes**

2½ cups all-purpose flour

½ cup sugar

1 tablespoon baking powder

½ teaspoon salt

1 cup milk

½ cup butter or margarine (1 stick), melted

1 large egg

1 teaspoon vanilla extract

1. Preheat oven to 400°F. Grease twelve 2½" by 1¼" muffin-pan cups.

2. In large bowl, with wire whisk, stir flour, sugar, baking powder, and salt. In medium bowl, with fork, beat milk, melted butter, egg, and vanilla until blended. Add liquid mixture to flour mixture; stir just until flour is moistened (batter will be lumpy).

3. Spoon batter into prepared muffin-pan cups. Bake until toothpick inserted in center of muffin comes out clean, 20 to 25 minutes. Immediately remove muffins from pan. Serve muffins warm, or cool on wire rack to serve later. Makes 12 muffins.

Each muffin: About 225 calories, 4g protein, 30g carbohydrate, 10g total fat (6g saturated), 41mg cholesterol, 312mg sodium.

JAM-FILLED MUFFINS

Prepare as directed (left) but fill muffin-pan cups one-third full with batter. Drop **1 rounded teaspoon strawberry or raspberry preserves** in center of each cup batter; top with remaining batter. Bake as directed.

BLUEBERRY OR RASPBERRY MUFFINS

Prepare as directed (left) but stir **1 cup blueberries or raspberries** into batter.

WALNUT OR PECAN MUFFINS

Prepare as directed (left) but stir ½ **cup chopped toasted walnuts or pecans** into batter. Sprinkle with **2 tablespoons sugar** before baking.

Basic Muffins with Variations

APPLE-OAT MUFFINS

....

Hearty oats and the sweet-and-spicy taste of apples and cinnamon make these muffins a great grab-and-go breakfast.

Prep: 15 minutes   Bake: 23 minutes

- 2 cups old-fashioned or quick-cooking oats, uncooked
- 1¼ cups all-purpose flour
- ½ cup packed brown sugar
- 2 teaspoons baking powder
- ¾ teaspoon baking soda
- ¾ teaspoon salt
- ½ teaspoon ground cinnamon
- 1 cup buttermilk
- 2 tablespoons vegetable oil
- 1 large egg, lightly beaten
- 1 cup shredded Golden Delicious or Granny Smith apples (1 to 2 medium)
- ½ cup walnuts, chopped

1. Preheat oven to 400°F. Grease 12 standard muffin-pan cups. In large bowl, combine oats, flour, sugar, baking powder, baking soda, salt, and cinnamon.

2. In medium bowl, with fork, beat buttermilk, oil, and egg until well blended; stir in shredded apples. Add apple mixture to flour mixture, and stir just until flour mixture is moistened (batter will be very thick and lumpy). Stir in chopped walnuts.

3. Spoon batter into prepared muffin cups. Bake 23 to 25 minutes or until muffins begin to brown and toothpick inserted in center of muffins comes out clean. Immediately remove muffins from pan. Serve muffins warm, or cool on wire rack to serve later. Makes 12 muffins.

Each muffin: About 210 calories, 5g protein, 33g carbohydrate, 7g total fat (1g saturated), 3g fiber, 18mg cholesterol, 320mg sodium.

CARROT-BRAN MUFFINS

....

Deliciously hearty and filled with fiber, these muffins will tide you over to your next meal.

Prep: 15 minutes plus standing   Bake: 30 minutes

- 1 cup milk
- ¼ cup vegetable oil
- 1 large egg, lightly beaten
- 1½ cups whole-bran cereal (not bran flakes)
- 1 cup shredded carrots
- 1¼ cups all-purpose flour
- ⅓ cup sugar
- 1 tablespoon baking powder
- ½ teaspoon salt
- ¼ teaspoon ground cinnamon
- 1 cup dark seedless raisins

1. Preheat oven to 400°F. Grease twelve 2½" by 1¼" muffin-pan cups.

2. In medium bowl, with fork, beat milk, oil, egg, cereal, and carrots until blended; let stand 10 minutes.

3. Meanwhile, in large bowl, with wire whisk, stir flour, sugar, baking powder, salt, and cinnamon. Add cereal mixture to flour mixture; stir just until flour is moistened (batter will be lumpy). Stir in raisins.

4. Spoon batter into prepared muffin-pan cups. Bake until muffins begin to brown and toothpick inserted in center of muffin comes out clean, about 30 minutes. Immediately remove muffins from pan. Serve warm, or cool on wire rack. Makes 12 muffins.

Each muffin: About 198 calories, 4g protein, 33g carbohydrate, 7g total fat (1g saturated), 21mg cholesterol, 309mg sodium.

NUTTY CARROT-BRAN MUFFINS

Prepare as directed above but substitute **golden raisins or dried cranberries** for the dark seedless raisins, if you like, or use a combination. Add ½ **cup chopped walnuts or pecans** in Step 2.

GOLDEN CORN BREAD

·····································

This slightly sweet batter can be baked into a tender square, muffins, or corn sticks.

Prep: 10 minutes   Bake: 20 minutes

1 cup all-purpose flour
¾ cup cornmeal
3 tablespoons sugar
1 tablespoon baking powder
¾ teaspoon salt
⅔ cup milk
4 tablespoons butter or margarine, melted
1 large egg

1. Preheat oven to 425°F. Grease 8-inch square baking pan.

2. In medium bowl, with wire whisk, stir flour, cornmeal, sugar, baking powder, and salt. In small bowl, with fork, beat milk, melted butter, and egg until blended. Add egg mixture to flour mixture; stir just until flour is moistened (batter will be lumpy).

3. Spread batter evenly in prepared pan. Bake until golden and toothpick inserted in center comes out clean, 20 to 25 minutes. Cut corn bread into 9 squares; serve warm. Makes 9 servings.

Each serving: About 178 calories, 4g protein, 25g carbohydrate, 7g total fat (4g saturated), 40mg cholesterol, 425mg sodium.

CORN MUFFINS

Grease twelve 2½" by 1¼" muffin-pan cups. Prepare as directed above but use **1 cup milk.** Fill each muffin-pan cup two-thirds full. Bake until golden and toothpick inserted in center of muffin comes out clean, about 20 minutes. Immediately remove muffins from pans. Serve warm, or cool on wire rack. Makes 12 muffins.

Each muffin: About 144 calories, 3g protein, 19g carbohydrate, 6g total fat (3g saturated), 31mg cholesterol, 322mg sodium.

CORN STICKS

Grease 14 corn-stick molds with vegetable oil. Heat molds in oven until hot, about 15 minutes. Meanwhile, prepare batter as directed (left). Spoon batter into hot molds. Bake until toothpick inserted in center of corn stick comes out clean, 15 to 20 minutes. Cool in molds on wire rack 10 minutes. Remove corn sticks from molds; serve warm. Makes 14 corn sticks.

Each corn stick: About 121 calories, 2g protein, 16g carbohydrate, 5g total fat (3g saturated), 26mg cholesterol, 273mg sodium.

SOUTHERN CORN BREAD

Prepare as directed (left) but place a 9- to 10-inch cast-iron skillet in oven while preheating. In Step 2 omit sugar, reduce baking powder to 1 teaspoon and salt to ½ teaspoon; add **¼ teaspoon baking soda,** and substitute **1 cup buttermilk** for milk. Spray hot skillet with nonstick spray; pour batter into skillet and spread evenly. Bake until a toothpick inserted in center comes out clean, 15 to 20 minutes. Cut corn bread into 8 wedges; serve warm. Makes 8 wedges.

Each wedge: About 243 calories, 7g protein, 35g carbohydrate, 8g total fat (4g saturated), 71mg cholesterol, 584mg sodium.

Southern Corn Bread

Quick Pecan Sticky Buns

QUICK PECAN STICKY BUNS

. . . .

These gooey treats usually take several hours to prep, since you have to wait for the dough to rise. Our no-fuss dough uses baking soda and powder for fast leavening, without losing any of the buttery cinnamon filling or pecan topping. The buns are ready in an hour.

Prep: 25 minutes plus cooling   Bake: 28 minutes

- ¼ cup plus ⅓ cup packed dark brown sugar
- 1½ teaspoons ground cinnamon
- 2 tablespoons honey
- 9 tablespoons butter, melted (do not use margarine)
- ¾ cup pecans, toasted and coarsely chopped
- 2¾ cups all-purpose flour
- ¼ cup granulated sugar
- 1½ teaspoons baking powder
- ½ teaspoon baking soda
- ½ teaspoon salt
- 1¼ cups buttermilk

1. Preheat oven to 425°F. Grease 9-inch round metal cake pan. In small bowl, combine ¼ cup brown sugar with cinnamon; set aside.

2. In 1-quart saucepan, heat honey, remaining ⅓ cup brown sugar, and 2 tablespoons butter on medium until mixture is blended and smooth, stirring occasionally. Pour into prepared pan and sprinkle evenly with pecans; set aside.

3. In large bowl, combine flour, granulated sugar, baking powder, baking soda, and salt. In small bowl, mix buttermilk and 5 tablespoons butter. With spoon, stir buttermilk mixture into flour mixture just until liquid is absorbed.

4. Turn dough onto lightly floured surface and knead 8 to 10 times or just until smooth, about 30 seconds. Pat dough into 12" by 9" rectangle. Brush dough with 1 tablespoon butter, then sprinkle with cinnamon-sugar mixture. Starting at one short end, roll up dough jelly-roll fashion. With seam side down, cut dough crosswise into 8 slices.

5. Place each slice, cut side down, on pecan mixture in cake pan; brush with remaining melted butter. Bake buns 28 to 30 minutes or until golden. Remove pan from oven. Immediately place serving plate over top of pan and invert onto plate, allowing topping to run down sides of buns. Remove baking pan. Cool buns slightly, about 10 minutes, to serve warm, or cool completely to serve later. Wrap any leftovers in foil, and store at room temperature up to 3 days. Makes 8 buns.

Each bun: About 445 calories, 7g protein, 57g carbohydrate, 22g total fat (9g saturated), 2g fiber, 38mg cholesterol, 485mg sodium.

CRANBERRY-ORANGE BREAD

....

Bake this tasty bread a day ahead to allow the flavors to develop and to make it easier to cut neat slices.

Prep: 20 minutes   Bake: 55 minutes

  1 large orange
2½ cups all-purpose flour
  1 cup sugar
  2 teaspoons baking powder
½ teaspoon baking soda
½ teaspoon salt
  4 tablespoons butter or margarine, melted
  2 large eggs
  2 cups cranberries, coarsely chopped
¾ cup walnuts, chopped (optional)

1. Preheat oven to 375°F. Grease 9" by 5" metal loaf pan. From orange, grate 1 teaspoon peel and squeeze ½ cup juice.

2. In large bowl, with wire whisk, stir flour, sugar, baking powder, baking soda, and salt. In small bowl, beat orange peel and juice, melted butter, and eggs until blended. With wooden spoon, stir egg mixture into flour mixture just until blended (batter will be stiff). Stir in cranberries and walnuts, if using.

3. Pour batter into prepared pan. Bake until toothpick inserted in center comes out clean, 55 to 60 minutes. Cool loaf in pan on wire rack 10 minutes; remove from pan and cool completely on wire rack. Makes 1 loaf, 12 slices.

Each slice without walnuts: About 223 calories, 4g protein, 40g carbohydrate, 5g total fat (3g saturated), 46mg cholesterol, 281mg sodium.

BANANA BREAD

....

For the best flavor, wait until your bananas are completely ripe and spotted but not blackened and soft.

Prep: 20 minutes   Bake: 1 hour

  2 cups all-purpose flour
¾ teaspoon baking soda
½ teaspoon salt
½ cup butter or margarine (1 stick), softened
½ cup granulated sugar
½ cup brown sugar
  2 large eggs
1½ cups mashed very ripe bananas (4 medium)
  1 teaspoon vanilla extract

1. Preheat oven to 325°F. Evenly grease 8½" by 4½" metal loaf pan.

2. In medium bowl, with wire whisk, stir flour, baking soda, and salt.

3. In large bowl, with mixer at medium speed, beat butter and granulated and brown sugars until light and fluffy. Beat in eggs, one at a time. Reduce speed to low; alternately add flour mixture and banana mixture, beginning and ending with flour mixture, occasionally scraping side of bowl with rubber spatula. Beat just until blended.

4. Pour batter into prepared pan. Bake until toothpick inserted in center comes out clean, about 1 hour. Cool loaf in pan on wire rack 10 minutes; remove from pan and cool completely on wire rack. Makes 1 loaf, 16 slices.

Each slice: About 197 calories, 3g protein, 32g carbohydrate, 7g total fat (4g saturated), 43mg cholesterol, 205mg sodium.

BANANA-NUT BREAD

Prepare bread as directed above but fold **1 cup walnuts or pecans (4 ounces),** coarsely chopped, into batter before baking.

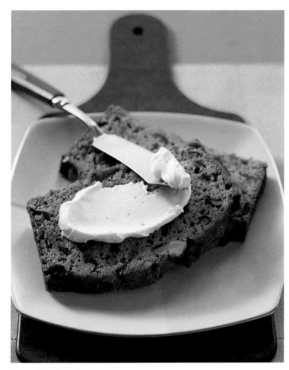

Date-Nut Bread

DATE-NUT BREAD

....

Serve slices of this dense, moist, old-fashioned favorite plain or slathered with cream cheese.

Prep: 20 minutes plus cooling
Bake: 1 hour 15 minutes

1½ cups chopped pitted dates
6 tablespoons butter or margarine, cut into pieces
1¼ cups boiling water
2 cups all-purpose flour
¾ cup sugar
1 teaspoon baking powder
½ teaspoon baking soda
½ teaspoon salt
1 large egg, lightly beaten
1 cup walnuts (4 ounces), coarsely chopped

1. In medium bowl, combine dates, butter, and boiling water; let stand until cool.

2. Preheat oven to 325°F and grease 9" by 5" metal loaf pan.

3. In large bowl, with wire whisk, stir flour, sugar, baking powder, baking soda, and salt. Stir egg into cooled date mixture. Stir date mixture into flour mixture just until flour is moistened. Stir in walnuts.

4. Pour batter into prepared pan. Bake until toothpick inserted in center comes out clean, about 1 hour 15 minutes. Cool in pan on wire rack 10 minutes; remove from pan and cool completely on rack. Makes 1 loaf, 16 slices.

Each slice: About 232 calories, 3g protein, 35g carbohydrate, 10g total fat (3g saturated), 25mg cholesterol, 192mg sodium.

ZUCCHINI BREAD

....

Everyone loves zucchini bread—especially the baker. It delivers lots of flavor with very little effort.

Prep: 20 minutes   Bake: 1 hour 10 minutes

1½ cups all-purpose flour
¾ cup sugar
2¼ teaspoons baking powder
½ teaspoon ground cinnamon
½ teaspoon salt
⅓ cup vegetable oil
2 large eggs
1½ cups shredded zucchini (1 medium)
½ cup walnuts (2 ounces), chopped
½ teaspoon freshly grated orange peel

1. Preheat oven to 350°F. Grease 8½" by 4½" metal loaf pan.

2. In large bowl, with wire whisk, stir flour, sugar, baking powder, cinnamon, and salt. In medium bowl, with fork, mix oil, eggs, zucchini, walnuts, and orange peel. Stir zucchini mixture into flour mixture just until flour is moistened.

3. Pour batter into prepared pan. Bake until toothpick inserted in center comes out clean, about 1 hour 10 minutes. Cool in pan on wire rack 10 minutes; remove from pan and cool completely on wire rack. Makes 1 loaf, 12 slices.

Each slice: About 209 calories, 4g protein, 26g carbohydrate, 10g total fat (1g saturated), 35mg cholesterol, 200mg sodium.

LEMON TEA BREAD

....

The combination of butter and sour cream makes this quick bread remarkably moist, and the lemon glaze helps to keep it that way.

Prep: 30 minutes   Bake: 55 minutes

Bread

    2   cups all-purpose flour
    ½   teaspoon baking powder
    ¼   teaspoon baking soda
    ½   teaspoon salt
    1¼ cups sugar
    4   large eggs
    1   small container (8 ounces) sour cream
    ½   cup butter (1 stick), melted (do not use margarine)
    1   tablespoon freshly grated lemon peel
    2   tablespoons fresh lemon juice

Glaze

    ⅓   cup sugar
    ⅓   cup fresh lemon juice

1. Prepare bread: Preheat oven to 350°F. Grease 9" by 5" metal loaf pan. Dust with flour.

2. In large bowl, with wire whisk, stir flour, baking powder, baking soda, and salt. In medium bowl, whisk sugar and eggs until blended. Add sour cream, butter, lemon peel, and lemon juice; stir until well mixed. Add sour cream mixture to flour mixture and fold together just until blended and no streaks of flour remain.

3. Pour batter into prepared pan, smooth top. Bake until toothpick inserted in center comes out clean, 55 to 60 minutes. Place pan on wire rack.

4. Prepare glaze: In cup, stir sugar and lemon juice. With thin wooden skewer, poke holes in hot bread and brush bread with glaze. Let cool completely in pan. Makes 1 loaf, 16 slices.

Each slice: About 235 calories, 4g protein, 32g carbohydrate, 10g total fat (6g saturated), 76mg cholesterol, 191mg sodium.

THE PERFECT COFFEE CAKE

....

The name says it all. Three tempting layers of a tender sour cream batter cushion two layers of a brown sugar, pecan, and cinnamon filling.

Prep: 30 minutes   Bake: 55 minutes

    1½ teaspoons baking powder
    1   teaspoon baking soda
    ¾   teaspoon salt
    3   cups plus 1 tablespoon all-purpose flour
    ¾   cup chopped pecans
    ⅓   cup packed brown sugar
    1¼ teaspoons ground cinnamon
    1½ cups granulated sugar
    ¾   cup butter or margarine (1½ sticks), softened
    2½ teaspoons vanilla extract
    3   large eggs
    1   container (16 ounces) sour cream
    1   cup confectioners' sugar
    4   to 6 teaspoons milk

1. Preheat oven to 350°F. Grease 12-cup Bundt pan; dust with flour.

2. In medium bowl, with wire whisk, stir baking powder, baking soda, salt, and 3 cups flour. In small bowl, combine pecans, brown sugar, cinnamon, and remaining 1 tablespoon flour.

3. In large bowl, with mixer at medium speed, beat granulated sugar, butter, and 2 teaspoons vanilla until creamy. Beat in eggs, one at a time. Alternately beat in flour mixture and sour cream, beginning and ending with flour mixture. Beat just until blended, occasionally scraping bowl.

4. Evenly spread 2 cups batter in prepared pan; sprinkle with half of nut mixture. Top with 2 cups batter. Sprinkle with remaining nut mixture, then top with remaining batter. Bake cake until toothpick inserted in center comes out clean, 55 to 60 minutes. Cool cake in pan on wire rack 10 minutes. With small metal spatula, loosen cake from pan; invert onto rack to cool completely.

5. Prepare glaze: In small bowl, stir confectioners' sugar, milk, and remaining ½ teaspoon vanilla until smooth. Drizzle glaze over cake. Makes 16 servings.

Each serving: About 410 calories, 5g protein, 51g carbohydrate, 21g total fat (10g saturated), 77mg cholesterol, 550mg sodium.

FRUIT-STREUSEL COFFEE CAKE

....

This delectable coffee cake can be made year-round with almost any seasonal fruit.

Prep: 30 minutes   Bake: 50 minutes

Streusel Topping
- ¾ cup all-purpose flour
- ½ cup packed brown sugar
- 1 teaspoon ground cinnamon
- 4 tablespoons cold butter or margarine, cut into pieces

Cake
- 2¼ cups all-purpose flour
- 1½ teaspoons baking powder
- ½ teaspoon baking soda
- ½ teaspoon salt
- ¾ cup butter or margarine (1½ sticks), softened
- 1½ cups granulated sugar
- 3 large eggs
- 1 cup milk
- 1 teaspoon vanilla extract
- 1¼ pounds ripe pears, apples, or peaches, peeled and thinly sliced; or nectarines or plums, not peeled, thinly sliced (3 cups); or fresh or frozen rhubarb, cut into 1-inch pieces (4 cups); or 1 pint blueberries

1. Prepare topping: In medium bowl, with wire whisk, stir flour, brown sugar, and cinnamon. With fingertips, blend flour mixture and butter until mixture resembles coarse crumbs.

2. Prepare cake: Preheat oven to 350°F. Grease and flour 13" x 9" baking pan. In medium bowl, whisk flour, baking powder, baking soda, and salt.

3. In large bowl, with mixer at low speed, beat butter and sugar until blended, frequently scraping bowl with rubber spatula. Increase speed to high; beat until light and fluffy, about 2 minutes, occasionally scraping bowl. Reduce speed to low; add eggs, one at a time, beating well after each addition.

4. In cup, combine milk and vanilla. With mixer at low speed, alternately add flour mixture and milk mixture to butter mixture, beginning and ending with flour mixture, beating until smooth.

5. Spread batter evenly in prepared pan. Arrange fruit slices on top, overlapping them slightly. Evenly sprinkle streusel topping over fruit. Bake cake until toothpick inserted in center comes out clean, 50 to 55

minutes. Cool in pan on wire rack 10 minutes to serve warm, or cool completely in pan. Makes 15 servings.

Each serving: About 355 calories, 5g protein, 52g carbohydrate, 14g total fat (8g saturated), 78mg cholesterol, 317mg sodium.

EASY CHRISTMAS STOLLEN

....

Expect all the flavor and richness of a traditional holiday sweet bread without the bother of yeast dough.

Prep: 25 minutes   Bake: 1 hour

- 2¼ cups all-purpose flour
- ½ cup sugar
- 1½ teaspoons baking powder
- ¼ teaspoon salt
- 8 tablespoons butter or margarine (1 stick)
- 1 cup ricotta cheese
- ½ cup candied lemon peel or coarsely chopped red candied cherries
- ½ cup dark seedless raisins
- ⅓ cup slivered blanched almonds, toasted (page 692)
- 1 teaspoon vanilla extract
- ½ teaspoon freshly grated lemon peel
- 1 large egg, lightly beaten
- 1 large egg yolk

1. Preheat oven to 325°F. Grease large cookie sheet.

2. In large bowl, with wire whisk, stir flour, sugar, baking powder, and salt. With pastry blender or two knives used scissor-fashion, cut in 6 tablespoons butter until mixture resembles fine crumbs. With spoon, stir in ricotta until mixture is moistened. Stir in candied lemon peel, raisins, almonds, vanilla, grated lemon peel, egg, and egg yolk until well mixed.

3. Turn dough onto lightly floured surface; gently knead dough 2 or 3 times. With floured rolling pin, roll dough into 10" by 8" oval. Fold oval lengthwise almost in half, so that edges do not quite meet.

4. Place stollen on prepared cookie sheet. Bake until toothpick inserted in center comes out clean, about 1 hour. Transfer to wire rack. Melt remaining 2 tablespoons butter and brush over warm stollen. Cool completely. Makes 12 servings.

Each serving: About 298 calories, 7g protein, 38g carbohydrate, 14g total fat (7g saturated), 67mg cholesterol, 211mg sodium.

PANCAKES

For thinner pancakes, add a little more milk to the batter.

Prep: 15 minutes   Cook: 4 minutes per batch

- 1 cup all-purpose flour
- 2 tablespoons sugar
- 2½ teaspoons baking powder
- ½ teaspoon salt
- 1¼ cups milk
- 3 tablespoons butter or margarine, melted
- 1 large egg, lightly beaten
  vegetable oil for brushing pan

1. In bowl, with wire whisk, stir flour, sugar, baking powder, and salt. Add milk, butter, and egg and stir until flour is moistened.

2. Heat griddle or 12-inch skillet over medium heat until drop of water sizzles; brush lightly with oil. Pour batter by scant ¼ cups onto hot griddle, making a few pancakes at a time. Cook until tops are bubbly, some bubbles burst, and edges look dry. With wide spatula, turn and cook until underside is golden. Transfer to platter; keep warm.

3. Repeat with remaining batter, brushing griddle with more oil if necessary. Makes 3 servings.

Each serving: About 388 calories, 10g protein, 46g carbohydrate, 19g total fat (10g saturated), 116mg cholesterol, 981mg sodium.

BLUEBERRY PANCAKES
Prepare as directed (above) but add **1 cup blueberries** to pancake batter.

BUCKWHEAT PANCAKES
Prepare as directed (above) but use **½ cup all-purpose flour** and **½ cup buckwheat flour.**

BANANA PANCAKES
Prepare as directed (above) but add **1 very ripe medium banana,** mashed (about ½ cup), and **¼ teaspoon baking soda;** use only **¾ cup milk.**

CORNMEAL PANCAKES
Prepare as directed (left) but add ¼ **cup cornmeal** to flour mixture.

BUTTERMILK PANCAKES
(Pictured on page 556)
Prepare as directed (left) but use only **2 teaspoons baking powder** and **½ teaspoon baking soda.** Substitute **1¼ cups buttermilk or 1 cup plain yogurt plus ¼ cup milk** for milk.

SOUR CREAM PANCAKES
Prepare as directed but substitute **1 small container (8 ounces) sour cream** and use only **¼ cup milk.**

WHOLE-GRAIN PANCAKES

Serve up some heart-healthy grains for a new brunch-time favorite.

Prep: 15 minutes   Cook: 15 minutes

- 2 ripe peaches, pitted and chopped
- ½ pint raspberries (1 cup)
- 1 tablespoon sugar
- ½ cup all-purpose flour
- ½ cup whole-wheat flour
- ½ cup quick-cooking oats (uncooked)
- 2 teaspoons baking powder
- ½ teaspoon salt
- 1¼ cups fat-free (skim) milk
- 1 large egg, lightly beaten
- 1 tablespoon vegetable oil

1. In medium bowl, combine peaches, raspberries, and sugar. Stir to coat; set fruit mixture aside.

2. Meanwhile, in large bowl, combine flours, oats, baking powder, and salt. Add milk, egg, and oil; stir just until flour mixture is moistened (batter will be slightly lumpy).

3. Spray 12-inch nonstick skillet with cooking spray; heat on medium 1 minute. Pour batter by scant ¼ cups into skillet, making about 4 pancakes at a time. Cook until tops bubble and some bubbles burst, and edges look dry. With wide spatula, turn pancakes and cook until undersides are golden. Transfer pancakes to platter. Cover; keep warm.

Whole-Grain Pancakes

4. Repeat with remaining batter, using more non-stick cooking spray if necessary. To serve, top with fruit mixture. Makes 12 pancakes or 4 servings.

Each serving: About 275 calories, 10g protein, 46g carbohydrate, 6g total fat (1g saturated), 6g fiber, 55mg cholesterol, 545mg sodium.

MAPLE SYRUP

Pure maple syrup is graded by color, which can range from pale brownish gold to an almost molasses hue. *Vermont Fancy* or *U.S. Grade A Light Amber* is mild and tastes best with foods that won't overpower its sweet, subtle flavor. *U.S. Grade A Medium Amber* and *U.S. Grade A Dark Amber* have a stronger taste and aroma and pair well with breakfast waffles and pancakes. *Grade A Medium* is the type most often found on store shelves. *U.S. Grade B* has an intense flavor that can stand up to the heat of cooking.

Once it is opened, store pure maple syrup in glass in the refrigerator, and use within 6 months. Unopened, it will keep indefinitely. Maple syrup also freezes well.

BUTTERMILK WAFFLES

....

Crisp yet fluffy, these are worth getting out of bed for. Top with butter, syrup, or your favorite fresh fruit.

Prep: 15 minutes   Bake: 4 minutes per batch

1¾ cups all-purpose flour
1½ teaspoons baking powder
 1 teaspoon baking soda
 ½ teaspoon salt
 2 cups buttermilk
 4 tablespoons butter or margarine, melted
 2 large eggs, lightly beaten

1. Preheat waffle baker as manufacturer directs.

2. In large bowl, with wire whisk, stir flour, baking powder, baking soda, and salt. Add buttermilk, melted butter, and eggs; whisk until smooth.

3. When waffle baker is ready, pour batter into center until it spreads to within 1 inch of edges. Cover and bake as manufacturer directs; do not lift cover while waffle is baking.

4. When waffle is done, lift cover and loosen waffle with fork. Serve immediately or keep warm in oven (place waffle directly on oven rack to keep crisp). Reheat waffle baker before pouring in more batter. If batter becomes too thick upon standing, thin with a little more buttermilk. Makes eleven 4" by 4" waffles or 4 servings.

Each serving: About 388 calories, 13g protein, 48g carbohydrate, 16g total fat (9g saturated), 142mg cholesterol, 1,065mg sodium.

PECAN WAFFLES

Prepare as directed above but add **1 tablespoon sugar** and **1 cup pecans (4 ounces),** chopped, to batter. Stir batter for each waffle before pouring.

SWEET MILK WAFFLES

Prepare as directed above but omit baking soda; use **1 tablespoon baking powder.** Substitute **2 cups milk** for buttermilk.

19
····

YEAST BREADS & SANDWICHES

YEAST BREADS

There's something magical about mixing flour and yeast with liquid and witnessing the transformation of the ingredients into a tempting loaf. Whether you enjoy the ritual of hands-on kneading or prefer the convenience of using a bread machine, it's always satisfying to make bread at home. In this chapter, you'll find sweet buns for breakfast, firm loaves to slice for sandwiches or toast, rolls for serving alongside main courses, and pizzas that will make a meal.

TYPES OF YEAST

Yeast is the organism that makes bread rise. It reacts with the natural sugars in flour to create carbon dioxide gas, which is trapped in the dough and forces it to expand.

Dry yeast comes in ¼-ounce packages, jars, and in bulk. One ¼-ounce package of dry yeast equals 2¼ teaspoons of fresh yeast.

Fresh yeast is available in foil-wrapped 1-ounce cakes. It is very perishable; refrigerate and use within two weeks. Fresh and dry yeast become activated when mixed with warm water (105° to 115°F). Let the water-yeast mixture stand for about five minutes. It should look creamy, which indicates that the yeast is alive.

Quick-rise yeast cuts the rising time of traditional yeast doughs by about 50 percent. This yeast requires very hot tap water (120° to 130°F) to be activated.

KNOW YOUR FLOURS

A variety of flours can be used for bread making. Different flours contain varying amounts of gluten, which is what gives dough its strength and elasticity. Wheat flours milled from hard winter wheat are high in gluten and great for bread making.

Bread flour is made entirely from hard wheat and makes delicious, chewy, crusty loaves.

All-purpose flour is a blend of hard and soft wheats and yields a more tender bread. All-purpose flour is available unbleached and bleached. Bleaching somewhat reduces the amount of gluten. You can use either bread or unbleached all-purpose flour for bread, but you will need more all-purpose flour as it absorbs less liquid.

Whole-wheat flour and rye flour are usually combined with bread or all-purpose flour in yeast doughs.

MIXING THE DOUGH

When mixing bread dough, use a large glass or ceramic bowl and a sturdy wooden spoon. You can also use a heavy-duty electric mixer; attach the paddle to make a soft dough, then switch to the dough hook to knead.

Flour and yeast are the basic ingredients in bread making, but other ingredients play a role. Salt slows the rising and enhances the flavor of bread. Fat (butter, oil, or eggs) adds richness, moistness, and softness to the crumb. Milk gives bread a tender, sweet crumb, and sugar promotes tenderness and a golden crust.

Because yeast works best in a warm environment, have all the ingredients at room temperature. The

---

Whole-Wheat-Walnut Bread (recipe page 577)

amount of flour needed to make a dough will vary according to the type of flour and the amount of humidity in the air (on a humid day, a dough will require more flour).

KNEADING THE DOUGH

Kneading activates the gluten in flour, which strengthens the dough. Knead in just enough flour to prevent the dough from sticking to the work surface. Doughs that are sweet and rich or contain whole-grain flours should be somewhat sticky. If kneading in a heavy-duty mixer, take care not to overknead; six to eight minutes is usually sufficient.

Place the dough on a lightly floured surface. To knead, fold one-fourth of the dough back onto itself, then push it down and away from you with the heel of your hand. Give the dough a quarter turn and repeat until the dough is smooth and elastic and tiny blisters appear on the surface, which will usually take from eight to ten minutes.

RISING AND SHAPING THE DOUGH

• Choose a bowl large enough to allow the dough to rise until doubled in volume. Grease the bowl lightly with butter, margarine, or oil. Gather the dough into a ball and place in the bowl; turn to coat the top. Cover the bowl with plastic wrap and place in a warm, draft-free spot.
• If you like, you can let the dough rise in the refrigerator for up to twelve hours. Before shaping the dough, let it stand at room temperature for about two hours, or until it loses its chill.

• The dough should rise until doubled. To test, press two fingers about ½ inch deep into the center of the dough. If the indentation stays, the dough has risen sufficiently.
• To punch the dough down, gently push your fist into the center to deflate it.
• The bread is now ready to be shaped. Place the dough on a lightly floured work surface, cover with plastic wrap, and let rest for 15 minutes.
• Grease the pans as directed in the recipe, add the bread, and loosely cover with plastic wrap. Let stand in a warm place until doubled in volume.

BAKING THE BREAD

Position a rack in the center of the oven and preheat for at least ten minutes. If baking two loaves at once, allow at least two inches between the pans.

To prevent bread from bursting during baking, most loaves are slashed with a serrated knife or single-edge razor blade before baking. The tops of loaves can be brushed with beaten whole egg for a golden crust, egg yolk for a dark brown crust, or egg white for a shiny crust. Bread is done when it pulls away from the sides of the pan and is nicely browned. If tapped on the bottom with your knuckles, the bread will sound hollow, and the sides of the loaf should feel crisp and firm.

COOLING AND STORING

Remove the bread from the pan and place, right side up, on a wire rack, away from drafts. If you must have warm bread, let it rest for at least 20 minutes before slicing; hot rolls, however, can be served immediately.

Be sure bread is completely cool before wrapping or freezing. Store soft breads in plastic bags and crusty breads in paper bags at room temperature for up to five days. Most breads freeze well for up to three months. Place in a heavy-duty zip-tight plastic bag or tightly wrap in heavy-duty foil. To thaw, let stand at room temperature for about one hour, or wrap the frozen bread in foil (with an opening at the top so steam can escape) and heat in a 300°F oven for about 20 minutes.

WHITE BREAD

···

The all-American bread: beautiful tall loaves for toast and sandwiches.

Prep: 25 minutes plus rising   Bake: 30 minutes

½ cup warm water (105° to 115°F)

2 packages active dry yeast

1 teaspoon plus ¼ cup sugar

2¼ cups milk, heated to warm (105° to 115°F)

4 tablespoons butter or margarine, softened

1 tablespoon salt

about 7½ cups all-purpose or bread flour

1. In large bowl, combine warm water, yeast, and 1 teaspoon sugar; stir to dissolve. Let stand until foamy, about 5 minutes. Add milk, butter, remaining ¼ cup sugar, salt, and 4 cups flour. Beat well with wooden spoon. Gradually stir in 3 cups flour to make soft dough.

2. Turn dough onto floured surface and knead until smooth and elastic, about 8 minutes, working in enough of remaining ½ cup flour just to keep dough from sticking.

3. Shape dough into ball; place in greased large bowl, turning dough to grease top. Cover bowl loosely with greased plastic wrap and let rise in warm place (80° to 85°F) until doubled in volume, about 1 hour.

4. Grease two 9" by 5" metal loaf pans. Punch down dough. Turn dough onto lightly floured surface and cut in half. Shape each half into rectangle about 12" by 7". Roll up from a short side. Pinch seam and ends to seal. Place dough, seam side down, in prepared pans. Cover pans loosely with greased plastic wrap and let rise in warm place until almost doubled, about 1 hour.

5. Meanwhile, preheat oven to 400°F. Bake until browned and loaves sound hollow when lightly tapped on bottom, 30 to 35 minutes. Remove loaves from pans; cool on wire racks. Makes 2 loaves, 12 slices each.

Each slice: About 187 calories, 5g protein, 34g carbohydrate, 3g total fat (2g saturated), 8mg cholesterol, 323mg sodium.

CINNAMON-RAISIN BREAD

Prepare as directed (left) but stir **2 cups dark seedless raisins** into yeast mixture with milk. Spread each rectangle with **2 tablespoons butter or margarine,** softened, leaving ½-inch border. In small cup, combine **⅓ cup firmly packed brown sugar** and **1 tablespoon ground cinnamon;** sprinkle evenly over butter. Roll up each loaf from a short side. Pinch seam and ends to seal. Makes 2 loaves, 12 slices each.

Each slice: About 244 calories, 5g protein, 47g carbohydrate, 4g total fat (2g saturated), 11mg cholesterol, 335mg sodium.

TROUBLESHOOTING

──────────

Dough Overrises in Bowl: To fix (otherwise, loaf could collapse in the oven or be heavy-textured), turn the dough onto a lightly floured work surface and knead for two to three minutes. Cover, let rest 15 minutes, then shape as directed.

Bread Is Too Pale: Place the loaf directly on the oven rack and bake for five to ten minutes longer.

Bread Is Dry and Crumbly: The dough contained too much flour or the dough overrose.

Bread Collapses in Oven: The shaped dough overrose in the pan before baking. Don't let dough rise above the pan's rim.

Bread Has Cracks: The dough contained too much flour or the pan was not large enough.

Bread Has Holes: The dough wasn't kneaded enough (it's almost impossible to overknead by hand), rising time was too long, or the dough rose in too warm a place.

OLIVE-ROSEMARY LOAVES

·········

This robust peasant loaf is flavored with Kalamata olives and fresh rosemary. Using high-gluten bread flour guarantees your baking success.

Prep: 30 minutes plus rising   **Bake:** 30 minutes

- 1½ cups warm water (105° to 115°F)
- 4 tablespoons extra-virgin olive oil
- 2 packages active dry yeast
- 1 tablespoon sugar
- 1 cup Kalamata or green olives, pitted and chopped
- 2 tablespoons finely chopped fresh rosemary
- 2 teaspoons salt
   about 5 cups bread flour
   or about 5¼ cups all-purpose flour

1. In large bowl, combine ½ cup warm water, 3 tablespoons oil, yeast, and sugar; stir to dissolve. Let stand until foamy, about 5 minutes. Stir in remaining 1 cup warm water, olives, rosemary, salt, and 4 cups flour until combined.

2. Turn dough onto lightly floured surface and knead until dough is smooth and elastic, about 8 minutes, working in enough of remaining 1 cup bread flour or 1¼ cups all-purpose flour just to keep dough from sticking.

3. Shape dough into ball; place in greased large bowl, turning dough to grease top. Cover bowl loosely with plastic wrap and let dough rise in warm place (80° to 85°F) until doubled in volume, about 1 hour.

4. Punch down dough. Turn dough onto lightly floured surface and cut in half; cover and let rest 15 minutes for easier shaping. Grease large cookie sheet.

5. Shape each dough half into 7½" by 4" oval; place 3 inches apart on prepared cookie sheet. Cover loosely with damp kitchen towel and let rise in warm place until doubled, about 1 hour.

6. Meanwhile, preheat oven to 400°F. Brush tops of loaves with remaining 1 tablespoon oil. With serrated knife or single-edge razor blade, cut three parallel diagonal slashes across top of each loaf. Bake until golden and loaves sound hollow when tapped on bottom, about 30 minutes. Cool on wire rack. Makes 2 loaves, 12 slices each.

Each slice: About 148 calories, 4g protein, 23g carbohydrate, 4g total fat (1g saturated), 0mg cholesterol, 296mg sodium.

WHOLE-WHEAT-OATMEAL BREAD

·········

This recipe makes two slightly flat breads with a sweet nutty flavor and dense texture.

Prep: 42 minutes plus rising   **Bake:** 35 minutes

- 2 cups warm water (105° to 115°F)
- 2 packages active dry yeast
- ½ teaspoon sugar
- ½ cup honey
- 4 tablespoons butter or margarine, softened
- 1 cup quick-cooking or old-fashioned oats, uncooked
- 1 tablespoon salt
- 4 cups whole-wheat flour
- 1 large egg
   about 2½ cups all-purpose flour
   or about 2 cups bread flour

1. In large bowl, combine ½ cup warm water, yeast, and sugar; stir to dissolve. Let stand until foamy, about 5 minutes. Stir in remaining 1½ cups warm water, honey, butter, oats, salt, and 2 cups whole-wheat flour until smooth. Stir in egg. Gradually stir in remaining 2 cups whole-wheat flour, then 2 cups all-purpose flour or 1½ cups bread flour.

2. On lightly floured surface, knead dough until smooth, about 7 minutes, working in enough of remaining ½ cup flour just to keep dough from sticking.

3. Shape dough into ball; place in greased large bowl, turning dough to grease top. Cover bowl loosely with plastic wrap and let rise in warm place (80° to 85°F) until doubled in volume, about 1 hour.

4. Punch down dough. Turn dough onto lightly floured surface and cut in half; cover and let rest 15 minutes. Grease large cookie sheet.

5. Shape each dough half into 7" by 4" oval; place on prepared cookie sheet. Cover loosely with damp kitchen towel; let rise in warm place until doubled, about 1 hour.

6. Meanwhile, preheat oven to 350°F. With serrated knife, cut three to five ¼-inch-deep crisscross slashes across top of each loaf. Lightly dust tops of loaves with all-purpose flour. Bake until loaves sound hollow when tapped on bottom, 35 to 40 minutes. Transfer to wire racks to cool. Makes 2 oval loaves, 12 slices each.

Each slice: About 177 calories, 5g protein, 33g carbohydrate, 3g total fat (1g saturated), 14mg cholesterol, 315mg sodium.

WHOLE-WHEAT-WALNUT BREAD

(Pictured on page 572)

Prepare as directed (left), **using ½ cup milk,** heated to warm (105° to 115°F), instead of water and only **1 package active dry yeast.** Stir in **1 cup warm water, 3 tablespoons butter or margarine,** softened, **2 tablespoons molasses, 1½ teaspoons salt, 2 cups whole-wheat flour,** and only **½ cup all-purpose or bread flour.** Then, gradually, stir in **¾ cup all-purpose or bread flour.** Proceed as directed, but after punching down dough in Step 4, knead in **2 cups walnuts (8 ounces),** toasted (see page 692) and coarsely chopped. In Step 5, reduce rising time to about 45 minutes. Preheat oven to 375°F. Just before baking, with sharp knife or single-edge razor blade, cut three 3-inch-long and ¼-inch-deep diagonal slashes across tops of loaves. Bake loaves about 30 minutes.

Each slice: About 155 calories, 4g protein, 17g carbohydrate, 9g total fat (2g saturated), 5mg cholesterol, 165mg sodium.

BREAD-MACHINE MULTIGRAIN LOAF

Bread machines have become the favorite appliance of many home bakers. This recipe uses the setting for a 1½-pound whole-wheat loaf. Be sure to add the ingredients according to your machine's instructions.

Prep: 10 minutes
Bake: per bread machine's instructions

- 2   cups whole-wheat flour
- 1   cup all-purpose flour
- ¼   cup bulgur wheat
- ¼   cup old-fashioned oats, uncooked
- 2   tablespoons toasted wheat germ
- 1½ teaspoons salt
- 1¼ cups buttermilk
- ¼   cup honey
- 3   tablespoons vegetable oil
- 1   package active dry yeast

Prepare recipe according to your bread machine's instructions. Makes 1 loaf, 16 slices.

Each slice: About 143 calories, 4g protein, 25g carbohydrate, 3g total fat (0g saturated), 1mg cholesterol, 240mg sodium.

BRIOCHE

Rich and buttery brioche, a classic in French bread making, rests overnight in the refrigerator and is put into a preheated oven the next morning in time for breakfast. A heavy-duty mixer is a must for the stiff, sticky dough. It makes excellent French toast and bread pudding.

Prep: 25 minutes plus rising and overnight to refrigerate   Bake: 30 minutes

- ¾   cup milk, heated to warm (105° to 115°F)
- 1   package active dry yeast
- 1   teaspoon plus ¼ cup sugar
- 4   cups bread flour or all-purpose flour
- 1   teaspoon salt
- 6   large eggs
- 1   cup butter (2 sticks), softened and cut into pieces (do not use margarine)

1. In large bowl of heavy-duty mixer, combine warm milk, yeast, and 1 teaspoon sugar; stir to dissolve. Let stand until foamy, about 5 minutes.

2. Stir in remaining ¼ cup sugar, 1 cup flour, and salt until blended. With mixer at low speed, beat in 1 egg. Continue beating, alternately adding remaining 3 cups flour and remaining 5 eggs until well incorporated. Gradually beat in butter until smooth.

3. Transfer dough to lightly buttered large bowl. Loosely cover bowl with greased plastic wrap and let rise in warm place (80° to 85°F) until doubled in volume, about 2½ hours.

4. Meanwhile, lightly grease two 8½" by 4½" metal loaf pans. Punch down dough. Divide dough in half; place in prepared pans. Loosely cover pans with lightly greased plastic wrap; refrigerate overnight.

5. Preheat oven to 350°F. Bake loaves until golden brown and toothpick inserted in center comes out clean, about 30 minutes. Remove loaves from pans; cool on wire racks. Makes 2 loaves, 12 slices each.

Each slice: About 188 calories, 5g protein, 19g carbohydrate, 10g total fat (6g saturated), 75mg cholesterol, 197mg sodium.

QUICK-AND-EASY ANADAMA BREAD

We've streamlined this early-American cornmeal-molasses bread by turning it into a batter bread and using quick-rise yeast.

Prep: 25 minutes plus rising   **Bake: 30 minutes**

- 3 cups all-purpose flour
- ⅓ cup cornmeal
- 1 teaspoon salt
- 1 package quick-rise yeast
- 1 cup water
- ¼ cup light (mild) molasses
- 3 tablespoons butter or margarine, softened
- 1 large egg

1. In large bowl, with wire whisk, stir 1 cup flour, cornmeal, salt, and yeast. In 1-quart saucepan, heat water and molasses over low heat until very warm (120° to 130°F). Meanwhile, grease 2-quart soufflé dish or deep casserole.

2. With mixer at low speed, gradually beat molasses mixture and butter into flour mixture just until blended. Increase speed to medium; beat 2 minutes, occasionally scraping bowl with rubber spatula. Beat in egg and 1 cup flour to make thick batter; continue beating 2 minutes, frequently scraping bowl. With wooden spoon, stir in remaining 1 cup flour to make soft dough.

3. Place dough in prepared soufflé dish. Cover loosely with plastic wrap and let rise in warm place (80° to 85°F) until doubled, about 1 hour.

4. Meanwhile, preheat oven to 375°F. Bake bread until browned and loaf sounds hollow when lightly tapped on bottom, 30 to 35 minutes. Remove loaf from soufflé dish; cool on wire rack. Makes 1 round loaf, 10 slices.

Each slice: About 219 calories, 5g protein, 38g carbohydrate, 5g total fat (2g saturated), 31mg cholesterol, 279mg sodium.

DOUBLE-CHEESE BATTER BREAD

This simple batter bread gets its fabulous flavor from shredded cheddar and freshly grated Parmesan cheese. It makes terrific toast.

Prep: 25 minutes plus rising   **Bake: 35 minutes**

- ¾ cup warm water (105° to 115°F)
- 1 package active dry yeast
- 1 teaspoon plus 1 tablespoon sugar
- 6 ounces extra-sharp Cheddar cheese, shredded (1½ cups)
- ¼ cup freshly grated Parmesan cheese
- ½ teaspoon salt
- 2½ cups all-purpose flour
- 2 large eggs

1. In large bowl, combine warm water, yeast, and 1 teaspoon sugar; stir to dissolve. Let stand until foamy, about 5 minutes. With wooden spoon or mixer at low speed, stir in Cheddar, Parmesan, remaining 1 tablespoon sugar, salt, and 1½ cups flour just until blended.

2. Separate 1 egg. Cover egg white and reserve in refrigerator. Beat remaining egg and remaining egg yolk into batter.

3. Stir batter vigorously or increase speed to medium and beat 3 minutes, frequently scraping bowl with rubber spatula. Stir in remaining 1 cup flour to make stiff batter that leaves side of bowl.

4. Cover bowl loosely with greased plastic wrap; let dough rise in warm place (80° to 85°F) until doubled in volume, about 1 hour.

5. Grease deep 1½-quart round casserole. Stir down batter; turn into prepared casserole. Cover loosely with greased plastic wrap; let rise in warm place until doubled in volume, about 45 minutes.

6. Meanwhile, preheat oven to 350°F. Beat reserved egg white; brush over top of loaf. Bake bread until browned and loaf sounds hollow when tapped on bottom, about 35 minutes. Remove loaf from casserole and cool on wire rack. Makes 1 loaf, 12 slices.

Each slice: About 185 calories, 8g protein, 22g carbohydrate, 7g total fat (4g saturated), 52mg cholesterol, 234mg sodium.

Breadsticks

BREADSTICKS

···

These breadsticks can be made well ahead. They keep perfectly for up to two weeks in an airtight container.

Prep: 40 minutes plus resting
Bake: 20 minutes per batch

- 2 packages quick-rise yeast
- 2½ teaspoons salt
  about 4¾ cups all-purpose flour
- 1⅓ cups very warm water (120° to 130°F)
- ½ cup olive oil
- 3 tablespoons caraway, sesame, or poppy seeds, or freshly grated Parmesan cheese

1. In large bowl, combine yeast, salt, and 2 cups flour. With wooden spoon, stir in very warm water; beat vigorously 1 minute. Stir in oil. Gradually stir in 2¼ cups flour. Stir in caraway seeds, if using. (If using other additions instead, add in Step 3.)

2. Turn dough onto lightly floured surface and knead until smooth and elastic, about 8 minutes, working in enough of remaining ½ cup flour just to keep dough from sticking. Cover dough loosely with plastic wrap; let rest 10 minutes.

3. Meanwhile, preheat oven to 375°F. Grease two large cookie sheets. Cut dough in half. Cover one half; cut remaining half into 32 equal pieces. Shape each piece into 12-inch-long rope; place 1 inch apart on prepared cookie sheets. If not using caraway seeds, sprinkle with sesame seeds, poppy seeds, or Parmesan.

4. Bake breadsticks until golden and crisp, about 20 minutes, rotating cookie sheets between upper and lower oven racks halfway through baking. Transfer to wire racks to cool. Repeat with remaining dough. Makes 64 breadsticks.

Each breadstick: About 52 calories, 1g protein, 7g carbohydrate, 2g total fat (0g saturated), 0mg cholesterol, 91mg sodium.

ROSEMARY-FENNEL BREADSTICKS
Prepare as directed but omit caraway, sesame, or poppy seeds or Parmesan. In Step 1, stir **2 teaspoons fennel seeds**, crushed, **1 teaspoon dried rosemary leaves**, crumbled, and **½ teaspoon coarsely ground black pepper** into dough. Proceed as directed.

SPECIAL BUTTERS FOR YEAST BREADS
——————————————

Try these delicious butters on your freshly baked bread.

MARMALADE OR STRAWBERRY PRESERVES BUTTER
In small bowl, with mixer at medium speed, beat 1 cup butter or margarine (2 sticks), softened, and ⅓ cup orange marmalade or strawberry preserves until blended. Cover and refrigerate up to one week. To use, let stand at room temperature 30 minutes for easier spreading. Makes about 1⅓ cups.

WHIPPED HONEY BUTTER
Prepare as directed for Marmalade Butter but omit marmalade and beat in 2 tablespoons honey and ⅛ teaspoon ground cinnamon. Makes about 1⅛ cups.

FRESH STRAWBERRY BUTTER
Prepare as directed for Marmalade Butter but omit marmalade and beat in ½ pint strawberries, hulled and crushed, and 3 tablespoons confectioners' sugar. Cover and refrigerate up to 2 days. Makes about 2¼ cups.

REFRIGERATOR ROLLS

....

Be sure to offer a basket of these soft, buttery rolls at your next holiday feast. (The dough can be made ahead and refrigerated overnight.)

Prep: 35 minutes plus rising   Bake: 15 minutes

1½ cups warm water (105° to 115°F)
  2 packages active dry yeast
  1 teaspoon plus ½ cup sugar
 ½ cup (1 stick) plus 2 tablespoons butter
      or margarine, softened
  2 teaspoons salt
      about 6 cups all-purpose flour
  1 large egg
      vegetable oil for brushing

1. In large bowl, combine ½ cup warm water, yeast, and 1 teaspoon sugar; stir to dissolve. Let stand until foamy, about 5 minutes. Stir in remaining 1 cup warm water, ½ cup butter, remaining ½ cup sugar, salt, and 2¼ cups flour. With wooden spoon or mixer at low speed, gradually beat in egg and ¾ cup flour; continue beating 2 minutes, scraping bowl frequently with rubber spatula. Stir in 2½ cups flour to make soft dough.

2. Turn dough onto lightly floured surface and knead until smooth and elastic, about 10 minutes, working in enough of remaining ½ cup flour just to keep dough from sticking to surface.

3. Shape dough into ball; place in greased large bowl, turning dough to grease top. Cover bowl loosely with plastic wrap and let rise in warm place (80° to 85°F) until doubled in volume, about 1½ hours.

4. Punch down dough and turn; brush with oil. Cover bowl tightly with greased plastic wrap and refrigerate overnight or up to 24 hours. (Or, if you like, after punching down dough, shape into rolls as in Step 5. Cover loosely and let rise until doubled, about 45 minutes, and bake as in Step 6.)

5. About 2½ hours before serving, remove dough from refrigerator. Grease 15½" by 10½" deep roasting pan. Cut dough into 30 equal pieces; shape into balls. Place balls in prepared pan; cover pan loosely and let rise in warm place until doubled, about 1½ hours.

6. Meanwhile, preheat oven to 400°F. Bake until golden and rolls sound hollow when lightly tapped on bottom, 15 to 20 minutes. Melt remaining 2 tablespoons butter. With pastry brush, lightly brush melted butter over hot rolls. Serve warm. Makes 30 rolls.

Each roll: About 147 calories, 3g protein, 23g carbohydrate, 5g total fat (3g saturated), 17mg cholesterol, 197mg sodium.

PARKER HOUSE ROLLS

Prepare dough as directed in Steps 1 through 4 (left). About 2½ hours before serving, melt ½ **cup (1 stick) butter or margarine** in large shallow baking pan. On lightly floured surface, with floured rolling pin, roll out dough ½ inch thick. With floured 2¾-inch round biscuit cutter, cut out as many rounds as possible. Knead trimmings together; reroll and cut out more rounds. Dip both sides of each dough round in melted butter; fold rounds in half and arrange in rows in prepared roasting pan, letting rolls touch each other. Cover loosely and let rise in warm place until doubled, about 1½ hours. Bake rolls 18 to 20 minutes. Serve warm, or cool on wire racks to serve later. Makes about 40 rolls.

Each roll: About 127 calories, 2g protein, 17g carbohydrate, 5g total fat (3g saturated), 18mg cholesterol, 165mg sodium.

OATMEAL-MOLASSES ROLLS

....

Topped with a butter-molasses glaze and sprinkled with oats, these light rolls look as good as they taste.

Prep: 1 hour plus rising   Bake: 45 minutes

  1 cup boiling water
  1 cup plus 2 tablespoons old-fashioned oats,
      uncooked
 ¾ cup warm water (105° to 115°F)
  1 package active dry yeast
  1 teaspoon sugar
  5 tablespoons butter or margarine, softened
 ⅓ cup plus 2 teaspoons light (mild) molasses
1½ teaspoons salt
      about 4¼ cups all-purpose flour

1. In medium bowl, pour boiling water over 1 cup oats, stirring to combine. Let stand until oats have absorbed water and mixture has cooled to warm (105° to 115°F), about 10 minutes.

2. Meanwhile, in small bowl, combine warm water, yeast, and sugar; stir to dissolve. Let mixture stand until foamy, about 5 minutes.

3. In large bowl, with mixer at low speed, beat 4 tablespoons butter until creamy. Add 1/3 cup molasses, beating until combined. Beat in oat mixture, yeast mixture, and salt just until blended. Gradually beat in 2 cups flour just until blended. With wooden spoon, stir in 2 cups more flour. Turn dough onto lightly floured surface and knead until smooth and elastic, about 5 minutes, working in enough of remaining 1/4 cup flour just to keep dough from sticking.

4. Shape dough into ball; place in greased large bowl, turning dough to grease top. Cover bowl loosely with plastic wrap and let rise in warm place (80° to 85°F) until doubled in volume, about 1 hour. Grease 13" by 9" baking pan.

5. Punch down dough. On lightly floured surface, cut dough into 18 equal pieces. Shape each piece into ball and arrange in prepared pan in three rows of six balls each. Cover pan loosely and let rise in warm place until doubled, about 1 hour.

6. Meanwhile, preheat oven to 350°F. Bake rolls until very lightly browned, about 30 minutes.

7. Melt remaining 1 tablespoon butter. Stir in remaining 2 teaspoons molasses.

8. After rolls have baked 30 minutes, remove from oven. Brush with molasses mixture and sprinkle with remaining 2 tablespoons oats. Bake rolls until golden, about 15 minutes longer. Serve warm, or cool on wire racks to serve later. Reheat if desired. Makes 18 rolls.

Each roll: About 183 calories, 4g protein, 32g carbohydrate, 4g total fat (2g saturated), 9mg cholesterol, 230mg sodium.

BASIC PIZZA DOUGH

Try making this dough the night before to save some time; double the recipe and freeze half to have on hand for another meal. All-purpose flour produces a light crust, and bread flour gives it a chewy texture.

Prep: 40 minutes plus rising   **Bake:** 15 minutes

1 1/4 cups warm water (105° to 115°F)
  1 package active dry yeast
  1 teaspoon sugar
  2 tablespoons olive oil
  2 teaspoons salt
    about 4 cups all-purpose flour
    or about 3 1/2 cups bread flour
    cornmeal for sprinkling

1. In large bowl, combine 1/4 cup warm water, yeast, and sugar; stir to dissolve. Let stand until foamy, about 5 minutes.

2. With wooden spoon, stir in remaining 1 cup warm water, oil, salt, and 1 1/2 cups flour until smooth. Gradually add 2 cups all-purpose flour or 1 1/2 cups bread flour, stirring until dough leaves side of bowl. Turn dough onto lightly floured surface and knead until smooth and elastic, about 10 minutes, working in enough of remaining 1/2 cup flour just to keep dough from sticking.

3. Shape dough into ball; place in greased large bowl, turning dough to grease top. Cover bowl loosely with plastic wrap and let rise in warm place (80° to 85°F) until doubled in volume, about 1 hour.

4. Punch down dough. Turn onto lightly floured surface and cut in half; cover loosely and let rest 15 minutes. Or, if not using right away, place dough in greased large bowl, cover loosely with greased plastic wrap, and refrigerate up to 24 hours.

5. Sprinkle two large cookie sheets with cornmeal. Shape each dough half into ball. On one prepared cookie sheet, with floured rolling pin, roll one ball into 14" by 10" rectangle. Fold edges in to form 1-inch rim. Repeat to make second pizza. Makes enough dough for 2 large pizzas, 4 main-dish servings each.

Each 1/8th dough: About 262 calories, 7g protein, 49g carbohydrate, 4g total fat (1g saturated), 0mg cholesterol, 584mg sodium.

CHEESE PIZZA

The champ of all pizzas. If you like, sprinkle the top with 1 teaspoon dried oregano or 2 to 3 tablespoons chopped fresh basil just before serving.

Prep: 40 minutes plus rising and resting
Bake: 15 minutes

½ recipe Basic Pizza Dough (page 581)
1 cup Marinara Sauce (page 254)
2 tablespoons freshly grated Parmesan cheese
4 ounces mozzarella cheese, shredded (1 cup)

1. Prepare pizza dough.

2. Meanwhile, prepare Marinara Sauce.

3. Shape pizza dough as directed. Sprinkle with Parmesan. Spread sauce over Parmesan and top with mozzarella.

4. Preheat oven to 450°F. Let prepared pizza rest 20 minutes. Bake until crust is golden, 15 to 20 minutes. Makes 4 main-dish servings.

Each serving: About 391 calories, 14g protein, 55g carbohydrate, 12g total fat (5g saturated), 25mg cholesterol, 899mg sodium.

MORE PIZZA TOPPINGS

To keep the crust crispy, scatter cheese over the dough before topping with other ingredients.

Sprinkle fresh herbs over the pizza just before serving. Try these delicious combinations:

• Grilled radicchio, cooked crumbled pancetta or bacon, crumbled goat cheese, chopped fresh sage.

• Sautéed cremini mushrooms, cooked sweet Italian sausage, thinly sliced fresh mozzarella cheese, dried oregano.

• Coarsely chopped grilled eggplant, marinated artichoke hearts, chopped plum tomatoes, shredded mozzarella cheese, fresh basil leaves.

• Thinly sliced mozzarella, crumbled gorgonzola, spoonfuls of ricotta, freshly ground black pepper, fresh basil leaves.

FOCACCIA

This bread's wonderfully chewy texture and fine crumb are the result of three risings. Sprinkle 2 tablespoons chopped fresh sage or 1 tablespoon chopped fresh rosemary over the focaccia just before baking, if you wish.

Prep: 25 minutes plus rising   **Bake:** 18 minutes

1½ cups warm water (105° to 115°F)
1 package active dry yeast
1 teaspoon sugar
5 tablespoons extra-virgin olive oil
1½ teaspoons table salt
3¾ cups all-purpose flour or 3½ cups bread flour
1 teaspoon kosher salt or coarse sea salt

1. In large bowl, combine ½ cup warm water, yeast, and sugar; stir to dissolve. Let stand until foamy, about 5 minutes. Add remaining 1 cup warm water, 2 tablespoons oil, table salt, and flour; stir to combine.

2. Turn dough onto floured surface and knead until smooth and elastic, about 7 minutes. Dough will be soft; do not add more flour.

3. Shape dough into ball; place in greased large bowl, turning dough to grease top. Cover bowl loosely with plastic wrap and let stand in warm place (80° to 85°F) until doubled in volume, about 1 hour.

4. Lightly oil 15½" by 10½" jelly-roll pan. Punch down dough and pat into prepared pan. Cover loosely with plastic wrap and let rise in warm place until doubled, about 45 minutes.

5. With fingertips, make deep indentations, 1 inch apart, over entire surface of dough, almost to bottom of pan. Drizzle with remaining 3 tablespoons oil; sprinkle with kosher salt. Cover loosely with plastic wrap; let rise in warm place until doubled, about 45 minutes.

6. Meanwhile, preheat oven to 450°F. Bake focaccia on lowest oven rack until bottom is crusty and top is lightly browned, about 18 minutes. Transfer focaccia to wire rack to cool. Makes 12 servings.

Each serving: About 201 calories, 4g protein, 31g carbohydrate, 7g total fat (1g saturated), 0mg cholesterol, 537mg sodium.

TOMATO FOCACCIA

Prepare as directed (left) but drizzle with only **1 tablespoon olive oil.** Arrange **1 pound ripe plum tomatoes,** cut into ¼-inch-thick slices, over top; sprinkle with **1 tablespoon chopped fresh rosemary or 1 teaspoon dried rosemary,** crumbled, and **½ teaspoon coarsely ground black pepper,** in addition to the **1 teaspoon kosher salt.** Bake as directed.

RED PEPPER FOCACCIA

Prepare as directed (left) but do not sprinkle with kosher salt. In 12-inch skillet, heat an additional **1 tablespoon olive oil** over medium heat. Add **4 red peppers,** sliced, and **¼ teaspoon table salt** and cook, stirring frequently, until tender, about 20 minutes. Cool to room temperature. Sprinkle over focaccia just before baking.

DRIED TOMATO AND OLIVE FOCACCIA

Prepare as directed (left) but increase kosher salt to **1½ teaspoons.** In Step 5, combine **½ cup Gaeta olives,** pitted, **¼ cup drained oil-packed dried tomatoes,** coarsely chopped, and kosher salt. Sprinkle over focaccia just before baking.

ONION FOCACCIA

Prepare as directed (left) but do not sprinkle with kosher salt. In 12-inch skillet, heat an additional **2 teaspoons olive oil** over medium heat. Add **2 medium onions,** sliced, **1 teaspoon sugar,** and **½ teaspoon table salt** and cook, stirring frequently, until golden brown, about 20 minutes. Cool to room temperature. Spread over focaccia just before baking.

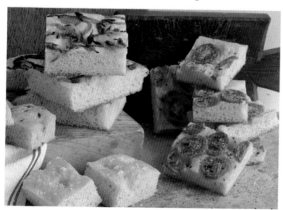

Assorted Focaccia

FRUIT FOCACCIA

....

A sweet take on traditional flatbread, this eat-with-your-hands dessert is easy to make using supermarket pizza dough.

Prep: 20 minutes
Bake: 20 minutes plus standing and cooling

- 1 pound fresh pizza dough, at room temperature
- 1 tablespoon olive oil
- 2 teaspoons butter or margarine, melted
- ¼ cup granulated sugar
- 1 cup blueberries
- 1 cup raspberries
  confectioners' sugar for dusting

1. Preheat oven to 425°F. Line 15½" by 10½" jelly-roll pan with parchment paper.

2. On lightly floured surface with floured rolling pin, roll dough to a 14" by 10" oval. Transfer to prepared pan and reshape into oval if necessary. Cover with clean kitchen towel and let stand 15 minutes.

3. In cup, mix olive oil and butter; brush over dough. Sprinkle dough with 2 tablespoons granulated sugar.

4. Bake dough 10 minutes. Remove from oven and top with blueberries and raspberries; sprinkle with remaining 2 tablespoons granulated sugar. Return focaccia to oven; bake 10 to 15 minutes longer or until fruit is juicy and dough is browned at edges.

5. Slide focaccia onto wire rack using parchment paper. Loosen bottom of focaccia with spatula and remove parchment paper. Cool slightly to serve warm, or serve at room temperature. To serve, sprinkle focaccia lightly with confectioners' sugar. Makes 8 servings.

Each serving: About 195 calories, 4g protein, 37g carbohydrate, 5g total fat (1g saturated), 2g fiber, 3mg cholesterol, 200mg sodium.

PISSALADIÈRE

A specialty of Nice, France, this pizzalike tart is usually served as a snack or appetizer, but it makes a nice supper or brunch dish too. You can prepare the dough in advance. Let it rise once, then freeze for up to three months. Defrost and follow the recipe.

Prep: 40 minutes plus rising
Cook/Bake: 55 minutes

- 1 cup warm water (105° to 115°F)
- 1 package active dry yeast
- 3 cups all-purpose flour
- 1¾ teaspoons salt
- 2 tablespoons olive oil
- 2 pounds onions, chopped
- 1 can (2 ounces) anchovy fillets, rinsed, drained, and coarsely chopped
- ⅓ cup pitted and halved Kalamata or Gaeta olives

1. In cup, combine ¼ cup warm water and yeast; stir to dissolve. Let stand until foamy, about 5 minutes.

2. In large bowl, with wire whisk, stir flour and 1½ teaspoons salt. Stir in yeast mixture, remaining ¾ cup warm water, and 1 tablespoon oil. Turn dough onto lightly floured surface and knead until smooth and elastic, about 8 minutes. Shape dough into ball; place in greased large bowl, turning to grease top. Cover bowl loosely with plastic wrap and let rise in warm place (80° to 85°F) until doubled in volume, about 45 minutes.

3. Meanwhile, in 12-inch skillet, heat remaining 1 tablespoon oil over low heat. Add onions and remaining ¼ teaspoon salt and cook, stirring frequently, until onions are very soft and golden, about 30 minutes. Remove from heat; set aside to cool.

4. Grease 15½" by 10½" jelly-roll pan. Punch down dough and pat into prepared pan. Cover loosely with plastic wrap and let rise 30 minutes.

5. Meanwhile, preheat oven to 425°F. With fingertips, make shallow indentations over surface of dough. Toss onions and anchovies and spread mixture over top. Place olives on onion mixture at 2-inch intervals. Bake on lowest oven rack until crust is golden, about 25 minutes. Cut into 32 squares. Makes 32 appetizers.

Each square: About 73 calories, 2g protein, 12g carbohydrate, 2g total fat (0g saturated), 1mg cholesterol, 205mg sodium.

SOFT PRETZELS

These soft pretzels, a specialty of Pennsylvania Dutch country, are best served warm with mustard. Freeze them after shaping, if you like. Let them thaw, then dip in the baking-soda mixture and bake as directed. The pretzels can be sprinkled with sesame or poppy seeds in addition to the salt.

Prep: 30 minutes plus rising   Bake: 16 minutes

- 2 cups warm water (105° to 115°F)
- 1 package active dry yeast
- 1 teaspoon sugar
- 1 teaspoon table salt
  about 4 cups all-purpose flour
- 2 tablespoons baking soda
- 1 tablespoon kosher or coarse sea salt

1. In large bowl, combine 1½ cups warm water, yeast, and sugar; stir to dissolve. Let stand until foamy, about 5 minutes. Add salt and 2 cups flour; beat well with wooden spoon. Gradually stir in 1½ cups flour to make soft dough.

2. Turn dough onto floured surface and knead until smooth and elastic, about 6 minutes, kneading in enough of remaining ½ cup flour just to keep dough from sticking.

3. Shape dough into ball; place in greased large bowl, turning dough to grease top. Cover bowl loosely with plastic wrap and let rise in warm place (80° to 85°F) until doubled in volume, about 30 minutes.

4. Meanwhile, preheat oven to 400°F. Grease two cookie sheets. Punch down dough and cut into 12 equal pieces. Roll each piece into 24-inch-long rope. Shape ropes into loop-shaped pretzels.

5. In small bowl, whisk remaining ½ cup warm water and baking soda until soda has dissolved.

6. Dip pretzels in baking-soda mixture and place 1½ inches apart on prepared cookie sheets; sprinkle with kosher salt. Bake, rotating cookie sheets between upper and lower oven racks halfway through baking, until browned, 16 to 18 minutes. Serve pretzels warm, or transfer to wire racks to cool. Makes 12 pretzels.

Each pretzel: About 167 calories, 5g protein, 33g carbohydrate, 1g total fat (0g saturated), 0mg cholesterol, 1,192mg sodium.

OVERNIGHT STICKY BUNS

....

Make these rich, yummy rolls the night before serving. Let them rise overnight in the refrigerator, then bake and serve for breakfast. You can wrap any leftovers in foil and freeze; reheat, still wrapped, in a 350°F oven for 15 to 20 minutes.

**Prep: 1 hour plus rising and overnight to refrigerate
Bake: 30 minutes**

Dough

- ¼ cup warm water (105° to 115°F)
- 1 package active dry yeast
- 1 teaspoon plus ¼ cup granulated sugar
- ¾ cup milk
- 4 tablespoons butter or margarine, softened
- 3 large egg yolks
- 1 teaspoon salt
  about 4 cups all-purpose flour

Filling

- ½ cup packed brown sugar
- ¼ cup dried currants
- 1 tablespoon ground cinnamon
- 4 tablespoons butter or margarine, melted

Topping

- ⅔ cup packed brown sugar
- 3 tablespoons butter or margarine
- 2 tablespoons light corn syrup
- 2 tablespoons honey
- 1¼ cups pecans (5 ounces), coarsely chopped

1. Prepare dough: In cup, combine warm water, yeast, and 1 teaspoon granulated sugar; stir to dissolve. Let stand until foamy, about 5 minutes.

2. In large bowl, with mixer at low speed, blend yeast mixture with milk, butter, remaining ¼ cup granulated sugar, egg yolks, salt, and 3 cups flour until blended. With wooden spoon, stir in ¾ cup flour.

3. Turn dough onto lightly floured surface and knead until smooth and elastic, about 5 minutes, working in enough of remaining ¼ cup flour just to keep dough from sticking.

4. Shape dough into ball; place in greased large bowl, turning dough to grease top. Cover bowl loosely with plastic wrap and let rise in warm place (80° to 85°F) until doubled, about 1 hour.

5. Meanwhile, prepare filling: In small bowl, combine brown sugar, currants, and cinnamon; set aside. Reserve melted butter.

6. Prepare topping: In 1-quart saucepan, combine brown sugar, butter, corn syrup, and honey; heat over low heat, stirring occasionally, until brown sugar and butter have melted. Grease 13" by 9" baking pan; pour melted brown-sugar mixture into pan and sprinkle evenly with pecans.

7. Punch down dough. Turn dough onto lightly floured surface; cover and let rest 15 minutes. Roll dough into 18" by 12" rectangle. Brush dough with reserved melted butter and sprinkle with currant mixture. Starting at a long side, roll up dough jelly-roll fashion; place, seam side down, on surface. Cut dough crosswise into 20 slices.

8. Place slices, cut side down, on brown-sugar mixture in prepared pan in four rows of five slices each. Cover and refrigerate at least 12 hours or up to 15 hours.

9. Preheat oven to 375°F. Bake buns until golden, about 30 minutes. Remove from oven. Immediately place serving tray or jelly-roll pan over top of baking pan and invert; remove pan. Let buns cool slightly to serve warm, or cool on wire racks to serve later. Makes 20 buns.

Each bun: About 291 calories, 4g protein, 42g carbohydrate, 13g total fat (5g saturated), 50mg cholesterol, 195mg sodium.

ORIGINS OF STICKY BUNS

German-speaking immigrants brought with them their recipes for beloved foods, including sweets. These buns were made popular in the nineteenth century by the Pennsylvania Dutch, who settled in various parts of Pennsylvania, but especially around Philadelphia. Cinnamon buns, sticky buns, stickies, *schnecken*, and icing-topped sugar buns are all similar and all scrumptious.

SANDWICHES

The first sandwich, created in 1762, was a matter of necessity. The Earl of Sandwich, an enthusiastic gambler, requested bread and meat dishes that he could consume while continuing to gamble, and at that moment the sandwich was born. Every culture has its sandwich: The Italians relish their panini and calzones, the Mexicans enjoy burritos, bagels and lox are a Jewish tradition, and the croque madame and croque monsieur are standard fare in Paris bistros. These days, you don't even need sliced bread to make a sandwich. It could just as easily be a filled and rolled-up flour tortilla. And the meat is optional too: No one thinks twice about eating a pita pocket filled with a crisp Greek salad or a vegetable frittata tucked between thin slabs of herbed focaccia.

You can perk up an old standard by adding a tasty new condiment like one of our flavored mayonnaises (try Ginger-Sesame Mayonnaise or Chipotle Mayonnaise at right), or by serving it on your own home-baked bread.

SAFE SANDWICHES

The brown-bag lunch is an American tradition, but it should be carefully packed to ensure that the contents remain tasty and safe to eat.

If you are making a lot of sandwiches, use this simple assembly-line technique: Line up the bread slices in rows, apply the spreads, top with the fillings, and cover with the remaining bread. Wrap the sandwiches tightly in waxed paper or foil, or place in zip-tight sandwich bags. Some ingredients, such as tomatoes, lettuce, and cucumbers, can make bread soggy, so it's best to wrap these items separately and to add them to the sandwich just before eating.

Sandwiches containing meat, poultry, fish, or eggs should not stand at room temperature for longer than two hours; warm temperatures encourage the growth of salmonella. Pack these sandwiches in insulated lunch boxes with portable ice packs to keep them at a safe cold temperature.

FLAVORED MAYONNAISE

It's easy to transform mayonnaise into a luscious condiment that will boost the flavor of any sandwich.

ROASTED-RED PEPPER MAYONNAISE

$1/2$ cup mayonnaise, $1/4$ cup finely chopped roasted red pepper, and 1 tablespoon chopped fresh parsley

LEMON MAYONNAISE

$1/2$ cup mayonnaise, $1 1/2$ teaspoons fresh lemon juice, 1 teaspoon freshly grated lemon peel, and pinch ground black pepper

GINGER-SESAME MAYONNAISE

$1/2$ cup mayonnaise, 2 small green onions, finely chopped, 1 tablespoon chopped fresh cilantro, 1 teaspoon minced, peeled fresh ginger, and $1/4$ teaspoon Asian sesame oil

CHUTNEY MAYONNAISE

$1/2$ cup mayonnaise, $1/4$ cup mango chutney, finely chopped, and 1 tablespoon chopped fresh cilantro

BASIL MAYONNAISE

$1/2$ cup mayonnaise, $1/4$ cup chopped fresh basil, and $1/8$ teaspoon ground black pepper

CHIPOTLE MAYONNAISE

$1/2$ cup mayonnaise, 1 finely chopped chipotle chile in adobo, 1 teaspoon adobo sauce, and $1/4$ teaspoon ground cumin

PESTO MAYONNAISE

$1/2$ cup mayonnaise and 4 teaspoons pesto

HORSERADISH MAYONNAISE

$1/2$ cup mayonnaise, 1 tablespoon bottled white horseradish, and 1 teaspoon fresh lemon juice

PICKLED JALAPEÑO MAYONNAISE

$1/2$ cup mayonnaise, $1/4$ cup chopped fresh cilantro, and 1 to 2 pickled jalapeños, finely chopped

HEALTH CLUB SANDWICHES

....

This carrot-sprout-and-bean-spread combo will satisfy your palate and ease your conscience.

Prep: 25 minutes   Cook: 2 minutes

- 2 tablespoons olive oil
- 2 teaspoons plus 1 tablespoon fresh lemon juice
- 1 teaspoon honey
- ⅛ teaspoon ground black pepper
- 3 carrots, peeled and shredded (1 cup)
- 2 cups alfalfa sprouts
- 1 garlic clove, finely chopped
- ½ teaspoon ground cumin
  pinch ground red pepper (cayenne)
- 1 can (15 to 19 ounces) garbanzo beans, rinsed and drained
- 1 tablespoon water
- 12 slices multigrain bread, lightly toasted
- 1 large ripe tomato (12 ounces), thinly sliced
- 1 bunch watercress, tough stems trimmed

1. In medium bowl, stir 1 tablespoon oil, 2 teaspoons lemon juice, honey, and ground black pepper until mixed. Add carrots and alfalfa sprouts; toss until mixed and evenly coated with dressing.

2. In 2-quart saucepan, heat remaining 1 tablespoon oil over medium heat. Add garlic, cumin, and ground red pepper and cook until very fragrant. Stir in garbanzo beans and remove from heat. Add remaining 1 tablespoon lemon juice and water; mash beans to a coarse puree.

3. Spread garbanzo-bean mixture on 8 toast slices. Place tomato slices and watercress over 4 garbanzo-topped toast slices. Top remaining 4 garbanzo-topped slices with alfalfa-sprout mixture and place on watercress-topped bread. Cover with 4 remaining toast slices. Cut sandwiches in half. Makes 4 main-dish servings.

Each serving: About 379 calories, 14g protein, 57g carbohydrate, 12g total fat (2g saturated), 0mg cholesterol, 545mg sodium.

Health Club Sandwiches

SLIM SANDWICHES

TEST KITCHEN TIP

A sandwich doesn't have to be calorie- and fat-laden. Replace high-fat mayonnaise with one of the reduced-fat varieties (stir in some chopped fresh herbs for a flavor lift). Or hold the mayo and spread your bread with naturally low-fat mustard or try a spread of non-fat yogurt mixed with a bit of mustard. Chutney, delicious by itself or when blended with mayonnaise or mustard, adds a sweet-and-spicy dimension to a sandwich.

Many lunch meats are high in calories and sodium. Look for alternatives such as grilled vegetables or skinless chicken breast, freshly roasted turkey breast, shrimp in low-fat dressing, or water-packed tuna. Cheese is another high-fat sandwich ingredient that should be enjoyed in moderation.

Instead of ordering your sandwich at the deli counter, take a stroll by the salad bar. There are lots of candidates for a terrific sandwich just waiting to be piled onto bread (or into a pita) and drizzled with low-fat dressing: Artichoke hearts, roasted peppers, peperoncini, sprouts, shredded carrots, asparagus, sliced tomatoes, and tofu are all smart choices.

CHICKEN CLUB SANDWICHES

....

This is a great way to use leftover turkey or chicken—you'll need about 2 cups shredded or sliced meat.

Prep: 20 minutes   Cook: 15 minutes

4   small skinless, boneless chicken breast halves
    (1 pound)
¼   cup flavored mayonnaise (page 586)
    or plain mayonnaise
8   slices bacon, each cut crosswise in half
12 slices firm white or whole-wheat bread
2   ripe medium tomatoes (12 ounces), thinly sliced
8   small romaine lettuce leaves

1. In 10-inch skillet, combine chicken and enough *cold water* to cover; heat to boiling over high heat. Reduce heat; cover and simmer until chicken loses its pink color throughout, 8 to 10 minutes. Drain and cool to room temperature.

2. Meanwhile, prepare flavored mayonnaise.

3. In 12-inch skillet, cook bacon over medium heat until browned. Transfer bacon to paper towels to drain.

4. Spread about 1 teaspoon mayonnaise on each bread slice; top 4 bread slices with tomato slices and lettuce.

5. Cut chicken breasts on diagonal into thin slices. Place 4 more bread slices, mayonnaise side up, on top of lettuce. Arrange chicken and bacon on top and cover with remaining 4 bread slices.

6. To serve, cut each sandwich on diagonal into quarters. Use frilled toothpicks to hold slices together, if you like. Makes 4 main-dish servings.

Each serving: About 513 calories, 38g protein, 47g carbohydrate, 18g total fat (4g saturated), 83mg cholesterol, 800mg sodium.

---

5 IDEAS FOR . . . FRENCH BREAD

The perfect baguette has a beautiful, crispy crust surrounding a light, chewy inside. Start with a 10-ounce loaf.

PANZANELLA SALAD

Preheat oven to 375°F. Trim ends from loaf and reserve for another use. Cut remaining bread into ½-inch cubes; place on cookie sheet and toast in oven 8 minutes. In bowl, toss 4 medium tomatoes, cut into ½-inch chunks, with 2 cups ½-inch seedless cucumber chunks and ⅔ cup balsamic vinaigrette. Add bread and 1½ cups torn and loosely packed fresh basil leaves; toss to coat. Serves 6.

SHRIMP AND BLACK BEAN PIZZA

Preheat oven to 450°F. Cut loaf horizontally in half; cut each half crosswise in half. Place on cookie sheet, cut sides up; spread with 1 cup well-drained mild black bean-and-corn salsa. Top with 8 ounces cleaned, cooked, and chopped shrimp, ¼ cup chopped fresh cilantro, and 1½ cups shredded pepper Jack cheese. Bake 6 minutes to heat through. Serves 4.

MONTE CRISTO

Cut loaf on extreme diagonal into 16 slices ½ inch thick. Set aside 8 slices. Spread remaining slices with 2 tablespoons spicy brown mustard; top with 8 ounces sliced ham, 4 ounces sliced Swiss cheese, and reserved bread slices. In pie plate, with fork, mix 2 large eggs, 2 tablespoons water, and 2 teaspoons spicy brown mustard. Dip sandwiches in egg mixture to coat well. Cook in 12-inch nonstick skillet on medium 12 to 15 minutes or until golden on both sides. Serves 4.

MAKE-AHEAD SUB

Drain 1 jar (12 ounces) giardiniera salad; chop. Cut loaf horizontally in half; spoon ⅔ cup chopped giardiniera on bottom. Top with 6 ounces each sliced salami and Provolone cheese, and remaining giardiniera. Replace top of bread. Cut sandwich into quarters and tightly wrap each in plastic wrap. Refrigerate 1 hour or overnight. Serves 4.

CHOCOLATE BREAD PUDDING

Trim ends from loaf and reserve for another use. Cut bread into ½-inch cubes; place in shallow 2½-quart baking dish. In saucepan, heat 1 cup milk, ½ cup sugar, and ⅛ teaspoon salt to simmering. Remove from heat; whisk in 1¼ cups dark chocolate chips, then 2 cups milk and 4 large eggs. Pour over bread; press bread with spoon to absorb liquid. Chill 1 hour. Preheat oven to 350°F. Heat kettle of water to boiling. Place baking dish in 13" by 9" pan. Press bread again. Add water to pan around dish. Bake 50 minutes, or until set at edges. Cool 30 minutes. Serves 8.

PAN BAGNAT

Tuna salad sandwiches á la française! It's best to make this large sandwich a day ahead to allow the juices to soak into the bread.

Prep: 30 minutes plus chilling

- 1 round loaf (8 inches) country-style bread (12 ounces)
- 1 garlic clove, cut in half
- ¼ cup extra-virgin olive oil
- 2 tablespoons red wine vinegar
- ¼ teaspoon salt
- ⅛ teaspoon ground black pepper
- 3 ripe medium tomatoes (1 pound), sliced
- ½ cup loosely packed small fresh basil leaves
- 1 tablespoon fresh mint leaves
- 1 can (6 ounces) tuna packed in olive oil, drained and flaked
- ⅓ cup Mediterranean olives, such as Gaeta or Kalamata, pitted and chopped
- 2 green onions, chopped
- 1 tablespoon capers, drained
- 1 large hard-cooked egg, peeled and sliced

1. Cut bread horizontally in half. Remove enough soft center from each half to make 1-inch shell. (Reserve soft bread for another use.)

2. Rub inside of bread halves with cut side of garlic. In cup, stir oil, vinegar, salt, and pepper until blended. Drizzle about one-fourth of oil mixture over garlic-rubbed bread.

3. On bottom half of bread, arrange one-third of tomato slices; drizzle with about half of remaining oil mixture, then top with half of basil and all of mint.

4. In small bowl, combine tuna, olives, green onions, and capers. Spoon tuna mixture over herbs; top with sliced egg. Arrange remaining tomato slices and remaining basil on top. Drizzle with remaining oil mixture. Replace top half of bread.

5. Wrap sandwich tightly in foil and refrigerate at least 4 hours or up to 24 hours before serving to blend flavors and let juices moisten bread. To serve, cut into 4 wedges. Makes 4 main-dish servings.

Each serving: About 396 calories, 16g protein, 31g carbohydrate, 25g total fat (3g saturated), 68mg cholesterol, 1,111mg sodium.

TURKEY AND MANGO ROLL-UPS

A lime-spiked curried chutney adds zip to this rolled sandwich. If you can't find lavash, divide the filling ingredients among four 8- to 10-inch flour tortillas.

Prep: 25 minutes plus chilling

- 1 large lime
- ¼ cup light mayonnaise
- 3 tablespoons mango chutney, chopped
- ½ teaspoon curry powder
- ⅛ teaspoon paprika
- 1 lavash flatbread (7 ounces)
- 1 medium cucumber (8 ounces), peeled and thinly sliced
- 8 ounces thinly sliced smoked turkey breast
- 1 medium mango, peeled and finely chopped
- 6 large green-leaf lettuce leaves

1. From lime, grate ¼ teaspoon peel and squeeze 1 tablespoon juice. In bowl, stir mayonnaise, chutney, lime peel and juice, curry powder, and paprika until blended.

2. Unfold lavash; spread evenly with mayonnaise mixture. Arrange cucumber slices over mayonnaise, then top with turkey, mango, and lettuce. From a short side, roll up lavash, jelly-roll fashion.

3. Wrap lavash roll in foil and refrigerate at least 2 hours or up to 4 hours to blend flavors and let bread soften. To serve, trim ends, then cut lavash roll into 4 pieces. Makes 4 main-dish servings.

Each serving: About 375 calories, 18g protein, 55g carbohydrate, 7g total fat (2g saturated), 29mg cholesterol, 939mg sodium.

CHICKEN GYROS

....

These traditional Greek sandwiches (pronounced JEER-oh) are most often made with spit-roasted thinly-sliced lamb. Our version features leaner chicken breasts, but keeps all the authentic taste.

Prep: 20 minutes   Cook: 5 minutes

- 1 teaspoon olive oil
- 1½ pounds skinless, boneless chicken breast halves, cut into 1-inch chunks
- ½ teaspoon dried oregano
- ½ teaspoon salt
- ½ teaspoon ground black pepper
- ¼ cup tahini (sesame seed paste)
- ¼ cup water
- 3 tablespoons non-fat plain yogurt
- 1 tablespoon fresh lemon juice
- 1 garlic clove, crushed with press
- ¼ cup loosely packed fresh cilantro leaves, chopped
- ¼ teaspoon ground red pepper (cayenne)
- 4 (6-inch) pitas
- 2 cups sliced romaine lettuce
- ½ seedless cucumber, chopped (1 cup)
- 1 large tomato (8 ounces), chopped
- 2 green onions, sliced

1. In 12-inch nonstick skillet, heat oil 1 minute on medium. Sprinkle chicken with oregano, ¼ teaspoon salt, and ¼ teaspoon black pepper, and toss to coat. Add chicken to skillet and cook 5 to 7 minutes or until chicken is no longer pink throughout. Transfer chicken to plate or bowl; cover with foil to keep warm.

2. Meanwhile, make tahini sauce: In small bowl, with wire whisk, combine tahini, water, yogurt, lemon juice, and garlic. Stir in cilantro, red pepper, ¼ teaspoon salt, and ¼ teaspoon black pepper. (Makes about ¾ cup tahini sauce.)

3. To serve, cut a piece from the side of each pita (about ¼ pita) and save for another use. Carefully open each pita pocket and fill with one-fourth each romaine, cucumber, tomato, chicken, and green onions. Top with tahini sauce; serve gyros with any additional sauce on the side. Makes 4 main-dish servings.

Each serving: About 360 calories, 34g protein, 41g carbohydrate, 6g total fat (1g saturated), 4g fiber, 64mg cholesterol, 695mg sodium.

OPEN-FACED STEAK AND MUSHROOM SANDWICHES

....

Thin slices of juicy steak topped with onions and mushrooms sautéed in butter and red wine are served on crusty French bread for this classic.

Prep: 15 minutes   Cook: 30 minutes

- 2 tablespoons butter or margarine, softened
- 1 tablespoon plus 1 teaspoon chopped fresh tarragon
- ³⁄₈ teaspoon ground black pepper
- 1 loaf (8 ounces) French bread, cut horizontally in half
- 3 teaspoons vegetable oil
- 1 beef flank steak (1¼ pounds)
- ¾ teaspoon salt
- 1 medium onion, thinly sliced
- 12 ounces mushrooms, trimmed and sliced pinch dried thyme
- ⅓ cup dry red wine

1. In small bowl, stir butter, 1 tablespoon tarragon, and ⅛ teaspoon pepper until well blended. Spread tarragon butter evenly on cut sides of bread. Cut each half into 4 pieces.

2. In heavy 12-inch skillet (preferably cast iron), heat 2 teaspoons oil over medium-high heat until very hot. Pat steak dry with paper towels and sprinkle with ¼ teaspoon salt and ⅛ teaspoon pepper. Add steak to skillet and cook 6 to 8 minutes per side for medium-rare or until desired doneness. Transfer steak to cutting board. Set aside.

3. Add remaining 1 teaspoon oil and onion to skillet; cook over medium heat, stirring frequently, until tender, about 5 minutes. Stir in mushrooms, thyme, remaining ½ teaspoon salt, and remaining ⅛ teaspoon pepper. Cook over medium-high heat until mushrooms are tender and liquid has evaporated, about 8 minutes. Stir in wine and boil 2 minutes. Remove from heat. Keep warm.

4. Holding knife almost parallel to cutting board, cut steak into thin slices across the grain; arrange on bread. Spoon mushroom mixture on top; sprinkle with remaining 1 teaspoon tarragon. Makes 4 main-dish servings.

Each serving: About 544 calories, 35g protein, 38g carbohydrate, 26g total fat (11g saturated), 89mg cholesterol, 946mg sodium.

CARAMELIZED ONION AND GOAT CHEESE PANINI

Assemble these delicious panini and make them hot and crunchy in a sandwich press, if you own one, or in a grill pan on the stovetop.

Prep: 15 minutes   Cook/Grill: 37 minutes

- 2 tablespoons olive oil
- 2 sweet onions (1 pound each), thinly sliced
- ½ teaspoon salt
- ¼ teaspoon ground black pepper
- ½ teaspoon chopped fresh thyme leaves
- 8 center slices (½ inch thick) country-style bread
- 4 ounces soft fresh goat cheese

1. In nonstick 12-inch skillet, heat oil on medium 1 minute. Stir in onions, salt, and pepper; cover and cook 15 minutes or until very soft, stirring occasionally. Uncover and cook 15 to 25 minutes longer or until onions are golden brown, stirring frequently. Stir in thyme; remove pan from heat.

2. Preheat sandwich press or grill pan on medium.

3. Meanwhile, assemble panini: Place 4 slices bread on work surface. Spread one-fourth of goat cheese on each slice and top with one-fourth of onion mixture. Top with remaining bread slices.

4. Place 2 panini in sandwich press and close top, or arrange them in a grill pan and place a heavy skillet (preferably cast iron) on top of panini and press down. Cook, turning once, 7 to 8 minutes or until bread is toasted and browned on both sides. Repeat with remaining 2 panini. Cut in halves or quarters to serve. Makes 8 appetizer servings.

Each serving: About 190 calories, 7g protein, 24g carbohydrate, 8g total fat (3g saturated), 3g fiber, 7mg cholesterol, 375mg sodium.

Assorted Panini

RED PEPPER AND PROVOLONE PANINI

Prepare panini as directed (left), but omit Step 1. In Step 2, while grill is preheating, in small bowl, combine **1 jar (7 ounces) roasted red peppers,** drained and sliced; ¼ **cup white wine vinegar; 1 clove garlic,** crushed with press; and ¼ **teaspoon ground black pepper.** Set aside 10 minutes; drain. In step 3, divide **6 ounces sliced Provolone, 4 ounces sliced Genoa salami,** and marinated red peppers evenly among 4 bread slices; top with remaining bread. Complete as in Step 4.

Each serving: About 215 calories, 11g protein, 17g carbohydrate, 11g total fat (5g saturated), 1g fiber, 28mg cholesterol, 675mg sodium.

MOZZARELLA, TOMATO, AND BASIL PANINI

Prepare panini as directed (left) but omit Step 1. In Step 3, divide **2 ripe plum tomatoes,** cored and sliced; **6 ounces sliced fresh mozzarella;** ½ **cup loosely packed fresh basil leaves;** ⅛ **teaspoon salt;** and ¼ **teaspoon ground black pepper** evenly among 4 bread slices. Top with remaining bread. Complete as in Step 4.

Each serving: About 145 calories, 7g protein, 17g carbohydrate, 6g total fat (3g saturated), 1g fiber, 17mg cholesterol, 230mg sodium.

PERFECTLY SIMPLE TOMATO SANDWICHES

....

These sandwiches are fabulous just the way they are, but we also like them with a few sprigs of watercress tucked in. Make them with absolutely ripe tomatoes.

Prep: 15 minutes

- 1 lemon
- ⅓ cup mayonnaise
- ¼ teaspoon ground coriander
- ¼ teaspoon salt
- ¼ teaspoon coarsely ground black pepper
- 1 large round or oval loaf (1 pound) sourdough or other crusty bread
- 2 pounds ripe tomatoes (3 large), thickly sliced

1. From lemon, grate ½ teaspoon peel and squeeze 1 teaspoon juice. In small bowl, combine mayonnaise, lemon peel and juice, coriander, salt, and pepper until well blended.

2. Cut eight ½-inch-thick slices from center of bread. (Reserve ends for another use.) Toast bread, if desired. Spread mayonnaise mixture on each bread slice. Arrange tomato slices on 4 bread slices; top with remaining bread slices. To serve, cut each sandwich in half. Makes 4 main-dish servings.

Each serving: About 392 calories, 9g protein, 52g carbohydrate, 18g total fat (3g saturated), 11mg cholesterol, 742mg sodium.

SMOKED SALMON SANDWICHES WITH DILL CREAM CHEESE

....

To turn this open-face sandwich into a heartier, more portable treat, top with an additional slice of pumpernickel that's been spread with cream cheese.

Prep: 15 minutes

- 1 small package (3 ounces) cream cheese, softened
- 1 tablespoon minced shallot
- 1 tablespoon capers, drained and chopped
- 1 tablespoon chopped fresh dill plus additional sprigs
- 1 teaspoon fresh lemon juice
- 4 slices pumpernickel bread
- 6 ounces thinly sliced smoked salmon ground black pepper
- 4 teaspoons salmon caviar (optional)

In small bowl, stir cream cheese, shallot, capers, chopped dill, and lemon juice until well blended. Spread evenly on bread slices and arrange smoked salmon on top. Sprinkle lightly with pepper. Place 1 teaspoon caviar on each sandwich, if you like, and top with dill sprigs. Makes 4 main-dish servings.

Each serving: About 207 calories, 12g protein, 17g carbohydrate, 10g total fat (5g saturated), 33mg cholesterol, 1,224mg sodium.

DOUBLE-TOMATO BRIE HEROES

Whether you call it a sub, hero, wedge, hoagie, grinder, Italian sandwich, po' boy, torpedo, or zeppelin, each of these cheese-, meat-, and vegetable–filled oblong sandwiches reflects regional culinary traditions and ethnic preferences. There is one element, however, they all share: They're simply delicious. For our Double-Tomato Brie Heroes we use fresh as well as dried tomatoes that have been marinated in lightly salted oil with herbs. If you use the unseasoned variety of dried tomatoes, you may want to sprinkle them with some salt.

In small bowl, combine 1 jar (6½ ounces) oil-packed dried tomatoes, drained and finely chopped, 2 tablespoons extra-virgin olive oil, and 2 tablespoons white wine vinegar. Spread dried-tomato mixture evenly on cut sides of 2 long loaves (8 ounces each) Italian bread, each cut horizontally in half. Slice 1 pound Brie cheese with rind left on and arrange on bottom halves of bread. Divide 1 cup loosely packed fresh basil leaves and tomato slices from 2 ripe medium tomatoes (12 ounces). Replace tops of bread. To serve, cut each hero crosswise into 4 pieces. Makes 8 main-dish servings.

CLASSIC ITALIAN HERO

If you feel the urge, build on the basic recipe by adding any of the ingredients listed below and/or whatever else you can think of.

Prep: 15 minutes

¼ cup vinaigrette of choice

1 large loaf (12 ounces) Italian bread

4 ounces thinly sliced hot and/or sweet capocollo, prosciutto, soppressata, and/or salami

4 ounces mozzarella cheese, preferably fresh, thinly sliced

shredded romaine lettuce or arugula, peperoncini, basil leaves, roasted red peppers, very thinly sliced red onions, pesto, olivada, and/or sliced ripe tomatoes

1. Prepare vinaigrette.

2. Cut bread horizontally in half. Remove enough soft center from each half to make 1-inch shell. (Reserve soft bread for another use.)

3. Brush vinaigrette evenly over cut sides of bread. Layer meats and cheese on bottom half of bread. Top with additional ingredients of your choice. Replace top half of bread. If not serving right away, wrap sandwich in foil and refrigerate up to 4 hours. Cut into 4 pieces. Makes 4 main-dish servings.

Each serving: About 430 calories, 20g protein, 36g carbohydrate, 23g total fat (7g saturated), 48mg cholesterol, 1,226mg sodium.

Classic Italian Hero

MUFFULETTA

This rich sandwich is a classic in New Orleans' French Quarter, where it's especially good at the Central Grocery. But you don't have to travel all that way; this recipe will "let the good times roll" at your house.

Prep: 25 minutes plus chilling

1¼ cups finely chopped celery with leaves

1 cup drained giardiniera (Italian mixed pickled vegetables), chopped

¾ cup green and black Mediterranean olives, such as Gaeta or Kalamata, pitted and chopped

⅓ cup chopped fresh parsley

1 garlic clove, minced

¼ cup olive oil

¼ teaspoon ground black pepper

1 round loaf (8 to 10 inches) soft French bread

4 ounces thinly sliced smoked ham

4 ounces thinly sliced Provolone cheese

4 ounces thinly sliced Genoa salami

1. In medium bowl, stir celery, giardiniera, olives, parsley, garlic, oil, and pepper until well mixed. Cover and refrigerate at least 4 hours or up to overnight to blend flavors.

2. Cut bread horizontally in half. Remove enough soft center from each half to make 1-inch shell. (Reserve soft bread for another use.) Onto bottom half of bread, spoon half of celery-olive mixture; layer ham, cheese, and salami on top. Spoon remaining celery-olive mixture over. Replace top half of bread.

3. Wrap sandwich in foil and refrigerate at least 4 hours or up to 24 hours to blend flavors and let juices soften bread. To serve, let stand at room temperature about 30 minutes, then cut into 6 wedges. Makes 6 main-dish servings.

Each serving: About 399 calories, 17g protein, 28g carbohydrate, 24g total fat (8g saturated), 41mg cholesterol, 1,615mg sodium.

CUCUMBER TEA SANDWICHES

Utterly English and perfectly delicious, these classic sandwiches are a necessity at a tea party. A V-slicer or mandoline will make the thinnest cucumber slices.

Prep: 20 minutes plus chilling

1 English (seedless) cucumber

½ teaspoon salt

5 tablespoons butter or margarine, softened

16 very thin slices white or whole-wheat bread

32 fresh mint leaves (optional)

1. Cut cucumber lengthwise in half and remove soft seed area in center. Cut cucumber crosswise into paper-thin slices. In colander set over bowl, toss cucumber and salt. Cover and refrigerate 30 minutes, stirring occasionally. Discard liquid in bowl. Pat cucumber slices dry with paper towels.

2. Lightly spread butter on each bread slice. Arrange cucumber on 8 buttered slices; place 1 mint leaf, if using, in each corner of bread. Top with remaining bread slices. Trim crusts and cut each sandwich on diagonal into quarters. Makes 32 tea sandwiches.

Each sandwich: About 36 calories, 1g protein, 4g carbohydrate, 2g total fat (1g saturated), 5mg cholesterol, 74mg sodium.

MAKE-AHEAD TIP FOR TEA SANDWICHES

To enjoy more time with your guests, make tea sandwiches ahead and store them as follows:

Line a jelly-roll pan with damp paper towels. Place sandwiches in the pan and cover with additional damp paper towels to keep the bread from drying out. Cover the pan tightly with plastic wrap and refrigerate up to four hours.

WATERCRESS AND RADISH TEA SANDWICHES

••••••••••••••••••••••••••••••••

These tea sandwiches look demure but have a pleasant peppery kick.

Prep: 20 minutes

3 tablespoons butter or margarine, softened
8 very thin slices white or whole-wheat bread
  pinch salt
  pinch ground black pepper
½ bunch watercress, tough stems trimmed
3 radishes, very thinly sliced

Lightly spread butter on each bread slice and sprinkle with salt and pepper. Arrange only very tender watercress sprigs on 4 buttered slices and top with radishes. Cover with remaining bread slices. Trim crusts and cut each sandwich on diagonal into quarters. Makes 16 tea sandwiches.

Each sandwich: About 39 calories, 1g protein, 4g carbohydrate, 2g total fat (1g saturated), 6mg cholesterol, 71mg sodium.

DILLED-EGG TEA SANDWICHES

••••••••••••••••••••••••••••••••

Use this recipe for large-size sandwiches as well as delicate tea sandwiches. They're tasty either way.

Prep: 40 minutes

3 large hard-cooked eggs, peeled and finely shredded
¼ cup mayonnaise
2 tablespoons chopped fresh dill
¼ teaspoon freshly grated lemon peel
¼ teaspoon ground black pepper
12 very thin slices white or whole-wheat bread

In medium bowl, stir eggs, mayonnaise, dill, lemon peel, and pepper. Spread evenly on 6 bread slices; top with remaining bread slices. Trim crusts and cut each sandwich into 3 equal rectangles. Makes 18 tea sandwiches.

Each sandwich: About 68 calories, 2g protein, 6g carbohydrate, 4g total fat (1g saturated), 37mg cholesterol, 95mg sodium.

CHEDDAR AND CHUTNEY TEA SANDWICHES

••••••••••••••••••••••••••••••••

This sweet-and-savory combination is a treat with a cup of tea or even a cocktail.

Prep: 15 minutes

3 tablespoons butter or margarine, softened
3 tablespoons mango chutney, finely chopped
8 very thin slices white or whole-wheat bread
4 ounces Cheddar cheese, shredded (1 cup)

In small bowl, stir butter and chutney until well blended. Spread evenly on bread slices. Sprinkle Cheddar on buttered side of 4 bread slices. Top with remaining bread. Trim crusts and cut each sandwich into 4 squares or triangles. Makes 16 tea sandwiches.

Each sandwich: About 78 calories, 2g protein, 6g carbohydrate, 5g total fat (3g saturated), 13mg cholesterol, 136mg sodium.

SMOKED SALMON TEA SANDWICHES

••••••••••••••••••••••••••••••••

Using two different breads for these sandwiches is a nice touch but not absolutely necessary.

Prep: 20 minutes

8 very thin slices white bread
8 very thin slices whole-wheat bread
6 tablespoons butter or margarine, softened, or whipped cream cheese
6 ounces very thinly sliced smoked salmon

Lightly spread butter on each bread slice. Arrange salmon on buttered side of white bread, trimming to fit. Top with whole-wheat bread. Trim crusts and cut each sandwich on diagonal into quarters. Makes 32 tea sandwiches.

Each sandwich: About 43 calories, 2g protein, 3g carbohydrate, 3g total fat (1g saturated), 7mg cholesterol, 166mg sodium.

20
····
DESSERTS

Our collection of scrumptious desserts is sure to tempt you: soufflés, meringues, custards, puff pastry desserts, pudding cakes, and other earthly delights. Many of the desserts rely on eggs for their distinctive textures, so here are some tips to help you with some basic techniques.

CUSTARDS

Custard, a cooked milk or cream mixture thickened with eggs and sweetened with sugar, can be baked for a dessert or cooked on top of the stove for a silky dessert sauce (called a stirred custard).

A moderate cooking temperature is necessary for baked custards, so they are cooked in a water bath (a roasting pan filled with hot water to come halfway up the sides of the cups), which insulates them from the oven's heat. For stirred custards, the yolks are gradually heated. A small amount of the hot liquid is stirred into the yolks, then the yolk mixture is stirred back into the hot liquid. This prevents the custard from curdling.

The center of a properly cooked custard will jiggle, as it will continue to cook as it cools. Insert the tip of a knife into the custard about 1 inch from the center; it should come out clean.

Custard sauces must be stirred constantly over low heat to prevent scorching and overcooking. The custard is cooked until thick enough to coat a spoon. Strain the custard into a bowl, then press a piece of plastic wrap directly onto the surface.

HIGH-RISING SOUFFLÉS

The secret to a beautifully risen soufflé isn't really that secret. It's all about perfectly beaten eggs whites. Separate the eggs while cold, then let them sit at room temperature until warm, so they will beat to their highest volume.

Beat the egg whites just until stiff—not dry. Fold about one-third of the whites into the batter to lighten it, then fold in the remaining whites.

Because soufflés need a blast of hot air to rise properly, be sure the oven is preheated thoroughly. A soufflé is done when puffed and golden brown, with a somewhat soft, barely set center. Once exposed to the air, a soufflé will keep its puff for only three to five minutes.

MAGICAL MERINGUES

Meringues are nothing more complicated than a beaten mixture of egg whites and sugar. There are two types of meringue, soft and hard, which simply depend on the proportion of sugar to egg whites. Soft meringue contains less sugar while hard meringue contains more sugar.

Never make meringue on a humid or rainy day, because it will absorb the moisture from the air and end up soggy or "weep." Beat room-temperature egg whites at high speed until soft peaks form. Then add the sugar, two tablespoons at a time, beating just until stiff, glossy peaks form. Check that the sugar has dissolved by rubbing a bit of the meringue between your fingers.

MERINGUE SHELLS

....

Fill these versatile shells with whipped cream or Lemon Filling (page 652) and berries, or with ice cream and chocolate sauce. Do not make meringues in humid weather: They will get soggy.

Prep: 15 minutes plus cooling   Bake: 2 hours

3   large egg whites
1/8   teaspoon cream of tartar
3/4   cup sugar
1/2   teaspoon vanilla extract

1. Preheat oven to 200°F. Line large cookie sheet with foil or parchment paper. In small bowl, with mixer at high speed, beat egg whites and cream of tartar until soft peaks form when beaters are lifted. Sprinkle in sugar, 2 tablespoons at a time, beating until sugar has dissolved. Add vanilla; continue beating until egg whites stand in stiff, glossy peaks when beaters are lifted.

2. Spoon meringue into 6 equal mounds on prepared cookie sheet, 4 inches apart. With back of tablespoon, spread each mound into 4-inch round. Make well in center of each round to form "nest."

3. Bake until meringues are firm and just begin to color, about 2 hours. Turn off oven; leave meringues in oven 1 hour or up to overnight to dry. If not leaving overnight, cool completely on cookie sheet on wire rack. Store meringue shells in airtight container. Makes 6 servings.

Each serving: About 106 calories, 2g protein, 25g carbohydrate, 0g total fat (0g saturated), 0mg cholesterol, 28mg sodium.

MINIATURE MERINGUE SHELLS

Preheat oven to 200°F. Line two cookie sheets with foil or parchment paper. Prepare as directed in Step 1 above. Drop meringue by rounded teaspoons, 2 inches apart, on prepared cookie sheets. With back of teaspoon, make well in center of each to form "nest" about 1 1/2 inches across. Bake until meringues are firm and just begin to color, about 1 hour. Turn off oven; leave meringues in oven 1 hour or up to overnight to dry. If not leaving overnight, cool completely on cookie sheet on wire rack. Store as directed. Makes 20 miniature shells.

Each serving: About 32 calories, 0g protein, 8g carbohydrate, 0g total fat (0g saturated), 0mg cholesterol, 8mg sodium.

PERFECT MERINGUE SHELLS

For symmetrically shaped meringue shells, mark circles on the foil with a toothpick. Use a saucer as a guide for large shells or a 1 1/2-inch jar cap or cookie cutter for miniature shells.

PAVLOVA

This Australian favorite was created to honor prima ballerina Anna Pavlova, who was renowned for her leading role in *Swan Lake*. Swanlike in its delicacy and pristine whiteness, it always gets rave reviews.

Preheat oven to 275°F. Line large cookie sheet with foil. Grease foil; dust with flour. Using a 9-inch round cake pan as a guide, with toothpick, trace a circle in center of foil. In small bowl, whisk 2/3 cup sugar and 1 tablespoon cornstarch. In large bowl, with mixer at medium speed, beat 4 large egg whites and 1/4 teaspoon salt until foamy. Beat in sugar mixture, 1 tablespoon at a time, beating well after each addition, until sugar has completely dissolved and whites stand in stiff, glossy peaks when beaters are lifted. Beat in 2 teaspoons distilled white vinegar and 1 teaspoon vanilla extract. Spoon meringue into circle on foil. With back of spoon, spread meringue to edge of circle, forming a "nest" with a 2-inch-high rim all around.

Bake until set, about 2 hours. Turn off oven; leave meringue in oven 2 hours. Cool completely on cookie sheet on wire rack.

In small bowl, with mixer at medium speed, beat 1 cup heavy cream and 2 tablespoons sugar to soft peaks. Beat in 1/2 teaspoon vanilla. To serve, spoon whipped cream into center of meringue and top with peeled, thickly sliced kiwifruit and sliced strawberries.

RASPBERRY JAM SOUFFLÉ

This impressive fat-free dessert is easier to make than you think—just fold store-bought fruit spread into beaten egg whites and bake. To do ahead, prepare and refrigerate soufflé mixture in soufflé dish up to three hours, then bake as directed just before serving.

Prep: 20 minutes   Bake: 15 minutes

- 2/3 cup seedless raspberry spreadable fruit (no-sugar-added jam)
- 1 tablespoon fresh lemon juice
- 4 large egg whites
- 1/2 teaspoon cream of tartar
- 2 tablespoons sugar
- 1 teaspoon vanilla extract

1. Preheat oven to 375°F. In large bowl, with wire whisk, beat fruit spread with lemon juice; set aside.

2. In medium bowl, with mixer at high speed, beat egg whites and cream of tartar until soft peaks form when beaters are lifted. Sprinkle in sugar, 1 tablespoon at a time, beating until sugar has dissolved. Add vanilla; continue beating until egg whites stand in stiff peaks when beaters are lifted.

3. With rubber spatula, gently fold one-third of beaten egg whites into raspberry mixture. Fold in remaining whites, just until blended. Spoon mixture into 1 1/2-quart soufflé dish; gently spread evenly.

4. Bake until soufflé has puffed and is lightly browned, and knife inserted 1 inch from edge comes out clean, 15 to 18 minutes. Serve immediately. Makes 6 servings.

Each serving: About 75 calories, 3g protein, 16g carbohydrate, 0g total fat, 1g fiber, 0mg cholesterol, 35mg sodium.

BANANA SOUFFLÉ
Prepare soufflé as directed but prepare banana puree instead of spreadable fruit. In blender or in food processor with knife blade attached, puree **2 very ripe medium bananas,** cut into large pieces, with **2 tablespoons sugar, 1 tablespoon fresh lemon juice** and **1/4 teaspoon ground cinnamon** until smooth. Fold beaten egg whites into banana puree and bake as directed.

CHOCOLATE SOUFFLÉS

Soufflés always make an impression. They are irresistible as individual soufflés and spectacular baked as one large dessert.

Prep: 20 minutes plus cooling   Bake: 25 minutes

- 1 1/4 cups plus 3 tablespoons granulated sugar
- 1/4 cup all-purpose flour
- 1 teaspoon instant espresso-coffee powder
- 1 cup milk
- 5 squares (5 ounces) unsweetened chocolate, chopped
- 3 tablespoons butter or margarine, softened
- 4 large eggs, separated, plus 2 large egg whites
- 2 teaspoons vanilla extract
- 1/4 teaspoon salt
  confectioners' sugar

1. In heavy 3-quart saucepan, combine 1 1/4 cups granulated sugar, flour, and espresso powder. With wire whisk, gradually stir in milk until blended. Cook over medium heat, stirring constantly, until mixture has thickened and boils; boil, stirring, 1 minute. Remove from heat.

2. Stir in chocolate and butter until melted and smooth. With whisk, beat in egg yolks until well blended; stir in vanilla. Cool to lukewarm.

3. Meanwhile, preheat oven to 350°F. Grease eight 6-ounce custard cups or ramekins or 2-quart soufflé dish; sprinkle lightly with remaining 3 tablespoons granulated sugar.

4. In large bowl, with mixer at high speed, beat egg whites and salt just until stiff peaks form when beaters are lifted. With rubber spatula, gently fold one-third of beaten egg whites into chocolate mixture; fold back into remaining egg whites just until blended.

5. Spoon into prepared custard cups or soufflé dish. (If using custard cups, place in jelly-roll pan for easier handling.) Bake until soufflés have puffed and centers are glossy, 25 to 30 minutes for individual soufflés, 35 to 40 minutes for large soufflé. Dust with confectioners' sugar. Serve immediately. Makes 8 servings.

Each serving: About 356 calories, 7g protein, 44g carbohydrate, 19g total fat (10g saturated), 122mg cholesterol, 178mg sodium.

ORANGE LIQUEUR SOUFFLÉ

....

This is perhaps the most popular and elegant of all soufflés. Infuse it with your favorite orange liqueur: Grand Marnier, curaçao, or triple sec.

Prep: 20 minutes plus cooling   Bake: 30 minutes

- 4 tablespoons butter or margarine
- 1/3 cup all-purpose flour
- 1 1/8 teaspoons salt
- 1 1/2 cups milk, warmed
- 1/2 cup plus 2 tablespoons granulated sugar
- 4 large eggs, separated, plus 2 large egg whites
- 1/3 cup orange-flavored liqueur
- 1 tablespoon freshly grated orange peel
  confectioners' sugar
  whipped cream (optional)

1. In heavy 2-quart saucepan, melt butter over low heat. Add flour and salt; cook, stirring, 1 minute. With wire whisk, gradually whisk in warm milk. Cook over medium heat, stirring with wooden spoon, until mixture has thickened and boils. Reduce heat and simmer 1 minute. Remove from heat.

2. With wire whisk, stir 1/2 cup granulated sugar into milk mixture. Gradually whisk in egg yolks, whisking rapidly to prevent curdling. Cool egg-yolk mixture to lukewarm, stirring occasionally. Stir in orange liqueur and orange peel.

3. Preheat oven to 375°F. Grease 2-quart soufflé dish with butter and evenly sprinkle with remaining 2 tablespoons granulated sugar.

4. In large bowl, with mixer at high speed, beat egg whites until stiff peaks form when beaters are lifted. With rubber spatula, gently fold one-third of beaten egg whites into egg-yolk mixture; fold mixture back into remaining egg whites just until blended.

5. Spoon mixture into prepared soufflé dish. To create top-hat effect (center will rise higher than edge), with back of spoon, make 1-inch-deep indentation all around top of soufflé about 1 inch from edge of dish. Bake until soufflé has puffed, is golden, and knife inserted 1 inch from edge comes out clean, 30 to 35 minutes. Dust with confectioners' sugar. Serve immediately. If desired, pass whipped cream to spoon onto each serving. Makes 8 servings.

Each serving: About 214 calories, 6g protein, 26g carbohydrate, 10g total fat (5g saturated), 128mg cholesterol, 162mg sodium.

Orange Liqueur Soufflé

RASPBERRY-BANANA TRIFLE

....

This beautiful dessert is easier to make than you think—store-bought pound cake and jam are the secret ingredients.

Prep: 1 hour plus chilling   Cook: 15 minutes

Cake
- 1 frozen pound cake (1 pound), thawed
- 6 tablespoons seedless red-raspberry jam

Custard
- 6 large eggs
- ³/₄ cup sugar
- ¹/₃ cup cornstarch
- 4 cups milk
- 4 tablespoons butter or margarine
- 2 tablespoons vanilla extract
- 3 large ripe bananas (1¹/₂ pounds), sliced

Topping
- 1 cup heavy or whipping cream
- 2 tablespoons sugar
  fresh raspberries and fresh mint leaves for garnish

1. Prepare cake: With serrated knife, cut crust from pound cake. Place cake on 1 long side; cut lengthwise into 4 equal slices. With small spatula, spread 2 tablespoons jam on top of 1 cake slice; top with another cake slice. Repeat with remaining jam and cake, ending with cake. Slice jam-layered cake crosswise into ¹/₄-inch slices, keeping slices together, then cut cake lengthwise in half down center. (You should have about 26 slices jam-layered cake cut in half to make 52 half slices.)

2. Prepare custard: In medium bowl, with wire whisk, beat eggs, sugar, and cornstarch; set aside. In 4-quart saucepan, heat milk just to boiling. While constantly beating with whisk, gradually pour about half of hot milk into egg mixture. Pour egg mixture back into milk in saucepan, and cook over medium-low heat, whisking constantly, until mixture thickens and begins to bubble around edge of pan; mixture will not boil vigorously. Simmer custard 1 minute, whisking constantly; it must reach at least 160°F. Remove saucepan from heat; stir in butter with vanilla.

3. Assemble trifle: In 4-quart glass trifle dish or deep glass bowl, place 2 rows of cake slices around side of bowl, alternating horizontal and vertical placement of cake slices to make a checkerboard design. Place some cake slices in a layer to cover bottom of bowl; top with one-third of sliced bananas. Spoon one-third of warm custard on top of bananas. Top with half of remaining bananas and half of remaining custard. Top with remaining cake, then bananas and custard. Cover surface of custard with plastic wrap to prevent skin from forming. Refrigerate trifle 6 hours or overnight.

4. Before serving, prepare topping: In small bowl, with mixer at medium speed, beat cream with sugar until stiff peaks form. Remove plastic wrap from trifle; top trifle with whipped cream and garnish with raspberries and mint. Makes 24 servings.

Each serving: About 240 calories, 4g protein, 28g carbohydrate, 12g total fat (5g saturated), 72mg cholesterol, 120mg sodium.

VARIATIONS ON A TRIFLE

Though there are many, many recipes for trifles (see the strawberry-rhubarb version on page 602), they probably have three elements in common: strips or cubes of cake for their base, a rich custard sauce for pouring between the layers, and fresh fruit. After that, whipped cream, sliced or slivered nuts, candied fruit, jam, and brandy or fruit-flavored liqueur are all popular add-ins. Here are some ways to vary our delectable trifle:

- Use plain or chocolate sponge cake or a fruit-flavored pound cake instead of the plain pound cake.
- Try orange, apricot, or strawberry jam instead of the raspberry jam.
- Substitute 3 cups of whole, sliced, or diced fresh fruit—strawberries, blackberries peaches, apricots, plums—for the banana.
- Drizzle the cake with a little brandy or orange-flavored liqueur before brushing it with jam.

STRAWBERRY-RHUBARB TRIFLE WITH AMARETTO CUSTARD

....

There's more to rhubarb than pie filling.

Prep: 40 minutes plus chilling   Cook: 20 minutes

- 3 cups whole milk
- 1¼ cups sugar
- ⅓ cup cornstarch
- ⅛ teaspoon salt
- 2 large egg yolks
- ¼ cup Amaretto or other almond-flavored liqueur
- 1¼ pounds rhubarb, trimmed and cut into ½-inch chunks
- 2 pounds strawberries, hulled and each cut into quarters (5 cups)
- ½ cup heavy or whipping cream
- 2 frozen ready-to-serve pound cakes (10 to 11 ounces each), thawed and cut into ¾-inch cubes

1. Prepare custard: In 4-quart saucepan, heat 2½ cups milk and ¾ cup sugar on medium just to boiling. Remove saucepan from heat. In medium bowl, with wire whisk, mix remaining ½ cup milk with cornstarch and salt until smooth; beat in egg yolks. Into yolk mixture, stir small amount of hot milk mixture; gradually stir yolk mixture back into milk mixture in saucepan. Cook on medium until mixture thickens and boils, stirring constantly. Remove from heat; stir in liqueur. Pour custard into clean bowl. To keep skin from forming as custard cools, press plastic wrap onto surface of hot custard. Refrigerate until cold, at least 3 hours.

2. While custard cools, in 12-inch nonstick skillet, cook rhubarb, one-fourth strawberries (1¼ cups), and remaining ½ cup sugar on medium 18 to 20 minutes or until mixture boils and thickens, stirring occasionally. Transfer to bowl. Let cool to room temperature, or cover and refrigerate until ready to use.

3. When ready to assemble: In bowl, with electric mixer on medium speed, beat heavy cream until soft peaks form. Gently fold whipped cream into chilled custard. In 3½-quart glass trifle dish or serving bowl, place half of pound cake cubes; spoon half of custard over pound cake. Spread half of strawberry-rhubarb mixture over custard, then half of remaining uncooked strawberries. Repeat with remaining pound cake, custard, strawberry-rhubarb mixture, and strawberries.

Cover and refrigerate at least 4 or up to 24 hours to blend flavors. To serve, spoon into individual dessert bowls. Makes 16 servings.

Each serving: About 340 calories, 5g protein, 49g carbohydrate, 14g total fat (8g saturated), 86mg cholesterol, 185mg sodium.

FRUIT CRISP

....

We love the flavor of pecans in the crisp topping, but you can use walnuts, hazelnuts, or almonds, if you like.

Prep: 20 minutes plus cooling   Bake: 40 minutes

- 1 lemon
- 2 pounds nectarines (about 6 medium), pitted and cut into thick wedges
- ½ pint (1 cup) raspberries
- 1 cup blueberries
- ¼ cup granulated sugar
- ⅔ cup packed brown sugar
- ½ cup all-purpose flour
- ½ teaspoon ground nutmeg
- 6 tablespoons cold butter or margarine, cut into pieces
- ½ cup old-fashioned oats, uncooked
- ⅓ cup chopped pecans
  vanilla ice cream (optional)

1. Preheat oven to 400°F. From lemon, grate ½ teaspoon peel and squeeze 2 teaspoons juice. In shallow 2-quart casserole or 8-inch baking dish, toss nectarines, raspberries, blueberries, granulated sugar, and lemon peel and juice until fruit is evenly coated.

2. In medium bowl, combine brown sugar, flour, and nutmeg. With pastry blender or 2 knives used scissor-fashion, cut in butter until mixture resembles coarse crumbs. Stir in oats and pecans; sprinkle evenly over fruit.

3. Bake crisp until top is golden and fruit is hot and bubbly, 40 to 45 minutes. Cool crisp slightly on wire rack. Serve warm with vanilla ice cream if you like. Makes 8 servings.

Each serving: About 300 calories, 3g protein, 51g carbohydrate, 14g total fat (6g saturated), 4g fiber, 25mg cholesterol, 100mg sodium.

CRÈME CARAMEL

A masterpiece of French dessert making: individual custards in their own caramel sauce.

Prep: 15 minutes plus cooling and chilling
Bake: 50 minutes

¼ plus ⅓ cup sugar
4 large eggs
2 cups milk
1½ teaspoons vanilla extract
¼ teaspoon salt

1. Preheat oven to 325°F. In heavy 1-quart saucepan, heat ¼ cup sugar over medium heat, swirling pan occasionally, until sugar has melted and is amber in color. Immediately pour into six 6-ounce custard cups or ramekins.

2. In large bowl, with wire whisk, beat eggs and remaining ⅓ cup sugar until blended. Whisk in milk, vanilla, and salt until well combined; pour mixture through fine mesh sieve into prepared custard cups.

3. Place custard cups in small baking pan; place on rack in oven. Carefully pour enough *very hot water* into pan to come halfway up sides of cups. Bake just until knife inserted 1 inch from center of custards comes out clean, 50 to 55 minutes. Transfer custard cups to wire rack to cool. Cover and refrigerate until well chilled, 3 hours or up to overnight.

4. To serve, run tip of small knife around edge of custards. Invert cups onto dessert plates, shaking cups gently until custards slip out. Leave inverted cup on plate for several minutes to allow caramel syrup to drip onto custards. Makes 6 servings.

Each serving: About 177 calories, 7g protein, 24g carbohydrate, 6g total fat (3g saturated), 153mg cholesterol, 177mg sodium.

LOW-FAT CRÈME CARAMEL

Here, low-fat milk replaces whole milk and 2 egg whites stand in for 2 whole eggs, yet the custard is still velvety and tastes as good as the higher-fat original.

Prep: 20 minutes plus chilling   **Bake: 40 minutes**

1 cup sugar
2 tablespoons cold water
2 large eggs plus 2 large egg whites
3 cups low-fat (1%) milk
1 teaspoon vanilla extract

1. Preheat oven to 350°F. Heat 4-quart saucepan of *water* to boiling on high to use for water bath later.

2. In 2-quart saucepan, heat ⅔ cup sugar with cold water on medium until melted and a light caramel color, swirling pan occasionally. Immediately pour caramel into eight 6-ounce custard cups or ramekins.

3. In large bowl, with wire whisk, beat eggs, egg whites, and remaining ⅓ cup sugar until well blended. Beat in milk and vanilla. Pour custard mixture into custard cups.

4. Place cups in large roasting pan (17" by 11½"); pour boiling water in pan until it comes halfway up sides of cups. Bake 40 minutes or until center of custard is just set. Remove custard cups from water in roasting pan; cool on wire rack. Cover and refrigerate 4 hours or until custard is well chilled.

5. To serve, with small metal spatula, carefully loosen custard from sides of cups. Invert each crème caramel onto dessert plate, tapping cup to help release custard. Leave inverted cup on plate for several minutes to allow caramel syrup to drip from cup onto custard. Makes 8 servings.

Each serving: About 155 calories, 6g protein, 29g carbohydrate, 2g total fat (1g saturated), 0g fiber, 57mg cholesterol, 75mg sodium.

CARAMEL

Always pour caramel into custard cups immediately. Otherwise, it will overcook and harden.

CRÈME BRÛLÉE

....

Its brittle caramelized top and velvety custard make this an ultimate indulgence.

Prep: 20 minutes plus cooling and chilling
Bake/Broil: 38 minutes

½ vanilla bean or 2 teaspoons vanilla extract

1½ cups heavy or whipping cream

1½ cups half-and-half or light cream

8 large egg yolks

⅔ cup granulated sugar

⅓ to ½ cup packed brown sugar

1. Preheat oven to 325°F. With knife, cut vanilla bean lengthwise in half; scrape out seeds. Into heavy 3-quart saucepan, add cream, half-and-half, and vanilla bean. Heat over medium heat until bubbles form around edge. Remove from heat. Remove vanilla bean.

2. Meanwhile, in large bowl, with wire whisk, beat egg yolks and granulated sugar until well blended. Slowly stir in hot cream mixture until well combined. Pour cream mixture into ten 4- to 5-ounce broiler-proof ramekins or a shallow 2½-quart casserole.

3. Place ramekins or casserole in large roasting pan; place pan on rack in oven. Carefully pour enough *very hot water* into pan to come halfway up sides of ramekins. Bake just until set (mixture will still be slightly soft in center), 35 to 40 minutes. Transfer ramekins to wire rack to cool to room temperature. Cover and refrigerate, at least 3 hours or up to overnight.

4. Up to 2 hours before serving, preheat broiler. Place brown sugar in small sieve; with spoon, press sugar through sieve to cover tops of chilled custards.

5. Place ramekins in jelly-roll pan for easier handling. With broiler rack at closest position to heat source, broil custard just until sugar melts, 3 to 4 minutes. Serve, or refrigerate up to 2 hours. The melted brown sugar will form a delicious brittle crust. Makes 10 servings.

Each serving: About 307 calories, 4g protein, 25g carbohydrate, 21g total fat (12g saturated), 232mg cholesterol, 38mg sodium.

BAIN MARIE

A *bain marie* (hot water bath) is the best way to ensure that delicate custard mixtures cook evenly. Here's how to do it: Place custard cups or baking dish in a baking or roasting pan. Place the pan on the oven rack. Pour in enough very hot water (not boiling) to come halfway up the sides of the dish. This method is sometimes used for cheesecakes and other egg-based dishes too.

GETTING TO KNOW GELATIN

Odorless, tasteless, and colorless, gelatin is used as a thickening agent in desserts. The most common form is powdered gelatin, which comes in individual envelopes. One envelope equals about 2½ teaspoons (¼ ounce) and will set about 2 cups of liquid.

Gelatin must always be dissolved. Sprinkle it over a small amount of cold liquid and allow to stand until it has softened and soaked up the liquid, about 5 minutes. Add the softened gelatin to the recipe's liquid; stir constantly over low heat until completely dissolved. To check that the gelatin has fully dissolved, lift a little into a spoon: There should be no visible crystals. Or, rub a bit of the gelatin between your fingers.

PUMPKIN CHEESECAKE CRÈME CARAMEL

This is a wonderful do-ahead alternative to pumpkin pie. Use a thin-bladed knife to make slicing easier.

Prep: 30 minutes plus cooling and chilling
Bake: 1 hour 10 minutes

1	orange
1¼	cups sugar
1	package (8 ounces) cream cheese, softened
1	cup can solid-pack pumpkin (not pumpkin-pie filling)
6	large eggs
1	can (12 ounces) evaporated milk
½	cup heavy or whipping cream
¼	cup orange-flavored liqueur
1	teaspoon vanilla extract
1	teaspoon ground cinnamon
	pinch ground nutmeg
	pinch salt

1. Preheat oven to 350°F. Fill kettle or covered 4-quart saucepan with *water;* heat to boiling over high heat.

2. Meanwhile, from orange, with vegetable peeler, remove 6 strips peel, about 3" by 1" each. With knife, trim off as much white pith as possible from peel. In 1-quart saucepan, heat orange peel, ¾ cup sugar, and *¼ cup water* to boiling over medium heat; cover and cook 5 minutes. Remove cover and cook until sugar mixture is amber in color, 1 to 2 minutes longer. Pour hot caramel into 9" by 5" metal loaf pan. With fork, remove and discard orange peel. (Hold loaf pan with pot holder to protect hands from heat of caramel.) Set pan aside.

3. In large bowl, with mixer on medium speed, beat cream cheese and remaining ½ cup sugar 2 minutes, occasionally scraping bowl with rubber spatula. Beat in pumpkin, then eggs, one at a time. Reduce speed to low; beat in evaporated milk, cream, liqueur, vanilla, cinnamon, nutmeg, and salt just until well mixed.

4. Pour pumpkin mixture through medium-mesh sieve over caramel in loaf pan, pressing it through with rubber spatula. Place loaf pan in 13" by 9" baking pan; place in oven. Carefully pour boiling water into baking pan to come three-quarters up sides of loaf pan.

5. Bake until knife inserted 1 inch from edge of custard comes out clean (center will jiggle), 1 hour 10 to 15 minutes. Remove loaf pan from baking pan to cool on wire rack 1 hour. Cover and refrigerate crème caramel at least 8 hours or overnight.

6. To unmold, run small metal spatula or knife around sides of loaf pan; invert crème caramel onto serving plate. Leave loaf pan in place several minutes, allowing caramel syrup to drip from pan onto loaf. (Don't worry if some caramel remains in loaf pan.) Makes 12 servings.

Each serving: About 280 calories, 7g protein, 28g carbohydrate, 15g total fat (9g saturated), 150mg cholesterol, 135mg sodium.

BREAD PUDDING

The combination of dark raisins, just a touch of cinnamon and nutmeg, and a splash of dark rum makes this pudding a classic. For best texture, be sure to use day-old bread.

Prep: 20 minutes plus standing and cooling
Bake: 45 minutes

½	cup dark seedless raisins
3	tablespoons dark rum or bourbon
½	cup sugar
¼	teaspoon ground cinnamon
⅛	teaspoon ground nutmeg
4	large eggs
2	teaspoons vanilla extract
3	cups milk
3	cups day-old French bread cubes (½ inch)

1. In cup, combine raisins and rum; let stand 15 minutes. Grease 8" by 8" glass or ceramic baking dish.

2. In large bowl, whisk sugar, cinnamon, and nutmeg. Whisk in eggs and vanilla until combined. Add milk to egg mixture and whisk until well blended. Stir in bread cubes. Let stand 15 minutes, stirring occasionally. Stir in raisin mixture.

3. Preheat oven to 325°F. Pour bread mixture into prepared dish. Bake 45 to 50 minutes, or until a knife inserted near center of pudding comes out clean. Let cool on wire rack. Serve warm or refrigerate and serve cold. Makes 8 servings.

Each serving: About 213 calories, 8g protein, 31g carbohydrate, 6g total fat (3g saturated), 119mg cholesterol, 164mg sodium.

TIRAMISÙ

....

Rich and moist but light-as-a-feather, this classic sweet is a favorite afternoon treat in Italy.

Prep: 35 minutes plus chilling

- 1 cup hot espresso or very strong brewed coffee
- 3 tablespoons brandy
- 2 tablespoons plus ½ cup sugar
- 18 crisp Italian ladyfingers (savoiardi; 5 ounces)
- ½ cup milk
- 1 container (16 to 17½ ounces) mascarpone cheese
- ¾ cup heavy or whipping cream
  unsweetened cocoa
  Chocolate Curls (page 653)

1. In 9-inch pie plate, stir coffee, brandy, and 2 tablespoons sugar until sugar has dissolved; cool to room temperature. Dip both sides of 9 ladyfingers into coffee mixture, one at a time, to soak completely; arrange in single layer in 8-inch square baking dish.

2. In large bowl, stir milk and remaining ½ cup sugar until sugar has dissolved. Stir in mascarpone until blended.

3. In small bowl, with mixer at high speed, beat cream until soft peaks form. With rubber spatula, gently fold whipped cream into mascarpone mixture until blended. Spread half of mixture over ladyfingers in baking dish.

4. Dip remaining 9 ladyfingers into coffee mixture and arrange on top of mascarpone mixture. Spread with remaining mascarpone mixture. Refrigerate 3 hours or up to overnight.

5. Meanwhile, prepare Chocolate Curls.

6. Just before serving, dust with cocoa. Cut into squares and spoon into goblets or dessert dishes. Garnish with curls. Makes 12 servings.

Each serving: About 323 calories, 4g protein, 22g carbohydrate, 23g total fat (15g saturated), 55mg cholesterol, 59mg sodium.

BLUEBERRY-LEMON TIRAMISÙ

....

In Italian, tiramisu means "lift me up." Here, blueberries, lemon, and yogurt replace mascarpone and chocolate for a light and lovely finale to a summer meal.

Prep: 20 minutes plus chilling overnight
Cook: 5 minutes

- 1 to 2 lemons
- 3¾ cups blueberries
- ¾ cup sugar
- 4 tablespoons water
- 1 container (17 to 18 ounces) non-fat Greek yogurt
- 1 package (3 ounces) ladyfingers
  mint sprig for garnish

1. From lemons, grate 1½ teaspoons peel and squeeze ¼ cup juice.

2. In medium saucepan, combine 1½ cups blueberries, ¼ cup sugar, and 1 tablespoon water. Heat on medium 5 minutes or until blueberries soften and juices thicken, stirring occasionally. Transfer to medium bowl and stir in 1½ cups blueberries. Set aside.

3. Prepare lemon syrup: In microwave-safe small bowl, combine ¼ cup sugar and remaining 3 tablespoons water. Cook in microwave on High 1 minute. Stir in 3 tablespoons lemon juice and 1 teaspoon lemon peel.

4. In medium bowl, stir together yogurt and remaining ¼ cup sugar, 1 tablespoon lemon juice, and ½ teaspoon lemon peel.

5. In 8-inch square ceramic or glass baking dish, arrange half of ladyfingers. Brush with half of lemon syrup. Spoon blueberry mixture evenly over ladyfingers. Arrange remaining ladyfingers over blueberries. Brush with remaining lemon syrup. Spoon yogurt mixture on top, spreading evenly. Cover and refrigerate overnight. To serve, top tiramisù with remaining ¾ cup blueberries and garnish with mint sprig. Makes 9 servings.

Each serving: About 165 calories, 7g protein, 34g carbohydrate, 1g total fat (0g saturated), 2g fiber, 23mg cholesterol, 90mg sodium.

Tip: We tested this recipe with both soft ladyfingers and hard (Italian-style) ladyfingers, which are sometimes called savoiardi, and had good results with both types.

If you use soft ladyfingers, separate them into halves before layering. Hard ladyfingers are each only one piece and do not need to be separated.

SLICED CITRUS WITH LEMON-LIME SYRUP

....

Serve this versatile fruit dish for brunch or dessert.

Prep: 20 minutes plus chilling   **Cook: 3 minutes**

- 1 to 2 lemons
- 1 lime
- ¼ cup sugar
- 2 navel oranges
- 2 clementines
- 2 red or white grapefruit

1. From lemons, grate 1 teaspoon peel and squeeze 3 tablespoons juice. From lime, grate ½ teaspoon peel and squeeze 1 tablespoon juice.

2. In 1-quart saucepan, combine lemon and lime juices and sugar; heat to boiling over medium-high heat. Reduce heat to low; simmer 1 minute. Remove saucepan from heat; stir in lemon and lime peels. Cover syrup and refrigerate until cold.

3. Meanwhile, cut peel and white pith from oranges, clementines, and grapefruit. Slice all fruit crosswise into ¼-inch-thick rounds. Arrange slices on deep large platter.

4. Spoon syrup over citrus. If not serving right away, cover and refrigerate up to 2 days. Makes 6 servings.

Each serving: About 95 calories, 1g protein, 24g carbohydrate, 0g total fat, 3g fiber, 0mg cholesterol, 1mg sodium.

Sliced Citrus with Lemon-Lime Syrup

GIVE IT A LIFT WITH CITRUS

Grated peel or juice can dress up almost anything, sweet or savory. Just a sprinkle or squeeze before serving can make the difference between a plain and a fancy dish. Here are some quick ways the GH test kitchen likes to use citrus.

GRATED PEEL

- Stir any type into rice pilaf to change it from simple to sumptuous.
- Sprinkle lime peel over vanilla ice cream for a zesty, fresh flavor.
- Toss orange peel with buttered carrots or roasted sweet potatoes.
- Mix lemon peel into plain sugar cookie dough to turn out a quick lemon cookie.

JUICE

- Squeeze a wedge of lemon or lime into a glass of cola, ginger ale, or tonic to cut the sweetness and enliven the flavor.
- Squirt lemon, lime, or orange juice over steamed shellfish or grilled chicken just before eating it.
- Add lemon juice to bottled salad dressing to give it a sprightly homemade taste.
- Drizzle lemon juice, rather than malt vinegar, over French fries.
- Squeeze lime juice into the center of an avocado half and sprinkle salt over all for a quick, healthy snack.
- Stir lime juice into canned black bean or lentil soup to add zip before serving.

GRATED PEEL AND JUICE

- Stir grated lemon peel and juice into store-bought mayonnaise for a tangy sandwich spread or a dressing for steamed asparagus.
- Grate any citrus peel into a bowl with a tablespoon or two of butter and add a squirt of juice plus a pinch of dried herb to make a citrus butter; toss with cooked vegetables.
- Combine grated orange peel and juice with marmalade, and stir into a fruit salad for a sweet treat.

PANNA COTTA WITH BERRY SAUCE

....

Panna cotta, which means "cooked cream" in Italian, is a custard that is served cold with a sauce.

Prep: 20 minutes plus chilling   Cook: 15 minutes

- 1   envelope unflavored gelatin
- 1   cup milk
- ½   vanilla bean or 1½ teaspoons vanilla extract
- 1¾ cups heavy or whipping cream
- ¼   cup sugar
- 1   strip (3" by 1") lemon peel
- 1   cinnamon stick (3 inches)
     Best Berry Sauce (page 511), made with raspberries
     fresh raspberries

1. In 2-cup measuring cup, evenly sprinkle gelatin over milk; let stand 2 minutes to soften gelatin slightly. With knife, cut vanilla bean lengthwise in half; scrape out seeds and reserve.

2. In heavy 1-quart saucepan, combine cream, sugar, lemon peel, cinnamon stick, and vanilla bean halves and seeds (do not add vanilla extract yet); heat to boiling over high heat, stirring occasionally. Reduce heat and simmer, stirring occasionally, 5 minutes. Stir in milk mixture; cook over low heat, stirring frequently, until gelatin has dissolved, 2 to 3 minutes.

3. Discard lemon peel, cinnamon stick, and vanilla bean from cream mixture. (Stir in vanilla extract, if using.) Pour cream mixture into medium bowl set in large bowl of *ice water*. With rubber spatula, stir mixture until it just begins to set, 10 to 12 minutes. Pour cream mixture into eight 4-ounce ramekins. Place ramekins in jelly-roll pan for easier handling. Cover and refrigerate panna cotta until well chilled and set, 4 hours or up to overnight.

4. Meanwhile, prepare Best Berry Sauce.

5. To unmold panna cotta, run tip of knife around edges. Tap side of each ramekin sharply to break seal. Invert onto dessert plates. Spoon sauce around each panna cotta and sprinkle with raspberries. Makes 8 servings.

Each serving without Raspberry Sauce: About 228 calories, 3g protein, 9g carbohydrate, 20g total fat (13g saturated), 76mg cholesterol, 37mg sodium.

Panna Cotta with Best Berry Sauce

BLUEBERRY SPICE WHOOPIE PIES

....

Popular for generations throughout New England, whoopie pies have become a bake-sale favorite in recent years. Here, fresh blueberries in a marshmallowy cream filling update this classic cake-like cookie.

Prep: 30 minutes   Bake: 11 minutes per batch

Cakes

   2 cups all-purpose flour
   1 teaspoon ground cinnamon
   ½ teaspoon ground ginger
   ½ teaspoon baking soda
   ¼ teaspoon ground nutmeg
   ¼ teaspoon salt
   ⅛ teaspoon ground cloves
   ¾ cup (1½ sticks) butter or margarine, softened
   1 cup packed light brown sugar
   1 large egg
   2 tablespoons light (mild) molasses
   ½ cup reduced-fat sour cream

Filling

   1 package (8 ounces) reduced-fat cream cheese
      (Neufchâtel)
   1 jar (7½ ounces) marshmallow creme
   2 cups blueberries plus additional for garnish

1. Prepare cakes: Preheat oven to 350°F. Spray three large cookie sheets with nonstick cooking spray. In medium bowl, mix flour, cinnamon, ginger, baking soda, nutmeg, salt, and cloves.

2. In large bowl, with mixer on medium-high speed, beat butter until smooth. Add brown sugar and beat 3 to 4 minutes or until creamy, scraping sides of bowl with rubber spatula. Add egg and molasses, and beat until well blended. With mixer on low speed, beat in flour mixture alternately with sour cream, beginning and ending with flour mixture, just until blended.

3. Spoon batter by heaping tablespoons onto prepared cookie sheets, 2½ inches apart (you should get 30 cakes). Bake cakes, one sheet at a time, 11 to 13 minutes or until cakes spring back when pressed lightly. Cool cakes in pan on wire rack 1 minute, then transfer with spatula to wire rack to cool completely. Cakes can be made up to one day ahead; wrap tightly in plastic wrap or foil and store at room temperature.

4. Prepare filling: In large bowl, with mixer on medium-high speed, beat cream cheese until smooth. Reduce speed to low; add marshmallow creme and beat just until blended, scraping beaters if necessary. Fold in blueberries. Spread ¼ cup filling on flat side of half of cakes. Top each with plain cake, flat side down, pressing lightly. If you like, garnish with additional blueberries pressed into side of filling. Makes 15 whoopie pies.

Each whoopie pie: About 320 calories, 4g protein, 44g carbohydrate, 15g total fat (9g saturated), 1g fiber, 55mg cholesterol, 260mg sodium.

CHOCOLATE FONDUE WITH FRUIT

....

A fun ending to any meal.

Prep: 15 minutes   Cook: 5 minutes

   6 squares (6 ounces) semisweet chocolate,
      coarsely chopped
   ½ cup half-and-half or light cream
   ½ teaspoon vanilla extract
   4 small bananas, each peeled and
      cut into ½-inch-thick slices
   2 to 3 small pears, not peeled, each cored and
      cut into ½-inch-thick wedges
   1 pint strawberries
   ½ cup finely chopped almonds, toasted

1. In heavy 1-quart saucepan, heat chocolate and half-and-half over low heat, stirring frequently, until chocolate has melted and mixture is smooth, about 5 minutes. Stir in vanilla; keep warm.

2. To serve, arrange bananas, pears, and strawberries on large platter. Spoon sauce into small bowl; place nuts in separate small bowl. With forks or toothpicks, have guests dip fruit into chocolate sauce, then into nuts. Makes 8 servings.

Each serving: About 249 calories, 4g protein, 36g carbohydrate, 13g total fat (5g saturated), 6mg cholesterol, 10mg sodium.

BROWNIE PUDDING CAKE

....

Two desserts for the price of one! The batter separates during baking into a fudgy brownie with a silky smooth chocolate pudding base.

Prep: 20 minutes   Bake: 30 minutes

- 2 teaspoons instant-coffee powder (optional)
- 2 tablespoons plus 1¾ cups boiling water
- 1 cup all-purpose flour
- ¾ cup unsweetened cocoa
- ½ cup granulated sugar
- 2 teaspoons baking powder
- ¼ teaspoon salt
- ½ cup milk
- 4 tablespoons butter or margarine, melted
- 1 teaspoon vanilla extract
- ½ cup packed brown sugar
  whipped cream or vanilla ice cream (optional)

1. Preheat oven to 350°F. In cup, dissolve coffee powder in 2 tablespoons boiling water, if using.

2. In large bowl, combine flour, ½ cup cocoa, granulated sugar, baking powder, and salt. In 2-cup measuring cup, combine milk, melted butter, vanilla, and coffee mixture, if using. With wooden spoon, stir milk mixture into flour mixture until just blended. Pour into ungreased 8-inch square baking dish.

3. In small bowl, thoroughly combine brown sugar and remaining ¼ cup cocoa; sprinkle evenly over batter. Carefully pour remaining 1¾ cups boiling water evenly over mixture in baking dish; do not stir.

4. Bake 30 minutes (batter will separate into cake and pudding layers). Cool in pan on wire rack 10 minutes. Serve hot with whipped cream, if you like. Makes 8 servings.

Each serving: About 238 calories, 4g protein, 43g carbohydrate, 7g total fat (5g saturated), 18mg cholesterol, 267mg sodium.

Brownie Pudding Cake

LEMON PUDDING CAKE

....

A tried-and-true dessert that is just plain wonderful served from the baking dish while steaming hot. Try the orange version too.

Prep: 20 minutes   Bake: 40 minutes

3 lemons

¾ cup sugar

¼ cup all-purpose flour

3 large eggs, separated

1 cup milk

4 tablespoons butter or margarine, melted

⅛ teaspoon salt

1. Preheat oven to 350°F. Grease 8-inch square baking dish. From lemons, grate 1 tablespoon peel and squeeze ⅓ cup juice. In large bowl, combine sugar and flour. With wire whisk, beat in egg yolks, milk, melted butter, and lemon peel and juice.

2. In small bowl, with mixer at high speed, beat egg whites and salt until soft peaks form when beaters are lifted. With rubber spatula, gently fold one-third of beaten egg whites into lemon mixture. Fold in remaining whites, just until blended. Pour batter into prepared baking dish.

3. Set baking dish in medium roasting pan; place on rack in oven. Carefully pour enough *very hot water* into roasting pan to come halfway up sides of baking dish. Bake until top is golden and set, about 40 minutes (batter will separate into cake and pudding layers). Cool in pan on wire rack 10 minutes. Serve hot. Makes 6 servings.

Each serving: About 256 calories, 5g protein, 32g carbohydrate, 12g total fat (7g saturated), 133mg cholesterol, 179mg sodium.

ORANGE PUDDING CAKE

Prepare as directed above but in Step 1 use **¼ cup fresh lemon juice, ¼ cup fresh orange juice,** and **2 teaspoons freshly grated orange peel.**

RICE PUDDING

....

Cooking the rice very slowly in lots of milk makes this pudding especially creamy. Serve with fresh berries.

Prep: 10 minutes   Cook: 1 hour 15 minutes

4 cups milk

½ cup regular long-grain rice

½ cup sugar

¼ teaspoon salt

1 large egg

1 teaspoon vanilla extract

1. In heavy 4-quart saucepan, combine milk, rice, sugar, and salt; heat to boiling over medium-high heat stirring frequently. Reduce heat; cover and simmer mixture, stirring occasionally, until rice is very tender, about 1 hour.

2. In small bowl, with fork, lightly beat egg; stir in ½ cup hot rice mixture. Slowly pour egg mixture back into rice mixture, stirring rapidly to prevent curdling. Cook, stirring constantly, until rice mixture has thickened, about 5 minutes (do not boil, or mixture will curdle). Remove from heat; stir in vanilla. Serve warm, or spoon into medium bowl and refrigerate until well chilled, about 3 hours. Makes 4 cups or 6 servings.

Each serving: About 234 calories, 7g protein, 37g carbohydrate, 6g total fat (4g saturated), 58mg cholesterol, 187mg sodium.

RICH RICE PUDDING

Prepare as directed above and refrigerate. In small bowl, with mixer at medium speed, beat **½ cup heavy or whipping cream** until soft peaks form. With rubber spatula, gently fold into rice pudding. Refrigerate until ready to serve, up to 4 hours. Makes 8 servings.

STICKY TOFFEE PUDDING

Long a British holiday tradition, this pudding, with its sticky caramel topping, is outstanding whatever the occasion. Serve it warm with whipped cream.

**Prep: 20 minutes plus standing and cooling
Bake/Broil: 31 minutes**

- 1 cup chopped pitted dates
- 1 teaspoon baking soda
- 1½ cups boiling water
- 10 tablespoons butter or margarine (1¼ sticks), softened
- 1 cup granulated sugar
- 1 large egg
- 1 teaspoon vanilla extract
- 2 cups all-purpose flour
- 1 teaspoon baking powder
- 1 cup packed brown sugar
- ¼ cup heavy or whipping cream
  whipped cream (optional)

1. Preheat oven to 350°F. Grease 13" by 9" baking pan. In medium bowl, combine dates, baking soda, and boiling water; let stand 15 minutes.

2. In large bowl, with mixer at medium speed, beat 6 tablespoons butter until creamy. Beat in granulated sugar until light and fluffy. Add egg and vanilla; beat until blended. Reduce speed to low; add flour and baking powder, beating to combine. Add date mixture and beat until well combined (batter will be very thin). Pour batter into prepared pan. Bake until golden and toothpick inserted in center of pudding comes out clean, about 30 minutes.

3. Meanwhile, in heavy 2-quart saucepan, combine brown sugar, cream, and remaining 4 tablespoons butter; heat to boiling over medium-high heat, stirring frequently. Boil 1 minute; remove saucepan from heat.

4. Turn oven control to broil. Spread brown-sugar mixture evenly over top of hot pudding. Broil at position closest to heat source until bubbling, about 30 seconds. Cool in pan on wire rack 15 minutes. Serve warm with whipped cream, if you like. Makes 12 servings.

Each serving: About 362 calories, 3g protein, 62g carbohydrate, 12g total fat (7g saturated), 50mg cholesterol, 259mg sodium.

VANILLA PASTRY CREAM

This versatile cream is used to fill many classic desserts, such as Cream Puffs (opposite). Be sure to cook the cream for the full two minutes, or it may not set up.

Prep: 5 minutes plus chilling   Cook: 10 minutes

- 2¼ cups milk
- 4 large egg yolks
- ⅔ cup sugar
- ¼ cup all-purpose flour
- ¼ cup cornstarch
- 1 tablespoon vanilla extract

1. In heavy 3-quart saucepan, heat 2 cups milk over medium-high heat until bubbles form around edge. Meanwhile, in large bowl, with wire whisk, beat egg yolks, remaining ¼ cup milk, and sugar until combined; whisk in flour and cornstarch until blended. Gradually whisk hot milk into egg-yolk mixture.

2. Return milk mixture to saucepan; cook over medium-high heat, whisking constantly, until mixture has thickened and boils. Reduce heat to low and cook, stirring, with wooden spoon, 2 minutes.

3. Remove from heat and stir in vanilla. Pour pastry cream into shallow dish. Press plastic wrap onto surface of pastry cream. Refrigerate at least 2 hours or up to overnight. Makes 2¾ cups.

Each tablespoon: About 31 calories, 1g protein, 5g carbohydrate, 1g total fat (0g saturated), 21mg cholesterol, 7mg sodium.

CHOCOLATE PASTRY CREAM

Prepare pastry cream as directed above but add **3 squares (3 ounces) semisweet chocolate** and **1 square (1 ounce) unsweetened chocolate,** chopped and melted, with vanilla. Makes about 3 cups.

Each tablespoon: About 44 calories, 1g protein, 3g carbohydrate, 3g total fat (2g saturated), 23mg cholesterol, 37mg sodium.

CHOUX PASTRY

This light, airy pastry is the basis for many glorious desserts, such as éclairs and cream puffs. Use the batter while it is still warm to get the highest puff possible.

Prep: 10 minutes   Cook: 5 minutes

½ cup butter or margarine (1 stick), cut into pieces
1   cup water
¼ teaspoon salt
1   cup all-purpose flour
4   large eggs

In 3-quart saucepan, combine butter, water, and salt; heat over medium-high heat until butter melts and mixture boils. Remove from heat. Add flour all at once and, with wooden spoon, vigorously stir until mixture leaves side of pan and forms a ball. Add eggs to flour mixture, one at a time, beating well after each addition, until mixture is smooth and satiny. Shape and bake warm dough as directed in following recipes.

One recipe: About 1,566 calories, 39g protein, 98g carbohydrate, 113g total fat (64g saturated), 1,098mg cholesterol, 1,763mg sodium.

CREAM PUFFS

If you like, fill these cream puffs with Vanilla Pastry Cream (opposite) instead of vanilla ice cream.

**Prep: 30 minutes plus standing and cooling
Bake: 40 minutes**

Choux Pastry (left)
Hot Fudge Sauce (page 510)
1   quart vanilla ice cream

1. Preheat oven to 400°F. Grease and flour large cookie sheet. Prepare Choux Pastry. Drop slightly rounded ¼ cups batter in 8 large mounds, 3 inches apart, on prepared cookie sheet. With moistened finger, gently smooth tops.

2. Bake until golden, 40 to 45 minutes. Remove puffs from oven; with tip of knife, make small slit in side of each puff to release steam. Turn off oven. Return puffs to oven and let stand 10 minutes. Transfer puffs to wire rack to cool completely. With serrated knife, cut each cooled puff horizontally in half; remove and discard any moist dough inside puffs.

3. Prepare Hot Fudge Sauce. To serve, place ½-cup scoop vanilla ice cream in bottom half of each cream puff; replace tops. Spoon Hot Fudge Sauce over puffs. Makes 8 servings.

Each serving: About 525 calories, 9g protein, 51g carbohydrate, 34g total fat (20g saturated), 202mg cholesterol, 339mg sodium.

CHOUX PASTRY

Choux pastry dough is unique because it is cooked twice: first on the stove and then in the oven. (Its original name was *chaud,* or "hot pastry," which eventually became *choux.*) The dough makes a light, airy, hollow pastry that is perfect for filling with ice cream, whipped cream, or pastry cream.

• When cooking the dough, be sure the butter is completely melted by the time the water comes to a full boil. If too much water evaporates, the dough will be dry.

• For the best results, use room-temperature eggs. Add them to the batter, one at a time, mixing well after each addition.

• For the highest puff, always shape and bake choux pastry dough while it is still warm.

• Bake the pastries until golden brown: Pale, undercooked pastries collapse when removed from the oven.

• Choux dough creates a lot of steam when baked: This steam needs to be released or the pastries will become soggy. As soon as the pastries are removed from the oven, use the tip of a small knife to cut a slit into the side of each one.

• Unfilled choux dough pastries can be frozen in heavy-duty zip-tight plastic bags for up to one month; simply recrisp in a 400°F oven for a few minutes before serving.

PRALINE CREAM PUFF WREATH

....

Also known as Paris-Brest (named in honor of the bicycle race from Paris to the city of Brest in Brittany and back), this is cream-puff dough baked in the shape of a bicycle wheel. It makes a festive dessert at Christmas.

Prep: 50 minutes plus chilling and cooling
Bake: 55 minutes

- 2 cups milk
- 3 large egg yolks
- ²/₃ cup granulated sugar
- 3 tablespoons cornstarch
- 2 teaspoons vanilla extract
   Choux Pastry (page 613)
- ¼ cup water
- ⅓ cup sliced natural almonds, toasted
- 1 cup heavy or whipping cream
- 1 tablespoon confectioners' sugar, plus
   additional for dusting

1. Prepare pastry cream: In heavy 3-quart saucepan, heat milk over medium-high heat until bubbles form around edge. Meanwhile, in medium bowl, with wire whisk, beat egg yolks, ⅓ cup granulated sugar, and cornstarch until well blended. Gradually whisk about half of hot milk into egg-yolk mixture. Whisk egg mixture into milk in saucepan and cook over medium heat, whisking constantly, until mixture has thickened and boils. Reduce heat to low and cook, stirring with a wooden spoon, 2 minutes.

2. Remove saucepan from heat; stir in vanilla. Pour pastry cream into medium bowl; press plastic wrap onto surface. Refrigerate until well chilled, 2 hours or up to overnight.

3. Meanwhile, prepare wreath: Preheat oven to 425°F. Grease and flour large cookie sheet. Using 8-inch cake pan or plate as guide, with toothpick, trace circle in flour on prepared cookie sheet. Prepare Choux Pastry.

4. Spoon dough into pastry bag fitted with ½-inch plain tip. Using tracing as guide, pipe dough in 1-inch-thick ring just inside circle. Pipe second ring outside of first, making sure dough rings touch. With remaining dough, pipe third ring on top of center seam of first two rings. With moistened finger, gently smooth dough rings where ends meet.

5. Bake wreath 20 minutes. Turn oven control to 375°F and bake until golden, about 25 minutes longer. Remove wreath from oven; with tip of knife, make several small slits in sides to release steam. Bake 10 minutes longer. Transfer wreath to wire rack and cool completely.

6. While wreath is baking, prepare almond praline: Lightly grease cookie sheet. In heavy 1-quart saucepan, combine remaining ⅓ cup granulated sugar and water; heat to boiling over medium-high heat, swirling pan occasionally, until sugar has dissolved. Boil mixture, without stirring, until amber in color, 5 to 7 minutes. Remove from heat and stir in almonds. Stir mixture over low heat just until it reliquifies. Immediately pour praline mixture onto prepared cookie sheet; spread with back of spoon to ½-inch thickness. Let praline stand on cookie sheet on wire rack until completely cool, about 10 minutes.

7. Break praline into small pieces. In food processor with knife blade attached, process praline to fine powder. With rubber spatula, gently fold praline into chilled pastry cream.

8. In small bowl, with mixer at medium speed, beat heavy cream and 1 tablespoon confectioners' sugar just until stiff peaks form.

9. With long serrated knife, slice cooled wreath horizontally in half; remove and discard moist dough from inside. Spoon or pipe pastry cream into bottom of wreath; top with whipped cream. Replace top of wreath. Refrigerate up to 2 hours if not serving right away. To serve, dust with confectioners' sugar. Makes 12 servings.

Each serving: About 326 calories, 7g protein, 26g carbohydrate, 22g total fat (11g saturated), 178mg cholesterol, 177mg sodium.

CLASSIC STRAWBERRY SHORTCAKES

·····································

It just wouldn't be summer without this classic dessert.

**Prep: 30 minutes plus cooling
Bake: about 15 minutes**

Shortcake Biscuits

2½ cups all-purpose flour
  1 tablespoon baking powder
  ½ teaspoon baking soda
  ½ teaspoon salt
  ⅓ cup plus 1 tablespoon sugar
  ½ cup (1 stick) cold butter or margarine,
     cut into pieces
  1 large egg, separated
  1 cup buttermilk

Sugared Strawberries

2½ pounds strawberries (8 cups)
  2 tablespoons sugar
  1 tablespoon water

Whipped Cream

  1 cup heavy or whipping cream
  2 tablespoons sugar
  1 teaspoon vanilla extract

Classic Strawberry Shortcake

1. Preheat oven to 425°F. Prepare shortcakes: In large bowl, combine flour, baking powder, baking soda, salt, and ⅓ cup sugar. Cut in butter.

2. In small bowl, with fork, beat egg yolk with buttermilk; stir into flour mixture just until mixture forms soft dough that leaves side of bowl.

3. On floured surface, with floured hands, knead dough 6 to 8 times to combine; pat dough to ¾-inch thickness.

4. Cut out shortcakes; place 1 inch apart on ungreased large cookie sheet. Press trimmings together; cut to make 8 biscuits in all.

5. In another small bowl, with fork, lightly beat egg white; brush on shortcakes. Sprinkle with remaining 1 tablespoon sugar. Bake 15 to

20 minutes or until golden. Cool on wire rack.

6. Hull strawberries, then slice. In large bowl, stir strawberries, sugar, and water. Let stand 15 minutes or refrigerate up to 4 hours.

7. Prepare whipped cream: In medium bowl, with mixer at medium speed, beat cream, sugar, and vanilla until stiff peaks form.

8. Split each shortcake horizontally. Place bottom halves on 8 dessert plates. Layer berries and cream over shortcake bottoms; replace tops. Dollop with cream and berries.

Each serving: 480 calories, 7g protein, 58g carbohydrate, 25g total fat (15g saturated), 4g fiber, 102mg cholesterol, 550mg sodium.

MULTIGRAIN SUMMER SHORTCAKES

....

Thanks to whole-wheat flour and rolled oats, this old-time classic is now diet-friendlier (and still delicious). Also boosting the health factor: swapping whipped cream for a yummy, just-as-satisfying combo of cream cheese and yogurt.

Prep: 20 minutes plus cooling   Bake: 12 minutes

Shortcakes
- ½ cup old-fashioned oats
- 1 cup all-purpose flour
- ½ cup whole-wheat flour
- ¼ cup packed light brown sugar
- 2 teaspoons baking powder
- ½ teaspoon salt
- ¼ teaspoon baking soda
- ¾ cup low-fat buttermilk
- 3 tablespoons canola oil
- 1 large egg

Berries
- 1 pound strawberries, hulled, each cut into quarters
- 1 cup blackberries
- 1 cup blueberries
- 1 cup raspberries
- 2 tablespoons granulated sugar
- 1 tablespoon fresh lime juice

Filling
- 4 ounces reduced-fat cream cheese (Neufchâtel), softened
- ⅓ cup confectioners' sugar
- 1 cup non-fat plain yogurt
- ½ teaspoon grated fresh lime peel

1. Prepare shortcakes: Preheat oven to 425°F. Spray large cookie sheet with nonstick cooking spray. Place oats in blender and blend until finely ground.

2. In large bowl, with wire whisk, combine ground oats, all-purpose flour, whole-wheat flour, brown sugar, baking powder, salt, and baking soda until blended. Break up lumps of brown sugar with fingers if necessary.

3. In small bowl, with wire whisk, mix buttermilk, oil, and egg until well blended. Add buttermilk mixture to oat mixture and stir just until blended.

4. Spoon dough by ¼ cups onto prepared cookie sheet, 3 inches apart, making 8 mounds. Bake 12 to 14 minutes, or until firm when pressed. Transfer shortcakes to wire racks to cool.

5. Meanwhile, prepare berries: In medium bowl, combine all berries, granulated sugar, and lime juice. (Makes 6 cups.) Set berries aside.

6. Prepare filling: In another medium bowl, with mixer at medium speed, combine cream cheese, confectioners' sugar, and ½ cup yogurt. With rubber spatula, gently fold in lime peel and remaining yogurt.

7. To serve, split shortcakes in half horizontally. Place a bottom half on each of 8 dessert plates. Spoon on filling and berries, then add shortcake top. Makes 8 servings.

Each serving: About 320 calories, 9g protein, 50g carbohydrate, 10g total fat (3g saturated), 6g fiber, 39mg cholesterol, 400mg sodium.

Tip: As delicious as these shortcakes are with berries, they're just as luscious with a blend of your favorite stone fruits. You'll need about 5 cups of chopped fruit.

Multigrain Summer Shortcake

NECTARINE AND CHERRY CRISP

••••••••••••••••••••••••••••

Two favorite summertime fruits become the perfect foil for the cookie-like topping.

Prep: 30 minutes
Bake: 1 hour to 1 hour 15 minutes

Nectarine and Cherry Filling

- ½ cup granulated sugar
- 3 tablespoons cornstarch
- 10 ripe medium nectarines (3 pounds), each cut in half, pitted, and cut into 6 wedges
- 1½ pounds dark sweet cherries, pitted
- 2 tablespoons fresh lemon juice
- 2 tablespoons cold butter or margarine, cut into small pieces

Oatmeal Topping

- 6 tablespoons butter or margarine, softened
- ⅔ cup packed brown sugar
- 1 large egg
- 2 teaspoons vanilla extract
- 1½ cups old-fashioned oats, uncooked
- ¾ cup all-purpose flour
- ¼ teaspoon baking soda
- ¼ teaspoon salt

1. Preheat oven to 375°F. Prepare filling: In large bowl, combine granulated sugar and cornstarch. Add nectarines, cherries, and lemon juice; toss until coated.

2. Spoon mixture into 13" by 9" baking dish; dot with butter. Place dish on foil-lined cookie sheet to catch any overflow during baking. Cover with foil; bake until mixture is gently bubbling, 40 to 50 minutes.

3. Meanwhile, prepare topping: In large bowl, with mixer at medium-high speed, beat butter and brown sugar until smooth. Add egg and vanilla; beat until fluffy. With spoon, stir in oats, flour, baking soda, and salt until mixed.

4. Drop topping by scant ¼ cups over bubbling fruit. Bake, uncovered, until topping has browned, 20 to 25 minutes. Cool slightly on wire rack to serve warm. Makes 12 servings.

Each serving: About 317 calories, 5g protein, 56g carbohydrate, 10g total fat (5g saturated), 38mg cholesterol, 162mg sodium.

FIGS IN PHYLLO

••••••••••••••••••••••••••••

These flaky-crisp crust cups are almost foolproof. All you do is drape ready-made sheets of phyllo around ramekins. Finish off this good-for-you Greek treat with yogurt, honey, and sliced figs.

Prep: 20 minutes plus cooling   Bake: 12 minutes

- 8 sheets (16" by 12" each) fresh or frozen (thawed) phyllo dough
- 3 tablespoons melted butter or margarine
- 1⅓ cups non-fat Greek yogurt
- 4 teaspoons honey
- 12 fresh ripe Calimyrna figs, each cut into quarters fresh mint sprigs for garnish

1. Preheat oven to 375°F.

2. On work surface, place 1 sheet phyllo; lightly brush with some butter. Place second phyllo sheet on top; lightly brush with some butter. Cut layered phyllo crosswise in half into two rectangles. Place one rectangle over the other, rotating it so that points of second rectangle are angled slightly away from points of first. Set 6-ounce custard cup or ramekin, right side up, in center of phyllo stack, and gather phyllo up around custard cup to form phyllo shell. (Make sure not to fold any phyllo over edge of custard cup.) Place phyllo shell with cup in 15½" by 10½" jelly-roll pan. Repeat with remaining phyllo sheets and butter to make 4 shells in all.

3. Bake phyllo shells 12 to 15 minutes or until golden brown. Cool in pan on wire rack 15 minutes; remove cups from shells. Cool shells completely on wire rack, about 45 minutes.

4. To serve, place shells on 4 dessert plates. Fill each shell with ⅓ cup yogurt, drizzle with 1 teaspoon honey, and top with quartered figs. Garnish with mint. Makes 4 servings.

Each serving: About 345 calories, 11g protein, 53g carbohydrate, 11g total fat (2g saturated), 6g fiber, 3mg cholesterol, 320mg sodium.

Tip: Phyllo dough can dry out and become brittle quickly. To keep dough moist, cover unused portion with a damp paper towel while working.

PEACH COBBLER

....

A true summer treat, bursting with the flavor of ripe peaches and topped with lemon-scented biscuits. Serve with rich vanilla ice cream or softly whipped cream.

Prep: 45 minutes   Bake: 45 minutes

Peach Filling

- 6 pounds ripe medium peaches (16 to 18), peeled, pitted, and sliced (13 cups)
- ¼ cup fresh lemon juice
- ⅔ cup granulated sugar
- ½ cup packed brown sugar
- ¼ cup cornstarch

Lemon Biscuits

- 2 cups all-purpose flour
- ½ cup plus 1 teaspoon granulated sugar
- 2½ teaspoons baking powder
- ¼ teaspoon salt
- 1 teaspoon freshly grated lemon peel
- 4 tablespoons cold butter or margarine, cut into pieces
- ⅔ cup plus 1 tablespoon half-and-half or light cream

1. Prepare filling: Preheat oven to 425°F. In nonreactive 8-quart saucepot, toss peaches with lemon juice; add granulated and brown sugars and cornstarch, tossing to coat. Heat over medium heat, stirring occasionally, until bubbling; boil 1 minute. Spoon hot peach mixture into 13" by 9" baking dish. Place baking dish on foil-lined cookie sheet to catch any overflow during baking. Bake 10 minutes.

2. Meanwhile, prepare biscuits: In medium bowl, combine flour, ½ cup granulated sugar, baking powder, salt, and lemon peel. With pastry blender or two knives used scissor-fashion, cut in butter until mixture resembles coarse crumbs. Stir in ⅔ cup half-and-half just until mixture forms soft dough that leaves side of bowl.

3. Turn dough onto lightly floured surface. With lightly floured hands, pat into 10" by 6" rectangle. With floured knife, cut rectangle lengthwise in half, then cut each half crosswise into 6 pieces.

4. Remove baking dish from oven. Arrange biscuits on top of fruit. Brush biscuits with remaining 1 tablespoon half-and-half and sprinkle with remaining 1 teaspoon granulated sugar. Return cobbler to oven and bake until filling is hot and bubbling and biscuits are golden, about 35 minutes longer. To serve warm, cool cobbler on wire rack about 1 hour. Makes 12 servings.

Each serving: About 331 calories, 4g protein, 69g carbohydrate, 6g total fat (3g saturated), 16mg cholesterol, 199mg sodium.

PLUM KUCHEN

....

The word kuchen, *which is German for "cake," is used to describe any number of fruit-topped or custard-filled desserts that have a yeast-batter or cake-batter base.*

Prep: 30 minutes   Bake: 35 minutes

- 5 large plums or 10 prune plums
- 1 cup all-purpose flour
- 1 teaspoon baking powder
- ¼ teaspoon salt
- 6 tablespoons butter, softened (do not use margarine)
- ⅔ cup plus 2 tablespoons sugar
- 2 large eggs
- ½ teaspoon vanilla extract
- ½ teaspoon ground cinnamon

1. Cut large plums into quarters and remove pits. If using prune plums, cut in half and remove pits. Preheat oven to 350°F. Grease a 9-inch square baking pan.

2. Whisk flour, baking powder, and salt in a small bowl. In large bowl, with electric mixer on medium speed, beat butter and ⅔ cup sugar until creamy, about 2 minutes. Beat in eggs one at a time until well blended. Beat in vanilla. With mixer on low speed, beat in flour mixture just until blended.

3. Spoon batter into prepared pan and spread evenly. Arrange plums, skin side down on batter. Combine remaining 2 tablespoons sugar and cinnamon in a small bowl; sprinkle over plums. Bake until toothpick inserted in center comes out clean, 35 to 40 minutes. Cool in pan on wire rack and serve warm or room temperature. Makes 8 servings.

Each serving: About 261 calories, 4g protein, 38g carbohydrate, 11g total fat (6g saturated), 78mg cholesterol, 231mg sodium.

LEMON-BLUSH NAPOLEONS

....

As luscious as bakery-bought Napoleons, these slimmed-down versions require zero dough diligence—the wafer-light layers are baked wonton wrappers.

Prep: 30 minutes, plus cooling   Bake: 12 minutes

- 24 (3¼" by 3") wonton wrappers (about half 12-ounce package)
- 2 tablespoons butter or margarine, melted
- 4 teaspoons coarse sanding sugar
- 2½ cups non-fat Greek yogurt
- ¾ cup lemon curd
- 6 cups raspberries (1½ pounds) confectioners' sugar for dusting

1. Preheat oven to 325°F. Grease two cookie sheets. Place 12 wonton wrappers in one layer on sheet of waxed paper. With pastry brush, lightly brush with melted butter and sprinkle 1 teaspoon sanding sugar over all. Turn wontons over; lightly brush with butter and sprinkle with 1 teaspoon sanding sugar. Place wonton wrappers on one cookie sheet between oven racks. Repeat with remaining wontons, butter, and sanding sugar.

2. Bake wonton wrappers 12 to 14 minutes or until golden on both sides, rotating cookie sheets between oven racks halfway through baking. With spatula, transfer to wire racks to cool. If not using baked wontons right away, store in tightly sealed container at room temperature up to 3 days.

3. In medium bowl, stir yogurt and lemon curd until blended.

4. To serve, arrange 8 baked wontons on 8 dessert plates (or place all 8 on large platter); spread 3 tablespoons of yogurt mixture on each. Arrange 9 raspberries per wonton on yogurt mixture. Repeat layering with 8 more wontons, yogurt mixture, and raspberries. Place remaining 8 wontons on top. Dust with confectioners' sugar to serve. Makes 8 servings.

Each serving: About 210 calories, 7g protein, 40g carbohydrate, 5g total fat (1g saturated), 6g fiber, 4mg cholesterol, 125mg sodium.

Tip: Sanding sugar can be found in the baking aisle of some supermarkets, or in specialty stores where cake-decorating supplies are sold.

RED FRUIT NAPOLEONS

(Pictured on page 596)

....

Store-bought butter-wafer cookies make preparing this tempting dessert easy.

**Prep: 15 minutes plus standing
Microwave: 1½ minutes**

- 1 pound strawberries
- 1 cup raspberries
- 2 tablespoons granulated sugar
- 3 ounces white chocolate, chopped
- ½ cup heavy or whipping cream
- 3 tablespoons sour cream
- 24 very thin oval waffle-shaped butter wafer cookies confectioners' sugar (optional)

1. Reserve 8 small strawberries for garnish. Hull and slice remaining strawberries. In medium bowl, combine sliced strawberries, raspberries, and granulated sugar. Let stand 15 minutes, stirring occasionally to allow juices to run.

2. Meanwhile, in microwave-safe medium bowl, heat chocolate in microwave oven on High 1½ minutes; stir until melted and smooth. Cool slightly.

3. In small bowl, with mixer at medium speed, beat heavy cream and sour cream until stiff peaks form when beaters are lifted. With rubber spatula, fold mixture into white chocolate just until combined.

4. To serve, place 1 cookie on each of 8 dessert plates; top with half of cream and fruit mixtures. Repeat layering. Top with remaining cookies; sprinkle with confectioners' sugar, if you like. Garnish with strawberries. Makes 8 servings.

Each serving: About 380 calories, 5g protein, 42g carbohydrate, 22g total fat (15g saturated), 2g fiber, 62mg cholesterol, 185mg sodium.

Fire-Roasted Nectarines

FIRE-ROASTED NECTARINES
....

Grilling intensifies the fruit's flavors, creating a sweet-and-smoky succulence. Garnish with a simple salsa of blueberries, strawberries, and raspberries.

Prep: 20 minutes   Grill: 5 minutes

- 2 cups strawberries (8 to 10 ounces), hulled and coarsely chopped
- ½ cup raspberries
- ⅓ cup blueberries
- 2 tablespoons sugar
- 2 teaspoons finely chopped crystallized ginger
- 1 teaspoon fresh lemon juice
  pinch salt
- 4 ripe medium nectarines, each cut in half and pitted

1. Prepare salsa: In medium bowl, mix strawberries, raspberries, blueberries, sugar, ginger, lemon juice, and salt. Set aside. (Makes 2 cups.)

2. Prepare outdoor grill for direct grilling on medium. Spray cut sides of nectarine halves with nonstick cooking spray. Place nectarine halves on hot grill grate and cook 5 to 6 minutes or until lightly charred and tender, turning over once.

3. To serve, in each of 4 dessert bowls, place 2 nectarine halves, cut sides up, and top with berry salsa. Makes 4 servings.

Each serving: About 130 calories, 2g protein, 32g carbohydrate, 1g total fat (0g saturated), 5g fiber, 0mg cholesterol, 35mg sodium.

Tip: No access to an outdoor grill? Nectarines can be cooked indoors on a ridged grill pan. Spray the pan with nonstick cooking spray and heat on medium until hot, then grill nectarines as directed.

APPLE-CALVADOS CREPES

....

These crepes can be filled with almost any seasonal fruit. If you can't find Calvados, French apple brandy, use applejack. If you prefer, you can substitute apple juice.

Prep: 50 minutes plus chilling   Bake: 5 minutes

12 Basic Crepes (page 237)

Apple Filling

5 tablespoons butter or margarine

3 pounds Golden Delicious apples (6 large), peeled, cored, and finely chopped

½ cup plus 1 tablespoon sugar

¼ cup Calvados or applejack brandy

1. Prepare Basic Crepes. Preheat oven to 400°F. To make filling, in 12-inch skillet, melt 4 tablespoons butter over medium-high heat. Stir in apples and ½ cup sugar; cover and cook until apples are soft, about 10 minutes. Remove cover and cook, stirring occasionally, until apples begin to caramelize, about 10 minutes. Stir in Calvados and remove from heat.

2. Spread scant ¼ cup apple filling down center of each crepe and roll up jelly-roll fashion. Arrange rolled crepes in single layer, seam side down, in shallow 3½- to 4-quart baking dish. Dot with remaining 1 tablespoon butter and sprinkle with remaining 1 tablespoon sugar. Bake until heated through, about 5 minutes. Makes 6 servings.

Each serving: About 488 calories, 7g protein, 64g carbohydrate, 22g total fat (13g saturated), 161mg cholesterol, 430mg sodium.

PLUM FILLING

In 12-inch skillet, melt 3 tablespoons butter or margarine over medium-high heat. Add **2½ pounds ripe plums (10 large),** quartered and pitted, **⅔ cup granulated sugar,** and **pinch ground cloves.** Cook, stirring occasionally, until plums are tender, 15 to 20 minutes. Fill crepes and bake as directed in Step 2, above

MIXED BERRY FILLING

In medium bowl, toss **1½ cups hulled and halved strawberries, 1½ cups blueberries, 1½ cups raspberries,** and **⅔ cup granulated sugar.** Fill crepes and bake as directed in Step 2 above.

BANANA FILLING

In medium bowl, toss **2 large ripe bananas, sliced, with ¼ cup packed brown sugar.** Fill crepes and bake as directed in Step 2 (left).

AUTUMN FRUIT COMPOTE

....

Poach a combination of dried fruits and fresh apples with just a touch of citrus and cinnamon for a satisfying compote. Serve after a rich entrée, such as pork or roast goose.

Prep: 20 minutes plus chilling   Cook: 25 minutes

1 orange

1 lemon

4 medium Golden Delicious or Jonagold apples, each peeled, cored, and cut into 16 wedges

1 package (8 ounces) mixed dried fruit (with dried plums)

1 cup dried Calimyrna figs (6 ounces)

½ cup sugar

1 cinnamon stick (3 inches)

3 cups water

1. From orange and lemon, with vegetable peeler, remove peel in 1-inch-wide strips. From lemon, squeeze 2 tablespoons juice (reserve orange for another use).

2. In nonreactive 4-quart saucepan, combine apples, mixed dried fruit, figs, orange and lemon peels, lemon juice, sugar, cinnamon stick, and water; heat to boiling over high heat, stirring frequently. Reduce heat; cover and simmer, stirring occasionally, until apples are tender, 15 to 20 minutes.

3. Pour fruit mixture into serving bowl; cover and refrigerate at least 4 hours to blend flavors. Serve chilled. Store in refrigerator up to 4 days. Makes 8 servings.

Each serving: About 211 calories, 1g protein, 55g carbohydrate, 1g total fat (0g saturated), 0mg cholesterol, 8mg sodium.

FROZEN DESSERTS

5-MINUTE FROZEN PEACH YOGURT

....

A food processor makes quick work of this dessert. Try it with strawberries, blueberries, or your favorite combination of flavorful frozen fruits.

Prep: 15 minutes plus standing

- 1 bag (20 ounces) frozen unsweetened peach slices
- 1 container (8 ounces) plain low-fat yogurt
- 1 cup confectioners' sugar
- 1 tablespoon fresh lemon juice
- ⅛ teaspoon almond extract

1. Let frozen peaches stand at room temperature 10 minutes. In food processor with knife blade attached, process peaches until fruit resembles finely shaved ice, occasionally scraping down side with rubber spatula.

2. With processor running, add yogurt, confectioners' sugar, lemon juice, and almond extract; process until mixture is smooth and creamy, occasionally scraping down side. Serve immediately. Makes about 4 cups or 8 servings.

Each serving: About 107 calories, 2g protein, 25g carbohydrate, 1g total fat (0g saturated), 2mg cholesterol, 20mg sodium.

....

This granita is a Neapolitan tradition. If you prefer, use decaffeinated espresso.

Prep: 10 minutes plus cooling and freezing

- ⅔ cup sugar
- 2 cups hot espresso coffee
  unsweetened whipped cream (optional)

In medium bowl, stir sugar and espresso until sugar has completely dissolved. Pour into 9-inch square metal baking pan; cool. Cover, freeze, and scrape as directed for granitas (page 625). Serve granita with whipped cream, if you like. Makes about 5 cups or 10 servings.

Each serving: About 53 calories, 0g protein, 14g carbohydrate, 0g total fat (0g saturated), 0mg cholesterol, 1mg sodium.

Tip: If you do not have an espresso coffeemaker, use 3 cups water and 1⅓ cups ground espresso coffee in an automatic drip coffeemaker.

ICE CREAM AND OTHER FROZEN DESSERTS

ICE CREAM: Dairy-rich ice cream is one of life's sweet indulgences. Most are prepared with an egg-custard base, which gives ice cream its incomparable texture. These ice creams may also be called frozen custard, French ice cream, or gelato. Philadelphia-style ice cream, which doesn't contain egg yolks, has a slightly icy texture that emphasizes the flavor of the cream.

ICES: Made from sweetened fruit purees or juices, ices are beaten with a mixer after an initial freezing to incorporate air and produce a lighter texture, then frozen again until firm.

FROZEN YOGURT: Made from either low-fat or fat-free yogurt along with fruit or flavorings; it has the creaminess of ice cream but without all the fat.

SHERBET: A frozen combination of fruit juice (usually citrus), sugar, and milk, cream, or egg whites.

SORBET: Smooth-textured sorbet is usually made from a sweetened fruit puree with no dairy products.

GRANITA: Italian in origin, granita has the same ingredients as sorbet, but it is chilled in a (baking) pan and stirred frequently during freezing to achieve a granular, icy texture (*granita* comes from the Latin word for "grain").

WATERMELON GRANITA

Seedless watermelon makes this a cinch to prepare.

Prep: 15 minutes plus cooling and freezing
Cook: 5 minutes

- 1 cup sugar
- ³/₄ cup water
- 1 large piece (5¹/₂ pounds) seedless watermelon
- 2 tablespoons fresh lime juice

1. In 2-quart saucepan, combine sugar and water; heat to boiling over high heat, stirring until sugar has dissolved. Reduce heat to medium and cook 1 minute. Set saucepan in bowl of ice water until syrup is cool.

2. Meanwhile, remove rind from watermelon and cut into chunks. In blender or in food processor with knife blade attached, puree melon, in batches, until smooth. With spoon, press puree through sieve into medium bowl; discard fibers.

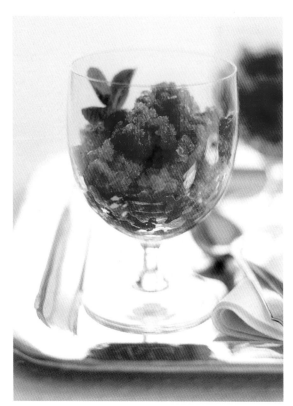

Bold Berry Granita

3. Stir sugar syrup and lime juice into puree; pour into 9-inch square metal baking pan. Cover, freeze, and scrape as directed for granitas (opposite). Makes about 9 cups or 18 servings.

Each serving: About 70 calories, 0g protein, 17g carbohydrate, 0g total fat (0g saturated), 0mg cholesterol, 2mg sodium.

BOLD BERRY GRANITA

Frosty, fruity, and fat-free, this heat-beating Italian ice doesn't require any special equipment.

Prep: 20 minutes plus cooling and freezing
Cook: 5 minutes

- 1 cup water
- ¹/₂ cup sugar
- 1 to 2 lemons
- 1 pound strawberries, hulled
- 1¹/₂ cups raspberries (about ³/₄ pint)
  fresh mint sprigs for garnish (optional)

1. Make sugar syrup: In 2-quart saucepan, heat water and sugar to boiling on high, stirring until sugar dissolves. Reduce heat to low and simmer, uncovered, 5 minutes. Set aside to cool slightly, about 5 minutes.

2. Meanwhile, from lemons, grate 2 teaspoons peel and squeeze ¹/₄ cup juice. In food processor with knife blade attached, blend strawberries and raspberries until pureed. With back of spoon, press puree through sieve into medium bowl; discard seeds.

3. Stir sugar syrup and lemon juice and peel into berry puree. Pour into 9-inch square metal baking pan.

4. Cover, freeze, and scrape as directed for granitas (opposite). Garnish with mint, if you like. Serve immediately. Makes about 5 cups or 10 servings.

Each serving: About 60 calories, 1g protein, 15g carbohydrate, 0g total fat, 2g fiber, 0mg cholesterol, 0mg sodium.

LEMON GRANITA

This simple, zesty granita has an invigorating tang.

**Prep: 10 minutes plus cooling and freezing
Cook: 10 minutes**

- 1 cup sugar
- 2 cups water
- 4 large lemons

1. In 2-quart saucepan, combine sugar and water; heat to boiling over high heat, stirring until sugar has dissolved. Reduce heat to medium and cook 5 minutes. Set saucepan in bowl of ice water until syrup is cool.

2. Meanwhile, from lemons, grate 2 teaspoons peel and squeeze ¾ cup juice.

3. Stir lemon peel and juice into sugar syrup; pour into 9-inch square metal baking pan. Cover, freeze, and scrape as directed for granitas (below). Makes about 4 cups or 8 servings.

Each serving: About 103 calories, 0g protein, 27g carbohydrate, 0g total fat (0g saturated), 0mg cholesterol, 1mg sodium.

GRANITAS

Cover and freeze the granita mixture until partially frozen, about 2 hours. Stir with a fork to break up the chunks. Cover and freeze until completely frozen, at least 3 hours or up to overnight. To serve, let the granita stand at room temperature until slightly softened, about 15 minutes. Use a metal spoon to scrape across the surface of the granita, transferring the ice shards to chilled dessert dishes or wine goblets without packing them.

TARTUFO

*These chocolate-coated ice-cream balls are intended to resemble truffles (*tartufo *means "truffle" in Italian).*

Prep: 30 minutes plus freezing

- 1 pint chocolate or vanilla ice cream
- 2 tablespoons brandy
- 6 maraschino cherries, stems removed
- 1 cup fine amaretti cookie crumbs (20 cookies)
- 1½ cups semisweet chocolate chips
- 4 tablespoons butter or margarine, cut into pieces
- 2 tablespoons light corn syrup

1. Place ice cream in refrigerator to soften slightly, about 30 minutes. Line small cookie sheet with waxed paper and place in freezer. In cup, pour brandy over cherries. Place amaretti crumbs on waxed paper.

2. Working quickly, with large ice-cream scoop (⅓ cup), scoop ball of ice cream. With ice cream still in scoop, gently press 1 cherry deep into center of ball; reshape ice cream around cherry. Release ice-cream ball on top of amaretti crumbs and roll to coat well. Place on prepared cookie sheet in freezer. Repeat to make 6 ice-cream balls. Freeze until firm, at least 1½ hours.

3. In medium bowl set over saucepan of simmering water, heat chocolate chips with butter and corn syrup, stirring occasionally, until chocolate and butter have melted and mixture is smooth. Remove pan from heat, but leave bowl in place to keep chocolate warm for easier coating.

4. Remove 1 ice-cream ball from freezer; place in slotted spoon and slip ice-cream ball into melted chocolate, turning quickly to coat thoroughly. Return to cookie sheet. Repeat with remaining ice-cream balls. Freeze until chocolate is firm, about 1 hour. If not serving right away, wrap in foil and freeze up to 1 day.

5. To serve, let tartufo stand at room temperature until slightly softened, about 10 minutes. Makes 6 servings.

Each serving: About 476 calories, 5g protein, 59g carbohydrate, 27g total fat (15g saturated), 36mg cholesterol, 133mg sodium.

TULIPES

....

For an elegant presentation at a dinner party or other special occasion, serve your favorite ice cream or sorbet in these delicate cookie shells.

Prep: 30 minutes   Bake: 5 minutes per batch

3 large egg whites
¾ cup confectioners' sugar
½ cup all-purpose flour
6 tablespoons butter, melted (do not use margarine)
½ teaspoon vanilla extract
¼ teaspoon salt
1 quart ice cream or sorbet

1. Preheat oven to 350°F. Grease large cookie sheet. In large bowl, with wire whisk, beat egg whites, confectioners' sugar, and flour until well blended. Beat in melted butter, vanilla, and salt.

2. Make 2 cookies by dropping batter by heaping tablespoons, 4 inches apart, on prepared cookie sheet. With narrow metal spatula, spread batter to form 4-inch rounds. Bake cookies until golden around edges, 5 to 7 minutes.

3. Place two 2-inch-diameter glasses upside down on work surface. With spatula, quickly lift 1 hot cookie and gently shape over bottom of glass. Shape second cookie. When cookies are cool, transfer to wire rack. (If cookies become too firm to shape, return them to cookie sheet and place in oven to soften slightly.)

4. Repeat Steps 2 and 3 with remaining batter. (Batter will become slightly thicker upon standing.) Store tulipes in single layer in airtight container at room temperature. To serve, place on dessert plates and fill with ice cream. Makes about 12 tulipes.

Each serving with ice cream: About 192 calories, 3g protein, 22g carbohydrate, 11g total fat (7g saturated), 35mg cholesterol, 155mg sodium.

SORBET-AND-CREAM CAKE

....

Here's a colorful dessert for a festive meal. Substitute raspberry and passion fruit sorbets, or your favorite flavors, for the strawberry and mango, if you prefer.

**Prep: 30 minutes plus freezing and chilling
Bake: 10 minutes**

1 cup vanilla wafer crumbs (30 cookies)
4 tablespoons butter or margarine, melted
½ teaspoon freshly grated lime peel
2 pints vanilla ice cream
1 pint strawberry sorbet
1 pint mango sorbet
1 pint lemon sorbet
1 ripe mango, peeled and sliced
   fresh raspberries

1. Preheat oven to 375°F. In 9" by 3" springform pan, with fork, stir wafer crumbs, melted butter, and lime peel until crumbs are evenly moistened. With hand, press mixture firmly onto bottom of pan. Bake crust 10 minutes. Place in freezer until well chilled, about 30 minutes.

2. Meanwhile, place 1 pint vanilla ice cream and strawberry, mango, and lemon sorbets in refrigerator to soften slightly, about 30 minutes.

3. Arrange alternating scoops of vanilla ice cream and strawberry, mango, and lemon sorbets over crust in two layers; with rubber spatula, press down to eliminate air pockets. Place in freezer until ice cream is firm, about 30 minutes.

4. Meanwhile, place remaining 1 pint vanilla ice cream in refrigerator to soften slightly. With narrow metal spatula, evenly spread vanilla ice cream over ice cream and sorbet layers. Cover and freeze until firm, at least 4 hours or up to 1 day.

5. To serve, dip small knife in hot water, shaking off excess; run knife around edge of pan to loosen cake. Remove side of pan; place cake on platter. Let stand about 15 minutes at room temperature for easier slicing. Decorate top of cake with mango slices and raspberries. Makes 20 servings.

Each serving: About 161 calories, 1g protein, 27g carbohydrate, 6g total fat (3g saturated), 18mg cholesterol, 63mg sodium.

RASPBERRY BAKED-ALASKA PIE

....

A showstopping dessert that is sure to win you applause.

Prep: 40 minutes plus freezing   **Bake:** 2 minutes

- 3   pints vanilla ice cream
- 2   packages (3 ounces each) soft ladyfingers, split in half
- 1/3 cup orange-flavored liqueur
- 1   package (10 ounces) frozen raspberries in syrup, slightly thawed
- 4   large egg whites
- 3/4 cup sugar
- 4   teaspoons water
- 1/4 teaspoon cream of tartar
- 1/4 teaspoon salt

ICE CREAM TREATS

MINI ICE CREAM SANDWICHES

Spread flat side of 2 chocolate- or vanilla-wafer cookies with thin layer of creamy peanut butter. Sandwich a small scoop of your favorite (slightly softened) ice cream between 2 peanut butter coated sides.

WAFFLES AND ICE CREAM

Lightly toast 1 frozen Belgian waffle. Top with vanilla ice cream or frozen yogurt and frozen (thawed) strawberries or raspberries in syrup.

ICE CREAM PARFAITS

Pour some almond-flavored liqueur over 1 scoop coffee ice cream. Top with whipped cream and crushed amaretti cookies.

ICE CREAM DRINK

In blender, combine 2 tablespoons orange-flavored liqueur with 2 scoops peach or vanilla ice cream; blend until smooth. Pour into tall glass and top with whipped cream.

S'MORE SUNDAE

Spoon 1 tablespoon fudge sauce over graham cracker. Top with 1 scoop chocolate ice cream and marshmallow topping.

---

1. Transfer ice cream to large bowl and place in refrigerator to soften slightly, about 30 minutes. Line bottom and side of 9-inch deep-dish pie plate with about two-thirds of ladyfingers, rounded side down, allowing ends to extend beyond pie plate rim. Drizzle with half of liqueur.

2. In medium bowl, crush raspberries. Drop dollops of raspberries over ice cream in large bowl; with knife, cut through raspberries and ice cream once or twice to create marbled effect. With large serving spoon, carefully transfer half of ice cream into pie plate, keeping marbled effect; place bowl of remaining ice cream in freezer. Arrange remaining ladyfingers on top of ice cream in pie plate; drizzle with remaining liqueur. Spoon remaining ice cream evenly over ladyfingers. Cover and freeze until firm, at least 4 hours.

3. In medium bowl set over saucepan of simmering water, with mixer at medium speed, beat egg whites, sugar, water, cream of tartar, and salt until soft peaks form when beaters are lifted or until temperature on thermometer reaches 160°F, 10 to 14 minutes. Place bowl on work surface; continue to beat egg whites until stiff peaks form when beaters are lifted, 8 to 10 minutes longer. With spoon, quickly spread meringue over top of pie, sealing meringue to edge and making decorative swirls with back of spoon. Freeze, uncovered, up to 6 hours.

4. To serve, preheat oven to 500°F. Bake pie until meringue is lightly browned, 2 to 3 minutes. Serve immediately. Makes 12 servings.

Each serving: About 281 calories, 5g protein, 45g carbohydrate, 9g total fat (5g saturated), 81mg cholesterol, 140mg sodium.

21

CAKES & FROSTINGS

This all-American dessert may be one of the most enduring images in the world of desserts. So, to satisfy everyone's sweet cravings, we offer cakes for every appetite and every occasion: gingerbread for the holidays, luscious cheesecakes for parties, tempting butter cakes for family suppers, and some of the most delectable chocolate cakes ever.

PERFECT CAKES EVERY TIME

The ingredients in cake recipes are carefully balanced, so it is essential that you precisely measure the ingredients and make sure that they are at room-temperature.

Butter You can usually use either butter or stick margarine, but butter has superior flavor. Soften the butter just until malleable.

Eggs We use large eggs to make our cakes. Chilled eggs don't beat to their maximum volume, so leave them out at room temperature after separating them.

Flour Although most of our recipes call for all-purpose flour, some use cake flour, which produces tender cakes. If you don't have cake flour, for every cup of cake flour, spoon 2 tablespoons of cornstarch into a 1-cup measure. Spoon in enough all-purpose flour to fill the cup, then level it off. When measuring flour, use the spoon-and-sweep method (see Basics, page 11).

Pans Always use the recommended pan size. Measure the pan if necessary. To line a pan, place it on a piece of waxed paper. Use a pencil to trace around the bottom edge and cut out the shape.

Greasing and Flouring If the recipe directs you, grease or grease and flour the pans. (Pans for foam cakes are not greased because these batters need to cling to the side of the pan as they rise.) Apply a film of vegetable shortening using a folded piece of paper towel. When greasing a Bundt pan, be sure to get into all the crevices, or use nonstick cooking spray. To flour a greased pan, sprinkle a tablespoon or so of flour into the pan, tilting it to coat the bottom and side. Invert the pan and tap out the excess.

Oven Know-How
Position the oven racks as directed, then thoroughly preheat the oven. When baking two cakes, place a rack in the center of the oven. If baking more cakes,

place the racks in the center and upper third of the oven. Stagger the pans so they are not directly above one another. Cake pans should never touch the sides of the oven or each other. For cakes baked in tube pans, position the oven rack in the lower third of the oven.

Vanilla Chiffon Cake (recipe page 643)

STORING CAKES

Always refrigerate cakes that contain fillings or frostings made with whipped cream, cream cheese, sour cream, yogurt, or eggs. Because of their high fat content, unfrosted butter cakes stay moist for two or three days at room temperature. Foam cakes contain little or no fat and dry out quickly; store at room temperature for up to two days.

To freeze butter cakes, place them, unwrapped, in the freezer until firm; wrap in plastic and then in heavy-duty foil. Frosted cakes can be frozen for up to two months; unfrosted cakes for up to six months. Do not freeze cakes with whipped-cream frostings or egg-based fillings. Foam cakes can be frozen in heavy-duty zip-tight plastic bags for up to three months.

BUTTER CAKES

These cakes rely on fat for moistness and richness. The fat must be beaten well with the sugar to provide an aerated base. Beat the butter-and-sugar mixture with an electric mixer on medium speed until light and fluffy, scraping down the side of the bowl as directed. Beat in the eggs, one a time, beating well after each addition.

Pour the batter into the prepared pans and gently tap the pans on a counter to break any large air bubbles. The cake is done when a toothpick inserted into the center comes out clean. Some cakes also pull away slightly from the side of the pan. Or lightly press the center of the cake with your finger; the top should spring back.

Cool the cake on a wire rack for ten minutes. Run a knife around the inside of the pan. Invert a second rack on top of the pan. Invert both racks along with the pan. Remove the top rack and the cake pan. Replace the top rack and invert the cake again, so it is right side up.

YELLOW CAKE

Make this versatile cake with shortening (for delicate flavor and crumb) or butter (for rich flavor). Either way, it will have the taste of old-fashioned goodness.

Prep: 45 minutes plus cooling   Bake: 30 minutes

- 2   cups all-purpose flour
- 2   teaspoons baking powder
- 1   teaspoon salt
- ½   cup vegetable shortening or ½ cup butter or margarine (1 stick), softened
- 1¼   cups sugar
- 3   large eggs
- 1   teaspoon vanilla extract
- 1   cup milk
  Chocolate Butter Frosting (page 650)

1. Preheat oven to 350°F. Grease and flour two 8-inch round cake pans or one 9-inch square baking pan, or line twenty-four 2½-inch muffin-pan cups with paper baking liners. (Preheat oven to 325°F if using 9-inch square pan.)

2. In medium bowl, with wire whisk, stir flour, baking powder, and salt. In large bowl, with mixer at medium speed, beat shortening and sugar until light and fluffy, about 5 minutes. Add eggs, one at a time, beating well after each addition. Beat in vanilla. Reduce speed to low; add flour mixture alternately with milk, beginning and ending with flour mixture. Beat just until smooth, frequently scraping bowl with rubber spatula.

3. Divide batter between prepared pans; spread evenly. Bake until toothpick inserted in center comes out clean, about 30 minutes for 8-inch layers, 40 to 45 minutes for 9-inch square cake, or 20 to 25 minutes for cupcakes. Cool in pans on wire racks 10 minutes. Run thin knife around layers to loosen from sides of pans; invert onto racks to cool completely.

4. Prepare Chocolate Butter Frosting. Place one layer, rounded side down, on cake plate. With narrow metal spatula, spread ⅔ cup frosting over layer. Top with second layer, rounded side up. Spread remaining frosting over side and top of cake. Makes 12 servings.

Each serving with Chocolate Butter Frosting: About 526 calories, 5g protein, 66g carbohydrate, 28g total fat (13g saturated), 87mg cholesterol, 421mg sodium.

ORANGE CAKE

Prepare cake as directed but add **1 teaspoon freshly grated orange peel** with vanilla. Frost with Fluffy White Frosting (page 652) or Orange Butter Frosting (page 650).

Each serving with Fluffy White Frosting: About 345 calories, 5g protein, 56g carbohydrate, 11g total fat (3g saturated), 56mg cholesterol, 312mg sodium.

Each serving with Orange Butter Frosting: About 494 calories, 5g protein, 77g carbohydrate, 19g total fat (8g saturated), 77mg cholesterol, 383mg sodium.

SILVER WHITE CAKE

Made without egg yolks, this cake has a pristine ivory color that can be accented by a variety of frostings. Try Peppermint Whipped Cream Frosting (page 651), or fill with Lemon Filling (page 652), then frost with Fluffy White Frosting (page 652).

Prep: 50 minutes plus cooling Bake: 30 minutes

- 2 cups cake flour (not self-rising)
- 2 teaspoons baking powder
- 1 teaspoon salt
- 4 large egg whites
- 1¼ cups sugar
- ½ cup vegetable shortening
- 1 teaspoon vanilla extract
- ¼ teaspoon almond extract
- 1 cup milk
  Chocolate Butter Frosting (page 650)

1. Preheat oven to 350°F. Grease and flour two 8-inch round cake pans.

2. In medium bowl, with wire whisk, stir flour, baking powder, and salt. In medium bowl, with mixer at high speed, beat egg whites until soft peaks form when beaters are lifted. Sprinkle in ¼ cup sugar, 1 tablespoon at a time, beating until sugar has dissolved and egg whites stand in stiff, glossy peaks when beaters are lifted.

3. In large bowl, with mixer at low speed, beat shortening and remaining 1 cup sugar until blended. Increase speed to medium. Beat in vanilla and almond extracts. Reduce speed to low; add flour mixture alternately with milk, beginning and ending with flour mixture. Beat just until smooth, occasionally scraping bowl with rubber spatula. Gently fold in beaten egg whites, one-third at a time, just until blended.

4. Divide batter between prepared pans; spread evenly. Bake until toothpick inserted in center comes out clean, about 30 minutes. Cool in pans on wire racks 10 minutes. Run thin knife around layers to loosen from sides of pans. Invert onto racks to cool completely.

5. Prepare Chocolate Butter Frosting. Place one layer, rounded side down, on cake plate. With narrow metal spatula, spread ⅔ cup frosting over layer. Top with second layer, rounded side up. Spread remaining frosting over side and top of cake. Makes 12 servings.

Each serving with Chocolate Butter Frosting: About 492 calories, 4g protein, 63g carbohydrate, 26g total fat (13g saturated), 34mg cholesterol, 423mg sodium.

FROSTING LAYER CAKES

Use a narrow metal spatula to spread frosting. It is easiest to frost a cake if it is elevated and can be turned. If you don't have a cake decorating stand, place the cake on a serving plate set on a large coffee can or inverted bowl.

Simply brush off any crumbs and use a serrated knife to trim away any crisp edges. Place the first layer, rounded side down, on the serving plate. To keep the plate clean, tuck strips of waxed paper under the cake, covering the plate edge. Spread the cake layer with ½ to ⅔ cup frosting, spreading it almost to the edge. Top with the second cake layer, rounded side up. Thinly frost the cake to set the crumbs and keep them in place; first coat the top of the cake, then the side. Finish the cake with a thicker layer of frosting. Where the top and side of the frosting meet, smooth it by sweeping and swirling the edge of the frosting toward the center of the cake. Then slip out the waxed paper strips and discard.

GOLDEN BUTTER CAKE

....

This classic layer cake is a good candidate for frosting, but it is so moist that it can also be baked in a tube pan, dusted with confectioners' sugar, and enjoyed plain.

Prep: 45 minutes plus cooling   Bake: 23 minutes

- 3 cups cake flour (not self-rising)
- 1 tablespoon baking powder
- ½ teaspoon salt
- 1 cup butter or margarine (2 sticks), softened
- 2 cups sugar
- 4 large eggs
- 2 teaspoons vanilla extract
- 1 cup milk
   Orange Butter Frosting (page 650)

1. Preheat oven to 350°F. Grease three 8-inch round cake pans. Line bottoms with waxed paper; grease and flour paper. Or grease and flour 9-inch fluted tube pan.

2. In medium bowl, with wire whisk, stir flour, baking powder, and salt. In large bowl, with mixer at medium-high speed, beat butter and sugar until light and fluffy, about 5 minutes. Add eggs, one at a time, beating well after each addition. Beat in vanilla. Reduce speed to low; add flour mixture alternately with milk, beginning and ending with flour mixture. Beat just until smooth, scraping bowl with rubber spatula.

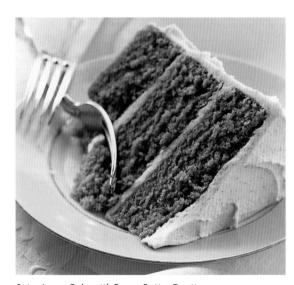

Spice Layer Cake with Brown Butter Frosting

3. Divide batter among prepared cake pans; spread evenly. Place two pans on upper oven rack and one pan on lower oven rack so that pans are not directly above one another. Bake until toothpick inserted in center comes out clean, 23 to 28 minutes for 8-inch layers, or 50 to 55 minutes for tube pan. Cool in pans on wire racks 10 minutes. Run thin knife around layers to loosen from sides of pans. Or, if using fluted tube pan, run tip of knife around edge of cake to loosen. Invert onto racks. Remove waxed paper; cool completely.

4. Prepare Orange Butter Frosting. Place one layer, rounded side down, on cake plate. With narrow metal spatula, spread ⅔ cup frosting over layer. Top with second layer, rounded side up, and spread with ⅔ cup frosting. Place remaining layer, rounded side up, on top. Spread remaining frosting over side and top of cake. Makes 16 servings.

Each serving with Orange Butter Frosting: About 472 calories, 4g protein, 70g carbohydrate, 20g total fat (12g saturated) 105mg cholesterol, 359mg sodium.

Each serving without frosting: About 315 calories, 4g protein, 43g carbohydrate, 14g total fat (8g saturated), 86mg cholesterol, 305mg sodium.

SPICE LAYER CAKE

Prepare as directed but use **2⅔ cups all-purpose flour, 2½ teaspoons baking powder,** and **1 teaspoon salt.** Add **2 teaspoons ground cinnamon, 1 teaspoon ground ginger, ½ teaspoon ground ginger,** and **¼ teaspoon ground cloves;** with wire whisk, stir until blended. In Step 2, use **1 cup granulated** and **1 cup dark brown sugar** and **5 eggs.** Omit vanilla. Bake 25 to 30 minutes. Proceed as directed, using Brown Butter Frosting (page 650). Makes 16 servings.

Each serving with Brown Butter Frosting: About 490 calories, 5g protein, 73g carbohydrate, 20g total fat (12g saturated), 116mg cholesterol, 360mg sodium.

PEANUT BUTTER CUPCAKES

....

These cupcakes are great for kids' parties. If you prefer, omit the chocolate topping and use your favorite frosting.

Prep: 10 minutes   Bake: 18 minutes

1³/₄ cups all-purpose flour
 1 tablespoon baking powder
 ¹/₂ teaspoon salt
 ¹/₂ cup creamy or chunky peanut butter
 ¹/₄ cup vegetable shortening
 ³/₄ cup sugar
 2 large eggs
 ³/₄ teaspoon vanilla extract
 1 cup milk
 1 bar (4 ounces) semisweet or milk chocolate, cut into 18 pieces

1. Preheat oven to 350°F. Line eighteen 2¹/₂-inch muffin-pan cups with paper baking liners.

2. In small bowl, with wire whisk, stir flour, baking powder, and salt.

3. In large bowl, with mixer at medium speed, beat peanut butter and shortening until combined. Add sugar and beat until light and fluffy, about 3 minutes. Add eggs, one at a time, beating well after each addition. Beat in vanilla. Reduce speed to low. Add flour mixture alternately with milk, beginning and ending with flour mixture, occasionally scraping bowl with rubber spatula.

4. Divide batter evenly among cups. Bake until toothpick inserted in center of cupcake comes out clean, about 18 minutes. Place 1 piece of chocolate on top of each cupcake; return to oven until chocolate melts, about 1 minute. With small metal spatula, spread chocolate over tops of cupcakes. Remove from pans and cool on wire rack. Makes 18 cupcakes.

Each cupcake: About 192 calories, 5g protein, 23g carbohydrate, 10g total fat (3g saturated), 26mg cholesterol, 193mg sodium.

APPLESAUCE SPICE CAKE

....

For a quick snack, make this easy cake. You may already have all of the ingredients on hand.

Prep: 20 minutes   Bake: 40 minutes

 2 cups all-purpose flour
1¹/₂ teaspoons ground cinnamon
 1 teaspoon baking powder
 ¹/₂ teaspoon baking soda
 ¹/₂ teaspoon ground ginger
 ¹/₄ teaspoon ground nutmeg
 ¹/₂ teaspoon salt
 ¹/₂ cup butter or margarine (1 stick), softened
 ¹/₄ cup granulated sugar
 1 cup packed dark brown sugar
 2 large eggs
1¹/₄ cups unsweetened applesauce
 ¹/₂ cup dark seedless raisins
      confectioners' sugar

1. Preheat oven to 350°F. Grease and flour 9-inch square baking pan.

2. In medium bowl, with wire whisk, stir flour, cinnamon, baking powder, baking soda, ginger, nutmeg, and salt.

3. In large bowl, with mixer at low speed, beat butter and granulated and brown sugars until blended. Increase speed to medium-high; beat until light and fluffy, about 3 minutes. Add eggs, one at a time, beating well after each addition. Reduce speed to low; beat in applesauce. Mixture may appear curdled. Beat in flour mixture until smooth, occasionally scraping bowl with rubber spatula. Stir in raisins.

4. Scrape batter into prepared pan; spread evenly. Bake cake until toothpick inserted in center comes out clean, about 40 minutes. Cool completely in pan on wire rack. To serve, dust with confectioners' sugar. Makes 9 servings.

Each serving: About 369 calories, 5g protein, 62g carbohydrate, 12g total fat (7g saturated), 75mg cholesterol, 383mg sodium.

APRICOT UPSIDE-DOWN CAKE

....

A nice riff on the traditional pineapple, and a great dish for a summertime get-together.

Prep: 25 minutes plus cooling   Bake: 35 minutes

- ½ cup packed brown sugar
- 8 ripe apricots, each cut in half and pitted
- 1¼ cups all-purpose flour
- ½ cup granulated sugar
- ¼ cup cornmeal
- 1¼ teaspoons baking powder
- ½ teaspoon salt
- ½ teaspoon baking soda
- ¾ cup low-fat buttermilk
- 2 large eggs
- 2 tablespoons butter or margarine, melted
- 2 tablespoons canola oil
- 1 teaspoon freshly grated lemon peel
- 1 teaspoon vanilla extract

1. Preheat oven to 350°F. Spray 10-inch cast-iron or ovenproof skillet with nonstick cooking spray. Sprinkle brown sugar evenly over bottom of skillet. Arrange apricot halves, cut sides down, over brown sugar.

2. In large bowl, whisk flour, granulated sugar, cornmeal, baking powder, salt, and baking soda until blended. In small bowl, whisk buttermilk, eggs, butter, oil, lemon peel, and vanilla extract until blended. Add buttermilk mixture to dry ingredients and fold with a spatula until just blended. Pour batter over apricots and spread to cover evenly.

3. Bake 35 to 40 minutes, or until toothpick inserted in center of cake comes out clean. Let cool in skillet on wire rack 10 minutes. Run knife around side of skillet. Place platter on top of skillet and carefully invert cake onto platter. Remove skillet. Cool cake slightly to serve warm, about 30 minutes. Makes 8 servings.

Each serving: About 290 calories, 5g protein, 49g carbohydrate, 8g total fat (1g saturated), 2g fiber, 62mg cholesterol, 365mg sodium.

Apricot Upside-Down Cake

PINEAPPLE UPSIDE-DOWN CAKE

....

We cut the pineapple slices in half to fit more fruit into the pan. Plums or apples make delicious variations (you won't need the pineapple juice).

Prep: 30 minutes   Bake: 40 minutes

- 2 cans (8 ounces each) pineapple slices in juice
- ⅓ cup packed brown sugar
- 8 tablespoons butter or margarine (1 stick), softened
- 1 cup cake flour (not self-rising)
- 1 teaspoon baking powder
- ¼ teaspoon salt
- ⅔ cup granulated sugar
- 1 large egg
- 1 teaspoon vanilla extract
- ⅓ cup milk

1. Preheat oven to 325°F. Drain pineapple slices in sieve set over bowl. Reserve 2 tablespoons juice. Cut 8 pineapple slices in half and drain on paper towels. Refrigerate remaining slices for another use.

2. In 10-inch oven-safe skillet (if skillet is not oven-safe, wrap handle with double layer of foil), heat brown sugar and 2 tablespoons butter over medium heat until melted. Stir in reserved pineapple juice and heat to boiling; boil 1 minute. Remove skillet from heat. Decoratively arrange pineapple in skillet, overlapping slices slightly to fit.

3. In small bowl, with wire whisk, stir flour, baking powder, and salt. In large bowl, with mixer at high speed, beat remaining 6 tablespoons butter and granulated sugar until fluffy, frequently scraping bowl with rubber spatula. Reduce speed to low; beat in egg and vanilla until well blended. Add flour mixture alternately with milk, beginning and ending with flour mixture. Beat just until blended.

4. Spoon batter over pineapple; spread evenly with rubber spatula. Bake until toothpick inserted in center comes out clean, 40 to 45 minutes. Run thin knife around cake to loosen from side of skillet; invert onto serving plate. (If any pineapple slices stick to skillet, place on cake.) Serve warm or at room temperature. Makes 8 servings.

Each serving: About 302 calories, 3g protein, 46g carbohydrate, 13g total fat (8g saturated), 59mg cholesterol, 267mg sodium.

PLUM UPSIDE-DOWN CAKE

Prepare as directed but substitute **1 pound plums** for pineapple. Cut plums into 1/2-inch-thick wedges. Heat brown sugar and 2 tablespoons butter in oven-safe skillet over medium heat until melted. Add plums and increase heat to high. Cook, stirring, until plums are glazed with brown-sugar mixture, about 1 minute.

APPLE UPSIDE-DOWN CAKE

Prepare as directed but substitute **3 large Golden Delicious apples (1 1/2 pounds)** for pineapple. Peel, core, and cut apples into 1/4-inch-thick wedges. Heat brown sugar and 2 tablespoons butter in oven-safe skillet over medium heat until melted. Add apple wedges and cook over high heat until apples are fork-tender and begin to brown, 7 to 8 minutes.

GINGERBREAD

....

Because it's mixed by hand, this gingerbread has a dense, chewy texture. For a more cakelike consistency, beat the batter with an electric mixer for two full minutes. (One important tip: Measure the water after it comes to a boil.)

Prep: 15 minutes   Bake: 45 minutes

- 2 cups all-purpose flour
- 1/2 cup sugar
- 2 teaspoons ground ginger
- 1 teaspoon ground cinnamon
- 1/2 teaspoon baking soda
- 1/2 teaspoon salt
- 1 cup light (mild) molasses
- 1/2 cup butter or margarine (1 stick), cut into 4 pieces
- 3/4 cup boiling water
- 1 large egg, lightly beaten

1. Preheat oven to 350°F. Grease and flour 9-inch square baking pan.

2. In large bowl, with wire whisk, stir flour, sugar, ginger, cinnamon, baking soda, and salt until blended.

3. In small bowl, combine molasses and butter. Add boiling water and stir until butter melts. Add molasses mixture and beaten egg to flour mixture; whisk until smooth.

4. With rubber spatula, scrape batter into prepared pan. Bake gingerbread until toothpick inserted in center comes out clean, 45 to 50 minutes. Cool in pan on wire rack. Serve gingerbread warm or at room temperature. Makes 9 servings.

Each serving: About 349 calories, 4g protein, 59g carbohydrate, 12g total fat (7g saturated), 51mg cholesterol, 324mg sodium.

APRICOT-PECAN FRUITCAKE

....

This light fruitcake has a mellow brandy flavor and is studded with chunks of tangy apricots and buttery pecans. You can make it up to one week ahead, but it's best to glaze it the day it's served.

Prep: 20 minutes plus cooling
Bake: 1 hour 10 minutes

1   pound dried apricot halves (2½ cups),
    cut into ½-inch pieces
2   cups pecans (8 ounces), coarsely chopped,
    plus ⅔ cup pecan halves
1   tablespoon plus 2 cups all-purpose flour
2   teaspoons baking powder
1   teaspoon salt
1   cup butter or margarine (2 sticks), softened
1¼ cups sugar
5   large eggs
½   cup brandy
1   tablespoon vanilla extract
⅓   cup apricot preserves

1. Preheat oven to 325°F and grease 9- to 10-inch tube pan.

2. In medium bowl, toss apricots and coarsely chopped pecans with 1 tablespoon flour. In separate medium bowl, with wire whisk, stir remaining 2 cups flour, baking powder, and salt.

3. In large bowl, with mixer at low speed, beat butter and sugar until blended. Increase speed to high; beat until light and fluffy, about 5 minutes, occasionally scraping bowl with rubber spatula. Reduce speed to low. Add eggs, brandy, vanilla, and flour mixture; beat until well blended, frequently scraping bowl. Stir apricot mixture into flour mixture.

4. Spoon batter into prepared pan; spread evenly. Arrange pecan halves on top of batter in two concentric circles. Bake until toothpick inserted in center comes out clean, 1 hour 10 to 20 minutes. Cool in pan on wire rack 10 minutes. Run thin knife around cake to loosen from side and center tube of pan; lift tube to separate cake from pan side. Slide knife under cake to separate from bottom of pan. Invert cake onto wire rack and remove center tube. Turn cake, right side up, onto rack to cool completely.

5. In 1-quart saucepan, heat apricot preserves over medium-high heat, stirring constantly, until melted and bubbling. Strain through sieve set over small bowl. With pastry brush, brush cooled cake with preserves. Or wrap cake and refrigerate up to 1 week, then brush with preserves before serving. Makes 24 servings.

Each serving: About 300 calories, 4g protein, 35g carbohydrate, 17g total fat (6g saturated), 65mg cholesterol, 233mg sodium.

CRANBERRY-RAISIN FRUITCAKE

Prepare as directed but substitute **2 cups walnuts (8 ounces),** toasted (page 692) and coarsely chopped, plus **⅔ cup walnut halves** for pecans and **1½ cups golden raisins plus 1 cup dried cranberries** for apricots.

APPLE-WALNUT BUNDT CAKE

....

This easy-to-make, dense cake is filled with apple chunks, tasty golden raisins (substitute dark raisins or dried cranberries, if you like), and a generous amount of walnuts.

Prep: 25 minutes plus cooling   Bake: 1 hour 15 minutes

3   cups all-purpose flour
1¾ cups granulated sugar
1   teaspoon baking soda
1   teaspoon ground cinnamon
¾   teaspoon salt
¼   teaspoon ground nutmeg
1   cup vegetable oil
½   cup apple juice
2   teaspoons vanilla extract
3   large eggs
1   pound Golden Delicious or Granny Smith apples
    (3 medium), peeled, cored, and coarsely chopped
1   cup walnuts (4 ounces), coarsely chopped
1   cup golden raisins
    confectioners' sugar

1. Preheat oven to 350°F. Grease and flour 10-inch Bundt pan.

2. In large bowl, combine flour, granulated sugar, baking soda, cinnamon, salt, nutmeg, oil, apple juice, vanilla, and eggs. With mixer at low speed, beat until well blended, frequently scraping bowl with rubber spatula. Increase speed to medium; beat 2 minutes,

scraping bowl. With wooden spoon, stir in apples, walnuts, and raisins.

3. Spoon batter into prepared pan; spread evenly. Bake until cake pulls away from side of pan and toothpick inserted in center comes out clean, about 1 hour 15 minutes. Cool in pan on wire rack 10 minutes. Run tip of thin knife around edge of cake to loosen. Invert cake onto rack; cool completely. Dust with confectioners' sugar. Makes 16 servings.

Each serving: About 408 calories, 5g protein, 54g carbohydrate, 20g total fat (3g saturated), 40mg cholesterol, 202mg sodium.

CARROT CAKE

Legend has it that George Washington enjoyed some carrot tea bread in 1783, and it remains one of America's favorite desserts.

Prep: 40 minutes plus cooling   Bake: 55 minutes

2½ cups all-purpose flour
  2 teaspoons baking soda
  2 teaspoons ground cinnamon
  1 teaspoon baking powder
  1 teaspoon salt
  ½ teaspoon ground nutmeg
  4 large eggs
  1 cup granulated sugar
  ¾ cup packed light brown sugar
  ½ cup vegetable oil
  ¼ cup milk
  1 tablespoon vanilla extract
  3 cups loosely packed shredded carrots
    (about 6 medium)
  1 cup walnuts (4 ounces), chopped
  ¾ cup dark seedless raisins
    Cream Cheese Frosting (page 652)

1. Preheat oven to 350°F. Grease 13" by 9" baking pan. Line bottom with waxed paper; grease paper. Dust pan with flour. Or grease and flour 10-inch Bundt pan.

2. In medium bowl, with wire whisk, stir flour, baking soda, cinnamon, baking powder, salt, and nutmeg.

3. In large bowl, with mixer at medium-high speed, beat eggs and granulated and brown sugars until blended, about 2 minutes, frequently scraping bowl

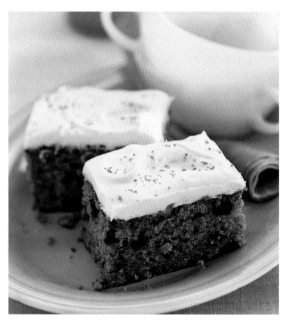

Carrot Cake with Cream Cheese Frosting

with rubber spatula. Beat in oil, milk, and vanilla. Reduce speed to low; add flour mixture and beat until smooth, about 1 minute, scraping bowl. With wooden spoon, fold in carrots, walnuts, and raisins.

4. Spoon batter into prepared pan; spread evenly. Bake until toothpick inserted in center comes out almost clean, 55 to 60 minutes for 13" by 9" cake or about 1 hour for Bundt cake. Cool in pan on wire rack 10 minutes. Run thin knife around sheet cake to loosen from sides of pan. Or, if using Bundt pan, run tip of knife around edge of cake to loosen. Invert onto rack. Remove waxed paper; cool completely.

5. Meanwhile, prepare Cream Cheese Frosting. Transfer cooled cake to cake plate. With narrow metal spatula, spread frosting over sides and top of cake. Makes 16 servings.

Each serving with Cream Cheese Frosting: About 486 calories, 6g protein, 70g carbohydrate, 22g total fat (7g saturated) 78mg cholesterol, 436mg sodium.

DELUXE CARROT CAKE

Prepare as directed but omit milk; fold in **1 can (8 to 8¼ ounces) crushed pineapple in unsweetened juice** with walnuts and raisins.

MOLTEN CHOCOLATE CAKES

···

When you cut into these warm cakes, their delectable molten centers flow out. You can assemble them up to 24 hours ahead and refrigerate, or freeze up to two weeks. If you refrigerate the cakes, bake them for ten minutes; if they are frozen, bake for 16 minutes. Serve with whipped cream or vanilla ice cream.

Prep: 20 minutes   Bake: 8 minutes

    4 squares (4 ounces) semisweet chocolate, chopped
    ½ cup butter or margarine (1 stick), cut into pieces
    ¼ cup heavy or whipping cream
    ½ teaspoon vanilla extract
    ¼ cup all-purpose flour
    ¼ cup sugar
    2 large eggs
    2 large egg yolks
       whipped cream or vanilla ice cream (optional)

1. Preheat oven to 400°F. Grease eight 6-ounce custard cups. Dust with sugar.

2. In heavy 3-quart saucepan, combine chocolate, butter, and cream; heat over low heat, stirring occasionally, until butter and chocolate melt and mixture is smooth. Remove from heat. Add vanilla; with wire whisk, stir in flour just until mixture is smooth.

3. In medium bowl, with mixer at high speed, beat sugar, eggs, and yolks until thick and lemon-colored, about 10 minutes. Fold egg mixture, one-third at a time, into chocolate mixture until blended.

4. Divide batter evenly among prepared custard cups. Place cups in jelly-roll pan. Bake until edge of cakes is set but center still jiggles, 8 to 9 minutes. Cool in pan on wire rack 3 minutes. Run thin knife around cakes to loosen from sides of cups; invert onto dessert plates. Serve immediately with whipped cream or ice cream, if desired. Makes 8 servings.

Each serving: About 281 calories, 4g protein, 20g carbohydrate, 22g total fat (12g saturated), 148mg cholesterol, 139mg sodium.

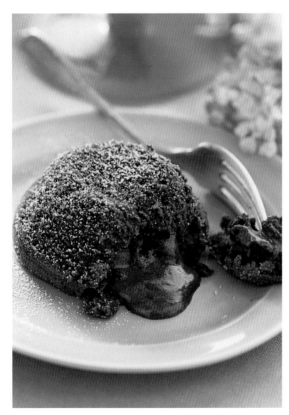

Molten Chocolate Cakes

CHOCOLATE BUTTERMILK CAKE

···

The deep chocolate flavor comes from unsweetened cocoa and the tender crumb from buttermilk.

Prep: 45 minutes plus cooling   Bake: 30 minutes

    2 cups all-purpose flour
    1 cup unsweetened cocoa
    1½ teaspoons baking soda
    ¾ teaspoon salt
    1½ cups buttermilk
    2 teaspoons vanilla extract
    1¾ cups sugar
    ¾ cup butter or margarine (1½ sticks), softened
    3 large eggs
       Classic Butter Frosting (page 650)

1. Preheat oven to 350°F. Grease two 9-inch round cake pans. Line bottom of pans with waxed paper; grease waxed paper. Dust with cocoa, shaking out excess.

2. In medium bowl, with wire whisk, stir flour, cocoa, baking soda, and salt. In 2-cup liquid measuring cup, mix buttermilk and vanilla; set aside.

3. In large bowl, with mixer at low speed, beat sugar and butter until blended. Increase speed to high; beat until creamy, about 3 minutes, occasionally scraping bowl with rubber spatula. Reduce speed to low; add eggs, one at a time, beating well after each addition. Add flour mixture alternately with buttermilk mixture beginning and ending with flour mixture. Beat just until blended, scraping bowl occasionally.

4. Divide batter between prepared pans; spread evenly. Bake until toothpick inserted in center of cake comes out clean, 30 to 35 minutes. Cool in pans on wire racks 10 minutes. Run thin knife around layers to loosen from sides of pans. Invert cakes onto racks to cool completely. Carefully remove and discard waxed paper.

5. Prepare Classic Butter Frosting.

6. Place one layer, rounded side down, on cake plate. With narrow metal spatula, spread ⅔ cup frosting over layer. Top with second layer, rounded side up. Spread remaining frosting over side and top of cake. Makes 16 servings.

Each serving without frosting: About 255 calories, 5g protein, 37g carbohydrate, 11g total fat (7g saturated), 65mg cholesterol, 360mg sodium.

CHOCOLATE TRUFFLE CAKE

······································

This exceptionally sinful chocolate dessert is easy to make, but it must be refrigerated for twenty-four hours before serving for the best flavor and texture. For the neatest slices, dip the knife into hot water before cutting each one.

Prep: 1 hour plus overnight to chill
Bake: 35 minutes

14   squares (14 ounces) semisweet chocolate, chopped
2   squares (2 ounces) unsweetened chocolate, chopped
1   cup butter (2 sticks; do not use margarine)
8   large eggs, separated
½   cup granulated sugar
¼   teaspoon cream of tartar
   confectioners' sugar

1. Preheat oven to 300°F. Remove bottom from 9" by 3" springform pan and cover with foil; wrap foil around back. Replace pan bottom. Grease and flour foil bottom and side of pan.

2. In heavy 2-quart saucepan, combine semisweet and unsweetened chocolates and butter; heat over low heat, stirring frequently, until melted and smooth. Pour chocolate mixture into large bowl.

3. In small bowl, with mixer at high speed, beat egg yolks and granulated sugar until very thick and lemon-colored, about 5 minutes. With rubber spatula, stir egg-yolk mixture into chocolate mixture until blended.

4. In separate large bowl, with clean beaters and with mixer at high speed, beat egg whites and cream of tartar until soft peaks form when beaters are lifted. With rubber spatula, gently fold beaten egg whites, one-third at a time, into chocolate mixture just until blended.

5. Scrape batter into prepared pan; spread evenly. Bake 35 minutes. (Do not overbake; cake will firm upon standing and chilling.) Cool completely in pan on wire rack; refrigerate overnight in pan.

6. Run thin knife, rinsed under very hot water and dried, around cake to loosen from side of pan; remove side of pan. Invert cake onto serving plate; unwrap foil from pan bottom and lift off pan. Carefully peel foil away from cake.

7. To serve, let cake stand 1 hour at room temperature. Dust with confectioners' sugar. Or dust heavily with confectioners' sugar over paper doily or stencil. Makes 20 servings.

Each serving: About 251 calories, 4g protein, 19g carbohydrate, 20g total fat (12g saturated) 113mg cholesterol, 126mg sodium.

LIGHT CHOCOLATE BUNDT CAKE

....

Satisfy your chocolate cravings with this low-fat treat. Skip the Mocha Glaze and save 45 calories and 11 carbs per serving.

Prep: 30 minutes plus cooling   Bake: 45 minutes

- 2¼ cups all-purpose flour
- 1½ teaspoons baking soda
- ½ teaspoon baking powder
- ½ teaspoon salt
- ¾ cup unsweetened cocoa
- 1 teaspoon instant espresso-coffee powder
- ¾ cup hot water
- 2 cups sugar
- ⅓ cup vegetable oil
- 2 large egg whites
- 1 large egg
- 1 square (1 ounce) unsweetened chocolate, melted
- 2 teaspoons vanilla extract
- ½ cup buttermilk
  Mocha Glaze (right)

1. Preheat oven to 350°F and grease 10-inch Bundt pan.

2. In medium bowl, with wire whisk, stir flour, baking soda, baking powder, and salt.

3. In 2-cup measuring cup, stir cocoa, espresso-coffee powder, and hot water until blended.

4. In large bowl, with mixer at low speed, beat sugar, oil, egg whites, and egg until blended. Increase speed to high; beat until creamy, about 2 minutes. Reduce speed to low; beat in cocoa mixture, melted chocolate, and vanilla. Add flour mixture alternately with buttermilk, beginning and ending with flour mixture. Beat just until blended, occasionally scraping bowl with rubber spatula.

5. Scrape batter into prepared pan; spread evenly with rubber spatula. Bake until toothpick inserted in center comes out clean, about 45 minutes. Cool in pan on wire rack 10 minutes. Run tip of thin knife around edge of cake to loosen from side of pan. Invert onto rack to cool completely.

6. Prepare Mocha Glaze. Place cake on cake plate; pour glaze over cooled cake. Makes 16 servings.

MOCHA GLAZE

In medium bowl, combine ¼ **teaspoon instant espresso-coffee powder** and **2 tablespoons hot water;** stir until blended. Stir in **3 tablespoons unsweetened cocoa, 3 tablespoons dark corn syrup,** and **1 tablespoon coffee-flavored liqueur** until blended. Add **1 cup confectioners' sugar;** stir until smooth.

Each serving with Mocha Glaze: About 280 calories, 4g protein, 53g carbohydrate, 7g total fat (2g saturated), 14mg cholesterol, 232mg sodium.

TYPES OF COCOA

Not all cocoas are created equal. There is a difference between natural and Dutch-process cocoas. Don't swap cocoa types and do not use mixes for hot chocolate drinks; use what is recommended in the recipe. Both types of cocoa have rich chocolate flavor, are equally delicious, and contain between 8 and 24 percent fat.

In our kitchens, we usually use natural cocoa because it is readily available. Its acidity works in tandem with the baking soda in a batter to create carbon dioxide bubbles, which leaven cakes. Dutch-process cocoa is treated with an alkali agent that neutralizes and removes some of the cocoa's acidity. The process was developed in the Netherlands in the mid-1800s, hence the name. This procedure changes the cocoa's chemical composition, so it doesn't need to be combined with baking soda. You'll find Dutch-process cocoa at specialty food stores and most supermarkets. Look closely at the label; some cocoas are alkalized even if the label doesn't clearly state it.

LEMON-POPPY SEED POUND CAKE

....

This tangy-sweet cake keeps well. Store poppy seeds in the refrigerator; they turn rancid quickly if stored at room temperature.

Prep: 25 minutes plus cooling   Bake: 1 hour 20 minutes

- 2 cups all-purpose flour
- 2 tablespoons poppy seeds
- ½ teaspoon baking powder
- ¼ teaspoon baking soda
- ¼ teaspoon salt
- 2 large lemons
- ¾ cup butter or margarine (1½ sticks), softened
- 1½ plus ⅓ cups sugar
- 4 large eggs
- 1 teaspoon vanilla extract
- ½ cup sour cream

1. Preheat oven to 325°F. Grease and flour 9" by 5" metal loaf pan.

2. In medium bowl, with wire whisk, stir flour, poppy seeds, baking powder, baking soda, and salt until combined. From lemons, grate 1 tablespoon peel and squeeze 3 tablespoons juice.

3. In large bowl, with mixer at low speed, beat butter and 1½ cups sugar until blended. Increase speed to high; beat until light and fluffy, about 5 minutes. Add eggs, one at a time, beating well after each addition, frequently scraping bowl with rubber spatula. Beat in lemon peel and vanilla. Reduce speed to low. Add flour mixture alternately with sour cream, beginning and ending with flour mixture; beat just until smooth.

4. Spoon batter into prepared pan; spread evenly. Bake until toothpick inserted in center comes out clean, about 1 hour 20 minutes. Cool in pan on wire rack 10 minutes. Run thin knife around cake to loosen from sides of pan. Remove from pan; place on rack set over waxed paper.

5. In small bowl, combine lemon juice and remaining ⅓ cup sugar. With pastry brush, brush mixture over top and sides of warm cake. Cool completely. Makes 16 servings.

Each serving: About 267 calories, 4g protein, 36g carbohydrate, 12g total fat (7g saturated), 80mg cholesterol, 178mg sodium.

VANILLA POUND CAKE

....

This delicate, finely textured pound cake is not as sweet as some. It's perfect with an afternoon cup of tea.

Prep: 20 minutes plus cooling   Bake: 1 hour

- 1½ cups butter or margarine (3 sticks), softened
- 2¼ cups granulated sugar
- 6 large eggs
- 1 tablespoon vanilla extract
- ¾ teaspoon salt
- 3 cups cake flour (not self-rising)
  confectioners' sugar

1. Preheat oven to 325°F. Grease and flour 10-inch Bundt pan.

2. In large bowl, with mixer at low speed, beat butter and granulated sugar just until blended. Increase speed to high; beat until light and fluffy, about 5 minutes, frequently scraping bowl with rubber spatula. Reduce speed to medium. Add eggs, one at a time, beating well after each addition. Add vanilla and salt. Increase speed to high; beat 3 minutes, scraping bowl. With wire whisk, stir in flour just until smooth.

3. Spoon batter into prepared pan; spread evenly. Bake until toothpick inserted near center comes out clean, 1 hour to 1 hour 10 minutes. Cool in pan on wire rack 10 minutes. Run tip of thin knife around edge of cake to loosen. Invert onto rack to cool completely. Dust with confectioners' sugar. Makes 20 servings.

Each serving: About 299 calories, 3g protein, 36g carbohydrate, 16g total fat (9g saturated), 101mg cholesterol, 247mg sodium.

FOAM CAKES

Foam cakes depend on whole eggs or egg whites for their airy texture. Angel food cake is light because it doesn't contain any fat; it gets its height from a large amount of beaten whites. Chiffon and sponge cakes contain beaten whole eggs or egg yolks, along with vegetable oil or melted butter. Patience is the key to success with foam cakes. If a recipe calls for the eggs to be beaten until thick and lemon colored, expect it to take from three to ten minutes. When the beaters are lifted, the egg mixture should form a thick ribbon.

How to Mix When combining the ingredients for these batters, fold them in with a rubber spatula. Cut down through the center of the batter, then draw the spatula across the bottom of the batter and up the side of the bowl. Flip the spatula over and draw it across the top. Give the bowl a quarter turn, and repeat until ingredients are blended.

How to Bake Bake the cake for the minimum recommended time, then check often for doneness.

How to Cool Cakes baked in tube pans are cooled upside down so they keep their shape. Invert the pan and insert it over the neck of a tall bottle or funnel (some pans have small feet), and cool completely. Sponge layer cakes are cooled just like butter cakes. Jelly-roll cakes are removed from the pan and rolled up with a towel.

BEATING EGG WHITES

The secret to light, even "heavenly" angel food cakes is properly beaten egg whites. Start with room-temperature egg whites to get the fullest volume. For "stiff glossy peaks" beat the whites until they form peaks that hold their shape when the beaters are lifted but are still moist. Overbeaten whites look lumpy and watery; there is no way to salvage them. Begin again with new egg whites.

ANGEL FOOD CAKE

···

Angel food cake, beloved for its clean flavor and light texture, has an added attraction—it's low in fat.

Prep: 30 minutes   Bake: 35 minutes

- 1 cup cake flour (not self-rising)
- ½ cup confectioners' sugar
- 1⅔ cups egg whites (12 to 14 large egg whites)
- 1½ teaspoons cream of tartar
- ½ teaspoon salt
- 1¼ cups granulated sugar
- 2 teaspoons vanilla extract
- ½ teaspoon almond extract

1. Preheat oven to 375°F. Sift flour and confectioners' sugar through sieve set over small bowl.

2. In large bowl, with mixer at medium speed, beat egg whites, cream of tartar, and salt until foamy. Increase speed to medium-high; beat until soft peaks form when beaters are lifted. Sprinkle in granulated sugar, 2 tablespoons at a time, beating until sugar has dissolved and egg whites stand in stiff, glossy peaks when beaters are lifted. Beat in vanilla and almond extracts.

3. Transfer egg-white mixture to larger bowl. Sift flour mixture, one-third at a time, over beaten egg whites; fold in with rubber spatula just until flour mixture is no longer visible. Do not overmix.

4. Scrape batter into ungreased 9- to 10-inch tube pan; spread evenly. Bake until cake springs back when lightly pressed, 35 to 40 minutes. Invert cake in pan onto large metal funnel or bottle; cool completely in pan. Run thin knife around cake to loosen from side and center tube of pan. Remove from pan and place on cake plate. Makes 16 servings.

Each serving: About 115 calories, 3g protein, 25g carbohydrate, 0g total fat (0g saturated), 0mg cholesterol, 114mg sodium.

CAPPUCCINO ANGEL FOOD CAKE

Prepare as directed but add **4 teaspoons instant espresso-coffee powder** and ½ **teaspoon ground cinnamon** to egg whites before beating; use **1½ teaspoons vanilla extract** and omit almond extract. In cup, **mix 1 tablespoon confectioners' sugar** with ⅛ **teaspoon ground cinnamon;** sprinkle evenly over cooled cake.

VANILLA CHIFFON CAKE

(Pictured on page 628)

....

All this tall, handsome cake needs is a dusting of confectioners' sugar and some fresh berries served on the side.

Prep: 20 minutes   Bake: 1 hour 15 minutes

2¼ cups cake flour (not self-rising)
1½ cups granulated sugar
1 tablespoon baking powder
1 teaspoon salt
¾ cup cold water
½ cup vegetable oil
5 large eggs, separated, plus 2 large egg whites
1 tablespoon vanilla extract
½ teaspoon cream of tartar
confectioners' sugar

1. Preheat oven to 325°F. In large bowl, with wire whisk, stir flour, 1 cup granulated sugar, baking powder, and salt. Make a well in center; add cold water, oil, egg yolks, and vanilla to well. With wire whisk, stir until smooth.

2. In separate large bowl, with mixer at high speed, beat egg whites and cream of tartar until soft peaks form when beaters are lifted. Sprinkle in remaining ½ cup granulated sugar, 2 tablespoons at a time, beating until sugar has dissolved and egg whites stand in stiff, glossy peaks when beaters are lifted. With rubber spatula, gently fold one-third of beaten egg whites into egg-yolk mixture, then fold in remaining egg whites until blended.

3. Scrape batter into ungreased 9- to 10-inch tube pan; spread evenly. Bake until cake springs back when lightly pressed, about 1 hour 15 minutes. Invert cake in pan onto large metal funnel or bottle; cool completely. Run thin knife around cake to loosen from side and tube of pan. Remove from pan and place on cake plate. Dust with confectioners' sugar. Makes 16 servings.

Each serving: About 217 calories, 4g protein, 31g carbohydrate, 9g total fat (1g saturated), 66mg cholesterol, 264mg sodium.

CITRUS CHIFFON CAKE

Prepare as directed (left) but substitute **1 tablespoon freshly grated orange peel** and **1 teaspoon freshly grated lemon peel** for vanilla, and substitute ½ **cup fresh orange juice** and ¼ **cup fresh lemon juice** for cold water. In small bowl, combine **1 cup confectioners' sugar, 1 teaspoon freshly grated lemon peel,** ¼ **teaspoon vanilla extract,** and about **5 teaspoons orange juice** to make smooth glaze. Spoon over cooled cake.

GOLDEN SPONGE CAKE

....

This cake is just perfect for soaking up fruit juices. Serve it with fresh fruit, or use it as a base for a shortcake or trifle.

Prep: 20 minutes   Bake: 15 minutes

¾ cup all-purpose flour
2 tablespoons cornstarch
3 large eggs
½ cup sugar
1 tablespoon butter or margarine, melted

1. Preheat oven to 375°F. Grease and flour 9-inch square baking pan.

2. In small bowl, with wire whisk, stir flour and cornstarch.

3. In large bowl, with mixer at high speed, beat eggs and sugar until thick and lemon colored and mixture forms ribbon when beaters are lifted, about 10 minutes, occasionally scraping bowl with rubber spatula. Fold in flour mixture until well blended, then fold in melted butter.

4. Scrape batter into prepared pan; spread evenly. Bake until cake is golden and springs back when lightly pressed, 15 to 20 minutes. Cool in pan on wire rack 10 minutes. Run thin knife around cake to loosen from sides of pan; invert onto rack to cool completely. Makes 8 servings.

Each serving: About 148 calories, 4g protein, 24g carbohydrate, 4g total fat (2g saturated), 84mg cholesterol, 39mg sodium.

JELLY ROLL

Jelly rolls are easy to make and look sensational on a decorative platter. Fill the roll with your favorite jam or tangy Lemon Filling (page 652).

Prep: 20 minutes plus cooling   Bake: 10 minutes

- 5   large eggs, separated
- ½   cup granulated sugar
- 1   teaspoon vanilla extract
- ½   cup all-purpose flour
-    confectioners' sugar
- ⅔   cup strawberry jam

1. Preheat oven to 350°F. Grease 15½" by 10½" jelly-roll pan. Line with waxed paper; grease paper.

2. In large bowl, with mixer at high speed, beat egg whites until soft peaks form when beaters are lifted. Sprinkle in ¼ cup granulated sugar, 1 tablespoon at a time, beating until egg whites stand in stiff, glossy peaks when beaters are lifted. Do not overbeat.

3. In small bowl, with mixer at high speed, beat egg yolks, remaining ¼ cup granulated sugar, and vanilla until very thick and lemon colored, 8 to 10 minutes. Reduce speed to low; beat in flour until blended. With rubber spatula, gently fold egg-yolk mixture into beaten egg whites just until blended.

4. Scrape batter into prepared pan; spread evenly. Bake until cake springs back when lightly pressed, 10 to 15 minutes.

5. Meanwhile, sift confectioners' sugar onto clean kitchen towel. When cake is done, run thin knife around edges of cake to loosen from sides of pan; invert onto towel. Carefully remove waxed paper. Trim ¼ inch from edges of cake. From a short side, roll cake up with towel jelly-roll fashion. Place rolled cake, seam side down, on wire rack; cool completely.

6. Unroll cooled cake. With narrow metal spatula, spread evenly with jam. Starting from same short side, roll up cake (without towel). Place rolled cake, seam side down, on platter and dust with confectioners' sugar. Makes 10 servings.

Each serving: About 163 calories, 4g protein, 30g carbohydrate, 3g total fat (1g saturated), 106mg cholesterol, 40mg sodium.

Jelly Roll

CHEESECAKES

There are two types of cheesecake: cream cheese and curd cheese. Some have a crust, which can be made of pastry dough, graham crackers, or cookies. The filling can be plain or flavored—for example, with citrus, chocolate, or pumpkin. To bake perfect cheesecakes, the cream cheese must be well softened. Let it stand for at least one hour at room temperature.

How to Bake To prevent the butter in the crust from leaking or to waterproof the cake if placed in a water bath, the outside of the pan is often wrapped with heavy-duty foil. Cheesecake should be baked until the center barely jiggles; it will firm up during cooling and chilling.

How to Cool To help prevent cracking during cooling, run a thin knife around the edge of the cheesecake as soon as the cheesecake comes out of the oven.

DELUXE CHEESECAKE

....

This is the classic New York–style cheesecake: very dense, rich, and baked in a pastry crust. Baking it at a low temperature and slowly cooling it in the oven are the keys to its perfect texture.

Prep: 45 minutes plus cooling and chilling
Bake: 50 minutes plus standing

- ½ cup butter or margarine (1 stick), softened
- 1½ cups sugar
- 3 large egg yolks
- 1¼ cups plus 3 tablespoons all-purpose flour
- 5 packages (8 ounces each) cream cheese, softened
- 5 large eggs
- ¼ cup milk
- 1 teaspoon freshly grated lemon peel

1. Preheat oven to 400°F. In small bowl, with mixer at low speed, beat butter and ¼ cup sugar until blended. Add 1 egg yolk and beat until well combined. Beat in 1¼ cups flour just until combined. Divide dough into almost equal parts; wrap slightly larger piece in plastic wrap and refrigerate.

2. Press smaller piece of dough onto bottom of 10" by 2½" springform pan. Bake until golden, about 8 minutes; cool completely in pan on wire rack.

3. Turn oven control to 475°F. In large bowl, with mixer at medium speed, beat cream cheese just until smooth; gradually beat in remaining 1¼ cups sugar. Reduce speed to low. Beat in eggs, remaining 2 egg yolks, milk, remaining 3 tablespoons flour, and lemon peel just until blended, occasionally scraping bowl with rubber spatula.

4. Press remaining piece of dough around side of pan 1 inch from rim (do not bake). Scrape cream-cheese mixture into crust. Bake 12 minutes. Turn oven control to 300°F; bake 30 minutes longer. Edge will be set, but center will still jiggle. Turn off oven; let cheesecake remain in oven 30 minutes.

5. Remove cheesecake from oven and place on wire rack. Run thin knife around edge of cheesecake to prevent cracking during cooling. Cool completely in pan on wire rack. Cover and refrigerate until well chilled, at least 4 hours or up to overnight. Remove side of pan to serve. Makes 20 servings.

Each serving: About 359 calories, 7g protein, 24g carbohydrate, 27g total fat (16g saturated), 160mg cholesterol, 233mg sodium.

OUR SUBLIME CHOCOLATE SAUCE

....

Some people think that you can't improve a classic. They obviously haven't tasted our sauce! It's a decadent topping for the Deluxe Cheesecake at left.

Prep: 5 minutes   **Cook: 10 minutes**

- 4 squares (4 ounces) unsweetened chocolate, chopped
- 1 cup heavy or whipped cream
- ¾ cup sugar
- 2 tablespoons light corn syrup
- 2 tablespoons butter or margarine
- 2 teaspoons vanilla extract

1. In heavy 2-quart saucepan, combine chopped chocolate, cream, sugar, and corn syrup; heat to boiling over high heat, stirring constantly. Reduce heat to medium. Cook at a gentle boil, stirring constantly, until sauce has thickened slightly, about 5 minutes.

2. Remove from heat; stir in butter and vanilla until smooth and glossy. Serve hot, or cool completely, then cover and refrigerate up to 1 week. Gently reheat before using. Makes about 1¾ cup.

Each tablespoon: About 83 calories, 1g protein, 8g carbohydrate, 6g total fat (4g saturated), 14mg cholesterol, 14 mg sodium.

Lemon-Ricotta Cheesecake

LEMON-RICOTTA CHEESECAKE

....

Serving this cake with fresh raspberries and thin strips of lemon zest is both beautiful and tasty.

Prep: 20 minutes plus cooling and chilling
Bake: 1 hour 25 minutes plus standing

- 4 large lemons
- 1 cup vanilla wafer crumbs (about 30 cookies)
- 4 tablespoons butter or margarine, melted
- 1¼ cups sugar
- ¼ cup cornstarch
- 2 packages (8 ounces each) cream cheese, softened
- 1 container (15 ounces) ricotta cheese
- 4 large eggs
- 2 cups half-and-half or light cream
- 2 teaspoons vanilla extract

1. Preheat oven to 375°F. Tightly wrap outside of 9" by 3" springform pan with heavy-duty foil. From lemons, grate 4 teaspoons peel and squeeze ⅓ cup juice. In pan, combine cookie crumbs, melted butter, and 1 teaspoon lemon peel; stir with fork until evenly moistened. With hand, press mixture firmly onto bottom of pan. Bake until crust is deep golden, about 10 minutes. Cool completely in pan on wire rack.

2. Turn oven control to 325°F. In small bowl, stir sugar and cornstarch until blended. In large bowl, with mixer at medium speed, beat cream cheese and ricotta until very smooth, about 5 minutes; slowly beat in sugar mixture. Reduce speed to low. Beat in eggs, half-and-half, lemon juice, vanilla, and remaining 3 teaspoons lemon peel just until blended, frequently scraping bowl with rubber spatula.

3. Pour cream-cheese mixture into cooled crust. Bake 1 hour 15 minutes. Turn off oven; let cheesecake remain in oven 1 hour longer.

4. Remove cheesecake from oven and transfer to wire rack; remove foil. Run thin knife around edge of cheesecake to prevent cracking during cooling. Cool completely in pan on wire rack. Cover and refrigerate until well chilled, at least 6 hours or up to overnight. Remove side of pan to serve. Makes 16 servings.

Each serving: About 324 calories, 8g protein, 25g carbohydrate, 22g total fat (13g saturated), 117mg cholesterol, 182mg sodium.

LIGHT CHEESECAKE

....

We lightened up this Big Apple classic simply by using low-fat and fat-free dairy products and streamlining the crust recipe.

Prep: 20 minutes plus cooling and chilling
Bake: 1 hour 15 minutes

³/₄ cup graham cracker crumbs

2 tablespoons trans-fat-free
   vegetable oil spread, melted

3 packages (8 ounces each) reduced-fat
   cream cheese

1 cup sugar

1 tablespoon cornstarch

1½ pints fat-free sour cream

1¼ teaspoons vanilla extract

2 large eggs plus 2 large egg whites
   assorted berries for garnish, optional

1. Preheat oven to 325°F. In 9-inch springform pan, stir crumbs with melted spread until moistened. With hand, firmly press mixture onto bottom of pan. Bake crust 15 minutes or until deep golden. Cool 5 minutes on wire rack.

2. Meanwhile, in large bowl, with mixer on medium speed, beat cream cheese until smooth. Combine sugar and cornstarch. Slowly beat sugar mixture into cream cheese. On low speed, beat in sour cream and vanilla. Add eggs and egg whites, one at a time, until blended.

3. Pour batter over crust in pan. Bake cheesecake 1 hour. Edge will be set, but center will still jiggle. Turn oven off; let cheesecake remain in oven 1 hour. Transfer to wire rack. Run thin knife around edge of cheesecake to prevent cracking during cooling. Cool in pan, about 2 hours. Cover and refrigerate 4 hours or overnight. Remove side of pan to serve. Makes 16 servings.

Each serving: About 255 calories, 8g protein, 26g carbohydrate, 13g total fat (7g saturated), 0g fiber, 59mg cholesterol, 250mg sodium.

Light Cheesecake

CHEESECAKE TOPPINGS

TEST KITCHEN TIP

Sometimes a delectable slice of plain cheesecake hits the spot, but there are also times when a bit of "gilding the lily" is called for. It is easy to dress up a cream cheese cheesecake without a lot of fuss. Here are some of our favorite ways:

• Top chilled cheesecake with hulled whole, halved, or sliced strawberries. Brush with ½ cup melted red currant jelly.

• Serve slices of cheesecake accompanied by a sauce-boat of our Sublime Chocolate Sauce (page 645). For a very special occasion, cover the top of the cheesecake with Chocolate Curls (page 653).

• Top chilled cheesecake with fresh raspberries or concentric circles of raspberries and blackberries. Serve with Best Berry Sauce (page 511).

• Top chilled cheesecake with ½-inch wedges of peeled ripe peaches. Serve with Sweetened Whipped Cream (page 511).

PUMPKIN CHEESECAKE

....

Pumpkin pie, move over. Here's a deliciously creamy dessert that is bound to become a new tradition at your next Thanksgiving dinner.

**Prep: 30 minutes plus cooling and chilling
Bake: 1 hour 25 minutes**

Crumb Crust
- 1 cup graham cracker crumbs
(8 rectangular crackers)
- 3 tablespoons butter or margarine, melted
- 2 tablespoons sugar

Pumpkin Filling
- 2 packages (8 ounces each) cream cheese, softened
- 1¼ cups sugar
- 1 can (15 ounces) solid-pack pumpkin (not pumpkin-pie filling)
- ¾ cup sour cream
- 2 tablespoons bourbon or 2 teaspoons vanilla extract
- 1 teaspoon ground cinnamon
- ½ teaspoon ground allspice
- ¼ teaspoon salt
- 4 large eggs

Sour Cream Topping
- 1 cup sour cream
- 3 tablespoons sugar
- 1 teaspoon vanilla extract

1. Preheat oven to 350°F. Tightly wrap outside of 9" by 3" springform pan with heavy-duty foil. In pan, combine graham-cracker crumbs, melted butter, and sugar; stir with fork until evenly moistened. With hand, press mixture firmly onto bottom of pan. Bake 10 minutes. Cool completely in pan on wire rack.

2. Prepare pumpkin filling: In large bowl, with mixer at medium speed, beat cream cheese until smooth. Slowly beat in sugar until blended, about 1 minute, frequently scraping bowl with rubber spatula. Reduce speed to low. Beat in pumpkin, sour cream, bourbon, cinnamon, allspice, and salt. Add eggs, one at time, beating after each addition, just until blended.

3. Pour pumpkin mixture into crust and place in large roasting pan. Place pan on oven rack. Carefully pour enough *very hot water* into roasting pan to come 1 inch up side of springform pan. Bake until center of cake barely jiggles, about 1 hour 10 minutes.

4. Prepare topping: In small bowl, with wire whisk, beat sour cream, sugar, and vanilla until smooth. Remove cheesecake from water bath (leave water bath in oven); spread sour-cream mixture evenly over top. Return cake to water bath and bake 5 minutes longer.

5. Remove cheesecake from water bath and transfer to wire rack; remove foil. Run thin knife around edge of cheesecake to prevent cracking during cooling. Cool completely in pan on wire rack. Cover and refrigerate until well chilled, at least 6 hours or up to overnight. Remove side of pan to serve. Makes 16 servings.

Each serving: About 307 calories, 5g protein, 29g carbohydrate, 19g total fat (11g saturated), 101mg cholesterol, 217mg sodium.

MARGARITA CHEESECAKE

....

Lots of fresh lime juice and zest and a generous amount of orange-flavored liqueur make this cheesecake special. To prevent a thick bottom edge of crust, first press crumbs onto the bottom of the pan, then pack crumbs against the side of the pan.

**Prep: 35 minutes plus cooling and chilling
Bake: 1 hour plus standing**

- 4 to 5 limes
- 1 orange
- 8 ounces vanilla wafer cookies (65 wafers)
- 7 tablespoons butter or margarine, melted
- 4 packages (8 ounces each) cream cheese, softened
- 1¼ cups sugar
- ¼ teaspoon salt
- 4 large eggs
- 1 container (8 ounces) sour cream
- ¼ cup orange-flavor liqueur or orange juice
orange and lime slices for garnish (optional)

Margarita Cheesecake

1. Preheat oven to 350°F. From limes, grate 1 tablespoon plus 2 teaspoons peel and squeeze ½ cup juice. From orange, grate ½ teaspoon peel. In food processor with knife blade attached, pulse vanilla wafers and 2 teaspoons lime peel to make fine crumbs (you should have about 2½ cups crumbs). In 9" by 3" springform pan, combine cookie crumbs and melted butter; stir with fork until evenly moistened. With hand, press mixture firmly onto bottom and 2 inches up side of pan. Tightly wrap outside of pan with heavy-duty foil. Bake crust 15 minutes. Cool completely in pan on wire rack.

2. In large bowl, with mixer at medium speed, beat cream cheese until smooth, occasionally scraping bowl with rubber spatula. Gradually beat in sugar and salt until blended. Reduce speed to low; beat in eggs, one at a time, sour cream, liqueur, orange peel, lime juice, and remaining 1 tablespoon lime peel just until blended and smooth.

3. Pour cream-cheese mixture into crust, making sure to scrape any peel on beaters into batter. Bake until cheesecake is set 2 inches from edge but center still jiggles, about 45 minutes. Turn off oven; let cheesecake remain in oven 1 hour longer.

4. Remove cheesecake from oven and cool completely in pan on wire rack. Cover and refrigerate cheesecake until well chilled, at least 6 hours or up to 2 days.

5. To serve, carefully remove side of springform pan. Let cheesecake stand at room temperature 30 minutes for better flavor. If you like, arrange orange and lime slices on top of cake for garnish. Makes 20 servings.

Each serving: About 335 calories, 6g protein, 23g carbohydrate, 25g total fat (15g saturated), 111mg cholesterol, 265mg sodium.

MILK CHOCOLATE CHEESECAKE

To ensure a creamy smooth texture, make sure that the cream cheese, eggs, and sour cream are at room temperature. About 30 minutes on the counter is all it takes.

Prep: 25 minutes plus cooling and chilling
Bake: 1 hour

- 1 package (9 ounces) chocolate wafer cookies
- 6 tablespoons butter or margarine, melted
- 2 packages (8 ounces each) cream cheese, softened
- ½ cup plus 2 tablespoons sugar
- ¼ teaspoon salt
- 3 large eggs, lightly beaten
- ¼ cup whole milk
- 2 teaspoons vanilla extract
- 1 bag (11½ ounces) milk chocolate chips, melted
- 1½ cups sour cream

1. Preheat oven to 350°F. In food processor with knife blade attached, pulse chocolate cookies until fine crumbs form. Add butter to crumbs and pulse several times to combine. Transfer cookie mixture to 9-inch springform pan. With hand, press firmly onto bottom and about 2 inches up side of pan. Bake 10 minutes. Cool completely in pan on wire rack.

2. In large bowl, with mixer at medium speed, beat cream cheese, ½ cup sugar, and ¼ teaspoon salt until smooth, about 2 minutes, scraping bowl with rubber spatula. Reduce speed to low. Add eggs, milk, and vanilla; beat just until blended, occasionally scraping bowl. Add chocolate and beat until combined.

3. Pour cream-cheese mixture into crust. Bake until cheesecake is set 2 inches from edge but center still jiggles, about 45 minutes.

4. In small bowl, stir sour cream and remaining 2 tablespoons sugar until sugar dissolves; set aside.

5. Remove cheesecake from oven. Gently spread sour-cream mixture evenly over top. Return cheesecake to oven and bake 5 minutes longer to set sour cream. Remove from oven and cool completely in pan on wire rack. Cover and refrigerate until well chilled, at least 6 hours or up to 3 days.

Each serving: About 315 calories, 5g protein, 27g carbohydrate, 22g total fat (12g saturated), 74mg cholesterol, 755mg sodium.

FROSTINGS AND FILLINGS

CLASSIC BUTTER FROSTING

....

This may be the simplest frosting to prepare but you'd never suspect so from its rich flavor.

Prep: 10 minutes

½ cup butter or margarine (1 stick), softened

1 package (16 ounces) confectioners' sugar

3 to 6 tablespoons milk, half-and-half, or light cream

1½ teaspoons vanilla extract

In large bowl, with mixer at medium-low speed, beat butter, confectioners' sugar, 3 tablespoons milk, and vanilla until smooth and blended. Beat in additional milk as needed for easy spreading consistency. Increase speed to medium-high; beat frosting until light and fluffy, about 1 minute. Makes about 2⅓ cups.

Each tablespoon: About 71 calories, 0g protein, 12g carbohydrate, 3g total fat (2g saturated), 7mg cholesterol, 26mg sodium.

LEMON BUTTER FROSTING

Prepare as directed but omit vanilla and use **2 tablespoons fresh lemon juice**, and **1 teaspoon freshly grated lemon peel**. Use only **1 to 2 tablespoons milk** as needed for easy spreading.

ORANGE BUTTER FROSTING

Prepare as directed for Lemon Butter Frosting but substitute **orange juice** for lemon juice and **orange peel** for lemon peel.

BROWN BUTTER FROSTING

In small skillet, over medium heat, cook butter until lightly browned; let cool. Prepare as directed.

WHITE CHOCOLATE BUTTER FROSTING

....

Use this sweet frosting on your favorite chocolate cake.

Prep: 15 minutes

1 cup butter (2 sticks), softened (do not use margarine)

2 cups confectioners' sugar

6 ounces white chocolate, Swiss confectionery bars, or white baking bars, melted and cooled

3 tablespoons milk

In large bowl, with mixer at low speed, beat butter, confectioners' sugar, white chocolate, and milk just until combined. Increase speed to high; beat until light and fluffy, about 2 minutes, frequently scraping bowl with rubber spatula. Makes about 3½ cups.

Each tablespoon: About 62 calories, 0g protein, 6g carbohydrate, 4g total fat (3g saturated), 9mg cholesterol, 37mg sodium.

CHOCOLATE BUTTER FROSTING

....

The combination of semisweet and unsweetened chocolates gives this frosting its perfect flavor balance.

Prep: 15 minutes

¾ cup butter (1½ sticks), softened (do not use margarine)

2 cups confectioners' sugar

1 teaspoon vanilla extract

4 squares (4 ounces) semisweet chocolate, melted and cooled

2 squares (2 ounces) unsweetened chocolate, melted and cooled

In large bowl, with mixer at low speed, beat butter, confectioners' sugar, and vanilla until almost combined. Add semisweet and unsweetened chocolates. Increase speed to high; beat frosting until light and fluffy, about 1 minute. Makes about 2½ cups.

Each tablespoon: About 75 calories, 0g protein, 8g carbohydrate, 5g total fat (3g saturated), 9mg cholesterol, 36mg sodium.

SILKY VANILLA BUTTER FROSTING

·······················

Butter is beaten into a flour-thickened base to make an exquisitely light and creamy frosting. Make sure the frosting base is completely cooled before beating in the butter.

Prep: 10 minutes plus cooling Cook: 8 minutes

- 1 cup sugar
- ½ cup all-purpose flour
- 1⅓ cups milk
- 1 cup butter or margarine (2 sticks), softened
- 1 tablespoon vanilla extract

1. In 2-quart saucepan, thoroughly combine sugar and flour. With wire whisk, gradually stir in milk until smooth. Cook over medium-high heat, stirring frequently, until mixture has thickened and boils. Reduce heat to low; cook 2 minutes, stirring constantly. Remove from heat; cool completely.

2. In medium bowl, with mixer at medium speed, beat butter until light and fluffy. Gradually beat in milk mixture; beat in vanilla. Makes about 3¼ cups.

Each tablespoon: About 55 calories, 0g protein, 5g carbohydrate, 4g total fat (2g saturated), 10mg cholesterol, 39mg sodium.

SILKY LEMON BUTTER FROSTING

Prepare as directed but substitute **1 tablespoon freshly grated lemon peel** for vanilla extract.

SILKY ORANGE BUTTER FROSTING

Prepare as directed but substitute **1 teaspoon freshly grated orange peel** for vanilla extract.

SILKY CHOCOLATE BUTTER FROSTING

Prepare as directed but use ¾ **cup sugar,** ¼ **cup all-purpose flour,** and **3 tablespoons unsweetened cocoa.** Gradually whisk in **1 cup milk** until smooth. Continue as directed but in Step 2 beat in **4 squares (4 ounces) semisweet chocolate, melted and cooled** with milk mixture and vanilla. Makes 3 cups.

Each tablespoon: About 64 calories, 0g protein, 6g carbohydrate, 5g total fat (3g saturated), 11mg cholesterol, 42mg sodium.

WHIPPED CREAM FROSTING

·······················

For the occasions when a cake needs no other embellishment than some freshly whipped cream.

Prep: 5 minutes

- 2 cups heavy or whipping cream
- ¼ cup confectioners' sugar
- 1 teaspoon vanilla extract or
- 2 tablespoons brandy or fruit liqueur

In small bowl, with mixer at medium speed, beat cream, confectioners' sugar, and vanilla until stiff peaks form. Makes about 4 cups.

Each tablespoon: About 28 calories, 0g protein, 1g carbohydrate, 3g total fat (2g saturated), 10mg cholesterol, 3mg sodium.

COFFEE WHIPPED CREAM FROSTING

Prepare as directed but dissolve **2 teaspoons instant-coffee powder** in **2 teaspoons hot water;** add to cream.

PEPPERMINT WHIPPED CREAM FROSTING

Beat cream as directed but omit sugar and vanilla extract. Fold in ¼ **cup crushed peppermint candy.**

COCOA WHIPPED CREAM FROSTING

Prepare as directed but use ½ **cup confectioners' sugar** and add ½ **cup unsweetened cocoa.**

CHOCOLATE GLAZE

·······················

Pour or spread the warm, never hot, glaze over cakes, cream puffs, or other desserts. The glaze will thicken and set as it cools.

- 3 squares (3 ounces) semisweet chocolate, coarsely chopped
- 3 tablespoons butter
- 1 tablespoon light corn syrup
- 1 tablespoon milk

In heavy 1-quart saucepan, heat chocolate, butter, corn syrup, and milk over low heat, stirring occasionally, until smooth. Makes about ½ cup.

Each tablespoon: About 100 calories, 1g protein, 9g carbohydrate, 8g total fat (5g saturated), 12mg cholesterol, 50mg sodium.

FLUFFY WHITE FROSTING

....

This irresistible marshmallowlike frosting is at its best the day it is made. If you're planning on frosting a chocolate cake, omit the lemon juice.

Prep: 15 minutes   Cook: 7 minutes

- 2 large egg whites
- 1 cup sugar
- ¼ cup water
- 2 teaspoons fresh lemon juice (optional)
- 1 teaspoon light corn syrup
- ¼ teaspoon cream of tartar

1. In medium bowl set over 3- to 4-quart saucepan filled with *1 inch simmering water* (bowl should sit about 2 inches above water), with handheld mixer at high speed, beat egg whites, sugar, water, lemon juice if using, corn syrup, and cream of tartar until soft peaks form and mixture reaches 160°F on candy thermometer, about 7 minutes.

2. Remove bowl from pan; beat egg-white mixture until stiff, glossy peaks form, 5 to 10 minutes longer. Makes about 3 cups.

Each tablespoon: About 17 calories, 0g protein, 4g carbohydrate, 0g total fat (0g saturated), 0mg cholesterol, 2mg sodium.

FLUFFY HARVEST MOON FROSTING

Prepare as directed but use **1 cup packed dark brown sugar** for granulated sugar and omit lemon juice.

CREAM CHEESE FROSTING

....

This is the classic frosting for carrot cake (page 637), but do try it with banana or spice layer cakes, too.

Prep: 10 minutes

- 2 small packages (3 ounces each) cream cheese, slightly softened
- 6 tablespoons butter or margarine, softened
- 3 cups confectioners' sugar
- 1½ teaspoons vanilla extract

In large bowl, with mixer at low speed, beat cream cheese, butter, confectioners' sugar, and vanilla just until blended. Increase speed to medium. Beat until smooth and fluffy, about 1 minute, frequently scraping bowl with rubber spatula. Makes about 2½ cups.

Each tablespoon: About 66 calories, 0g protein, 9g carbohydrate, 3g total fat (2g saturated), 9mg cholesterol, 30mg sodium.

LEMON FILLING

....

This vibrant pucker-producing filling is popular. It makes enough to fill two or three cake layers.

Prep: 15 minutes plus chilling   Cook: 8 minutes

- 3 large lemons
- 1 tablespoon cornstarch
- 6 tablespoons butter, cut into pieces (do not use margarine)
- ¾ cup sugar
- 4 large egg yolks

1. From lemons, grate 1 tablespoon peel and squeeze ½ cup juice. In 2-quart saucepan, with wire whisk, mix cornstarch and lemon peel and juice until blended. Add butter and sugar. Heat to boiling over medium-high heat, stirring constantly; boil 1 minute.

2. In small bowl, lightly beat egg yolks. Into egg yolks, beat ¼ cup hot lemon mixture; pour egg mixture back into lemon mixture in saucepan, beating rapidly to prevent curdling. Reduce heat to low; cook, stirring constantly, until mixture has thickened (do not boil), about 5 minutes. Pour into medium bowl. Press plastic wrap onto surface. Refrigerate until chilled, at least 3 hours or up to 3 days. Makes about 1 cup.

Each tablespoon: About 93 calories, 1g protein, 11g carbohydrate, 6g total fat (3g saturated), 65mg cholesterol, 46mg sodium.

GANACHE

Ganache is a thick, creamy chocolate filling meant to be slathered between layers of your favorite cake.

Prep: 15 minutes plus chilling

- 1 cup heavy or whipping cream
- 2 tablespoons sugar
- 2 teaspoons butter or margarine
- 10 squares (10 ounces) semisweet chocolate, chopped
- 1 teaspoon vanilla extract
- 1 to 2 tablespoons brandy or orange- or almond-flavored liqueur (optional)

1. In 2-quart saucepan, combine cream, sugar, and butter; heat to boiling over medium-high heat. Remove saucepan from heat.

2. Add chocolate to cream mixture and with wire whisk, whisk until chocolate melts and mixture is smooth. Stir in vanilla and brandy, if using. Pour into jelly-roll pan and refrigerate until spreadable, at least 30 minutes. Makes 2 cups.

Each tablespoon: About 74 calories, 1g protein, 6g carbohydrate, 6g total fat (3g saturated), 11mg cholesterol, 6mg sodium.

CHOCOLATE GARNISHES

CHOCOLATE CURLS

Use these curls to garnish ice cream, cakes, and pies.

Prep: 15 minutes plus chilling

- 1 package (6 ounces) semisweet chocolate chips
- 2 tablespoons vegetable shortening

1. In heavy 1-quart saucepan, combine chocolate chips and shortening; heat over low heat, stirring frequently, until melted and smooth.

2. Pour chocolate mixture into foil-lined or disposable 5¾" by 3¼" loaf pan. Refrigerate until chocolate is set, about 2 hours.

3. Remove chocolate from pan. Using vegetable peeler and working over waxed paper, draw blade across surface of chocolate to make large curls. If chocolate is too cold and curls break, let chocolate stand about 30 minutes at room temperature until slightly softened. To avoid breaking curls, use toothpick or wooden skewer to transfer.

CHOCOLATE LEAVES

Use only nontoxic leaves, such as lemon, gardenia, grape, magnolia, nasturtium, rose, and violet, which are available at some florist shops.

Prep: 30 minutes plus chilling

- 12 lemon leaves or other nontoxic leaves
- 1 package (6 ounces) semisweet chocolate chips
- ¼ cup vegetable shortening

1. Wash leaves in warm soapy water; pat thoroughly dry with paper towels.

2. In heavy 1-quart saucepan, combine chocolate chips and shortening; heat over low heat, stirring frequently, until melted and smooth.

3. With pastry brush or small metal spatula, spread layer of melted chocolate mixture on underside (back) of each leaf (underside will give more distinct leaf design). Place chocolate-coated leaves, chocolate side up, on waxed paper–lined cookie sheet. Refrigerate until chocolate is firm, about 30 minutes.

4. With cool hands, carefully and gently peel each leaf away from chocolate.

> **TOXIC LEAVES**
>
> Do not allow these leaves to come in contact with chocolate or any other foods: amaryllis, azalea, caladium, daffodil, delphinium, dieffenbachia, English ivy, hydrangea, jonquil, larkspur, laurel, lily of the valley, mistletoe, narcissus, oleander, rhododendron.

22

PIES & TARTS

Whether a pie is bursting with seasonal fruit, filled with creamy custard, or crowned with meringue, you can always count on one thing: It will be delicious. Of course, a tender, flaky crust is one of the most important elements. There's no mystery to making a fine crust: Just follow our easy mixing and rolling techniques, and you'll find that it's as . . . easy as pie.

INGREDIENTS

The flavor and texture of a baked piecrust depend on two main ingredients: flour and fat. For the tenderest crust, use all-purpose flour.

The single most important factor in the quest for tender pastry is the fat. Butter gives a dough rich flavor, crispness, and color; vegetable shortening makes it flaky. We use butter and shortening to give piecrust the best qualities of each. To keep the fat in the dough chilled and firm, use ice water to bring the ingredients together. And be sure both the butter and shortening are well chilled. The pieces of fat should hold their shape. The kitchen should be cool, too. If you must make pie on a hot day, chill the flour.

MIXING THE DOUGH

• A pastry blender is the best utensil for blending fat and flour. But you can also use two dinner knives, scissor-fashion, to cut in the fat until the mixture resembles coarse crumbs. Using a fork to toss, combine the mixture, then sprinkle in the water, 1 tablespoon at a time, mixing lightly after each addition, just until the dough is moist enough to hold together.

• Shape the dough into one or more disks, depending on the recipe. Wrap each disk in waxed paper or plastic wrap and chill for at least 30 minutes or up to overnight. If it's been chilled overnight, allow the dough to stand at room temperature for about 30 minutes to soften it slightly or it will crack when rolled out.

ROLLING OUT THE DOUGH

To prevent sticking, dust the work surface lightly with flour. Rub the rolling pin with flour, too. If you wish, sprinkle a little flour on top of the dough. Start in the center and roll out the dough, rolling up to—but not over—the edge. Give the dough a quarter turn. Repeat until you have an even round. If the dough tears, just moisten the edges and press them together.

THE PERFECT FIT

Use a glass pie plate or a dull metal one. We use a standard 9-inch pie plate for most of our pies. Some fruit pies call for a deep-dish pie plate (9 inches wide by 1½ to 2 inches deep). For tarts, use a fluted pan with a removable bottom.

There are two ways to transfer rolled-out dough to a pie plate or tart pan: Loosely roll the dough onto the rolling pin, position the pin at one side of the pie plate, and unroll the dough. Alternatively, fold the rolled-out dough into quarters, set it into the pie plate, and unfold.

Fit the dough into the pie plate by gently easing it onto the bottom and against the sides with your fingertips. Never stretch the dough to fit, or the crust may

Deep-Dish Peach-Berry Pie (recipe page 666)

shrink during baking. To help reduce shrinkage in single-crust pies, chill the piecrust for 10 to 15 minutes before baking.

DECORATIVE PIE EDGES

These borders are the perfect way to add a professional finish to homemade pies.

Forked Edge Trim the dough edge even with the rim of the pie plate. With floured fork tines, press patterns into the dough edge at even intervals.

Fluted Edge Trim the dough edge, leaving a 1-inch overhang. Fold the overhang under; form a stand-up edge. Place the thumb and forefinger of one hand, ½ inch apart, on the outside of the pastry edge; pinch the dough into a V shape. With the forefinger of your other hand on the inner side of the pastry edge, push the dough to define the shape. Repeat.

Turret Edge Trim the dough edge, leaving a 1-inch overhang. Fold the overhang under; form a stand-up edge. With a knife, cut the dough at ½-inch intervals. Fold the dough pieces down, alternating toward and away from the rim.

Appliqué Edge Prepare Pastry Dough for 2-Crust Pie (opposite). Roll out the dough for the bottom crust and place in the pie plate as directed; trim the edge even with the rim of the plate. Roll out the remaining disk of dough ⅛ inch thick. With a floured small knife or small cookie cutter, cut out small leaves or hearts. Lightly brush the dough edge with water. Gently press the shapes, slightly overlapping them, onto the dough edge to adhere.

Crimped Edge Trim the dough edge, leaving a 1-inch overhang. Fold the overhang under; form a stand-up edge. Push one index finger against the inside edge of the rim; with the index finger and thumb of the other hand, pinch dough to flute. Repeat all around the edge, leaving ¼ inch between each flute.

PIE TOPS

Prepare Pastry Dough for 2-Crust Pie (right). Roll out the dough for the bottom crust and place in the pie plate as directed; fill. Roll out the remaining disk into a 12-inch round; proceed as directed below.

Window Center the dough round over the filling. Trim the edge, leaving a 1-inch overhang. Form a stand-up edge and make a decorative edge (left). Cut a 4-inch X in the center of the top crust; gently fold back the points to make a square opening.

Lattice With a pastry wheel or small knife, cut the dough round into ½-inch-wide strips. Moisten the edge of the bottom crust with water. Evenly space half of the pastry strips across the top of the pie; press at both ends to seal. Place an equal number of strips on top at a right angle. Trim the edge, leaving a 1-inch overhang, then moisten and press the strips. Turn the overhang over the ends of the strips. Form a high stand-up edge and make a decorative edge.

Appliqué Center the dough round over the filling. Trim the edge, leaving a 1-inch overhang. Form a stand-up edge and make a decorative edge (left). Roll out the trimmings. Use a small knife dipped in flour to cut free-form shapes. Brush the undersides of the dough shapes with water; place, moistened-side down, on top of the pie.

BAKING IT RIGHT

To catch any overflow, bake the pie on a sheet of foil with the edges crimped, or place on a foil-lined cookie sheet. Bake the pie in the lower third of the oven so the bottom crust crisps and the top doesn't overbrown (if the top is browning too fast, cover it loosely with foil, opposite).

Before serving, always cool fruit pies on a wire rack so the filling can set.

STORING PIES

Fruit pies can be covered and stored overnight at room temperature. For longer storage, refrigerate. Meringue pies are best the day they are made. Pies with cream or custard fillings should be refrigerated as soon as they are cool. Refrigerate leftovers.

PASTRY DOUGH FOR 2-CRUST PIE

·······································

Every cook should know how to make a from-scratch piecrust. Our perfect recipe gets its flavor from butter and its flakiness from vegetable shortening.

Prep: 15 minutes plus chilling

- 2¼ cups all-purpose flour
- ½ teaspoon salt
- ½ cup cold butter or margarine (1 stick), cut into pieces
- ¼ cup vegetable shortening
- 4 to 6 tablespoons ice water

1. In large bowl, with wire whisk, stir flour and salt. With pastry blender or two knives used scissor-fashion, cut in butter and shortening until mixture resembles coarse crumbs.

2. Sprinkle in ice water, 1 tablespoon at a time, mixing lightly with fork after each addition, until dough is just moist enough to hold together.

3. Shape dough into two disks, one slightly larger than the other. Wrap each disk in plastic wrap and refrigerate 30 minutes or up to overnight. (If chilled overnight, let stand 30 minutes at room temperature before rolling.)

4. On lightly floured surface, with floured rolling pin, roll larger disk into 12-inch round. Roll dough round onto rolling pin and ease into pie plate, pressing dough against side of plate. Trim edge, leaving 1-inch overhang.

Reserve trimmings for decorating pie, if you like. Spoon filling into crust.

5. Roll remaining disk of dough into 12-inch round. Cut ¾-inch circle out of center and cut 1-inch slits to allow steam to escape during baking; center dough over filling. Or make desired pie top (opposite). Fold overhang under; make decorative edge (opposite). Bake as directed in recipe. Makes enough dough for one 9-inch 2-crust pie.

Each ⅒th pastry: About 235 calories, 3g protein, 23g carbohydrate, 15g total fat (7g saturated), 25mg cholesterol, 210mg sodium.

FOOD PROCESSOR PASTRY DOUGH

In food processor with knife blade attached, pulse flour and salt to mix. Evenly distribute butter and shortening on top of flour mixture; pulse just until mixture resembles coarse crumbs. With processor running, pour **¼ cup ice water** through feed tube. Immediately stop motor and pinch dough; it should be just moist enough to hold together. If not, with fork, stir in up to **2 tablespoons additional ice water.** Refrigerate and roll as directed.

SHORTENING PASTRY DOUGH

Prepare as directed but use **¾ cup vegetable shortening** and omit butter; use **1 teaspoon salt.**

VINEGAR PASTRY DOUGH

Prepare as directed but substitute **1 tablespoon distilled white vinegar** for 1 tablespoon ice water.

PROTECTING TOP AND EDGES OF PIECRUST

───────

Fold a 12-inch square of foil into quarters. With scissors, cut out an 8-inch round from middle. Unfold foil and place over pie, folding foil edges around piecrust to cover it.

Place a 12-inch square of foil over pie. Fold foil edges around piecrust to cover it.

PASTRY DOUGH FOR 1-CRUST PIE

....

Chilling a piecrust before baking helps it retain its shape.

Prep: 15 minutes plus chilling

1¼ cups all-purpose flour

¼ teaspoon salt

4 tablespoons cold butter or margarine, cut into pieces

2 tablespoons vegetable shortening

3 to 5 tablespoons ice water

1. In large bowl, with wire whisk, stir flour and salt. With pastry blender or two knives used scissor-fashion, cut in butter and shortening until mixture resembles coarse crumbs.

2. Sprinkle in ice water, 1 tablespoon at a time, mixing lightly with fork after each addition, until dough is just moist enough to hold together.

3. Shape dough into disk; wrap in plastic wrap. Refrigerate 30 minutes or up to overnight. (If chilled overnight, let stand 30 minutes at room temperature before rolling.)

4. On lightly floured surface, with floured rolling pin, roll dough into 12-inch round. Ease into pie plate, gently pressing dough against side of plate.

5. Make decorative edge (page 656) as desired. Refrigerate or freeze until firm, 10 to 15 minutes. Fill and bake as directed in recipe. Makes enough dough for one 9-inch crust.

Each 1/10th pastry: About 123 calories, 2g protein, 13g carbohydrate, 7g total fat (4g saturated), 12mg cholesterol, 104mg sodium.

PASTRY FOR 9-INCH TART

Prepare as directed but use **1 cup all-purpose flour,** ¼ teaspoon salt, **6 tablespoons cold butter or margarine,** cut into pieces, **1 tablespoon vegetable shortening,** and **2 to 3 tablespoons ice water.** In Step 4, roll dough into 11-inch round. Ease dough into 9-inch tart pan with removable bottom. Fold overhang in and press dough against side of pan so it extends ⅛ inch above rim. Proceed as directed. Makes enough pastry for one 9-inch tart shell.

Each ⅛th pastry: About 151 calories, 2g protein, 13g carbohydrate, 10g total fat (6g saturated), 23mg cholesterol, 160mg sodium.

PASTRY FOR 11-INCH TART

Prepare as directed but use **1½ cups all-purpose flour,** ½ **teaspoon salt,** ½ **cup cold butter or margarine** (1 stick), cut into pieces, **2 tablespoons vegetable shortening,** and **3 to 4 tablespoons ice water.** In Step 4, roll dough into 14-inch round. Ease dough into 11-inch tart pan with removable bottom. Fold overhang in and press dough against side of pan so it extends ⅛ inch above rim. Proceed as directed. Makes enough pastry for one 11-inch tart shell.

Each 1/12th pastry: About 148 calories, 2g protein, 13g carbohydrate, 10g total fat (5g saturated), 21mg cholesterol, 175mg sodium.

PREBAKED PIECRUST OR TART SHELL

....

For the best flavor and texture, be sure to bake the piecrust until evenly golden.

Prep: 15 minutes plus chilling   Bake: 20 minutes

1 recipe Pastry Dough for 1-Crust Pie, Pastry for 9-Inch Tart, or Pastry for 11-Inch Tart (left and above)

1. Prepare pastry dough as directed through chilling.

2. Preheat oven to 425°F. Use dough to line 9-inch pie plate, 9-inch tart pan with removable bottom, or 11-inch tart pan with removable bottom. If using pie plate, make decorative edge. If using tart pan, finish edge as directed in recipe. Refrigerate or freeze until firm, 10 to 15 minutes.

3. Line pie or tart shell with foil; fill with pie weights or dry beans. Bake 15 minutes. Remove foil with weights; bake until golden, 5 to 10 minutes longer. If shell puffs up during baking, gently press it down with back of spoon. Cool on wire rack. Fill (and bake) as directed in recipe. Makes 1 piecrust or tart shell.

GRAHAM CRACKER-CRUMB CRUST

....

For the freshest flavor, make your own cookie crumbs.

Prep: 10 minutes   Bake: 10 minutes

1¼ cups graham-cracker crumbs (9 rectangular
      graham crackers)
  4 tablespoons butter or margarine, melted
  1 tablespoon sugar

1. Preheat oven to 375°F. In 9-inch pie plate, with fork, mix crumbs, melted butter, and sugar until crumbs are evenly moistened. Press mixture firmly onto bottom and up side of pie plate, making small rim.

2. Bake 10 minutes; cool on wire rack. Fill as recipe directs. Makes one 9-inch crust.

Each ¹⁄₁₀th crust: About 105 calories, 1g protein, 12g carbohydrate, 6g total fat (3g saturated), 12mg cholesterol, 137mg sodium.

CHOCOLATE WAFER-CRUMB CRUST

Prepare as directed but substitute **1¼ cups chocolate-wafer crumbs (24 cookies)** for graham-cracker crumbs.

Each ¹⁄₁₀th crust: About 108 calories, 1g protein, 12g carbohydrate, 7g total fat (3g saturated), 13mg cholesterol, 130mg sodium.

VANILLA WAFER-CRUMB CRUST

Prepare as directed but substitute **1¼ cups vanilla-wafer crumbs (35 cookies)** for graham-cracker crumbs.

Each ¹⁄₁₀th crust: About 92 calories, 1g protein, 9g carbohydrate, 6g total fat (3g saturated), 12mg cholesterol, 80mg sodium.

MAKING COOKIE CRUMBS

TEST KITCHEN TIP

To make cookie crumbs, place the cookies in a heavy-duty zip-tight plastic bag and crush them with a rolling pin or meat mallet. You can also use a food processor or blender. For about 1 cup crushed cookie crumbs, use twenty 2¼-inch chocolate wafers, 14 gingersnaps, 22 vanilla wafers, or 7 rectangular plain or chocolate graham crackers.

DOUBLE BLUEBERRY PIE

....

In our version of this old New England recipe, we maximize the blueberry flavor by stirring raw berries into the cooked filling. To make it easy for casual summer entertaining, we've paired it with a simple gingersnap crust.

Prep: 30 minutes plus chilling   Bake: 8 minutes

1²⁄₃ cups gingersnap cookie crumbs
       (about 25 cookies)
   5 tablespoons butter or margarine, melted
   2 tablespoons plus ½ cup sugar
   2 tablespoons cornstarch
   2 tablespoons cold water
   3 pints blueberries
      whipped cream (optional)

1. Preheat oven to 375°F. In 9-inch pie plate, with fork, mix cookie crumbs, melted butter, and 2 tablespoons sugar until moistened. With hand, press mixture firmly onto bottom and up side of pie plate. Bake 8 minutes. Cool on wire rack.

2. Meanwhile, in 2-quart saucepan, blend cornstarch and water until smooth. Add half of blueberries and remaining ½ cup sugar to cornstarch mixture; heat to boiling over medium-high heat, pressing blueberries against side of saucepan with back of spoon. Boil, stirring constantly, 1 minute. Remove from heat; stir in remaining blueberries.

3. Pour blueberry filling into cooled crust. Press plastic wrap onto surface and refrigerate until thoroughly chilled, about 5 hours. Serve with whipped cream, if desired. Makes 10 servings.

Each serving: About 241 calories, 2g protein, 42g carbohydrate, 8g total fat (4g saturated), 16mg cholesterol, 201mg sodium.

CLASSIC APPLE PIE

....

For the best flavor, fill this pie with a combination of apples, such as Gala, Granny Smith, and Golden Delicious. You can also use half brown sugar and half granulated sugar.

Prep: 45 minutes plus chilling and cooling
Bake: 1 hour 20 minutes

Pastry Dough for 2-Crust Pie (page 657)

²/₃ cup sugar

2 tablespoons all-purpose flour

½ teaspoon ground cinnamon

⅛ teaspoon salt

3 pounds cooking apples (9 medium), peeled, cored, and thinly sliced

1 tablespoon fresh lemon juice

1 tablespoon butter or margarine, cut into pieces

1. Prepare pastry dough as directed through chilling.

2. In large bowl, with wire whisk, stir sugar, flour, cinnamon, and salt. Add apples and lemon juice; gently toss to combine.

3. Preheat oven to 425°F. Use larger disk of dough to line 9-inch pie plate. Spoon apple filling into crust; dot with butter. Roll out remaining disk of dough; cut center circle and 1-inch slits to allow steam to escape during baking. Place over filling and make decorative edge.

4. Place pie on foil-lined cookie sheet to catch any overflow during baking. Bake 20 minutes. Turn oven control to 375°F; bake until filling bubbles in center, about 1 hour longer. If necessary, cover pie loosely with foil during last 20 minutes of baking to prevent over-browning. Cool on wire rack 1 hour to serve warm, or cool completely to serve later. Makes 10 servings.

Each serving: About 369 calories, 3g protein, 55g carbohydrate, 16g total fat (8g saturated), 28mg cholesterol, 251mg sodium.

VERY BLUEBERRY PIE

Prepare as directed above but use **¾ cup sugar, ¼ cup cornstarch,** and a **pinch salt,** and substitute **6 cups blueberries (about 3 pints)** for apples. In Step 3, dot filling with **2 tablespoons butter or margarine,** cut into pieces. Bake and cool as directed.

Each serving: About 374 calories, 4g protein, 53g carbohydrate, 17g total fat (8g saturated), 31mg cholesterol, 253mg sodium.

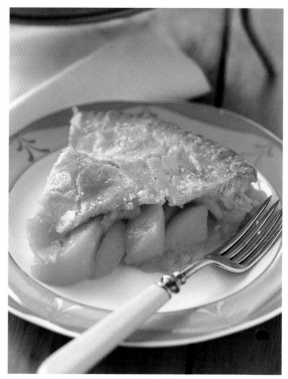

Peach Pie

PEACH PIE

Prepare as directed (left) but use **¾ cup sugar, ¼ cup cornstarch,** and a **pinch salt,** and substitute **3 pounds ripe peaches (9 large),** pitted, peeled, and sliced (7 cups), for apples. In Step 3, dot filling with **2 tablespoons butter or margarine,** cut into pieces. Bake and cool as directed.

Each serving: About 360 calories, 4g protein, 52g carbohydrate, 16g total fat (8g saturated), 28mg cholesterol, 236mg sodium.

RHUBARB PIE

Prepare as directed (left) but use **1½ cups sugar, ¼ cup cornstarch,** and a **pinch salt,** and substitute **2 pounds rhubarb,** trimmed and cut into ½-inch pieces (7 cups), for apples. In Step 3, dot filling with **2 tablespoons butter or margarine,** cut into pieces. Bake and cool as directed.

Each serving: About 387 calories, 4g protein, 59g carbohydrate, 16g total fat (8g saturated), 28mg cholesterol, 239mg sodium.

DEEP-DISH APPLE PIE

....

People with a passion for piecrust will appreciate this double-crust delight: Flaky layers of dough encase a sweet, tender apple filling. Yum!

Prep: 45 minutes plus chilling and cooling
Bake: 1 hour 10 minutes

Pastry

2½ cups all-purpose flour
½ teaspoon salt
10 tablespoons cold butter or margarine (1¼ sticks), cut into pieces
6 tablespoons vegetable shortening
6 to 7 tablespoons ice water

Apple Filling

⅔ cup sugar
⅓ cup cornstarch
½ teaspoon ground cinnamon
¼ teaspoon ground nutmeg
¼ teaspoon salt
3½ pounds Granny Smith, Golden Delicious, and/or Braeburn apples, each peeled, cored, and cut into 16 wedges
1 tablespoon fresh lemon juice
2 tablespoons butter or margarine, cut up
1 large egg white, lightly beaten
1 teaspoon sugar

1. Prepare pastry: In food processor with knife blade attached, blend flour and salt. Add butter and shortening, and pulse until mixture resembles coarse crumbs. Sprinkle in ice water, 1 tablespoon at a time, pulsing after each addition, until large moist crumbs just begin to form.

2. Shape dough into two balls, one slightly larger. Flatten each into a disk; wrap each in plastic wrap and refrigerate 30 minutes or overnight. (If chilled overnight, let stand 30 minutes at room temperature before rolling.)

3. Meanwhile, preheat oven to 400°F. Place cookie sheet on rack in lower third of preheating oven to bake pie on later. Prepare apple filling: In large bowl, combine sugar with cornstarch, cinnamon, nutmeg, and salt. Add apples and lemon juice, and toss to coat evenly.

4. On lightly floured surface, with floured rolling pin, roll larger disk of dough into 12-inch round. Ease dough into 9½-inch deep-dish glass or ceramic pie plate, gently pressing dough against side of plate. Trim dough edge, leaving 1-inch overhang; reserve trimmings. Spoon apple mixture into pie crust; dot with butter.

5. Roll remaining disk for top crust into 12-inch round. Place over filling in bottom crust. Trim pastry edge, leaving 1-inch overhang; reserve trimmings. Fold overhang under; make decorative edge (page 656). Brush crust with some egg white. Reroll trimmings. With knife or cookie cutters, cut out apple and/or leaf shapes; arrange on pie. Cut short slashes in top crust to allow steam to escape during baking. Brush cutouts with egg white, then sprinkle crust and cutouts with sugar.

6. Bake pie 1 hour 10 minutes or until apples are tender when pierced with knife through slits in crust. Cover pie loosely with foil during last 20 minutes of baking to prevent overbrowning. Cool on wire rack 3 hours to serve warm, or cool completely to serve later. Makes 10 servings.

Each serving: About 455 calories, 4g protein, 61g carbohydrate, 23g total fat (11g saturated), 4g fiber, 39mg cholesterol, 330mg sodium.

Deep-Dish Apple Pie

DEEP-DISH APPLE COBBLER

....

A cobbler is a traditional fruit casserole with a biscuit topping. This version, with apples, bubbles with homespun charm and flavor.

Prep: 30 minutes   **Microwave/Bake:** 43 minutes

Cobbler Crust

  1   cup all-purpose flour
1½   teaspoons baking powder
 ¼   cup plus 1 tablespoon sugar
  3   tablespoons cold butter or margarine,
       cut into ½-inch pieces
 ½   cup plus 1 tablespoon heavy or whipping cream
 ⅛   teaspoon ground cinnamon

Apple Filling

  1   lemon
2½   pounds Granny Smith, Golden Delicious,
       and/or Gala apples, peeled, cored,
       and cut into ½-inch-thick wedges
 ⅓   cup sugar
  2   tablespoons cornstarch
 ⅛   teaspoon salt

1. Prepare cobbler crust: In medium bowl, combine flour, baking powder, and ¼ cup sugar. With pastry blender or using two knives scissor-fashion, cut in butter until mixture resembles fine crumbs. Add ½ cup cream and stir with fork until dough comes together.

2. Gather dough into ball and place on lightly floured sheet of waxed paper. With floured rolling pin, roll dough into 9-inch round. Slide waxed paper onto cookie sheet and refrigerate dough until ready to use. In cup, mix cinnamon and remaining 1 tablespoon sugar; set aside.

3. Preheat oven to 400°F. Prepare apple filling: From lemon, grate ½ teaspoon peel and squeeze 1 tablespoon juice. In large bowl, toss lemon peel and juice with apples, sugar, cornstarch, and salt. Transfer apple mixture to 9½-inch deep-dish glass or ceramic pie plate. Cover with waxed paper and cook in microwave oven on High 8 minutes or until apples are fork-tender, stirring well halfway through cooking.

4. Immediately, while filling is hot, remove dough round from refrigerator and, with the help of the waxed paper, invert dough over apple mixture. Peel off paper. Cut 4-inch X in center of round; fold back points to make square opening. Brush dough with remaining 1 tablespoon heavy cream; sprinkle with cinnamon-sugar.

5. Bake pie 35 to 40 minutes or until filling is bubbling in center. If crust is browning too quickly, loosely cover pie with foil after 25 minutes. Cool pie on wire rack. Makes 12 servings.

Each serving: About 195 calories, 2g protein, 32g carbohydrate, 8g total fat (5g saturated), 2g fiber, 24mg cholesterol, 110mg sodium.

EASIEST APPLE PIE EVER

....

We'll never tell! Store-bought piecrust and a filling pre-cooked in the microwave make this pie fast and easy—and absolutely delicious.

Prep: 10 minutes   **Bake/Microwave:** 22 minutes

  1   frozen deep-dish piecrust
 ½   cup chopped pecans
 ¼   cup all-purpose flour
 ¼   cup packed brown sugar
  2   tablespoons butter or margarine
  1   large egg white
 ¼   cup granulated sugar
  2   tablespoons cornstarch
 ½   teaspoon ground cinnamon
  3   pounds Granny Smith, Golden Delicious,
       and/or Gala apples, each cored, peeled,
       and cut into 8 wedges
  1   tablespoon fresh lemon juice
       vanilla ice cream for serving (optional)

1. Preheat oven to 375°F. While crust is thawing at room temperature for 15 minutes, mix pecans, flour, and brown sugar in bowl. Work in butter with fingertips until mixture resembles coarse crumbs. Set aside.

2. Prick bottom and sides of crust with fork. Bake 12 to 15 minutes or until lightly golden. Immediately brush bottom and sides of hot crust with light coating of egg white. Reset oven to 425°F.

3. Meanwhile, in large bowl, combine granulated sugar, cornstarch, and cinnamon. Toss in apples and lemon juice. Cover with waxed paper and microwave on High 12 minutes, stirring halfway through. Spoon filling into crust. Sprinkle pecan topping over filling.

4. Bake pie 10 to 12 minutes or until topping is golden. Cool on wire rack. Serve with vanilla ice cream, if you like. Makes 10 servings.

Each serving: About 290 calories, 3g protein, 43g carbohydrate, 12g total fat (3g saturated), 3g fiber, 7mg cholesterol, 120mg sodium.

Tip: For a true homemade presentation, use our trick to transfer the store-bought crust from its foil pan to a 9-inch pie plate: Gently fold back the foil around edge of the frozen crust and pull slightly on the crust to remove it. Place it in the pie plate and thaw as directed. Before filling the crust, use your fingertips to press lightly on the thawed dough to mold it into the shape of the pie plate.

Strawberry Cheese Pie

DELUXE CHEESE PIE

This is like a scrumptious classic cheesecake, but it's made in a fraction of the time.

Prep: 20 minutes plus cooling and chilling
Bake: 45 minutes

Graham Cracker-Crumb Crust (page 659)
1½ packages (8 ounces each) cream cheese, softened
½ cup plus 2 tablespoons sugar
2 large eggs
½ teaspoon vanilla extract
1 container (8 ounces) sour cream

1. Preheat oven to 350°F. Prepare crust as directed. Cool on wire rack.

2. In medium bowl, with mixer at low speed, beat cream cheese and ½ cup sugar until smooth, occasionally scraping side of bowl with rubber spatula. Add eggs and vanilla; beat just until combined.

3. Pour cheese filling into cooled crust. Bake until set, about 30 minutes.

4. Blend sour cream and remaining 2 tablespoons sugar. Spread evenly over hot pie. Bake until set, about 5 minutes. Cool pie on wire rack. Refrigerate at least 2 hours for easier slicing or up to overnight. Makes 10 servings.

Each serving: About 337 calories, 6g protein, 27g carbohydrate, 23g total fat (14g saturated), 102mg cholesterol, 262mg sodium.

STRAWBERRY CHEESE PIE

Prepare as directed but omit sour-cream mixture; cool pie completely. Arrange **1½ pints strawberries,** hulled and cut in half, on top of pie. In small saucepan, heat **⅓ cup red currant jelly** over medium-low heat until melted and bubbling; brush over strawberries.

TART CHERRY PIE

....

If you see tart (sour) cherries in your farmers' market, buy enough to make several desserts and freeze the extra cherries for later use.

Prep: 1 hour plus chilling
Bake: 1 hour 20 minutes

Pastry Dough for 2-Crust Pie (page 657)
- 1 cup sugar
- ¼ cup cornstarch
  pinch salt
- 2¼ pounds tart (sour) cherries, pitted (4½ cups)
- 1 tablespoon butter or margarine, cut into pieces

1. Prepare pastry dough as directed through chilling.

2. Preheat oven to 425°F. In large bowl, with wire whisk, stir sugar, cornstarch, and salt. Add cherries and toss to combine.

3. Use larger disk of dough to line 9-inch pie plate. Spoon cherry filling into crust; dot with butter. Roll out remaining disk of dough; cut out center circle and 1-inch slits to allow steam to escape during baking. Place dough over filling; make decorative edge (page 656).

4. Place pie on foil-lined cookie sheet to catch any overflow during baking. Bake 20 minutes. Turn oven control to 375°F; bake until filling bubbles in center, 1 hour to 1 hour 10 minutes longer. Cover pie loosely with foil during last 20 minutes of baking to prevent overbrowning. Cool on wire rack 1 hour to serve warm, or cool completely to serve later. Makes 10 servings.

Each serving: About 381 calories, 4g protein, 57g carbohydrate, 16g total fat (8g saturated), 28mg cholesterol, 239mg sodium.

FROZEN TART CHERRY PIE

Prepare as directed above but use **1¼ cups sugar, 1 bag (20 ounces) frozen tart cherries,** thawed (with their juice), and **⅓ cup cornstarch.**

CANNED CHERRY PIE

Prepare as directed but use **2 cans (16 ounces each) pitted tart (sour) cherries packed in water.** Drain; reserve ½ cup cherry juice. In medium bowl, combine **¾ cup sugar, ¼ cup cornstarch, ⅛ teaspoon ground cinnamon,** and **pinch salt.** Add reserved cherry juice, cherries, and **½ teaspoon vanilla;** toss to combine.

LEMON MERINGUE PIE

....

Here is our favorite recipe for this all-time classic lemon masterpiece, crowned with billowing meringue.

Prep: 45 minutes plus chilling and cooling
Bake: 30 minutes

Pastry Dough for 1-Crust Pie (page 658)
- 4 to 6 lemons
- 1½ cups sugar
- ⅓ cup cornstarch
- ¼ teaspoon plus pinch salt
- 1½ cups water
- 3 large eggs, separated, plus 1 large egg white
- 2 tablespoons butter or margarine, cut into pieces
- ¼ teaspoon cream of tartar

1. Prepare pastry dough as directed through chilling.

2. Preheat oven to 425°F. Use dough to line 9-inch pie plate; make decorative edge (page 656). Refrigerate or freeze until firm, 10 to 15 minutes.

3. Line pie shell with foil; fill with pie weights or dry beans. Bake 15 minutes. Remove foil with weights; bake until golden, 5 to 10 minutes longer. If pastry puffs up during baking, press it down with back of spoon. Cool on wire rack.

4. Meanwhile, from lemons, grate 1 tablespoon peel and squeeze ¾ cup juice; set aside.

5. In 2-quart saucepan, combine 1 cup sugar, cornstarch, and ¼ teaspoon salt; stir in water. Cook over medium heat, stirring constantly, until mixture has thickened and boils; boil 1 minute. Remove from heat.

6. In small bowl, whisk egg yolks. Stir in ⅓ cup hot cornstarch mixture until blended; slowly pour yolk mixture back into in saucepan, stirring rapidly to prevent curdling. Place pan over low heat; cook, stirring constantly, until filling is very thick, about 4 minutes. Remove from heat; stir in butter, then gradually stir in lemon peel and juice until blended. Pour into cooled pie shell.

7. Turn oven control to 400°F. In small bowl, with mixer at high speed, beat egg whites, cream of tartar, and pinch salt until soft peaks form when beaters are lifted. Sprinkle in ½ cup sugar, 2 tablespoons at a time, beating until sugar has dissolved and egg whites stand in stiff, glossy peaks when beaters are lifted.

8. Spread meringue over filling to edge of pie shell. Decoratively swirl meringue with back of spoon. Bake until meringue is golden, about 10 minutes. Cool on wire rack away from drafts. Refrigerate at least 3 hours for easier slicing or up to 2 days. Makes 10 servings.

Each serving: About 321 calories, 4g protein, 52g carbohydrate, 11g total fat (5g saturated), 82mg cholesterol, 224mg sodium.

PILGRIM PUMPKIN PIE

....

For those who prefer a spicy pie, add $^1/_8$ teaspoon ground white pepper, or serve with softly whipped cream flavored with ground ginger.

Prep: 25 minutes plus chilling
Bake: 1 hour 10 minutes

Pastry Dough for 1-Crust Pie (page 658)
1 can (15 ounces) solid-pack pumpkin (not pumpkin-pie filling) or 2 cups mashed cooked pumpkin (page 429)
1 can (12 ounces) evaporated milk
$^3/_4$ cup packed brown sugar
2 large eggs
1 teaspoon ground cinnamon
$^1/_2$ teaspoon ground ginger
$^1/_2$ teaspoon salt
$^1/_4$ teaspoon ground nutmeg

1. Prepare pastry dough as directed through chilling.
2. Preheat oven to 425°F. Use dough to line 9-inch pie plate; make high stand-up edge. Refrigerate or freeze until firm, 10 to 15 minutes.
3. Line pie shell with foil; fill with pie weights or dry beans. Bake 15 minutes. Remove foil with weights; bake until golden, 5 to 10 minutes longer. If shell puffs up during baking, gently press it down with back of spoon. Turn oven control to 375°F.
4. In large bowl, with wire whisk, mix pumpkin, evaporated milk, brown sugar, eggs, cinnamon, ginger, salt, and nutmeg until well combined. Place piecrust-lined pie plate on oven rack; carefully pour in pumpkin filling. Bake until knife inserted 1 inch from edge comes out clean, about 50 minutes. Cool on wire rack at least 1 hour or up to 6 hours. Makes 10 servings.

Each serving: About 267 calories, 6g protein, 36g carbohydrate, 11g total fat (6g saturated), 66mg cholesterol, 282mg sodium.

PUMPKIN CHEESECAKE PIE

....

Don't wait for a holiday to try this irresistibly tasty pie; it's a great finish to any autumnal meal.

Prep: 30 minutes plus chilling and cooling
Bake: 1 hour

Pastry Dough for 1-Crust Pie (page 658)
1 package (8 ounces) reduced-fat cream cheese (Neufchâtel), softened
$^1/_2$ cup granulated sugar
$^1/_4$ cup packed brown sugar
1 can (15 ounces) pure pumpkin puree (not pumpkin-pie filling)
1 teaspoon ground cinnamon
$^1/_2$ teaspoon ground ginger
$^1/_4$ teaspoon ground nutmeg
$^1/_4$ teaspoon salt
3 large eggs
$^1/_2$ cup heavy or whipping cream
2 tablespoons molasses
1 teaspoon vanilla extract

1. Prepare pastry dough as directed through chilling.
2. Preheat oven to 400°F. Line pie shell with foil and fill with pie weights, dry beans, or uncooked rice. Bake pie shell 15 to 20 minutes or until set. Remove foil and weights and bake 5 to 8 minutes longer or until shell is golden. If shell puffs up during baking, gently press it down with back of spoon. Remove crust from oven to cool slightly. Lower oven heat to 350°F.
3. Meanwhile, prepare cheesecake filling: In large bowl, with mixer on medium speed, beat cream cheese and sugars until smooth. Add pumpkin, cinnamon, ginger, nutmeg, and salt; beat until blended, occasionally scraping bowl with rubber spatula. Add eggs, cream, molasses, and vanilla; beat until well blended, occasionally scraping bowl. Pour filling into hot pie shell.
4. Bake pie 40 to 45 minutes or until filling is puffed and set at edges but still jiggles slightly in center. Cool completely on wire rack, then cover and refrigerate at least 6 hours or until firm and well chilled. Makes 12 servings.

Each serving: About 300 calories, 6g protein, 31g carbohydrate, 18g total fat (9g saturated), 2g fiber, 92mg cholesterol, 240mg sodium.

DEEP-DISH PEACH-BERRY PIE

(Pictured on page 654)

··

We love to prepare this pie with a mix of berries, but it is equally delicious with only one or two types of berries.

Prep: 40 minutes plus chilling and cooling
Bake: 35 minutes

Crust

- 1 cup all-purpose flour
- 1½ teaspoons baking powder
- ¼ cup plus 1 tablespoon sugar
- 3 tablespoons cold butter or margarine, cut into pieces
- ½ cup plus 1 tablespoon heavy or whipping cream
- ⅛ teaspoon ground cinnamon

Fruit Filling

- ½ cup sugar
- ¼ cup cold water
- 2 tablespoons cornstarch
- 2 pounds ripe peaches (about 5 medium), pitted and cut into 1-inch pieces
- 3 cups assorted berries (1 cup each blueberries, blackberries, and raspberries)

1. Prepare crust: In medium bowl, combine flour, baking powder, and ¼ cup sugar. With pastry blender or two knives used scissor-fashion, cut in butter until mixture resembles fine crumbs. Add ½ cup cream and stir with fork until dough comes together. Gather dough into ball and place on lightly floured sheet of waxed paper. With floured rolling pin, roll into 9-inch round. Slide waxed paper onto cookie sheet; refrigerate dough. Mix cinnamon and remaining 1 tablespoon sugar.

2. Prepare filling: Preheat oven to 400°F. Place cookie sheet lined with foil in oven. In 4-quart saucepan, stir sugar, water, and cornstarch until cornstarch dissolves. Add peaches; heat to boiling over medium-high heat, stirring often. Reduce heat to low; simmer, stirring often, 2 minutes. Remove from heat; stir in berries. Pour filling into 9½-inch deep-dish pie plate.

3. Immediately remove dough from refrigerator and, using waxed paper, invert over fruit. Peel off paper. Cut 4-inch X in center of round; fold back points to make square opening. Brush dough with remaining 1 tablespoon cream; sprinkle with cinnamon sugar.

4. Place pie on foil-lined cookie sheet to catch any overflow. Bake until fruit is bubbly in center, 35 to 40 minutes. If necessary, cover pie loosely with foil during last 10 minutes of baking to prevent overbrowning. Cool pie on wire rack. Makes 8 servings.

Each serving: About 310 calories, 3g protein, 51g carbohydrate, 11g total fat (7g saturated), 35mg cholesterol, 130mg sodium.

PECAN PIE

··

This southern classic couldn't be any richer or more delicious.

Prep: 25 minutes plus chilling and cooling
Bake: 1 hour 5 minutes

Pastry Dough for 1-Crust Pie (page 658)
- 1¾ cups pecan halves (7 ounces)
- ¾ cup dark corn syrup
- ½ cup packed brown sugar
- 4 tablespoons butter or margarine, melted
- 1 teaspoon vanilla extract
- 3 large eggs

1. Prepare pastry dough as directed through chilling.

2. Preheat oven to 425°F. Use dough to line 9-inch pie plate; make decorative edge (page 656). Refrigerate or freeze until firm, 10 to 15 minutes.

3. Line pie shell with foil; fill with pie weights or dry beans. Bake 15 minutes. Remove foil with weights; bake until golden, 5 to 10 minutes longer. If shell puffs up during baking, gently press it down with back of spoon. Cool on wire rack. Turn oven control to 350°F.

4. Coarsely chop 1 cup pecans. In large bowl, with wire whisk, mix corn syrup, brown sugar, melted butter, vanilla, and eggs until blended. Stir in chopped pecans and remaining ¾ cup pecan halves.

5. Pour pecan filling into cooled pie shell. Bake until filling is set around edges but center jiggles slightly, 45 to 50 minutes. Cool on wire rack at least 1 hour for easier slicing. Makes 12 servings.

Each serving: About 353 calories, 4g protein, 38g carbohydrate, 22g total fat (7g saturated), 74mg cholesterol, 177mg sodium.

CHOCOLATE PECAN PIE

Prepare as directed (left) but use ¾ **cup packed dark brown sugar** and add **2 squares (2 ounces) unsweetened chocolate,** melted, to filling with butter.

BANANA CREAM PIE

....

A vanilla wafer–crumb crust is our favorite for this pie, but if you love the combination of chocolate and bananas, use the Chocolate Wafer–Crumb Crust variation.

Prep: 30 minutes plus cooling and chilling
Bake: 10 minutes

Vanilla Wafer–Crumb Crust (page 659)

- ¾ cup sugar
- ⅓ cup cornstarch
- ¼ teaspoon salt
- 3¾ cups milk
- 5 large egg yolks
- 2 tablespoons butter or margarine, cut into pieces
- 1¾ teaspoons vanilla extract
- 3 ripe medium bananas
- ¾ cup heavy or whipping cream

1. Prepare crust as directed. Cool completely.

2. Meanwhile, prepare filling: In 3-quart saucepan, combine sugar, cornstarch, and salt; stir in milk. Cook over medium heat, stirring constantly, until mixture has thickened and boils; boil 1 minute.

3. In small bowl, with wire whisk, lightly beat egg yolks; beat in ½ cup hot milk mixture. Slowly pour egg-yolk mixture back into milk mixture, stirring rapidly to prevent curdling. Cook over low heat, stirring constantly, until mixture has thickened, about 2 minutes.

4. Remove saucepan from heat. Add butter and 1½ teaspoons vanilla; stir until butter melts. Transfer mixture to medium bowl. Press plastic wrap onto surface. Refrigerate, stirring occasionally, until cool, about 1 hour.

5. Slice 2 bananas. Spoon half of filling into crust. Arrange sliced bananas on top; spoon remaining filling evenly over bananas. Press plastic wrap onto surface; refrigerate at least 4 hours or up to overnight.

6. To serve, prepare topping: In small bowl, with mixer at medium speed, beat cream and remaining ¼ teaspoon vanilla until stiff peaks form; spread over filling. Slice remaining banana; arrange around edge of pie. Makes 10 servings.

Each serving: About 367 calories, 6g protein, 41g carbohydrate, 21g total fat (12g saturated), 162mg cholesterol, 216mg sodium.

COCONUT CREAM PIE

Prepare as directed but omit bananas; fold ¾ **cup sweetened flaked coconut** into filling before spooning into crust. Refrigerate and top with whipped cream as directed. To serve, sprinkle with ¼ **cup sweetened flaked coconut,** toasted.

EASY EGGNOG PUMPKIN PIE

....

For a special finish, top each serving with a dollop of whipped cream sprinkled with pumpkin-pie spice.

Prep: 20 minutes plus chilling and cooling
Bake: 1 hour

Pastry Dough for 1-Crust Pie (page 658)

- 1 can (15 ounces) pure pumpkin (not pumpkin-pie filling)
- 1¼ cups prepared eggnog
- ⅔ cup sugar
- 1½ teaspoons pumpkin-pie spice
- ¼ teaspoon salt
- 3 large eggs

1. Prepare pastry dough as directed through chilling.

2. Preheat oven to 375°F. Use dough to line 9-inch pie plate; place on foil-lined cookie sheet.

3. In large bowl, with wire whisk, mix pumpkin, eggnog, sugar, pumpkin-pie spice, salt, and eggs until combined. Pour pumpkin mixture into piecrust (mixture will come up almost to top of crust).

4. Bake until filling puffs up around edges and center is just set but not puffed, about 1 hour. Cool completely on wire rack. Refrigerate until ready to serve. Makes 12 servings.

Each serving: About 165 calories, 3g protein, 23g carbohydrate, 7g total fat (3g saturated), 69mg cholesterol, 150mg sodium.

CHOCOLATE CREAM PIE

....

Dessert doesn't get better than a traditional chocolate cream pie.

**Prep: 35 minutes plus cooling and chilling
Bake: 10 minutes**

Chocolate Wafer-Crumb Crust (page 659)
- ³/₄ cup sugar
- ¹/₃ cup cornstarch
- ¹/₂ teaspoon salt
- 3³/₄ cups milk
- 5 large egg yolks
- 3 squares (3 ounces) unsweetened chocolate, melted
- 2 tablespoons butter or margarine, cut into pieces
- 2 teaspoons vanilla extract
- Chocolate Curls (page 653; optional)
- 1 cup heavy or whipping cream

1. Prepare crust as directed. Cool completely.

2. Meanwhile, in heavy 3-quart saucepan, combine sugar, cornstarch, and salt; whisk in milk until smooth. Cook over medium heat, stirring constantly, until mixture has thickened and boils; boil 1 minute.

3. In small bowl, with wire whisk, lightly beat egg yolks. Beat ¹/₂ cup hot milk mixture into beaten egg yolks. Slowly pour egg-yolk mixture back into milk mixture, stirring rapidly to prevent curdling. Cook over low heat, stirring constantly, until mixture is very thick or until temperature on thermometer reaches 160°F.

4. Remove saucepan from heat and stir in melted chocolate, butter, and vanilla until butter melts and mixture is smooth. Pour hot chocolate filling into cooled crust; press plastic wrap onto surface. Refrigerate until filling is set, about 4 hours.

5. Meanwhile, make Chocolate Curls, if using.

6. To serve, in small bowl, with mixer at medium speed, beat cream until stiff peaks form; spoon over chocolate filling. Top with chocolate curls, if desired. Makes 10 servings.

Each serving: About 417 calories, 7g protein, 38g carbohydrate, 28g total fat (16g saturated), 171mg cholesterol, 329mg sodium.

Chocolate Cream Pie

APPLE CRUMB SQUARES

....

A tender butter crust; a generous filling of cooked apples, raisins, and brown sugar; and a walnut and brown sugar topping make this dessert irresistible.

Prep: 1 hour plus cooling   Bake: 1 hour

Crumb Topping
- 1 cup all-purpose flour
- 1 cup pecans or walnuts, coarsely chopped
- ¹/₂ cup butter or margarine (1 stick), slightly softened
- ¹/₂ cup light or dark brown sugar
- 1 tablespoon vanilla extract
- 1 teaspoon ground cinnamon

Crust
- 3 cups all-purpose flour
- ¹/₃ cup granulated sugar
- ¹/₄ teaspoon salt
- ³/₄ cup cold butter or margarine (1¹/₂ sticks)

Apple Filling

- 4 pounds green cooking apples, such as Granny Smith, peeled, cored, and cut into ½-inch pieces
- 4 tablespoons butter or margarine
- ¾ cup raisins or dried currants
- ½ cup packed light or dark brown sugar
- ¾ teaspoon ground cinnamon
- 1 tablespoon plus 2 teaspoons cornstarch
- 3 tablespoons fresh lemon juice

1. Prepare topping: In medium bowl, with fingertips, mix flour, pecans, butter, brown sugar, vanilla, and cinnamon until mixture comes together. Shape into a ball; wrap in plastic wrap and refrigerate.

2. Preheat oven to 375°F. Lightly grease sides of 15½" by 10½" jelly-roll pan.

3. Prepare crust: In large bowl, with fork, mix flour, granulated sugar, and salt. With pastry blender or two knives used scissor-fashion, cut in butter until mixture resembles fine crumbs. With hand, press crumb mixture evenly onto bottom of prepared pan.

4. Bake crust until golden brown (crust may crack slightly), 20 to 24 minutes.

5. Meanwhile, prepare filling: In nonstick 12-inch skillet, cook apples, butter, raisins, brown sugar, and cinnamon over medium heat, stirring occasionally, until apples are very tender and most of liquid from apples has evaporated, 25 to 30 minutes. In cup, mix cornstarch and lemon juice. Stir lemon-juice mixture into apple mixture and cook, stirring, until mixture thickens. Remove skillet from heat.

6. Spread apple mixture over hot crust. Break crumb topping into chunks and scatter over apple mixture. Bake until topping browns, about 40 minutes. Cool completely in pan on wire rack.

7. To serve, cut lengthwise into 4 strips, then cut each strip crosswise into 6 squares. Makes 24 squares.

Each square: About 315 calories, 3g protein, 42g carbohydrate, 16g total fat (8g saturated), 33mg cholesterol, 155mg sodium.

FROZEN KEY LIME PIE

Quick, refreshing, and light—what more could you ask for in a summer dessert?

Prep: 20 minutes plus cooling and freezing
Bake: 10 minutes

Graham Cracker-Crumb Crust (page 659)
- 4 limes
- 1 can (14 ounces) sweetened condensed milk
- 1 cup heavy or whipping cream

1. Prepare crust as directed. Cool completely.

2. From limes, grate 1 tablespoon peel and squeeze ½ cup juice. In large bowl, with wire whisk, stir condensed milk and lime peel and juice until well blended.

3. In large bowl, with mixer at medium speed, beat cream until stiff peaks form. Fold whipped cream, one-third at a time, into lime mixture just until blended.

4. Pour mixture into cooled crust. Cover and freeze at least 3 hours or up to 1 month. Before serving, let pie stand 10 minutes at room temperature for easier slicing. Makes 10 servings.

Each serving: About 319 calories, 5g protein, 36g carbohydrate, 18g total fat (11g saturated), 59mg cholesterol, 196mg sodium.

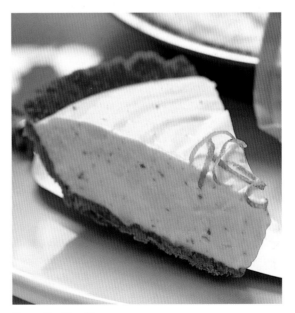

Frozen Key Lime Pie

DARK CHOCOLATE-WALNUT CARAMEL PIE

....

This oh-so-decadent pie, made with dark chocolate, creamy caramel, and toasted walnuts, is well worth the calorie splurge. Perfect for your next special occasion.

Prep: 45 minutes plus cooling and chilling
Cook: 15 minutes

- 1 cup sugar
- ¼ cup water
- 1¼ cups heavy or whipping cream
- 8 squares (8 ounces) semisweet chocolate, cut up
- 2 tablespoons butter or margarine
- 2 teaspoons vanilla extract
- 1¾ cups walnuts (7 ounces), toasted and coarsely chopped
  Prebaked Piecrust for 1-Crust Pie (page 658)

1. Prepare piecrust as recipe directs, but bake crust about 2 minutes longer after removing pie weights or until deep golden. Cool pie shell on wire rack at least 15 minutes.

2. In heavy 3-quart saucepan, heat sugar and water on medium-high until sugar dissolves and turns amber, 15 minutes, swirling pan occasionally.

3. Meanwhile, in microwave-safe 1-cup liquid measuring cup, heat ¾ cup cream in microwave on High 45 seconds or until warm. Place remaining ½ cup cream in refrigerator to chill for whipping later.

4. Remove saucepan from heat. Stir in warm cream until smooth caramel forms (sugar syrup will stiffen when cream is added). Stir in chocolate and butter until completely melted. Stir in vanilla extract and 1½ cups walnuts.

5. Pour warm chocolate filling into pie shell. Cool 1 hour on wire rack, then cover and refrigerate at least 3 hours or until set.

6. When ready to serve, in medium bowl, with mixer on medium speed, beat remaining ½ cup cream until soft peaks form. With metal spatula, spread whipped cream on top of pie, leaving ½-inch border all around. Sprinkle with reserved walnuts. Makes 12 servings.

Each serving: About 500 calories, 6g protein, 40g carbohydrate, 37g total fat (15g saturated), 3g fiber, 53mg cholesterol, 130mg sodium.

Dark Chocolate-Walnut Caramel Pie

CHOCOLATE-CARAMEL WALNUT TART

....

This tart is a grown-up take on the mile-high pie at left, but equally luscious. The pastry can be prepared, baked, and frozen up to one week ahead of time. Thaw it at room temperature before filling.

Prep: 40 minutes plus chilling and cooling
Bake: 30 minutes
Prebaked Tart Shell for 11-Inch Tart (page 658)

- 1 cup sugar
- ¼ cup water
- ¾ cup plus 1 cup heavy or whipping cream
- 2 bars (4 ounces each) bittersweet chocolate, chopped
- 2 tablespoons butter or margarine
- 2 cups walnuts (8 ounces), lightly toasted and chopped
- 2 teaspoons vanilla extract
  walnut halves

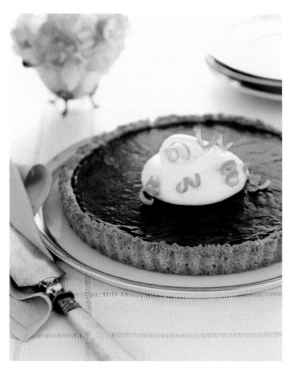

Chocolate Macaroon Tart

1. Prepare pastry dough as directed through baking and cooling.

2. Prepare filling: In heavy 3-quart saucepan, heat sugar and water over medium-high heat, swirling pan occasionally, until sugar is melted and amber in color, about 10 minutes. Remove from heat. Stir in cream until a smooth caramel forms. Stir in chocolate and butter until melted. Add chopped walnuts and vanilla and stir to combine.

3. Pour warm filling into cooled tart shell. Refrigerate until set, at least 3 hours.

4. To serve, remove side of pan. In small bowl, with mixer at medium speed, beat remaining 1 cup cream until stiff peaks form. Garnish tart with whipped cream and walnut halves. If not serving right away, refrigerate up to one day. Makes 12 servings.

Each serving: About 505 calories, 6g protein, 42g carbohydrate, 38g total fat (16g saturated), 48mg cholesterol, 160mg sodium.

CHOCOLATE MACAROON TART

....

This sophisticated tart comes together with surprisingly little time or effort.

Prep: 15 minutes plus cooling and chilling
Bake/Cook: 20 minutes

- 1 package (10 ounces) soft coconut macaroon cookies
- 1 cup heavy or whipping cream
- 8 squares (8 ounces) semisweet chocolate, chopped
- 2 tablespoons orange-flavored liqueur, such as Grand Marnier or Triple Sec
- 1 teaspoon vanilla extract
- ½ teaspoon confectioners' sugar
- 1 navel orange, for garnish

1. Preheat oven to 350°F. Spray 9-inch tart pan with removable bottom with nonstick cooking spray. In food processor with knife blade attached, pulse macaroons until fine crumbs form. Sprinkle crumbs into prepared pan. With hand, press crumbs onto bottom and up side of pan. Bake crust 10 to 12 minutes or until golden-brown; cool completely on wire rack (about 30 minutes).

2. In 1-quart saucepan, heat ¾ cup cream to boiling on medium. Remove from heat. Add chocolate; with wire whisk, whisk until melted and smooth. Stir in liqueur and vanilla. Pour chocolate mixture into tart shell. Refrigerate 2 hours or until set.

3. When ready to serve, in small bowl, combine sugar and remaining cream. With electric mixer on medium speed, beat cream until soft peaks form.

4. With vegetable peeler, from orange, remove 3" by ½" strip of peel. With paring knife, scrape off and discard white pith from peel; very thinly slice peel lengthwise. One at a time, wrap each strip around chopstick or pencil and hold 10 to 15 seconds or until curled. Garnish tart with whipped cream and citrus curls. Makes 12 servings.

Each serving: About 265 calories, 3g protein, 29g carbohydrate, 16g total fat (11g saturated), 2g fiber, 27mg cholesterol, 65mg sodium.

CHOCOLATE TRUFFLE TART

So unbelievably decadent, all you'll need is one thin slice!

Prep: 20 minutes plus chilling and cooling
Bake: 40 minutes

Pastry for 9-Inch Tart (page 658)

6 squares (6 ounces) semisweet chocolate, coarsely chopped

½ cup butter or margarine (1 stick)

¼ cup sugar

1 teaspoon vanilla extract

3 large eggs

½ cup heavy or whipping cream
softly whipped cream (optional)

1. Prepare pastry dough as directed through chilling.
2. Preheat oven to 425°F. Use dough to line 9-inch tart pan with removable bottom. Trim edge even with rim of pan. Refrigerate or freeze until firm, 10 to 15 minutes.
3. Line tart shell with foil; fill with pie weights or dry beans. Bake 15 minutes. Remove foil with weights; bake until golden, 5 to 10 minutes longer. If shell puffs up, gently press it down with back of spoon. Cool in pan on wire rack. Turn oven control to 350°F.
4. Meanwhile, in heavy 2-quart saucepan, melt chocolate and butter over very low heat, stirring frequently, until smooth. Add sugar and vanilla; stir until sugar has dissolved. In small bowl, with wire whisk, lightly beat eggs and cream. Whisk ⅓ cup warm chocolate mixture into egg mixture; stir egg mixture back into chocolate mixture in saucepan until blended.
5. Pour warm chocolate filling into cooled tart shell. Bake until custard is set but center still jiggles slightly, about 20 minutes.
6. Cool in pan on wire rack. When cool, remove side of pan. Refrigerate until chilled, about 4 hours. Serve with a dollop of whipped cream, if desired. Makes 12 servings.

Each serving: About 306 calories, 4g protein, 22g carbohydrate, 24g total fat (14g saturated), 103mg cholesterol, 206mg sodium.

APPLE TARTE TATIN

This caramelized apple tart—a classic French dessert—is baked in a skillet. Serve it warm with ice cream.

Prep: 1 hour 10 minutes plus chilling
Bake: 25 minutes

Pastry for 9-Inch Tart (page 658)

6 tablespoons butter or margarine

1 cup sugar

1 tablespoon fresh lemon juice

3¾ pounds Golden Delicious apples (9 medium), peeled, cored, and each cut in half

1. Prepare pastry dough as directed but roll into 12-inch round. Transfer to cookie sheet; refrigerate.
2. Preheat oven to 425°F. In heavy 10-inch skillet with oven-safe handle (if skillet is not oven-safe, wrap handle in double layer of foil), combine butter, sugar, and lemon juice; cook over medium-high heat until butter melts and mixture bubbles. Place apples in skillet, overlapping them. Cook 10 minutes, turning apples to cook evenly. Carefully turn apples rounded side down; cook until syrup has thickened and is amber in color, 8 to 12 minutes longer. Remove from heat.
3. Place chilled dough on top of apples in skillet; fold edge of dough under to form rim around apples. With knife, cut six ¼-inch slits in dough to allow steam to escape during baking. Bake until crust is golden, about 25 minutes.
4. When tart is done, place large platter on top. Wearing oven mitts to protect your hands, quickly turn skillet upside down to unmold tart. Cool 30 minutes to serve warm, or cool completely to serve later. Makes 10 servings.

Each serving: About 342 calories, 2g protein, 52g carbohydrate, 16g total fat (9g saturated), 37mg cholesterol, 198mg sodium.

PEACH TARTE TATIN
Prepare as directed above but substitute **3¾ pounds ripe-firm peaches (11 medium),** peeled, halved, and pitted, for apples. Bake and cool as directed.

PEAR TARTE TATIN
Prepare as directed but substitute **3¾ pounds ripe-firm Bosc pears (about 7),** peeled, cored, and cut lengthwise in half, for apples. Bake and cool as directed.

BUTTERY APRICOT TART

....

The pastry for this spectacular tart can also be prepared in a food processor with the knife blade attached: Combine the sweet pastry dough ingredients and pulse just until the dough comes together.

Prep: 20 minutes plus cooling
Bake: 1 hour 10 minutes

Sweet Pastry Dough

1¼ cups all-purpose flour
¼ cup sugar
¼ teaspoon salt
7 tablespoons butter or margarine, cut up

Apricot Filling

¼ cup sugar
1½ teaspoons all-purpose flour
1½ pounds apricots (8 to 10 large), each cut in half and pitted
2 tablespoons plain dried bread crumbs
2 tablespoons chopped shelled pistachios

1. Preheat oven to 375°F.

2. Prepare pastry dough: In medium bowl, with wire whisk, stir flour, sugar, and salt. With pastry blender or two knives used scissor-fashion, cut in butter until mixture resembles coarse crumbs. With hand, press dough together in bowl.

3. Transfer dough to 11-inch fluted tart pan with removable bottom. Press dough onto bottom and up side of pan. Trim edge even with rim of pan. Bake shell 20 minutes.

4. Meanwhile, prepare filling: In medium bowl, stir sugar and flour; add apricots and toss to coat.

5. Sprinkle hot tart shell with bread crumbs. Arrange apricot halves, cut sides down, in shell. Bake tart until shell is golden and apricots are tender, 50 to 55 minutes. Cool tart in pan on wire rack.

6. To serve, carefully remove side of pan. Sprinkle tart with pistachios. Makes 8 servings.

Each serving: About 265 calories, 4g protein, 37g carbohydrate, 12g total fat (7g saturated), 29mg cholesterol, 200mg sodium.

WARM BANANA-PECAN TART

....

To minimize last-minute preparation, bake the crust up to two days ahead. Prepare the toasted-pecan cream up to one day in advance and refrigerate. Then simply assemble the tart just before serving.

Prep: 1 hour plus chilling   Bake/Broil: 32 minutes

Pastry for 11-Inch Tart (page 658)
½ cup pecans, toasted
½ cup plus 1 tablespoon sugar
3 large egg yolks
1 tablespoon cornstarch
¾ cup half-and-half or light cream
2 tablespoons butter or margarine, cut into pieces
1 teaspoon vanilla extract
5 ripe medium bananas (about 2 pounds)

1. Prepare pastry dough as directed through chilling.

2. Prepare pecan cream: In blender or in food processor with knife blade attached, process pecans and ¼ cup sugar until pecans are very finely ground.

3. In small bowl, stir ¼ cup sugar, egg yolks, and cornstarch until blended. In 2-quart saucepan, heat half-and-half to simmering over medium-high heat. While whisking constantly, gradually pour about half of half-and-half into egg-yolk mixture. Return egg-yolk mixture to saucepan and cook over low heat, stirring constantly, until mixture has thickened (do not boil), 4 to 5 minutes. Stir in pecan mixture, butter, and vanilla until butter melts. Transfer pecan cream to medium bowl. Press plastic wrap onto surface and refrigerate at least 30 minutes or up to overnight.

4. Meanwhile, preheat oven to 425°F. Use dough to line 11-inch tart pan with removable bottom. Trim edge even with rim of pan. Refrigerate or freeze until firm, 10 to 15 minutes.

5. Line tart shell with foil; fill with pie weights or dry beans. Bake 15 minutes. Remove foil with weights; bake until golden, 5 to 10 minutes longer. If shell puffs up during baking, gently press it down with back of spoon. Turn oven control to broil.

6. Cut bananas on diagonal into thin slices. Arrange slices, overlapping slightly, in tart shell. Spoon chilled pecan cream over bananas and sprinkle with remaining 1 tablespoon sugar. Cover edge of shell with foil. Place at position closest to heat source and broil until top is lightly caramelized, 1 to 2 minutes. Carefully remove side of pan. Serve warm. Makes 12 servings.

Each serving: About 315 calories, 4g protein, 36g carbohydrate, 18g total fat (8g saturated), 85mg cholesterol, 203mg sodium.

DOUBLE-BERRY LINZER TART

To give this Austrian tart holiday flair, we've added fresh cranberries to the traditional raspberry jam.

Prep: 30 minutes plus chilling   Bake: 40 minutes

- 1 cup cranberries
- ¼ plus ⅓ cup packed brown sugar
- ¼ cup cranberry-juice cocktail
    pinch plus ¼ teaspoon salt
- ¾ cup seedless raspberry jam
- ⅔ cup hazelnuts (filberts), toasted and skinned (page 692)
- 1¼ cups all-purpose flour
- 6 tablespoons butter or margarine, softened
- 1 large egg
- ½ teaspoon vanilla extract
- ¼ teaspoon baking powder
- ¼ teaspoon ground cinnamon
    confectioners' sugar (optional)

1. In nonreactive 1-quart saucepan, combine cranberries, ¼ cup brown sugar, cranberry-juice cocktail, and pinch salt; heat to boiling over medium-high heat. Reduce heat to medium; cook, stirring occasionally, until cranberries pop and mixture has thickened slightly, about 6 minutes. Stir in raspberry jam; refrigerate until cool, about 30 minutes.

2. Meanwhile, in blender or in food processor with knife blade attached, process hazelnuts and ¼ cup flour until nuts are very finely ground.

3. In large bowl, with mixer at low speed, beat butter and remaining ⅓ cup brown sugar until blended. Increase speed to medium-high; beat until light and fluffy, about 3 minutes. With mixer at medium speed, beat in egg and vanilla until smooth, about 1 minute. Reduce speed to low. Add hazelnut mixture, remaining 1 cup flour, baking powder, cinnamon, and remaining ¼ teaspoon salt; beat just until combined.

4. With floured hands, press two-thirds of dough onto bottom and up side of 9-inch tart pan with removable bottom. Trim edge even with rim of pan. Wrap tart shell and remaining dough in plastic wrap and refrigerate until disk of dough is firm enough to shape, about 30 minutes.

5. Preheat oven to 400°F. Spoon cooled filling into tart shell. On lightly floured surface, divide remaining dough into 10 equal pieces. With floured hands, roll each piece into 8½-inch-long rope. Place 5 ropes, 1½ inches apart, across top of tart. Place remaining 5 ropes at right angle to first ropes to make lattice pattern. Or, if desired, weave dough ropes to create "fancy" lattice pattern (see photo below). Trim ends of ropes even with edge of tart and press ends to seal. With hands, roll any dough trimmings into ¼-inch-thick ropes. Press ropes around edge of tart to make finished edge. If ropes break, press pieces together.

6. Bake until filling bubbles and crust is lightly browned, about 40 minutes. Cool in pan on wire rack at least 1 hour. When cool, carefully remove side of pan. Dust with confectioners' sugar, if desired. Makes 10 servings.

Each serving: About 290 calories, 4g protein, 43g carbohydrate, 12g total fat (5g saturated), 40mg cholesterol, 175mg sodium.

Double-Berry Linzer Tart

FRESH STRAWBERRY CREAM CHEESE TART

· ·

This easy fruit tart is so versatile that it also tastes good topped with raspberries, blueberries, or even grapes, instead of strawberries. Make it with whatever fruit is in peak season.

Prep: 30 minutes plus chilling and cooling
Bake: 20 minutes

1½ cups all-purpose flour
¼   teaspoon salt
⅓   cup plus 3 tablespoons confectioners' sugar
10 tablespoons butter or margarine (1¼ sticks), chilled and cut into ½-inch pieces
1   teaspoon vanilla extract
3   tablespoons ice water
6   ounces reduced-fat cream cheese (Neufchâtel), softened
½   cup reduced-fat sour cream
3   tablespoons chopped crystallized ginger
1½ pounds strawberries, stems and leaves discarded and each berry cut lengthwise in half

1. In food processor with knife blade attached, combine flour, salt, and ⅓ cup sugar; pulse until blended. Add butter and pulse until mixture resembles coarse meal. Add vanilla, then ice water, 1 tablespoon at a time, pulsing until moist clumps form. Gather dough into ball; flatten into disk. Wrap in plastic wrap and refrigerate until firm enough to roll, at least 1 hour. (If chilled overnight, let dough stand 30 minutes at room temperature before rolling.)

2. Preheat oven to 375°F. On large sheet of parchment paper, with floured rolling pin, roll dough into 12-inch round. Using 11-inch dinner plate as guide, and with sharp knife, cut 11-inch round from dough; discard trimmings.

3. Transfer round, still on parchment, to large cookie sheet. Press and pinch all around the edge to create a decorative fluted border. Refrigerate or freeze, still on cookie sheet, about 10 minutes to firm dough slightly.

4. Bake dough 20 to 25 minutes or until golden. Place cookie sheet on wire rack and cool crust completely, about 20 minutes.

5. Meanwhile, in medium bowl, with spoon, mix cream cheese, sour cream, crystallized ginger, and remaining 3 tablespoons sugar until blended. Spread cream cheese mixture on cooled crust. Arrange strawberries, wide ends down, in concentric circles to cover cream cheese mixture. Makes 8 servings.

Each serving: About 315 calories, 5g protein, 30g carbohydrate, 20g total fat (12g saturated), 2g fiber, 57mg cholesterol, 285mg sodium.

Fresh Strawberry Cream Cheese Tart

Frozen Fruit Tart

FROZEN FRUIT TART

....

With a melt-in-your mouth filling that blends low-fat vanilla ice cream and mango sorbet, this tart recalls the straight-from-childhood taste of a Creamsicle.

Prep: 40 minutes plus cooling and freezing
Bake: 8 minutes

- 8 graham crackers (5" by 2½" each)
- 2 tablespoons whole natural almonds (with brown skin still on)
- 1 tablespoon sugar
- 1 tablespoon canola oil
- 1 tablespoon honey
- 2 teaspoons water
- 1½ cups light vanilla ice cream, such as slow- or double-churned
- 1½ cups mango or passion fruit sorbet
- 3 ripe nectarines, each pitted and cut into 8 wedges
- 2 ripe plums, each pitted and cut into 8 wedges
- 1 cup raspberries

1. Preheat oven to 350°F. Prepare crust: In food processor with knife blade attached, pulse graham crackers until fine crumbs form. Add whole almonds and sugar; pulse until almonds are finely chopped. In cup, mix canola oil, honey, and water; drizzle over crumb mixture. Pulse until crumbs are evenly moistened. Press crumb mixture onto bottom and up side of 9-inch round tart pan with removable bottom.

2. Bake crust 8 to 10 minutes or until set and lightly browned at edges. Cool completely in pan on wire rack.

3. Remove ice cream and sorbet from freezer; let stand at room temperature 10 minutes or until slightly softened. Spoon scoops of ice cream and sorbet alternately into tart shell, pressing with back of spoon to smooth; cover and freeze until firm, at least 4 hours or overnight.

4. Carefully remove side of pan and place tart on round platter. Arrange circle of nectarine wedges on top of tart 1 inch from edge, then circle of plum wedges inside nectarines. Mound raspberries in center of tart. Serve immediately. Makes 8 servings.

Each serving: About 235 calories, 3g protein, 39g carbohydrate, 6g total fat (1g saturated), 3g fiber, 8mg cholesterol, 110mg sodium.

WHAT ELSE CAN IT DO? MELON BALLER

Use this not-so-humdrum multitasker to save time, reduce waste, or add a decorative flourish. Here's how:

• Remove the seeds from fruit. Rotate the tool around the centers of halved apples or pears to evenly dig out only the core.

• Shape petite meatballs from your favorite ground-meat mixture. Brown them in a sauté pan and serve as an appetizer, or toss with spaghetti and sauce for the kids.

• Form perfectly round mini cookies with the dough of your choice. Just reduce your usual baking time by 1 to 2 minutes. The bite-size treats make a smart, portion-controlled snack; or tie a handful into a festive packet for a cute impromptu gift or party favor.

• Serve up sorbet in style. Mix and match scoops of flavors and colors and arrange them in a dish; freeze until serving time.

LEMON TART

....

This tangy French-style tart can be served on its own or accented with fresh berries. Be sure to make a high pastry rim to contain all the delicious filling.

Prep: 25 minutes plus chilling and cooling
Bake: 50 minutes

Pastry for 9-Inch Tart (page 658)
4 to 6 lemons
4 large eggs
1 cup granulated sugar
⅓ cup heavy or whipping cream
confectioners' sugar

1. Prepare pastry dough as directed through chilling.

2. Preheat oven to 425°F. Use dough to line 9-inch tart pan with removable bottom; press dough up side so it extends ¼ inch above rim of pan. Refrigerate or freeze until firm, 10 to 15 minutes.

3. Line tart shell with foil; fill with pie weights or dry beans. Bake 15 minutes. Remove foil with weights; bake until golden, 5 to 10 minutes longer. If shell puffs up during baking, gently press it down with back of spoon. Cool tart shell in pan on wire rack. Turn oven control to 350°F.

4. From lemons, grate 1½ teaspoons peel and squeeze ⅔ cup juice. In medium bowl, with wire whisk, beat eggs, granulated sugar, and lemon peel and juice until well combined. Whisk in cream.

5. Carefully pour lemon filling into cooled tart shell. Place tart on foil-lined cookie sheet to catch any overflow during baking. Bake until filling is set but center still jiggles slightly, about 30 minutes. Cool completely on wire rack. Just before serving, dust with confectioners' sugar. Makes 8 servings.

Each serving: About 324 calories, 5g protein, 40g carbohydrate, 17g total fat (9g saturated), 143mg cholesterol, 195mg sodium.

PEACH-RASPBERRY GALETTE

....

A galette is a little more casual than a pie but just as tasty. The combination of sweet and juicy fresh peaches and flavorful raspberries is a perfect match.

Prep: 30 minutes plus chilling   Bake: 45 minutes

Pastry Dough
1½ cups all-purpose flour
¼ teaspoon salt
½ cup cold butter (1 stick), cut into pieces (do not use margarine)
4 to 6 tablespoons ice water

Peach-Raspberry Filling
3 tablespoons cornstarch
¾ cup plus 1 tablespoon sugar
1½ pounds peaches (4 to 5 medium), peeled and cut into thick wedges
½ pint raspberries
2 tablespoons butter, cut into small pieces (do not use margarine)
1 large egg white, lightly beaten

1. Preheat oven to 425°F.

2. Prepare pastry dough: In medium bowl, with wire whisk, stir flour and salt. With pastry blender or two knives used scissor-fashion, cut in butter until mixture resembles coarse crumbs. Sprinkle in ice water, 1 tablespoon at a time, mixing with hands after each addition until dough is just moist enough to hold together (it will feel dry at first). Shape dough into a disk. Wrap in plastic wrap and refrigerate 30 minutes.

3. Line large cookie sheet with parchment paper. On floured surface, roll dough into 13-inch round (edge may be uneven). Transfer dough round to prepared cookie sheet.

4. Prepare filling: In large bowl, with wire whisk, stir cornstarch and ¾ cup sugar. Add peaches and raspberries; gently toss until fruit is evenly coated.

5. Spoon filling onto dough, leaving 2½-inch border; dot with butter. Fold border of dough over filling, pleating edges and leaving an opening in center. Pinch dough to seal any cracks. Brush dough with egg white; sprinkle with remaining 1 tablespoon sugar.

6. Place two sheets of foil under cookie sheet; crimp foil to form rim to catch any overflow during baking. Bake until crust is golden brown and filling is gently bubbling, 45 to 50 minutes. As soon as galette is done, use long metal spatula to loosen it from parchment to prevent sticking. Cool 15 minutes on cookie sheet, then slide galette onto rack to cool completely. Makes 8 servings.

Each serving: About 345 calories, 4g protein, 49g carbohydrate, 16g total fat (10g saturated), 41mg cholesterol, 235mg sodium.

PLUM FRANGIPANE TART
······································

Use either red or black plums for this tart. Frangipane, a rich almond, butter, and sugar mixture, is a classic partner for plums.

**Prep: 30 minutes plus chilling
Bake: 1 hour 10 minutes**

Pastry for 11-Inch Tart (page 658)

1 tube or can (7 to 8 ounces) almond paste, crumbled

4 tablespoons butter or margarine, softened

½ cup sugar

¼ teaspoon salt

2 large eggs

2 teaspoons vanilla extract

¼ cup all-purpose flour

1¼ pounds ripe plums (5 large), pitted and each cut into 6 wedges

1. Prepare pastry dough as directed through chilling.

2. Preheat oven to 425°F. Use dough to line 11-inch tart pan with removable bottom. Trim edge even with rim of pan. Refrigerate or freeze until firm, 10 to 15 minutes.

3. Line tart shell with foil; fill with pie weights or dry beans. Bake 15 minutes. Remove foil with weights; bake until golden, 5 to 10 minutes longer. If shell puffs up during baking, gently press it down with back of spoon.

4. Meanwhile, in large bowl, with mixer at low speed, beat almond paste, butter, sugar, and salt until almond paste is crumbly. Increase speed to medium-high and beat until well blended, about 3 minutes, frequently scraping bowl with rubber spatula. (There may be some tiny lumps.) Add eggs and vanilla; beat until smooth. With wooden spoon, stir in flour.

5. Pour almond-paste mixture into warm tart shell; spread evenly. Arrange plums in concentric circles over filling. Bake until golden, 50 to 60 minutes. Cool in pan on wire rack. When cool, carefully remove side of pan. Makes 12 servings.

Each serving: About 342 calories, 6g protein, 37g carbohydrate, 20g total fat (8g saturated), 66mg cholesterol, 274mg sodium.

CRANBERRY-ALMOND TART

Prepare as directed but omit plums. Bake almond filling until golden, about 20 minutes. Cool in pan on wire rack. In 2-quart saucepan, combine **1 cup cranberries, ¾ cup sugar, ⅓ cup water,** and **½ teaspoon freshly grated orange peel;** heat to boiling over high heat. Reduce heat; simmer until cranberries pop and mixture has thickened slightly, about 5 minutes. Stir in additional **2 cups cranberries;** set aside until cool. When cool, carefully remove side of pan; spoon cranberry topping over almond filling.

PEELING PEACHES

TEST KITCHEN TIP

Our favorite method for peeling peaches is to submerge them, a few at a time, in boiling water for about 15 seconds (no longer or they will start to cook). With a slotted spoon, immediately transfer them to a large bowl of ice water. One at a time, lift out the peaches and slip the skin off. Here's a good method to use if the peaches are perfectly ripe: Put the tip of a paring knife into the stem end and peel away the skin in strips. Whatever you do, don't peel a ripe peach with a vegetable peeler; you'll bruise the delicate flesh.

23

COOKIES & CONFECTIONS

Cookies are one of the simplest and most delicious treats you can make. Here is our collection of favorite recipes and tips to help guarantee your baking success.

TYPES OF COOKIES

• Bar cookies couldn't be easier. Mix up some dough, spread it in a pan, then bake, cool, and cut.
• Drop cookies are made by dropping spoonfuls of soft dough onto cookie sheets.
• Molded cookies are made from a stiff dough that is formed into balls, logs, pretzels, or other shapes or baked in individual molds.
• Pressed cookies are made from a stiff dough that is squeezed through a cookie press or pastry bag.
• Refrigerator cookies (also called icebox cookies) begin with a chilled stiff dough that is sliced and baked.
• Rolled cookies are made from a stiff dough that is rolled out into a thin layer, then cut into shapes.

COOKIE SHEET SAVVY

Good-quality cookie sheets are one of the secrets to perfect cookies. Heavy-gauge metal cookie sheets that have a dull finish turn out the most evenly browned cookies; aluminum is ideal. Double-thick insulated cookie sheets discourage overbaking and are a good investment. Dark cookie sheets can overbrown the bottoms of cookies. If your cookie sheets are old and discolored, line them with foil. Better still, purchase new ones.

The air in your oven should circulate freely around the cookie sheets, which should be at least 2 inches smaller in length and width than your oven. Cookie sheets should be rimless (or have only one or two turned-up edges) for the best air circulation.

Grease cookie sheets only when a recipe directs you to. Some cookies have a high fat content, so greasing isn't necessary. Vegetable shortening is better than butter for greasing cookie sheets because butter sometimes browns as it melts in the oven. Nonstick cookie sheets and silcone nonstick baking liners are good alternatives to greasing and flouring.

For an even coat when greasing is required, use a crumpled piece of paper towel. To flour a cookie sheet, sprinkle the greased sheet evenly with a little flour, then tap off the excess. For easy cleanup, line cookie sheets with foil (dull side up).

Never place cookie dough on a hot cookie sheet; a hot cookie sheet will melt the dough before it has a chance to set. Always let cookie sheets cool between batches. If the recipe calls for greased sheets, regrease for each batch.

BAKING SUCCESS

• While butter and margarine are interchangeable in some cookie recipes, for the best flavor and texture, use butter.
• If you prefer margarine, make sure it contains 80 percent fat. Spreads (diet, whipped, liquid, or soft) have a high water content, which produces tough cookies that lack flavor.

Chocolate Wows (recipe page 689)

• For the tenderest cookies, once the flour has been added, mix the dough just until blended.

• Use a measuring spoon to scoop up equal portions of dough to make consistently shaped cookies that will bake in the same amount of time.

• For drop cookies, place spoonfuls of dough 2 inches apart unless the recipe directs otherwise.

• Dust the work surface lightly and evenly with flour before rolling out dough. Rub the rolling pin well with flour to keep it from sticking to the dough, or lightly dust the top of the dough with flour.

• When rolling out chilled dough, roll out one portion at a time; keep the remaining dough covered in the refrigerator.

• If a chilled dough cracks when rolled, let it stand at room temperature to soften slightly, then try again.

• For evenly baked cookies, bake one sheet of cookies at a time in the center of the oven. If you want to bake two sheets at a time, position the racks in the upper and lower thirds of the oven. Then, halfway through baking, rotate the cookie sheets between the upper and lower oven racks (unless directed otherwise) and also rotate them front to back.

• Bake cookies for the minimum suggested baking time, then check for doneness. If not done, watch them carefully for the remainder of the time to avoid overbaking.

• Unless a recipe directs otherwise, cool cookies briefly on the cookie sheet to firm slightly, then transfer to wire racks to cool completely; hot cookies are too soft to be moved immediately to racks. Cool bar cookies completely in the pan before cutting.

STORING COOKIES

Store soft and crisp cookies in separate containers with tight-fitting covers. Crisp cookies that soften can be recrisped in a 300°F oven for three to five minutes. Soft cookies can be kept soft by adding a piece of apple or bread to the container; change it every other day or so. (This technique also works for soft cookies that have hardened.) Store bar cookies in the pan they were baked in, tightly covered with foil or plastic wrap.

To freeze baked cookies, cool them thoroughly. Place them in airtight containers, cushioned with crumpled waxed paper, if necessary. If the cookies have been decorated, freeze them until hard in a single layer on a cookie sheet, then pack for storage, separating the layers with waxed paper. To thaw, unwrap the cookies and let stand for about ten minutes at room temperature.

To freeze unbaked cookie dough, wrap tightly in heavy-duty foil and store in a container. For refrigerator cookies, wrap the logs of dough in heavy-duty foil. Freeze for up to six months; thaw in the refrigerator. Remember to label and date each package.

CHOCOLATE AND COCOA

Because of its unique flavor and smooth texture, chocolate is an essential component in all kinds of sweets, including candies. There are many different kinds of chocolates, and they are rarely interchangeable. See Chocolate and Cocoa Powder, page 688.

Chocolate has two enemies: water and high heat. If a single drop of water gets into chocolate while it's melting, the chocolate can "seize" (form a dull, thick paste). Chocolate melted over heat that is too high clumps and becomes grainy, so melt it over low heat.

To chop chocolate, use a sharp, heavy knife and a dry, clean cutting board. Chop into ¼-inch pieces.

To melt chocolate, place the chopped chocolate in a heavy-bottomed saucepan; stir frequently over low heat until melted, watching carefully to avoid scorching. Or place the chocolate in the top of a double boiler over very hot, not simmering, water and stir until melted. Or place it in a microwave-safe bowl and microwave at 50 percent power, stirring at intervals.

Store chocolate and cocoa powder in a cool, dry place. "Blooms," or pale streaks that may appear, will not affect the chocolate's performance or taste.

GOOD HOUSEKEEPING'S FUDGY BROWNIES

···

Ultrarich with lots of deep, dark chocolate flavor, these brownies are fabulous with or without our praline icing. For a moist, fudgy texture, do not overbake.

Prep: 10 minutes   Bake: 30 minutes

1¼	cups all-purpose flour
½	teaspoon salt
¾	cup butter or margarine (1½ sticks)
4	squares (4 ounces) unsweetened chocolate, chopped
4	squares (4 ounces) semisweet chocolate, chopped
2	cups sugar
1	tablespoon vanilla extract
5	large eggs, beaten

1. Preheat oven to 350°F. Grease 13" by 9" baking pan. In small bowl, with wire whisk, stir flour and salt.

2. In heavy 4-quart saucepan, melt butter and unsweetened and semisweet chocolates over low heat, stirring frequently, until smooth. Remove from heat. With wooden spoon, stir in sugar and vanilla. Add eggs; stir until well mixed. Stir flour mixture into chocolate mixture just until blended. Spread batter evenly in prepared pan.

3. Bake until toothpick inserted 1 inch from edge comes out clean, about 30 minutes. Cool completely in pan on wire rack. When cool, cut lengthwise into 4 strips, then cut each strip crosswise into 6 pieces. Makes 24 brownies.

Each brownie: About 206 calories, 3g protein, 26g carbohydrate, 11g total fat (6g saturated), 60mg cholesterol, 121mg sodium.

PRALINE-ICED BROWNIES

Prepare brownies as directed; cool. In 2-quart saucepan, heat **5 tablespoons butter or margarine** and **⅓ cup packed brown sugar** over medium-low heat until mixture has melted and bubbles, about 5 minutes. Remove from heat. With wire whisk, beat in **3 tablespoons bourbon or 1 tablespoon vanilla extract plus 2 tablespoons water;** stir in **2 cups confectioners' sugar** until smooth. With small metal spatula, spread topping over room-temperature brownies; sprinkle **½ cup pecans,** toasted and coarsely chopped, evenly over topping. Cut brownies lengthwise into 8 strips, then cut each strip crosswise into 8 pieces. Makes 64 brownies.

Each brownie: About 297 calories, 3g protein, 39g carbohydrate, 15g total fat (8g saturated), 66mg cholesterol, 147mg sodium.

Praline-Iced Brownies

COCOA BROWNIES

....

Whenever you get a chocolate craving, you can whip up these easy saucepan brownies on the spur of the moment.

Prep: 10 minutes   Bake: 25 minutes

- ½   cup all-purpose flour
- ½   cup unsweetened cocoa
- ¼   teaspoon baking powder
- ¼   teaspoon salt
- ½   cup butter or margarine (1 stick)
- 1   cup sugar
- 2   large eggs
- 1   teaspoon vanilla extract
- 1   cup walnuts (4 ounces), coarsely chopped (optional)

1. Preheat oven to 350°F. Grease 9-inch square baking pan. In small bowl, with wire whisk, stir flour, cocoa, baking powder, and salt.

2. In 3-quart saucepan, melt butter over low heat. Remove from heat and stir in sugar. Stir in eggs, one at a time, until well blended; add vanilla. Stir flour mixture into sugar mixture until blended. Stir in walnuts, if using. Spread batter evenly in prepared pan.

3. Bake until toothpick inserted 2 inches from center comes out almost clean, about 25 minutes. Cool completely in pan on wire rack.

4. When cool, cut into 4 strips, then cut each strip crosswise into 4 pieces. Makes 16 brownies.

Each brownie: About 132 calories, 2g protein, 17g carbohydrate, 7g total fat (4g saturated), 42mg cholesterol, 110mg sodium.

FUDGY LOW-FAT BROWNIES

....

Moist, chocolaty, and low-fat. Need we say more? Serve with cold skim milk for a delicious treat that won't overload your daily calorie count.

Prep: 15 minutes   Bake: 18 minutes

- 1   teaspoon instant espresso-coffee powder
- 1   teaspoon hot water
- ¾   cup all-purpose flour
- ½   cup unsweetened cocoa
- ½   teaspoon baking powder
- ¼   teaspoon salt
- 3   tablespoons butter or margarine
- ¾   cup sugar
- 2   large egg whites
- ¼   cup dark corn syrup
- 1   teaspoon vanilla extract

1. Preheat oven to 350°F. Grease 8-inch square baking pan. In cup, dissolve espresso powder in hot water; set aside. In large bowl, with wire whisk, stir flour, cocoa, baking powder, and salt.

2. In 2-quart saucepan, melt butter over low heat. Remove from heat. With wooden spoon, stir in sugar, egg whites, corn syrup, vanilla, and espresso until blended. Stir sugar mixture into flour mixture just until blended (do not overmix). Pour batter into prepared pan.

3. Bake until toothpick inserted in center comes out almost clean, 18 to 22 minutes. Cool completely in pan on wire rack.

4. When cool, cut into 4 strips, then cut each strip crosswise into 4 pieces. If brownies are difficult to cut, use knife dipped in hot water and dried; repeat as necessary. Makes 16 brownies.

Each brownie: About 103 calories, 2g protein, 19g carbohydrate, 3g total fat (2g saturated), 6mg cholesterol, 88mg sodium.

BLONDIES

These scrumptious bars, sometimes known as butter-scotch brownies, are a pecan lover's dream.

Prep: 10 minutes   Bake: 30 minutes

- 1 cup all-purpose flour
- 2 teaspoons baking powder
- 1 teaspoon salt
- 6 tablespoons butter or margarine
- 1¾ cups packed light brown sugar
- 2 teaspoons vanilla extract
- 2 large eggs
- 1½ cups pecans (6 ounces), coarsely chopped

1. Preheat oven to 350°F. Grease 13" by 9" baking pan. In small bowl, with wire whisk, stir flour, baking powder, and salt.

2. In 3-quart saucepan, melt butter over low heat. Remove from heat. With wooden spoon, stir in brown sugar and vanilla; add eggs, stirring until well blended. Stir flour mixture into sugar mixture just until blended. Stir in pecans. Spread batter evenly in prepared pan.

3. Bake until toothpick inserted 2 inches from edge of pan comes out clean, about 30 minutes. Do not overbake; blondies will firm as they cool. Cool completely in pan on wire rack.

4. When cool, cut lengthwise into 4 strips, then cut each strip crosswise into 6 pieces. Makes 24 blondies.

Each blondie: About 159 calories, 2g protein, 21g carbohydrate, 8g total fat (2g saturated), 25mg cholesterol, 179mg sodium.

COCONUT BLONDIES

Prepare as directed above, stirring in ¾ **cup flaked sweetened coconut** with pecans.

CHOCOLATE CHIP BLONDIES

Prepare as directed through Step 2 above; let batter stand 15 minutes. Stir in **1 package (6 ounces) semi-sweet chocolate chips.** Proceed as directed.

LEMON-CRANBERRY SHORTBREAD

Not your grandmother's shortbread, these glazed melt-in-your-mouth bars are festive enough for the holidays and pretty enough for afternoon tea.

Prep: 30 minutes plus standing
Bake: 35 minutes

- 2 to 3 lemons
- ¾ cup cold butter (1½ sticks), cut into pieces (do not use margarine)
- ¼ cup granulated sugar
- 1½ cups confectioners' sugar
- 2 cups all-purpose flour
- ½ cup dried cranberries

1. Preheat oven to 300°F. Line 13" by 9" metal baking pan with foil, extending foil over rim.

2. From lemons, grate 2 tablespoons plus ½ teaspoon peel and squeeze 2 tablespoons plus 1 teaspoon juice.

3. In food processor with knife blade attached, blend butter, granulated sugar, ½ cup confectioners' sugar, 2 tablespoons lemon peel, and 1 tablespoon lemon juice until creamy. Reserve remaining lemon peel and juice for glaze. Add flour and pulse until dough begins to come together. Add cranberries and pulse until evenly mixed into dough (most cranberries will be chopped, a few will remain whole). With hand, press dough evenly onto bottom of prepared pan.

4. Bake until edges are lightly browned and top is pale golden, 35 to 40 minutes. Cool completely in pan on wire rack.

5. When shortbread is cool, in small bowl, with spoon, stir remaining 1 cup confectioners' sugar, 1 tablespoon lemon juice, and ½ teaspoon lemon peel until smooth, adding some of remaining 1 teaspoon juice, if necessary, to obtain a good spreading consistency. Spread glaze over shortbread. Let stand until glaze sets, about 30 minutes.

6. Remove shortbread from pan by lifting edges of foil; transfer to cutting board. Cut lengthwise into 3 strips, then cut each strip crosswise into 12 bars. Makes 36 bars.

Each bar: About 90 calories, 1g protein, 13g carbohydrate, 4g total fat (3g saturated), 11mg cholesterol, 40mg sodium.

CARAMEL-PECAN BARS

···

These easy-to-make bar cookies were inspired by the popular bite-size candies that resemble little turtles.

Prep: 1 hour plus cooling and chilling
Bake: 25 minutes

Cookie Crust

- ³/₄ cup cold butter (1½ sticks), softened (do not use margarine)
- ³/₄ cup confectioners' sugar
- 1½ teaspoons vanilla extract
- 2¼ cups all-purpose flour

Caramel-Pecan Filling

- 1 cup packed light or dark brown sugar
- ½ cup honey
- ½ cup butter (1 stick), cut into pieces (do not use margarine)
- ⅓ cup granulated sugar
- ¼ cup heavy or whipping cream
- 2 teaspoons vanilla extract
- 1½ cups pecans (6 ounces), toasted (page 692) and coarsely chopped

Topping

- 2 ounces semisweet chocolate, melted

1. Preheat oven to 350°F. Grease 13" by 9" metal baking pan; line pan with foil, extending foil over rim.

2. Prepare crust: In large bowl, with mixer at medium speed, beat butter, confectioners' sugar, and vanilla until creamy, about 2 minutes. Reduce speed to low, gradually beat in flour until evenly moistened (mixture will resemble fine crumbs). With hand, firmly pat crumbs evenly onto bottom of prepared pan.

3. Bake until lightly browned, 25 to 30 minutes. Transfer pan to wire rack.

4. Prepare filling: In 2-quart saucepan, combine brown sugar, honey, butter, granulated sugar, cream, and vanilla; heat to full rolling boil over high heat, stirring frequently. Reduce heat to medium-high; set candy thermometer in place and continue cooking, without stirring, until temperature reaches 248°F or firm-ball stage (when small amount of mixture dropped into very cold water forms a firm ball that does not flatten upon removal from water).

5. Sprinkle pecans evenly over warm crust. Pour hot caramel over nuts. Cool in pan on wire rack 1 hour or until caramel is room temperature and has formed a skin on top.

6. With fork, drizzle melted chocolate over caramel layer. Cover and refrigerate until cold and chocolate has set, at least 1 hour.

7. When cold, remove from pan by lifting edges of foil; transfer to cutting board. Cut lengthwise into 6 strips, then cut each strip crosswise into 8 bars. Let stand at room temperature to soften slightly before serving. Makes 48 bars.

Each bar: About 140 calories, 1g protein, 16g carbohydrate, 8g total fat (4g saturated), 15mg cholesterol, 55mg sodium.

LINING PAN WITH FOIL

———————

Invert the baking pan so it is bottom side up. Mold a length of foil, shiny side facing out, over the pan, pressing the foil firmly to set the shape. Lift up the foil.

Turn the pan right side up. Lower the foil "pan" into the baking pan; smooth it out to create a tight fit.

THE PERFECT LEMON BAR

···

A tender cookie crust and a silky smooth fresh lemon filling makes these bars perfect.

Prep: 25 minutes plus cooling   Bake: 40 minutes

- ³/₄ cup butter (1½ sticks), softened (do not use margarine)
- 2¼ cups all-purpose flour
- ²/₃ cup plus 1 tablespoon confectioners' sugar
- 3 to 4 large lemons
- 6 large eggs
- 2 cups granulated sugar
- 1 teaspoon baking powder
- ³/₄ teaspoon salt

1. Preheat oven to 350°F. Grease 13" by 9" baking pan. Line pan with foil, extending foil over rim; lightly grease foil.

2. In food processor with knife blade attached, pulse butter, 2 cups flour, and ²/₃ cup confectioners' sugar until mixture is moist but crumbly. Dough should hold together when pressed between two fingers. Sprinkle mixture evenly into prepared pan. Bake until lightly browned, 20 to 25 minutes.

3. Meanwhile, prepare filling: From lemons, grate 2½ teaspoons peel and squeeze ²/₃ cup juice. In large bowl, with wire whisk, beat eggs. Add lemon peel and juice, granulated sugar, baking powder, salt and remaining ¼ cup flour; whisk until well blended.

4. Whisk filling again and pour over hot crust. Bake until filling is just set and golden around edges, 18 to 22 minutes. Transfer pan to wire rack. Sift remaining 1 tablespoon confectioners' sugar over warm filling. Cool completely in pan on wire rack.

5. When cool, remove from pan by lifting edges of foil; transfer with foil to cutting board. If you like, trim edges. Cut lengthwise into 4 strips, then cut each strip crosswise into 8 pieces. Makes 32 bars.

Each bar: About 145 calories, 2g protein, 22g carbohydrate, 6g total fat (3g saturated), 52mg cholesterol, 126mg sodium.

HONEY GRANOLA BREAKFAST BARS

···

Instead of eating overly sweet and high-fat store-bought granola bars, we highly recommend making your own. These are quickly mixed in one bowl.

Prep: 15 minutes   Bake: 30 minutes

- 2 cups old-fashioned oats, uncooked
- 1 cup all-purpose flour
- ³/₄ cup packed light brown sugar
- ³/₄ cup dark seedless raisins
- ½ cup toasted wheat germ
- ³/₄ teaspoon ground cinnamon
- ³/₄ teaspoon salt
- ½ cup vegetable oil
- ½ cup honey
- 1 large egg
- 2 teaspoons vanilla extract

1. Preheat oven to 350°F and grease 13" by 9" baking pan.

2. In large bowl, with wooden spoon, stir oats, flour, brown sugar, raisins, wheat germ, cinnamon, and salt until blended. Stir in oil, honey, egg, and vanilla until well combined. With wet hand, pat oat mixture evenly onto bottom of prepared pan.

3. Bake until light golden around edges, 30 to 35 minutes. Cool completely in pan on wire rack.

4. When cool, cut lengthwise into 4 strips, then cut each strip crosswise into 4 pieces. Makes 16 bars.

Each bar: About 242 calories, 4g protein, 39g carbohydrate, 9g total fat (1g saturated), 13mg cholesterol, 119mg sodium.

CONFECTIONERS' SUGAR

Confectioners' sugar is a blend of very finely ground sugar and some cornstarch to prevent lumps. The addition of cornstarch notwithstanding, confectioners' sugar often contains small lumps. We recommend sifting it after measuring.

CHEWY OATMEAL-CHOCOLATE-CHERRY COOKIES

For chewy cookies, bake the minimum time; for a crispy treat, bake a few minutes longer.

Prep: 35 minutes plus cooling
Bake: 12 minutes per batch

1½ cups all-purpose flour
2 teaspoons baking soda
½ teaspoon salt
¾ cup granulated sugar
¾ cup packed brown sugar
¾ cup butter or margarine (1½ sticks), softened
2 large eggs
2 teaspoons vanilla extract
3 cups old-fashioned oats, uncooked
1 cup dried tart cherries or raisins
1 package (6 ounces) semisweet chocolate chips (1 cup)

1. Preheat oven to 350°F. Grease large cookie sheet. In small bowl, with wire whisk, stir flour, baking soda, and salt.

2. In large bowl, with mixer at medium speed, beat granulated and brown sugars and butter until creamy, occasionally scraping bowl with rubber spatula. Beat in eggs, one at a time, beating well after each addition. Beat in vanilla. Reduce speed to low; gradually beat in flour mixture just until blended, occasionally scraping bowl. With wooden spoon, stir in oats, dried cherries, and chocolate chips.

3. Drop dough by rounded measuring tablespoons, 2 inches apart, onto prepared cookie sheet. Bake until tops are golden, 12 to 14 minutes. With wide spatula, transfer cookies to wire racks to cool. Repeat with remaining dough. Makes about 54 cookies.

Each cookie: About 100 calories, 1g protein, 15g carbohydrate, 4g total fat (2g saturated), 15mg cholesterol, 100mg sodium.

CHOCOLATE AND COCOA POWDER

TEST KITCHEN TIP We always use pure chocolate products and avoid artificially flavored compound (summer) coatings or premelted chocolate, all of which include large amounts of vegetable fats.

UNSWEETENED CHOCOLATE is simply ground cocoa beans. Professionals call it chocolate liquor. It's not very tasty on its own, so it is combined with sugar and other ingredients in recipes.

BITTERSWEET CHOCOLATE has been sweetened, but the amount of sugar varies greatly from brand to brand. Some list the percentage of chocolate liquor on the label. A brand with 70 percent will be more bitter than one with 64 percent. Most European chocolate bars are bittersweet, and some bittersweet chocolate is now produced in the U.S.

SEMISWEET CHOCOLATE is similar to bittersweet chocolate, although it is usually a bit sweeter. It is available in individually wrapped one-ounce squares and in bulk. It can be used instead of bittersweet chocolate.

SWEET CHOCOLATE is usually sold under a brand name (and used to make German chocolate cake). Do not confuse it with bitter- or semisweet chocolate.

MILK CHOCOLATE contains dried milk powder and a high proportion of sugar. It is essentially an eating chocolate—it is not usually used for baking.

WHITE CHOCOLATE is not really a chocolate but rather vanilla-flavored, sweetened cocoa butter (a by-product of chocolate processing), although some brands substitute vegetable fat for the cocoa butter.

UNSWEETENED COCOA POWDER provides the rich chocolate flavor in many desserts. There are two kinds: *natural* and *Dutch-process*; check the label. In baking, they are not interchangeable. They react differently when mixed with baking soda or baking powder. However, for a cup of hot cocoa, use your favorite.

NATURAL COCOA POWDER is the most common cocoa in American kitchens. Unless stated otherwise, it is the one we used for the recipes in this book.

DUTCH-PROCESS COCOA POWDER has been treated with an alkali to mellow cocoa's natural bitterness and to give baked goods a darker color.

CHOCOLATE WOWS

(Pictured on page 680)

After one bite of these decadent cookies, you will understand why we call them "Wows."

Prep: 20 minutes   Bake: 13 minutes per batch

- ⅓ cup all-purpose flour
- ¼ cup unsweetened cocoa
- 1 teaspoon baking powder
- ¼ teaspoon salt
- 6 squares (6 ounces) semisweet chocolate, chopped
- ½ cup butter or margarine (1 stick)
- 2 large eggs
- ¾ cup sugar
- 1½ teaspoons vanilla extract
- 2 cups pecans (8 ounces), chopped
- 1 package (6 ounces) semisweet chocolate chips (1 cup)

1. Preheat oven to 325°F. Grease two large cookie sheets. In small bowl, with wire whisk, stir flour, cocoa, baking powder, and salt.

2. In heavy 2-quart saucepan, melt chopped chocolate and butter over low heat, stirring frequently, until smooth. Remove from heat and cool.

3. In large bowl, with mixer at medium speed, beat eggs and sugar until light, about 2 minutes, frequently scraping bowl with rubber spatula. Reduce speed to low. Add cooled chocolate mixture, flour mixture, and vanilla; beat just until blended. Increase speed to medium; beat 2 minutes. Stir in pecans and chocolate chips.

4. Drop batter by rounded teaspoons, 2 inches apart, on cookie sheets. With small metal spatula, spread batter into 2-inch rounds. Bake until tops are shiny and cracked, about 13 minutes, rotating cookie sheets between upper and lower oven racks halfway through baking. Cool 10 minutes on cookie sheet. With wide spatula, transfer cookies to wire racks to cool completely.

5. Repeat with remaining batter. Makes about 48 cookies.

Each cookie: About 102 calories, 1g protein, 9g carbohydrate, 7g total fat (3g saturated), 14mg cholesterol, 45mg sodium.

CHOCOLATE CHIP COOKIES

Who can say no to this classic cookie?

Prep: 15 minutes   Bake: 10 minutes per batch

- 1¼ cups all-purpose flour
- ½ teaspoon baking soda
- ½ teaspoon salt
- ½ cup butter or margarine (1 stick), softened
- ½ cup packed brown sugar
- ¼ cup granulated sugar
- 1 large egg
- 1 teaspoon vanilla extract
- 1 package (6 ounces) semisweet chocolate chips (1 cup)
- ½ cup walnuts, chopped (optional)

1. Preheat oven to 375°F. In small bowl, with wire whisk, stir flour, baking soda, and salt.

2. In large bowl, with mixer at medium speed, beat butter and brown and granulated sugars until light and fluffy. Beat in egg and vanilla until well combined. Reduce speed to low; beat in flour mixture just until blended. With wooden spoon, stir in chocolate chips and walnuts, if using.

3. Drop dough by rounded tablespoons, 2 inches apart, on two ungreased cookie sheets. Bake until golden around edges, 10 to 12 minutes, rotating cookie sheets between upper and lower oven racks halfway through baking. With wide spatula, transfer cookies to wire racks to cool completely. Repeat with remaining dough. Makes about 36 cookies.

Each cookie: About 80 calories, 1g protein, 11g carbohydrate, 4g total fat (2g saturated), 13mg cholesterol, 79mg sodium.

WHITE CHOCOLATE-MACADAMIA COOKIES

Prepare as directed but substitute **¾ cup white baking chips** for semisweet chocolate chips and **1 cup chopped macadamia nuts (4 ounces)** for walnuts, if you like.

Each cookie: About 110 calories, 1g protein, 11g carbohydrate, 7g total fat (3g saturated), 13mg cholesterol, 84mg sodium.

PEANUT BUTTER COOKIES

....

Great as an afternoon snack or as a special treat to sneak into a brown-bag lunch. If you like, instead of crosshatching the cookies with a fork, lightly press mini nonmelting chocolate-covered candies into the top of each cookie before baking.

Prep: 15 minutes   Bake: 15 minutes per batch

1¼	cups all-purpose flour
1	teaspoon baking soda
¼	teaspoon salt
1	cup creamy peanut butter
½	cup butter or margarine (1 stick), softened
½	cup packed brown sugar
¼	cup granulated sugar
1	large egg
½	teaspoon vanilla extract

1. Preheat oven to 350°F. In small bowl, with wire whisk, stir flour, baking soda, and salt.

2. In large bowl, with mixer at medium speed, beat peanut butter, butter, brown and granulated sugars, egg, and vanilla until combined, occasionally scraping bowl with rubber spatula. Reduce speed to low. Add flour mixture and beat just until blended.

3. Drop dough by heaping tablespoons, 2 inches apart, on two ungreased large cookie sheets. With fork, press crisscross pattern into top of each cookie.

4. Bake until lightly browned, 15 to 20 minutes, rotating cookie sheets between upper and lower oven racks halfway through baking. With wide spatula, transfer cookies to wire racks to cool completely.

5. Repeat forming and baking with remaining dough. Makes about 36 cookies.

Each cookie: About 100 calories, 3g protein, 9g carbohydrate, 6g total fat (2g saturated), 13mg cholesterol, 114mg sodium.

---

5 IDEAS FOR . . . PEANUT BUTTER

News flash: This staple spread isn't just for kids' lunch boxes anymore. It adds protein and flavor to family meals from breakfast to dinner—and makes a great dessert. For best results, use the regular or reduced-fat creamy variety, since the oil in must-stir natural types may separate out.

STUFFED FRENCH TOAST

In pie plate, with fork, beat 2 large eggs with ½ cup milk. Spread ½ cup peanut butter on 8 slices firm white sandwich bread. Diagonally slice 1 banana and arrange on 4 bread slices; top with remaining bread to make 4 sandwiches. Dip in egg mixture to coat. In 12-inch nonstick skillet, melt 1 tablespoon butter or margarine on medium. Add sandwiches and cook 6 minutes or until golden on both sides. Drizzle with maple syrup. Serves 4.

AFRICAN-STYLE CHICKEN

In 12-inch skillet, heat 1 tablespoon oil on medium-high. Add 1¼ pounds skinless, boneless chicken thighs, cut into 1-inch cubes; cook 8 minutes, stirring often. Add 1 tablespoon curry powder; cook 1 minute, stirring. Stir in 1½ cups roasted-garlic pasta sauce, 1 can (15 to 19 ounces) rinsed and drained garbanzo beans, ¾ cup water, and ½ cup peanut butter; heat to boiling. Cover; simmer on low 5 minutes. Stir in 2 tablespoons chopped fresh cilantro. Spoon over rice. Serves 4.

ASIAN NOODLES

In saucepot, cook 12 ounces fettuccine as label directs, adding 1 package (10 ounces) shredded carrots and 1 package (6 ounces) snow peas during last 2 minutes of cooking. Reserve ½ cup cooking water; drain fettuccine mixture. In same saucepot, blend ½ cup peanut butter, ½ cup low-fat ginger vinaigrette, and add reserved cooking water. Add fettuccine mixture; toss well. Serves 4.

NO-BAKE COOKIES

In saucepan, cook ½ cup corn syrup with ⅓ cup sugar on medium 3 minutes or until sugar dissolves. Stir in 1 cup peanut butter until blended. Remove from heat; stir in 3 cups whole-grain cereal flakes until coated. Drop by rounded tablespoons onto waxed paper; cool. Store at room temperature in airtight container. Makes 2 dozen.

SWIRL BROWNIES

Prepare 1 box (19 to 20 ounces) brownie mix as label directs for 9-inch square pan. In bowl, stir ½ cup peanut butter, ¼ cup confectioners' sugar, 1½ tablespoons melted butter, and 1 large egg until smooth. Dollop peanut butter mixture onto brownie batter in pan; swirl with knife. Bake according to directions. Makes 16.

SOUR CREAM COOKIES

....

Fresh lemon peel brings out the richness of these cookies.

Prep: 15 minutes   Bake: 10 minutes per batch

- 1   cup all-purpose flour
- ¼   teaspoon baking soda
- ¼   teaspoon salt
- 6   tablespoons butter or margarine, softened
- ½   cup sugar
- ½   cup sour cream
- 1   teaspoon freshly grated lemon peel
- ½   teaspoon vanilla extract

1. Preheat oven to 350°F. Grease two cookie sheets. In small bowl, stir flour, baking soda, and salt.

2. In large bowl, with mixer at medium speed, beat butter until creamy. Gradually add sugar and beat until light and fluffy. Beat in sour cream, lemon peel, and vanilla. Reduce speed to low; beat in flour mixture just until blended.

3. Drop dough by rounded teaspoons, 1 inch apart, on prepared cookie sheets. Bake until set and golden around edges, 10 to 12 minutes, rotating cookie sheets between upper and lower oven racks halfway through baking. Cool 1 minute on cookie sheets; with wide spatula, transfer cookies to wire racks to cool completely. Repeat with remaining dough. Makes about 36 cookies.

Each cookie: About 49 calories, 0g protein, 6g carbohydrate, 3g total fat (2g saturated), 7mg cholesterol, 46mg sodium.

ALMOND MACAROONS

....

We've rolled classic macaroons in sliced almonds for extra texture and an elegant presentation.

Prep: 20 minutes   Bake: 18 minutes

- 1   tube or can (7 to 8 ounces) almond paste, cut into 1-inch pieces
- ⅓   cup confectioners' sugar
- 1   large egg white
- ½   cup sliced natural almonds

1. Preheat oven to 325°F. Evenly grease and flour large cookie sheet.

2. In small bowl, with mixer at low speed, beat almond paste until crumbly. Add confectioners' sugar and egg white; beat until well blended (dough will be wet and sticky).

3. Place almonds on waxed paper. With lightly floured hands, roll dough into 1-inch balls. Roll balls in almonds, gently pressing to coat. Place balls, 1 inch apart, on prepared cookie sheet. Bake until golden, 18 to 20 minutes. With wide spatula, transfer cookies to wire racks to cool completely. Makes about 30 cookies.

Each cookie: About 50 calories, 1g protein, 5g carbohydrate, 3g total fat (0g saturated), 0mg cholesterol, 3mg sodium.

COCONUT MACAROONS

....

These chewy flourless cookies, a traditional Passover dessert, are good any time of the year.

Prep: 10 minutes   Bake: 25 minutes

- 3   cups flaked sweetened coconut
- ¾   cup sugar
- 4   large egg whites
- ¼   teaspoon salt
- 1   teaspoon vanilla extract
- ⅛   teaspoon almond extract

1. Preheat oven to 325°F. Line two cookie sheets with parchment paper or foil.

2. In large bowl, stir coconut, sugar, egg whites, salt, vanilla, and almond extract until well combined.

3. Drop batter by rounded teaspoons, 1 inch apart, on prepared cookie sheets. Bake until set and lightly golden, about 25 minutes, rotating cookie sheets between upper and lower oven racks halfway through baking. Cool 1 minute on cookie sheets; with wide spatula, transfer cookies to wire racks to cool completely. Makes about 42 cookies.

Each cookie: About 41 calories, 1g protein, 6g carbohydrate, 2g total fat (2g saturated), 0mg cholesterol, 32mg sodium.

CHOCOLATE COCONUT MACAROONS
Prepare as directed, stirring **2 tablespoons unsweetened cocoa** and **1 square (1 ounce) semisweet chocolate**, grated, into coconut mixture.

ALMOND CRESCENTS

These classic holiday favorites are great for gift giving. Butter is essential to the exquisite texture and flavor. If you like, they can be shaped into 1-inch balls instead.

Prep: 45 minutes plus chilling
Bake: 20 minutes per batch

- 1 cup blanched whole almonds (4 ounces), lightly toasted (right)
- ½ cup granulated sugar
- ¼ teaspoon salt
- 1 cup butter (2 sticks), softened (do not use margarine)
- 2 cups all-purpose flour
- 1 teaspoon almond extract
- ½ teaspoon vanilla extract
- ¾ cup confectioners' sugar

1. In food processor with knife blade attached, process almonds, ¼ cup granulated sugar, and salt until almonds are very finely ground.

2. In large bowl, with mixer at low speed, beat butter and remaining ¼ cup granulated sugar until blended, occasionally scraping bowl with rubber spatula. Increase speed to high; beat until light and fluffy, about 3 minutes. Reduce speed to low. Gradually add flour, ground-almond mixture, almond extract, and vanilla and beat until blended. Divide dough in half;

wrap each piece with plastic wrap and refrigerate until dough is firm enough to handle, about 1 hour, or freeze about 30 minutes.

3. Preheat oven to 325°F. Working with one piece of dough at a time, with lightly floured hands, shape rounded teaspoons of dough into 2" by ½" crescents. Place, 1 inch apart, on two ungreased cookie sheets.

4. Bake until lightly browned around edges, about 20 minutes, rotating cookie sheets between upper and lower oven racks halfway through baking. With spatula, transfer cookies to wire racks set over waxed paper. Immediately dust confectioners' sugar over cookies until well coated; cool completely. Repeat with remaining dough. Makes about 72 cookies.

Each cookie: About 58 calories, 1g protein, 6g carbohydrate, 4g total fat (2g saturated), 7mg cholesterol, 34mg sodium.

WALNUT OR PECAN CRESCENTS

Prepare crescents as directed but substitute **1 cup walnuts or pecans** (not toasted) for almonds and omit almond extract.

HAZELNUT CRESCENTS

Prepare crescents as directed but substitute **1 cup toasted, skinned hazelnuts (filberts)** for almonds and omit almond extract.

TOASTING NUTS

TEST KITCHEN TIP

Toasting nuts brings out their flavor and, in the case of nuts such as hazelnuts, facilitates removal of the skins.

To toast almonds, pecans, walnuts, or hazelnuts, preheat the oven to 350°F. Spread the shelled nuts in a single layer on a cookie sheet. Bake, stirring occasionally, until lightly browned and fragrant, about 10 minutes. Toast hazelnuts until the skins begin to peel away. Let the nuts cool completely before chopping.

To skin hazelnuts, wrap the still-warm toasted nuts in a clean kitchen towel and let stand for about 10 minutes. Using the towel, rub off as much of the skins as possible (all of the skin may not come off).

Almond Crescents

JUMBO GINGERSNAPS

....

The ginger-molasses flavor in these crackle-top cookies is just perfect. Their generous size makes them especially festive, but you can also make smaller cookies.

Prep: 20 minutes   Bake: 15 minutes

- 2 cups all-purpose flour
- 2 teaspoons ground ginger
- 1 teaspoon baking soda
- ½ teaspoon ground cinnamon
- ½ teaspoon salt
- ¼ teaspoon ground black pepper (optional)
- ¾ cup vegetable shortening
- ½ cup plus 2 tablespoons sugar
- 1 large egg
- ½ cup dark molasses

1. Preheat oven to 350°F. In medium bowl, with wire whisk, stir flour, ginger, baking soda, cinnamon, salt, and pepper if using.

2. In large bowl, with mixer at medium speed, beat shortening and ½ cup sugar until light and fluffy. Beat in egg until blended, then beat in molasses. Reduce speed to low; beat in flour mixture just until blended.

3. Place remaining 2 tablespoons sugar on waxed paper. Roll ¼ cup dough into ball; roll in sugar to coat evenly. Repeat with remaining dough to make 10 balls in all. Place balls, 3 inches apart, on ungreased large cookie sheet. Or, for small cookies, roll dough into balls by slightly rounded tablespoons and place 2 inches apart on two ungreased cookie sheets.

4. Bake until set, about 15 minutes for large cookies or 9 to 11 minutes for smaller cookies, rotating cookie sheets between upper and lower oven racks halfway through baking. Cookies will be very soft and may appear moist in cracks. Cool 1 minute on cookie sheets on wire racks; with wide spatula, transfer cookies to wire racks to cool completely. Makes 10 giant cookies or about 30 small cookies.

Each cookie: About 323 calories, 3g protein, 42g carbohydrate, 16g total fat (4g saturated), 21mg cholesterol, 258mg sodium.

RASPBERRY LINZER THUMBPRINTS

....

These cookies have all the flavor and texture of a classic Austrian linzer torte: a nutty crust and a raspberry jam filling.

Prep: 45 minutes plus cooling
Bake: 20 minutes per batch

- 1 cup hazelnuts (filberts), toasted and skinned (opposite) plus ⅓ cup, not toasted
- ½ cup sugar
- ¾ cup butter or margarine (1½ sticks), cut into pieces
- 1 teaspoon vanilla extract
- ¼ teaspoon salt
- 1¾ cups all-purpose flour
- ¼ cup seedless raspberry jam

1. Preheat oven to 350°F.

2. In food processor with knife blade attached, process 1 cup toasted hazelnuts and sugar until nuts are finely ground. Add butter, vanilla, and salt and process until blended. Add flour and process just until evenly combined. Remove knife blade and press dough together with hands.

3. Finely chop remaining ⅓ cup hazelnuts; spread on waxed paper. Roll dough into 1-inch balls (dough may be slightly crumbly). Roll balls in nuts, gently pressing to coat. Place balls, 1½ inches apart, on two ungreased large cookie sheets. With thumb, make small indentation in center of each ball. Fill each indentation with ¼ teaspoon jam.

4. Bake until lightly golden around edges, about 20 minutes, rotating cookie sheets between upper and lower oven racks halfway through baking. With wide spatula, transfer cookies to wire racks to cool completely.

5. Repeat with remaining balls and raspberry jam. Makes about 48 cookies.

Each cookie: About 74 calories, 1g protein, 7g carbohydrate, 5g total fat (2g saturated), 8mg cholesterol, 42mg sodium.

LEMON ICEBOX COOKIES

···

This dough is wonderful to have on hand in the freezer so you can bake fresh cookies whenever you wish. It's also the base for three delicious variations.

Prep: 20 minutes plus chilling
Bake: 10 minutes per batch

1²/₃ cups all-purpose flour
   1 teaspoon baking powder
 ¼ teaspoon baking soda
 ⅛ teaspoon salt
   3 lemons
 ½ cup butter or margarine (1 stick), softened
 ¾ cup sugar
   1 large egg yolk

1. In medium bowl, with wire whisk, stir flour, baking powder, baking soda, and salt. From lemons, grate 1 tablespoon peel and squeeze 2 tablespoons juice.

2. In large bowl, with mixer at medium speed, beat butter and sugar until light and fluffy. Beat in egg yolk and lemon peel and juice until combined. Reduce speed to low; beat in flour mixture just until blended.

3. Divide dough in half. On waxed paper, form one piece of dough into 12-inch log. Repeat with remaining dough. Wrap each log and refrigerate overnight, or freeze until very firm, at least 2 hours.

4. Preheat oven to 375°F. Grease and flour two large cookie sheets or line with parchment paper or foil. Cut 1 log crosswise into ¼-inch-thick slices. Place slices, 1 inch apart, on prepared cookie sheets.

5. Bake until set and golden brown around edges, 10 to 12 minutes, rotating cookie sheets between upper and lower oven racks halfway through baking. With wide spatula, transfer cookies to wire racks to cool completely. Repeat with remaining dough. Makes about 96 cookies.

Each cookie: About 25 calories, 0g protein, 3g carbohydrate, 1g total fat (1g saturated), 5mg cholesterol, 21mg sodium.

LEMON-WALNUT ICEBOX COOKIES

Prepare as directed, stirring **1 cup walnuts (4 ounces)**, finely chopped, into dough after adding flour.

Each cookie: About 33 calories, 0g protein, 4g carbohydrate, 2g total fat (1g saturated), 5mg cholesterol, 21mg sodium.

LEMON-ANISE ICEBOX COOKIES

Prepare as directed, beating **2 teaspoons anise seeds** into dough with lemon peel.

ORANGE ICEBOX COOKIES

Prepare as directed but substitute **1 tablespoon freshly grated orange peel** and **2 tablespoons fresh orange juice** for lemon peel and lemon juice.

COCONUT COOKIES

···

Adding flaked coconut to the rich dough adds texture as well as flavor to these melt-in-your-mouth gems.

Prep: 20 minutes   **Bake: 15 minutes per batch**

2¾ cups all-purpose flour
   1 teaspoon baking powder
 ½ teaspoon salt
   1 cup butter or margarine (2 sticks), softened
   1 cup sugar
   1 large egg
   2 tablespoons milk
   1 teaspoon vanilla extract
1½ cups flaked sweetened coconut

1. Preheat oven to 325°F. In medium bowl, with wire whisk, stir flour, baking powder, and salt.

2. In large bowl, with mixer at medium speed, beat butter and sugar until light and fluffy. Beat in egg, milk, and vanilla. Reduce speed to low; beat in flour mixture just until blended. Stir in coconut (dough will be crumbly). With hands, press dough together.

3. Drop dough by rounded teaspoons, 2 inches apart, on two ungreased cookie sheets. With fork, press crosshatch into each cookie, flattening to ¼-inch thickness. Bake until edges are lightly browned, 15 to 17 minutes, rotating cookie sheets between upper and lower oven racks halfway through baking. With wide spatula, transfer cookies to wire racks to cool.

4. Repeat shaping and baking with remaining dough. Makes about 72 cookies.

Each cookie: About 45 calories, 0g protein, 5g carbohydrate, 2g total fat (2g saturated), 7mg cholesterol, 41mg sodium.

HERMITS

∙∙

These spicy fruit bars date back to New England's clipper-ship days and got their name from their long-keeping quality. Sailors would stow them away "like hermits" for snacking on during their extended voyages.

Prep: 20 minutes plus cooling   Bake: 13 minutes

- 2   cups all-purpose flour
- 1   teaspoon ground cinnamon
- ½   teaspoon baking powder
- ½   teaspoon baking soda
- ½   teaspoon ground ginger
- ¼   teaspoon ground nutmeg
- ¼   teaspoon salt
- ⅛   teaspoon ground cloves
- 1   cup packed brown sugar
- ½   cup butter or margarine (1 stick), softened
- ⅓   cup dark molasses
- 1   large egg
- 1   cup dark raisins
- 1   cup pecans (4 ounces), toasted (page 692) and coarsely chopped (optional)

1. Preheat oven to 350°F. Grease and flour two large cookie sheets.

2. In medium bowl, with wire whisk, stir flour, cinnamon, baking powder, baking soda, ginger, nutmeg, salt, and cloves.

3. In large bowl, with mixer at medium speed, beat sugar and butter until light and fluffy. Beat in molasses until blended. Beat in egg. Reduce speed to low; beat in flour mixture just until blended, occasionally scraping bowl with rubber spatula. With wooden spoon, stir in raisins and pecans, if using, just until combined.

4. Divide dough into quarters. With lightly floured hands, shape each quarter into 12" by 1½" log. Place 2 logs, about 3 inches apart, on each cookie sheet.

5. Bake until logs flatten and edges are firm, 13 to 15 minutes, rotating cookie sheets between upper and lower racks halfway through baking. Cool logs on cookie sheets on wire racks 15 minutes. Transfer logs to cutting board. Slice each log crosswise into 8 cookies. Transfer cookies to wire racks to cool completely. Makes 32 cookies.

Each cookie: About 105 calories, 1g protein, 19g carbohydrate, 3g total fat (2g saturated), 15mg cholesterol, 80mg sodium.

BUTTERSCOTCH FINGERS

∙∙

When butter and brown sugar are combined, there's an almost magical transformation into the flavor we know as butterscotch. Here, pecans are added for texture.

**Prep: 30 minutes plus chilling and cooling
Bake: 12 minutes per batch**

- 2⅓   cups all-purpose flour
- 1½   teaspoons baking powder
- ½   teaspoon salt
- 1   cup butter or margarine (2 sticks), softened
- 1   cup packed dark brown sugar
- 1   large egg
- 1   teaspoon vanilla extract
- ¾   cup pecans, chopped

1. In medium bowl, with wire whisk, stir flour, baking powder, and salt.

2. In large bowl, with mixer at medium speed, beat butter and sugar until creamy, occasionally scraping bowl with rubber spatula. Beat in egg and vanilla. Reduce speed to low; beat in flour mixture just until blended, occasionally scraping bowl. With wooden spoon, stir in pecans.

3. Shape dough into 12" by 3¾" by 1" brick. Wrap brick in plastic wrap and refrigerate until firm enough to slice, at least 6 hours or overnight. Or freeze about 2 hours. (If using margarine, freeze brick overnight.)

4. Preheat oven to 350°F. Grease large cookie sheet.

5. With sharp knife, cut brick crosswise into ⅛-inch-thick slices. Place slices, 1 inch apart, on prepared cookie sheet. Bake until edges are lightly browned, 12 to 14 minutes. Transfer cookies to wire rack to cool.

6. Repeat with remaining dough. Makes about 96 cookies.

Each cookie: About 65 calories, 1g protein, 7g carbohydrate, 4g total fat (2g saturated), 11mg cholesterol, 55mg sodium.

Meringue Fingers

MERINGUE FINGERS

....

These ethereal meringue cookies are dipped into chocolate, which gives them fabulous flavor.

Prep: 25 minutes plus cooling   Bake: 1 hour

- 3   large egg whites
- ¼   teaspoon cream of tartar
- ⅛   teaspoon salt
- ½   cup sugar
- 1   teaspoon vanilla extract
- 2   squares (2 ounces) semisweet chocolate, chopped
- 1   teaspoon vegetable shortening

1. Preheat oven to 200°F. Line two large cookie sheets with foil or parchment paper.

2. In small bowl, with mixer at high speed, beat egg whites, cream of tartar, and salt until soft peaks form when beaters are lifted. Beating at high speed, gradually sprinkle in sugar, 2 tablespoons at a time; beat until sugar has dissolved. Add vanilla; continue beating until meringue stands in stiff, glossy peaks when beaters are lifted.

3. Spoon meringue into pastry bag fitted with ½-inch star tip. Pipe meringue in 3-inch lengths, 1 inch apart, on prepared cookie sheets.

4. Bake cookies until set, about 1 hour, rotating cookie sheets between upper and lower oven racks halfway through baking. Cool 10 minutes on cookie sheets on wire racks; then, with spatula, transfer cookies to wire racks to cool completely.

5. When cookies have cooled, in heavy 1-quart saucepan, melt chocolate and shortening over low heat, stirring frequently, until smooth; remove from heat. Dip one end of each cookie into melted chocolate; let dry on wire racks set over waxed paper. Makes about 48 cookies.

Each cookie: About 16 calories, 0g protein, 3g carbohydrate, 0g total fat (0g saturated), 0mg cholesterol, 10mg sodium.

HOLIDAY COOKIE DOUGH

....

Smart cookies are strategic about holiday baking. If your goal is to whip up a diverse assortment of goodies in record time, then share in our flour-power secret: one do-it-all dough, like our triple-tested version below. It's quick to make and can turn out many different types of delicious—and distinctive—cookies, all sure to hit the sweet spot with family and friends.

Prep: 10 minutes

2³/₄ cups all-purpose flour
¹/₄ teaspoon baking soda
¹/₄ teaspoon salt
1 cup (2 sticks) butter, softened (do not use margarine)
³/₄ cup sugar
1 large egg
1 teaspoon vanilla extract

1. On waxed paper, combine flour, baking soda, and salt.

2. In large bowl, with mixer on medium speed, beat butter and sugar 1 minute or until creamy, occasionally scraping bowl with rubber spatula. Add egg and vanilla; beat until well mixed. Reduce speed to low; gradually beat in flour mixture just until blended, occasionally scraping bowl.

3. Follow directions on this page through page 701 for your choice of cookie.

Tip: This simple dough, the starting point for all our holiday cookie recipes, calls for butter—no substitutes—because butter not only gives the best flavor in baked goods, but it also makes the dough much easier to work with. Margarines and spreads are often too soft to produce a cookie that can be rolled or shaped without difficulty.

CRANBERRY-ORANGE SPICE COOKIES

....

Crystallized ginger and pumpkin pie spice give these cookies an autumn-inspired zing that draws cookie lovers from near and far!

Prep: 40 minutes plus freezing and cooling
Bake: 14 minutes per batch

Holiday Cookie Dough (left)
¹/₂ cup dried cranberries, finely chopped
¹/₄ cup crystallized ginger, finely chopped
2 teaspoons grated fresh orange peel
1 teaspoon pumpkin pie spice
3 tablespoons green sugar crystals
3 tablespoons red sugar crystals

1. Begin preparing Holiday Cookie Dough. In Step 2, stir in cranberries, ginger, orange peel, and pumpkin pie spice along with flour until well mixed. Divide dough in half.

2. On lightly floured surface, with hands, shape each half into 10-inch-long log. Using hands or two clean rulers, press each log into 10-inch-long squared-off log. Wrap each in plastic wrap and freeze until firm enough to slice, 2 hours or refrigerate overnight. (Logs can be frozen up to 1 month.)

3. Preheat oven to 350°F. On sheet of waxed paper, place green sugar. Unwrap one log and press sides in sugar to coat. Cut log into ¹/₄-inch-thick slices. Place slices, 1 inch apart, on ungreased large cookie sheet. Bake cookies 14 to 16 minutes or until golden. Transfer cookies to wire rack to cool. Repeat with red sugar and second log.

4. Store cookies in tightly sealed container at room temperature up to 1 week or in freezer up to 3 months. Makes about 60 cookies.

Each cookie: About 70 calories, 1g protein, 9g carbohydrate, 3g total fat (2g saturated), 0g fiber, 12mg cholesterol, 50mg sodium.

FIG-FILLED MOONS

....

Here, our Holiday Cookie dough is filled with a sweet and wholesome mixture of orange, dried fruit, walnuts, and honey.

Prep: 1½ hours plus chilling and cooling
Bake: 12 minutes per batch

Holiday Cookie Dough (page 697)
1 large orange
5 ounces dried Mission figs, stems removed (about 1 cup)
½ cup walnuts
¼ cup raisins
¼ cup honey
1½ teaspoons ground cinnamon
1 large egg, lightly beaten
coarse sugar crystals (optional)

1. Prepare Holiday Cookie Dough. Divide dough into 3 pieces. Flatten each piece into a disk; wrap each in plastic wrap. Refrigerate dough at least 2 hours or overnight, until firm enough to roll.

2. Meanwhile, from orange, grate ½ teaspoon peel and squeeze 3 tablespoons juice. In food processor with knife blade attached, combine orange peel and juice, figs, walnuts, raisins, honey, and cinnamon. Pulse until fig mixture is well blended but still has a coarse texture. Cover and set aside until ready to use.

3. Preheat oven to 350°F. Between two sheets of waxed paper, roll a disk of dough ⅛-inch thick. Remove top sheet of waxed paper. With floured 2½-inch scalloped round biscuit or cookie cutter, cut out as many cookies as possible. Wrap and refrigerate trimmings to reroll later.

4. With spatula, carefully place cookies, 1 inch apart, on ungreased large cookie sheet. Spoon 1 level measuring teaspoon fig filling onto center of each cookie. Fold each cookie in half over filling; brush with egg. Sprinkle with sugar crystals if you like. (If dough becomes too soft to work with at any time, place in freezer 10 to 15 minutes to firm up.)

5. Bake cookies 12 to 15 minutes or until tops are golden-brown. Transfer cookies to wire rack to cool. Repeat with remaining dough, dough trimmings, fig filling, and egg.

6. Store cookies in tightly sealed container at room temperature up to 1 week or in freezer up to 3 months. Makes about 48 cookies.

Each cookie: About 100 calories, 1g protein, 13g carbohydrate, 5g total fat (3g saturated), 1g fiber, 20mg cholesterol, 65mg sodium.

MEXICAN WEDDING COOKIES

....

Unlike other recipes for similar cookies, this one calls for the cookies to be rolled in confectioners' sugar once cooled; if they're still warm, the coating will get sticky.

Prep: 30 minutes plus cooling
Bake: 13 minutes per batch

1½ cups pecans (6 ounces)
3 tablespoons plus 1½ cups confectioners' sugar, sifted
Holiday Cookie Dough (page 697)

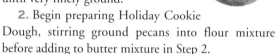

1. In food processor with knife blade attached, pulse pecans with 3 tablespoons confectioners' sugar until very finely ground.

2. Begin preparing Holiday Cookie Dough, stirring ground pecans into flour mixture before adding to butter mixture in Step 2.

3. Preheat oven to 350°F. Shape dough by rounded measuring teaspoons into 1-inch balls. Place balls, 1½ inches apart, on ungreased large cookie sheet. Bake cookies 13 to 15 minutes or until bottoms are browned and tops are light golden. Let stand on cookie sheet 2 minutes to firm up slightly, then transfer to wire rack to cool. Repeat with remaining dough.

4. Place confectioners' sugar in pie plate. Roll cooled cookies in sugar to coat, twice if desired.

5. Store cookies with sheets of waxed paper between layers in tightly sealed container at room temperature up to 1 week or in freezer up to 3 months. Makes about 96 cookies.

Each cookie: About 60 calories, 1g protein, 7g carbohydrate, 3g total fat (1g saturated), 0g fiber, 8mg cholesterol, 30mg sodium.

Tip: Make sure cookies are cool before rolling in confectioners' sugar; if they're still warm, the coating will get sticky.

STAINED-GLASS ORNAMENTS

....

Tasteful—and tasty—edible ornaments to hang on your tree. Avoid red-and-white swirled peppermint candies—they won't melt in the oven.

Prep: 1½ hours plus chilling and cooling
Bake: 10 minutes per batch

Holiday Cookie Dough (page 697)
1 bag (6¼ ounces) hard candy, such as sour balls

1. Prepare Holiday Cookie Dough; divide into three pieces. Flatten each piece into a disk; wrap each in plastic wrap. Refrigerate at least 2 hours or overnight, until firm enough to roll.

2. While dough is chilling, place each color hard candy in separate heavy-duty plastic bag. Place a bag on towel-covered work surface or floor. With meat mallet or rolling pin, lightly crush candy into small pieces about the size of coarsely chopped nuts, being careful not to crush until powdery. Repeat with remaining bags of candy.

3. Preheat oven to 350°F. Line large cookie sheet with foil. Between two sheets of waxed paper, roll a disk of dough ⅛ inch thick. Remove top sheet of waxed paper. With 3- to 4-inch holiday-shaped cookie cutters, cut out as many cookies as possible. Place, 1 inch apart, on prepared cookie sheet. Cut out centers of cookies with 1½- to 2-inch cookie cutters. Remove and refrigerate trimmings and cutout centers.

4. Bake cookies 7 minutes. Remove cookie sheet from oven; fill each cookie's center with ½ teaspoon crushed candy. Return to oven and bake 3 to 4 minutes longer or until cookies are lightly browned and candy is melted. Cool cookies completely on cookie sheet on wire rack before removing with metal spatula. Repeat with remaining dough, trimmings, and candy.

5. Store cookies in tightly sealed container at room temperature up to 2 weeks or in freezer up to 3 months. Makes about 60 cookies.

Each cookie: About 70 calories, 1g protein, 10g carbohydrate, 3g total fat (2g saturated), 0g fiber, 12mg cholesterol, 50mg sodium.

Tip: To hang cookies as ornaments from tree, before baking, use a skewer to poke a small hole in each unbaked cookie. After baking and cooling, thread ribbon, string, or nylon fishing line through the hole.

CHOCOLATE RASPBERRY THUMBPRINTS

....

Thumbprint cookies are so versatile, lending themselves to many flavor combinations. In this version, chocolate and raspberry make winning sweet-tart partners.

Prep: 40 minutes plus cooling
Bake: 14 minutes per batch

Holiday Cookie Dough (page 697)
2 squares (2 ounces) unsweetened chocolate, melted
¼ cup unsweetened cocoa
1¼ cups (5 ounces) sliced natural almonds (with brown skins), coarsely chopped
½ cup seedless red raspberry or apricot jam

1. Preheat oven to 350°F.

2. Begin preparing Holiday Cookie Dough. In Step 2, beat in chocolate and cocoa with egg and vanilla extract. With hands, shape dough by rounded measuring teaspoons into 1-inch balls. Place sliced almonds in pie plate or on sheet of waxed paper; roll balls in chopped almonds to coat.

3. Place balls, 1½ inches apart, on ungreased large cookie sheet. With thumb or handle of wooden spoon, make small indentation in center of each ball. Fill each indentation with about ¼ teaspoon jam. Bake cookies 14 to 15 minutes or until jam is bubbly and cookies are baked through. Transfer to wire rack to cool. Repeat with remaining balls and jam.

4. Store cookies in tightly sealed container, putting sheets of waxed paper between layers, at room temperature up to 3 days or in freezer up to 3 months. Makes about 84 cookies.

Each cookie: About 65 calories, 1g protein, 7g carbohydrate, 4g total fat (2g saturated), 1g fiber, 9mg cholesterol, 35mg sodium.

WHITE-CHOCOLATE-DIPPED PEPPERMINT STICKS

....

These peppermint sticks look beautiful and taste even better! Leave out a dish of them when trimming the tree or relaxing by the fire with a mug of hot cocoa.

**Prep: 1 hour plus freezing and cooling
Bake: 11 minutes per batch**

Holiday Cookie Dough (page 697)
- 1/4 teaspoon peppermint extract
  green and red paste food coloring
- 5 ounces white chocolate, melted
- 6 green or red starlight mints, crushed

1. Prepare Holiday Cookie Dough. Divide dough in half; transfer half to another bowl. Stir peppermint extract into 1 portion of dough. Divide peppermint dough in half; transfer half to another bowl. Tint 1 portion green, the other red.

2. Preheat oven to 350°F. Line 9-inch square metal baking pan with plastic wrap, extending wrap over 2 sides of pan to form handles. Pat plain dough in pan. Freeze 10 minutes. Pat green dough over half of plain dough; pat red dough over other half of plain dough. Freeze 10 minutes.

3. Lift dough from pan using plastic wrap; place on cutting board. Cut dough into thirds so that one piece is all red on top, one is all green on top, and piece (from middle) is half red and half green. Cut each third crosswise into 3/8-inch strips. Twist strips and place, 1 1/2 inches apart, on ungreased cookie sheet. Bake 11 to 13 minutes or until golden brown. Transfer to wire rack to cool. Repeat.

4. Dip one end of each cookie into white chocolate and place on waxed paper. Sprinkle chocolate with crushed mints. Refrigerate cookies 15 minutes to set.

5. Store cookies in tightly sealed container with sheets of waxed paper between layers at room temperature up to 1 week or in freezer up to 3 months. Makes about 60 cookies.

Each cookie: About 75 calories, 1g protein, 9g carbohydrate, 4g total fat (3g saturated), 0g fiber, 13mg cholesterol, 50mg sodium.

CHOCOLATE PINWHEELS

....

Three kinds of chocolate make these cookies a triple-threat. Perfect for the choco-holics on your gift list!

**Prep: 30 minutes plus freezing and cooling
Bake: 10 minutes per batch**

Holiday Cookie Dough (page 697)
- 1/3 cup miniature semisweet chocolate chips
- 1/4 cup confectioners' sugar
- 1 square (1 ounce) unsweetened chocolate, melted
- 2 tablespoons unsweetened cocoa powder
- 2 tablespoons all-purpose flour

1. Prepare Holiday Cookie Dough. Divide in half; transfer half to another bowl. Stir chips, sugar, chocolate, and cocoa into one half. Stir flour into plain dough half.

2. On sheet of waxed paper, roll chocolate dough into 14" by 10" rectangle. Repeat with plain dough. Leaving plain rectangle on waxed paper, pick up and place it, dough side down, on top of chocolate rectangle so that edges line up evenly. Peel off top sheet of waxed paper. If dough is too soft to work with, refrigerate 10 minutes. Starting from long side, tightly roll rectangles together, jelly-roll fashion, to form log, lifting bottom sheet of waxed paper to help roll. Cut log crosswise in half. Wrap each half with plastic wrap and freeze 2 hours or refrigerate overnight.

3. Preheat oven to 350°F. With sharp knife, cut one log (keep other log refrigerated) crosswise into 1/4-inch-thick slices. Place slices, 2 inches apart, on ungreased large cookie sheet. Bake cookies 10 to 12 minutes or until lightly browned. Transfer to wire racks to cool. Repeat with remaining log.

4. Store cookies in tightly sealed container at room temperature up to 1 week or in freezer up to 3 months. Makes about 48 cookies.

Each cookie: About 90 calories, 1g protein, 10g carbohydrate, 5g total fat (3g saturated), 0g fiber, 16mg cholesterol, 60mg sodium.

Tip: If waxed paper wrinkles when you roll out the dough, peel off paper and replace it before continuing.

APPLE PIE SPICE RUGELACH

....

These filled and rolled crescent-shaped cookies are a Hanukkah tradition. Our version features a moist and spicy walnut–apple butter filling.

Prep: 1½ hours plus chilling and cooling
Bake: 15 minutes per batch

Holiday Cookie Dough (page 697)
- ⅓ cup all-purpose flour
- 1 cup dried currants
- ⅔ cup walnuts or pecans, finely chopped
- ¼ cup packed brown sugar
- 1½ teaspoons apple pie spice
- 3 tablespoons granulated sugar
- ½ cup plus 1 tablespoon apple butter

1. Prepare Holiday Cookie Dough, stirring additional ⅓ cup flour into dry ingredients in step 1. Divide dough into four equal pieces. Flatten each piece into a disk; wrap each disk with plastic wrap. Refrigerate dough 4 hours or overnight, until firm enough to roll.

2. Meanwhile, in small bowl, mix currants, walnuts, brown sugar, and 1 teaspoon apple pie spice. In cup, mix granulated sugar with remaining ½ teaspoon apple pie spice.

3. Preheat oven to 350°F. Between two sheets of waxed paper, roll one disk of dough into 9-inch round. Remove top sheet of waxed paper. Spread dough with 1 heaping measuring tablespoon apple butter and sprinkle with ½ cup fruit mixture, leaving ¼-inch border around edge.

4. With pizza wheel or sharp knife, cut round into 12 wedges. (If dough becomes too soft to work with, place in refrigerator 10 to 15 minutes to firm up.) Starting at wide end, roll each wedge jelly-roll fashion. Place cookies, point side down, 1 inch apart, on ungreased large cookie sheet; shape into crescents. Brush tops lightly with water and sprinkle with some spiced sugar. Bake cookies 15 minutes or until golden brown. Transfer to wire rack to cool. Repeat with remaining dough disks, fruit mixture, and spiced sugar.

5. Store cookies in tightly sealed container, putting waxed paper between layers, at room temperature up to 2 weeks or in freezer up to 3 months. Makes about 48 cookies.

Each cookie: About 125 calories, 1g protein, 18g carbohydrate, 5g total fat (3g saturated), 1g fiber, 15mg cholesterol, 65mg sodium.

HAZELNUT-CHOCOLATE SANDWICH COOKIES

....

A real yuletide yummy: two tiny cookies sandwiched with a rich and luxurious filling of hazelnuts and chocolate.

Prep: 1½ hours plus cooling
Bake: 9 minutes per batch

Holiday Cookie Dough (page 697)
sugar for pressing cookies
- ⅓ cup hazelnuts, toasted and chopped
- ¾ cup hazelnut-chocolate spread

1. Prepare Holiday Cookie Dough.

2. Preheat oven to 350°F. With hands, shape dough by level measuring ½ teaspoon into balls. Place balls, 2 inches apart, on ungreased large cookie sheet. Dip bottom of flat-bottomed glass in sugar; use to press each ball into 1-inch round, dipping again in sugar as needed. Sprinkle half of the rounds with hazelnuts. Bake cookies 9 to 10 minutes or until edges are golden brown. Transfer to wire rack to cool. Repeat.

3. Assemble sandwich cookies: Spread flat sides of plain cookies with ½ teaspoon hazelnut-chocolate spread. Top each with a nut-covered cookie, top side up, pressing lightly.

4. Store cookies in tightly sealed container with sheets of waxed paper between layers at room temperature up to 1 week or in freezer up to 3 months. Makes about 72 sandwich cookies.

Each cookie: About 65 calories, 1g protein, 7g carbohydrate, 4g total fat (2g saturated), 0g fiber, 10mg cholesterol, 45mg sodium.

CLASSIC SUGAR COOKIES

....

Our tender, delicate butter cookie is sure to become a favorite in your house. Decorate with colored sugar or Ornamental Frosting (right), if you like.

Prep: 1 hour 30 minutes plus chilling
Bake: 12 minutes per batch

- 3   cups all-purpose flour
- ½   teaspoon baking powder
- ½   teaspoon salt
- 1   cup butter (2 sticks), softened (do not use margarine)
- 1½   cups sugar
- 2   large eggs
- 1   teaspoon vanilla extract

1. In large bowl, with wire whisk, stir flour, baking powder, and salt. In separate large bowl, with mixer at low speed, beat butter and sugar until blended. Increase speed to high; beat until light and fluffy, about 5 minutes. Reduce speed to low; beat in eggs and vanilla until mixed, then beat in flour mixture just until blended, occasionally scraping bowl with rubber spatula. Shape dough into four equal disks; wrap each disk and refrigerate overnight, or freeze until firm enough to roll, at least 2 hours.

2. Preheat oven to 350°F. On lightly floured surface, with floured rolling pin, roll one piece of dough until slightly less than ¼ inch thick; keep remaining dough refrigerated. With floured 3- to 4-inch cookie cutters, cut dough into as many cookies as possible; reserve trimmings for rerolling. Place cookies, 1 inch apart, on two ungreased large cookie sheets.

3. Bake until golden around edges, 12 to 15 minutes, rotating cookie sheets between upper and lower oven racks halfway through baking. With wide spatula, transfer cookies to wire racks to cool completely.

4. Repeat with remaining dough and trimmings. Makes about 72 cookies.

Each cookie: About 61 calories, 1g protein, 8g carbohydrate, 3g total fat (2g saturated), 13mg cholesterol, 47mg sodium.

JAM-FILLED SUGAR COOKIES

Prepare, chill, and roll dough as directed (left). With 2½-inch fluted round or other decorative cutter, cut dough into rounds; with smaller cutter (1 to 1¼ inches), cut out and remove centers from half of rounds. Reserve centers for rerolling. Bake as directed; cool completely. Using **1 cup seedless raspberry jam,** warmed, spread whole rounds with thin layer of jam. Top with cutout rounds. Makes about 36 cookies.

Each cookie: About 144 calories, 2g protein, 23g carbohydrate, 5g total fat (3g saturated), 26mg cholesterol, 98mg sodium.

ORNAMENTAL FROSTING

....

This glossy, hard-drying frosting is often made with raw egg whites, but we prefer meringue powder, which is available at supermarkets and baking supply stores.

Prep: 5 minutes

- 1   package (16 ounces) confectioners' sugar
- 3   tablespoons meringue powder
- ⅓   cup warm water
     assorted food colorings (optional)

1. In large bowl, with mixer at medium speed, beat confectioners' sugar, meringue powder, and water until stiff and knife drawn through mixture leaves path, about 5 minutes.

2. If desired, tint frosting with food colorings. Keep tightly covered to prevent drying out. With small metal spatula, artists' paintbrushes, or decorating bags with small plain tips, decorate cookies with frosting. (You may need to thin frosting with a little warm water to obtain good spreading or piping consistency.) Makes about 3 cups.

Each tablespoon: About 39 calories, 0g protein, 10g carbohydrate, 0g total fat (0g saturated), 0mg cholesterol, 2mg sodium.

GINGERBREAD CUTOUTS

....

For tree decorations, before baking, make a hole in each cookie with a drinking straw. After baking, tie a loop of nylon fishing line through the hole of each cookie for easy hanging.

Prep: 45 minutes plus cooling and decorating
Bake: 12 minutes per batch

½ cup sugar
½ cup light (mild) molasses
1½ teaspoons ground ginger
1 teaspoon ground allspice
1 teaspoon ground cinnamon
1 teaspoon ground cloves
2 teaspoons baking soda
½ cup butter or margarine (1 stick), cut into pieces
1 large egg, beaten
3½ cups all-purpose flour
Ornamental Frosting (left)

1. In 3-quart saucepan, combine sugar, molasses, ginger, allspice, cinnamon, and cloves; heat to boiling over medium heat, stirring occasionally with wooden spoon. Remove from heat; stir in baking soda (mixture will foam up). Stir in butter until melted. Stir in egg, then flour.

2. On floured surface, knead dough until thoroughly blended. Divide dough in half; wrap one piece in plastic wrap and set aside.

3. Preheat oven to 325°F. With floured rolling pin, roll remaining piece of dough slightly less than ¼ inch thick. With floured 3- to 4-inch cookie cutters, cut dough into as many cookies as possible; reserve trimmings. Place cookies, 1 inch apart, on two ungreased large cookie sheets. If desired, with drinking straw or skewer, make ¼-inch hole in each cookie for hanging.

4. Bake until brown around edges, about 12 minutes, rotating cookie sheets between upper and lower oven racks halfway through baking. With wide spatula, transfer cookies to wire racks to cool completely. Repeat with remaining dough and trimmings.

5. When cookies are cool, prepare Ornamental Frosting; use to decorate cookies as desired. Allow frosting to dry completely, about 1 hour. Makes about 36 cookies.

Each cookie without frosting: About 93 calories, 1g protein, 15g carbohydrate, 3g total fat (2g saturated), 13mg cholesterol, 100mg sodium.

CHEWY FRUIT BARS

....

Wrap up these wholesome bars individually for your kids' lunchboxes—and toss a couple into your own bag, too.

Prep: 20 minutes plus cooling   **Bake:** 25 minutes

2½ cups all-purpose flour
¾ teaspoon baking soda
1 teaspoon ground cinnamon
¼ teaspoon salt
1 cup (2 sticks) butter, softened (do not use margarine)
1½ cups packed dark brown sugar
2 large eggs
1 teaspoon vanilla extract
1 cup walnuts (4 ounces), chopped
1 cup pitted dried dates, chopped
1 cup dried tart cherries
½ cup dried apricot halves, chopped
½ cup golden raisins
confectioners' sugar for dusting (optional)

1. Preheat oven to 350°F. Line 15½" by 10½" jelly-roll pan with foil, leaving an extra 2 inches foil at each end to serve later as handles; grease foil.

2. On waxed paper, combine flour, baking soda, cinnamon, and salt. In large bowl, with mixer on medium speed, beat butter and brown sugar 1 minute or until creamy, occasionally scraping bowl with rubber spatula. Add eggs one at a time; add vanilla and beat until well mixed. Reduce speed to low; gradually beat in flour mixture just until blended, occasionally scraping bowl. Add walnuts, dates, cherries, apricots, and raisins to dough, stirring until blended (dough will be thick).

3. With floured fingers, press dough evenly into prepared pan. Bake 25 to 28 minutes or until surface is browned and toothpick inserted in center comes out clean. Cool completely in pan on wire rack. Remove from pan, using foil handles, and place on cutting board. With long, sharp knife, cut lengthwise into 4 strips, then cut each strip crosswise into 12 bars.

4. Store cookies in tightly sealed container with sheets of waxed paper between layers at room temperature up to 1 week or in freezer up to 3 months. Sprinkle with confectioners' sugar before serving, if you like. Makes 4 dozen cookies.

Each bar: About 145 calories, 2g protein, 23g carbohydrate, 6g total fat (3g saturated), 1g fiber, 24mg cholesterol, 70mg sodium.

COOKIE JIGSAW

....

If you want to make the puzzle ahead of time, it's best to wrap and freeze undecorated pieces, then unwrap, thaw completely, and follow decorating directions.

Prep: 1 hour 15 minutes plus cooling and decorating
Bake: 30 minutes

lightweight cardboard or sturdy paper
for pattern template
2½ cups all-purpose flour
1½ teaspoons baking powder
¼ teaspoon salt
¾ cup butter or margarine (1½ sticks), softened
¾ cup sugar
1 large egg
1 tablespoon milk
2 teaspoons vanilla extract
¾ cup light corn syrup
assorted decorations: green, red, white, yellow, and blue sugar crystals; chocolate sprinkles; multicolor, white, and star-shaped candy décors; and small round yellow candies

1. On cardboard or paper, draw a Christmas-tree template 10 inches high (from tip of tree to top of trunk) and 10½ inches wide (at base of tree above trunk), with a 1-inch high by 2-inch wide trunk. Cut out template and set aside.

2. Preheat oven to 325°F. Grease and flour large cookie sheet. In medium bowl, with wire whisk, stir flour, baking powder, and salt.

3. In large bowl, with mixer at medium speed, beat butter and sugar until creamy. Beat in egg, milk, and vanilla until well blended (mixture may look curdled). Reduce speed to low; beat in flour mixture just until blended. Pat dough into small rectangle.

4. Place dough in center of cookie sheet. With floured rolling pin, roll dough into 13" by 11" rectangle. Bake 15 minutes.

5. Transfer cookie sheet to wire rack. Center tree template lengthwise on warm cookie. With knife, cut around template into cookie; remove template, leaving tree outline. Press floured 1½-inch star-shaped cookie cutter into cookie at top of tree; remove cutter, leaving star outline. Press floured 1-inch round cookie cutters into tree in several places, leaving ornament outlines. Press 2½-inch star cutter into remaining cookie around tree, leaving star outlines.

6. Cut tree into various geometrically shaped puzzle pieces, being careful not to cut into ornament outlines. Cut remaining cookie around tree into puzzle pieces, being careful not to cut into star outlines.

7. Return cookie sheet to oven and bake until cookie is light brown, 12 to 14 minutes longer. Transfer cookie sheet to wire rack; cut through all designs and pieces. Cool cookie puzzle on cookie sheet 10 minutes. Carefully slide puzzle, in one piece, onto wire rack; cool completely.

8. To decorate: In 1-quart saucepan, heat corn syrup to boiling over medium heat, stirring frequently. Boil, stirring, 1 minute. Remove round ornament pieces from tree; brush tree and trunk with corn syrup. Sprinkle tree with green sugar crystals to coat, then attach small round yellow candies as desired. Sprinkle with or dip trunk into chocolate sprinkles. Brush ornament pieces with corn syrup; sprinkle with or dip into choice of colored sugar crystals or décors. Remove star decorations from around tree; brush with corn syrup and sprinkle with or dip into yellow sugar crystals. Brush puzzle pieces around tree with corn syrup; sprinkle with blue sugar crystals, then sprinkle lightly with white and star-shaped décors. Reheat corn syrup if it becomes too thick.

9. Allow puzzle pieces to dry completely, about 1 hour. When pieces are dry, reassemble puzzle on large tray to serve, or store puzzle in tightly covered container at room temperature up to 1 week. Makes about 42 cookies.

Each cookie: About 95 calories, 1g protein, 15g carbohydrate, 4g total fat (2g saturated), 15mg cholesterol, 80mg sodium.

Cookie Jigsaw

APRICOT-RASPBERRY RUGELACH

....

A tender cream cheese dough gives these rugelach traditional taste and texture.

Prep: 1 hour plus chilling   Bake: 35 minutes

- 1 cup butter or margarine (2 sticks), softened
- 1 package (8 ounces) cream cheese, softened
- ¾ cup granulated sugar
- 1 teaspoon vanilla extract
- ¼ teaspoon salt
- 2 cups all-purpose flour
- 1 cup walnuts (4 ounces), chopped
- ¾ cup dried apricots, chopped
- ¼ cup packed brown sugar
- 1½ teaspoons ground cinnamon
- ½ cup seedless raspberry preserves
- 1 tablespoon milk

1. In large bowl, with mixer at low speed, beat butter and cream cheese until creamy. Beat in ¼ cup granulated sugar, vanilla, and salt. Beat in 1 cup flour. Stir in remaining 1 cup flour just until blended. Divide dough into 4 equal disks. Wrap each disk and refrigerate until firm, at least 2 hours or up to overnight.

2. Prepare filling: In medium bowl, combine walnuts, apricots, brown sugar, ¼ cup plus 2 tablespoons granulated sugar, and ½ teaspoon cinnamon until well mixed. Line two large cookie sheets with foil; grease foil.

3. On lightly floured surface, with floured rolling pin, roll 1 disk of dough into 9-inch round; keep remaining dough refrigerated. Spread 2 tablespoons preserves over dough. Sprinkle with ½ cup walnut mixture, gently pressing so that nuts adhere. With pastry wheel or sharp knife, cut dough into 12 equal wedges. Starting at curved edge, roll up each wedge. Place, point side down, ½ inch apart, on prepared cookie sheet. Repeat with remaining dough, one disk at a time.

4. Preheat oven to 325°F. In cup, with fork, stir remaining 2 tablespoons granulated sugar and remaining 1 teaspoon cinnamon. With pastry brush, brush rugelach with milk. Evenly sprinkle cinnamon-sugar on top.

5. Bake until golden, 35 to 40 minutes, rotating cookie sheets between upper and lower oven racks halfway through baking. With wide spatula, immediately transfer rugelach to wire racks to cool completely. Makes 48 rugelach.

Each rugelach: About 116 calories, 1g protein, 12g carbohydrate, 7g total fat (4g saturated), 16mg cholesterol, 67mg sodium.

MOLASSES

During the sugar refining process, the juice that is extracted from sugarcane or sugar beets is boiled down to a syrupy mixture from which sugar crystals are removed. The syrup that remains is molasses.

Whether or not molasses is sulphured or unsulphured simply depends on whether sulphur dioxide was used in the processing of the molasses. Unsulphured molasses has a milder, cleaner flavor. Store molasses in a dark, cool place for up to one year.

LIGHT MOLASSES comes from the first boiling of sugar syrup. It has a light color and mild flavor and is often used as a pancake/waffle syrup as well as for baking.

DARK MOLASSES comes from the second boiling and is darker, not as sweet, and thicker than light molasses. It is the molasses used to flavor baked goods such as gingerbread and for Indian pudding and baked beans.

BLACKSTRAP MOLASSES comes from the third boiling of sugar syrup. It is very dark, a bit bitter, and rather thick.

Brandy Snaps

BRANDY SNAPS

••

*Make these elegant lacy cookies in dry weather—
otherwise they will be sticky.*

Prep: 25 minutes   Bake: 5 minutes per batch

½   cup butter (1 stick; do not use margarine)
3   tablespoons light (mild) molasses
½   cup all-purpose flour
½   cup sugar
1   teaspoon ground ginger
¼   teaspoon salt
2   tablespoons brandy

1. Preheat oven to 350°F. Grease large cookie sheet.

2. In 2-quart saucepan, melt butter with molasses over medium-low heat, stirring occasionally, until smooth. Remove from heat. With wooden spoon, stir in flour, sugar, ginger, and salt until blended and smooth; stir in brandy. Set saucepan in bowl of hot water to keep warm.

3. Drop 1 teaspoon batter on cookie sheet; with small metal spatula, spread in circular motion to make 4-inch round (during baking, batter will spread and fill in any thin areas). Repeat three times more, placing rounds 2 inches apart. (Do not place more than 4 cookies on sheet.)

4. Bake until golden brown, about 5 minutes. Cool 30 to 60 seconds on cookie sheet on wire rack, just until edges have set; then, quickly flip cookies over.

5. Working as quickly as possible, roll each cookie around handle (½-inch diameter) of wooden spoon. If cookies become too hard to roll, return to oven briefly to soften. As each cookie is shaped, slip off spoon handle and cool completely on wire racks. Repeat with remaining batter. Makes about 24 cookies.

Each cookie: About 72 calories, 0g protein, 8g carbohydrate, 4g total fat (2g saturated), 10mg cholesterol, 64mg sodium.

ALMOND-ANISE BISCOTTI

....

Soaking the anise seeds in liqueur softens them and releases their delicious flavor.

Prep: 25 minutes plus cooling   Bake: 55 minutes

- 1   tablespoon anise seeds, crushed
- 1   tablespoon anise-flavored apéritif or liqueur
- 2   cups all-purpose flour
- 1   cup sugar
- 1   cup whole almonds (4 ounces), toasted (page 692) and coarsely chopped
- 1   teaspoon baking powder
- ⅛   teaspoon salt
- 3   large eggs

1. Preheat oven to 325°F. In medium bowl, combine anise seeds and anise-flavored apéritif; let stand 10 minutes.

2. Meanwhile, grease large cookie sheet.

3. In large bowl, with wire whisk, stir flour, sugar, chopped almonds, baking powder, and salt. With wire whisk, beat eggs into anise mixture. With wooden spoon, stir egg mixture into flour mixture until blended. Divide dough in half. On prepared cookie sheet, with floured hands, shape each half into 15-inch log, placing them 3 inches apart (dough will be sticky).

4. Bake until golden and toothpick inserted in center comes out clean, about 40 minutes. Cool 10 minutes on cookie sheet on wire rack, then transfer logs to cutting board.

5. With serrated knife, cut each log crosswise on diagonal into ¼-inch-thick slices. Place slices, cut side down, on two ungreased cookie sheets. Bake 15 minutes, turning slices over once and rotating cookie sheets between upper and lower oven racks halfway through baking. With spatula, transfer biscotti to wire racks to cool completely. Makes about 84 biscotti.

Each biscotto: About 33 calories, 1g protein, 5g carbohydrate, 1g total fat (0g saturated), 8mg cholesterol, 12mg sodium.

CHOCOLATE AND HAZELNUT TRUFFLES

....

Use the best chocolate you can find to give these truffles European flair. If you wish, add 2 tablespoons of coffee, orange, or almond liqueur to the melted-chocolate.

Prep: 25 minutes plus chilling

- 8   ounces bittersweet chocolate or 6 squares (6 ounces) semisweet chocolate plus 2 squares (2 ounces) unsweetened chocolate, coarsely chopped
- ½   cup heavy or whipping cream
- 3   tablespoons butter, cut into pieces and softened (do not use margarine)
- ⅓   cup hazelnuts (filberts), toasted and skinned (page 692), finely chopped
- 3   tablespoons unsweetened cocoa

1. Line 8½" by 4½" loaf pan with plastic wrap; smooth out wrinkles. In food processor with knife blade attached, process chocolate until finely ground.

2. In 1-quart saucepan, heat cream to simmering over medium-high heat. Add to chocolate in food processor and puree until smooth. Add butter and process until smooth.

3. Pour chocolate mixture into prepared pan; spread evenly. Refrigerate until cool and firm enough to handle, about 3 hours.

4. Remove chocolate mixture from pan by lifting edges of plastic wrap. Invert chocolate block onto cutting board; discard plastic wrap. Cut chocolate lengthwise into 4 strips, then cut each strip crosswise into 8 pieces. (To cut chocolate easily, dip knife in hot water and wipe dry; repeat as needed.) With cool hands, quickly roll each square into ball. Roll 16 truffles in chopped hazelnuts and remaining 16 truffles in cocoa. Place in single layer in waxed paper–lined airtight container. Refrigerate up to 1 week, or freeze up to 1 month. Remove from freezer 5 minutes before serving. Makes 32 truffles.

Each truffle: About 66 calories, 1g protein, 5g carbohydrate, 6g total fat (3g saturated), 8mg cholesterol, 13mg sodium.

CHOCOLATE-WALNUT FUDGE

. . . .

This rich and creamy fudge couldn't be easier to make.

Prep: 25 minutes plus chilling

1 pound bittersweet chocolate or 16 squares (16 ounces) semisweet chocolate, chopped

1 can (14 ounces) sweetened condensed milk

1 cup walnuts (4 ounces), coarsely chopped

1 teaspoon vanilla extract

⅛ teaspoon salt

1. Line 8-inch square baking pan with plastic wrap; smooth out wrinkles. In heavy 2-quart saucepan, melt chocolate with condensed milk over medium-low heat, stirring constantly, until smooth. Remove from heat.

2. Stir in walnuts, vanilla, and salt. Scrape chocolate mixture into prepared pan; spread evenly. Refrigerate until firm, about 3 hours.

3. Remove fudge from pan by lifting edges of plastic wrap. Invert fudge onto cutting board; discard plastic wrap. Cut fudge into 8 strips, then cut each strip crosswise into 8 pieces. Layer between waxed paper in airtight container. Store at room temperature up to 1 week, or refrigerate up to 1 month. Makes 64 pieces.

Each piece: About 67 calories, 1g protein, 8g carbohydrate, 4g total fat (2g saturated), 2mg cholesterol, 13mg sodium.

SUGAR SYRUP TEMPERATURES

Many candies are made with sugar syrup. Measuring the temperature of sugar syrup accurately is crucial in candy making. For the best results, always use a candy thermometer. When attaching the thermometer to the pan, be sure the tip of the thermometer doesn't touch the bottom of the pan.

When cooking a sugar syrup, crystals form on the side of the saucepan. They must be dissolved, otherwise the candy may be grainy. Rub a pastry brush that's been dipped into cold water against the sugar crystals to wash them into the syrup. Repeat all around the inside of the saucepan until no sugar crystals remain.

BUTTER-NUT TOFFEE CRUNCH

. . . .

This classic candy is perfect for gift-giving during the holidays. You can purchase festive packaging at your local party store.

Prep: 15 minutes plus cooling   Cook: 25 minutes

1¾ cups sugar

⅓ cup light corn syrup

¼ cup water

1 cup butter or margarine (2 sticks)

2 cups walnuts (8 ounces), lightly toasted (page 692)

2 squares (2 ounces) unsweetened chocolate, chopped

2 squares (2 ounces) ounces semisweet chocolate, chopped

1 teaspoon vegetable shortening

1. In heavy 2-quart saucepan, combine sugar, corn syrup, and water; heat to boiling over medium heat, stirring occasionally. Stir in butter. Set candy thermometer in place and continue cooking, stirring frequently, about 20 minutes or until temperature reaches 300°F (hard-crack stage).

2. Meanwhile, lightly grease 15½" by 10½" jelly-roll pan. Finely chop walnuts.

3. Remove saucepan from heat. Reserve ⅓ cup walnuts; stir remaining walnuts into hot syrup. Immediately pour mixture into prepared jelly-roll pan. Working quickly, spread evenly with spatula. Cool candy completely in pan on wire rack.

4. Prepare chocolate glaze: In small saucepan, melt chocolates and shortening over low heat, stirring until smooth. Remove saucepan from heat; cool slightly.

5. Lift out candy in one piece and place on cutting board. With metal spatula, spread warm chocolate evenly over candy; sprinkle with reserved walnuts. Let stand until chocolate sets, about 1 hour.

6. With knife, break toffee crunch into serving-size pieces. Layer between waxed paper in airtight container. Store at room temperature up to 2 weeks. Makes about 1¾ pounds candy.

Each ounce: About 195 calories, 2g protein, 18g carbohydrate, 14g total fat (6g saturated), 19mg cholesterol, 75mg sodium.

INDEX

ACKNOWLEDGMENTS

A book of this scope takes the efforts of many people to make it a reality. Along with those who worked on this edition, I'd also like to thank the people who brought the previous editions of this book to life. Frank Bennack and Ellen Levine for the green light to do it right—and in color! Deborah Mintcheff, Lisa Brainerd Burge, and Rick Rodgers, shapers of chapters; Fraya Berg, Allison Dewine, Sandy Gluck, Wendy Kalen, Lori Longbotham, Maryanne Marinelli, Gina Miraglia, Paul Picciuto, Carol Prager, Sarah Reynolds, Samantha Seneviratne, Marianne Svec, and Rosanne Toroian, food lovers all, who produce delicious recipes that work.

TO COLLEAGUES AT GOOD HOUSEKEEPING: Rosemary Ellis, Sarah Scrymser, Jennifer Cook, Courtney Murphy, Bill Swan, Sara Lyle, Sharon Franke, and Samantha Cassetty: Thanks for your discerning eyes, sage counsel, and general cheerleading. To my test kitchen colleagues Genevieve Ko, Cathy Lo, Jessica Fox, and Sherry Rujikarn: Thank you for fabulous new recipes, well-educated palates, and most especially for being such an enthusiastic, ready-for-anything team!

TO OUR BOOK TEAM: Publisher Jaqueline Deval, Project Editor Sarah Scheffel, editorial alumni Marisa Bulzone and Maryanne Bannon, and Pamela Hoenig, reviser of the Canning & Freezing chapter: Thank you all for approaching every word, recipe, taste, photo, and query with enthusiasm and a fresh eye. My thanks also to Chris Thompson, Art Director, who in concert with Roberto de Vicq Cumptich, and Margery Greenspan of MG Design gave us a wonderful anniversary cover and an updated interior design.

TO OUR FRIENDS IN THE FOOD INDUSTRY: National Cattleman's Beef Association, National Pork Producer's Council, National Chicken Council, American Egg Board, California Fig Advisory Board; California Tree Fruit Agreement; National Center for Home Food Preservation: Thank you for all your help in clarifying product information, cooking techniques, and food safety practices.

FOR ADVICE ON TABLE ETIQUETTE: Cardel Ltd. and Tiffany & Company.

IT WAS A JOY TO WORK WITH SO MANY GIFTED PEOPLE.

—SUSAN WESTMORELAND
Food Director, *Good Housekeeping*

PHOTOGRAPHY CREDITS

JAMES BAIGRIE: Pages vii (top center), x (bottom center), vix (bottom center), xxi (top left), 36, 39, 45, 106, 117, 232, 269, 292, 298, 339, 373, 385, 492, 538, 617, 621, 624, 634, 647, 677 (top)

CHRIS BAIN: Pages xxvii, xxxv (right)

MARY ELLEN BARTLEY: Page 375, 692

MONICA BUCK: Pages v (left), vi (right), 164, 180, 260, 295, 300

CORBIS IMAGES: Ocean, xxxv; Ariel Skelley, xxxiv; Snowflake Studios Inc., xiii (top center); Rainer Berg/Westend 61, xxxiii (left)

TARA DONNE: Pages vii (left), vii (right), 75, 184, 309, 432, 477 (bottom), 607

PHILIP FRIEDMAN/STUDIO D: Pages 38, 428 (bottom), 677 (bottom)

GETTY IMAGES: Chris Alack, xvii (right); Eric Audras, xxii; Paul Bradbury, xxvi; Maren Caruso, xxxvi; George Doyle, xxxii; Don Farrall, xxiii (left); Thomas Grass, xxxi; Carlos Hernandez, xxviii; Mint Images/ Helen Norman, xxx; Finn O'Hara, xxix; Brett Stevens, xxxiii (right); Kate Whitaker, xvi (right); Tanya Zouev, xvii (top center)

BRIAN HAGIWARA: Pages v (middle), viii (left), x (right), xi (bottom center), xiii (bottom center), xiii (right), xiv (top center), xv (left), xxi (bottom left), 5, 6–8, 11–12, 20, 31, 94, 144, 148, 153–155, 157, 160, 166, 172–173, 176–178, 181, 190, 197, 199, 201, 203, 206, 209, 211, 214–215, 217–219, 221–222, 278, 306, 310, 312, 318, 327, 335, 343, 364, 368, 370, 372, 376, 380, 472, 476, 477 (top), 481, 490, 500, 502–503, 510–511, 625–626

LISA HUBBARD: Pages xi (top center), 446, 455, 596, 654

ISTOCKPHOTO: Ursula Alter, xxiv (bottom left); Igor Dutina, xxv (bottom right); Floortje, xxiv (right); JL Gutierrez, xxv (top left); Karpix, xxxvii (left); Robyn Mac, xxv (top left), xxv (top right); Peter Polak, xxiii (right); Shipfactory, xxxvii (right); pages 192, 414 (right), 421, 439

FRANCES JANISCH: Page 676

JOHN KERNICK: Pages 131, 428 (top)

YUNHEE KIM: Pages xxi (bottom right), 233, 323, 571, 661, 670

RITA MAAS: Pages v (right), vi (center), viii (top center), ix (right), x (center), 5, 30, 41, 49, 88, 91, 227–228, 231, 237, 241, 277, 280, 291, 297, 304–305, 315, 386, 388–391, 393–396, 398–399, 401–409, 411–412, 414 (left), 415–420, 424, 426, 429–431, 433–435, 437, 443, 512, 515–516, 518, 527–528, 530–532, 534–535, 616, 705

KATE MATHIS: Pages ix (left), xiv (left), xv (center), xvi (left), xviii, 35, 39, 42, 61, 112, 236, 246, 273, 302, 438, 479, 536, 542, 544, 546–547, 549, 550–551, 565, 671

ALISON MIKSCH/FOOD PIX: Page 28

ELLIE MILLER: Pages 697–701

NGOC MINH NGO: Page 336

STEVEN MARK NEEDHAM: Page 696

CON POULOS: Page 265

DAVID PRINCE: Pages 108, 478

THERESE RAFFETTO: Page 224

ALAN RICHARDSON: Pages 130, 344, 351, 423

KATE SEARS: Pages vi (left), viii (right), 159, 324, 340, 367, 482–483, 591

SHUTTERSTOCK: Elena Elisseeva, xxiv (top left)

STOCKFOOD: Leigh Beisch Photography, ix (center), vix (left), Michael Marquand, x (top center)

ANN STRATTON: Pages viii (bottom center), xii (left), xii (right), xiii (left), xvi (bottom center), xvii (left), xvii (bottom center), 5, 50, 53, 56–57, 65–66, 70, 76, 83, 85, 243–245, 248–249, 271, 448–450, 453–454, 456–463, 465, 467–471, 600, 603–604, 608, 610, 613–615, 656–658, 660, 663, 668–669, 673, 675

MARK THOMAS: Pages vii (top center), xxi (top right), 59, 94, 99–100, 114, 120, 122, 127, 132, 135, 137, 141–142, 250, 253, 259, 274–275, 308, 314, 331, 349, 352, 497, 556, 558–560, 562, 564, 567, 570, 572–575, 578–579, 582–583, 587, 589, 593, 628–629, 632, 637–638, 642, 644, 646, 680, 683, 686, 689, 692, 706–707

ANNA WILLIAMS: xii (center)

METRIC EQUIVALENT CHARTS

The recipes that appear in this cookbook use the standard United States method for measuring liquid and dry or solid ingredients (teaspoons, tablespoons, and cups). The information on this chart is provided to help cooks outside the U.S. successfully use these recipes. All equivalents are approximate.

METRIC EQUIVALENTS FOR DIFFERENT TYPES OF INGREDIENTS

A standard cup measure of a dry or solid ingredient will vary in weight depending on the type of ingredient. A standard cup of liquid is the same volume for any type of liquid. Use the following chart when converting standard cup measures to grams (weight) or milliliters (volume).

Standard Cup	Fine Powder (e.g., flour)	Grain (e.g., rice)	Granular (e.g., sugar)	Liquid Solids (e.g., butter)	Liquid (e.g., milk)
1	140 g	150 g	190 g	200 g	240 ml
3/4	105 g	113 g	143 g	150 g	180 ml
2/3	93 g	100 g	125 g	133 g	160 ml
1/2	70 g	75 g	95 g	100 g	120 ml
1/3	47 g	50 g	63 g	67 g	80 ml
1/4	35 g	38 g	48 g	50 g	60 ml
1/8	18 g	19 g	24 g	25 g	30 ml

USEFUL EQUIVALENTS FOR LIQUID INGREDIENTS BY VOLUME

1/4 tsp =				1 ml
1/2 tsp =				2 ml
1 tsp =				5 ml
3 tsp =	1 tbls =		1/2 fl oz =	15 ml
	2 tbls =	1/8 cup =	1 fl oz =	30 ml
	4 tbls =	1/4 cup =	2 fl oz =	60 ml
	5 1/3 tbls =	1/3 cup =	3 fl oz =	80 ml
	8 tbls =	1/2 cup =	4 fl oz =	120 ml
	10 2/3 tbls =	2/3 cup =	5 fl oz =	160 ml
	12 tbls =	3/4 cup =	6 fl oz =	180 ml
	16 tbls =	1 cup =	8 fl oz =	240 ml
	1 pt =	2 cups =	16 fl oz =	480 ml
	1 qt =	4 cups =	32 fl oz =	960 ml
			33 fl oz =	1000 ml = 1 l

USEFUL EQUIVALENTS FOR DRY INGREDIENTS BY WEIGHT

(To convert ounces to grams, multiply the number of ounces by 30.)

1 oz =	1/16 lb =	30 g
4 oz =	1/4 lb =	120 g
8 oz =	1/2 lb =	240 g
12 oz =	3/4 lb =	360 g
16 oz =	1 lb =	480 g

USEFUL EQUIVALENTS FOR COOKING/OVEN TEMPERATURES

	Fahrenheit	Celsius	Gas Mark
Freeze Water	32° F	0° C	
Room Temperature	68° F	20° C	
Boil Water	212° F	100° C	
Bake	325° F	160° C	3
	350° F	180° C	4
	375° F	190° C	5
	400° F	200° C	6
	425° F	220° C	7
	450° F	230° C	8
Broil			Grill

USEFUL EQUIVALENTS FOR LENGTH

(To convert inches to centimeters, multiply the number of inches by 2.5.)

1 in =		2.5 cm
6 in =	1/2 ft =	15 cm
12 in =	1 ft =	30 cm
36 in =	3 ft = 1 yd =	90 cm
40 in =		100 cm = 1 m

FOOD EQUIVALENTS

Bacon, 16-ounce package, diced, cooked	1½ cups pieces		Cottage cheese, 8 ounces	1 cup
Beans, dry 1 pound 1 cup	2 cups 2 to 2½ cups cooked		Couscous, 1 cup	about 2½ cups cooked
Berries	See individual varieties.		Crackers, crushed graham, 7 5" by 2½" crackers saltine, 28	about 1 cup fine crumbs about 1 cup fine crumbs
Blackberries, 1 pint	about 2 cups		Cranberries, 12-ounce bag	3 cups
Blueberries, 1 pint	about 3 cups		Cream, heavy or whipping, 1 cup	about 2 cups whipped cream
Bread crumbs, dried 8-ounce package	2¼ cups		Cream cheese 3-ounce package 8-ounce package	6 tablespoons 1 cup
Bread crumbs, fresh 1 slice bread	½ cup bread crumbs		Currants, dried, 5 ounces	about 1 cup
Butter or margarine ¼-pound stick 1 pound	½ cup or 8 tablespoons 4 sticks or 2 cups		Dates, dry, pitted, 10-ounce container	about 2 cups
Cabbage, 1 pound coarsely sliced	about 4 to 5 cups		Egg whites, large 1 1 cup	about 2 tablespoons 8 to 10 egg whites
Celery, 1 medium bunch sliced/diced	about 4 cups		Egg yolks, large, 1 cup	12 to 14 egg yolks
Cheddar cheese, 4 ounces	1 cup shredded		Flour, 1 pound all-purpose cake whole-wheat	about 3½ cups about 4 cups about 3¾ cups
Cherries, 1 pound	about 2 cups pitted			
Chicken, cooked 2½-pound to 3-pound chicken, diced meat	about 2½ cups		Gelatin, unflavored, to gel 2 cups liquid	1 envelope
Cocoa, unsweetened, 8-ounce can	2 cups		Green or red bell pepper, 1 large	about 1 cup chopped
Coconut, flaked, 3½ ounces	1⅓ cups		Hominy grits, 1 cup	about 4½ cups cooked
Cookies, crushed chocolate wafers, 20 2¼-inch gingersnaps, 15 vanilla wafers, 22	about 1 cup fine crumbs about 1 cup fine crumbs about 1 cup fine crumbs		Honey, liquid, 16 ounces	1⅓ cups